CROSS-EXAMINATION: SCIENCE AND TECHNIQUES

Larry Pozner
Denver, Colorado

Roger J. Dodd
Lake Park, Georgia

SECOND EDITION

QUESTIONS ABOUT THIS PUBLICATION?

For CUSTOMER SERVICE ASSISTANCE concerning replacement pages,
   shipments, billing, reprint permission, or other matters,

> please call Customer Service Department at 800-833-9844
> email *customer.support@lexisnexis.com*
> or visit our interactive customer service website at *www.lexisnexis.com/printcdsc*

For QUESTIONS or FEEDBACK concerning this publication,

> please call: 800-446-3410 ext.7522
> or email: *lncps@lexisnexis.com*

For **information on other LEXISNEXIS MATTHEW BENDER publications**,

> please call us at 800-223-1940
> or visit our online bookstore at *www.lexisnexis.com/bookstore*

ISBN: 978 0-327-16434-0

Second Printing

Matthew Bender & Company, Inc.
Editorial Offices
701 E. Water Street
Charlottesville, VA 22902
800-446-3410
www.lexisnexis.com

Product Number 6598511

(Pub. 65985)

DEDICATION

To James W. Barley, for the person that he was, and to Matthew A. Dodd and Andrew J. Dodd, for the persons they will become.

Roger J. Dodd
Lake Park, Georgia

To Raedel, who quietly told me to stop talking about it and go downstairs and write it. And to my daughters, Quinlan, Briana, Whitney, and Madison. Daddy will come upstairs now.

Larry S. Pozner
Denver, Colorado

FOREWORD

This is simply the best book on the art and science of cross-examination ever written. Before I contemplate a major cross-examination in a criminal case or a deposition of a significant witness in a civil case, I literally go back to this book to stimulate my thinking. I give this book to all my law students, lawyers who work with me, and even my own children who have used it to great effect during their mock trial competitions during high school and college. Looping (on cross and direct), using trilogies, pyramiding trilogies upon trilogies, repeating a question to the witness who won't answer and other control techniques for the runaway witness, organizing by the chapter method, sequencing, and sliding off objections have all become indispensable concepts for teachers of trial practice.

Larry and Roger are wonderful teachers and terrific lawyers. But better still, they were smart enough to steal and refine all the good techniques employed by colleagues at the NACDL's National College of Criminal Defense Lawyers. We are all indebted for this marvelous piece of larceny because it takes real talent to organize and communicate the accumulated wisdom of your betters in an effective way.

When I began practicing law and teaching in law school more than 30 years ago, it was conventional wisdom that good cross-examination was the product of talent — it couldn't really be taught. The best one could do, following Irving Younger's Ten Commandments of Cross-Examination (which were really eight commandments), was to minimize one's losses. Larry Pozner and Roger Dodd have fundamentally changed the pedagogy. Good cross-examination, even great cross-examination, can be taught. Just follow the rules outlined in this seminal book and you can do better than just avoid disaster — you can win your case.

Barry Scheck
New York City, New York
October 28, 2004

FOREWORD TO FIRST EDITION

I have reviewed in depth the completed manuscript of *Cross-Examination: Science and Techniques*, authored by my two friends and colleagues, Roger J. Dodd and Larry S. Pozner, both being distinguished trial lawyers who have labored long in many grueling legal battles to protect the accused and sustain Constitutional rights.

As all of the readers of this book will instantly recognize, Constitutional rights have been seriously eroded within the past twenty years. We have seen *Leon* which has almost signalled a repeal of the Fourth Amendment. For the first time in the history of Anglo-American jurisprudence a coerced confession can be considered harmless error. With the affirmance of *Mistretta v. United States*, our Title III Federal Judges have been virtually stripped of any real sentencing discretion. The list gets longer at every session of the U.S. Supreme Court.

Cross-examination is without a doubt the most effective tool that remains in an advocate's arsenal, and as of yet it is still alive and well. Along with the almost lost art of skillful oratory, it can still lead to victory in many cases. It remains, as Justice Holmes once said, "the greatest locomotive for the discovery of the truth."

This is a monumental work, and every practitioner who has an interest in cross-examination should have this volume close at hand.

Bobby Lee Cook
Summerville, Georgia
May 5, 1993

ACKNOWLEDGMENTS

Edwin Jackson is truly a soldier. His formal title is Senior Director of Publishing for LexisNexis. Beyond what his title might imply, he has soldiered with us through the chilled winds of an early morning in Toronto, through the sweltering heat of Phoenix, and everywhere in between over the North American continent. He is the bungee cord that has connected us to LexisNexis and it is his flexibility that has resulted in us writing this Second Edition eleven years after the First Edition was published.

We have learned much. We thank our clients, co-counsel, and witnesses over the last eleven years, many whose names we cannot recall.

More importantly, we thank our misguided opponents, judges who have produced sleepless nights, and witnesses who have tested us in evil, unnatural ways. We learned more from you. Be assured that we will not forget your names.

Larry's acknowledgments concerning this Second Edition: I need to acknowledge and thank some people without whom this Second Edition would have been far more difficult and far less productive. First, my thanks to the members of my law firm of Hoffman Reilly Pozner and Williamson, LLP. You have inspired me beyond measure. Thank you for welcoming a solo criminal defense lawyer into a team-based commercial litigation practice. And thank you also for understanding why I can never abandon the practice of defending the citizen accused.

To Christian Monson, I am deeply indebted to you for your dedication and good cheer in reviewing and cleaning up the chapter drafts and for your tact when suggesting that perhaps something could be explained a little better (translation: What in the world are you saying?), edited a little more closely (translation: All right already, you made the point), or held back as needing further development (translation: Now here is a truly bad idea). Now go to law school.

To Roger Dodd, my co-author and lecture partner of more than a decade: There are only two people who can understand how we can work together. You and I. What an unlikely pair we are. So be it.

Finally, to my civil trial partner for the last 15 years, Dan Reilly. Trial work can be an enormously exhilarating experience and it can be a miserable experience. We have shared both.

There are only two people who can understand how we can work together. You and I. Wait, I think I see a pattern here. Anyway, the career of a trial lawyer is a scrapbook of courtroom experiences. My scrapbook is full of memories of the two of us collaborating on a truly bizarre array of trials including deranged bounty hunters, an insurance company run by crooks, dog food bags, and the ownership of an NFL franchise. Who could ask for a more exciting career? Thank you. Much that I have learned from you is in this book.

Roger's acknowledgments concerning this Second Edition:

Jeannie Lankford suffered through the First Edition with Roger. Unbelievably, she is still here without complaint through the Second Edition. Kim McCoggle has assisted Jeannie throughout. Kim has carried the load this go around. Her good-hearted chuckle and shake of the head complements Jeannie's belief. What a team. To my frail but angelic mother, Dorothy Dodd, who insisted throughout my life that I had something to say when the rest of the world had other thoughts, thank you. She is a daily inspiration.

SPECIAL NOTE AND DISCLAIMER

The spirit of this book is one of shared learning. The authors' goal is to pass along to the trial bar any useful forms of the many techniques of cross-examination that have been used by skillful advocates for many generations. Those advocates in turn undoubtedly learned them from their predecessors. By analyzing these techniques and setting forth certain guidelines that are successfully used, the authors assume that other trial lawyers will take them, improve upon them, and pass them down yet again. Hence, these techniques are the invention of need and the property of all who would make use of them.

In order to illustrate the operation of these techniques, certain examples have been set out. In keeping with the spirit of this book, these materials are not representative as the work of any one particular lawyer. The authors have freely drawn upon the trial experiences of a great many lawyers. In some instances, fact, events, witnesses, and cross-examinations have been created in order to illustrate a particular technique. In other instances, factual cases have been drawn upon as the inspiration for a particular illustration. Nonetheless, even in those situations, the names, dates, places, and events have been modified for teaching purposes, and the resulting transcripts should not be understood in the least as actual transcripts of cases, but should be accepted solely in this spirit in which they are offered — hypothetical illustrations of the science and techniques of cross-examinations that might be employed in a courtroom setting.

TABLE OF CONTENTS

Chapter 8.   THE ONLY THREE RULES OF CROSS-EXAMINATION

Chapter 1

PHILOSOPHY AND OVERVIEW OF THE SCIENCE OF CROSS-EXAMINATION

SYNOPSIS

§ 1.01　A Book for Real Lawyers with Real Problems

Trial work is incredibly hard work and cross-examination is the hardest aspect of trial work. But there are techniques that can make cross-examination easier. There are techniques that can make cross-examination more productive. There are also techniques that elevate the importance of cross-examination. This book discusses and analyzes many of the techniques of modern cross-examination. Although the book is copyrighted, the techniques are not. The authors neither invented them, nor own them. The techniques of modern cross-examination belong to any trial lawyer.

The authors are trial lawyers, not scholars. If you came looking for legal citations to assist in the task of cross-examination, buy another book. This book will not help in a situation in which a judge ignores legal standards and refuses to allow a lawyer to cross-examine a witness. This book is not about academic exercises, the history of cross-examination, or the literature of cross-examination. It does not contain famous cases or war stories.

This book is not about case law. It is about trial work. It is about the importance of facts in the trial process. The first fact: Trial work is special. Trial lawyers are special. That is not to say that other legal work is less important, but it is to say that only a trial lawyer can appreciate what another trial lawyer endures during trial. Trial work is hard work. It is emotional work. It is mentally and physically draining. This book does not make light of trial work. It does not insult our brothers and sisters of the trial bar by implying that any of us have mastered our craft, that any of us are completely confident of our abilities, or that we have learned all that we need to learn about trial work. There is always more to learn.

§ 1.02　Cross-Examination Is a Necessary Part of the Search for the Truth

Our system of justice does not blindly accept witness testimony. Every witness who takes the stand is subject to cross-examination. That says something about what our culture believes. It believes that the truth is best found if all testimony is subject to a searching inquiry by the opposing counsel. But if the lawyer is to aid the truth-finding process with her cross-examination questions, she must use methods designed to uncover the truth, expose the partial truth, and challenge the credibility of a witness who has reason to distort the truth. If the simple question, "Are you sure?" was enough, this book would be unnecessary. Cross-examination techniques exist to ferret out facts that may have been omitted, obfuscated, or overstated. Some might suggest that this theory of cross-examination begins with a cynical outlook toward the fact-finding process. The response is that this theory of cross-examination begins with a realistic outlook toward the fact-finding process. The search for the truth has not changed.

Ever since trials have been reported, cross-examination has been featured as a vital portion of the trial. Socrates, while representing himself against his accuser, Miletus, is said by Plato to have cross-examined him long and well.

Wigmore said:

> For the two centuries past, the policy of the Anglo-American system of evidence has been to regard the necessity of testing by cross-examination, the "truth" of direct examination as an essential portion of the trial. Not even the abuses, the misunderstandings, and the puerilities which are so often found associated with cross-examination have availed to nullify its value. It may be that in more than one sense, it takes the place in our system which torture occupied in the medieval system of the civilians. Nevertheless, *it is beyond any doubt the greatest legal engine ever invented for the discovery of truth.*

5 Wigmore, Evidence § 1367

(Chadborn Rev. 1794)

In America this right was considered so essential that it was incorporated into the confrontation clause of the Sixth Amendment of the United States Constitution.

The right to cross-examine is inherently embodied in the right to a fair trial. While not directly referenced in the Constitution, innumerable cases insist that for a fair trial, civil litigants must have the right to cross-examine.

§ 1.03   Cross-Examination: The Science, Not the Art

"Science" is historically a term seldom applied to the task of cross-examination. Francis Wellman, in the most widely-read book on cross-examination (*The Art of Cross-Examination*, Macmillan Company, 1903; republished in 1936), continuously refers to cross-examination as an "art." The preface cautions: "Nor have I attempted to treat the subject (of cross-examination) in any scientific, elaborate or exhaustive way; but merely to make some suggestions upon the art of cross-examination . . . ."

The problem with thinking of cross-examination as an art is that the term is deceivingly inaccurate. Moreover, if cross-examination is an art, it stands to reason that it would be very difficult to teach its techniques. After all, a student can be taught art appreciation but she can hardly be taught how to be an artist. "Art" may be pleasing to those who prefer to think of themselves as courtroom artists, or to those whose egos require that they separate themselves from mere mortal lawyers. When applied to the task of cross-examination, "art" is misleading. Referring to cross-examination as an art conveys the erroneous message that some trial lawyers have the talent to cross-examine while others don't. It assumes cross-examination has no rules or fixed reference points. It cannot be taught or learned, but only viewed in wonderment and awe. A master of the "art" of cross-examination spins marvelous tales, befuddles the witness, and miraculously emerges with incredibly damaging omissions. Supposedly, this is performed in mysterious ways that mere lawyers cannot possibly comprehend, let alone learn.

This book wholly and flatly rejects such narrow and self-congratulatory thinking. Good cross-examination is the work of a studied legal technician skilled in the methods of witness examination. There are facts to be introduced, points to be made, theories to be supported, and opponent theories to be undermined. All of these things are accomplished through questions that introduce facts. Thorough preparation, mastery of technique, and execution of a solid plan produce more courtroom victories than all the flash, glitz, and strokes of supposed courtroom brilliance combined.

Cross-examination is a science. It has firmly established rules, guidelines, identifiable techniques, and definable methods, all acting to increase the cross-examiner's ability to prevail. The elements of successful cross-examination can be described, practiced, and learned. Willing trial lawyers can acquire and develop those skills.

Certainly, all cross-examiners experience occasions when the cross-examination goes beautifully. The best-prepared attorneys frequently make cross-examination appear easy, or at least easier. But it is preparation supported by scientific principles of cross-examination that paves an easier path through the cross-examination of an adverse witness.

§ 1.04   Control Under Trial Conditions

Even though cross-examination is a science, it is not performed under laboratory conditions. It comes about under the most difficult of circumstances. The opponent and the witnesses to be cross-examined are there to defeat the cross-examiner's best efforts. The courtroom is controlled at various times by various forces: the judge, the jury, the client, the client's family, the opponents, opposing parties, and witnesses. There are many forces competing for control. Cross-examination is the phase of trial in which the trial advocate is least in control. In opening statement and closing argument, the lawyer is allowed to perform with little or no interruption or fear of contemporaneous contradiction. Where voir dire is allowed, the give and take between lawyer and prospective juror is seldom rancorous or hostile. In direct examination, the lawyer is working with a witness rehearsed by the lawyer and who ordinarily agrees with the lawyer's goals. None of these circumstances describe cross-examination.

While historically all authors agree that controlling the witness is critical to a good cross-examination, there is precious little written about how to develop that control. Control is the central concept of this work. Methods of establishing courtroom control through cross-examination are the baseline of these materials. There are, however, many procedural and environmental factors that aid the cross-examiner's quest for courtroom control.

Unlike voir dire, opening statements, and closing arguments, cross-examination rarely has time restrictions. To unduly restrict the time needed for cross-examination would violate fundamental due process fair trial rights.

The cross-examiner controls all aspects of questions asked. The cross-examiner controls the number of questions asked and the speed with which the questions are put to the witness. The cross-examiner controls the witness's duration on the stand. The cross-examiner may compel the witness to move about the courtroom by referring to demonstrative aids. The cross-examiner may compel the witness to remain seated. It is fair to say that this is the phase of the trial in which the advocate is freest in the courtroom.

§ 1.05   Rethinking the Goals of Modern Cross-Examination

Cross-examination has historically been viewed as an effort in damage control. Too much time and teaching has reinforced the notion that cross-examination is a dangerous thing to be forgone or sharply limited. As a result, the process of cross-examination has been viewed as combat. Past techniques were geared for battles with the witness. They were premised on the notion that a witness called by the opponent is only to be beaten down or minimized, and seldom to be gainfully employed as a provider of constructive information for the cross-examiner's theory of the case. It has been drummed into all trial lawyers that every witness called by the opponent is predisposed to obstruct the cross-examination by interruption, denial, and confusion. As a result of such teaching, too many lawyers believe developing the truth through cross-examination is too arduous. It is better to wait for the friendly witness who can be taken through a direct examination.

Certainly there are elements of attack within some cross-examinations. But more fundamentally, cross-examination is an opportunity to elicit favorable facts as opposed to simply attacking unfavorable testimony. The modern advocate must condition herself to expose and develop the truth of the case through witnesses called by the opponent

Cross-examination is how an advocate shows a witness's direct testimony is out of context, exaggerated, or simply false. More than that, cross-examination is a unique opportunity to build the cross-examiner's theory of the case and to insert helpful facts into the story. This relieves the cross-examiner of the burden of building a case solely through the cross-examiner's witnesses and client.

§ 1.06　The State of Modern Cross-Examination

Any objective observer viewing trials, particularly viewing cross-examinations, would state that the field of cross-examination is generally in a state of disrepair. This is not because cross-examination is an art and there are too few artists practicing law. The problem is that law schools have abandoned the task of training competent trial lawyers. The profession has generally failed to dissect the field of cross-examination and learn its components. By calling it "art," lawyers were in essence instructed, "You either have it or you don't."

At the beginning of the 20th century, John W. Davis, in the foreword to *The Art of Cross-Examination*, stated:

> There are, as Mr. Wellman points out, *no set rules* that will fit all situations unless in deed it be the one that he reinforces with his quotation from Josh Billings: "When you strike 'ile,' stop boring; many a man has bore clean through and let the 'ile' run out of the bottom." (Emphasis added.)

When examined, in fact, this "ile" rule is not a helpful rule at all. The cross-examiner only knows that she has violated the rule after it has been violated — not a useful guideline.

Francis Wellman, in *The Art of Cross-Examination*, cautions:

> In all of your cross-examinations, never lose control of the witness; confine his answers to the exact questions you ask. He will try to dodge direct answers or if forced to answer directly, will attempt an antiqualification or an explanation that will rob his answer of the benefit it might otherwise be to you.

As critical as this advice may be, no direction or suggestion is offered on *how* the advocate can control the witness by narrowing the field of possible evasion. No suggestion is given as to how the advocate can reliably introduce facts through a hostile witness by correctly structuring the question. No rules are given as to how the advocate discourages and responds to the unresponsive answer. But there are techniques to accomplish these goals. These techniques result in better control of the areas of cross-examination and better control of witnesses (even those who seek to be beyond control).

It is not enough to tell trial lawyers what not to do. It is a decidedly inefficient form of instruction to educate lawyers to recognize when things have gone wrong without simultaneously teaching methods to diminish the chances that things will go wrong. It is impossible to learn how to cross-examine by learning only what the lawyer must not do. It is equally impossible to become a better cross-examiner by being repeatedly told that control is essential, without being schooled in the techniques needed to establish and maintain witness control. Such techniques do exist and have existed for centuries. Perhaps, they were set aside in the quest to turn cross-examination into an ego contest or an attempt to "beat" the witness. There exists a body of cross-examination techniques that not only safely produce useful material, but also provide methods to take advantage of unexpected opportunities offered by the witness. This book is built on that fundamental premise.

§ 1.07   The Ten Commandments of Cross-Examination: A Turning Point

A history of American cross-examination unequivocally shows that for 200 years, no organized effort was made to discover and define the set of principles that underlie successful cross-examinations. Judge Irving Younger's inspiring lecture, "The Ten Commandments of Cross-Examination," stands as an initial effort to codify some rules of successful cross-examination.

This superb and entertaining lecture at last awakened interest in the science of cross-examination. However, as a teaching device, "The Ten Commandments," had severe limitations. "The Ten Commandments" contained many admonitions that the cross-examiner would recognize that she had broken only *after* breaking the commandment. Instructing the lawyer not to ask one question too many is akin to instructing the tennis player to not miss their first serve. While the advice is undoubtedly correct, its accomplishment is more difficult. The cross-examiner recognizes this important commandment right after she has breached it. There is no success awarded for that late recognition.

Nonetheless, "The Ten Commandments" served to acquaint large numbers of trial lawyers with the concept that successful cross-examination has identifiable guidelines. It was a beginning. The profession owes a debt to Judge Younger for his pioneering work in teaching trial advocacy. Trial lawyers must now take the next step by recognizing, analyzing, and discussing the modern techniques of cross-examination.

§ 1.08   Attaining Basic Competency in an Era of Fewer Trials

In the past, the popular conception was that trial skills could only be learned in trial. Years of trial work were required before basic competency could be reached in the skill of cross-examination. The implication was that an indeterminate number of clients would suffer as the cross-examiner learned her trade.

This book flatly rejects that view as unrealistic and pessimistic. Maybe it was true in a different time. If so, it was advice based on an adversary system that had room for an enormous number of small trials. It also required many unsuspecting clients. There was a time when the courts were open to the small commercial or personal injury trial. Many more cases went to trial and the cases were small enough that they provided a suitable training ground. With the advent of what is termed "tort reform" and the creation of tort thresholds that require a minimum amount of damage in order to bring a personal injury action, opportunities for small civil trials dried up.

In the criminal arena, the creation of public defender systems has had an unintended consequence on the trial bar. In the time before the proliferation of public defender systems, many lawyers in private practice were appointed to defend criminal cases. The advent of public defender systems in the 1970s meant that the vast majority of criminal cases were funneled into a much smaller number of full-time criminal defense attorneys. While public defender systems greatly serve the interests of criminal justice, lawyers now have fewer opportunities to establish their trial skills in criminal cases.

However, trial is not the exclusive venue in which to learn the techniques of cross-examination. Trial work and cross-examination, in particular, call upon specific skills. And those skills can be acquired without sacrificing clients or decades to the task.

Trial lawyers are confronting the happy realization that there are methods for the preparation and delivery of predictably successful cross-examinations. These methods can be defined, explained, and learned. As a result, a studious trial lawyer can dramatically improve her abilities as a cross-examiner through methods that are not exclusively or even predominantly confined to the courtroom.

§ 1.09   Identifying the Building Blocks of Successful Cross-Examinations

A cross-examiner who studies and follows the only three rules of cross-examination (chapter 8), prepares properly for the hearing (see chapters 3-7, 9-11), and who organizes her cross-examinations around a theory of the case (chapter 2), through the use of the chapter method (chapter 9), will become not merely a competent cross-examiner, but a truly formidable cross-examiner.

The science of cross-examination does not operate on hunches. The science of cross-examination does not depend on oratorical tricks and showmanship. The science of cross-examination relies on the marshaling of facts in support of a series of previously identified goals. It recognizes the importance of the formation of questions designed to efficiently introduce facts necessary to prove or support those goals and the logical sequencing of those questions. These techniques are aimed at bolstering a defined theory of the case or undermining the opponent's theory of the case.

The science of cross-examination equips the cross-examiner with the ability to predict where and how a witness will seek to evade, while simultaneously equipping the cross-examiner with techniques to limit the evasions and minimize the effect of witness evasions. This is not to say that the "unknown" will be eliminated from the trial. The infinite variations of human behavior mean that the unpredictable will sometimes occur in cross-examination. But with solid cross-examination techniques, the advocate can sharply reduce the likelihood that the witness will respond in an unpredictable or harmful fashion. Moreover, within the science of cross-examination there exists a body of techniques to take advantage of the witness who offers up unanticipated answers (see chapter 26, *Loops, Double Loops, and Spontaneous Loops*).

Much in the same sense that higher mathematics cannot be learned without having an understanding and ability to add and subtract, the scientific techniques of cross-examination require that the basic building blocks be mastered before more advanced levels can be understood and properly applied in the courtroom.

For instance, the ability to perform a trilogy (to impress upon the jury a certain goal or theme fact) (see chapter 25, *Trilogies*) is dependent on the use of the only three rules of cross-examination (see chapter 8, *The Only Three Rules of Cross-Examination*). A spontaneous loop is a tremendously effective technique to silence runaway witnesses and to make the cross-examination appear brilliantly off-the-cuff (see chapter 26, *Loops, Double Loops, and Spontaneous Loops*). This technique also requires adherence to the three rules, development of the theory of the case (see chapter 2, *Developing a Theory of the Case*), and the proper preparation of the cross-examination material (see chapter 9, *The Chapter Method of Cross-Examination*).

§ 1.10   Science Versus Art

Trial lawyers who steadfastly rely on the basic building blocks of cross-examination can frequently elevate the effectiveness of their cross-examinations. In essence, the goal of the accomplished cross-examiner is not to create a single beautiful cross-examination, or to develop the ability to occasionally devastate a witness on cross-examination. The goal of this book is to raise the advocate's success rate in each and every cross-examination. The object is to score on the factual points. Consistent and confident execution of the basic techniques of cross-examination creates the aura of a devastating cross-examiner. However, the objective of a solid trial lawyer should not be to devastate the occasional witness. To make witness devastation a goal is to place the ego needs of a cross-examiner over the factual needs of the case. Cross-examination is not a contest between the witness and the lawyer. Cross-examination is simply another opportunity to build or teach her case.

The reliance on basic techniques of cross-examination is the surest way to become known as an excellent cross-examiner. Although, it is not the cross-examination war story that is the goal of the mature advocate. Resulting cross-examinations may be less dramatic but victories will be easily apparent. The lawyer can become a truly formidable advocate without resorting to showmanship or risky strategies. In fact, the truly formidable advocate renounces showmanship as a weapon. She approaches each cross-examination with knowledge of the purposes of that cross-examination, employs a cross-examination plan designed to establish particular factual goals, and uses the techniques of cross-examination most helpful in establishing those factual goals.

When methods of cross-examination are refined into a science and techniques appropriately applied by the cross-examiner, the cross-examiner is free to listen better in the courtroom and to take advantage of unexpected opportunities. Less time is spent considering what to ask and how to ask it, as those questions have been settled on by cross-examination preparation techniques (chapters 5-7 and chapter 10). Mastery of the techniques permits the cross-examiner to work with such confidence that the cross-examiner is now free to consider additional factors such as voice, movement, and phraseology. Trial lawyers free the talent within by applying the scientific approach to cross-examination preparation and delivery.

§ 1.11   Application to All Trial-like Settings

This book presents a detailed treatment of cross-examination techniques. It does not differentiate between jury or court trials or between trial and non-trial evidentiary hearings. The same principles of cross-examination preparation and delivery can be used in all settings in which a witness gives testimony and is subject to cross-examination. Granted, there are undoubtedly times in depositions and other pre-trial hearings in which the lawyer runs different risks than at trial. This means that on selected occasions, the lawyer can employ a different set of techniques within a non-trial hearing. For the sake of brevity, the book will often speak of the effect of a particular technique on a jury. More accurately, however, these techniques are equally useful in any cross-examination encounter occurring under the rules of trial.

§ 1.12   Overview of Comprehensive Analysis

The book studies and discusses at length the integral relationship of cross-examination to the theory of the case and the development of themes, theme lines, and theme phrases of the case.

Because no cross-examination can hope to be effective without thorough and complete preparation, a large portion of the book deals with the overlooked techniques of cross-examination preparation.

The book suggests that it is helpful to conceptually develop the case in a different order than trial or historical conceptual paradigms. This book presents a method of preparation and organization that centers on the development of the cross-examination and then builds outwards both toward jury selection and toward closing argument and instructions. This method of preparation permits much faster preparation. It is suggested that it is also the most realistic and comprehensive method of preparing for trial.

§ 1.13   Why the Advocate Can't Wait Until Closing to Win the Case

> The issue of a cause rarely depends on a speech (opening statements and closing arguments) and is but seldom even affected by it, but there is never a cause contested, the result of which is not mainly dependent upon the skill with which the advocate conducts his cross-examination.

Lord Brougham

To put it in a more modern way, the lawyer closes for show, but she crosses for dough. Most often, the outcome of the trial depends on cross-examination, be it a civil or criminal case. Even good opening statements are ineffective unless supported by facts developed at trial. Closing arguments come too late. The jury is too sophisticated to be swayed by arguments advanced in a closing that are unsupported by facts developed on cross-examination. Juries and judges require and desire facts.

§ 1.14   Drawbacks of Closing Argument Preparation Systems

Some trial lawyers have been taught that it is best to prepare a trial through the reverse preparation system (that is, preparing the closing argument first and working backwards). Such a system has major drawbacks.

Closing argument-centered preparation is unduly time-consuming. Trial lawyers can often construct a closing argument even as early as the first client meeting. The problem is that as the other side develops its theory of the case, the advocate's closing argument must be modified, restructured, and in some cases abandoned because of "facts" that are indisputable. If these "facts" are destructive of the trial lawyer's closing, then her closing *must* be modified, restructured, or abandoned.

These modifications leave the trial lawyer with little preparation of value. Hours of preparation can yield precious little usable material. This process of elimination (to find the best closing argument) becomes time-consuming and frustrating to overburdened trial lawyers.

§ 1.15   Advantage of Cross-Examination-Centered Trial Preparation

On the other hand, when the major cross-examinations are thoroughly understood and prepared, the theory of the case and its theme phrases inevitably follow. A powerful closing argument flows naturally from the planned cross-examinations. Preparation of the major cross-examinations of the case exposes the indisputable facts that the trial lawyer must address. The lawyer preparing for trial must also evaluate what facts will realistically be available to the other side through the direct testimony of her own witnesses. From this preparation of the major cross-examinations and analysis of the cross-examination of her witnesses, a stronger closing argument will develop.

By working backwards from the planned cross-examinations, it will become very easy to develop the powerful theory-driven, fact-intensive opening statement. From the opening statement flow the issues to be discussed with a jury in voir dire.

The direct examinations are then developed as enhancements and supplementation of the facts admitted through the cross-examinations. Instead of relying solely on the cross-examiner's own witnesses to support a theory of the case, the trial attorney views the opponent's witnesses as equal opportunities to develop her theory of the case. (It must be noted that only prosecutors are saddled with the task of relying primarily on direct examinations to build their case. However, every technique discussed in this book is equally useful to a prosecutor faced with the important and difficult task of cross-examining the defendant or the witnesses called in support of the defendant with little or no discovery.)

§ 1.16   Preparation Enhances All Techniques

Preparation is still the single best trial technique. This book embraces this philosophy and therefore spends considerable time discussing methods and techniques for the preparation of cross-examinations. The systematic preparation of cross-examination encompasses the organization of cross-examination, including, the organization of the file, trial notebook, exhibits, documents, and chapters of cross-examination. Because of the chapter format of cross-examination, which builds upon the materials created through cross-examination preparation systems, the amount of time lost from haphazard searches, unorganized materials, and lack of focus is dramatically reduced.

The techniques of cross-examination can both reduce associated risks from cross-examination and produce greater opportunities to establish favorable facts for the cross-examiner's theory of the case. A detailed analysis of impeachment techniques and multiple techniques to control the runaway witness is presented in depth. The risks of redirect and recross, and using recross to produce theme results also are discussed.

Having established and developed these fundamental building blocks of cross-examination, the book will then discuss techniques useful in the delivery of cross-examination, including using silence, loops, trilogies, and primacy and recency.

§ 1.17   The Advantages of Consistent Labeling of Techniques — Communicating in the Language of Trial Work

Lawyers use labels. They use the word "cross" as shorthand for cross-examination of a witness. Personal injury lawyers use the shorthand "P.I." as an abbreviation for personal injury litigation. Criminal defense lawyers use "P.C." as shorthand for probable cause in a criminal case.

In other professions and trades, there is shorthand labeling for various activities that that trade performs. Any electrician knows what a "220" is, just as any carpenter knows what a "two by four" is. These are labels that permit persons within a profession to communicate quickly and accurately.

The volatility and spontaneity of trial work requires that lawyers be able to communicate quickly and accurately. Throughout this book, techniques will be labeled and those labels will be used in a uniform manner. There is a reason for this. There is no extra time in trial preparation or trial. Lawyers need to be able to communicate with each other concerning useful techniques that might be employed in the cross-examination of a particular witness.

For example, lawyers who become accustomed to thinking and talking in terms of "chapters" of cross-examination have a better ability to picture such chapters, and to create an appropriate chapter of cross-examination under very stressful conditions.

The "sequences of cross-examination" is now a phrase understood by cross-examiners, and as a result, a lawyer can suggest to her co-counsel a change of sequence and be understood. The words "loop," "trilogy," "spontaneous loop," and "safe haven" all becomes terms that can be employed in trial as they become part of the cross-examiner's standard vocabulary.

This critical need for quick, accurate shorthand communication demands these terms to be used uniformly at trial so that lawyers can communicate accurately in the hectic environment of trial work. Throughout this book, such terms will be defined on its first usage. Thereafter, whenever that term is used, it will be in accordance with that definition.

§ 1.18 Successful Cross-Examination Is More Dependent on Facts Than Personality

Obviously these techniques are designed to improve cross-examination skills in the courtroom in front of a jury. Not only do they teach the jury, they minimize the need for judge's involvement during the cross-examination. These techniques are founded on the right to cross-examine or to use leading questions while simultaneously diminishing the role of glitz, showmanship, or any other courtroom trickery. A cross-examination style based upon mastery of the facts relaxes the judge and makes for a more persuasive presentation to the jury. As these techniques point out, the cross-examiner can give appropriate emphasis to critical points without the need to raise her voice. The techniques of modern cross-examination depend upon well-understood teaching methods not force of personality.

§ 1.19 Shorter Questions = Quicker Trials

When experienced cross-examiners are presented with the only three rules of cross-examination (see chapter 8, *The Only Three Rules of Cross-Examination*), and particularly the one fact per question rule, they often ask: "Do judges really let you get away with such a slow presentation?"

The answer is yes. Judges allow this kind of presentation because the method is not slow. An organized cross-examination designed to accomplish a series of specific goals moves more quickly. There is purpose. There is rhythm. By phrasing questions in the short, concise, one-fact per-question manner, the cross-examination actually moves faster. By forming groups of questions in the chapter method (see chapter 9, *The Chapter Method of Cross-Examination*), the advocate avoids skipping from one area to another and then skipping back to a partially developed topic requiring additional questions in order to be fully developed.

The rule of one new fact per question means that there are no compound questions, and therefore no objections to compound questions. The use of leading questions means that there is no real confusion on the part of the witness as to what was asked. Experienced trial judges recognize the difference in a trial conducted by a lawyer employing modern techniques of examining witnesses. Judges recognize that the cross-examination portion of the case moves with precision toward identifiable goals of importance.

By developing the witness examinations around an articulable theory of the case the lawyer can establish clear-cut goals. She can develop those goals in a fact-by-fact method, so that the judge is not put into a position to guess where the cross-examination is going, whether a goal has been reached, or whether certain facts have been developed that would support a conclusion to be argued in closing.

More often than not in non-jury settings, judges will advise cross-examiners to "break down the question into smaller parts" when a witness seems to have trouble answering a longer question. This is the same philosophy that gave birth to the one fact per question rule. Judges have praised this scientific approach, inasmuch as it eliminates needless rambling.

§ 1.20   Cross-Examination: Danger and Opportunity

The Chinese pictograph for "crisis" is made up of two other pictographs: "danger" and "opportunity." So, too, the crisis of cross-examination represents both danger and opportunity.

All trial lawyers, from the neophyte to the veteran, experience cross-examination as a form of crisis control. Physically, cross-examination raises the pulse rate and the blood pressure. Mentally, it produces anxiety, perhaps even fear. This is normal. After all, the opponent puts up the witness for a purpose. In all likelihood, that purpose was achieved in the direct testimony.

§ 1.21   Controlling the Danger

All cross-examiners see the danger attendant to the process of cross-examination. Few recognize all the opportunities that cross-examination provides.

The first and best method of controlling the danger is detailed in the material dealing with preparation. Preparation is the single best method of controlling the dangers of cross- examination. Having fully prepared, the lawyer can move into positive side of cross-examination: taking advantage of opportunities.

The central focus of the advocate must be organization of the cross-examination and control of the witness. These are accomplished through the preparation systems combined with the three rules of cross-examination. The three rules of cross-examination must become a brain stem function for the cross-examiner.

The cross-examiner must instinctively revert to declaratory statements ending with a question mark. She must use the one-fact-per-question approach, designed to accomplish a specific goal in a logical manner, moving from the general to the specific.

Whether the cross-examiner has months or mere minutes to prepare, the cross-examiner will mentally and, if time allows, physically prepare chapters of cross-examination, to organize and orient the cross-examination in an understandable manner for the jury. All case preparation is explored from the viewpoint of the theory of the case. Theme lines are developed early and often.

§ 1.22   Techniques Designed to Enhance Opportunities and to Highlight the Most Important Facts Developed in Cross-Examination

One of the chief downsides to the outdated and defensive views of cross-examination is that it proscribed methods supposedly designed to avoid damage to the cross-examiner's case. While this is unquestionably an important aspect of cross-examination, too often the cross-examiner was so preoccupied with not being harmed on cross-examination that she overlooked the tremendous opportunities provided by cross-examination for the production of favorable information that supported the cross-examiner's theory.

There are techniques designed to allow a fact finder to better understand the important facts being scored by the cross-examiner. Looping, beginning with the construction of a basic loop, and moving to the development of double loops, and finally the recognition and crafting of spontaneous loops is the first of many advanced techniques that are based on the basic building blocks of cross-examination. If the building blocks are well established and developed, the more advanced techniques will be readily learned and applied.

Trilogies are wonderfully effective in cross-examination, establishing a theme fact and making it unforgettable. The concept of trilogies is adaptable equally well to opening statements and closing arguments.

Numerous other advanced techniques are developed and discussed using rules of construction and examples. These techniques are born from an understanding and mastery of the basic building blocks of cross-examination. These advance techniques include primacy and recency, diminishing and building the issue, creation and uses of silence, voice, movement, body language, timing, theme congruency, and juxtaposition. Specific applications of the scientifically developed techniques, both basic and advanced, are then provided for the reader.

Finally, exercises are provided to gain experience without the traditional requirement of doing so while on the lawyer is on her feet in actual trial at the expense of a client. These exercises, as highlighted by "cluster cross," were developed and continue to be developed as a method not only to learn, but completely master the basic scientific building blocks of cross-examination, and practice and learn the more advanced techniques before the would-be cross-examiner has ever uttered a question under fire in the courtroom.

§ 1.23   Achieving the Value of Preparation

It must be emphasized that the preparation to perform a technique allows a lawyer to make that technique her own. Instead of thinking of trial as the only place to learn how to do trial work, this book advocates that techniques be practiced before trial so that they will feel natural when used in trial. The preparation systems and cross-examination techniques discussed throughout this book can be practiced and learned outside of trial so that they can be employed easily in a trial. Like all other skills, cross-examination preparation and delivery systems are best mastered by repetition. The cross-examiner acquires the skills more quickly by practicing the techniques in non-trial hearings where witnesses must be examined through cross-examination. The more a lawyer practices these techniques outside of trial, the easier the lawyer will find it to use these techniques in trial.

§ 1.24   Scientific Methods of Cross-Examination Interlock to Create a System of Cross-Examination

An important goal of this book is to provide an integrated, scientific method of cross-examination. The chapter method of cross-examination explains how the logical development of one chapter supports and interconnects with other chapters of cross-examination. The progress of each chapter makes it more likely that the subsequent chapters will produce favorable answers that are immediately understood and appreciated by the fact finder. The basic rules of cross-examination provide all the structure needed to employ the more advanced techniques of cross-examination. The scientific preparation of cross-examination supports the ability to control the field of cross-examination and thereby use the hostile witness to establish important facts.

The techniques of leading question formation support the cross-examiner's control of the witness. Each technique has a purpose and a place in the trial plan. The employment of a particular technique of cross-examination often provides the foundation for more advanced techniques.

No technique is particularly difficult to learn. Each technique is easily learned alone and used under the stressful conditions of trial work. Any technique that is complicated is, for that very reason, an invalid technique. Trial work is tough enough without introducing hyper-technical theories of cross-examination. Advanced cross-examination is often nothing more than the recognition and use of cross-examination techniques appropriate to the situation. It is often helpful to study the material of one chapter or technique in conjunction with another chapter or technique. To aid in this process, when discussing any particular technique there is frequently noted where in the book other related material can be found (see chapter 12, *Employing Primacy and Recency*).

§ 1.25   The Snowball Effect of Sound Preparation Systems Accompanied by the Employment of Fundamental Techniques of Cross-Examination

The use of scientific preparation systems and sound techniques of cross-examination have a snowball effect on opponents, their clients, and their witnesses. Most lawyers practice in a relatively limited geographic area. Now, aided by computer databases, it is possible to track the career and reputation of an opponent who has come from far way to try this case. The word gets out that certain lawyers are "excellent" cross-examiners. When this word gets out, opponents don't look forward to having their witnesses face that cross-examiner. Opponents do not look forward to having to engage in the taking of testimony against that type of cross-examiner. It would perhaps be unfair to call this technique the intimidation of opponents, but it is fair to call it a reality that lawyers evaluate the abilities of their opponents when they evaluate their case for trial.

The preparation system and techniques in this book lead to the cross-examiner's control of the witness and a seemingly natural ability to group together favorable facts in order to tell the many stories that combined to make up a case. As a result, opponents who have learned to rely on flashy techniques in the ability to talk glibly with little preparation come to understand that those skills will not match up well with a lawyer who relies on intensive preparation.

§ 1.26   Strategic Value of This System at Trial

Opponents can recognize the ability of the cross-examiner to skillfully control both the witness and the subject matter examined upon in the cross-examination. As a result, the opponent must continually analyze and re-evaluate the risks of calling each of their witnesses. Opponents exposed to these systems understand that there are problems with virtually every witness, and that the skillful cross-examiner is likely to find those problem areas and seize upon them.

As a result of this realization it is not unusual for the structure of a trial to change dramatically, not simply because of what the jury hears but also because of what the jury never hears. Often an opponent declines to call a witness out of the realization that the cross-examination would be so effective that the value of the witness would be destroyed or that the points to be made with the witness are likely to be outweighed by the points that can be made by the cross-examiner.

The trial lawyer must always bear in mind that the easiest evidence with which to deal is the evidence that did not come in. From a cross-examiner's viewpoint, witnesses who never take the stand cannot help the opponent.

§ 1.27   The Techniques of Cross-Examination Encourage Outbursts by the Witness

When the cross-examiner controls the flow of information through leading questions, and through the chapter method of cross-examination, frustration builds up in the witness. This frustration is vented through vocal outbursts by the witness. A witness seldom blurts out something calculated to help their side of the case. The witness who cannot control his emotions in a courtroom cannot effectively persuade a jury. The technique of spontaneous looping, discussed at length in chapter 26 is built around the recognition that hostile witnesses frequently provide the most useful information when they are attempting to dodge a question or respond with anything other than a "yes" answer.

In preliminary matters, and particularly in recorded statements and depositions, a tightly controlled examination leads the witness to a frustration level that gives birth to spontaneous outbursts. These outbursts provide additional opportunities for the cross-examiner to learn more facts, which can be used to craft better chapters of cross-examination. The old adage that people don't make good decisions when they are angry or frustrated certainly applies on the witness stand. The cross-examiner must listen closely for helpful information contained in these outbursts. This information can then be followed up by closed-ended questions to take advantage of this new information.

§ 1.28   Use of the Only Three Rules in Framing Pleadings

The three fundamental rules of cross-examination are applicable to pleadings as well as to trial. Take, as a starting point, Rule 8 of the Federal Rules of Civil Procedure. "General Rules of Pleadings" states that "[a] pleading which sets forth a claim for relief, whether an original claim, counterclaim, cross-claim, or third party claim . . . shall contain . . . *a* short plain statement of the claim . . . ." (Emphasis added.)

It is easy for a plaintiff's lawyer to plead civil cases in a style that sets forth one specific fact per numbered paragraph. In that way, when an answer is received the plaintiff knows exactly what is and what is not admitted.

An example of the old way:

3.

The plaintiff was traveling south on Ashley Street, the defendant was traveling north on Ashley Street and the defendant negligently ran into the plaintiff's vehicle.

Answers and Defenses

3.

The allegations in Paragraph 3 are denied.

In the former example, the plaintiff is left with a general denial of the paragraph and does not know what he or she now must prove factually. But consider the following form of pleading on the same matter:

Allegations	Answers and Defenses
3. The Plaintiff was traveling south on Ashley Street.	**3.** The allegation in Paragraph 3 is admitted.
4. The Defendant was traveling north on Ashley Street.	**4.** The allegation in Paragraph 4 is admitted.
5. The Plaintiff's and the Defendant's cars collided.	**5.** The allegation in Paragraph 5 is admitted.
6. The Defendant was negligent in colliding with the Plaintiff.	**6.** The allegation in Paragraph 6 is denied. The Defendant specifically denies any and all acts of alleged negligence.

In this example, the plaintiff now has an admission in three of the four paragraphs. There is now no issue as to the location of the plaintiff's vehicle, the location of the defendant's vehicle, and the fact that the vehicles collided. The only issue now to be presented is whether the defendant was negligent.

This pleading was developed in conjunction with the cross-examination rule of one fact per question. If there is only one fact per paragraph in a pleading, that fact will either be admitted or denied. If there is only one fact per question, the witness must either admit or deny the fact. In both cases, the lawyer knows exactly what the witness is admitting or denying. Both in pleading and in cross-examining, the scientific approach frames issues better and allows the lawyer to better control the field of inquiry.

§ 1.29   The One Fact Per Question Method of Framing Motions

This technique of setting forth the pertinent facts, one new fact at a time, is equally applicable to motions. If motions to suppress, or motions in limine, or even motions to continue, are set out in one fact for each numbered paragraph, the judge can quickly understand what factual issues are in dispute and what factual issues are conceded. The judge may now request the opponent to respond orally, paragraph by paragraph. This deprives the opponent of the opportunity to give a long, rambling, non-responsive answer. This factual approach simplifies the judge's chores. If presented in a persuasive factual sequence, this better ensures a favorable ruling to the pleader.

If the court realizes that the first five paragraphs of a six-paragraph motion are admitted, then the court, by common sense, begins to realize that there must be some merit to the motion. The pleader should fashion all pleadings to maximize the admissions in order to help convince the court that the motion has merit.

This book's application goes far beyond the obvious application to questioning witnesses in front of a jury. It becomes an outline to the practice of trial work.

§ 1.30   Time-Saving Aspects of Cross-Examination-Centered Preparation

Every lawyer wishes she had more time to prepare. A lawyer only has a given period of time to prepare. As a result, time must be most profitably used. Less time wasted is the equivalent of having more time. Using the systems of cross-examination-centered preparation saves time. Preparation time is decreased, since areas not related to the opposing theories of the case are not explored. Whatever preparation time available is devoted to identifying and preparing for goals obtainable through cross-examination. Therefore, more time is left for productive purposes. The method of framing cross-examination questions is simple and certain, reducing considerations about how to phrase a question, in what order to place questions, or how to organize the cross-examination. That has been taken care of by the three rules (see chapter 8, *The Only Three Rules of Cross-Examination*), the chapter preparation (see chapter 10, *Page Preparation of Cross-Examination*) and the appropriate sequence of presentation (see chapter 11, *Sequences of Cross-Examination*) of the cross-examination. This is left for creative thought.

§ 1.31   Preparation Leads to Greater Creativity

The scientific approach frees the cross-examiner to devote more time and creative energy to the presentation of cross-examination. A lawyer at the podium who is searching for the next area, who is trying to frame up the next question, or who is trying to remember other facts that could be of use, is ill-equipped to rise to her greatest level of proficiency. A lawyer who approaches the cross-examination with facts organized in the chapter method is far more confident and therefore far more able to listen to answers and make spontaneous judgments concerning strategy, voice, pace, and movement.

The scientific approach to cross-examination frees the creative energies inside the cross-examiner in a way that permits the cross-examiner to have the time and energy to utilize the more sophisticated techniques of cross-examination. See chapter 17, *Impeachment by Omission*, chapter 21, *Creation and Uses of Silence* and chapter 22, *Voice, Movement, Body Language, and Timing*. Secure in the material she has prepared, the cross-examiner is free to consider how best to present the material.

§ 1.32   Adding Technique to Technique to Build Cross-Examination

The modern techniques of cross-examination may be learned step by step. Each technique builds in part on the others. It is a total system. A simple technique, once learned and mastered, supports a more advanced technique.

Once the techniques can be performed consistently, the level of cross-examination is raised. It can be raised yet again by the use of conscious, motivational word choices, and conscious use of combinations of the techniques.

§ 1.33   Techniques Are Not Used to Accomplish Style Points

Much has been made about the value of employing scientifically based techniques of cross-examination. A word of warning, however. It is the effect of the techniques that is sought, not recognition of the techniques themselves. The fine cross-examiner seeks results, not merely style points. Few of these techniques will be recognized for the skills that they are. The reward is that the lawyers, judges, opponents, witnesses, juries, and clients will recognize the products of good cross-examination.

The thought needed to frame a beautiful trilogy will be lost on everyone else in the courtroom, save the cross examiner. The technique of the trilogy concept may be lost, but the effect will not be lost on the jury. The reality of the intense devotion of time and energy before the cross examination ever began will be lost on all. It is not in the least necessary that others recognize the specific techniques. The greatest tribute to any cross examiner is the verdict in favor of her client. The science and techniques set forth in this book are designed to assist in attaining that goal.

§ 1.34   Acknowledging the Difficulty of Cross-Examination

None of this is meant to imply that cross-examination is easy. But it can be made easier. The preparation of cross-examination cannot be eliminated, but it can be made shorter. Cross-examination cannot be made perfect, but it can be made more productive. All of these things can be accomplished through systems of preparation and techniques of delivery. If, after considering the material in this book, these techniques remain unclear, the fault is with the authors not the readers.

§ 1.35   Summary

Cross-examination is much more science and application of technique than it is art. The ability to cross-examine superbly (not just competently) can be taught, learned, and practiced. This book is devoted to that task.

Chapter 2

DEVELOPING A THEORY OF THE CASE

SYNOPSIS

§ 2.01 A Definition of a Theory of the Case

A theory of the case is a cogent statement of an advocate's position that justifies the verdict he or she is seeking. A theory of the case is not necessarily cast in the words that will be used with the jury, but words that are heard in the lawyer's mind as the case is prepared. The goal of the trial plan is to create factual support for the advocate's theory of the case. A secondary but important goal of the trial plan is to create factual attacks on the opponent's theory of the case.

Just as an artist paints a picture from a fixed perspective, so must the lawyer prepare the case from the perspective of his or her theory of the case. If the advocate has no theory of the case, she would have no unifying focal point to the various portions of the case, from voir dire through instructions. The theory of the case is not a strategy — it is a philosophy. It is the reasoning by which the advocate is entitled to the verdict she is seeking. The theory of the case is advanced through the trial strategy. That is, to say, all phases of the trial, from jury selection through closing argument, are executed in a manner designed to assist the fact finder in understanding and accepting the advocate's theory of the case.

The different phases of the trial interlock to advance the theory of the case. Jury selection is designed to acquaint the possible jurors with the theory of the case (to the real but limited extent that jury questioning can do so), to allow the possible jurors to discuss events in their lives that tie to the advocate's theory of the case, and eventually to select as jurors those individuals who appear most inclined to accept the advocate's theory of the case. The opening statement must unambiguously communicate the advocate's theory of the case and outline the facts that will support that theory. It must also communicate facts that hurt the opponent's theory. The factual support for a lawyer's theory of the case comes through the examination of witnesses, whether on direct examination or cross-examination, and the introduction of exhibits. Closing argument allows the lawyer to again clearly articulate the theory of the case and to package for the fact finder the facts that support that theory of the case. The lawyer is now able to discuss how the facts interact with the court's instructions of law to justify the verdict sought by the advocate.

The instructions of law are also a component of theory of the case. The instruction conference, although out of view of the jurors, is an important battleground over the theory of the case. Counsel seeks instructions of law that make the facts proved legally relevant to the verdict sought.

§ 2.02 A Theory of the Case Must Be Adopted Long Before Trial

Only by adopting a theory of the case can a lawyer prepare for trial. Only by adopting a theory of the case can a lawyer meaningfully conduct the various phases of a trial. Only by understanding a theory of the case can a fact finder appreciate the significance of the facts produced by an advocate and apply those facts to the instructions of law given by the court.

Trial advocacy does not begin when the parties announce they are ready for trial. The lawyer has come to court to advocate a position. Further, that position must be understood long before trial. The position may be thought of as a theory of the case.

The law permits a lawyer to try a lawsuit even if the lawyer has failed to adopt a well-defined theory of the case. The law cannot require good advocacy. Any lawyer is permitted to pick a jury, give an opening statement, examine and cross-examine witnesses, and give a closing argument. When lacking a theory of the case, voir dire, opening statement, direct and cross-examination, and closing argument are all seemingly unrelated elements of a trial. A lawyer may be technically proficient in the various aspects of trial. But lacking a unifying theory of the case, such a lawyer can win style points only, not the verdict. The verdict belongs to the advocate who has provided the fact finder with a theory of the case and has armed the fact finder with the facts necessary to support that theory. Lacking a theory of the case, the phases of trial are but academic exercise of the right to trial without a unifying purpose. In order to be successful, each part of trial must interconnect to support a fixed theory of the case understood by both the advocate and the fact finder.

§ 2.03   The Best Theories of the Case Reflect Common Life Experiences

The best theories of the case are those that are consistent with ordinary experiences felt by jurors. By selectively refreshing those memories and emotions during voir dire, the jurors are reminded that the dominant emotion of the case is an emotion that they too have felt under parallel (though not necessarily similar) circumstances.

For instance, assume the case involves an allegation of breach of fiduciary duty. Few jurors can be counted on to understand the term and to have experience with it. However many jurors have been in the situation where they very much counted on someone with superior knowledge to guide them in a matter of importance. Many jurors will also have experienced the feeling of having been let down. A prospective juror given the opportunity to talk about that life experience will recall the feeling of counting on somebody and the feeling of helplessness and even betrayal when their reliance on that person proved to be misplaced. An open-ended question in voir dire that allows a juror to talk about any such type of life experience will promote within that juror the dominant emotion of the plaintiff's case.

Assume an investment company is charged with intentionally failing to get its clients out of a failing investment. The defense is that the failure of the investment is obvious only in hindsight. A voir dire question might be: "Have you ever been second guessed or Monday morning quarterbacked about a decision you made?" The lawyer is attempting to selectively refresh a memory of an episode in which the person did the best he could with the information he had, but through no fault of his own made an erroneous judgment. Worse, the person suffered criticism by people who were not fair and who did not have to make the judgments on the spot. Now, after the situation is all too clear, those parties perceive that the solution was obvious and clues were missed.

Any prospective juror who has endured such an unpleasant experience and who recalls that episode will immediately be put into the frame of mind that understands both the defendant's theory of the case and the dominant emotion of that theory.

§ 2.04 The Theory of the Case Is the Factual Goal; the Trial Strategy Is That Combination of Techniques and Methods Adopted to Advance the Theory of the Case

The theory of the case is different than the strategy that advances that theory. The lawyer must adopt a theory of the case in order to craft a trial strategy designed to advance that theory of the case. In fact, a lawyer must adopt a theory of the case law before trial, since both formal and informal discovery, motion practice, pleadings, and virtually every other facet of pre-trial work should be designed to advance the theory of the case.

Just as an opponent may go to trial without a theory of the case, an opponent could have a theory of the case but lack any strategy whatsoever. An opponent with a theory but with no strategy engages in questioning that is not goal oriented, or in a voir dire that deals with issues that have nothing to do with the issues to be tried. Such lawyers use closing argument to attack the testimony of various witnesses as if the attack alone was the goal of the case. They fail to marshal the evidence in support of the particular theory of the case. During jury selection, lawyers ask jurors about their children or where they work. Often, these topics are unlikely to influence the jurors' perceptions of the lawyer's theory of the case and waste the lawyers' time. The lawyer may have a theory of the case, and he may have a strategy, but the two don't come together.

Conversely, some lawyers try cases with a strategy, but with no theory of the case. They cross-examine to prove every inconsistency, though they put up no affirmative notion of what it is their side is saying. Such lawyers simply lash out at everything proved by the opponent without regard for whether those facts have any bearing on the outcome sought by the cross-examining party.

Without benefit of a theory of the case, there is no unifying tactic, hub, or nexus to build the strategy around. Hence, the individual parts of the case are not only unrelated to each other, but also may prove to be internally inconsistent. Without a theory of the case, the lawyer might cross-examine on incompatible theories, such as identity of the defendant as the perpetrator and insanity of the defendant. All too often, insurance defense lawyers fight both liability and damages, when, in reality, they would have been better off conceding liability, and pitching the battle on the damage issue alone.

A theory of the case is the single dominant concept that links all other aspects of the trial. This overall philosophy guides the strategy of the trial. Its support is the goal of all trial tactics the trial lawyer adopts. By developing a theory of the case, counsel is able to define the field of battle. The theory of the case tells the lawyer what battles must be fought and what issues are immaterial to the outcome of the dispute.

§ 2.05　Developing a First Draft Theory of the Case

While it is very difficult to successfully try a case unguided by a theory of the case, it is not at all difficult to craft a theory of the case. While it is true that an advocate's theory of the case will go through several refinements, in most situations, an advocate will begin developing a useful theory of the case upon first hearing the client's recitation of the facts. Of course, this first client meeting can only acquaint the lawyer with a tiny fraction of all of the facts of the case, but the viewpoint of the client will likely lead to the first rough formulation of the theory of the case. Whether it is, "I acted in self-defense" or "If they had told me the truth I never would have invested" or "He stole from Peter to pay Paul" or "He cheated us so, of course, we fired him," the client can often (though unconsciously) articulate the starting point for the theory of the case. While the lawyer will refine the theory the case over time, even the act of refinement is based on an analysis of the facts available integrated into the working theory of the case.

The first draft of the theory of the case may be stated as broadly as, "The doctor did not do the tests necessary to diagnose my client's illness" or "The doctor was in a hurry, and that is how the bowel got perforated during surgery." In commercial litigation, the initial attempt at a theory might be, "The landlord is hiding all kinds of unrelated expenses under the guise of common area maintenance fees, and thereby jacking up my client's rent." In criminal defense work, a review of the facts may lead to a theory such as, "The snitch was about to go to prison until he made up a story about the defendant confessing" or "It was the deceased who kept advancing and pushing the fight, forcing my client to shoot in self-defense."

How can even a first draft theory of the case be adopted until all the facts or at least most of the facts are known? The answer is that the facts can only be understood in relationship to a proposed working theory of the case. Without a theory of the case, the facts may be understood individually but not collectively. In science, this is expressed as a hypothesis, which may become a theory. It is the goal of the lawyer to package the facts in groupings that support a theory of the case. The lawyer can only analyze her ability to successfully create these factual groupings if the lawyer can envision the points the lawyer wishes to make. Without a working theory of the case, the lawyer may well recognize packages of facts that prove a conclusion. But that conclusion may be of no value in relationship to what will eventually be the theory of the case. For instance, the facts may show that a witness is tremendously vulnerable on his version of a meeting. But that meeting may have no significance to the claims of the plaintiff, or the defenses that will eventually be advanced. Few lawyers can afford to study every fact as if they are of equal importance. By adopting a first draft theory of the case, the lawyer can review facts with a critical eye, and be more able to recognize the facts that are important and worth further development.

§ 2.06 Analysis of the Thought Process to Create a Theory of the Case

When discussing how to develop a case theory efficiently, it is sometimes difficult to conceptualize the thought process. Begin by locating facts beyond change. A likely starting point to find facts beyond change is in places where the facts, by definition, cannot change. Documents, photographs, tangible evidence, physical evidence, audio and videotapes, and the natural laws (e.g. gravity) are likely starting places.

Analyze the testimony of all potential witnesses to find additional potential facts beyond change. Remember — *beyond change* does not mean difficult to change — it means *impossible*.

Determine if the facts beyond change give rise to inferences beyond change that then in and of themselves become facts beyond change.

During this process, "feel" the dominant emotion or passion created by these facts. The dominant emotion or passion will be discerned while finding facts beyond change. It will color and influence the facts beyond change, and, in most cases, will become a fact beyond change itself. The 'feel' is from the juror's perspective not the lawyer's.

Taking these facts beyond change that include the dominant emotion of the case and coupling them with the legal principles permitted, a theory of the case will now begin to develop. In developing the theory, the facts beyond change must be consistent and run with the grain of the theory, not contrary to or against the theory. Likewise, the theory must be supported by the legal principles with which the court will instruct the jury.

A theory will then be distilled or broken down into a theme or themes that are consistent with each other. Themes perhaps can best be described as human experiences that we all have that parallel, but may not be similar to, the parties' human experience in this case. In this way, jurors can be made to "feel" the position of the advocate's client.

Themes are further distilled into theme lines. That is, they are made into memorable sentences, phrases, or words that crystallize and capture the essence of the theme and the theory. These theme lines will be integrated and used repetitively through voir dire, opening, direct, objections and responses to objections, closing, and, most importantly, the advocate's cross-examinations and resistance of the opponent's cross-examinations.

Whenever possible, these theme lines will be coupled with and used in connection with facts beyond change. In this way, the theme lines are made believable because of their connection with facts beyond change.

This thought process becomes a positive feedback cycle in the sense that facts beyond change start the cycle but are also incorporated into the last stage of the cycle. Because trial lawyers deal with human beings and human experiences, and because trials take place not in the past but in the present, this circular type evolution is not stationary. It is a self-generating process that continues throughout the trial and moves in a direction. It is a positive feed-back system.

The key to the proper theory of the case is identifying the proper, dominant emotion of the case so that as the theory evolves in the case, it will evolve in the direction of the dominant emotion of the case. This will further heighten the effectiveness of the advocate's theory. See chart below.

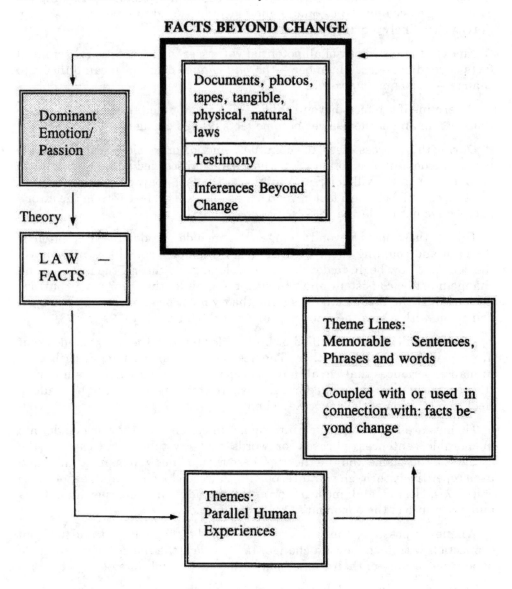

FACTS BEYOND CHANGE

Dominant Emotion/ Passion

Documents, photos, tapes, tangible, physical, natural laws

Testimony

Inferences Beyond Change

Theory

L A W — FACTS

Theme Lines: Memorable Sentences, Phrases and words

Coupled with or used in connection with: facts beyond change

Themes: Parallel Human Experiences

§ 2.07   Using a Mock Closing Argument as a Method to Shape a First Draft Theory of the Case

In order to develop a first draft theory of the case, it is only necessary to begin to think in terms of how the advocate will persuade the fact finder. It is sometimes helpful to think backwards from a closing argument. Upon first hearing the client's version of the facts the advocate might ask themselves, "If I had to argue the case right now what would I say to a jury?" Undoubtedly the answer will lack the fine detail provided by discovery and trial, but the broad outline of the argument is apparent soon after meeting with the client. If the lawyer can begin making closing arguments in her head, the lawyer is on her way to developing a theory of the case.

For those who encounter some difficulty in identifying a draft or working theory of the case, this closing argument thought process is a helpful method. Other lawyers may find it more efficient to think in terms of cross-examinations to be given and to be defended against. It may be that the theory first developed is later modified or discarded. But the method of developing a theory is not changing, only the lawyer's prediction of its success. If the lawyer begins to modify the theory, soon she hears herself giving different closing arguments. The case has not changed, only the realization that other facts have taken on greater importance, and some facts believed to be very important are now less important or even unimportant. As the theory of the case changes, different facts are elevated in their importance. As the facts are developed before trial the lawyer better gauges her ability to successfully argue her proposed theory of the case. As facts that support the theory are developed, the advocate's case becomes stronger. As the advocate realizes she has insufficient facts to support her theory, or when she realizes that the facts available could recast it to a different theory, the theory evolves and changes. This is a natural process in the evolution of the case before trial. It is not a natural or successful process during trial. Once trial commences it is extraordinarily difficult to change the lawyer's theory of the case.

While developing a theory of the case the lawyer must simultaneously envision the opponent's theory of the case. The lawyer does not get to pick her opponent's theory of the case, but she must recognize that theory and prepare the cross-examinations that will attack that theory. The key phrase is "attack that theory." Not "attack that witness." Witnesses are not attacked. Opponent's theories are attacked. The harmful or incomplete testimony of the witness may be challenged. The credibility of the witness can be tested. The motive, interest, or bias of the witness may be revealed. But these are not attacks on the witness so much as they are attacks on the information the witness seeks to convey.

The goal of cross-examination is no different than the goal of any other portion of the trial: introduce testimony and exhibits in a manner that allows the fact finder to immediately comprehend how those facts support the theory of the case or undermine the opponent's theory of the case. The difference between cross-examination and the other portions of the case is that cross-examination offers unusual opportunities and challenges in building support for the cross-examiner's theory of the case.

Cross-examinations can be both constructive and destructive. The portions of cross- examinations that are termed destructive are those that attack the opponent's theory of the case. The constructive element of cross-examination is the use of the opponent's witnesses to build the advocate's theory of the case (see chapter 11, *Sequences of Cross-Examination*). As will be discussed, whether constructive or destructive, cross-examination is designed to teach the important facts to the fact finder. The important facts influence the opposing theories of the case.

§ 2.08 The Theory of the Case as a Guide to Discovery and Investigation

One of the hallmarks of civil litigation is the ability of the two sides to engage in formal discovery processes including depositions, interrogatories, and requests of documents and items. It is extraordinarily difficult to engage in a meaningful discovery process until a draft theory of the case has been formulated. The discovery process works best and is most economically conducted when it is aimed at proving a defined theory of the case, or attacking the opponent's presumed or announced theory of the case. The lawyer cannot ask a corporation to produce all documents on all issues. Even if it were possible to do so, the result would be stacks of useless paper. Instead, the advocate first formulates a theory of the case before envisioning what types of documents might exist to support that theory, and which witnesses need to be deposed to prepare for the likely cross-examinations on that theory of the case and on the opponent's theory of the case. This concept of theory-driven discovery bears further discussion (see chapter 4, *Cross-Examination-Focused Investigation*). What is important at this juncture is the realization that it is the contrasting theories of the case that drive pre-trial preparation including the conceptualization of the cross-examinations necessary and available.

How does the lawyer begin to conceptualize cross-examinations when trial may be months, even years away? Alternatively, how does she conceptualize cross-examinations when she has no discovery or only a very short time from opening a file until trial? As soon as a theory is conceived, the advocate may begin the process of conceptualizing the cross-examinations that will be needed. Trial lawyers instinctively do this and it is a healthy instinct. It may be a function of a law school education that the lawyer is schooled to view both sides at issue and to be capable of arguing either side. What is important is that the advocate adopts a starting position to think about how she would argue the case and how the opponent is likely to argue the case.

Of course it may not be possible to script the cross-examinations, but it is never too soon to mentally play out or outline what witnesses or types of witnesses will need to be cross-examined and where those cross-examinations are likely to be productive. The advocate should always keep in mind that cross-examinations are a vehicle to build her theory of the case as much as they are a vehicle to damage the opponent's theory of the case. As a result of this two-sided function of cross-examination, it is critical to envision the theory of the case likely to be advanced by the opponent. In other words, she needs to understand the opponent's theory of the case so that she can envision what information the opponent will need to produce in direct examinations to support his theory of the case. By conceptualizing where the opponent must go, the advocate can begin to conceptualize the weaknesses in the likely stories to be heard in the envisioned direct examinations.

§ 2.09   Civil Theories Must Encompass Liability, Proximate Causation, and Damages

It must be remembered that civil cases have theories that encompass liability, proximate causation, and damages, though sometimes one of these issues are far less in dispute. In a commercial case the plaintiff's theory of the case may be stated as: "The defendant stole my software program and cost me millions of dollars." The defense might counter with an initial theory of the case: "We did not steal your software program and anyway your software was never very successful."

In a commercial case, the plaintiff might start with a theory, "I had a right of first refusal to buy back the business, but the defendant sold the business without telling me. I want my business back." The defense might begin with a theory, such as, "The right of first refusal did not apply under the circumstances." The defense might have an alternative theory: "Even if we had given you notice of our intention to sell the business, you did not have the funds necessary to match the offer so you were not damaged."

In a products liability lawsuit, the plaintiff might begin with a theory: "Your snowmobile was defectively designed to start with the throttle open. As a result, when using it, it started with an enormous jerk and threw me off causing my horrible injuries." The defense might counter by conceding: "The plaintiff's injuries are indeed horrible, but the design is appropriate for sports use, and the plaintiff was careless in his remounting and starting of the vehicle following a fall."

§ 2.10   Understanding the Two Opposing Theories of the Case Allows the Advocate to Know Which Facts Are Worth Fighting Over

Everything previously stated about the futility of casting a theory in opposition to a fact beyond change (see § 2.20, below), is true of witnesses as well as lawyers. A witness compelled to testify in opposition to a fact beyond change, damages her own credibility. Similarly, the advocate who requires one of her own witnesses to testify in opposition to a fact beyond change, damages her own witness's credibility. The cross-examiner may wish to set up cross-examinations where the impeachment of a witness occurs not through the testimony of another witness, but through a document, photograph, or other exhibit that will be judged by the jury to be a fact beyond change.

In this way, while the witness may leave the stand feeling secure that he has testified forcefully and accurately, the jury perceives his testimony to contradict a fact beyond change. Credibility is thereby diminished. By way of example, look at the analysis of witness/hit man's testimony concerning how he murdered the victim. If the witness testified that he stood at the head of the victim and stabbed her twice, compare the coroner's report that verified the police photographs showing the assailant stood to the side of the victim and stabbed her four times. The reports and photographs will be facts beyond change. Even though the witness may testify to whatever length and with whatever degree of certainty he wishes, to the extent that the testimony contradicts the photos and coroner's report, his testimony cannot and will not be believed. The witness loses credibility.

If the lawyer's theory is self-defense and identification is conceded, there is nothing productive in "proving" that the witness saw a man six feet four, even though the defendant is five feet seven. The height issue by itself is an irrelevant issue in the face of an admission of identity. However, if the witness is going to testify to his perceptions of other parts of the fight, and those perceptions hurt the theory of self-defense, then the cross-examiner may wish to cross-examine on the six feet four/five feet seven discrepancy. The purpose is not for showing misidentification, but for showing the general inability of the witness to correctly perceive all facts.

By doing so, the advocate has converted the five feet seven stature of the defendant into a fact beyond change by conceding the defendant's identity as the perpetrator, *and forced the witness to testify against the fact beyond change.* By describing the height of the assailant as being six feet four, the witness's credibility has been put in opposition to a fact beyond change — the actual height of the defendant. While that loss of credibility in relationship to the height issue is of no factual consequence to the theory of the case, the loss of credibility spills over to other aspects of the witness's testimony. The fact finder may ask: "If the witness can be so wrong on that one piece of the description, how wrong could he be on the other facts he claimed to have seen?"

In a domestic relations case, all persons questioned, including the husband's accountant, will testify that the wife is a kind, soft-spoken, gentle, retiring, and easily intimidated person. The wife presents herself in this way in her testimony. But the husband has a different story to tell. The wife's attorney is only too happy to give the husband the opportunity to do so. The wife's attorney casts great doubt on the husband's general credibility by cross-examining the husband on his view. By saying that his wife is better described as a "combative personality," and "a woman who is loud, obnoxious, and offensive to everyone who meets her," the husband's credibility is put against the facts beyond change that will be testified to by each other witness including witnesses perceived to be on the husband's side of the case. In this manner, the husband's witnesses appear to be contradicting the party that has called them. The overall effect is that the husband will lose credibility on other issues as his version of this fact (his wife's demeanor and personality) is disbelieved by the fact finder.

§ 2.11   Relationship of Theory to the Likely Standard or Uniform Instructions of Law

When adopting a theory of the case, counsel must be cognizant of the applicable law. A successful theory of the case must be consistent with both the law and the facts beyond change. In fact, a theory of the case describes counsel's position on how the facts and law come together to justify the outcome being sought.

The theory of the case must incorporate the instructions of law likely to be given. In every case there are predictable standards or uniform instructions of law that the lawyer can anticipate in her first moments of work on the case. A review of the judge's standard or uniform charge book will make obvious certain instructions that will be given. In developing a theory of the case, the lawyer must be mindful of these stock instructions, as they offer guidance as to where the lawyer should aim her case theory.

A theory of the case that has great emotional appeal, but which finds no support in the instructions is destined to fail. The advocate cannot adopt a theory of the case simply because it sounds good or because it incorporates the best facts available. Those facts must be made relevant by the applicable law. The power of a fact stems primarily from its legal significance as defined by the instructions, its logical ability to support the advocate's theory of the case, or alternatively, its logical ability to undermine the opponent's theory of the case. If the fact is otherwise significant in the context of both the instructions of law and the theory of the case, then its emotional impact will enhance the value of that fact. But lacking legal relevance and a tie to the theory of the case, a highly emotional fact may bother a fact finder but it will not compel the decision.

For instance, there are uniform instructions on the credibility of witnesses, the burden of proof, and the elements of every tort. It is useful for the advocate to gather the uniform instructions that are likely to apply to the case. This task is not enormously time-consuming but is enormously helpful in developing a theory of the case. The earlier it is done, the better. Both in criminal and civil actions, uniform instructions tell the lawyer what the party must prove. A failure to prove any one of the elements of the crime, or the cause of action must result in a defense verdict on that claim. Thus the prosecution or the plaintiff must adopt a theory of the case that incorporates these legal requirements.

§ 2.12   Instructions Help Refine the Working Theory

For instance, if the plaintiff is alleging trademark infringement, a likely uniform instruction that must be incorporated into the theory of the case will be:

"Likelihood Of Confusion" — Instruction No. 55

In determining whether there is or will be a likelihood of confusion as to origin, sponsorship, endorsement, or affiliation caused by the use of the word _____ by both Plaintiff _____ and Defendants _____, or any of them, in connection with _____, you may draw on your common experience as citizens of the community. In addition to the general knowledge you have acquired throughout your lifetimes, you should consider the following factors, which are described, in the following instructions:

(1)   Degree of similarity between the marks;

(2)   The strength or weaknesses of the marks in question;

(3)   Intent of the Defendants;

(4)   Product and marketing similarities;

(5)   Degree of care;

(6)   Evidence of actual confusion.

These six factors are not the only factors you may consider. Further, no one factor is determinative. No one factor or consideration is conclusive, but each aspect should be weighed in light of the total evidence at the trial. The marks are not compared side-by-side, but are compared singly as consumers would encounter the products in the marketplace. It is the overall impression of the mark that you should consider.

Now the lawyer knows of six areas of facts to develop, investigate, and cross-examine. These six general areas will undoubtedly lead to other areas of facts that deserve the cross-examiner's attention.

§ 2.13   Instructions That Are the Basis of Certain Theories

Uniform instructions alone are the bedrock of some theories, especially in criminal cases where the burden of proof is upon the government to prove guilt beyond a reasonable doubt. The credibility of prosecution witnesses is often the chief issue in contention. In these cases, the instruction on the credibility of witnesses is a required instruction. A sample of that instruction:

Credibility of Witnesses

You may have to decide what testimony to believe. You should carefully consider all of the testimony given and the circumstances under which each witness has testified.

Consider each witness' knowledge, motive, state of mind, demeanor, and manner while on the stand. Consider the witness' means of knowledge, ability to observe, and strength of memory. Consider also any relationship each witness may have to either side the case; the manner in which each witness might be affected by the verdict; and the extent to which, if at all, each witness is either supported or contradicted by other evidence in the case. You should consider all facts and circumstances shown by the evidence to affect the credibility of the witness' testimony.

You may believe all the testimony of a witness, or part of it, or none of it.

In a case in which the theory of the case is, in its most general terms, "misidentification," this credibility of witness instruction is of tremendous assistance. It instructs the jury that inconsistencies in a witness's testimony can themselves produce a reasonable doubt. Although the lawyer must do a great deal more work to flesh out the theory of the case by making it more precise and fact descriptive than "misidentification," the ultimate theory is greatly assisted by this uniform instruction.

Similarly, if it is to be argued that a witness has intentionally lied as to a material fact, many states have an instruction that warns jurors that a witness who was found to be lying in one aspect of his testimony can be disregarded in all other aspects of his testimony. This instruction applies to all types of cases.

§ 2.14 The Relationship of Theory of the Case to Special Instructions

Special instructions are instructions that can only be obtained upon a showing of applicability.

In a medical malpractice case, where more than one physician was part of the team caring for the plaintiff, plaintiff's counsel, under appropriate facts, may offer the following special instruction:

Liability of Physicians Acting Jointly

When two or more physicians expressly or impliedly agree to work with each other to treat or care for a patient's injury or condition, each physician is legally responsible to the patient for any negligence of any of the other physicians arising out of and within the scope of their agreement to treat or care for that injury or condition.

The number of possible special instructions is enormous. It is not for the court but for the advocate to seek the instruction that might apply to the particular matter being litigated. The earlier that counsel can identify such special instructions, the more easily counsel can craft a theory of the case that finds solid support in the law. This interplay between special instructions and the creation of a winning theory of the case is very important. Special instructions can make a theory of the case possible, and they can make a theory of the case stronger.

The special instructions that could benefit an advocate's theory of the case must be recognized and calculated into the trial strategy before the case begins, not after the evidence has been concluded and the fight about instructions begins. Instructions will only be given when they are made appropriate by the facts already adduced during trial. Therefore a trial lawyer must be mindful of the special instructions she will seek in developing the cross-examinations, and secondarily, the direct examinations. The trial lawyer must prove sufficient facts to justify the giving of the special instructions. For instance, there are several special instructions that can be obtained if defense counsel is able to introduce a sufficient showing of facts in support of those instructions.

§ 2.15   Vague Theories: A Roadmap to Disaster

The theory of the case, while it cannot be an elaborate position on all of the facts, is something more than a conclusory statement such as, "There exists reasonable doubt" or "Plaintiff has proved her case by a preponderance of the evidence." Or even, "The plaintiff has proved the defendant ran the stop sign, which caused the accident, and thereby injured the plaintiff." Such theories are too vague to serve as a focusing mechanism for winning trial strategies. As will be later discussed (see chapter 8, *The Only Three Rules of Cross-Examination* and chapter 9, *The Chapter Method of Cross-Examination*), conclusory statements create no pictures. People remember cases by their mental images. The powerful theory of the case should be stated in such a way as to create a mental image that is favorable to the proponent of that theory.

When conclusory statements are used as a substitute for theory, or when a theory of the case is stated in legalisms, there is nothing remotely memorable about such a "theory" because it is pure lawyer talk. It does not compel a juror to any emotion or passion and it does not remind them of any parallel human experience. The successful theory must be case specific. Generalizations and conclusory statements will not suffice. Jurors need some handle on how the facts of this particular case compel a particular decision. In the absence of such specificity, there truly is no theory of the case. Therefore, the lawyer is incapable of identifying what facts will lead toward the chosen theory.

In criminal cases, the ultimate non-theory is: "The defendant is not guilty." This is no theory at all, but a purely conclusory statement. Theories such as, "The evidence does not prove guilt beyond a reasonable doubt," offer no guidance as to the critical facts to be produced in cross-examination. Such conclusory statements create no mental image. They do not assist the jurors in recalling any particular facts of the case. Similarly, this naked conclusion does not assist the lawyer in excluding facts or areas that are irrelevant to the theory.

The theory of the case must be factually specific enough to narrow the scope of the cross-examinations the lawyer needs to deliver, and to provide a sense of direction or goal in each of the components of the cross-examination (see chapter 9, *The Chapter Method of Cross-Examination*). The theory of the case must also be specific enough to allow the jurors to integrate the facts they are going to hear in the cross-examination into a theory of the case that they understand. In other words, the fact finder must understand the theory of the case so that an answer (fact) can be immediately appreciated in the context of that theory of the case. It is the goal of the trial lawyer to place a theory of the case before the fact finder with sufficient specificity so that the answers elicited on cross-examination can immediately be appreciated for their effect on the advocate's theory of the case.

When a vague theory is created, the case is left adrift. By leaving open any course of action, the lawyer compels herself to follow no particular course of action. The cross-examinations wander since they have no focal point. Cross-examination becomes a series of unrelated attacks on the witness. Some lawyers term this maximizing flexibility. It is nothing of the sort. It is simply the lack of a defined goal.

When theories drift, cross-examinations lack focus and jurors become confused over what the lawyer is trying to prove. Since the jurors do not comprehend the goal, they cannot tell if the goal has been achieved. Juries do not vote for what they do not understand. Juries do not vote for confusion. The advocate's lack of clarity is penalized by the jury's verdict. The theory of the case must be understood so that the fact finder can choose to adopt it. It is inappropriate and unrealistic to ask the fact finder to assemble the facts into their own theory of the case.

§ 2.16 Them Theories Versus Us Theories

In criminal law, where the burden of proof is upon the government, it is easiest for defense counsel to frame theories that discuss "them" rather than "us." A "them theory" focuses on the government's evidence. It is an attacking theory. In contrast, an "us theory" focuses on the defendant's version of the story or the defendant's witnesses. The advantage of a "them theory" is that it reminds the jurors that the burden of proof is upon the government and not the defense. In contrast, by focusing upon the defendant's version of the facts, an "us theory" has the tendency to psychologically shift some burden to the defense. The chief danger of an "us theory" is that it can cause the jurors to vote on whether to believe the defendant and his or her witnesses. For this reason, in criminal cases, "them theories" are preferred over "us theories." The ultimate "us theory" is alibi. It focuses the jury on the issue of whether the defendant has *proved* his presence elsewhere.

In civil law, where the burden of proof is only by a preponderance of the evidence, there is still an often-overlooked advantage to "them theories." To the extent that an advocate focuses on the weaknesses in the opponent's case, or on facts admitted by opponent's witnesses, there is greater credibility to her argument.

This is true because the introduction of favorable facts in cross-examination allows the advocate to remind the jury that it was not her witness who has testified to the favorable fact, but a witness called by the opponent. Furthermore, a fact adduced in cross-examination is less subject to attack (and, at times, impossible to attack) by the opponent on redirect examination (see chapter 14, *Redirect and Recross Examination*).

While an opponent is permitted to impeach his own witness, the reality is that he has already tried to establish the credibility of that witness on direct examination, and subsequent attacks to impeach the witness appear unfair to the jury. The only other attack approach is for the opponent to lead his own witness or explain by leading questions on redirect. Neither is very effective (see chapter 14, *Redirect and Recross Examination*). Furthermore, an opponent faced with the task of selectively discrediting a portion of his own witness's testimony runs afoul of the doctrine of primacy and recency. The last thing the jurors will hear will be the opposition trying to convince them of the loss of credibility of his own witness (see chapter 12, *Employing Primacy and Recency*).

§ 2.17 Using Words and Voice That Fit Theory

A theory of the case has its own emotional level (see chapter 22, *Voice, Movement, Body Language, and Timing*). The cross-examination on the lying witness is an entirely separate emotion from the cross-examination on the mistaken witness. Entrapment in a drug case involving a young defendant allows more of a self-righteous indignation than does self-defense that leads to the death of another. On the civil side, defense of an auto accident case resulting in fatalities must be keyed at a lower emotional level than a defense in which no one is hurt.

In determining the appropriate voice or emotion for a cross-examination, the cross-examination must factor in the jury's perceptions concerning the witness, the mood the lawyer wishes to create within the courtroom, and the emotional content of the theory of the case. When in doubt, the cross-examiner is better served by less emotion in all situations. The jurors' perception of a witness are important, but, to a great extent, predictable. A witness who is indeed the victim of a crime will arouse the jury's sympathy. While that witness might be proven to be mistaken, the method of proof must be gentler because the witness has already been victimized. The jury will not tolerate a second victimization. Children and the elderly are psychologically protected by the jurors. While they may be discredited, it must be done with subtlety and gentleness. The witness must be left with self-respect.

On the other hand, the witness who would lie is perceived by the jurors as fair game for far more punishing cross-examination. The mood can be more aggressive, though the words and voice tone must still be within the bounds of courtroom decorum. The cross-examinations may be more abrupt, the pace of questions can be quicker, and control in general can appear to be tighter.

While the jurors will not protect an expert witness, they expect experts to be dealt with a degree of professional respect. Conversely, because the expert is expected to be able to fend for herself, questioning can be vigorous, and control can be tight (and appear to be tight). In general, a more intense emotional level of cross-examination can be tolerated than with that of a sympathetic lay witness.

§ 2.18 A Theory of the Case Is Always Fact Dependent

Every theory of the case is factually driven, regardless of its nature. The vitality of a theory of the case is judged by the strength of the facts that support that particular theory coupled with the law that recognizes the consequences of sustaining that theory. When lawyers say that they have a cold winner on the law, what they really mean is that they have facts of such high quality that a fair application of the law (the instructions) must inevitably lead to a successful verdict. (A lawyer claiming this has usually misjudged the strength of his case, but that is another book.)

Although a theory of the case may begin development based only upon a client interview, the theory of the case is adopted with the knowledge that theories must remain fluid in the face of changing facts. Developing facts may strengthen a theory, modify it, or extinguish its vitality. The process is a bit like the chicken and the egg riddle. What comes first? Does the advocate develop a theory of the case and then search for facts that support it or does the advocate develop the facts and then fashion a theory of the case to fit those facts? The answer is that the theory of the case is responsive to the facts, but it must be developed long before all or even most of the facts are known.

The case begins with a client with a problem. The problem must be understood before the trial lawyer can adopt a theory of the case. The trial lawyer must know the client's position before calculating a trial plan designed to support that position. In most cases the client is able to articulate his position. For example:

- "I shot in self-defense."

- "I intended to pay for it but hadn't gotten to the checkout counter yet."

- "We fired him because he did bad work not because of his age."

- "The product was a piece of junk that exploded in my face."

- "If he used the product the way it was intended this never would have happened."

And so it goes from shoplifting cases to corporate antitrust actions, from drunk driving prosecutions to insurance premium class actions, the first interview is sufficient to arm the advocate with a working theory of the case. The advocate begins work based on that theory of the case. The next step is to develop the facts to aid that theory. The advocate also envisions the opponent's theory of the case. From this point forward, the lawyer's quest is to gather facts that support that preferred theory. However, the facts that are gathered strengthen or weaken that theory. Theories are responsive to the facts available. The facts are not manipulated or forced into fitting a pre-selected theory. This process of working from a theory to the available facts make sense. The client does not announce, "We did it now you tell us why we did it." More often, the client describes why he did something (and his unconscious theory of the case).

Simultaneously, the trial lawyer envisions the opponent's theory of the case. In order to develop the destructive aspect of cross-examinations, counsel seeks facts that will undermine the opponent's theory. A scientifically prepared case does not involve a study of the facts to see what theory emerges but rather a search for facts that support a particular working theory of the case.

In analyzing facts, the lawyer need judge them not only for themselves but also for the inferences to be fairly drawn from them. If more than one inference can be drawn from an anticipated fact, then the lawyer is given greater leeway in developing her theory. If, on the other hand, only one clear inference can be reasonably drawn from a fact or set of facts, the advocate must utilize that one inference as much as if the inference were itself a fact. The lesson of trial work is that many facts can be viewed as helping both sides. In fact the advocate learns to adopt seemingly bad facts as if she were proud of them. A good theory of the case does not evade or ignore bad facts but accommodates seemingly bad facts so that they can be seen as supporting the lawyer's theory of the case.

Once a theory is postulated, trial counsel will discover that many of the facts of the case are neutral facts. They are facts that neither conflict with nor support that theory. So long as the theory remains the same, the lawyer need not fight these facts or their inferences. However, if the theory is changed, the advocate must reanalyze facts that were first thought to be neutral to determine if they have now become negatives or positives to the new theory. Conversely, the advocate must constantly scrutinize supposedly neutral facts to see if there is a way of utilizing those facts and the inferences to be drawn from them into the chosen theory. Throughout this process, the lawyer is constantly seeking to convert "neutral" facts into facts that support the theory. While the incorporation of neutral facts into the theory is a helpful goal, such facts are not the limiting or driving forces in the development of a theory of the case. The facts that most limit the lawyer in the development of a theory of the case are "facts beyond change." (see § 2.20, below.)

§ 2.19   Cross-Examination Is a Critical Opportunity to Advance a Theory of the Case

Cross-examination does not occur in a vacuum. The lawyer does not cross-examine simply to show that she can do so. And cross-examination does not occur simply because a direct examination has been concluded. The lawyer does not cross-examine because she has the right to do so but because she needs to do so. She cross-examines not simply to disprove a point. She cross-examines because cross-examination offers her superb opportunities to advance her theory of the case. The lawyer needs to advance her theory of the case throughout trial. Cross-examination is simply another opportunity to establish facts that assist in supporting her theory of the case.

Cross-examination preparation systems are designed to prepare lawyers to engage in cross-examinations best suited to accomplishing those goals. (see chapter 5, *Cross-Examination Preparation System 1: Topic Charts*; chapter 6, *Cross-Examination Preparation System 2: Sequence of Events Charts*; and chapter 7: *Cross-Examination Preparation System 3: Witness Statement Charts*.) The techniques of cross-examination are designed to assist in delivering cross-examinations that accomplish those goals. However, neither the science nor the techniques of cross-examination can assist in accomplishing the goals of a cross-examination unless those goals are linked to a theory of the case. The theory of the case provides the goals not only for the overall strategic texture of the cross-examination, but the individual examinations themselves. By developing a theory of the case, the lawyer knows which facts need to be proved and which inferences must be put in a position to be forcefully argued at the close of the case.

§ 2.20   Facts Beyond Change — A Definition

Facts beyond change are facts that will be believed by the jury as fair, accurate, and highly relevant regardless of best efforts to dispute or modify them. After all, that is why they are called facts beyond change. Facts beyond change are the givens of a lawsuit. In a positive sense, facts beyond change are the structure that supports and channels the theory. The negative consequence of a fact beyond change is that it limits the possible theories of the case. Any successful theory of the case must either incorporate all facts beyond change, or be neutral to them. That is, a theory must either build upon the facts beyond change, or stand in harmony with them. A successful theory of the case can never contradict a fact beyond change, because, if the fact finder is confronted with a theory and an actuality (a fact beyond change), and the two cannot exist simultaneously, the fact finder must decide the case in accordance with the actuality (the fact beyond change).

Remember, a fact beyond change is one that will not be diminished by an effective cross-examination. If cross-examination can affect the fact finder's perception that the fact is fair or accurate or relevant, the fact is capable of dispute and is no longer a fact beyond change.

§ 2.21   Recognizing the Most Telling Facts Beyond Change

Source of facts beyond change include documents, photographs, scientific tests, other tangible items, and the laws of nature. These facts are less disputable than witness testimony, which is somewhat subject to human frailties. That is not to say that test results must be accepted as infallible; they are not. Once verified, they are more likely to be accepted by a jury as a fact beyond change. In a civil case, if appropriate investigation determines that the client's car left 96 feet of skid marks before impact, the fact is indeed 96 feet. There may be room to interpret the meaning of the skids, but a theory of the case that relies on the client never applying her brakes is simply not viable. The client obviously saw, heard, or perceived something, hit her brakes for some reason, and left the 96 feet of skid marks. That is a fact beyond change. It will not go away. The theory must incorporate it or at least accommodate it.

In a contract case, assume that all agree that the document that represents the contract is not fraudulent. Consequently, the words of the document become facts beyond change. One may seek different interpretations of the document, but there will be no room to assert that the document does not exist, or that the parties did not sign it. The existence of the contract becomes a given of the case — a fact beyond change. It serves to limit the possible theories of the case for the advocate who seeks to dispute it. A successful theory must incorporate this fact as positive to the theory or make that fact neutral by accommodation.

§ 2.22   A Quick Guide to Finding Facts Beyond Change

One of the most important aspects of developing a theory of the case is the recognition of the relevant facts beyond change. Once these facts beyond change are found, the worth of a proposed theory quickly advances or recedes.

As a starting place to find facts beyond change, the trial lawyer is advised to scrutinize documents, photographs, videotapes, audiotapes, and other exhibits or tangible items. While the interpretations of such items may be argued, often the existence of the item itself enormously influences the available theories.

For instance, no matter how well the advocate cross-examines, the images on a photograph will not change. The advocate may argue concerning the accuracy of the photograph, or its interpretation, but in the absence of strong evidence of faking or altering the scene, a photograph "testifies" eloquently about its own content.

Similarly, in a contract case, the contract itself is likely to be a fact beyond change. Its meaning may be debated, but the document itself is likely to be the starting point for many theories and the destruction or limitation of many other theories. Tangible items are not the only place facts beyond change can be found, but they are a good starting place.

In commercial litigation, the documents produced by the respective sides are often the source of the most relevant facts beyond change. Assume a memo was drafted that originally stated, "We should tell our dealers to call their customers and replace the part." Further assume that this memo was passed up the chain of command and a superior inserted by handwriting the word "not" so that the memo now read, "We should not tell our dealers to call their customers and replace the part." Further assume that as a result of the change, the dealers were not called concerning the part.

It is a fact beyond change that the memo originally advised a course of conduct, that a superior completely changed the recommendation, and that the changed recommendation was followed. In adopting a defense theory of the case, the corporation must embrace the change of advice. It is foreclosed from arguing that no one was aware of the potentially defective part or that no corporate executive believed notice to the dealers was appropriate. The defense is saddled with several facts beyond change all stemming from a single document. Those facts beyond change must be taken into consideration when fashioning the theory.

§ 2.23   Investigate Thoroughly Before Conceding Any Fact to Be a Fact Beyond Change

Remember, inasmuch as facts beyond change effectively limit the advocate's theory of the case, the cross-examiner must be diligent in researching their accuracy. The lawyer must utilize objectivity in evaluating each fact's capability of belief. When facts are assumed to be beyond change, the lawyer has limited herself. If facts can be shaken by cross-examination or weakened in any other way, they are *not* facts beyond change. The advocate takes the lazy way out assuming facts to be beyond change without attempting to test their true nature. The lawyer take a fool's way out when a theory is adopted that contradicts facts beyond change based on the stubborn and unrealistic hope that the fact beyond change will be overlooked or disbelieved.

§ 2.24 Neutral Facts Beyond Change

In any lawsuit, there are literally thousands of facts that are beyond change, but most of them have no particular value to the case. For instance, in a certain case, it may be completely indisputable, yet wholly irrelevant, that an event happened at night, or that it happened in the city, or that it happened on a Tuesday. On the other hand, these same facts may be critical in some other kinds of lawsuits. While these may be facts beyond change, if they have no consequence to the case, they neither compel nor prohibit a particular theory of the case. The fact that they will always be believed is overcome by the fact that they will never be believed to be relevant to the decision-making process.

§ 2.25 Core Facts Beyond Change

In any lawsuit, there are, however, a small core of facts beyond change that are critical to the process of shaping a successful theory of the case. For example, in a homicide case, if a prosecution witness claims the defendant is found at the scene of the homicide with a gun in his hand minutes after the homicide occurred, these findings alone are meaningful. However, if that prosecution witness can be shown to have a motive to fabricate, or if that witness has other credibility problems or is contradicted by other witnesses, that testimony concerning the defendant should not be viewed as a fact beyond change. It is only when the cross-examiner determines that the circumstances are such that this testimony will always be believed that that testimony creates a fact beyond change.

The fact beyond change is not that the defendant committed the homicide but only that the defendant was found at the scene of the homicide with a gun in his hand, minutes after the homicide occurred. The advocate must examine these facts to see what inference can be drawn from them. Even these facts beyond change do not prove that the gun now was the murder weapon. Depending on where the scene of the crime might be, it could be normal that the defendant was there within minutes. In fact it might be that dozens of other people were there. However, if the opponent can add other facts beyond change, such as the gun that was found was the murder weapon, the scene was quite remote, and no other people were in the vicinity, the facts beyond change dramatically limit the defendant's possible theories of the case. Certainly self-defense is still available, as is insanity or accident. Indeed, suicide is still theoretically available as part of the theory of the case.

A defense that asserts that the defendant was somewhere else (alibi) is not now available. Misidentification of the defendant as the perpetrator is out of the question; the defense is left with self-defense, accident, defense of third persons, but not alibi or misidentification. For example, if a neutral third-party witness says that no other persons were around the two when the shooting occurred, and if that person is judged to be credible in the face of what can be perceived as the finest attacks on credibility on that limited issue, the facts beyond change have now ruled out the defense that "another person did it." Now, add that the witness saw the defendant aim at the deceased, heard the gun go off, and that the gun tests show no operating difficulties in the gun.

The defense will likely discard the theory of accidental shooting. By objectively viewing the whole panoply of facts beyond change, the defense may well find that there are sufficient facts beyond change that require the defendant to rule out all potentially successful defenses except self-defense. All other theories have been eliminated at this stage.

§ 2.26   Inferences Beyond Change

Besides facts beyond change, the lawyer must also consider inferences beyond change. Certain facts, grouped together, lead the jury to an inference or to multiple possible inferences. The jury may be instructed on inferences. An inference is a finding deduced from the existence of other facts. When the deductive process leads a fact finder to only one possible inference, that is an inference beyond change. If there is only one possible inference from a grouping of facts, or only one inference that a jury will take away from a group of facts, that inference itself becomes a fact beyond change. For instance, in a case in which there will be substantial uncontradicted testimony concerning a series of recent fights between two marriage partners, the existence of bad blood between these spouses is an inference beyond change. The existence of animosity between the two, existing up to and including the day of the homicide, can and will be reasonably deduced from the facts. The inference of bad blood is now a fact beyond change.

As was true with facts beyond change, inferences beyond change are truly limited to those circumstances where any and every reasonable juror will arrive at the identical conclusion and will draw the identical inference. If jurors can draw differing inferences with the aid of cross-examination and other testimony, counsel is no longer faced with an inference beyond change. She is faced with one of the classic reasons for cross-examination. Do not be too quick to concede an inference beyond change. It is quite possible that through the discovery and investigation process, counsel can marshal sufficient evidence to take what appears to be an inference beyond change and convert it into a disputed item or even into an inference beyond change that now plays in favor of the side that originally feared that inference.

§ 2.27   Contradictory Facts Do Not Defeat True Facts Beyond Change

Facts beyond change are limited to what their name expresses: a fact that will be believed in a certain manner even in the face of contradictory evidence. Of course, there are some facts beyond change for which no contradictory evidence exists. There is only one version of the fact. Both sides acknowledge it so it is easily recognizable as a fact beyond change.

A conceptually more difficult problem is recognizing that contradictory facts do not defeat a true fact beyond change. If they could defeat a fact beyond change, then the fact beyond change wasn't a fact beyond change in the first place. Example: If after analyzing all of the supporting information, the lawyer comes to the conclusion that the third-party witness will be believed on the issue of the defendant as perpetrator of an assault, then the fact that the defendant has a decent cross-examination as to identification will not assist. If the cross-examination was strong enough to overcome the third-party witness, then the identification would not be a fact beyond change, but would be a fact capable of change. On the other hand, if the cross-examination and other supporting evidence can potentially cause a fact finder to doubt the identification, then the third-party identification is not a fact beyond change but is simply another fact in dispute.

If it is concluded for a variety of sound factual reasons that the neutral witness will be believed on this issue of identification, then the defendants use of an identification defense is not only useless, it is of negative value to its proponent. The lawyer's credibility is destroyed by seeking to advance any theory flatly contradicted by a fact beyond change. Unbelievable theories must not be used despite their allure when first investigated. The allure comes from facts that are contradictory.

A fact beyond change limits the theories available but does not destroy the ability to craft a winning theory. The lawyer searches for and recognizes facts beyond change so that she will not draft a theory of the case that is contradicted by a fact beyond change. In a slip and fall case, assume the plaintiff claims he slipped and fell as a result of walking across an incompletely mopped up puddle of shampoo. At the beginning of the case the defendant may not have sufficient information to make a judgment as to whether that is indeed what happened. At that point, the available theories of the case include alternative theories on the source of the plaintiff's injuries. However, during the investigation of the case it may become clear to defense counsel that the plaintiff's story of what caused the fall will be accepted by the jury. At that point the reason for the fall becomes a fact beyond change.

Defense counsel may argue otherwise to the jury, but if a reasoned analysis is that the argument must fail, then that element is a fact beyond change. The right to argue a point does not change the fact.

In a jurisdiction where conduct is admissible in a domestic relations case, the facts that the defendant's husband is a wonderful father who takes care of his children and is supportive to the children emotionally will not defeat a fact beyond change in a separate area of the case. Assume, in that same case, that documents clearly show that the husband has fraudulently conveyed to his mother $350,000 worth of certificates of deposit two days before he filed for divorce. The fact finder will find, as a fact beyond change, that the husband intended not to permit the wife to have access to these funds. The fact finder will find as a fact beyond change that the transfer was intended to defeat the wife's alimony claim in the impending divorce action. The husband's conduct as a father will not alter the hiding of the money.

In a criminal case, if facts beyond change, including direct and circumstantial evidence, eliminate all defenses except self-defense, the fact that the defendant gave a statement to the police denying that he was involved in the shooting is of no assistance to the theory. Defense counsel cannot, with credibility, rest a defense on the statement because that defense will run contrary to facts beyond change. Furthermore, use of that statement by the lawyer weakens the defense, as it puts the defendant in a position of advocating a defense contrary to facts beyond change. Although the statement may be admissible, both the client's credibility and the lawyer's credibility will be hurt when an attempt is made to use the identification issue as part of the theory of the case. It would be easier to explain away the defendant's panicky assertion of, "I didn't do it," than to run counter to facts beyond change. This same seemingly exculpatory statement by the defendant is in reality a fact of assistance to the prosecution's version of the case. This is so, even though the defendant's statement does not admit anything that the prosecution needed. However, the defendant, through the statement, is asserting a position contradicted by facts beyond change. It thus hurts the defendant's own credibility. If the opponent puts into evidence that statement, the advocate must suffer some damage, but it may be overcome. If, on the other hand, the advocate chose to introduce and rely on that assertion as part of her theory of the case, the advocate of this unacceptable position suffers a larger loss of credibility.

By further way of example, in a child sexual assault case, assume the child has related a coherent and consistent story of touching over the outer clothing. Further assume that an independent, credible witness saw this occur and that therefore the story is not only capable of belief, but *will* be believed despite the best attempts to impeach it. In such a case, the defense is better off adopting a theory that makes use of the touching and explains it in some non-sexual manner, rather than adopting a theory that is hinged on a denial of the touching. Choosing theories in this method takes courageous counsel, but the alternative is to adopt an oratorically arguable, but factually unwinnable theory.

§ 2.28   Facts Beyond Change Affect a Theory Only to the Extent That the Conceded Fact Impacts the Theory

A fact beyond change limits the available theories of the case only to the extent that the fact beyond change impacts a particular theory. A fact may be a bad fact, but it may leave open inferences necessary to support a theory of the case. For example, take the case of a blood alcohol test of the defendant taken shortly after a car accident. The initial hypothesis of the case might be based on the assumption that the lab work quantifying the defendant's blood alcohol level can be successfully challenged. If this is true, the blood alcohol level is no longer a fact beyond change. If, however, after diligent research and preparation, the insurance company lawyer comes to the conclusion that the blood work will indeed be accepted as that of the defendant, and that the test was correctly performed, then the blood alcohol level becomes a fact beyond change. The cross-examiner may have available a series of questions concerning other, better tests that could have been done, or chain of custody issues, but such questions are not useful. To ignore this while developing the theory is self -deceptive and case destructive. However, concession of this fact beyond change still leaves the lawyer with room to argue that the plaintiff was not injured by this collision. Thus, even the acceptance of a fact beyond change may leave ample room to craft a successful theory of the case.

§ 2.29 Neutralizing Facts Beyond Change — Drafting a Theory of the Case That Accommodates Facts Beyond Change

The recognition of a fact beyond change does not in itself limit a theory of the case. Counsel must first determine whether she can live with the fact beyond change. In other words, does the preferred theory allow for the existence of that particular fact beyond change? If so, the fact beyond change has not limited the theory. It is for this reason that counsel seeks to recognize the facts beyond change and then accommodate them within the theory. In essence the lawyer is saying: "I can live with that."

Example: The defendant is accused of insuring his business partner for $1 million before arranging to have her murdered. At the very inception of the case, certain facts become unmistakably clear: (1) the defendant did insure his business partner for $1 million; (2) she was murdered; (3) the defendant was living a lifestyle way beyond his means.

A successful theory of the defense must explain why the defendant would take out a $1 million insurance policy on his partner. It must give a reason for his partner to have been murdered other than for his own personal benefit. His spendthrift lifestyle must be accommodated within the theory. An appropriate theory of the case may be that the defendant greatly valued the services of his business partner. Since he always purchased the biggest and best of anything, he was more likely to buy a $1 million dollar policy than a $100,000 policy. This theory of the case has more chance of success than one that states that buying a $1 million policy was appropriate given the financial situation of the parties.

The "buy the biggest" theory does not contradict the facts beyond change, nor does it embrace some of them while accommodating others. Indeed these are bad facts beyond change but a theory can be designed that is consistent with such facts. Initially, accommodating "bad" facts seems to weaken the theory, but accommodating the facts is necessary to make the theory more believable. However, it is believable only if there are facts that support the supposition that the defendant greatly valued the business expertise of his partner and that defendant's style of business was consistent with the purchase of a $1 million insurance policy rather than one for a lesser amount.

When seeking to neutralize facts beyond change, the advocate does not change the nature of the facts. She only seeks to change the harm those facts inflict on the theory. Instead of fighting those facts, an effort is made to accommodate them within the theory. The hope is that the very fact beyond change that first hurt the theory now has an inference attached to it that can help the theory or at least be theory-neutral.

Take the case of the defendant standing over the dead victim with the murder weapon in his hand. A lawyer could postulate some bizarre and factually unsupported theory as to why the defendant just happened to be in possession of the smoking weapon, but argue that the defendant had nothing to do with the shooting. A better theory will, instead, concede the defendant shot the victim. The theory will show that a reasonable inference is that having performed the shooting in self-defense, the defendant felt no need to flee. He was willing to stay at the scene and await the arrival of the police. The opponent may well scoff at that assertion, but at least now the theory has posited different inferences and explanations to be drawn from the fact beyond change. More importantly, some of those inferences favor the defendant. The facts beyond change have not been changed, but they have been accommodated within the theory of the case. To the limited extent possible, they have been neutralized.

§ 2.30   Theories Must Accommodate Facts Beyond Change

It is the theory of the case that accommodates the facts beyond change, not vice versa. Facts create theories, facts support theories, facts limit theories, and facts extinguish theories. The facts come first, and the theory follows. But once a theory is postulated it must make use of facts. A theory of the case can make a fact important but a theory cannot create facts. Of course, discovery and investigation are designed to uncover the facts that breathe life into a theory (see chapter 4, *Cross-Examination-Focused Investigation*). Having adopted a theory, some facts become more important than others. The facts are not changing, only their value relative to the theory. The theory of the case allows the fact finder a framework in which to understand the facts. Without a theory of the case the fact finder might hear the answer but not understand its significance. With the aid of a theory, the fact finder can immediately integrate an answer in to the decision-making process. As a result while the facts do not change, their impact upon a jury is changed depending on the theory advanced by the advocate. In order to gain the value of an understood theory of the case the fact finder must understand the theory before the cross-examinations begin. Explanations in closing argument of the importance of facts come too late to achieve full advantage of the facts.

While a theory of the case may make a fact beyond change less relevant, or perhaps even irrelevant, its relevance is revitalized as soon as the theory contradicts the fact. A theory that contradicts a fact beyond change will harm the theory. A successful theory of the case cannot beg the fact finder to ignore facts that will be believed. This begging for ignorance is a fantasy. Advocates may show the fact finder why the facts either support the theory (positive), or do not harm the theory (neutral). An advocate can never successfully argue against facts beyond change.

The advocate is reminded that a fact beyond change that is productive of alternative inferences, one of which supports the advocate's theory, is a fact not at odds with the theory of the case. It is for the advocate to establish the likelihood that the favorable inference is more accurate. In order to win the battle of alternative inferences, cross-examination is used to bring out additional facts that relate to the fact beyond change.

§2.31 Incorporating Facts Beyond Change into a Theory of the Case

The best theories, meaning theories of the case most likely to succeed, are theories built upon facts beyond change. To the extent that there are facts beyond change within the record that clearly support the advocate's theory, they may be the most powerfully persuasive facts to the fact finder. Note that the opponent also must seek to accommodate these facts beyond change into his theory or face the inevitable failure that occurs when facts beyond change contradict theory.

In developing a theory of the case, it is vitally important that all information be searched for facts beyond change that could possibly aid the proposed theory. To the extent that the case theory rests on facts beyond change, the advocate has put an opponent in the position of having to respond to the advocate's theory of the case. The opponent must now either craft a theory of the case that is dependent upon the disbelief of the advocate's facts beyond change (and in so doing he must fail if the facts beyond change are truly facts beyond change), or he must craft a theory of his case that accommodates the facts beyond change developed by the advocate. An adversary who fails to face up to an opponent's facts beyond change in adopting her own theory is doomed to failure. He will be forced to argue a theory that can only succeed if a jury does not believe a fact beyond change. In other words he must ask a jury to be illogical or to ignore facts that will be perceived as both accurate and relevant. This is too much to ask of the jury.

As an example in a civil case, assume that there is an automobile accident. The defendant struck the plaintiff's slower truck from behind. The defendant admits the truck was slower, admits that she saw it, and admits it was properly in the right-hand lane. It would appear that liability is clear based on these facts beyond change. But the defendant also shows that another car, going much faster, forced her back into the right lane after she began to pass the truck. Now those same facts beyond change are inconsistent with the defendant's theory of the case.

Within any particular case, there will be found both positive and negative facts beyond change. Facts that initially appear positive or negative should be studied to see how they can be integrated into the advocate's theory and how they will likely be employed by the opponent.

Example: Assume a search of the defendant yields drugs. Assume that the entire issue is whether the defendant consented to a search of her suitcase. In addition, assume the following facts beyond change: When the defendant was first stopped, she protested. She refused to sign a "Miranda" form. The officers never advised her of her right to leave without being searched. She offered some minimal physical resistance. She pulled her suitcase towards her. At no time did she manifest an attitude of cooperation.

While the officers will always testify that they had consent (itself a conclusion), these additional facts beyond change can create an unmistakable picture of a lack of cooperation. These detailed facts make the officers' assertion of her cooperation less credible. As this example shows, starting with facts beyond change, the lawyer may craft a motion to suppress and argue favorable inferences from what first appeared to be negative facts beyond change.

In a domestic relations case where the wife alleges that the husband had a chronic drinking problem for the last six years of their marriage, this may be first viewed as a negative fact beyond change in the case. However, this fact may be coupled with the additional facts beyond change, such as the husband was passed over for promotion just prior to the time his drinking problem began, and that the husband continued to do poorly financially for the remaining six years of the marriage until the filing of the divorce decree. While some would argue that the drinking problem is a negative fact, it may be viewed favorably in the context of being able to show the fact finder that this husband has not and cannot produce sufficient income to financially pay alimony to the wife.

In a homicide case in which the defendant is accused of second-degree murder, the coroner's report showing five bullet wounds to the deceased is a negative fact beyond change to a self-defense theory. The same coroner report shows that all of the wounds are contact or near contact. These may at first appear to be a very negative fact beyond change. However, in comparing the bullet wounds to the defendant's statement to the police that the victim had jumped on him and was on top of him when the defendant fired upward into him, the coroner's report is in accordance with the statement. The facts are consistent with the defendant's statement.

In this sense, the angle of the wounds, and the distance at which they have been fired, are not now negative facts beyond change, but positive facts beyond change. It is dependent upon the manner, perspective, or context in which the facts are viewed. A slightly different manner, perspective, or context changes the same "fact" from negative to positive. This view of the facts permits the lawyer to argue to the jury that the defendant, if he made up this story, could not have come up with a version that would fit a coroner's report created weeks later. The coroner's report, initially thought to contain numerous bad facts beyond change, in essence now verifies the truthfulness of the defendant's version of events.

§ 2.32   Facts Beyond Change — Making Facts Positive

If a lawyer can take a fact beyond change and use it within her theory, the opponent's sting is removed. Trial lawyers, too often, see the negative facts beyond change. Put another way, lawyers see the factual problems with the case. The advocate should not shrink from examining what would appear to be bad facts, but should instead re-examine those facts from as many angles as possible in order to determine if they can be viewed as positive facts or at least neutral facts. The object of this exercise is to take what the opponent considers to be his best facts and weave them into the theory of the case, thereby depriving the opponent of the power of those facts. As a result of this process there may develop situations where each side claims a fact beyond change as theirs, supporting their conflicting theories. That is a tolerable state of affairs.

It is often the case that both sides claim a fact beyond change. This results in multiple inferences that can be drawn from a fact beyond change. In such a circumstance the advocate might lose the battle of inferences as to that fact, but still prevail in the verdict. More often, the jury withholds judgment as to which inference is correct and moves on to decide the case on firmer ground including other facts beyond change and other inferences from such facts.

§ 2.33   Facts Beyond Change Are Proven in Cross-Examinations

It is in cross-examination rather than direct examination that the facts beyond change are best proven. A fact finder expects that a witness in direct examination will support the side of the case responsible for calling that witness. This expectation of a bias in favor of the side calling the witness does not hold true for witnesses taken on cross-examination, or witnesses called for purposes of cross-examination. Here the expectation is that the witness will admit a fact helpful to the cross-examining lawyer only if that testimony is factually accurate. As a result, it is better to establish facts beyond change through the mouth of a witness perceived by the fact finder to be aligned with the opponent.

Assume in a copyright infringement case the plaintiff alleges that the defendant wrongfully made use of the copyrighted name of plaintiff's product. Assume the plaintiff testifies that the name of his product was widely known in the industry and that he had displayed his product at trade shows also attended by sales executives of the defendant corporation. At this point there is a disputable inference whether the defendant was aware of the product name being used by the plaintiff.

However, if plaintiff's attorney cross-examines one or more sales executives of the defendant corporation, either by calling that witness in their case in chief or by cross-examining that witness after they have been called by the defendant, and establishes that indeed the defendant sales executive was aware that plaintiff was marketing that product under that name, the defendant no longer has the option of arguing that it was unaware of the fact. Knowledge on the part of the defendant of the existence of the product, and the name under which it was being marketed are now facts beyond change.

The defendant is not foreclosed from other defenses, including that the product name was generic, or that the plaintiff's copyright was improperly obtained, or that the manner in which the defendant used the name did not amount to a copyright infringement. However, the fact beyond change established in cross-examination has limited the available theories of the case. That limitation may be small, but it is real. Attorneys on both sides of the case must now consider that limitation in building their opposing theories of the case.

§ 2.34   The Emotional Component of Objections and Responses to Objections

Objections and the responses to objections are often voiced in an emotional tone that is unjustified. The court does not need the tone of voice in order to understand the objection or the response. In fact the court is likely to disapprove of the undue display of emotion in what is essentially a very cryptic legal argument in front of jurors. In the courtroom where everything is magnified, an angry tone of voice may well communicate things that the lawyer did not intend to communicate. It is better to tone down the objection and the response. Likewise, the tone of the cross-examiner's objections and responses to opponent's objections should be consistent with the dominant emotion to be displayed in support of the cross-examiner's theory of the case. No matter how angry the cross-examiner may be in stating the objection, or in responding, she must resist showing that emotion if it is inappropriate in the context of the theory of the case.

§ 2.35   Emotional Elements of a Theory of the Case

Every theory of the case has its own emotional level or pitch. Some theories contain elements of righteous indignation, some are pitched at the level of common sense and quiet deliberation, some theories generate confusion and uncertainty (often useful in defense of criminal cases), and others generate sadness. It is necessary for the advocate to articulate the theory of the case to others in and outside of the office so that the advocate can best gauge the emotional components of the theory of the case. Sometimes the theory of the case causes the advocate to be highly emotional when the content of the theory is far less emotional. It is very dangerous to present a theory of the case at an emotional level that is unjustified by that theory. It is far better to use a voice that underplays the emotion of any theory. This allows the jurors to individually experience the theory at their own emotional level. If the advocate can determine the proper emotional pitch of the theory, and if the supporting facts allow and encourage the jurors to experience that emotion as they hear the testimony, the jurors are emotionally in tune with the theory of the case. Then a vote in the lawyer's favor feels right to the jurors. The emotional pitch of a theory of the case can be termed the "dominant emotion" of the case. If that emotion can be identified and used as the dominant emotion, the theory of the case becomes far more acceptable to the jury.

All too often lawyers attempt to sway jurors with emotion rather than fact. This is a singularly bad error. The emotional content of a theory may add sting to otherwise good facts but emotion will never be substitute for facts. Fact finders often view a lawyer's use of emotion as a camouflage for weak facts. On the other hand, powerful facts will generate the necessary emotion without the lawyer's assistance. Trial is and should be fundamentally about facts not feelings. The lawyer must learn to trust that the facts will generate the appropriate response and feelings among listeners. The lawyer cannot force that response.

There is an additional problem that comes from advocating an emotional response to the facts. The more a lawyer relies on emotion, the more likely the lawyer will be out of tune with some jurors. People prefer to select their own emotional response to a situation rather than have another person dictate to them the emotion they should feel. Why then does a lawyer seek to identify the dominant emotion of their theory of the case? The goal is to try to identify how neutral fact finders will feel about certain facts. Those facts that will generate the strongest emotional response are facts that need to be highlighted and relied on within the advocate's theory of the case.

§ 2.36 Identifying the Dominant Emotion of the Theory of the Case

It is likely that in the first interview with the client the lawyer will feel some emotional response to the story. However, this first rendition of the facts is likely to be so tilted in favor of the client as to be unreliable. The first opportunity to reliably determine the dominant emotion is during the discovery phase of the case. Whether a civil or a criminal matter, the lawyer should be acutely aware of her own emotions as she reads depositions, reports, records, or interviews. Does the lawyer become angry with the doctor who missed the diagnosis? Does the lawyer feel skepticism at the explanations of the opponent, but profoundly sad at the senseless death or injury of a party? Is she sympathetic to the victim who seems confused in his or her facts?

In all manner of cases, in reading even the preliminary discovery, the lawyer must be cognizant of the emotions generated by those facts. It is equally important to recognize the facts that generate an emotional response in favor of the opponent. As the opponent's case unfolds in the courtroom, that emotion will likely emerge. If the advocate is going to skillfully deal with the opponent's theory of the case the advocate must be prepared to skillfully deal with the emotional response likely to be generated by that theory. In other words it is unfair and unwise to ignore the reality that the opponent's case will generate emotions negative to the lawyer's theory of the case or emotions positive to the opponent's theory of the case. That which is foreseen can be defended against. As was true of facts beyond change, the best method of coping with powerful emotions generated by the opponent's case is to co-opt or accommodate them as the emotion of the lawyer's case. If a fair reading of the facts warns the advocate that the opponent's case will generate tremendous sadness or a sense that the defendant's conduct has created an enormous tragedy, it is better to craft a theory of the case that incorporates that sadness and sense of tragedy.

Even where little or no discovery exists, a discussion with the client or witness concerning the facts of the case will generate some feel for the emotion. These are the same emotions that the jurors are likely to feel when they hear the facts related in the courtroom. While there may be instances when these emotions can be deflected, it is far better to inject these emotions into the theory of the case rather than fight them. Through this process, the dominant emotion of the case is determined. While searching intellectually for the dominant emotion, the lawyer must be open emotionally to feel it. While facts should be appreciated for what they logically prove a complete analysis of a case includes consideration of how the case will feel, what emotions are likely to be generated in the telling of the facts.

The lawyer must seek to mold the dominant emotion into part of the theory of the case. An entrapment defense is, in essence, the feeling of "that's not fair." Self-defense is based on fear, and assault on a bully is based on anger or better, on humiliation. Some medical malpractice cases have at their heart the greed of caregivers, while others are generated by a feeling the doctor was well-meaning but inexperienced at the procedure. Some are predicated on mistakes allegedly made by well-meaning but overworked institutions. The defense of a malpractice case may concede that a bad result was obtained and that the plaintiff is indeed greatly injured but that the team of caregivers should not be blamed because medical science is imperfect. The lawyer must see how the case feels and attempt to ingrain that feeling into the theory of the case.

§ 2.37   Emotion Becomes Fact

In so doing, an effort is made to transform the emotion of the theory of the case into a "fact" of the case. The advocate tries to make the jurors feel that dominant emotion, through the presentation of the facts. When jurors feel betrayed, angry, cynical, or any other emotion that has been targeted as part of the theory, they are determining the "fact" of the emotional aspect of the case to be valid. The object is to make the jury feel as the client did.

By integrating the dominant emotion into the theory of the case the advocate is creating a courtroom environment in which the fact finder can emotionally respond to the facts in a manner similar to how the client has responded to those same facts. This allows the fact finder to validly conclude that the client's emotional response was appropriate. The jurors are feeling what the client was feeling. In the closing argument, the argument (theory of the case) to be made is in tune with what the jurors are already feeling. The jury's emotional receiver, their humanity, is in tune with the theory of the case. They are therefore more receptive to the lawyer's theory of the case.

The opposite is true of the opponent who is advancing a theory incongruent with the dominant emotion of the case. That theory simply does not "feel" right to the jurors. That problem alone will not deprive the opponent of a favorable verdict but it will present obstacles. The chief obstacle is that the emotion experienced by the jurors stems from facts not oratory. The facts are being perceived in a particular way that produces the dominant emotion.

By arguing a theory that denies the dominant emotion, the opponent is in essence arguing for a different interpretation of the facts. In order to assist the jurors or allow the jurors to feel the targeted dominant emotion in all phases of the case, the lawyer must move them toward the dominant emotion. The lawyer moves the fact finder toward the dominant emotion by recognizing the facts within her theory of the case that produce that emotion, by making those facts important to the theory of the case, and by proving those facts to the satisfaction of the jurors. By doing so, the lawyer is moving the fact finder toward acceptance of a critical "fact" of the theory.

§ 2.38   The Dominant Emotion Can Only Be Determined by Phrasing the Theory of the Case in Lay Terms Based on the Facts, Not in Legal Phrases

A theory of the case must be phrased in language commonly used, not in the language of the law. When the lawyer uses the language of the law she has oversimplified the theory of the case. By thinking of the theory of the case in language used in everyday communication the lawyer will more easily identify the dominant emotion of that theory.

If the lawyer phrases a theory of the case in the language of the law she can too easily misjudge the dominant emotion produced by that theory. For instance the defense of a product liability case based on a failure of the product under a freak set of circumstances will produce an emotional pitch that is different than a defense of a product liability case based on a consumer's completely foolish use of a product. In the first instance the dominant emotion may be sadness and a sense of unreality that so bizarre a thing could have occurred. In the latter example the defendant's theory of the case may contain the same elements of sadness but also includes the emotion that the plaintiff has brought this tragedy upon himself. Yet both may be characterized as "tragic cases."

This example shows an instance where what might be thought of in similar legal terms is in reality two differing theories of the case producing very different dominant emotions. This situation is not all unusual. The use of legal words to describe a theory of the case gives very little guidance to the emotional aspects of the case. Not every homicide or assault case defended on the legal basis of self-defense will produce the same emotional response or a fact finder. Depending on the actions of the alleged victim, the jurors may feel abject sympathy, complete loathing, or anything in between.

Counsel must look deeper than the legal name of their defense in order to understand the dominant emotion of the case. For instance, in the defense of an assault case based upon self-defense, the fact finder may feel fairly positively about the alleged victim. That is to say, the lawyer may realize that the fact finder will not view the alleged victim as a "bad" person or a person who deserved to be assaulted. But this feeling alone will not drive the verdict. If it is predicted that the jurors will feel some sense of sorrow, some sense of loss or some sense of sympathy for the alleged victim, a defense theory of the case must take that into consideration. It should be presented not to fight against that dominant emotion but to incorporate that emotion in the theory of the case. The theory must strive therefore to make this sorrow part of the theory of the case. Word selection, tone of voice, and physical gestures must be more in tune with sorrow than with anger. The advocate must discuss how the victim unfortunately brought this upon himself, that the victim had opportunities to stop the fight but didn't, or that the victim created an appearance that was misunderstood and thereby brought about his own death.

In closing argument, the lawyer will say things such as, "We are not here to say (the alleged victim) was a bad person or that he deserved what happened. But we are here to talk about why it happened, what role he had to play in it and how the law treats his actions." If all of this were first suggested in closing argument that is far too late to begin to cope with the dominant emotion of the case. The cross-examinations themselves must be voiced in a manner similar to the tone being used in the closing argument. The questions would remain as leading and the facts brought out just as forcefully. But the voice is one tinged with understanding and a bit of sorrow.

On the other hand, in another case defended on the same legal concept of self-defense, where it can be fairly presented that the alleged victim was a bully who goaded, insulted, and otherwise hounded the defendant into the act of self-defense, the emotional content of the theory is sharper. The facts have changed, the likely perception of the jurors concerning the alleged victim has changed and as a result the dominant emotion has changed.

There is room for the lawyer to cross-examine with a sharper tone of voice. The pace of questions can be quicker and the tone of the cross-examination can be more forceful. This is not a license to be ugly or unduly emotional towards a witness. But there is license to conduct the same cross-examination in a slightly elevated emotional pitch. The lawyer can display far less understanding of the actions of the alleged victim and far less sorrow for the consequences of the episode. Under these facts, while the defense theory using generic legal terms might properly be titled "self-defense," more specifically it may be thought of as, "He brought it on himself." Therefore the lawyer may seek to generate within the jury a different emotion than the sadness that was part and parcel of the theory in the previous self-defense example.

In comparing the two self-defense cases, the recitation of facts in opening statement can and should be used to create within the jurors differing dominant emotions. The dominant emotion can be generated in an entirely proper opening statement by the techniques of selecting, compiling, and accentuating specific facts, aided only slightly, if at all, by the tone of voice. Remember always that the courtroom magnifies any display of emotion (see chapter 13, *The Relationship of Opening Statement to Cross-Examination*). Counsel is advised always to underplay the emotions of a case. If the facts are recited in a powerful way, assembled to paint specific and fitting pictures of a bully who is goading the defendant, the facts alone will convey the dominant emotion. It is through the powerful recitation of facts that the jury is guided toward the dominant emotion of the theory. If the facts can validly generate the emotion, the fact finders will feel it, even if the lawyer can't and won't argue it.

Assume in a breach of an employment contract suit that the employer has terminated the employee. The employee claims that termination was based on improper considerations, but the defense alleges just cause. In legal jargon the case may be termed a "wrongful termination case." The effect of using legal terms is to mask the underlying factual and emotional scenario that characterizes a true theory of the case. This legally phrased scenario may be susceptible to a wide spectrum of possible dominant emotions. In fact, at first blush, many trial lawyers would say there is no emotion in a termination of contract case. But of course there is. When additional facts beyond change are considered, it is readily apparent that, in fact, there are dominant emotions.

In the first scenario, assume that the employer terminated the employee two weeks before Christmas and that the facts beyond change would show that the timing was intentional. The timing was intentional to send a "signal" to the other key employees that they, too, could be terminated if production did not increase. This calculated termination prior to a major holiday creates a dominant emotion or passion of "unfairness," or "ruthlessness," and "profit at any cost."

In the second scenario, the employee is terminated two weeks before Christmas. But the employer will testify, and it is a fact beyond change, that the employer did everything in his power to keep the employee on, including taking substantial cuts in earnings by the employer, borrowing money at the bank, and making efforts to find the employee a similar position with competitive corporations. In this context, the dominant emotion certainly would not be "ruthlessness" or "profit at any cost," but more of an understanding tone coupled with a firmness based on "the employer gave his word when he signed the contract." While this may be a firm statement, it is made with understanding and without vindictiveness.

Both are breach of contract cases. Both rely on documents and timing that will not change, but each calls for a different emotional pitch. Quite clearly what differs in the examples are the facts of the case, which in turn drive different emotional responses. The lesson is that it is insufficient to postulate a theory of the case in purely legal terms, such as "breach of contract," "self-defense," "contributory negligence," etc. Instead counsel must conceptualize her theory of the case in more particular terms such as, "We did everything we could," "He brought it on himself," or "He never should have used the product this way." By characterizing the theory of the case in lay language on specific facts, counsel can more accurately determine the dominant emotion of that theory.

§ 2.39 Our Cross-Examination — Emotion

Of course, cross-examination presents an enormous opportunity to generate the dominant emotion. In fact, it is the single best opportunity to do so because cross-examination is where the lawyer develops the greatest tension between conflicting facts. The interaction between the lawyer and the witness is itself so productive of emotion that the time is ripe for the development of the target emotion so long as the lawyer has realized what emotion needs to be generated. The voice, the sequence of questioning, the lawyer's body movements, all give the jury insight into how the lawyer feels about a particular set of facts. That alone will not convince the jurors to adopt the dominant emotion, but it helps. The lawyer can, moreover, style her questions, choice of words, and mood to create within the courtroom the emotion that the lawyer has targeted. If the lawyer is quiet and understanding as she asks leading questions, or if there is a show of anger at the situation that the lawyer alleges was created by the opponent, the lawyer gives an emotional context to the facts. The advocate must make sure that the emotional context is in keeping with the chosen theory of the case. The choices of emotions and the means of expressing them must be made in accordance with the dominant emotion of the case, which must, in turn, be coordinated with the theory of the case.

§ 2.40   Employing the Dominant Emotion from Voir Dire to Closing Argument

For too many years, lawyers have viewed closing argument as not only the best, but the sole phase in which to create and express the dominant emotion of the theory of the case. In fact, properly presented facts will generate the appropriate emotions. Any voir dire that discusses the issues in the case may provide an outlet for the dominant emotion of the theory of the case. The facts are discussed in opening statement. They contain facts from the body of both direct and cross-examinations. There are ample opportunities throughout the trial to give voice to the dominant emotion. It is suggested that the resolution of the case rarely depends on the closing arguments (see chapter 1, *Philosophy and Overview of the Science of Cross-Examination*). Waiting until closing argument to inject the proper emotion is too late. There is a need to create in the jury the dominant emotion of the theory long before closing argument, although closing argument can and should act as a reaffirmation of that emotion.

When voir dire is available, it can be used to help ingrain the dominant emotion of the theory. One of the principle goals of voir dire is to seek within the jurors' life experiences those events that have as their common denominator the dominant emotion of the defendant's theory of the case. By eliciting discussion of such life experiences, the jurors are required to think of personal situations that produced the same emotion characterizing the advocate's theory of the case. As early as voir dire, before the jurors have been selected, the advocate may begin to inject into the trial the dominant emotion. By doing so, the advocate will raise the jurors' level of awareness of the circumstances that have caused them to feel that emotion in the affairs of their own life.

§ 2.41   Changing Facts Beyond Change: The Use of Motions in Limine — Civil Applications

To review: A fact beyond change is a fact that will be believed by the jury as accurate regardless of the best efforts to dispute or modify it. But in order for the fact finder to form that judgment the fact must be introduced at the trial or hearing. As discussed, the consequence of a fact beyond change limits or channels the available theories of the case. If the lawyer removes a harmful fact beyond change, the advocate simultaneously opens up the available theories of the case. The motion in limine is a method of potentially removing harmful facts beyond change.

In civil cases, the motion in limine remains an entirely appropriate vehicle to employ in shaping the theory of the case. Though often based on evidentiary rules rather than constitutional grounds, the motion in limine's application is identical to a motion to suppress in criminal law; it limits the evidence available to an opponent or expands the evidence for the lawyer's theory of the case. The consequence of winning a motion in limine is to either weaken the foundation of an opponent's theory of the case or to remove an impediment to the theory of the case proposed by the proponent of the motion. Just as discovery provides additional facts with which to fashion theories and to block the opponent's theories, the motion in limine seeks to withdraw or add facts useful to the opponent or harmful to your theory of the case. Thus, counsel should make use of the motion in limine to preclude the admission of harmful evidence. Simultaneously counsel should explore methods of incorporating that evidence into their theory of the case, or neutralizing that evidence.

§ 2.42 Using the Motion in Limine to Add Evidence in Support of a Theory of the Case

A motion in limine is not always designed to limit evidence; it can be designed to seek a pre-trial ruling permitting the admission of evidence. When finding evidence that supports the lawyer's theory of the case, but that may be ruled inadmissible, it is necessary to create ways of verifying its admissibility. The motion in limine seeking the admission of evidence needs to be heard as far before trial as possible. The ruling will have consequences on the theory of the case in the overall trial tactics including the scope of the cross-examinations.

Many judges put off such rulings until shortly before trial and at times even until trial has commenced. This makes for a great deal of uncertainty, but such is life in the courtroom. A theory of the case cannot safely be predicated on the belief that counsel will prevail in the motion in limine. In other words the theory of the case must be able to rest on other facts whose admissibility is not in question. By winning the right to admit the evidence subject to the motion, counsel expands the available theories of the case, or creates additional facts in support of that theory or obtains additional facts useful in undermining the opponent's theory of the case. By admitting additional evidence, the good theory of the case can be dramatically strengthened, or a non-viable theory may be reborn and made viable.

§ 2.43 Request for Admissions Can Shape Facts Beyond Change

In civil cases, requests for admissions and for authentication of documents can be a powerful tool to be used early in the discovery process before the opposing counsel has learned or understood the advocate's theory of the case. By the careful wording of the request for admissions using detailed and descriptive facts, as well as identification and request for authenticity of documents or photographs, the opposing counsel can be forced unwittingly to stipulate to facts beyond change that will greatly enhance the advocate's theory of the case. On the other hand, the admissions to certain facts or authentication of certain documents may well put in jeopardy theories of the case that lend themselves to the opponent, but which the opponent has not yet identified as being a viable theory of her case.

§ 2.44   Changing Facts Beyond Change — The Role of Criminal Motion Practice

If a fact beyond change is a fact that, if testified to, will be believed by the jury in spite of efforts by opposing counsel, how then can a fact beyond change be changed? In criminal cases, the goal can be achieved through motion practice. A motion to suppress evidence is a motion to delete certain facts beyond change.

The worst part of a drug case is normally the defendant's possession of the drug. In many cases, it would be a fact beyond change. That is to say, after the agents testify, a jury will believe that the defendant did possess the illegal drug. However, that will only be a fact beyond change if the opponent is permitted to get in the evidence of the defendant's possession of the substance.

In many cases, the defendant's confession is a fact beyond change. This narrows the available theories. Even if the confession is explainable, that a confession was made is itself a fact beyond change.

To the extent that a motion to suppress evidence succeeds in whole or in part, these facts beyond change disappear from the lawsuit. Since the suppressed facts are never available to the fact finder, they cannot be facts in dispute. They cannot be facts of the lawsuit. They cannot be facts beyond change.

The absence of drugs in a drug case is almost always fatal to the prosecution. The absence of a confession in other cases may open wide the available theories of the case. For this reason, in a criminal case, defense counsel must zealously search out facts subject to motion practice, such as suppression of an identification, an item of evidence, a confession, or similar evidence. The motions are the greatest method of broadening the available theories of the case, while simultaneously eliminating the opponent's best facts beyond change.

Prosecutors also have access to a motion practice that can alter the facts to be heard by the fact finder. For instance prosecutors have increasingly sought to admit evidence of similar transactions. This is fertile ground for both the prosecution and defense motion practice. When a prosecutor seeks the admission of similar transactions, the effect is to add an enormous number of harmful facts with which the defense must now contend. The motion, if granted, has added additional support for the prosecution's case.

A prosecution motion to admit evidence may impact defendant's available theories of the case or it may simply make the current theory of the case more difficult for the opponent to establish. For instance, by admitting a series of similar transactions to prove identification, the government seeks to deprive the defense of the ability to argue identity successfully. Showing that the defendant committed an earlier crime, and showing the similarities of that crime to the present crime, the government hopes to establish the identity of the defendant as the perpetrator of both crimes. While a misidentification theory of the case may still remain arguable, it is greatly injured by the similar transactions evidence. A successful motion in limine, defeating the use of a similar transaction, may revitalize a theory of the case based on mistaken identification by eliminating certain facts beyond change.

When the prosecution seeks the admission of statements of a codefendant, or the right to call an expert to interpret the meaning of supposedly code words the defendant has said over the telephone, the prosecution is asking to add facts, and in some instances moving to add facts and inferences that can become so strong that they become facts beyond change.

§ 2.45 Motions to Block Emotional Aspects of Case

Another use of the motion in limine is to block the admission of evidence that damages the emotional aspects of a theory of the case. Ordinarily, the cross-examiner seeks to generate certain emotions consistent with her theory of the case. For instance, if counsel is seeking to portray his client as frightened, confused, or weak, the opponent will likely offer evidence that portrays him as confident and strong. A motion in limine precluding the admission of such evidence leaves open to the cross-examiner the ability to create her target emotion (vulnerability), which in turn enhances the theory of the case dependent upon the existence of that emotion.

§ 2.46 Prioritizing Motion Practice and Pre-trial Discovery by Effect on the Theory of the Case

In a perfect world, infinite time and resources would be available to explore every theory, fully litigate every motion, and fully investigate every fact. The world of the trial lawyer has never been and will never be one of infinite time and resources. Energies must be focused.

In developing a theory of the case for a civil or a criminal trial, time and effort must be directed to those areas most likely to advance the theory of the case. Translating this to pre-trial discovery and motion practice, the following can be said: If the best theory of the case is blocked by the existence of a fact, or can be made substantially better by the introduction of a fact, it is worth all the time to develop a motion or request for admission that precludes the introduction of the undesired fact, or to develop a motion or request for admission that permits the inclusion of that fact. By prevailing in this single endeavor, the lawyer more favorably alters the course of trial than through use of the same time and energy in an attempt to prepare a theory of the case that is blocked by a fact beyond change, or which is fatally lacking supporting facts.

It may take 25 hours of preparation to try a drug possession case and an additional 25 hours to prepare fully and try the motion to suppress the drugs. Assuming counsel truly does not have available time to do both, and assuming that the drug case is solid and easily proven, counsel would be better off fully preparing and litigating the motion to suppress evidence, as its success erases the need to spend any hours in trial preparation. Conversely, its failure dramatically limits the theories available to the defense. Viewed another way: The same hours devoted to the motion practice could potentially produce a dead certain winner, while, assuming admission of the drugs, the hours spent in trial preparation produces, at best, a skillful loss.

In order to prioritize among the many pre-trial endeavors that deserve the lawyer's time, the lawyer must look at which motion has the greatest affect on the theory of the case. In theory the advocate may file an endless array of discovery motions or litigate all of the motions that may be conceived. But in a world of finite resources, the lawyer must allocate her time and money resources to those motions whose success most profoundly affects the theory of the case. By so doing, the lawyer spends her efforts in areas most likely to affect the outcome of her case.

In a personal injury case based on an automobile accident case where the insurance defense attorney's theory of the case rests upon the fact that the plaintiff's injuries suffered in his collision are much more minor than are being portrayed, less time should be spent as to the "fault" or liability concerning the collision. Much time and much precise investigation will be committed to the diagnosis and proximate cause of the alleged injuries and to the medical condition of the plaintiff before the collision.

§ 2.47   Converting the Theory of the Case into a Theme — Theme Lines, Phrases, and Words

A theory of the case is the concise statement that the lawyer spoke to herself in defining how to convince a jury of the rightness of her position. But, that statement, short as it might be, can sometimes be too cumbersome to convey to a jury. In order to use a theory of the case as a persuasive tool, it is often possible and useful to convert the theory of the case into a theme phrase. The theme distills the essence of the theory of the case into a short refrain capable of being formed into a question on cross-examination.

A theory of the case might have only one theme that distills the essence of that theory. A theory of the case may have multiple themes that, when coupled together, distill the essence of the theory of the case. If the theory supports multiple themes, the themes must be consistent and capable of being interwoven together to completely support the theory. The theory may be distilled further in that the theme becomes stated in a theme line, phrase, or word capable of capturing and making memorable the theme, and therefore the theory.

Theme lines can be sentences, phrases, or simple words. Themes may be distilled further into theme lines, phrases, or words. That does not necessarily mean that a simple word, phrase or theme line will represent the entire theme or theory. In other words, theme lines, phrases, and words are shorthand efforts to state a theme and theory, but may not capture all of the theory in a shorthand presentation. They will only represent that theory.

One of the most memorable examples in turning a theory into a theme is found in Dr. Martin Luther King's speech delivered in the march on Washington, August 28, 1963. The portion of his speech best remembered, and, in fact, the words that have come to best symbolize Dr. King's work, are set out below:

> I say to you today, my friends, so even though we face the difficulties
> of today and tomorrow, *I still have a dream*. It is a dream deeply rooted

in the American meaning of its creed, "We hold these truths to be self-evident, that all men are created equal."

I have a dream that one day on the red hills of Georgia, sons of former slaves and the sons of former slave owners will be able to sit down together at the table of brotherhood.

I have a dream that one day even the state of Mississippi, a state sweltering with the heat of injustice, sweltering with the heat of oppression, will be transformed into an oasis of freedom and justice.

I have a dream that my four little children will one day live in a nation where they will not be judged by the color of their skin, but the content of their character.

I have a dream today!

I have a dream that one day down in Alabama — with its vicious racists — with its governor having his lips dripping with the words of interposition and nullification — one day right there in Alabama, little black boys and black girls will be able to join hands with the little white boys and white girls as sisters and brothers.

I have a dream today!

I have a dream that one day "every valley shall be exalted and every hill and mountain shall be made low. The rough places will be made plain and the crooked places will be made straight, and the glory of the Lord shall be revealed, and all flesh shall see it together."

In presenting his cause to the nation and to the world, Dr. King's theory was clearly that America ought to offer liberty and justice equally to all people regardless of race. As a vehicle for advancing his theory, he adopted the phrase, "I have a dream." That phrase symbolized not only the fact that racial equality was still missing in America, but also the hope that it could be achieved. His effectiveness in synthesizing a very complex theory into a memorable theme and a theme line is borne out by the fact that in the United States, and many parts of the world, people who never heard the speech, nor have ever read it, can identify the theme, "I have a dream," and correctly translate its meaning into their own words. In this way "I have a dream" has been transformed into a theme and a theme line symbolizing the much more complex theory. When that theme line is heard, people immediately envision the facts of racial injustice and the hope for a fairer world, upon which the theory is built.

In a complex copyright infringement action based on the alleged copying of copyrighted software, the defense theory of the case was that the software allegedly copied had very little marketplace value. Therefore the damages, if any, are quite small. A key component of the defendant's cross-examination was the fact that although many demonstration packages of the software were made available to potential customers relatively few customers bought a license to use the software. Of the few who purchased the license to use the software, even fewer chose to renew their license. This can be converted into the theme phrase: "Those that try it don't buy it."

In the appropriate self-defense case the phrase, "He just kept coming," may well communicate the best aspects of the theory of the case.

In a case predicated on the conduct of certain mutual funds managers who allowed after hours trading in violation of their prospectus and to the detriment of their other customers a theme phrase might be: "But they let them do it any way."

Once a theory of the case has been reduced to a theme, that theme can be used in the course of the cross-examination of witnesses associated with the opponent (see chapter 26, *Loops, Double Loops, and Spontaneous Loops*).

§ 2.48   Common Themes in Cases

In self-defense cases, cross-examiners often claim the theory that the victim was the initial aggressor. A theme, or one of the themes, was that the defendant retreated, but the aggressor continued the attack. Possible theme lines might be, "But he didn't stop," "But he wouldn't stop," "But he just kept coming," or "He kept pushing it." In order to create these themes, the cross-examiner must search for and develop facts within the case that permit the lawyer, through cross-examination, to demonstrate that the victim didn't stop the action, refused to stop the action, or kept initiating action. The cross-examiner is seeking to create opportunities to require opposing witnesses to admit or verify a theme line, which verifies the theme, which verifies the theory. After establishing the appropriate facts that made the theme line true, the cross-examiner adds a leading question that incorporates the theme line, and forces the witness to give an admission as to that theme line. By this method, facts are introduced that support the theory of the case. The cross-examiner then makes the theory more memorable by forcing admission of the selected theme line by witnesses to verify the accuracy of the theme statement. In this way, facts beyond change become inextricably interwoven with the theory.

In a contract case where one party is insisting that the contract be performed and the other party is attempting to have the contract declared null and void, a possible theme line might be: "She gave her word," "Her word is her bond," or "A contract is a promise."

In a road wreck case where the defendant was highly intoxicated, a theme line of plaintiff's counsel might be, "She knew she would have to drive home, but she kept on drinking," or "She knew she was drunk, but she got in the car anyway."

In a domestic relations case where custody is an issue, a theme line for the wife may be, "She always put the children first," or "Whatever sacrifice it took, the children always had as good as she could provide."

§ 2.49   Integration of Theory of the Case Throughout the Case

Themes, theme lines, phrases, or words are key phrases that synthesize and symbolize the theory of the case. Themes can be repeated in the opening statement, direct examination, cross-examination, and closing argument. To be effective, a theme must encapsulate the more complex theory so that the very uttering of the theme line, phrase, or word calls to the jurors' minds the essence of the theory of the case.

Having researched the facts in order to prepare opportunities to introduce the theme line in cross-examination, the lawyer begins its use *no later* than opening statement. In opening statement, the lawyer will set forth her facts with great particularity. The theme line is then added as an emphasizing statement. In this way, the theory of the case is cemented in the jury's mind in the opening statement, and the theory, as expressed in theme lines, theme phrases, and theme words, becomes familiar, comfortable, and, thus, more memorable.

The following short section of opening statement shows introduction of the theme:

> James Donaldson came to the door. It was a screen door. He could see out. He could see Danny. And James Donaldson could have stopped there, but he didn't. He shoved open the screen door and ran outside. He could have stopped there, but he didn't. He ran at Danny. He ran fifty-one feet down the sidewalk toward Danny. He could have stopped at any point — but he didn't. And as he got closer to Danny, he made his hands into fists. And he cocked back his right arm. He still could have stopped, but he didn't. And he brought his right arm back, by his ear to get ready to hit Danny. Still he could have stopped, but he didn't. And finally, as he came charging into Danny, fists at the ready, five foot seven, sixteen-year-old Danny pulled out the knife and he stabbed six foot one, twenty-two-year-old James Donaldson. He stabbed this bigger, older man who so many times could have stopped, but didn't.

But opening statement is sometimes not the first opportunity to establish a theme line, or the first opportunity to put across to the jury the theory of the case. Voir dire, where available, should be used to introduce both the theory and its theme line or theme lines. Although in voir dire the lawyer cannot announce theme lines and theory to a jury, by asking questions of the jurors that compel them to discuss situations in their own lives to which the theme line would be equally applicable, the lawyer has introduced to the jurors the key concept that shall be brought alive throughout the case.

Of course, in closing argument, the lawyer is free to use the theme lines, phrases, and words. The best use of it is as a summary line following a recitation of groupings of facts that made its use appropriate. After the lawyer has discussed with the jurors the supporting facts that prove out the theory of the case, the lawyer can then state the theme line, such as, "But he didn't stop." In this way, the theme of the case can be made the dominant discussion point of jury deliberations. Furthermore, this method solidifies the theme line in the jurors' minds as it symbolizes the key aspects of the cross-examination. Therefore, any juror who recites or remembers the advocate's theme line or slogan will recall the outlines of the theory that translates the best cross-examination materials. The facts have been organized around the theme line so that a fact finder recalling the theme phrase will automatically recall the advocate's best factual evidence.

In any case in which inconsistencies in the key witness's statement are productive of the best theory of the case, a theme line such as, "Now she can explain it," "The facts changed," "But the truth changed," or "Now he has changed his mind," all serve to remind the jurors of the numerous inconsistencies in the testimony of the key witnesses. Once again, the mechanism for inserting these theme lines into the case remains the same. Foreshadowing in voir dire (when possible), announcement in opening statement, admission and repetition in cross-examination, affirmation in direct examination (when used) and revitalization in closing argument.

All of the theme lines discussed thus far are a straightforward shorthand statement for a theory of the case. When the lawyer is attacking the credibility of a witness based upon multiple inconsistencies in his or her statements, a theme phrase such as, "But the truth changed," is shorthand for the shifting nature of the witness's recollection.

§ 2.50   Mocking/Sarcastic Theme Lines (With or Without the Accompanying Tone of Voice)

A word of great caution: The use of a sarcastic or a mocking voice creates very real and substantial risks of lowering the credibility of the lawyer. As is often the case it is far better to allow the facts to speak for themselves rather than to overlay the facts with a tone of voice or manner that some jurors and judges may find objectionable both in the legal and communicative sense.

There is, however, a technique, a method of putting up a theme line that gently mocks the opponent's version while simultaneously summarizing the advocate's theory of the case. In appropriate cases, the lawyer can use irony, underplayed sarcasm, or a slight mocking tone in developing a theme line that successfully symbolizes the theory of the case while simultaneously pointing out the weakness of the opponent's theory. An example of such a mocking theme is found in Shakespeare's *Julius Caesar*. Following the assassination of Caesar, his loyal friend, Mark Antony, sought the permission of Brutus to speak over the body of Caesar. Brutus permitted Mark Antony to do so only on the express condition that Mark Antony not cast any blame on Brutus and the other assassins. Mark Antony agreed to this and in his speech (read: closing argument), he scrupulously observed the agreement:

> Friends, Romans, countrymen, lend me your ears!
> I come to bury Caesar, not to praise him.
> The evil that men do lives after them,
> The good is oft interred with their bones;
> So let it be with Caesar. The noble Brutus
> Hath told you Caesar was ambitious;
> If it were so, it was a grievous fault,
> And grievously had Caesar answer'd it.
> Here, under leave of Brutus and the rest
> *For Brutus is an honorable man,*

So are they all, all honorable men,
Come I to speak in Caesar's funeral.
He was my friend, faithful and just to me;
But Brutus says he was ambitious,
And Brutus is an honorable man.
He had brought many captives home to Rome,
Whose ransoms did the general coffers fill;
Did this in Caesar seem ambitious?
When that the poor have cried, Caesar hath wept;
Ambition should be made of sterner stuff:
Yet Brutus says he was ambitious,
And Brutus is an honorable man.
You all did see that on the Lupercal
I thrice presented him a kingly crown,
This he did thrice refuse. Was this ambition?
Yet Brutus says he was ambitious,
And sure he is an honorable man.
I speak not to disprove what Brutus spoke,
But here I am to speak what I do know.
You all did love him once, not without cause;
What cause withholds you then to mourn for him?
O judgment! thou [art] fled to brutish beasts,
And men have lost their reason. Bear with me,
My heart is in the coffin there with Caesar,
And I must pause till it come back to me.

William Shakespeare, *Julius Caesar*, III, ii, 75-109.

At the conclusion of Mark Antony's speech in which he literally abided by the command that he cast no blame upon the assassins, and indeed repeatedly called them honorable men, the citizens of Rome turned on Brutus and his co-conspirators, causing Brutus to take his own life.

Whether civil, domestic, or criminal, adept cross-examiners may achieve the same figurative result by repeatedly putting before the jury evidence of a witness's ability and willingness to lie. By repeatedly establishing that the witness has lied in the past to satisfy his needs, and has lied to many types of people under many types of situations, the jury is led to the conclusion that the credibility of this witness is so low that a verdict based upon this witness' testimony is unjustified. In such instances, the lawyer may chose to adopt Mark Antony's stratagem and create a theme in praise of the "truthful" character of such a witness. Such a theme could be, "You are an honest man," "We have your word on it," or "You wouldn't lie to us." By requiring the witness during cross-examination to repeatedly admit his lies, call himself a liar, and explain why he has lied to better his position, the cross-examiner has established credibility to use any one of the theme phrases previously mentioned. The cross-examiner could further parallel Shakespeare's writings by reminding the jury: "My opponent says Mr. Jones wouldn't lie to you." In this manner, by repeatedly referring to the "truthful" character of the witness, the lawyer reminds the jurors of the wholesale lack of credibility of that witness. Furthermore, use of such a theme phrase focuses the jury's attention on the opponent's efforts to win based upon the supposed truthfulness of that witness.

This leaves the opponent the unenviable task of either arguing against that fact beyond change (a potential failure), or arguing that the witness *is* ready, willing and able to lie, but is not lying this time. All of this is done well within the bounds of ethics and decorum, as the cross-examiner has not termed the witness a liar and has, in fact, repeatedly said the opposite. In arriving at that verdict, every time any juror mentions the theme phrase, it will reawaken memories of the lies told by the witness, the deceptions engineered by the witness, and the people victimized by the witness. The jury will see their verdict as a judgment on the credibility of the witness. The credibility of the witness potentially becomes the only issue in the case.

In a commercial litigation case, the corporate defendant may well urge as part of its theory of the case that it was only employing its customary business practices. This then could lead to an opponent's repeated questioning cross-examination, "It was just business as usual?" The tone of voice can be completely neutral but the content or message of that theme phrase is that harmful or inappropriate conduct is a routine matter in the course of conducting the defendant's business.

§ 2.51   Integrating the Theme of the Case

Inserting theme lines throughout the case integrates the theory of the case from voir dire through instructions. In every phase of the case, opportunities are created to express the theory of the case and ingrain that theme. In voir dire, discussion is had with the jurors concerning their own life experience, which hopefully generated within them parallel emotions and concepts to that which the lawyer will express in the theory of the case. In opening statement, the lawyer can announce and articulate the theme as the jury is given a detailed preview of the facts to come, using theme lines as punctuation points. Care will be taken to express the theme line in such a way that it cannot be ruled argumentative. Theme lines such as: "But he didn't stop," or "now it has changed," or "when it would benefit him, he has lied" are all fair game. They express what the evidence will show rather than the lawyer's comment upon the evidence. They are tied to facts beyond change.

It is in cross-examination that the theory and theme lines become most visible to the jurors. The thrust of the cross-examination is to support the theory of the case. But in cross-examination, the cross-examiner also encounters the best opportunities to ingrain theme lines. It is in cross-examination that the lawyer can cause opposing witnesses to affirm the cross-examiner's theme lines and require a "yes" answer to such theme phrases as: "But now it has changed," "So you lied," "You are just a good businessman," "You are an honest man, aren't you," "You love your family, but . . .," "But you didn't stop," "You lied when it would . . .," or any other such theme line.

When the opponent cross-examines witnesses who support proponent's theory, the witnesses will know the theme lines, phrases, and words that are the key to the proponent's case. The witnesses' use of these lines will make difficult or impossible an effective cross-examination.

In closing argument, jurors are reminded of the theme. A theme line properly integrated causes the jurors to remember the critical areas of cross examination where the opposing side admits the theory that was tied to that theme line. The instructions then verify for the jury that there is a legal basis for proponents theme. Whether it is the credibility of witnesses instruction, preponderance of the evidence, elements of neglect, a special instruction on the right to defend one's self based on apparent necessity, "duress," or "choice of evils," there is some instruction that contains within it a reference to the concepts embraced by the chosen theme line and the theory.

In this manner, the theory of the case has been ingrained through every stage of the trial. Tactical avenues have been created to permit expression of the theme in each phase. The entire case is organized around the theory of the case, and this sense of cohesion or purpose permits the jury's attention to continually focus on the best aspects of the case from the cross-examiner's point of reference. Eventually, use of the theme lines reminds the jurors of the points earlier scored during the course of the trial.

Chapter 3

INTRODUCTION TO THE STRATEGY, PREPARATION, AND ORGANIZATION OF CROSS-EXAMINATION

SYNOPSIS

§ 3.01   Recognizing the Need and Value of a Cross-Examination Preparation System

There is a unifying thought that travels through every concept in this system: Preparation above all other things makes better trial lawyers. Better preparation of the case will inevitably produce better cross-examinations. This, in turn, permits better opening statements and better closing arguments. If the lawyer wishes to give better cross-examinations, preparation is essential. But it is not enough to say the lawyer must prepare. There are techniques for preparation of cross-examination, just as there are techniques for the delivery of cross-examination. There is a science to preparation.

It is preparation more than any other factor that makes a lawyer steady in the courtroom. Preparation is the quiet work in the office and in the mind that leads to the very visible sense of control in the courtroom. The advocate who desires to become a great cross-examiner has only to better prepare their cross-examinations. Courtroom power stems largely from pre-trial preparation.

Lawyers have sometimes said that a particular cross-examination just wrote itself. What they probably meant is that they could envision what needed to be written, so the writing of the cross-examination seemed to flow. The better the advocate envisions her theory of the case, the easier it is to prepare the necessary cross-examination chapters. But cross-examination chapters don't write themselves. A disciplined lawyer writes them.

Undoubtedly each advocate will be called upon at various times to deliver many cross-examinations without thorough, written preparation. That does not mean that this is the preferred method of preparing to cross-examine. Undeniably, when the time comes to cross-examine, every lawyer can stand up and ask questions. But the unfocused asking of questions is not so much cross-examination as discovery by trial. An unfocused cross-examiner is much more likely to resort to browbeating, nit picking, or some style of cross-examination designed to gratify one's ego. When the questions are not prepared around the theory of the case and the material is not organized into chapters, the cross-examination is not a path to success. It is a wander in the woods. The task of the cross-examiner is to make use of the facts available. A cross-examination without organization results in an uneven use of the facts available. This is not a method. It invariably becomes a painful process for both attorney and client. Many points may be scored, but many points are missed. Worse, many points score against the lawyer. Many chapters may go well, but many unnecessary battles are fought and lost. There is a better way. Special problems and techniques of cross-examination without discovery are discussed in chapter 27, *Cross-Examination Without Discovery*.

§ 3.02   There Must Be Efficiency in Lawyer's Preparation Time

The starting point of the science of cross-examination is the development of a first draft of the theory of the case (see chapter 2, *Developing a Theory of the Case*). After developing a theory of the case, the advocate can engage in the systematic cataloging of facts currently available. This sequence of theory development followed by factual review permits the lawyer to appreciate just what facts are available and useful to that theory of the case. At this point, the lawyer can engage in the systematic course of discovery and investigation in order to add further facts necessary to strengthen that theory of the case and to fill in the gaps in the catalog of existing facts.

A fundamental principle of cross-examination preparation is that it permits the cross-examiner to better utilize the facts and evidence available. A fact available but not noticed or not understood during the pre-trial preparation will not be usable within the cross-examinations. Indeed, a great deal of the science of cross-examination is the better utilization of facts that were always available. A lack of theory-based preparation of cross-examination chapters leads to the inadequate use of the facts available. Techniques that give added emphasis to the total facts available will be discussed. But first and most fundamentally, the lawyer must begin her preparation of cross-examination by determining what facts are likely available for use in creating strong cross-examinations built around a recognized theory of the case.

The trial lawyer is always looking for the one fact that will make the case, or the fact will lead to the unraveling of the opponent's case. However, before investing time and money looking for new facts, the skilled advocate must first evaluate the facts that already exist within the file. These may be facts brought in by the client, or in criminal cases, the facts that an opponent must disclose upon request. The trial lawyer should first evaluate what facts have been collected before she begins spending her time and money on supplementing that collection of facts. There are systems that make the cataloging of available facts much easier, less time-consuming, and more productive. These systems are enhanced by additional methods of gathering facts necessary to fill out the desired chapters. On top of these preparation systems are techniques of converting the material into usable pages of cross-examination (see chapters 5, 6, and 7).

Is it possible to have too much discovery? Is it possible to have too many facts? The answer unfortunately is yes and no. It is possible to gather too much evidence. The problem is not the bulk of the evidence, but the value of that evidence in relationship to the contrasting theories of the case. It is easily possible to acquire a multitude of facts of little use. It is very hard to acquire too many facts in support of a focused theory of the case.

It is a waste of time, money, and energy to engage in an unfocused discovery that is designed to uncover facts that relate only tangentially, if at all, to the chapters of cross-examination necessary to build the theory of the case or to attack the opponent's theory of the case.

This may occur because the advocate has not focused on the cross-examinations necessary to win the case. This in turn happens because the advocate has not focused her discovery efforts around her theory of the case. Whether the case is civil or criminal, small or large, the first task is to create a draft theory of the case. She must then understand the currently available facts to determine how they assist in building the chapters necessary to support that theory of the case or how they assist in undermining the opponent's theory of the case. Finally, she must employ discovery or investigation efforts designed to further strengthen the theory of the case or to further undermine the opponent's theory of the case.

§ 3.03   The Preparation System Must Be Simple to Operate

A useful preparation system is required to accomplish the goals of analyzing the facts available and employing discovery or investigative efforts designed to support the advocate's theory of the case or to attack the opponent's theory of the case. In order to be useful to a busy trial lawyer, any preparation system must be efficient. It is highly inefficient and time-consuming to depend on a non-system "system" in which counsel, while reading the discovery, makes notes of particular facts or aspects of the case, and then having compiled notes on that aspect or that issue, rereads the discovery looking for all of the versions or facts relating to another issue. This "system" requires the lawyer to read the discovery as many times as there are issues to be studied. While the repetitious review of discovery would eventually permit a trial lawyer to prepare for cross-examination, it is so wasteful of precious time that it is a system only for the lawyer with but a single case to prepare. A lawyer using this non-system can only survive if she is being paid hourly, and if she has a client who has money to burn.

In the real world, the only systems that are affordable are those that allow the lawyer to simply reduce discovery, in whatever quantity, into groupings of facts that can be quickly and easily used to draft cross-examinations. The system must be accurate so that it picks up the nuances of the facts related by the witnesses, groups them in some logical way, and puts them into a format so that the facts may be immediately transferred to paper in the course of writing the cross-examination chapters.

In the event of a witness denial, the rules of impeachment require that the lawyer be ready to confront a witness with the time, place, and person to whom they made a statement and the text of their former statement on that fact. Each of the three systems discussed in this book have been developed to meet all of these requirements.

§ 3.04 The Search for Relevant Facts and Inconsistencies

Even a moderately experienced lawyer, reading discovery a single time, gains a sense of the case. That is not to say that any lawyer, regardless of experience, can read the discovery a single time and know the nuances of the cross-examinations. In fact, the contrary is true. The more voluminous the discovery, the less likely it is that the factual nuances can be detected or appreciated. The process of reading discovery yields, at most, an overall feel of the case. While this overall sense of the case minimally equips a lawyer to cross-examine with a moderate amount of preparation, the lawyer cannot yet cross-examine thoroughly or scientifically. Much important material is lost to the cross-examiner either through lack of recognition or lack of development.

Creating cross-examinations through multiple readings of discovery is both an inefficient and ineffective method of preparing for cross-examinations. Mastery of the facts cannot be achieved through multiple readings of discovery. While the repetitious reading of discovery, even if possible, will undoubtedly help a lawyer recognize important facts, the process does very little to integrate the facts into usable stories or chapters. The relationship of one fact to another is easily lost. Until the facts gained through discovery are organized in a systematic format, it is likely that much of the valuable information in the discovery will remain hidden.

The organization of the facts must occur through a systematic method that groups facts together in a meaningful way. All the facts or versions of the facts that bear on a particular chapter need to be brought together so that a skillful lawyer can determine how to use those facts to build a chapter. In addition, when facts are brought together around a central theme the advocate can recognize the internal (given by the same witness) and external (in comparison with other witnesses) inconsistencies within the facts. Of course, the ability to make these external factual comparisons requires that the versions of facts offered by other witnesses be similarly grouped into a systematic format.

The systematic organization of facts permits the advocate to recognize another form of external inconsistency: inconsistencies with tangible or physical evidence. To be efficient, a cross-examination preparation system must permit a comparison of a witness's version of a fact with any physical or tangible evidence bearing on that fact. All these comparisons are based on logic.

§ 3.05   The Search for Facts of Assistance

A useful cross-examination preparation must accomplish far more than illustrate inconsistencies. Inconsistencies are largely useful in attacking the credibility of a witness but are less useful in constructing factual pictures that teach the fact finder. The lawyer needs cross-examination preparation systems that also find and reorganize facts to assist the advocate's theory of the case.

In a medical malpractice case, it is essential that counsel know the exact explanation that the opposing expert witness has given by opposing counsel concerning the conduct of the doctor. If the alleged negligence is a failure to diagnose a condition, the lawyer needs to know each opportunity the defendant had to observe something that could have assisted in arriving at the correct diagnosis. The lawyer would also want to know the facts for every opportunity the defendant had to have additional tests, or make additional observations that would have led to the correct diagnosis. In addition, the lawyer would want to find and study any instance when the expert witness has delivered a paper, given a speech, testified, or discussed in any way, whether in writing or orally, the issue of diagnosis of such conditions and/or the failure to diagnose such conditions. The expert witness's position on this fact can then be grouped together in individual portions to be analyzed in comparison with one another. The opinions and writings of the expert may also be compared with the missed opportunities available to the defendant to correctly diagnose the condition.

Similarly, in a misidentification defense, if the witness says that a purse snatching took place on a very dark street, the number of times and the different ways in which the witness described the dark street all may be of assistance to defense counsel. The witness's discussions of this "fact" or "issue" need to be found and grouped together, just as much as the witness's various versions of how tall the robber might have been, and whether the robber had any tattoos, facial scars, or other identifying marks. The number of items under study can be small or large, but the preparation system must remain simple. Any cross-examination preparation system is designed to accommodate the facts and group them into an understandable and usable format.

In the absence of a preparation system, counsel must rely on her memory in reading discovery to recognize the various versions of facts that are consistent and inconsistent with the theory of the case. Even if the case isn't overly complex, reliance on memory alone is foolhardy.

§ 3.06   The Search for Useful Topics: The Need for a Theory of the Case

Skillful cross-examinations are not requests for free-flowing narratives concerning all the events of the case. Instead, cross-examinations are a series of leading questions grouped to prove a series of goals of importance to the theory of the case. As will be discussed at length, these groupings of questions may best be thought of as chapters (see chapter 9, *The Chapter Method of Cross-Examination*). Cross-examination consists of chapters that undermined the opponent's case and the chapters that support the cross-examiner's theory of the case. Hence, categorizing discovery in terms of topics as discussed by each witness is a system suited to the preparation of winning cross-examinations. The organization of the facts around topics facilitates the process of breaking the topics in to chapters. The chapters can then be arranged and performed in a tactically meaningful proper sequence. However, all of the techniques of cross-examination depend on the lawyer's adopting a theory of the case and arranging facts to support that theory. In order to begin preparing any cross-examination, the lawyer must first envision the theory of the case (see chapter 2, *Developing a Theory of the Case*).

In a domestic relations case, where custody and division of assets are at issue, undoubtedly there will be multiple issues concerning the conduct of both parties. If, in the alternative, the custody portion of the case has been stipulated, the topics concerning conduct will only be relevant as they relate to the remaining issue concerning the division of assets. In this scenario, it is likely that many custody chapters would be meaningless and chapters concerning only financial issues will be the focus to which most preparation efforts are concentrated.

If a misidentification case is to be tried, the cross-examination chapters deal with identification issues rather than self-defense or entrapment chapters. If, in the alternative, the theory relies upon self-defense, then identification issues become largely unimportant. Indications of poor identification may still remain relevant to lower the credibility of a preceding witness on the issue of self-defense. The lawyer must focus her attention and preparation only on the facts or areas that the lawyer might profitably explore in the course of developing the theory of the case and the areas that can be fruitfully explored to undermine the opponent's theory of the case.

The lawyer must prepare to advance a particular theory. Cross-examinations prepared in the absence of a theory require the lawyer to prepare too many diverse chapters, spend too much time, prepare the wrong chapters, or prepare not deeply enough in critical areas. All of these alternatives cause enhanced risk at trial to the lawyer.

What follows are cross-examination preparation systems designed to take a little or a lot of discovery and reduce it to a useful, organized body of information. It should be properly categorized and available for the drafting of the chapters of cross-examinations, which will all be aimed at advancing the lawyer's theory of the case.

§ 3.07   Ease of Operation

The best cross-examination preparation system is easy to use. There are not two sets of preparation systems: a set of systems for the well-funded cases, or in cases where the lawyer has the luxury of unlimited time and another set for the rest of us. On the contrary, the systems discussed are all methods that can be used by any lawyer, regardless of her level of experience, to achieve a very high level of cross-examination preparation in a relatively short amount of time. Of course, the amount of time varies with the amount of factual evidence that must be digested and the complexity of the cross-examinations attempted. It is the goal of any useful preparation system to minimize the amount of time needed for cross-examination preparation, and to maximize the level of factual understanding that can be obtained given the amount of time available.

The less experienced the lawyer will ordinarily derive the most immediate benefit from a thoughtful preparation system. First, the less experienced lawyer has often been working with no system, so the use of any preparation system allows this lawyer to enjoy a more dramatic learning curve. The less experienced lawyer offers little resistance to the notion of preparation systems. She has not yet developed the dangerous attitude that cross-examination is a matter of feel and that preparation desensitizes the lawyer's touch with the facts.

On the other hand, the more experienced lawyer is in a better position to appreciate the power that flows from thorough preparation. Having once missed or forgotten a key point, having one time misplaced the fact needed to impeach smoothly from a prior statement, or in any other way having suffered from a lack of complete mastery over the facts, the experienced lawyer knows the value of a thorough preparation system. Furthermore, each of these systems operates scientifically to reduce the amount of time necessary to systematically digest discovery to the minimum possible amount of time.

The trial lawyer of any level of competence also appreciates the value of thorough preparation when she experiences the sense of calm and control that comes from preparation. Once a lawyer has enjoyed a great cross-examination based on thorough preparation, she becomes a believer in the idea that preparation, above all else, yields better cross-examinations.

For those who employ associates, law clerks, or paralegals, the less experienced lawyer or the non-lawyer working under the supervision of the trial lawyer may operate each of the three systems presented. Because these systems operate in a logical, scientific, and learnable method, non-lawyers operating in support of the lead counsel can become proficient in using the systems. The systems operate on thoroughness and detailed examination of facts, not on some artistic "feel" that only the brilliant or intuitive may have.

A word of caution, however. Any person assisting the trial lawyer in preparing for a cross-examination must understand both the preparation system and the necessity of absolute accuracy and thoroughness. If the lawyer does not have complete faith in the work product of the assistant, the lawyer will find herself repeating the preparation and wasting all the time and energy that went into the initial preparation performed by the non-lawyer.

§ 3.08　　Moving from a Cross-Examination Preparation System to the Writing of the Cross-Examination

The advocate's task is not to create a miscellaneous information cataloging system but to create a cross-examination preparation system. These systems are designed so that the facts useful to cross-examination can be located, cataloged, and then moved directly from the cataloging process to the page preparation of cross-examination (chapter 10). A cross-examination preparation system is most beneficial in its ability to group together the facts bearing on a particular issue. Once the system accomplishes this, its usefulness has not been exhausted. The organization and resulting in-depth learning of the facts, was worth the effort alone. However, the system proves its ultimate worth as it is employed to draft the cross-examinations themselves.

The concept of "writing" the cross-examination deserves explanation in definition. "Writing" may be more formalized for some lawyers than for others. There are various schools of thought on the extent of the "writing" necessary in the preparation of cross-examination. While these differing schools of thought will be discussed in later chapters, there is much room for flexibility in how much of a cross-examination to write down. However, for the present, it is sufficient that "writing" be understood as the physical assembly of information necessary to conduct cross-examinations in the chapter method for use during the trial.

The meticulous preparation of cross-examinations is done in order to carry out the chapter method of cross-examination (chapter 9). There is a bit of the chicken and egg aspect to this method of preparation. In order to understand why there is a need to employ a cross-examination preparation system, it is helpful to understand the chapter method of cross-examination. On the other hand, to carry out the chapter method of cross-examination, it is necessary to have employed some system to recognize and develop detailed the facts that permit the drafting of cross-examination chapters.

Above all else, keep this thought in mind: Effective cross-examination is not based upon the retelling of a story; it is based upon the systematic study and presentation of facts relating to particular chapters of the story (see chapter 9, *The Chapter Method of Cross-Examination*). Cross-examination is best limited to the chapters that are helpful in supporting a theory of the case or in undermining the opponent's theory of the case. As a next step, the chapters of cross-examination will prove most helpful when they are placed in powerful sequences (see chapter 11, *Sequences of Cross-Examination*).

Thus far, the systems have been discussed in terms of digesting materials gained in discovery. However, the systems do not end there. Once all the facts available through discovery have been systematically cataloged, these same systems expand to incorporate those additional facts obtained through other forms of investigation. It is not only unnecessary, but counterproductive, to duplicate the system with another parallel system that accounts for materials generated through informal methods of discovery including interviews, and materials obtained through searches of electronic databases such as LexisNexis. Such additional materials need to be kept in the same form, and in the same place as the facts culled from the formal discovery process so that counsel may immediately recognize the contradictions, errors, omissions, or consistency of the facts. Furthermore, in order to fluidly make the transition from the cataloging of facts to the drafting of cross-examination, all facts potentially relating to a particular issue or chapter need to be kept in one place.

In this method, good facts are far more likely to be recognized and far harder to overlook. The systematic approach to cross-examination preparation culminates in an advocate who is far better prepared with the chapters necessary to successfully undertake the cross-examinations and who is more confident in her ability to do so.

Chapter 4

CROSS-EXAMINATION-FOCUSED INVESTIGATION

SYNOPSIS

§ 4.01 Theory of the Case as Guide to Pre-trial Discovery and Investigation

Trial lawyers love facts. That's good. They love all the facts. That's bad. There are facts that don't matter. Collecting them, cataloging them, and remembering them take time, money, and memory. The lawyer is going to run out of all three before running out of available facts. It would be better to save time, money, and effort for the facts that really matter.

Which facts matter? There is a big difference between facts for trial and raw data. All the facts are data but the jury is not in need of raw data. The jury is looking for refined data. The jury needs the facts that will help it decide the case. They need facts that inform.

What facts will help the jury decide the case? The jury needs the facts that help it decide the issues in contention. The jury needs facts that inform about the elements of the opposing theories of the case.

Cross-examination is a series of goal-oriented exercises. So are the tasks of discovery and investigation. (For ease of reference the formal procedural methods of discovery and the informal methods of investigation will be referred to throughout this chapter as investigation. Investigation encompasses both.) Both discovery and investigation are concerned with the cross-examiner's need for facts. But the cross-examiner does not seek all the facts. The goal of a well-managed investigation is not to know everything about everything, which is unnecessary and counterproductive. The quest of cross-examination-focused investigations is to know as much as can be known about topics that are needed for the trial.

What is worth knowing depends upon the theory of the case selected by the advocate and the theory of the case selected by the opponent. Suppose a personal injury action in which the initial investigation strongly indicates liability will be conceded because the defendant who was speeding on an icy road lost control of his car and hit the plaintiff from behind. The defense of the case will involve the analysis of damages. Similarly, in a self-defense case, identification is a given. Money spent investigating the credibility of witnesses whose only role is to identify the defendant is money wasted.

In every case there are a number of facts that do not vitally bear on the cross-examiner's theory of the case. Investigating such issues wastes time and effort. Investigations must be performed with the same sense of purpose as cross-examinations. The effort must be directed toward defined goals. In order to define the goals of the investigation, a theory of the case must be developed that tells the lawyer what things will be disputed, what things are needed to be proved, and what things are needed to be highlighted in order to prevail.

§ 4.02 Investigation Defined

"Investigation" as used here means the process of using both informal and formal discovery (in civil cases depositions, interrogatories, requests for admissions, and others). "Discovery" and "investigation," are in some ways interchangeable. The real difference lies in the fact that "discovery" is largely open for the opponent to view while investigation can leave an advocate prepared in areas unknown by the opponent.

§ 4.03 Cross-Examination-Focused Investigation

Cross-examination-focused investigation is designed to develop facts useful in developing the chapters of cross-examination. The chapters are in turn developed as a method of forwarding the theory of the case. Without a theory of the case it is impossible to meaningfully define issues to be investigated, impossible to properly prioritize among the areas to be investigated, and impossible to mark the progress of the investigative result. The advocate should use the theory of the case as the rudder to guide all investigative and discovery efforts. A quick check of a contemplated investigative or discovery request is to ask, "If I find what I hope to find, how much value would it have to my theory of the case?" In other words, the advocate must be careful to spend her limited time and financial resources seeking the information most likely to make the difference.

If the lawyer is defending a criminal case on the basis of identification, then issues relating to self-defense are irrelevant. The investigations seeking to disclose which party is the initial aggressor, what words were spoken between the parties, or who was armed with a weapon, are beside the point if the defense is going to say to the jury that the client was not present. If the defense is utilizing an insanity defense, issues of identification and the nature of the weapon are completely irrelevant. Perhaps very little of the homicide itself needs to be investigated. Those parts of the crime deserving of investigation include anything before, during, or after the episode that could strengthen the insanity defense. Of course, an enormous proportion of the investigative effort lies in a thorough investigation of the client's psychiatric and social history.

Similarly, in a products liability case, the lawyer may be willing to concede that the plaintiff was badly injured in an accident involving a jet ski, but may completely deny that the jet ski was defective in any way. It may well be the assertion of defense counsel that the accident that caused the injuries was the fault of the defendant. In that case, comparatively little investigation will be spent on the injuries. Much investigation will apply to the liability issue. On the other hand, the lawyer might concede that the accident was the defendant's fault, and that the plaintiff has been correctly tested and diagnosed, but that the injuries pre-existed. Then the investigation will *not* focus on this collision, but on the plaintiff's medical and injury history. In every instance, without a theory, the lawyer is left to investigate the universe of possibilities; neither time nor money permits such extravagances. With a theory, concerted effort, and sharp focus will apply to only those issues that touch on the theory.

Just as facts beyond change narrow the theory the lawyer may adopt, the theory adopted narrows the scope of the investigation. By concisely creating a theory of the case, many areas of possible investigation are ruled out while simultaneously focusing the investigation on the issues that can support the theory.

In fact, the most productive investigations are finely tuned to coincide with the most important issues within the theory of the case. It is insufficient to direct an investigation based upon a theory that the jet ski is a defectively manufactured product. The first issue is what is the nature of the defect? Is the plaintiff's counsel saying that this entire model of jet skis contained a particular defect? If so, then investigation of the design and engineering of that particular vehicle is important, but only insofar as it uncovers evidence relating to the design and engineering defect of that one part of the vehicle alleged to be defectively designed. If it is the throttle mechanism that is alleged to be at fault, then investigations of how the gas tank was manufactured are inconsequential.

A discovery request for all the engineering drawings on all the component parts is poorly calculated to produce facts useful for cross-examination. But a discovery request for how the throttle mechanism was designed for other models produced by this manufacturer may be worthwhile. In addition, an investigation of how the throttle mechanism was designed for other models sold by other manufacturers may also be helpful. Craft a theory. Then craft a discovery and investigation designed to uncover the facts of greatest significance to that theory. The most direct proof of the theory is preferred.

§ 4.04   The Danger of Non-Goal Directed Investigations

Investigating without a theory is not only wasteful, it is also unlikely to produce satisfactory results since the investigative effort is not focused on uncovering those facts most useful to proving the specific theory. There is, moreover, a separate and distinct harm that comes from investigating without a theory or investigating in a manner inconsistent with a theory. Witnesses are misled, and potentially, the lawyers are also misled. When an investigator spends time on issues unrelated to the theory, she generates false issues in the witness's mind. The witnesses resist when there is no need to resist real issues, because they are confused concerning the direction of the lawyer. Another problem of non-goal directed investigation is that the cross-examiner can develop wonderful facts that solidly prove things that have no great bearing on the competing theories of the case. But having spent so much time and effort in mastering those facts the cross-examiner feels compelled to use them. The result can be a richly detailed story of no great significance.

For example, in a civil case, the theory is that the plaintiff was injured when his brakes malfunctioned. The lawyer may not be troubled by the fact that as a result of this mechanical malfunction, the plaintiff/client ran a red light. In this theory, the fact that the client ran a red light may be accepted. On the other hand, had the lawyer not first developed a theory of the case, it is foreseeable that the lawyer could dispatch an investigator or take depositions designed to challenge the assertion that the client ran the red light. Not only is this a waste of time and effort, it is confusing to witnesses and misleads them as to the real issues. As the lawyer struggles to challenge the credibility of the witness who saw the client ran the red light, the lawyer diminishes the opportunity to use that witness in favor of the true theory of the case. If investigation moves in the wrong direction or moves in no particular direction, it actually undermines the lawyer's ability to establish the case by inserting into the witness's mind false issues and by diverting his attention from the facts that need to be discussed. This misdirection subtly impeaches the lawyer's credibility by bringing into dispute matters that the lawyer has neither intention nor need of disputing.

§ 4.05 Benefits of Cross-Examination-Focused Investigation in Civil Cases

It is obvious why a criminal defense lawyer would prepare the investigation based on her likely cross-examinations of prosecution witnesses. Often the cross-examinations are the entire defense case. Less obvious is why a civil lawyer, whether plaintiff's counsel or a defendant's lawyer, would conduct cross-examination-focused investigation. The answer is that cross-examination-focused investigation is an efficient method of preparing a civil case.

Evidence produced from the opponent's case (the opponent's witnesses), be it a civil or a criminal case, is more believable to a jury than if that same evidence is produced from the proponent's witnesses. It is only common sense that if the opponent's witnesses agree with the proponent's evidence, the jury is more apt to believe that evidence. That is why the word "admissions" bears such a special place in American trial jurisprudence. This is formalized in the Civil Practice Act in regard to requests for admissions.

The reverse is equally true: Admissions made by the proponent's witnesses that support or assist the opponent's theory of the case will be thoroughly believed by the jury to the detriment of the lawyer who called the witness. This does not mean that the proponent will refrain from offering all of the evidence that will support her theory of the case through her witnesses. She will. But the fact of the matter is that the jury will believe testimony extracted under cross-examination more quickly and more often than it will believe the same information coming from a witness closely aligned with the lawyer who calls the witness for purposes of direct examination.

There is another fundamental reason why civil cases benefit from a cross-examination-focused method of investigation. Under the civil rules, the plaintiff can build her case by calling the defendant's witnesses. Generally speaking, witnesses who are aligned with the opposing party may be called for purposes of cross-examination. The plaintiff may often put on the bulk of her case through witnesses employed by the defendant. This is especially true in all forms of commercial litigation. The plaintiff must be prepare to win the case through those cross-examination's as often only by witnesses employed by or aligned with the opposing party can provide the facts necessary to demonstrate liability.

Similarly, the defense in a civil case will most often need to cross-examine the plaintiff, the plaintiff's expert, and the other witnesses called by the plaintiff long before the defense is granted the procedural opportunity to call its own witnesses. The case may be largely decided by then. Any attack on damages should have been mounted during the plaintiff's case. Often, the conduct of the plaintiff or the plaintiff's agents has great bearing on liability. In any event, civil cases are greatly dependent on cross-examination.

Because of the central importance of cross-examination to both sides of a civil lawsuit, lawyers investigate and use discovery in a method that extracts as many admissions from the opponent's witnesses and clients as possible, thus making the cross-examiner's theory of the case more easily proved. Similarly, the prepared lawyer guards against calling witnesses to establish a point, knowing that, as to other points, her witness will have to testify adversely to her theory of the case.

Once these two general classes of evidence have been thoroughly investigated, the well-prepared civil lawyer moves on to the evidence that can be produced through her witnesses that will enhance the admissions gathered from the proponent's case. The skillful lawyer also works diligently at the production of evidence through her own case that will qualify or weaken any admissions that her own witnesses will make against her theory of the case.

§ 4.06   Three-Step Analysis of Investigation

Having created a theory of the case, and envisioned the opponent's theory of the case, the advocate may take the first step of cross-examination-focused investigation. She can determine what facts or types of information could exist which would most affect the strengths of the opposing theories of the case. It is important to aim the initial discovery efforts directly at uncovering those facts.

The analysis of what admissions will be forced from the proponent's case is a second, but equally important, step of the investigative process. The trial lawyer must evaluate what facts the opponent will be able to generate through the cross-examination of the trial lawyer's witnesses.

The third step is to find and develop evidence through the trial lawyer's own witnesses that in the first instance will support the trial lawyer's theory of the case, and in the second instance weaken any admission that will be obtained from the trial lawyer's case that will support the opponent's case.

§ 4.07   Investigation Based on Needs: Working Toward the Chapters of Cross-Examination

Once the lawyer has developed a theory of the case, the lawyer is in a position to broadly recognize the chapters of cross-examination that will be needed to support that theory of the case and undermine the opponent's theory of the case. The advocate should assess the strength of the facts obtained through discovery by sorting the facts through any cross-examination preparation system. (see chapters 5, 6, and 7 laying out various cross-examination preparation systems.) Having compared the facts available to the facts necessary, the lawyer can find the weaknesses in her own case and the strengths of the opponent's case that must be further attacked. The lawyer is now in a position to recognize areas in what additional facts will most influence the cross-examinations. The trial lawyer can also recognize areas in which facts are needed to strengthen her witnesses' credibility on points that will be in contention.

Counsel may realize that, as to a critical event, her evidence is insufficient. For instance in a copyright infringement action where both liability and damages are at issue, defense counsel may be working from a theory that, even if there were infringement, the item infringed had never proved profitable for the plaintiff's company. It is easy to recognize the chapters demonstrating that lack of profitability will be very helpful to the defendant's theory of the case.

Defense counsel needs to aim discovery at the production of documents that proved that lack of profitability. But if defense counsel only asks for the tax returns of the plaintiff's business, and if that business sells many types of software, the lack of profitability of the business as a whole does not equip defense counsel for the detailed cross-examination's necessary to show the lack of profitability of this particular product. The cross-examiner needs different documents and deposition testimony designed to ferret out the facts necessary to win this issue.

At the beginning of a case, before even a database search has been run, the lawyer almost certainly has inadequate knowledge of the credentials of opposing counsel's expert. After a database search, and perhaps even after obtaining the expert's report and resume, the cross-examiner may realize that the expert has excellent credentials in general. But the cross-examiner may decide to still question the experience of the expert in the narrow field that is the subject of this lawsuit. A witness who is an acknowledged expert in the field of stock broker conduct may have no valid experience upon which to offer an expert opinion addressing the duties of a stock broker acting as an insurance agent. By envisioning the cross-examination the advocate desires to give, the discovery process can be aimed precisely at the issues most likely to be productive.

Assume the advocate knows the story previously related by a witness. The lawyer does not know if that version is accurate. The lawyer must examine what parts of the expected testimony need to be challenged. The lawyer should analyze whether the story has inconsistencies, whether there are holes in the story, and what might be in the story that can be used to bolster the advocate's theory of the case. In order to take the next step in developing the cross-examinations, the advocate must move from the development of the theory of the case to recognition of the specific areas of the planned cross-examinations. What helps? What hurts? What probably does not matter? What cannot be changed?

Is the job of the lawyer to focus the investigation on answering these questions for better or for worse? In either event, lawyer should know the information earlier rather than discovering the truth during trial. Investigation may provide the facts that the lawyer desperately needs in order to complete her chapter of cross-examination of a witness. Alternatively, theory-directed investigation may warn the lawyer that the honest and provable answer will be contrary to the theory of the case. It is far better to find this out during the investigative phase of the case than in the middle of the trial. Evidentiary surprises in trial are hard on lawyers. Discovery by trial is hard on clients.

§ 4.08   The Role of Investigation in Refining a Theory of the Case

The theory of the case guides the investigation, but as the investigation deepens, as hoped for, chapters materialize or evaporate, as different facts of the case strengthen or weaken the theory of the case. Cross-examination-focused investigation not only eliminates unwelcome surprises at trial, but also permits the trial lawyer time to use her energy and efforts to refine the theory of the case, or, in the unusual situation, to completely modify the theory of the case early in the investigation/discovery phase. At this time that facts beyond change are clearly identified, and the trial lawyer knows well in advance of trial whether the theory of the case is usable, possible, and believable.

The closer the lawyer can come during the early phases of the case in identifying the gaps in the cross-examination chapters, the more focused she can make the investigation. In a sense, this is a process of elimination. That is, the trial lawyer attempts to eliminate all gaps in the cross-examination chapters. As each gap is eliminated, the focus of the investigation is more narrowly refined until no gaps remain.

Likewise, the trial lawyer eliminates unfavorable evidence that can be developed through the cross-examination of her own witnesses in this same process. The more focused the investigation, the more likely the lawyer is to come up with answers. The more answers she has, the more likely she will be able to fashion more powerful cross-examinations. The cross-examiner must first, through the process of discovery and investigation, eliminate as many of the gaps as possible in the cross-examination of her witnesses and the cross-examination of opponent's witnesses.

It is then time to enhance the cross-examination of opponent's witnesses and enhance the ability of the proponent's witnesses to withstand cross-examination. If investigation is done in a disorderly manner and is not cross-examination-focused, too often a workable, believable theory of the case is developed too late in the investigative/discovery process. There remains not enough time, energy, or money for the enhancement of the theory of the case through cross-examination of the opponent's witnesses and strengthening the proponent's witnesses to resist cross-examination.

As a result of the cross-examination-focused investigative method, the investigative process/theory development is ongoing throughout the case. As chapters are drafted and redrafted (see chapter 9, *The Chapter Method of Cross-Examination*), the lawyer continually folds in the new information she obtains through investigation. The new information may change a particular chapter and may thereby generate yet another investigative need. Once the results of the investigation are fed back into the preparation system and the cross-examinations, the lawyer often discovers that a new area of inquiry is necessary. Hence, investigation produces results that drive further investigation. All the time the lawyer is honing her theory, sharpening cross-examinations, discarding chapters that will no longer work (an equally important function), and generating further investigative issues that may produce new chapters. This relationship is diagrammed below:

Chart 1

The Role of Investigation in Developing
a Theory of the Case

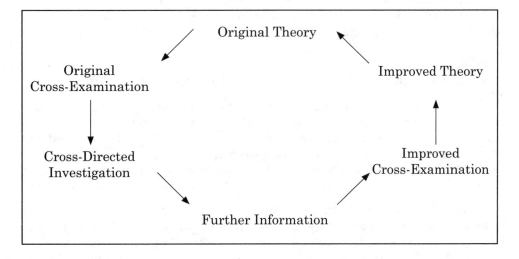

§ 4.09   The Refinement of Investigative Objectives

In order to recognize the needs of the investigation, the lawyer must envision the cross-examinations she desires to perform. The earlier the lawyer can begin outlining the cross-examination on both sides of the case, the earlier she can detect the weaknesses that must be fixed. The weaknesses that cannot be fixed need to be incorporated within the theory. Weaknesses that become facts beyond change that are fatal to the theory require the theory be changed.

The more finely detailed the theory of the case, the more the lawyer can hone her investigation, which will provide even better direction to the investigation, and hence produce useful facts more quickly.

It is therefore efficient to begin thinking in terms of the cross-examinations necessary to establish a particular theory before beginning the investigation. This is largely an exercise in logic. What logically should exist if the advocate's theory of the case is true? Or, if the lawyer assumes the theory of the case to be correct, what evidence should be findable? For instance, if the plaintiff alleges that the defendant ruined his business, costing him hundreds of thousands of dollars in damages, then in theory the records of the business should show a robust financial statement, a steady flow of work, a dependable workforce, many successfully completed contracts, and more. These or similar indicia of success should exist if the plaintiff's theory is accurate.

If it is the defense theory that the business was failing and that the plaintiff suffered minimal damages, then logically there should be tangible evidence of financial weakness or other indicators that the business was doing poorly. The anticipated cross-examinations contain many chapters designed to cause the plaintiff and his supporting witnesses to concede facts showing that the business was of no great value. The investigative effort must first be directed at the various types of business records that would show success or failure. Opinion evidence of competitors or expensive expert evaluations are not only secondary to such an investigation, they are far less likely to carry the necessary cross-examination chapters. A simple set of timesheets showing that the plaintiff had laid off workers over the months before the alleged liability-producing event or had reduced employee hours would more effectively tell the story.

§ 4.10   Example of Theory-Directed Investigation

In a homicide case, the defense alleges that the client acted in self-defense based on a longstanding fear of a man who had threatened him many times. The deceased's threats concerned money the client owed to the deceased. On the evening of the homicide, the deceased began to abuse the defendant verbally. The defendant then took a knife out and told the deceased to leave him alone. The deceased lunged at the defendant and the defendant stabbed him.

This scenario, though suggestive of self-defense, is not yet ready for a cross-examination-focused investigation. It is not enough to suggest that the theory of the case is self-defense. Many more questions must be answered before an exact theory of the case, supported through the cross-examination-focused investigation, can be produced for the jury. Can the defense produce witnesses to the prior threats? If the defense can produce witnesses to that effect, can those witnesses withstand the government's cross-examination? Are those witnesses impeachable? Are those witnesses impeachable as to other unrelated events that will be admissible? Was the defendant aware of the prior threats? Does the law of the state require the defendant be aware of the prior threats, or are they admissible on a separate ground, such as proving who the initial aggressor was? What was the precise nature of the prior threats? How recently had they occurred? Did the deceased track the defendant down to the bar? Had he been stalking him? How many other people were in the bar? Had the deceased been drinking? Had the defendant been drinking? What were the deceased's words to the defendant?

Obviously, the more the lawyer can turn a general theory of the case (self-defense) into a specific theory of the case (self-defense motivated by fear of the deceased because of prior threats), the more the lawyer can investigate toward producing specific facts about the specific theory. This specific investigation and discovery produces themes and theme phrases (see chapter 2, *Developing a Theory of the Case*). These theme phrases, when identified early in the investigation, become theme phrases used by the cross-examiner throughout interviews, depositions, or pre-trial motion hearings. These theme phrases will become phrases adopted by the witnesses (see chapter 26, *Loops, Double Loops, and Spontaneous Loops*).

While the investigation may not provide all the answers, it is worth the time, effort and expense. Knowing what the lawyer will be unable to prove is as valuable as knowing what can be proven.

§ 4.11 Civil Applications of Cross-Examination-Focused Investigations

Cross-examinations have a positive aspect in that the chapters of cross-examination can be used to build the cross-examiner's theory of the case. Cross-examination chapters can be designed to cast doubt upon the opponent's theory of the case. As the lawyer strengthens her cross-examination material, simultaneously strengthening her theory of the case, she weakens her opponent's theory. This is true in all cases — criminal, civil, commercial, and matrimonial.

It must be the primary goal of the lawyer to investigate along paths designed to improve the material available for cross-examination. The lawyer begins with a proposed theory. As she develops it through cross-examination, the theory remains largely the same but becomes more plausible, provable, and persuasive. Certainly some parts of the theory become so strong that it is wise to make those factual chapters a focal point of the case. That is not a change of theory so much as a change of emphasis on selected parts of the theory. The cross-examiner may well be arguing the same theory, but now predicates her argument on the areas or chapters that she can factually dominate while underplaying the importance of areas that have not panned out as well. Thus cross-examination, in all cases, adjusts the theory of the case, which in turn focuses the cross-examination even more narrowly.

In the civil context, a cross-examination-focused investigation is driven by two fields of cross-examination. The first consideration is investigation designed to strengthen the cross-examinations that the trial lawyer will conduct against her opponent's witnesses. These are the most telling cross-examinations for the theory of the case and should receive the first and greatest attention. The second consideration involves cross-examinations that will be conducted by the opponent against the proponent's witnesses. Of course, these cannot be ignored, but they should receive the second consideration in the investigation.

If the trial lawyer has prepared thoroughly for her cross-examinations of her opponent's witnesses, many important facts will be admitted by the opponent's witnesses. Every admission by the opponent's witness effectively removes a cross-examination of the advocate's witness on that point. Chapters that go well in the cross-examination of the opponent's witnesses have the effect of narrowing the areas that an opponent can challenge. After all, it was his witness that admitted that fact. To cross-examine the advocate's witness on that point requires that the opponent essentially argue to the jury that his witness was wrong or lacked credibility. Establishing important points through the opponent's witnesses makes the job of preparing the proponent's witnesses much easier.

§ 4.12   Criminal Case Applications of Cross-Examination-Focused Investigations

In a criminal context, the preparation and investigative style of the trial lawyer is somewhat different. The prosecutor is forbidden to call the defendant to the stand. The prosecutor must build her case through direct examinations. As a result, a theory-directed investigation by the prosecution must be aimed at strengthening the direct examinations of the prosecution witnesses. In that regard it is still quite helpful if the prosecutor will envision the likely cross-examinations of her witnesses. Criminal defense lawyers have only to establish a reasonable doubt. A prosecutor should study the proposed direct examination chapters in order to determine the weaknesses in the case. An investigation designed to shore up the weaknesses is very much a theory-directed investigation.

Because the burden of proof is so heavily against the prosecution, criminal defense lawyers frequently do not put up witnesses to testify. Therefore the vast majority of the cross-examination-focused defense investigation applies only to those cross-examinations that defense counsel will conduct of the opponent's witnesses. Here the issue is not simply to find that gaps in the anticipated direct examinations. While criminal defense counsel is advised to study the likely direct examinations and direct her investigation toward the weaknesses in the prosecution case that alone will not suffice.

Criminal defense counsel must still have an articulable theory of the case. "The defendant is not guilty" is not a theory of the case. "There exists a reasonable doubt" is not a theory of the case. If the criminal defense counsel is contending that there has been a misidentification then defense counsel must investigate in that specific area. In other words, defense counsel would be looking for the lighting conditions, the time of the occurrence, how long the event took, and other linked factors. The theory of the case might be better stated as, "There has been a misidentification because this crime happened so quickly under such poor lighting conditions." The investigation of a criminal defense case requires the advocate to search for facts that strengthen the defense theory of the case. In that regard, a criminal defense investigation is quite similar to the investigation conducted by a civil advocate.

§ 4.13   Theory → Investigation → Improved Theory: A Positive Feedback System

Because of this inextricable linking of investigation to cross-examination, the better the lawyer envisions the cross-examination chapters she wishes to use, the more focused the resulting investigative effort. This process of cross-examination-driven investigation results in a positive feedback system. The more refined the cross-examination goals, the more refined the investigation. As the investigation becomes more refined and goal-directed, the results become much more useful in creating more detailed and factually powerful cross-examinations.

The cross-examiner must remember that cross-examination is an avenue to prove things, not simply to disprove things. The cross-examiner must not neglect the areas that can be developed through an opposing witness without opposition. It may well be that the opposing witness wishes not to cooperate. But if the facts are laid out for the witness and he knows that he cannot safely deny the facts, he finds himself repeatedly providing answers that support the cross-examiner's theory of the case.

There is a simple method of directing an investigation calculated to strengthen both a theory of the case and its component chapters of cross-examination. Often a lawyer laments, "If only I had the following fact." That critical fact might well be obtainable through a properly focused investigation. It is one thing to mourn a theory that, after investigation, cannot be fully supported. It is quite another to mourn the theory that could have prevailed had the lawyer only turned her investigation toward sustaining the theory. The more the lawyer understands the details of the cross-examination she would like and needs to give, the more she can drive the investigation toward filling in those detailed factual unknowns.

§ 4.14 The Earlier the Lawyer Can Envision the Cross-Examinations, the Earlier She Can Direct a Productive Investigation

One of the hardest lessons for a trial lawyer to learn is that things done late do not yield the same benefits as the same things done early. A few hours spent on the drafting of cross-examination weeks before trial produces an entirely different result than the identical number of hours spent on the development of cross-examination the weekend before trial. Armed with rough drafts of the cross-examinations the lawyer wishes to give, the lawyer is sure to spot weaknesses. The cross-examiner finds areas that require further factual support, areas of ambiguity in the evidence, and areas where further attack is possible.

Spending time drafting cross-examinations before critical depositions is even more beneficial. Knowing what the lawyer needs for trial, the deposition can include far more pinpoint questioning designed to flesh out the most important issues in the case. The cross-examiner can come out of the deposition understanding the factually strong and weak parts of her case. With time and effort, the cross-examiner can cure these weaknesses or at least learn that they cannot be cured in time to adjust the theory of the case. On the weekend before trial, weaknesses cannot be cured. In fact, often in civil litigation, the discovery cut off date may be one or more months in advance of trial. That is not to say that rough draft cross-examinations must be written weeks or even months in advance, but if that were to occur, it would be no sin. The earlier the recognition of the factual goals, the better the trial lawyer is positioned to find the necessary facts to support those goals. The earlier the cross-examiner realizes that some battles cannot be won, the earlier the cross-examiner can build a theory that makes it unnecessary to fight those battles.

Realistically, first draft cross-examinations can certainly be conceived and outlined long in advance of trial. The fact of the matter is that most lawyers begin mentally drafting the cross-examinations shortly after the first interview with the client. These mental drafts are refined after reviewing the discovery. It is at that time that the investigative plan ought to be conceived, and the execution of it begun more formally. Hence, the first step in cross-examination-driven development is to conceive the general nature of the cross-examinations (it is here that facts beyond change are found) and the resulting theory of the case. It is necessary to then move into an evaluation of the discovery available and update continuously, even as the cross-examinations are delivered.

§ 4.15   Civil Cases: The Optimum Order of Formal Discovery

Civil depositions and requests to produce documents are extraordinarily effective in preparing for cross-examinations. The greatest value of these two discovery devices is ordinarily achieved by using the two in a particular order. The most productive order is to obtain the documents before engaging in the depositions. In that way, the deposition can be much more trial-like. Armed with the documents, the advocate can discuss with the witness what was said in any document and why it was said. The cross-examiner can determine who was in the chain of creation of the document. The cross-examiner can obtain insight into the thinking of the organization or person. Armed with documents, the cross-examiner can compel admissions because the witness is confronted with the documents.

As always, the more a lawyer demonstrates concrete knowledge of the facts, the less a witness feels free to deny facts or to attempt any manner of deception. Documents prepared outside of litigation are almost always more honest than the witnesses who will later try to explain them. The documents serve as a can opener to the truth. Counsel should always try to obtain the most pertinent documents before undertaking the depositions. An additional advantage of this sequence of discovery is that the documents sometimes disclose the name and role of the witness who needs to be deposed.

§ 4.16   Cross-Examination-Focused Depositions

Depositions need to target the theory of the case. The theory of the case is advanced through specific chapters of cross-examination. The deposition is the single best opportunity to polish those chapters. While there is room for open-ended questioning in depositions, much of the value of a deposition is derived from specific questions driving at establishing specific facts that support the theory of the case. The deposition can also be used to ingrain the themes of the leading questions of the case. Not only will the witness admit to the facts asked in the specific question, he will be admitting those theme phrases for later use at trial.

Interestingly enough, witnesses often subscribe to and make their own theme phrases that support the theory of the case so that those lines can be placed into the cross-examinations of those witnesses (see chapter 26, *Loops, Double Loops, and Spontaneous Loops*).

Depositions too often fall into a chronological recitation of questions that all end up asking the same question: "What happened next?" This general meandering through the investigative/discovery phase of the lawsuit squanders opportunities to find and create hard-edged answers to relevant issues that a cross-examination-focused investigation/discovery process would have created. Rather than the cross-examiner simply traveling through the same old "canned" interrogatories followed by open-ended "what happened next" questions at deposition, the cross-examiner can be much more specific.

When minimal discovery and investigation is available before a deposition, a larger portion of the deposition must be open-ended. There must be an invitation extended to the witness to give enough facts upon which to base a more specific cross-examination. But this does not mean that the cross-examiner will make every question open-ended. It does not mean that theme phrases need to be abandoned.

§4.17 The Value and Techniques of Open-Ended Questions at Depositions

Open-ended questions generate narrative responses. Narrative responses contain a great deal more information than can be obtained by leading questions. That is why there is room in a deposition for open-ended questions. Open-ended questions seek information, which is certainly one of the purposes of a deposition. But even the asking of open-ended questions employs a technique. Assume the cross-examiner understands a supposed fact, event, or explanation to be a certain way before the deposition but does not believe that fact, event, or explanation. In the deposition, the cross-examiner should ask only open-ended questions about that fact, event, or explanation. In this way, the witness is offered the broadest possible opportunity to change or vary with the previous or expected explanation. If the cross-examiner repeats anything to a witness in the form of leading questions, that cross-examiner makes it easy for the witness to merely verify the previous version. The cross-examiner is advised not to accept the previous unfavorable version of fact as accurate and therefore not to repeat it to the witness as a leading question.

The cross-examiner should closely follow the resulting longer answers to open-ended questions. As always, if the current version of any event or fact is more helpful than a previous version, the cross-examiner should immediately lock it in and build a chapter designed to show why the current version being given in the deposition is accurate. In this scenario, the current version is more helpful than a previous version that may have been obtained either from this witness, from another witness, or from a document. But the witness should not be impeached with the prior version as to do so implies that the prior version is the more accurate version.

The cross-examiner should compare the narrative answers with the cross-examiner's theory of the case. Within the long narrative answer there may be dozens of facts. The cross-examiner is listening for those facts which fit into the planned chapters of cross-examination. Whenever any part of an answer supports in any way the theory of the case, that portion of the answer needs to be pulled out of the long narrative answer, rephrased and repeated in a leading question to clarify and solidify that specific fact.

This technique is done to create clarity for the sake of potential impeachment and in order to cement in the mind of the witness the answer that is preferred. This can be accomplished by focusing additional questions on the desired part of the narrative answer, by asking additional leading questions that support the important fact or scenario, or by repeating the fact or phrases that the lawyer wishes to reinforce. This latter technique will be done in a closed-ended (leading) fashion, spontaneously looping the witness (see chapter 26, *Loops, Double Loops, and Spontaneous Loops*).Thus, all discovery and investigation will be cross-examination-driven.

§ 4.18   Problems and Benefits of Interrogatories and Request for Admission

Interrogatories can be useful, but they are not a replacement for depositions. It is true that an interrogatory asking for all of the details of an event will provide the lawyer an answer, but it has also provided the witness with an unbelievable amount of time and assistance in crafting that answer. Interrogatories are best used to locate other witnesses, documents, dates, or other facts that are not subject to interpretation.

Request for admissions undoubtedly will contain theme phrases that will support the trial lawyer's theory of the case. Such a phrase might be, "failed to obtain . . ." or "failed to notice . . ." or any other such phrase that can be attached to a hard-edged fact. If admitted (and if they are asked in the request for admissions, they are facts that the trial lawyer knows must be admitted), not only is the fact admitted, but the theme phrase will be admitted and be ready for use in cross-examination of that witness at trial. Requests for admission can also be used as a substitute for stipulations. Important dates, financial data, organizational charts, and other fixed events or facts can be handled either through a request for admission or stipulation. For instance, if a currency has been used in a case other than the American dollar, a conversion rate table stipulated to or admitted by the opponent will obviate the necessity for a chapter on the conversion rate.

If the case is about the fluctuating price of a commodity or a security, an admission or a stipulation as to date and price will save the lawyer a great deal of time that would otherwise have been used in the creation of one or more chapters on those facts. Again, by focusing in advance of trial on the facts that need to be proved for the theory of the case, counsel can better find discrete factual areas where an admission or a stipulation will ease the burden of cross-examination. It may be that such facts could not have been disputed by a witness, but that would still require the cross-examiner to perform a chapter to establish those facts. It is far better to hold those facts out of cross-examination and establish them through the very minimal effort of request for admission or stipulation.

§ 4.19 Criminal Law: Evaluating the Government's Investigation

In all criminal prosecutions, the burden is on the government. The failure of the government to establish proof beyond a reasonable doubt results in a defense verdict. Therefore, criminal defense practice is in the first instance a reactive process. The government, whether federal, state, or local, generates the criminal lawsuit, which must be based upon documented evidence of guilt. The filing of a criminal charge must be accepted at face value: The government is saying that it knows something that causes them to believe that the defendant engaged in a particular forbidden act. Since the government is going to have the burden of proof, in theory, it ought to know quite a bit about the facts before filing the case.

Before spending defense time and money investigating the case, defense counsel must first analyze what has been gathered by the prosecution and is available to the defense.

Assuming some discovery is forthcoming, the first task is to catalog and digest what has been obtained from the prosecution during the initial stages of discovery. It is critical that the lawyer fully dissect what the prosecution found in its investigation in order to develop the initial drafts of cross-examination, to organize the investigative effort, and to support the motion practice, including pursuing both additional discovery, motion practice, and potential discovery violations.

§ 4.20 Tracking Criminal Case Discovery

In most state court criminal actions, discovery is both limited in quantity and informally handled. In many states discovery is available on demand. The defense asks for discovery as allowed by law and the prosecutor photocopies the file and sends it over. There is a problem lurking in such an informal procedure. It is difficult for defense counsel to know if she has received all the discovery. It also is difficult to key such discovery in to the source column of the prepared pages of cross-examination (see chapter 10, *Page Preparation of Cross-Examination*). For instance, several police officers may have filed police reports, and the result is that there are several police reports marked page 1. As a result, when preparing cross-examinations counsel might note as a source "P. RPT. 1." Because there are several police reports this identification can prove misleading. Worse, often one or more law enforcement agents might file several reports so the source code would need to include the agent's name, the date of the report, and the page of the report. In addition, it can be difficult to remember and find any particular police report. The solution is to impose a system on discovery so that **any** particular page can be located instantly.

In civil and criminal cases, the best way to keep track of discovery is to Bates label each page of discovery. In that way, no two pages have the same number. Instead, every page has a discrete Bates number. Ideally, the opponent would provide discovery with the Bates number already on the page. If the opponent is unwilling to do so, counsel should ask the court to require the prosecution to number the pages as they are made available to the defense. This system does not include transcripts that are separately numbered.

Why go to this trouble? And what does this system have to do with cross-examination? Simplicity is a requirement for any system that will withstand the craziness of a courtroom. In trial, it can be very difficult to find even the most obvious and important report. If every page has its own Bates number, then that number can be used as a further indicator of a source of a fact. Source could then show the officers named, the date of the report the page of the report and the Bates number. If counsel has kept together a complete set of discovery in Bates order, any page can instantly be found and used in the courtroom.

Below is the outline of this process:

1) Ask the opponent to number his file in the lower right corner of each sheet. Numbering can be done by hand or with a hand stamp. In jurisdictions where the defense is charged with the responsibility of photocopying the prosecutor's file, the defense lawyer, investigator, or paralegal can easily insert the number before photocopying.

2) Obtain photocopies of the prosecution discovery after the numbers have been inserted on the prosecutor's file.

3) Make an index of what is contained in each page or group of pages.

People v. Neal Fine

Discovery Index

1-22	Police Repts.
23-35	Witness File
36-46	Rap Sheets
47-48	Neal Fine
49-56	Police Witness File
62	Lab Reports
57-66	Norm Fine
67-82	Property/Evidence
83-84	Witness File
85	Misc.
86	Driver's License — Fine
87	Diagram of Scene
88	Stmt. — Castillo (See 119)
89	Stmt. — David Wooley
90	Stmt. — David Eder (See 118)
91	Stmt. — Bob Brown
92	Stmt. — Bruce Smith
93	Stmt. — Janice Sands (See 117)
94-97	Stmt. — Nesbitt
98	Stmt. — Danny Eder (See 116)
99	Witness File
100	Stmt. — James Smith

101-115	Lab Reports
116	Stmt. — Danny Eder (See 98)
117	Stmt. — Janice Sands (See 93)
118	Stmt. — David Eder (See 90)
119	Stmt. — Castillo (See 88)
120-123	Stmt. — Greg White
124-134	Police Rpts.
135	Police Witness File
136	Witness File
137	Stmt. — Ron Bank (See 157)
138-140	Police Witness File
141	Bank's diagram
142-153	Stmt. — James Ray
154-155	Stmt. — James Ray
156	Police Witness File
157	Stmt. — Ron Bank (See 137)
158	Witness File
159-164	Police Reports
165-166	Transcript of Defendant's Stmt.
167-170	Transcript of Bruce Smith
171-176	Transcript of Brown
177-182	Property/Evidence
183-201	Lab Reports
202-226	Med Reports — Ray
227	Med Release — Brown
228	Med Release — Eder

4) When additional discovery becomes available, request the opponent to number the pages, beginning with the next number in order. At all costs try to avoid receiving a second batch of discovery that begins with the number 1. The lawyer will find that she has gotten the opponent to number his original pages of discovery, or if he has done that for them before photocopying, they are much more willing to number consecutively number discovery.

5) In the event that the opponent is unwilling to participate in this very simple mutually protective system of discovery, number your own file in consecutive order and send a confirming note back to the opponent:

August 9, 2004

Ms. Carol Stein
Chief Deputy District Attorney
Gunnison, Colorado

Re: People v. Bellow, 04CR 45

Dear Ms. Stein:

This will confirm that on January 9, 2004, I received from your office initial discovery in this case. I have numbered those pages consecutively 1-53. I would appreciate it if you would number your file accordingly so that we may easily compare files at a later date to ensure that I have not inadvertently failed to obtain all available discovery.

Sincerely,

The lawyer may also ask the court to order that pages be numbered to eliminate any potential problems. Judges are receptive to the idea, since it eliminates many discovery issues later.

6) In order to check the completeness of the discovery, at appropriate times, ask the opponent for the last number in his discovery file, and compare it to the last number on the lawyer's list. This way, the lawyer can ensure that her file is identical to the opponent's file. In the event of a discovery dispute, a simple comparison of page numbers will be sufficient to settle the issue.

§ 4.21   Discovery Index: Large Amounts

It is beyond the purview of this chapter to discuss the myriad of problems associated with the modern phenomena of the mega case. However, since these cases are appearing more often, some word should be said on the discovery process in such cases: The more discovery obtained, the more necessary an indexing system. As the discovery becomes large, the tendency is to abandon any system, as the amount of effort required to systematize the discovery itself becomes a significant time and expense item. This is exactly the wrong response to massive discovery.

Some indexing system needs to be in place. It can be by witness, by topic, or by number stamp. It is vitally necessary to chronicle what has been received, since without some form of index, not only is it likely that discovery will be misplaced, but it is virtually impossible for defense counsel to prevail in proving a discovery violation. If counsel cannot adequately describe what has been received, counsel cannot adequately identify what is missing.

§ 4.22   Digesting the Discovery

After obtaining discovery and indexing it, the next task is to make use of it. Cross-examination preparation systems described later (see chapters 5, 6, and 7) are all methods of digesting discovery — putting it into a format by which it would be understood to be fashioned into cross-examinations.

§ 4.23   Creating Investigative Checklists

Investigative checklists are an easy and efficient method of beginning the investigative process. While it is likely the longer the discovery, the longer the checklist, it is also true that the longer the discovery, the more necessary the checklist. Do not be afraid to create very long checklists, as the process of prioritization will, of necessity, cut down the number of items investigated. If the lawyer has a limited budget, investigation has to be organized and prioritized.

Cross-examination-focused investigations are designed to search for the facts that will most strengthen the hoped-for chapters of cross-examination. In order to efficiently search for facts through formal discovery procedures or informal investigations, it is necessary that the lawyer know the facts she would like to find. In order to look for an answer, the lawyer must first understand the leading question she would like to ask at trial. The more the lawyer has considered the likely chapters of cross-examination, the easier the lawyer can draft brief notes of what additional facts need to be established.

Four separate investigative checklists are set out in Charts 2, 3, 4, and 5. They will be referred to illustrate the principles set forth above.

This first example shows how the advocate preparing a particular chapter can easily outline the additional facts needed to make that chapter work. In this case the advocate is preparing for a trial alleging an infringement of a trademark. One of the chapters the advocate would like to use at trial concerned the amount the defendant spent in an effort to promote a brand that allegedly infringed on the plaintiff's brand.

Chart 2

Partial Investigative Checklist: Chapter on year 2003 marketing plan

Was there a written marketing plan for year 2003?

How much was budgeted for marketing the product?

How much was spent on marketing the product?

How was it spent?

Break out spending by the marketing media chosen including TV, radio, point-of-purchase, mailers, etc.

Were stores paid to stock their product? If so, how much? Is there a list?

How many mailers were mailed?

Get a copy of each form of mailed advertisement.

What was the mailing list?

(Etc.)

A survey of this list will not be surprised at the entries. In fact, any lawyer faced with the task of building a chapter showing the massive marketing done by the defendant could come up with a great many additional questions. That is precisely the point. The advocate will find it quite easy to work backward from the picture the lawyer wishes to point toward the questions that need to be asked in order to gather the facts necessary.

The more the lawyer can list the chapters she would like to do at trial, the easier it becomes to create a cross-examination-focused investigation. This kind of very informal outline can be used as a guide to the request for production of documents, such as production of any marketing plan for the product, the crafting of specific interrogatories seeking a purely factual answer such as the number of coupons mailed, and the deposition questions such as which department came up with the idea of paying retailers to stock the product.

§ 4.24   A Second Checklist

This second example is a different form of investigative checklist. This checklist stems from discovery already obtained. In either a civil or a criminal setting, once discovery begins to flow the advocate will find it quite useful to review those documents and generate follow-up questions or request for production based on issues raised through a reading of the discovery obtained to date. This technique is simply recognition of the fact that any one part of discovery will often cause the advocate to recognize the need for additional discovery or the need to draft chapters, which make use of facts found in the discovery to date.

Chart 3

Partial Investigative Checklist working backward from discovery documents

Homicide Case — Theory of the defense is that the government informant (Donald) is the murderer

413. When Donald tried to buy the Mercedes with the money he got from the sale of the truck, he purchased it from the Inn of Imports. They have a credit application that lists Donald's employment as P.R. Mineral. Please find the application.

414. Radar, PH 13:22 says P.R. Mineral was bought by Double States, Inc., which was Tim and Audrey McKinnon's corporation. Please get corporate documents to verify this.

415. Radar, PH 17:20 says that he found the left half of the frame rail in the Fairplay Mill. Check with Detective Radar. I think he means right half.

416. Detective Radar, PH 19:13 says he's had conversations with Mrs. Lilly Donner. Ask for discovery.

417. Personally inspect Donner logbook now found in property.

418. Radar talks about the occasion when he was looking for Donald and Donald came screeching around the corner pulling up to the house. This was the time when Don was surprised to see Radar and produced some phony titles that he tried to con Radar into looking at. See: PH 22:20.

419. Note to Jan on the McKinnon bonds: tell me how long he stayed in jail before posting the bond after he was brought back the first time, what jail he was in, and let's get a copy of his call record. Let's also get a copy of his visitor record.

420. We'll need copies of the minute orders in the Durango case to show that Donald failed to appear on the day of the trial.

421. Radar, PH 35:3 is a story by Donald on exactly where the grave is. Note that he knows how many rows of wheat in, and the kind of detail that can only be gotten by having paid close attention as opposed to the state of shock with his head hidden as he claims.

422. Radar, PH 36:4 Donald gives a description of how to find the grave. Radar PH 37:17 is more on finding the grave. Note Donald's story about having to go back and look at the lights at night. Let's go look at the lights at night.

Chart 4

Partial Investigative Checklist

Divorce Case — Spouse thought to be hiding marital assets

50. Go to County Court Records Department and check property log for Ralph's name or Ralph transferring property to either his parents or the girlfriend, Tami Maes.

51. Subpoena bank records for Ralph to look for large withdrawals possibly transferring them to parents or Tami.

52. Get income tax records from client. If they filed separately, see if she also has copies of Ralph's income tax records.

53. Compare interrogatory answers with supporting documents.

54. Husband was federally employed, get balance of retirement account. See if he has ever drawn on it for a house loan, etc. See if he ever transferred any to an IRA or other retirement-type account. Try to get percentage of his contribution to retirement that would have been refunded upon his resignation and track where that money went (i.e., personal bank account, CD. etc).

55. Drive by Ralph's parents' house and girlfriend's house. Look for any missing assets (boat, car, motorcycle) visible from the outside. Try to do this between 5:30-6:00 p.m. when they may be coming home from work and have the garage open.

56. Try to find old boyfriends of Tami. We may be able to get information from one of them if there was a nasty breakup when Ralph came into the picture.

57. Likewise, talk to client about Ralph's friends or previous friends that might have knowledge of these missing assets and may have heard Ralph talking about them at some time.

58. Check with the bars, restaurants Ralph frequents, both while he and client were together and with Tami. Possibly someone remembers hearing or seeing something from our list of missing assets.

59. Check with the health club Ralph belongs to for anyone hearing or seeing Ralph with a new car, motorcycle, etc., or if anyone heard him bragging about assets his "wife" was not going to get.

60. Ralph and Sherri's daughter is 18. She is quite articulate. Can we/Should we put her on the stand to discuss her college plans and financial needs?

61. Sherri has been taping some of her phone calls from Ralph, after they split. He sometimes calls while drunk and usually says that if she doesn't cook his dinner tonight, he'll fight her over every cent. Do we win points from the calls, or do we lose by virtue of having stooped to taping him?

62. Do a Lexis search on Ralph — debts, assets, transfers.

§ 4.25   Summary

The cross-examination-focused investigation will make the investigation and discovery process more efficient, more clearly focused, and directed at actual trial preparation. It takes less time. It organizes the material better. It permits the trial lawyer to have a better night's sleep prior to trial, knowing that what could have been done was done. Cross-examination-focused investigation eliminates much waste and creates more benefits. It leaves the lawyer better prepared to advance the theory of the case.

Chapter 5

CROSS-EXAMINATION PREPARATION SYSTEM 1: TOPIC CHARTS

SYNOPSIS

§ 5.01   The Value of Organization by Topic

Cross-examinations are a series of goal-oriented exercises; each designed to make a particular point. This method is referred to throughout the book as the chapter method of cross-examination. Each chapter of cross-examination is built around logically related facts that are established through leading questions or the grouping of questions establishing a goal. The goal is not confined to the last question of the chapter, but can be thought of as the entire picture that is painted by the accumulation of facts within the chapter.

In order to move efficiently from undigested facts to the prepared cross-examination chapters, it is necessary to envision the case in very small increments. How small the increment needs to be depends on the relationship of that item to the theory of the case. Some topical increments can be rather large when they bear little relationship to the theory of the case, or are not in dispute. Some topics need to be broken down minutely because they are critical to the theory of the case or they may be very much in dispute. The more important the topic is to the theory of the case, the greater the detail must be devoted to it. As a result, the more important the topic, the more likely it needs to be subdivided into even smaller parts so that each part may be separately proved as fully as possible. The cross-examiner cannot afford to leave out facts in those areas of greatest importance.

In order to efficiently undertake a topic method of preparation, it is necessary that the cross-examiner devise a first draft theory of the case. It is also necessary that the cross-examiner recognize the opponent's theory of the case. Having done this, the advocate is now in a position to recognize the topics of likely importance, and to begin to sort the available facts into those topics. Simultaneously, the advocate is equipped to recognize topics of no importance, and therefore skip any preparation in these areas.

For instance, in a malpractice case based on a failure to diagnose, the critical opportunity to diagnose allegedly occurred on a Wednesday, December 12. But Wednesday, December 12, in and of itself played no part in either of the opposing theories of the case. It would be unnecessary to gather the facts that prove the events took place on Wednesday, December 12. On the other hand, if either one of the opposing theories of the case attaches importance to the day or the date, then the advocate who needs to establish the importance of that date needs to gather the facts that can prove that date.

Similarly, it may not be significant that there was a lightning storm and the lights flickered off and on at one point during the surgery. On the other hand, if part of the theory of the case is that the surgeon attempted to do something very intricate and important during the time the lights were flickering off and on, then the proponent of that theory would want to know a great many details about that episode, and would undoubtedly write several chapters dealing with the flickering lights, the lack of vision, the necessity for vision at that moment, exactly what part of the surgical procedure was occurring at that moment, as well as other related facts. What information is important is dependent on what the lawyer wishes to prove. Until a goal is set, it is difficult, if not impossible, to recognize the chapters that advance the case toward that goal.

Whether the advocate uses a computer program to compile related facts, note pads, index cards, or some other method, the process is still the same. The available facts are taken from their source material and placed into a topical organization so that the advocate might see the available facts organized by topic.

When doing this by hand, the cross-examiner begins with a lot of empty pages. On a computer, the best way to begin is in an outline program. It is not necessary for the advocate to write out the names of the topics she is looking for within the facts. A general understanding of the topics comes from her recognition of the theories of the case. What is important is that the advocate be able to spot facts that need to be saved within the preparation system. Of course, in recognizing the contrasting theories of the case, the advocate will envision many of the most important topics before beginning the review of the formal or informal discovery. However, while reading the facts, the advocate is likely to see a finer breakdown of topics in the most important areas. In addition, facts may suggest to the cross-examiner additional topics, which can be prepared as potential areas of cross-examination.

Even the most perceptive lawyer will find it difficult to conceive of all the chapters of cross-examination weeks or months in advance of trial. Happily, it is unnecessary for the cross-examiner to do so. The most efficient method of digesting large quantities of facts is not to pre-conceive of the topics in any more than a general sense. It is important that the cross-examiner be able to spot the chapters as they are encountered in discovery. In other words, knowing the general theory of the case allows the cross-examiner to review discovery and recognize facts of significance. The object of this preparation technique is to extract those useful facts from discovery and bring them together in the creation of the chapters of cross-examination.

§ 5.02 Definition of "Discovery"

"Discovery," as used here, includes the material made available by the opponent in either criminal or civil cases. Discovery, in most civil cases, is formalized: interrogatories, depositions, requests to produce documents, requests for admissions, and the right of inspection are the customary forms of civil discovery. This is augmented by independent investigation. The lawyer's independent investigation often includes private interviews with potential witnesses and searches of electronic databases. In discussing the creation of topic chapters, the term "discovery" includes both the facts gained through the formal discovery process as well as any facts gained through an independent investigation.

In criminal cases, where discovery is generally more restrictive than in civil cases, defense counsel must push for as much discovery as possible and must then turn toward motion practice to generate additional discovery (see chapter 4, *Cross-Examination-Focused Investigation*). All results, regardless of where they are derived, are sources for the topic organizational system.

§ 5.03   Topic Pages Make Facts Accessible, Comprehensible, and Usable

Once a case has generated more than even a few pages of discovery no lawyer can hope to remember all the facts in detail *and* remember where that fact was found. A fact becomes accessible when the advocate can immediately identify the page where the fact appears. But even more is required to make a fact accessible. What the advocate needs is the ability to see the relationship among facts. The creation of topic pages begins that process. By putting onto a topic page all facts that relate to that small topic, the cross-examiner can see how those facts support or fail to support the topic. The grouping of facts on a topic page allows the lawyer to quickly judge the strength of the evidence currently available to prove a particular point. That is the turning point in the process of transforming data into presentable evidence or facts. The facts are now comprehensible. Because the facts on a particular point can be found on the appropriate topic page, and because that topic page carries the source of the fact, the cross-examiner can move quickly into the cross-examination drafting process.

§ 5.04   The Contents of a Topic Page

The topic page should contain facts in a form immediately capable of insertion into a cross-examination chapter. That does not mean that every topic page will be converted into a chapter because after review the cross-examiner will undoubtedly find many topics unworthy of cross-examination. In addition, some topics may have such minor value that merely a single question is necessary. Other topics may need to be combined or divided. What is important is that the topic page conveys all the information a cross-examiner would find necessary if she chose to use that material inside any chapter of cross-examination.

§ 5.05   A Topic May Generate Facts Sufficient to Fill More Than One Page of Preparation Materials

The creation of a topic page is the intermediate step between undigested data and completed cross-examination chapters. The creation of chapters is discussed at length in chapter 9, *The Chapter Method of Cross-Examination* and chapter 10, *Page Preparation of Cross-Examination*. The finished chapters of cross-examination should be prepared one chapter per page. However, in the preparation of a topic page it may well be that the useful facts under a single topic require more than one page. Although the facts that relate to a single topic require more than one page of preparation materials, throughout this chapter, those pages of facts will still be referred to as a single topic page.

It is entirely acceptable at this stage of the development of a proposed cross-examination chapter for the facts to consume more than one page. Counsel should recognize that a single topic requiring multiple pages of facts will likely support more than one chapter at trial. This is simply recognition that the material may be best handled by a finer breakdown of topics at trial.

As always, that breakdown will only occur if the facts, when presented in greater detail, create additional support for the theory of the case. It is quite possible to have multiple pages of facts on a topic at the preparation stage but decide later that there are relatively few facts of significance deserving proof at trial. If an individual topic requires several pages of facts, and those facts break into separate sections or chapters, each supporting the theory of the case, the result at trial will be a chapter bundle. The creation of a chapter bundle is the result of recognizing that the material is so voluminous that it is necessary to break the material into several related trial cross-examination chapters.

For instance, assume a single topic in the topic page preparation system is titled: "Selling furniture to the Horton Co." The single sale is not the heart of the matter but solely one example of problems the plaintiff encountered in selling their goods. That one topic may generate two or three pages of facts. That multi-page conglomeration of facts is sufficient for cross-examination preparation purposes. However, when it comes time to draft the cross-examination chapters, counsel must study the multiple pages of facts under this topic in order to determine whether the facts should be broken down further into separate topics. The answer is wholly dependent on the theory of the case, the opposing theory of the case, and the value of the facts in relation to that theory of the case.

§ 5.06   The Contents of a Discrete Topic Page

The minimal contents of a discrete topic page should include:

1.   Name of witness whose testimony is under scrutiny.

2   The title or brief description of the topic discussed on this page.

3.   Each statement of the witness or fact on that particular topic.

4.   The source of the fact.

Each of these entries deserves discussion:

1. The name of the witness.

Each topic page carries the name of the witness because that same topic may need to be replicated for one or more witnesses. Working on the assumption that things get mixed up, the advocate is advised that something as simple as entering the name of the witness at the top of a topic page can save a lot of time and aggravation later. In fact, the moment at which the information is needed is likely the moment the advocate is least in the mood to cope with missing, misfiled, or ambiguous information.

2. The title or brief description of the topic.

The value of this topic page method is to break facts into their logical groupings. A topic such as "the fraud" is not a chapter. It's a case. Each topic page must be small enough to be useful. The cross-examiner needs to be able to find very specific information useful in creating a single chapter. Each topic page carries the name of the topic on that page. That name or topic may well become the name of a chapter using that material.

3. The facts relating to that topic.

Of course, the value of the topic page is that it contains the facts or testimony relating to that particular topic as related by one witness. This is truly the process of cross-examination preparation as this process of gathering closely related facts is critical to building each individual chapter designed to prove one central goal, or to create one picture of importance. By moving these closely related facts out of voluminous discovery and on to a single topic page, they immediately become accessible, comprehensible, and usable. These are three critical attributes of any cross-examination preparation system.

4. The source of that fact.

A fact whose source cannot be found may be a fact wasted. If the advocate drafts a leading question designed to use that fact and the witness denies that fact, the cross-examiner needs the ability to immediately find the source of that fact for purposes of impeachment. Moreover, in many jurisdictions a fact asserted in a prior inconsistent statement may now come in as substantive evidence. In other words, if the cross-examiner cannot find the source of a disputed fact she loses not only the opportunity to impeach, but also the evidentiary value of that prior statement and also a piece of her credibility. That is a lot to lose for failing to note a source.

§ 5.07   Special Systems in Documenting Sources

By now the advocate is aware of the necessity of repeatedly and accurately noting the source of a fact. This process is easy so long as the advocate sticks to a single system and realizes that in times of great stress (like the rest of the lawyer's career) the advocate must be able to instantly and correctly interpret that system.

It is easy if there is a single witness and a single deposition. Then the code for a fact found in the deposition of that witness at page 106 line 12 can be shown as Dep 106:12, D 106:12, or simply 106:12. But as the depositions pile up and the other forms of source material are added, something more elaborate is required. Here are a few suggestions for a system with the firm realization that every lawyer can create her own set of codes so long as that code makes sense and is used consistently.

If in a deposition, note the page and line of that deposition. If there are multiple days of depositions from a single witness it is imperative that the court reporter be instructed in advance to number the pages sequentially beginning with 1. There is nothing as prone to confusion than multiple volumes of a witness's deposition, each beginning with page one. Each volume number should be followed by page number and line number. The resulting source code would be: Purden v4, 863:9 has no experience computing taxes.

The meaning of this code is that the witness will admit that he has no experience computing taxes. That fact is found in the Purden deposition, volume 4, page 863, line 9.

If in a transcript other than a deposition, such as the transcript of a preliminary hearing, a code showing the source, i.e., "P.H." for preliminary hearing is needed.

Some hearings have names that should not be used in front of a jury. For instance, the transcript that result from a motion to suppress should not be referred to as "the hearing on the defense motion to suppress." Similarly, referring to a "*Daubert* hearing" may make sense in a trial to the court, but it would be a poor method of referring to a transcript in front of the jury. The name of the hearing is not critical to a foundation, but the date, place, and people in attendance and the fact that the witness was under oath are critical.

§ 5.08 Special Systems in Documenting Exhibits as Sources

Depositions and reports, while rich in facts, are hardly the only sources of facts useful for possible cross-examination chapters. The exhibits in a case are all possible sources of facts as well. Virtually everything that can be marked as an exhibit would only be marked if it had evidentiary value. Items have evidentiary value only when they provide a fact or an inference. The facts of importance in any item of evidence should be keyed in to the appropriate topic page.

Start with the most obvious of examples: documents. Lawyers engage in great discovery battles in order to obtain documents. Prosecutors send law enforcement agents out with subpoenas and search warrants to obtain documents. Criminal defense lawyers file discovery motions with the goal of obtaining additional documents. The value of these documents is measured by the facts contained in the document. As much as transcript testimony, the facts contained in documents must be made accessible, comprehensible, and useful. The important facts in the document need to be sifted into the appropriate topic page. In some instances, the topic page may be filled with a series of facts obtained from a particular document.

Assume a party suggests as part of her theory of the case that the opponent was desperately in need of money. Further assume that part of the proof on this issue is a bank loan with a heavy payment schedule. The topic page might well be titled "the American Big Bank loan" or "owing $18 million." Whatever the name of the chapter, if there are facts of importance that counsel may wish to prove, the lawyer needs to establish the source of those facts. It is insufficient to merely note on the page "see Exhibit 473." Any fact of importance concerning that loan needs its own specific source. Set out below is a topic page "owing $18 million."

January 1998. Owing $18 million

Ex 473 (21) B	January 16, 1998
Ex 473 (1)	from American Big Bank
§ 7	
Ex 473 (5)	$18,453,095 9% interest
§ 15	
Ex 473	9% interest
	16 payments payable quarterly $1,153,318 per quarter
	($18,453,095 divided by 16 payments)
Ex 473 (3)	plus interest (9% on declining balance) beginning April 16, 1998
§ 4	

In this way even complex documents can be broken down into their compo-nent facts and placed on the appropriate topic page. It may occur that some-thing in Exhibit 473, the bank loan document, could touch upon another topic. For instance if the bank loan had been secured by a cosigner, that fact may well appear on this topic page dealing with the loan, and again on a topic page discussing the relationship of the witness with the person who was the cosigner of the loan.

Complex cases frequently require many exhibits, and many of the exhibits have multiple pages. The resulting source codes reflect that complexity but are still easily understood. For instance, Ex. 473 means trial exhibit 473. Exhibits that are documents within a great many pages need the second set of numbers (21) meaning page 21 of Ex. 473. Even then, business documents can be very difficult to follow. The designation § 7 translates to paragraph 7 on page 21 of Ex. 473.

But not all business documents have paragraph numbers. In such instances, it is very helpful to at least create a code so that the lawyer knows approxi-mately where on the page that fact can be found. In this example the lawyer has adopted "T" for the top one third of the page, "M" for the middle one third of the page, and "B" for the bottom one third of the page.

What matters is that there is a system. The advocate is urged to create a source code system used repetitively (no matter the type of the case) so that extra is not spent either creating a new system or trying to remember the workings of the system created.

§ 5.09 Creating Topic Pages on a Computer

The topic pages can be created directly on to the computer with little effort. The computer will be used as simply a very large pad of paper. Once again, it is unnecessary and counterproductive to try to envision the titles of chapters for the topic pages. Place topics on the computer. Then search discovery for the information to fill each topic page as the facts appear.

A simple method:

1. Open the computer program to any outline function.

2. Search the first page of discovery for the first fact that deserves to be on a topic page.

3. Figure out a name of the topic page that makes sense.

4. Go into the outline function and type the title of the topic page.

5. On that titled topic page enter the fact and the appropriate source code.

6. Find the next fact deserving of entry into any topic page.

7. In the outline function type the title of a new topic page.

8. On that titled topic page enter the fact and the appropriate source code.

Now just keep spotting facts and creating new topic pages, while reviewing the pages of discovery in order until the facts of value are digested into their appropriate topics. In the outline function, every time a new topic is spotted a new topic page is created in the outline. The advocate is invited to temporarily number the topics and create a chart of the numbers, or to rearrange the topics into chronological order or other groupings. The important factor is to separate the facts into their appropriate topics for use in creating chapters of cross-examination.

It is possible to move information or answers directly from transcripts to the topic pages. The transcripts need to be on disk. The process of reviewing the transcript pages remains the same. When the lawyer finds a fact that should be placed on a topic page, the lawyer can move the material directly from the transcript and on to the topic page by selecting the transcript material needed and copying it with the copy function, under the edit menu. Then simply place the cursor on the fact column of the topic page and use the paste function. Be sure to source each entry.

§5.10   Coping With Document Intense Litigation

Truly massive discovery creates truly massive document review efforts. It is beyond the scope of this book to discuss the various systems available to cope with extreme discovery. Suffice it to say the documents will need to be read and the team of people reading will need to be working toward the same topic pages. Multiple people can review documents and put the facts in to a topic page system but it is critical that there be coordination concerning what facts are important and the names of the topics being searched.

§5.11   A Sample of Some of the Chapters in a Multi-Topic Breakdown

In order to give a better picture of what a topic breakdown might look like, the following is provided. These topics come from a copyright infringement case and all deal with the potential cross-examination of a single witness. The witness is aligned with the plaintiff. He is in charge of sales for the plaintiff and is expected to testify that the allegedly infringed upon computer software was of great value. The defense cross-examination is designed to show that software had only nominal value and the software never enjoyed a strong market. The cross-examination is also intended to specifically demonstrate that certain large companies who purchased licenses to use the software did so only in limited quantities. After trying the software, they failed to renew their license. Here's a partial listing of the topics that the facts could be sorted into:

Definitions/Descriptions

SoftPRO vs. SoftPRO Plus

SoftPRO Central vs. SoftPRO Enterprise

Current Version of SoftPRO

Is SoftPRO a Blank Screen?

Record keeping of SoftPRO Sales

Versions of SoftPRO

Agreement with GK

Why GK Did Not Meet Expectations

Call Center Agreement with Shawn for GK Agreement

GK's Switch from Call Center to SoftPRO Central

Hum's Role in GK Negotiations

Star's Role in GK/Shawn Call Center Agreement

LTCC's Role in Call Center

GK Deal vs. Mn Mutual Deal

Kittenmark's Prospects

Why Did Star Get Involved with Kittenmark?

Star's Role in Developing & Changing SoftPRO/SoftPRO Plus

Confidentiality Agreement Between Kittenmark and Star

§ 5.12 Examples of Topic Pages Filled Out With Facts and Sources

Witness: Hag

Definitions/Descriptions

Source	Facts	Notes
Vol. 1 27:7-10	"SoftPRO Plus was a version — it was a model of SoftPRO that offered two internal models of a taxable asset or an annuity to fund long term care insurance. . . ."	
Vol. 1 27:11	"SoftPRO has an annuitization of an existing annuity. So you take a deferred annuity and begin taking payments off of it to fund life insurance that allows a client to leave more assets to their heirs. But it also included the annuitization model, the CD model and systemic withdrawal from an asset, and it included a qualified plan, pension plan, IRA type model. And it did not include any consideration for long term care funding, to fund long term care like SoftPRO Plus did."	
Vol. 1 39:23 40:1	"Merchant account is when you do business on the Internet and put your credit card number in. It travels to a merchant account, which is then tied to a bank account."	
Vol. 1 103:20-22	Authorize.net = authorizes credit card for validity to see if it's stolen	
Vol. 1 257:5-7	"SoftPRO Plus is a relatively small piece of the pie. It's a specialized industry because it focuses on long term care."	

Witness: Hag

SoftPRO vs. SoftPRO Plus

Source	Facts	Notes
Vol. 1 29:5-7	"SoftPRO Plus is still around, but we haven't sold it, per se, in long time because the capabilities were integrated into SoftPRO. . . . It's more generic also."	
Vol. 1 29:11-19	SoftPRO vs. SoftPRO Plus: ". . . it helps you maintain that software a lot easier when you have one product with switches that say turn on this option or that option or that option. So when you're maintaining software, you're only maintaining one set of source codes. . . . So eventually it became a product. And based on options at generation time, you turned on different models."	
Vol. 1 29:20-22	Q: "So there's only one source code for all the SoftPRO and SoftPRO products right now?" A: "In the BaseO version, that's correct"	
Vol. 1 30:11-14	The source code that is used today was first created in the SoftPRO Plus project and he was integrating with SoftPRO, he added more BaseO code to create that there is today	
Vol. 1 45:8-11	By fall of 2000, had merged the SoftPRO Plus and the SoftPRO together	

§ 5.13   Topic System's Usefulness in Finding and Documenting Inconsistencies

The topic page system of cross-examination preparation is an excellent method to prepare for the chapters of cross-examination needed to attack the credibility of a witness or to attack the credibility of a story told by multiple witnesses. The customary credibility cross-examination places a great deal of emphasis on finding and exploiting internal inconsistencies (that is, inconsistencies in various versions of an event as related by a single witness), external inconsistencies (that is inconsistencies which occur when multiple witnesses described a single event in differing ways), inconsistencies with physical facts, and other ways in which the testimony of the key witnesses can be shown to be contradictory. The topic method of cross-examination preparation is well suited to this task. In addition, the credibility of a witness may be attacked by showing the bias, interest, or motive of the witness. The gathering of facts along these topics allows the advocate to move the facts very efficiently from the topic pages into prepared chapters of cross-examination.

Presume an issue of eyewitness identification. Identification issues are often thought of as occurring in the criminal context, and they are ordinarily thought of as relating to the identity of the defendant. This is too limited a definition. "Identification" really means "perception." Perception issues occur often in civil cases on identification of things or events rather than persons. For instance, in a car accident case, the description of how a collision occurred may be the critical aspect of the suit. In a product defect case, eyewitness testimony concerning what the plaintiff was doing with the product at the time of the allegedly damage producing event may be the critical issue.

In a variety of civil contexts it may be necessary to successfully cross-examine the witness concerning his perceptions. This type of cross-examination is based on chapters relating to credibility issues. A cross-examiner seeking to establish a lack of credibility as to the eyewitness testimony will need to study and digest the facts along topics designed to challenge the credibility of certain aspects of the witness's story. This form of cross-examination will be based on such things as internal inconsistencies, lack of opportunity to observe, vagaries in descriptions, and other factors leading a jury to the conclusion that the information given by the witness cannot be trusted. In any case in which eyewitness testimony may need to be discredited, the cross-examiner must first analyze what the witness claims to have observed. Finally, the lawyer will need to analyze the witness's opportunity to observe. In addition, the lawyer will need to take into account the witness's version of each part of the event as compared to the observations of other witnesses, the laws of nature, any available documentary or physical evidence, and common sense.

In this criminal case example, the prosecution's case is based upon an eyewitness identification. This identification in turn is based upon the physical description of the perpetrator, as related by the eyewitness. For ease of explanation, this chapter will focus on a criminal identification case. The initial set of topic pages will focus on possible identification issues: height, weight, body hair, head hair, pants, shirt, jewelry, scars, etc. See Chart 1, below.

Below is a listing of a few of the possible identifying factors requiring factual research prior to cross-examination in the misidentification defense. However, before studying the list the advocate should bear in mind the fact that it is not necessary to have such a list in advance of the construction of the topic pages. The cross-examiner has no way of knowing which of these topics may be mentioned within the discovery or the investigation. It often proves more efficient for the lawyer to simply begin the process of cataloging the facts by topic by studying a single page of discovery and sorting onto a topic page any facts relating to the description of the alleged perpetrator.

Chart 1

Potential topics relating to identification

Height	Tattoos
Weight	Scars
Clothing	Nose
Age	Eyes
Facial Hair	Teeth
Head Hair	Voice
Glasses	Accent
Glasses Frame	Shoes
Contact Lenses	Socks
Skin Color	Hat
Gun Color	Gun Size
Gun Style	Body Build

As can be seen from this list, the number of possible topics in an identification case is quite large. Furthermore, any one of these items could have enormous significance as to guilt or innocence. For instance, if the defendant has a gold front tooth and, after a face-to-face robbery, the sole victim/witness fails to describe a robber with a gold front tooth, that omission alone could produce a reasonable doubt as to guilt. Conversely, if the witness describes a robber with a gold front tooth, and the defendant has no gold front tooth, the entire prosecution case may fail on that issue alone.

How is the lawyer to decide on the topics that should be made into topic pages? The topics of importance are derived from her theory of the case and the opposing theory of the case. If the theory of the case is that the defendant was indeed present, but was only attempting to take back something that belonged to him, the failure of a witness to see the defendant's gold tooth is of far less importance. It may still be a topic of interest in that the failure to detect the gold tooth might assist in showing that the witness did not have a good opportunity to observe the entire transaction, or that the witness is wrong on a myriad of details and cannot be trusted as to any portion of his story which hurts the opposing theory of the case.

Clearly, the topics will differ from case to case, as the theory of the case shifts. Although there can be expected some duplication of topics in most identification cases, a standard list of topics will not be efficient. The proper way to employ the topic system is to work directly from the discovery itself, not from the universe of possibilities of topics. That universe of possible topics is far too broad to be of use. The lawyer must begin her preparation with that which is described by the witnesses in this case.

Any topic on an identification factor that has come up anywhere in discovery or investigation needs to have its own topic page. Each topic index page must be limited to those pieces of information dealing with that single factual category. For example, "What did the robber look like?" is far too broad a topic. A physical description must be broken down into all of its components, including height, weight, eyes, hair, scars, marks, or other identifying topics.

Additional topic pages should be made for every descriptive topic recounted by a victim/witness. For instance, if an identification witness describes a weapon, a getaway car, or even a peculiar odor about the perpetrator, a topic page must be prepared containing all descriptions given by the witness of these topics. Internal or external inconsistencies on these issues can accumulate to undermine the credibility of the witness just as much as inconsistencies on issues of description of the suspect.

§ 5.14   Building Topic Pages

The object is to create a system that allows the advocate to read discovery a single time while building the topic pages. In a case that generates only a small amount of discovery or documents it may be possible (but inefficient) for the lawyer to review the entirety of discovery a single time before beginning the process of creating the topic pages. Even If the discovery is voluminous, counsel certainly has a draft theory of the case in mind. Working from that draft theory of the case, the lawyer is ready to begin filling out the topic pages.

Every case develops its own set of topics, so the topics used in one identification case will vary from the topic pages of a prior identification case. Topic pages will be built by moving facts out of case discovery and onto appropriate topic pages while neither losing nor adding anything in the transplanting. Remember, the lawyer's job is transplanting *not* translating. Complete accuracy is attainable and must always be demanded. It is critical that in the process of moving the information out of discovery and on to the appropriate topic page that testimony is not changed. This is critical because the words that are on the topic page become the leading questions of cross-examination.

The danger of translation is that in response to a leading question the witness may deny that he said a particular thing. The cross-examiner, working from the written chapter of cross-examination would believe that she had quoted the witness directly from the discovery, only to find during the act of impeachment that the cross-examiner has in some way changed the wording from the discovery to the topic page. By translating the facts, the question has become inaccurate for the prepared chapter of cross-examination. In this process the cross-examiner risks losing credibility with the jury and will undoubtedly lose confidence in her own system. The facts that are pulled out of discovery must not be altered in the process.

While the example that follows is drawn from a criminal case, the system works equally well in civil cases. Simply substitute the civil discovery; i.e., deposition, answers to interrogatories, etc., for the criminal items discussed.

Step One: Work from Source Documents to the Creation of Topic Pages

Take the first page of discovery in a criminal case, often a police report detailing the offense, begin at the top and look for every piece of information that touches upon the broad issue of identification if that is the theory of the case, or upon any other issue in which the lawyer may be interested.

Assume there is a single victim/witness who will testify to identification. There may be other witnesses, including police officers and lay people who will testify to surrounding issues, but only one witness will testify to identification. A full set of identification topic pages must be built for this identification witness. If there is more than one identification witness, a separate set of identification topic pages is required for each witness.

Each index page should show the witness's name and the topic of the page.

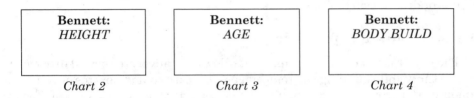

Bennett:	Bennett:	Bennett:
HEIGHT	AGE	BODY BUILD
Chart 2	Chart 3	Chart 4

Assuming there is only one identification witness, Scott Bennett, the cross-examiner needs to create a full set of identification pages showing every item of identification as related by Mr. Bennett. Here, for instance, Chart 2 deals with witness Bennett, and the limited topic of "Height"; Chart 3 deals with the same witness, but the different topic of "Age." This system continues for each additional topic perceived by this witness. Inconsistencies will ordinarily form the basis of the successful cross-examination of the identification witness, but other facts described by the identification witness are equally useful. For instance, the witness may have described the weapon, the getaway car, and the door from which entry was made. All are particularly useful topics for cross-examination, and, therefore, require their own topic index page.

In scanning the first page of discovery in this example, the offense report (see Chart 5, below), a transfer is begun into the topic page system of all information that deals with issues in which the lawyer might be interested. In this first page, or source document, the lawyer finds a block of information in which the officer has apparently asked the witness for a description of the robber (see Chart 6). These answers are in categories and can be easily placed onto the index page, and thus the page system begins.

Chart 5
First Source

Page 1 of 5 Pages

DENVER POLICE DEPARTMENT

OFFENSE REPORT

CFS No

☐ City Property or Personnel Involved

☒ Original Rept
☐ Additional Rept

Offense Report No 92-1601523

EVENT

Offense Type: Robbery - Business - Gun

How Complaint Received: ☐ Phone ☐ Radio ☐ On-View ☐ Station

Date and Time of Offense (Thru/In between)

Date 7 / 20 / 92 (TM1) 24 Hr Time 22:55 Day

(DT2) and Date / / (TM2) 24 Hr time Day

☐ (1) Daylight ☐ (2) Dark ☐ (3) Unk

Location: 66514 W Hilfax St

Apt No | Floor | Precinct | Type of Premises: Business Speedy Burrito #512

VICTIM

Name (First MI Last or Firm): Speedy Burritto

Sex | DOB | Race | Height | Weight | Marital Status

Address Res | City | State | Zip | Phone

Bus Add | Bus Pho 321-1234

Hospital | Ambul No | Attendant | Physician

No Vict | Injury/Other Victims

REPORTED BY

☐ Victim ☐ Officer ☐ Other | Name: Scott Bennett | Relationship to Victim | Age | Sex

Address Res: 2900 Race Ave | City: Denver | State: CO | Zip: 80219 | Phone: 757-5432

Bus Add: 66514 W Hilfax St | Bus Phone: 321-1234

Other Comments

SUSPECTS

Name/Alias | Add | City | State | Zip

Sex	Age	Race	Height	Weight	Hair	Eyes	Hair Style	Build	Glasses	Brd/Must	DOB
M	30	blk	73"	150	blk	brn	afro	hvy			

Comments on scars, tattoos, clothing description, other physical characteristics

VEHL.

Vehicle of Suspect: V Make: Chevy | V Model: Geo | V Year: 1990 | V Style: 2-dr | Veh Shade Lt Dk | Veh Color: green | V Top Color: green | Vin

Vehicle of Victim: Lic Number | Lic Year | Lic State | Lic Type | V Ident Characteristics

WITNESS

Name: Rodney Paxton | Add: 4647 E Bellaire | City: Aurora | State: CO | Zip: 80123 | Phone: 345-6789 | Sex: M | Age: 33 | Race: W

Bus Add: 66514 W Hilfax St Speedy Burrito | Bus Phone

WEAPON

Weapons (Make, Type, Cal, BBL, Serial No) or Describe Other Evidence Seized/Tool(s) used: 2-4 inch blue steel semi-automatic pistol.

NARRATIVE

Point of Entry or Where Attacked | Method of Entry/Attack

Victim's Statement

Witness Statement

Scene Investigation (Prior to crime, during/mo, after/suit, misc)

Burg Entry ☐ (1) Forcible ☐ (2) No Force ☐ (3) Att Forcible | Vehicle Entry ☐ (1) Force ☐ (2) No Force

Robbery ☐ (1) Armed ☐ (2) Strong armed | Assault ☐ (1) Gun ☐ (2) Knife ☐ (3) Other Weapon ☐ (4) Other Aggr ☐ (5) Other

STOLEN PROPERTY

No	Qty	Article	Type/Model/Size/Cal	Brand/Make	Serial No	Color	Est Value	EDP Code

Value of ▶	Currency	Jewelry	Furs	Clothing	Misc	Total Value ▶

ADMIN

Officer Taking Report: M. Bates, L. R. Wiley | Off No: 1122-3340

Investigator Assigned

Date and Time of Making Report: Date 7 . 20 . 92 24 Hr Time 29:15

Operation ID Yes ☐ No ☐

Agency Notified

I affirm this information is true and Correct. Signed

Read and Approved by

DPD 250 (1-77)

Chart 6

SUSPECTS

Name/Alias | Add. | City | State | Zip

Sex	Age	Race	Height	Weight	Hair	Eyes	Hair Style	Build	Glasses	Brd./Must.	DOB
M	30	blk	73"	150	blk	brn	afro	hvy			

Comments on scars, tattoos, clothing description, other physical characteristics

Chart 7, below, displays identifying information provided by the witness to the reporting officer, concerning the description of the robber.

Chart 7

Descriptive items available within page 1 of the police report.		
age	eye color	weapon
race	hair color	weapon color
sex	hair style	weapon size
height	build	
weight		

For purposes of illustration, concentration will be on the building of the "height" page. While this is just one of many topics to be covered, the building of topic pages is replicated for each topic and each witness.

From page one of the police report (Chart 5), it is clear that the officer has obtained a description of the height of the robber. The lawyer is ready to begin the topic page, which will carry each description given by witness Bennett of the height of the robber.

Chart 8

Bennett: *Height*
73″ (6-1)

The height, 6'1″, is taken off the source document (Chart 6) and put on the Bennett-Height page (Chart 8).

Because of the rules of impeachment, the lawyer also needs to show on the index page where in the discovery she found the points of information being transferred onto the topic pages. The lawyer must therefore write the source of the information "offense report, page 1/5." (See Chart 10, upper left hand corner.)

Chart 9

Bennett: *Height*   Off Rpt. p.1/5
73″ (6-1)

A trial lawyer must always assume that the witness may forget, deny or change this description no matter how often they were consistent before trial. Thus, the topic page must contain all other types of information needed for the laying of a foundation to introduce a prior inconsistent statement: the date the statement was given, and the person to whom given (see Chart 5, lower right hand corner). Now these are added to the topic page so that now the page is complete as to this one version of the witness's description of height.

Chart 10, below, graphically sets out how the lawyer has taken the necessary information off a source document and transplanted it to a topic page.

Chart 10

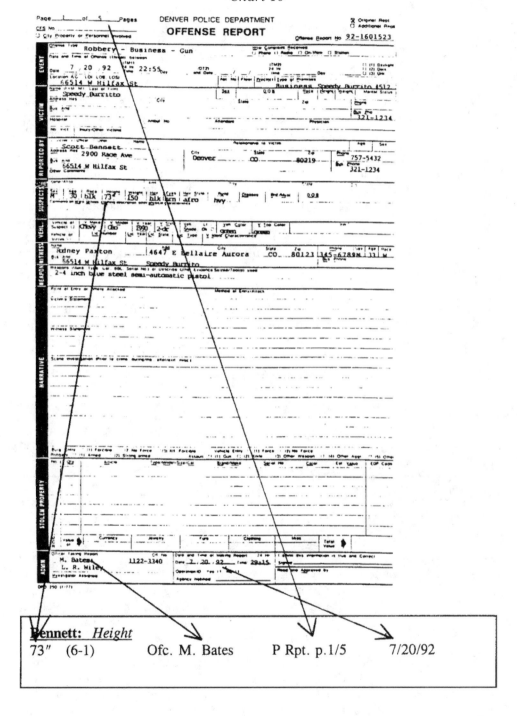

Bennett: *Height*
73″   (6-1)   Ofc. M. Bates   P Rpt. p.1/5   7/20/92

This, then, is an overview of the process by which the lawyer transfers a *single description* point of a *single fact* from the source document onto the index page guard.

Step Two: Build Topic Pages by Exhausting All Useful Information on Each Single Page of Discovery Material Before Moving to the Next Page of Source Material.

At this point, the lawyer has *not* completed this topic page. The lawyer has only completed the first entry onto the topic page. In order to complete the topic page, the lawyer must find every description of height given by this witness in all of the discovery material. Finally, the lawyer will also eventually add on a reference to client's actual height.

In order to accomplish this, the lawyer does not need to, and should not go through the stack of discovery looking for every height description. Such a method would force the lawyer to reread every page of discovery innumerable times as she builds each topic page. That is a gross misuse of precious time. Instead, the lawyer should go through the remainder of the first page of discovery, copying onto the appropriate topic page each "fact" dealing with any other topic of the identification issue or any other topic in which she is interested.

As the lawyer builds a set of identification topic pages from this first page of discovery, the other identifying descriptions given on page 1 of the police report (Chart 5) require the generation of additional topic pages at this point.

Chart 11

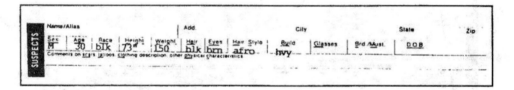

That is, the items in Chart 11 alone would require the lawyer to create entries on separate entitled topic pages for "age," "hair style," and "build."

There are always a great many facts that are not in dispute. Such facts do *not* require a topic page. For instance, the witness says the robbery happened at Speedy Burrito. Unless something comes up to cast doubt on this, the issue is not worth reducing to a topic page. Similarly, the race and sex of the robber are not in dispute, and therefore, no topic page need be made — unless it should later occur that this or another witness disputes that the robber was a black male.

When all of the facts gathered from the first page of discovery have been transferred onto appropriate topics pages, the lawyer will begin on the next page. Counsel must now work through all offense reports, police supplements, preliminary hearing transcripts, grand jury testimony, suppression hearing transcripts, defense interviews, statements by any third persons who have also discussed that topic with that witness, and all of the discovery, whether formal or informal.

§ 5.15   Digesting Second and Subsequent Source Documents

The same process just completed for the first source document is repeated for the second and subsequent source documents. In this example, Chart 12 shows a partial page out of the Second Source Document, a preliminary hearing transcript .

Chart 12
Second Source
Partial Preliminary Hearing Transcript

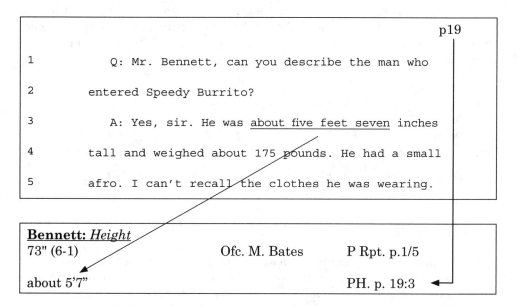

The height (about 5′7″) is transplanted to the height page. Note the exact quote is moved. Nothing is added. Nothing is deleted. The foundational information is transferred, including, in this case, the exact page and line number, and that it was at the preliminary hearing (PH.). While the prosecutor's name, title, and date of statement are included in Chart 13, by coding the lawyer can shorten the transfer.

Chart 13, below, shows the height page with the addition of a description of height found in the preliminary hearing transcript, including all identifying information.

Chart 13

Bennett: *Height*			
73" (6-1)	Ofcr. M. Bates	Off. Rpt. p.5	7/20/92
about 5'7"	DA: Simpleton	PH. p.19:3	11/15/92

§ 5.16   Tracking Imprecise Descriptions

Often a witness will not give a precise answer concerning a fact or issue, but will in some indirect way describe the fact or characteristic. Such information is as much a form of identification or assertion as a more precise answer and may prove equally useful. Such descriptions are subtler and more difficult to catch. For instance, suppose the witness stated: "I was standing right across from him and I had to look up." That phrase is pertinent to the height topic, though not as precise an answer as 5'7". It needs to go on the height topic page, as an identical quote (see Chart 14).

Chart 14

Bennett: *Height*			
73" (6-1)	Ofcr. M. Bates	Off Rpt. 1/5	7/20/92
about 5'7"	DA: Simpleton	PH. p.19:3	11/15/92
We were standing in front of each other and I had to look up.		HRG. 78:21	2/20/93

In any case, civil or criminal, in which the perceptions of a witness are in question, any topic in which the witness has been given an opportunity to show inconsistency, confusion, or an inability to observe or recall a detail is fertile for cross-examination. Besides the raw descriptive data of the assailant, other topics can be of equal importance in casting doubts on the credibility of the witness. Perhaps the victim is confused about where it happened, when it happened, how long it took, how many participants were involved or what was taken. All of these issues require separate topic index pages. Descriptions of the weapon, words spoken by the assailant, the color or model of the getaway car, and all other things that can be shown to be inconsistent, or unlikely to have occurred in the sequence or manner suggested by the victim/witness, are useful to the lawyer, and therefore she needs to keep track of them.

Regardless of the nature of the case, as to each and every subject that may be of interest, a separate topic page should be prepared so that the facts found in discovery may be distilled onto the pages. Remember, a topic page entry is incomplete unless the source page and line number or number of the page of discovery is noted so that the fact can be instantaneously relocated. Never assume the factual entry will be easy to relocate. In the stress of the courtroom, it is not.

§ 5.17   Coding the Topic Pages for Source

A single document or transcript may be the source for a great many entries on many different topic pages. The lawyer may repetitively write the date of the hearing or report, the name of the reporting person, or, in the case of court hearings, the names of the judge and the district attorney who were also present, as these items are needed each time in order to lay a proper foundation for impeachment. As a short cut, it is useful to make a summary source page detailing the foundation information as to each of these discovery documents. In that way the topic page need only say "PH" for preliminary hearing, or "Mtn Hrg" for motion hearing, and the page and line, while the source code page will show that the preliminary hearing was conducted November 15, 1992, in courtroom 111 before Judge Frey, and deputy district attorney Larry Simpleton.

Chart 15

Bennett: SOURCE CODES FOR SOURCE DOCUMENTS		
Off Rpt	Ofcr. Mike Bates	7/20/92
PH Ct 111	Judge Frey/DA Simpleton	11/15/92
Def. Interv.	(D.I.) Bob Lucas	1/12/93
MTN HRG. Ct 17	Judge Hutt/DA Hines	2/20/94

Having created a source page, the lawyer can now greatly reduce the amount of source information needed to properly show on the topic entries:

Chart 16

Bennett: *Height*			
73″ (6-1)	Off. Rpt.	1/5	7/20/92
about 5'7"	PH	19:3	11/15/92
We were standing in front of each other and I had to look up.	MTN HRG.	78:21	2/20/93

However, even when using this source code page, it is absolutely critical that every notation on the topic pages have the name and page number of the source document. Page and line should be used wherever possible (see Chart 16, entries 2 & 3). If no line number is available, at least the portion of the page should be noted "[arrow up]" showing on the upper half of page or "[arrow down]" showing on the lower half of page, or any other helpful codes. It is always harder to find the information in trial than the lawyer would think.

Multiple Witnesses Single Topic Comparison

Chart 17

Bennett: *Build*	
160-175	P. Rpt. p.2/5
175-180	PH 80:21
Pretty good shape	PH 80:25
Trim	PH 81:4, 81:1

Chart 18

Dudley: *Build*	
Medium to heavy	Off. Rpt. 2/5
Very heavy set, big belly	PH 63:14-20
protruded all the way around	

Chart 19

Paxton: *Build*	
Little stockier than LSP	PH 25:23
Could not tell shape the guy	Mtn. Hrg. 31:6
was in	

§ 5.18   Tracking the "Non-Answer" Answer

If a witness, when asked about a particular topic, says, "I didn't see it," "I've forgotten," or "I'm unsure," or any other words along these lines, that answer needs to appear on the appropriate topic page, as well (see Paxton's page, above). Such statements may prove inconsistent with other testimony of that witness or another witness on that topic. Such "non-answers" are also useful in crafting a cross-examination that requires the witness to repeatedly answer, "I can't remember" or "I didn't see." This may be the safest of crosses, and equally telling or helpful to the cross-examiner (see chapter 20, *Dealing With the "I Don't Know" or "I Don't Remember" Witness*).

Occasionally, the lawyer discovers in her source material no answer whatsoever. The answer isn't, "I didn't see it," but a blank where an answer could have been written, or a failure to describe something that elsewhere the witness does describe. Such a failure to describe a fact requires both a notation on the appropriate topic page and further investigation. For instance, in the initial police offense report (Chart 5), which formed the first source page for the topic pages, there is a blank under "glasses" and a blank under "beard/mustache" (see Chart 5, Bennett's description). During the initial reading of discovery, done to verify the theory of the defense, the lawyer may have mentally noted whether a "glasses" or "beard and mustache" description was given.

This information should be noted on the appropriate page (see Chart 20). If a description of that item is ever given by that witness, then the failure to give such a description to the police officer in the course of the offense report is something that must be noted on the proper topic page (see Chart 21). A failure to report to the officer a description of these items is inconsistent with later giving a description of that topic. The blanks found in descriptions may translate to either the answer, "None" or "I don't know." Further clarification may be required.

Chart 20

Bennett: *Glasses*	
No info given	Off. Rpt. 1
I think he had wire-framed glasses	PH. 17:6

Chart 21

Bennett: *Items Absent*	
Glasses: No description	Off. Rpt. 1
Tattoos: No description	Off. Rpt. 1/5

Furthermore, if the lawyer recalls and notes that another witness saw glasses or a beard or mustache, the theoretical "none" answer by this witness sets up an external inconsistency. Compare Chart 21, above, with Chart 22, below. Once again witness Bennett has given internally inconsistent answers and has given answers inconsistent with witness Paxton.

Chart 22

Paxton: *Glasses*	
Black framed	P. Rpt. 1/5
Heavy black	PH. 56:19

§ 5.19 Tracking "Did Not See" and "None" Answers

The process and necessity of tracking definitive information provided by a witness and tracking "non-answers" of the witness has been presented. There is another type of answer—the answer in the negative. Answers in the negative are answers in which the witness affirmatively admits a lack of knowledge on a particular topic, i.e., "I didn't see if he was wearing glasses." Just as was true from the other forms of answers, the lawyer must keep track of such negative answers in order to be prepared to impeach with them or to bring them out in cross-examination as a means of showing how little the witness saw or recalls.

§ 5.20 Tracking Facts on Which All Information Is in the Negative

There are invariably a great many topics that the witness did not see or describe in the discovery, the hearings, or the pre-trial investigation. It is help-ful to create a general topic page for all of the items that are consistently not seen, or those seen, but not remembered (see Chart 23, below). Later, if a specific fact becomes significant or is contradicted by this or another witness, the "didn't see" answer can be transferred to the appropriate witness/topic page (see Chart 24). In this way, the cross-examiner is shielded from the requirement to reread all of the discovery. This "did not see" page can now also serve as the basis of a cross-examination on what was not seen (see Chart 25).

Chart 23

Bennett: *Did not see / Can't remember*	
Shirt — Can't recall	Off. Rpt. 2/5
Hair style — I couldn't really see it	PH. 20:13
Shoes — I didn't see them	PH. 33:2

Chart 24

Bennett: *Shirt*	
Can't recall	Off. Rpt. 2

§ 5.21   Generic Topic Pages

There are some pieces of important data that do not fit conveniently into any one topic, but are important to a great many topics. For instance, the opportunity to observe the robber is important as to every single item of description given by the witness. However, it is too time consuming and redundant to put that information on topic page after topic page. Therefore, it is easier to create a single topic page such as "Opportunity to Observe" that contains upon it all appropriate information. See Chart 25, below.

Chart 25

Bennett: *Opportunity to Observe*	
The store was real well lit.	Off. Rpt. p. 3
He walked right up to me and was standing across the counter from me.	Supp. p.7
I didn't see him walk in the door and the first time I noticed him was when he walked up and asked for the money.	Supp. p. 9
The whole robbery took no more than two minutes and then he turned and ran out.	PH. 19:60

Note, however, that when filling out such generic pages, such as "Opportunity to Observe," if the lawyer happens upon an inconsistency, the information is now deserving of its own topic page. Inconsistencies on any topic rate their own page, since each area of inconsistency may well be worth its own chapter of cross-examination (see chapter 9, *The Chapter Method of Cross-Examination*).

For instance, if at one point the witness states that the robbery took no more than 30 seconds, but at another point the lawyer finds a claim by the witness that the whole thing took about five minutes, such material is worthy of its own topic page (see Chart 26). The lawyers might call it "duration of robbery" or some other term that reminds her of what she is talking about, but any meaningful inconsistency is worth its own topic page, since inconsistencies are of utmost importance to the cross-examiner.

Chart 26

Bennett: *Duration of Robbery*	
30 seconds	Off. Rpt. p.5
It took about five minutes	PH 19:12

§ 5.22 Coding In Externally Verifiable Facts

A completed topic page will immediately show any internal inconsistencies (inconsistencies within the statements given by that witness on any topic). By comparing completed topic pages of more than one witness in the same topic, the lawyer has identified one form of external inconsistency. Further work is needed to locate and show other forms of external inconsistencies.

Externally verifiable facts include, but are not limited to, other witness descriptions, exhibits, documents, photographs, drawings, videotapes, audiotapes, experiments, physical evidence, tangible evidence, and the verifiable laws of nature such as time of sun- rise and the direction in which a landmark is located.

The significance of much of the information on a particular topic page can only be appreciated when compared to the defendant, or to some other externally verifiable fact. For instance, if the client has a prominent facial scar, there deserves to be a topic page on that characteristic, so the lawyer can enter onto that topic page every single instance where the witness has been given an opportunity to describe the face of the assailant, but made no mention of a scar. This remains true even if the direct question of a scar did not arise. The witness can explain all she wants that she was not directly asked about that fact. But jurors may doubt that a person who stood face-to-face with a robber, described him and picked his picture later, did not notice or mention the facial scar; or having noticed it, failed to tell anyone about it.

In other instances, while all of the entries on a particular topic page may be consistent with each other, and even consistent with other witnesses, they, of course, must be considered in relationship to absolutely unquestionable realities. In a criminal case based on identification testimony, the defendant's physical characteristics will generally fall into the category of physical evidence. If a witness consistently describes the assailant as being in good shape and the client has a noticeable beer belly (which was not recently acquired), then that aspect of the witness's description is very relevant to a theory of the case based on misidentification. Every instance where the witness has said something about the assailant being in good shape may be externally inconsistent with the client's actual build. Hence, every one of those descriptions needs to be noted on the topic page, regardless of the fact that they are consistent with each other. Similarly, in civil cases, what the witness perceived, and the consistency of those perceptions, may be at odds with reality: The stop sign the witness insists was not there, the "hill" that does not exist, or the patient's spiking temperature.

§ 5.23   Sourcing External Facts

In order to make the necessary comparison of a witness's version of facts to any externally verifiable fact, it is necessary to code in information somewhere on the topic page concerning that fact. It too needs to have a source. If the only source of that information is the client, the lawyer is mentally boxing herself in needing to call the client to the stand. Not all cases make that the most favored position to be in. In a civil case where the client may be called in any event, the lawyer is boxing herself into dependence on the client's credibility in order to establish that particular fact. It is far better to look for ways to independently prove the external facts than to rely solely upon the client. For instance, on the height page. Assume the lawyer can develop an inconsistency between the description given by a witness and the height of the client, and further assume that the lawyer wants the jury to know the height of the client. It is important to mark the height of the client on the witness height page along with a source that can introduce that evidence. Example:

Chart 27

Bennett: *Height*			
73" (6-1)	Ofcr. M. Bates	Off. Rpt. 1/5	8/30/83
about 5'7"	DA: Simpleton	PH. 19:3	11/15/83
We were standing in front of		MTN HRG.	78:21
each other and I had to look up.			
Pretty tall – at least 6 feet.		Def. Int.	p.3
5'8"	**client**	**Booking slip**	**9/15/83**

§ 5.24   Facts from Other External Sources

So far, the witness topic pages have assumed the witnesses to be live people. However, there are many occasions in both civil and criminal cases when facts speak for themselves, though a witness must take the stand to introduce the fact. For instance, the coroner's report shows: (1) the blood alcohol of .20; (2) three stab wounds to the back; or (3) a bullet trajectory entering the chest and angling upward exiting in the back. All of these topics themselves are facts that need to be coded into appropriate topic pages. In a civil case, the highway diagrams, the accident scene diagrams, the pathology lab report are all facts from external sources that need to be coded into the appropriate topic pages.

Similarly, in a contract case, a document may use a particular phrase. If this is a fact having some bearing on the case, it needs to be coded into the appropriate page. In a products liability case, another example may be a warning label on a machine, or a user's manual that either contains a particular warning, or omits a particular warning. Language, or lack of language is itself a fact and best yet, is a fact beyond change. The document says what the document says, the photo shows what the photo shows, and the number of stab wounds noted in the autopsy is almost surely the number of stab wounds. These facts may contradict the witness, either by their introduction in raw form or by their introduction through the testimony of the witness, such as a coroner interpreting the fact. Similarly, the physical dimensions and mechanical characteristics of a machine are fixed facts. Testimony inconsistent with these physical characteristics is testimony that can be exposed as unbelievable. In all such instances, the lawyer must move the facts, the documents, exhibits, and reports onto the appropriate topic pages. In a civil wrongful death action:

Chart 28

Distance of Collision from Intersection	
The car hit him in the middle of the intersection.	Witness Mackey PH. p.3:9 (Preliminary Hearing of Defendant)
The car "hit the guy that died" right under the red light The body fell "right there"; "no movement."	Mackey Depo. p.22:7
Body found on sidewalk 36 feet from corner.	Coroner's Report p.7
Only blood stains from 32-34 feet from corner.	State Accident Lab Rpt. 4 p.2

As Chart 28 indicates, Mackey's testimony is consistent in his version of events, yet inconsistent with both the anticipated testimony of the coroner and the anticipated testimony of the investigative lab technician. These external inconsistencies can either be coded directly onto the appropriate topic page or they can each have their own page (see Charts 29 and 30 below).

Chart 29

Coroner Whitney: *Distance of Collision from Intersection*	
Body found on sidewalk 36 feet from corner	Det. Police Rpt. 6/14

Chart 30

Investigative Lab: *Distance of Collision from Intersection*	
Blood stains from 32-34 feet from corner	Jim McHughs Rpt. 3/6

In this way, the lawyer looks at external facts as witnesses. In the same way that witnesses testify, documents, photographs, and measurements can communicate. Though all may require an interpreter, they are as much testimony in the case as the words spoken by witnesses. Therefore, they need to be coded into the topic pages so that the lawyer can find both instances where witnesses are inconsistent with external facts, and instances where witnesses are consistent with external facts.

§ 5.25   Summary of the Preparation Technique

At the conclusion of this process, the lawyer has taken all of the information in discovery, added information gained in hearings and transcripts of any kind, added material derived from investigation, and then systematically grouped the material together by topic so that the lawyer now has categorized and systemized the information available.

Thousands of facts have been chiseled down into a few dozen pages. It is within these pages that the lawyer has the majority of the facts needed to prepare tight, accurate, penetrating cross-examinations. In writing the cross-examinations, the lawyer will refer almost exclusively to these pages, rather than to the discovery from which they were distilled (see chapter 10, *Page Preparation of Cross-Examination*). Remember, even if many of the pages generated reveal no inconsistencies, they must be retained. They may have tremendous value at trial. No trial lawyer can ever predict when a witness will vary a story or detail that has previously been thought to be rock solid. This will be further discussed in chapter 16, *Eight Steps of Impeachment by Inconsistent Statement*.

Chapter 6

CROSS-EXAMINATION PREPARATION SYSTEM 2: SEQUENCE OF EVENTS CHARTS

SYNOPSIS

§ 6.01   Sequence of Events Charts

A goal of any cross-examination preparation system is to provide a systematic analysis for the advocate's use. In that regard, it makes no difference which system an advocate uses so long as that system adequately equips the lawyer to understand the interrelationship of the facts of the case, see their application against the competing theories of the case, and prepare for the drafting of appropriate cross-examination chapters in an efficient manner.

There are several ways to analyze the facts of a case. In the previous chapter the method used was to break down a case into many small topics. While there might be some relationship between one topic and another, the topics are separately analyzed and prepared in a system that allowed the advocate to regroup the facts as appropriate. In contrast, the preparation technique employed in a sequence of events charts is based upon breaking a case into events. Events are ordinarily a larger subdivision of the case compared with chapters. The theory and general method of preparation using the sequence of events chart is parallel to those used in the topic page method. Of course, the most critical events may themselves eventually be studied at the individual fact level, but the initial breakdown is along the line of occurrences in the case. Sequence of events charts are useful in preparation of both small and large scale commercial litigation, personal injury cases, domestic cases, and intent defenses in criminal cases.

§ 6.02 Most Appropriate Usage

The type of case most susceptible to a sequence of events analysis involves the testimony of multiple witnesses examining a single event. Most personal injury cases can benefit from this type of analysis. Commercial litigation cases also are amenable to an event level analysis. Many forms of domestic relations litigation, including custody and visitation disputes, could benefit from an event level analysis. In contrast, credibility cases in which a single witness relates his perceptions of an event lend themselves more readily to topic index pages, since the elements of fact perception or identification are so readily divisible into finite topics.

§ 6.03 Steps of the System

There are three parts to this type of organization: First, the lawyer will adopt a preliminary chart breaking the case into the sequence of important events; second, the lawyer breaks down each portion of each event using the topic page system; and third, the lawyer charts each witness' observations (see chapter 7, *Cross-Examination Preparation System 3: Witness Statement Charts*) within the topics that make up each event sequence.

Just as was true in the topic index page system, in order to accomplish the first step, the sequence of events must be detailed enough that each part of the sequence is small enough to be a workable piece of information. If the sequence of events reads: 1) Events before the fight; 2) The fight; and 3) Events after the fight, there really is no sequence of events chart. "The fight" is simply too broad to be understood without a much more elaborate breakdown no matter how short its duration. Similarly, "before the fight" and "after the fight" are not events at all but general time spans in which many events occurred.

In a commercial dispute, the advocate is looking for events far more discrete than the time frames negotiating the contract, signing the contract, or the breach of the contract. In order to be useful in drafting cross-examinations, the lawyer must create a far more detailed event breakdown.

Time frames (that is, blocks of time with specific reference to finite and minute events) are a good place to start, as opposed to time spans. For ease of illustration and because of a basic human understanding of self-defense, an analysis of this system of cross-examination preparation will be done as applied to self-defense cases. Within the most important events, the advocate should pay attention to the nuances, the second-by-second actions of the fight (or other event) during which self-defense arises or fails to arise. The system is applicable equally to domestic relations conduct cases (truly a series of events) and to civil cases in general, particularly personal injury actions and commercial cases.

§ 6.04   Example of System Application

Example: Two men come out of a bar. They have been drinking and arguing, and a fight may be coming. The defendant returns to his automobile. His reasons are ambiguous. The victim comes out of the bar door toward the defendant. The victim speaks. The defendant reaches over into his glove compartment, gets a gun, stands up, and shoots the victim.

The cursory recitation of facts may suggest a weak self-defense case, but proper charting of the full sequence of events may reveal otherwise. Analysis of each time frame is essential to proper charting of the events in a sequence of events preparation system. The analysis for purposes of this example will begin with the actions from the bar door outward. That is not to say that the actions within the bar are meaningless. Almost certainly, those actions or events will have enormous significance, but they are themselves the subject of a separate sequence of events breakdown.

For each time frame to be studied, the advocate should break down each movement or movements within it. This analysis gives an overview of a breakdown. Note, however, the breakdown can (and will in most instances) be in more detail. A slower procession through the time frame movements would take place.

The defendant leaves the bar. Is he running or walking?

The victim leaves the bar. Is he running or walking?

As the defendant is leaving, the victim is yelling. What is he yelling?

The defendant gets in the car. Which door? Is he getting in the driver's door with his keys in his hand, or is he getting in the passenger door (which is strange, unless his intention is to get to the glove compartment where he has the gun)?

Assuming the defendant enters through the driver's door, how many steps behind is the victim?

At what pace is the victim moving?

What is the victim saying?

What is the defendant saying?

When the defendant reaches across for the gun, where is the victim?

Is the door open or closed?

When the defendant reaches the gun, where is the victim now?

What is he saying?

What is he doing?

Where are his hands?

Defendant shoots. From where? At what angle?

Having received these answers, the sequence of events in time frame movements may look like this:

The defendant walks out of the bar.

The defendant walks toward the car.

The victim comes out of the bar.

The victim is yelling.

The victim runs toward the defendant.

The defendant scrambles to open the driver door.

The victim keeps running.

The defendant falls across the front seat, reaching for the gun.

The victim is almost to the car, still running, now yelling threats.

The defendant grabs the gun, yelling, "Leave me alone!"

The victim reaches in the car.

The defendant shoots upward while lying on his back on the front seat.

(The degree of breakdown depends on the facts, the amount of preparation time, and the theory of the case. It is sufficient to say that the greater the breakdown of events, the better the understanding of the nuances of the case.)

Now the lawyer must create topic page for each of the finite facts within each time frame of the sequence of events before the event chart can be created. For instance:

Chart 1

Witness Trujillo: Car Keys		
"Keys in hand" when reached car-door	Off. Report p. 1 Bates 0004	9/13/03
Keys in "right hand at wheel of car"	Det. Epps Interview 4:14	10/20/03
"Keys were found in the ignition"	Det. Brown Report p. 3 Bates 0124	10/20/03
"Keys were in ignition"	Tow-Truck report p. 2 (Hollender) Bates 0152	10/20/03

§ 6.05   Topics within Events

When studying a sequence of events in preparation for cross-examination, it is important to realize that "events" are as capable of reduction into finite facts just as the components of the description given by the witness in the identification case. The lawyer should reduce events into topic pages in the same way that hard-edged facts such as height and weight in Preparation System 1 were separately tracked.

For instance, in the self-defense case, the event sequence shows a verbal argument after leaving the bar. But the topic pages need to be far more detailed. The more detailed the specific facts that are obtained, the easier it is to formulate "one fact per question" questions on cross-examination. The one-fact-per-question method, with such detailed specific facts, leads the jury naturally to the conclusions that support the theory of the case.

The victim speaks: Did the victim say something particularly derogatory or threatening? What was that exact sentence? Tone? When was it said in relationship to other sentences and action? Did the defendant reply? Again, for sake of analysis, assume that the client says the victim said, "I'm gonna kick your ass." The lawyer will need a topic page for threats made by the victim. There may even need to be multiple pages for threats. For instance, threats in the bar, threats outside the bar, or a more thorough breakdown.

On any specific topic page, the lawyer must place not only the defendant's version of such threats, but the version given by every other witness to that event or portion of events. In this way, as was true in the illustrations given of the topic page system in chapter 5, the lawyer can compare all of the witness's versions as to a single fact in one glance. The lawyer can also put the topic pages into chronological order so that she can retrace the sequence of events of the case without flipping endlessly through discovery. The greater the number of witnesses to an event, the greater the necessity for the use of topic event pages in a sequence of events chart.

Now assume that there was some pre-fight ugliness between a criminal defendant and the deceased. The two parties argued back and forth in public, and the fight then moved outside. By this point, certain witnesses had seen some portions of the fight. Other witnesses saw different portions of the fight. The lawyer is in need of a step-by-step, time frame sequence of events. These are then broken down into individual facts. There is great significance to such facts as to who took the first step, what the client said at that point, when the client went to the car, what door he entered, the pause between pointing the gun, and shooting the gun. As to each of these, the lawyer needs a factual breakdown showing every witness's version of each time frame movement of the action.

The synopsis of depositions in civil cases, particularly when witnesses tend to ramble, is much more useful to the cross-examiner when done in chronological order of case events. Using an event method of synopsizing the depositions is more efficient, as it eliminates the necessity to flip through various pages of the deposition (or pages of the synopsis of the deposition) to find all references to a particular topic within the case events. The deposition synopsis can then be formed into the topic cards.

§ 6.06   Time and Motion Studies as Models for Event Charts

The best way to envision this kind of event breakdown is to envision the time and motion studies that were popular in the 1930s. In a time and motion study, the individual movements made by a worker in order to assemble a part or product were studied in minute detail so that social scientists could compute how to make the work progress smoother, reduce the number of steps required, and lower costs of production, all the while speeding up production.

The lawyer's goal is to understand the time and motion of the event (in this example, a criminal episode) and to assemble it before the jury in such a way as to show the justification for the defendant's ultimate actions. By visualizing the episode as a film, this system breaks the tape down frame by frame so each frame may be studied and catalogued in great detail. This also keeps the sequence of events in chronological order.

By breaking down the episode into component parts, the lawyer is better able to show the jury seemingly minute events that may take on greater factual and legal significance when examined in detail within the context of the overall picture or episode. Breaking down each event in minute detail becomes extremely important in giving the cross-examiner the option or ability to emphasize or de-emphasize the significance of any selected time frame movement.

The same general rules that were laid out in the previous chapter apply to these topic pages as well. The lawyer will obtain individual facts for each witness and place them on topic pages, noting in exact language each statement made by the witness concerning that particular fact, to whom or in what setting the statement is made, and identify or source the information by page number, line number, date and persons involved. In the event that a witness is present but fails to observe something that happened, that failure to observe should be equally noted on the appropriate topic page. For instance in Chart 1 above, Witness Trujillo saw the car keys in various ways. However, the witness "didn't see them" after the defendant entered the vehicle. This is noted equally as being just as important as the earlier observations. Particularly in light of the fact that Detective Brown then finds the keys in the ignition of the vehicle as "physical evidence" and notes it in his supplemental report.

The failure of the witness to see the keys becomes stronger and supports the defendant's theory of the case that he intended to leave the scene. That is, he placed them in the ignition. In the event a witness hears or sees something, but is ambiguous in his answer, that ambiguity should be noted exactly on the appropriate page. Again using the example of Witness Trujillo in the previous chart (Chart 1), the witness noted, "keys in hand" but did not note which hand. While this appears to be not ambiguous, the ambiguity becomes readily apparent when the witness can now identify in the interview with Detective Epps the fact that the keys were in "the right hand at wheel of car." This ambiguity initially is often seen by a jury as a sign of honesty by the witness, rather than imprecision. The more careful qualification illustrates witness precision when pressed for more details on what must have appeared to be an unimportant fact.

§ 6.07   Coding In Non-Testimonial Evidence

Of equal and sometimes greater importance is what non-testimonial evidence will "say" about a particular fact. If the client says that the deceased smashed a beer bottle during the argument, the analysis of the discovery on this issue will only be complete if the topic card contains observations by witnesses or law enforcement agents concerning the presence or lack of presence of broken glass at the crime scene. If the detective found a broken beer bottle in the bar, the detective is as much a witness to that fact in the case as if he has been there and witnessed the breaking of the bottle.

Similarly, if the broken glass is photographed, or better yet, taken into evidence, its physical presence "testifies" on a material issue in the case and needs to be noted on an appropriate topic page. For instance, Witness Trujillo's chart concerning the car keys (Chart 1) notes that the investigating officer, Detective Brown, found the keys in the ignition to the vehicle after he arrived at the scene. The fact that the keys were in the ignition may well be a most significant fact, showing that the defendant intended to drive away when he entered the vehicle. It can be effectively argued that a person in the rush of pre-battle preparations would not take the time to place the keys to the vehicle in the ignition. The keys in the ignition may well become a cornerstone to the self-defense theory of the case. This one single fact could strongly lead the jury to a conclusion that supports the theory of the case.

Assume for a moment that the keys in the ignition are not noted or photographed, but the police tow truck driver is capable of testifying that the keys were in the ignition. This piece of physical evidence can be introduced by the tow truck driver. Defense counsel can argue that the detective, by failing to note, photograph, or obtain the keys from the ignition, overlooked a valuable piece of evidence, which when compiled with other errors and omissions by the detective, greatly affect his credibility. The insertion of physical evidence into a topic page system is done recognizing that physical evidence testifies at least as well as people. In fact, in a great many instances, physical evidence testifies with greater clarity and certainty than witnesses.

As chapter 2, *Developing a Theory of the Case*, points out, physical evidence and documentary evidence (that is, things that cannot be changed), as opposed to testimony of witnesses (which is always subject to change by use of different words, inflections, and tones) are tremendously powerful pieces of evidence. Certainly, personal injury lawyers have long known that physical evidence moves a jury to award greater damages when it supports their theory of the case. Introduction of a duplicate of the surgical rod and metal screws used to repair a compound fracture allow the jury to "feel" the pain of surgery and hospitalization more than a recitation of what was done. Domestic relations lawyers realize that photographs of the residence of the parties often speak with great clarity and in such a way that could never be verbalized by the lawyer concerning the financial condition and lifestyle of the parties before the separation.

A great many criminal defense lawyers have learned that sorry truth while defending a case in which the witnesses are weak on their identification, but the defendant's fingerprint is found at the scene. The converse is equally true. In an adult sexual assault case, a victim might testify that the defendant grabbed her forcefully and ripped her clothes in the course of forcing her submission to sex. However, the absence of any torn clothing, missing buttons, or any other damage to her clothing testifies quite powerfully in opposition to that witness and must be noted in the appropriate places on the appropriate topic cards.

Again, when inserting physical evidence of any type onto a topic page, it is necessary to note the witnesses who will be able to testify to those facts, such as investigating detectives, laboratory technicians, or booking desk officers. For instance, the live witnesses in Witness Trujillo (Chart 1) are Detective Brown and the tow-truck driver Hollender. Detective Brown was the investigating officer who came on the scene after the death. He observed the keys in the ignition. He made a note of that location. Detective Brown's name is noted on the appropriate topic page as to being able to verify the keys in the ignition. Additionally, the tow-truck driver, Hollender, noted that the keys were in the ignition at the time of the tow. His name and observations are found on the appropriate topic page, as well as were in his report he made his observations.

Just as was the case in topic pages based on witness testimony, the lawyer must indicate the document and page number in discovery (or the actual present location if an exhibit) where this material can be found. Using the example of the car keys (Chart 1), the notation is made that the car keys are mentioned on the supplemental report dated October 1, 2003, on page 3 of 5 pages in the lower half of the page.

In the event that the detective had not mentioned the car keys, but the tow truck driver could testify to the fact that they were in the ignition and actually has the car keys in his possession now, that should be noted on the topic card so that counsel can decide whether to issue a subpoena duces tecum for the production of the car keys to be introduced as an exhibit.

§ 6.08   Highlighting Events within a Sequence

In any particular case, the lawyer's first attempt to break the case into a sequence of events may not result in the most powerful version of a sequence of events. The lawyer may ask, "How can this be?" If the sequence is in doubt, it can be litigated. If it is certain, the lawyer is stuck with it. While the lawyer cannot change the sequence of events, she can increase or decrease the importance and impact of various events by how she chooses to phrase and group them together. If the client has been in the wrong or makes a bad impression in early events (using the self-defense example), consider starting the cross-examination of the sequence with the first critical event that takes place after the earlier series of less useful events or harmful events viewed from the theory of the case (see chapter 11, *Sequences of Cross-Examination*).

Similarly, if, after the fight, the client does things that are not to his credit, it is foolish to dwell on them in cross-examination. Will that mean that an opponent will not find them and examine on them? No. It means that when the lawyer is interviewing or questioning witnesses prior to trial, preparing the cross-examination, or giving the opening statement, the lawyer will be emphasizing those critical parts of the sequence that are the best or most favorable for her theory of the case. Sequence and depth of presentation subtly convey to both witnesses and jurors the cross-examiner's belief as to the key events in the case. While the jury will not forget the other events, they certainly will not talk about them in as great a detail as they would if they thought those were the critical events of the case. In this way, the cross-examiner can gently reshape the nature of events, emphasizing some events by examining them in minute detail while de-emphasizing others by grouping them together in broader forms of examination.

§ 6.09   An Example of the Use of Detail to Emphasize a Topic

An example is taken from a domestic relations case. The parties had been married 22 years. They have raised three children, all of whom are above18. The husband has struck the wife with an open hand on one occasion during the marriage.

If the cross-examining lawyer wanted to emphasize the fact that the husband struck the wife, a detailed cross-examination of that blow would include each party's position in a particular room just prior to the blow. Details should include all of the following: The husband raised his hand, the husband pulled his hand back behind his ear, the husband swung forward with his right hand to strike the wife, it was done with the intention of striking the wife in the face, the blow landed on the left cheek of the wife, the wife was propelled into the couch two feet from where she was standing before being struck, the wife began to cry, the wife's left cheek began to turn red in the shape of a handprint, the wife covered her face, and the husband's hand stung from the blow.

By examining this one incident in such minute detail, the cross-examiner can emphasize this incident in a memorable fashion to make it appear much greater than if the cross-examiner chose to de-emphasize the impact of this fact.

If the cross-examiner wishes to de-emphasize the effect of this slap to the face, time would be spent on detailing the fact that the parties had been married 22 years and been through a lot together. The cross-examiner would point out that the parties had endured good and bad times, including times when the parties' children were injured or in trouble, times when the parties had good financial periods, times when the parties had poor financial periods, times when the parties had great stresses upon them, and times when the parties were angry with each other.

The cross-examiner would then put into context that despite all of these events, in 8,030 days of marriage, the husband had only struck the wife one time. It was only an open hand blow, it caused no broken bones, required no trip to the hospital, and resulted in no permanent injury. In this way, the cross-examiner would de-emphasize the importance of this unfortunate conduct by putting it into context with other events.

Although bad facts are not going to disappear, much of the sting may be taken out of them by this method of grouping and de-emphasizing bad events (see chapter 23, *Diminishing or Building the Point*).

§ 6.10   Grouping Events with Theme Phrases

Several events can be regrouped and presented as one event and given a theme phrase that has impact on the theory of the case. In the self-defense example, by characterizing the movement as "the defendant retreats," the cross-examiner influences the word choices of witnesses.

Similarly, when a defendant threatens, but does not strike, these actions are labeled a "warning" rather than a "threat." By titling an event with a theme phrase and using that theme phrase in pre-trial interviews and hearings, the lawyer influences the witness's perceptions about the event. The word choices of the witnesses are directly affected (see chapter 26, *Loops, Double Loops, and Spontaneous Loops*). When the theme phrase is then applied to the topic during trial by the cross-examiner, and hopefully by the witness, the desired perception, as evidenced by the theme phrase, is communicated to the jury. This concept is not new. Prosecutors have long referred to complaining witnesses as "victims" when in fact the entire trial concerned whether the person was indeed a victim.

§ 6.11   Creating Event Titles That Benefit the Theory

Throughout the leading question format, the description of an item or event is first in the hands of the cross-examiner. As an example, a plaintiff's lawyer may refer to his client's injury as a cut, but if fair would rather talk about the injury in terms of "the scar." These phrases can become theme lines to be used throughout cross-examination, rather than being thought only appropriate for closing argument.

The lawyer should examine the particular set of facts in a simple case to visualize how a sequence chart can be created and utilized. A criminal case example is given, but the concept applies equally as well to civil cases. In this sequence, the defendant (Jim) is driving on a busy downtown street. A young man walks off the sidewalk while making small talk with his friends. He is also making rude comments to women passersby. The defendant has to hit his brakes. There is no collision, but insulting words are exchanged. The defendant/driver gets out. There is more verbal confrontation. As it begins to appear that blows will be forthcoming, the defendant/driver pulls a gun, fires a shot, hitting nobody, then quickly fires a second shot that strikes the "victim" (Concorde) in the chest. Defendant/driver immediately gets back in his van and leaves the scene. Victim dies at the scene. Based on these events, the first draft of the sequence of events chart looks like this:

Chart 2

Defendant: Jim Roark   Deceased: Roy Concorde
Sequence of Events (A Failed First Attempt)
1. Concorde before accident
2. Van almost hits Concorde
3. Van stops/Defendant exits
4. Confrontation
5. Shooting
6. Defendant into van and leaves

There are many problems with this first attempt at a breakdown of the case. A great deal of time is spent on the sequence leading up to the shooting, and the "fight" or "shooting" represents only one part of the six-part sequence. Anyone can tell from looking at this chart that the defense case is not going to benefit by a prolonged discussion of events 1, 2, 3, and 6. Furthermore, an attempt to create topic cards for this overly broad breakdown of events leads to an overly broad view of critical events. For instance, examine the versions given by witnesses Foenum, Clark, and Minson of "The Shooting" (Chart 3). Some hear one shot, some see only the second shot, some know about what preceded it, and some do not. It is difficult to meaningfully compare statements of each witness. This inevitably leads to open-ended cross-examination in which an improperly prepared defense lawyer invites witnesses to re-testify to "what you saw" or "what happened next."

Chart 3

Multiple Witness Comparison
Chart on One Element
"The Shooting"
(First Version)

Witness:

1. Kendal

Hears angry voices and a gunshot; see victim grab side.

2. Maiden

Hears car backfire; 3-5 seconds later hears small caliber handgun, doesn't see who has gun, "first thinks it's Mr. Doors."

3. Foenum

"I turned away and heard a shot (blank or starter pistol)," saw all parties on sidewalk; saw victim come at defendant and swing coat at him; defendant backs up towards van; sees .22 in defendant's hand, sees defendant point at and shoot victim, sees victim grab side; 10-15 seconds between shots.

4a Clark
4:50 p.m. statement

Defendant fires 1 or 2 warning shots at victim's party then without provocation shoots directly at victim.

4b Clark
6:50 p.m. statement

Hears small caliber shot; looks and sees defendant exchanging "abusive words" with group; sees defendant exchange words with Doors, also a short shoving match with Doors; Doors retreats 20-25 ft., leaving victim in line of fire, defendant raises pistol calmly to waist level and fires; 8-10 seconds between shots.

5. Hahn

Hears one shot and see Mexicans continuing to go after defendant; hears second shot and sees that a short Mexican has been shot.

6. Guadalupe

Defendant fires first shot at John Doors who is in street on other side of victim; fires 2nd shot at victim, gun in right hand, defendant about 5 ft. from victim when shot.

7. Riley

Defendant while backing up pulls gun and shoots twice.

8. Doors

Defendant points gun at witness and fires, witness thinks gun has blanks and goes at defendant again; defendant shoots victim in chest.

The ability to conduct a precise cross-examination is lost through such generalized charts. The lawyer cannot control the witness, since the lawyer is not in control of the facts. In a breakdown of the shooting, witness by witness, the lawyer will see "the shooting" as a far more complex matter rather than a single event (see Chart 3). Greater precision in the analysis of the breakdown leads to greater precision in the selection of chapters (see chapter 9, *The Chapter Method of Cross-Examination*), and to greater precision in questions and word choice in the questions (see chapter 8, *The Only Three Rules of Cross-Examination*). This precision permits detailed factual development of the cross-examiner's theory of the case.

As a comparison of Chart 3 and Chart 4 shows, the original breakdown of events unproductively lumped together a great many finite events under the single title "Shooting." If the lawyer is going to build cross-examinations around a self defense theory, she must break down both the "confrontation" and "the shooting" into their component events and then de-emphasize the harmful earlier and later events so that the sequence and detail play to the advantage of the cross-examiner's theory of the case. If the lawyer begins to fashion the cross-examinations based upon the first breakdown (Chart 3), the lawyer would be forced to emphasize why the defendant got out of his van in the first place. Unhelpful emphasis would also be given to why he got back in and drove away. Based on the first breakdown, in all likelihood the lawyer would inadequately study and explain the sequence of events related to the confrontation itself.

Chart 4

Sequence of Events (Improved Version)
People v. Jim Roark
Victim: Roy Concorde

Gang walking/talking/harassing
Concorde walks off curb
Jim (in van) almost hits Concorde
Jim out of van

1. Jim/Concorde confrontation
2. Doors joins in
3. Jim retreats
4. Shot # 1 by Jim (the warning shot)
5. Concorde keeps coming
6. Shot # 2 (fatal)

Jim into van
Jim drives away

§ 6.12   Compression and Expansion

The Sequence of Events Draft II (Chart 4) illustrates the concept of compressing the sequence of events in areas that are not particularly helpful, while expanding the sequence of events in the areas where greater detail is critical to the theory of the case. Gone are the events that precede the face-to-face confrontation. In their place, "the shooting" has been expanded into five separate events. If the lawyer's self-defense theory is to prevail, she must find within the expanded version of "the shooting" the details that can assist. Hence, this portion of the sequence of events must be studied in the greatest detail.

Chart 5

Draft II Charting a Sequence of Events

POOR	BETTER
1) Victim before accident	1) Jim/Concorde confrontation
2) Van/accident	2) Doors joins in
3) Van stops/defendant exit	3) Jim retreats
4) Confrontation	4) Shot #1 (The warning shot)
5) Shooting	5) The gang keeps coming
6) Post Shooting	6) Shot #2

Is this fair? Yes it is. While the lawyer cannot avoid a discussion of what happened prior to the fight, it is certainly not something a lawyer wants to emphasize with the witnesses. The more time spent interviewing witnesses on these details, the more the witnesses are going to remember these events in detail and report the details in court.

Particularly in civil cases where the lawyer has the opportunity to depose opposing witnesses by means of cross-examination, the focus of this lawyer's questioning becomes critical. As the lawyer's questioning focuses the witness on certain events within a series of events, the witnesses must reorganize their own thoughts and rethink the context in which all other events have occurred in light of the questioning as to the events focused upon by the lawyer.

If the lawyer were to conduct a "what happened next" form of deposition, the witness is not led to this reanalysis or into placing the events he saw into the context of other events that he may or may not have seen or incorrectly were told about by others. This fact-driven and carefully focused type of deposition refocuses the deposition in such a way as to require original thought by the witness.

In this example, "the shooting" is at the heart of the theory of the case. If the lawyer breaks that event apart, she can keep track of the witnesses item by item and show it in greater detail: 1) how the fight escalated needlessly and 2) how the deceased was responsible for the escalation.

Is this breakdown wholly accurate? Not yet. There are many sub-issues (time frame movements) within each of the events. For instance, now that the lawyer has broken down the overly broad category, "the shooting," into its components, she can take the witnesses' statements and break them into the same components so that the shooting unfolds sequentially. The lawyer can see each witness's version of each of the components of the fight. This breakdown of facts into a comparison chart is useful, not only in preparing the courtroom cross-examination, but also during the interviewing or deposing witnesses. Quite simply, witnesses who came upon the scene at the end of the fight, not knowing what preceded it, have their perceptions colored or skewed by the gaps in their knowledge.

This sequence of events analysis allows the lawyer to understand when the witness began observing the event. This in turn permits the lawyer to analyze the flow of events from the eyes of the witness. In this sense, the lawyer now has a much better understanding of why the witnesses are saying what they are saying. As a result, the lawyer is better able to accurately predict how the witness's story will be modified.

If the cross-examiner can put herself into the shoes of the witness, the cross-examiner can better appreciate the witness's perception of what the witness saw. Because a particular witness may know nothing about what caused the defendant's actions at event 4 (Shot # 1) and prior to event 4, the witnesses will assume that the defendant's actions were purely malicious. In the course of pre-trial interviewing or cross-examination, when witnesses are shown that other witnesses saw earlier critical incidents, they understand "their" facts in a different context. As a result, they often become far less hostile. They understand the theory and often volunteer new "facts" to support it.

The sharpness or anger goes out of some of the witness's testimony at events (2) "Doors joins in," (3) "Jim retreats," (4) "the warning shot" and (5) "the gang keeps coming." All these events serve to explain event (6) "shot # 2." Having been made aware of these earlier events, it becomes comprehensible to the witness (and simultaneously to the jury) that there are good reasons for the defendant's actions at event 6, "shot # 2."

Equally important to the cross-examination preparation is the realization that a witness who sees relatively few of the events of a case may be the most critical witness in establishing the cross-examiner's theory. Examine sequences 2, 3 and 4 of Chart 4. Witnesses who see only these three topics, or any one of them, but cannot testify in the least concerning the defendant's later actions, can still establish the first aggressive actions by the victim and his friends. Such a witness, working from an admittedly incomplete body of facts, can build a context in which the later events can be better understood and fully appreciated by the jury.

One of the side benefits of using a witness who has an incomplete knowledge of all of the facts of the case is that there is little downside risk for the cross-examining lawyer. This witness truly cannot volunteer "new" facts detrimental to the cross-examiner's theory of the case because this witness admittedly does not know additional facts.

§ 6.13 Non-Witnesses as Witnesses

The cross-examiner should always scrutinize "non-witnesses" to determine if they are potentially helpful witnesses. Non-witnesses are those witnesses who have not seen, heard, or observed an event likely to have captured the hearing, sight, and knowledge of any reasonable person. The fact that these things were not observed, heard, or seen may well be used by the cross-examiner to water down or blunt the testimony of those who claimed to have seen the events. For this reason, a chart showing each witness's version of a particular event must include witnesses who state they did not see that particular event.

§ 6.14　Sequencing

Ordinarily lawyers think of events in chronological order. So do witnesses. So do juries. That does not mean that each witness should be cross-examined chronologically as to events, even when certain events or portions of events are being skipped over. Unless the jury would be unable to follow a cross-examination other than in chronological order, the cross-examiner should always consider cross-examination in non-chronological order (see chapter 11, *Sequences of Cross-Examination*).

What becomes of the topics that have been left out of the sequence? They do not disappear. The opponent is not so foolish as to overlook the defendant's getting out of the van or the defendant's driving away afterward. But, through a strong opening statement and a well-directed cross-examination, the lawyer can lay out in a systematic fashion the best sequence of events. This sequence makes perfect sense, it is accurate, and the witnesses are comfortable discussing it.

In this example, the lawyer might begin the cross-examination on Chart 4, event 1 of the sequence and proceed through event 6, and perhaps even use a chart to aid the jury in talking about and thinking about the six-part sequence that the lawyer has designed. Assuming the lawyer has utilized this breakdown of events in her pre-trial interviews or depositions, the witnesses themselves will gravitate toward the chosen sequence and will abbreviate their discussion of the events before and after that sequence because they simply no longer find them as important as they might have originally.

As each witness is led through the cross-examination, the jury begins to focus on the six-part sequence. If the lawyer elects to simultaneously create or use a chart of events, all eyes will turn to it as the lawyer fills it with the testimony of each witness as to each of the numbered events. The chosen sequence, while not excluding the prosecution's reference to other items, diminishes the importance of those other items. Through cross-examinations, foreshadowed by a factual detail-dominated opening statement, "the fight," as broken down into the six parts, becomes the focal point of the case. While the defendant's unfortunate actions of getting out of the van and leaving after the fatal shot will not disappear, they will not become the focus of the case.

§ 6.15　Applying the Sequence of Events Method to Large Scale or Complex Civil Litigation

A good system should work as a well in a large case as in a small case. The system may require some minor adaptation, but there is no reason why a sequence of events breakdown cannot and should not be applied to large scale or factually complex civil litigation. In fact, the more witnesses or the more complex the case, the more compelling it is to use a sequence of events breakdown.

The process of understanding a complex case can be daunting. There can be so many witnesses, so many exhibits, and so many events that it seems there is no convenient way to master the facts. In fact, regardless of the number of witnesses or events or exhibits, a breakdown of the case into a sequence of events will disclose the important areas suitable for cross-examination.

§ 6.16   Beginning the Breakdown of the Complex or Large Scale Case

The breakdown of a multiyear series of events involving dozens of witnesses is not materially different than the breakdown of a fight case lasting five minutes and involving half a dozen people. The lawyer must stay focused on sequence of events. But how does she put together a sequence of events when depositions are ongoing, document discovery is in process, and the case may be in litigation for years before trial? How can the lawyer know what all the events will be? The answer is that the lawyer sometimes cannot know or does not need to know all of the events in order to begin the preparation system. To be certain, the lawyer should have a very good idea of the sequence of events by talking to her own client. In civil litigation, especially complex litigation, the client ordinarily has employees who were involved and who help fill in the likely series of events. Armed with even this preliminary outline, the lawyer can easily create a case event preparation system that prepares the largest case for cross-examination and trial.

§ 6.17   Page by Page Deposition Summaries: A Failed System

For years lawyers have either summarized their own depositions or enlisted the aid of others to handle this important task. The method ordinarily used to summarize a deposition is to either (a) chronologically summarize the important testimony on a per page basis or (b) to chronologically note when a topic is discussed and note the page and line number where that discussion begins and ends. Set out below is a single page of a deposition summary using that second method of summarization and sourcing. The work product is accurate and it is well done. In the complex or multi-witness case it is also of very little use. This preparation system is very time-consuming, yields a product largely unsuitable for cross-examination preparation purposes, and provides at best a very murky understanding of a complex case.

Chart 6

464:15-465:14	At one point, there was a special rollout window provision. This was common in the industry at the time.
465:15-469:4	Exhibit 694 is identified as a policy for a single premium deferred annuity. Every CSM single premium deferred annuity sold during the time GGH owned the company, guaranteed the initial rate for three years. After the first three years, on the anniversary date, the client would receive

a letter from CSM, giving the client the rate for the coming year. That guaranteed provision gave people the right to get out of the CSM single premium deferred annuity with no surrender penalty, if on any anniversary, that letter they got in the mail said for the coming year they were going to receive more than 1 percent below the initial guarantee. After year 3 and before getting to year 8, there is a window to get out free for every single annuity holder under this contract. To get a client out free, all a broker had to do was to compare the rate being promised on the anniversary to the rate originally promised in the contract.

469:5-471:2   Serey worked with the contract everyday.

471:3-472:15   Howard had a standard business card that you ordered through company stock. Serey never saw a business card that said Howard Boxe Insurance Agent. The brokers were more of a financial planner and he would not expect them to limit themselves like that.

472:16-473:1   A purchase of an annuity is part of an investment portfolio.

473:2-475:18   In all the time Serey was with CSM, he never put an ad out to the general population about CSM annuities. The most likely scenario was a client saying to a broker, I'm looking for an investment and the broker would say let me tell you about CSM single premium deferred annuities.

475:19-477:7   From 1998 through 2003, CSM had very little name recognition in the general population of America

477:9-481:24   Serey does not recall that in 2001, he began to experience complaints that led him to investigate how Southshore was interpreting the rollout provision. Serey believes that the intent of the rollout window was that any year that CSM offered a renewal rate more than 1 percent different in the initial three-year guarantee, the client may rollout without penalty. He did not believe that meant there was a certain time period within which to do it. As far as Serey knows, every Howard client who bought a single premium deferred annuity during the time that GGH owned that company, got the benefit of that provision. It was never brought to Serey's attention that any policyholder that might have exercised that provision wasn't granted that provision at any time. Serey agrees that everybody who was in that clause could get out free. Serey knew exactly what this provision meant.

This type of summary has limited use when a case revolves around a single witness. Even then there are severe limitations to this form of fact indexing. As a cross-examination preparation tool, it has limited application even assuming there are no other witnesses.

The deposition summary notes are chronological but not by event. Instead, the chronology is simply whatever order or lack of order was adopted by the deposing lawyer. In addition it is quite likely that some topics will be touched upon in multiple places in a single deposition. But this form of deposition summary does not gather the related facts in one place. Instead, the advocate must review the entire deposition summary and try to find where important issues are discussed. Then, in order to prepare cross-examination chapters, the lawyer must realign the testimony into the appropriate event or topic groupings. This requires the lawyer to adopt yet a second system to help straighten out what the first system did not accomplish. Even if a lawyer was supremely organized and took depositions in the chapter method, witnesses at depositions are likely to volunteer answers that touch upon earlier or later chapters. As a result, the lawyer will be jumping around the entire deposition summary searching for facts that relate to each other.

Unfortunately that is just the beginning of the problem. This form of deposition summary provides both too much and too little to be of use in gaining a thorough understanding of the case and for cross-examination preparation. The too much is the length of the summary. This deposition summary provides too little detail to be of use in the immediate crafting of cross-examination chapters. The title "summary" is accurate and it is damning. Leading question cross-examinations cannot be based on summaries but have to be based on hard-edged facts. In turn, those facts must be capable of immediate and independent proof should the witness did not have the fact contained in the leading question. This ability is fundamental to the task of impeachment by inconsistent statement. This form of summary provides too little in the way of highly detailed fact with a readily identifiable page and line source.

This form of summary also provides too much information. If the lawyer looks at these long entries, she will see that a great many useful facts may end up in a single paragraph. These facts may be related in the broadest sense, but are not broken down to the topic level necessary to facilitate the preparation of individual chapters of cross-examination. If the lawyer finds a fact of importance in one of these paragraphs contained in the summary, the lawyer must inevitably turn to that page of the deposition in order to read the exact quote, to make note of the exact page and line source, and then put that fact into a separate cross-examination preparation system where that fact can be seen in context with the other facts to which it relates.

In all likelihood, a lawyer provided with deposition summaries in this form will be forced to adopt a second system, usually a topic page system, in order to be in a position to prepare individual chapters of cross-examination for this witness. When time is running short and nights are running long, and advocates are trying to create chapters of cross-examination from this form of deposition summary, they will curse the system, the person tasked with creating the deposition summaries, and the person who encouraged the lawyer to apply to law school.

And all the failings of this form of deposition summary are in a case where there is only a single key witness. The lawyer hasn't even begun to discuss the difficulty of comparing the testimony of one witness versus the testimony of several other witnesses on the same fact or event.

But not to worry, there is a system that is relatively easy to employ. It is far more efficient. It requires less time and it will yield far greater benefits. It is the sequence of events charts as adapted for complex or large scale litigation.

§ 6.18 Steps in Building Sequence of Events Charts Tracking the Testimony of Multiple Witnesses

The system begins with the same raw data, the deposition of a single witness. However the summarization must be in a different form. Counsel should begin with a mental picture of the end product desired. What is needed in the complex or multi-witness case is a preparation system that allows the lawyer to view each of the events in chronological order:

(1) To be able to compare the testimony of each witness concerning that event.

(2) To be able to study the documents most important to that event.

(3) As to each document, to be able to compare the testimony of each witness concerning that document insofar as that document relates to that one event.

(4) As to each testimonial entry, the page and line of the deposition where that fact can be found.

In this way the lawyer can immediately see what every witness has said about each important event, what the documents say about that event, and what the witnesses say about the documents. This is a system that makes complexity understandable. This system is not only an efficient method of deposition summarization, but is truly a master guide to the case.

Of course it would be rare if a single deposition covered all the events or topics of importance in the case. That is not a problem. The system only wants to know what this witness can contribute concerning an event or topic. It will concern itself with the next witness after that deposition is taken or other discovery is developed. Assume there are fifty critical events stretching over ten years. Neither the number of events nor the span of years matters. The case must be digested in bite-sized pieces. It is impossible to immediately understand the whole. It is possible to understand each of the parts one at a time. If the first deposition covers events 1, 2, 7, 13, 36, 45, and 49, then the testimony of the witness as to each of these events will be listed under the title of that event. This is no different than the system that was employed earlier in the chapter concerning a relatively small criminal case. Within each of these events the important facts will be noted along with their source page and line.

Set out below is a single page from a case summary showing the testimony of several witnesses on a single topic or event.

If and when the witness discusses an exhibit in relation to an event, that portion of the testimony relating to that exhibit and that event will be placed under that event title. If the witness discusses a document in relation to two separate events, then that document should be referenced under each of those separate events and the testimony of the witness that relates some portion of that document to that topic or event should be listed under that topic or event.

Chart 7

NEGOTIATION PROCESS

The First Meeting

<u>Chris Smith</u>

- Says he first discussed selling **MONEY AMERICA** Ltd. to Rybinski in March or early April of 2001 during a meeting in the Fisher Building in Detroit. Just a one hour meeting between himself and Rybinski. No one else present. 7:2-8:2

- He doesn't have any record of the meeting. 4:4-8:2

- Smith doesn't remember any specifics about his meeting with Rybinski in Detroit. 5:15-5:16

- Shortly after the meeting in Detroit discussions began between Rybinski's people and Smith's people. 5:17-24

<u>Augustus Rybinski</u>

- Rybinski went to Detroit to meet with Smith. He didn't meet with anyone else. He believes this meeting occurred in early April of 2001, but it might have been in very late March of 2001. 19:25-23:15

- Rybinski says that he didn't meet Cynthia Kueen on that trip. 19:16-22

- Rybinski says that he and Smith met in his office and then went across the street and had dinner. Spent about an hour and a half over dinner. Smith discussed his potential interest in selling the company, and Rybinski discussed his potential interest in buying the company. 19:10-24

- When dinner was over . . . so was the meeting. 19:25-20:10

Cynthia Kueen

- Kueen's recollection is that Rybinski made "the first pass" at Smith to buy MONEY AMERICA Ltd. 13:7-12

- She then says that she doesn't know who contacted who first. 13:13-20

- She doesn't recall what the price was. 18:14-21

Set out below is a single page from a case summary showing how testimony concerning an exhibit is accommodated within the sequence of events charts.

Chart 8

Exhibit 32 — Letter from Ernest-Young Financial to Wang

Augustus Rybinski

- Rybinski agrees that the letter appears to be information that EY letter provided to Wang at his request regarding Rybinski's financial information. He believes that the letter was given to Smith. 40:7-40:19

Dan Beck

- He was not involved in analyzing whether Rybinski had the financial ability to do the deal. 6:3-7, 12-16

Wan Wang

- Wang says that Rybinski really wanted to do the acquisition of MONEY AMERICA Ltd. on his own and Wang was concerned that financial burden would be too heavy for him alone. Wang says that he expressed those recollections to Kueen in their conversation. 16:8-17:6

One witness at a time, one document at a time the case summary is built. On any particular day the cross-examiner is prepared to understand what the testimony is on any point. To the extent that the case summary can be kept current, it becomes an immediate guide to deposition preparation. A lawyer who knows what each witness has said thus far about an event or a document can immediately discover whether the witness currently being deposed is inconsistent with any previous testimony.

Set out below is a portion of the table of contents of the sequence of events charts notebook.

Chart 9

I. SMITH'S DECISION TO SELL 148

    A.   WHY HE SOLD 148

II. RYBINSKI/SMITH NEGOTIATIONS 164

    A.   INITIAL CONTACT 164

    B.   THE FIRST MEETING 166

    C.   FOLLOW-UP TO FIRST MEETING 167

    D.   NEGOTIATIONS IN DETRIOT 169

        1.   Lunch Meeting Between Rybinski and Smith 185

        2.   Smith's Concerns about Rybinski's Financial Ability 186

        3.   Negotiations — Purchase Price 198

        4.   Tax Issues 206

        5.   Rybinski's Advisors and Negotiating Team 220

III. THE AGREEMENT 228

    A.   FORM OF THE TRANSACTION 230

    B.   WHO DRAFTED IT 235

        1.   Who Drafted the FG 241

    C.   MEANING OF THE FG 244

        1.   Exclusion of Minority Interest 253

    D.   DEFINITION OF SUBSIDIARY 273

    E.   PAYMENT TERMS OF THE AGREEMENT 276

IV. MARCH 2004 CLOSING 281

    A.   SECURITY AGREEMENT 288

        1.   Section 4.1 of Security Agreement — Grant of Security Interest in the Partnership 292

        2.   Default Provisions 296

            a.   Section 9.22 297

            b.   Section 10.36 298

    B.   MISC. CLOSING DOCUMENTS 301

The key to the application of the sequence events charts to complex or multi-witness cases is to break down testimony of each witness by topic, not by page. In turn, the method to efficiently break down the testimony of a witness by topic is to distribute the material on any one-page of the deposition into its appropriate topics before moving to the next page of the deposition. It is completely unnecessary to pick an important topic and review the entire deposition looking for facts on that topic. Instead, the advocate need only take the useful facts on the first page and sort it into its topics, and proceed a page at a time until the deposition material is exhausted.

In order to be of optimum use this resulting case summary should be indexed in multiple fields. Below are the fields, which optimally should be used:

The players: a description of the critical people or entities involved in the case.

Chart 10

I. THE PLAYERS 1

A. SMITH 1

1. Who He Is as a Person 1
2. Who He Is as a Father/Husband 3
3. Who He Is as a Business Person/Employer 6
4. Relationship with Rybinski 9

B. SMITH ENTITIES 12

1. Smith Sewage Company 12
2. Smith Natural Ltd. 12

C. PAUL RYBINSKI 28

1. Who He Is as a Person 28
2. Who He Is as a Business Person/Employer 29
3. Relationship with Chris Smith 30
4. Who He Is as the Owner MONEY AMERICA Ltd 31

The events: this is the heart of the case summary using the sequence of events system. The events are listed in chronological order. An example of a sequence of events charts as found above at Chart 8 notice: An event may be broken down into many subparts. An example of a single event broken down into multiple subparts is the event titled MONEY AMERICA Ltd. — The Smith Years.

Chart 11

I. MONEY AMERICA Ltd. — THE SMITH OWNERSHIP 104

A. FORM OF OWNERSHIP 104

B. SMITH'S ADVISORS DURING HIS OWNERSHIP OF MONEY AMERICA LTD 104

C. FEELINGS ABOUT OWNING THE COMPANY 107

D. BANKING RELATIONSHIPS 107

E. HIS CONTRIBUTION TO THE SUCCESS OF THE COMPANY 109

The exhibits: any exhibit important enough to make it into the summary should be listed in the index of exhibits and of course the pages on which it is referenced should be listed. The exhibits need to be listed by number, brief description, and date.

Chart 12

**CASE SUMMARY
INDEX OF EXHIBITS**

Exhibit 63 — Affidavit of Chris Smith — 10/25/03 6

Exhibit 68 — Easy Money Financial Statement of Chris Smith 24, 657

Exhibit 73 — Letter from Morten to Wendel Smith — November 3, 2003, 24

Exhibit 40 — Third restated and amended agreement of limited partnership between Rybinski and MONEY AMERICA Ltd. 33, 271

Exhibit 25 — MONEY AMERICA Ltd. Third restated and amended agreement of limited partnership — April 2, 2002, 40, 525

Exhibit 60 — Excerpt from 2002 Partnership Return filed by MONEY AMERICA Ltd. and J5 44, 407

Exhibit 61 — Amended 1077 U.S. Partnership Return 44, 407

Exhibit 162 — 2002 U.S. Partnership Return for MONEY AMERICA Ltd 44, 407

§ 6.19   Summary

In this pre-trial preparation system, the cross-examiner must evaluate and break down each event in substantial detail. While the breakdown will be chronological, the cross-examination itself should be performed in a favorable sequence. Then, as the cross-examiner learns the topic card pre-trial preparation system, each fact within those events or each topic will be further broken down witness by witness. It is through this careful analysis that fast moving events can be slowed down so that careful, detailed analysis can be made.

Once this analysis is made, the cross-examiner can consciously and intelligently make decisions as to what events will be emphasized and what events will be de-emphasized for the jury. In this process of breaking down events, theme phrases will occur to the cross-examiner.

Chapter 7

CROSS-EXAMINATION PREPARATION SYSTEM 3: WITNESS STATEMENT CHARTS

SYNOPSIS

§ 7.01   A Preparation System for a Key Witness with Multiple Statements

There are many cases in which the heart of the opponent's case is built around the testimony of a very small number of critical witnesses. Often the direct and cross-examination of a single witness will likely dominate the deliberations. Because of the importance of that single witness or those few important witnesses, it may have been possible to focus the case investigation around that witness or those few important witnesses. If the witness is a witness for the prosecution in a criminal action, it is quite possible the prosecution has taken a very long witness statement, may have placed the witness in front of the grand jury, or may have interviewed the witness on more than one occasion.

In any case in which a few witnesses have great importance and have given more than one statement concerning the events, a useful preparation technique is to create a witness statement chart for each of those witnesses. The witness statement chart is a method designed to keep track of and compare the many statements given by a single witness as to a series of events.

§ 7.02   The Statements of a Witness: A Definition

This preparation system speaks in terms of the statements of a witness. That phrase should be viewed in its broadest context. Most lawyers tend to think of the statement of a witness as an interview or a deposition transcript. However, witnesses speak on a matter to a variety of mechanisms. The statements of a witness are contained not only in his deposition and interview, but also in documents that contain the expressions of that witness. If a witness has written a report, clearly that is recognizable as a statement of the witness. If a witness has authored a memo, an e-mail, or any other document that contains words or thoughts that can fairly be attributed to that witness, those too are the statements of that witness. Witnesses also talk to other witnesses. When one witness (A) relates what another witness (B) said or did, that too is the statement of witness (B).

§ 7.03   Likely Scenarios for the Application of Witness Statement Charts

In personal injury/auto collision cases, the plaintiff and the defendant are often the most knowledgeable about liability events. They may each have given multiple statements to police officers, interrogatories, and at depositions. In the domestic case, each party is the most knowledgeable witness involved for the respective sides. When the marriage is to be dissolved, even if the marriage has only lasted a short period of time, the quantity of information available from one witness is enormous. The inner workings of a marriage are normally inquired into great detail. In a personal injury case, when a plaintiff is asking for substantial damages, the defense is always inclined to pick through the plaintiff's life in great detail for reasons why the jury should not award that kind of money.

In criminal law, this situation also describes "snitch" cases, as well as other forms of assaultive conduct. When an insider turns state's evidence, frequently the prosecution or its law enforcement agents will listen with infinite patience to whatever inside stories the "turned" witness has to tell. Prosecutors so love getting a look at the seamy underbelly of crime that they keep the tape recorders running, the grand jury asks all the questions they have been saving from twenty years of television watching, and the police run out to the jail to do multiple debriefings. The result is a pile of discovery generated by a single key witness. Similarly, in all matters of assault or violent crimes, the complaining witness has often made numerous statements to law enforcement agents and at hearings.

In commercial litigation, the key witness or witnesses are often easy to spot and are therefore rigorously deposed. That then is likely the most extensive statement of the witness. But in addition, key witnesses are often the authors of many documents, which should also be understood as the statements of that witness. If a deposition is taken of the key witness, and later discovery surfaces that permits the cross-examiner to re-depose the witness, the result may be multiple statements of a witness as to the same events. In addition, that witness may have been deposed on the same general topics in related lawsuits. The subject of the lawsuit may have been a matter of interest to a governmental agency such as the Securities and Exchange Commission, the Consumer Product Safety Council, the National Association of Securities Dealers, a State Attorney General's office, or any of the myriad of governmental and quasi-governmental agencies that take testimony or require written responses to inquiries. All of this is mentioned to suggest that the cross-examiner be alert to the possibility that the witness has given additional statements on the subject matter of litigation, though perhaps not under the caption of this case. Every such statement can be intensely important in providing cross-examination material or facts.

In all such cases, the first task of the cross-examiner is to understand in detail the many statements of the witness. In order to prepare for the cross-examination of a witness who has given many statements or who has been involved in the preparation of many documents, which can be attributed to that witness, the lawyer must prepare and digest a large volume of information. There are techniques that work well in such circumstances. The most exhaustive and reliable method is the witness statement chart.

§ 7.04   Using Witness Statement Charts to Build a Theory of the Case

As will be discussed at length, witness statement charts are extremely useful in finding all manner of inconsistencies. However, cross-examination is not solely or even primarily about attacking the witness's story. A primary message of this book is that cross-examination is an opportunity to build the cross-examiner's theory of the case using witnesses called by an opponent. Once the statements of the opponent's important witness or witnesses are placed into witness statement charts by event, the cross-examiner may find areas in which the witness has said things that will support the cross-examiner's theory of the case. These are areas where the cross-examiner can safely ask leading questions using the information gained from the charts. The charts confirm facts that the cross-examiner will develop. In that way, the charts are part of the process of building a case not simply part of the process of attacking the opponent's case. In order for the witness statement charts to accomplish this, it is important that all statements of a witness on a topic of interest are included in the charts, no matter how minor, so that the cross-examiner will have available the factual building blocks of a successful chapter.

§ 7.05   Charting the Life Events of the Witness and Other Seemingly Collateral Matters

If the cross-examiner intends to challenge the credibility of a witness, impeachment as to his background is especially effective. The lawyer can chart what the witness has said about himself, his jobs, his personal background, his educational accomplishments, and other historical data. Below are listed some additional places the advocate might check in order to see what representations have been made by a witness about himself, his educational, or work background.

Resumes
Statements on tax returns
Statements on bank loan applications
Divorce records
Newspaper articles
Business advertising materials
Submissions to licensing boards
Job applications
Custody hearings
Credit reports
Military records

All of the information the witness gives about himself are not only statements of a witness, but are statements of a particularly personal nature. A witness can be forgiven for misperceiving an event. The witness will likely not be forgiven for forgetting the fact that they were fired from a job. A witness may forget a fact, but later recall it. A witness will not so easily be excused for recalling a college degree they did not obtain. Charting the life events of a witness through the various paper trails that every person leaves behind can reveal some of the finest impeachment material within a credibility cross-examination.

Using a witness statement chart concerning the life events of the witness as a cross-examination preparation technique to chart should not be confined to the con man, criminal defendant, or "snitch" witness. The newspapers are full of stories of Ph.D.'s who really aren't, of charity board members with professional licensure issues, of wheeler-dealers who can claim ownership to a real estate empire while actually being in default on their bank loans. A healthy dose of skepticism will serve the advocate well. Some of the most highly regarded members of the community may well have told different stories of their upbringing, their education, their military service and medals, even their marriages and number of children. Charting what a witness has said about his own life events are worth the effort if the case must focus on the credibility of this particular witness.

Witnesses who must manufacture awards, invent college degrees, change the university from which they actually graduated, or give themselves exaggerated job titles can be exposed as lacking credibility long before the facts of the case itself are delved into. For instance, in his many debriefings by the government, a snitch might claim a rather elaborate employment or educational history. It may be worth charting these so as to set these against other records generated by defense investigation that prove these rather collateral assertions to be outright lies.

§ 7.06 Purpose of a Witness Statement Chart (Criss-Cross Chart)

A witness statement or criss-cross chart is a method of quickly comparing all versions of an event as related by a single witness. Where such a witness has given multiple statements of the critical events of the lawsuit, it becomes quite difficult to find and compare all versions given by the witness on any one topic.

This cross-examination preparation method is not confined to instances where there is a single witness at the heart of the lawsuit. In any case where a single important witness has given multiple statements, this method of preparation yields a tremendous insight into the vulnerabilities of that witness. This preparation system can be used any time any witness has given multiple statements concerning a series of events. The criss-cross chart breaks each full statement into its component events and then pastes them up, event by event, so that by consulting a single page of the criss-cross chart, the cross-examiner can read every version of an event ever given by that witness.

§ 7.07 Dividing Statements into Events

In chapter 6, *Cross-Examination Preparation System 2: Sequence of Events Charts*, the importance of recognizing that a civil action, a car collision, or a crime is made up of a series of intertwined events was discussed. Similarly, when creating charts of the multiple statements of a single witness, it is necessary to break those lengthy statements into a series of separate statements concerning individual topics or events.

Examine a simple personal injury case: A single witness sees the collision of two cars at a traffic-light controlled intersection. The case will rise or fall on that witness's testimony. At a minimum, the witness's statement concerning the accident could be divided into four events: (1) the view of the plaintiff's car before the collision; (2) the view of the defendant's car before the collision; (3) the view of the traffic light before the collision; and (4) the view of the collision. The cross-examiner might divide the collision into a greater number of events, depending on other events or topics, which the cross-examiner chooses to study. The cross-examiner could choose to break down a simple traffic light collision in a much more detailed fashion, including positions of other vehicles prior to the collision, speed of each car, the weather that day, distracting noises or other visual events, the position of the various vehicles after the collision, statements made by the occupants after the collision, and all other facts of the events leading up to the collision.

One of the first jobs of the cross-examiner is to envision the many ways in which a statement may be broken down into its component topics or events. Suffice to say, there is practically no event of importance that cannot be broken into smaller chunks; and, certainly, no case that cannot be broken into a great many events.

Chart 1 below sets out some of the key events of an extremely complex murder for hire scheme. The defendant is charged with the contract murder of his wife. The alleged hit man has confessed, been convicted, and is testifying for the government. The case, broken into its key events, is as follows:

Chart 1

The Events Used to Break Down the Statements of the Cooperating
Prosecution Witness (Hit Man)

1. First meeting of the defendant.
2. Begin booking bets from the defendant.
3. Check out the defendant's financial condition.
4. Meet the defendant at his office.
5. Continue booking bets.
6. Early morning phone call.
7. Clandestine meeting with defendant.
8. Solicitation to commit murder.
9. Defendant discusses private jet trips.
10. Second meeting to discuss homicide.
11. Hit man's proposal.
12. Defendant discusses insurance of wife.
13. Defendant's proposal of payments to the hit man.
14. Defendant pays hit man.
15. Establishment of the date for the murder.
16. Defendant lays out his alibi.
17. Hit man's first attempt.

18. Hit man's preparation for the kill.

19. Failure of attempt number 1.

20. Defendant phones hit man.

21. Defendant proposes an additional murder.

22. Thanksgiving day phone call.

23. Defendant sets up alibi.

24. Hit man prepares second attempt.

25. Hit man to the house.

26. Entry into the house.

27. Victim's clothing.

28. Hit man uses phone.

29. Victim receives phone call from the defendant.

30. Hit man pulls gun.

31. Hit man orders victim to bedroom.

32. Victim on bed.

33. Stabbing.

34. Ransack room.

35. Leave the house.

36. Dispose of knife and gloves.

37. Hit man tries to set up alibi.

38. A.M. phone call from a friend — defendant's wife found dead.

39. Defendant's check bounces.

40. Meeting with defendant.

41. Hit man hires collection goon.

42. Collector torches the car.

43. Phone calls to the defendant.

44. Defendant sets up meeting.

45. Meeting with defendant concerning insurance.

46. More meetings with the defendant to collect money.

47. Get defendant to sign a note.

48. Preparation of the note.

49. Defendant skips town.

50. Hit man tells police defendant owes him lots of money.

51. Police begin investigating hit man.

52. Hit man tries to get a loan against the note.

53.   Hit man files collection case on the note.

54.   Hit man arrested — separate robbery.

Note: Those are not all the potential cross-examination chapters (see chapter 9, *The Chapter Method of Cross-Examination*) in the case, nor are they even a list of all the potential cross-examination chapters dealing with the hit man. In fact, the hit man has numerous prior felonies, was receiving immunity on several crimes aside from this murder, and had myriad other problems requiring the preparation of multiple chapters of cross-examination on credibility issues alone. The above chronological list of events, however, represents the breakdown of the critical events in the hit man's statements concerning the crime itself. Using this list of events, a witness statement chart can be prepared. This chart is built on the witness's various statements on each of these events so that the witness's version of these events can be compared to other statements by this witness.

§ 7.08   Using a Witness Event Chart to Expose Internal Inconsistencies

The first benefit derived from a witness statement is that it exposes internal inconsistencies. Internal inconsistencies are inconsistencies within the various statements made by a single witness. Because the chart compares each version or description of an event to each other, description of that same offense given by that one witness, a witness event chart will immediately expose any change of story as to any single event. Softer forms of internal inconsistencies will also surface. An example of the softer internal inconsistency is a statement such as, "I don't know" or "I don't remember," versus a firm articulation of recalling an event.

§ 7.09   Witness Statement Charts Document Sources for Leading Questions and for Impeachments

Witness statement charts allow the cross-examiner to draft leading questions whose answers are well documented and can, therefore, be sourced. Furthermore, if, during trial, the witness was to suddenly and unexpectedly change his story concerning any particular topic, the witness statement or criss-cross chart could immediately be consulted and used to impeach the witness with all prior versions given by the witness on that topic.

The example below displays the charting of topic 41 in the above, "Hit man hires collection goon," in the sequence of topics. It discloses a minor inconsistency:

Hit Man Hires Collection Goon

Dec. 9 Statement to DA	Dec. 11 Grand Jury Testimony	Witness Notebook	March 25 Police Interview
Page 15 Q: When did you first meet Don Sales? A: As I recall, it was late September, early October, but I'm not positive when I met him. Q: And how did you meet him? A: I met him through Lance Berry. Q: For what purpose? A: Well, initially it was to do pointing and drywall work.	Page 46 Q: Who is Sales? A: Fellow by the Name of Don Sales. Q: How did you happen to first meet Mr. Sales? A: I went to a friend of mine by the name of Lance Berry and I said to him, "I have a fellow that owes me some gambling money and he's not paying me And I really need it. I need to show him some force, show him that I'm not going to screw around with him. Give me some ideas." At Page 47 this point he said to me "Your man Sales is the guy."	Page 23 Hired Sales to do drywall work. Promised him $500 after the job was done.	Page 7 I hardly don't know him. I think I may have met him once through a friend but I can't recall for sure.

§ 7.10   Application of Sequence Events Charts in Commercial Litigation

The utility of sequence of events charts is not in the least limited to criminal litigation. In fact, a great many commercial cases at their heart have one or two key witnesses for the opponent. The techniques of cross-examining a high-ranking corporate executive are no different than the techniques employed for the cross-examination of any other witness. The same preparation systems can be employed to yield the same advantages. A commercial litigation will find that a sequence of events charting of the key corporate witness for the plaintiff or the defendant is very useful in developing a portion of the chapters of cross-examination.

Below is a sequence of events charts drawn from a commercial case. The case involved allegations against a stock brokerage firm relating to its monitoring of its clients' investments in a company once entirely owned by the brokerage firm. The chart breaks the case into more than 40 separate events. The multiple statements made by the critical corporate executive, who was deeply involved in the activities, that were at the heart of the lawsuit. For a variety of procedural reasons, including the fact that important documents continually surfaced after the witness was first deposed, the witness was required to give multiple depositions.

1. Chris Adams' background in insurance

2. Adams' job at GON

3. Adams' reason for leaving GON in 2004

4. Financial Services — Adams' Job at Harman

5. Did Adams ever learn that Smith was suggesting that someday clients get out of GON?

6. Smith tells others to get out of GON

7. Ability to track rollouts

8. Did Samantha Kruop tell Adams that GON had problems?

9. Did Samantha Kruop advise Adams she was getting out of GON?

10. Talking with Kruop — Contradiction

11. "As a result of this new association, we have gained greater financial strength"

12. How did Adams learn of Drop in 2002 from B + to B?

13. Wires sent to Branch Offices

14. Oct. 2002 Memo — Adams adding word "NOT"

15. Adams' knowledge of VestFine

16. Adams' knowledge that Oxford group charged $2 million management fees

17. Morning Accent paragraph — RE: Arkansas Law

18. Who told Adams that insurance industry had guarantee provisions that underwrite any possible loss?

19. Chris Adams' action upon learning that credit rating had dropped because of an operation loss at GON?

20. Meeting with Nick Neckry/Nistim

21. What was discussed with Nick Neckry?

22. Adams' understanding of Nistim background

23. Request for additional information from Nistim

24. Adams keeps in touch with Nistim

25. Rollout of variable annuity portfolio

26. Anti-twisting

27. Rollovers at $500,000 a day

28. Adams' definition of run on the bank

29. Adams certain that if there was a run on the annuities to cash them in on GON, that GON couldn't do it

30. Did Adams tell brokers to rollover into A + companies?

31. Howard Harman market any Southeast Product after 10-30-02

32. How did Adams monitor GON?

33. Due diligence

34. Did Adams have anyway of knowing where GON was chartered?

35. Monitoring GON charter?

36. Did Adams notify anyone within Howard Harman system after GON was no longer chartered in Arkansas?

37. Concern about company move to South Dakota

38. Difficulties in communicating GON

39. State of California banned GON

40. When did Adams sell his annuity?

41. When did Adams first have info of problems with GON?

42. Circumstances when clients are to be contacted as to investments that are jeopardized?

43. Why clients buy annuities?

44. Shock of 8/01 Financial statements

45. Adams becomes investment executive 12-23-02

§ 7.11   Other Applications of Sequence of Events Charts

Breaking into events the statements of a child is particularly difficult, as children tend to wander a great deal in their statements, and their interviews are not nearly as tightly controlled as interviews with adults. Therefore, rather than name a particular episode, it is often easier to divide the allegation into a series of questions or events:

Chart 2

Sequence of Events: Sexual Assault on a Child

1. Night of the Nutcracker.

2. Fight over TV show.

3. Room where it happened.

4. Showing Jerry her dress.

5. Pinned her down.

6. Started wrestling.

7. Clothes on.

8. Jerry inserts fingers.

9. Sally goes to her room.

10. Hit him with toy tennis racket.

11. Jerry says don't tell anyone.

12. Sally after the incident.

13. Babysitter Charlie did it also.

14. Charlie pulled pants down.

15. Telling mom about Charles.

16. Telling mom about Jerry.

In making a criss-cross chart, flexibility is the key. Events can be named or divided in any way that logically assists in breaking down the stories given by the witness charting the statements. In the above example of a child molestation case, an alternative method of charting the statements is by breaking the story down into a series of questions. Chart 2, when broken into questions, would appear as follows:

Chart 3

Attentive Method of Breaking Down Sequence of Events,
Sexual Assault on Child

1. When first incident occurred.

2. Where first incident occurred.

3. What Jerry said afterwards.

4. What Sally calls her rectum.

5. What ice cream had to do with the incident.

6. What started the argument between Sally and the Jerry.

7. What Jerry did to her.

8. Events leading up to the second touching.

9. What happened the second time Jerry touched her.

10. Where the touching happened.

11. Where Sally was when it happened.

12. What she did after the touching.

13. What happened with her other babysitter.

14. When did it happen.

15. When told her mother.

Note: These are neither the questions the cross-examiner would ask at trial. Nor are these the chapters of cross-examination (see chapter 9, *The Chapter Method of Cross-Examination*), and certainly the topics are not in the sequence that the cross-examiner would use at trial. These topics are simply dividing lines to be used in breaking the story of a child witness into component parts.

A much more detailed breakdown needs to be done in certain areas, i.e., Topic 9, "What happened the second time." An individual chapter of cross-examination might well be the fight over the TV show. In fact, the fight over the TV show might become a focus issue for the defense and could result in the writing of several chapters, i.e., "Sally watching TV, Jerry changes channel to news," "Sally and Jerry fight over the change." As there were inconsistencies in the child's version of where the assault took place, this, too, could form its own chapter or chapter bundle of cross-examination and might well be its own event in a criss-cross chart.

§ 7.12 Choosing the Topics to Be Charted

Not every word of an important witness is worth studying. There can be a great deal of introductory comments, extraneous stories, and background information having nothing to do with the case, or dealing with matters not in dispute. Such material may be omitted from the topic chart. However, in those cases in which the cross-examiner must allege that the witness is fabricating the testimony, she may find it beneficial to chart the witness's most innocuous comments.

§ 7.13 The Value of Charting Seemingly Collateral Matters

If an advocate is using a witness statement chart to prepare for cross-examination of a witness it is likely that the cross-examiner feels the need to challenge the credibility of that witness. When a lawyer is going to make a major part of her cross-examination an attack on credibility, the lawyer best prepare any chapter that might yield the opportunity to impeach the witness. These seemingly collateral areas often are extremely fertile ground for cross-examination. The credibility of the witness can often be greatly diminished by joining impeachments on major events with impeachments in minor matters, areas not directly related to the lawsuit, but contained in witness narratives.

In other cases that are dependent principally on the testimony of a single witness, quite often the charts can be confined to statements directly pertaining to the issues in dispute. While the merely mistaken witness may be completely honest and accurate in explaining preliminary events, inconsistencies as to the critical events are generally the most fertile ground to explore. The inconsistencies will show that the witness has either mistakenly described the occurrence or is, for some less honorable reason, changing his story.

Chart 4 below is taken from a case of sexual assault on an adult female. The allegations resulted in both the filing of criminal charges and a civil suit. The male and female know each other, and the conversations and occurrences that lead them to get together at her apartment are judged to be consistent and not worthy of indexing. This is not to say they are worthless for cross-examination. In fact, they have significant value to the defendant's theory of the case. However, since the complaining witness's statements are consistent with each other and consistent with the defendant's version of events, no criss-cross chart has been created for those pre-apartment statements. There will be plenty of informational cross-examination on those facts. Instead, only the scene inside the apartment from entry through departure is charted. MJ is the alleged victim. DB is the defendant. Below is listed the series of events of the alleged rape:

Chart 4

Incidents on 4/9/04

Arrival

    1.   Arrival

    2.   House Tour

    3.   Mixing Drinks

    4.   Couch — Small Talk

Initial Contact — Floor

    5.   On Floor — DB Plays with Hair

    6.   On Floor — DB First Use of Force

    7.   On Floor — DB Second Use of Force

    8.   MJ Crawling — DB Exposure and Hand Contact

    9.   On Floor — DB Kisses

   10.   On Floor — DB Lying Down

Bathroom

   11.   MJ Follows Defendant into Bathroom

   12.   Contact in the Bathroom

Bedroom

   13.   Entry into Bedroom

   14.   DB Moves to Bed

   15.   DB Undresses

   16.   MJ Undresses

   17.   1st Penetration

   18.   Question of Pregnancy

   19.   2nd Penetration

   20.   3rd Penetration

   21.   MJ Tries to Leave Bed

   22.   DB Takes Shower

   23.   DB Talks to MJ

   24.   DB Departs

§ 7.14 Moving Statements onto Charts

Witness statement charts can be easily assembled by hand or by using computers. The goal is to create an easy method of comparison. The form the lawyer uses is a personal preference and is secondary. Whether prepared by hand or by computer, there are steps in the creation of a statement comparison chart (criss-cross chart).

Step 1: Break the case down into the events that will be studied.

Step 2: For each event to be charted create an event page, entering the title of the events at the top of the page.

Step 3: If working by hand, divide into columns with one column for every statement the witness has given, and an additional blank column for certain notes the lawyer may need to add later. If the witness has given three statements, the lawyer will need four columns (see Chart 5, below). If working by computer no fixed columns need to be created, though the statements will be transferred electronically. In the case of depositions, it is important that the deposition transcript be obtained in ASCII format so that specific pages and lines can be electronically transferred onto the appropriate topic page. When importing material from any transcript or report, the material must be placed under a heading showing the date of that statement or other source. In the case of a statement taken from a document, the date of the document and its exhibit number should be included. If the document has a name, it should be included in the source heading.

If working by hand, statements can be reduced on a photocopier so that they can be physically cut and pasted on to the appropriate topic sheet. Care must be taken that the statement is pasted under its appropriate date, title, or exhibit number.

Chart 5

Preparing to Chart a Set of Statements from a Single Witness

Preliminary Hearing August 17, 2003	Initial Police Report May 7-8, 2003	Suppression Hearing Nov. 16, 2003	Notes

Below is a list of statements made by the complaining witness in the sex assault case outlined above:

1. OFFENSE REPORT: 7-1-04 Statements by Lori James to Officer Kohler.

2. SUPPLEMENTAL POLICE REPORT: 7-1-04 Statements by Lori James to Officer Kohler.

3. POLICE REPORT: 7-8-04 Statements by Lori James to Bob Harding (Counselor at Youth and Victims).

4. POLICE REPORT: 7-29-04 Statements by Lori James to Officer Barro.

5. POLICE REPORT: 7-29-04 Statements by Lori James to Bob Harding.

6. PRELIMINARY HEARING TRANSCRIPT: 2-19-05 Testimony of Lori James.

Step 4: Under a column showing the date of a statement or deposition, exhibit number, or document name, transfer the useful information from that one source on to the corresponding topic sheet.

A single deposition, statement, or exhibit may yield useful information on all of the topics to be studied, on some of the topics, and rarely on none of the topics. Ordinarily it is best to create witness statement charts in chronological order. The process is the same as that outlined in chapter 5, *Cross Examination Preparation System 1: Topic Charts*. Counsel, or the person to whom the task is delegated, should first break the earliest statement into its component sections based on the event break down envisioned by the lawyer. The process, as always, is not to read a deposition or statement looking for any particular event, but instead to start the first page and take off of that page anything that belongs under a particular event. When the useful material on the first page of a deposition or statement or document has been exhausted, attention should be paid to the next page. The process is repeated one page at a time until all useful items within a deposition, statement, or exhibit have been moved onto the appropriately titled event page.

Chart 6 below shows how a single topic page will accommodate multiple statements by a witness.

Chart 6

Lori James Topic:_____			
1. Offense Report: 7/1/04 Statements to Officer Kohler	2. Police Report: 7/8/04 written Stmt. to Detective Harding	3. Transcript: 2/19/05 Preliminary Hearing Testimony	4. Mtns. Hrg 4/21/05

Step 5: Expanding the witness statement charts to accommodate all the statements on one subject.

In a multi-party civil case where one witness may make many statements, or be the author of many documents bearing on an event, more than one sheet of paper may be required to list the several statements given by that witness. Within reason, the size of the paper is discretionary, as all of the lawyer preparation systems are designed primarily for office use while preparing the cross-examination. If necessary, more than one sheet of paper may be used to display the multiple statements by a witness on any one topic. Conceivably, the witness may have authored many documents, which have portions bearing directly on a single event. That fact alone or in conjunction with other depositions and statements may necessitate the use of multiple sheets of paper to keep track of all of the statements of a witness on that one topic. However this situation must be distinguished from the situation that occurs when the topic breakdown is too large so that any one topic encompasses too much material. When the lawyer realizes that the initial breakdown of a topic was too broad, the proper corrective action is simply to break that topic into smaller topics, and to then re-divide the witness statements into the correspondingly smaller topics.

When multiple events are commingled in one long entry, the purposes of the criss-cross chart are hindered. For the chart to work best, it must be broken down into small enough events so that the lawyer preparing cross-examination can quickly understand the witness's multiple versions of an event and find any inconsistencies.

Step 6: Create a tabbed notebook for ease of reference

Because counsel will be using these charts repeatedly in preparing the cross-examination, it is best that they be put in a notebook with tab numbers or tab names for events. These charts are ordinarily not used in actually performing the cross-examination in the courtroom. However, there are occasions when the cross-examiner will need to consult these charts during trial (see § 7.26), so the charts should not be so cumbersome that the cross-examiner cannot take them into and use them in court.

Chart 7 shows a section of a preliminary hearing transcript. This particular discussion might be copied into the event "offering a drink." If that discussion has relevance, it belongs on its own topic page. If it has no relevance, no topic page should be made for it.

Chart 7

8	A: Well, we went into the living room and he sat his
9	coat down, and I said, "Well, make yourself at home."
10	And as we started to sit, I said, "Oh, can I get you
11	something to drink? I've got all kinds of things. Is there
12	anything that you'd like?"
13	And I started walking to the kitchen, and he followed,
14	and he said, "Well, what have you got?"
15	And I said, "Well, I've got soda pop, I've got wine, I've
16	got rum, I've got Amaretto." I said, "Really anything. What would
17	you like?"
18	And he said, I'll have a rum and Coke."
19	And I said, "Okay." And I said, "The rum's brand new."
20	I said, "You take what you feel comfortable with."
21	And he said, "Do you have diet pop?"
22	And I said, "Yes, I do."

§ 7.15   Creating Identically Formatted Pages for Limited Source Material

If there are only two or three source statements, then each page of a witness statement chart can be built along an identical format:

(1) Create one fixed column for every occasion on which the witness had given a statement;

(2) Label each column with the name (and usually the date) of the source statements;

(3) Keep one additional column blank, for lawyer's notes; and

(4) After creating a properly formatted page with columns properly labeled the lawyer can reproduce the formatted page to create as many topic pages as necessary. Chart 5, above, shows a formatted page, ready for use in inserting statements. Note how the formatted page contains the date and name of each statement. No matter how many statements, there must be a separate column for each occasion in which the witness has made a statement.

§ 7.16   Use Non-Formatted Pages When Many Sources Will Need to Be Displayed

Civil litigation frequently produces more statements and more documents containing statements than are ordinarily found in criminal cases. There are exceptions. White-collar criminal cases frequently have all the appearances of the document-intensive civil case. Whether the case is civil or criminal, when there are great many documents authored by a witness, or a great many statements by that witness, counsel should not try to create a pre-formatted topic page showing each of the dates of statements and each of the document numbers. The reason the formatted page is unnecessary is that a great many of the documents will contain no reference to most of the events in the chart. On the other hand, there may be a profusion of documents that all speak to a very small number of the events in the chart.

While the lawyer will follow the system of creating a topic page for each event in the witness statement chart, each individual topic page should only carry the headings of the statements or exhibits actually used in dissecting the statements of the witness as to that topic. For instance, if the witness has written seven different documents, which referred to a single event, has been deposed as to that event, the topic page for that event will contain eight headings, one for each source statement and an extra column for lawyer notes. The next topic in the sequence may only have two sources of statements by the witness, one document and one deposition and only need three columns.

In complex events, or in cases where there are extensive depositions or exhibits containing much detail, it may be that the charting of a single event requires more than one page. When this happens, the lawyer should carefully scrutinize the event to see if it is, in reality, more than one event. When a single event requires more than one page, it is still easy to read the pages and find inconsistencies in versions of the story. When this happens, simply continue the creation of an additional page. Chart 8, below, shows one column only of a multi-statement chart referred to earlier in Chart 6. As Chart 8 demonstrates when a witness has given a voluminous description of a single event, it may be necessary to use more than one page to paste up that one event, as described in the course of a single statement.

Chart 8

Lori James		Event: Mixing Drinks (Page 1)	
5. Police Report: 7-29-02 Stmts to Ofcr. Harding	6. Deposition: 2-4-03	7. Transcript: 2/19/03 Preliminary Hearing Testimony	NOTES
		Page 32 8 A. Well, we went into the living room and he 9 sat his coat down, and I said, "Well, make 10 yourself at home."	
Lori James		Event: Mixing Drinks (Page 2)	
5. Police Report: 7-29-02 Stmts to Ofcr. Harding	6. Deposition: 2-4-03	7. Transcript: 2-19-03 Preliminary Hearing Testimony	NOTES
		Page 100 17 Q: It's 2 o'clock in the afternoon and Mr. 18 Bernard comes over at your invitation; is that 19 right?	

§ 7.17   Chronological Analysis of Statements Includes Previous Direct and Cross-Examinations

The assembler should ordinarily display all of the witness's statements in chronological order. The oldest statement will ordinarily appear on the left side of the page so that in the process of reading across the page the lawyer can better envision how the story has changed over time.

The goal is to disassemble one entire witness statement and reassemble it by event. Note that a witness may discuss a single event on multiple occasions within one full statement. In civil depositions, preliminary hearings and criminal motions hearings, the witness may have spoken about a topic in both direct examination and cross-examination. Both sets of answers need to be pasted up in the same column under the appropriate source label (i.e., Dep. 12/5/02). In such cases, some code must be inserted on the statements to show whether the statement was made on direct examination or cross-examination. This code will be helpful in writing and laying foundations for impeachments (see Chart 9).

Chart 9

Lori James

Floor – Plays With
Hair

Police Rpt. 7-1-02 Stmts.	Deposition 2-4-03 Stmts.	Prelim. Hrg. Testimony 2-19-03	Police Rept. 7-29-02 Stmts.
Page 2 Victim stated at this time Mr. Bernard came and sat on the floor next to her and that she was kneeling on both knees and that Mr. Bernard was stretched out on the floor, propped up by his right arm. At this time Mr. Bernard started touching victim's hair, victim told him to stop. However he continued and stated that her hair smelled nice and asked her what she used on it. Victim told him what she used and asked him why he was doing this since he was married. Victim stated that at this time Mr. Bernard stated, "Oh I forgot until you mentioned it." At that time Mr. Bernard pulled victim's hair tight with his right hand and started kissing the victim. She stated she told him to stop.	Page 18 Q: So that's where you were when what happened now? A: Well, he came up behind me and sort of laid on his arm on the floor and started lifting my hair, playing with it. Page 20 Q: Okay. Would you show me then and describe for us what he was doing with your hair. A: He was lifting it, and twirling, playing with it. Q: Was he pulling on it? A: Not at that time, no. Page 21 A: I just turned and looked at him. He said "Your hair smells nice. What do you use on it?" And I said "What?" and he Said "What do you use on your hair? It smells nice." and I said "Finesse. Why?" He said "Well, it smells nice. I wouldn't know that." Page 22 Q: Then what happened? Q: He just stayed down next to you? A: Beside, yes.	Direct Page 34 A: And I no more than put the CD in, and he was kind of leaning, laying behind me, and he started playing with my hair. Page 35 Q: And what did you do when he started playing with your hair? A: I just kind of looked at him strange, and he said "Your hair smells nice. What do you use on it?" Page 36 And I said, "Finesse. Why?" And he said, Well, I wouldn't know that. I was just curious. It smells very nice. Q: Then what happened? A: Well, when he was playing with my hair, the next thing I knew, he had grabbed my hair, back of my neck and pulled me towards him and started kissing on me. Cross Page 103 Q: As you're turning on the music, Jim got up from the couch, came over and sat. Q: You did not resist his doing that? A: No.	Page 4 James was kneeling at her stereo and Bernard came up next to her. Bernard laid on his left side, as James was at the stereo. They had made a comment about Leon Redbone and as James was turning The stereo on Bernard kind of sat up and started playing with her hair. James turned and looked as Bernard asked "What do you use on your hair?" James told him it was Finesse and asked why. Bernard stated that he did not know about things like that. Bernard then grabbed James by the hair right by the back of the neck. Bernard turned James' head toward him and started kissing her. Page 5 Brown asked James how she started to feel and if she was starting to feel uncomfortable and James stated yes. James states that she then put her left hand on Bernard's chest and pushed him away. James told Bernard that if he came over for this reason, he had the wrong impression.

Make sure when moving sections of testimony out of statements and into the appropriate column to make a note on the testimony as to what page and position (line number if possible) from within the statement it is taken (see page numbers on Chart 9 above). Caution: recitations of testimony are incomplete if they lack proper documentation of their source. Just as the lawyer had to document sources on her topic pages, she must document sources as precisely as possible on the witness statement chart. Hence when moving material from transcripts, make sure, at that point, to add page and line to the material relocated to the topic page. Sourcing of a particular response will become absolutely critical in the process of page preparation of cross-examination (see chapter 10, *Page Preparation of Cross-Examination*), and in impeachment by inconsistent statement (see chapter 17, *Impeachment by Omission*). The clearer and more detailed the source, the greater efficiency in writing the cross-examination and the more effective the cross-examiner during trial.

§ 7.18   Adding Additional Topics to the Charts

When the lawyer has taken apart the entire first statement of the witness there is a completed "base" version of events. The lawyer is now ready to review the next statement. The process is repeated. The second statement is analyzed for statements concerning the same topics or events previously focused on. Where such a statement is found it is entered on the appropriate topic or event page. In reading a subsequent statement or document, the lawyer may come across a new topic worthy of page. If this topic had been found in the first statement, and had been recognized as important, that the topic page would already have been prepared. Assume that this topic did not come up in the first statement. The topics initially selected for the witness statements chart are not permanent and unchangeable. If a new topic should emerge it is simply necessary to create a new topic page and of course on that page to enter any statements of the witness concerning that topic.

§ 7.19   Dealing With "Blanks" or Things Not Said

Often in litigation the witness has given one statement, which is his longest, most complete statement. In civil cases this is ordinarily the deposition of the witness. In criminal cases it may be a preliminary hearing transcript, or interview by detective, or a statement by the defendant or witness to law enforcement. Other statements will not contain as many facts. When a witness has described something in his longest statement and does not describe it or has not asked about it in other statements, leave a blank in the column labeled for that other statement, showing that on that date, nothing was said about that topic. This means that if the lawyer reads the witness's factual version of an event or topic in the longest column, and does not see a factual version in the second column, but does in the third, the matter never came up in statement two, but did in statement three.

In Chart 10, below, note that while the witness has described "mixing drinks" in two statements, there is a blank in column 3, showing that the witness did not discuss this issue in the course of that statement.

Similarly, the lawyer may discover events described in later statements that were never discussed in the longest statement. Of course, an event chart will still need to be created. However, since no mention of the event occurred within the base statement, that column will remain blank. Other statement columns will be filled in with the witness's version of that event.

In reading the statements, the lawyer may even realize there is an event or topic not accounted for in the original chart of events. In such instances, the lawyer will need to create a new topic page for that newly-found event or topic and enter the appropriate portions of the witness's statements as she did with all other events or topics. All facts relating to the newly identified topic are entered, and the title of the new topic needs to be entered at the appropriate place in the sequences of events list.

When the set of charts is finished, they should be tabbed. Topic tabs may be placed along the edge of the page identifying the critical fact or event covered on that page. If preferred, the criss-cross chart may be indexed, and numbered dividers can be used to separate and identify the topic pages in the notebook of charts. The tabs will aid the lawyer in quickly locating the desired topic. The lawyer has now created a statement book or criss-cross chart on that witness. At a glance, the lawyer can analyze any aspect of the story, no matter now many statements the witness has given. There is no need to leaf through transcripts, police interviews, and court hearing transcripts. By locating the tab of the events or topics in which the lawyer is interested, the cross-examiner can immediately review all the versions of the topic or event given by the witness, as all facts concerning each event or topic will be contained on that tabbed page.

Chart 10

Lori James   Topic: MIXING DRINKS

Sup. Police Report 7-1-02 Stmts.	Police Rpt. 7-8-02 Stmts.	Police Rpt. 7-29-02 Stmts. 2/19/03	Prelim. Hrg. Testimony
Page 2 Victim offered Mr. Bernard a drink and it was decided that he would have a rum and coke if the victim had some wine. Victim stated that she gave Mr. Bernard the rum bottle and he asked for a diet coke. Victim stated that Mr. Bernard had to open the wine bottle for her and after that she poured herself some wine. Victim stated that she sat on the floor, played some tapes, and she and Mr. Bernard talked about music artists.		Page 4 James asked Bernard if he wanted a drink and Bernard got up and stood by the kitchen. Bernard stated he would like a rum and coke if she (James) would have some wine. Bernard fixed the drink and opened the wine for James. James then returned to the couch and sat in the middle.	Page 32 A. We went into the living room and he sat his coat down, and I said, "Make yourself at home." As we started to sit I said, "Oh, can I get you something to drink? I've got all kinds of things. Is there anything that you'd like?" I started walking to the kitchen and he followed and said "What have you got?" I said "I've got soda pop, wine, rum, Amaretto. Anything. What would you like?" He said "I'll have a rum and coke." I said "The rum's brand new, you take what you feel comfortable with." He said "Do you have diet pop?" and I said yes. Page 33 He said "Diet pop seems to cut the smell of alcohol and I have an appointment this afternoon."

§ 7.20   Discovery of Internal Inconsistencies

What has the witness event chart accomplished so far? By reading across, the lawyer can find any inconsistencies between any of the statements of the same witness, no matter how many versions the witness has given. All of the versions of each event are now organized and sourced. The lawyer need only consult the appropriate tab in order to review the witness's multiple accounts of any fact or topic. There is no longer a need for time-consuming searches through volumes of statements in order to find a topic or compare versions (see Chart 11). This is just the beginning of the usefulness of the criss-cross chart.

§ 7.21   Showing a Change of Chronology

Occasionally, a witness will tell the same story but will change the order in which events occurred. This form of inconsistency, although rare, is as useful in impeachment as an internal inconsistency. Changes of chronology are as much an "inconsistent statement" as if the witness had changed the underlying facts themselves. The lawyer needs a method by which she can keep track of changes of chronology, since they can be important for showing how an event developed and for impeachment by inconsistent statement. Changes in chronology will show up two ways on the charts.

The easiest way is one in which the change occurs within the body of a single topic.

Chart 11

Chronological Inconsistencies Apparent Before Trial

Elaine Cantor   KED COMES IN

Transcript 3/26/02	Eleven-page hand-written statement	12/2/90 Statement to Cops 2:40 a.m.	Notes
11 and that's when Ked comes storming in, and he started yelling and he pointed at me and he asked where Dave was and Dave—I Don't—I turned my back to finish putting on my jewelry and Dave, I guess, stood up. I'm not sure Because he was behind me. And that's when Ked started yelling at him, he was calling him a long-haired—is it all right to say it? Q: Yes. 11A: He called him a long-haired (obscenity), he said don't you ever laugh at me again, and that's when the first blast went off.	4 "Where's that longhaired (obscenity) in the truck" 4 I'm not sure Ked grabbed Dave or not but I think he did and he started to yell "Don't you ever laugh at me again you long hair—that's when the first shot went off.	4 Q: Did Ked say anything before he fired any of the shots? A: No, I heard the shot then go off, and then he said something about him laughin' at him.	

Chart 12

Internal Inconsistencies Apparent Before Trial — Change of Chronology

Fred Mills   CALL TO BILLY

Preliminary Hearing 2/24/03	Police Statement 1/10/04	Notes
P12:6 I was deep in debt. I'd been losing a lot of money gambling, and I was in way over my head. I called Billy and said Jeez, I've got to come up with some bucks and he said—"Well, if you want to take a little trip for me." I told him I'd call him back. P14:12 Well, I knew I had an interest payment coming up Friday to Colton and it was 5% a week on $9000, so I thought I'd see if I could get Colton to let me slide for a few more days. But he wouldn't go for it so then I had to call Billy back.	P9 I was up to my ears in hock. I had a bad run in the games and I needed to cover my losses. I'd borrowed $9000 from Colton at 5% per week and I knew I couldn't pay it. So I called him and asked, you know, can I slide a week or so and he said no way. P10 So I called up Billy so I told him the situation and he says, yeh, maybe there is something I can do to make some bucks—maybe I could run a little errand, you know, take a trip for him, pick up some drugs.	

When the body of the topic stays consistent, but the events occur in different order, the chart must be annotated to show the change in chronology. In order to analyze the problem of charting a change of chronology, assume there are but three facts or topics being analyzed: A, B, and C. Further assume that in the earliest statement, the witness says the facts happened in this order: A, B, C. Further assume that in the second statement, the witness says the events happened in the order A, C, B. Any change in chronology can easily be picked up by the lawyer because the lawyer has created the charts in chronological order. If the lawyer creates the charts starting with the earliest statement on the left and then entering additional statements by the witness on that topic in chronological order in each column, when working across from the base column, the change of chronology becomes apparent.

§ 7.22   Discovery of External Inconsistencies: Charting Other Witness

Witness statement charts are extremely helpful in spotting external inconsistencies. That is, inconsistencies between the statement of one witness and the statement of another witness on the same topic. A comparison of the separate witness statement charts by themselves will accomplish this. No more is necessary then comparing the witness statement charts of two or more witnesses on the same topic. However, it may be useful for the lawyer to leave room to note such external inconsistencies. A blank column will be placed to the far right of the page. This column may be left unlabeled, or may be labeled Trial, Tactics, or Notes. After all witness statements are pasted up, this column can be put to several uses.

The lawyer has now digested the star witness's story in all its versions, showing all internal inconsistencies. Even if the witness has been internally consistent he may be contradicted by another witness or by physical, tangible, or documentary facts. The lawyer should look for inconsistencies with other witnesses first. The reason to concentrate first on this kind of inconsistency is because of the damage this type of inconsistency does to the opponent. When two or more witnesses identified with the opponent are inconsistent with each other, the result is not only a diminution in the credibility of one of those witnesses, but also a diminution in the credibility of the opponent's case. The opposing lawyer now has the unenviable task of explaining to a jury which of his witnesses is to be believed on an important issue.

§ 7.23   Shortcuts to Finding Inconsistencies Between Witnesses

It is not necessary to create full witness statement charts for every witness. However, if a lawyer chooses to do this, a method for doing is found in the previous chapter, sequence of events charts. Assume that the lawyer has not chosen to do this but has instead concentrated her efforts on digesting all of the statements of the one critical witness. After pasting up each version of the star witness's story, it is now far easier to read discovery concerning other witnesses and find the inconsistencies with the star witness's testimony. While it is possible to do a cut and paste as to all other witnesses who have given statements concerning any of the topics or events in the witness statement chart, this may not be worth the time expenditure.

Seldom are there massive quantities of discovery on witnesses other than the target witness. It may prove easier and less time consuming to pick up a less important witness statement and read it while following along through the star witness statement charts. At this point, having created the charts, the statements of the target witness are well known to the cross-examiner. Consequently, it is very easy for the cross-examiner to recognize instances in which another witness differs with the target witness as to any important event or fact. When the comparison witness differs with the target witness, turn to the appropriate topic page in the criss-cross chart and in the "notes" column make a note of the impeaching witness's statement. This note should be put along side the specific fact that is impeached. The note must include all sourcing, i.e., the comparison witness's name, date of statement, and page, and line, of the statement.

Chart 13

Example: Single Page Taken from a
Witness Statement Chart
Showing External Inconsistencies Apparent
Before Time of Trial
Subject: Taking the Trailer Back

Mike McAllister   Taking The Trailer Back

1/22/02 Stmt. To Det. Kirby	3/16/02 Stmt. to Det. Sadar	Prep Notes
Page 23 A: I took the trailer back at about 9:30 a.m. Q: Where? A: That rental Shop . . . Time Rentals. Q: What makes you think it was 9:30? A: I seen them all working when I got there, so it must've been about 9:30 or so. Q: What did you do? A: I took them that trailer and I left. That's it.	Page 51 I got up the next morning kinda late . . . I took that trailer back to that rental place, you know, . . . Time Rentals . . . Had to be around 9:15 or so. They was all workin' so it must've been maybe 9:15, 9:30.	See statements of Rick Edwards and William Lockhart, Time Rental's employees. Rick Edwards's 3/15/03 Stmt. P.5 I opened Time Rentals that morning. The trailer was there at 7:30 when I arrived. That Mike guy came in around noon and paid us to move a truck frame off our trailer and on to some other trailer. William Lockhart 5/15/02 Stmt. P2 I got to work about 8:00, the usual time. The trailer was sitting on the street when I came in. About noon, some guy came in and wanted a truck frame lifted off our trailer.

§ 7.24   Discovering External Inconsistencies: Charting In Physical Evidence

There is a third kind of inconsistent statement that the charts will reveal. This is also the second kind of external inconsistency. There is an external inconsistency when any witness takes the position that is contradicted by physical evidence or by a document. Once the witness statement charts has been prepared for the primary witness, the statement of that witness shall be compared to all the other evidence in the case, and any additional external inconsistencies can be recognized.

After the target witness's story has been separated into the topics of the witness statement charts, the lawyer can efficiently scan all of the exhibits or possible exhibits — photos, documents, objects — to see if any "speak" a different version of a fact than the versions given by the target. If so, then in the "notes" column, the cross-examiner will write "see exhibit _____," or a description of the possible exhibit, what it shows, where it is found in discovery and through whom it may come into evidence.

Chart 14

Inconsistencies with Exhibits Apparent Before Time of Trial Cross Keyed with Impeaching Exhibits

Statement to DA:	Grand Jury Testimony	Notes
December 9, 2002	December 11, 2002	

P33 Q: And which side of her body from looking at her, her being flat down, which side of her body did you stab her on? A: The first blow was on the right side of her body on the back corner side. Q: All right. Above the waist? A: Yes. Q: Below the right shoulder blade or left shoulder blade, which — . . . It would be the right shoulder blade, I, I believe just below it. P31: A: As I recall, I stabbed her three times, two or three.	P36 Q: What portion of her body were the other stab wounds in? Where else did you stab her? A: As I recall there were two on the right side of the body and one on the left. Q: Was the knife pointed up and down from head to toe or across from side to side? A. Side to side. Q: Are you sure of that? A: Almost positive, yes, although I can't be dead sure. Those few moments I recall the first blow and then it's hard for me but as I recall the knife was pointed, the sharp edge was going toward me. I held it in my right hand. Q: Do you recall how many times you stabbed her? A: As I recall it was three. It might have only been two. Again, that point is very difficult.	See Exhibits D & E. Ex. D & E: Autopsy Photos show 5 wounds, all made by person standing at her head. Coroner, Dr. Toll, will testify 5 stab wounds, all from person at her head, not at side.

Chart 14 shows the components of a single topic "in a witness statement chart" that are consistent with each other, but inconsistent with both exhibits and the anticipated testimony of another witness.

§ 7.25   The Chart's Use in Drafting Cross-Examinations

The completed and annotated criss-cross witness chart now shows internal inconsistencies among the many statements given by the witness. It shows external inconsistencies with witness and exhibits. It shows changes in chronology as well. All of these inconsistencies, as well as the witness's version of all other key facts, have been sourced. All of this information will be used in drafting the cross-examination of the primary witness. The lawyer is now free to select the inconsistencies of value to the cross-examiner's theory of the case. Exploitation of any inconsistency in cross-examination is dependent on the theory chosen.

Witness statement charts are used to write cross-examinations. They allow the lawyer to pinpoint and develop chapters for cross-examination. In writing cross-examinations, the lawyer is armed with the exact words of the witness, and the source of that information. Through the charts, the lawyer knows the source document for every statement and the page, page position, and perhaps even the line. The statement charts can now be used to develop the chapters of cross-examination (see chapter 9, *The Chapter Method of Cross-Examination*). Using this criss-cross chart of the star witness, the lawyer can draft cross-examinations on the chapters that she thinks are important, on the inconsistencies, both internal and external, and the other chapters she thinks are important. See chapter 9, *The Chapter Method of Cross-Examination* and chapter 10, *Page Preparation of Cross-Examination.*

Knowing where the witness has remained consistent as to a topic is also valuable. Since the ideal leading question is one to which the cross-examiner knows the answer, the chart is a treasure trove of leading questions because the cross-examiner knows what the witness has said on any topic and exactly where the witness has said it. This sourcing of even the most basic and consistent information will provide the backbone for the page preparation of cross-examination (see chapter 10, *Page Preparation of Cross-Examination*).

§ 7.26   Use of Witness Statement Charts in Court to Impeach New Stories

The cross-examiner will cross-examine from material drawn from the witness statement charts, but ordinarily she will work from the prepared chapters of cross-examination rather than from the raw charts themselves. The charts are preparation materials but they are not finished chapters. Furthermore the charts can be unwieldy and contain too little context information to fill out an entire chapter. However, for reasons to be discussed, the cross-examiner should take the criss-cross chart to court every time, as it can instantly provide timely information necessary for cross-examination.

It should again be pointed out that inconsistencies are only one of the many kinds of chapters useful in cross-examination. It may well be that the lawyer will use the witness statement charts to draw out the many favorable facts with which the witness agrees, thereby supporting the cross-examiner's theory of the case. In this sense, the witness statement charts are confirmatory. They further show if the witness has been consistent with that fact.

When a witness has given enough statements to justify this kind of preparation effort, it is likely the opponent is going to have that key witness on the stand for quite a while. This one witness is likely to testify to a great deal of information.

The prepared lawyer does not need to write down very much of the information given on direct examination. Virtually all of the testimony should be in accord with the statements found in the chart. However, any time a witness gives a new (different) version of a fact, whether it occurs during the direct examination or cross-examination, the lawyer need only leaf through the chart book to the properly tabbed page of the event in question and write in the spare right-hand column, the newest version.

Chart 15

Jane Smith   HOME/GO TO BED

First Trial: May 7-18, 2001	Preliminary Hearing: Dec. 27, 2000	Statement to Police: Nov. 16, 2000	Notes
125 A: He took us home, and I went upstairs and checked on Bobby, and Mindy and Rich were in my room and I cried for a while. 199 Q: When you returned home that was around 2:00, right? A: Yes. Q: In the morning. Did you go to sleep shortly thereafter? A: Yes.	11 Q: And where did you go from there? A: To my apartment. Q: Okay, what happened when you got back to the apartment? A: I cried for awhile and then went to sleep. Q: When you got home that evening, where did you go? A: Upstairs and checked on my son. Into my room, Mindy and Rich were in my room. I went downstairs and slept on the floor. Q: Where did you do your crying? A: I don't know.	(questioning by Det. Dean) 8 A: The cab arrived and took us home and I cried for maybe two or three hours and Bobby didn't wake up that night, which was strange.	Direct Exam 10:15 a.m. before recess "And then I went downstairs and he raped me."

The lawyer may elect to have co-counsel, a law clerk, or a secretary sitting in the back of the courtroom keeping track of this information so that she is not disturbed at counsel table. But even if the lawyer keeps the chart, it is certainly possible to find the correct page rather quickly and jot a note on the new fact.

§ 7.27 Direct Testimony and Cross-Examination Changes (New Changes)

When a witness on direct or cross-examination changes his story, it may well be that the change itself is worth exploiting as another inconsistency in the testimony. This is especially true if the witness has testified unequivocally on prior occasions and now changes those facts dramatically.

Assume the witness has consistently told the same story as to a certain fact. As a result, the lawyer may not have written a chapter of cross-examination for this issue. If in the course of trial a new story to this fact pops up, the lawyer can immediately cross-examine the witness on each of the prior inconsistent statements on all versions of that fact, using that page of the criss-cross chart. Even though the cross-examiner has not written this cross-examination, the criss-cross chart shows every prior version of that fact given by the witness and gives the lawyer the foundation chapter (sourcing material), including the date of the statement and the page.

Chart 16

No Inconsistencies Before Trial
New Inconsistencies Occur During Cross-Examination

Thanksgiving Day Phone Call

DA Interview December 9, 2002	Grand Jury Testimony December 11, 2002
Q: Okay. On Thanksgiving Day of 1999, did you have any telephone conversations or personal meetings with Don Howes? A: I had a telephone call from him. Q: All right. Would you tell me what that telephone call was about? A: He called Bob Barton's home, whom they were having Thanksgiving dinner with. He called to get in line on the Detroit football game, which Detroit plays every Thanksgiving Day, And bet the game. Q: So in fact, on Thanksgiving Day, you had a conversation with Mr. Howes where he placed a bet. A: That's correct. Q: All right. During that telephone conversation or any other telephone conversation that day, did you have any discussions with Mr. Howes on the killing of his wife? A: No. excuse me. Let me back up. During the telephone conversation that I had with Don on Thanksgiving Day, he did indicate to me at that time that he was leaving town the next day, and he also asked me as I recall something together, and it is this call that the Friday.	A: The next conversation that we had concerning that, to my recollection, was on Thanksgiving Day. Q: Okay. Where were you when this conversation took place? A: I was at my home. Q: And how did you come into contact with Mr. Howes? A: Don called me from Bob Barton's home. Don called me and asked me for the line on the Detroit game which Detroit plays every Thanksgiving Day. Q: Did you have some further discussion in this phone conversation about a meeting or anything further to do with the plan to kill Mrs. Howes? A: He asked about the game first of all and bet the game. He also implicated to me—indicated at that time that he was going to be out of town the next day for the weekend and he hoped very much that everything could be accomplished that all the arrangements could be made. And I said, "Yes, they can." And he said, "We need to get together." And I said "Fine." to the effect of we need to get tentative meeting was set up for Friday.

As an example, Chart 16 shows a page of a chart titled "The Thanksgiving Day Phone Call." Although the topic is important to the opponent's theory of the case, the witness has always been consistent in this story, and the story as it stands before trial contains no good information for the cross-examiner's theory of the case. As a result, no chapter of cross-examination has been prepared. However, in the course of cross-examination on another chapter, the witness now unresponsively speaks of the Thanksgiving Day call and adds the statement: "He called me on Thanksgiving Day and he told me I had to go through with it, because he knew where my wife and kids lived, and he would kill them."

Under these circumstances, even the quickest and most experienced trial lawyer feels icy cold. Ordinarily, it would be nearly impossible to impeach forcefully on this new version. About the best the lawyer could do was to say, "Isn't it true, this is the first time you have ever said any such thing?" Then the lawyer must sit back and hope that the hostile witness chose to admit that it was a new version. All too often, the witness replies, "No, I've brought this up before." And why shouldn't he say that? After all, the witness is already making up new facts; a few more won't matter.

Through the application of proper preparation techniques, the cross-examiner should no longer fear the new story. Now, through the criss-cross chart, the cross-examiner is fully armed not only to survive the new story, but to turn it into a major impeachment of the witness.

Through preparation of the witness statement charts, the lawyer is literally and in great detail prepared for the new story — whatever it may be. Should a witness change a story, the lawyer can impeach on it immediately. The lawyer need not leaf through transcripts to find the exact quotes, the lawyer does not have to swear at herself for not having prepared a cross-examination on that issue, and the lawyer does not have to panic. At some convenient point in the cross-examination, perhaps after a recess to quickly recheck the criss-cross chart, the lawyer may begin to impeach the witness. This is especially easy, in that the criss-cross chart tabbed book is composed of reductions of actual transcripts, or of cut and paste statements, so it is as if the lawyer is reading from the transcripts. Should the lawyer elect to do so, the page and line notations within the witness statement chart book permits the lawyer to pick up the appropriate transcripts or reports and immediately points out the impeaching location to the witness.

Through the use of witness statement charts, the lawyer has seized control of the courtroom and has reminded the jury and the witness that she is in control of the facts. She is, therefore, in control of the case. The lawyer has asserted her mastery of the facts, and even if she is surprised during cross-examination by a new version, she can meet and refute that version almost instantly.

§ 7.28 Summary

These charts have tremendous visual and demonstrative evidence type effects in front of a jury. When a witness statement chart is laid out, and it is obvious to the witness and to the jury that the cross-examiner is using the chart to impeach the witness with specific facts and with specific quotes from each of the prior statements, the overall effect is completely intimidating to the witness and completely reassuring to the jury.

The advocate should never fear being exposed as well prepared. Any time a witness or a juror recognizes that the advocate has taken great care to learn the facts, the credibility of the advocate is increased. Simultaneously, the anxiety of the witness is increased. Preparation has a profound effect on a witness who understands that the lawyer knows every word the witness has said about a point. That witness is far more likely to agree to the truthful leading question and far less likely to try to deceive or in any way evade.

A properly prepared criss-cross chart allows a cross-examiner, armed with an encyclopedic knowledge of the witness's prior statements, to face even the toughest, most prolific witness. Both safe leading questions and impeaching inconsistencies can be mapped out long in advance, allowing the lawyer to draft chapters confidently (see chapter 9, *The Chapter Method of Cross-Examination*) and source answers (see chapter 10, *Page Preparation of Cross-Examination*). Now, fully prepared, the cross-examiner is free to listen carefully to the testimony and apply the advanced techniques that make the prepared cross-examiner appear artful.

Chapter 8

THE ONLY THREE RULES OF CROSS-EXAMINATION

SYNOPSIS

§ 8.01 "Great" Cross-Examination: A Misleading Term

Too often stories are told of a cross-examiner who has taken great risks, used open-ended questions, cross-examined without real preparation, and yet somehow won the case. It is suggested that the case was won despite the lack of preparation and technique. And even inside of that winning case, the advocate may have accomplished her cross-examination goals in perhaps two out of the five witnesses who were cross-examined. And all of that was on a great day. On a normal day, poor preparation leading to unnecessary risk-taking is a recipe for disaster. Even if the ill-prepared or ill-trained lawyer was somehow able to adequately cross-examine four out of five witnesses, the fifth witness may cause the case to unravel.

A lawyer whose best technique is her ability to look good while performing badly is not a great cross-examiner. A less dramatic performance of well-prepared material presented in a manner that minimizes risk to the examiner's case while maximizing the damage done to the opponent's case is truly wonderful cross. A word to those who practice in areas where little time for preparation may be available. The application of techniques discussed in this chapter will dramatically elevate the ability of the cross-examiner to obtain favorable admissions, provide support for the theory of the case, and minimize the ability of the witness to take the cross-examination into undesirable areas.

The task is not to make cross-examination into breathtakingly difficult and daring adventures, but to make the difficult task of cross-examination appear easier. The cross-examiner must strive for the consistency of success that comes from preparation advanced by sound technique. Success in cross-examination is an imprecise determination, but can be summarized as the accomplishment of the factual goals set out by the cross-examiner. Few cross-examinations accomplish every goal, but with the sound application of techniques, the advocate can expect to accomplish far more of her goals than would have been accomplished without the application of the science and techniques of cross-examination.

Just as the physicians' creed begins: "First, do no harm," the cross-examiner's creed must be: "First, do no harm to your client's case on cross-examination." There is an element of risk-taking in every cross-examination. Sound application of techniques can reduce the risks of cross-examination, but never extinguish the risks. One of the hallmarks of great cross-examination is the systematic application of techniques employed to establish the greatest amount of helpful information while minimizing the risks inherent in cross-examination.

Often an advocate claims numerous victories of witness destruction on cross-examination. However, a review of the entire transcript of cross-examination reveals that while points were scored against the witness, the cross-examiner became bloodied in the process because the witness scored equally valuable points against the cross-examiner.

The object of cross-examination must be to score as many useful points as possible while minimize the ability of the witness to score points against the cross-examiner's case.

The conventional wisdom is that if a witness has done no damage to the cross-examiner's case, a lawyer might elect to forgo asking questions. If no questions are asked, certainly the witness can score no additional points. However, even in circumstances where no damage has been done, it may be that the witness could testify to several additional facts that aid the cross-examiner's case (see chapter 11, *Sequences of Cross-Examination*). Thus, even the witness who has done no damage may need to be cross-examined. In any event, the skillful cross-examiner views every witness as an opportunity to introduce testimony that supports the advocate's theory of the case. Simultaneously, the cross-examiner seeks to employ techniques designed to minimize the opportunities for the witness to enhance his previous testimony or to open up new areas that will damage the cross-examiner's positions.

§ 8.02   Great Cross-Examination Teaches

Cross-examination is not an exercise based on emotion, presence, and oratory. It is not the cross-examiner showing the witness and all of those who observe, (but primarily the witness) that the cross-examiner is smarter, quicker, louder, more demonstrative, or more fearsome. It is about teaching the cross-examiner's theory of the case to the fact finder. Why is it necessary to tell cross-examiners what cross-examination is not about? Because each cross-examiner views the cross-examination as pitting her skills, her preparation, her intelligence, and her techniques against those of the witness. This is true in a sense. The focus of cross-examination should be on the cross-examiner, but the witness can steal that focus. But in a larger sense, cross-examinations are not about a performance by an advocate, but rather the teaching of facts that are critical to the cross-examiner's theory of the case.

Lawyers who believe that cross-examinations are intellectual endeavors rebel against the idea of teaching. They want it to be a contest of egos. However, the jury does not vote on which lawyer "looks good" or which lawyer performed eloquently. Rather, the jury is called upon to vote on a theory of the case. When the lawyer realizes that a cross-examination teaches the cross-examiner's theory of the case, pressure is reduced. The focus is shifted from the cross-examiner's ego to the cross-examiner's ability to convey to the listeners the logic behind the cross-examiner's theory of the case. Once the focus is shifted from the cross-examiner as lawyer to cross-examiner as teacher, the focus becomes conveying understandable presentations that guide the fact finder in real time.

§ 8.03   Cross-Examiner's Control of Themselves

Every lawyer wants to be able to conduct an effective cross-examination. How can this be accomplished? Decidedly not through incredible talent, luck, or instinct, but rather through control. Thankfully it is not only the talented artist of a lawyer who can control while on cross-examination. The lawyer must be in control of her own emotions first (see chapter 22, *Voice, Movement, Body Language, and Timing*) before she can hope to control her material or the witness. Cross-examination of any witness produces an adrenaline rush in the lawyer unequalled by other portions of the trial. Because the focus is on the cross-examiner, this rush of adrenaline is natural. It will not go away with more years at the bar or more trials under the belt. The cross-examiner must become accustomed to dealing with this physiological and psychological change in herself. She must come to understand that the adrenaline will flow, emotions will become heightened, and the natural tendency of the trial lawyer to be aggressive will become more pronounced. Witnesses do not voluntarily comply on cross-examination. Cross-examiners want them to comply. It is a setting for conflict. With the understanding and use of a cross-examination system that does not place reliance on emotion, physical presence, or intellectual gymnastics, this surge of adrenaline can be controlled and used to the cross-examiner's advantage.

The system propounded in this text is not based on oratory, flamboyance, demonstrative abilities, or acting skills. Rather, it is based on simple rules designed to teach the fact finder the theory of the case well. It is also designed to teach the witness that disruption of the orderly introduction of facts to the jury will receive a negative reaction. Further, it will teach that the witness complying with the orderly presentation of facts to the jury will receive positive feedback. The sanctions will be that the witness is forced to verify the truthful facts sought to be established by the cross-examiner. This process may require endurance and pain by the witness but it will happen. On the other hand, the witness who honestly admits facts that help the cross-examiner's or hurt the opponent's theory of the case will be rewarded by the cross-examiner moving on to new facts and not punishing the witness for failure to admit desired facts.

§ 8.04 Great Cross-Examinations Eliminate Distractions

Cross-examinations that are full of distractions to the fact finder cannot be considered great. If the fact finder cannot learn the lesson being taught by the cross-examiner, the effort is not superior. As in any learning environment, distractions need to be minimized for a true teaching paradigm to be in place.

In the courtroom, distractions are numerous. The opponent has the right to object. The judge then rules. The cross-examiner is not asking questions during this process. The judge has the ability to object. Again the cross-examiner is not asking questions and the fact finder is distracted. The witness has the ability to object in numerous ways. The witness can state that he does not understand the question. The witness can answer questions not asked or answer the question that is asked in an unresponsive manner. All of these are distractions.

Equally important, the cross-examiner can distract the fact finder unintentionally. By talking too loudly, using an aggressive demeanor, or using a demonstrative or emotional appeal, the jury or judge is distracted from learning the cross-examiner's theory of the case. What is needed on cross-examination is a reasonable tone by the cross-examiner and effective techniques that eliminate objections from the opponent and the judge.

§ 8.05   When to Say "No Questions on Cross, Your Honor"

The conventional wisdom of a generation ago was that if a witness had done no damage to the cross-examiner's case on direct examination, the lawyer should elect to ask no questions. That logic was completely defensive in nature. It entered the cross-examination with the premise that the cross-examiner would lose the cross-examination. Instead, trial lawyers must focus on the positive that can come out of teaching the case through the opponent's witnesses.

Assume that a fact (the color of the car was blue) could be established through the cross-examiner's own witness on direct examination or through the opponent's witness on cross-examination. Which would be better? If the cross-examiner chooses to prove the fact through her own witnesses on direct examination, the jury is left with a common sense notion that the cross-examiner's own witness would support her theory of the case. However, if the cross-examiner elicits from the opponent's witness that same fact, the jury will give the information greater credibility and weight.

As proof of this statement, think of what the opponent can say in closing argument should the cross-examiner prove that fact through her own witness. The opponent would clearly be able to say: "Witness X testified that the car was blue. What would you expect that witness to say when called by the cross-examiner?" However, if the opponent's own witness testified that the car was blue, the opponent would never say: "My witness testified that the car was blue. What would you expect my witness to say?"

Trial lawyers must now understand that questions on cross-examination are verbal requests for admissions. Once admitted by the other side, these requests are sacrosanct and beyond dispute. There is an added advantage, of course, that the cross-examiner is the one teaching primarily on cross-examination since the cross-examiner is talking most of the time. Contrast that with the fact that the cross-examiner is asking open-ended questions and the cross-examiner's witnesses on direct are doing most of the talking and most of the teaching on direct examination.

What then should the cross-examiner be asking if the opponent's witness on direct has not hurt the cross-examiner nor given much support to the opponent's theory of the case? Cross-examination is always available in two areas. First and foremost, any fact that the witness on cross-examination can give that would support the cross-examiner's theory of the case should be exploited fully and taught as completely and thoroughly as possible. Second, any fact that hurts the opponent's theory of the case should be inquired into on cross-examination. Both of these areas for cross-examination should be exploited. Consequently the times when the cross-examiner will utter the words, "No questions on cross-examination, Your Honor," will be very few and very far between.

§ 8.06 Relationship of the Three Rules to Time

The three rules of cross-examination are designed to maximize the amount of factual information coming before the jury in the shortest amount of time. Juries have changed in the last decade. We all have. Each of us demands more information quicker than ever before. All of us multitask more than we ever have before. With the advent of the Internet, each of us insists on having access to tremendous amounts of data in the shortest amount of time possible. Who among us would wait thirty seconds for our computer to boot up? Less than ten years, thirty seconds would have been a trivial amount of time to have access to the tremendous resources on the Internet or databases such as LexisNexis. Now, thirty seconds is an interminable amount of time to wait for the door to open to that information. Juries have become impatient. How best to satisfy this impatience? Through cross-examination. The cross-examiner using the three rules can get more detailed and precise testimony in front of the jury in the least amount of time possible.

As a component of this relationship of cross-examination to time, the trial lawyer must understand that the more important a fact or series of facts are to the theory of the case, the more time the jury expects to be spent on those facts. If facts are not important to the theory of the case, no time should be spent on developing those facts. Remember, time is the measure of importance in the courtroom, not the oratory inflection or volume of the cross-examiner's voice. Importance equals time.

§ 8.07 Relationship of Cross-Examination to Anxiety and Confidence

Each cross-examiner performs better when her confidence is higher. When a cross-examiner is confident, the words come easier. When she is confident, the thoughts come quicker. When she is confident, the goal appears obtainable.

Anxiety impedes the processing of information. Anxiety destroys confidence. Anxiety undermines confidence. Anxiety leads to frustration, anger, embarrassment and fear.

This goes for witnesses too.

With the three rules of cross-examination and other techniques in this text, the cross-examiner's confidence can remain at a high point while the confidence of the witness is eroded and replaced with anxiety. The three rules are designed to keep the lawyer's confidence at a high level while keeping the anxiety level of the witness at a high level. Said a different way, the rules are designed to keep the lawyer's confidence high and her anxiety low, while keeping the anxiety of the witness high and his confidence low.

The relationship between the witness and the cross-examiner is an inverse ratio. When the cross-examiner's confidence is high, the witness's confidence is low. When the cross-examiner's anxiety is high, the witness's anxiety is low. When a witness's anxiety is high and his confidence is low, he is less likely to carefully select words to explain his position. He is less likely to offer additional information to explain his position. He is less likely to volunteer new testimony. Ultimately, the witness is less likely to tailor his testimony, whether in the obvious form of "lying" or in the less obvious form of carefully orchestrating his testimony to fit into the theory of the opponent's case.

§ 8.08   Real Time Learning in Cross-Examination

The three rules are designed to permit the fact finder to learn the cross-examiner's theory of the case and to understand effective attacks upon the opponent's theory of the case in real time. Real time is defined as being the instant when the questions and answers are spoken in trial. The opposite of real time is to suggest that the jury will only understand the significance of a question and answer in the closing argument, or worse, in the jury room. The jury must understand the significance of the questions and answers at the time of trial. It is only through the building of these facts, one at a time, that the fact finder can appreciate the significance of the testimony and the relationship of that testimony to other testimony that has come before this witness and will come after this witness.

The jurors must be able to say to themselves, "I understand why the lawyer is asking this question and I understand the significance of the admission." Juries vote for what they understand.

§ 8.09   Achieving Control and Real Time Understanding through the Form of the Question

Human beings learn best when the learning seems easy or simple. The student does not readily absorb complex teachings. Whether the student is in the courtroom in the form of a jury and judge or whether the student is found somewhere else, learning small parts is easier than learning complexities.

Consequently, the cross-examiner must heed the admonitions of military philosophers like Napoleon and Von Clausewitz. Why military philosophers? Trials are nothing more than civilized versions of warfare. Both warfare and trial work, particularly cross-examinations, are filled with emotion and fright. That emotion is felt not only by the witness, but also by the cross-examiner.

Napoleon said: "A great general is one who does the average thing when all those around him are filled with emotion and fright."

Karl von Clausewitz said: "Everything in war is simple, but the simplest thing is difficult."

The lawyer who attempts to do great cross-examinations by taking "great risks" and exercising her personal presence to force a witness into admissions is following a road full of pitfalls and distractions. She doesn't teach the fact finder the needed information for the verdict. However, the lawyer who repeatedly and predictably performs solid, understandable cross-examinations, that some peers mistakenly call average, is the great cross-examiner. Consistently good cross-examinations equal great cross-examinations in the combat of trial. More cases are won and fewer cases lost because of this cross-examination. It is because juries understand the cross-examiner's theory of the case. With that understanding, they produce the "right" verdict. Juries need not marvel at the skills and bearing of the cross-examiner.

§ 8.10   The Historical Context of the Only Three Rules of Cross-Examination

For more than one hundred years, and informally for centuries before, trial lawyers have attempted to understand what made a good cross-examination. An effort was made to define those factors and place them into rules so that others could learn and replicate the good cross-examinations for future use. A generation ago, Irvin Younger gave the dramatic lecture of the Ten Commandments of Cross-Examination. Unfortunately, there are few cross-examiners who can remember ten things while up on their feet presenting a cross-examination.

A more in-depth analysis of those Ten Commandments reveals that many of them are placed in the negative (e.g., don't ask one question too many). Unfortunately when a rule is placed in the negative, the practitioner only realizes the rule has been violated after the rule has been violated and not before the damage has been done. This chapter sets out the foundation methods of obtaining control of the witness question by question. There are only three rules. That is something that can be remembered even in the middle of a cross-examination. The rules are all positive. Something that leads the cross-examiner to understand the rule before it is violated and the damage is done. Finally, the rules apply to every type of case, whether jury trial, a judge trial, an arbitration panel, or mediation. The rules apply in civil cases, criminal cases, administrative cases, and domestic relations cases. Consequently, because the rules have universal application, the rules afford the cross-examiner a predictability of result in any kind of setting. Because the rules provide predictable responses, results can be replicated. The cross-examiner is no longer required to learn a new system of cross-examination when venturing into a different factual setting. The rules are: (1) leading questions only, (2) one new fact per question, and (3) a logical progression to one specific goal.

§ 8.11   Rule 1: Leading Questions Only

The Federal Rules of Evidence and the rules of evidence of all states, permit leading questions on cross-examination (Fed. Rules Evid. Rule 611 (c); 28 U.S.C.A.). Simultaneously, the right to use leading questions is almost wholly denied the direct examiner. This is the fundamental distinguishing factor of cross-examination. It is the critical advantage given the cross-examiner that must always be pressed.

Despite this incredible opportunity, many lawyers do not take advantage of this rule and insist on asking open-ended questions. This is unnecessary at best and foolhardy at worst. A skillful lawyer must never forfeit the enormous advantage offered by the use of leading questions.

The "leading questions only" technique means that, in trial, the cross-examiner must endeavor to consistently phrase questions that are leading. No matter what the reason or rationale, a non-leading question introduces far greater dimensions of risk and occasions far less control than a question that is strictly leading.

One of the greatest risks occasioned by the use of open-ended questions is not the answer that may be given to that question. The answer may be perfectly acceptable to the cross-examiner. However, by asking the open-ended question, the cross-examiner has failed to consistently train the witness to give short answers to leading questions and not to volunteer information. By teaching inconsistently, with every open-ended question the cross-examiner sows the seeds for later problems in the cross-examination. As will be discussed, cross-examiner must teach a consistent lesson to the witness: The cross-examiner will pose the question and the witness may verify or deny the suggested fact. The consistency of teaching through the repetitive form of the leading question is fundamental to the goal of witness control.

§ 8.12   Leading Questions Allow the Cross-Examiner to Become the Teacher

If the lawyer is to teach the case, the lawyer must demonstrate that she understands the case. The leading question positions the cross-examiner as the teacher, while the open-ended question positions the cross-examiner as a student. Through the open-ended question it is the witness who becomes the teacher. The open-ended question focuses courtroom attention on the witness. The leading question focuses attention on the cross-examiner. The cross-examiner seeks that attention not for ego gratification, but for purposes of efficiently teaching the facts of the case. The cross-examiner/teacher using leading questions places the cross-examiner in control of the flow of information. The leading question also allows the cross-examiner to select the topics to be discussed within the cross-examination. These topics will be referred to throughout the book as the chapters of cross-examination.

§ 8.13   Use Short Declarative Questions

Leading questions are often defined as questions that suggest the answer. This is too broad a definition. True leading questions do not merely suggest the answer; they *declare* the answer.

Review the following three questions:

1) How do you feel about drinking?

2) Do you like to drink?

3) You like to drink?

Most lawyers will recognize the first question is not a leading question. There is no answer suggested in the question. It is completely open-ended, allowing the witness to respond in any manner that he or she chooses.

There are many experienced trial lawyers who would argue that the second question, "Do you like to drink?" is a leading question, as it indicates that the person should respond only with a monosyllable. It is not, however, a leading question for cross-examination. It does not *require* the desired answer. It does not *declare* the answer.

The third question, "You like to drink?" is leading, and unquestionably more confining and suggestive of the answer desired than question number one or two.

Why is this? The answer is quite simple. The fact that question number three begins with a non-verb means that it will be more closed-ended, more conducive to a restricted, monosyllabic answer. Especially when phrased as a statement, it *tells* the witness to answer with the answer the questioner requires. It *declares* the answer.

If the question mark is taken away from question three, it would be a short declarative sentence. Leading questions on cross-examination must be short declarative sentences. While the court reporter will type them all with a question mark at the end, the cross-examiner's voice need not even inflect a questioning tone.

§ 8.14   Declarative Questions Give Understanding to the Jury

The accomplished cross-examiner asks questions the way Ernest Hemingway wrote:

> Maybe today. Every day is a new day. It is better to be lucky. But I would rather be exact.

The Old Man and the Sea

The cross-examiner does not ask questions the way James Joyce wrote:

> And by that way went the herds innumerable of bellwethers and flushed ewes and shearling rams and lambs and stubble geese and medium steers and roaring mares and polled calves and longwools and storesheep and Cuffe's prime springers and culls and sowpigs and baconhogs and the various different varieties of highly distinguished swine and Angus heifers and polly bullocks of immaculate pedigree together with prime premiated milchcows and beeves: and there is ever heard a trampling, cackling, roaring, lowing, bleating, bellowing, rumbling, grunting, champing, chewing, of sheep and pigs and heavyhooved kine from pasturelands of Lusk and Rush and Carrickmines and from the streamy vales of Thomond, from McGillicuddy's reeks the inaccessible and lordly Shannon the unfathomable, and from the gentle declivities of the place of the race of Kiar, their udders distended with superabundance of mild and butts of butter and rennets of cheese and farmer's firkins and targets of lamb and crannocks of corn and oblong eggs in great hundreds, various in size, the agate with the dun.

Ulysses

Each of us was exposed to Hemingway and James Joyce. Unquestionably, each had talent. Unquestionably, each wrote beautifully. Which one was understood more quickly?

Juries and judges understand when a leading question is put in a declarative style. The fact proposed is immediately understandable. It is learnable in real time.

Take question three from the preceding section: "You like to drink?" If Hemingway were to ask this question, he would use two questions rather than one. The understanding for the jury would be more precise and more immediate. The resistance from the witness would be minimized:

4) You drank?

5) You like it?

Examine what has been accomplished with breaking the question down to a more understandable form. The witness is given a question about drinking and responds. Once the witness has said "yes," the witness must say that he likes it or subjects himself to ridicule, humiliation, or at the very least illogical thought.

§ 8.15　　Dealing With Witnesses Who Don't Want to Answer

Most cross-examiners have encountered a witness who feigned a lack of understanding that the leading question requires a response. The lawyer asks: If the witness doesn't answer, what do I do?

First, that is a rare situation. Yes, there are some witnesses who will pretend they do not understand that they are being asked to verify or deny the truthfulness of the fact within the leading question. But these witnesses are rare and are almost always witnesses who have testified a great many times before and who are marked advocates of the position taken by the lawyer who called them to the stand.

First, consider the vast majority of witnesses. They come to court reluctantly perhaps only once in their lives. These witnesses are not interested in game playing. They want to tell their story, answer the questions, and get off the witness stand. If they are schooled in the method of examination based on leading questions, they will freely and quickly provide answers to those questions. For these witnesses, it is imperative that the cross-examiner teach consistently. It is imperative for the cross-examiner to use leading questions exclusively so that the witness will understand that that is the exclusive method by which witnesses are to be cross-examined.

The use of leading questions to establish facts is not confined to the courtroom. In every day conversations most people do not speak in perfectly grammatical sentences. People use shorthand. They don't necessarily even finish their questions. The flow of the conversation establishes a context. In everyday life people understand each other even when the grammar or punctuation would earn a failing grade on an English final. Think about it. In everyday life, we do not add ". . . don't you?" to our sentences. At the last social function you attended, people did not ask questions such as, "You want a drink, don't you?"

There may be the rare judge who interrupts and offers that your declarative question is not, in fact, a question. In this case, occasionally add the "... don't you?" or other introductory or concluding phrase that turns the declarative question into a true question. This will undoubtedly satisfy the bench. Experience has taught that this method is so conversationally common that interruptions from the bench soon stop.

There are four ways to retrieve an answer using this short declarative question if an answer is not quickly forthcoming.

§ 8.16   Five Ways to Retrieve Answers

There are at least five ways to retrieve an answer using a short declarative question if an answer is not quickly forthcoming.

(a)   *Voice Inflection*

In everyday conversation, people do not use such ending phrases as "... don't you?" The questioner raises her voice to a higher pitch (a voice inflection) and pauses at the end of a question. That is the listener's cue to answer the question. This is the best, and most often used technique to obtain an answer. It's natural for everyone: witness, lawyer, jury, and judge.

(b)   *Pause (silence)*

Judges will not allow witnesses to remain silent in the courtroom. The courtroom is a formal atmosphere, but it is still a social exchange. Human beings do not like silences in conversations. The judge knows that lawyers ask questions and witnesses give answers. The jury and the witness know this as well. If a question has been posed, the witness must answer it. Most judges will tell the witness to answer the question. Most non-professional witnesses will answer the question in any case without prompting. The witness will be embarrassed by the silence and fill it, often before the judge intervenes.

(c)   *Pause (silence) and Point*

Expert witnesses and professional witnesses sometimes learn obstructive behavior. One of these behaviors is to avoid responding to a declarative question and stare back at the cross-examiner in response to the question. For those witnesses, a more aggressive approach is required. Remember however to minimize some of the aggressive nature with body language.

The witness who, in response to declarative questions, only stares at the cross-examiner needs to be goaded in some nonverbal way. The witness is being nonverbal so the cross-examiner may reply in kind. The cross-examiner can try the "pause and point" technique.

For example, the cross-examiner has put a perfectly simple, straightforward question to the witness: "That is not in your report?" The witness responds by staring balefully at the cross-examiner. There is silence in the courtroom. The judge raises her head to see what is amiss. The cross-examiner, while never losing eye contact with the witness, points to the witness with her right forefinger. A similarly encouraging gesture can be made, less aggressively, with an open hand. By nature, the witness understands immediately an answer is called for and supplies the desired "yes."

Remember, no one likes to be embarrassed. Silence embarrasses people; it makes them uncomfortable. Pointing tells everyone who is causing the silence.

The "pause and point" method has taught many a willfully recalcitrant witness to respond. The witness soon realizes that it is easier to answer than to be pointed at and embarrassed.

(d)   *Tag Lines*

While "tag lines" should ordinarily be reserved for oratorical emphasis (see chapter 13, *Employing Primacy and Recency*), occasionally it is appropriate to add such phrases as ". . . didn't you?", ". . . isn't that correct?", or ". . . right?" to prime the pump. This lets the witness know that the cross-examiner will be using this form of question, and the witness is required to give answers. Beware: The overuse of a tag line for *any purpose* will rob it of its power (see chapter 13, *Employing Primacy and Recency*).

(e)   *Establish the Rules of the Game*

There are those rare witnesses who resist answering unless the judge orders them to answer. Professional witnesses — that is, witnesses who spend much of their lives testifying (expert witnesses, investigators, police officers) — are often trained to just stare at the cross-examiner if the question is not phrased as a question, or to answer by saying, "Is that a question?"

If the witness asks, "Is that a question?", then the answer, of course, is "yes." Add no more. The witness is then faced with remembering the question before his interruption. Inevitably, the witness will ask, "What was the question?"

Q: You did not tell him he was free to leave?

A: Is that a question?

Q: Yes. (Long pause)

A: What was the question?

Q: You did not tell him he was free to leave?

The jury now understands that it was a question and now realizes that the witness was intentionally being difficult. For the dramatic effect this technique has on a witness's behavior, see chapter 19, *Controlling the Runaway Witness*.

§ 8.17   Avoid Enemy Words That Give Control to the Witness

The adept cross-examiner *never* uses questions that begin with the following:

1) Who

2) What

3) When

4) Where

5) How

6) Why

7) Explain

These words create the polar opposite of closed-ended questions. These words invite uncontrolled, unpredictable, and perhaps unending answers. These words *invite the witness to seize the action*, to become the focal point of the courtroom. They take the jury's mind off the fact the cross-examiner is trying to develop and allow the witness to insert a mishmash of facts, opinions, and stories designed to focus the jury on the issues the witness thinks are most important.

Cross-examiners are not journalists looking to present both sides of a story. Cross-examiners are not interested in having the witness explain everything that the witness wishes to explain. Cross-examiners strive to highlight those portions of the witness's testimony that are helpful to the cross-examiner's theory of the case.

There are those who maintain that they are so skillful that they can pose open-ended questions, the answers to which will always be of assistance. These lawyers are fond of saying, "I didn't care how she answered," or "There were no possible answers that could hurt me." In response, those lawyers have only eliminated the answers they have thought of. None of us are so omniscient that we can confidently state that we have eliminated every possible negative answer. There are truly bad answers and non-responsive answers awaiting the open-ended question. Why take that unnecessary chance? This applies to the most experienced trial lawyer as well as the novice. No one outgrows this advice.

For example, the cross-examination of the government's major witness — an admitted "large-scale drug smuggler" for the drug cartel in a federal criminal prosecution — was proceeding well as a result of the very thorough and controlled questioning by a very skillful lawyer. One slip into the enemy words, however, devastated the cross-examiner:

Q: How much cocaine did you import into the United States?

A: With the assistance of your client or without his assistance?

The flip side of that coin is, why give up the advantage of the leading question? If, in fact, the cross-examiner has eliminated all other possible answers, why take the chance in asking anything but a leading declarative question, which dictates the answer? Remember to always control the witness. Keep the focus of the questioning on the cross-examiner instead of the witness.

§ 8.18　　What Happens When Those Words Are Used

In a large, well-publicized federal drug money laundering case, an excellent cross-examiner cross-examined one of the government's major witnesses as to his prior inconsistent statements made under oath.

The examination of prior inconsistent statements under oath lasted for more than 90 minutes. During that hour and the half cross-examination, the witness was asked solely leading questions to which the verifiable answer was "yes." The jury was completely repulsed by this witness's testimony.

At the end of this solid, workmanlike cross-examination, the experienced trial lawyer asked: "Can you *explain* to this jury, why, after taking an oath, after swearing to God to tell the truth, you lied repeatedly?" (Emphasis added.) Even though this was a witness who was completely cowed, the witness, having been given an opening, took advantage of it: "In the beginning, I lied to keep my money. But as I came to know your client better, I began to lie to keep my life. I lied then, because I realized he would kill me and he would kill my family, he would do anything to anybody if it helped him."

In one careless question, by use of one of the enemy words, this cross-examiner gave control over to the witness and thereby undid the painstaking work of painting the witness as liar under oath. The picture had been well-painted, only to be ruined by asking the witness for an explanation.

§ 8.19　　Open-Ended Questions Encourage Long-Winded Answers Even to Later Leading Questions

Of course, not every witness can respond so spontaneously in a devastating manner to a single open-ended question, but that is no reason to run the risk. In fact, the risk of a bad answer to that particular question is only one of the risks created by the open-ended question. A far greater risk is that the cross-examiner is now teaching inconsistently. By mixing open-ended and close-ended questions, the cross-examiner is, in effect, instructing the witness that it is completely permissible or expected that the witness will volunteer long explanations to the cross-examiner's questions. The result of this inconsistent teaching is that the witness can no longer be counted on to give short answers even to the simple leading questions. Seen in this regard, every open-ended question damages the cause of witness control so zealously sought by the cross-examiner.

§ 8.20　　Mood and Emphasis

Another great advantage of the leading question is that it permits the cross-examiner to choose the emotion of the answer and the facts to be stressed. When leading questions are used, the cross-examiner can ask in a cold, hard, factual tone of voice, in a matter-of-fact tone, with sarcasm, or with incredulity. The choice belongs to the cross-examiner. If the witness is left to choose, it is unlikely that the opposing witness will independently adopt the favored tone of voice. Yet, the cross-examiner can create the tone of the facts by using tone of voice to set the emotional stage, allowing the witness only the right to answer "yes."

§ 8.21 Word Selection, Tone of Voice, Word Emphasis

Similarly, by use of the leading question, the cross-examiner can use her voice to place the emphasis on the selected words.

The open-ended question results in the following:

Q: Did you put that in your report?

A: No, I didn't.

The leading question, on the other hand, results in the same words, but with a different emphasis:

Q: In your 27-page report, you never mentioned any such thing?

A: No, I didn't.

In the leading question, the cross-examiner controls word selection, tone of voice, and word emphasis. All of these devices of persuasion are forfeited when the cross-examiner offers up the open-ended question.

§ 8.22 Word Selection

One of the most important benefits of the leading question permits the cross-examiner to select the words to describe the events to be discussed in the question. Most witnesses do not carefully consider their words nor carefully select words to describe what they are testifying. Normally, just as in everyday life, the witness offers the best word they can think of at the time. This may help the opponent's theory of the case or may be neutral. The one predictable statement that could be made is that the word will not be selected to consciously help the cross-examiner's theory of the case.

By use of a leading question, the cross-examiner controls the word selection and may more descriptively and vividly describe that which has occurred.

Compare the following two questions:

1) You saw a man lying on the side of the road?

2) You saw a man hurled from the car?

The first question describes with some precision a potential plaintiff in a personal injury suit. But when compared with the more descriptive word "hurled" in the second question, the first question is colorless.

The lawyer's conscious use of word selection can make the fact finder, both judge and jury, react differently to the explanation of events by the witness. Beyond that, careful word selection makes the witness feel differently about himself and his role in the activities.

Do not be discouraged if a witness, particularly a professional expert witness, will choose to disagree with a vivid but fair word selection.

Example:

Q: You saw a man <u>hurled</u> from the car?

A: I would not call it that counselor.

Initially this response may cause the cross-examiner to rethink her vivid descriptive word. Once she has determined that it is a fair word to describe the actual facts and events, it is then up to her to make the fact finder and the witness realize that the word is fair and will not be abandoned.

Q: You saw the man exit the car?

A: Yes.

Q: He did not voluntarily exit?

A: No.

Q: He exited through the window?

A: That's true.

Q: He exited through the side window?

A: Yes.

Q: That side window was rolled up when he exited?

A: Yes.

Q: He exited through the window head first?

A: Yes.

Q: His head broke through the window as he exited?

A: Yes.

Q: The man was hurled from the car?

A: That's correct counselor.

Once the trial lawyer determined that the descriptive word that she used was a fair, accurate, and vivid word, the non-answer is dealt with more detailed questioning, more precision, and more time. Do not abandon the vivid word.

§ 8.23   Word Selection Describes Theory

When the cross-examiner carefully selects words to describe her theory of the case, the cross-examiner never has to verbalize or have the witness agree to the conclusion that represents the theory of the case. As an example, in nine questions the cross-examiner by word selection conveys to the jury her entire theory of the case:

Q: She confided in you that this was her life savings?

A: Yes.

Q: She cautioned you that her goal was safety?

A: Yes.

Q: She was sixty-six years old?

A: Yes.

Q:. She was on a fixed income?

A: Yes.

Q: She was retired?

A: Yes.

Q: She was on a fixed income?

A: Yes.

Q: She told you it was her nest egg?

A: Yes.

Q: She told you it was her life savings?

A: Yes.

Q: She told you it was all the money that she had?

A: Yes.

Does the cross-examiner need to explain to the jury that the plaintiff was a conservative investor?

§ 8.24   Rule 2: One New Fact Per Question

The scientific method provides that the experimenter has a controlled environment and adds one variable at that time to that environment to determine the effect of that variable.

For example, the controlled environment of ten kilograms of pressure per square inch will raise the known object 3.2 centimeters off the platform. The experimenter then adds twenty kilograms per square inch to the controlled environment and concludes that this variable will raise the known object 5.4 centimeters. Under the scientific method, if the experimenter changes two variables at the same time, the experimenter would be confused as to the cause of the result, and no dependable findings or conclusions would result. If the experimenter had added twenty kilograms per square inch pressure and two kilograms weight to the known object, the experimenter could not be certain which variable produced the greater result.

Cross-examiners need acceptable conclusions supported by facts to work successfully. They need to add only one new fact per question. This is a critical component in the quest for witness control. By placing only a single new fact before a witness, the witness's ability to evade is dramatically diminished. Simultaneously, the ability of the fact finder to comprehend the significance of the fact at issue is greatly enhanced.

§ 8.25   A Time-Honored Method to Teach the Fact Finder

Dr. Seuss, in his classic work *Hop on Pop*, repeatedly used the smallest component, a single word, and expanded it only so far as necessary to create a simple sentence:

Hop

Pop

We like to hop.

We like to hop on top of Pop.

Stop. You must not hop on Pop.

This teaching method is exactly that necessary to "teach" the witness to answer only "yes." The jury best learns a case this way, too.

Three questions are offered as an example:

1)   See Spot?

2)   See Spot run?

3)   See Spot run home?

The initial question discusses one fact. Each succeeding question contains one additional or new fact to be added to the body of facts established by previous questions.

By this method, the scope of the fact at issue is sharply controlled. As a result of the tight control over the scope of the question, the permissible scope of the witness's answer is tightly controlled.

§ 8.26   Vague, Equivocal or Subjective Words Do Not Not Count as Facts

It is not always possible to ask questions confined to hard-edged facts. Occasionally, we must ask questions that characterize facts. The facts demanded by these questions are not as sharply defined. The use of any adjective increases the risk of the question:

Q: You kicked him?

Q: You kicked him three times?

Q: You kicked him three times as hard as you could?

In this example, it appears that the examiner is adding only one new fact per question to control the witness. However, the examiner has run an increased risk in question three.

Vague, equivocal, or subjective words are more difficult to control than hard facts. If, on cross-examination, this question were put to an uncooperative witness, the answer might be something to the effect of: "What do you mean by 'as hard as I could'?" The more difficult witness would simply answer "no."

The cross-examiner has created this problem by posing this subjective question. Should the witness choose to quarrel with the adjective "hard as I could," there would be time-consuming, distracting, and unproductive sorting out of the facts in the question. The examiner would be required to determine which one of the facts the witness refused. Or, as so often happens, with simply no time to straighten out the muddle, the question is abandoned. One loose, equivocal fact can make the entire sentence broad and equivocal. Example:

Q: You caught the ball?

A: Yes.

Q: You caught the red ball?

A: Yes.

Q: You caught the red ball well?

A: What do you mean by "well"?

By asking only a single new fact per question, the cross-examiner can isolate the fact in dispute in each case. Although the cross-examiner was careful to ask one new fact per question, the cross-examiner asked a fact ("well") that was subjective. The description of how the ball was caught is in dispute. That is clear because the cross-examiner had only one new fact in each question. That fact has already been isolated and now it can be addressed.

The proof of the validity of moving one fact per question is simple. If the cross-examiner asks the question, "You caught the red ball well", first and received the answer, "No", what would the cross-examiner instinctually do? The cross-examiner would go back and prove that section of questions one fact at a time.

Q: You caught the ball?

A: Yes.

Q: You caught the red ball?

A: Yes.

Q: You caught the red ball well?

A: No.

Q: You did not catch it well?

A: No.

By using one new fact per question, the cross-examiner has isolated the dispute to one fact — that fact being "well". Unfortunately, that fact is vague and subjective. Because it is vague and subjective, the cross-examiner must now clarify that fact for the jury.

Even this clarification is not terribly difficult because there was no time-consuming discussion about what fact was in dispute.

Q: You caught the red ball well?

A: No. What do you mean by "well"?

Q: You caught it with one hand?

A: Yes.

Q: You did not drop it?

A: True.

Q: You did not bop it or fumble it?

A: True.

Q: You caught it cleanly?

A: Yes.

Q: You caught the red ball well?

A: Yeah, pretty well.

Clarification comes from more detailed, more precise facts that give a cleaner, crisper picture of the events that occurred.

§ 8.27   Fixing the Vague Question

Isolate the Fact in Dispute

Often, when the cross-examiner has encountered a "no" answer, she is unsure as to what fact the denial applies. This is a problem of the cross-examiner's creation. By including in any question more than one new fact, she has created a situation in which a denial can apply to more than one fact. In such instances, the cross-examiner must first back up and start the chain of questions back at the last fact to which she has gotten an affirmative answer:

Q: You saw the blue car come around the corner, and sped through the red light?

A: No.

This compound question contains five facts and one adjective. There are five possible "facts" to which the answer "no" might apply. Now the examiner must decipher to what "no" refers: The color of the car? The speed of the car? The color of the light? Whether the witness saw anything at all? Even if the opponent does not object on the basis of compound questions, the witness has just as effectively done so by answering "no." If the lawyer has established *any* of these facts, she must now back up to the last fact established, re-establish it and then continue one new fact at a time:

Q: You did see a car?

A: Yes.

Q: It was blue?

A: Yes.

Q: The blue car came around the corner?

A: True.

Q: It drove through the red light?

A: True.

Q: As it drove through the red light, it was speeding?

A: It depends on what you mean by speeding.

By backing up to the last *safe* point in the above sequence, the cross-examiner can now begin the process of isolating the fact in dispute. The cross-examiner can now concentrate her efforts on clarifying that issue.

In addition, many times the lawyer immediately assumes that a negative answer to a compound question means the witness is fighting the cross-examiner about something that must be proven. As the following exchange shows, often the witness is not fighting the lawyer about what she must prove, only about her word choice in describing certain things:

Q: You saw a car go through the light?

A: Yes.

Q: The light was red for the car?

A: Yes.

Q: The car that was speeding through the red light was blue?

A: No.

Q: No, it wasn't speeding?

A: No, it was gray. (Pause.) Well, it could have been light blue.

Q: Well, a light blue or gray car was speeding through the light?

A: Yes.

In this case, the word choice was "gray" rather than "light blue." It may be that this simply doesn't matter. (However, one may appropriately ask the cross-examiner why was the question asked, if the color of the car truly did not matter?) The witness may not be disagreeing about anything of relevance, and the cross-examiner may be able to accept the answer. However, it would serve the cross-examiner well to be careful of this witness, as he has shown not only the willingness to dispute facts, but the ability to potentially prevail in the dispute.

§ 8.28   Redefine the Disrupted Issue Using Objective Facts

If a disputed issue can be redefined by the use of objective facts, do so. Objective facts are most easily understood by the jury and the easiest method to eliminate the problem:

Q: He was a good distance away?

A: I would not say "a good distance."

Q: He was ten feet away?

A: Yes.

Q: The distance of the light pole from the curb?

A: About ten feet.

By asking the question with the detailed fact of "ten feet away," and providing the additional detail that this is the distance from the light pole to the curb (still only one fact, just a concrete description), the cross-examiner is serving the witness with notice that the cross-examiner has gone out and measured that distance. The cross-examiner is also providing a form of definition for the equivocal phrase "a good distance away."

§ 8.29 The More Detail the Better

The subjective conclusion frequently provides the witness an easy method to dodge the question. Example:

Q: You owed a lot of money to the bank?

A: I don't know that I would consider it a lot. (The solution is to provide details where details are available.)

Q: You owed the bank $11,853,000?

A: Somewhere in that neighborhood.

If in fact the cross-examiner can supply details, the cross-examiner should do so. Witness how the addition of detail enriches this description:

Q: You sent the research memo to every stockbroker?

Q: There are 458 stockbrokers brokers employed by your company?

A: About that many.

The addition of the detail of "458" illustrates to the witness and to the jury that the lawyer has researched the facts, and that the lawyer knows more about the issue than the witness. The witness is more likely to agree to offer up "yes" answers when faced with that kind of detail.

§ 8.30 Subjective Interpretation

It is occasionally necessary to ask a question that calls for a subjective interpretation. However, even in such cases, by offering an alternate subjective interpretation, the witness may be forced to agree with the cross-examiner's subjective description:

Q: The streetlight on that corner is a 450-watt bulb?

A: I'm not sure.

Q: The streetlight was very bright?

A: Yes.

By starting with a fact specific reference (450 watt bulb), the cross-examiner demonstrates that she knows the details. The witness may not agree with the detail, but will almost always agree with the cross-examiner's subjective characterization or interpretation after being given those details (". . . the light was very bright").

§ 8.31   Faster, Cleaner Crosses

It has been asked whether judges will permit this kind of meticulous questioning. Not only do judges permit this method, they encourage it.

Empirically tested, this method results in faster cross-examinations, simply because there is no debate about what has been asked. No time is consumed in colloquies or objections to the form of the question:

Q: You caught the red ball well?

A: What do you mean by "caught the ball well"?

Q: You caught the red ball?

A: Yes.

Q: You caught it with one hand?

A: Yes.

Q: You did not drop it?

A: True.

Q: You did not bobble it or fumble it?

A: True.

Q: You caught it cleanly?

A: Yes.

Q: You caught the red ball well?

A: Yeah, pretty well.

If the cross-examiner asks a question with a vague, subjective word, the witness will turn the tables on the cross-examiner; that is, the witness begins asking the questions ("What do you mean by 'caught the ball well'?"). In this situation the cross-examiner must exercise greater care and be more detailed with the facts to prove the subjective characterization. Often this can be done by putting the word in context, by detailed elimination of other subjective standards that the cross-examiner does not wish to prove. Redefining an equivocal fact can also be done by meticulously adding detail to the picture:

Q: The lighting was very bright?

A: It depends on what you mean by very bright.

Q: From where you were standing, you could see people's faces across the street?

A: Yes.

Q: You could plainly see the color of the cars going through the intersection?

A: Yes.

Q: The light was bright enough that you could count the number of people in the cars?

A: Yes.

Q: The light was bright enough that you could have read a newspaper?

A: I suppose so.

At this point, it is not necessary to re-ask the initial question, since the jury appreciates just how bright it was. The witness has been required to affirm alternative, objective definitions, or facts that cumulatively equal "the light was very bright." Putting subjective interpretation into context by specific facts makes for cleaner cross-examination.

§ 8.32   The Three-Step Method to Fix the Equivocal, Vague Question

1. Back up to safe facts already established.

2. Move forward one fact at a time so as to identify and isolate the "fact" being disputed.

3. Eliminate all subjective standards, or, in the alternative, by detailed facts, point to the only subjective standard that would be logically permissible or plausible.

§ 8.33   Avoiding the Compound Question Avoids Objections

This method of asking only one fact per question also assists in meeting objections. As discussed, when the cross-examiner asks only one fact per question, she avoids having to interpret the meaning of a "no" answer. Similarly, when avoiding compound questions, counsel sidesteps multi-tiered objections that include objections to the form of the question, thus allowing counsel to better meet any forthcoming objection. Witness this interchange:

Q: You were charged with murder in this case as well?

A: Yes.

Q: So in exchange for your testimony, you have worked out some kind of back room deal that will keep you out of prison or at least the State might not ask that you go to prison?

Opp.:   Objection. That is a compound question. It calls for a conclusion on the part of the witness, and also it is argumentative.

Q: Your Honor, I believe I have a right to show motive, interest, or bias.

Judge: Sustained.

(Whereupon appellant's counsel did not pursue this completely valid and important line of cross-examination.)

The objection was only to the form of the question and not the substance of the question. Counsel's argument to the trial court supported and justified the question as to the substance and his reason for asking it, but did not address the form of the question. The trial court, in repeating its ruling, did not prevent appellant's counsel from continuing this line of questioning in a proper form. Had counsel broken the question into its component parts, the cross-examiner could easily have established the facts of the plea bargain and its likely consequence on the sentence that could be imposed on the witness. The objection could easily have been overcome. In fact, it could have been avoided had counsel placed before the witness a series of leading one-fact questions.

§ 8.34 The "Close Enough" Answer

Be wary of answers that seem "close enough" to the subjective standard in the question. Because the cross-examiner has asked a subjective fact, and because the answer is further qualified by the witness, the cross-examiner may be stepping further away from the goal to be established, not closer to it.

Q: The man was tall?

A: Pretty tall.

Or

Q: The product was losing money?

A: It was not performing as well as we would have liked.

Now where is the cross-examiner? There were problems enough with "tall" in the first question. Now, the equivocal answer "pretty tall" is even more fraught with ambiguity. If "tall" is truly a fact to be established, the cross-examiner would do better to back up and use the Three-Step Method in order to establish the goal before moving elsewhere.

Similarly, by allowing the witness to dodge the question as to whether the product was losing money, the cross-examiner is left with a very muddy picture. Even though the question is sufficiently precise, the imprecise answer is unacceptable. The cross-examiner should seek to quantify the loss or at least to establish the fact that the product was losing money. Whether the witness believes the product was performing adequately or inadequately is not the point of the question. The answer really amounts to the witness rephrasing the question. This should not be permitted.

§ 8.35 How Not to Fix the Bad Question

Don't Argue with the Witness over Subjective Terms

Q: You were disappointed in the sales of the product?

A: What do you mean by "disappointed"?

Q: You know what I mean.

This is not a question. The jury will realize that the cross-examiner is arguing about a subjective issue and will hold it against the cross-examiner, not the witness.

Don't Comment on the Problem

This is true, no matter how suave the lawyer may believe her comment to be:

Q: I can't believe that you don't know what "disappointed" means.

Or

Q: Are you telling this jury that you do not know what the word "disappointed" means?

This response shows the frustration of the cross-examiner but does not advance the fact-finding process. The cross-examiner asks such a question because the cross-examiner believes that the jury will not accredit this answer. In this regard to cross-examiner is probably correct. It is for that very reason that the cross-examiner need not drop to the level of the witness and engage in an unnecessary and petty line of questioning. Instead, the cross-examiner should attempt to replace the subjective description with an objective fact or facts:

Q: You were disappointed in the sales of the product?

A: I don't know what you mean by "disappointed."

Q: You had projected first-year sales of the product to be in excess of $12 million?

A: Really our hope, not totally a projection but more of a desire or goal. And even then that would be our best case scenario.

Q: Total first-year sales of the product were $3,256,753.

A: Yes, slightly more than $3 million.

Counsel has wisely avoided a fight about the word "disappointed." Instead, by showing a more detailed factual projection versus the factual results, the fact finder can easily draw its own inference, and that inference is inescapable. The company must have been disappointed in the sales.

Avoid the Frontal Assault on the Answer That Denies a Subjective Description

Q: You blistered him for even suggesting that the investors be warned?

A: No.

Q: No? You did!

All of these approaches convey to the jury and witness that the cross-examiner is frustrated, which only exacerbates a bad situation. Remember, it was probably the cross-examiner who created the situation by ignoring the rule of "one new fact per question." The subjective conclusion of the cross-examiner is not a fact. If the cross-examiner had confronted the witness with the actions taken by the witness, the words used by the witness, and the voice employed by the witness, then one fact at a time the point could have been made that the corporate executive "blistered" his subordinate for even suggesting that the investors be warned. Even if the witness created the problem, in order to take advantage of the reluctance to answer, the lawyer must remain calm and return to the "one new fact per question" technique.

If it becomes painfully obvious by the elimination of other subjective standards and by rephrasing the question one fact at a time that the witness is being willfully recalcitrant, then the jury will observe it and hold it against the witness. The cross-examiner's task is to get the answer. The jury will provide the necessary emotional sting through its judgment on the credibility of this witness.

§ 8.36   Never Abandon the Valid and Necessary Leading Question

The cross-examiner should not abandon the valid and necessary question. If the fact was unnecessary or if the form of the question was objectionable there is no need to battle to save the point. (If the fact was unnecessary, it should not have been asked in the first place.) But if the fact was important to the theory of the case and the form of the question was appropriate, the cross-examiner sends a wrong signal by abandoning the question in the face of an evasive answer. To do so is to encourage the witness to further evade. Abandoning the question, even if that fact can be established by another witness, runs the risk of implying to the jury that the question asked is unimportant or incorrect. Worse, it teaches the witness that if the lawyer is confronted with difficult responses, she will abandon that line of questioning. Neither lesson should be taught to the jury or the witness.

§ 8.37   Facts, Not Conclusions, Persuade

The second rule of one fact per question tightly controls the witness. The witness has before him but a single new fact. It is hard for the witness to express confusion or be evasive. Moreover the jury is more easily educated by this technique of factual presentation. Because the facts are so detailed and because the facts are presented one at a time, the jury will reach the conclusion to which the facts inevitably point. The jury will embrace the same logical conclusion suggested by the cross-examiner.

One might say, the technique of one fact per question is akin to planting acorns in a jury box, not oak trees. Remember it is the lawyer, not the jury, who is intimately familiar with the facts. The jury must be slowly and carefully be brought to the conclusion sought by the advocate. It is far safer to let the jury reach its own conclusion based on the facts rather than demanding that conclusion from a hostile witness. The structure of one fact per question meticulously builds the picture so that the jury reaches the cross-examiner's desired conclusion, even though the conclusion itself may never be put to the witness. See chapter 9, *The Chapter Method of Cross-Examination* and chapter 10, *Page Preparation of Cross-Examination*.

§ 8.38   Conclusions, Opinions, Generalities, and Legalisms Are Not Facts

Cross-examiners always feel the need to move faster in a trial. Judges become impatient. Juries send signals of boredom. Witnesses show a willingness to become uncontrollable. All of these facts make the cross-examiner want to move quicker. Unfortunately cross-examiners tend to think that moving to conclusions, opinions, generalities, and legalisms makes for faster movement. When studied, conclusions, opinions, generalities and legalisms do not move the case along faster. Worse, they inadequately teach the cross-examiner's theory of the case.

Individual, precise, detailed facts will always trump or overcome a conclusion, opinion, generality, or legalism. The reason? Facts (multiple and precise) paint a mental image. Conclusions, opinions, generalities, and legalisms paint no image at all.

§ 8.39   Conclusions Are Not Facts

Q: Only a wealthy man could live at that address?

A: I wouldn't call myself wealthy.

The lawyer has created a problem for herself by falling into word usage that is conclusionary. It results in a distraction to the cross-examination and does not teach the details necessary for the jury to come to the conclusion that the witness is wealthy. The cross-examiner moves to facts and away from the conclusion to fix the problem:

Q: You are not poor?

A: No.

Q: A poor man does not wear Armani suits?

A: No.

Q: A poor man does not ski in the Alps?

A: No.

Q: A poor man does not drive a 2004 Mercedes?

A: No.

Q: A poor man does not travel over 100,000 miles a year for pleasure?

A: No.

Q: A poor man does not own three homes?

A: No.

Q: A poor man does not have his third home in Aspen, Colorado?

A: No.

§ 8.40   Opinions Are Not Facts

In a personal injury case involving an eighteen-wheel truck, the defendant truck company produced an expert who was qualified over objection of the plaintiff. The expert witness gave the opinion that the defendant driver was not fatigued at the time of the collision. The cross-examiner realized that it was impossible to argue with an opinion. (Simply because every person has one and is entitled to it.) The cross-examiner realized that attacking the facts upon which the opinion was based was a more effective attack on the opinion itself. Example:

Q: Doctor, you said on direct examination that the driver was not fatigued?

A: That is correct counselor.

Q: The defendant had driven ten straight hours?

A: True.

Q: He had driven from Louisiana to Georgia?

A: True.

Q: He had driven Interstate 10 and Interstate 75 — nothing but interstate?

A: True.

Q: He had driven over 627 miles straight through?

A: True.

Q: He had never left the seat of that cab?

A: That's true.

Q: He hadn't stopped to stretch?

A: That's true.

Q: He had not stopped for coffee?

A: True.

Q: He had not stopped to use the bathroom?

A: True.

Q: He had never turned off the engine?

A: Yes.

Without ever directly attacking the opinion of the expert, the cross-examiner has successfully attacked that opinion.

§ 8.41   Generalities Are Not Facts

Trial lawyers fall into generalities when they become fatigued. Instead of being precise, as the trial lawyer knows she must be, she generalizes. Generalizing always creates a problem for the trial lawyer. Example:

Q: You caught the red ball well?

A: I wouldn't say well.

The trial lawyer realizes her error and immediately become precise and detailed:

Q: Well you did catch the ball?

A: Yes.

Q: You caught it with one hand?

A: Yes.

Q: You didn't drop it?

A: True.

Q: You did not bobble it?

A: True.

Q: You didn't fumble it?

A: True.

Q: You caught it cleanly?

A: Yes.

Q: You caught it cleanly and never broke stride?

A: Yes.

The jury has a much more vivid picture of what happened. That picture more closely resembles the picture in the cross-examiner's mind.

§ 8.42   Legalisms Are Not Facts

Not only do legalisms fail to teach the trial lawyer's theory of the case, they are often met with appropriate objections. In a personal injury case coming out of a collision between an eighteen-wheel commercial truck and a car, the defendant was asked on cross-examination:

Q: You were negligent?

A: No.

Opp.: Objection. He asked for a legal conclusion.

Judge: Sustained.

The lawyer moves into one true fact at a time to better prove and teach her theory of the case:

Q: It was dark, but you didn't slow down?

A: No.

Q: It was raining, but you didn't slow down?

A: No.

Q: The road was slick, but you didn't slow down?

A: No.

Q: The traffic was heavy, but you didn't slow down?

A: No.

Q: The traffic was bumper to bumper, but you didn't slow down?

A: No.

Q: You were passing every car that you come up to, but you didn't slow down?

A: Yes.

The jury may not understand negligence. The jury does understand someone who would not slow down.

§ 8.43 Creating Impact One Fact at a Time

By establishing one fact at a time, the cross-examiner achieves another laudable goal: The cross-examiner adds impact to the answers. By letting each fact have its own moment of revelation, the jury is allowed to concentrate on the development of the picture long before the whole picture is revealed. Example:

Q: You saw the six-foot, five-inch, 225-pound guy with the bloody fists beat down the five-foot, seven-inch, 155-pound boy with the bloody face?

This question was put to the state's only eyewitness to an assault. The answer received was "yes." The cross-examiner was elated. In one fell swoop, she had gotten an admission to numerous favorable facts. In the process, however, she deprived herself of the opportunity to create a truly memorable picture of self-defense.

The reason this question and answer never impressed the jury was because the jury was not given the time to absorb the eleven facts.

Q: You (1) saw the (2) six foot, five inch (3) 225-pound (4) guy with the (5) bloody (6) fists (7) beat down the (8) five foot, seven inch (9) 155-pound (10) boy with the (11) bloody face?

Had the individual facts been put to the eyewitness a single fact at a time, the cross-examiner would have had 11 times as many opportunities to use voice and emphasis to create drama. The cross-examiner could choose the pace of each individual question, building emotion, and creating interest as the individual facts piled up. Slowly, inexorably, the picture emerges of the much bigger man beating mercilessly on the much smaller boy. For example:

Question 1:

Q: You saw the fight?

A: Yes.

Question 2:

Q: John, the big guy, was fighting?

A: Yes.

Question 3:

Q: John was six-feet, five-inches tall?

A: Yes.

Question 4:

Q: John is a big man?

A: Yes.

Question 5:

Q: Dave is only five-feet, seven-inches?

A: Yes.

Question 6:

Q: Dave is a much smaller boy?

A: Yes.

Question 7:

Q: John weighed 225 pounds?

A: Yes.

Question 8:

Q: Dave is 155 pounds?

A: About that.

Question 9:

Q: John was a much bigger person.

A: Yes.

Question 10:

Q: John was a much heavier person.

A: Yes.

Question 11:

Q: And then John was hitting Dave?

A: Yes.

Question 12:

Q: He was hitting Dave with his fists?

A: Yes.

Question 13:

Q: He was hitting Dave in the face?

A: Yes.

Question 14:

Q: John was hitting Dave, and his fists were bloody?

A: Yes.

Question 15:

Q: And as you watched, you saw the blood on Dave's face?

A: Yes.

Question 16:

Q: You saw John beating down on Dave, in the face, with his fists?

A: Yes.

The eleven individual facts now consume a total of sixteen questions. Note that the cross-examiner used more questions than the number of facts within the initial compound question to establish all of the desired facts. Sometimes it takes many more questions than the number of facts. As discussed earlier in dealing with subjective questions, it may take multiple questions to establish just one important descriptive word or fact. Sometimes the added questions are simply ways of adding interest or better filling out the picture. In this example, the cross-examiner has been able to expand the material by use of summary questions and looping facts already introduced (see Chapter 26, *Loops, Double Loops, and Spontaneous Loops*).

§ 8.44   Infusion of Emotion Question by Question

The "one fact per question" technique allows the cross-examiner to infuse various emotions on a question-by-question and fact-by-fact basis. In each question the cross-examiner has created the flexibility necessary to drive the jurors emotionally into the story. It is for the cross-examiner to determine which facts to serve with a change of voice or an emotional inflection that signals the fact finder to the importance of that particular fact.

In contrast, when there are multiple new facts stuffed into a single question, it becomes exceedingly difficult to place different emotional tones on different facts. The multi-fact question was already too cumbersome, and the addition of changes of voice, tone, and emphasis would be preposterous. In the example above, the last, sixteen-part breakdown of the facts presents the facts more in a more digestible manner. Not every fact deserves an emotional overlay. In fact, relatively few facts should receive extra emphasis. When every fact is implied to be extremely important, it becomes extremely difficult for the fact finder to accurately pick out which fact is truly the most important.

By asking one new fact per question, the picture of violence is made more graphic then could be provided by any conclusory statement. There is a true sense of drama to the unfolding scene. The jury is given time to absorb the picture. This evidence is brought to the fore of the jury's mind.

Generally speaking, the more subjective the fact to be established, or at the other end of the spectrum, the more complex the fact to be established, the more careful and detailed the questioner must be. Therefore, the questioner must ask multiple questions to establish facts at either end of the spectrum.

When the cross-examiner compresses too many facts into one question, the lawyer becomes sloppy with his or her word usage. There are too many facts to deal with, so the cross-examiner cannot select adequately descriptive words. As the questions improperly encompass multiple new facts, there is a tendency to minimize the descriptive words. To the cross-examiner, the question already seems overly long, and the addition of descriptive detail only serves to further complicate the question. Hence, by enlarging the field of inquiry within the question, the cross-examiner has simultaneously diminished the ability of the sentence to create a vivid word picture. The technique of one new fact per question provides the solution. Each individual question has to be short enough to allow the cross-examiner the flexibility to infuse the descriptive words helpful in explaining that fact.

By presenting one fact per question to the jury, not only is the jury led step by step to the ultimate conclusion for the completion of that factual picture, but the cross-examiner has the freedom to concentrate on individual emotionally evocative facts within each question. The more concentrated the focus of the individual question, the more opportunity for descriptive, emotion-inducing word choices. Just as the jury can better envision the picture because of a more regulated flow of facts, the jury can better sense the desired emotion created by better word selection. The one new fact question permits the examiner to better control this flow of facts.

§ 8.45   Word Selection Made Easier by Envisioning the Event

While presenting one fact per question, the cross-examiner must make certain that the words used are adequate to create the desired case scenario. There is a technique to aid the cross-examiner in selecting the descriptive words that can make the picture clearer and the facts more vivid. If the cross-examiner will form a mental image of what she is seeking to describe, and then present that mental image through leading questions, the result is a series of leading questions of finer texture. The cross-examiner wishes the fact finder to see the picture, so it would only stand to reason that the cross-examiner must first see that picture:

Q: You saw the big boy hit the little boy?

A: Yes.

Compare that question with the following question that adds no new facts to the question, but is intended to heighten the image of the fight's unfairness by painting a more vivid picture:

Q: You saw the big boy beat on the little boy?

"Beat" is a more powerful and descriptive word than "hit." "Beat on" not only shows stronger impact than "hit," it emphasizes the height and size advantage that ultimately will be played out fact by fact to the jury. By seeing the fight in greater detail, the cross-examiner can describe, through leading questions that same fight in greater detail.

Q: He pounded Dave with his fist?

Q: He punched him in the ribs?

Q: He smacked him in the face?

The cross-examiner must strive to use descriptive words to describe accurately the facts questioned upon. The descriptive words will come naturally to mind when the cross-examiner will look into her own head to see the event.

§ 8.46 Labeling

In this age where more and more information is floods our senses daily, jurors and judges find it difficult to remember names and events. Word selection is critical in labeling all major witnesses, all major pieces of evidence, and all major events within the theory of the cross-examiner's case. In the example above, Jim is labeled "the big boy" and Dave is labeled the "little boy". The action is labeled a "beating" (beat on). These are fair, reasonable descriptions of what happened that vividly illustrate the cross-examiner's theory of the case. For more on labeling, see chapter 26, *Loops, Double Loops, and Spontaneous Loops.*

§ 8.47 Rule 3: Break Cross-Examination into a Series of Logical Progressions to Each Specific Goal

Cross-examination of a witness is not a monolithic exercise. Instead, the cross-examination of any witness is a series of goal-oriented exercises. The third technique of the only three rules of cross-examination is to break the cross-examination into separate and definable goals.

Each section of cross-examination must have a specific goal. It must be so specific and so clear that the cross-examiner, if asked at any time without notice (as judges are inclined to do), can identify the factual point she is seeking to make. Another way of envisioning this is to view cross-examination as a series of pictures that must be painted.

The vast majority of cross-examinations have multiple specific goals (see Chapter 9, *The Chapter Method of Cross-Examination*). However, the cross-examiner should proceed a chapter at a time in order to establish a single identifiable goal at a time. Cross-examination is a series of specific goals. Each goal, in turn, must be developed individually and fully before proceeding to the next specific goal.

Too often advocates envision the cross-examination of a witness as having a single, overriding goal such as:

- "destroying the credibility of the witness."

- "showing the defendant drove negligently."

- "proving the defendant robbed the store."

To think of cross-examination in such a manner is to make exceedingly difficult the preparation and presentation of the cross-examination. It is too big. Furthermore, the advocate will notice that these are all conclusory goals, not factual goals. Cross-examination is ideally suited for the establishment of factual goals. Cross-examination is ill-suited for the establishment of conclusory goals. Setting aside for the moment the fact that jurors are unpersuaded by conclusions, witnesses called by the adversary are extremely unlikely to agree with the cross-examiner's conclusions. It is therefore improper and unnecessary to conceive and plan cross-examination in such global terms. Instead, it is far easier and more productive to engage in the technique of breaking down every cross-examination into its individual factual goals. As the lawyer accomplishes those factual goals, the fact finder is led to the appropriate and desired conclusion.

There are two reasons for developing specific factual goals. First, it is easier for the jury to follow any line of questioning if it clearly and logically progresses to a specific goal. An organized presentation that is broken down into several individual points invites attention. Even a reluctant listener can focus attention when there is clear sense of organization and defined points being made by the speaker.

The second value in breaking cross-examination into individual factual goals, is that it allows the judge to know where the cross-examiner is proceeding so that she will permit the cross-examiner to continue. Long gone is the age when a trial was a civic event. Trials are now statistics. Judges want cross-examiners to "move it along." There is undoubtedly a general right to cross-examine witnesses. But that is insufficient. There must be a reason to cross-examine the witness. Before rising to cross-examine, the advocate must have firmly in mind the individual goals of that cross-examination.

A wonderful by-product results when the cross-examiner clearly has specific goals every time she is requested by the court to identify those goals. Eventually the trial judge and the opponent learn that, for this cross-examiner, there is always a specific goal. When in doubt, opponents will not object, nor will judges sustain the objection if made. This gives the cross-examiner even greater latitude in her examination.

Each specific goal within a cross-examination should either assist the cross-examiner in building her theory of the case, or assist the cross-examiner in undermining the opponent's period of the case. It is unnecessary and unwise to pursue factual goals that do not impact the contrasting theories of the case.

§ 8.48 From the Very General to Very Specific Goals

A logical progression dictates that the issue to be developed must proceed from the very general to the specific goal. Think of it as a funnel. The general questions funnel the witness to specifics.

Witnesses will find it easier to agree to general issue questioning before they are brought to specifics. This is true particularly when specific facts will be harmful to the witness. The witness will not respond in a monosyllable manner to the question unless that entire issue has been developed from the general to the specific.

A witness is unlikely to admit at the onset of cross-examination that he is a chronic liar. However, a series of facts may well establish that the witness can understand why people would lie, has been in situations where a lie benefited the witness, and has lied in those situations. The cross-examiner should start out generally and proceed slowly and methodically, one fact at a time, to the specific goal of establishing that the witness is a "liar." The cross-examiner is advised to recall that "liar" is a conclusion, and one that the witness is unlikely to adopt. That is not the goal of the cross-examination chapter. The goal is to provide the fact finder with sufficient facts by which they may infer that the witness is a liar. The technique, as always, is to provide facts to the witness through leading questions making it more likely that the witness will give truthful "yes" answers. The cross-examiner should strive to score the points factually, leaving it up to the fact finder to draw the appropriate inference.

§ 8.49 General Questions Lock in and Make Easy the Specific

The following cross-examination contains questions indicating that the witness is willing to lie:

Q: In December the police questioned you about this case?

A: Yes.

Q: You told Det. Wylie you knew nothing about the case?

A: Yes.

Q: That was not the truth?

A: No, it wasn't.

Q: Instead of telling the police the truth, you chose to lie?

A: Yes.

Q: You did not want to tell him the truth?

A: No.

Q: The truth was likely to get you in trouble?

A: Yes.

Q: So you lied?

A: Yes, I did.

Q: The reason you lied was because you believed a lie would help you?

A: Yes.

Q: You are willing to lie if a lie will help you?

A: Yes.

Q: You are a liar?

A: On occasion.

Q: On occasion when you need to be?

A: True.

The questions set out above are not necessarily the only ten questions in this line of questioning. It may take twenty questions to move the witness to the point of giving in to the cross-examiner's goal. The goal may be accomplished logic dictates that the witness will admit that which is logical or appear to the fact finder by developing admissions to various misrepresentations previously told by the witness. Such an examination may end as follows:

Q: You are a talented liar?

A: Yes.

Q: You can make up and tell lies very quickly?

A: Yes.

Q: You can think of elaborate lies and work on them a long time?

A: Yes.

Q: You are the best liar that you know?

A: Yes.

A witness's body language may tell as much as his answers. At the end of the above examination, a carefully questioned witness, when asked if he is the best liar he knows, will not shrink, hesitate, or act defensively towards the jury. The witness will act as if he were proud of his status as a liar. The jury will not be proud of him.

§ 8.50 Proceeding from the General Question One Fact at a Time Makes the Specific Answer Inescapable

The following line of questions illustrates the point that one fact at a time progresses logically and inevitably, both for the witness and the jury:

Q: When you got back to the apartment you noticed you were missing your lighter?

A: Yes.

Q: You discussed it missing that night?

A: Yes, a little.

Q: It was the lighter you had used to light a cigarette when you got into the van?

A: Yes.

Q: It was a metal lighter?

A: Sure.

Q: You realized that it had spilled from your purse?

A: Yeah.

Q: You figured out it was left in the van?

A: Yes.

Q: And that your fingerprints on that lighter were going to lead the investigation to you?

A: Yes.

§ 8.51 The General to the Specific Creates Interest

This method of questioning can make the mundane issue of the size of the carry-on bag in a drug courier profile case interesting:

Q: Airlines have regulations that are backed up by federal law on what size of bag you can carry on the plane, don't they?

A: Yes.

Q: It has to fit under the seat?

A: Yes.

Q: Or in the overhead compartment?

A: Yes.

Q: And you have been on these airlines that travel in our country?

A: Yes.

Q: There is not a lot of room under the seats.

A: Correct.

Q: The overhead compartments are small?

A: True.

Q: So the bags that were carried onto the plane would have to fit legally under the seat or in the overhead compartment?

A: That's true.

After that line of questioning, each juror can visualize the size of the bag that travelers have become accustomed to fitting under the seat or in the overhead compartment. The idea is to make the jury see, hear, or otherwise "sense" the evidence. They must "experience" that evidence.

§ 8.52   The More Difficult the Witness, the More General the Chapter Must Start

By proceeding from the general to the specific one fact at a time, the cross-examiner is putting the witness in the dilemma of answering general questions before the witness knows where the general questions will lead to specifically. More experienced witnesses, professional witnesses, and expert witnesses are more adept at realizing where the specifics factual goals may lie when a general question is introduced. Consequently, that witness will begin to fight the cross-examiner intentionally at the very beginning of general questions.

There is a technique to disarm this type of witness. It is to start more generally.

In a divorce action, the defendant husband is a CEO of a Fortune 500 company and has been deposed both in this and previous marriages on several occasions. He has testified in domestic relations trials on three occasions, and has been deposed and testified over thirty times in commercial settings. The cross-examiner chose to begin the cross-examination as generally as possible:

Q: Your name is Clyde Simpson?

A: Yes.

Q: You are married?

A: Yes.

Q: You are married with two children?

A: Yes.

Q: You are married with two children and both are boys?

A: Yes.

In a divorce case, it is hard to imagine a more general start than a question concerning whether the witness is actually married.

§ 8.53   Checklist for Rules

Trials are difficult affairs, and cross-examinations are undoubtedly the most tension-producing of its phases. In order to achieve a smooth flow of testimony from an opponent's witness while simultaneously avoiding objections to the form of the question, a checklist is offered.

When the witness becomes unresponsive, when the cross-examiner receives an answer that is contrary to what she expected to receive, when there is an objection or interruption of some kind, or when cross-examination suddenly becomes "bogged down," the most likely explanation is that the cross-examiner is seeking to establish more than one fact per question.

Concentrate on the question that produced an unfavorable response, back up, and do the following:

1. Refer back to the question asked immediately before the last question.

2. Re-ask that question.

3. Identify all of the facts contained in the question that produced the unfavorable response.

4. Then add only one fact per question to the original question, until the fact denied is isolated.

This method may seem slow or tedious. It requires the cross-examiner to remember two former questions — the question that did not receive the unfavorable result and the one that did. This is a hard task to do with only one fact per question. It is worse with multiple fact questions. However, it is the best way to work out of the situation.

§ 8.54   The "Yes" Answer Is the Most Understood Response

The techniques discussed in the only three rules of cross-examination are designed to produce a great many "yes" answers. When the cross-examiner has placed a fact before the witness and the jury through a leading question, the "yes" answer efficiently allows the fact finder to understand what has been proven. The short leading question followed by the short verification is the best teaching method. All answers other than "yes" require more concentration and risk more misunderstanding. That is not to say that in order to be successful the cross-examiner must always get a "yes" response. As will be discussed, there are other ways of making important points even when a witness denies the leading question.

Phrasing a question so that the desired and expected answer is "yes" is a far more efficient method of teaching. Dr. Herbert H. Clark, a psychologist at John Hopkins University, has performed studies that show that the average person takes forty-eight percent longer to understand a sentence that uses a negative than to understand a positive or affirmative sentence.

It is very difficult to comprehend a question phrased in the negative answered in the negative. Example:

Q: That document wasn't provided to the investors?

A: No.

What has the witness said? It is true that with a little concentration the listener may realize that the witness has confirmed that the document was not provided to the investors. But the chance for misunderstanding is greater, as is the concentration needed to assimilate the information. That is not to say that a question phrased in this manner is impermissible, or represents poor technique. Where possible, the question should be put to the witness in such a way that the desired and expected answer is "yes."

If the cross-examiner wants the jury to remember Mr. Kay, a witness who is a liar, she will phrase every question so that the answer must be "yes," so that the jury remembers, "Yes, he is a liar."

Picking up our prior example:

Q: You lied to the police?

A: Yes.

Q: You lied to your probation officer?

A: Yes.

Q: You lied to your wife?

A: Yes.

Q: You lied to the bank?

A: Yes.

Conclusion? He is a liar. If, in a divorce case, the cross-examiner wants the jury to remember that the husband viewed the wife (his client) as a wonderful mother, all questions will be put to that witness in such a way as to receive a "yes" answer.

Q: Your wife was a volunteer when the children were in Boy Scouts?

A: Yes.

Q: Your wife was President of the Parent/Teachers Organization?

A: Yes.

Q: Your wife always placed the children first?

A: Yes.

Conclusion? What a wonderful mother!

§ 8.55   The Technique of Seeking a "No" Response

As noted, there are some specific, important exceptions to the customary technique of phrasing leading questions designed to elicit an affirmative response. There are occasions in which one of the goals of the cross-examiner is to establish the absence of evidence, of things not done, of missed opportunities, or some other scenario characterized by a lack of facts.

One exception to the "yes" principle is the witness that has done nothing to add to this case, from the point of view of the cross-examiner's theory of the case. The cross-examiner wishes to convince the jury to *remember nothing* said by this witness or to think of the witness as a person who said or did nothing. This witness contributed nothing to the case. Remember, people do not understand negatively phrased questions half as well as they do affirmatively phrased questions. By phrasing the question so that every answer is "no," the cross-examiner leaves the jury with the impression that this witness did nothing, this witness contributed nothing, and that this witness was a "zero" in this trial.

Reduce Confusion for Jury and Appeal

There is another important reason to phrase questions to the witness in the negative. If the question must be phrased with confusing language to receive a "yes," do not try to receive an affirmative response. Example:

Q: Isn't it true that you did not take the time to dust for fingerprints?

A: Yes.

That is very confusing to the jury. It is better to ask the "No" witness a series of questions requiring a negative answer:

Q: You did not take the time to collect their specimens?

A: No.

Q: You did not take the time to try to lift the fingerprints?

A: No.

Q: You did not take the time to take the fingerprints from the wallet?

A: No.

Q: You did not take the time to do any of those things?

A: No.

Through this method of phrasing questions in such a way as to require the witness to answer "no," the cross-examiner can accurately and forcefully paint the picture of a witness who did nothing.

The appellate record is much easier to read if the "no" witness is treated in such a way as to give "no" answers. The double negative sentences required to receive a "yes" have been eliminated.

§ 8.56 Seeking the "No" Answer in Order to Marginalize the Witness

There is another technique that calls upon the cross-examiner to deviate from the standard technique of seeking affirmative replies. The focus of this technique is to "marginalize" the witness by factually demonstrating that he has had little or nothing to do with the critical facts of the case. "Marginalization" of a witness is far different **from** the previous technique in which the point of the cross-examination was to show that the witness was involved in the case, but failed to do many important things in the case. In both circumstances the cross-examiner is intentionally seeking "no" answers, but the goals of the cross-examination chapters are different.

The cross-examiner seeks to show that the witness has had no real contact with the important elements of the case. The way to do so is to ask a series of leading questions showing that the witness was not there, did not participate, did not review the facts at issue, or was otherwise inconsequential:

Q: You were not at the meeting of October 9, 2004?

A: No.

Q: You had no role in the selection of the product name?

A: No.

Q: You had no role in designing the advertising campaign?

A: No.

Such a series of questions, though more cumbersome then a simple, affirmatively stated fact, leads to the desired picture of a witness who is a "zero" in the case. A short series of such negatively phrased questions will ordinarily prove sufficient to make the point. The advocate is cautioned that this technique must be used sparingly. The list of things any witness did not do or did not see is infinite. The witness should only be shown to be uninvolved in the most important aspects of the case, and only then for the purpose of showing that the witness was really out of the loop of importance. This technique shows the witness has been called more for show than substance.

§ 8.57   Making Sure to Receive a "Yes" Where "Yes" Is Really the Answer

When confronted with these controlling techniques, some hostile witnesses will seek to evade by attempting to skirt giving the admittedly truthful "yes." Example:

Q: You show $400.00 per month more living expenses now than you did in your statement two months ago?

A: Okay.

Q: By "okay," you mean "yes?"

A: Yes, sir.

Or

Q: You show $400.00 per month more living expenses now than you did in your statement two months ago?

A: Okay.

Q: By "okay," you mean "yes?"

A: Okay.

Q: Yes?

A: Yes.

The witness has attempted to answer the question that deserves a simple "yes" by substituting "okay." It is not a big difference, but it is an important difference. Cross-examiners must require preciseness of themselves and their witnesses. "Okay" is less precise than "yes." The problem is easily rectified. A simple clarification elicits the unambiguous "yes" answer.

Similarly, some witnesses enjoy answering questions with the slang "uh huh" or a nod of a head. Each time, a simple "yes?" or "your answer is yes?" will elicit the required answer. Another way of compelling the witness to answer is to remind the witness that "uh huh" requires translation:

Q: You signed the contract?

A: Uh huh.

Q: By "uh huh" you mean "yes?"

A: Yes.

While this seems trivial, the overriding lesson is that the cross-examiner must strive to teach accurately and consistently. "Yes" is a more accurate answer. Encouraging the witness to respond with crisp answers reminds the witness that there is a system to make cross-examination proceed more quickly. Simultaneously, by rejecting slang, nodding, or other imprecise answers, the cross-examiner applies a sanction that discourages the witness from further giving such imprecise answers.

§ 8.58 "If You Say So" Answer Helpful But Still Requires Interpretation

There are locations within a cross-examination in which it becomes clear to a witness that the cross-examiner is asking leading questions based on facts capable of establishment by the cross-examiner. In other words, the witness concedes that the cross-examiner is correctly relating the facts. Alternatively, it may become clear to the witness that the witness has a poorer memory of the details then does the cross-examiner. In such circumstances a witness may respond to a leading question with the answer, "If you say so" or "I will take your word for it." This is a helpful response, but it still requires interpretation or verification to ensure that the answer is understood as "yes."

The lawyer's response can be a clarifying question along the lines of: "You agree my question correctly states the fact?" or "I have told the truth?" or "That was the truth" or "You will take that as the truth from me?" This will invoke the "yes" answer. This type of answer from a witness is of great importance. More so than a simple "yes," this answer communicates to the jury that the witness is willing to vouch for the credibility of the cross-examiner. The credibility of the cross-examiner is thereby enhanced.

However, if the witness uses the phrase, "If you say so," as a shorthand for, "I don't know, and I don't care to take the time to become certain," this is the equivalent of a denial. In such a circumstance the cross-examiner is advised to turn down the "if you say so" answer and proceed to independently prove the truth of the statement through a document, deposition, or some other source. If there is no independent proof available with which to confront the witness, the lawyer can again resort to the phrase, "By that you mean 'yes?'" It is important that the fact finder understand that the witness has been treated fairly and that the cross-examiner has fairly stated the facts within the leading question.

The same technique is useful with the "No" witness. "Uh uh," a shake of the head, or "I suppose not" all require a further question:

Q: Your answer is "no?"

A: My answer is "no."

§ 8.59   Requiring the Unequivocal Answer for Impeachment and Appeal

Except for the "No" witness, requiring a "yes" satisfies the judge that the witness has responded and makes the answer clear for appeal. At the trial level, it also makes the answer clear for any future impeachment. Impeachment of a witness when the transcript reads "uh huh" inevitably results in the witness saying that the "uh huh" (yes) really should be "uh uh" (no). The same is true with the infamous transcript notation: witness indicated in the affirmative. The witness only has to say that she shook her head and did not nod her head.

§ 8.60   The Techniques of the Only Three Rules Can Lead to Unexpectedly Honest Answers

The cumulative effect of the use of the modern techniques of cross-examination is to encourage the witness to tell the truth more quickly and more often. An additional and very important reward for the use of such techniques is that the witness may begin to concede honest answers to leading questions that the cross-examiner could not independently prove. In other words, cross-examination has proven so successful that the witness is willing to admit even harmful facts in circumstances where the cross-examiner believes the question to be accurate, but cannot directly impeach a "no" answer.

Once the witness is conditioned to rapidly verify the leading questions, the cross-examiner is in a better position to take risks. The cross-examiner can ask leading questions for which no independent proof is available, but for which the she has a good faith basis of belief.

Assume that an important document has been changed. The cross-examiner believes that the superior instructed the subordinate to make the change. However, there are no independent witnesses to the conversation, and the only way to prove the fact is through an admission by one or the other of the two people involved. The cross-examiner may choose to address the issue in this way:

Q: When you came out of the meeting, the memo had changed?

A: Yes.

Q: The meeting involved only you and your boss?

A: Yes.

Q: It was changed because your boss ordered you to change it?

At this point the witness might deny the truthfulness of the assertion. If the chapter has been set out with a logical progression of facts toward this fact, it may be possible or even likely that a jury will conclude that this is precisely what occurred despite the denial of the witness. In a best-case scenario, the witness may see the logic of the progression of facts and concede the truthfulness of the leading question. With the application of sound cross-examination techniques including the employment of the only three rules of cross-examination, the chapter method of cross-examination (chapter 9) in employing the science and techniques of sequencing the chapters of cross-examination (chapter 11), the cross-examiner will enjoy many of these moments.

§ 8.61   Self Correcting the Cross-Examiner's Honest Mistakes

In the heat of cross-examination it may inadvertently occur that the cross-examiner asks a leading question, believing the fact to be true, to which the witness erroneously agrees. Either at that point in the cross-examination or subsequently during the cross-examination of that witness, the cross-examiner may realize that the leading question has misstated the fact. This is a dangerous state of affairs. The situation is markedly different than the example above in which the cross-examiner has asked the leading question, believing it to be true, but depending on the honesty of the witness to establish the fact. But what happens if the witness agrees with the factual premise of a leading question, but that answer is demonstrably erroneous? The erroneous answer, though seemingly helpful, must be corrected by the cross-examiner.

The credibility of the cross-examiner must transcend all other tactical considerations. Once the cross-examiner loses credibility with the fact finder, even the most accurate of leading questions will produce skepticism among the jurors or out right mistrust on the part of the judge. The right to use leading questions does not include the right to intentionally or inadvertently mislead the witness. If the cross-examiner asks a leading question, and thereafter realizes that she has inadvertently stated a fact, both ethically and tactically, the best course is to correct the error. This often happens because the cross-examiner thinks a document says something it doesn't or has mistakenly performed a mathematical computation, or has misunderstood something said by another witness. There is no great harm in making such an error, but there is great harm in trying to capitalize on the error. The best approach is to simply straighten it out when it is discovered:

Q: Your company never made a profit?

A: No.

(Sometime later in the cross-examination the advocate realizes this was erroneous.)

Q: Earlier I suggested to you, your company had never made a profit and you agreed that was true. I want to correct myself. In fact, in the period 1996 – 2003, there was one year when your company did make a profit?

A: I'm not sure.

Q: In the year 2001, your company did make a profit of approximately $56,000?

A: Yes, I think so.

While there are many ways to phrase the correction, the cross-examiner cannot allow a demonstrably false leading question to stand. The opponent will almost certainly pick up on the error and one of the first things that the cross-examiner will hear in the redirect examination is this:

Q: Do you remember when (the cross-examiner) suggested to you that your company had never made a profit?

Once that has happened, it is too late for the cross-examiner to recapture her creditability. The opponent now has the right and the ability to demonstrate that the cross-examiner has posed a leading question suggesting a fact that is untrue. The fact that the witness agreed to it is not of assistance to the cross-examiner. In fact, the fact that the witness affirmed a fact demonstrably untrue serves to undermine all of the "yes" answers given by that witness. After all, if the cross-examiner could get the witness to say "yes" when the answer was honestly "no," how many times did the cross-examiner get away with this kind of intimidation?

It is not worth it. The credibility of the cross-examiner has been most strongly undermined by the actions of the cross-examiner. Conversely, if the cross-examiner discovers that she has erroneously stated a fact, and then expeditiously brings it to the attention of the witness, the credibility of the cross-examiner is salvaged. It may even be enhanced.

The trial lawyer must always remember this is but one case in an entire career. Cases come and go. Some are won and some are lost, but reputations for honesty and fair dealings are made slowly. No case is worth the advocate's reputation. In fact, a reputation for honesty and integrity will likely cause the court to permit the cross-examiner wider latitude in cross-examinations to come.

§ 8.62   The Three Rules — Building Blocks for Advanced Techniques

It cannot be stressed enough that these three rules are the basic building blocks for all future advanced techniques. If the lawyer can perform the three building block techniques in every question, she can advance to the more artistic techniques. Each new technique builds upon the solid foundational techniques of : (1) leading questions only; (2) one new fact per question; and (3) building toward a specific goal.

Chapter 9

THE CHAPTER METHOD OF CROSS-EXAMINATION

SYNOPSIS

§ 9.01   The Chapter Method Defined

There is a structure to the materials gathered and the questions asked within any cross-examination. The term "chapter method" is meant to reinforce the understanding that the cross-examination of any witness is not a flowing discussion with a single unifying purpose. Instead the advocate must think of the cross-examination of any witness as a series of small discussions (chapters) on individual topics of importance to the cross-examiner. Cross-examination in the chapter method seldom flows. Instead it moves from topic to topic, not necessarily in chronological order. It virtually never covers everything a witness might know about the case. Chapters sometimes relate to each other. Sometimes the transition from one chapter to another chapter amounts to an abrupt jump to a completely separate area of the case. What can be said is that there is a beginning and an end to each chapter. The beginning and the end of each chapter are largely mapped out before the cross-examination begins. The chapters are designed to maximize the good evidence available. As a result, chapters do not trail off. They end crisply. A chapter that has not accomplished its purpose using the best facts available is not likely to get better through additional questions. If the best evidence didn't work, the second best evidence or the unknown evidence is likely to produce worse results.

A trial is a book of information. The individual witness examinations are themselves large accumulations of information. (Parts of the books.) The individual topics within the cross-examinations are the chapters of the book.

Each chapter has a designed purpose or goal. The jurors can understand the purpose of each chapter as the cross-examiner assembles related facts into one logical sequence, designed to paint one picture. The chapter method is the polar opposite of the freewheeling style of cross-examination. The chapter method of cross-examination is designed as the optimum teaching model in an adversary system. An advocate working without benefit of the chapter method of cross-examination can establish many important facts, but does so in no particular order. As a result, the jurors must reassemble the facts in order to understand the points being made by the cross-examiner.

§ 9.02 Chapter Defined

Cross-examination is a series of goal-oriented exercises. Each of these individual exercises is a cluster of related facts grouped to establish one particular point useful to the questioning party. The chapters of cross-examination are each composed of a series of goal-focused, leading questions. Any one topic of cross-examination will be presented through one or more chapters of cross-examination.

Of course, within any cross-examination, there are many types of goals, each accomplished by a chapter or a grouping of chapters (chapter bundle). For instance, the goal of a chapter may be to prove existence of a fact or a scenario, to build a sufficient body of facts from which may be deduced a helpful inference, to introduce facts that will weaken the fact finder's belief in a fact or scenario suggested by the opponent, or to establish facts that affect the credibility of a witness. Once the advocate becomes comfortable with the concept that the cross-examination of every witness is a series of goal-oriented questions, the lawyer should recognize that the logical form of a series of goal-oriented questions is a chapter. Each chapter is itself a goal-oriented device designed to marshal together a group of facts that leads the jury to make a favorable conclusion on a particular issue or fact, even if that conclusion is not admitted by the witness. Each chapter has an individual theme that supports the theory of the case. Each chapter has its own beginning and ending.

§ 9.03 The Definition of a Chapter Bundle

A chapter bundle is a grouping of related chapters that need to be used together in order to create a full picture of a topic. A single topic within a cross-examination may well require several chapters. For instance, in a civil suit alleging that a customized computer software program was defective and therefore need not be paid for, the topic of whether the software was defective may require a great many chapters each focusing on one of the various alleged defects within the program. In addition, there would almost certainly be one or more chapters detailing the consequences of each of those defects.

§ 9.04 The Chapter Method Gives the Cross-Examiner Control of the Topics of Cross-Examination

The chapter method is a controlled, pinpoint series of factual explorations of topics selected by the cross-examiner. The chapter method suggests and demands that the cross-examination be a controlled series of questions designed to accomplish well-defined goals. Those goals in turn support the advocate's theory of the case or undermined the foundation of the opponent's theory of the case.

Using the chapter method of cross-examination, the lawyer selects for discussion only those areas she believes to be necessary and fruitful. The lawyer divides those areas into individual chapters. She can then draft cross-examinations that develop within each chapter all of the facts that drive the jury to the acceptance of the goal in that chapter (see chapter 10, *Page Preparation of Cross-Examination*).

The chapter method of cross-examination is built upon the realization that cross-examination is very much a positive endeavor, not simply a defensive reaction to direct examination. Cross-examination in the chapter method is decidedly not an opportunity to repeat or explain the direct examination. Direct examinations ordinarily require the witness to recite in chronological order all of the events of a topic or topics, so that the witness has told an entire story. In contrast, cross-examinations are selective revelations in individual areas of the story. Many of these chapters of cross-examination address parts of the story that have been completely omitted or parts that require greater focus. However, many parts of the story will be ignored because they are unproductive or unnecessary.

§ 9.05   The Chapter Method Gives the Cross-Examiner Witness Control

Not every part of the opponent's story is capable or deserving of attack. There are parts of the direct examination that potentially help the cross-examiner, and there are parts that cannot successfully be disputed. There are other parts of the direct examination that simply do not matter. It is critical that the cross-examiner work from a method that ensures only the topics of importance to the cross-examiner will be discusses.

The chapter method is fundamental to the process of witness control. The witness was called by the opponent. If left to pick his own topics for discussion, the witness is likely to take the jury into areas calculated to help the opponent. On the other hand, far greater witness control would be established by a method of offering leading questions only. By grouping questions into narrow fields of inquiry selected by the cross-examiner, the result is far greater control over matters discussed by the witness.

The chapter method recognizes that the cross-examiner is not going to attack or retell the entire story of the direct examination. The cross-examiner is going to attack, introduce, or highlight only portions of it. She will undoubtedly agree with many facts testified to on direct examination. As to these facts, she may choose to offer no cross-examination. In some instances, some cross-examination will occur as to agreed facts, not to weaken a factual assertion but to highlight these agreeable facts. That is done in order to put those admitted facts into context and show the fact finder that those facts have greater significance than given by the opponent. In such instances, the purpose of cross-examination is not to cast doubt upon such facts, but to make sure that these facts indeed come to the attention of the jurors, so that they can appreciate the significance of those facts in an alternative context — the context created in cross-examination.

Often there are a whole series of questions asked in direct examination that will go unchallenged for a different reason. They simply have no significance to the cross-examiner's theory of the case. The tendency in all direct examinations, both civil and criminal, is to "tell a story." As a result, direct examinations tend to cover much more material than is truly useful or at issue in the case. The skillful cross-examiner will let most of these facts go without comment, as most of these facts assist neither side. But the cross-examiner should still listen for "spontaneous loops" and theme phrases (see chapter 2, *Developing a Theory of the Case* and chapter 26, *Loops, Double Loops, and Spontaneous Loops*).

Modern cross-examination uses the chapter method to both attack the opponent's theory of the case and to support the advocate's theory of the case. Too much of the literature of the field has focused on cross-examination as a destructive device whose only purpose is primarily to attack the direct examination testimony. This is an old-fashioned and overly defensive view of cross-examination. Indeed there are chapters of cross-examinations solely destructive in nature. They are intended to harm the credibility of the opponent's case. It is entirely appropriate to build chapters that expose inconsistencies. As always, this is a selective process. The cross-examiner does not invite open-ended testimony of the witness, but requires the witness to admit or discuss particular facts that are selected by the cross-examiner.

§ 9.06 The Chapter Method Builds Support for the Advocate's Theory of the Case

A witness may well know many additional facts not brought out on direct examination that help the cross-examiner's theory of the case. There are phrases that assist the theory of the case for the cross-examiner. These facts will be exploited, highlighted, and made more memorable to the jury. This is the use of cross-examination as a method of building the cross-examiner's theory of the case.

The selective attack may be positive in nature. That is, the presentation of facts may require the witness to agree with the theory of the cross-examiner's case, or the presentation of facts through this witness may greatly undermine a witness to be presented by the opponent later in the trial. These positive cross-examinations or "constructive" cross-examinations are also selective. They do not tell an entire story, but only portions of it.

There is a "proving" aspect to cross-examination. To the extent that there is a gap in the story being told by the opponent, a skillful cross-examination may insert into the case the facts, which fill that gap and thereby "prove" some further aspect of the story. A skillful cross-examiner may redirect by using those facts presented by the opponent and adding certain facts to them to redirect the conclusions that the jury will form.

§ 9.07 A Chief Advantage of the Chapter Method: Better Use of the Available Facts

There are distinct advantages to adopting the chapter method of cross-examination. Chief among them is that the chapter method encourages a disciplined approach to the understanding and use of facts. It is a system of organization and presentation that will work in every type of case, every type of personality, and in every trial venue whether it is a jury trial, a court trial, or arbitration. The chapter method encourages the lawyer to conduct more exhaustive analyses of the available facts. There is a difference between knowledge of the facts and an analysis of the facts. A lawyer can know the facts without ever having completed an analysis of the facts. An analysis suggests that the facts have been compared one to the other, have been reorganized, and have been grouped in logical packages, so that different or stronger conclusions may be drawn from those same, otherwise innocuous, facts.

A more systematic analysis of the available facts will permit the lawyer to sort the facts in support of a particular proposition into bundles or groupings of related facts. These bundles of related facts (chapters) permit the jury to enjoy a real-time understanding of the significance of facts to the cross-examiner's theory of the case. As a bonus, the chapter method of cross-examination gives counsel the freedom to quickly and easily order and reorder the sequences of the cross-examination (see chapter 11, *Sequences of Cross-Examination*). The chapter method gives topical and emotional control over the cross-examination to the cross-examining party, rather than to the witness. It permits a lawyer to engage in cross-examining hostile witnesses in areas (chapters) of the lawyer's choosing, while avoiding and eliminating opportunities for the witness to maneuver the cross-examination into areas (chapters) of the witness's choosing.

§ 9.08 Purpose of a Chapter

A chapter is a group of leading questions designed to accomplish a goal. The facts within a chapter are presented through the leading questions in a logical sequence. The goal of a chapter may be to highlight a fact, to dispute or weaken a fact, to introduce a new fact, to affect either positively or negatively the credibility of a witness (not necessarily the witness being questioned), and always to allow the jurors to gain an understanding of the significance of the facts in relation to the opposing theories of the case. A chapter might simultaneously accomplish more than one of these goals. A chapter is only worth doing if it advances the advocate's theory of the case or it undermines the opponent's theory of the case. Embodied within this rule is the concept that a chapter that diminishes the credibility of an opposing witness simultaneously diminishes the credibility of the opponent's theory of the case.

The purpose of drafting a chapter is to use the best available admissible evidence to push a jury toward the recognition of a well-defined, fact-specific goal. A chapter is performed to establish one goal or complete one picture. In the process of establishing the goal, the lawyer often establishes many subsidiary points. The cross-examiner is trying to communicate an image. A series of leading questions puts before the jury many facts, each one contributing to the intended image or goal. While seeking to establish a goal or paint a picture of an event, the advocate may simultaneously affect the credibility of a witness. For example, the process of impeachment by inconsistent statement establishes the goal of demonstrating that the prior statement of the witness was more believable. Simultaneously by establishing that the witness has previously testified in a manner inconsistent with their current testimony, the advocate has scored a subsidiary goal of diminishing the credibility of the witness.

A chapter is composed of a logical sequence of questions designed to reduce the lawyer's risk while increasing the comprehension and impact of the evidence. A logical sequence of leading questions within a chapter requires that the lawyer move the jury and the witness through a progression of related facts. It is the job of the cross-examiner to compile the facts that relate to each other so that the jury is not burdened with the responsibility of assembling the facts established by the cross-examination chapter. The goal fact is not necessarily the culmination of all the supporting facts but simply the last fact in the logical sequence of facts on a point. The important concept is that each chapter is an organized sequence of leading questions designed to put into a context the significance of the goal of that chapter. The facts of a chapter are its context. They are the details that flesh out the desired picture.

The goal of a chapter may assist in the establishment of a goal in conjunction with the cross-examination (or possibly the direct examination) of another witness. By way of example, a fact to be highlighted through witness A may achieve its importance only when considered in conjunction with a fact disputed during the cross-examination of witness B. Simultaneously, that fact highlighted during the cross-examination of witness A may indeed affect the credibility of witness B. Therefore, two goals are accomplished. In this way, a single chapter may accomplish more than one goal, even though the information within the chapter only establishes a single goal-fact.

§ 9.09 Breaking Cases into Understandable Parts

"Divide each problem into as many parts as possible; that each part being more easily conceived, the whole may be more intelligible."

Descartes, *Discourse on Method* (1637).

An entire case contains an enormous amount of information. No judge or jury can learn the entire case at once. Even a simple case is made out of an enormous number of separate parts, which have come together to create the issues and events in dispute. The chapter method allows the trial lawyer to divide even the most complex case into individual parts such that the jury can understand those smaller parts and thereby gain an understanding of the entirety of the case.

A crime, a contract case, an auto accident, a divorce, or virtually anything leading to a lawsuit, is not a single fact or event, but a group of facts and events that together form the case. In order to recognize the facts the lawyer will dispute, highlight, or create (put into context), the lawyer needs first to break cases into their component parts so that they may be studied individually. Charts 1, 2, and 4 of chapter 7, *Cross-Examination Preparation System 3: Witness Statement Charts* are all examples of breaking crimes into events.

Below is a representation of a simple homicide, first presented with a very broad-brush overview:

Barbie and Ken have been living together. Barbie says she is broke. Ken suggests she prostitute herself with Ken acting as her pimp. They go out one night. Ken arranges with a man to have sex with Barbie. Before the man can have the sex, Ken kills him. Barbie subsequently reports Ken to the police.

Although this is an accurate overview of the case, it is the barest outline of the case. It is worthless to the cross-examiner, since the lawyer is left with many questions, such as: "What is the nature of their relationship?", "Did they know the man?", "Did Barbie see the murder?", "How did the murder occur?" The facts of the case are too few, too compressed, and too conclusory to be useful in preparing cross-examination.

In order to find the vulnerabilities of a case, the lawyer will first break the case into smaller parts so the facts of each event can be examined closely. Within these facts there may be many opportunities for successful cross-examination, but the lawyer cannot find them without first breaking down this case into its component parts.

Here then is a second, more detailed, telling of the facts:

Barbie and Ken have been living together for a few weeks. Also living with them was Barbie's girlfriend, Midge. Barbie is the single mother of an infant child. Barbie is on welfare and receives Aid to Dependent Children and food stamps. According to Barbie, on the night in question, she was broke, had no food for her baby, and her baby was starving. Ken suggested that she commit one or more acts of prostitution to raise some money. She agreed to do this solely out of desperation.

Ken and Barbie left the house and walked around in a part of Cleveland where prostitutes are frequently contacted. First, they stopped by a hotel where a friend of Barbie's worked. She and the friend had a social conversation, after which Barbie and Ken left.

Barbie committed her first act of prostitution in a deal negotiated by Ken. Barbie and Ken then went to the Beef Bowl where they ate some dinner. They then went back on the street, at which time Ken negotiated a second act of prostitution with a man in a white van. Barbie and Ken got in the van, and they drove to a secluded area. As Barbie was climbing into the back of the van to get undressed, Ken pulled out a knife and killed the man. He then took the man's money, and he and Barbie fled. A few blocks away they got into a taxi and went back to the house.

Barbie was quite upset and cried herself to sleep. The next day she saw a news broadcast on the homicide, read a newspaper report of it, and decided to call the police. She called a police officer that she has known for some time. The cop came to the house and arrested Ken for the homicide.

This second version is a more useful case narrative. A case narrative is a story told as a series of parts. Each part is, in turn, made up of numerous facts. This expanded case narrative allows the lawyer to better view the story as a series of individual facts, but the events still need a further division into fact chapters. In order to find opportunities for cross-examination, the lawyer must further dissect the story as grouping of facts.

§ 9.10 The Development of Chapters: The Process

After the lawyer has broken down the major components of a case into smaller parts, the lawyer should be in a position to recognize facts, groups of facts, and parts that may be suitable for examination. These will need to be studied at their chapter level. A quick method of recognizing potential chapters is to use a part process.

1. Divide the case into its important scenarios. A single scenario may be composed of many events.

2. Divide the important scenarios into their component events. A single good event may contain many good issues.

3. Analyze the component events for issues of assistance. A single good issue may require more than one chapter.

Apply these steps to a commercial case involving an allegation that a corporation hid from its investors its declining financial health. This case is brought by shareholders. This case involves the criminal prosecution of the corporate executives. The overall theory of the case may be that in order to keep its share price up, the corporation deceived the market. But the proof of that theory is dependant upon a great many factual scenarios. One of those scenarios involved a meeting in which an outside auditor reported very troubling financial news concerning the corporation to the chief financial officer of the defendant corporation. Within that meeting, the outside auditor reported many facts concerning several bookkeeping irregularities. Those irregularities were themselves composed of several erroneous or impermissible bookkeeping entries.

Follow the three-step analysis in reviewing a single scenario.

1. A single important scenario:

The meeting between the outside auditor and the chief financial officer.

2. A single component event in that important scenario:

The outside auditor reported on the bookkeeping entries relating to sales of computers to XYZ Corp.

3. A single good issue inside of that one component discussion may deserve development through more than one chapter:

Within the bookkeeping entries of that single sale of computers to XYZ Corp., the following bookkeeping irregularities were noted:

Chapter: The sale was booked the last day of the corporate year, but the contract was not signed until 20 days into the following corporate year.

Chapter: The sale was booked in an amount that far exceeded the actual dollar value of the contract.

Chapter: The computers, which were sold, both counted as an asset in the year-end inventory, and simultaneously the value of the amount allegedly due from the sale of these computers was counted as an asset.

This type of analysis is at the heart of the chapter method of cross-examination. Instead of talking in global terms about bookkeeping irregularities, the cross-examiner produces factual evidence of the bookkeeping irregularities, explaining the significance of each irregularity and allowing the jurors to come to their own conclusion that this was fraudulent conduct.

§ 9.11   The Most Important Topics Ordinarily Deserve the Most Detailed Presentations

The cross-examiner will soon find that the most important topics or areas within a case ordinarily require more than one chapter in order to create the several pictures or establish the several goals within that topic or area. Within each chapter are the leading questions, which minutely form the picture or establish the goal. The most important topics will ordinarily require the most detailed factual presentations. In the above example, the topic of the meeting and fee revelation to the CFO that there were bookkeeping irregularities are absolutely critical to the theory of the case. It follows that this subject deserves a richly detailed presentation requiring many chapters.

The form of the question to the CFO is not: "Did the outside auditor tell you about any financial irregularities?" Such a question is far too broad and deeds control of the facts to the witness for discussion. The form of the question is not: "Isn't it true that the outside auditor told you about some problems with the XYZ contract?" This question, while slightly more specific, provides no clear picture of the facts upon which the case must be built. The correct form of the question is far more narrow. There is a chapter that sets up the importance of the outside auditor. That chapter is constructed using specific facts that paint a clear picture of the definition and importance of an outside auditor. There is a chapter that proves the importance of the meeting. This chapter is constructed with leading questions that provide facts that paint a clear picture that the meeting was important. What is next needed is a chapter that exposes the conversation concerning the computer sale to XYZ. And then there is a single chapter that discusses the entire sub-issue of booking the sale before it actually occurred. This will be followed by a chapter that lays out factually the separate issue of booking the sale in an amount that was inflated. There is a single chapter that lays out factually the double counting of the computers as both an asset and as a sale.

This may seem like it will take a long time to accomplish, but a chapter could be less than a dozen facts. The facts are put into leading questions so the process of establishing a single chapter may only amount to a minute or two of courtroom time. The pictures created by such a detailed presentation in areas important to the theory of the case are truly quite stunning. Too often the backhanded compliment to a good cross-examiner is: "Sure it went well. You had great facts." In reality, the compliment should be: "Sure it went well. You made excellent use of the facts you had."

If there were 50 such transactions, the cross-examiner might at some point begin to shorten the chapter presentations as to each of the frauds. But at first the cross-examiner would establish why these bookkeeping entries distort the financial picture of the company. In order to establish the prosecutor's theory of the case, it is critical that the jury be educated as to why such bookkeeping entries are impermissible. Once these types of chapters are used, it is not necessary to repeat those same chapters in relation to other alleged frauds that use the same pattern. It is necessary that each fraud be given attention. They cannot be grouped into a single chapter called: "Isn't it true you booked a lot of things erroneously?" The heart of the theory of the case is the individual events alleged to be fraudulent and the chapters that reveal the facts at that level.

§ 9.12   Recognizing Events Suitable for Cross-Examination

The cross-examiner may have many chapters, which are suitable for cross-examination, but she still needs to cull the best. A matter may be capable of being cross-examined upon, but still not be worthy of being cross-examined. "Suitable for cross-examination" does not mean that the lawyer must inevitably cross-examine on these issues, groups of facts, or specific facts. It means only that an area appears to be a likely area for cross-examination. In order to be a likely area for cross-examination, the event must have within it a fact or facts that: (1) cast doubt on an opponent's assertion; (2) are likely to be conceded by the opponent yet need to be highlighted or more firmly placed in the proper context; (3) are likely to be omitted in direct examination but needs to be added to the picture, since it assists the lawyer's theory of the case; or (4) reflect upon the credibility of a witness. In all instances, in order to qualify as a potential area for cross-examination, a topic must contain a fact or facts that assist the lawyer in developing her theory of the case. This then is only a preliminary screening of the facts. A more thorough analysis is required to actually deliver the cross-examination chapter.

§ 9.13   Possible Chapters of Cross-Examination Deserve Preparation, Even Though They May Later Be Dropped

After the lawyer begins developing her potential chapters of cross-examination, she will often reserve judgment on some chapters initially thought to be useful. Perhaps the potential chapters do not bear directly enough on the theory of the case or perhaps they are too tangential to be of assistance. Perhaps further investigation needs to be done to discover facts that, if added to the area under study, would make the chapters in this area useful in cross-examination.

As the lawyer begins a deeper study of the facts, she will inevitably find topics that she originally passed over that she now recognizes as useful. Fear not, as nothing that has been done so far in cross-examination preparation is permanent. The addition or deletion of areas of cross-examination is still easily accomplished.

§ 9.14   Events or Areas Versus Chapters

Bear in mind that identifying the events of a case is not the equivalent of identifying the chapters of cross-examination. Creating a list of the events of a case does not create the chapter for cross-examination, as this broad breakdown is still far too large to be studied carefully. A list of the events of a case may well suggest possible areas for cross-examination but the lawyer must find within these events the chapters that require detailed exploration before the jury.

In surveying the events of a case, the lawyer is looking for facts that can be used to build her theory of the case. Simultaneously, the lawyer is looking for weaknesses or in the opponent's theory of the case, i.e., any suggestion that further inquiry is merited. Such weaknesses represent overall concepts of cross-examination and are not in themselves a cross-examination. For instance, on first reading the narrative of Barbie and Ken, the lawyer may well recognize the implausibility of the central feature of Barbie's story: Because her child was starving, she decided to turn to prostitution. Yet the mother has family in the city and knows people who live in the multi-unit apartment building. The explanation causes the lawyer to realize she needs to cross-examine in this general area, although the exact form of chapters of the cross-examination is undetermined.

§ 9.15   Examples of Preliminary Analysis of Chapter Development in a Particular Case

The development of chapters is altogether a natural act for a trial lawyer. It is virtually impossible for a trial lawyer to hear a client's story without beginning to think of the chapters she will need in both direct and cross-examination. Perhaps the lawyer is unaccustomed to recognizing the topics as chapters. But cases always break into chapters and the most relevant chapters ordinarily suggest themselves after the advocate formulates a first draft. The analysis considers the theory of the case likely to be advanced by the opponent. The lawyer need only play out in her head what the trial will look like in its broadest terms. Within each case there are some topics or events that by their very nature indicate their importance to cross-examination and signal the need to formulate a specific chapter or chapters of cross-examination.

In a domestic relations case where the wife is asking for alimony and child support, the cross-examiner immediately knows that there will be a chapter or chapters concerning the husband's assets and liabilities.

In a personal injury lawsuit resulting from a car collision, the cross-examiner (whichever side of the case she may be on) will know that there will be multiple chapters on liability, and, in all likelihood, multiple chapters on each statute allegedly broken that resulted in the collision. Each injury deserves its own development. A single injury may require several chapters in order to be fully explained.

In an eyewitness examination, inconsistency as to items of description will automatically cause a lawyer to begin to think in terms of chapters on inconsistencies. Each area of inconsistency, such as height, weight or, facial hair, deserves its own chapter or chapters.

In a self-defense case, the angry words spoken by the deceased will be recognized as forming the basis for a chapter or chapters on cross-examination. When defending a case built around the testimony of an immunized "flip" witness, the snitch's prior bad acts will, of course, be recognized as fertile areas (multiple chapters) for cross-examination.

In a copyright infringement case, the extent of the copyright will need to be examined for purposes of liability. The damages aspect of the case will necessitate studying the history of sales of the copyrighted materials.

In the defense of a wrongful discharge claim, the work history of the fired employee may require many chapters. If there was a single precipitating event, a single straw that broke the camel's back, that event will probably require the development of several chapters.

§ 9.16   Putting Facts into Context

Not every chapter is suggested by a consideration of the broad outlines of the case. Some chapters only appear after the advocate has engaged in a detailed analysis of the facts. There are some facts or groups of facts that take on significance only when viewed in juxtaposition or comparison to other facts, testimony or exhibits. For example, take the following fact pattern:

A witness who has turned State's evidence asserts that he got involved with the defendant in this crime before the defendant begged him to go along and help on some aspect of the crime, and based on their friendship he did so.

Found elsewhere in the discovery is a debriefing of that cooperating witness where he claims that he hated the defendant, ever since the defendant beat him up in a bar fight a couple of years prior to the crime.

The first paragraph of the story, when viewed in isolation, may be insignificant to the theory of the case, or the lawyer may consider that the negatives of cross-examining on this issue outweigh the positives. However, when the two paragraphs are compared, the lawyer realizes that both events may deserve cross-examination, as they relate to each other and make implausible the witness's story as to why he cooperated with the defendant in this crime. In effect, the greater the witness's description of the bar fight and his resulting hatred of the defendant, the more unlikely the witness's story of why he went along with the defendant on this crime.

In any event, after reflecting on the significance of various facts or areas of the case and determining which may be useful for the exploration in cross-examination, the lawyer moves to the next step, breaking chapters out of the analysis.

§ 9.17   Breaking Chapters Out of the Analysis

The tendency of less experienced trial lawyers is to examine in global terms (headlines, generalities, conclusions, or summaries). Frequently, the less experienced the lawyer, the more global the cross-examination. A global cross-examination is a cross-examination that seeks to sum up a point of view about the facts, rather than establishing the facts with such specificity that the jury can come to that conclusion on its own. An example of a global cross-examination is this question: "You were driving negligently?" The more global the cross-examinations, the fewer facts are used within the leading questions. Instead, the cross-examiner asks the witness to agree with the cross-examiner's conclusion. The fewer facts relied upon to build a chapter, the more risks the cross-examiner runs in terms of receiving unfavorable answers and failing to advance favorable facts. Global methods of cross-examination deprive the cross-examiner of control (see chapter 8, *The Only Three Rules of Cross-Examination*). By proceeding one detailed specific fact at a time, the cross-examiner provides herself self-discipline in moving slowly and thoroughly, but methodically, through the best material available.

In order to move from the global form of cross-examination to the chapter form of cross-examination, it is necessary to break a case into identifiable goals. Each goal of cross-examination will require at least one chapter of cross-examination, though some goals may be accomplished only through a group of chapters known as bundles (see chapter 11, *Sequences of Cross-Examination*). The mental movement from the overview of the case to the narrow focus on finite goals of cross-examination is accomplished by examining cases first as component parts and then examining these component parts of the case as potential chapters.

An event, topic, or component part of the case is a major section of the case. Some sections of the case will be neutral to the theory of the case. Some sections will be positive or favorable to the theory of the case. Some sections will be negative or unfavorable to the theory of the case. Analyzing the case information in another light, some facts will appear to be unassailable. Other facts will appear to be subject to great dispute.

A single large event can in turn be seen as a series of smaller events. Each small event may be worthy of cross-examination deserving of at least one chapter. By using the chapter method, the cross-examiner will analyze more thoroughly the individual facts that may be developed within each chapter. By doing this, the cross-examiner may find smaller, more detailed chapters within a negative chapter that are in fact positive to the theory of the case.

Chapters are built one question at a time, but they are not just one question or one fact. They are a series of questions and a series of facts that lead logically to the one factual goal. One "event" may contain many chapters, many helpful factual goals.

§ 9.18 Even Bad Events May Contain Good Facts Deserving of a Chapter

A criminal defense lawyer is defending a case based on a theory of missed identification. If a witness picks the defendant out of a photo lineup, that can be viewed as harmful to the defense. However, if the witness has been told, before coming down to view the lineup, that the police have a suspect ("we have arrested the man"), and they want to see if the witness can pick him out of the lineup, then that is evidence worth its own chapter. Those facts may be worthy of examination because they show that when the witness went down to the police station, she felt a need to pick somebody out of the lineup because the police had "the man."

Further, when the witness appears at the lineup, if there are six people in it, and two simply do not fit the description given by the witness, the defense lawyer may have two additional chapters on how those people could easily be excluded.

Assume the witness views the lineup for five to ten minutes before circling any number. That unusual length of time may itself be worthy of a chapter of cross-examination. If, after the witness circles a number, the officer says something in confirmation such as, "You've done well," or "Yeah, that's what we thought," it is yet another chapter. The police have clearly indicated to the witness that she has picked correctly. Of course this means the witness should keep picking that individual throughout the remainder of the case. How many chapters could an able lawyer generate out of a single part of the case (the lineup)? The lawyer could have as many chapters as she can find positive or helpful. The lawyer has as many chapters as she has distinguishable goals.

In this example, it first appears that the lineup component part of the case would be negative or unfavorable to the theory of the case. Undoubtedly the opponent will take the witness through the lineup selection during the direct examination. Indeed, the fact that the witness picked the defendant out of the lineup is a bad fact. But a more detailed analysis by the cross-examiner has developed multiple chapters that in fact are favorable to the theory of the case. It can put the opponent in a position of having to explain to the jury why his presentation of the larger issue in direct examination did not deal more particularly with the multiple details of the cross-examination.

In another example, the defendant has been arrested for driving under the influence of alcohol. One large part of the prosecution case involves roadside sobriety tests, a series of physical tests and observations supposedly designed to allow the officer to determine if the driver is likely driving under the influence of alcohol.

One of the standard roadside tests is called the "heel to toe" test. In this test, the officer requires the driver to walk a prescribed number of steps down an imaginary or real line, beginning with the foot designated by the officer. The officer instructs the driver that after taking the prescribed number of steps, the driver is to turn around, begin with a designated foot, and walk another prescribed number of steps. All of this is to be accomplished with the driver's arms at his sides. Officers explain to the jury that this test is a test of memory and a test of coordination and balance. Very frequently the officer testifies in direct examination in conclusory form: "The witness failed the heel to toe test." Or the officer testifies that the witness failed the heel to toe test because of particular enumerated errors: "On steps six and seven the defendant lost his balance and had to raise his arms to stay on the line."

Assume that the defendant cannot contradict that assertion but does challenge the notion that he "failed" the heel to toe test or that the test was even a valid indication of whether he was driving while intoxicated. The cross-examiner might well begin with a study of the terrain where the test was conducted. Was this test ordered on the roadside of a busy highway with 18-wheeled trucks whizzing by at 70 miles an hour? Was this test ordered on an uneven and unpaved shoulder of the road, or on gravel? Was there a real line or only an imaginary line? Did the officer keep flashing all of the lights of his cruiser during the tests? Was the defendant walking toward several sets of high beams hitting him in the face while doing the test? Was it raining or snowing during the test? These and many more facts may be assembled into one or more convincing chapters that factually display the difficulty for any driver of performing this test at this location. Such facts would lead to one or more chapters on the site of the test and the testing circumstances.

Those chapters concerning the site of the test and the conditions of the test do not even touch upon the test itself. If the defendant was told to take nine steps before turning around, and did take nine steps before turning around, then the defendant perfectly passed the memory part of the test. If the defendant was told to begin with his left foot, and did begin with his left foot he perfectly passed that part of the test. If the defendant was told that after reaching the end of the line he should turn to his right before coming back, and he did turn to the right, he perfectly passed that part of the test. If the defendant was told that after turning he was to take six steps toward the officer, and the defendant did take six steps toward the officer he perfectly passed that part of the test. As can be seen, it may be that the advocate must concede some or even many facts to the opponent. But even in a scenario being used by the opponent to his supposed advantage, there may well be a great many facts that assist the cross-examiner. The appropriate method is to examine any scenario in detail in order to find those facts that may be assembled to form a coherent picture of assistance to the cross-examiner. In the above scenario, there may well be one or more chapters concerning the things done right by the defendant that paint a picture sharply at odds with the incomplete picture painted by the direct examination. The cross-examiner is reminded that no fact in isolation can create the vivid pictures created by chapters. The cross-examiner must gather the facts that relate to each other to build a chapter designed to accomplish a single goal. There may well be several goals that can be accomplished by breaking down the heel to toe testing performed by the officer.

§ 9.19 Chapter Size

How big is a chapter? A chapter is only as big as the number of good facts available to accomplish a single goal. Cross-examiners must train themselves to think in greater detail. In court the lawyer can always back up to a more general presentation, but it is very difficult to start with only a very skeletal notion of a chapter and develop the appropriate leading detailed questions at the podium. Within an event there is often more than one point of importance. When there is more than one goal that can be obtained through discussion of an event or topic, it is likely that there is more than one chapter that needs to be considered for cross-examination. It is impossible to decide how far to break down a part or topic of the case until the lawyer understands how many favorable facts are contained in that part. In addition, it is impossible to decide how far to break down a topic of the case until she understands the importance of that topic to the competing theories of the case.

Example: With the advent of video cameras it has become uncomfortably common to see images of law enforcement agents beating a person taken into custody. Examine this scenario for chapters that might be created by the defense, and then for chapters that might be created by the prosecution.

The actual beating of the suspect (other events such as the chase, the stop, the aftermath, the communications are not considered here) is an event that can easily be divided into a great many separate chapters, based upon the portion of the beating administered by each police officer. However, if the lawyer was trying to show the jury the viciousness and senselessness of the beating, it would be possible to separately cross-examine on minute facts concerning each of the separate blows. By stopping the videotape after each blow, the skillful cross-examiner could cross-examine each of the police officers on each blow that was administered.

Having discussed the lack of rationale for that blow, the force of that blow, the aim of that blow, the officer's selection of billy club or kick (and other areas related to each blow), the cross-examination could move to the next blow, which would be the next chapter. That would not take into account any of the other aspects of the case deserving of chapters. It may be said that that is overkill. A cross-examiner might choose to perform any detailed chapters on the particular blows or particular weapons used or particular kicks that followed the movement or lack of movement by the suspect. Certainly, the cross- examination of an officer concerning his role in the beating would take far more than a single chapter called "the beating."

Look at the same scenario in the hands of the defense lawyers representing the law enforcement agents. It is highly unlikely that a defense lawyer would cross-examine the citizen who was beaten to discuss the various kicks and blows administered by the police. However, the defense lawyer may use the same videotape to show in slow motion the various movements or gestures of the suspect potentially reaching for a weapon, becoming aggressive, or any other action that could show that the suspect was never under control and was unwilling to submit to a more peaceful form of arrest. Such a cross-examination would be broken down into chapters. It would be less efficient and less dramatic to perform all of that material in a single chapter titled, "you resisted" or "you were always in control of the situation."

§ 9.20   Draft Chapters Backwards

A helpful way to approach the development of chapters is to engage in a four-step process designed to efficiently move the advocate from chapter concept to chapter completion. It is easy to think of the process in this way: draft chapters backwards. Below is a diagram of the process followed by a description of the four steps:

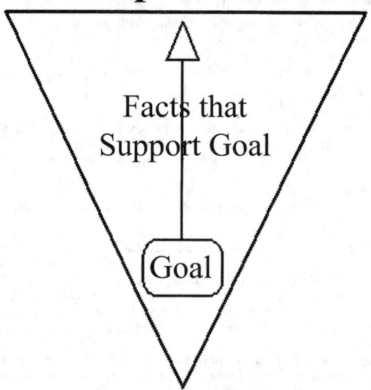

Draft Chapters Backwards

Facts that Support Goal

Goal

One: Identify any one single factual goal to be achieved in the course of the cross-examination that is congruent with the theory of the case.

Two: Review cross-examination preparation materials for all facts that lead toward acceptance of that single factual goal.

Three: Draft a single chapter that covers those facts, leading to the factual goal as set out.

Four: If, while in the course of drafting a chapter an additional worthwhile goal is identified, separate that goal and its supporting material into its own chapter.

Many successful trial lawyers have informally adopted the chapter method of cross-examination, often without recognizing it as a system. This simple technique of chapter building permits lawyers to move with precision toward her goals. Most experienced lawyers will find that they are already using portions of the chapter system. Such lawyers will rediscover that adoption of the rest of the system or formalizing the system will be quite natural and convenient. Less studied lawyers wander from topic to topic and thereby adopt ill-defined goals, never marshalling all of the supportive facts at any one place. This lack of a preparation system becomes apparent during the cross-examination when the lawyer is forced to skip back and forth among areas of cross-examination as the lawyer remembers some of the things (facts) previously left out. Lawyers using a disorganized approach flit from topic to topic, never knowing what has been established and never confident that she has made her point. These lawyers often are interrupted by objections of , "Cumulative" or "Asked and answered," and rulings by the judge to "Move it along."

§ 9.21 The Building of a Chapter, Step One: Select a Specific Factual Goal

Select a single factual goal to be achieved in the course of the cross-examination that is within the theory of the line of questioning.

Trial is not a discovery device. Skillful lawyers do not simply stand up and begin asking questions; they ask them with a well-thought out purpose. The purpose is always to advance the chosen theory of the case or to undermine the opponent's theory of the case.

Trial victories are virtually never the result of a single point beautifully made. Most cases are won through an accumulation of facts that teach a coherent story that is supported by the applicable law. Similarly, the credibility of a witness, or of an entire case is seldom killed with a single blow. The credibility of witnesses and cases bleed to death from a thousand little pinpricks. In cross-examination, the trial lawyer will highlight some facts already admitted by the witness and add certain facts that the lawyer forces the witness to admit, thereby creating for the jury a factual conclusion or inference that favors the theory of the case.

Central to the concept of the chapter method of cross-examination is the recognition that each individual factual goal must be proven separately, even though it may have a very close relationship to similar goals. For instance, if it is important to show the robber had no facial scars, then that individual topic has its own chapter and is written up separately from all other chapters dealing with other aspects of the robber's description. In a non-chapter system, the lawyer would be tempted to approach the podium with a piece of paper or note card that says something like:

Description

blue jeans

facial scars

height

body build

Working from such a poorly organized and abbreviated set of notes, the lawyer is likely to cross-examine on these issues generally, but the lawyer would do so with decreased opportunity to clearly establish her goals. Lack of chapter preparation increases the risk that the trial lawyer will not recall all of the preliminary facts that make the goal less objectionable, more persuasive, and more believable. When the lawyer minimally asks the preliminary questions required to set up the goal, she increases the risk that she will fail to include all the useful information available or that the witness will give an unanticipated or unfocused answer that she is unprepared to impeach immediately.

Through the three rules of cross-examination, the witness is closely hemmed in by the very narrow scope of the leading questions that formed the chapter. If the witness is not handled through leading questions, the witness is more likely to resist giving affirmative answers. If that result were not bad enough, a lack of leading questions deprives the lawyer of the ability to convey to the jury her mastery over the facts. The introduction of facts, which do not logically relate to each other, lessens both the jury's and witness's perception that the cross-examiner is in control of the case. Successful chapters always depend on factual detail. That factual detail is best handled through detailed notes. Through lack of detail and specificity, the trial lawyer fails to reassure the juror that, in matters of credibility, it is safest to agree with the trial lawyer's version of the facts.

§ 9.22   Detailed Notes for Detailed Chapters

In addition, working from inadequately prepared notes decreases the lawyer's opportunity to convince the jury of the theory of the case. Without inadequate notes, the trial lawyer's questioning becomes unfocused and uncertain. When chapters (and their goals) are not handled crisply, witnesses are encouraged to fight back. Often, facts that support the lawyer's theory are omitted under the pressures of the moment. As a result, goal answers are not firmly anchored by all available supporting facts, and jurors are thereby permitted to remain uncertain concerning the trial lawyer's goal-facts.

Take a very common area of cross-examination: A prior felony conviction of the prosecution witness. In order to disarm the cross-examination, the prosecution will elicit from his witness that he has indeed been convicted of a felony. On cross-examination, the cross-examiner is permitted to re-establish that the witness has been convicted of a felony. A rudimentary approach to this issue produces this abbreviated exchange:

Q: Now Mr. Jones, you have been convicted of a felony?

A: Yes, I was.

Q: In fact, in 1988, you were convicted of robbery?

A: Yes.

Q: You got sent to prison for four years?

A: That's true.

In this interchange, it can be recognized that there is adherence to many of the fundamental rules of cross-examination. There is a goal: Establishment of the prior felony conviction. There is questioning toward that specific goal. All questions are in the leading question format. The answer to every question is "yes," and the goal-fact is established: Proof of the felony conviction.

However, in the larger sense, the truncated nature of this chapter results in the failure to establish one goal and the under-achievement of a second goal. While the lawyer has minimally accomplished the informational goal — repetition of the fact of a felony conviction, the lawyer has done so without impact. The felony conviction is a cold fact; it inspires no great inferences. There is nothing particularly damaging in this chapter, save the naked fact of the felony conviction of robbery resulting in a prison sentence.

Furthermore, the better reason for performing this chapter is to damage the credibility of the witness, so as to persuade a jury that this witness is not to be trusted. Perhaps the jurors will not like the witness, and the witness is probably doomed never to be hired by any of the jurors to run their cash register. However, the cross-examination material is rather boring and is so inadequately detailed as to be nothing more than an informational exercise. The summary nature of the chapter has robbed the chapter of its potential emotional impact by failing to generate drama. It fails to illustrate the meaning of this material in the larger picture of the credibility of the witness.

All of these deficits can be overcome when the lawyer recognizes that the topic of the prior felony conviction offers the lawyer more than one chapter's worth of evidence. Each chapter requires a fuller airing. This evidence could be broken into smaller components, and each component should then be fully developed into a chapter. In such a manner, the cross-examiner offers the jury a more detailed, factual context in which to appreciate the significance of what the lawyer is trying to communicate.

In the present example of the prior felony conviction, the cross-examiner may choose to break the prior felony into four separate but related chapters:

Prior felony

(a)   The facts of the armed robbery;

(b)   The deal;

(c)   The sentence; and

(d)   The time served.

Here then is an example of an abbreviated possible cross-examination of those chapters of a prior felony conviction:

(a) *You Are an Armed Robber* (Chapter Heading)

Q: On April 16, 1988, you needed some money?

Q: So you took a gun?

Q: A .44 magnum revolver?

Q: You loaded it with six bullets?

Q: You went into the "Little Mom and Pop" drug store?

Q: At the corner of 6th and Downing?

Q: You put that loaded .44 magnum into the face of a 58-year-old woman?

Q: You threatened her?

Q: "Give me all of the money, or I'll blow your brains all over the wall" were your words?

Q: She gave you her money?

Q: So you didn't pull the trigger?

Q: You ran out of that drug store and ran down an alley?

Q: You were running away when the police captured you?

(b) *You and the Prosecutor Plea Bargained -or- You Got a Deal* (Chapter Heading)

Q: The police caught you running away from the robbery?

Q: They caught you with your gun?

Q: They caught you with her money?

Q: And the 58-year-old victim could identify you?

Q: You were charged with felony theft?

Q: That felony carried up to 16 years in prison?

Q: You were charged with armed robbery?

Q: That means that you robbed somebody using a gun?

Q: And that is exactly what you did?

Q: That felony carried up to 32 years in prison?

Q: But you didn't plead guilty to felony theft?

Q: You didn't plead guilty to felony armed robbery?

Q: Even though you were guilty of both felonies?

Q: Instead, the prosecution dismissed the felony theft case completely?

Q: And then, on the armed robbery charge, they reduced it to simple robbery?

Q: That means that they dropped the gun out of the case?

Q: What the government did for you was to make it just as if you had no gun at all?

Q: Because of that plea bargain, you were not facing up to 16 years on felony theft because that felony had been dismissed?

Q: And you were not facing up to 32 years on the armed robbery?

Q: That had been dropped down to robbery without a gun?

Q: And that smaller crime only carries 16 years?

Q: You were now only facing 16 years?

(c) *The Sentence* (Chapter Heading)

Q: Because the felony theft charge was dismissed by the government, you didn't have to serve a single day for the crime?

Q: For felony theft, instead of serving up to 16 years in prison, you got zero?

Q: For your robbery of a 58-year-old lady, you weren't facing 32 years in prison?

Q: The prosecution cut in half what you were facing?

Q: But you didn't even get 16 years?

Q: Not even 10 years?

Q: Not even 5 years?

Q: In fact, you went to court and asked for probation?

Q: You didn't want to do any time in prison?

Q: You asked the judge to give you no prison sentence at all?

Q: After threatening an innocent 58-year-old woman with "Give me all your money or I'll blow your brains all over the wall," you asked for probation?

Q: You told the judge that you deserved probation?

Q: And while the judge did not give you probation, she gave you only four years as your sentence?

(d) *The Time Served* (Chapter Heading)

Q: Even then you thought four years was too much?

Q: You filed a motion for reconsideration and you told the judge that she should cut your sentence?

Q: But she stuck by it?

Q: So you had a four-year sentence for pulling a .44 magnum gun in the face of a 58-year-old woman and threatening to kill her?

Q: But you didn't serve four years?

Q: You did less than 22 months; 1 year and ten months?

Q: After originally facing 16 years for felony theft and 32 years for armed robbery, you did 22 months; 1 year and then 10 months?

By breaking down the "prior felony conviction," the component part of the case, into more detailed chapters, the cross-examiner has thoroughly proven to the jury why it should not believe this witness, and why this witness has motivation to assist the prosecution. But the cross-examiner also has gone well along the way to creating a feeling that this witness is not right. The way the jury feels about the witness is often more important than the intellectual response.

There are those who will say that they won't be permitted to delve so deeply into a prior felony. For such lawyers, there are a variety of answers: Prepared cross-examiners get more latitude than do unprepared wanderers. Judges reward precision and preparation. Juries appreciate these same qualities. Furthermore, no matter how little of this additional material the lawyer gets in, it is a great deal more punishing to the witness than a bare bones cross-examination that lets the witness off with a naked confirmation (a rehash of direct) of the felony conviction and the four-year sentence.

§ 9.23   Examples of Chapters in a Domestic Relations Case

In a domestic relations setting, which can be a jury or a non-jury trial, the cross-examiner must convince the jury that the defendant husband is wealthy in order to support the plaintiff/wife's claim for child support, equitable division of property, and periodic alimony. Without the chapter method, the cross-examiner could establish what would appear at first brush to be a rather strong admission from the defendant in one question:

Q: You are wealthy?

A: Yes.

In a theoretical world, that admission would be sufficient to sustain a large verdict against the defendant husband in all three areas of financial prayers in the lawsuit (child support, equitable division of property, and alimony).

Trials are not conducted in a theoretical world. They are conducted in front of people who want to feel that they have done right and want to feel that they had sufficient factual grounds to justify their award.

The cross-examiner could break down the overall component of the case (wealth) into many other categories:

WEALTH
(1)   Land
(2)   Cars
(3)   Vacation Home
(4)   Marital Home
(5)   Bank Accounts
    (a)   Nations Bank
    (b)   First Union Bank
    (c)   Wells Fargo Bank
    (d)   Citibank
(6)   Retirement Funds
(7)   Profit Sharing
(8)   Gun Collection

LIABILITIES
(1)   Less Than 10% Of Assets
(2)   No Contingent Liabilities

In this rather elementary breakdown, the cross-examiner has greatly enhanced her ability to cross-examine successfully and to convince the jury of the magnificent wealth of the defendant.

As each of these chapters are more thoroughly developed, they may in time be split into more detailed multiple chapters. For instance, the chapter on cars may divide into three chapters of its own:

CARS
(1)   2004 Mercedes
(2)   1990 Jaguar
(3)   2003 Land Rover

As these examples bear out, the establishment of a goal is enhanced by a systematic approach whereby the overall part, topic, or event is divided into chapters. This remains true whether the finder of fact is a judge or a jury. Each chapter drives toward its own conclusion.

§ 9.24   Example of a Series of Potential Chapters in a Commercial Case

In this next example an investment executive (Sharp) must be cross-examined concerning his failure to monitor an investment. This failure to monitor is the foundation of the lawsuit. As a result, the cross-examination of the single witness would have a great impact on the likelihood of success. The cross-examination preparation might yield more than 200 potential chapters of cross-examination. The actual cross-examination might require a full day and more than 100 chapters of cross-examination. The partial listing of some of the chapters that might be prepared for this witness includes the following:

Selected potential cross-examination chapters for James Sharp:

Job is to do diligence on investments.

Sharp decided which companies were strong enough to be sold to clients.

Sharp's job to monitor safety of ABC insurance company.

Sharp surveyed the insurance market on a constant basis.

Sharp was the only person employed by the defendant to monitor the safety of ABC insurance company.

Brokers were told to call Sharp with insurance questions.

Sharp determined what information the brokers received.

Clients deserved correct information.

Clients look to their brokers for correct information.

Brokers look to Sharp for correct information.

Sharp monitored ABC on behalf of the brokers' clients

Sharp relationship with Kane.

Kane tells Sharp to get clients out of ABC.

Sharp never warned brokers Kane felt ABC unsafe.

Sharp relationship with Rogers.

Rogers told Sharp he was getting his clients out of ABC.

Sharp told his boss about Kane and Rogers concerns.

Sharp learns ABC lost $3 million.

Sharp learns ABC took high management fees.

Sharp learns ABC paid extraordinary dividends to its owners (management).

Sharp learns ABC sold to new owners.

Sharp learns ABC no longer trying to sell insurance.

These are just a sampling of the many chapters that might be prepared for a single witness. The purpose in laying out these chapter titles is to make clear that the cross-examination of a witness is best accomplished in chapters, each chapter making a single point, establishing a single factual goal or picture. The chapters are not complex, though the accumulation of chapters is the best method for proving a complex story.

§ 9.25 Example of a Series of Chapters Necessary to Portray a Complex Character Impeachment

A more complex example of the need to divide the matter into its component chapters and how to make that chapter division is found in the following scenario:

Fact Pattern: The prosecution calls a snitch witness. As part of their plea negotiations, they have promised the snitch not to file a particular case against him. That case involves a complex fraud: The snitch applied for a bank loan to buy an eighteen-wheel over-the-road truck, purportedly to haul coal. He filled out a fraudulent bank application claiming that he had a contract to haul coal. His loan application also listed several small trucks as assets. He got a $55,000 bank loan for the truck and operating expenses. The bank closed the loan, the defendant took the check for the truck to his friend, who signed it as if the friend had sold him a truck. In fact there was no truck. The defendant used a portion of the bank loan to buy insurance coverage on the non-existent truck. He made none of his loan payments. He then reported the truck as stolen and collected on the insurance, which went to repay the bank loan. Through this complex scheme, the snitch made about $50,000 in the swindle.

All of this evidence could be covered as part of a single chapter of cross-examination on this witness's deal. As part of the chapter on "the deal," the lawyer could simply require the witness to admit that he committed a fraud and is getting immunity for the crime. However, the elaborate nature of the fraud is extremely critical to the lawyer's closing argument: This is a person lacking in credibility; that the witness is a person experienced in lying, cheating and stealing; and that this witness is a person capable and willing to mislead jurors as much as he was willing to mislead bankers, insurance companies, and the police who took the police report on the stolen truck. Hence, to milk those facts for more value, it can be broken down into, at least, the following chapters:

Example of a single crime (immunized) planned and executed by the snitch:

a) The Loan Application (full of lies)

b) The Loan Payment Schedule (promises made were really lies, as snitch had no intention of repaying loan)

c) Loan Payments Made (none — no intention of keeping word)

d) $48,000 to Tumbleweed (got friend to sign check as if defendant had bought a truck — a big lie)

e) Insuring the Truck (insurance application is all lies — there is no truck)

f) Reporting the Theft (big lie — even names a real person as a scapegoat, showing snitch's ability to concoct false story blaming real people and places)

g) Collecting the Insurance (snitch solves a lie with a lie — gets insurance company to use its money to repay bank, and thereby bail out snitch who has paid nothing on the loan)

h) Just Keep on Trucking (snitch runs a con to get out of a con and, having cheated everyone, keeps the $50,000 from the original bank loan as profit from his ability to lie, cheat, and steal)

By breaking this one fraudulent scheme into its component chapters, the lawyer shows the jury that in actuality there are a number of crimes (and more lies), including defrauding the bank, defrauding the insurance company, conspiracy, and filing a false police report.

This chapter breakdown permits the lawyer to explore and reveal the snitch's ability to lie convincingly to sophisticated business people and police, all according to a plan that nets the snitch a great profit. In chapter (f), "Reporting the Theft," the lawyer recognized an opportunity to prove through cross-examination that the snitch can use real people and places to concoct a wholly fictitious set of events, which he can then sell to the police. The worth to the lawyer's closing argument of such detailed chapters is incalculably high.

§ 9.26   Give Each Chapter a Title

Each chapter concerns itself with one factual goal. The materials collected for chapters are not miscellaneous, but facts related to each other. The chapter stands for a logical proposition. That proposition is the title of that chapter. Chapter titles create a very organized method of preparing not only cross-examination, but opening statements and closing arguments as well. Because the cross-examiner has identified all of the chapters that are favorable to her theory of the case, she can use the same topics in closing argument. Chapter headings also assist the cross-examiner in jury voir dire.

In the domestic relations example discussed earlier in this chapter, the cross-examiner first viewed a potential subpart of the case as "wealth." This was further broken down into specific assets. Finally, a part of it was broken down into three vehicles. By simply reviewing the chapter heading from the cross-examination, the cross-examiner will be prepared to give a factual opening statement about a 2004 Mercedes, 1990 Jaguar, and a 2003 Land Rover. No longer will the cross-examiner, who is pressed for time, have to speak in abstract or global terms (for example: "a bunch of cars") about subjects that are important to the theory of the case. Both in opening statement and in closing argument, the cross-examiner can be extremely fact-specific by reviewing her chapter headings.

§ 9.27   The Building of a Chapter, Step Two

Review cross-examination preparation materials for all facts that lead toward acceptance of the single factual goal of each chapter.

This stage is dependent upon material discussed in chapters 5, 6, 7, and 8 — all of which discuss preparation systems. This may seem to pose a chicken and egg dilemma. Can discovery material be sorted into useful categories before goals of cross-examination have been decided upon or are goals to be determined after preparation materials have been surveyed? The answer is that the first reading of discovery, coupled with a client interview, yields a generalized theory of the case. This initial concept of a theory of the case suggests the most obvious goals and these goals in turn generate the initial search for cross-examination preparation materials. Then, as the attorney begins to sort the discovery into factual groupings in support of identified goals, more potential goals will be recognized. This in turn generates additional groupings of preparation materials.

In theory, the case would remain the same throughout the preparation stage, but preparation of cross-examination is not a static event with fixed boundaries. As chapters are developed, they will suggest other chapters. As investigative tasks are completed, additional facts will become available that will hopefully make new goals possible, and old goals more likely to achieve (see chapter 4, *Cross-Examination-Focused Investigation*).

As the lawyer recognizes a chapter to contain more than a single goal, she will divide it into multiple chapters, each requiring its own page preparation. As can be seen, the process of drafting chapters for cross-examination is a dynamic system. It constantly leads the attorney in positive feedback circles, from preparation materials to establishment of goals to the recognition of further goals that require further groupings of facts in support of that goal.

The lawyer will find that this process intuitively feels right. When creating chapters, the lawyer can feel the case coming together and can hear herself performing the cross-examinations. As the lawyer digests the preparation materials and then moves the materials into the chapter pages, the lawyer can very accurately gauge the strength of the theory of her case and the weaknesses of the opponent's theory. A lawyer looking at her prepared chapters can find the factual gaps that deserve further discovery or investigation. By being able to focus her discovery or investigative efforts, the lawyer inevitably creates a more efficient discovery or investigation process both in terms of time and money spent.

§ 9.28   The Chapter Method Gives Clarity to an Event

How can the lawyer recognize facts that lead toward acceptance of a factual goal? If the lawyer views a chapter as a very brief documentary film on one small scene, the lawyer is looking for those additional facts that give the scene more depth and texture. The task is to find facts to make the picture more vivid for the fact finder. In cross-examination, ambiguity is the cross-examiner's enemy. Each fact must be placed into a context that will assist the fact finder in understanding and accepting the fact goal of that chapter.

If the cross-examiner desired that a particular factual event remain muddy or testimony remain ambiguous, the cross-examiner would not have cross-examined on it in the first place. Chapters, by their very nature, give clarity to an event. Once the cross-examiner chooses to cross-examine on a particular subject, the cross-examiner has elected to establish that fact goal more clearly than if it was discussed in direct examination.

It may well be that the picture presented through cross-examination will conflict with a previous picture drawn on direct examination, and thus create an ambiguity to the fact finder as to the reality of that fact. The cross-examiner prevails on that issue when the jury finds the picture she has painted to be more vivid and more believable. Facts are the tools for these tasks. The purpose of the chapter is to amalgamate related facts around a central point for the fact finder.

§ 9.29   Vivid Chapters Showing the Strong Factual Support for a Prior Inconsistent Statement Cause Jurors to Accept the Prior Statement as More Accurate

This painting of an alternative picture is the very nature of impeachment by inconsistent statement (see chapter 16, *Eight Steps of Impeachment by Inconsistent Statement*). The opponent has sought to paint a clear picture of a fact that hurts the cross-examiner's case. In cross-examination, the lawyer wants the witness to establish a prior version of the fact with great clarity, in order to blur the focus of the initial picture painted in direct examination. Impeachment by inconsistent statement is similar to a double exposure of the film. The picture may itself have been well defined, but after the cross-examination there is a double exposure that makes the fact finder's vision less certain.

Ordinarily, the cross-examiner's task in preparing a cross-examination is to find facts that make a particular picture clearer for the fact finder. The cross-examiner may choose to highlight a fact, produce a new fact, impeach an old fact. In each instance while doing so, the cross-examiner establishes not only the chapter's factual goal, but also provides the fact finder with all available admissible facts that will lead the fact finder to believe in the accuracy of that goal-fact.

§ 9.30   The Building of a Chapter, Step Three: Accumulating the Facts in Support of the Goal

The most efficient way to construct a chapter is to envision the single factual goal or the picture the cross-examiner is to paint and gather the facts to support that goal. In the chapter method of cross-examination, the cross-examiner needs to draft a single chapter that covers those facts leading to each individual factual goal.

Examine a point that can be established through a single chapter. The opponent has called an expert in the field of psychiatry. In hopes of strengthening the credibility of that expert, the opponent has brought out the fact that nine separate papers authored by the expert have been published in various psychiatric journals. The import of this information is that the jurors should accept the witness as a credentialed expert in the field of psychiatry. Of course, this is not the only qualification of the witness as an expert. There are many other chapters relating to the qualifications of this witness, but the number of publications is certainly an item that assists the opponent in establishing the credibility of their expert.

The cross-examiner may have many goals for the cross-examination of this expert. It may well be that the cross-examination will consume a substantial amount of courtroom time. Nonetheless, the cross-examination must reveal itself one goal at a time. There is ordinarily no single chapter of cross-examination that will dispose of the expert and his opinion, or that will convert the expert into a witness helpful to the cross-examiner's side of the case.

However, theoretically there might exist a chapter titled: "You really aren't a psychiatrist." The exploration of the fact that the witness never went to medical school, assumed a false identity, and committed fraud posing as a doctor, is worthy of more than one chapter. But all of that is largely theoretical. A cross-examiner armed with this accumulation of facts should take a deep breath and enjoy the prolonged chapter method of cross-examining the witness into oblivion. But, that is a very theoretical problem.

Back to the real world. Good cross-examination is detailed and methodical. The cross-examiner undoubtedly has many goals but they must all be taken one at a time. In this above scenario one of the larger goals of the cross-examination is to weaken the credibility of the witness as a method of undermining confidence in the psychiatric opinion expressed by the witness. One of the individual chapters available to the cross-examiner is based upon the fact that none of the nine publications addressed the topic of psychiatric diagnosis. This is a single chapter which groups together the available facts designed to minimize the importance of the fact that the witness/expert has been published nine times. The credibility of a witness is enhanced or diminished by factual chapters. This chapter is an example of that concept.

Chapter: Publications

Q: You placed everything you published in your resume?

Q: You are particularly proud of your articles?

Q: Publishing and article shows where your interests lie?

Q: Doing research in that area helps develop your expertise in that area?

Q: From 1996 to 2004, you have published nine articles?

Q: Every one of your articles was about hospital administration?

Q: In fact, all of your articles were about hospital administration in a tax-supported institution?

Q: Your articles are all about this single narrow administrative issue?

Q: None of your articles addressed psychiatric diagnosis?

End of chapter. That's all there is. There is not a conclusion: "So, you are not really an expert in psychiatry?" The chapter has scored what was available to be scored. That is the value of the chapter. The cross-examiner has assembled sufficient facts to demystify the expert on the single point that his publications mark him as a person whose opinion on a psychiatric diagnosis is very much to be trusted. Yes, the expert might still be credible. Yes, there is a great deal more to do. But the fact that the expert has been published nine times no longer carries the power it once did.

The opponent is less likely to try to use that fact to bolster the credibility of his witness. A jury is far less likely to consider the fact that the witness has been published at all bearing on the credibility of the witness's opinion on the issue of psychiatric diagnosis. There are undoubtedly more individual chapters that undermine the credibility of the witness. Each will be performed. Each chapter will use the available facts to prove a single factual goal. The accumulation of chapters will diminish the credibility of the witness and will undermine the jurors' confidence in the expert opinion. No one chapter is a witness killer. The accumulation of chapters may not be particularly dramatic. But a methodical chapter method approach accomplishes the overall goals of cross-examination are best most dependably.

§ 9.31   Conclusions May Normally Be Disputed, But Facts That Support the Conclusion May Not Be Disputed

Normally, a conclusion sought by the cross-examiner is capable of great dispute. By cross-examining in the chapter method, the cross-examiner can present an accurate picture of facts that compel the fact finder to agree with the cross-examiner's desired conclusion without ever asking the witness to agree with that desired conclusion. This is accomplished through chapters establishing factual goals that are themselves incapable of dispute.

For example, in a commercial case the cross-examiner wishes to show the jury that the opposing party/witness was at a specific time under great financial pressure. The witness will never concede that conclusion. In fact, he can be counted on to vigorously dispute it. Cross-examining in the chapter method shows that there is no need to offer up that conclusory question and engage in the fight that will inevitably occur. Instead, the technique most helpful is to factually demonstrate various aspects of the financial situation of the opposing party/witness at the time in question. Listed below are some of the chapters of the cross-examiner might develop in order to win the disputed issue:

Chapter: In 2000 you borrowed $12 million from Great National Bank.

Chapter: The payments on the $12 million loan were as follows.

Chapter: The money was borrowed to finance your acquisition of the Box Co.

Chapter: The plan was to use money coming from your coal contract to make the loan payments.

Chapter: The value of the coal contract.

Chapter: The payments expected from the coal contract.

Chapter: But in 2001 the coal contract was canceled.

Chapter: In May 2001 you missed your quarterly loan payment to the bank.

The cross-examination would continue with a series of chapters factually demonstrating the financial crisis facing the opposing party/witness in 2001.

As this list of chapters shows, the cross-examiner can best make a disputed point by displaying the chapters of facts that paint the picture. Each chapter is factually accurate. The hostile witness is left with the very difficult task of answering yes but wanting to explain why yes does not matter. The cross-examiner is best advised to ignore the explanations and stick to proof of the facts. It is completely unnecessary to ask the witness to agree with the fact finder's desired conclusion that the witness was under great financial pressure in the spring of 2001. Instead, the cross-examiner must be satisfied that the systematic grouping of facts within each chapter will allow the jury to arrive at the desired conclusion regardless of the witness's protests. The advocate is reminded that the direct examination or redirect examination denial of the witness is merely a conclusion and conclusions can't paint a picture. The cross-examiner's facts are far more vivid and are far more dependable than the mere rhetoric of the witness. What a chapter factually proves is far more powerful than what a witness orally denies in a conclusion.

§9.32 Chapters Are About Facts, Not About Conclusions

If the cross-examiner wishes the witness to establish a fact, it is not sufficient just to ask the witness for the goal in the form of a conclusion. If the cross-examiner wishes to show that the defendant owed a fiduciary duty to the plaintiff, it is largely ineffective to merely ask the hostile witness, "Isn't it true that you owed a fiduciary duty to my client?" Asking conclusions is a poor substitute for proving facts. If a fiduciary duty exists, it exists because factually the elements of a fiduciary duty can be proved through chapters of cross-examination. The proof of fiduciary duty would require a chapter bundle, each chapter designed to factually support one of the legal elements of fiduciary duty. It may be that the witness on the stand can only testify to two of the five elements. That witness would then only be taken through those two chapters. The other chapters designed to factually prove the elements of a fiduciary duty would be reserved for other witnesses who are in a position to respond to those leading questions.

Even if a hostile witness can be counted on to affirm the cross-examiner's conclusory question, the affirmative answer, standing alone, is insufficient to create the factual context necessary to make the point. Asking one question, "You are a sophisticated businessman?" on cross-examination, and receiving a favorable admission is insufficient to persuade a fact finder to make a determination with enough clarity and with enough emphasis to reward the cross-examiner. In order to effectively teach a point, the cross-examiner must provide the judge or jury with the many individual facts that help the jury to be certain of a goal fact. The chapter method marshals all the facts that will assist in proving or supporting that picture or answer. The chapter on a single topic makes clearer the pictures the cross-examiner is seeking to point out.

On the other hand, if the cross-examiner wishes to prove that the witness is uncertain of a fact or did not observe a particular thing, the cross-examiner must marshal all available and admissible evidence that support the inference that the witness could not or did not see a particular thing. For this reason, facts that do not at first appear to be related to each other can be of great assistance in supporting each other once the goal-fact of the chapter has become clearly identified.

§ 9.33   One Question Is Never a Chapter

Facts must be established in sufficient context so that a jury will accept the goal-fact as having been proved. A single leading question can never fully create a dependable context. A group of facts can create context. A group of facts can create a believable picture.

It is never enough just to receive a favorable answer to a goal fact question. The goal must be supported with the strongest available factual details. The factual details that support the proposition give the jurors the strongest basis to accept the inference suggested by a chapter (see chapter 10, *Page Preparation of Cross-Examination*).

Anyone who has tried a case knows the frustration of a juror coming up to the lawyer after the case and saying: "You are a good lawyer, and if I ever get in trouble I will call you, but you had nothing to work with." An equally experienced lawyer will know the satisfaction of having properly developed fact goal chapters when a juror will approach the lawyer after a trial and say: "You are an okay lawyer, but that case was easy."

It is the purpose of the cross-examiner to make the critical decisions easy for the jury by providing such detailed and multiple supporting facts that the decisions seem inevitable or at least fully supported by the facts. The chapter method of cross-examination preparers the lawyer to establish many important facts through witnesses called by the opponent. A fact admitted by an opponent is more easily accredited by the jurors than if the same fact or testified to by a witness aligned with the cross-examiner's side of the case.

§ 9.34   Separate Chapter — Separate Development

In the course of negating, highlighting, or creating a goal-fact, the lawyer must almost always first establish many subsidiary or supporting facts. For instance, a simple goal of establishing that a witness saw a blue car requires not simply the question, "You saw the blue car?" Example:

Q: You were standing on the street corner?

A: Yes.

Q: It was daylight?

A: Yes.

Q: You saw a car?

A: Yes.

Q: It caught your attention at that moment?

A: Yes.

Q: The car was blue?

A: Yes.

This group of leading questions requires the witness to admit all four facts so as to more firmly establish the goal-fact that the witness saw a blue car. This method of questioning is discussed at length in chapter 8, *The Only Three Rules of Cross-Examination*. The short introductory questions are designed to flesh out the context for the goal fact. Having introduced the supporting material, the lawyer has more firmly established the accuracy of the fact that the car was indeed blue.

§ 9.35   Drafting Chapters: Putting Facts into Context

A goal can be a literal fact. But often the goal is to create within the jury a "feeling" about a fact. The "fact" is itself made up of innumerable subsidiary or supporting facts. For instance, in a chapter called, "Promises Made by the Government," the literal fact is the criminal witness got a deal in exchange for immunized testimony. The witness undoubtedly will concede that and may well have done so on direct examination. The lawyer's more significant goal is to compel the jurors to be skeptical of this witness's testimony.

What then is the lawyer establishing with her chapter? The lawyer is first putting the "fact" of a deal into context. A well-drafted chapter fills out for the fact finder the context in which the fact matters.

Assume a defendant is arrested for theft, but no stolen money is found on him. This is a fact. It could be the single most critical fact in the case or it could be of no great significance, depending on the context. Was the defendant approached moments after the bank robbery because he fit the description of the bank robber? Was the defendant arrested four weeks later after a photo identification? Only by knowing the context of the fact can the lawyer, and ultimately the jury, appreciate the significance of the fact.

To understand the significance of a fact, the lawyer must study it in its context. The chapter method provides the context for each factual goal. In the chapter, "Promises Made by the Government," the goal-fact may be the deal. But perhaps the context the defense lawyer hopes to exploit is the lopsidedness of the deal. The witness was caught red-handed. The witness was facing an enormous prison sentence and he no longer needs to fear that prison sentence because prosecutors promised to take care of it for him. These numerous subsidiary facts must all be established in order to provide a context in which the goal-fact can be appreciated.

Some chapters have a second, and equally important, purpose: Establishing a feeling or an emotional reaction to the facts. This concept that facts generate feelings has been discussed in the materials dealing with the dominant emotion of the case (see chapter 2, *Developing a Theory of the Case*). Generating a particular emotion about the facts is an additional goal of some chapters.

For example, "Promises Made by the Government" is as much designed to upset the jury concerning the dealings between the prosecutors and the drug dealing witness, as it is to convey the factual information of the chapter. In fact, there are instances in which it could be argued that the emotional goal is superior to the factual goal. When the lawyer can require the snitch to spell out how he lied, cheated, and deceived people, proving how the snitch accomplished his crime is subsidiary to the goal of convincing the jury of his complete lack of scruples and his genius at manipulating facts and inventing lies. The emotional reaction by the jury will be felt long after the factual reasons fade away.

§ 9.36   The Building of a Chapter, Step Four: If, While Drafting a Chapter, an Additional Goal Is Identified, Separate That Goal and Its Supporting Material into Its Own Chapter

By reading the foregoing material, it is obvious that chapters are developed by breaking events or issues into smaller goals that become identified as chapters. When is any subject sufficiently broken down? The answer is mathematical, but the mathematical equation is an expression of the theory of the case.

Trial mathematics:

- Every topic has a value.

- That value can range from virtually zero to supremely important.

- To recognize the value of a particular topic, consider how much that topic helps the cross-examiner's theory of the case or how much that topic undermines the opponent's theory of the case.

- A topic having the greatest impact on the opposing theories of the case deserves the greatest time and attention.

An example of the application of this formula will undoubtedly assist. In an earlier example, the cross-examiner needed to establish that the opposing party was in deep financial trouble in the spring of 2001. If the establishment of that financial crisis would have a great impact on the competing theories of the case, then the available material demonstrating that financial crisis is deserving of a multi-chapter presentation. That portion of the cross-examination is deserving of great time and attention. A bank loan requiring periodic payments would get its own chapter. A missed payment in that time frame would deserve its own chapter. The forced sale of the witness's assets at distress prices would deserve its own chapter. If there are more individual items or events that can assist the cross-examiner in proving or portraying the financial crisis in the spring of 2001, then the cross-examiner needs to develop more chapters that use those facts.

If a bank loan entered into by the witness years before has some bearing on the financial plight of the witness in 2001, then that bank loan deserves a chapter of cross-examination as well. But if a bank loan entered into years before has no bearing on the financial plight of the witness, then that loan deserves no mention. Even if that loan was defaulted on 10 years ago, if that fact or event has no relevance to an issue in this case, then it is undeserving of time on cross-examination. If, on the other hand, the witness were to testify on direct examination or on cross-examination that he had excellent credit and had never defaulted on a loan, then a "default" chapter would suddenly be of relevance.

§ 9.37   In Matters of Importance, a More Exacting Breakdown Is Preferred

Empirical observation teaches that trial lawyers will err on the side of not analyzing and breaking down facts. Having developed a theory of the case and understood the opponent's theory of the case, the trial lawyer is better equipped to recognize the topics of greatest importance. It is suggested that trial lawyers break down the most important topics in great detail. The best evidence deserves the greatest time and attention in the trial. It is a very simple process to decide to combine two potential chapters into one larger chapter on very short notice, rather than attempt to break down one chapter into two smaller chapters on short notice.

The domestic relations example earlier that broke down the general topic of the divorce case concerning the husband's "wealth" into various assets is an illustration of how the trial lawyer will identify additional goals as a chapter is being developed.

First, while analyzing the case, the lawyer identifies the large topic or general category of "wealth." Upon reflection, the lawyer breaks it down further into various assets including "cars." Given the fact that the trial lawyer wants to provide transportation to his client in one of the three cars available, and given the fact that each of the cars is valued in excess of $40,000, the lawyer then decides to break the chapter down further into three individual chapters. When this is done, all of the supporting material or factual information concerning each chapter (each car in this case) is placed into that individual more detailed chapter.

In the criminal example concerning the lineup, it can be seen that even general chapters that appear to be negative (unfavorable to the trial lawyer's theory of the case), often bear fruitful analysis that supports the theory of the case when the details are more closely examined and analyzed.

In chapter 10, *Page Preparation of Cross-Examination*, the trial lawyer learns what a chapter looks like when written out. When the chapter method is combined with the page preparation method, the trial lawyer gains a much firmer visual understanding of the chapter method.

When in doubt, analyze the material more closely for a more refined focus. Events are understood only in a context. And jurors make decisions between two competing inferences by comparing the facts that support each alternate inference.

§ 9.38   How to Avoid Spending Time on Unproductive Chapters

Can the lawyer break the evidence down too far and into too much detailed information? Yes, the breakdown can become too small. What is deserving of the greatest attention is the evidence that has the greatest impact on the theory of the case. A chapter having no bearing on the opposing theories of the case has no business being done at all. If an event happened on Wednesday, or it happened on December 9, but the day or date have nothing to do with the contrasting theories of the case, there is no reason to discussed those facts and certainly no reason to develop a chapter concerning the day or date.

If the educational background of the witness has no bearing on the case or on the credibility of that witness then there is no reason to discuss that background. There are many areas of discovery that can be recognized before trial as having no impact on the case. One of the advantages of the chapter method of cross-examination is that it allows the lawyer to skip over large amounts of fact that can be analyzed as undeserving of attention at trial.

Time not spent preparing for irrelevant issues is time saved. That time can then be used to more fully develop chapters that matter to the theory of the case. When faced with a potential topic of cross-examination, the cross-examiner need only compare that topic to the competing theories of the case and ask what difference it would it make if that topic were established well? In order to be of value, the topic or proposed chapter must have impact on the two competing theories of the case or on the credibility of a witness. Topics or chapters that accomplish none of these things are not worthy of the cross-examiner's time and attention.

Chapter 10

PAGE PREPARATION OF CROSS-EXAMINATION

SYNOPSIS

§ 10.01   One Chapter = One Page

A chapter is a sequence of questions designed to establish a goal. It there-fore makes sense that each chapter of cross-examination be composed sepa-rately from every other chapter. The chapter method of cross-examination is weakened by drafting multiple chapters on a single page. The best form of preparation for chapter method cross-examination is to devote one page to each chapter.

By drafting no more than one chapter per page, the lawyer encourages her-self to fill out the chapter with all the facts necessary to put the goal into its context. The lawyer pushes herself to fully develop the important facts in each chapter. Sometimes the sheer embarrassment of looking at a half-empty sheet of paper drives the lawyer to think of other facts that might enhance the chapter. When a chapter runs more than one page, the lawyer is often forced to recognize that she really has multiple chapters that are being unprofitably combined.

A corollary to the rule that each chapter deserves its own page is that no chapter should require two pages. Undoubtedly there will be occasions when a topic requires multiple chapters (a chapter bundle). But when the strong facts consume more than one page it is very likely that the material would be better presented as two separate chapters with two smaller goals. Another practical problem with having a chapter longer than a page or placing two chapters on a page is that in the heat of a courtroom battle, it is easy to forget the follow-up questions on a second page.

Turning a page seems the easiest thing in the world until an opponent is objecting, a hostile witness is attempting to evade, and the judge is becoming impatient. When two or more chapters are placed on a single page, it is more likely that material will be omitted or addressed in the wrong order. Chapters need to be separately drafted for another distinct reason: Individually-drafted chapters can be reorganized in infinite combinations to create the most power-ful sequence of presentation (see chapter 11, *Sequences of Cross-Examination*). When chapters are separately drafted and placed one per page, the lawyer can add, delete, and change the order of chapters at any time prior to and even during trial. When multiple chapters are combined on a single page, the lawyer has locked herself into a sequence of presentation. Some lawyers might scribble a note on such a page indicating that a certain chapter is to be deleted or performed later. However, in the heat of trial, it is hard enough to do what was planned. It is almost impossible to recall what the lawyer intended to skip and which subject she intended to revisit. Multiple chapters on a single page encourage the lawyer to cover each chapter even if the lawyer later determines that one of those chapters should be abandoned.

This description implies each page is a series of leading questions all ordered around a single chapter and leading to a specific goal. By posing these leading questions to the witness, the lawyer seeks to compel a series of "yes" answers, thus establishing the goal of that chapter. Establishing the goal of the chapter in turn enhances the theory of the case.

§ 10.02 Multiple Chapters on One Page: A Recipe for Confusion

When two chapters are placed on one page and the lawyer attempts to integrate the direct examination, exhibits, and other "happenings" at trial, the page becomes a series of arrows, scratched-out directions, a list of priorities and stage notes that are indecipherable. This becomes confusing and frustrating at trial:

Chart 1

Source	Questions	Notes
	Chapter I. Good Father	
Deposition 43/13	"pretty good"	"OK"
Deposition 44/1	"certain activities"	
Deposition 2/9	"thought of self"	
Deposition 116/8	"worked long hours"	
	Chapter II. Good Husband	
Deposition 16/14	"most of the time"	"Not good"
Deposition 16/22	"better with children"	
		Photo of Family

Chart 2

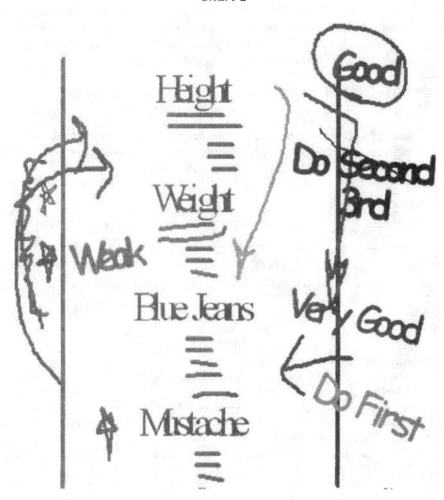

These two examples of pages of cross-examination (Chart 1 and Chart 2) are samples of the confusion that comes from the failure to adopt a cross-examination preparation system. There is so much going on the courtroom that the last thing the advocate needs is the stress of trying to remember what she was thinking when she wrote those cryptic notes. The advocate is warned: More colored pens will not make a system. Colored tabs on the side of pages will not improve the situation but instead create yet another confusing system within a system.

§ 10.03   Prepared Pages of Cross-Examination: It's the Show, Not the Safety Net

Many lawyers believe that it is possible to perform good cross-examinations without a script. This is undoubtedly true. It is also possible for a visitor to find her way in a city without a map, but it would be quicker and safer if she had one. It would be even easier if she had studied the map and outlined a route in advance.

The page preparation of cross-examination ensures that the lawyer will move toward a single goal at a time and that she will present to the fact finder the best facts on that topic. Again, without a prepared page of cross-examination the lawyer is more likely to ask the goal questions without filling in all the available supporting facts. In addition individual page preparation is the best technique of ensuring that the lawyer will complete a selected goal before moving to another goal.

The lawyer works from a script in cross-examination, so she can avoid the "Oh no!" syndrome. All attorneys who have worked without full preparation of their cross-examination chapters have suffered this result. The first variation of the syndrome: The lawyer has done what she perceives to be a brilliant cross-examination. The witness has been wrung dry of useful information. The lawyer confidently tells the judge, "No further questions." The witness is excused. After he has left the courtroom, the lawyer returns to counsel table where she looks down at her list of things she was to cover and sees one or more that she forgot completely to address. The lawyer says to herself, "Oh no!" (or worse).

The syndrome also manifests itself at or near the time of closing argument. The trial has concluded and the lawyer is drafting final notes and mentally rehearsing her summation. The lawyer realizes that she has forgotten to put into evidence a fact or a chapter upon which she intended to rely on closing argument. Now it is too late. A chapter that the lawyer failed to get into evidence is a group of facts that do not exist for closing argument. As a result, the case has been weakened by the advocate's own actions, not the actions of opposing counsel. Who knows what would have been the added effect of the fifth point had the lawyer just taken the time to outline the chapters properly.

Less-than-fully prepared cross-examinations overlook facts. Questions not asked are the equivalent of facts thrown away and arguments squandered. Inevitably, even the best-prepared lawyers will forget to write some things and ask some things in trial. This is the penalty all lawyers pay for being human. The lawyer does not need to add to that list of errors and omissions those things that the lawyer could have cured through thorough preparation of a script for each chapter of cross-examination.

§ 10.04 Thinking of Cross-Examination in Terms of Chapters

Each chapter is a finite goal. For instance, take a personal injury case about a car collision. If the lawyer has done her topic cards and finds that she has an important inconsistency concerning what the driver saw immediately before the accident, and that previous version is more helpful than a later version given by the same witness, there will be a cross-examination chapter on what the driver saw immediately before the accident. This will be drafted as a single chapter on a single page.

Further assume that the witness heard something of importance immediately before the accident. There will not be a chapter titled: "What the driver saw and what the driver heard immediately before the accident." Those will be two separate chapters. The lawyer must completely finish one chapter in her cross-examination before going to another chapter. In order to make sure that the lawyer has done this, she drafts a single chapter and dedicates a sheet of paper to each chapter. The chapter has a chapter heading at the top of the sheet. It has every question on that chapter in an appropriate order on that single page.

§ 10.05   The Three Critical Questions That Must Be Instantly Answerable by the Cross-Examiner

Cross-examination is mentally and physically exhausting affair. And that's on a good day. There are a lot of decisions to be made during the cross-examination. In the midst of all of the stress, the advocate is trying to guide a hostile witness through a large quantity of facts with the intent of proving several very important goals. What is most needed is a cross-examination system and set of techniques that allows the cross-examiner to remain focused and in control of the cross-examination regardless of the situation. At any moment in the cross-examination the cross-examiner must be able to answer the three fundamental questions of cross-examination:

1. Where am I?

2. Where am I going?

3. How am I going to get there?

Each of these critical questions will now be examined. The techniques of page preparation of cross-examination will answer each question fully.

First: Where am I? Cross-examination is a series of goal-oriented exercises. At any point in the cross-examination the advocate needs to be able to immediately determine what goal she is developing. "Where am I?" represents that moment when the cross-examiner either shifts focus to a new chapter or loses focus due to some distraction. Because the cross-examination does not necessarily proceed in chronological order, and because the cross-examiner ordinarily wishes to avoid certain topics, cross-examinations are not a stream of consciousness event (see chapter 11, *Sequences of Cross-Examination*). The cross-examiner has planned the chapters that she wishes to cover and placed them into persuasive sequences. The cross-examiner does not have the time, energy, or need to memorize either the chapters or the sequences in which they should be used. Instead, every chapter will carry its title at the top of the page. Each chapter will be confined to only one page. Two chapters will never appear on the same page. In order to answer the question, "Where am I in this cross-examination?" the cross- examiner need only glance at the top of the page and she will be instantly oriented to the subject she for cross-examination.

Next: "Where am I going?" This question is shorthand for the goal the cross-examiner is seeking in the chapter. It identifies the goal. Often the goal is signified by the title at the top of the page, such as "Pullman had no background in insurance" or "the formula in the software is taken directly from the IRS code." But the question "where am I going" also signifies that there is an ending point.

Finally: How am I going to get there? This is an extremely difficult question for the unprepared cross-examiner to answer. It is the failure to have an answer to this question that causes cross-examination to meander and to open up areas that are harmful to the cross-examiner. But through the technique of page preparation the cross-examiner knows at any moment exactly how she intends to get the information called for by this chapter. The facts to be adduced are listed on the page itself. No matter how stressful the courtroom environment is, the cross-examiner need only look down to remind herself of the leading questions to be asked and to follow that script to its completion. Of course there is room to change questions, add facts, drop questions that seem unnecessary, and customize the chapter based on the circumstances. But these changes in judgments become so much easier because the cross-examiner has a firm starting point or outline of how to conduct this chapter of cross-examination.

Armed with the chapters of cross-examination and using the page preparation techniques in this chapter, the cross-examiner can instantly answer the three questions: Where am I? Where am I going? How do I get there? The cross-examiner will therefore always feel grounded. Knowing the answers to these questions allows the cross-examiner to think about more important issues, like those that can only be decided as the cross-examination occurs. A lawyer who feels grounded at the podium is a lawyer in control of the case.

§ 10.06 Degrees of Written Chapters: Room for Flexibility

It is appropriate to note here (and it will be demonstrated in several examples) that there are different schools of thought on how to prepare the page for cross-examination. Most attorneys will accept the technique that one chapter = one page. Where possible, every question should be sourced. Where differences occur is the degree to which the details of the cross should be written.

Some advocates are more comfortable writing every key factual question they intend to ask in each chapter of the cross-examination. Devotees to this school prefer thorough preparation and absolute indexing of each question. Certainly these attributes are helpful and desirable at trial.

In contrast, some lawyers believe that outlining thoroughly and sourcing every individual question is the preferable method. This method encourages flexibility and spontaneous creativity in the wording of individual questions within the outline of the chapter. It sacrifices a degree of preparation, but is not stifling.

Neither school is right or wrong. Each lawyer, depending on her personality, style, and experience will locate the method that works best for her. The lawyer should find her comfort zone. That is not to say that the lawyer must subscribe to only one of these two schools. Certainly one school of thought can be applied to one witness and the other to the very next witness. The critical factor is that some substantial planning of the content of each chapter is called for in order to maximize the opportunities available in cross-examination.

§ 10.07   Form of the Columns on the Page

When it comes to drafting the page of facts or outline of questions within certain parameters to be discussed, the choice is up to the individual. As a starting technique it is advantageous to divide each page into three unequal columns: One wide column for the questions or outline of the questions to be asked, a second narrow column for the source of the answer, if known, and a third column for tactical comments, notes on use of exhibits, stage directions, quotes from direct examination, and quotes from prior cross-examination.

In setting up the page, the cross-examiner should choose the order of columns that feels best. After experimentation, one or the other method will seem more natural. One method uses the column on the left side of the page for the source, the larger middle column is used for the questions or outline of questions for cross-examination, and the column on the right hand of the page is reserved for tactical comments and quotes. See method 1, below.

An alternative page format uses the column on the left side of the page for tactics, a narrow middle column for sourcing, and the right hand column for the cross-examination questions or outline of questions. See method 2, below.

Lawyers are encouraged to use either format or any other format with which they are comfortable.

Four samples of alternative page layouts

Method 1

Bennett (Witness)		
Sourcing	HEIGHT (Chapter Title)	Tactics
	(Leading Questions)	

Method 2

Bennett (Witness)		
Tactics	Sources	HEIGHT (Chapter Title)
		(Outline of Questions)

Method 3: Some lawyers drop the source column altogether and simply put the source in parentheses following the leading question or outline of questions. See method 3 below.

Method 3

Bennett (Witness) HEIGHT (Chapter Title)	Tactics
You were face-to-face with the robber? (Leading Questions) (77:9) (Source)	

Method 4: Some lawyers who have the benefit of great quantities of discovery find that their courtroom presentations are so heavily dependent on their pre-trial preparation that any notes they might take in direct examination are of minor consequence only. They therefore develop their cross-examination pages using only a column for the facts they wish to assert and the column for the sources, where available.

Method 4

BENNETT **CROSS-EXAMINATION**	
SOURCE	HEIGHT (Chapter Title)
	(Leading Questions)

§ 10.08 Leading Questions Format

Each cross-examination chapter is a series of leading questions. The importance of preparing cross-examination as a series of leading questions cannot be overemphasized (see chapter 8, *The Only Three Rules of Cross-Examination*). A page of cross-examination questions is a page of answers. Hence, what the lawyer is really drafting is not a series of questions, but factual statements or facts the lawyer wishes to establish. It is the lawyer's desire that the witness agree with these factual statements. In addition, the lawyer has many techniques that damage a witness who answers other than with a "yes" (see chapter 19, *Controlling the Runaway Witness*, chapter 26, *Loops, Double Loops, and Spontaneous Loops*, and chapter 16, *Eight Steps of Impeachment by Inconsistent Statement*).

Below is an example of the questions column in a single chapter in a multi-chapter cross-examination where the general theory of the case is misidentification. This chapter concerns itself only with the witness's (victim's) version of the height of the robber:

Height of the Robber (Chapter title)

Q: You were face-to-face with the robber?

Q: You were standing directly across the counter from him?

Q: The robbery took several minutes?

Q: You looked the man up and down?

Q: And you noticed you had to look up at him?

Q: You are 6' tall yourself?

Q: You found yourself looking up at a man taller than you?

In a driving under the influence case, where the theory of the case is that improper subjective observations are being coupled with unreliable objective evidence, the next example shows the question column of a single chapter on *one* of the inaccuracies of the Breathalyzer:

The 2100: 1 Ratio is only an Average (Chapter title)

Q: You are certified as an Intoxilyzer operator?

Q: You must take a course to get that certification?

Q: Requirements of that course are set out by the Health Department?

Q: Their rules determine what's in the course?

Q: Principles of breath testing and physiology of breathing are taught in that course?

Q: You know that it is the alcohol in blood that affects you?

Q: Breath testing is a way of trying to find out how much alcohol is in the blood?

Q: The reason it assumes that is because there is an average relationship of breath to blood in people's bodies?

Q: But of course people's bodies are all different?

Q: If you took the average height of every body in this room you might come up with 5'6"?

Q: That doesn't mean everyone is 5'6"?

Q: In fact, most people aren't 5'6"?

Q: They're either more or less?

Q: Same with breath-to-blood ratio?

Q: The Intoxilyzer assumes everybody's breath-to-blood ratio is 2100 to 1?

Q: But 2100: 1 is just an average?

Q: Most people are either higher or lower?

Q: But Intoxilyzer assumes everybody is 2100 to 1?

Q: If a particular person's breath-to-blood ratio is less than 2100 to 1, the Intoxilyzer will give an inflated reading of the BAC?

Q: You have no idea if the defendant's breath-to-blood ratio is 2100 to 1?

The next example is drawn from a sexual assault case. The complaining witness is a 16-year-old female who alleges that her schoolteacher had sex with her on numerous occasions. The defense theory is that the complaining witness is psychologically disturbed and seeking attention. She is seeking revenge on a teacher who was friendly to her but now is no longer friendly.

This chapter immediately follows a chapter in which the expert witness has described the victim as complaining about a previous (claimed) rape while the victim was in the hospital. This previous claimed rape is now conceded by the victim never to have occurred.

The general goal of this chapter is to show that the complaining witness suffers inadequately treated victimization fantasy.

Victimization Fantasy (Chapter title)

Q: Fair to call this (falsely alleged hospital rape) a victimization fantasy?

Q: A very intense and very real one?

Q: A psychological name for it is a dissociate episode?

Q: Certainly possible that this is not the only time in E's life when she has had one of these?

Q: In fact, you know about other times that it has happened to her?

Q: One of the reasons you had for keeping her in the hospital when you evaluated her progress on August 16 was that she might have more of them?

Q: If she's going to have problems perceiving reality, you would rather have her in the hospital?

Q: But you had to let E out of the hospital on September 6, 1991?

Q: The reason for that was her insurance coverage had run out?

Q: You really would have liked for her to stay in the hospital longer?

Q: You can't cure someone of borderline features and problems with reality in three weeks, can you?

Q: It is possible for someone to have these episodes of blurring fantasy and reality when there isn't a psychologist around to convince them it was unreal?

Q: You agree that if a person had a fantasy that she believed was true and rather than anyone telling her it was unreal, people told her it was true, her belief that it was true could solidify?

The fourth example comes from a commercial case. In this example, a high-ranking employee had written a letter citing facts concerning a product, stating the product was defective and denouncing the conduct of his company. That letter has now come to light through discovery, and at trial the employee will attempt to back away from the letter. This particular chapter attempts to portray the very contentious meeting that occurred between the employee and his superior as a result of the letter.

The Ron Lane Meeting (Chapter title)

Q: Ron Lane was angry?

Q: He told you that your letter did not make people in Chicago headquarters happy with you?

Q: You discovered that the management of Blaine was angry at you for putting these facts in writing?

Q: Ron Lane made it clear to you that you were being called in because of your letter?

Q: The meeting lasted an hour and a half to two hours?

Q: It was not a pleasant meeting?

Q: Ron Lane used obscenities?

Q: Ron Lane yelled?

Q: Lane said that this letter about how Blaine handled the engineering problems in the Blaine 2000 all terrain vehicle (ATV) was a more serious matter then you understood it to be?

§ 10.09   Safely Asking Questions to Which the Answer Is Not Known

Cross-examiners ask leading questions on cross-examination. The advocate's ability to teach the case is built around the use of leading questions in cross-examination. Witness control is predicated upon the use of leading questions. The historic maxim of cross-examination is: "Never ask a question to which you do not know the answer." But this rule is both misunderstood and misapplied.

The misunderstanding comes from too narrow an application of the term "know the answer." This shorthand phrase implies that the cross-examiner must have proof that the witness has previously admitted this fact or be armed with a witness or exhibit capable of impeaching the witness should she deny the leading question fact. This limitation on cross-examination is so restrictive and so negative in connotation that, as to some critical issues, the cross-examiner is left with little or nothing to ask. This is not a rule that can be used if it is interpreted so narrowly.

Certainly in this age of limited discovery not all answers can be known prior to trial. In criminal law this is particularly true since the defense ordinarily faces significant discovery limitations and the prosecution must contend with discovery limitations. In addition, the Fifth Amendment shields defendants from having to make any statement until the moment they choose to take the witness stand. In addition, discovery limitations are becoming more frequent in civil cases. In many arbitrations, few depositions are taken. In every forum regardless of the amount of discovery available, it is impossible for pre-trial preparation to document every fact needed for the cross-examinations.

This often cited advice is better understood as a caution that the cross-examiner should not take unnecessary risks. In this sense the rule is of some assistance. If the definition of "know the answer" is broadened to include situations where a particular answer may not be independently provable, but may be logically indicated, then the advice has far greater utility. By constructing chapters using what facts are known in combination with the facts that logically flow from those known facts, leading questions can be asked to which the answer is less than certain but predictable. The applications of the techniques of the only three rules are instrumental in substantially reducing the risk inherent in any question to which the answer cannot be independently proved.

If the cross-examiner has carefully proceeded within a chapter from the general to the specific, many leading questions can be asked to which the only logical answer will have been learned by the cross-examiner by the time the question to which the answer is not known is asked. The third rule of the only three rules is that questions should follow the logical sequence to a specific goal. If the cross-examiner constructs a series of questions so that the answer to any one question is logically deducible from the previously admitted facts, then the witness must either answer the question with a logical "yes." Or he risks deny the leading question and providing an illogical answer. Illogical answers harm the witness's credibility. Furthermore, logical fact finders are incapable of confidently picturing the illogical response. In other words, while the witness is free to answer illogically, the minds of the fact finders will continue to process information logically. Any fact or series of facts that logically leads to another fact will cause the fact finder to picture the logical answer.

The cross-examiner encourages a witness to answer honestly through a variety of techniques, including the grouping of leading questions in a logical sequence. Another very important technique that reduces the risk of asking leading questions to which the answer cannot be documented is to document as many other facts as possible so that if a witness denies a leading question to which the answer is known, the cross-examiner can immediately impeach the answer. Through this method the witness is taught that it is the witness who incurs risk by denying the leading question. The witness cannot be sure of what answer he may have previously given in a deposition, what facts may have been previously provided by other witnesses, or what facts may be ascertained from documents.

Every time the witness denies a leading question and is immediately impeached, the witness is schooled in the danger of denying a fact when that fact is true. The techniques of impeachment are discussed at great length in this book (see chapter 16, *Eight Steps to Impeachment by Inconsistent Statement*, chapter 17, *Impeachment by Omission*, and chapter 18, *Advanced Impeachment Techniques*). Within the science and techniques of page preparation is a technique critical to witness control in the ability to instantly impeach. That technique is referred to as "sourcing the answer."

§ 10.10 "Sourcing the Answer"

"Sourcing" is the process of finding and entering the designation of where, within the materials, a particular answer can be found. Knowing the answer, and knowing where the answer can be documented, is the highest plateau of witness control. When the lawyer knows and can document the answer to a leading question, she erases any fear that the witness will successfully deny the leading question, plead a lack of memory, or substitute a different answer. While witnesses can still attempt all of these evasions, they are unlikely to do so because of the high degree of control the lawyer has gained through use of this technique. Furthermore, they cannot successfully engage in these evasions because the lawyer is now prepared to impeach on anything other than the answer "yes."

This physical preparation for the possibility of impeachment represents a quantum leap in control of the witness. The lawyer's ability to prepare at this high level is derived from the cross-examination preparation systems discussed in chapters 5, 6, and 7.

In each preparation system discussed, the lawyer gathered facts not only of the multiple versions of a fact or event given by the witness, but also the specific location in discovery of each version. At that point, the lawyer had created a preparation system in which she had "sourced the answer." Now, when preparing the pages of cross-examination, the lawyer need only add to the leading question a notation as to the source of the answer that is suggested by the leading question.

For instance, in the lawyer's preparation for a civil trial of a wrongful death case she may have prepared a topic card on how fast the defendant driver was going when he first saw the truck (see chapter 5, *Cross-Examination Preparation System 1: Topic Index Cards*). The index card might appear as follows:

SUE SHANE	SPEED WHEN FIRST SAW TRUCK
Unsure of speed limit	Interrogatory No. 26
Looked at speedometer just a minute before	P. Rpt. p.3
Saw going 45 mph	P. Rpt. p.3
Thought going 45 mph	Dep. 126:21

In the cross-examination of the driver, the lawyer established a chapter on when the driver first saw the truck, and in that chapter, the lawyer is going to ask a series of questions to prove that single issue. One of those chapters will be how fast she was driving when she first saw the truck. That chapter includes the leading questions: "You looked down at your speedometer?" and "You saw that you were going 45 miles per hour?" The lawyer knows that the answers should be "yes" because the preparation system establishes that fact.

In order to properly source the question on the lawyer's page preparation of cross-examination, the lawyer will systematically fill the page of a chapter with all of the sources for as many of the answers as the lawyer can within the body of the chapter.

As it would appear in Method 2, for example, on a single page of paper, the lawyer has the leading questions that make up this single chapter. Of course, they are not questions as much as they are facts. Now, to the left of that group of questions, the lawyer may draw a line creating a column running down the middle of the page. In this column, the lawyer should write the source for as many of these facts as can be found in discovery. The safest cross-examinations are those in which the lawyer has a source for the most important facts within the chapter, though there will often be leading questions to which the facts have never been established previously. The more facts that the lawyer can "source," the safer the cross-examination chapter.

Take the first example above, when, through a series of leading questions, the lawyer established the height of the robber. Now, working from one of the cross-examination preparation systems, the lawyer feeds into this middle column the source for each of the facts to be established.

Chart 3, below, illustrates the page preparation of a single topic, "Height of the Robber," documenting the source of each of the answers.

Chart 3

Source and Question Portion of Chapter

Bennett NOTES	SOURCE	Height of Robber
	Suppression Hearing 77:9	You were face-to-face with the robber.
	Police Rpt. P3 T	You were standing directly across the counter from him.
	PH 20:12	The robbery took several minutes.
	S HRG 23:11	You looked the man up and down.
	PH 20:14	You noticed you had to look up to him.
	PH 36:21	You are 6' tall yourself.
	S HRG 79:4	The robber was taller than you.
	PH 36:12 SHRG 22-5	You found yourself looking up at a man taller than you.

The result of this process of "sourcing the answer" is that the lawyer is now instantly prepared for an impeachment by inconsistent statement. The lawyer has literally prepared for the worst-case scenario. If the witness were to say to a leading question, "No, I wouldn't agree with that," or "Gee, I don't think that's correct," or "I cannot recall," the lawyer is immediately prepared to impeach. The source notes in the source column tell the lawyer where, within even the largest file, the lawyer can find that precise answer.

The master source card tells the date of the hearing, report location, and the persons present (see chapter 5, 6, and 7 on preparation systems). Because of the lawyer's preparation, she may now immediately impeach by laying an appropriate foundation. This instant and seemingly effortless impeachment reassures fact finders that the lawyer is the best guide to the facts.

Simultaneously the immediate impeachment of the witness schools him in the risks of denying a leading question. This preparation technique establishes and reinforces credibility with judges as they instantly recognize that the cross-examiner is well prepared.

In addition, judges grant more leeway for additional impeachments once they recognize that a witness has been successfully impeached (see generally chapter 11, *Sequences of Cross-Examination*). Finally, immediate impeachments by inconsistent statement strike fear in the heart of opponents. They are weaponless in this battle. A correctly handled impeachment offers no valid objection. The opponent completely understands that the cross-examiner is not troubled by evasive answers, but in fact uses the opportunity to both establish the fact desired and to impeach the witness. The opponent becomes far less confident that his witness can answer the redirect examination questions without tripping and thereby opening up other opportunities for impeachment by inconsistent statement. This realization impacts the willingness of the opponent to engage his witness in any redirect examination.

The preparation technique of sourcing the fact allows the lawyer to avoid the anxiety of the unexpected answer. The lawyer no longer fears the loss of the goal itself or loss of momentum.

§ 10.11   Know Where to Find the Fact

Cross-examiners operating without sourcing the facts are easy to spot. After getting the unexpected denial, the lawyer utters the hollow phrase, "Your honor, may I have a moment?" They are at the podium. Meanwhile, the jury is focused on the confrontation between the witness and the cross-examining lawyer, and with all of this tension coursing through their bodies, with everyone staring at them, and with their client wondering how badly this is going to hurt her case, the lawyer begins to desperately comb through exhibits, transcripts, or answers to interrogatories. Every second spent in the fruitless search for the expected answer is painful. It will take a whole lot longer for the cross-examiner to find the impeaching material than most people can endure.

The more desperate lawyers say something like, "Isn't it true you've said something different before?" And of course, the lawyer gets back a flat "no" or "I don't think so, not to that question" from the witness who can sense lack of confidence, weakness, and fear in the cross-examiner. Most of the time, the lawyer tries to bravely cover up the utter agony and embarrassment by saying, "Well, I'll come back to that." Not likely. The lawyer is not going to come back because she is not prepared to come back. There may never be an opportunity to come back. The strength of the chapter has been spent. Actually, the strength of the chapter has been wasted.

Because of inadequate preparation (representing just one small shortcut), the cross-examiner has, at least as to this point, turned victory into defeat. The lawyer has embarrassed herself at having lost the point. She has yielded the momentum of the cross-examination to the witness and she has proven her own fallibility to the jury. The client and the case are hurt, while the witness is strengthened. The witness has unfairly denied a point and has gotten away with it. This encourages further obfuscations.

In general, the lawyer has lost control and credibility at the same time. Worst of all, the lawyer has suffered all of those negative consequences on a point where the lawyer was right. Please take note of that lesson: The lawyer has suffered grave damage to her case by questioning on an area in which the truthful answer was indeed "yes." If the lawyer can do that kind of damage to her credibility when she is right, imagine what damage the lawyer could do to her case when she is wrong. The point is that because of a failure to source the fact, the lawyer might as well be wrong. For all the jury knows, the lawyer was wrong. Having been wrong, the lawyer's credibility is now suspect.

§10.12 Sourcing the Answer: Eliminating Risky Business

All of this damage could have been avoided, and the situation could have been turned substantially to the lawyer's advantage by sourcing the leading question. When the lawyer has written out the source of the fact next to the leading question, the minute a witness denies, dodges, or feigns a lack of recollection, the lawyer can begin her systematic attack through impeachment:

Q: You noticed you had to look at the robber?

A: Well, I wasn't exactly taking a survey. He had a gun in my face.

Or

A: No, I don't think I had to look up at him, I looked more across at him.

Or

A: I can't recall.

Impeachment begins:

Q: You came to this court for another hearing in this case?

Q: It was on July 1, 1992?

Q: The prosecutor, Ms. Brewsterman, was there asking questions?

Q: We were in Courtroom T on the first floor of this building (etc., establishing the foundation). (Cross-examining attorney visibly reading from transcript.)

Q: You were asked, by Prosecutor Brewsterman at page 20, line 12: Did you get a look at the man? Your answer at page 20, line 14: "Yeah, I did, and

I gave him a good look up and down, and I noticed that I had to look up to him." (Cross-examiner goes on to complete impeachment.)

The contrast between the two scenarios is dramatic. In one, the cross-examiner is working without having sourced the fact. In the other, the cross-examiner is working from a sourced chapter of examination. For the fully prepared cross-examiner, something electrifying has happened. Although the point itself was not major, the very act of impeachment has bestowed a string of benefits upon the cross-examiner. First, the witness is brought up short. He has been defeated easily. The attempt to deny, evade, or alter the answer has immediately been defeated by impeaching the witness with his own previous answer. The witness now must confirm having given the previous answer. Instead of losing a point, the cross-examiner has scored the original point (the goal of the question or chapter) and has simultaneously enjoyed the bonus of lowering the credibility of the witness, which is the consequence of a successfully performed impeachment.

§ 10.13   Always Source

The cross-examiner cannot always predict when the opportunity to impeach will be offered. Sourcing the fact is a technique not reserved for the most important chapters or the most important facts within the chapters. Sourcing a fact should become a matter of habit or routine. While the task might have been difficult at a point in the lawyer's development when they did not use the chapter method of preparation, once the lawyer has adopted any of the cross-examination preparation systems and he is transitioning that material into chapters, the source for a fact is immediately at hand and can easily be noted as the chapter is written. Below is an example of a typical chapter adequately sourced:

Firing Francine

Notes	Source	
	Depo 91:15	You fired Francine on July 2, 2004?
	91:17	You were her immediate supervisor?
	167:11	You fired her abruptly?
		There was no warning?
		There was no probationary period?
	168:15	You had a few notes scrawled on a piece of paper?
		You read the note?
		And that was the end of it?
		Francine asked if she could discuss it?
		You said no and walked out of the room?
		Francine tries to get her personal items

Notes	Source	
		Before you walked out Francine asked if she could go back and collect her personal things from her desk?
	167.21	You told her she was not allowed to go back to her office?
		You did not even allow her to pick up her personal items?
		You had one of your guards bring Francine her purse?
	168:12	2 or 3 days later you let her back into the building with a guard?
		The guard stood beside her while she cleaned out her desk?
		Then the guard escorted her out of the building?

As can be seen, not every fact has a source. Many times the cross-examiner knows or believes a fact because her client or another witness has related that fact. Sometimes the cross-examiner knows a fact because it is logical for that fact to exist. It is not critical that every fact in a chapter be sourced. It is critical that the facts that can be sourced are sourced.

§ 10.14   Other Benefits of Sourcing the Fact

By sourcing the fact, the cross-examiner is preparing to broaden the field of cross-examination. This occurs through the special psychodynamics of trial. Judges appreciate and reward prepared lawyers. Judges acknowledge lawyers who are on a roll. Judges recognize when a cross-examination is going well. The cross-examiner who appears prepared to immediately impeach is the cross-examiner who will likely later be rewarded when she moves into areas of impeachment that may draw an objection. A judge who has previously observed successful impeachment of this witness is more likely to allow further inquiries into credibility (see chapter 11, *Sequences of Cross-Examination*).

A successful impeachment captures the attention of the jury. As one impeachment follows the other, the jury gives its silent approval for the lawyer to continue to impeach.

In contrast, the lawyer who has the material but is unprepared to impeach and who botches the easy opportunities to impeach often finds herself stopped by a judge. The true reason for the ruling is not so much because the impeachment was collateral, but because there is no longer a belief that the lawyer can efficiently accomplish the impeachment in any event.

A judge has many discretionary calls to make in the course of trial. The surest way to encourage calls that go the cross-examiner's way is to take advantage of every opportunity to demonstrate thorough preparation, pinpoint cross-examination, and steady advancement toward meaningful goals.

§ 10.15   The Drama of Instant Impeachment

When the cross-examiner has sourced a fact and suddenly encounters a full or partial denial of the sourced fact, the end result will always be the opportunity for a successful impeachment of the witness. The cross-examiner has the opportunity to impeach but not the necessity. There may be those changes of story that assist the cross-examiner and therefore do not call for an impeachment. There may be situations in which the fact is judged to be so minor or the impeachment so complex, that the cross-examiner, for some tactical reason, chooses not to impeach.

When the cross-examiner elects to impeach using a prior inconsistent statement contained in a deposition or a document, there is an interesting byproduct to this technique. When a witness tries to deny the truth of the leading question, and the cross-examiner immediately begins impeachment from a document, there is an undeniable urge on the part of the opponent to grab the cited transcript, chart, or report. Should the opposing counsel have some difficulty locating the document, so much the better. It graphically illustrates the opponent's diminished degree of preparation. This in turn demonstrates the opponent's lack of factual control, which can prove fatal when the jury deliberates on which version of the case is to be trusted.

Assume that opposing counsel can quickly find his transcript or report. He will hurriedly shuffle through the pages to find the page and line to which the cross-examiner has referred. The jurors' eyes turn toward opposing counsel, expecting to hear a loud objection. They, along with the witness, are wondering if the opponent will stand up and say something along the order of, "Your Honor, nothing like that appears in this transcript." Or, "Your Honor, counsel is completely misquoting the former testimony of the witness." They are waiting and wondering, but that is not what they are going to hear because exactly at the page and line of the document the cross-examiner has specified will be the information that she has demanded of the witness in the leading question. Now, that portion of the drama having been played out, the cross-examiner may take the document in question and confront the witness, requiring him to acknowledge his prior inconsistent answer.

After the cross-examiner has acted out this mini-drama several times in a case, there are some opponents who will forgo searching their documents and resources to verify the fact that the lawyer is suggesting through her leading question. When this happens, and the jury notices that the opponent no longer tries to retrieve a transcript or document, the jury understands the opponent to be saying, in essence, "If that lawyer says it, it's true." At that point, the cross-examiner has established even greater credibility with the fact finder, witness, and even with opposing counsel.

Sometimes, the opponent chooses to verify every reference cited by the cross-examiner. The jury will watch as the opponent searches for the cited material and then choose not to object. Each of these mini-dramas is further verification to the jury that the cross-examiner is superbly in control of the facts.

This drama is not lost on the witness, who notices that the lawyer who put him on the stand, is unable to protect him from the cross-examiner. This encourages the witness to save himself by granting the lawyer the "yes" answer that the leading question first demanded. This, in turn, decreases risk for the remainder of the cross-examinations. All of these benefits stem from one simple technique — sourcing the question.

§ 10.16 Tracking the Witness's Direct Examination

The fourth benefit derived from drafting no more than one chapter per page is the ability to integrate new answers or facts produced during the opponent's direct examination of the witness or facts developed earlier on in cross-examination. When chapters are separately prepared, the lawyer can easily add notes, quotations, or new questions directly into the subject matter where they belong. As a result, the lawyer avoids taking a page or two of mixed notes on a variety of subjects during direct examination, which then leads the lawyer to partially cross-examine the witness on a variety of issues, none fully developed. In the resulting confusion, facts are taken up out of context and chapters are less than fully developed. Under these circumstances, the cross-examiner will often ask questions suggested by the notes taken during direct examination and then return to the same area of inquiry later when the opponent's prepared chapter is reached in the sequence of cross. By then, however, all semblance of control, precision, or sequence is lost. For all of these reasons, the best method is: a page of cross-examination equals a chapter of cross-examination.

When a witness is on direct examination there ought to be little reason to take notes. His direct examination should be the same old story. It ought to be what the lawyer has anticipated hearing, it ought to run along familiar lines, and it ought to have been accurately predicted in advance. Both the bad parts and the good parts ought to be very much in accordance with what the cross-examiner anticipated when she wrote her cross-examinations. It is therefore not necessary to take notes over the entire course of a witness's direct examination.

There are, on the other hand, some portions of the direct examination that the lawyer may want to document. It is for this reason that the lawyer makes a third column along the side of the prepared page of cross-examination (see diagrams below). In this third column the lawyer will keep track of what may be called "tactical issues." The first tactical issue may deal with the witness's direct examination.

Chart 4

Method 1

Source	Chapter Title	Tactics
	Cross-Examination Questions	

Method 2

Tactics	Source	Chapter Title
		Cross-Examination Questions

§ 10.17   Responding to the Witness's Direct Examination

It may occur that a witness changes a story during his direct examination. It may be a new statement inconsistent with a previous statement, a fact that has never been asserted previously, or any other thing upon which the lawyer wishes to cross-examine. When such change occurs in the course of direct examination, the lawyer needs only to turn quietly to her chapters of cross-examination to locate the prepared chapter of cross-examination to which this material relates. Having located the appropriate chapter, the lawyer needs only make a note in the tactic column on the new information and then, when the lawyer cross-examines in this chapter, the new material is a visible reminder to consider cross-examining concerning this new material.

Of great importance is the fact that the new story will be found precisely where it belongs — on the page of prepared questions that deal with that issue, and that contain the sources for the facts on that very issue. In this way, instead of accumulating on one page a string of unrelated notes on several issues arising in the direct examination, each note finds its way to the proper location within the chapter page that relates to that note.

While it is critical to pay attention to the witness's direct examination, it is not particularly difficult to find the appropriate chapters in the prepared pages to insert a new issue. As direct examinations almost always proceed in chronological order, it is easy to follow the direct examination. Since the cross-examiner is listening for issues, it is easy to page through the chapters of cross-examination, though those chapters are almost certainly not in chronological order (see chapter 11, *Sequences of Cross-Examination*). If the cross-examiner is uncomfortable taking even a moment to turn to the prepared chapters to make a notation in the appropriate page, the lawyer may resort to the system of keeping notes on new items or reminder slips of any kind on a separate piece of paper. However, these notes should be transferred to the appropriate chapters of cross-examination at the next available recess (see chapter 9, *The Chapter Method of Cross-Examination*).

Whatever else recesses are for, they are not for relaxation of counsel. Transferring direct examination notes onto appropriate cross-examination chapters or looking through cross-examination preparation materials for inconsistent answers or source locations of impeachment material, or otherwise ingraining new materials into the cross-examinations are but some of the things to be performed during recesses.

Chart 5 below shows the use of the "tactics" column to record a witness's helpful testimony given on direct examination. This exact quote, properly recorded in the tactics column, can be retrieved by the cross-examiner when performing this chapter and looped back to the witness. Because the quote is recorded where it needs to be, its usefulness to the cross-examiner will be increased.

Chart 5

Method 1

Witness **Bennett** Source	Height of the robber	Tactics
SHRG 77:9	You were face to face with the robber?	
Police Rpt. P. 3	You were standing directly across the counter from him?	"I was no more than 3' from him."
PH 20:12	The robbery took several minutes? And you looked the man up and down?	
PH 20:14	And you noticed you had to look up at him?	
PH 36:21	You are 6' tall yourself?	
SHRG 79:4	The robber was taller than you?	
SHRG 22:5	The robber was 6'3"?	

Method 2

Witness **Bennett** Tactics	Source	Height of the robber
"I was no more than 3' from him."	Suppression Hearing 77:9	You were face to face with the robber?
	Police Rpt. P. 3	You were standing directly across the counter from him?
	PH 20:12	The robbery took several minutes? And you looked the man up and down?
	PH 20:14	And you noticed you had to look up at him?
	PH 36:21	You are 6' tall yourself?
	SHRG 79:4	The robber was taller than you?
	SHRG 22:5	The robber was 6'3"?

In chart 6 below, the notes column contains a new answer, given on direct examination, which is contradictory to the prepared script:

Chart 6

Method 1

Bennett Source	Height	Notes
SHRG 79:4	The robber was taller than you?	"The robber was shorter than me."

Having noted the new inconsistency in the notes column of the correct chapter, when reaching that chapter during cross-examination, the properly prepared lawyer may confidently confront the witness on this new and dramatic change of testimony. The lawyer can then use the witness's exact words as a jumping off point for impeachment. This is only one of several ways to handle this impeachment. See chapter 16, *Eight Steps to Impeachment by Inconsistent Statement* for other methods.

§ 10.18 Responding to the Witness's Earlier Cross-Examination Answers

Often when a cross-examination is going well, a witness will offer bait (see chapter 30, *Recognizing and Controlling Bait*) to entice the lawyer into changing the lawyer's predetermined sequence of cross-examination. Cross-examiners working without scripted cross-examinations too often take the bait for fear that if they do not do so, they may forget to return to the baited issue. The lawyer armed with prepared chapters of cross-examination will easily resist the bait. That lawyer will take a second or two to leaf through the cross-examination chapters, locate the appropriate place within the appropriate chapter to mark the offered quote, and then return to the sequence of cross-examination outlined before trial ever started. If necessary, the cross-examiner can code a quote with a D or an X in the tactics column to indicate whether that quote was from the witness on direct or cross-examination.

By using the tactical issues column to note a witness's exact words, whether given in direct or cross-examination, the lawyer is equipped to capitalize on the quote, either on cross-examination or in closing argument.

Chart 7

Bennett Source	Height	Notes
P. Rpt. P3	You were standing directly across the counter from him?	D "I was not more than 3' from him." "I was so close I could smell his breath."

Perhaps this new statement contains a better or more favorable recitation of facts than the cross-examiner previously possessed. In that case, the lawyer might want to loop off the exact words of the witness (see chapter 26, *Loops, Double Loops, and Spontaneous Loops no boldface*) or even spontaneously loop (delayed) off the statement by in essence forcing the witness to reassert the desired phrase during cross-examination.

As an example of the spontaneous loop the lawyer asked:

Q: You were standing directly across the counter from him?

A: Yes.

Q: When you were standing so close to him that you could smell his breath, you were no more than three feet away?

A: Yes. (This is a delayed spontaneous loop from the direct examination.)

§ 10.19 Keying In the Exhibits for Use as Impeachment

Exhibits have multiple uses in a cross-examination. Their placement on a page is dependent on how they will be used. If the exhibit is being used as the source of an impeachment, the trial exhibit number, page, and line should be noted in the source column. In this use, the exhibit is the functional equivalent of a deposition. It contains the previous statement of the witness. Below is a representation of a chapter demonstrating how exhibits can be keyed in as sources of a fact:

Chart 8

SOURCE	ANOTHER PART TO TYUR DEAL
	September 2000 as part of the sale of JY Ltd. to TYUR you formed a new private company, JY Ltd. (bought back name).
Ex. A-5 (6) **¶ 15**	You owned 90% of company.
Ex. A-5 (6) **¶ 15**	Charles Moore, the Executive V.P., owned 3.2%.
	You knew private company JY Ltd. brought back many properties from TYUR.
Ex. A-5 (7)	1) Kola (U.S.) 2) A resort property in Mexico 3) A Gulfstream III jet 4) Furniture, vehicles (your car collection), 12 other cars in Montreal, office space
Ex. B article	5) Spare parts for the Gulfstream jet 6) A contract to buy an even more deluxe Gulfstream jet 7) Lease on top 3 floors of skyscraper Provencal building in downtown Montreal 8) 2 furnished suites in NYC 9) A Cadillac in Japan
	And your company gets a coal commission contract.

§ 10.20 Building Chapters Designed to Admit an Exhibit

Some exhibits go in by stipulation. In fact, this is becoming increasingly common in both civil and criminal cases for the court to require the parties to meet in advance of trial and narrow their objections to exhibits. Some exhibits go in with relatively little effort. The foundation for the exhibit is simple and straightforward. The witness can lay that foundation and the opponent really does not believe he can block the admission of the exhibit, or intend to object to its admission. In such instances the exhibits can be shown in the body of the prepared page with the simple note "mark and introduce Exhibit 17, the nursing notes."

However, there are those situations in which the introduction of the exhibit is itself the purpose for the chapter. In such circumstances, it is important that a chapter be written to lay the foundation or do anything else necessary to accomplish the admission of the exhibit. Below is an example of a chapter written for the express purpose of admitting an exhibit:

Chart 9

SOURCE	Intro of E-5: Game plan for default (overcoming attorney/client privilege)
Ex. E-5	You were afraid Mr. Harlan would default on his payment to you. So afraid that you wanted a game plan for default. That game plan is contained in Exhibit E-5. E-5 was written at your request.
E-5: pg. 1 Bates: 02759	You made it on June 1st. You shared E-5 with your management team. Your management team were business people, not lawyers. E-5 was not modeled by an attorney/client communication. And it is fact E-5 was distributed to your employees so they would know which percentages needed to have liens placed on them.
Ex. E-5	Move to admit E-5.

§ 10.21 Keying In Exhibits as a Tactical Reminder

Another use of the notes or tactics column is to key in exhibits. It may be that the cross-examination can benefit from showing a witness a particular exhibit. It may be that a particular exhibit must be introduced through this witness. It may be that an exhibit can be impeached or explained through this witness. In all of these events, this tactics column can be used to remind the cross-examiner of the exhibit to be introduced or discussed.

The chapter below is designed to impeach a portion of the story of a high school student who claims to have had multiple consensual sexual experiences with her principal. The school janitor has been called by the prosecution to establish seeing the two together at school long after classes were over. This cross-examination chapter is designed to impeach the girl's story that the sex acts took place in certain locked rooms. Note the use of the tactics column to key in a useful exhibit.

Chart 10

Goal: Show inconsistencies between testimony and physical evidence

HEAD CUSTODIAN SHAW SOURCE	DOORS	NOTES
	You are the head custodian at Fitzmunkers Middle. You were in the late 1990 and early 91. Familiar with work that was done on doors and locks over the last few years. Back in late 2000 the lock on the office nurses' bathroom door didn't work. That was because back in 1999 the lock on the door to the main office didn't work but the nurse's bathroom lock did so they were switched. You personally saw to it that the lock was switched. To do this, you created a work order.	
	More important to be able to keep the office locked than the bathroom.	Introduce work order — EX.11
	Aware that it was common for the principal and the office staff to use the bathroom in the health office. So they were all aware that the lock didn't work.	
4-2	You had a conversation with Mr. Hardin when he first became principal in fall of 1990 about the locks.	
4-2	Remember telling him that lock on bathroom in health office didn't work.	
	You are also familiar with the lock on the door to the principal's office. It requires a key. Can only be locked from the outside. No button or keyhole on the inside.	

While the introduction of an exhibit often forms its own chapter, once an exhibit is in evidence, discussions concerning it require a stage note within a chapter prompting the lawyer on when and how to make use of the exhibit.

Chart 11

Example: Page Preparation of Chapter Involving an Exhibit

Ms. Farr	The Lighter	Tactics
Preliminary Hearing 12-7:25	When you got back to your apartment you noticed your lighter was missing.	
PH 167:4	That night or the next morning you discussed it being missing with Midge.	
PH 167:15	It was the lighter you had used to light a cigarette when you got into the van.	
	It was a metal lighter. In fact this is your lighter.	Show her ex _____
PH 167:9	You realized it was in the van — that it had spilled from your purse.	
PH 167:19	You believed that your prints were on it.	
PH 167:22	And that your prints on that lighter were going to lead the police to you.	

Similarly, there are times that the lawyer marks an item for identification, but it may not be introduced. For instance, items may be shown to a witness for purposes of impeachment or as demonstrative evidence. The court may ask that the item be marked for identification so that the record is complete. That same item, whether it is a transcript containing an inconsistent statement, a record used to refresh the witness's recollection, or any other type of document that is not going to be introduced, is still a prop that needs to be set in place. This tactics column is the appropriate place to keep notes concerning such exhibits and props.

The chapter below is prepared as part of the impeachment on a "snitch" witness. It deals with several exhibits that may be shown to the witness in telling the story of a prior fraud committed by this witness. Hopefully, the snitch will admit the truth of the leading question, but should he hesitate, the appropriate exhibit is keyed in, ready for use.

Chart 12

Example: A Chapter of Cross-Examination Keyed With Exhibits for
Identification Purposes

Mark Nautiluss (Snitch) SUBJECT – THE INSURANCE FRAUD GETTING THE LOAN		
Source		*Tactics*
Cooling GJ 5:22	9/18/82 you went to People's Bank and asked for a $50,000 loan	see Cooling GJ 5:22 GJ Ex 17 loan app. ID ———
Cooling GJ 5:23 PH 154:17	You said you need $ to purchase over road tractor/trailer for your coal loading business	
	They made you a $55,000 loan	GJ Ex. 18: loan 11/9/82 pkg p1 ID # ——— GJ Ex 18: loan pkg p7 ID # ———
	The money was to purchase a new Kenworth Tractor and some cash for operating expenses.	GJ Ex 18: loan pkg p3 ID # ———
Cooling GJ 10:1	The bank wanted to inspect the 1982 Kenworth, but you said your dealer had not received it yet.	
Cooling GJ 10:10	So, bank gave you one ck for $48,000 to Tumbleweed Ent. for 1982 Kenworth.	GJ Ex. 19: Bank ck ID # ———
Cooling GJ 10:16	And bank gave you a ck for $7,000 for operating expenses.	GJ Ex. 20: Bank ck ID #

Sometimes the note in the tactics column is not about an exhibit to be used during the cross-examination or an item to be marked for identification when shown to the witness, but is a reminder to counsel of the existence of a piece of evidence that will contradict what the witness is saying. The lawyer may want to key in the note about the exhibit just as a reminder that the lawyer is setting the witness up for impeachment through either the previous or upcoming use of that exhibit.

By way of example, examine a case involving a witness who allegedly murdered the defendant's business partner so that the defendant might recover some insurance. One of the chapters of the cross-examination involves the witness's description of where he stood as he stabbed the victim lying in his bed. While preparing the witness statement charts, it was noted that the alleged hit man's description of the homicide did not match the coroner's report and photographs, either in the number of stab wounds, or in the place where the assailant must have been standing in order to inflict the stab wounds.

The witness is not going to be confronted with these differences. To do so would only point up the inconsistency to the witness and perhaps allow the witness to give a credible explanation. Part of the theory of the case is that the alleged hit man is not the hit man at all, but is covering up for a far bigger conspiracy not involving the defendant. Therefore, a chapter that demonstrates the alleged hit man's unfamiliarity with the homicidal act is a benefit to the lawyer. The lawyer has prepared that cross-examination chapter from the witness statement or criss-cross chart. To track this process, see chapter 7, *Cross-Examination Preparation System 3: Witness Statement Charts.*

Chart 13

The Stabbing		
Source		*Tactics*
GJ 12/11/81 p 36	You were standing by his left side.	
DA	You held the knife in your fist so that the sharp edge was facing toward you.	(demonstrate with rubber knife)
GJ 12/11/91 p 36	The first time you stabbed	
DA 12/9/81 p 33	him was on the right side.	
GJ 12/11/81 p 36	You believe it entered his right lung.	
GJ 12/11/81 p 34	You raised up the knife	
DA 12/9/81 p 36	and plunged it in full length.	
DA St 12/9/81 p 31	You stabbed him 3 times.	Pres EX _____, _____, _____, photos of deceased 5 stab wounds all made by person at his head
GJ 12/11/81	From side to side — across his body.	Pros Wit Dr. Toll (Coroner) Make sure details of wounds in Ev. during cross of Dr. Toll Chapters: # of wounds Direction of wounds Where assailant prob standing

§ 10.22　Tracking Inconsistencies with Other Witnesses

On those occasions when the cross-examination of one witness is done to set up an impeachment of another witness, or *by* another witness, it is important to make note of the fact that the current testimony or chapter is part of a two-witness impeachment. In such instances, the chapter the lawyer is doing may not make sense to the jury, even though they have heard the testimony of both witnesses. In the tension of trial, it is even possible for the cross-examiner to lose track of how a particular chapter will be used to frame up an inconsistency with another witness. In such instances, it is helpful to make notes in the tactics column, adding in the text from another witness or in some way noting that another witness has or will testify inconsistent with the material found within this witness's chapter.

Chart 14

SOURCE	1992 NEGOTIATIONS BEGIN WITH GARY GOUNDERY
EK 304:4-10	You admit that you sent Hank Putter to negotiate with Gary Goundery in 2000 about Gary Goundery's purchase of Rust Financial?
EK 304:3-307:8	And it's your testimony that you allowed Putter to do this, even though you had no interest in selling Rust Financial to Mr. Goundery?
GG 10:16	And you were aware Hank Putter and Gary Goundery flew to S.C. to work out the details of the contract with Hank Putter concerning the negotiations to sell 100% of your interest in Rust Financial.
	You are still trying to hold off bankruptcy of your business EKJU (US)
GG 30:23	Hank Putter would suggest direct calls to you from Gary Goundery.
GG 31:1	Hank Putter would relate your specific requests on negotiable items.
GG 31:7	Hank Putter made it clear that he was in regular conversations with you.
	Many phone calls, much exchange of information and you kept assuring Gary Goundery team that your revenue and expense projections were reasonable.
EK 304:4	"I was not particularly interested in this, and so I did not take an active participation in the exercise myself."
GG 22:13	But at the same time you tried to communicate with real time pressure to get deal closed.
GG 30:17	It was a 4-month period of negotiations leading up to the final session July 4, 2000, weekend in Madison.
	But there was one last step: the buyer gets to look at the detailed financial records of the business

By way of further example, see the notes concerning Coroner Toll set out in the "tactics" column of the preceding murder trial example.

Chart 15

Traffic Reconstructionist Lindy		
Source	NO SKID MARKS	Tactics
Dep 1/12	You investigated the scene?	
Dep 4/4	You looked for skid marks?	
Dep 4/6	You found none? None on the road?	Ex._____ Photo from Tech I. Corbit showing skid marks
	None on the curb? None on the sidewalk?	Ex. _____ (Skid marks on road, curb, sidewalk)
Dep 63/19		Plaintiff expert Corbit: "They were faint because it was black rubber on blacktop pavement, but I have no doubt they are skid marks."

§ 10.23   Customary Order of Questions within a Chapter

The most frequent purpose of a chapter of cross-examination is to introduce or highlight a particular fact or to create a vivid picture of a particular moment or event. Although establishment of this goal-fact or picture may often serve to impeach the witness, a chapter that introduces or highlights a fact that impeaches a witness takes a form different from that of a chapter devoted to impeachment by inconsistent statement. The form of a chapter designed to impeach by inconsistent statement will be discussed separately (see chapter 16, *Eight Steps to Impeachment by Inconsistent Statement*).

The introduction or highlighting of a fact through cross-examination can best be accomplished through an ordering of questions that begins with the general area of questioning within the chapter, and moves to the specific. It is ordinarily envisioned as an inverted triangle:

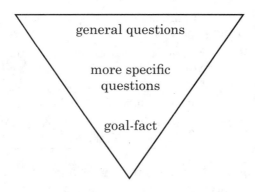

When it is said that a chapter begins with the general and moves to the specific, it is meant that the chapter begins with a series of questions that establishes the broad nature of the topic and then, through a series of leading questions, pulls the witness down an ever-narrowing path until, at the conclusion of the chapter, the witness answers the specific question that proves the goal. The chapter below exemplifies this frequently employed format:

Chart 16

Example of General to the Specific

Type of Case:	Employee Sues Employer Claiming Sexual Harassment Overall
Goal:	To discredit the complaining witness's allegation that on several occasions the employer took her into his office during work hours and locked the door so that he could engage in sexual activities with her.

The Employer's Secretary		
	DOORS NOT LOCKED	
	Your desk is immediately to the left of Mr. Lewis' door.	Show diagram Defendants Ex. 9
	Your desk is less than 3 feet from his doorway.	
	Your desk is perpendicular to his door. So when you are seated at your desk you can see into his door. His door has a lock. It is a push button lock. It makes a distinctive "click" when it is pushed or locked.	

Chart 17

Type of Case: DUI
Area of Inquiry: Roadside examination
Specific Area: Improper administration of the Horizontal Gaze
                 Nystagmus Test
Goal: Undermine police officer's expertise

DUI Officer Bloomingdale	Horizontal Gaze Nystagmus Test
	Method of Conducting Horizontal Gaze Nystagmus Test When you give HGN you look for three different things in each eye. Look for whether the eye follows pen smoothly. Then look to see if the eye jerks when it is all the way to the side. Then look to see at what angle the eye begins to jerk. Means you have to move the pen in front of each eye a number of times.
DMV Hrg. 28:23	And when you gave the test to Mr. S. you moved the pen at the same speed each time.
	But that's not the right way to give the test, is it?
DUI ENF Man p12	The Colorado manual on correct procedures for roadside test says you're supposed to move the pen at a high speed when checking for smooth pursuit.
DMV Hrg 29:16	But you are to move pen at half that speed when checking for the angle the jerking begins.
DUI ENF Man p16	And the State of CO DUI ENF Man says if you move the pen at the wrong speed you will mistake the normal movement of the eye for nystagmus. In other words if you give the test incorrectly you will think you see nystagmus when it really isn't there. You did not give the test in accordance with the manual. Since you moved the pen at the same speed each time, then you did at least half that test incorrectly.

Also refer to the other examples in this chapter, as they show that the common sequence of questions within a page or chapter of cross-examination, are moving from the general to the specific. All have in common the same structure: First, the cross-examiner establishes the opportunity for the witness to observe an event or understand an event. Then there is a narrowing of the questions to show an ability to observe and understand events in this particular situation. Finally, there is the observation or goal-fact itself.

Alternatively, the chapter begins with the general statement of principles or a general orientation to the scene. The chapter proceeds with more finally detailed facts and concludes with a completion of the picture. This is quite often the form of a chapter of cross-examination. The goal of such a chapter is not to win a battle with the witness but to use the witness as a method of educating the jurors on important fact or issue. The chapter may well contain no facts, which are in dispute. The power of the chapter is not in the confrontation with the witness, but in the use of a hostile witness to establish facts that assist the cross-examiner's theory of the case. Recall, a fact admitted by the opponent's witness is a fact that can no longer easily be disputed by the opponent.

Furthermore a fact admitted by the opponent's witness is one less fact that must be proved by a witness called by the cross-examiner. If there are fewer facts, which must be proved by a witness called by the cross-examiner, the fewer opportunities there are for that witness to fumble or create an opportunity for productive cross-examination by the opponent. It is no minor accomplishment to craft a series of chapters that allow the cross-examiner to establish many facts of importance and paint many necessary pictures all without encountering a "no" answer.

§ 10.24 Use of Theme Phrases as a Secondary Goal of a Chapter

Ordinarily once the picture is completed, or a goal fact is established, the chapter has ended. The goal of the chapter is always placed at the bottom. However, there is a specific technique in which the specific answer or specific goal-fact of a chapter is followed by another question. This additional leading question is often a question designed to insert the theme phrase. In such instance, the chapter truly has two goals: Establishment of the fact, and establishment of verification of the theme phrase upon which the lawyer intends to capitalize in closing argument. An example of such a chapter, moving from the general to the specific, and then ending with the theme phrase follows:

Chart 18

Witness: Snitch
Goal: Destroy credibility through character attack
Chapter: Willingness to involve innocent wife in lies for snitch's own benefit

Mary A. Dennis worked at the United States Trays of Snarp Association in Chicago.	General introductory material
You knew that because Mary A. Dennis is your wife.	
She didn't know about the scheme. She wasn't part of the fraud.	Specific questions designed to demonstrate witness's ability to cheat and lie

She was just a handy name. An easy way to handle things. She had no idea you were doing this. She didn't get the money. She didn't cash the checks. You cashed the checks. You signed her name. That's forgery.	
You just kind of pulled your wife down into the middle of your own crimes.	Chapter goal: witness's total lack of morals
You put your wife in a position where she would be arrested.	Theme phrase of "you put your wife in a position . . ." also used
You put your wife in a position where she would be charged.	
You put your wife in a position where she would be convicted.	
You put your wife in a position where she could go to prison.	
Fifty-six times.	
It was dishonest.	Establishment of theme
But it was good for your business. It was good for you.	Theme phrases: ". . . good for your business"; "good for you"

In the example below drawn from a trademark infringement action, the cross-examiner wishes to establish a goal fact that a high ranking corporate employee had reason to believe that his company would be infringing on the trademarked name of a competing cat food, but that he cared so little for the rights of the plaintiff that he proceeded anyway. That goal alone makes the chapter quite valuable. Equally important is the use of this chapter to establish the theme phrase, "It wasn't your problem." The resulting chapter accomplishes both its factual goal and the added goal of theme integration.

Using the Name Purrcat — Not Your Problem (Chapter title)

Q: Arden Heller told you that there was a cat food on the market named Purrcat?

Q: And Purrcat was a direct competitor to your cat food?

Q: You didn't call the legal department and say, guys, we're putting Purrcat on our bags?

Q: You didn't call Moffat, the head of marketing and tell him we're putting Purrcat on your bags?

Q: You didn't call anybody?

Q: You just rolled it out?

Q: Tens of thousands of bags with Purrcat on them?

Q: Because using Purrcat on your bags wasn't your problem?

§10.25 Creating a Strong Inference as the Goal

Besides the factual goal, in some instances there is an unstated additional goal of a chapter: creating an inference — the conclusion that the jury is to arrive at, concerning that witness. Such a goal inference is in reality a conclusion and a conclusion will not directly be asked of the witness, since the witness will likely be unwilling to admit this inference or conclusion.

A common chapter that employs this technique is a "things-not-done" cross-examination, or a "things-done-incorrectly" cross-examination. To ask the witness at the conclusion of the chapter if he can verify that he has screwed up the case or has conducted the investigation poorly or incompletely, is to force the witness into a situation where they will give an explanation. The lawyer may rather let the jury come to its own conclusion as to how well the case has been investigated.

In such instances, the conclusion that the lawyer wishes the jury to draw from the testimony will not be asked of the witness. Instead, it is a conclusion or inference that the jurors are likely to draw from the hard-edged facts that can be introduced through the cross-examination chapter. The inference is built upon facts, not persuasion. If the chapter provides the facts then the jurors will likely come to that conclusion on their own. While the lawyer might discuss such inferences or conclusions during closing argument, by that point in the case, the battle over the inference has largely been decided.

To obtain the jurors agreement with the desired conclusion or inference, the lawyer must follow the customary format of building a chapter from the general to the specific. This following chapter is an example of a factual chapter of whose goal it is to support an inference.

Below is an example from a civil case about a securities investment that has gone bad. The stockbroker for the investor complained to management that the research department of the brokerage firm had provided incomplete and misleading information to the stockbrokers in an attempt to bolster the price of the stock. After receiving the complaint the brokerage firm took two actions. It paid back the investors the money they had lost, and it levied a substantial fine against the stockbroker. The fine was allegedly for some unspecified violation of securities rules.

The purpose of the cross-examination chapter was to drive the inference that the fine was a way of warning this and other stockbrokers not to complain or take a position adverse to the interests of the company. At the time of the cross-examination the stockbroker still worked for the brokerage firm and was unwilling to taking a position adverse to the brokerage firm. However, a fact-based chapter that compels an inference does not require a hostile witness to change his attitude, only that he honestly answer factual questions. Although this chapter is part of a chapter bundle which explains the entire sequence of complaint letters and actions by the brokerage firm. While only one of the chapters within the bundle is presented, it is possible to see how the facts point to the inference that the actions by the brokerage firm were retaliatory and not based on a violation of rules or industry standards.

Chart 19

Alleged compliance violation

Exhibit 50 (letter)	In June 2002 you wrote your first letter of complaint?
	You received no reply from your company?
Exhibit 53 (letter)	In January 2003 you wrote another letter about this investment?
	Again, you heard not a word of reply from your company?
depo 112:21	Mary Allen, the head of compliance, never called?
	She never told you in any way that you had violated any rule?
186:07	Your client did not even know you had written these letters?
186:19	You wrote these letters solely because you had your customer's best interests in mind?
190:22	You never believed telling your brokerage firm how you analyzed a situation was any violation of a securities law?
190:25	Telling your brokerage firm how you saw the facts was the exercise of your judgment is an investment executive?
199:9	The National Association of Securities Dealers never wrote you saying that you had violated any rules?
199:15	The Securities and Exchange Commission never wrote you that you had violated any rules?
201:18	In fact the head of your compliance department, Mary Allen, never even talked to you about your letters?
202:19	Instead what happened was that you wrote a third letter setting out the facts as you saw them?
Exhibit 57 212:11	That is when your boss Norm Spiegel called you in and said you were fined $75,000?

Such a factual chapter used in conjunction with other chapters (a chapter bundle) that educate the jurors on the letters of complaint and the settlement with the client is the most effective way of equipping the jurors to accept the inference that the broker was fined for speaking out. Through this entire chapter that hostile witness is never asked to agree with the inference but is only asked to agree with the factual leading questions.

Another example of a factual chapter designed to compel an inference is called: "Investigating defendant's whereabouts at time of arson." It concerns a detective sent to interview a homeowner who is suspected of burning down his house. The theory of the defense is that the police department always assumed the defendant to be guilty and never investigated anyone other than the defendant. Regardless of the evidence, the police intended to charge the defendant with the crime.

Cross of the Investigator:

Investigating defendant's whereabouts at time of arson

Q: You do not know what time the fire on April 11, 1991, was called in, was reported?

A: No, I don't.

Q: You do not know the person who called in the first report of the April 11, 1991 fire?

A: No, I don't.

Q: It was part of your assignment to see if you could find out where Robert Lucans was at the time of the fire on April 11, 1991?

A: No.

Q: You interviewed him about where he was at the time of the fire?

A: Yes.

Q: And you interviewed his family?

A: Yes.

Q: About the events of April 11, 1991?

A: Yes.

Q: You were assigned to interview Robert Lucans and his family about the events of April 11, 1991?

A: Yes.

Q: And it could have been that you would have developed evidence that would prove he couldn't have been at the house at the time of the fire?

A: My purpose was to gain information.

Q: You were sent out on this case as part of the investigation of an arson of April 11, 1991?

A: Yes.

Q: Robert Lucans was a suspect in that?

A: Yes, he was.

Q: You wanted to know his whereabouts at the time of the fire?

A: Yes.

Q: The fact of the matter is you interviewed him because he could have been the perpetrator of the arson?

A: He could have been.

Q: You needed to know his whereabouts at the time of the arson?

A: Yes.

Q: The purpose of the interview was to pin down his whereabouts at the time of the arson?

A: Yes.

Q: That was your assignment?

A: My assignment was to interview him.

Q: About that subject?

A: About his whereabouts right after the fire.

Q: And at the time of the fire?

A: Yes.

Q: And you didn't know the time of the fire?

A: I didn't know.

The investigating detective, sent to check out the defendant's alibi, did not know when the fire started or even when it was called in. He may well have an explanation for how he could interview the defendant concerning his whereabouts at the time of the fire, but that fact he will never be asked. Instead, the cross-examiner will save the issue until closing argument — when the witness is no longer able to drum up an excuse or scenario to explain the curious method of investigation.

§ 10.26   Planning Chapter Bundles

It may take several chapters to explain one event in a case. When several chapters are required to tell a full story (see chapter 11, *Sequences of Cross-Examination*), each chapter within the bundle should be built using the same inverted triangle form in which the chapter is headlined with the general proposition or statement of fact and progress toward increasingly specific questions until the goal is established or the picture painted. In addition, this grouping of chapters together may form the inverted triangle, moving from the general propositions in the first chapters to the specific and most important facts in the concluding chapter. For example, in cases involving the testimony of an expert witness, it is often important in the early chapters to show exactly how a thing should be done, and then in the later chapters to show how the thing was done. The outline of how this multi-chapter presentation moves from the general to the specific is outlined below:

Witness: Expert in child abuse case

Goal: Undermine expert opinion that abuse has occurred.

Chapters: 1. Not all injuries are the product of abuse

                  2. Factors that experts look for to determine if child
                     abuse has occurred

                  3. Type of medical examinations needed to determine if
                     abuse occurred

                  4. Lack of such examination in this case

The questions contained within chapters 3 and 4 of this chapter bundle are set out so that the sequence of chapters moving toward the goal may be seen. (For trial, each chapter will be prepared on a separate page.)

Chart 20

Chapter 3 — Information needed to determine if abuse occurred:

You want full medical histories

You want all medical reports

You want a complete physical

Sometimes type of injury may tell you how it occurred:

Fingerprint from a slap

Scalding water creating a burn

Cord marks from a whipping

Marks made by a coat hanger

X-rays

Lab data

Incidents that happen in the past, or the lack of past incidents

You have to do a very thorough and careful evaluation using these tests and interviews to determine if abuse occurred

---

Chart 21

Chapter 4 — Diagnosis without an examination:

Never saw Melissa in person

Never spoke to her by phone

Never had your staff examine Melissa

Never reviewed CAT scans

Never reviewed X-rays

Never reviewed head measurements

Never saw the results of any medical tests performed on Melissa

Never got any lab results

Never saw a single medical report that chronicled any other examinations of Melissa

---

Within chapter 3 the questioning moves from the general to the specific, but the whole sequence of the four chapters also moves from the general to the specific:

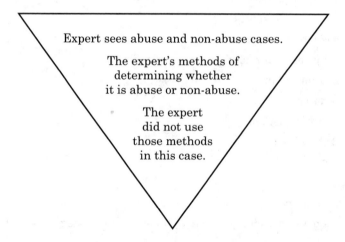

§ 10.27   Preparing Credibility Chapters

While the visible primary goal of a chapter may be to introduce or highlight a fact, often the unspoken goal of a chapter is to affect the credibility of the witness. Even in such instances, the lawyer will find herself establishing a factual point as she is working toward a more generalized goal of affecting credibility. The lawyer uses a series of facts to paint the picture, but the true apex of the triangle or the goal of the chapter, is the creation of a goal-feeling about the witness. This is often accompanied by the establishment of a theme phrase. Two examples of such chapters are set forth below:

In this first example, the city auditor has testified that he believed that the defendant Raceway was charging too much for tickets, but that he remained silent because the city gained increased tax revenue. It is the position of the defendant that the auditor studied the contract and actually came to the conclusion that Raceway was within their rights and that no violation was occurring. Of course, the hostile witness will never agree with that conclusion. While the cross-examiner would undoubtedly perform several chapters dealing with the contract itself, this particular chapter is designed to reflect on the credibility of the witness:

"I do not audit things that do not make the city money."

The city charter establishes the position of auditor?

The auditor is the general accountant for the city?

It is your job to make sure the city fairly and accurately accounts for the money it owes and the money that is owed to it?

You pride yourself on your integrity?

Your job is to be fair and accurate no matter who it helps?

The matter who it hurts?

But in direct examination you said your job is to look out for the city's financial interest?

You say you did not audit what Raceway was charging for admission because you thought they were charging too much?

It is your position that if a company has a contract with the city but they violate that contract by charging people too much, so long as the city makes more money it's not your job to blow the whistle?

In fact, you would say it is your job to keep quiet?

So Raceway charged too much for tickets, and the city collected too much in the tax on the tickets, that is something you wanted to ignore?

Chart 22

Witness: Snitch — Drug Conspiracy
Goal: Damage credibility by impeachment on character issues
Chapter: Cross-examination on being a loan shark

Money Lender

You are a money lender, aren't you, Mr. Arden?

You loan your money out.

And you ask a reasonable return on your investments.

You ask 30% a week.

120% a month.

1,500% a year.

So a $1,000 loan from you costs $15,000 in interest a year.

Plus, of course, the original $1,000.

That's called loan sharking, isn't it?

That's just good business.

If somebody wants to pay it, why not let him, right?

You never promised it was a good rate.

You never promised it was a fair rate.

But if somebody is desperate enough, your attitude is: Why not?

---

§ 10.28   Format for Expert Witness Chapters

In a series of chapters formed in sequence to prove that an officer has not investigated properly, that an expert has not tested or analyzed properly, or in any other sequence of chapters performed with a goal of showing things not done, or things done improperly, the general format of the chapter is:

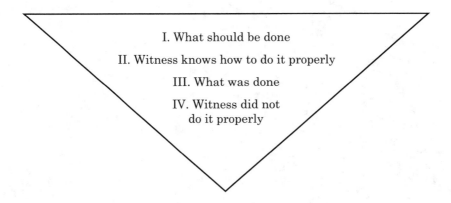

I. What should be done

II. Witness knows how to do it properly

III. What was done

IV. Witness did not
do it properly

In the event that the expert witness denies part II — so much the better for the cross-examiner. After gaining that very damaging admission, the lawyer could still press ahead to establish parts III and IV.

If chapters I, II, and, III are done well, it may not be necessary or prudent to perform chapter IV. It is in the case by inference that the cross-examiner may elect to discuss chapter IV in closing argument, when the witness is no longer in a position to explain away the errors and omissions.

If a lawyer were cross-examining an expert witness in an attempt to show that while they did certain things, they did not do them in accordance with the proper procedures, the inverted triangle formed by the sequence of chapter is as follows:

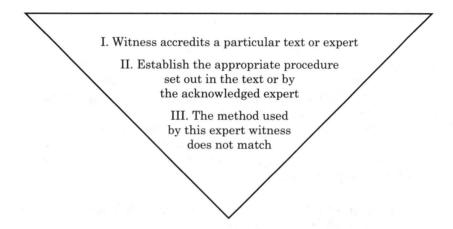

§ 10.29 Not Necessary That Witness Recognize Goal-Facts

Often the witness does not appreciate the significance of the goal-fact toward which the lawyer is driving in the cross-examination. This occurs because the witness does not realize that another witness, or some item of physical evidence, contradicts the witness's assertion. It is not necessary that the witness understand that the lawyer is driving toward a goal or that the lawyer has achieved the goal. It is only necessary that the jury understand the significance of the fact admitted or testified to by the witness.

In such instance, the triangle form of questioning remains the same, though the witness the does not sense the value of the goal achieved. The chapter can be diagramed in the customary way.

Although the witness does not necessarily feel the pinch of the narrowing triangle, the jury appreciates the significance of the goal thereby established. It is to the lawyer's advantage that the witness does not recognize the goal. The lawyer is likely to encounter a less directed fight by the witness. That is, the witness may still resist leading questions were possible, but the fight is not properly aimed, since the witness is unsure where the cross-examination is heading. It appears to the jury that the witness is just being hard to get along with.

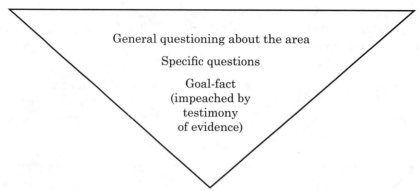

General questioning about the area

Specific questions

Goal-fact
(impeached by
testimony
of evidence)

Such chapters can look innocuous on their face. A witness can be led into a series of answers that is directly contradictory to the statements of another witness on the same topic. Opposing counsel, who has called both witnesses, realizes the damage being done but is helpless. The leading questions are not objectionable. The witness is not being impeached and therefore feels comfortable with his answers. But the jurors understand the significance of the chapter. A portion of the story of the opponent is now disputed by two witnesses called by the opponent. Such chapters often go rather smoothly, though they are very effective impeachments.

§ 10.30   Sequence of Questions Impeaching With an Inconsistent Statement

Impeachment by inconsistent statement is a subject of such importance that it is discussed at length in chapter 16, *Eight Steps of Impeachment by Inconsistent Statements*. This discussion is limited to the sequence of questions in a chapter designed to impeach with an inconsistent statement.

The ordinary rule of moving from the general to the specific applies in such chapters. However, the introductory material at the top of the triangle may be the introduction, in some form, of the current version of a fact about to be impeached. The lawyer may begin by putting in some form of the witness "today's version" of a fact and then proceed through the general introductory questions (foundation impact questions) before arriving at the goal of the chapter — introduction of the prior inconsistent statement. This can be diagramed as follows:

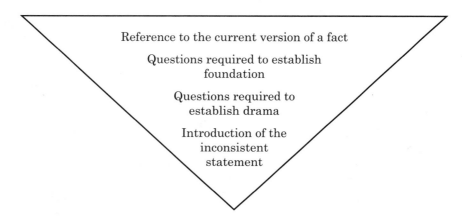

Reference to the current version of a fact

Questions required to establish
foundation

Questions required to
establish drama

Introduction of the
inconsistent
statement

Keep in mind, however, that there is an eight-step process to impeach by inconsistent statement (see chapter 16, *Eight Steps to Impeachment by Inconsistent Statement*).

In written form, an abbreviated form of such an impeaching chapter might read as follows:

Chart 23

Differing Stories on Why Embezzle from TBC	
	On 3/25/86 when D.A. Inv. Abe Hendrickson interviewed you (to get you ready to testify for this case), you had a new story:
	This fraud arose out of your bookmaking activities.
Bertolli st to Hendrickson 3/25/86 p.19	Some execs at TBC had lost on some football bets and they would not pay, but they did authorize you to steal the money for the corporation.
	[Use of Foundation Questions]
(Bob Cantor, Pres, TBC)	And when you were caught you told your employers a story.
	A story on why you needed to cheat them to defraud them to lie to them.
Police rpt. 8/10/85 p.21T (st of Bob Cantor)	Your story:
	You needed to steal the money because you were getting a divorce and you need the money to pay bills.
(D.A. Inv. A. Hendrickson)	A different story for a different audience.

Chapter 11

SEQUENCES OF CROSS-EXAMINATION

SYNOPSIS

§11.01 The Strategy of Sequencing Cross-Examination Chapters

One of the great benefits derived from the preparation of cross-examination in the chapter method is the ability to order and reorder the chapters into sequences selected by the cross-examiner. Advocates too often ignore the virtues of planning the order of cross-examination. As a result, many cross-examinations are approached in a random sequence or in the lock-step sequencing produced by a purely chronological approach. In order to derive the greatest benefit from the chapter method of cross-examination, it is helpful to perform the chapters of cross-examination using a strategy. There are many persuasive sequences possible and there is never one best sequence. The strategy of sequencing a cross-examination is built upon the notion that the same chapters of cross-examination performed in a more persuasive order produce better results. The cross-examination can be enhanced by the order in which its parts are presented.

The science and techniques of sequencing the chapters of cross-examination are built around the notion that the most important issues to be exploited are unlikely to have occurred chronologically. For instance, if chronological order were used in cross-examination, impeachment chapters would be performed as they occur within the chronological sequence of the story. By the time the best impeachments occur, the jury may well have already decided the witness is credible.

If, on the other hand, the chapters of the cross-examination are placed in an order selected by the advocate, the cross-examiner can choose to perform the strongest impeaching chapters early in the cross-examination, and thereby diminish the credibility of the witness at an earlier point within the cross-examination. The value of such a sequencing technique is that jurors are most attentive and are most disposed to critically examine the credibility of the witness at the beginning of a cross-examination. All damage done to the credibility of the witness through early chapters of cross-examination may well carry over through the remainder of the cross-examination. In other words, by lowering the credibility of the witness at an early point in the cross-examination, the advocate derives benefits throughout the cross-examination. In fact, when the advocate runs into hostile answers in later chapters, the jury is likely more skeptical of the answers as a result of the impeaching chapters that have already been performed. This is but a single example of the benefits to be gained by sequencing the chapters of cross-examination in the most persuasive order.

The strategy of sequencing a cross-examination is integrally tied to the concept that the cross-examining party, through the use of planned sequences, can cause a jury to pay greater attention to certain facts. This strategy also can keep a hostile witness off balance and more efficiently attack a witness's credibility or demonstrate motive, interest and bias. The cross-examiner can use sequences to establish greater control of the witness and thereby diminish the risk that the witness will answer non-responsively in more difficult areas of cross-examination.

The techniques of placing chapters into planned sequences of cross-examination uses psychological principles, including primacy and recency and the Skinnerian principle that behavior is molded by consequences.[1]

Just as it is foolish to believe that the first 12 jurors into the box are as good as a jury carefully selected with a theory of the case in mind, it is naive to believe that any random order of cross-examination is as good as a planned order of cross-examination. The Hollywood movie industry — the world's greatest storyteller — uses flashbacks, cutaways, close-ups, and a myriad other techniques to generate and hold audience interest.

The skillful cross-examiner can employ the courtroom equivalent of these techniques. Happily, there are an endless variety of alternative sequences that may be assembled to create an entire cross-examination. The important concept is that a planned sequence is more likely to produce a desired result that any unplanned sequence. Fashioning a persuasive sequence of cross-examination is another weapon in the skillful cross-examiner's arsenal. To the degree that it is ignored, it is a weapon wasted.

§ 11.02   Sequences Designed to Heighten Impact

The science and techniques of sequencing are first and foremost methods of aiding the fact finder in understanding the facts and how they support the advocate's theory of the case. Placing chapters into a desired sequence heightens the impact of the cross-examination material. The cross-examiner does this by using techniques that give more prominence to certain specific facts and chapters.

The placement of a chapter in a sequence, or the placement of a chapter bundle in the overall cross-examination does not alter the content of those chapters of cross-examination. Instead, the selection of a sequence is designed to enhance the impact of a chapter or chapter bundle. A part of the strategy of placing chapters into planned sequences is to derive greater bang for the buck — to make the material more meaningful to the jury than if it had been presented randomly.

§ 11.03   Sequences Designed to Enlarge the Scope of Admissibility

The strategy of some cross-examinations is to expand the areas in which cross-examination may occur. Certain sequences have the effect of broadening the permissible areas of impeachment by demonstrating to the court that the witness is capable of being impeached. When the cross-examiner fairly impeaches a witness, this successful impeachment strengthens the legal ability of counsel to impeach in more abstract or collateral areas. In other words, a lawyer asking for a discretionary ruling that permits further impeachment is more likely to earn that ruling if the advocate has already successfully impeached the witness. Trial lawyers know the feeling of "being on a roll."

---

1   B.F. SKINNER, THE BEHAVIOR OF ORGANISMS (1938).

When this happens, it is noticed by the judge and the jury as well. A lawyer on a roll has a far better chance to move into new areas of impeachment.

Some sequences of cross-examination are designed to enhance the ability of the lawyer to pursue chapters of cross-examination, which might otherwise be objected to and sustained as collateral. For instance, if the advocate wishes to pursue matters that seem remote in time and circumstance to the issues being tried, it is incumbent upon the lawyer to provide the court with a framework through which the court can understand the relationship of the remote material to the issues to be decided. The opening statement provides an excellent opportunity to make clear the relationship between supposedly collateral evidence and the chapters the court will readily acknowledge being material.

When performing these chapters that may seem remote at first, the cross-examiner should use introductory phrases that alert the court to the time between this chapter and later chapters that are relevant. For instance, if the cross-examiner wishes to show an event in 1990 during the trial of a contract in 2002, it is a very helpful technique to introduce that 1990 chapter or chapter bundle with some phrase such as, "Certain business decisions you made in 1990 had a direct impact on your financial position in 2002?" Such an introductory phrase alerts the judge that the evidence that follows is tied to issues in the case and forms part of the advocate's theory of the case.

§ 11.04 Sequences Designed to Control the Witness

A third distinct strategy of cross-examination sequencing is to provide the cross-examining lawyer with methods of encouraging the witness to honestly answer affirmatively, to discourage the witness from providing unresponsive answers, and to bring back under control a runaway witness who is attempting to steer the cross-examination into areas of his own choice. Certain sequencing techniques work to suppress the will of the witness to contradict or evade by redirecting the witness into safe areas of inquiry.

Not every chapter of cross-examination comes off as planned. There undoubtedly will be occasions when the witness scores or fends off the cross-examiner's attack. Sometimes the cross-examiner may have foreseen this possibility, while at other times the damage is unexpected. One of the uses of sequences is designed to control the witness and to provide the cross-examiner with a safe passage back into dependable chapters when the cross-examination goes awry.

§ 11.05 Relationship of Sequencing to the Chapter Method

Placing chapters in any strategic sequence is another method of exercising control over the witness and the courtroom. The chapter method of cross-examination, accomplished through page preparation of cross-examination, is the foundation that makes possible the sequencing of cross-examination. Therefore, creating powerful sequences of chapters is a technique that belongs only to the prepared lawyer in employing the chapter method of cross-examination preparation. See chapter 9, *The Chapter Method of Cross-Examination* and chapter 10, *Page Preparation of Cross-Examination*.

The chapter method of cross-examination discussed the necessity of building a series of goal-oriented chapters, each designed to establish one particular factual goal useful to the cross-examining party. Having divided the cross-examination materials into chapters, written each chapter individually and placed one chapter only on each page (see chapter 10, *Page Preparation of Cross-Examination*), there is now a system ideally suited to the task of placing cross-examination materials into selected sequences. Because each of the chapters has been individually prepared, there is flexibility to position chapters in the order judged to be most effective. The lawyer is no longer tied to a chronological presentation. The lawyer may take up issues in whichever sequence seems most likely to generate the emotions she wishes the jurors to feel when hearing the facts. By abandoning a purely chronological approach to cross-examination the advocate can save material to craft a strong attack both early and late in the cross-examination. Risky material can be interspersed with strong material that has the effect of lowering the risk that a witness will answer not responsively. In general, the cross-examiner can take advantage of the preparation to keep the witness off stride while simultaneously keeping the jury's attention and interest.

§ 11.06   Do Not Repeat or Follow the Direct Examination Sequences

A cross-examiner who adheres to an old fashioned format of taking a few notes made during direct examination is likely to cross-examine in whatever order the notes were written. This random assortment of notes leaves to chance the impact created by cross-examination. Below is an example of the cross-examination performed from rough notes with no thought of the science and techniques of sequencing:

Chart 1

Unplanned Cross-Examination Sequences
1. Who are you?
2. You were the driver of a car on September 12, 1992?
3. Where had you been that night?
4. Who were you with?
5. What drinking/How much?
6. Route home
7. Intersection of 5th and Cherry Streets?
8. Hit station wagon?

Too often, the cross-examiner believes she can manipulate and reformulate her sequence of topics by drawing arrows or making notes in the margin of the list of topics. While this may be of some use in the law office setting, such hieroglyphics do not serve the lawyer well in the stressful environment of trial:

Chart 2

Planned Cross-Examination Sequences
5. What drinking/How much?
3. Where had you been that night?
6. Route home?
7. Intersection of 5th and Cherry Streets?
8. Hit station wagon?
4. Who with?

An attorney using the list in Chart 1 will likely cross-examine the defendant/car driver on his entire story in chronological order. In that way, the story will unfold without regard to persuasive impact. For instance, the extremely critical area "what drinking/how much" may come 15 or 20 minutes into the cross when it would have greatest impact as the very first chapter performed. Chart 2 shows a planned method of cross-examination.

§ 11.07 The Chapter Method Lets the Lawyer Emphasize Important Material

A further sin of such an unplanned sequence is that it gives as much emphasis on who was with the defendant as to how much he as drinking. Since everything will be covered in the story, everything receives approximately the same weight.

§ 11.08 The Chapter Method Lowers the Risks of Transitioning into Chapters to Be Avoided

Furthermore, working from cross-examination notes as opposed to chapters, limits the ability of the lawyer to move crisply from pre-selected topic to pre-selected topic (chapter to chapter). In the heat of trial, even the most practiced lawyer may forget which areas have been fully developed, which areas the lawyer intended to get back to, and which areas have been completely omitted. In fact, it is far more likely that the advocate will be eventually slip into the "what happened next?" mindset. In other words, in times of stress the cross-examiner will often lose her way and wander into undesired topics.

§ 11.09 The Chapter Method Creates Flexibility

The chapter method is infinitely more flexible than even the best general cross-examination notes. The chapter method permits the speedy integration of new materials gained on direct examination, reordering of cross-examination sequence, deletion of chapters no longer thought to be useful, and reclaiming of chapters that have earlier been set aside when they were then thought to be unproductive. Inasmuch as separate chapters have been created, each designed to highlight, support, or undermine a single goal or concept of importance; the individual page preparation of those chapters gives the cross-examiner ultimate flexibility. When a witness offers up on direct examination a new story or a new fact of importance, the cross-examiner can put one note onto the appropriate chapter page, rather than leaving the note in the margin of a sheet of paper that refers to 10 or 20 chapters. Then when the advocate stands up to perform the cross-examination, the note will be where it is needed — on the page of the chapter to which it relates.

In advance of trial, the cross-examiner may write a chapter that appears quite useful, only to find that the chapter has lost its viability after a particularly good explanation is given in direct examination. Under such circumstances, the individual chapter can simply be pulled out of the stack of chapters and set aside. There is no need for crossing out and interlineations with arrows and numbers, all of which will only serve to confuse the lawyer during trial.

The converse is equally true: The lawyer may write a chapter in the office hoping that something will occur in the trial that will allow the advocate to use the facts in that chapter. Perhaps it is an impeachment that seems collateral. However, an answer of a witness during trial may well make that prepared chapter not only admissible, but also extremely valuable. Having written the chapter, the cross-examiner can insert that chapter into the cross-examination at the time and place desired.

There are occasions when there is room for a witness to either admit or deny a fact, and the chapter will only become useful depending on the position taken by the witness. In such circumstances, the lawyer may have a prepared chapter at counsel table so that if the circumstances warrant, it can be inserted into the proper sequence of cross-examination. All of these options can be accomplished when the facts of cross-examination have been broken down into chapters and each chapter has been independently prepared.

§ 11.10   The Chapter Method Is Part of a Total System

Using the cross-examination preparation system, combined with page preparation of cross-examination, counsel is prepared to take advantage of the changing dynamics of the cross-examination. As the witness tries to bob and weave, the cross-examining lawyer can fall back on a system that can accommodate changes in tactic, changes in emphasis, and changes in testimony. In all ways, the chapter method affords the cross-examining lawyer ultimate control over the sequence and content of the examination to be performed.

§ 11.11   The Science and Techniques of Sequencing: Guidelines, Not Rules

What follows are the strategic and tactical considerations for handling the common decisions of cross-examination sequences. It must be stressed that these are guidelines, not rules. They suggest sequencing techniques that are designed to work in the majority of cases, whether civil or criminal, divorce or contract. However, in certain situations, a skillful cross-examiner may elect to ignore one or more of these guidelines and *adopt* a different sequence. This is as it should be. The critical point is the realization that there are strategic and tactical considerations to sequences of cross-examination. The goal is not to follow any rigid pattern, but to develop a useful pattern for the case at hand.

The selection of a sequence is dependent on too many variables to be termed "rules." The amount and quality of material available, the degree of hostility of the witness, the placement of this witness in the order of witnesses, all influence the sequences the cross-examiner might choose to employ. However, for the most part, these guidelines describe the solutions to the most frequently encountered issues in determining a persuasive sequence.

§ 11.12   Begin the Cross-Examination With the Chapters Previously Selected as the Opening Sequence

The doctrine of primacy is critical to the selection of an opening sequence of chapters. Cross-examiners strive, above all else, to have an impact in the opening moment of a cross-examination. To this end, counsel has selected truly meaningful chapters. This could be a chapter or chapter bundle that strongly supports the advocate's theory of the case or that demonstrably weakens the foundation of the opponent's theory of the case. The chapter may demonstrate a clear bias or perhaps unmask a full-blooded lie. Many of the guidelines of the sequencing of the cross-examination address the need to score factual points early in the cross-examination with simple, comprehensible, and undeniably admissible facts. A cardinal rule must be that one must not abandon the well-thought out opening sequence of cross-examination in favor of some recently hatched idea.

Why would this happen? Why would a cross-examiner abandon the well-thought out sequences of cross-examination planned in advance of trial? The answer is that the cross-examiner is often attempting to respond to the just concluded direct examination. In fact, most cross-examiners take notes of the direct examination. While this is not a bad exercise, abandoning prepared chapters in favor of cross-examining from those notes of direct examination is a mistake. This is termed "chasing the direct examination." When a cross-examiner chases the direct examination she takes on the chapters developed by the direct examiner as the cross-examination game plan. But the direct examination cannot be the best game plan for the cross-examination. It is virtually impossible that the direct examiner placed his chapters in order that are most advantageous to the cross-examiner. While the direct examination notes have utility, that utility is as an addendum to the prepared chapters of cross-examination, not as a substitute for the cross-examiner's game plan.

There is another way in which the cross-examiner can mistakenly be induced to abandon the prepared opening sequence of the cross-examination. Quite often the last chapter of the opponent's direct examination establishes some goal of use to the direct examiner. In fact, it would be shocking if that were not true. The cross-examiner frequently has an emotional reaction (usually anger) to that evidence, or believes that she has the ability to solidly rebut that proof. Perhaps the cross-examiner has a prepared chapter or chapter bundle that directly takes on that issue. For any of these reasons the cross-examiner is induced to immediately take on the opponent's last chapter.

Regardless of the reason, this is almost certainly an erroneous strategy. If the cross-examiner indeed has a well-prepared chapter, that chapter can be taken up at its appropriate time within the sequence of the cross-examination. The appropriate time to use the prepared chapter is when it was planned for. That has not changed because the opponent has concluded their direct examination in this same area. If the cross-examiner is responding out of emotion or she is trying to one up the opponent by proving the cross-examiner's ability to successfully take on this subject matter, the cross-examiner is now giving in to ego. The best course of conduct is to proceed with the cross-examination as planned. Even if the sequences of cross-examination deserve some adjustment, that adjustment should be made during a recess. Decisions as to sequence made on the fly are seldom as sound as the strategy that was calculated in the calm before trial. The cross-examiner should begin the cross-examination with the sequence of chapters that the cross-examiner planned to use before becoming agitated by the direct examination. The advocate must be reassured by the knowledge that she will eventually get to those prepared chapters that effectively confront the testimony that produced the emotional response.

§ 11.13   Begin the Cross-Examination With Chapters That Are Predictably Safe

The cross-examiner should always begin the cross-examination with well-developed chapters in which the advocate has confidence. The cross-examiner should save for later the development of new chapter discovered during the direct examination. As a corollary to this guideline the cross-examiner should resist the temptation to realign the sequences of the cross-examination chapters based upon the notion that her creative passion and genius suggests that the chapters can be worked into a new and stronger sequence. If new or better evidence has the makings of some truly memorable chapters, they will not disappear. If, with the passage of time, they still seem like a good idea, there will be time available to perform them (see chapter 14, *Redirect and Recross Examination*).

It is critically important to seize control of both the topics of cross-examination and the demeanor of the witness at the onset of the cross-examination. If, instead, the cross-examiner offers up a sequence of chapters not well thought out, a likely outcome is a firefight with the witness in which the cross-examiner cannot cleanly establish his goals. This initial failure to establish control of either the topics or the manner in which the witness is encouraged to answer the leading questions will do a great deal to boost the willingness of the witness to fight through the remainder of the cross-examination. Furthermore, while a clean, solid chapter or chapter bundle at the beginning of the cross-examination establishes the cross-examiner's control of the courtroom, the failure to do so encourages opponents and judges to begin to obstruct the rhythm of the cross-examination. Above all else, the cross-examiner must first establish control of both the witness and the chapters to be covered by employing the only three rules of cross-examination and by cross-examining in the chapter method. These techniques allow the cross-examiner to clearly establish important facts and to cleanly to get on a roll in the opening sequences of cross-examination.

§ 11.14   Do Not Use Chronological Order in Confrontational Cross-Examinations

Chronological order is the preferred device for the storyteller who has the task of explaining the entire picture. That is generally the direct examiner's role. The cross-examiner is not interested in the entire story, but only in selected portions of the story. In addition, the cross-examiner may be interested in presenting parts of the story that were entirely omitted by the direct examiner. Even as a method of direct examination, chronological order has its weaknesses. As a method of sequencing cross-examinations, it is decidedly deficient and can prove quite harmful. Confrontational cross-examinations depend upon the lawyer's ability to draw out of the witness admissions that he would prefer not to give. In some instances, the cross-examiner can anticipate that the witness is going to flatly deny the leading question. But in other cases, the witness may try to explain his answer in such a way as to harm the examining lawyer's theory of the case.

§ 11.15   Damages of Chronological Order

The use of chronological order has several side effects, none of which are desired by the cross-examiner. When cross-examination is done in chronological order, there is a tendency to get into areas that there was no intention of cross-examining on at all. This happens because the questioner is tempted to or falls into the "what happened next" mode of examination. Even if the questioner avoids this crutch, the witness often does not. The chronological sequence of cross-examination encourages the witness to volunteer "what happened next." Remember, cross-examination is performed only on chapters selected by the cross-examiner, not the witness.

There is an additional danger to cross-examining a witness using a chronological order of chapters. The witness, knowing full well what is coming up next, can give as little or as much emphasis to the material as the witness chooses, thus stealing from the cross-examiner the ability to highlight or downplay facts. The witness can then comment further on topics in which the cross-examiner either has no interest or a negative interest. Even if discussion of a topic does not hurt the cross-examiner, there will be many topics that simply have no relevancy to the theory of the case. They are a distraction. By introducing into the cross-examination volumes of evidence having no bearing on the theory of the case, the cross-examiner has muddied the picture desired for the jury. Such cross-examination mixes trash with the treasure and leaves for the jury the task of sorting out the items of importance.

Another risk of chronological cross-examinations is that by giving the witness time to realize what issues he is likely to face, the witness can begin mentally working on the explanation he will need. Cross-examination must be done with impact. The witness must be thrust into the middle of a very difficult situation with no time to consider avenues of escape. If there is to be impeachment upon an inconsistent statement, the examiner must immediately engulf the witness in the impeaching chapter without giving them any warning of what is coming.

Finally, by cross-examining in chronological order, the lawyer has abandoned every other guideline set out in this chapter on the sequences of cross-examination. It is virtually impossible that a chronological sequence of chapters will satisfy the other guidelines, such as showing bias, interest, or motive early, or developing risky areas only after establishing control. In a confrontational cross-examination, nothing worthwhile is gained by performing the overall cross-examination in chronological order.

§ 11.16   Avoid Using Chronological Order in Informational Cross-Examinations

There may be an occasion when the chronological approach to informational cross-examination is appropriate, but it would only be on those occasions where a witness is purely informational. A witness is purely informational when the witness knows a limited number of facts, and as to each and every fact he will readily admit the fact. For example, an eyewitness may have seen only one thing, one part of an event, or only heard one short conversation. A police officer may have had but a single role: to guard a crime scene so that no one entered. Such narrow witnesses are rare. If everything the witness had to say had been helpful to the cross-examiner, the opponent, in all likelihood, would not have called the witness in the first instance.

More often, a cross-examination will have only portions that are informational; cross-examinations will tend to be a blend of information and confrontation. Even when a witness knows and will freely admit many facts of assistance to the cross-examiner, normally the witness knows some harmful facts as well. By avoiding chronological order, even in informational cross-examinations, the cross-examiner better controls the witness and denies the witness the easy opportunity to insert undesired information unrelated to the chapters of cross-examination selected by the advocate.

Even in purely informational cross-examinations, where there is no impeachment or confrontation to be done, the cross-examiner must guard against the unresponsive answer. Through the careful selection of chapters sequenced in a particular order, the responses are funneled toward only the information desired and the opportunity to offer the surprise answer is eliminated. Just as is true with the confrontational witness, the facts the "informational" witness will freely admit are likely of differing weights or importance. The guidelines that assist in highlighting a fact have equal applicability. In an informational cross-examination, the cross-examiner must order the sequence of chapters so as to begin with a very important fact and to end with a very important fact. Regardless of the form of the cross-examination, to proceed in chronological order is to make the cross-examination less interesting than it might be and, simultaneously, run the risk that some areas that were not intended to be opened up will be discussed because either the lawyer or the witness moved into a "what happened next" mode.

Having recognized the distinction between informational and confrontational portions of cross-examination, the lawyer can easily envision the different dynamics of the two forms of cross-examination. There are then guidelines that can be applied to these changing dynamics that help the cross-examiner determine an appropriate sequence in which to do cross-examinations that contain both confrontational and informational materials.

§11.17 When Developing a Longer Story Utilizing a Chapter Bundle, Develop This Portion of the Story in Chronological Order

There are times when chronological order, within a confrontational or informational cross-examination, is entirely appropriate. For instance, chronological order may be quite useful and appropriate when developing the existence of motive, interest, or bias, when showing the commission of another crime. It is also useful in developing a sequence of the chapters concerning the topic of a prior felony conviction or the granting of immunity. In this case, internal chronological order provides a framework of understanding for the jury. That is to say, it may well be best to show how the witness sought immunity in this case or how the witness developed a bias toward your client by telling that story in chronological order. However, that chapter bundle need not be performed at the chronological point at which that occurred within the entire sequence of the overall cross-examination.

Similarly, in describing how a particular corporate decision was arrived at, how a meeting proceeded, or how a scientific test was done, chronological order is the sensible method. In other words, within a chapter bundle, chronological order is the appropriate way to sequence the chapters of that bundle. But again, the bundle itself does not have to be used at the place within the cross-examination where, chronologically, that topic or event occurred.

Some topics simply cannot be split up, or they will make no sense. This customarily occurs when there is a series of events in a case that make sense only when seen in relationship to each other. For instance, with a personal injury action, a chapter about the moments before impact, a chapter on the actions and inattention of the driver before impact, a chapter on the first view of the car about to be struck, and the chapter concerning the speed the defendant-driver was traveling all fit together. While there could be a rare circumstance where these chapters should be separated, they really are a bundle of chapters (see chapter 9, *The Chapter Method of Cross-Examination*).

In a commercial case the development and circulation of a particularly important memo may have great meaning and involve many chapters. In order for the overall topic to make sense and to get the most benefit from the evidence it is necessary that the chapters concerning this one memo be performed one after the other. A great deal of context will be lost if these chapters are separated and spread over the course of the cross-examination. This grouping of chapters is a chapter bundle.

Chapter bundles are groups of chapters that must be done together in order to complete a coherent picture of a single event. It is still important to present each chapter fully, and to prove its factual goal. However, each chapter cannot be understood in isolation, but needs to be performed in a sequence with the other chapters in its bundle. Cross-examining counsel assists the jury in keeping the chapter bundle together because, while each chapter may have its own goal, that goal can best be understood when seen by the jury in connection with the other goals of the other chapters within the chapter bundle.

Because of the time needed to develop a group of chapters or a bundle, no quick impact is obtainable. That is to say, the impact that the cross-examiner hopes to derive from a strong opening sequence or a powerful closing sequence ordinarily cannot be achieved by cross-examining on facts contained within a chapter bundle. Since the full power of the bundle comes about only after the complete story is seen, chapter bundles are generally best performed in the middle of cross-examinations, between sequences that score quick, hard points. Impeachments from transcript, prior inconsistent statements, and testimony that is markedly inconsistent with that of other witnesses or that of tangible evidence, such as documents or photographs, all score more quickly and cleanly than the material contained in a chapter bundle. Therefore, those portions of cross-examination that must be handled through chapter bundles should be sandwiched by other chapters that move quicker and more fluidly.

§ 11.18　Integrate the Theme Early and Often

The importance of developing a theme is discussed at length in chapter 2, *Developing a Theory of the Case*. Having decided upon a theme during pre-trial preparation, begin ingraining that theme in the jury's mind as early as possible. One or more chapters of the cross-examination should contain the theme phrase or its variants. One of these chapters should be performed early in the cross-examination, preferably near the very beginning of the cross-examination.

When the witness is a critical witness and the theme revolves around inconsistent statements by that witness, impeaching by inconsistent statement is an excellent manner to begin the cross-examination. This is equally true in cross-examination of the spouse in a divorce case and the cross-examination of the defendant driver in a personal injury case. Whether the issue is one of contract or criminal law, or any other dispute, with careful selection of theme chapters sequenced in a particular order, the witness's responses are funneled toward only the information desired and the opportunity to offer the surprise answer is reduced.

Where the theme is that a particular witness has reason or motivation to deceive, a chapter telling that he has deceived in the past is a very useful early chapter. If mistaken identification is part of the theme, a theme line such as, "It happened so quickly," can be brought home by an initial chapter on things not seen because they happened too quickly. This same theme line—"it happened so quickly" — can be used in a variety of personal injury cases as part of the cross-examination of a defendant who is alleged to have caused the accident. In a cross-examination on self-defense, some action or words by the victim that helped create the apparent necessity for self-defense allows the lawyer to lay the theme in the initial chapter. In a child custody case, where one parent did not make it to several events of importance for the child, a theme line such as, "You couldn't find the time," can be set up and introduced in a very early chapter of the cross-examination.

By performing a theme chapter at the very onset of the cross-examination, the advocate leads the jury to more vividly recall that portion of the cross-examination. The early use of a theme chapter sets a tone for the entire cross-examination to come, which in turn sets a tone for the overall case (see chapter 12, *Employing Primacy and Recency*).

The advocate should ingrain the theory of the case and theme into chapters of cross-examination frequently if possible. In a personal injury action, if the goal of the cross-examination is to discredit the defendant's "independent medical examination", the lawyer might cross-examine over a series of chapters in which the defense doctor formed some objective sign of injury consistent with the diagnosis made by plaintiff's expert. The theme line could be: "Dr. Cohen found spasms in the neck muscles and you looked; and you now cannot agree. . . ." Or when speaking of the plaintiff's complaints: "She tells us her arm tingles and you are not surprised. . . ." By repeating these phrases throughout the cross-examination, each time linked to an appropriate and admitted fact, the theme of the cross-examination will be fully ingrained in the minds of the jurors.

If the cross-examiner intends to compel the witness to call himself a liar, it is best to get him to do so as often as possible throughout the cross-examination. If the theme is that the victim could have stopped the fight, but escalated it at every opportunity, chapters containing that theme ("But you didn't stop. . .") could be spread throughout the cross-examination.

In a breach of contract case, plaintiff's counsel might purposefully begin the cross-examination by showing a single instance where a particular item called for by the contract was not built or supplied as specified. The proof may be attached to a theme line such as: "the words of the contract say high grade carpet, but the delivery was medium grade," or "your customer cared enough to spell it out in the contract, but . . . ." When this form of proof and phrase is repeated throughout the cross-examination, the phrase first heard by the jury in the cross-examination takes on major significance.

Regardless of the nature of the theme, within reason, the more repetitions of the theme phrase, the greater its recognition and viability during jury deliberations. Of course, it is possible to beat to death a theme phrase by overuse. The cross-examiner must have the self-control and the confidence to firmly establish the phrase and then move on.

§ 11.19 When Attacking Credibility, Attack Very Early in the Cross-Examination

In general, when attacking credibility, the attack should begin early in the cross-examination so as to destroy the impression of credibility before the witness has an opportunity to bolster his own credibility. The more time a witness has to develop his credibility, the more effort and material will be required in cross-examination to reverse the jury's initial impression.

Of course, the witness has had an opportunity to develop his credibility during his direct examination. Even the immediate attack on the credibility of a witness, at the onset of cross-examination, comes late in the sequence of the examination of that witness. The witness has already enjoyed an easy opportunity to build their credibility through the direct examination. In order to combat this, the cross-examiner, aiming to diminish credibility, must begin the process in opening statement. By attacking credibility before direct examination has begun, the cross-examiner reverses the order of attack and leaves the direct examiner with the task of trying to build credibility that has already been severely undermined. By using opening statement to reveal the facts which undermined the credibility of a witness, the credibility established by the direct examiner is always less formidable than would have been the case without the punishing opening statement.

If the theory of the case involves showing that a witness is mistaken, demonstrating the mistake or change of stories begins to undermine the credibility at once. Human fallibility leads to mistakes. The cross-examiner should show the fallibility of this witness by pointing out changes of story, demonstrating that parts of the witness's story are inconsistent with physical facts, or by proving that the witness contradicts the story of another witness or exhibit. In this way, the initial impression formed by the jury is that this witness is mistaken or at least that the witness's story is to be doubted in as much as the initial cross-examination has substantiated multiple mistakes or contradictions in their story.

If the cross-examiner intends to show a witness is willfully testifying falsely, the lawyer usually derives the greatest benefit by exposing a fabrication in an early chapter of cross-examination. No good can come from permitting the witness to build up further credibility before beginning the attack on credibility. The attack on credibility must begin early in the cross-examination, and the best method of attack is through one or more chapters that demonstrate a fabrication or deception. The lie that is exposed need not necessarily concern a fact in this case. It can be a lie from a previous civil law suit, a distortion or fabrication on a resume or curriculum vitae, a lie to get out of a debt. Whatever the form of the lie, if the cross-examiner is going to suggest that a witness is intentionally deceiving the fact finder, the advocate should show early in the cross-examination that the witness has lied.

In a medical malpractice case based upon a failure to diagnose, plaintiff's counsel discovered subtle but significant alterations in medical records. By impeaching on these alterations first, the credibility of the defendant/doctor may be too damaged to benefit from the favorable testimony of several experts to the effect that the missed diagnosis did nothing to alter the patient's chances of recovery.

In a personal injury case, the plaintiff claims great psychological damage from having ingested some pieces of glass found in the eggs served by the defendant's restaurant. When asked in her deposition the state of her marriage, her answer was "just about perfect." In fact, at the time of the deposition she was separated from her husband and had obtained a temporary restraining order against him. While the husband was not a witness to the case, defense counsel's establishment of the deceitful deposition answer is likely to undermine her credibility as to all future answers. As a result the objective evidence of her injury may still prevail but the witness's lack of credibility will likely allow the jury to award a lesser amount of damages. Fact finders find a way to punish parties who do not tell the truth.

§11.20 Show Bias, Interest, or Motive Early in the Cross-Examination

When a witness has a pronounced bias or motive for testifying, it is best to reveal it early in the cross-examination. Again, by revealing bias, interest, or motive to the jury in the opening statement, the advocate preconditions the jury to disbelieve or withhold judgment about belief during the direct examination. The jury will factor in the demonstrated bias throughout the cross-examination.

There are other advantages to be gained by the early use of chapters that demonstrate a motive, interest, or bias of the witness. A witness whose motive, interest, or bias is exposed is likely to become even more nervous concerning his own testimony. The response of the witness to revelation of his motive, interest, or bias varies from witness to witness but may include the following:

- The witness may become defensive in his answers, trying overly hard to justify the testimony he is giving.

- The witness may become self-doubting and hold back on damaging information in hopes of being perceived as less biased.

- The witness may become argumentative or overly aggressive in reaction to the attack on his motives, interest, or bias and thereby offer up even more evidence of his bias.

All of these reactions play to the advantage of the cross-examiner, by coloring the juror's perception of the testimony yet to be heard.

The lawyer must recognize that jurors are engaged in a moment-by-moment judging of the credibility of a witness. Throughout the cross-examination the jurors may be rejecting certain pieces of testimony while accepting others. If the advocate can actually demonstrate a bias, interest, or motive by placing those chapters near the beginning of the cross-examination, the advocate can tilt jurors toward disbelief or reasonable doubt before they have even heard the subsequent chapters of information.

§11.21 When Numerous Impeaching Chapters Are Available, Take the Cleanest Impeachment First

Impeachments occupy a special importance in cross-examination. A fact admitted by an opposing witness carries more weight than a fact testified to by the lawyer's own witness. This is true because the jury well knows that the witness would not give up the fact willingly, since his motivation runs contrary to the lawyer's theory. A fact eventually admitted over protest is given even more weight by the jurors, as is a fact admitted by a witness called by the opposition, which the witness in some way worked to hide or deny. This is as true in civil cases as in criminal cases. A fact that is admitted by an opponent or a person aligned with an opponent, has greater credibility than the same material testified to by the cross-examiner's witnesses. Jurors believe some witnesses will shade the truth, but they do not believe that witnesses will shade the truth to hurt their own cause.

Two very powerful purposes are served by those chapters of cross-examination that impeach the witness. First, the impeaching sequence forces the admission of a disputed fact. Additionally, the admission of the fact is directly harmful to the credibility of the witness (see chapter 16, *Eight Steps of Impeachment by Inconsistent Statement*). Impeachments, however, carry with them their own dangers. A simple leading question deserving of a "yes" answer is itself safer and easier than the impeaching question. Often the significance of the impeachment can only be understood after a detailed series of preliminary questions within the chapter. Impeachments on inconsistent statements require the laying of an appropriate series of foundation questions (a chapter bundle), and these questions in turn must be more skillfully drafted with great attention to detail and phraseology. For these reasons, there are special guidelines to the sequencing of impeaching chapters.

An impeaching chapter may itself be the opening chapter of cross-examination. An impeaching chapter may set up the theme or need to go first to establish motive, interest, or bias. However, when several impeaching chapters are available, there are some guidelines to help put the impeaching chapters into a sequence likely to have the greatest impact on the witness and the jurors.

§ 11.22   Set Up Impeachments from Transcripts With Chapters That Accredit the Court Reporter

There are some sequences of chapters that work well to introduce chapters of impeachment from transcripts. First, the lawyer needs to engage in techniques that accredit the transcript process. Jurors, after all, are strangers to the legal process and they are not in the least familiar with verbatim transcripts of testimony. They do not have a working knowledge of the shorthand reporting system and many are quite skeptical that a court reporter can accurately take down all of the words being spoken.

Depending on the sophistication of the witness, he too may doubt the ability of a court reporter to accurately take testimony. In order to reassure the jury as to the accuracy of the transcripts being used, and to reduce the risk that a witness can dispute the accuracy of a transcript, there is a technique available. Somewhere early in the case, perhaps in voir dire or early in the examination of the witness, the cross-examiner should look for a reason to ask the court reporter to read back the previous question. For instance, in voir dire, if opposing counsel objects to a question, and the court overrules the objection, the lawyer might ask the court reporter to read back to the prospective juror the question just asked.

The jurors immediately compare what they have just heard read back to them with what they remember the question to have been and realized that the two memories are identical. In this way, the jurors get some insight into the shorthand reporting system. The lawyer has enhanced the credibility of the court reporter. This same technique can be used at any occasion in which there is some interruption in the proceeding, allowing the cross-examining party to request a read back by the court reporter.

Another technique of accrediting the court reporter, done for an entirely separate purpose, is using the court reporter to control the runaway witness (see chapter 19, *Controlling the Runaway Witness*). In this technique, the lawyers asks the court reporter to read back to an evasive witness her exact question, thereby transferring her question into a question by a member of the court's own staff. While the primary goal of this technique is to establish control over the witness, it simultaneously reminds the jurors that the court reporter's notes are both official and accurate. Both objectives can be achieved by these techniques.

§ 11.23 Perform the Most Relevant Impeachment Before Using Less Relevant Impeaching Chapters

When several impeaching chapters are available, it is best to lead with those impeachments that most directly bear on the theory of the case. Lead with the most relevant evidence before using evidence that is less relevant to the theory of the case. Relevant evidence is defined as evidence having any tendency to make the existence of any fact that is of consequence to the determination of the action more probable or less probable than it would be without the evidence (Federal Rules of Evidence, Rule 401).

"Relevancy," as the Federal Rules uses the term, means a great deal more than that = the classical definition. The most relevant material in a cross-examination is the concedingly admissible material of greatest import to the cross-examiner's theory of the case. In applying this guideline, the issue facing the cross-examiner is not "can it come in?" but, among all the things that are admissible, which impeachment most benefits the theory of the case? It is in that special sense that the term "relevant" is used in this guideline.

This guideline is in accordance with the guideline of primacy. Furthermore, by leading what will become several chapters of impeachment with the most relevant impeachment, the cross-examiner more effectively begins the destruction of the credibility of the witness, thereby proving to the judge and the jury that there are flaws in the story of the witness and that cross-examining counsel has the evidence to expose those flaws. The effect of lesser impeachments is heightened by the fact that they follow one or more very relevant chapters of impeachment. Then, when the cross-examiner moves into less relevant impeachments (impeachments on more collateral matters), such chapters are less likely to draw objection and more likely to keep the jurors' attention, since the lawyer has previously demonstrated the factual weaknesses in the testimony of this witness. In addition, a witness who has been successfully impeached on undeniably material matters is fair game for other impeachments increasingly farther a field.

The first set of impeaching chapters establishes many psychological points of use in further impeachments. Both the judge and the jury now know that cross-examining counsel is prepared and able to impeach the witness. This means the "permission" to attempt further impeachments will not cost the court a lot of wasted time. Counsel has proven the ability to get the job done efficiently and fairly. Of equal importance is that cross-examining counsel has demonstrated that the witness is worthy of impeachment. The first successful chapters of impeachment serve to take the witness down a notch in the eyes of the fact finder. Now the witness is seen as vulnerable on the facts; additional attempts by the cross-examiner to impeach the witness are received by the court with more favor.

Had counsel instead elected to impeach on the more collateral matters first, she runs the risk of a sustained objection or of the jury thinking that such impeachments are unfair or of no great significance. By the time she gets to the major impeachment, she risks having lost momentum and indeed having lost some of her material by way of material objection.

§ 11.24   Regardless of Importance, Use Clearly Admissible Chapters of Impeachment Before Attempting Impeachments That Might Be Ruled Inadmissible

When numerous impeaching chapters are available, first use those chapters of impeachment that are undeniably admissible. In this way, cross-examining counsel generates momentum for the cross-examination by leading with evidence that does not provoke an objection. By using clearly admissible chapters of impeachment first, the impeaching evidence rolls in to begin the damage of the witness. By scoring with chapters that crisply and fairly impeach the witness, the lawyer makes the witness's credibility subject to further attacks, and thereby psychologically broadens the bounds of admissibility. The witness who has been successfully impeached on several items is more vulnerable to attack when the lawyer reaches chapters at the edge of admissibility. Given that judges have broad discretion at the edges of relevancy, solid impeachments lay the groundwork to show the judge that the cross-examiner is prepared to further impeach, and that the witness is worthy of further impeachment. Once the witness has been impeached several times, the judge is encouraged to rule the witness fair game for additional impeachment. Judges are less protective of witnesses whose credibility has already been fairly called into question. And judges are aware that the jurors' must make a determination as to the credibility of each witness, and that the credibility of this witness is now the subject of fair and effective attack.

By taking the most admissible impeachments first, the cross-examiner weakens the witness, conditions the judge, and alerts the jury that a full and fair attack on credibility is under way, and that the lawyer is armed to win that battle.

§ 11.25 Use the Most Easily Conducted Impeachment Before Attempting Complex Impeachments

Where several chapters of impeachment are available or where more than one impeaching sequence is directly relevant and clearly admissible, the cross-examiner benefits from using the most easily conducted chapters of impeachment first. In this way, counsel can cleanly impeach very early in the cross-examination. The goal of witness control is furthered.

Some impeachments, though relevant and admissible, are cumbersome. The story may be difficult to tell, the significance of the answer may be unclear without further elaboration, or the impeachment may only have meaning when considered in conjunction with testimony not yet introduced. For any of these reasons, some chapters of impeachment are simply more difficult to perform than others. In such instances, it is advantageous to begin with impeachment that can be cleanly performed. In this way, the witness is immediately put on notice that the cross-examiner is able to impeach easily.

If, on the other hand, the cross-examiner were to begin with a relevant and admissible but cumbersome chapter on impeachment, the cross-examiner runs the risk of becoming bogged down in the laying of foundations, arguments over the words of the impeachment, or other hurdles that the witness or opposing counsel can put before the lawyer. Having not yet developed a track record of control over the witness, the cumbersome nature of the impeachment encourages the witness to fight. This heightens the risk that opposing counsel will interpose objection.

§ 11.26 Behavior Is Molded by Consequences

Behavior is molded by consequences. Every successful impeachment leads the witness to a better understanding that the best way to avoid further embarrassment is to concede the truth. This fear on the part of the witness becomes stronger the more times punishment through impeachment has been administered by the cross-examiner. The cross-examiner establishes greater control and thereby lowers risk through preparation for possible impeachment. A witness who has already been impeached based on an inconsistent answer, a witness who has already been hemmed in by a series of tight, leading questions, a witness who has tried to evade answering only to be brought up short, has learned at every step to be more wary of the questioning party and less willing to challenge the leading question.

The lesson to be learned is that the cross-examiner must first establish control over a witness through safe chapters. Safe chapters are chapters in which the impeaching evidence has already been discovered, chapters in which the answer to the leading questions is documented in discovery, chapters in which the motive, interest, or bias of the witness becomes evident, or any other chapters that, when properly formed up, will require pre-determined, helpful answers from the witness. In this way, the early chapters of the cross-examination serve to "train" the witness. Then a more risky chapter may be approached. Whatever the degree of risk of the new chapters, a lasting effect of impeachment has lowered that risk.

§ 11.27   Disperse Solid Impeachments

When several impeachments are available in transcripts or other documents, it is ordinarily advantageous to intersperse such solid impeaching chapters throughout the cross-examination. In order to appreciate the significance of this technique, the cross-examiner must bear in mind the effect of impeachment on the witness. Quite often, the witness does not see the impeachment coming. The witness may not recall his prior testimony. The witness may not realize he is at odds with an exhibit or with another witness. Even if the witness understands that he is about to give an answer that can be impeached, the act of impeachment itself has a sting.

Witnesses never enjoy the experience of being impeached and it is likely they never get used to it. Every time a witness is impeached, a scar is left on the memory of the witness. The witness is led to understand that, when in doubt as to a fact, it is likely the cross-examiner has correctly stated the fact in the leading question. A witness who has been impeached will modify his behavior to lessen the chances that he will again be impeached. By disbursing impeachments throughout the cross-examination, the witness is unsure which leading question, or which chapter may be the foundation for the next impeachment. Before denying a leading question the witness must weigh the likelihood of impeachment. This is a very difficult process for most witnesses and the difficulties are compounded by the speed at which facts are placed before the witness through use of the only three rules of cross-examination. In summary, successful impeachment chapters interspersed throughout a cross-examination keep a witness off balance and encourage the witness to be more honest in their answers.

§ 11.28   Disperse Impeachments Using Documents (Paper Is Power)

Every successful impeachment results in a sanction against the witness. But there is special power in an impeachment based upon a document. In this regard, the power of transcripts must first be understood. Impeachment through an inconsistent statement documented in a transcript of the witness's testimony is relatively quick, safe, and powerful. The witness has said something today that is at odds with their documented former answer. The witness will have an extremely difficult time denying the accuracy of the transcript. Furthermore, the laying of the foundation for use of the transcript can itself be a powerful sequence of questions. Throughout that sequence, there is no room for an unresponsive answer. A lawyer can move confidently through foundation and into impeachment, score the point, and move on. As a result of these characteristics, such sure-fire and effective chapters should be interspersed so that they can be used to back up more risky areas.

Similarly, any impeachment that may be accomplished using a photograph, a memo, a physical exhibit, or any other item of evidence that is tangible is an impeachment to be treasured. The memo, the e-mail, and the letter all speak louder than the words of the witness. They testify that the witness is being inaccurate. The tangible form of the impeaching item lends additional power and drama to the impeachment and as a result, the scar left by the impeachment is deeper. The witness retains in his memory the picture of the moment he was exposed as being inaccurate. The jurors also have a better picture of the impeachment as they can recall a physical item that was used as part of the impeachment. As can be seen, paper is power. Not only has the cross-examiner accomplished the ordinary goals of an impeachment, the cross-examiner has simultaneously promoted the importance of the document or piece of evidence used to impeach the witness.

§ 11.29 Impeachments That Occur Spontaneously During the Cross-Examination Are Opportunities to Establish Risky Material

The guidelines above discuss the value of disbursing planned impeachment chapters throughout the cross-examination. However, the properly sourced page preparation of cross-examination offers the cross-examiner multiple additional opportunities for impeachments (see chapter 10, *Page Preparation of Cross-Examination*). These are not properly seen as impeachment chapters, but are actually impeachments taking place within a planned chapter. These kinds of impeachments are a speed bump on the road to the goal. The cross-examiner had not planned for the witness to change his answer, but the cross-examiner had a source document upon which to base an impeachment. The award is an instant, unplanned, or spontaneous impeachment.

This form of impeachment has the identical effect on a witness as other impeachments: The witness becomes unsure of himself and more likely to accept the truthfulness of the cross-examiner's leading question. At this moment of self-doubt the witness is weakened. It is at this moment that the cross-examiner might choose to ask the more risky question. Of course, she uses the leading question/one new fact per question techniques. The risk taken is ordinarily that the cross-examiner believes she knows the answer, but that she cannot prove the answer independently. In other words, the cross-examiner must depend upon the truthfulness of the hostile witness to reveal or affirm a fact that hurts that witness's position. In this moment of self-doubt, created by a spontaneous impeachment in an area where the witness thought he could safely fight, the witness is more likely to concede such a fact.

§ 11.30 Cross-Examine on Collateral Issues Once the Opportunity Arises, Rather Than at a Fixed Point in the Cross-Examination Sequence

There are some chapters and topics that counsel would love to cross-examine on, but that may be ruled collateral by a judge. A ruling that a topic is "collateral" often is made because the court does not appreciate the tie between the objected to chapter and an issue within the case. In order to increase the ability to cross-examine in these areas and to avoid objection by an opponent or overcome the objection if made, the cross-examiner must look at these areas of cross-examination as targets of opportunity. The target of opportunity is an area upon which the lawyer would cross-examine *if* the witness offers an opening. However, when preparing the cross-examination it may appear that the area is risky or not factually ripe for impeachment. In such a situation, the cross-examiner does not begin the cross-examination with the fixed intent to cross-examine in this chapter, but plans to cross-examine upon it only if the witness offers some answer (often a non-responsive answer) that touches upon the target area.

Then, using the witness's response as an entry, the cross-examiner can move into the prepared chapter that was not sequenced.

It is neither necessary nor appropriate to fix these chapters within the sequence of cross-examination. Instead, the lawyer should have them ready, waiting for the witness to give some answer, which promotes their admissibility. While it is indeed the witness that creates the opportunity to change our sequence, this is not an exception to guidelines that suggest a lawyer be hesitant to change a sequence based upon the answer of a witness. The lawyer chooses when to change the sequence by watching for opportunities and taking on new chapters only after doing everything possible to minimize the risks.

In order to prepare for the cross-examination in these collateral areas, counsel must draft the cross-examination chapters on the arguably collateral issue in advance and then wait for the witness to say something in direct examination or in cross-examination that opens or tangentially touches upon the issue.

For instance, the witness may have been suspected of arson, but charges were dropped for lack of evidence. It is going to be almost impossible to cross-examine on this chapter unless the witness opens the area of arson. During the cross-examination of the witness, while doing a recap of the witness's prior felony convictions, the witness testifies: "Sure, I've done some stuff I'm not proud of, but nothing dangerous like robbery, arson, or murder."

If counsel is going to get to a cross-examination on the witness having previously burned down his own building in an attempt to collect insurance, the time is now. She should immediately move to the chapters that were previously written concerning the witness's suspected arson case. By volunteering any information on the issue of arson, the witness may have done enough to stall an objection by the opponent, and at a minimum it clearly provides the cross-examiner with a basis to combat the objection. Judges are not hesitant to rule that a witness or attorney has "opened the door," and at the very least, the witness has created the opportunity to perform the very short cross-examination in the collateral area before being ordered to move on, as counsel now has an undeniable good faith basis to begin using the previously prepared materials on the issue of arson. Even if objection is interposed and sustained, the jury will be aware that on this collateral issue, counsel is prepared to challenge the witness's credibility. The witness will get that same message.

There are other occasions in which collateral material may be converted to fully admissible material by a chance comment by the witness. The well-prepared lawyer prepares for and recognizes opportunities for cross-examination in areas where opponents and witnesses sensed danger. For instance, quite often opposing lawyers in direct examination seek to introduce their witness to the jury and try to humanize them by having the witness relate a little of their life history. To the extent that this history contains some fruitful areas of untruths, the witness has made the untruth on a collateral matter admissible by opening the area on direct examination. This fatal slip by a witness in the first five minutes of her direct examination, when both she and the prosecutor believe themselves to be totally without risk:

Q: (By the prosecutor) Where did you work after that?

A: I was an aide at Charmco Nursing Home for about a year.

Q: What did you do there?

A: I took care of the old people and helped get them dressed and made beds and just generally helped in their care.

Q: And why did you leave that job?

A: My mother got sick and had to have an operation, so I quit to stay home and take care of her.

Undoubtedly, both the prosecutor and the witness thought this to be a most innocuous and risk-free area, designed to cause the jury to think well of the witness, who would soon be testifying that she witnessed the defendant murder a man. It was a tiny throwaway line by the witness designed to bolster credibility, but in reality it opened a collateral area of impeachment — the witness's work history at Charmco Nursing Home.

The lawyer has prepared for this by investigating the work history of the witness. Perhaps it will be necessary to immediately send out an investigator to check on the work history of the witness or to subpoena duces tecum the employment file of the witness. Whatever the mechanism, a new area of potential inquiry has been opened, and depending on the results of the quick investigation, the lawyer might seize upon the issue. In this instance, the trip by the investigator to the nursing home produced an employment file that showed that the witness had not quit her job at the nursing home to take care of her mother but had been fired. Furthermore, while she sought in direct examination to create a picture of herself as a sensitive and caring aide to the elderly, in reality she was fired for abusing patients and coming to work high on drugs. These are materials that may well have been so collateral as to be wholly inadmissible. Now, through the direct examination of the witness, they have become material, and she may be cross-examined on this area using the employment records. As a result of a small slip by the witness in an area that seemed safe, some of the most damaging impeachment can now be performed.

Note, however, that even if counsel had possessed this employment file before beginning the cross-examination, and even if the witness had given this false testimony at a pre-trial hearing, the material is still more collateral than other testimony contained in the cross-examination. It has a greater risk than other evidence contained in the cross-examination, and it likely lacks the full impact of better evidence contained in the cross-examination.

In order to best introduce the evidence at some appropriate point in the cross-examination, it is necessary to remind the witness of the previous testimony, allowing her again the opportunity to tell the jury the story that counsel now knows to be false, a story the cross-examiner is about to impeach. In this way, counsel reminds the court as well that this is a repetition of previous testimony under oath, and is therefore fair game for cross-examination.

§ 11.31   Develop Risky Areas Only After Establishing Control of the Witness Through Safe Chapters

To some extent, the application of each rule of the only three rules, aided by the page preparation of cross-examination, represent significant steps toward establishing control over the witness. The proper application of preparation and techniques for forming the questions and the chapters has the inescapable effect of driving home to the witness the fact that the cross-examining party is thoroughly prepared on the facts, capable of punishing any erroneous, evasive, or inconsistent answer, and that no objection can stop the cross-examination.

There will always be those areas of cross-examination that pose risks for the questioner. This can occur because the cross-examining lawyer is acting with incomplete discovery, because the witness has a plausible explanation to counter the thrust of the cross-examination chapter or because the witness has previously demonstrated a willingness to provide a non-responsive or runaway answer. A witness who is demonstrated a willingness to engage in behavior designed to dodge the truthful answer to a leading question is a witness who has signaled the increased risk of any chapter that is not fully sourced. If, for any of these reasons, a particular area of cross-examination appears to be risky, the risk can be decreased, and at times eliminated, through the advantageous sequencing of chapters.

As discussed in chapter 8, *The Only Three Rules of Cross-Examination*, one of the greatest benefits to the cross-examiner is the use of leading questions to establish control over the witness and the resulting examination. A witness who has been schooled in the advantages of the "yes" answer, and who has learned the dangers of impeachment is a witness less likely to take risks in their subsequent answers. When a witness realizes that the cross-examiner may well be able to impeach a less than completely honest answer, most witnesses become more reluctant to shave the truth or fence with the cross-examiner. The leading question coupled with appropriate immediate impeachment when the witness denies a sourced fact, teaches the witness the dangers of answering anything other than "yes" when "yes" is the truthful answer.

Plaintiff's counsel in a personal injury case must cross-examine the defendant's medical expert. The expert will testify that plaintiff should not be experiencing the kinds or degrees of pain of which she complains. It is likely that no cross-examination will change that opinion. However, by first establishing the appropriateness of the tests run by plaintiff's doctors, and then discussing the results they obtained in the defense expert's tests, the cross-examiner is in a better position to take up the tests *not* run by defendant's expert witness. Yes, the defense expert can explain why those tests were not run, but the explanation follows powerful chapters on tests that played in favor of the plaintiff. In addition, if the defense expert has been impeached, and chapters demonstrating a motive, interest or bias have been completed a hostile witness is noticeably less inclined to pick a fight, to explain at length, or to dodge the leading question.

It is incorrect to think that the witness is "lulled" into giving the desired answer. In fact, nothing about this cross-examination sequence lulls the witness; instead the truthful series of leading questions fatigues the witness and breaks down their desire to dispute the leading questions of the cross-examining party. The constant flow of leading questions, impeachments, and forced truthful admissions has the effect of breaking down the will of the witness to fight the lawyer. The cross-examiner must keep in mind that the tones of the questions need not be aggressive, only their content. It is the facts that ultimately defeat the witness, not the tone of voice in which they are asked.

It is essential that by the time the risky area is hit upon, the witness has already painfully learned the apparent futility of disputing the truth of the leading question. Through such a sequence, where chapter after chapter of safe material is first performed, and where the safe material within a risky chapter is first performed, the cross-examining attorney has lowered the risk that a witness will unfairly deny the truth as stated in the leading question.

§ 11.32 The Cross-Examiner May Build Her Own Credibility Through a Series of Strong Chapters Based Upon Leading Questions, Before Risky Areas

Thus far, the dynamic has been analyzed from the standpoint of the cross-examiner and the witness. It is important to fold in the perceptions of the jury. They have witnessed chapter after chapter of winning evidence. For the most part, the witness has been forced to concede "yes" answers. In some instances, the witness has given an answer with some assurance on direct examination, only to find himself on cross-examination impeached with an inconsistent statement. In some instances, the witness has been forced to give facts that contradict other witnesses or that contradict physical or tangible evidence. Throughout all of these chapters, it has become apparent to the jury that the cross-examining lawyer has an encyclopedic knowledge of the case.

She is systematically proceeding through the case proving point after point, even though the witness may be hostile. The jury too must not be alerted to the risk inherent in a particular chapter. They too become accustomed to the lawyer completing her goal and increasingly skeptical of the witness's explanations as the lawyer repeatedly wins the battle with the witness chapter after chapter. When the risky area is approached, should the witness still have the strength to begin the fight, he does so with decreased credibility. His explanation, his dodge, or his alternative fact seems less credible. By proper sequencing of chapters, the lawyer has decreased the chance that the witness will give the undesired answer, and has simultaneously decreased the likelihood that the jury will believe the undesired answer.

§ 11.33   Chapters That Are Risky, Either Because of Issues of Materiality, Admissibility, or Complexity Become Easier If Taken After the Witness Is Under Control

This guideline is the product of the previous guidelines. Within a cross-examination there is a sequence for risky chapters and there is a method of expanding the boundaries of impeachment. Cross-examining counsel can decrease risk and expand the parameters of admissibility by demonstrating to the court her control of the facts, the ability to move efficiently and appropriately through the methods of impeachment, and that the witness is deserving of impeachment.

A judge, having realized these facts, is far more likely to let the lawyer move through discretionary chapters, since the judge is now aware that the cross-examining party has a method and the ability to carry it off. The cross-examiner's preparation is rewarded, in that demonstrable preparation encourages the judge to grant greater leeway in admissibility and in the time available to impeach. The lawyer that wanders in her cross-examination may even find herself curtailed from reaching admissible matters as she simply used up the available airtime allotted to her in the judge's mind. On the other hand, when dealing with the prepared lawyer who moves efficiently through the evidence and is seemingly always on a roll, a judge is far more willing to grant leeway, knowing that the attorney has a goal in mind and is moving diligently toward that goal.

§ 11.34   Do Not Give Verbal or Behavioral Cues That a Chapter Has Increased Risk

In introducing a chapter with increased risk, it is important that the cross-examining attorney cross-examine in a style that is consistent with the safe chapters previously performed. It is a mistake to hesitate or become equivocal. It is especially unwise to start leading questions with verbs (see chapter 8, *The Only Three Rules of Cross-Examination*), to change from a form of question that seeks a "yes" to a form of questioning that seeks a "no" answer.

It is very important that the cross-examiner use a tone of voice that is consistent with the tone that has been adopted in the immediately previous chapters. A weaker tone or a tone that implies uncertainty alerts the witness. By cross-examining in a style that is consistent with the immediately previous chapters the witness is not alerted to the fact that the cross-examiner has moved out of safe, though punishing chapters, and into an area where the witness might have the upper hand. Similarly, the risk of a chapter is decreased by opening the chapter with as safe a sequence of leading questions as possible so as to establish control within the parameters of the chapter before hitting upon the riskier facts.

§11.35 When Anticipating an Undesired "No" Answer, Precede That Question With a Question on a Parallel Issue That Will Result in a "Yes" Answer

At times the cross-examiner will ask a leading question to which she would like the answer to be "yes," but fully expects to receive a "no" answer. The "no" is unwanted, though it seems unavoidable. These events tend to be critical issues where a ``yes" answer would so verify the cross-examiner's theory of the case that the witness cannot afford to give it. Usually these questions can be spotted by the tendency on the part of the cross-examining lawyer to lead the question with a very forceful: "Isn't it true . . . (issue)?" Lawyers somehow believe that if they are more forceful in their phrasing, the witness will change his answer; in effect believing that a theory of the case can be yelled into life. They are wrong.

Voice, movement, and timing are not substitutes for facts (see chapter 22, *Voice, Movement, Body Language, and Timing*). Assuming the cross-examiner lacks suitable evidence to solidly impeach the ``no" answer, she still may need to indicate to the jury that the ``no" is deceptive and is not to be believed. There is a technique for accomplishing this task: Build a chapter around the anticipated "no" answer, placing the "no" issue at the end of the chapter. The cross-examiner will then lead up to the anticipated negative answer by a sequence of leading questions on parallel facts that are going to produce "yes" answers. Then, the "no" is juxtaposed with material that makes the "yes" answer seem more believable.

For example, take the case where the theory is that the snitch was actually the drug dealer. The cross-examiner's key question is that the car load of marijuana intercepted by the police belonged to the snitch, not the defendant. The witness in direct testimony states that the intercepted load belonged to the defendant. The planned cross-examination question is: "It was your load that the police intercepted in March 2002?"

Now applying this guideline, the cross-examiner can end up having fully anticipated the "no" answer to this key question, but the cross-examiner can begin to undermine the "no" by a series of leading questions on parallel facts making the anticipated "no" answer appear untruthful:

Q: You have been smuggling loads of marijuana for four years?

A: Yes.

Q: You have gotten away with it dozens of times?

A: Yes.

Q: In January, 2001, you smuggled a load of marijuana from El Paso to Denver?

A: Yes.

Q: It was your load?

A: True.

Q: You were the driver?

A: Right.

Q: In September of 2001, you smuggled a load from Los Angeles to Denver?

A: Yeah.

Q: It was your load?

A: Yeah.

Q: You were the driver?

A: Yeah.

Q: In January of 2002, you smuggled a load of marijuana from Salt Lake City to Denver?

A: That too.

Q: It was your load?

A: True.

Q: You were the driver?

A: Yes.

Q: In March, 2002, you were caught smuggling a load of marijuana from Tucson to Denver?

A: Yes.

Q: It was your load?

A: No.

Q: You were the driver?

A: Yes.

The "no" answer remains. However, by foreshadowing the "no" with a series of questions on parallel episodes in which the answer was "yes," the attorney has shown the jury why the "no" answer is not fully credible. The answer fails the plausibility test of the jury. The cross-examiner has properly and succinctly demonstrated to the jury that this last load was nothing different than previous episodes, the only distinction being that the witness is unwilling to tell the truth about this episode.

§ 11.36 Prepared Chapters Countering the Power of the Opponent's Case Are Best Performed in the Middle of Cross-Examination

The opponent has evidence that works well for him, too. After all, if the cross-examiner has all the weapons, there isn't much of a lawsuit. In the real world, however, there is the problem of what to do when some of the cross-examiner's chapters must take on facts that are very much to the favor of the opponent.

Why would a cross-examiner enter into such chapters, since they play to the power of the opponent? While it may be that no clean, solid impeachment is possible, some cross-examination around the edges of such material may be necessary in order to weaken the impact of the opponent's presentation. It may be that some exploration is required so as to not leave the material completely un-rebutted and thereby concede defeat. In such instance, when the cross-examiner is attacking against the power of the opponent's case, it is best to sequence these chapters of impeachment have been performed, and before exhausting all of the cross-examiner's chapters.

In this way, the damage has been done to the credibility of the witness *before* the cross-examiner must take on the witness in areas of strength. In addition, by not leaving such difficult chapters for the end of cross-examination, the advocate is capable of inflicting additional damage *after* the difficult chapters have been completed. It is critical that the cross-examiner leave herself with strong material to use to reestablish any control and loss of momentum created by taking on the witness in areas where the witness has a strong chance of prevailing. Therefore, when counsel is forced by circumstances to take on a witness in chapters in which the witness has the upper hand, the cross-examiner must hold in reserve strong chapters to stop the flow of negative information, should it occur.

§ 11.37 Never Lead or Conclude a Cross-Examination With a Risky Chapter

The many dangers of impeaching in risky areas have been discussed. Methods of decreasing the risk have been discussed. However, the skillful cross-examiner, understanding the dangers and having done what she can to decrease the risks, must still abide by another guideline: Do not attempt to begin or conclude a cross-examination with a risky chapter.

No matter how strong a start or finish this risky chapter would be, it is not worth the risk. If used to lead the cross, this encounter will set the tone for the entire cross to come. If the witness "wins" on this first encounter, he will discover the benefits of being combative and will, therefore, revert to a combative posture throughout the cross-examination. Worse, the jury immediately sees the fallibility of cross-examining counsel — hence the cross-examiner's credibility is immediately and perhaps irretrievably lost.

If used to conclude the cross, all of the best "witness stopper" chapters have now been spent elsewhere in the cross-examination. The impeachments have been used, the biases shown. Now, if the conclusion of the cross-examination goes poorly, the cross-examiner has no safe route, but must dig in and fight to salvage the conclusion. Gone is any hope of ending on a high note. In its place is at best a long and tedious battle to escape humiliation at the hands of the witness. The witness ends on a high note, not the lawyer. Redirect is encouraged.

Risks, if they must be run, should be run in the middle of cross-examinations where there is time and material to dispel the damage that might be done by the witness. Cross-examinations must begin and end predictably. The purpose of the first and last sequence of cross-examination is not to undo the witness (which is almost never achieved); it is to score a point of true value. This is no time for risky business. Start and end with a safe chapter.

§ 11.38 In Long Cross-Examinations, Treat Each Day or Half-Day as a Separate Cross-Examination

Some cross-examiners of a single witness are time-consuming, but critical to the success of the lawsuit. Such a cross-examination may require several hours or more. In any cross-examination that proceeds for any great length, the jury may lose its focus, and some of the drama may be dissipated simply by the duration of the examination. The cross-examiner may counteract this loss of focus and drama by reverting back to the guidelines, which discussed laying a theme early and often, and interspersing impeachment chapters to keep the attention of the jury. The cross-examiner is free to reorder chapters during recesses including after a lunch break, or after an overnight recess. After such a recess, the jurors are undoubtedly feeling refreshed, but the emotions built in the courtroom have dissipated.

Assuming the lawyer has finished the sequence of chapters she was performing before the recess and has concluded a topic and is not in the middle of a topic, the lawyer should commence a resumed cross-examination with a chapter that once again scores a point with impact as soon as possible (primacy). The cross-examiner must grab the jurors and draw them back into the mood created before the recess.

If counsel has been cross-examining the credibility of the witness as being mistaken, this is best accomplished by immediately impeaching after the break on an inconsistent statement. When accusing a witness of willfully deceiving the jury, the chapter that introduces another lie told by the witness will best accomplish this purpose. If counsel has a chapter that contains within it the theme phrase, immediately after a recess is an excellent opportunity to use such a chapter.

In this way, the cross-examiner has refreshed the jury's recollection that this witness has been skillfully under attack throughout the cross-examination. In accordance with the principles of primacy and recency, a new attacking chapter coming immediately after a recess, strikes the jury as particularly important. Through this reshuffling of chapters, the jury is given the opportunity to reflect that it seems that this witness is forever being caught in contradictions, lies, or is in other ways impeached.

§ 11.39 Once Cross-Examination Has Begun, Be Reluctant to Change the Predetermined Sequence

The cross-examiner must have confidence in the sequence of chapters established prior to commencing the cross-examination. However, the witness cannot be counted on to stick with the cross-examiner's script. To the contrary, an effective cross-examination often forces the witness to try to jump to other areas or chapters. Chapters that he believes will be safer (see chapter 30, *Recognizing and Controlling Bait*). It often happens that the witness jumps into chapters that counsel intended to cross-examine upon in any event, though the chapters were intended for use later in the sequence. It is tempting to immediately jump from a chapter underway and follow the witness into the other chapter touched upon by a witness in order to show the witness that the lawyer can impeach on that as well. However, to do so allows the witness to dictate the cross-examiner's sequence of cross-examination.

This is a most dangerous practice. Every chapter had its own goal, and its own pattern of questions necessary to establish that goal (see chapter 9, *The Chapter Method of Cross-Examination*). By allowing the witness to lure questioning counsel into jumping out of a partially completed chapter into a new chapter, counsel has permitted the witness to move the lawyer away from the systematic completion of the goal of the chapter then being performed. This means that later, the cross-examiner must come back and pick up the pieces of the broken chapter. This process will almost certainly compromise the power of that chapter. Moreover, a great risk is run that the lawyer will fail to return to the chapter and thereby lose the goal altogether.

When the cross-examiner chases a witness into an area picked by the witness or allows a witness to drag the cross away from the prepared sequence, the result is that the cross-examiner has ceded control back to the witness. This remains true even if the witness drags the cross-examiner into another chapter that was already prepared. While it is tempting to make the leap as a way of showing the jury and the witness that the cross-examiner can control even the unexpected, there are methods by which the skillful cross-examiner can complete the current chapter and simultaneously express her ability and willingness to take up the newly raised matters.

Assume the witness, in the midst of answering questions in one chapter, volunteers a partially or fully non-responsive answer that brings up another chapter. The best course of conduct is to ignore the bait and to stick with the game plan. Any other response psychologically encourages the witness to offer up additional bait. At most, the cross-examiner may assure the witness of the cross-examiner's control by saying:

Q: You have brought up the (new subject). We will get to that in due course, OK?

Even this response may concede too much control to a witness. The preferred course is for the cross-examiner to discourage the witness from offering any bait designed to take the lawyer to a chapter selected by the witness. That can be best accomplished by an ignoring the attempts by the witness to set his own agenda for the cross-examination.

If the witness should jump into a new chapter that is among the cross-examiner's best material, there is a technique not only to remind the witness of the cross-examiner's control, but also to heighten the impact of that coming chapter. The cross-examiner can say to the witness, "You agree that this topic is important?" The cross-examiner can then go to the blackboard or large writing pad and write the name of the chapter or the topic brought up by the witness. The cross-examiner can then assure the witness that she will get back to that. The jury will now wait with anticipation to see what will occur when cross-examining counsel returns to this area. Of course, upon the return, the cross-examiner must be able to score solid points to impeach in these chapters, as the cross-examiner now has impliedly promised that this material will be of significance to the theory of the case.

Having used any of these techniques to deflect the suggestion of the witness that the cross-examination go into a different area, the cross-examiner must then follow up immediately with the leading question she had next planned to ask in the chapter he was currently performing. In this way, the witness is cautioned that his attempt to drag counsel away from the prepared chapters will not work. Counsel will punish the witness for his non-responsive answer. Through these techniques, the witness's apprehension of the upcoming cross-examination has been heightened. The jury, rather than believing the lawyer to be unprepared, is reassured that she is so well prepared that she intends to take the witness back to this additional area. While never abandoning the sequence of cross-examination, counsel has assured the jury and intimidated the witness. Both the jury and the witness realize that examining counsel would not have made the commitment to get back to the volunteered material at a later time were counsel not confident of her ability to master the additional chapters as well.

§ 11.40   Never Let a Witness Force a Change in Sequence

Prior to trial, when all the lawyer's powers of concentration are focused, the lawyer has placed the chapters into what is believed to be the most persuasive sequence. Now, in the heat of trial, during direct or cross-examination, the witness has said some truly angering or new things or seems to be volunteering all kinds of openings that fit very nicely with written chapters that counsel had intended to perform at some later time. There is a natural tendency to jump from what was planned to what the witness is now talking out of a desire to show the witness that counsel is prepared in that area and can one-up the witness. The cross-examiner must resist the temptation and stick to the chapter sequence the lawyer has prepared, while observing the following guidelines (see chapter 30, *Recognizing and Controlling Bait*).

§ 11.41   Cross-Examining Counsel May, for Good Reason, Change a Sequence

Sometimes, through no action of the witness, the lawyer may come to the conclusion during the cross-examination that a change of sequence is in order. It may happen that a new answer has been given in direct examination that promotes the value of a previously planned chapter. Under such circumstances it is both acceptable and safe to reorder the chapters before standing up to cross-examine. This thoughtful decision, made prior to commencing the cross-examination, ordinarily leads to better results than a spontaneous decision to reorder the chapters made during the actual cross-examination.

Another situation that can generate a voluntary change of sequence is an answer containing information that can be immediately used against the witness. This information, be it a fact or a phrase, can be spontaneously looped by the cross-examiner (see chapter 26, *Loops, Double Loops, and Spontaneous Loops*). A cross-examiner who chooses to spontaneously loop an answer does so based upon the belief that the value of the loop can best be realized by immediate repetition of the word or phrase used by the witness. Having made this election, cross-examining counsel should exploit the spontaneous loop material. Then return to the scripted chapter in which she was previously working.

In the midst of cross-examination there are more things that can go wrong than can go right through a reordering of chapters. Have faith. If the chapters are left in the sequence in which they were planned, the cross-examiner will inevitably get to all of the material eventually and will get to the material in an order that in calmer times seemed to make good sense.

§11.42 When a Witness Volunteers a "New" Area of Cross-Examination That Relates to the Chapter Being Performed, Counsel May Choose to Examine on Those Materials at Once

When a witness volunteers an answer within a chapter that relates to that chapter, it may make sense to impeach the witness immediately on that new answer or to cross-examine on that new material. There is, of course, an increased risk in doing so because the material is new. The cross-examiner is less prepared on that issue than the issue previously scripted. Nonetheless, if the new material directly relates to the chapter in which the cross-examiner is then working, the risk is decreased.

This is true because the cross-examiner presumably has a safe sequence of questions within the chapter to fall back on. The cross-examiner can rely upon the material originally written for the chapter so that if the deviation from the chapter does not produce results, the original material is available as a path to safety. Depending upon the material available to the cross-examiner, it may be possible to immediately take on and successfully counter the new material within the chapter before returning to the remainder of the chapter.

However, the cross-examiner must be reminded that "new" material is a form of bait offered by the witness. If the chapter was solid before the material was volunteered, it should be completed as written. Counsel may be better off not chasing the new material but forcing the opponent to either inquire into it using open-ended questions on redirect. In this way, the cross-examiner is allowing even more time to consider whether to and how to take on the new material (see chapter 30, *Recognizing and Controlling Bait*). The advocate should remember that if the "new" material does not relate to the chapter then being performed, but relates instead to a upcoming chapter. The cross-examiner should not chase the witness into the new material.

§ 11.43 Before or During Cross-Examination, the Cross-Examiner May Safely Abandon or Add Previously Written Chapters

Simply because the cross-examiner has written a chapter does not mean that the cross-examiner must perform the chapter. Sometimes the direct examination settles an issue. The chapter written to exploit that issue may no longer be necessary, useful or safe. For any such reason, it is entirely acceptable to put aside prepared material. Similarly, sometimes chapters are prepared that seem to lack vitality. They may have been written with the hope that the witness will make a mistake, open a door, or otherwise create a circumstance in which the chapter can be pursued. If, within the direct examination or the cross-examination, circumstances change and the stored chapters appear to have utility, it is also appropriate to pick them up from the table and add them to the cross-examination being performed.

This flexibility can only occur through a lawyer's thorough preparation, backed up by a cross-examination preparation system (see chapters 5, 6, and 7). As was pointed out in the discussion of witness statement charts (see chapter 7, *Cross-Examination Preparation System 3: Witness Statement Charts*), the witness may have been entirely consistent on a point prior to trial, yet may alter his testimony during direct or cross-examination. It is, of course, entirely appropriate, to cross-examine on this new inconsistency, using the previously prepared witness charts or topic cards to impeach the witness on his change of story. In such an event, the attorney may be cross-examining solely from the raw witness charts or topic cards, so once again, the absolute accuracy of the cross-examination preparation system must be stressed.

Having elected to cross-examine on this new area, the cross-examiner should perform the new chapters of cross-examination at an appropriate point consistent with the other guidelines previously discussed. Another word of caution: It is extremely to use newly-developed chapters as the initial or the concluding chapters of a cross-examination.

§ 11.44 Keep a Safe Chapter to Use When the Witness Has Enjoyed a Moment of Success

Throughout the cross-examination, counsel attempts to reduce risk and establish control over the witness. Nonetheless, it must be acknowledged that there are some chapters that are risky. As a result, there are some chapters that are not going to go as well as planned. In such circumstances, it is understandable that the cross-examiner feels a momentary diminution of control and the witness feels a greater willingness to combat the cross-examiner. In such circumstances, it is wise to have a backup — a chapter that is predictably safe and easy to accomplish. This chapter can be thought of as a "cork."

The cork chapter is set aside for use when the unexpected occurs — when the witness scores in a way the cross-examiner might not have foreseen and when the cross-examiner needs a moment to get themselves and the witness back under control. The cork is dependable. It scores its planned goal and gives the cross-examiner the needed time and the positive momentum necessary to move safely back into the planned chapter sequences.

Chapters that are built around clean and crisp impeachments from transcripts or documents are excellent corks. A planned impeachment chapter provides the lawyer with an easy and safe way of moving back into control of the witness and reestablishing in the jurors' minds that this witness is on the run. If counsel has been stung in the preceding chapter or if the jury is wondering whether the preceding chapter has scored, by moving quickly into the safe impeachment from transcript, the lawyer implies to the jury that she is not the least harmed by the previous answers. The impeaching chapter demonstrates that the cross-examiner is inexorably chipping away at the credibility of the witness. Used in this manner, solid impeaching chapters act as a cork on the witness. The dependable material can be drawn on to stem the flow of damaging information spewing forth from the witness. The witness will moment ago was on the attack is now again on the defensive. Left alone the witness might be emboldened to again try to challenge the cross-examiner. Cross-examining counsel should apply a solid impeachment that forces the witness to back off.

A cork chapter need not be a chapter built around impeachment. Alternatively, a cork chapter can be fashioned out of any material that is clearly relevant to the opposing theories of the case, and is simple and straightforward enough that the goal of the chapter is predictably obtainable. The power of such chapter is not that it has enormous impact but that it has predictable utility and safety. The cross-examiner uses this chapter to prove a goal and show the witness that the witness's just concluded the experience of the beating cross-examiner was nothing more than a momentary glitch. The effect on the witness is to demonstrate that nothing will dissuade the cross-examiner from establishing the points she deserves.

§11.45 Using Cork Material Immediately Before the Planned Concluding Chapters of Cross-Examination

In the event that the cross-examination of the witness goes better than anticipated, or even in areas where the witness was thought to have power but does not turn the tide against cross-examining counsel, the cork chapters can be moved toward the end of the cross-examination to end the cross-examination with multiple impacts. Of course, a cork chapter, if not needed as a cork, still maintains all of its vitality and must be used before the end of the cross-examination. The cross-examiner must never waste the chapter. But in the midst of a difficult cross-examination, it is comforting to know that one or more powerful "cork" chapters are available in an emergency.

§11.46 Close Cross-Examinations With a Theme Chapter

As discussed in chapter 12, *Employing Primacy and Recency*, cross-examining counsel should strive to close the cross-examination with a chapter that makes a firm imprint on the jurors. The cross-examiner should save a chapter of importance and impact to close her cross-examination. A chapter that again makes use of factual material to repeat the theme is one possible method of the ending a cross-examination.

In a case built on mistaken identification, the theme of "but now it has changed" linked to changing descriptions can be used to its best advantage by performing an impeaching chapter on a part of the description as the initial chapter, and then performing an impeaching chapter on another part of the description as the final chapter of cross-examination. In this way, the first and last chapters the jurors hear are facts about the witness changing his description of the robber.

In a commercial case, where the plaintiff claims the defendant omitted certain information or warnings, a concluding chapter that shows one more omission is an effective way of concluding the cross-examination. In a commercial case in which the defendant seeks to show the lack of factual support for the plaintiff's theory, a final chapter that displays another source of information and of support for the plaintiff's theory brings home to the jury that the facts are missing.

§ 11.47   Close the Cross-Examination Using the Chapter or Chapters Written as the Closing Sequence

The cross-examiner will have found some group of chapters in which she has great faith. Based upon thorough preparation, she believes the evidence to be solid, safe, and powerful. For these same very good reasons, the cross-examiner has selected the concluding chapter or group of chapters. As counsel moves toward the conclusion of the cross-examination, she emotionally imagines how great it will be to end on a high note.

While this is true, the cross-examiner should stick with predictably solid chapters, rather than take chances with some riskier chapters that could result in a bigger impact or none at all. The risk is too high and the return too low to justify abandoning the well-thought-out concluding chapters in favor of the new, "inspired" chapters.

Assuming there are solid reasons to perform the new chapters, it is far better to integrate them into the existing sequences, leaving for last the prepared chapter sequence. By inserting the newly conceived or highly risky chapters into some midpoint in the cross-examination, there will still be time to recover momentum and control should it fail to work. The lawyer will have available material with which to finish on a guaranteed strong note.

§ 11.48   End With a Power Chapter

No risks should be run in the final chapter of a cross-examination. It is important that the cross-examination of a witness went well. It is unnecessary and unlikely that the cross-examination will end spectacularly. That should not be the goal of the advocate. What is important is to end the cross-examination crisply. The conclusion of a cross-examination is not the time to take chances. The cross-examiner does not want to end her cross-examination with a fight concerning the admissibility of a statement.

Similarly, the final chapter of cross-examination should be evidence that will not draw any other type of objection. The last chapter does not deserve a special tone of voice simply because it is the last chapter. Such a dramatic change in tone often produces the objection "argumentative." If a court were to rule the last chapter inadmissible, either in whole or in part, the advocate has suffered a self-inflicted wound. It would have been better to have run that risk at an earlier point in the cross-examination so that if the chapter were ruled inadmissible, there would be recovery time through other strong chapters.

Even if the advocate wins the evidentiary battle, her momentum will have been slowed. Some of the impact of the last chapter will be lost. Counsel must strive to end the cross-examination with purely admissible material performed concisely. Counsel wants to create a clean, powerful final point. The meandering question that allows for a bulky answer that trickles in is to be avoided. The last chapter and especially the last sentence of the last chapter call for affirmative responses that paint a picture that is of use to the theory of the case. It is now time to sit down.

The psychological principle of recency teaches that the lawyer must leave the jurors with a strong final impression. Among the strongest final impressions is reserving a lie for the liar or a final inconsistency for the mistaken witness (see chapter 12, *Employing Primacy and Recency*). As part of the cross-examiner's attempt to ingrain a theme (see chapter 2, *Developing a Theory of the Case*), the final sequence of cross-examination is an excellent opportunity to repeat the theme. For the purely mistaken witness, a final "now the facts have changed" make an excellent ending line for the cross-examination. For the lying witness, immunized by the government, who has repeatedly changed his story, a final "we have your word on it" may be enough to remind the jury that this is a person who has lied to many people on many occasions. In the custody case, a final "but you couldn't find the time" is a damning conclusion to a series of missed opportunities to interact with the children. In the personal injury case, the last sentence of the last chapter of the cross-examination on defendant's expert witness/doctor may be:

Q: And she complained of a pain in the small of her back?

Q: And that is exactly what you would expect from this collision?

All of these guidelines apply to a final sequence of cross-examination that has immediate impact, that is to say, a sequence of cross-examination in which the points being scored are apparent to the jury at the time they are scored.

§ 11.49 It Is Permissible to Conclude With a Chapter Whose Importance Will Only Become Evident in Relation to the Testimony of a Previous or Later Witness

Not all successful cross-examinations result in immediate gratification for the cross-examiner. There are those cross-examinations in which the cross-examiner may choose to use the final chapter as a sequence to score a point against a previous witness or to set up a major point to be scored by a later witness. Whether the witness is a police detective, a construction foreman, a treating doctor, or a school teacher, it is often quite advantageous to end their seemingly benign testimony with the firm establishment of a fact that will take on great significance only when contrasted with or added to the testimony of another witness.

The fact being set may often be an impeachment in which one witness called by the opponent testifies in a fashion dramatically opposite the testimony of another witness called by the opponent. Eventually this impeachment may prove quite important to the jury. But if the chapter will only be understandable after a later witness testifies, this technique of concluding the cross-examination will come across as weak. If a previous witness has already testified and provided the set-up for this concluding chapter, the jury will have a greater chance of recognizing the importance of this chapter. Nonetheless, unless the point is very important and its significance immediately recognized by the jury, such a chapter is best placed neither first nor last in the sequences of cross-examination.

Lawyers have long been schooled that the last chapter should have great impact, but that precept has been overstated, leading to a dangerous misunderstanding. The last chapter is the final point, not necessarily the best point. Cross-examinations end because the good evidence has been exhausted. Even the best chapter of cross-examination will never alone win the case. It is unwise to self-impose great pressure on the cross-examiner to end the cross-examination with some case breaking revelation. The object of the last chapter of cross-examination is simply to score another useful goal.

It is a rare occurrence where the import of the answer and the impact of the evidence will not be understood by the jury until they have heard information from another witness. Only then will they realize through that additional witness the impact of the previous answer. Under such circumstances, the witness himself does not understand that a point has been scored. This may seem dramatic, but this scenario is not ideal.

Any time the answer cannot be immediately integrated into the theory of the case by the fact finder, there is a heightened risk that the jurors will not understand or remember the answer. In order to link up the answer from one witness to the answer provided by another witness, it is best to make the link during opening statement. In this way, the jurors can understand why the question was asked, and why the admission was gained long before the second witness takes the stand to complete the picture or tie up the point. It does not matter that the first witness fails to understand the point being built by the cross-examiner. It is only important that the fact finder have that understanding.

For instance, in a personal injury case, the defendant driver has maintained from the first moment that the narrowing of the street width forced her to veer, resulting in a sideswipe of plaintiff's car. While she will testify in a most positive fashion on this point, plaintiff's counsel will next call the investigating police officer, who will testify in detail to the fact that the road does not narrow at all. In such circumstances, the defendant driver has no idea that her last answer on cross-examination is a setup for the destruction of her credibility. She will not be on the stand when the importance of this answer is revealed; she may not even be in the courtroom. Nonetheless, the eventual worth of this answer is so high as to justify its use as the closing sequence of the cross-examination.

Similarly, an informational cross-examination concluding chapter is done precisely in order to set up a point that will only become important in light of later testimony. For ease of comparison, simply reverse the order of witnesses in the above example. The police officer was to testify first. A powerful conclusion to her testimony would be to take the officer through her measurements of the roadway. The cross-examiner could end by establishing that there is not so much as an inch of change in the width of the roadway. Cross-examining counsel could then call the defendant for purposes of cross-examination and begin the cross-examination by eliciting from the defendant her story that the swerve was made necessary by a sudden narrowing of the roadway.

Chapter 12

EMPLOYING PRIMACY AND RECENCY

SYNOPSIS

§ 12.01 The Concept of Primacy

Psychology teaches that the first words a listener hears will be the words that the listener more easily remembers. Human experience and common sense reinforce the notion that a first impression is a lasting impression. Our mothers told us: "You only have one chance to make a first impression." This concept is called "primacy."

The advocate has unparalleled opportunity to make important points in the first few minutes of a cross-examination. The jury's attention is highly focused during the opening chapters of a cross-examination.

§ 12.02 The Concept of Recency

The field of psychology teaches that there is another equally identifiable and compelling principle called "recency." The principle of recency holds that the last words a listener hears will also be long remembered. Again, human experience validates this psychological concept. It is therefore important that the cross-examiner uses strong chapters in the concluding portions of a cross-examination.

§ 12.03 The Advocate Should Employ Both Psychological Tools

There is no need for trial lawyers to reconcile these concepts or to attempt to decide which is the more enduring: "primacy" or "recency." Trial lawyers can use both concepts to their advantage in every trial, hearing, or conversation. The most easily recognized application would be in cross-examination.

§ 12.04 Applications of Principles of Primacy and Recency to Cross-Examination

The principles of primacy and recency have at least three applications in the field of cross-examination. Their first application is to the sentence structure of each question. The second application of these principles addresses the structure of the individual chapter of cross-examinations. The third applies to the structure, organization, and content of the entire cross-examination of each witness.

§ 12.05 Sentence Structure

As was discussed within the three rules of cross-examination (chapter 8), each leading question should be a short declaratory statement with a question mark. The doctrines of primacy and recency provide further reasons why each of the cross-examiner's questions need be factual statements. They should not contain repetitious prefixes ("Isn't it true that . . .") or suffixes (". . . isn't that true?"). There are other such phrases: ". . . correct?" ". . . isn't that right?" "isn't it a fact . . .?" These are but a few examples of repetitive phrases.

The skillful repetition of any word or phrase gives greater emphasis to a word or phrase. This is helpful when using a theme word or phrase (see chapter 2, *Developing a Theory of the Case*). On the other hand, if the cross-examiner repeatedly uses certain words or phrases that do not assist the theory or theme line, then the repetition is useless to the cross-examiner or, worse, a mind-numbing habit.

An example of the misuse of a "tag line" comes from one page of a civil deposition:

Q: You are barely sixteen, isn't that right?

A: Yes.

Q: You have not had your driver's license long, isn't that right?

A: Yes.

Q: You have not driven any car except your father's, isn't that right?

A: No, I also drive the driver's education car at the high school.

Q: All right. You have only driven two cars in your entire driving history before this collision; your father's and the Driver's Education car, isn't that right?

A: Yes.

Q: Your father's car is a Toyota Celica hatchback — a small car, isn't that right?

A: Yes.

Q: The driver's education car at the high school is a car — not a truck, isn't that right?

A: Yes.

Q: The vehicle you were driving in this collision was a jacked-up, big-wheeled pickup truck, isn't that right?

A: Yes.

A lawyer reading aloud these questions and answers would quickly hear the problem created by the unthinking repetition of any such phrase. This is an unfortunate distraction as it is the information within the leading question that should draw the attention of the listener. Any such phrase desensitizes the listener to the other words and phrases of the sentence and numbs the mind. The sound of the questions becomes stilted and no one could blame a listener who decided to tune out.

If the boring, repetitive nature of such phrases were not bad enough, these monotonous words draw even greater attention because they are inevitably used at the beginning or at the end of the question. In essence, the least important words dominate the primacy and recency factors of the sentence. The facts become the mushy middle.

§ 12.06 Fact Finders Are Turned Off by Wasted Words

Primacy and recency teach that listeners will find it easier to both listen and understand the facts that they hear at the beginning and at the end of the question. Therefore, if such phrases as: "Isn't it a fact?" "Isn't it true?" or "Let me ask you this," are used the cross-examiner is not only being repetitious without good purpose (these are merely reused crutches for lawyers to "load" the next question), but the lawyer is also defeating and abusing the principal of primacy. Lawyers use primacy against themselves by encouraging the jury, through repetitious desensitizing, not to listen to the beginning of the question. That means that the jury won't listen to any of the question. The jury turns off.

§ 12.07   Utilizing Primacy and Recency in the Question

Phrases such as "Would you agree. . ." at the beginning of the sentence or "Isn't that correct?" at the end of the sentence are merely oratorical crutches used by lawyers to buy time while the lawyer is mentally loading the next question. The advocate has probably gotten into the habit of using these "no meaning" phrases as a time-filling device. The lawyer who instead steps to the podium with prepared chapters needs far less filler. A lawyer with prepared questions will find that the crutch impede the flow of the cross-examination. Having no real or psychological need to buy time, the lawyer will find it relatively easy to banish these words from the ordinary sentence structure of a cross-examination question.

In order to take advantage of the doctrines of primacy and recency, the advocate must eliminate these oratorical crutches and depend instead on the clean, crisp presentation of facts in each question. In accordance with the concept of primacy and recency, the lawyer should endeavor to keep sentences short so that the listener need not sift through a great many words in order to find the fact of importance. In essence, most cross-examination sentences can be made so short that there is no middle. There is only a brief set up of the desired fact. Below are some questions that demonstrate how wasteful and misleading can such crutch phrases be:

Recency Wasted

Q: You just turned sixteen, isn't that right?

A: Yes.

Q: You got your driver's license in May, isn't that right?

A: Yes.

Q: You have not driven any car except your father's, isn't that right?

Recency Utilized

Q: You just turned sixteen?

A: Yes.

Q: You got your driver's license in May?

A: Yes.

Q: You have not driven any car except your father's?

Primacy Wasted

Q: Isn't it true you just turned sixteen?

A: Yes.

Q: Isn't it true you got your driver's license in May?

A: Yes.

Q: Isn't it true you have not driven any car except your father's?

Primacy Utilized

Q: You just turned sixteen?

A: Yes.

Q: You got your driver's license in May?

A: Yes.

Q: You have not driven any car except your father's?

As can be seen, without the crutch phrases the questions are shorter and clearer. The concepts of primacy and recency are not wasted.

§ 12.08 Fear That the Witness Will Not Answer

The habit of ending sentences with: "Isn't that right?" or "Isn't that correct?" or "Didn't you?" or other similar phrases can also be a habit developed by the cross-examiner who doubts that the witness will answer the leading question. The advocate who has fallen into this method of coaxing a response has actually signaled her own discomfort with the leading question method of cross-examination. The form of the question needs to be leading. While there is room for the occasional use of such ordinarily wasted phrases, there is no room to change the style of questioning into a form of questioning admitted to be boring and repetitive. Similarly, beginning sentences with such phrases stem from a fear that the force of the question alone will not compel a "yes" answer.

The advocate needs alternative methods to encourage the witness to respond to the leading questions that do not contain such an introduction or tag line.

§ 12.09 Techniques That Teach Witnesses to Answer Leading Questions

[1] Use Voice Inflection to Signal the End of the Question

Witnesses must be trained to respond to the system. There are several devices that can be used to encourage a witness to recognize the declarative sentence as a cross-examination question calling for an answer.

Voice inflection is the most natural way of encouraging a witness to respond. It is the convention used in everyday speech patterns. In a social conversation, a person asking the question will often simply raise the inflection of her voice on the last word. She is putting a benefit emphasis on the last word to imply the question mark. By tying a change in voice inflection at the conclusion of the sentence the advocate tells the witness the question is concluded and the witness should now reply to the question asked.

[2] Use Silence

The use of silence is a second technique of encouraging and teaching a witness the proper method of complying in the courtroom setting. When a witness hesitates to answer or refuses to answer a question put to them, the cross-examiner should patiently wait for the answer. An answer will come (see chapter 8, *The Only Three Rules of Cross-Examination*). The reason why an answer will come is that the silence creates tension in the courtroom. It is clear to the fact finder that the question has been asked, so the judge or jury will ordinarily turn their attention to the witness. The witness will realize that attention is now being focused on them and they will endeavor to end the silence by providing an answer. Once a witness has been so conditioned, he is very likely to live by this practice through the remainder of the case.

The witness has internalized the pace and style of cross-examination questioning and will now respond with an answer. Meanwhile, the question has not been injured with a tag phrase such as: "Correct?"

[3]   Plant a Flag

A third technique of conditioning a witness to respond to the leading question is to properly use one of the introductory phrases or taglines as flag planting device. This method actually encourages the appropriate use of phrases previously branded as primacy or recency wasters. But with proper use, such phrases have great power. A flag-planting device calls special attention to the fact being asked. If the cross-examiner introduces a leading question with a phrase such as "the fact is," it will draw the attention of the fact finder. Because the phrase has not been used with the other questions, it signals to a juror that this question is especially important. Similarly, by ending an important leading question with a phrase such as "Isn't that right?" or "Correct?" the advocate has planted a flag on that question. The advocate has used the phrase in such a way as to say to the jurors that they should listen closely to this question and answer.

For example, the cross-examiner could finish a chapter on important information not communicated to a person deserving of such information (such as an investor, a law enforcement agency, a prospect of employer, etc.). Using this technique that final question could be: "But the fact is, you never gave that information to the (appropriate person or agency)?" Or, "you never gave that information to the (appropriate person or agency), isn't that correct?"

The use of these previously shunned phrases as flag-planting devices is dependent on the cross-examiner not using such phrases when they are unnecessary. By reserving the use of these phrases for the important questions, the utility of the phrase is preserved.

[4]   Explain the Rules of the Court

There is one category of witnesses most likely to profess that they do not understand they are being asked questions. The professional witness is the one witness most likely to wait in silence after the cross-examiner has concluded her question. After the silence has built to an uncomfortable level, this witness will innocently or not so innocently inquire: "I'm sorry. Was that a question?"

Of course this witness knows that it was a question. The witness is attempting to force the cross-examiner out of her system. The cross-examiner should not give in to either the suggestion that the leading questions be changed to open-ended questions or that each question be induced with some repetitive phrase such as "is that correct?" The cross-examiner is also cautioned not to fence with the witness. The easiest and most proper method of combating this strategy is to immediately reply to the question asked by the witness:

Q: You never ran that test?

A: I'm sorry, was that a question?

Q: Yes.

That's it. That is the most straightforward way of saying to the witness that he is to respond to the leading question in the form being used by the cross-examiner. The cross-examiner is tempted to say to the witness: "Of course they are questions. You've been in court 50 times, and you know that full well these are questions." The cross-examiner is advised to refrain from such responses. They are distractions. They reduce the cross-examiner to the level of the witness who is game playing and who may be spotted by the jurors as game playing.

When the cross-examiner simply responds "yes," the witness inevitably is forced to ask: "What was the question?" This shows the jury that the witness was not listening.

§ 12.10 Application of Primacy and Recency to Chapter Sequence

Having accepted the psychological underpinnings of primacy and recency, the cross-examiner should now structure the cross-examination in such a way that both the first chapter and the last chapter of cross-examination are powerful and important chapters for the jury to remember. Remember, powerful does not imply anything more than the fact that these chapters establish a point of importance. The point need not be the ultimate point or even a dramatic point. It should simply be a point that clearly supports the advocate's theory of the case or unmistakably undermines the opponent's theory of the case. Chapter 11, *Sequences of Cross-Examination*, provides detailed guidance on this tactical issue.

A reminder: In general, if important information can only be understood in conjunction with several prior chapters (a chapter bundle) (see chapter 10, *Page Preparation of Cross-Examination* and chapter 11, *Sequences of Cross-Examination*), then it should generally be retained as part of the last chapter sequence. On the other hand, those chapters that will negatively affect credibility should be performed at the beginning of cross-examination so that its impact will carry over through the remainder of the cross-examination.

§ 12.11   Application to Individual Chapter Construction

While not every chapter is enormously important, whatever value the chapter has is enhanced by adherence to the doctrines of primacy and recency. Taking these two concepts and applying them to each chapter of the cross-examination, the cross-examiner will want to begin and end each chapter with important information. This can be accomplished by introducing a chapter with a single fact or concept of importance to the overall understanding of the goal of the chapter and concluding the chapter with a leading question establishing the goal-fact of the chapter. The goal of the chapter is not necessarily the establishment of a single pivotal point. The goal of the chapter is often simply the crisp conclusion of a grouping of facts that paints the important picture. It is the chapter as a whole that accomplishes such a goal. For instance, if the lawyer is trying to show that a meeting was very important, it may require that five or six facts create such a picture. The last question provides a nice capstone to the chapter, but the goal was really accomplished by the grouping of facts.

As the goal of a chapter is reached, the cross-examiner may add a voice change or appropriate gesture or movement to highlight the goal fact obtained. These techniques of voice, timing, and movement complement the doctrine of recency and reinforce for the jury the importance of the material (see chapter 22, *Voice, Movement, Body Language and Timing*). Now, having obtained the goal of one chapter, through change of voice or timing, use of a moment of silence, or a movement to or away from the podium, counsel can begin the new chapter with a firm and fair question in a new subject and thereby reinforce the primacy of that material.

The following example is a chapter in the cross-examination of an expert witness in a sexual assault upon a child case. This chapter is part of a chapter bundle of which the overall goal is to force the expert to admit that the victim suffers from borderline personality disorder, as opposed to post-traumatic stress disorder. This particular chapter is designed to provide the definition of borderline personality disorder and show that the victim fits that definition. Analyzing the structure of the chapter, note that the first leading question is extremely important to the issue (that some people have difficulty telling the difference between fantasy and reality). Having established the central concept (primacy), the cross-examiner works through the chapter to the critical end: This doctor signed off on a medical chart in which she said the child suffered "borderline features" (recency). Example:

Q: It is certainly possible for some people to have difficulty telling the difference between fantasy and reality?

A: Yes.

Q: The human mind can do that?

A: Yes.

Q: Some people do that much more than others?

A: Yes.

Q: People with certain kinds of mental disorders or illnesses do it a lot?

A: Yes.

Q: There are many different kinds of mental disorders people can have?

A: Yes.

Q: Just like there are many kinds of physical disorders?

A: Yes.

Q: Mental disorders have names just like physical disorders?

A: Yes.

Q: One of the mental disorders where people have problems telling the difference between fantasy and reality is a thing called borderline personality disorder?

A: Yes.

New chapter

Q: You met Elizabeth at Strawberry Valley Medical Center?

A: Yes.

Q: You were on the staff there?

A: I was.

Q: Strawberry Valley Medical Center is a mental institution?

A: It is a hospital setting in which we treat people who might be experiencing some type of mental disorder.

Q: Elizabeth was involuntarily admitted to this mental institution?

A: That is my memory.

Q: Elizabeth was involuntarily admitted to this mental institution because she needed treatment for a mental illness?

A: It was thought that she might benefit from treatment.

Q: Elizabeth was in this hospital because she needed treatment?

A: Yes.

Q: There was a team of doctors and nurses that was treating Elizabeth, and you and that team had regular conferences?

A: Yes.

Q: At the end of each conference, the team would fill out a form discussing how Elizabeth was doing and what to do next?

A: Yes.

Q: (Showing exhibit) That's the conference form concerning Elizabeth for August 23, 1991?

A: Yes.

Q: It has signatures of all the team members at the bottom?

A: Yes.

Q: Including your signature?

A: Yes.

Q: There is a space at the bottom to put the justification for Elizabeth's continued stay at the hospital?

A: Yes.

Q: Some things are listed there?

A: Yes.

Q: The first one of those things is borderline features?

A: Yes.

The next example is taken from the cross-examination of a government informant. This particular chapter deals with one of the informant's prior crimes and is part of a chapter bundle in which the earlier chapters explain exactly how, through a complex scheme, the witness defrauded his employer. The purpose of this final chapter is to expose the witness's inconsistent versions of why he committed the crime. Then hook that to the theme phrase, "different stories for different audiences." In evaluating the primacy and recency in the chapter, note that the cross-examiner leads with a dramatic portion of the crime: the day the witness was caught. The chapter then proceeds to funnel through the inconsistent statement and down to the theme phrase:

Q: On January 11, 1985, the auditors discovered your fraud?

A: Yes.

Q: They walked into your office and confronted you with the bogus invoices?

A: Yes.

Q: They were right. You were cheating?

A: Yes.

Q: And when you were caught, you told your employers a story?

A: Yes.

Q: A story on why you needed to cheat them?

A: Yes.

Q: A story on why you needed to defraud them?

A: Yes.

Q: A story on why you needed to lie to them?

A: Yes.

Q: Your story: You needed to steal the money because you were getting a divorce and you needed to pay bills.

A: Yes.

Q: But on 3/25/86, when the D.A.'s investigator interviewed you (to get you ready to testify for this case), you had a new story?

A: Yes.

Q: This fraud arose out of your bookmaking activities?

A: Yes.

Q: Some execs at TBC had lost money to you on some football bets, and they would not pay up, but they did authorize you to steal the money from the corporation.

A: Yes.

Q: Those were different stories?

A: Yes.

Q: For different audiences?

A: Yes.

The advantages of primacy and recency in constructing chapters should not be ignored even when a chapter is informational, rather than confrontational.

The following example was drawn from a case in which it was alleged that a school principal had been involved in sexual misconduct with one of his students on multiple occasions. The prosecution called the school's head custodian to testify primarily on the fact that he had seen the principal and the student together in the building after hours. Defense counsel questioned the custodian on a different issue, one involving the student's allegation that she had sex with the principal in the bathroom of the health room and in his office, and that on each occasion he was careful to lock the doors from the inside.

The janitor was a neutral witness, who has only to tell the truth, regardless of who it benefits or harms. As a result, the following chapter is not done in a confrontational style, but an informational one. The chapter concludes with an exposure of physical evidence contradicting the witness:

Q: You are familiar with work done on the doors and locks over the last few years?

A: Yes.

Q: The reason is you are the head custodian at Fitzmunkers Middle?

A: Yes.

Q: You were there in late 1990 and early 1991?

A: Yes.

Q: Back in late 1990, the lock on the health room door didn't work, is that correct?

A: Yes.

Q: That was because back in 1989 the lock on the door to the main office didn't work, but the nurse's bathroom lock did, so they were switched?

A: Yes.

Q: It was more important to be able to keep the office locked than the bathroom?

A: Yes.

Q: You were aware that it was common for the principal and the office staff to use the bathroom in the health room?

A: Yes.

Q: So they were all aware that the lock didn't work?

A: Yes.

Opp.: Objection. Speculation.

Court: Sustained.

Q: You had a conversation with Mr. Hardin when he first became principal in the fall of 1990 about the locks?

A: Yes.

Q: You remember telling him that lock didn't work?

A: Yes.

Q: You are also familiar with the lock on the door to the principal's office, correct?

A: Yes.

Q: It requires a key to lock?

A: Yes.

Q: There is no keyhole on the inside?

A: Correct.

Q: There is no locking button on the inside?

A: Correct.

Q: It can only be locked from the outside?

A: Yes.

Q: There is no way to lock the door from the inside?

A: Correct.

It is useful to begin a chapter with a question that focuses the interest of the jurors on a particular topic. Of course, not every first or last question of a chapter will be riveting. There isn't that much good material in a case and most of the issues to be discussed on cross-examination are not tremendously dramatic. However, working with what is available, the cross-examiner should strive to open the chapter by focusing attention on the topic of the chapter and close the chapter with the strongest goal-fact of the chapter. Using this format, the cross-examiner has taken advantage of the doctrines of primacy and recency in constructing individual chapters.

Voice, tone, movements, and silence are all devices to aid the often difficult transition from one subject matter chapter to the next subject matter chapter. It is perfectly all right that the judge and jury see and realize that the lawyer is moving from one chapter to the other. The chapters do not all have to fit together seamlessly.

§ 12.12   Application of Primacy and Recency to Trial Recesses

Breaks in the trial for brief recesses or lunch diffuse the attention of the jurors. They must be brought back into the case after the break, especially after a long recess. The advocate should be willing to restructure her sequence of chapters in order to begin strong at the beginning of the day and after each break, as well as end strong prior to each break and at the end of the day (see chapter 11, *Sequences of Cross-Examination*).

Most judges run their courtroom on predictable time schedules. Trial judges are not averse to telling lawyers, if asked, what their trial schedule will be for any given day. If the trial judge customarily will begin at 9:00 a.m., take a break at 10:30 a.m., continue after the break until noon, commence after lunch at 1:30 p.m., take the afternoon break at 3:00 p.m., and finish at or about 5:00 p.m. This is vital information for the cross-examiner.

If the cross-examiner is forearmed with this information, the cross-examiner can modify the sequence of cross-examination or regulate the time used to go through the material so that power chapters are used to begin the day and to finish just before a break (see chapter 11, *Sequences of Cross-Examination*).

The cross-examiner can then select a powerful chapter to begin the next session of court and another to finish just before lunch, and so on throughout the day.

If the case is such that there will be multiple witnesses and many short cross-examinations, the cross-examiner can still use the judge's timetables to her advantage by lengthening or shortening the middle sections of the cross-examination, so that the pre-planned, powerful cross-examination will occur just before a break, before the lunch hour, or, in the best of all cases, before the close of that day.

§ 12.13   Increasing the Judge's Confidence and the Lawyer's Credibility

Utilizing these principles of primacy and recency in structuring the day's cross-examination, a lawyer is able to inform the court at sidebar that a cross-examination is intended to last approximately thirty minutes. She can ask if the court would consider breaking for the lunch hour at 12:15 a.m. rather than at noon, so that the cross-examination is not divided into two parts. If the cross-examiner has credibility with the court, this request is often granted.

When dealing with judges who are less flexible in regard to recesses, the cross-examiner can then make an intelligent, well-reasoned decision as to whether to "fill" the middle chapters of the cross-examination, so that after the recess, the cross-examination can resume with enough good material remaining to allow the lawyer to "reopen" with a powerful chapter (primacy) and develop the remaining material in such a way as to close with a power chapter (recency). In this way, the cross-examiner can not only fit her cross-examination in the court's schedule, but also can also subtly encourage the court to modify a day's schedule in ways that allow the cross-examiner to make best use of the doctrines of primacy and recency.

In addition, the employment of the doctrines of primacy and recency raise the anxiety level of the witness. A witness experiencing greater anxiety has less psychological ability to dodge and weave through the questions. Greater anxiety produces more straightforward and accurate responses. Because the questions are short, they make it clear exactly what fact the cross-examiner is suggesting. Because the facts are built up rapidly through a logical sequence, the witness has less time to contemplate methods of evading the question.

Those tag lines that the lawyer once used to buy time while thinking of the next question also provided the witness with thinking time. Because the lawyer now cross-examines from prepared pages of cross-examination, the facts come more quickly and the witness has far less time and ability to calculate methods of deception.

Chapter 13

THE RELATIONSHIP OF OPENING STATEMENT TO CROSS-EXAMINATION

SYNOPSIS

§ 13.01 Introduction

[1] Recognize the Power of the Opening Statement

Cross-examination consists of a series of goal-oriented chapters, each designed to reinforce the advocate's theory of the case or undermine the opponent's theory. A proper opening statement not only introduces the advocate's theory of the case to the fact finder, but also initiates the process of persuasion by familiarizing the fact finder with the most important chapters of the cross-examination to come. Naturally, the critical chapters of the advocate's direct examinations will also be highlighted in the opening statement. As will be seen in this chapter, emphasizing the important chapters of cross-examination are more important in the opening statement than doing the same for the direct examination chapters of the advocate's own witnesses.

[2] Parameters of This Chapter

The goal of this chapter is to show how cross-examination defines openings. Opening statements pre-sell the subsequent testimony of both favorable and adverse witnesses, along with admissions by witnesses on cross-examination. Generalized descriptions of how to give opening statements are left to others. Therefore, this chapter will focus on the factual importance of proper opening statements: how opening statements strengthen cross-examinations, key components of persuasive opening statements, and the relationship of opening statements and cross-examination to closing arguments. Several cross-examination techniques and oratorical devices most profitably adopted from cross-examination for use in opening statements will be offered.

§ 13.02 Effect of Opening Statement on the Judge — Earning More Room to Cross-Examine

The trial lawyer enhances her credibility by illustrating to the judge, as well as to the jury, an intimate familiarity with the operative facts and the ability to articulate detailed facts that allow a fair presentation of the case. In that regard, it is crucial that the judge understand what the lawyer considers to be the important aspects of the case. Quite often, even a well-prepared judge cannot envision how the facts will come together to establish a claim or a defense. A judge left to speculate on the importance of a particular line of questioning may disallow the line of questioning at the time of the cross-examination. The judge may erroneously entertain the objection "irrelevant" because the judge cannot envision how the chapter fits into the cross-examiner's theory of the case. Alternatively, the judge may urge the lawyer to hurry the cross-examination, causing the lawyer to shorten the presentation of important material. Stated in a positive light, once the judge understands the factual goals of the cross-examiner, and how those factual goals will be accomplished through various witnesses, the judge is more likely to permit the cross-examiner latitude to accomplish those factual goals.

The trial lawyer has lived with the case far longer than the judge. Too often, the trial lawyer thinks it is obvious how a particular line of questioning aids in establishing the lawyer's theory of the case. However, many important chapters can appear to others as irrelevant, innocuous, or too lengthy. The opening statement built to illustrate the trial lawyer's theory by extensively utilizing facts in support of the theory, will greatly aid the judge in appreciating the reasoning behind the various chapters of cross-examination.

Observe an example from a commercial case: The plaintiff sold his business to the defendant in 2003. The sales contract included a representation that the defendant was the sole purchaser of the business. The plaintiff now alleges that the defendant was buying the business as a representative of a group of investors. The plaintiff contends the value of the business has dramatically increased. Plaintiff sues for fraud, seeking rescission of the contract. The defendant denies plaintiff's claim of fraud, stating that he bought the business solely for his own account, though later other investors became involved. The defendant also challenges the materiality of the alleged false representation, stating that the plaintiff would have sold the business in any event, as the plaintiff was desperately in need of money. The defendant intends to cross-examine the plaintiff on his several failed business deals in the period 1999-2003. Once the court understands that these chapters directly attack the materiality element of fraud, their admissibility becomes obvious.

The opening statement needs to make the link between the plaintiff's earlier failed business deals and the need to sell the subject business in 2003. An insufficient opening statement on this issue could leave the judge with the impression that these chapters on failed business deals amount to little more than an attack on the business acumen of the plaintiff (a peripheral issue at best). On the other hand, when the cross-examiner gives a detailed opening statement linking these failed business deals in earlier years to the plaintiff's urgent need to sell this business, both the court and the jury can appreciate the relevance and the importance of these chapters. The factually-detailed, theory-driven opening statement allows the judge and jury to better understand the cross-examiner's theory of the case, but also encourages the judge to grant the cross-examiner more latitude to prove these failed business deals during the course of the cross-examination.

The inherent power of the opening statement to bolster the impact of subsequent cross-examination is as undervalued as it is unrecognized. The failure to recognize the power of the opening statement begins with the fact that many lawyers underestimate the tremendous opportunity and value of making a strong opening statement at all. The opening statement provides an opportunity to persuade. Some trial lawyers who do give some level of importance to opening statements nonetheless consider their development and preparation to be the last task before trial starts. Even those trial lawyers who understand the full value of opening statements use them as a method of "examining" witnesses in advance of calling them, rushing their presentation so that they can get down to the business of taking "real" evidence once the trial gets under way.

The truth of the matter is that the opening statement is far more valuable a persuasive tool than the closing argument. Twenty-five minutes of strong opening statement will prove more valuable than fifty minutes of equally strong closing argument. This makes perfect sense in the real world. Each person worries about making a good first impression, not necessarily making a good last impression. The first impression in front of the jury is the most important opportunity to tell the theory of the case to the fact finder.

A well-crafted opening statement leaves many jury members presuming the rightness of the advocate's position. Even those jurors not fully committed to their vote at the outset will have a mental map of the road that the advocate wants them to travel to the desired verdict. When a theory-driven and fact-based opening statement is matched against an opponent's weak opening statement, the opponent is left with the necessity of dissuading fact finders of what they have already begun to believe. The lawyer's strong opening statement must be overcome before the opponent can even begin to persuade the fact finder of the worthiness of his own case. In this way, the skillful, powerful opening statement gains an immediate introductory advantage in the task of persuasion.

§ 13.03   Opening Statement Is / ~~Is Not~~; And Even If Opening Statement Is Not Evidence, It Is Persuasion

[1]   The Opening Statement Is Used to Persuade

Jurors are routinely instructed that what the attorneys say in opening statement is not evidence. In addition, in trials to the court, arbitrations, and pre-trial hearings, the fact finder is undoubtedly aware that opening statements are not evidence. Trial novices will likely agree that no evidentiary consequences, good or bad, flow from opening statements since opening statements are not evidence. Nonetheless, opening statement furthers the process of persuasion.

It is the written law that opening statements are not evidence. Judges tell that to jurors, just as they always tell jurors that they are not to form any opinions about the case until the taking of evidence has concluded and deliberations have begun. The intention of these instructions is valid. The instruction itself recognizes that people begin forming beliefs about the case based on what they hear in opening statement. Experience teaches that people begin to form impressions, working hypothesis, if not full blown theories, as to what has happened and who is right and who is wrong, from the very beginning of the case and before sworn testimony begins. Strong opening statements are theory driven, fact intensive, and organized by chapter. Opening statements are designed to persuade, not to give an impartial overview of the evidence. The overall purpose of the opening statement is to give the advocate an opportunity to gather preliminary votes.

Example: In a civil trial over a disputed contract, the case settled after jury selection and opening statements. The defendant's opening statement was very factual, detailing how the plaintiff had failed to comply with the contract. Reacting to the opening statements alone, a juror approached the defendant after the court instructed the jury that the case had settled and the jury was dismissed, and said, "I hope you didn't pay that rascal [the plaintiff] any money." Is this surprising? Not at all. All people are accustomed to making decisions on the available information. Jurors, even judges, come to the courtroom eager to find out what happened, who was right, and who was wrong. The process of deciding a dispute begins subtly but instantly during attorney-conducted voir dire. It is in full gallop by the conclusion of opening statements.

[2]   Voir Dire: When Persuasion Once Began and May Still Begin in Some Jurisdictions

When attorney-conducted voir dire was the rule rather than the exception, the battle of persuasion began in jury selection. Sadly, the federal courts, and many state courts as well, now place severe time and other limitations on voir dire or offer only the inadequate substitute of judge-conducted voir dire. Even when attorney-conducted voir dire is permitted, objections are sustained or even initiated by the court to questions that touch on the lawyers' theories of the case.

Whether such rulings help in the "discovery of truth" is beside the point. It is the real world in which trial lawyers must live.

As a result of the emasculation of voir dire, the opening statement has become the principal technique of non-testimonial persuasion. Opening statement was always an important tool. Now it is even more important. Opening statement is more available than voir dire. As a persuasive technique, it is more timely than closing argument. It is more persuasive than instructions. A strong opening statement is the trial lawyer's first opportunity to compel the fact finder to contemplate the theory of the case and appreciate how it will be factually supported.

§ 13.04   Persuasion: Affecting Credibility Through Opening Statement

The credibility of the lawyer and her witnesses is paramount to persuasion. Jurors are instructed to judge the credibility of each witness. An opening statement organized by chapter can and should condition the jury to believe or disbelieve the witnesses they are about to hear, before those witnesses ever take the stand.

By human nature, fact finders judge the credibility of the advocates as well. Trial lawyers who give concise, fact-intensive, and well-organized opening statements that clearly explain their theory of the case gain credibility. Even with attorney-conducted voir dire, a newly sworn jury does not understand the nuances of the case. The detailed recitation of key facts in opening statement tells the jury that this lawyer is prepared, that this lawyer understands the facts in detail, and that this lawyer can explain the facts in a way that assists the jurors in understanding how the facts support the advocate's theory of the case. The lawyer giving such an opening statement becomes a trusted guide to the evidence.

Common experience outside the courtroom teaches that when people must stop for directions, they believe and are therefore willing to follow directions that are clear and detailed. Nebulous or confusing directions may be accurate, but the listener will not feel a sense of certainty and will follow these directions reluctantly, if at all. In fact, under this common scenario, the listener may well stop again soon to ask directions from a different person. The listener has graphically demonstrated a lack of trust in their first guide.

Good directions: Make a right hand turn at the third intersection. There is a traffic light at that corner. Travel 2.4 miles to a red light. There is a grocery store on the right hand corner. Make a left at that light. It is the third house on the left. It is yellow. Poor directions: Hang a left at the first traffic light you come to. Go down a ways, not very far, and there is some sort of store at the corner. Make a left. It is somewhere on that block or the next block.

Whose directions would the listener confidently follow? Who would the listener ask directions from in the future? Transport this scenario to the courtroom.

Included is a portion of a weak and unpersuasive opening statement on the credibility of the plaintiff in a commercial case: "You're going to hear from Mr. Thomas. Yes, he will say his company was badly damaged by the defendant's conduct. But the evidence will show a different story. The evidence will show that his company never did very well. You are going to hear evidence to challenge his version of damages. In fact, the evidence will show that he really wasn't injured."

The same material covered more persuasively: "Wayne Thomas will ask you to give him $500,000 in damages. He will tell you that that is the amount of money he lost due to what he claims was a violation of his copyright. Wayne Thomas will tell you that if Acme had not marketed its software program, in 2003 he would have sold tens of thousands of copies of his software program.

He claims his company would have made more than a half million dollars in profit. So let us look at the evidence of just how well his company, Money Mine, had performed in the two years it existed before the Acme software went on the market.

In 2001, Money Mine revenues were $52,300. But Money Mine expenses were $78,800. Money Mine lost $26,500. How many copies of the Money Mine software were sold in 2001? Not tens of thousands of copies. Not even thousands of copies. The plaintiff sold 632 copies.

In 2002, Money Mine revenues were $61,500. But Money Mine expenses were $89,400. Money Mine lost $27,900. How many copies of the Money Mine software were sold in 2002? Not tens of thousands of copies. Not even thousands of copies. The plaintiff sold 721 copies."

There is a great deal more that would be said in this opening statement. But just this brief snippet shows how devastating a picture can be painted with facts rather than empty conclusionary rhetoric. Do not tell the fact finders that the evidence will convince them of the rightness of the lawyer's position. Instead tell the fact finders the lawyer's position and the facts that support the position. The fact finders will be convinced. They will embrace their own conclusion.

Credibility is primarily a fact-based judgment. While jurors are instructed that they may use the demeanor of a witness as an aid in judging credibility, such indirect clues are less important (and less understood) than the direct method of judging the story that the witness relates. Jurors will first ask, "Does the story make sense?"

It is not enough to tell the jury that "a witness will testify that..." or "the evidence will show that..." Fact finders learn from the detailed recitation of facts, compiled in such a way as to tell a story and to paint a mental picture (see chapter 8, *The Only Three Rules of Cross-Examination*). If the lawyer wants the fact finder to believe a particular person as to a particular fact, the advocate must provide enough supporting detail so either the person or the story, or, ideally, both the person and the story, are invested with particular credibility.

Compare two approaches:

Example 1:

The evidence will show that Henry Hawkins admitted that his company, A.B. Cobb, withheld vital information from its clients. Henry Hawkins admitted this to his friend. His friend will testify. He will tell you what Henry Hawkins said to him about this critical issue. Henry Hawkins will deny he ever said it but you will have an opportunity to decide for yourself who is telling the truth.

Example 2:

James Snow worked with Henry Hawkins for six years. They rose together through the ranks of management. Both are now senior vice presidents. They shared responsibility for several projects. They came to trust each other, professionally and personally. Their families exchanged Christmas presents.

They and their spouses occasionally shared dinners together. So it was not out of the ordinary when Henry called James one day in the fall of 1994 and asked if he could spare a little time to talk with him. What struck James as unusual was Henry's specific request that they meet outside of the office building. Henry picked the place — the Portland Athletic Club. James marked his daily calendar, "Lunch with Henry, PAC 11:30 a.m." James remembers the meeting. Henry was unusually nervous. He picked at his food. He seemed distracted. He even lit up a cigarette — something James had not seen Henry do in almost two years. James waited until Henry was ready to talk, and finally that moment arrived. Henry began shaking. "Remember the SUJITSO bond offering? Well, there were problems. Big problems. It looks like the bonds may not be so good. It seems the research department failed to perform some basic financial checks before selling those bonds."

"Well," asked James, "Why not just get the clients out?" And James remembers Henry's reply. "That's what I asked management and I was told, 'No way, no way. ABCO clients own a majority of those stocks, and if we tell them to get out, the stock prices will drop through the floor. Somebody will start asking questions about why we sold these shares in the first place. When that happens, ABCO is going to end up in court and our research department personnel will look like morons.'"

Yes, James Snow well remembers that meeting and the words "our research department personnel will look like morons." But what will Henry Hawkins say? He will testify. Because we will call him to testify. Henry Hawkins will tell you that he can't remember using those words. He can't recall even discussing SUJITSO shares with James Snow. In fact, he can't even recall the lunch — not the Portland Athletic Club nor the phone call. He can't recall any of these events.

What does the second version of this brief portion of the opening statement accomplish that the first version does not? It has painted a factual picture of the lunch meeting. The fact finder has specific times, places, and even words. The advocate has organized this portion of the opening statement around the prepared chapters of cross-examination of Henry Hawkins, and has used a fact-intensive chapter presentation to sell the credibility of her witness while diminishing the credibility of a witness, Henry Hawkins, all without arguing whom to believe. By offering details that reveal the factual strengths or weaknesses inherent in a witness's testimony on a particular issue, the lawyer provides the fact finder with a logical and just method for reaching conclusions that the lawyer wants the fact finder to reach.

In the previous example concerning the conversation between James Snow and Henry Hawkins, both are senior vice presidents at ABCO. Would you be more inclined to believe James Snow or Henry Hawkins? In that short portion of the opening statement, the credibility of James Snow is elevated and the credibility of Henry Hawkins is deflated. It is done by facts, not conclusions.

The alternative, saying, "S (Snow) and H (Hawkins) will disagree, but you will find S is more believable," is both factually unsupported and objectionable. It is merely a statement of personal opinion, not a fact. See 13.21, *Handle Objections to the Opening Statement.* A solid chapter of facts culminating in a particular point builds the foundation for credibility. In the above example, the cross-examiner could launch a far more effective attack on the credibility of H (Henry Hawkins) by citing facts that are likely to cause a fact finder to doubt the credibility of H. If H has given contradictory versions of events, reveal those contradictions to the jury. If H has authored documents that tell a different story than H will relate in court, tell the jury about the documents. If H has a motive, an interest, and a bias, tell the jury the facts. In all instances, give the jurors the facts. Make it possible for the jurors to arrive at their own conclusion, supported by the lawyer's facts.

The advocate creates immediate credibility by the techniques she uses to deliver the opening statement and by the factual content of the opening statement. Opinions and sweeping generalities are improper in opening statements. When one lawyer consistently explains the case through the vivid use of facts organized around understandable topics, that lawyer is building her own personal credibility as well as the credibility of her case (see chapter 9, *The Chapter Method of Cross-Examination*). The advocate's credibility rises from a well-organized, factually-specific, and persuasive delivery of the theory of the case in the opening statement. Juries do not accept lawyers' conclusions, opinions, or generalities (see chapter 8, *The Only Three Rules of Cross-Examination;*). Juries desire facts upon which to form their own perceptions, conclusions, and opinions.

The fact finder does notice who is confident about the facts and who has an organized delivery. Most importantly, if the lawyer hopes for the fact finder to accept her theory, she must explain it in enough detail so that the fact finder can follow the theory through recognizable chapters. Counsel cannot afford to leave the jury guessing at what she will try to prove or disprove, or what facts are important. Don't leave the fact finder guessing. Tell the full factual story in the opening statement.

§ 13.05 Application of Primacy to Opening Statement

The psychological principle of primacy — what the fact finder hears first, the fact finder is more likely to believe and remember the longest — strongly suggests that the advocate must give a persuasive opening statement at the beginning of trial (see chapter 12, *Employing Primacy and Recency*).

The parallel principles of primacy and recency (the psychological principle that the fact finder will believe and remember best what was heard last) strongly suggest that the beginning portion and the conclusion of the opening must be important to the lawyer's theory of the case, well thought out, and strongly delivered.

In the event there are multiple parties aligned on one side of the case (usually defendants), the lawyer will be best off giving the first opening statement for her side of the case. The second best position is to give the last opening statement of the parties aligned on that side of the case. Obviously, the rules of procedure dictate who goes first and who goes last in a simple one-party plaintiff and one-party defendant case. However, when there are multiple plaintiffs or multiple defendants, a trial lawyer needs to strive for the strategic value of being the first or last to deliver her opening statement. When given the choice, the trial lawyer should always choose the first position, as a fact finder does get bored, confused, or distracted. No matter how persuasive the last statement, fact fatigue will have set in.

§ 13.06 The Relationship Between Opening Statement and Cross-Examination

The goal of opening statement is not to cause the fact finder to keep an open mind. Bluntly stated, the purpose of the opening statement is to aid in winning the case rather than simply explaining the case. Too often, trial lawyers are conditioned to expect interruptions and objections, such as, "She is arguing the case," or 'Opening statements are not evidence and counsel is giving the jury their opinion of the evidence." As a result, lawyers tiptoe shyly through their opening statement, hoping at best to outline the case without tripping off an objection. Valid objections are eliminated by the techniques in this chapter. Proper opening statements do not draw objections as the lawyer has no need to 'argue" the facts. Instead, by grouping facts through the chapter method, the facts argue that the lawyer's side is the more believable. At best, opening statements are both much more and much less than an encyclopedic explanation of all of the evidence and witnesses in the case.

On the more side: Opening statements are a vehicle to sell the advocate's theory of the case, enhance the credibility of the advocate's witnesses, undermine the opponent's theory of the case, and attack the credibility of the opponent's witnesses. In the course of accomplishing these goals, by dwelling on well-organized facts arranged around a central theory of the case, the trial lawyer's credibility is reinforced.

On the less side: The advocate need not discuss every witness or every issue in opening statement. Just as the lawyer cross-examines only on selected material, the opening statement points only to the critical issues in the case. The lawyer needs to determine "where the case breaks," that is, the area of the factual dispute that must be won if the lawyer is to prevail. The advocate will inevitably spot these battles long before trial. Within the opening statement, the trial lawyer must deliver the deepest, most detailed factual presentation in precisely these areas.

If the goals of focusing on the theory and selectively enhancing or attacking credibility sound the same as the goals set forth for cross-examination, that is because they are the same. Opening statements are given for the same reasons that cross-examinations are conducted. Both are a means of communicating the facts to the jury. Both are an opportunity to persuade. Both are times when the cross-examiner is talking the vast majority of the time. Their differences, however, hold the key to the successful opening statement.

Use of the opening statement as a persuasive technique offers several distinct advantages over the other phases of the trial. All trial lawyers understand that the testimony of witnesses on both direct and cross-examination is fraught with hazards. Witnesses do not always explain the facts succinctly. Witnesses may offer facts that do not make sense until linked with other facts introduced by later witnesses. Witnesses fight. Opponents interrupt with objections. The opening statement has none of these disadvantages. The advocate controls the sequence and rhythm of the opening statement. It is not dictated by the order of witnesses. The opening statement brings together pieces of evidence from many sources and groups them into understandable chapters. In this manner, the bulk of the case can be set forth in pertinent detail in a fraction of the time necessary to adduce the live testimony. Opening statements have the added benefit of being uninterrupted by the unresponsive or tangential statements of witnesses. In fact, the supreme benefit of a proper opening statement is that it is a concise and persuasive recitation of the key evidence, choreographed by the advocate in a manner helpful to the advocate.

To achieve this potential, the facts that need to be communicated in the opening statement must be distilled from the far larger number of available facts. Given enough time, a trial lawyer could literally tell the jury all the testimony that the jury was about to hear. While it might explain the case, it definitely would not explain the case persuasively. The best techniques of opening statements, like those of cross-examinations, have little to do with quantity and a great deal to do with focus. Just as in cross-examinations and, to a lesser extent, direct examinations, in opening statements, the advocate should utilize time in accordance with the importance of the facts addressed. Remember, in the courtroom, importance is measured by the time spent on the subject matter, not the volume or oratorical flair of the lawyer. When the lawyer speaks calmly, factually, and forcefully in the advancement of a recognizable theory of the case, the jury is alerted as to the key issues of the case. The opening statement is a literal compression of the case. A case that will take a day might entail an opening statement of 15 minutes. A matter that may be on trial for two or three weeks may be covered in an opening statement of 90 minutes. The selection of the facts to be discussed is crucial. To the extent that certain chapters of cross-examination are critical to the theory of the case, they are critical chapters in the opening statement. The chapters of an opening statement must help the fact finder focus on how the lawyer is going to win. From the fact finder's point of view, the opening statement assists in deciding the case. At a minimum, the opening statement provides the fact finder with a system or context in which to view the facts. The fact finder does not absorb all the facts, but absorbs the key pictures that come together in a cohesive theory of what really happened and how that equals a verdict. Therefore, the first measure of the quality of an opening statement is the degree to which it results in an individual fact finder's understanding of the advocate's theory of the case.

The value of an opening statement is measured by the degree to which it causes an individual fact finder to prejudge or, in the case of a more cautious juror, to favorably consider the merits of the lawsuit from the advocate's point of view. When successful, the opening statement will cause even the fair-minded fact finder to say, "If you prove what you've promised, I think you should win." This state of mind is referred to as "conditional commitment." When a fact finder entertains "conditional commitment," that fact finder is silently saying, "If you can prove the facts you have told me about, I am prepared to decide the case your way." The fact finder is not making an unconditional guarantee, as the salient facts must be produced as promised to the opening statement. It is not always possible to bring a fact finder to a state of "conditional commitment" but that is certainly the goal. The goal often heard in opening statement, "Keep an open mind" is not the goal desired by the lawyer. The opponent who uses that phrase is simply fearful that the other side's opening statement will overpower his case. He betrays his fear by asking the jury to remain neutral. But people do not remain neutral in the face of the facts promised in opening statement. They cannot help to begin to pre-judge the case, based on the assumption that these promised facts will be produced.

§ 13.07   The Relationship of Opening Statement to Direct Examination

Opening statements incorporate those portions of the direct testimony that are critical to the theory of the case. Remember, however, that a fact finder is much more likely to believe an admission of an opposing witness than the self-serving and predictable testimony of the trial lawyer's own direct witnesses. Although opening statements must often present facts that the advocate's own witnesses will substantiate, the opening should place emphasis on the cross-examination and the admissions by the other side's witnesses. In other words, focus on admissions of opponents, in preference to testimony that the lawyer's own witnesses will reiterate.

If a key point is proven by the lawyer's own witnesses and is admitted by the opposing witness, the lawyer should use both forms of evidence in opening statement — stressing the solid admission and backing it up with direct examination testimony.

Example 1:

> Ladies and gentlemen, Homer, the defendant, will testify that he was not at any of the locations at which the United States Government will tell you that the conspiracy occurred. More importantly, and even more significantly to you, each of the Government's witnesses (both of them), all of whom were at those locations where the Government tells you that the conspiracy occurred, will say that they never saw the defendant present, never heard of the defendant being present, and that they have no evidence to give you that the defendant was present at any one of those locations.

Note: Accent was put on the defendant's testimony, but below the admissions by the Government witnesses are stressed. The burden is lifted from the defendant, Homer. This fact now appears as an admission.

Example 2:

Ladies and gentlemen, two of the Government's witnesses will admit on cross-examination that the defendant was never at any of the locations where the Government alleges that the conspiracy took place. Of course, Homer, the defendant, is also going to say this. He was not at any of the locations where the conspiracy took place.

§ 13.08   Emotion in Opening Statement

This pre-judgment by jurors in reaction to her opening statement — which the stock legal instruction decries but the advocate craves — should not be based on an emotional pitch. While it would be nice if the lawyer could cause the fact finder to feel a particular way about the case, a fact finder's emotional reaction to the evidence is difficult to predict. It is difficult to maintain a particular emotion up to the time that the jury actually votes, be it hours, days, or weeks later. A successful case cannot be premised purely, or even largely, on an emotional pitch. Certainly, the opening should spark a reaction, but that reaction should be driven by the logic of the situation. Stated differently, the facts recited in a particular area may compel a juror to feel angry, but it is the grouping of the facts that drives the emotion, not the urging of counsel or the emotion of counsel. A tightly-crafted, fact-intensive opening statement may generate a predictable and desirable range of emotions within the fact finders. But even if it doesn't, the fact intensive opening statement should generate a belief about the key issues in the case. The goal is to create a predisposition as a result of the facts recited. Any emotional reaction to the facts recited is simply a byproduct.

By way of example, envision a prosecutor's opening statement in a simple drunk driving case in which there was no accident. The prosecutor should compile the facts so as to leave no doubt that the defendant was driving and had been drinking, and that consumption of alcohol had affected his ability to drive. Once this picture has been painted, the jurors should all come away convinced of these critical facts. Depending on strategy and presentation, which includes phrasing, timing, and word choice, the fact finders may experience emotional reactions that could range from strong disapproval to anger. If each fact finder is at least conditionally committed to voting guilty, regardless of their individual positions on the emotional spectrum, the opening statement has succeeded.

However, if the prosecutor sets out with the goal of persuading each juror to feel anger at the defendant for his conduct, she has assumed an unnecessary burden and risk — that some jurors will not respond with the desired emotion and will therefore come away from the opening statement lacking the conditional commitment to a guilty verdict. By making a particular emotion a goal of the opening statement, the advocate has made that "emotion" a fact in dispute. Jurors who do not feel that target emotion, are not likely to be persuaded by the theory that stands behind it. Further, the advocate has confused the issues by elevating an emotion to a degree of proof. Those jurors who come up short on that emotion will feel themselves out of synch with that fact.

In all cross-examinations, the advocate compiles facts in an attempt to compel desired conclusions. The lawyer uses facts combined with the judicious use of voice and timing to generate the appropriate emotion. The same works well in opening statements. In fact, the lawyer can be more effective in opening statements because she is able to spell out facts from different witnesses' testimony and weave those facts into an overall picture. In cross-examination, trust is placed in the grouping of facts, not the oratory or emotional delivery. Opening statements must share this trust. Emphasize facts not emotion.

§ 13.09   Opening Statement in Non-Jury Trials — Same Rules Apply But More So

The informality of bench trials, motions hearings, preliminary hearings, temporary injunctions or orders, or alternative dispute resolutions often deludes the lawyer into believing that no opening statement is necessary. Sometimes the judge, or mediator, or arbitrator will signal to the lawyers that opening statements will not be helpful, suggesting that they can pick the case up "on the fly." It is unlikely, however, that judges will fully understand the gist of the case solely from the pleadings. It often seems that the legal issue is straightforward, e.g., whether there was a contract, a fraud, or negligent conduct. However, the facts always come together in strange and unique ways. The judge may have heard a hundred preliminary injunction hearings based on breach of employment contract, but she hasn't heard the facts in counsel's case. A brief recitation of the key facts coupled with a clear communication of your theory of the case will aid, not bore, the court. The persuasive facts needed in order to prevail, are not fully understood without a proper context. The opening statement provides that context.

No case is immediately understandable without an appropriate opening statement. Every case needs "explaining." No presentation of evidence ever flows in purely chronological order. Cases do not proceed evenly with one level wholly constructed before the next level of evidence is introduced. Certain witnesses tell their entire story in one sitting, but much of what they say has importance only if understood in context. Without an appropriate theory-driven, fact-intensive opening statement, the fact finder is left to either guess at the context or remember all the facts for subsequent mental insertion into a context later to be learned. When? In closing? Or worse, after the court has taken it under advisement for days or weeks?

Judges and arbitrators want the advocate to know that they can follow the case without the benefit of opening statements. Even if the lawyer gives the fact finder the benefit of the doubt, she needs to remember that teaching the fact finder how to follow the facts in context is only one of the goals of opening statements. Persuading the fact finder is the ultimate goal, and by skipping the opening statement, the advocate makes absolutely no progress toward winning the case. By voluntarily giving up the right to opening statement, the attorney gives up an opportunity to persuade the judge.

If the other side wishes to grant deference to the intelligence and professionalism of the judge by waiving the opening statement, so be it. Equal respect for intelligence and position can be shown by giving a concise, fact-intensive opening presentation that educates the fact finder and begins the task of persuasion. Does the giving of an opening statement to a judge show disrespect? No. The lawyer shows disrespect to the fact finder by being unprepared to try her case. The well-crafted opening statement acknowledges the all-important role of fact finders, whether they are jury, judge, mediator or arbitrator. It is designed to assist them in their task. The rule is simple: It's show time. Get up and start winning your case. Give a strong, fact-intensive opening statement every time.

§ 13.10   The Construction of Opening Statement: The Three Rules of Opening Statement

The lawyer goes to trial with the goal of persuading the fact finder to vote her way. The opening statement must reveal to the fact finders the essential facts that compel them to accept her theory of the case. She came to court to win this lawsuit, not merely to explain it. In order to get the most value from the opening statement, she must deliver theory-driven, chapter-organized, and fact-intensive openings.

Three elements are necessary to the structure of the successful opening statement:

(1) Construct the opening statement around the lawyer's theory of the case;

(2) Base the opening statement on chapters of witness examination; and

(3) Present fact-intensive descriptions of the events that create pictures, not generalizations.

Structuring a powerful opening statement is simple if counsel has prepared the case using the chapter method. Successful opening statements (defined as openings that move the fact finder toward conditional commitment to the theory) have a great deal more to do with structure than with oratory. As with cross-examination, oratorical devices such as loops, trilogies, and theme lines can add great impact. But what is true of cross-examination is also true of opening statements — use of the chapter format to support a specific theory and organized communication of the detailed facts are of dominant consideration.

§ 13.11   Theory-Driven Opening Statement

Particular jurors are selected because the lawyer believes that they are the persons most likely to accept her theory of the case. The lawyer believes these fact finders are most likely to respond to the facts that the lawyer intends to produce in cross-examinations (and to any direct examinations that are necessary). The opening statement offers the advocate an uninterrupted opportunity to talk to these jurors.

What is the advocate going to tell them? They must be told the advocate's theory of the case. By educating the jurors about the theory of the case, the advocate provides them with a framework or point of reference for the otherwise seemingly unrelated facts that are going to be adduced through witness examinations.

It is important that the fact finders understand the theory of the case before witness examinations begin. This is especially true in cases where any significant portions of the theory are dependent on facts adduced through either the cross-examination of an opponent's witnesses or through the questioning of certain "adverse" witnesses for purposes of cross-examination. While direct examinations often tell a coherent chronological story, cross-examinations are designed to highlight or introduce only selected chapters of the story. Cross-examinations are most often disjointed and nonchronological. Generally, in cross-examination the advocate must cover small increments of the story, and even then, the strategy of sequencing most often dictates a non-chronological approach (see chapter 11, *Sequences of Cross-Examination*). It is crucial that the lawyer structure her opening statement around a cognizable theory of the case so that, as the facts are developed in cross and direct, the fact finder can immediately, in real time, recognize the significance of the facts being made and place those facts into context.

It is the theory of the case that gives direction to the cross and direct examinations. It is that same theory that must give direction to the opening statement. The goal is to win votes up front — even if only conditional votes. To keep these votes, the lawyer must verify the opening statement by introducing the facts through the testimony of witnesses, and the introduction of exhibits. A theory of the case provides a fixed point by which the fact finder can judge the evidentiary progress being made by the advocate. Knowing the theory, the fact finders are able to say to themselves, upon hearing the cross-examination, "I see where you're going." When the jurors hear the recitation of the facts, they are in the position to say, "Now I see how you're going to get there." Jurors need to understand where the lawyer is going (the theory of the case), as well as how he is going to get there (facts).

In order to put across the theory, it is not necessary to boldly announce, "Our theory is that . . ." or "We submit that . . ." Instead, the lawyer needs only to collect and present individual facts in such a way that the theory becomes obvious. For example, if a theory of the case and an opening statement based on that theory are truly effective, the lawyer need not say: "This is a divorce case. The wife, who is the plaintiff, is asking for alimony, and child support. If she does not get at least $2,000 month, her situation and that of her children will become desperate." The reason for the request for relief, the need, and even the consequences of a lesser award, become obvious from the proper recitation of facts.

Example:

> This case is about a man who ten years ago married a girl when she was eighteen years of age. They had a child, Alicia, a beautiful and bright child. The mother dropped out of school to nurture the child. Since the parties needed an income while the father continued his graduate school studies — first a Master's degree and then a Ph.D. — the mother worked as a teacher's aide in the public school system. Her schedule permitted her to take care of the child, and there was a daycare center at the school. Not much income, but enough. Once the husband received his Ph.D., the mother continued to work as a teacher's aide, and through the husband's early days of teaching, the mother continued to nurture Alicia because her schedule was the same as the child's. Now the husband is a full-time professor teaching early childhood education, earning a fine salary of $82,000 per year, with benefits, and lifelong job security, commonly referred to as " tenure." This man has now decided to abandon his family — a family that consists of a wife and child who still adore him, to live with a recent student of his who is nine years his junior. Younger, fresher, and better educated than his present wife.
>
> Despite his education and his understanding of education, he says that his wife and the mother of his child should receive no alimony, no educational allowance, and no security. He feels that she should get out and work a "real job" to better support their child regardless of the child's schedule. (More details to follow in the balance of the opening statement.)

Intensive use of facts without generalizations, conclusions, opinions, or legalisms "explain" the case to the fact finder while "arguing" or persuading the fact finder at the same time. Intensive fact presentations are not argumentative in the legal sense. Objections to them fail. The facts argue themselves.

§ 13.12   Theme Lines and Facts

The proffering of multiple pertinent facts followed by the repetition of theme and lines is an effective way of persuasively presenting a jury with the theory of the case and familiarizing them with the facts that support that theory. Examples of several theme lines are discussed in chapter 2, *Developing a Theory of the Case.*

For example, in defending a criminal case based on a self-defense theory, the trial lawyer will want to relate several instances where the alleged victim encouraged further contact, and at the conclusion of each of these mini-episodes (see chapter 9, *The Chapter Method of Cross-Examination*), the trial lawyer can firmly inform the jury in a theme line: ". . . but Don Cobb didn't let it rest. Instead, Don Cobb came at Jimmy again.' The words "self defense" are not part of the theme line in this example. Clearly, however, the jury is educated that it is the alleged victim who was the initial aggressor. The jury is led to understand, through use of multiple facts in each mini-episode (chapter), that Don Cobb "didn't let it rest" (a theme line) and that Don Cobb "came at Jimmy again" (another theme line).

In a civil case in which the defense is conceding liability, but where the defense's theory is that damages are minimal, defense counsel can persuasively advance her theory by undercutting several important issues impacting damages with the summary thematic statement: "And when her doctor administered the straight leg raise test he found nothing objectively wrong... and when her doctor administered the Babinsky test, he again found nothing objectively wrong."

If defense counsel tells the fact finder the details of the many types of tests performed on the plaintiff, and that the many tests failed to confirm the complaints (her doctor 'again found nothing objectively wrong"), the fact finder cannot help but understand the theory of the case. The fact finder is now well equipped to appreciate the significance of the cross-examinations of the plaintiff and the cross-examinations and direct examinations of the various experts. Those examinations will lead to the goal conclusion that all the physicians were unable to point to any objective finding that supports the subjective complaints of the plaintiff.

In opening statement, the skilled advocate will use specific detailed facts pulled from the upcoming cross-examinations to prove the theory of the case. There is no need to resort to generalizations. Generalizations are statements lacking in facts. Because the generalizations provide no facts, generalizations provide no pictures. Generalizations lead to argumentative statements, argumentative statements lead to sustained objections, and sustained objections in opening statement tend to frustrate the ability of the advocate to get across her theory or her supporting facts. A frustrated lawyer who has started to generalize will inevitably drop into the improper technique of giving her own personal opinion. All of this is ineffective. By using specific detailed facts, the facts themselves coupled with theme lines lead the jury to form their own opinions built on the advocate's facts. No arguments, no objections, and nothing to be sustained.

Take, for example, a battered spouse syndrome-murder case in which the following conclusions are offered.

Poor Example:

"T. Davis, the defendant, was terrorized by his father. T. Davis was so terrorized that he had to do what he did. It was justified."

Better Example:

Night was when the strange things would happen. T. Davis would be asleep sometimes when his father came home. Sometimes he would be awake. A great storm would roll through the little house on Florence Street in San Diego. Nothing would be safe. No one would be spared. A hurricane of emotion. A typhoon of words and activity would rattle anything in its path. Joe Davis would be drunk again. Or high on drugs. Or something. "I brought you into this world, and I can take you out."

The first example is an opening statement with no picture, nothing to visualize, and nothing to remember. The latter is more fact-intensive. It paints a number of mental images that create a memory that won't go away when the opening statement has been concluded.

§ 13.13   Using the Chapter Method to Craft an Opening Statement

The lawyer who has organized her cross-examinations (and any necessary direct examinations) using the chapter method (see chapter 9, *The Chapter Method of Cross-Examination*) is instantly and effortlessly prepared to give a powerful, theory-driven opening statement. In preparing to examine witnesses by chapters, the lawyer has automatically outlined the opening statement. All that remains to prepare the opening statement is to put the chapters into the order that makes the most sense for a fact finder at the opening statement phase of the case.

From the previous civil example, where the insurance defense lawyer concedes liability, five cross-examination chapters dealing with lack of objective evidence to support damages might be headed as follows:

(1) X-Rays — Negative

(2) MRI — Negative

(3) Straight Leg Raise Test — Negative

(4) Patient Climbing on Table — Without Substantial Difficulty

(5) Patient Walking Down Hallway Away from Doctor — Gait Appears Normal

The lawyer uses these chapters as an outline to talk to the jury in a fact-intensive manner. It is unnecessary for the lawyer to draft an outline in great detail or write out her opening statement in its entirety. She can remember the details of the facts and verbally embellish the simple outline presented above, because she has already written the individual chapters for cross-examination to be used on the plaintiff's doctor and on the plaintiff. An example of this portion of the opening statement could look like this:

The plaintiff, Betty Googe, complained of back pain and so her doctor, being a careful and compassionate man, ordered x-rays of her back. Those x-rays were negative. They revealed no broken bones. They revealed no injuries. The doctor found absolutely nothing objectively wrong. Plaintiff, Betty Googe, continued to complain about pain in her back and so her doctor, being a careful and compassionate man, ordered an expensive MRI test. It too was negative. It did not reveal any broken bones. It did not reveal any injuries. The doctor found absolutely nothing objectively wrong.

Of course, the doctor had already performed what doctors refer to as a "straight leg raise test," which is a test designed to determine whether or not there are abnormalities or problems or injuries to someone's back. Betty Googe's straight leg raise test was negative, indicating no injuries. Again, the doctor found absolutely nothing objectively wrong.

Doctors observe their patients in more ways than just performing tests on them. That is, they watch their patients get on and off the table in the examination room. Ms. Googe's compassionate and careful doctor noted that she could get on and off the table without substantial difficulty. In other words, she could climb up and climb down without showing any back pain. Absolutely nothing objectively wrong. The doctor also observed her walking away from the examination room, walking down the hallway, and the doctor noted and thought enough of it to note it in his records, that Betty Googe's gait (that is, the way that she walked) appeared to be normal, as if she had no back problems. No injuries. Absolutely nothing objectively wrong.

§ 13.14   Sequences of Chapters in Opening Statement

The sequence of chapters presented in opening statement is likely to be substantially different from the sequence the lawyer will adopt for the cross-examinations (see chapter 11, *Sequences of Cross-Examination*). If the lawyer presents a theory-driven, factually-detailed opening statement, the lack of chronological order of chapters used in cross-examination will not be confusing to the fact finder. While opening statements need not present the case in chronological order, a likely method is to discuss one element of the case fully, then link that element to other parts of the case which may have happened earlier or later. Within the opening statement — individual issues discussed chronologically and centered around a theory of the case — explain, put into context, and orient the judge and jury to the cross-examinations to come. By the time the fact finders hear the cross-examination of a particular witness, they will have heard both the logically arranged opening statement and the direct examination of that witness. As a result, they will be able to follow the story even though the cross-examination may be (and in all likelihood will be) conducted in a non-chronological sequence, completely omitting many unhelpful sections of the direct testimony.

By using the chapter method and giving a fact-intensive, well-organized opening statement, which in all likelihood will contain chronological presentations of the highlighted areas (chapter bundles), the lawyer not only persuades the jury, but also provides a fixed point of reference for understanding the non-chronologically sequenced cross-examination. Not only are the individual cross-examinations almost always non-chronologically arranged for the reasons set out in Chapter 11, but the presentation of witnesses during trial does not necessarily follow a chronological pattern. As the presentation of witnesses may well be non-chronological, generally, a chronological and sequence-based opening argument is even more important.

§ 13.15   Give a Fact-Intensive Opening Statement

Of these three elements, the one most often lacking in opening statements is the intensive use of favorable facts. Unfortunately, this deficit simply cannot be cured by oratorical devices. Loops (chapter 26), trilogies (chapter 25), and voice and movement (chapter 22) all have their limits. These techniques provide power only when used to highlight particularly helpful facts. By themselves, these techniques have no significance. Interesting words, phrases, and tones and voice may mark the advocate as articulate, but it is the recitation of facts that is persuasive. Between the facts or the flourishes, the best teaching lawyer always relies on the facts to win the case. On the other hand, the fact-intensive opening statement needs few embellishments to ensure its success.

Building the persuasive, fact-intensive opening is an easier task once the cross-examination chapters have been developed by the lawyer. The lawyer must abandon generalities, conclusions, legalisms, and opinions and concentrate on the specific facts that support the chapters that have already been prepared. There is no persuasive value in saying in a firm voice, "We will prove the defendant drove in a negligent (a legalism) manner, in fact, in a wanton and callous (legalism #2) manner." These are conclusory statements only. They give the jury nothing to envision, no facts to rely on, and no story to believe in. A fact finder cannot be persuaded by such conclusory phrases, as these phrases provide the fact finder with no facts upon which to base a judgment. The lawyer must provide the judge or jury with facts that support the conclusion she wishes them to embrace. The jury or judge can thus form their own conclusions and opinions, and these conclusions and opinions will not be easily challenged or changed — by anyone. A direct, chapter-organized presentation of the facts that graphically shows negligence, for example, is far more valuable than all the preaching and posturing of the most articulate lawyer who speaks in lawyeristic generalities about concepts of due care and the reasonable man standard.

Example of an opening statement example based on facts rather than conclusions:

> The night was dark. The clouds were low. There was a misty rain. The traffic that night was unusually heavy for so late an hour. The defendant, barely nineteen, had not driven this road before — not in good weather and certainly not in conditions of a dark, cloudy, and rainy night with heavy traffic. Burt Baker, the defendant, knew that he was tired, knew that he was fatigued, and knew that he was distracted by other worries. Defendant Burt Baker will admit that those worries that distracted him from paying complete attention also drove him to drive faster and faster as the night got later and later. Defendant Burt Baker will admit, and the physical evidence will show, that he didn't just break the speed limit, in fact, he was speeding at least twenty-two miles over the speed limit.

> Defendant Burt Baker will admit that Mary Jo's car was not the first car that he tried to pass. He will also admit that when he went to pass this car, he saw that the double yellow line was just up ahead. This is the manner in which defendant Burt Baker drove his vehicle head on into Sally Luke's vehicle.

In an example where the driver was drunk, it is not enough to tell the jurors, "We will prove the defendant drove in an intoxicated condition." The phrasing is stilted, the story is conclusory, and the impact is negligible. Sadly, the lawyer undoubtedly had available all the ingredients of a truly compelling opening on this aspect of the case.

Example:

> It was just a few minutes before midnight when Dan Caplan finished his last frosted mug of beer. He had started drinking at about 9:45 that Friday night, and he had one drink after another for that entire two hours. Dan Caplan decided to get in his car and drive home. In fact, he will tell you that having swallowed the equivalent of eight cans of beer, he felt just fine. His blood-alcohol level an hour after the collision was .196, putting him at more than twice the legal limit.

If jurors are given the facts, they will inevitably begin forming their own mental pictures, conclusions, and opinions. Given facts on the primary issues of a theory, the jury may adopt the lawyer's theory, or one that is sufficiently similar. If the jury adopts the theory, the ensuing cross-examinations will serve to verify what the jurors already believe to be true. The mental pictures may not be identical to the ones in the lawyer's mind, but they will be similar enough to carry the day.

A lawyer is not permitted to "argue" her case in opening statement. However, the facts that the lawyer reveals, the order in which the lawyer discusses them, and the emphasis the lawyer gives them, are all permissible devices that teach the theory of the case and "argue" for a certain result. For example, if the advocate is championing a medical malpractice case based on a failure to diagnose, the opening statement should contain several chapters that reveal the opportunities the physician had to diagnose the illness, and the list of telling facts that were available to the defendant/doctor. These should include how, when, and where the non-diagnosis or missed diagnosis occurred, and should describe the damages that flowed from the failure to diagnose. As a capstone to each one of these missed opportunities to diagnose, plaintiff's counsel might well choose to add a theme phrase such as: "But Dr. McDermott did not put the slide under the microscope. He did not see the dangerous cancerous cells,' or "Since Dr. McDermott saw no cancer, Cheryl McGill got no treatment."

A very short theme trilogy might include:

(1) Dr. McDermott saw no cancer.

(2) Cheryl McGill got no warning.

(3) The tumor grew uninterrupted for another month.

While the text (the detailed facts) of the chapters for cross-examination provides the text of the opening statement, it is certainly not necessary to provide the fact finder with every fact that the lawyer intends to adduce through the witnesses. Equipped with the chapters as an outline for the opening statement, the advocate will recall enough of the specifics to flesh out a sufficiently detailed opening statement covering all of the important issues relating to the advocate's theory of the case.

No persuasive technique is more helpful than a fact-intensive opening statement. All of the argument is provided by the facts. The well-organized facts argue themselves. It becomes completely unnecessary (and remains completely objectionable) to tell the jurors how to vote. The jurors have already formed their first impression of the facts, and they are already drawing their own conclusions. This technique of fact-intensive opening statement advances the credibility of the advocate's case long before the jurors have heard the first witness. In a larger sense, the fact finder has already heard from the witnesses before they have been called.

§ 13.16   Trilogies in Opening Statement

The trilogy technique (see chapter 25, *Trilogies*) can be utilized in opening statements and closing arguments as well as in cross-examination. While the chapter headings of important cross-examinations provide the advocate with an outline for the opening statement, the trilogies may highlight the substance of that outline.

It is important to remember that trilogies seldom occur naturally, and should often be scripted before trial. The successful execution of this technique requires practice. The more often an advocate uses trilogies, the easier this execution will become. Practice may and should be used outside the courtroom (see chapter 25, *Trilogies*).

Using the example above where the plaintiff alleged injury, and the defense theory is to minimize the plaintiff's damages, the following trilogy may be available:

(1) The patient had subjective complaints, so the doctor examined her.

(2) The patient had subjective complaints, so the doctor performed an MRI.

(3) The patient had subjective complaints, but the MRI revealed nothing objectively wrong.

In this next example from a commercial case, the plaintiff alleges that he would not have sold his business but for a misrepresentation on the part of the defendant. While the defense denies any fraud, as a further defense, the lawyer intends to show that any fact which may have been misrepresented was immaterial to the transaction. Defense counsel intends to argue that the plaintiff would have sold his business at that time and for that price due to (1) the extremely lucrative offer made by the defendant; (2) that this offer contained terms which were very advantageous to the plaintiff from a tax minimization perspective; and (3) Plaintiff's dire need for money. In opening statement the trilogy may be introduced as follows:

The facts will show that Mr. Jenkins always intended to do this deal. He got everything he needed:

- The right price.

- The right terms.

- The right time.

The lawyer may see better ways to phrase this trilogy. There are many other ways to construct the sentences. However phrased, the trilogy needs to get across the theme that this deal was going to happen anyway as it was so beneficial to the plaintiff. Of course, standing alone, the trilogy is merely conclusory, and thus unpersuasive. The lawyer must factually support each of the three prongs of the trilogy within the opening statement. Where will this material come from? The material will come from the written chapters of cross-examination. It will demonstrate that the plaintiff negotiated a great price that resulted in a huge profit and that he negotiated terms that allowed him to greatly minimize his tax liabilities. It will also demonstrate that he desperately needed the funds in order to save other businesses that he thought had more value. In other words, the lawyer may well have several chapters built into three chapter bundles that establish each of these factual goals. This material may take substantial time to introduce during cross-examination, but it can be very brief and very well summarized with the above trilogy. Giving the factual basis in opening moves quickly and smoothly. Using primacy to foreshadow those facts with the use of the trilogy in opening or by using recency to highlight the facts previously given in opening, lets the jury learn the memorable phrase and the facts that support it. The jury can be expected to remember the trilogy. This will give them the framework to better understand the chapters of cross-examination in these extraordinarily important areas. In fact, having introduced the trilogy in opening statement, it is extremely likely that the jurors will be listening for factual support for the trilogy prongs during the testimony.

§ 13.17   Loops in Opening Statement

Loops and spontaneous loops are discussed in detail in chapter 26. In order to effectively use loops in an opening statement, the lawyer must have decided that certain words and phrases are helpful to her theory of the case and has planned to emphasize them through the use of looping in cross-examination. The opening statement is an opportune time to introduce the jury to those words and phrases that will feature prominently in the cross-examinations to come. The psychology of primacy teaches that it is better to introduce those words and phrases of emphasis as early in the case as possible and to use them consistently throughout.

Again, examine the example of an injured plaintiff. In pursuing the defense goal of minimizing the plaintiff's damages, the defense advocate knows that she will be using the phrase "nothing objectively wrong" in her cross-examination of the plaintiff and in her cross-examination of the plaintiff's doctor. The opening statement provides a forum in which the advocate can introduce this phrase and familiarize the jury with it. In this way, the advocate introduces not only the chapter and the text of the chapter, but the specific power phrases that she will be using in her direct and cross-examinations.

The individual party, or an agent of the corporate party, is often present during the opening statement. Often, words of emphasis that the advocate uses in opening statement will unintentionally be picked up and used by the opponent or, more often than not, by the witness (party or agent) in direct or cross-examination answers. For example, in a federal drug conspiracy trial, the United States government immunized the pilot of the plane, Placido Gomez Fernandez. Mr. Fernandez became one of the government's major witnesses against the defendant. The defendant's lawyer in opening statement referred to Placido Gomez Fernandez as the "drug pilot' or "illegal drug pilot" every time his name was mentioned — a total of five times in a relatively short thirty-minute opening statement by the defense attorney.

As is so often the case, the government's supervising agent, who was assisting the United States Attorney with the presentation of evidence, had listened to the opening statement. When the government called the supervising agent to testify, and asked the agent about the witness, Placido Gomez Fernandez, the agent of his own volition volunteered the answer: "Oh yes, you mean the drug pilot.' This certainly did not help the government's case, but it was understandable that the agent had been influenced by the repetitive use of this phrase in the defendant lawyer's opening statement.

If the phrase or word of emphasis is helpful to the opposing party's theory of the case, why would that witness ever incorporate that word into his testimony? If used properly by the advocate giving the opening statement, then the emphasized word or phrase takes on additional power; power that evokes an emotion, a response, and a mental photograph. Even though the witness intellectually knows he should not use that word or phrase, the witness often does. To the jury, it will appear that the lawyer is spontaneously looping (see chapter 26, *Loops, Double Loops, and Spontaneous Loops*) the answer of the witness, but in reality the lawyer has induced the witness to use the word or phrase. That word or phrase has been pre-sold by her strong opening statement.

§ 13.18 Spontaneous Loops

The process of spontaneous looping as it relates to the cross-examination of the witness has been described at length in chapter 26, *Loops, Double Loops, and Spontaneous Loops*. The principles of spontaneous looping can be applied in limited situations in opening statement. When the opponent gives his opening statement first or has conducted voir dire, he may use a word or phrase that benefits the lawyer's side of the case. Opposing counsel may go too far in defending the position of his client. He may go too far in describing the position of the advocate's client. He may overplay with what the evidence will show and by so doing he may paint a picture that he cannot and will not be able to support factually. Those attorneys who have not carefully prepared and structured their opening statements or voir dire open the door for an alert trial lawyer to loop a phrase or word that he has used in his voir dire questions or in his opening statement.

Just as a skilled trial lawyer would not delay using a spontaneous loop in a cross-examination (see chapter 26, *Loops, Double Loops, and Spontaneous*

Loops), the advocate should immediately use the spontaneous loop technique in her opening statement to nail down that the opponent has in fact conceded a word or phrase of emphasis. This word or phrase of emphasis can now be used by the advocate to assist, bolster, and be incorporated into the advocate's theory of the case in opening statement.

For example, in a civil case where the plaintiff is complaining of residual pain and physical limitations due to a hip injury from an automobile collision, consider the instance where the insurance company's defense lawyer inartfully says in voir dire: "The plaintiff is claiming continuing pain and suffering.'

The advocate for the plaintiff, who is carefully listening to the voir dire (as opposed to discussing potential jury strikes with colleagues), incorporates the phrase "the plaintiff is claiming..." into her opening statement. In the appropriate chapters, she says:

> The plaintiff, Ruth, is claiming residual pain, but the plaintiff will not be the only person to claim or prove this. Dr. Mirratta will testify about degenerative changes in the hip. Dr. Mirratta will tell you that these changes are the result of the collision. Dr. Mirratta will tell you that these changes make the ball of the hip uneven instead of smooth as nature intended it. Dr. Mirratta will tell you that an x-ray of the ball of the hip of Ruth (and you will see a copy of the x-ray of the ball of that hip so that you can see for yourself) looks like an outline of the Rocky Mountains rather than the smoothness that was intended. Dr. Mirratta will tell you that with each move of the hip, the peaks and valleys that were caused by the collision cause Ruth to feel pain. These peaks and valleys will not lessen with age, but will become higher and lower, thus creating more pain. That is the pain that the plaintiff is claiming.

Examine the consequences of an overzealous plaintiff's lawyer in a commercial setting. The plaintiff is a former employee of the defendant. He was employed under a contract that specified that once he left the employment of the defendant, he was prohibited from using any trade secrets of his former employer. The employer claims that the identities of the clients are trade secrets. The former employee/plaintiff brings a declaratory judgment action (tried to the court, or to an industry arbitration panel) seeking a ruling that the identities of former clients are not trade secrets. One of the elements of a trade secret is that the business must have made reasonable efforts to protect the alleged trade secret. When plaintiff's counsel oversells the lack of evidence on this point, he opens himself up for a spontaneous looping in defendant's opening statement.

Plaintiff's counsel opening statement: "What efforts did the defendant make to protect the identities of the clients? These lists were kept on computer, and any sales representative could get into the computer and copy the list of clients of any other sales representative."

Defendant's counsel opening statement: "What efforts did the defendant make to protect the identities of the clients? According to the plaintiff, 'any sales representative could get into the computer and copy the list of clients of any other sales representative.' In fact, that is untrue. The defendant spent over $3 million devising a security system for its computer system. The defendant developed a seven-part security system for its computers. Any sales representative could get into the computer, IF they had the private login code number of the other representative. Any sales representative could get into the computer, IF they had the private log in code phrase of the other representative. Any sales representative could get into the computer, IF they had the laptop computer belonging to the other sales representative, because the computer system had a safeguard that only allowed a sales representative to use his password and his code number from his own computer. Any sales representative could get into the computer, IF . . . ."

A fact finder will recognize that plaintiff's counsel has badly oversold his theory on this element of trade secret law after the defense attorney's second or third repetition of the phrase, "Any sales representative could get into the computer, IF...." The fact finder is now acutely conscious of that fact and is primed to receive the evidence showing the multiple layers of protection built into defendant's computer system. Undoubtedly, plaintiff's counsel now regrets ever using the phrase, "Any sales representative could get into the computer . . . ." The unfortunate phrase has been spontaneously looped by the opponent within her opening statement, and as is always true of spontaneous loops, the phrase has been highlighted, the issue has been pinpointed, and the creator of the spontaneous loop has focused attention on an issue of importance that she will win.

Listen to the words or phrases the opponent uses in voir dire or in his opening statement. An unwary, ill-prepared, or overexcited opponent may offer an opportunity to use a spontaneous loop that can substantially advance the trial lawyer's theory of the case, or which could be used to effectively attack the opponent's theory of the case.

The above examples are built on a premise that the opponent has given an opening statement prior to her opening statement. What can be done when the advocate's opening statement precedes that of her opponent, and the opponent uses some word or phrase that she wishes to spontaneously loop? Her opportunity for opening statement is gone. But her opportunity to spontaneously loop the words of an opposing counsel has just begun. Those ill chosen words or phrases may be used effectively in the cross-examination of the opponent's witnesses, or with her own witnesses.

Example: "Mr. Jones (plaintiff), in order for any sales representative to get into the computer and take the list of another sales representative, he would need to possess the other sales representative's laptop computer?" The cross-examiner would then follow up with a series of leading questions along the same lines, each demonstrating another factual fallacy to the assertion of plaintiff's counsel that "any sales representative could get in to the computer, if . . . ." The spontaneous loop based on an opponent's unsupportable assertion in opening statement will be used in her closing argument. Under such circumstances, her use of the spontaneous loop brings the fact finder back to that time in opening statement when the opponent made the assertion or promise that she has now factually rebutted over and over again.

Keep in mind that it is not just an assertion that the trial lawyer can knock down or show to be untrue that she may wish to spontaneously loop. The opponent may make a concession within his opening statement that she wishes to spontaneously loop as well. Again, the spontaneous loop of an opponent's statement may take place in her opening statement, the cross-examination of the opponent's witnesses, through the direct examination of witnesses, and in her closing argument. It becomes one of the themes.

§ 13.19   Reveal Opponent's Inconsistencies in Opening

When an important part of the strategy of the lawyer is the exploitation of inconsistencies in the opponent's case, there are sound tactical reasons to reveal those inconsistencies in the opening statement. A preemptive strike at opening statement is important, as a trial lawyer should expect even a moderately skillful opponent to have anticipated the inconsistencies. There is not much the opponent can do, however, about inconsistencies already contained within a witness's pre-trial statements.

The lawyer prepared with cross-examination chapters built around solid inconsistencies, should reveal the inconsistencies, in opening statement in order to fully exploit their persuasive potential. Lawyers ordinarily explore inconsistencies as a method of attacking the credibility of the witness. Telling the fact finder about the important inconsistencies will serve to weaken the credibility of that witness <u>before</u> the witness even takes the stand. If the lawyer hides the inconsistencies out of fear that revelation in opening statement will allow the opponent to remedy the problems, she will have bypassed the opportunity to weaken the opponent's case.

A lawyer hesitates to air the inconsistencies in her opening statement because she fears the opposing lawyer will alert the witness to an inconsistency and thereby encourage the witness to change his story. If the opponent rises to the bait, inconsistency is not lost but multiplied. A documented contradiction does not disappear when a witness changes his story a second, third, or fourth time. All that the witness has done is add an additional inconsistency, and so a changed story favors the impeaching party, not the party being impeached. Furthermore, by changing his story during trial, the witness opens a new line of impeachment on the fact that he is changing his story (again) during trial. This will seldom prove reassuring to the jurors, who judge the witness's credibility.

The trial lawyer must expose the inconsistency up front, during the opening statement. In such a situation, the opponent is forced to deal with the trial lawyer's theory, and this distracts the opponent from advancing his own theory. Every time an opponent spends part of his opening statement explaining why the inconsistencies exist, he is using precious time and energy talking about the trial lawyer's theory of the case. He is arguing with the jury that they should not be persuaded by your case, but in so doing, he is not advancing his own case. Armed with demonstrably inconsistent statements that will be used in cross-examination, the lawyer must exploit them in detail in opening statement.

Example:

> Within minutes of the robbery, Mrs. Eidlestein told the police that the defendant had light brown hair "that was kind of long." Within two hours of that statement, the police brought Tommy James back to Mrs. Eidlestein's store. Mrs. Eidlestein will tell you that he was "bald as a cue ball," but that he was the robber. She will tell you that she has seen cue balls. She will tell you that she knows that they are smooth, glossy, with absolutely no hair on them and certainly not light brown hair "that was kind of long."

Further, as a result of having heard in opening statement that the witness has changed her story on one or more facts, the fact finder will likely be more cautious in accepting other uncontradicted parts of the witness's testimony. The witness then takes the stand as "damaged goods," having been tainted by these contradictions and inconsistent statements that damage credibility. Additionally, by revealing in opening statement prepared cross-examination chapters on motive, interest, prejudice, and bias, the lawyer has pre-conditioned the jury to be skeptical of the opponent's direct examination, long before the cross-examiner has had her turn to cross-examine on these issues.

§ 13.20 Voice, Movement, and Emotion

The cross-examination techniques of voice, movement, and emotion are discussed in detail in chapter 22. These techniques have equal application to opening statements.

A word of caution: the advocate must guard against expressing so much emotion in the opening statement that the opponent (rightly or wrongly) makes the objection 'argumentative." Even if the words are not argumentative, an overly emotional pitch may lead the judge to believe that they are. Many judges react to the emotional level of a lawyer's statement of facts without judging whether the content itself is argumentative. There is, however, plenty of room for the creative attorney to use voice variation, tone, and timing in a fact-intensive presentation.

Low emotion, a quiet voice, and subtle and confined gestures are generally most effective in any case in the courtrooms of America today, and this is especially true in the opening statement. Remember, the advocate has lived the case for days, weeks, months, perhaps even years, but the jury is just being introduced to the case. The lawyer cannot show anger or other emotion at the outset, as the jurors do not yet understand her anger or other emotion. The jury must be led slowly up to the desired emotional level. It is easy for the advocate to initially exceed the jury's capacity to feel emotion with unrestrained movement, voice, or tone. Through the careful choice of emphasis words and theme lines, the advocate can strike the correct and acceptable emotional pitch without having to resort to the high risk/low gain use of highly emotional content or grand gestures in opening statements. When in doubt, underplay emotion in opening.

§ 13.21   Handle Objections to the Opening Statement

The most common objection in opening statements is that the advocate is "arguing" the case. Judges inevitably rule in words to the effect: "Counsel, don't argue your case. Members of the jury, opening statements are not evidence, they are only an outline of what the lawyer thinks the case will be about." This ruling is given whether or not the judge thinks the lawyer is arguing the case — it is the stock ruling.

This ruling is correct. What is more important is that the fact-intensive, theory-driven opening statement makes objectionable argument completely unnecessary and counterproductive. The stock ruling should not affect the lawyer's opening statement. However, the interruption caused by the objection and by the judge's stock ruling will distract the jury and diminish the full impact of the opening statement. Everything that needs to be done in a powerful opening statement can be done well within the rules. Don't stray from the facts.

By giving fact-intensive, well-organized (by chapters), theory-driven opening statements based on the chapter method, there is no need for the lawyer to resort to generalities, conclusions, legalisms, or opinions. As a result, there is no opportunity to object. The silent objections that juries often feel, but have no ability to voice ("Boring," "I'm lost," or "Why is this important?"), are also rendered meaningless by the fact-intensive presentation built around chapters of anticipated cross and direct examinations.

If an objection is made, simply return to the factual presentation. Immediately following the objection, use the more detailed facts. The advocate may want to say: "The evidence will show..." as a lead in to the facts. The strength is found in the facts not in the lead in ceremonial phrase. When an objection is made the trial lawyer should use it as a springboard to become more fact focused, and restrain herself from appeals to emotions or using generalities, conclusions, opinions or legalisms. When in doubt, the more detailed the facts the better.

§ 13.22   Never Waive Opening Statement

Never waive your opportunity to give an opening statement. The opening statement is an unparalleled opportunity to influence the fact finders, so why would an attorney give it up? The argument in favor of situational waivers is usually predicated upon the assertion that the lawyer's case is too weak to be discussed. If that is true, then it is all the more reason to give as strong an opening as possible in order to try to win the case. After all, if the lawyer has already decided that she is likely to lose, it is time to take more risks, not fewer. Most jurors equate waiver with silence, and silence with weakness or, worse, with concession. When an advocate is offered the opportunity to tell her side of the story and she passes it up, the clear implication is that the lawyer has no story to tell and no strong disagreement with what has been or will be presented by the opponent. A situation may hypothetically exist where waiving opening statement makes sense, but we have not yet found that situation.

§ 13.23   Factual Openings Gain More Than They Give Away

Waiving an opening statement sounds like an effective way of hiding the strengths of your case from your opponent. Alternatively, lawyers sometimes rationalize that it would be better to waive or reserve their openings in order to keep their strong case or theory secret. Of all the purported reasons to reserve or waive opening, this is the most seductive. It sounds better than most justifications given for waiving opening statement, but it is wrong.

The overriding problem with the tactic of hiding the theory of the case from the opponent is that the advocate will be hiding her case from the fact finder as well. The net result is that the fact finder hears only one side, and it isn't the trial lawyer's. The price of concealment comes too high, even if the advocate manages to create some confusion or uncertainty on the part of the opponent.

In any event, there is great reason to doubt the primary premise of this tactic — that an advocate can successfully hide her theory from an opponent. There are, after all, only limited theories of the case available to an advocate, and in most cases the major strong and weak points of the case are already known to both sides. If an opposing lawyer is so poorly prepared that he has not focused on the advocate's theory, he is already ill-equipped to combat that theory.

By allowing the opponent unchallenged access to the jurors' minds in opening statement, the lawyer has unnecessarily promoted the opponent's credibility. The first and only objective of trial must be to win over the jurors, not to embarrass or confuse the opponent. The advocate can best accomplish that task by giving her opening statement and detailing for the jury the factual reasons to vote her way. If her theory of the case is strong, a fact-intensive, chapter-organized opening statement makes it stronger.

§ 13.24   Plaintiffs and Prosecutors Must Always Give an Opening Statement

It is impossible to conceive of a situation in which the party bringing the case would pass up the opportunity to brag about the case. Either a plaintiff or a prosecutor got this trial started and bears the burden of persuasion. The plaintiff/prosecutor surely must have a theory of the case and is about to call witnesses in support of that theory. Plaintiff's/prosecutor's counsel has no excuses and no options. She must open. If she doesn't, defense counsel will present his opening argument unchallenged, and will then dominate battlefield.

§ 13.25   The Defense Must Open Now, Not Later

It is the defense lawyer, civil or criminal, who theoretically has the option of reserving his opening statement until the beginning of his own case. The problem with this logic is that the beginning of the defense case is thought to come only after the end of the opponent's case. To forfeit to the opponent the quest for persuasion is never a wise tactic. The plaintiff/prosecutor has given her opening statement, told the jury members where to focus their concentration, and informed the jurors on the decisive issues of the lawsuit. The plaintiff's/prosecutor's opening will boost the credibility of her witness while undermining the credibility of the defense. Having gotten all the persuasive advantages of her opening, she can move forward to put up the evidence that will verify all the things the jury was already conditionally committed to as a result of hearing the opening statement. There is only one sensible technique that responds to the opponent's opening. The defense must reciprocate in kind by giving a fact-intensive, theory-driven, chapter-organized opening statement. The defense must work on obtaining a conditional commitment or at least on having the jurors hold off on committing at all. The defense case begins with the first cross-examination, not the defense's first witness.

In accordance with the doctrine of primacy, whether plaintiff or defense, whether the trial is criminal or civil, whether it is being tried to a judge or a jury, the lawyer must give her opening statement at the first possible opportunity. "Flexibility" is not gained by reserving the opening statement. A delayed opening statement abandons the field of persuasion to the opponent. She can then present her entire case without any of the persuasive impediments caused by the opponent's opening statement. This one-sided persuasive void leaves the jury with a clear understanding of the opponent's case, and no understanding of the advocate's.

Forget any advice about keeping options open by reserving opening statement. This is not a strategy; it is a dodge. A trial advocate's options are always limited. That is why trial lawyers study the facts that cannot change in order to develop the best potential theory of the case (see chapter 2, *Developing a Theory of the Case*). If the phrase "keeping my options open" means leaving the lawyer in a position to later advance one of several "possible" theories or for "playing for the fumble," she is setting herself up to perform a series of unfocused or contradictory cross-examinations. Under this scenario, counsel won't have any credibility left by the time she gives her reserved opening statement.

Perhaps counsel is thinking of reserving her opening with the hope of later developing a theory of the case. Set aside the question of how the lawyer picked a jury without having a theory of the case. Set aside the fact that the lawyer must cross-examine with no theory in mind. A lawyer working (and particularly cross-examining) without a theory of the case is not in a position to win the trial. That lawyer has nothing to teach the fact finder. Such a lawyer is not an effective advocate of any positive position. She is reduced to the role of hacking at the opponent's evidence, hoping that one of her blind thrusts will hit a vital organ and gravely damage the opposition.

The jury, and much more likely, the judge, perceives the lack of direction of this approach and the confusion caused by the lawyer's random and inconsistent attacks on the facts. The jury is likely to miss any rare shots that do hit the mark. A lawyer who lacks a theory of the case lacks sufficiently grouped evidentiary goals, and is left to conduct poorly focused direct examinations as well.

Some lawyers will tell of the time they reserved their opening statement and something wonderful and wholly unexpected developed during the opponent's case. They then took advantage of this development in their reserved opening statement. These lawyers, having once filled an evidentiary inside straight (poker), are doomed to bet against the odds for the rest of their careers. It is hoped such lawyers become our opponents.

If a defense lawyer is involved in a multiple defendant case, he might convince the judge to permit one or more defendants to reserve their opening statement, and have the other defendants proceed with their opening statements immediately following the opponent's opening. In this way, the defendant can have the benefits of both primacy (early opening) and recency (late opening) (see chapter 12, *Employing Primacy and Recency*), provided all defendants share a common theory. It is not likely that this will happen, but if the lawyer does not ask, it will never happen.

§ 13.26   Opening + New Developments = New Closing

Trials do take unexpected turns. The fact-intensive, theory-driven opening statement does not impede the ability to take advantage of new developments. It only serves to highlight for the jury the unusual twist the case has taken. After all, if the new development is something the lawyer wished she could have opened on, it must be something bad for her opponent and helpful to her theory of the case. The jury will see this and give full credit to the value of the new information. Because of the opening statement, the jury will be better equipped to understand the significance of the new development.

For example, suppose an insurance defense lawyer had intended to concede liability, or at least to argue it softly, choosing instead to open on damages. Then new evidentiary developments offer a solid argument on liability, as well as damages. The lawyer's original opening statement has not limited her ability to forcefully argue the newly developed liability issue in closing argument. In fact, the opening statement attacking the damages aspect of the case has served its purpose and has drawn the jury's attention to the flaws in this critical area. The jury has better understood the cross-examination chapters on that area. The fact that the opponent's direct examination chapters on liability have developed poorly, or that the cross-examination chapters on liability have gone unexpectedly well is no cause to wish that the insurance defense attorney had reserved her opening statement. A reserved opening would not have benefited her as to damages or liability. It would have come too late to take advantage of the solid cross-examinations on either damages or liability. The lawyer would have only gained the illusion of flexibility at the cost of persuasion. This is a trade never worth making.

§ 13.27   The Relationship of Opening Statement to Closing Argument

Assuming that the advocate has given a fact-intensive, theory-driven opening statement organized by the chapter method, how does this affect the closing argument? The closing argument will look very much like the opening statement, but will be given even more persuasively, by supplying conclusions, advancing counsel's interpretation and inferences (not opinion), and giving the jury the benefit of memorable phrases and words drawn from the testimony. The common thread of a consistent theory of the case, identified in opening statement, verified through testimony, and reviewed in closing argument, is not a bad thing. Internal consistency will help the case. The closing argument may include argument and will clearly be more dramatic, in the conventional sense of that word, and should be at least as persuasive as the opening statement.

But the closing argument seeks a different kind of persuasion. Because of the systematic approach of the chapter method, strengthened by a fact-intensive and theory-driven opening statement, the trial lawyer is no longer saddled with the responsibility of pulling together the entire case in the closing argument. Because of the opening statement, the fact finder understood where the case was aimed, and could therefore track the advocate's progress toward proving the case. The closing argument helps remind a fact finder where the case was proved, it may explore and explain inconsistencies in the owner's presentation of facts. But the closing argument no longer stands alone as the method of explaining why a particular verdict is justified. Through this method, the closing argument is introduced, strengthened, and made more effective and persuasive by a fact-intensive opening statement. The opening statement promises facts, the witness examination verifies facts, and the closing argument adds up the facts and empowers the jury to deliver the desired verdict based not on argument or oratory, but on a systematic compiling of the facts.

§ 13.28   Use of Demonstrative Exhibits in Opening Statement

If the cross-examiner intends to use demonstrative exhibits within the cross-examinations, strong consideration should be given to the use of those exhibits within opening statement. If there is doubt that the judge will permit it, ask in advance. Experience teaches that most judges will permit that which helps the jury understand, as long as not argumentative of its own nature. Demonstrative exhibits differ from trial exhibits in that they are not intended to be admitted into evidence, but their display and use is sanctioned as a method of compiling, distilling, or arraying other admissible facts.

Strong demonstrative exhibits do what the name implies: They demonstrate an important concept by pulling together facts that may come from many witnesses or many documents. Often, demonstrative exhibits that may be used during the cross-examination may be used with great effect in opening statement. For instance, if the cross-examiner wishes to demonstrate how the shares of the company were held at various times, a pie chart might prove quite useful with the witness. If the cross-examiner wishes to demonstrate how badly a stock was performing, or the continual decline in income of a particular witness, a bar graph or line would be appropriate. In these instances, the demonstrative aid would also be used with the witness. Instead of the lawyer merely talking the jury through a particular point, the point is graphically demonstrated by a demonstrative exhibit accompanied by a discussion or explanation of the evidence that will be introduced to validate that exhibit.

There are other occasions in which the demonstrative aid will not be used in cross-examination, but can effectively and ethically be used in opening statement. In opening statement, the cross-examiner will often wish to highlight the important parts of the testimony of many witnesses. In order to assist the jury in keeping track of these important points, the cross-examiner might fashion a demonstrative aid showing the name of a witness to be cross-examined, perhaps their position in the case or in the entity suing or being sued, followed by bullet points of the key admissions expected to be gained on cross-examination. This outline of the testimony of the witnesses will not be used during the cross-examinations, but can prove very effective in alerting the jurors to the highlights of the cross-examinations to come. Care must be taken to fashion such a demonstrative aid in a manner that is not argumentative. The title of an employee/witness should be accurately shown. The witness should not be referred to as "the outcry witness," or "the whistleblower," or any other such subjective description. To do so is to invite objection to the use of the demonstrative aid in opening statement as unduly argumentative. The demonstrative aid serves only to better equip the lawyer to present and teach the facts.

The cross-examiner may often want to demonstrate that people close to a particular party will offer testimony that disagrees with that party (see Chart 1, below). In such an instance, the cross-examiner may fashion a demonstrative aid that places within a circle, the name of the key witness or opposing party. The cross-examiner could then surround that name with the names of witnesses who would seem to be aligned with that party, but who will give up important testimony on cross-examination that contradicts or undermines the key witness/opposing party. Such a demonstrative aid might be entitled "the people closest to (name of key witness)." Alternatively, the board could be titled "(name of witness) closest business advisers." Whatever the situation, there are many ways to build such a demonstrative aid.

In each case the cross-examiner would place around the name of the key witness the names of close associates who are expected to offer damaging testimony against their friend or business associate within the cross-examination. In opening statement, the cross-examiner graphically demonstrates how the closest associates of a particular person will fail to fully support their friend's/business associate's assertions. This demonstrative aid alerts the fact finder that the opponent's case is undermined even by people aligned with the opponent.

At the same time this demonstrative aid serves as a springboard for the cross-examiner's discussion of the particular damaging evidence that the advocate intends to bring forward during the cross-examination of these particular witnesses. This is another instance in which a demonstrative aid may be used in opening statement, but likely will not be used in cross-examination. Instead, the demonstrative aid helps summarize a particular aspect of the cross-examinations.

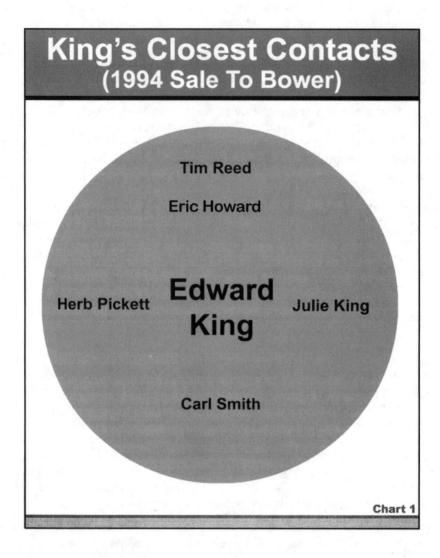

§ 13.29   Use of Timelines in Opening Statement

Timelines are one of the best and most frequently employed examples of a demonstrative exhibit. A timeline is often employed to orient the witness and the fact finder to where a fact fits into the sequence of important facts. The timeline may often be up during much of the trial, but it is not itself an admissible document. The entire timeline can be profitably previewed for the fact finder within opening statement. In fact, it is at this point in the case that the timeline may be most useful, as it efficiently conveys to the fact finder how the facts will come together to support the cross-examiner's theory of the case. The facts that fill the timeline may come into evidence through multiple witnesses spread over several days or weeks of testimony. Any one witness may provide only a few of the facts and dates, and may provide facts that do not flow chronologically. In other words, the witness may add important facts at greatly separated times on the timeline. If a fact finder can only see the development of the timeline as its facts are introduced in the cross (and direct) examinations, the timeline loses much of its utility. The timeline, used in this manner, rather resembles the television quiz show Wheel of Fortune. The fact finder is asked to continually guess what the finished timeline will say. The cross-examiner is far better off displaying the finished timeline in opening statement and explaining its meaning to the case at that point. Of course, it remains the duty of the cross-examiner to fill in the timeline through testimony and other admissible documents.

The opening statement explains the evidence and the witness examinations are designed to verify counsel's opening statement. Similarly, the timeline is counsel's submission of the most important facts accompanied by the date or sequence of those facts. Before developing the timeline, the cross-examiner has created the chapters that will introduce those facts and dates. The cross-examiner who has prepared evidentiary sourced chapters of cross-examination (see chapter 10, *Page Preparation of Cross-Examination*) is well prepared to build a demonstrative timeline. The evidentiary sourced chapters of cross-examination then become instrumental in securing the permission of the court to use a timeline as a demonstrative aid in opening statement.

The opponent can be expected to try to block the cross-examiner's use of the timeline. The most frequent objection to the use of a timeline in opening statement is that it is an inaccurate statement of the facts, or based on speculation as to what the testimony will show. Judges are attentive to these objections. There is limited utility to the bald statement of the cross-examiner/proponent of the timeline, to the effect that all of these facts and dates are accurate. A far better way to ensure the ability to use the timeline in opening statement is to show the evidentiary source on the timeline for each of the items displayed. If the cross-examiner intends to prove that the opposing party took the particular action on a particular date, then the timeline should show the event, the date, and the exhibit number of the document that will establish those facts. When the cross-examiner intends to prove an event through testimony, the timeline should show the fact or event, the date, and the name of the witness who will testify to that fact. Below (see Chart 2) is a representation of an evidentiary sourced timeline drawn from a medical malpractice case:

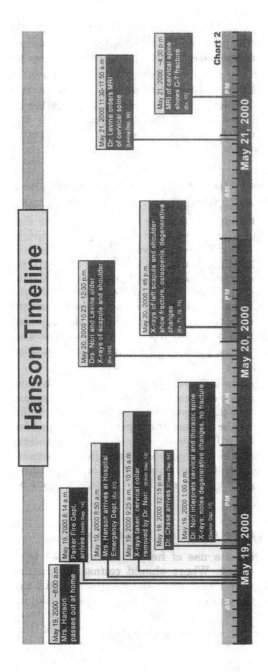

The sourced timeline dramatically alters the likely ruling of the court and the credibility of the demonstrative aid. When a judge is called upon to rule on the opponent's objections that the facts described are incorrect or unsupported by the evidence, the sourced timeline immediately shows the judge that each of the items will be supported by an exhibit or a witness. An additional benefit, and one that should not be underrated, is the effect on the credibility of the proponent. The timeline tells the jury and the judge that counsel is well prepared to establish her theory of the case, and that the facts line up to support that theory.

Some lawyers find that the exhibit numbers or witness names on the timeline may serve to complicate the picture. In such case it is advisable to prepare for the judge an 8 1/2 x 11 inch version of the timeline showing the exhibit numbers and witness names. A full set of the original or a small version (8 1/2 x 11) should be available for the judge.

§ 13.30   Use of Transcripts in Opening Statement

The advisability of revealing the inconsistencies within the testimony of a witness, including the inconsistent statements made by a witness was discussed in § 13.19. As an adjunct to that process, the cross-examiner needs to consider how transcripts of testimony may be effectively used in the opening statement. Of course, counsel is entitled to discuss with jury the various inconsistencies of a witness. But can counsel use the actual transcripts? The safest course is to ask permission of the court. The permission sought should be limited. If there are a few questions and answers, or better yet, a single question and answer critical to the theory of the case, counsel should alert the court that counsel wishes to use a demonstrative aid such as a blowup of the question-and-answer as it occurred in the deposition or other pre-trial hearing.

This highlighting of a point should be reserved for truly important issues. There is no value in graphically demonstrating one or a series of prior inconsistent statements solely because they are inconsistent. There may well be value in discussing these inconsistencies in the course of an opening statement for the same reasons the inconsistencies will be explored in cross-examination. However, the act of blowing up a single inconsistency magnifies the importance of that particular inconsistency. If it is not critically important, counsel misleads the fact finder by putting such great emphasis on that particular inconsistent statement.

§ 13.31   Use of Trial Exhibits in Opening Statement

Counsel should strongly consider the use of her most important trial exhibits within the opening statement. Where should counsel begin the process of selecting the best exhibits? The answer is contained within the chapters of cross-examination. To the extent that one or more trial exhibits will be the focus of attention in a critical cross-examination, the more counsel should consider displaying that exhibit in opening statement. By doing this, counsel permits the fact finder an opportunity to learn to understand the exhibit, and to understand the cross-examination that will occur around that exhibit. But why not wait until cross-examination to use the witness to explain the exhibit? Answer: Because the trial lawyer is better at explaining the exhibit.

By previewing the exhibit with the fact finder, the trial lawyer highlights the importance of that exhibit. By explaining the exhibit, counsel may shorten the number of cross-examination questions required to explain the exhibit to the fact finder. Furthermore, the use of the exhibit in the trial lawyer's opening statement may well affect the opponent's direct examination of their witness.

The jury has seen the exhibit before the direct examination. The jury under-stands that lawyer's theory concerning the exhibit. If the opponent chooses not to discuss the exhibit, the jury will frequently view that omission as a sign of weakness or fear. If, on the other hand, the opponent decides he must try to soften the force of the exhibit by discussing it with his witness, he gives more weight to the exhibit. More time spent in court on any matter means more importance is attached to it. Time is the measure of importance.

In addition, there is always the chance that the witness will fumble in his response, thereby making the situation worse. To those timid trial lawyers who would say that the use of an important exhibit in opening statement will unnecessarily alert the opponent to the advocate's "take" on that exhibit, and signal to the opponent of her intention to use the exhibit in cross-examination, the response to this is the same general response to any notion that the best evidence should ever be hidden. The good opponent has figured out by trial what are the important exhibits and how they will be used. If the document is good, its value should not be diminished because an opposing witness sees it coming. If it is hidden from the opponent, it is hidden from the fact finder. An exhibit hidden from the fact finder cannot possibly help teach and persuade the fact finder.

The trial lawyer, contemplating an upcoming cross-examination, has firmly decided that she likes this exhibit. That is why counsel intended to cross-ex-amine on it. That is why the lawyer is considering its use in opening state-ment. If she doesn't like the exhibit, or if she is not confident that it aids her in proving her theory of the case, or attacks the opponent's theory of the case, she will not elevate its importance by using it in her opening statement. In other words, devote time in opening statement only to the strongest exhibits.

There is an evidentiary bridge to be crossed before the trial lawyer makes use of an exhibit in opening statement. The exhibit must undoubtedly be admis-sible. The best way to ensure its admissibility is through pre-trial stipulations as to certain exhibits, or pre-trial rulings on the admissibility of certain exhib-its. One of the unwritten rules of trial work is that what is sauce for the goose is sauce for the gander. If the lawyer wishes to use selected exhibits in her opening statement, and she seeks the cooperation of her opponent, she must be willing to extend the same degree of cooperation concerning the exhibits he might wish to use. This does not mean that she should refrain from objecting to objectionable exhibits. It does mean that the two sides should work together to create a list of exhibits that are absolutely going to come in during the trial. An important side benefit of this approach is that it may make unnecessary many foundation questions for exhibits to which there is a stipulation.

Do not attempt to use an exhibit in opening statement that may not be admissible. Do not run the risk, even if it is a good-faith risk. Do not allow opponents to use within opening statements any exhibits whose admissibil-ity remains in question. Always ask an opponent to review all exhibits they intend to use in their opening statement.

Judges have two forms of rulings or exhibits in opening statements. Some judges rule that no attorney may use any exhibit that is not stipulated to.

Other judges take a more sporting approach by ruling that counsel may use any exhibits they believe to be admissible, but that counsel runs the risk that if the exhibit is not admitted, the court will later instruct the jury that the exhibit was improperly used and should not be considered. No one wants to be on the receiving end of such an instruction. In other words, play it by the book.

§ 13.32   Use of Witness Video Testimony in Opening Statement

Technology has changed trial work in a myriad of ways. One aspect of technology that has impacted cross-examination is the availability of videotaped or digitized depositions in civil (and some criminal) cases, and videotaped confessions or witness statements in some cases. Trial counsel may be tempted to play a portion of a videotaped answer or statement within the opening statement. It would seem a logical step forward in the techniques of opening statement in that, trial counsel certainly would be allowed to tell the jury the anticipated testimony of a witness, or the admission of a defendant in a criminal action. Since this is undoubtedly true, shouldn't the lawyer be permitted to show the statement instead of merely discussing the statement? The answer: Ask the court for permission. Even assuming the statement is undoubtedly admissible, a great many judges will likely decline permission to show a videotaped excerpt of the statement or deposition of a witness or a party, on the grounds that to do so would be to unduly highlight one particular piece of evidence. Of course, it is one of the goals of opening statement to highlight particular pieces of evidence. Nonetheless, judges are hesitant to turn opening statements in the direction of Hollywood productions.

The trial lawyer is more likely to secure permission to show a small number of short excerpts as opposed to either a large number of video clips, or a single video excerpt of substantial length. Counsel should be mindful of the fact that the jury will attach great weight to what ever video clip is shown. Therefore, if given the opportunity, counsel is advised to use only a video clip of great significance. Furthermore, the video clip must be so clear in its meaning that the fact finder can immediately appreciate the significance of the witness statement. Said another way: If the lawyer must explain why the witness's words are important to the verdict desired, the clip is not worth showing in opening statement.

§ 13.33   Time Savings Resulting from Chapter-Based Openings

No lawyer has enough time. Few can say that they get prepared early. Whether the lawyer is a public defender who just has moments and perhaps days to prepare for a trial or an advocate with months and years to focus on a few cases, time disappears and deadlines creep up.

Happily, the three key elements to preparing an opening statement are the same key elements to preparing a closing argument. These same three key elements are developed in large part by developing, concentrating, and focusing on cross-examinations. This is not to say that direct examination should be ignored; obviously, it should not. However, at least theoretically, direct examinations are cooperative efforts between the witness and lawyer. If the advocate places reliance on her ability to successfully cross-examine the opponent's witness to win her case and to persuade the fact finder, then that intensity of preparation directly advances the advocate's ability to give an effective, organized, and persuasive opening statement and closing argument.

The advocate who intensely prepares for cross-examination chapters has prepared much, if not all, of her opening statement since:

- The chapter headings of important cross-examinations serve as the outline for the opening statement.

- The detailed, specific, individual facts that have been developed to cross-examine the opponent's witnesses serve as the text of the chapters of the opening statement.

- The trilogies and loops that will be used in the cross-examinations will also be used and introduced in the opening statement.

- The theory of the case will run throughout the trial consistently.

That same preparation serves well the closing argument. The time saved in this method is substantial. Specifically, experience teaches that fully one-third of the normal preparation time for trial can be eliminated by this type of preparation. Not only is this opening statement method and technique effective and persuasive, but just as importantly, it gives the advocate more time to prepare efficiently for trial. It gives the advocate with limited time (all of us) the ability to devote our time to the preparation of the witness examinations. No matter what we believe about the value of opening statements and closing arguments, they will never rise to the value of the witness examinations. Producing the facts will always be more important than discussing the facts or arguing the facts. Our advice: Spend the bulk of your time preparing your chapters of cross-examinations and direct examinations. Work backwards from your chapters to craft your opening statement and then finally your closing argument.

Chapter 14

REDIRECT AND RECROSS EXAMINATION

SYNOPSIS

§ 14.01 "Here We Go Again"

"Just a few questions on redirect examination, Your Honor," says the opponent. Do not be misled by the statement. Whether she intends to take a minute or an hour, the redirect examiner always prefaces the redirect examination with, "Just a few questions Your Honor." These words produce apprehension in every cross-examiner, regardless of age, experience, or confidence level. The fear is that the redirect examination will somehow destroy the effect of a well-constructed cross-examination. Fortunately, the fear is unfounded.

The techniques that produce logical, goal-oriented chapters of cross-examination all serve to impede the opponent's ability ruin a solid cross-examination. Because most opponents are psychologically compelled to attack the cross-examination chapters that hurt them most, they are attacking the areas least vulnerable to successful redirect examination. As a result, the cross-examiner is often able to anticipate the likely areas of redirect examination. She is, thus, in a better position to spot opportunities to conduct a limited but helpful recross examination of the witness.

§ 14.02 The Law of Redirect Examination

The rules of redirect examination are fairly standard throughout the United States. It is not within the scope of this book to analyze the law of the various states and federal courts, but solely to set forth the science and techniques that enable the cross-examiner to form the examinations necessary to maximize her chances to win. Those include the cross-examinations and the recross examinations.

One of the hallmarks of a solid cross-examination is its tendency to leave the opponent unwilling to attempt the redirect examination for fear the damage will only be compounded. If a redirect examination occurs, it is because of the harm done by the cross-examination. In fact, the law recognizes that this is the principal goal of a redirect examination. One of the better expressions of the principal rule of redirect examination is:

> The basic function of redirect examination is to enable the witness to explain and clarify any relevant matters in his or her testimony which have been weakened, confused or obscured by cross-examination and to rebut the discrediting effect of any damaging statements or admissions or to correct any wrong impression that may have been created.

Easter v. State, 815 S.W.2d 924, 926 (Ark. 1991).

Redirect examination can ordinarily only develop testimony that touches upon the same subjects covered in the cross-examination. Correspondingly, recross examination can only deal with those subjects addressed in redirect examination. Because of these legal constraints, the cross-examiner need not fear redirect examination. She can look forward to the possibility of recross examination.

§14.03 The Law of Recross Examination

As to the scope of recross examination, the state and federal districts fall into one of two general rules. Again a thorough law search is beyond this book's scope. The more limited rule is that the party's cross-examination must be limited to *new matters* brought out on redirect examination. See, e.g., *State v. Vigil*, 571 P.2d 423, 424 (N.M. 1977); *State v. Faulkner*, 381 N.E.2d 934, 936 (Ohio 1978); *Green v. U.S.*, 718 A.2d 1042, 1061 (D.C. 1998). The broader view is that recross examination may embrace *all matters* testified to on redirect examination. See, e.g., *People v. Ciari*, 540 P.2d 1094, 1097 (Colo. 1975); *People v. Franklin*, 552 N.E.2d 743, 752 (Ill. 1990); *State v. Cordeiro*, 56 P.3d 692, 723-724 (Haw. 2002).

The law of recross examination is topic specific. The cross-examiner who has prepared the original cross-examination using the chapter method is, in the vast majority of recross examinations, equally prepared to recross *should it be necessary*. Quite often no further examination will be necessary.

Under the techniques advocated in this book, there are no generic cross-examinations. Instead of rambling "discovery by cross-examination," using the established techniques of cross-examination will result in a series of goal-directed chapters of cross-examination designed to further the theory of the case (see chapter 9, *The Chapter Method of Cross-Examination*). Using logically-constructed, goal-directed chapters, with the chapters arranged to take advantage of the techniques of cross-examination sequencing, the cross-examiner will find that she has made more points and has a sequence (see chapter 11, *Sequences of Cross-Examination*). The sequences of cross-examination will be designed in part to lower the confidence, desire, and ability of the opposing party to proceed with a redirect examination.

§ 14.04 Good Cross-Examinations Restrict the Opponent's Ability to Conduct Meaningful Redirect Examinations

As a result of the chapter method of cross-examination (see chapter 9, *The Chapter Method of Cross-Examination*), the cross-examiner has chosen the ground upon which the redirecting attorney must fight. Not only has the cross-examiner chosen the battlefield, she has developed and completed a cross-examination in those selected areas. Since the redirect examination must take place on this ground, any redirect examination must concern itself with chapters that have been attacked by the cross-examination.

The problem faced by the redirecting lawyer is that the cross-examination did not seek unsupported conclusions. Because each chapter of cross-examination was built upon a logical sequence of facts, the redirecting lawyer's attack upon the goal of that chapter requires the redirect examiner to challenge the many supporting facts. In other words, the redirect examiner cannot merely ask the witness to retract or modify a single "yes" answer. To do so leaves the fact finder with the memory of all the "yes" answers to the supporting facts. Because each chapter of facts has its own context and logic, the attempted redirect examination requires an attack on the entire context rather than on a single answer. Before engaging in any redirect examination, the redirect examiner must weigh his ability to successfully guide his witness through a series of open-ended questions in an area the witness has in all likelihood already handled poorly. The aim is to cause the witness to retract, modify, or explain a series of logical answers just recently testified to on cross-examination.

To successfully attack a single chapter is a formidable task. But when the redirect examiner is concerned about the damage done by a series of chapters, the difficulties are multiplied, as are the opportunities to accrue further damage through unanticipated answers. An effective redirect examination can no longer merely ask the witness to reconsider and change one isolated answer. The witness would be required to reconsider and change multiple answers. Most lawyers faced with the opportunity and risks of redirect examination choose not to ask the witness to make so many revisions.

The opponent who attempts to run the risk of redirect examination finds his witnesses generally unwilling or unable to take on such a heavy testifying burden. To reconsider and explain an entire group of answers requires great effort. Furthermore, the witness is now physically and mentally at his weakest point. Testifying is hard work. Few witnesses get stronger the longer they are on the stand. Compounding the fatigue factor is the element of spontaneity. The redirect examination was neither planned nor scripted. The witness has given many answers on direct examination, followed by many answers during the cross-examination. Now faced with an unrehearsed series of open-ended questions, it is difficult for the witness to concentrate on the answers that the redirect examiner wishes to have modified or explained. Indeed, every new question provides an opportunity for the witness to go further astray, or to verify and solidify a helpful answer given to the cross-examiner.

Compounding the difficulties is the changed demeanor of the redirect examiner. The redirect examination is taking place because opposing counsel is unhappy with the damage done by the cross-examination. As a result, the redirect examiner often approaches his witness with a demeanor markedly different than during the direct examination. Often he displays a sense of exasperation as the witness has given up answers not anticipated or desired by the direct examiner. His witness accurately reads his lawyer's exasperation as a sign that the witness has displeased the lawyer. This breeds tension between the witness and the lawyer at the very time when the witness is least able to comprehend the problems caused by the cross-examination answers. Alternatively, many lawyers undertaking a redirect examination find themselves angry with the opposing cross-examiner. Believing that the cross-examiner has unfairly attacked or confused the witness, the redirect examiner displays anger. Although the anger is directed at the cross-examiner, witnesses often misread that the anger is being directed at them for their answers. This emotional setting is hardly calculated to induce confidence on the part of the witness. In fact, any change in demeanor on the part of the redirecting lawyer serves as an additional impediment to a successful redirect examination. As can be seen, there are a great many barriers to the successful redirect examination following the well-constructed cross-examination. It is the redirect examiner who should feel most apprehensive undertaking such a task.

§ 14.05 Proper Sequencing of Original Cross-Examination Limits Redirect Examinations

The science and techniques of sequencing of the chapters of cross-examination are covered in chapter 11, *Sequences of Cross-Examination*. However, several of those sequencing guidelines should be reviewed to understand their desired effect on redirect examination. In particular, a selected group of techniques are aimed at creating a successful conclusion to the cross-examination of a witness: "Close Cross-Examination With a Theme Chapter"; "End With a Power Chapter"; "Never Lead or Conclude a Cross-Examination With A Risky Chapter"; "Never Let the Witness Force A Change In Sequence." Each of these guidelines is designed for the cross-examiner to finish the cross-examination in a positive light. By finishing the original cross-examination in this "best case scenario," the cross-examiner wins the last chapter. Winning the last chapter is of paramount importance. The last chapter does not have to be dramatic, but it must be won. If the chapter is lost, or if the cross-examination has ended in an argument rather than a concession, opposing counsel is emboldened to undertake a redirect examination. On the other hand, a solid chapter anchoring a cross-examination discourages the opposing party and his witness. Neither the lawyer nor his witness enjoys the prospect of a redirect examination, possibly to be followed by a recross examination.

If the witness or the opposing counsel is disillusioned with the performance of the witness in the last chapter of the cross-examination, that disillusionment will discourage any desire to redirect, which may lead to further damaging admissions by the witness. However, when the cross-examination ends in a dispute, the opponent is encouraged in the notion that his witness can successfully fight his way out of the admissions made during cross-examination. A redirect examination is now more likely to follow. The wise cross-examiner follows the guidelines of sequencing. When she does this, she eliminates many redirect examinations before they start.

§ 14.06   Predicting Scenarios When Redirect Examination Will Occur

The results of a cross-examination can be best seen as a spectrum of possibilities. At one end, the cross-examination was successful. The witness was shown to be unbelievable and the jury accepted that showing. The witness supported the cross-examiner's theory of the case and the jury accepted that showing. The witness undermined the opposing party's theory of the case and the jury accepted that showing. In each of these scenarios, the cross-examination has gone well. On the other extreme, the cross-examination has gone badly when the witness has successfully resisted the cross-examiner. The jury believes the witness more than ever.

In the middle ground, there are two more possibilities. One is that the cross-examination went mostly well. Although there were certain weaknesses in the cross-examination, the cross-examiner controlled the witness and brought out the points that the cross-examiner was required to develop through this witness in order to support the cross-examiner's theory of the case. The cross-examination hurt the witness and the opponent's theory when possible. However, the witness scored points for the other side as well.

The fourth possible result of a cross-examination (the other middle ground possibility) is that the cross-examination primarily went poorly. While the cross-examiner may have completed certain missions and showed the witness to be unreliable on certain points, much of the damage done by the witness in direct examination remained unrebutted. The witness largely controlled the examination. The witness remained believable to the jury in most material respects.

Given these four possible general results of cross-examination, it can be accurately predicted when the opposing attorney will want to engage in a redirect examination of the witness.

§ 14.07   The Successfully Cross-Examined Witness

When the witness fared poorly on cross-examination, ordinarily only the inexperienced opponent will engage in a redirect examination. Why? The witness has proven unable to successfully carry the burden of a cross-examination. To engage in a redirect examination under the circumstances, is to subject his witness to a great many additional questions over many chapters, all the while risking further damage from the already weakened witness. The opponent must contend with the notion that this witness has already done damage, and additional questions may produce answers capable of further exploration in a recross examination. If the opposing attorney actually attempts to redirect, the cross-examining attorney must view it as an additional opportunity to bring out more material useful to the cross-examiner's side of the case. Under the circumstances the cross-examiner should have little fear of the redirect examination. However, the cross-examiner is advised to dramatically limit any recross examination to areas already prepared or to forgo recross examination as unnecessary. "No new adventures" is a good phrase to keep in mind. When a witness has done poorly, a competent opponent ordinarily wants nothing more than to get his witness off of the stand as soon as possible. If there is no redirect examination, recross examination is unnecessary. No new testimony. No new harm. The cross-examination has accomplished its goals.

§ 14.08 The Unsuccessfully Cross-Examined Witness

Now examine a different point on the spectrum. The witness has performed very well on cross-examination. If the witness has done well upholding his version of events, it is only the inexperienced or greedy attorney who will attempt to redirect the witness. At first blush, it may appear that skipping redirect in this circumstance would be a missed opportunity by the attorney. But, upon reflection, it is clear that it is by far the safer course since any redirect examination holds new opportunities for disaster.

The value to the redirect examiner of emphasizing already well-established positions that have survived the first cross-examination is greatly outweighed by the danger of receiving a new and unanticipated answer. The potential upside of additional questioning is outweighed by the danger of exposing the witness to a second cross-examination. If the witness withstood the first cross-examination, it makes no sense to expose him to a second opportunity for cross-examination. Most experienced trial lawyers will not court the low gain/high risk inherent in exposing the witness to a second cross-examination.

Conversely, if an opponent should run those risks, from the cross-examiner's viewpoint, there is little to lose. Having lost the first round decisively, the cross-examiner may well be pleased by the prospect of a redirect examination. In all likelihood, the worst facts have already been cultivated by the opponent. A redirect examination may well provide answers the cross-examiner can use or successfully attack. Under such circumstances, the chief task of the cross-examiner is to listen closely to the redirect examination searching for those limited opportunities to assist the cross-examiner's theory of the case, or to attack the opponent's theory of the case. Any recross examination must have well-defined goals. Every chapter attempted in such a recross examination should be built on solid material. Of course, the recross examination is limited to new material brought out during the redirect examination. This should be a very small area. The object of the cross-examiner is to take advantage of no more than a handful of high gain/low risk opportunities.

This new "wading-in" must be restricted to any worthwhile high gain/low risk opportunities. The cross-examiner has had time to reflect on why the cross-examination did not go well. The cross-examiner has had the opportunity to refine the list of potential chapters. The cross-examiner has had an additional opportunity to hear and observe the witness on redirect examination, which may have been the source of additional recross examination material. This is truly a second chance for the cross-examiner, but it is sharply limited.

§ 14.09   The Middle Ground Witness

If the cross-examiner has largely scored the necessary points through cross-examination, the opposing attorney may well feel that it is time to reemphasize those few points that the witness has won from the cross-examiner. This is particularly true if the cross-examiner has lost the final chapter of that cross-examination. The witness has just experienced a second wind.

By allowing this second wind, the cross-examining attorney has violated multiple guidelines of sequences (see chapter 11, *Sequences of Cross-Examination*). The redirecting attorney now has every reason to believe that his witness can reiterate that testimony quickly on redirect examination, and thereby re-establish the appearance of credibility. The opponent will believe that this permits the witness to appear stronger to the jury. In this scenario, the cross-examiner should expect a redirect examination. When it comes, it will come on a chapter not won by the cross-examiner, but in a chapter largely won by that witness. Of course, since this chapter has gone fairly well for the witness, it is the opponent who runs the risk of a bad answer or new material. The cross-examiner must listen attentively to see if the witness offers new facts or a different answer that make for a successful chapter of recross examination.

If the witness has mostly won the cross-examination, the redirecting attorney has multiple opportunities to redirect in those safe areas, in an attempt to further establish for the jury that the witness has prevailed. Any redirect examination will likely reemphasize those areas that were best handled by the witness. Every one of these redirect examination chapters has as much downside risk for the opponent as potential gain.

In the event the witness has been successful in the final chapter of the cross-examination contrary to the sequencing designed by the cross-examiner (see chapter 11, *Sequences of Cross-Examination*),no boldface it is most likely that the redirect examination will start with the witness's victory in the last chapter of the original cross-examination. The cross-examiner should not start the recross examination on that same chapter that served as the final chapter of the original cross-examination. There simply is too much risk in this area. Unfortunately the cross-examiner is emotionally enticed to start with the last chapter that was lost. The cross-examiner is advised to find other chapters worthy of recross examination.

Many of the cross-examination of chapters that go badly are because of an unresponsive answer that has taken the cross-examiner by surprise. When this happens, the cross-examiner either ignores the unresponsive answer or deals with it poorly, which emboldens both the witness and the opposing attorney to build a redirect examination on the unresponsive answer. More often than not, this unresponsive answer is "new" testimony previously unheard by the cross-examiner.

The opposing attorney arms the cross-examiner and furnishes an opportunity to the cross-examiner by bolstering the "new" testimony in redirect examination. Why? The cross-examiner now has additional time to consider how to conduct the cross-examination on the "new" evidence. One of the favored techniques to deal with this phenomenon is through the use of Spontaneous Loops (see chapter 26, *Loops, Double Loops, and Spontaneous Loops*). This will be explained in further detail below.

§14.10 The Process of Elimination

From the cross-examiner's viewpoint, it is unlikely that there will even be redirect examination offered if the cross-examination has gone extremely well or extremely badly. If the cross-examiner was successful, why fear the redirect examination? And, if the cross-examination on the whole has failed (this may sound fatalistic), the narrowed grounds of recross examination should not produce any worse results. Although more pain may need to be endured, recross examination offers an opportunity to better handle the witness.

It is in the two middle areas that a more realistic effort will be made to rehabilitate the witness on redirect examination. Because the cross-examination was neither an all-out win nor an all-out loss, the redirecting attorney takes a substantial risk by redirecting. This is not a risk that most redirecting attorneys believe or recognize. The cross-examiner must capitalize on the risk.

§14.11 The Redirecting Attorney's Greatest Risk: Lack of Preparation

Of the many risks run by the redirecting attorney, the major one is lack of preparation — both on the part of the lawyer and his witness. This lack of preparation produces four types of opportunities for the cross-examiner once redirect begins.

(a) The redirecting attorney must again use open-ended questions, often in areas not thoroughly rehearsed with the witness. The witness, having no clear idea of tactics, may be left with the impression that his first (and perhaps helpful) answer on cross-examination did not please the redirecting attorney. He may now use the redirect examination as an avenue of change, thereby falling squarely into the trap of recross examination. A new change in story equals a new chapter or chapters for recross examination.

(b) Opposing counsel may attempt to perform a redirect examination based on steering the witness to essential "conclusion answers" or "general answers" (see chapter 8, *The Only Three Rules of Cross-Examination*). The redirect examination lawyer may attempt to steer the witness into these conclusions or general pronouncements by using leading questions. The more subtle approach is to steer the witness into affirming their previous position taken in direct examination. This affirmation is usually stated in conclusory form. Example:

On redirect, the lawyer asked:

Q: On cross-examination, you were identified as the Vice President in charge of all contracts?

A: That is true, I am the Vice President in charge of all contracts.

Q: Was there a contract in this case?

A: No.

Q: You are sure of that?

A: Yes.

Q: No question about it?

A: No. There was no contract.

Even when not led to the conclusion or general statement, the redirect examination gives no factual basis upon which these conclusions or general pronouncements are made.

This type of redirect examination opens the door for the cross-examiner to perform double loop chapters, which are rich in factual detail to expose the weakness of the conclusion or general statement (see § 14.28, below). Alternatively, in as much as the redirect examiner is depending on conclusions rather than facts, the cross-examiner may elect to perform no further cross-examination. It must be recalled that the original chapters of cross-examination were written to maximize the cross-examiner's opportunity to introduce and highlight favorable facts. When the cross-examiner has been successful, there is virtually no good reason to repeat any of these chapters or engage in any recross examination.

(c) Frequently, another important risk occurs when the witness does not confine his answers to neat areas that were clear-cut wins on the cross-examination. No matter how experienced, sophisticated, or prepared witnesses appear, they still do not understand chapters. Neither do they comprehend the respective theories of case. Both of these weaknesses may be exploited by the recross. If the redirecting question is loosely phrased, the off-target answer may reopen for the cross-examiner areas that were not won or not touched on by the witness in the original cross-examination. The new material may be just the material needed by the cross-examiner to take a chapter that did not work as well as hoped and convert it on recross to a powerful chapter. Alternatively, the new material may create the opportunity for a new chapter, where no chapter was previously possible before the ill-conceived redirect examination.

(d) Finally, the overly broad answer may open up entirely new areas for recross examination. Sometimes, the cross-examiner has set aside a chapter of prepared cross-examination, since it did not appear strong enough. The loose answer given to an open-ended question in redirect examination may so strengthen the unused chapter that it is now converted into a new and major point on recross examination. It is already prepared. It is ready for controlled presentation.

§ 14.12   Two Objections for the Cross-Examiner to Redirect Cross-Examination

As soon as the cross-examiner hears the words "redirect examination," she should immediately mentally (if not physically) note two objections that may well be made repeatedly during the redirect examination. Some lawyers choose to prepare a page of their trial notebook listing legal citations and the objections.

§ 14.13   Beware of Leading Questions on Redirect

A redirect examination doesn't enjoy new Rules of Evidence. Open-ended questions were not permitted on the original direct examination. They are no more permissible on redirect examination. The redirect examination is occurring because the opponent's case has been injured by the cross-examination. As a result, the redirect examiner will want to minimize his risks. A new series of open-ended questions will not minimize risks. Redirect examination invariably means that the redirecting attorney will attempt to lead the witness. Leading questions have propelled the just completed cross-examination. The opponent's urge to resort to leading questions to quickly move the witness through a rehabilitating "redirect" examination is understandable. Furthermore, open-ended questions always entail more risk than leading questions. It is no wonder that the redirecting attorney will ordinarily resort to leading questions in an attempt to shore up the sagging credibility of his case and to avoid the witness from doing any more damage.

The cross-examiner must be prepared to object immediately to the use of leading questions occurring in the redirect examination. To be sure, the ruling is discretionary with the court. If the court rules that the attorney may lead on redirect examination, it is likely not reversible error. However, the cross-examining lawyer must seek the ruling. The objection must be made at the very first substantive instance of leading on redirect examination. Lawyers are routinely permitted to lead as to introductory materials designed to set up further questioning. It is a tactical error to object to leading questions on undisputed facts that form a foundation for the substantive questioning to come. Even though the question may be leading, the court will likely overrule the objection in such an instance. This will spur the opponent into a greater use of leading questions. The cross-examiner will enjoy greater tactical success by waiting for the first leading question in a substantive and disputed area of fact. Then the objection should be stated crisply. If there is no objection, it encourages a redirect examination conducted by leading questions.

Leading questions can quickly insert bad answers into the case. Worse, by allowing the redirect examiner to use the leading question, it is opposing counsel who is testifying rather than the witness. Even the slowest of witnesses can understand that if they just say "yes" they will have pleased their lawyer. If the opponent gets away with leading questions, he will be emboldened. The damage to the cross-examiner mounts at an alarming rate. Cross-examiners must make the objection, even if the court has ruled that it will permit some leading on redirect. Some leading questions hurt more than others because they suggest answers that the witness was unlikely to have come up with on his own. Now, having received an instruction from his lawyer as to where he is to go with his answers, the witness can be counted on to carry out the goals of that chapter. For this reason it is imperative that the cross-examiner not permit leading questions to substantive facts in dispute. As painful as it might be, even if the court were to overrule an early objection as to the leading nature of a preliminary question, cross-examining counsel must not give up. Keep objecting as the leading questions become more significant. Object early, but remember to re-object as the leading questions touch upon more significant issues. The objections will remind the court that while leading questions are sometimes permitted as to foundational issues, opposing counsel is now far from such introductory issues.

The leading question usually begins innocuously.

Q: Mr. Burnham has just finished his cross-examination of you?

A: Yes.

Q: In particular, he asked you about the existence of the contract?

A: Yes.

Q: Let me direct your attention to those questions and answers.

A: Okay.

But soon, emboldened by the successful use of leading questions in these preliminary matters, redirecting counsel may attempt to use leading questions on the substantive issues:

Q: You said you had reviewed the contract?

A: Yes.

Q: But you had reviewed section 4.16?

A: Yes.

Cross-examination has now proceeded beyond foundation matters. If the cross-restore examiner does not now object, more significant leading questions will follow. More often than not, this is a fundamental error. The cross-examiner must make the opposing attorney earn all facts on redirect.

A second and less important reason for making and remaking the leading objection is to affect the jury's perception of what is occurring. The jury understands that it is not fair for the witness's own lawyer to testify for his witness. The jury wants the words to come out of the witness's mouth, not his lawyer's mouth, especially if the witness has admitted to damaging facts on cross-examination. The jury wants to hear the witness's explanation.

After a judge is reminded, through objection, that this is a *redirect* examination, the judge is less willing to permit the use of leading questions. When a judge sustains an objection to the use of leading questions on redirect examination, it is not unusual for the redirecting lawyer to abandon the redirect examination. This happens because the witness is already in trouble. The witness's cross-examination answers have created real problems for the side that called him. In the original cross-examination, he has made damaging admissions, testified to new facts, or exposed his own inconsistencies. Furthermore, as a result of skillful questioning in accordance with the only three rules (chapter 8) and the chapter method of cross-examination (chapter 9), the *witness does not know* when his admissions have greatly aided the cross-examiner's theory of the case (see chapter 2, *Developing a Theory of the Case*) or materially damaged the opposing lawyer's theory.

The resulting situation is fraught with added dangers to the redirecting lawyer. Stripped of the availability of leading questions, he must approach a fatigued, distracted, and often demoralized witness. Every open-ended question now risks a further bad answer or "off the wall" explanation that will permit more damaging recross examination.

Under these circumstances, the redirecting lawyer will often quietly withdraw after being denied the use of leading questions. Some attorneys will continue the redirect examination, but will give up on the first occasion when the witness answers badly. The redirecting lawyer knows that he is digging himself a deeper hole. Every new unexpected answer, every affirmation of a previous damaging fact, *every failure to give the hoped-for answer* to an open-ended question means even more time will have to be spent just getting back the ground newly lost. Many, if not most, redirecting lawyers quickly calculate that the odds of success are getting worse, and the effort needed is getting greater.

Open-ended questions work best with the fully prepared witness. Now the redirect examination must delve into areas in which the calling party did not prepare the witness. While this is especially true when the cross-examiner has examined with confrontational purposes to the direct examination (see chapter 11, *Sequences of Cross-Examination*), it is also true whenever the chapters of cross have developed new facts or expanded inconsistencies contrary to the testimony of other witnesses of which this witness is ignorant. Where the witness does not know that he contradicts another witness or physical fact, there is little motivation to retreat from the answer already given on cross-examination.

The well-planned cross-examination, executed by efficiently employing the chapter method and accompanying techniques, leaves a wounded witness in the middle of a minefield. It takes a special kind of genius or an ordinary fool to rush in to save the witness, armed only with open-ended questions. The redirect is therefore often abandoned midstream. An abandoned redirect examination is extremely helpful to the cross-examiner. In fact, an abandoned redirect examination is often more helpful than a redirect that never commenced. The abandoned redirect reaffirms for the jury that the cross-examination did great damage, and that the witness is beyond rehabilitation. There is an added advantage. Once the redirect has ended — even after only one question — the cross-examiner has the right to recross on the abandoned redirect. However, there is no advantage in having the last word, only in having the *best* word. There is scant reason to tamper with the lawyer's own successful cross-examination. Recross examination is decidedly not an opportunity to repeat chapters of cross-examination. When the opponent abandons his redirect examination midstream, the victory has been achieved, at least as to that witness.

§ 14.14   Examination Beyond the Scope of Cross-Examination

The second objection that the cross-examining lawyer must be prepared to use repeatedly is that the redirect examination is beyond the scope of the cross-examination. The reason that this objection must be made repeatedly is that the objection is *fact specific*. Generally the law requires that redirect examination not go beyond the bounds of the new material raised in the cross-examination. A redirect examination is not an opportunity for the opponent to repeat his direct examination. A redirect examination is not synonymous with, "I think I can do this better." However, those bounds are factual. The judge must make a factual determination each time an objection is made as to whether the question calls for factual information in areas beyond the bounds of the cross-examination. Once a judge has overruled the objection "Beyond the scope of the cross-examination," the cross-examiner has been advised that the opponent may conduct a redirect examination on that particular topic only. This is not a license for the opponent to redirect without objection on every topic. When the opponent attempts a redirect examination on a different area that the cross-examiner believes has already been covered in the original examination, the objection, "beyond the scope" should be repeated.

§ 14.15   The Value of the Chapter Method in Recognizing and Making Objections

The chapter method of cross-examination (see chapter 9), and the only three rules of cross-examination (see chapter 8), are very helpful in controlling redirect examination. The cross-examiner is thoroughly familiar with her theory of the case. The cross-examiner will know exactly what chapters were developed. The cross-examiner will know exactly what specific individual facts were developed within each chapter of cross-examination. The cross-examiner can refer the court with specificity not only to what chapters were covered but what specific facts were developed. This is impressive not only to the court and to the opponent, but to the jury.

Many courts do not permit speaking objections. Instead, cross-examining counsel will be left with, "Objection, beyond the scope of the cross-examination." However, because the areas covered by the cross-examination are so well identified by the chapter method, the court is in a far better position to recognize a redirect examination that has proceeded beyond the cross-examination. The chapter method communicates factual control of the case. Simultaneously, the chapter method arms the lawyer to recognize when the opponent is pursuing a line of questioning unauthorized by the Rules of Evidence.

When the judge sustains an objection to material "beyond the scope," the redirecting lawyer is badly hurt. The problem probably cannot be cured by rephrasing or by laying a better foundation. In all likelihood, the area is now off limits for good. The redirecting lawyer is blocked by the courtroom's toughest wall — the trial judge's ruling. The reaction is predictable — abandonment of at least the area objected to, and quite possibly abandonment of the entire redirect effort. Again, the effect of an aborted redirect examination that attempted to go outside the scope of the cross-examination is devastating.

The purpose of the redirect was for the opposing lawyer to finish on a high note. If the cross-examiner can defeat that without ever asking a question, the momentum has shifted again to the cross-examining lawyer.

When the cross-examiner makes the objection as to "beyond the scope of the cross-examination," that cross-examining lawyer should be prepared to cite a case from that jurisdiction on the scope of redirect examination. Of course, the judge is aware of this principle of law, but the use of the case name tells the judge, the opponent, and, most importantly, the jury that the cross-examiner was prepared for this eventuality. The cross-examiner did the necessary research specifically to stop this kind of impermissible effort. Find the case once. Use it for a career.

§ 14.16 Properly Wording the Objection

The words of this objection must be selected carefully to best convince the judge that further redirect in the area that the opposing lawyer wants to develop will greatly lengthen the trial.

Example:

> Your Honor, this is outside the scope of the cross-examination. As you will remember, Your Honor, I developed five specific areas on cross-examination, and this was not one of them. Further, if Your Honor permits redirect examination in this new area, it will lead to *"a whole new can of worms"* that we will have to cross-examine on at length.

If necessary, approach the bench to review for the court the precise areas upon which the cross was conducted. Judges are always favorably impressed with attorneys who show tangible signs of preparation. Once again the chapter method of preparation yields benefits for the cross-examining lawyer.

Judges do not want "a whole new can of worms" to deal with in a trial. It ends up being a mini-trial within a trial. The judge wants finality to the issue. The judge wants to move it along. The easy way to bring about finality is to cut it off sooner rather than later. If the judge permits redirect on an issue, then she must permit a very thorough and comprehensive recross examination on that issue. This is a right that is held both by civil parties and criminal defendants. The judge is well aware that it can be reversible error should she restrict the recross examination. Restricting redirect has never led to reversible error. In this case, sustaining the objection is an easy decision.

§ 14.17 Redirect Examination to Combat the Cross-Examiner's Cheap Shot

One likely reason for a successful redirect examination stems from the cross-examiner taking a cheap shot at the witness. When the cross-examiner establishes a point by some tricky questioning that omits or misrepresents central facts, the opponent will use a detailed redirect examination to point out that the image formed in cross-examination is not a fair position to take with the witness. The cross-examiner improperly misled the fact finder.

The redirect will be designed to show this and weaken the credibility of the cross-examiner.

The cheap shot can also be by way of a question that was asked by the cross-examiner and successfully objected to by the opposing attorney. The opposing attorney is permitted to develop by further questioning that there is a reasonable explanation for the innuendo that was cast by the objectionable question. He is permitted to point out that the objectionable question was a misleading and unprofessional effort at cross-examination.

Using the science of cross-examination carried out by the specific and defined techniques, the cross-examiner *never* needs to take a cheap shot. The skillful cross-examiner depends on preparation and skill to prove her chapters. Juries appreciate questions that create reasonable disputes as to the facts. However, juries have an intuitive ability to recognize a cheap shot. Judges are swift to recognize the cheap shot for what it is, and they are swift with a response. The response is ordinarily to give great latitude to the opponent to combat the cheap shot. When in redirect examination, the opposing attorney offers a reasonable explanation for the misleading impression created by the cheap shot question. The credibility of the cross-examiner is weakened and the judge is far more likely to grant even greater latitude through the rest of the redirect examination.

Under these circumstances, the redirect examination is effective. The offending cross-examiner is left with neither recross nor personal credibility on the issue, and deservedly so.

§ 14.18   Witness Vindication on Redirect/Exploring the Cross-Examiner's Cheap Shot

The overall effect of this kind of redirect examination is devastating. The damage to the cross-examiner cannot be overemphasized. The witness appears to be fully vindicated because the cross-examination (now rebutted in redirect examination) is shown to be unfair and unreasonable. Moreover, the witness appears to be the victim of an unscrupulous attack by a lawyer who has "put words in the witness's mouth." The fact finder is equally a victim having been misled. Under such circumstances it is the cross-examining lawyer rather than the witness who has lost credibility. The cheap shot exposes the cross-examiner as a person not to be trusted. This is fatal to the cross-examiner's case. No one trusts teachers or guides that mislead.

An example of a cheap shot:

Q: You say you loved your children?

A: Yes.

Q: But you didn't go to your daughter's soccer tournament on the Fourth of July?

A: No, but . . . .

Q: There are no buts about it, you didn't go?

A: No. No, I didn't. But you have to understand . . . .

Q: You didn't go?

Opp.: Objection, the cross-examiner is interrupting the witness.

Judge: Sustained. Restate your question and permit the witness to answer.

Q: Well, I will move on to another area, Your Honor.

The lawyer who depends on trickery will be happy with the impression now created. The honest, prepared lawyer fears the reasonable explanation that will be developed with devastating effect on redirect examination.

Redirect begins:

Q: You were asked on cross-examination if you loved your children?

A: Yes.

Q: Do you?

A: Yes, I do.

Q: You were asked whether or not you went to your daughter's soccer tournament on the Fourth of July?

A: Yes, and I tried to explain why I didn't go.

Q: Tell the jury why you didn't go to the game.

A: It was because I was in the hospital with my mother.

Q: Were you in the hospital or was your mother?

A: It was my mother. She was dying. I explained to Jamie (the daughter) that I could not go to her soccer tournament because her grandmother was close to death. She didn't really want to play the game, but her father insisted that the game was more important. I am really not criticizing that decision. Jamie could not have helped my mother much nor me at that point in her hospitalization.

Q: Did you discuss all of this with Jamie before you made the decision to stay in the hospital with your mother?

A: Yes, we talked about it at length. She understood that I needed to be with my mother. She said that she felt the same obligation, and we had a long discussion about this. This was one of those difficult decisions that she would be faced with the older she became. I told her she would have conflicting obligations, in this case one to her grandmother, and on the other hand the obligation to a team that was relying on her.

Q: Did your husband participate in this discussion?

A: No, he told the child that it was a simple decision, one that she need not worry about, and that I was being overly dramatic.

Q: How long did you stay in the hospital with your mother?

A: I had been with her three days before the soccer tournament. I stayed with her the day of the soccer tournament. She passed away that evening. I still feel that I made the right decision being with my mother.

The explanation in this case not only shows the cheap shot for what it was, that is, the mother clearly would have been with her child barring the imminent death of her mother. But it shows more. It shows the mother's dedication to both her child and her mother. It shows that the mother had discussions with the child about difficult decisions that will have to be made in life concerning family, morals, and values. The redirect examination showcases the mother's maturity and wisdom. It shows the morals and value system of the mother. It also speaks in great depth of the lack of love, morals, and values of the father. Finally, it shows the cross-examiner as a misleading scoundrel. Such is the price to be paid when the cross-examiner's cheap shot is exposed on redirect examination.

§ 14.19   Avoiding This Type of Redirect Examination by Avoiding the Cheap Shot Cross-Examination

Should this type of redirect examination scare a cross-examiner? Yes. Is it devastating to the cross-examiner? Yes. Should the cross-examination ever take a cheap shot in the hope that there will be no redirect or that the redirect will not clear up the misleading impression created by cross-examination? *Never.*

The firmness of that answer is dictated by both ethics and tactics. The cheap shot endangers the validity of all the good work done by the cross-examination. It gambles all, including the reputation for credibility of the cross-examiner, for shallow victories of little consequence. The cheap shot exposed in one trial is remembered for many trials to come. That judicial memory never well serves the cross-examiner nor her future clients.

§ 14.20   Redirect Examination on Objectionable Matters

A cheap shot on cross-examination may also be ruled as "opening the door" to redirect examination materials that were previously inadmissible.

In a products liability case, the law is clear in the jurisdiction that other injuries caused by this product to separate and unrelated potential plaintiffs after the date of the injury complained are inadmissible. Further, the law is clear that subsequent remedial actions as to the product that is the subject of the product liability case are inadmissible.

On cross-examination, the following cheap shot is taken:

Examiner:	You did not take this product off the market after the plaintiff's injury?
Opponent:	Objection, this deals with after-the-fact information, Your Honor.
Court:	I will permit it as the outer edge of cross-examination. Move along.

Examiner: You did not take it off the market, but you changed the product?

Opponent: Objection.

Court: Sustained.

Examiner: You didn't take it off the market and you knew other people were
. . .

Opponent: Objection.

Court: Sustained.

When the cross-examination was completed, a side bar conference was held. The opposing attorney requested the court to permit a limited redirect examination concerning the implications raised in the questions that were ruled inadmissible. A request for a limiting instruction was also made. The court instructed the jury that questions are not evidence, and if the court sustained objections to the questions, then the jury should not consider them. Further, the court instructed the jury that a limited redirect examination would be permitted to discuss the fact that the machine had not been taken off the market.

Redirect examination:

Q: On cross-examination, you were asked whether or not the product had been taken off the market?

A: Yes.

Q: Your answer was that it had not?

A: That is correct.

Q: And that was true even though this man claims to have been hurt by the product?

A: Yes, we continued to market it. As with all of our products, our company philosophy is that we will continue to evaluate and research and develop better methods and better products to help our customers. The Product Safety Council unanimously approved of this. They ruled it was fine. No problem.

The judge will invariably refuse recross examination on this same issue, as redirect examination was allowed solely to clear up the issue unfairly raised by the cross-examiner. In this situation, the cross-examiner should not have ventured into the area and will not be permitted to rebut the redirect examination. This is the likely outcome to a cross-examiner who unfairly raises an issue. The opponent will be allowed great latitude to clear up the issue, and the cross-examiner will be foreclosed from advancing the issue.

Another example in a typical objectionable cheap shot cross-examination:

Q: You talked to your lawyer before the deposition?

A: Yes.

Q: Your lawyer told you what to say?

A: No.

Q: You discussed the case with him?

A: Yes.

Q: That discussion was about the details in this case?

A: Yes.

Opposition: Objection. Your Honor, with all due respect, this is getting into the area of attorney/client privilege, and I would ask that the Court rule before any other questions are asked that it is covered by the privilege and should not be inquired into.

Court: Ms. Cross-Examiner, you are entering an area that you know is covered by attorney/client privilege. Unless you want to make a proffer to the court, I will instruct you not to inquire further.

Q: No proffer is necessary Your Honor, I will move on. (Addressing the witness.) Your position is that you don't want to discuss in front of this jury what you and your lawyer talked about before the deposition?

A: Well, I guess not. That is supposed to be private, isn't it?

Q: That is what I thought. I will move along. Now at the deposition, you said. . .

On redirect examination, the opposing attorney handled the situation as follows:

Q: You were asked about our conversations before the depositions. Did we have them?

A: Yes.

Q: Did I tell you that they were private and confidential?

A: Yes.

Q: Did I give you any advice on how to answer questions at the depositions?

A: Yes.

Q: What did I tell you?

A: You told me to tell the truth, no matter what.

Q: Did I tell you anything further?

A: Only to tell the truth. I had a strong case.

The science and techniques of cross-examination presented in this book contain no advice on how to craft an unfair cross-examination. There is absolutely no need for cheap shots. In fact, cheap shots are counterproductive to effective and credible cross-examination. The elimination of cheap shots in the cross-examination sharply limits an opponent's ability to engage in a success-ful redirect examination.

§ 14.21 Recross Examination: A Very Limited Field

A redirect examination should not be feared. More often than not, redirect examination is an admission that the cross-examination has scored important points. The two primary objections used to control any redirect examination have been reviewed. A chapter-based cross-examination restricts the field of redirect examination. Ordinarily, no recross examination is required or sug-gested. The method of conducting any necessary recross examination is dis-cussed next.

Recross examination is an extremely limited area of inquiry. The cross-ex-amination has gone well. There is no need to repeat it. Recross examination is limited to chapters that are necessary and winnable. Before standing up to engage in a recross examination, the cross-examiner must internally ask three questions: "Is this necessary? What is the goal? Can it be accomplished?" A recross examination should be undertaken only when the cross-examiner is satisfied with her own answers to these three questions.

§ 14.22 Guideline One: Limited Recross Examination to Prepared Chapters

If the cross-examiner determines that a limited recross examination is nec-essary, the science and techniques of cross-examination still apply. The recross examination needs to proceed by chapters, using leading questions and intro-ducing one new fact per question. Questions should be arranged in a logical sequence to prove a specific factual goal. But when can these chapters be writ-ten? Ordinarily, the chapters must be outlined in the courtroom during the redirect examination. They may not be pretty, but some organization is better than no organization. Only recross on prepared chapters. The preparation may be hurried and in an outline form only. There may not be much time to prepare a chapter for recross examination, but it is essential that the cross-examiner have a firm plan detailing what she wishes to accomplish through the recross examination, what facts she has with which to accomplish the goals, and the clear calculation that those goals are worth accomplishing.

This in-court calculation becomes more complicated in multi-party cases. In the case of multiple parties where a redirect examination may have dealt with chapters of cross-examination that the cross-examiner individually did not present for her party, that lawyer ordinarily will not recross on those areas. Even in that situation, recross examination will deal only with a cross-ex-amination previously prepared by the cross-examiner (compare chapter 11, *Sequences of Cross-Examination*).

§ 14.23   Guideline Two: Refer Specifically to Original Cross-Examination Chapter

Any recross examination should refer in a very specific way to the original cross-examination. It is neither sufficient nor useful to ask: "Didn't I ask you on cross-examination . . .?" This is too general a reference for the jury to come back to the original, controlled cross-examination. The jury must be oriented to that specific area of cross-examination to which the lawyer refers. This is relatively easily accomplished because of the chapter method of cross-examination. The cross-examiner knows the order of the cross-examination chapters delivered, so specific reference can be made to the chapter topic.

Example:

Q: Do you recall that during my cross-examination, you and I discussed the fact that you read the contract before signing it?

A: Yes.

Q: Specifically . . .

§ 14.24   Guideline Three: Use of Transcripts in Recross Examination

If daily transcripts are developed, it makes it much easier to orient the witness to a previous area of inquiry and an exact answer. Simply present the witness with the cross-examination testimony.

Undeniably, daily transcripts are rarely available. However, there is no prohibition from having a court reporter type up a page or two of cross-examination in preparation for a limited recross examination. The chapter organization of cross-examination will permit the lawyer to refer the court reporter to the presentation in such a way that she can actually find and prepare a very short section of the cross-examination quickly. All court reporters note the time of witnesses taking the stand, recess, and adjournments. If the lawyer can specify where and when the subject was raised in the cross-examination, the court reporter can more easily locate the specific factual reference. In this age of computer-aided word recognition, it is all the easier for the cross-examining lawyer to assist the court reporter in locating one or two pages of critical cross-examination.

§ 14.25   Guideline Four: Use the Second Chair Lawyer During the Examination

In the event that there is a second-seat lawyer (or non-lawyer assistant), one of the jobs of the second-seat lawyer (or non-lawyer) is to note the approximate time that the cross-examining lawyer or the redirect examining lawyer starts a new chapter. In as much as the cross-examination was conducted using chapters, and the redirect examination was limited, it is relatively easy to spot the chapter breaks in the testimony (see chapter 11, *Sequences of Cross-Examination* and chapter 9, *Chapter Method of Cross-Examination*). The second-seat lawyer will know the chapters to be covered on cross-examination. The second-seat lawyer will also know the sequence or order in which the chapters will be presented as well as the goal of each chapter. Noting these down as they are developed, as well as the time of day and any other special occurrences (circumstances that would stand out in the jury's mind, including, but not limited to, breaks or unusual events that occurred during the trial), will greatly assist the lead counsel for recross examination in orienting the jury specifically to the original cross-examination. The longer the trial and the more parties involved, the more important it is for this orientation process so the jury will remember. The lawyer intimidates when she can say: "I asked you on cross-examination at 11:17 a.m. this morning . . .?"

§ 14.26 Guideline Five: Theme Lines

In recross examination, return immediately to theme lines that were developed and presented to the jury in the original cross-examination (see chapter 2, *Developing a Theory of the Case*). There is no need to resort to the painstakingly detailed chapters used in the original cross-examination. Instead of re-developing each chapter, a fair summary of the prior testimony or a truncated chapter and the quoting of a theme line will bring the witness and the jury back to the important admissions on cross-examination.

On redirect examination:

Q: You are sure that the defendant is the person who robbed you?

A: Yes.

Q: And that is true even if the six different changes occurred?

A: Yes.

Q: Why is that?

A: Well, I just know that it is him. I know that my story changed those six times. I know that I was off on the height, the weight, the facial hair and those other things that Ms. Hart pointed out, but I just know that it is him. I just know that it is him.

On recross examination, begin immediately with theme lines:

Q: You admit to this jury that your story already changed six times?

A: Yes.

Q: You admit that your story already changed on the robber's height?

A: Yes.

Q: You admit that your story already changed on the robber's weight?

A: Yes.

Q: You admit that your story already changed on the robber's facial hair?

A: Yes.

Q: You admit that your story already changed on the time of day?

A: Yes.

Q: You admit that your story already changed on the lighting of the room?

A: Yes.

Q: You admit that your story already changed on the clothes of the person who robbed you?

A: Yes.

Despite the conclusion "I know that it is him," the jury is again shown the facts developed and highlighted by the theme line, "You admit that your story has already changed."

The use of a chapter containing theme lines authorizes the recross examining lawyer to deliver a mini closing argument. This provides the lawyer the opportunity to teach her theory of the case in real time. The jury hears the closing argument before it is ever given.

§ 14.27   "The Conclusion Coupled With an Excuse" as the Purpose for Redirect Examination

(a) Many redirect examinations are conducted to give reasonable "explanations" to cheap shots or misleading questions on cross-examination. If these areas are eliminated, then the most profitable avenues of redirect examination have been eliminated.

(b) The scientific method of cross-examination, particularly the technique of one fact per question in a logical progression culminating in a specific and identifiable goal, persuades the jury and the opponent that there are no reasonable explanations for the facts developed in the redirect chapters.

Put another way, a successful cross-examination does not ask for conclusions by the witness, but develops and requires the witness to supply individual specific facts upon which the jury will come to the desired and logical conclusion.

As a result of this fact-intensive chapter method of proof, redirect examination does not provide an "explanation" of the conclusion it offers, only an "excuse." This form of redirect examination insists on the conclusion despite the facts. For instance, the witness may have been taken through multiple chapters demonstrating circumstances that proved a product safety device was both necessary and inexpensive. Nonetheless, on redirect examination, the witness is asked, "Did you feel any safety device was necessary?" Of course, the witness is expected to answer, "No." This is a conclusory form of redirect examination, and should not be feared. In fact, it cannot be countered. Regardless of the strength of the cross-examination, the witness is entitled to stick by his conclusion. What the witness is not entitled to is credibility on that issue.

Often the conclusion is accompanied by an excuse as to why the conclusion is true even in the face of contrary facts. The facts previously admitted by the witness hems him in. As he squirms to evade the obvious and fair conclusion, the jurors recognize the literal and psychological difference between fair "explanation" on redirect examination and an "excuse." This redirect offers great opportunity for recross.

A redirect chapter offering a conclusion coupled with an excuse appears in this form:

Q: On cross-examination, Ms. Hart (the cross-examiner) said that your story had changed as to six separate facts on the eyewitness identification?

A: Yes.

Q: You are sure that the defendant is the person who robbed you, aren't you?

Opposition: Objection, leading.

Court: I will permit limited leading.

Q: You are sure that the defendant is the person who robbed you?

A: Yes.

Q: And that is true even if the six different changes occurred?

A: Yes.

Q: Why is that?

A: Well, I just know that it is him. I know that my story changed those six times. I know that I was off on the height, the weight, the facial hair, and those other things that Ms. Hart pointed out, but it all happened very quickly, and I was confused. But I will never forget it. I just know that it is him.

Here the witness gives no factual reason why he "knows" that it is the defendant, only that he is sure. This "excuse" ignores the inconsistencies developed in the factual cross-examination on six different occasions. Instead, it offers a blanket conclusion. The excuse is so conclusory that recross examination is unnecessary. Remember, there is no recross examination that can compel the witness to give up their conclusion no matter how absurd. However, the redirect examination did not alter the facts that made that conclusion unbelievable. But if recross is needed, handle the conclusion coupled with an excuse with a double loop chapter.

§14.28 Using a Double Loop Chapter to Exploit the Opportunity Created by a Redirect Examination Built on a Conclusion Coupled With an Excuse

Often the redirect examination becomes a series of conclusions or general pronouncements unsupported by facts. This form of redirect examination ignores the facts developed during the cross-examination. Facing such a redirect examination, the cross-examiner may elect not to perform additional recross examination. Recalling that facts trump conclusions and that conclusions create no images, the cross-examiner may well conclude that the redirect examination failed to overcome the damage done by the cross-examination. If the cross-examiner decides to engage in a brief recross examination, one technique is to develop a series of short chapters that use the double loop technique.

The double loop technique is explained in detail in chapter 26, *Loops, Double Loops, and Spontaneous Loops*. Essentially, it is the comparison of one fact against another. That comparison shows that the facts should not simultaneously exist. Most effective double loop chapters compare a detailed fact with a general pronouncement or conclusion. When this occurs, the conclusion suffers in a series of short, double loop chapters using individual facts to severely damage the conclusion.

Review the preceding example shown in § 14.27, in which the redirect is a conclusion coupled with an excuse. The recross examination could be:

Q: You have stated on redirect examination that the defendant, Bobby, is the person who robbed you?

A: Yes.

Q: You have already admitted that Bobby's height is not the same height as the person who robbed you?

A: That's true.

Q: You claim the defendant is the person who robbed you, even though the height of the person who robbed you is different than Bobby's?

A: Yes.

Q: You have admitted that Bobby's weight is not the same weight as the person who robbed you?

A: That is true.

Q: The person who robbed you weighed over 200 lbs?

A: True.

Q: Bobby's weight is closer to 150 lbs?

A: I see that.

Q: You claim that Bobby is the person who robbed you even though his weight is fifty pounds less than the person who robbed you?

A: Yes.

Q: The person who robbed you had long sideburns and a little goatee?

A: Yes, I am pretty sure he did.

Q: You have admitted that Bobby does not now nor has he ever to your knowledge had long sideburns or a small goatee?

A: Not that I know of.

Q: You claim that Bobby is the person who robbed you, even though he has never had long sideburns nor a small goatee to your knowledge?

A: Yes.

Q: You have admitted that the person who robbed you had on blue jeans?

A: Yes.

Q: When Bobby was shown to you within fifteen minutes of the robbery, he had on black pants?

A: True.

Q: You claim that Bobby is the person who robbed you even though the color of his pants were the wrong color within fifteen minutes of the robbery?

A: Yes.

Q: You have admitted that the person who robbed you had on a yellow T-shirt?

A: Yes.

Q: You have admitted that the shirt worn fifteen minutes after the robbery was a collared shirt?

A: Yes.

Q: The shirt was also white not yellow?

A: Yes.

Q: You claim that Bobby is the person who robbed you even though his shirt was different in the collar and the color than the person who robbed you within fifteen minutes of the robbery?

A: Yes.

The individual facts will trump the witness's conclusion.

§ 14.29   Recall of "New" Facts on Recross Examination

Sometimes a witness, on redirect examination, will suddenly and inexplicably "recall" important facts completely absent from any of his previous testimony. If handled property on recross examination this "new self help" will further impeach the witness.

Redirect examination:

Q: You said on cross-examination that you signed the contract, but the person who is shown as the notary public did not actually witness you signing the document?

A: Yes.

Q: But you did sign the contract?

A: Yes. And I didn't mention this before (not on direct examination nor on cross- examination nor before trial), but, you know, the plaintiff knew that the notary public was not there, and he told me that he did not care. I never mentioned it because I didn't think that it was important, but since it has been brought up, he knew it and he didn't care.

Recall of new facts during redirect examination is one of the classic excuses offered after a thorough and effective cross-examination. The jury seldom believes such excuses. More often than not, the jury further disregards the witness's testimony. Again, the cross-examiner may choose to leave unexamined the newly recalled facts on the basis that the jury is unlikely to accept them. On the other hand, it is hard to walk away from the new information fact.

The cross-examiner might perform several very short chapters detailing the number of times the witness had an opportunity before and during trial to mention the newly recalled facts, and a complete failure of the witness to have disclosed them before. Because of the cross-examination preparation systems and the chapter method, the cross-examiner can handle the new facts with ease. Inasmuch as the new facts concern an area of importance (otherwise, why is the witness desperate to insert the new facts?), it is likely that a chapter had previously been written and used to cover that "area of factual" material. In other words, the cross-examiner probably has a chapter in the deposition, preliminary hearing, interview, or elsewhere where this fact should have been disclosed, but wasn't. If there was a chapter showing the absence of the new facts, simply summarize the chapter previously performed, showing that the witness's answers on the previous occasions were inconsistent with the new facts now being asserted.

By way of example, examine this scenario in a commercial case. The plaintiff has been vigorously cross-examined on his business ethics, or lack thereof. An example of his allegedly greedy and self-serving behavior was his demand for many lavish perks as part of his sale of a business. The original cross-examination contained several chapters detailing this list of perks. The lawyer's judgment was that the material scored well with the jury. As has been discussed, strong chapters of cross-examination often push opposing lawyers into unrehearsed and ill considered redirect examinations.

Redirect examination:

Q: Now, Mr. Holoen, finally, you were asked about your desire to retain those items in that consulting agreement which Ms. Williams described as perks. Do you remember those questions?

A: Yes.

Q: Mr. Holoen, that particular agreement was assignable and transferable to any party you might choose, wasn't it?

A: Yes.

Q: And Ms. Williams asked you about that, didn't she?

A: Yes.

Q: Did you have an intention when you entered into that consulting agreement that was the reason why you requested of Mr. Clark what Ms. Williams calls perks?

A: Yes.

Q: And would you tell The Court and jury what that was?

A: As a result of the experience that I had — I had gone through, and was going through with my child, it was my intention to set up the foundation, which I did subsequently, that would serve the purpose with — that had the intended purpose of helping others who ran into the same kind of problem that I did or also being a value to teachers, parents, friends of people with problems, etc. Even during my tenure in the Tigers, the ability to use the franchise, the asset, whether we gave seats to people who supplied the coaches with cars, different suppliers to the club, in many different ways, they liked it. They liked to travel with the team. They liked to have tickets to the games, be able to go down to the sidelines, also tremendously valuable assets for auction purposes, being able to auction off so many seats to the Super Bowl for the purchase of the charity, as you know. So that was why it was assignable. They didn't know what the charity was going to be called at that point, nor did I know exactly what its first functions would be. But I knew what its intent was going to be. What, in fact, happened was, as we know, that interest was canceled. But, in the process of it being canceled, the purchase price was increased by —

Q: You're talking about the purchase price with Mr. Clark?

A: Yes, sir.

Q: Go ahead.

A: The purchase price was increased by approximately $2 million U.S. dollars. And then later, in 1985, after I had been paid that, that $2 million was the initial founding seed money that I put into the Holoen Substance Abuse Foundation.

Q: Thank you, Mr. Holoen. Thank you, Your Honor.

Court: Ms. Williams, do you have any questions?

Recross Examination:

Q: So as I understand it, Mr. Holoen, there was a plan all along that all of these requirements in the consulting agreement were there so you could give them to some charitable use?

A: To a charity to be formed that had not been formed.

Q: And you knew that all along, that's what you intended to do?

A: Yes.

Q: That's a very vivid memory you have of how all the Bowl tickets, all of the passes, all of the seats in the owner box. Those were always in your mind clearly as part of a package you intended to present to charity?

A: Yeah. I didn't divorce myself from being a part of that because you would be a host to the — for example, if we held a charity auction in Vancouver, and people would bid on that, it wouldn't come unattended to Mr. Clark's box. So I couldn't say that I wouldn't use a seat. I don't mean to say that.

Q: But, certainly, it was a well-constructed plan you had all along?

A: Ms. Williams, I don't know how well constructed it was.

Q: It's a very vivid plan you had?

A: Yeah. This was not a minor subject to me.

Q: I understand. It was a major subject to you?

A: My child's health? Yes.

Q: Let me read to you what you said under oath July 10–July 9, 2001. Question by Mr. Jones. "Do you remember wanting to have some type of consulting agreement with Joe Clark and the Tigers when you sold the team?" Your answer: "Yes. I remember that it was contemplated in the original agreement. Question: Why did you want it?" Your answer: "I can't recall the exact reasons at this time. Question: Could you remember any reasons?" Your answer: "No. Stated differently, I don't recall why my team of advisors and I believed that was how we arrived at this agreement. Question: Do you remember whether you were going to get paid? Answer: No, I don't. Question: Or how much you were going to get paid. Answer: No, I don't. Question: Or any other perks you would have gotten? Answer: No, I don't remember." You didn't remember any of those things under oath, did you?

A: I didn't remember them then, no.

Q: And at page 353, line 4, "I'm looking at Exhibit 65 on page 2, section 2-B-1. Question: Do you recall asking Joe Clark as part of this consulting agreement to agree to allow you — to have exclusive use of box 209 A with three parking spaces in the red area for all football games, including playoff games? Your answer. "No. I do not recall that." Question by Mr. Jones, "Do you remember asking Joe Clark to agree to provide you at no cost, two seats in the coaches' section on all flights made by the Tigers in connection with two seats in the owners' box and six seats in the stands for each away game played by the Tigers? Do you remember asking for that? Answer: I don't recall this. You don't recall any of this?"

A: The document itself I couldn't even recall. Ms. Williams, I didn't recall all of these things because it isn't what happened. I do recall what I did with the foundation . . .

Q: Why don't we summarize it this way. You were under oath, sir, for two full days, and never have you said anything remotely like what you just said about this consulting agreement?

A: I agree with that, Ms. Williams. If, on the other hand, the matter was previously beyond dispute, and hence a chapter had never been prepared, it is likely that somewhere in the cross-examination preparation materials is a draft chapter, an index card, or topic chart showing the witness's statements surrounding this now-contested issue (see chapter 5, *Cross-Examination Preparation System 1: Topic Charts*). Because the matter had not been contested before trial, no chapter may have been prepared. But in ruling out the need to prepare the chapter, the cross-examination preparation materials still remain. The cross-examining counsel needs only to return to the raw preparation materials to find the index card, witness statement chart, or other preparation device that contained not only the witness's pronouncements on the point now at issue, but also the page and line in discovery where those answers can be found. As was pointed out during the chapters on preparation systems, these preparation materials can be relied upon in an emergency to lay the appropriate foundation leading to the thorough impeachment by omission of the witness on the new facts asserted.

§ 14.30 Recross Based on a Spontaneous Loop from Redirect Examination

[1] Introduction

This chapter began by noting that redirect examination is more likely and recross examination may be more necessary, when there were mixed results on the original cross-examination. That is, both the cross-examiner and the witness scored important points, and the opposing counsel believes the witness can further aid the case through a redirect examination. In performing the redirect examination, opposing counsel must proceed with open-ended questions, with the necessary result that the witness is called upon to give answers far broader than "yes" or "no." Every answer is another opportunity for the witness to fumble and provide further facts that can be converted by the cross-examiner into a spontaneous loop.

[2] Spontaneous Loops from Redirect Testimony

A witness who has undergone attempted impeachment with inconsistencies seems to be a good candidate for redirect examination. This is deceptive, since the problem of inconsistencies is never easily cured. First, inevitably the witness will give additional information on redirect examination as to the inconsistencies. In all likelihood, the witness will offer some excuse that will assist the recross examining lawyer with additional information to use.

Listening to redirect examination is every bit as important as listening to the original direct examination. While a cross-examiner may, by body language, imply to the jury that this is all old news of no great import, the cross-examiner must be fully alert. If additional information is given that would be helpful to the recross examiner, the new answer can be immediately used to fashion one or more spontaneous loop chapters to be performed in recross examination. The best technique of capitalizing on new information is to link the testimony by spontaneously looping the new answers (see chapter 26, *Loops, Double Loops, and Spontaneous Loops*).

In a civil case, the plaintiff has testified and put up all his evidence, including medical testimony. The defendant has testified on direct and has been cross-examined. Now, on redirect, the defendant remembers, for the first time, that the plaintiff volunteered that "she wasn't really hurt" as the two parties stood on the side of the interstate waiting for the state trooper. A recross examination using a spontaneous loop technique of the newly remembered information and the technique of theme lines may go like this:

Q: Sir, you just told your lawyer for the first time that you "remembered" Molly Gumble saying that she wasn't hurt on the side of the road after the collision?

A: Yes.

Q: You just remembered that today?

A: Yes.

Q: You just remembered that when your lawyer questioned you the second time?

A: Yes.

Q: You didn't remember it when the lawyer questioned you the first time?

A: No.

Q: You didn't remember it when I questioned you the first time?

A: No.

Q: You didn't remember it when I questioned you before trial at your deposition?

A: No.

Q: You didn't remember it when the investigating officer filled out his collision report?

A: No, I didn't think of it at that point.

Q: You didn't remember it after the lawsuit was filed, requesting money for these injuries?

A: No, I guess I didn't.

Q: You didn't remember it when Molly took the stand and testified to the pain in her lower back?

A: No.

Q: You didn't remember it when Molly took the stand and testified to the pain that radiated into her left foot?

A: No.

Q: You didn't remember it when Molly testified as to how she could not pick up her two-year-old because of that pain?

A: No.

Q: You didn't remember it when she testified she couldn't have sex because of that pain?

A: No.

§14.31 Delaying the Opportunity to Recross

If, on redirect examination, the witness escapes without providing any new information helpful to the cross-examiner and offers no new information harmful to the cross-examiner, then, recross is unnecessary. The recross examining lawyer must compare those points on which the witness hurt the cross-examiner on the *original* cross-examination with those chapters that the cross-examiner originally won. The chapters already made in cross-examination will not evaporate under the heat of the redirect. Done well, they are ingrained in the minds of the jurors. When the cross-examiner tries to rehash favorable material, it is the cross-examiner who may suffer any less favorable answer.

§14.32 Problems Associated With Multiple Parties and Multiple Cross-Examinations and Their Solutions

Particular problems arise when there have been multiple cross-examinations of a witness by multiple parties. Not every cross-examiner is prepared and not every cross-examination is skillfully conducted. For the well-prepared and skillful cross-examiner, one of the more frustrating aspects of multi-party cases is to be involved in a trial where attorneys for co-parties do not conduct similarly methodical cross-examinations.

Sometimes a cross-examiner delivers a well-prepared and controlled cross-examination, only to listen to counsel for another party deliver an uncontrolled rambling cross-examination that skips from one area to another. The cross contains global accusations, but does not develop the facts one by one. There is no discernable theory.

If the opposing lawyer chooses to redirect the witness under these conditions, the opposing lawyer will concentrate on the sloppy and more freewheeling cross-examination that may well have produced some stunning admissions, but also produced some devastating answers. The problematic answers also affect the controlled, disciplined, and prepared cross-examiner.

§14.33 Pre-trial Strategy/Trial Options for Multiple Parties

If foreseen, this problem can be discussed *before* trial with named co-party counsel. Once the trial starts, the other named co-parties' cross-examination is beyond the control of the cross-examiner. There are no satisfying solutions to damage caused by sloppy cross-examination.

The problem of the freewheeling cross-examination must be discussed between counsel before trial. In the give-and-take of the discussion, the wise cross-examiner attempts to secure the first cross-examination. Going first, the most prepared cross-examiner can inflict the greatest amount of damage on the opponent's theory of the case. All of the inconsistencies in the testimony of the witness can be revealed, and in general, the greatest damage can be done to the credibility of the witness before any other lawyer needs to attempt her cross-examination. This will leave a weaker witness and an easier route to a successful cross-examination for every successive cross-examiner (see chapter 12, *Employing Primacy and Recency*). The same primary cross-examiner will then have the right to conduct the first recross examination. This places the cross-examiner in the best position to protect her client and to protect the clarity of her cross-examination. It also leaves the most prepared lawyer in the position to affect the outcome of the case for other parties with similar interests.

In the best-case scenario, performing the first original cross-examination immediately after the direct examination and having the right to frame the first recross examination (if necessary) permits the careful cross-examiner the opportunity to factually develop carefully chosen chapters to teach the jury in real time the cross-examiner's theory of the case (primacy). Whatever happens thereafter will have less effect on that original first cross-examination.

Likewise, the strongest position on recross examination is the first position. A recross examination has the potential to backfire on the cross-examiner and on all others whose interests are similarly aligned. Therefore the better course is to allow the strongest lawyer to perform the recross examination so as to limit the recross examinations that other lawyers might have been tempted to undertake. It is better to go first and eliminate problems rather than to go last and solve new problems created by poorly executed or unnecessary recross examinations. The first position is the best opportunity (primacy) to undo whatever damage the redirect, and more often than not, the potential recrosses, have done to the original cross-examination.

In the event that pre-trial agreements with counsel have not been reached, the cross-examiner must endure other party's potentially sloppy cross-examination. The controlled cross-examiner now faces the prospect of damaging redirect examination and damaging recross examinations by other parties. Nonetheless, there are several options for the cross-examiner. The skillful cross-examiner may choose to stay out of the fight completely. The cross-examiner may look at the situation and decide that the damaging material dumped on the other cross-examiner did not spill over to her client. In such a circumstance, she may decide not to recross. This is based on the hope to isolate the damage to the other cross-examiner and her party. An alternative method is to attempt to salvage the situation by recross examination that will benefit not only the cross-examiner's client, but the other cross-examiner's client as well. There is a substantial risk to this decision. The cross-examiner cannot afford to be identified with the other party and the other cross-examiner.

§ 14.34   When to Stay Silent and When to Attempt to Clean Up Co-Counsel's Errors

There is a mechanism to determine when to stay away and when to venture in. If the cross-examiner has not previously developed a chapter of cross-examination on areas that are now the subject of redirect examination, she should not enter into recross examination of those areas. Having originally chosen not to cross-examine in those areas meant that the lawyer decided the area was not conducive to a productive cross-examination. In addition, the area that the lawyer originally chose not to tackle on cross-examination, has now been stomped on by less thoughtful counsel for co-parties. The resulting answers will be more difficult than ever to clean up.

Perhaps the opponent's redirect examination is in an area that the careful cross-examiner had targeted as a chapter in her original cross-examination. Now another party's lawyer has made the advocate's results less effective through his cross-examination of that area. This, too, is a very difficult decision. If the cross-examiner can disassociate her client from the bad answers received by the other cross-examining attorney, it is still best not to recross examine. Later, in closing argument, counsel can argue that the client is not associated with those issues. If that disassociation is not possible, recross examination is in order. Trials are not environments that lead to clear cut choices. There is often the requirement for the cross-examiner to weigh multiple factors before making a decision. This is one of them.

§ 14.35   The Value of the Chapter Method to the Task of Recrossing in Multiparty Cases

When the cross-examining lawyer has targeted certain facts as a necessary chapter for cross-examination, realistically she is locked into performing the chapter even if the chapter area has been made chaotic. Regardless of the order in which the cross-examiner tackles the recross examination, the skillful cross-examiner must stay true to the original chapters of the cross-examination, supplemented by any spontaneous statements made by the witness during the original cross-examinations, the redirect, and any prior recross examinations. This is true even if the chapter or chapters may seem confused or chaotic.

Clarity of thought and conciseness of questioning are essential at this stage. The only three rule rules of cross-examination (chapter 8) have not changed. The chapter method is not obsolete (chapter 9). Revert to the scientific approach and fundamental techniques that characterized the original cross-examination in this area. Slowly *rebuild* the chapter or chapters factually that were dismembered by less skillful cross-examiners. When in doubt, use more detailed facts to accomplish this rebuilding. Resist the urge to cut to the bottom line or specific goal-fact. Patiently build the chapters one question at a time, one fact per question. While this may seem repetitive, it is refreshing to the jury who has seen a formerly clear image blurred by imprecise questioning in too many other cross and redirect examinations.

Multi-party cross-examinations by unskilled lawyers are frustrating and can cause good lawyers to lose close cases. Do not be affected by the other lawyer's panic attacks. The best way to make the best of a bad situation is to stay true to the chapter method of cross-examination.

§ 14.36   Never Again Fear Redirect Examination

It is clear that the better the original cross-examination, the less likely that the opponent will want to expose his client to recross examination. If the witness performed poorly, an experienced opponent tries to recover through another witness. If the witness performed poorly and the opponent is redirecting, the damage likely cannot be undone. In some cases, it can be worsened. If the opponent chooses to redirect a witness, remember that the cross-examiner has many tactical advantages on her side. Redirect examination is restricted to those areas upon which the witness was cross-examined. Using the chapter method of cross-examination, the cross-examining attorney is far more organized to handle any recross examination. The facts are before the cross-examining attorney and the parameters of those chapters are clearly defined.

The cross-examining attorney is armed with two potent weapons to disrupt and to cause her opponent to abandon a redirect examination — objections as to leading questions and objections as to outside the scope of the cross-examination. The cross-examiner will remember that the opponent has a communication problem with the witness. If the opponent did not have this problem, it would be unnecessary to redirect the witness.

When the opponent chooses to redirect a witness, the cross-examiner will concentrate on theme chapters as much as possible. She will listen for spontaneous loops available from the redirect examination when "new" information is added. She will apply the double loop chapter when the witness gives conclusion coupled with an excuse. The cross-examiner will use both double loop chapters and spontaneous loop chapters to carry the witness into theme chapters. Recross can be an early opportunity to give a mini closing argument.

Chapter 15

DESTROYING SAFE HAVENS

SYNOPSIS

§ 15.01   Identifying and Destroying Safe Havens

In the lexicon of cross-examination, a safe haven is a time worn excuse used by a witness to avoid arriving at the factual destination the lawyer is driving toward in her chapter. It is most often recognized as an excuse given by the witness as to why something was not done, was not important, or was never said before. In general, safe havens are the experiential or predictable ways a witness seeks to interrupt the logical flow of questions within a chapter so as to avoid having to testify affirmatively to the goal question or questions that conclude the chapter.

For instance, in criminal law's most common safe haven situation, an officer testifies to a fact found nowhere in his reports. As the lawyer moves from the general to the specific, setting up the importance of police reports and arriving at the absence of a mention of the critical fact in this report, the cross-examiner can anticipate the witness will look for a way out — a way to explain the absence of an important item in the police report. This way out is the safe haven for the witness. The witness has historically resorted to this way out over the years to successfully explain away such problems. There are a number of safe havens available to such a witness: lack of time, reports are only summary in nature, another officer would cover that fact, or lack of resources.

Whether the witness is an expert witness, civilian, law enforcement officer, or lay witness, he prefers to make himself look better than worse. Human beings will not behave much differently in a courtroom than they would outside one. That is to say, they will seek an excuse for actions or inactions that make them look bad. Winning the case is a laudable goal, but avoiding humiliation is a more critical psychological goal for most witnesses.

Both the witness's search for safe havens and the havens themselves are predictable. Either by experience or by logic, a cross-examiner can foresee the likely excuses to be interposed by the witness. Often, the cross-examiner thinks that these excuses ring hollow, and therefore makes no provision to address the excuse. Sometimes the cross-examiner, upon receiving the excuse, will do battle to try to back the witness away from the excuse. Neither of these tactics is ideal for success.

In the first place, jurors are strangers to courtrooms. Since they have not heard the same excuses over and over, jurors are more willing to believe that incidents get left out of reports, tests are not done, or any other excuse tossed out by the witness. If the lawyer desires the jurors to give no credit to the excuse, the lawyer needs to give the jurors solid factual reasons for skepticism.

On the other hand, the notion that the lawyer can back the witness away from an excuse already explained puts too much pressure on post-excuse cross-examinations. The excuse has been given and the lawyer is now questioning a witness who understands the need to preserve the excuse. This is a very difficult task, which will take time, energy, and risk. Even after a decent cross-examination concerning the excuse, jurors may still believe the excuse.

When the cross-examiner prepares to embark upon a cross-examination in which it can be anticipated that a witness may attempt to avoid the thrust of a chapter by seeking refuge in a safe haven, the optimum method of cross-examination is to block the safe haven before it is used. Alternatively, the cross-examiner can design the chapter so that the excuse, if offered, will lack credibility. Both techniques are accomplished by a series of questions performed before the witness appreciates the need for the safe haven. In order to accomplish this, the cross-examiner needs to add to the sequence of questions within a chapter a series of leading questions designed to block the effective use of a safe haven. For every safe haven that must be closed, there is a separate series of questions designed to accomplish the task.

§ 15.02 Each Safe Haven Has Its Own Chapter

Each of these series of questions may be seen as their own chapter designed to accomplish the unspoken goal of destroying a safe haven. These chapters in turn must be inserted into the sequence of chapters (chapter bundle) prior to the point the witness clearly perceives the ultimate goal of the chapter bundle. A diagram of this process is as follows:

The process is readily understood by comparing the cross-examination to a long hallway with doors. The goal-fact is obtainable only at the end of the hallway. The cross-examiner must, through leading questions, guide, pull, and prod the reluctant witness down the hallway until he is forced to confront the goal-fact or goal feeling and acknowledge its truthfulness. Safe havens are exits along the hallway. The lawyer must move the witness beyond safe havens before the witness sees the goal fact. If, on the other hand, the lawyer asks the goal question before she has closed the safe havens, the witness will deny the validity of the goal question and then resort to a safe haven (excuse) that has been left open. The diagram of this follows:

A short illustration of the chapter designed to block a safe haven:

> In a criminal case, the investigating officer claims at trial that the defendant made a very inculpatory statement when he was arrested. That statement appears nowhere in the police officer's report. The lawyer intends to cross-examine to show that the inconsistency between the officer's current recollection and a complete absence of such inculpatory statement in the report. The lawyer can anticipate that the officer will rely upon some excuse for not putting it in the report. She can foresee three excuses: (a) this report is a summary only and not every fact in the case was put into the report; (b) the arrest went down under unusual circumstances and there was not time to fill out a complete report; or (c) at the time he did not appreciate the importance of the statement.

The goal is to not only expose the inconsistency by omission, but to do so in a way that destroys the credibility of the officer's new version of events. If the cross-examiner is to accomplish the goal-fact (omission of the key statement) and the goal inference (the officer lacks credibility), the cross-examiner must first close off the safe havens.

Without revealing to the officer the goal of the cross-examination, the cross-examiner first asks a series of leading questions designed to show that the officer is well trained in the performance of his duties. Within that bundle of chapters would be a chapter on the importance of written reports.

The next chapter would concern itself with the fact that he had adequate time the night of the arrest, either at the scene or at the station house to write a complete report and that there were no physical or mental obstructions that kept him from writing a complete report.

The cross-examiner should next frame a chapter in which she establishes the need to put into a report those items that might reasonably ever be of consequence in the case. The lawyer would only then demonstrate that a confession is an item of paramount importance in any criminal case. Only after doing all of these preparatory chapters, each sealing off a safe haven, would the lawyer go into the report itself to show that the officer now states that there was a confession. However, nowhere in the reports is there any mention of a confession.

At this point, the historically safe reasons (safe havens) available to the officer for why the confession is not in the report has already been disavowed by the officer. The lawyer has taken the officer through a series of chapters, and in essence, required him to forsake his safe havens before he appreciated his need for a safe haven. Only when the lawyer has blocked all the foreseeable safe havens will she begin questioning directly toward the goal that makes the safe haven a necessity. By preparing the sequence of questions and chapters in such a way, the lawyer has blocked the witness's use of safe havens, and thus leaves the naked truth that:

(a) it could have been in the report;

(b) it should have been in the report;

(c) if it happened, it would have been in the report; and

(d) it is not in the report.

If the lawyer leaves a safe haven open and asks her goal question, the witness will jump for the safe haven. The lawyer has then left herself with the difficult task of dragging the witness out of the safe haven. Why then does the lawyer think that she can cause the witness to forsake the safe haven by questioning in advance of revelation of the ultimate goal question? The answer lies in a combination of psychology and sequencing.

§ 15.03 The Techniques of Destroying Safe Havens

When a witness has seen the lawyer's ultimate goal and needs a safe haven, he goes into it in order to save himself. Witnesses resort to safe havens in order to make themselves look better or to give themselves an explanation for an answer or conduct that on its face looks implausible or unprofessional. The psychodynamics of this situation are clearly that the witness must cling to the safe haven. On the other hand, if the lawyer approaches the chapters that seal off safe havens in advance of the revelation of her goal, the lawyer can create a scenario in which the witness relinquishes the safe haven in order to make himself look better. The cross-examiner is using the same dynamic (but in a different sequence) that would have gotten him into trouble to avoid trouble. The cross-examiner is using the witness's sense of self-protection from the affirmative answers to early questions that will have the effect of later denying the witness the safe haven he needs. The sense of professionalism and the desire to look good encourage witnesses to use the safe haven.

The lawyer accomplishes this by forming a series of leading questions, the essence of which is that the witness is a good witness, a good professional, a thorough person, and that he knows how to do things well. And in this case, he did perform well. The witness may look for the reason for the questions, but can find no harm in a continuing series of admissions to behaving like a professional. Similarly, with the lay witness, the witness can find no harm in admitting that he had an opportunity to observe and fully relate what he observed.

The key to this technique is to pose to the witness a series of leading questions to which the witness wants to answer "yes" rather than "no." The motivation is for the witness to look good. Everyone wants to look good. Witnesses in trials are no different. The cross-examiner can ask an officer:

Q: You are a professional law enforcement officer?

Q: Part of your professional duties is to fill out police reports?

Q: There are courses at the Academy that stress the importance of filling out reports accurately?

Q: You know other officers are going to rely on your reports?

Q: And you know that over the course of your career you will have thousands of cases?

Q: You want to keep accurate records of what happened in your cases?

Q: You want to keep accurate records of what happened because it would be unrealistic to think you could memorize all of the important facts of all of your cases?

Q: And because other people who were not there will only know what happened by referring to your report you know how to prepare accurate reports detailing the important facts?

Q: You wanted to prepare an accurate report detailing the important facts?

Q: You had the time to prepare an accurate report?

This chapter invites the officer to the exalted role of a professional. Care must be taken to do this chapter in a voice that is neutral. If the voice of the cross-examiner is aggressive or angry it will tend to tip off the witness that there is something wrong with the report. These questions are asked in an off-handed or neutral manner as if to imply, "Of course you are a professional. Of course you to look that time to do with well." Then the officer sees no reason to dodge. After all, every answer simply verifies that the witness is professional and behaved like a professional.

There are as many forms to this chapter as there are excuses to be offered. If the likely excuse is a lack of time, then the cross-examiner must seal off that safe haven with questions that show that the officer did take the time and would never leave without properly documenting the facts. For the surgeon, if the excuse likely to be offered by an expert is that he ran a test but failed to note it in his report, then the chapter needs to include facts that paint the expert into a corner in which he admits to the importance of accurate reports, and that he would never leave out something important. Every chapter that commits a witness to a course of conduct or professionalism that is at odds with some excuse has the effect of making it far less likely the witness will resort to that excuse. If he does, the excuse is less likely to be believed.

Similarly with a lay witness who wants to say that he forgot to tell an officer something or that the officer never asked, the lawyer can draft a series of chapters designed to show that the witness wanted to be thorough and accurate, and he was dealing with an officer that was eager to receive the information. This same principle holds true for prosecutors. This same principle holds true in commercial litigation.

A corporate executive or employee might be tempted to offer an excuse during cross-examination that he never thought a particular fact was important, that he forgot about that fact, or any other excuse that he will need to come up with to explain conduct or lack of conduct. In such a case, the technique is to write chapters that do not alert the witness to the need for the excuse but instead lock him into a story of professionalism, care, diligence, or some other set of traits and actions that have the effect of denying the witness the safe haven before he recognizes the need for it.

There is no psychological damage to the witness giving the lawyer a "yes" answer. In fact, the witness views himself as enhancing his credibility with such answers. Later, when the lawyer gets to the goal question and the witness needs the safe haven, it is too late. He has already explained to the jury that none of the excuses he now needs could exist in this case.

§ 15.04   The Sequence of Denying Safe Havens

Timing is important. It is critical that safe havens be destroyed before the witness perceives the need for them. In fact, it is not necessary to destroy the safe haven immediately prior to performing the goal chapter. It is often advantageous to destroy safe havens as a preliminary matter in the cross-examination then move to the impeaching statement later. In fact, since there may be several impeachments from inconsistent statements, a single set of chapters that destroy safe havens early in the cross will effectively deny the witness safe havens for a series of impeachments to be performed throughout the remaining cross-examination (see chapter 11, *Sequences of Cross-Examination*).

In this way, the witness is not alerted that the lawyer is setting up impeachments early in the cross-examination. The witness is at ease because the cross-examiner seems to be asking a sequence of "easy" questions. Because these questions come before the lawyer has attacked the credibility of the witness, the witness is comfortable with the cross-examiner at that point. It is the intuitive witness who can perceive that there will be an impeachment down the road that necessitates using of a safe haven.

§ 15.05   Dealing With the Professional Witness Who Keeps Safe Havens

There is the rare witness — almost always the professional witness — who holds tight to his safe havens knowing that potential excuses may come in handy later. Such a rare witness might volunteer a negative answer to a preliminary question in an attempt to hang onto a safe haven. But since that effort comes long before the goal chapter has been revealed, this in itself appears disingenuous to a jury. Furthermore, the witness who tries to guard his safe havens closely must volunteer answers about his lack of professionalism, lack of opportunity to observe, and lack of time to relate adequately. In so doing, he brings greater damage to his credibility than the lawyer might have scored in the goal chapter itself. Of course the goal chapter will still be performed later, but the lawyer is now alerted as to which safe haven the witness will seek for asylum.

§ 15.06   Baiting a Witness into a Safe Haven

There will be a time when the skillful cross-examiner wishes to leave open a selected safe haven for the witness. The cross-examiner does this for a reason. When the witness perceives the need for the safe haven, he will predictably run to the refuge (safe haven) purposely left open.

Why would a cross-examiner do such a thing? The cross-examiner does it only as a device for causing increased impeachment of the witness. The lawyer must leave open only a safe haven that she can thoroughly and unquestionably destroy with surrounding facts or witnesses. This advanced technique is set up as follows: Systematically destroy all but one safe haven. The lawyer then scores impeachment points by revealing an inconsistency or establishing the goal. The witness then attempts to diminish the value of what the lawyer has achieved by running to the safe haven. The lawyer thereafter systematically impeaches the excuse to show that the witness fraudulently used the safe haven. What the witness perceived to be a safe haven was, in reality, a trap. Of course, the value of this technique is predicated upon the ability to spring the trap. The cross-examiner's evidence as to the fraudulent nature of the safe haven must be unassailable by the opponent. If there is a risk that the jury could still perceive the safe haven to be honest, then the lawyer must revert to the originally suggested sequence and destroy the safe haven before the witness seeks its use.

A scenario in which the cross-examiner baits a safe haven follows: The witness has made a new statement as to a critical fact that is inconsistent with his entire position. The lawyer leaves open one safe haven. The witness, in fact, never made the earlier statement and that the person hearing it and noting it in a report has been wholly incorrect. The lawyer knows in advance that this reporting witness is very credible witness and will say in no uncertain terms that the report reflects exactly what the witness said.

§ 15.07 Allowable Safe Havens

There are some occasions in which the lawyer wishes to leave a safe haven open for the witness to use without attack. The lawyer does this because the safe haven selected by the witness in itself assists the cross-examiner's theory of the case. The reason for encouraging a witness to use a safe haven is that the safe haven speaks against the thrust of the opponent's case and supports the cross-examiner's theory of the case.

An example of this technique is provided in the following scenario:

> An accident investigation expert comes to the scene of a fatal auto accident. She undeniably possesses the ability, the dedication, and the necessity to perform a highly competent scene investigation. The lawyer finds within her reports that the witness has erroneously measured several critical distances and items at the scene.

The lawyer could close or attempt to close all of her safe havens and reveal the inconsistencies, thus impeaching the witness's credibility. However, in talking with the witness beforehand or in some pre-trial hearing, the lawyer has learned that he was under pressure to get the job done quickly because the accident took place on a major highway and traffic was backing up. The sequence of chapters the lawyer might use in order to encourage use of a safe haven that assists that theory of the case is to establish the expert's expertise, training, and desire and need to do the job correctly.

Through all this, the lawyer has left intact the chosen safe haven — the very important job was performed incorrectly because superiors put time demands on her that were inconsistent with her doing the job properly. The lawyer allows the witness to give the excuse for her errors, and thereafter leads the witness through a thorough explanation of the excuse.

In this way, the lawyer has used the safe haven to further destroy credibility and to enhance the theory. By showing all the wrong measurements, the lawyer has scored all the points she could have scored through this method of impeachment alone. In addition, the lawyer has enhanced the value of the impeachment by showing that the witness blames other law enforcement agents for her not getting the job done correctly. In turn, the lawyer can expect the jury to be less than sympathetic to a government that prosecutes an individual, but has not given the government's own expert enough time to conduct the investigation properly. The errors and the excuses for the errors represent two shots at the credibility of the witness. The lawyer has fired both barrels of the credibility shotgun and scored on both themes.

The psychodynamics of encouraging the use of a safe haven is quite parallel to the psychodynamics that would have occurred had the lawyer left the safe haven open inadvertently. The witness feels the lash of impeachment and consequent embarrassment and lack of self-esteem. The witness wishes to save himself and to diminish the sting by seeking to explain away her error.

The lawyer then offers a suggestion of a safe haven, making it clear in voice and manner that the lawyer believes it to be a true safe haven. The witness happily takes the predictable path into the safe haven. The lawyer is then able to safely cross-examine to show why this safe haven is appropriate. Such a cross-examination helps to establish the validity of the safe haven. Once this is done, every question again verifies that the witness should not feel bad because the blame should be cast on others. The witness is again happy to comply with these leading questions because these questions are bailing out the witness's own professionalism. Although he is doing so at the cost of others and, ultimately, at the cost of the side that called him, the witness will protect himself. Experts can be quite vulnerable to this technique. Experts can be counted on to preserve their own self-image.

Chapter 16

EIGHT STEPS OF IMPEACHMENT BY INCONSISTENT STATEMENT

SYNOPSIS

§ 16.01 Impeachment

One of the hallmarks of cross-examination is the act of impeachment. Cross-examination exposes the weakness of the opposing party's witness. One of the best methods to expose those weaknesses is through impeachment. There are many forms of impeachment, including bias, interest, prejudice, inconsistency with another witness, inconsistency with the physical evidence, cataloging things not done, inconsistency with common sense, and the revelation of omissions and inconsistent statements.

Whether the witness is determined to be honestly mistaken or willfully deceitful, impeachment is the vehicle to expose that to the fact finder. Of all of the forms of impeachment, impeachment by inconsistent statement is the most frequently utilized technique. Mastery of this technique is essential to effective cross-examination.

§ 16.02 Identifying the Eight Steps

There are eight distinct steps in the process of impeachment by inconsistent statement. Each step has its purpose. Some are legally required as part of a foundation and some are done as a matter of technique. By presenting all the legally required steps thoroughly and by adding the other techniques, the cross-examiner maximizes the effect of the impeachment.

1. Uncover or find the inconsistency;

2. Physically prepare the cross-examination on inconsistency;

3. Establish the current version of the testimony to be impeached;

4. Tie the witness to the current version of the fact to be impeached;

5. Equate or translate the versions;

6. Expose the inconsistent statement;

7. Maximize the damage or effect; and

8. Listen for useful volunteered information at trial.

These eight steps are inviolate. If completed each time, in order, successful impeachment will result. There are occasions when some of the eight steps may be performed in an abbreviated fashion. Nonetheless, these eight steps are the required structure for effective impeachment. This is not to say that the cross-examiner cannot add impact to her impeachment by carefully selecting words and developing detailed, precise chapters designed to maximize the effect of any impeachment. But without the eight steps, no matter how powerfully worded, the impeachment runs the risk of being unsuccessful and thereby undermining the credibility of the cross-examiner.

§ 16.03 Step 1 — Uncover or Find the Inconsistency

Techniques for discovering and documenting inconsistent statements are discussed in chapters 5, 6, and 7. Through the application of these systematic techniques, all witness statements made prior to trial have been broken down, collated by topic, and digested as to importance. As a result of the application of the systems, the cross-examiner has uncovered each inconsistency in the witness's previous discussions of the facts. Identifying "each" inconsistency is different than identifying the "big" or "important" inconsistency. "Each" means every inconsistency, whether important or not. The cross-examiner may not recognize that an inconsistency is "important" or "big" at the time of digesting the discovery. The inconsistency should be tracked in any event. The cross-examiner must leave herself in a position to make that determination as the case develops during the trial. This method ensures no inconsistency will be overlooked. The cross-examiner can continue her preparation for trial confident that if needed, the source material for the impeachment is readily available.

§ 16.04 Uncovering and Sourcing the Opportunity and Necessity for Accuracy by the Witness

When dealing with impeachment by inconsistent statements as opposed to all other types of impeachments, there is an additional step in preparation. For each statement, document, report, deposition, non-jury hearing, or interview conducted before trial, the cross-examiner should also prepare a separate note page of the trial notebook documenting where the witness has either been given the oath, or has, in any way, been cautioned concerning the necessity to give completely accurate information to the best of his abilities.

§ 16.05 At the Deposition

Oath and Verification Chart

T-2, L4–10	OATH
T-5, L20–T6, L24	ADMONITION
T-392, L16	"UNDERSTOOD ALL QUESTIONS"
T-392, L18	"GAVE HONEST ANSWERS"

For instance, in a deposition, the cross-examiner should note the page and line numbers where the witness was given the oath. In the chart above those are: T-2, L4-10 oath (read this code as transcript page 2, lines 4 through line 10 — the oath administered).

The cross-examiner should also note the admonition given by the deposing lawyer to the deponent of how important it is that the deponent understands all of the questions (on the above chart see T-5, L20–T6, L24 admonition). It is worth noting exactly where the deposing counsel cautioned the deponent that if he did not understand the questions, then it is the deponent's obligation to tell the deposing lawyer that he does not understand a question.

As a tactical note, it is wise to caution every deponent that if the deponent does not alert the questioning lawyer of any confusion concerning the questions, it would be "fair" for the deposing lawyer to assume (and for a jury that may hear all or a portion of the deposition to assume) that the deponent's answers were complete, responsive, and honest answers to the questions (for example: T-5, L20–T6, L24 admonition of the importance of the deposition):

Q: As I am sure your lawyer has told you, a deposition is a very important process in this lawsuit?

A: Yes.

Q: You understand that the questions are given to you under oath and your answers are given under oath?

A: Yes.

Q: Each of your answers is recorded word for word by the court reporter?

A: Yes.

Q: You realize, of course, that it is extremely important that you understand all of my questions?

A: Of course.

Q: And the reason that is so critical is that we need to understand all of your answers?

A: Yes.

Q: If at any time I do not understand your answers, I will stop and have you clarify. Would that be fair?

A: Yes.

Q: If at any time you do not understand my questions, I want you to stop and tell me that you do not understand them. Would that be fair?

A: Yes, that is fair.

Q: And whether or not you understand the questions means whether or not you have heard it, whether or not you understood the words in it, whether I mumbled so that you could not understand what I said, whether you were unfamiliar with certain words, do you understand that?

A: Yes.

Q: Is that a fair way to handle it?

A: Yes.

Q: It would be fair for all of us to assume that your answers are true, correct, and accurate to my specific question, unless you tell me that you did not understand the question. That would be fair?

A: Yes, I understand.

In order to complete this technique, the cross-examiner should ask, as the last two questions of the deposition or hearing:

Q: Have you understood each of my questions?

A: Yes.

Q: And have your answers been honest, complete, and truthful?

A: Yes.

Deposing counsel should not overlook the importance of the deposition review, correction process, and the correction sheet sent to the deponent. It is important to note the place and manner where these last opportunities for correction were explained to the deponent.

§ 16.06   Look for Signatures on Government Reports

On a collision report, a police report, or other government report, there is a line for the officer to sign attesting to the report. Often such report forms have item numbers for each critical piece of information including a line number for the space in which the officer attests to the report. In such instances, the cross-examiner's preparation should not only refer to the report (Police Rept. of 6/15/93, p.51), but reference should also be made to the line number (i.e., Line 32, [bottom of the page]) where the signature is located.

In government reports, there inevitably is a separate line item for "approval' by a supervisory official. Likewise, the cross-examiner will have not only the document number, but the line item number for the approval (Police Rept. of 6/15/92, p.1 — Line 33).

Federal and State tax returns contain not only a signature line, but also an attestation that the information is provided under penalty of perjury. A myriad of other government forms contained the same language. The cross-examiner should be careful to review all government forms for this language as the fact of its existence can lend tremendous impact to the impeachment of a witness concerning a statement inconsistent with the statement previously provided under oath.

§ 16.07   Statements, Interviews, and Private Reports

A statement or interview form often requires the signature of the person making that statement or giving that interview. Again the cross-examiner should have the document number, including the page number and the location (upper 1/3-"T", middle 1/3-"M", bottom 1/3-"B"). For a more detailed discussion, see chapter 10, *Page Preparation of Cross-Examination.*

§ 16.08   Purpose of Sourcing the Authenticity of the Statement

This extra level of preparation is done for two reasons. First, in the tension and stress of the courtroom it is quite easy to misplace or overlook necessary materials. It is incredibly hard to search through reports, interview notes, government documents, or pages of depositions under the scrutiny of the court and jury. If the necessary information is well documented, it is easier for the cross-examiner to find the specific item that the cross-examiner must locate.

There is a second reason to fully document the witness's verification of an earlier statement. This reason is built upon the appearance of the cross-examiner's credibility to the jury, judge, the opponent, and, perhaps most importantly, to the witness being impeached. When the cross-examiner can routinely, with no significant effort, locate the signature or other stamp of authenticity and recite its source, such specificity intimidates the witness. The unspoken suggestion is that the cross-examiner knows all, and that in times of doubt the witness is best served by affirming the leading question of the cross-examiner.

§ 16.09 Step 2 — Physical Preparation of the Cross-Examination

Once the inconsistencies have been uncovered and the verifying information developed, the physical preparation of the cross-examination becomes relatively straightforward. As is true of all areas of potential cross-examination, an impeachment by inconsistent statement is developed by chapters. Each impeachment by inconsistent statement requires at least one, and normally several, separate chapters (see chapter 9, *The Chapter Method of Cross-Examination*). Each answer to be obtained on the series of questions is written in the form of a leading question. Where the answer is known, the source of the answer is documented.

This systematic procedure is designed to wring the greatest impact out of the impeachment by inconsistencies. The cross-examiner is never blessed with enough true inconsistencies. Therefore, none can be wasted. Each impeachment must be maximized.

Once each chapter demonstrating an inconsistency has been developed, the organization of the chapters will then be conceptualized and put in proper sequence (see chapter 11, *Sequences of Cross-Examination*). Because each chapter is committed to only one page, the chapters can be organized and reorganized prior to trial. Where necessary, they can also be reorganized as additional information is gathered during direct examination and during earlier portions of cross-examination.

While there is general agreement that cross-examinations greatly benefit from being written, there is substantial flexibility as to how much and in what form each chapter must be written. Some cross-examiners believe the writing of each answer to be obtained from each question is the most effective method. Others confine their written chapters to an outline that highlights the significant answers to be obtained. The longer form is a true cross-examination script and the other is more akin to an outline. The cross-examiner is free to experiment and develop the style of chapter preparation that most suits the needs and style of the cross-examiner.

§ 16.10 Incorporating the Inconsistency into the Trial Notebook

In any style of chapter preparation, it is imperative that the exact inconsistency and the exact location of that inconsistent statement be noted.

The chart below gives a series of examples:

Chapter: Car Color

		Direct Testimony
Dep T-3: 16 (Blue Notebook)	"The car was blue."	"GREEN" (TIME:9:45 a.m.)

D-3 ↓ (Black Notebook)	The car was "unknown" color.
D-5 ↑ Videotape, 0962	"I'm not sure." Shrugged shoulders and smiled, no response.

Examine the examples from the chart above in the order they appear. Each shorthand entry is explained. The answer, "The car was blue,' is an exact quote. It will be found in the witness's deposition transcript page number 3, line 16. The deposition will ordinarily be kept separate from the written chapters of cross-examination. One reason for use of separate notebooks is that it gives a visual signal to the jury and the witness that the cross-examiner has studied the previous statements of the witness. In addition, after the first use of the deposition notebook to accomplish an impeachment the witness understands the meaning of the advocate's movement to retrieve the transcript. Thereafter, whenever the separate notebook is retrieved, the witness and the jury are placed on notice that an inconsistency will be brought out. An impeachment will be preformed. There will be a silence created when the cross-examiner must go to the notebook, whether it is at the podium or at counsel table (see chapter 21, *Creation and Uses of Silence*).

The answer that the car was an "unknown" color will be found in document 3 (D-3) contained in the black notebook. In the case of many documents, the exhibit number should be marked. In the event that the pages have been Bates numbered, that number should appear in the source column as well. The arrow pointing down (↓) signifies that there are no line numbers on the document, but that it is in the lower half of the document. While the arrow is not as exact as a line number, it has at least eliminated half of the page that ordinarily would have to be scanned or read. Any other code developed by the cross-examiner may be substituted. However, some code for location is quite helpful, since even one page of a transcript or a document is too much to survey when searching for an inconsistency during trial.

The answer, "I'm not sure," will be contained in document number five (D-5) in the upper half of the page, as shown by the arrow (↑). Since there is no notebook designation, it is found in the same notebook as previously referenced immediately above that notation in the cross-examiner's notes. Again, if in exhibit number is available before trial, that number should be used in the source column. If an impeachment is from a multi-page exhibit, it is even more important that the Bates number be used in addition to the exhibit number. Hence, an impeachment from a voluminous document marked as an exhibit might be noted this way: def Ex 241, Bates156. This would mean that within defendant's exhibit number 241 at Bates number 156, the impeaching statement will be found.

The answer, "shrugged shoulders and smiled, no response," is only a non-verbal response. In this age of video and digital cameras, when all jurors are members of the TV or digital generation, videotape depositions are common in the courtroom. Unfortunately, this has led to sloppiness on the part of lawyers. Since the lawyer can see the physical response of the witness to the question (i.e., shrug), the lawyer feels she has received a solid answer. However, because the answer is in nonverbal form, its later use for impeachment becomes far more problematic. It is extremely difficult to impeach using such a response. It is necessary that at the time the responses made before trial that the lawyer ask the witness to translate the response into words so that the transcript may be used later as the basis for impeachment by inconsistent statement.

In any pre-trial matter, hearing, deposition, or interview, nonverbal responses to questions should be immediately clarified so as to require the witness to speak his answer, thereby making the record useful:

Q: Did you see the car?

A: Yes.

Q: What color was the car?

(Witness shrugs shoulders.)

Q: It looked to me like you just shrugged your shoulders.

A: I did.

Q: I take that to mean that your answer is that you don't know the color of the car.

A: Yes, that's what I meant.

Or

Q: When you just shrugged your shoulders, did that mean that you don't know the color of the car?

A: Yes.

§ 16.11   Impeaching from Tapes and DVDs

Now that video and digital cameras are cheap, easy to use, and reliable, they are increasingly used in the interview or deposition process. For example, police agencies use video cameras in questioning witnesses or suspects. Especially in allegations of crimes against children, videotaped statements are common. In criminal cases, defense counsel is virtually never present when the witness (or defendant) is being questioned. As a result there is no opportunity to require the witness to translate his or her nonverbal response into a spoken format. Civil depositions are more frequently taped. This can be costly, therefore careful consideration should be given as to which depositions are deserving of videotaping. Civil investigations sometimes make use of video-taped interviews.

Having failed to translate physical responses promptly into verbal forms, or when confronted with a DVD or videotape already made, the cross-examiner must develop techniques to impeach from this form of "video transcript." If the cross-examiner will be cross-examining or impeaching from a DVD, CD, video, or audiotape, the cross-examiner must prepare using a method designed to allow efficient impeachment using the tape. By far the simplest and most effective method of impeaching from a videotape or DVD is to pre-select the portions that might be useful for impeachment and to place those separate statements on separate mini tapes or DVD slices that each contain but a single statement. In this way each very short tape or slice is useful in demonstrating a single inconsistent statement. There is no need to hunt through a longer tape to find the necessary passage that impeaches the witness. There is nothing more distracting to the jury or embarrassing to the cross-examiner than a failed attempt to cue the right footage. Every attempt thereafter becomes a defeat and a sign of incompetence. If the inconsistency is finally located, its impact is lessened. Worse, there are times when a cross-examiner will simply give up and move on. This is the, "I'll get back to that," method of non-impeachment. It is unlikely that the cross-examiner will ever get back to it. Embarrassment prohibits the return.

Many deposition tapes are now coded in an MPEG format. With the counter, the exact inconsistency can be located by a digital number. The cross-examiner must use foundation questions concerning the making of the DVD, CD, video, or audiotape. These are just the same as the foundation questions for any other document. Then the witness should be told, before the tape is turned on, exactly how the cross-examiner is going to impeach:

Q: And then at counter 0958, I asked you, "Did you see the car?" and your answer was "yes."

A: Yes, I did see the car.

Q: I then asked you, "What color was the car?" and your answer, at counter 0962, was to shrug. (Lawyer plays for witness the exact part of the DVD or tape showing that question and the visual response.)

At this point the witness must be asking himself what kind of lawyer knows the exact counter number for each question and response on the tape. The answer? A properly prepared one.

Regardless of the form in which an inconsistency is found, the exact documentation of the location of each inconsistency is at least as important as the physical comparison of the inconsistency itself. If the cross-examiner cannot find it and prove it, the inconsistency does not exist for the fact finder. The fact finder is left only with the version now testified to by the witness. If the inconsistency cannot be demonstrated, the witness's credibility escapes undamaged by the implied but unproven inconsistency. Simultaneously the unproven inconsistency damages the credibility of the lawyer who suggested but could not produce it.

§ 16.12   Step 3 — Establish the Current Version of the Testimony to Be Impeached

Of all the steps, this is the least difficult. In almost all cases, the current version of a fact was established in direct examination or was established through a leading question or was volunteered unresponsively earlier in cross-examination. The new version is frequently volunteered because the new version is favorable to the opponent and detrimental to the cross-examiner. Frequently, the cross-examiner can anticipate the introduction of the statement in the direct testimony because it has surfaced in some pre-trial hearing or statement. The index cards and the charts have picked up the fact that the change in the story has taken place.

In order to maximize the impact for the upcoming impeachment of the witness, the cross-examiner needs to remind the jury one more time of the current version normally stated in the direct testimony. This is the exception to the ordinary rule that the cross-examiner should avoid repeating the harmful portions of the direct testimony. There are two separate techniques for accomplishing this step.

§ 16.13   State or Summarize the Text to Be Impeached

Restating the direct examination is potentially dangerous to the cross-examiner. Any repetition of harmful information has the effect of reminding the fact finder of that testimony. Restating is, however, necessary to thoroughly set up the impeachment. In fact, this step requires that the fact finder be reminded of the testimony to be impeached. The entire chapter that contained the direct testimony to be impeached does not have to be presented; only the particular fact to be impeached upon must be repeated.

For example, the witness testified at a pre-trial hearing that he saw truck tire skid marks and, in fact, he saw them "quite clearly." However, in his previous statement to the investigating officer, he stated that he had not seen any skid marks. The lawyer might choose to repeat verbatim his testimony in this way: "On direct examination, you claimed you saw skid marks — in fact, you claim you saw them 'quite clearly'." When the cross-examiner chooses to restate the direct examination, the cross-examiner must take care to use the exact quotation from the direct testimony so that the jury will remember that moment in the direct examination. Only extract the minimum verbiage from direct examination to set up the impeachment. Do not repeat the entire direct examination chapter.

§ 16.14   Summarize Rather than Restate Direct Testimony That Is Explosive

Summarizing the direct testimony is preferred, however, when the direct testimony is quite powerful — when it provides very strong negative images against the cross-examiner's theory of the case, it is better to summarize. Example: The direct testimony was a vivid account of how the defendant ran a red light and slammed into a parked car, killing the occupant. The original version of the testimony is that the witness only heard the screech of brakes and then saw the accident. He did not remark on who had run the red light. Here the lawyer might isolate and summarize the facts necessary to set up the inconsistent statement by asking only: "You are telling us today that you saw a car run the red light?" Note, even when using this technique, the cross-examiner must not abandon the fundamental rules of cross-examination (see chapter 8, *The Only Three Rules of Cross-Examination*). The cross-examiner should still put the question to the witness in the form of a leading question. To do otherwise is to invite a recounting of the entire harmful story!

The cross-examiner must *fairly* summarize the witness's direct testimony as to the fact to be impeached. Any effort by the cross-examiner to be unfair in the characterization or summary of that testimony will result in the loss of credibility to the cross-examiner. It may also evoke empathy or sympathy for the witness. This is exactly the opposite effect that impeachment should create. It is therefore ill advised to reword the statement of the witness or in any way tamper with the words used by the witness.

Once again, this does not mean that the cross-examiner must quote the entire direct testimony or the entire scenario into which the impeachment fits, or even the entire answer that contained the inconsistency. It only means that the cross-examiner should use the exact quote as to the inconsistent fact at issue. The exact words can be placed in context through a fair summarization of the direct testimony so that the jury can recall in what context the words were spoken.

In the following example, the plaintiff has testified that she witnessed her former boyfriend brutally stab and kill a man. According to her, the stabbing took place as the victim tried to get out of his van. The cross-examiner intends to establish that this alleged attempt to get out of the van is inconsistent with an earlier statement of the witness. For obvious reasons, the cross-examining lawyer does not want to offer the witness an opportunity to repeat her testimony about the stabbing details itself. Consequently, the cross-examining lawyer will not include in the foundation questions any of the "stabbing" testimony:

Q: As I understand your testimony, Mr. Polidori tried to get out of the van, but couldn't?

A: Brett said, "Give me all your money." He said, "I will if you will let me out."

Q: He could not get out?

A: No.

Q: Your testimony now is that he never left the van?

A: That's what happened.

Q: You can recall that vividly, is that right?

A: Yes, as far as I can remember.

Q: Your memory is not vague on that, is it?

A: No.

Q: You recall it specifically?

A: I do.

Q: There's not any question about it, is there?

A: As far as I recall.

Q: You have testified under oath before concerning this, haven't you?

A: Yes.

Q: And you were asked before, in May of 1999, what you saw, isn't that correct?

A: Yes.

Q: Ms. Wright, I am at page 163 starting at line 10 of the transcript of May of 1999. You were asked this question: "Question: Did he get out of the van once the van was parked in the alley? Answer: Yes. Question: Did he get all the way out of the van? Answer: Yes, he was on the ground. Question: And how long did he stand outside the van? Answer: About five seconds." That was your was, in fact, your answer in May of 1989?

A: Yes, sir.

Q: Now you remember testifying that Mr. Polidori was completely out of the van?

A: Yes, that's what I said.

Q: For a full five seconds?

A: Yes.

§ 16.15   Phrases That "Set Up" Impeachments

While establishing the current version to be impeached, the cross-examiner can simultaneously fuse the question with a subtle cue to the jury (and to the judge) that the testimony the jury is about to hear repeated is inaccurate.

An example of establishing the current version of a mistaken witness:

Q: Mr. Jones, as I understand it you now believe the man you remember robbing you was six foot, three inches?

Or

Q: As I understood your testimony on direct examination, your latest thought is that the man who robbed you was six foot, three inches?

Or

An example of establishing the current version of a dishonest witness:

Q: Let me see if I understand this: Now you are telling this jury that you saw Tom hit Alan over the head? (aggressive)

Or

Q: Let me see if I understand today's version of events . . . (more aggressive)

Or

Q: What you are now saying is today's truth is that you saw Tom hit Alan? (extremely aggressive)

Each of the passages is a "set up" phrase. It is a code for: "This is a different story." Using these flag-planting phrases, the cross-examiner has put before the jury the specific fact to be impeached. The cross-examiner signals to the jury that she is not bringing up the subject merely to verify the direct testimony, but is instead rephrasing the testimony as an issue to be disputed. The cross-examiner has established with the jury and the witness the pattern for impeachment by inconsistent statement.

The cross-examiner can also use her body to establish with the jury and the witness a pattern for impeachment by inconsistent statement. If the cross-examiner will move to a particular place before revealing the inconsistent statement, that motion will soon be understood as a signal that any inconsistency of the witness is about to be exposed. By moving consciously to a different location (even if it is only one step), the cross-examiner signals that a different phase of cross-examination is beginning. This movement in itself both signals the jury and heightens the impact of an impeachment by inconsistent statement.

Because the lawyer has used opening statement to impress upon the jury the critical inconsistencies in the testimony of the witness, the jury has no difficulty in recognizing both the existence and the importance of the inconsistencies. All of these inconsistencies were picked up by a cross-examination preparation system used to prepare for trial. As a result of the integrated trial plan that allows the trial lawyer to recognize and focus on the chapters of greatest importance to the competing theories of the case, the cross-examiner has revealed in opening statement at least the major inconsistencies that the cross-examiner intends to prove. Whether the cross-examiner intends to brand the witness as mistaken or intentionally deceitful, the jury has learned through voir dire and opening statement that the credibility of the witness will be challenged. The jurors have been told the basis for that challenge; whether the basis is motive, interest, bias, or inconsistent statements.

One of the advantages of highlighting to the jury in opening statement the major inconsistencies that the cross-examiner expects to develop is that the jurors are alerted to these inconsistencies before ever hearing the direct testimony of the witness. Therefore, when the witness testifies on direct examination, the jury has been forewarned not to accept the story at face value. Instead, the jury is more inclined to suspend judgment on the credibility of that direct testimony version until such time as the jury hears the cross-examination on that subject.

This technique again exploits the doctrine of primacy. By revealing documented inconsistencies in opening statement the first impression received by the jurors concerning the credibility of the witness is a negative one. This impression remains unless the witness overcomes it. In short, the witness is beginning his direct testimony with a credibility deficit rather than the credibility surplus.

§ 16.16   Step 4 — Tie the Witness to the Current Version to Be Impeached

The witness has given today's version of the truth as "advertised' by the opponent's opening statement. If the opponent has failed to discuss this aspect of the witness's testimony, so much the better. In this event it is the cross-examiner who has the opportunity to disclose the fact of the inconsistency to the jury. Then, in cross-examination the cross-examiner will figuratively tie the new version of the story around the witness's (and hopefully the opponent's) neck so that the witness and the opponent's case appears to be established only if that new version is accepted. Once the witness has been forced to readopt his latest version as being completely truthful, the cross-examiner has, in effect, tied an important part of the credibility of the witness and the opponent's case to the believability of that particular piece of testimony. By this technique it appears to the jury that much of the opponent's case is staked on the credibility of the particular statement about to be impeached.

The goal is to teach the jury that the accuracy of the entire story is in question because critical parts of that story have changed. The jurors will receive a standard instruction in virtually every jurisdiction that reminds them that in judging the credibility of a witness they may fairly reflect upon whether that witness has been impeached. Impeachments by inconsistent statement will likely be viewed as important events reflecting on the truthfulness and credibility of both the impeached witness and the side that called that witness.

The witness can be required by the cross-examiner to tell the jury that his direct testimony is accurate. In this way, the witness will be committed to the accuracy of his soon-to-be impeached testimony. The cross-examiner can irretrievably bind the witness to his direct testimony on a particular point in a series of leading questions designed to show that the witness has no question concerning the accuracy of this direct examination on this particular point.

This method seems to contradict the cross-examiner's purpose in showing that the witness is unreliable. The contrary is true. By tying the witness to his direct testimony that will be contradicted by an earlier statement by the same witness, the impeachment is more astonishing.

In the face of a witness who claims to be certain, the jury will not understand why the direct testimony is not consistent with other statements made by the witness. In fact, the more certainty the witness has asserted on direct examination, the more unlikely the jury is to accept the fact that the story has changed. Then, when the facts surrounding the initial observation and the initial telling of the story are revealed to the jury (see chapter 9, *The Chapter Method of Cross-Examination*), the version of events given prior to trial will be more believable to the jury than the latest version given upon direct examination.

Such a technique of impeachment, done once, raises some doubts in the minds of jurors. When this technique of impeachment is done repeatedly over the course of a cross-examination it leads to outright juror skepticism. After all, the cross-examiner has demonstrated several times that the witness is sure of a fact, but yet totally at variance with his earlier position on the identical issue. When the cross-examiner continually exposes that the story recited in the direct testimony is full of changes, it undermines the ability of the opponent to argue "certainty" of the witness to the jurors or judge.

§ 16.17   Example of Tying the Witness to the Direct to Build Drama

The following is an example from a contract case in which the issue is whether certain signatures were notarized by people present when the signatures were actually placed on the document. The cross-examiner's position is that they were not. On direct examination, the witness testified in general terms that the witnesses' signatures were all properly placed on the document. On cross-examination, the witness will be confronted with a previous statement that the people who signed as witnesses were *not* in the room when the contract was signed. In the initial part of the impeachment, the cross-examiner ties the witness irretrievably to the scene of the signing of the contract:

Q: You had only signed one contract in your life?

A: Yes.

Q: It was the first professional football contract you had ever signed?

A: Yes.

Q: It was one of the high points of your life?

A: Yes, it was the high point of my life.

Q: The high point of your life?

A: Yes.

Q: It was an unforgettable experience?

A: Yes.

Q: That moment is frozen in your mind forever?

A: Yes.

Q: You can remember the room you were in?

A: Yes.

Q: It was the office of Abe Kane?

A: Yes.

Q: You can remember the day that it occurred, April 12, 1996?

A: Yes.

Q: You can remember the time of the day, about noon?

A: Yes.

Q: You can remember who was in the room?

A: Yes.

Q: Sharon Steinberg and Steve Steinberg were in the room?

A: Yes.

Q: You will never forget those people?

A: That's true.

At this point, the jury can well envision the signing of the contract. There is a vivid image in the jurors' minds. The cross-examination has painted an image that is potentially harmful to the cross-examination. It is at this point that the cross-examiner will reveal the real picture (the inconsistency that the witnesses were not in the room) and show to the jury that the direct testimony is only an illusion:

Q: You claim that your signature was notarized by this Sharon Steinberg and Steve Steinberg?

A: Yes.

Q: That is why you remember them being in the room?

A: Yes.

Q: The fact of the matter is, they were not in the room?

A: What?

Q: The fact of the matter is that you previously said under oath that they did not notarize your signature when you signed the documents?

A: Did I say that?

Q: You had your deposition taken in my office on the 13th day of July 2001?

A: Yes.

Q: Your lawyer was there?

A: Yes.

Q: He had carefully instructed you about what the deposition would be about?

A: Yes.

Q: He had told you that I would be asking you questions?

A: Yes.

Q: That you would give answers?

A: Yes.

Q: And that it was all done under oath?

A: Yes.

Q: That each word that we said would be taken down word for word by the certified court reporter?

A: Yes.

Q: He told you that we would be talking about that contract?

A: Yes.

Q: You were placed under oath?

A: Yes.

Q: You were placed under oath in the transcript on page 2, lines 4 through 10?

A: Yes.

Q: In the transcript, page 5, line 20 through page 6, line 24, I particularly gave you an admonition to make sure that you understood every one of my questions and that if you did not, that you would tell me that you did not, correct?

A: Correct.

Q: At page 56 line 17, you said: "The Steinbergs were not there. They didn't see nothing." Correct?

A: . . . looks like it.

Q: In fact, I told you that if you didn't tell me otherwise, I would assume that you understood my questions and you told me in your words that was fair?

A: Yes.

Q: At the end of the deposition at page 392, line 16, you told me that you understood all of my questions?

A: Yes.

Q: Your able lawyer was there for all of that?

A: Yes.

The picture carefully constructed on direct examination has now been shattered.

§ 16.18   Tying the Expert to the Direct Examination Testimony

The next example comes from the cross-examination of an expert witness called in the prosecution of a sexual abuse of a child case. The doctor has described in direct examination a finding that is contained nowhere in her report. That portion of the direct examination where this was revealed follows:

Q: (By the prosecutor) Did she call your attention to anything?

A: No.

Q: Tell us what you found?

A: Basically, everything was fairly normal. Her vaginal opening was normal sized. She did have a little — what I would call a nick on the vaginal ring, right about 6:00.

Q: Now, is it on the hymen, or the vaginal opening?

A: Vaginal opening.

Q: And could you give us, in your experience, the variety of things that could cause that?

A: (The witness answers in such a way as to imply it is from penetration by a finger, which is similar to the accusation being made by the child.)

Cross-examination follows:

Q: Doctor Hall, isn't it true that Anna never complained to you in the course of this alleged "hand in the pants incident" that she got cut or nicked?

A: No, she said, "It hurt. He hurt me." She never said "I was cut, ow."

Q: She never said, "I bled?"

A: Uh huh.

Q: No?

A: No.

Q: When you examined the vaginal opening, you did not detect any redness?

A: No, I didn't.

Q: This was just two days after the alleged sexual assault?

A: Yes, about that.

Q: In fact, during that examination, you did not find any evidence of any abnormality?

A: No, I wouldn't say that. I found that nick.

Q: And, of course, that nick was of enormous significance to you?

A: Well, I wouldn't say enormous, but it certainly was significant.

Q: What made it significant was the child's allegation that she had been sexually assaulted?

A: Yes.

Q: And in fact, her allegation that Jerry had stuck his finger into her vagina?

A: Yes, I had been told that, though not necessarily in those words?

Q: So you knew exactly what you were looking for?

A: I was looking for any evidence of abnormality.

Q: When you found this nick, you knew you had found an abnormality?

A: Well, yes.

Q: And in your mind, you knew this was a major piece of evidence in an investigation of a potential sexual assault?

A: Well, yes, I thought it was significant.

Q: It was certainly significant enough that it registered on you the minute you saw it?

A: Yes, as soon as I could detect it.

Q: As soon as you could detect it, you knew it was an item of significance in your evaluation of the child's allegations?

A: Yes, I thought it was or could be.

Q: On August 25, 2000, you were in this courtroom for some hearings in this case?

A: I don't recall the date, but yes, I was here.

Q: You do recall that the prosecutor was Cynthia Wright?

A: Yes, who is here.

Q: And I was here asking you questions?

A: Yes.

Q: Judge Matthews was on the bench right where she is today?

A: Yes, she was here.

Q: And we were talking about this very case?

A: Yes, that's what we did.

Q: In fact, we were talking about your findings in this case.

A: Yes, among other things.

Q: And I asked you at page 32, line 6: "What did your examination include?" Your answer: "I examined her vaginal area and her rectal area, though I did a cursory examination of the rest of her body as well, those were my major areas of concern." And at page 32, line 10: "Did you find any evidence of abnormality?" Your answer at page 32, line 11: 'No." At page 32, line 15: "What treatment did you prescribe?" Your answer: "None." At page 32, line 17: "Why was that?" Your answer: "There were no injuries

— no treatment was necessary." Doctor, I have handed you a copy of your transcript and I ask you to verify that those were the questions I asked you, and those were your answers under oath?

A: Yes.

The cross-examiner ties the expert to the direct testimony by not only locking in the word "nick," but by giving the fact finder the reasoning why the word "nick" was so significant to the doctor. The cross-examiner establishes that the doctor wasn't doing a general examination, but rather a specific sexual assault examination specifically looking for injury. The "nick" appearance becomes more significant in this context.

§ 16.19 Tying the Witness to Emotional and Dramatic Testimony

The following example of tying a witness to the statement is taken from the criminal context:

Q: It must have been very frightening?

A: Yes.

Q: I am sure that it made quite an impression on you?

A: Yes.

Q: There was really no mistake in what happened?

A: That's true.

Q: You watched as Tom picked up the hammer?

A: Yes.

Q: You watched Tom hit Joe over the head three times?

A: Yes.

Q: You stared at the whole thing?

A: Yes.

Q: It is burned into your mind?

A: Yes.

Q: That picture will not go away?

A: Never.

At this point, the cross-examiner must immediately and dramatically shift to the prior version, in which the witness claims never to have seen any of these things (see §16.32, below).

This technique of marrying the witness to the current version initially appears to be terribly damaging to the cross-examiner. But if the impeachment by inconsistent statement is effective, the damage will not fall upon the cross-examiner but diminish the credibility of the witness and the credibility of the opponent's case. By making the witness appear certain before revealing the inconsistency, the revelation of the inconsistency in great detail has a powerful impact on the jury.

§ 16.20   Develop a Chapter Using Facts That Indicate the Earlier Impeaching Version Is More Believable

When using this technique, the cross-examiner must always make certain that the earlier version is the more believable of the two versions. Otherwise, the effort to tie the witness to the current version will backfire. This is accomplished by not merely revealing the inconsistent version itself, but by revealing two other critical aspects enhancing it and its believability:

(1) The original observation was made under circumstances whereby the witness could be expected to be accurate; and

(2) The previous recitation by the witness was made under circumstances where the witness would want to be accurate and honest.

It is not just the naked fact of a differing version that must be proven; it is that there logically should *not* be a change on this issue. By requiring the witness to testify to facts that prove (1) and (2) above, when the lawyer shows that the change has occurred she shows that the earlier version is more trustworthy.

This step is an important step and is therefore deserving of a very complete chapter. The goal of the cross-examiner is to establish that the earlier version is the version to be believed. Therefore any fact that shows that the witness wanted to be accurate, needed to be accurate, had the opportunity to be accurate, and asserted the facts as accurate, aids the cross-examiner in establishing the reliability of the earlier version.

§ 16.21   Step 5 — Equate or Translate the Conflicting Versions

Sometimes the inconsistency between two versions of a fact is so clear that no translation is needed. Such stark inconsistencies make for very powerful impeachments. The very words of the witness in the first statement directly contradict the words of the witness in his newest version. In such a circumstance no juror can miss the fact that the witness has testified two different ways on two different occasions. However, there are those inconsistencies that require additional work in order for the jury to best envision how the statements are inconsistent. For example: Assume the direct testimony is that the armed robber was five foot, six inches tall, but the statement contained in the police report, is that the robber was six foot three. These descriptions are both in feet and inches. Hence there is no need for equating or translating the versions.

However, there are times that the direct testimony must be equated or translated in such a way as to make the inconsistency clear.

Assume that on direct testimony the witness states the armed robber was five foot, six inches tall. In the police report the same witness said: "He was taller than me, I looked up to him." The cross-examiner must equate or trans-late these versions:

Q: The floor you were standing on was level?

A: Yes.

Q: There were no steps?

A: No.

Q: You are about six feet tall?

A: Yes, I am six feet and one-half inches.

As can be seen, equating or translating often requires the cross-examiner to have performed further investigation. As soon as the cross-examiner reads the police report and finds that the robber was described as being "taller than me," the cross-examiner must investigate to determine the height of the wit-ness. She must make sure that the witness and robber were standing on the same level surface. The investigation must ensure that there are no reasons why the earlier statement does not mean exactly what it says: "I looked up at him." Translation: "He had to be taller than 6' ½'".

§ 16.22   Equating or Translating "I Don't Know"

A more subtle context of equating or translating comes up when a witness has said in a pre-trial statement that the witness "does not know" a particular fact. Such an equivocal statement requires a certain amount of translating in order to set up the impeachment:

Q: You told us in your deposition at page 49, line 36 that, "I don't know the height of the armed robber"?

A: Yes.

Q: You said that because you could not accurately judge the height of the robber?

A: Yes.

Q: If you had been able to judge the height of the robber, you would have given it to the police?

A: Of course.

Q: In fact, you wanted to describe the robber as best you could?

A: Yes, I wanted him to get caught.

Q: And if you had been able to estimate the height of the robber, you wanted to give that estimate to the officers so they could look for that robber?

A: I wanted them to look for the robber anyway.

Q: But you didn't give the officers the height of the robber because you didn't know the height of the robber?

A: Right.

Q: You did not know if the robber was five feet?

A: I wasn't sure.

Q: You didn't know if the robber was six feet?

A: I guess.

Q: You just didn't have the opportunity to observe the robber's height?

A: True.

The cross-examiner has required the witness acknowledge that he didn't know the height of the robber because he never got a good look at the robber (see chapter 20, *Dealing With the "I Don't Know" or "I Can't Remember" Witness*). Whenever and however the witness has equivocated pre-trial answers, the cross-examiner must equate or translate that equivocation into more exact concepts. Any words that are nebulous, subject to interpretation, or subjective, must be translated into precise concepts for the impeachment to work well.

§ 16.23   Step 6 — Expose the Inconsistent Statement

After tying the witness to the current version, the next thing that the cross-examiner must do is create a change of atmosphere in the courtroom. A certain mood has been built in the courtroom by not only permitting the witness to testify to the version of the fact presented in the direct testimony, but also by irretrievably binding the witness to it. The cross-examiner may have created a sense of tension or expectation that there is more to be said on this subject.

Since the judge and jury know that the cross-examiner is prepared and consistently questions in a goal-directed manner, they sense there is meaning to this repetition of a portion of the direct examination. Because of a detailed opening statement, the jury knows the witness has been inconsistent on several key issues. It may well be that the cross-examiner has foreshadowed this impeachment by explaining the inconsistent versions within the opening statement. If so the jurors understand that this is one of the inconsistencies discussed. If not, the jurors may have observed from the body language and set-up questions that the witness is about to be confronted with another inconsistency. Having learned to recognize the code phrases that set up impeachment, the jurors are primed to hear the impeachment. The fact finder has seen and now understands the pattern of impeachment.

§ 16.24   Using Silence to Signal the Fact Finder That an Impeachment by Inconsistent Statement Is About to Occur

The cross-examiner must now signal to the judge and jury a change in attitude and direction. There are several devices available to accomplish this. With the merely mistaken witness, the cross-examiner can change the pace of the examination. The tone of voice might become more matter-of-fact. The cross-examiner may display a puzzled look. Perhaps the cross-examiner will look down at the prepared chapter as a method of preparing to retrieve the impeaching document.

With the dishonest witness, the cross-examiner can markedly change her tone of voice. The voice can change from understanding or nonchalance to a lower, more pointed voice. The cross-examiner can stare directly at the witness.

In either case, drama can be built by simply taking a moment to slowly and purposefully return to counsel table to retrieve the first impeaching document, exhibit, or transcript. If that material is close by the cross-examiner, the cross-examiner should carefully locate the precise page of the transcript, document, or notebook that will create silence to heighten the drama (see chapter 21, *Creation and Uses of Silence*).

This retrieval of impeachment material, whether from counsel table or from a notebook located near the podium, may only take a matter of seconds, but it will draw the jury's attention to the purpose of the cross-examiner.

Keep in mind the process of "locating" the exact page of the transcript or the file from counsel table does not require any elaborate search. Because the impeachment has been sourced within the page preparation of that chapter of cross-examination, it is unnecessary for the lawyer to go through numerous files, documents, or pages. The location of the inconsistent statement has been documented before trial and the cross-examiner can now efficiently retrieve the necessary transcript or exhibit and turn to the exact page and line number before returning her full attention to the witness. The cross-examiner is primed and ready to expose the inconsistency.

§ 16.25   Signal the Fact Finder by Physical Movement

Any change of the cross-examiner's physical location can signal the change in the tone and importance of the examination. For instance, if the cross-examiner normally works directly behind the podium, the cross-examiner might move to the side of the podium when exposing the inconsistent statement. A physical change of position signals to the judge and jury (and to the witness) that a new level of inquiry is occurring, and with it comes a new demeanor on the cross-examiner's part.

§ 16.26   Do Not Overlook or Minimize the Foundation

A proper foundation must be laid for the exposure of the inconsistent statement. This is true whether the witness is merely mistaken or is to be branded as deceitful. The rules require that the witness be oriented to the prior statement. By orienting, the witness should be told who was involved, when and where it occurred, and what was said. This is true whether or not there is a requirement to actually show the witness the prior statement. Even if the rules did not require this "orientation," the inherent sense of fairness of juries demands a fair degree of orienting.

Once a foundation for a deposition has been properly laid, continued use of that deposition requires only a cursory foundation. Few judges will require the cross-examiner to endlessly repeat when the deposition was taken, who was present, etc., when such facts have previously been established. In such a circumstance the cross-examiner might simply state, "Let us again turn to your testimony on this point when we talked about this in January 2004 at your deposition." There is no precise formula for such an abbreviated foundation and the cross-examiner is invited to put the emphasis on that part of the foundation that seems most important.

§ 16.27   Foundation as a Tactical Weapon

Mechanically doing what the rules require may be sufficient legally, but wholly insufficient factually. The cross-examiner must convert the required foundational questions into tactical weapons. The pace, phrasing, and tone of the foundational questions provide information to the jurors about the importance of the upcoming impeachment and the attitude of the cross-examiner (see chapter 22, *Voice, Movement, Body Language, and Timing*).

Because it is the prior statement that the lawyer wants the jury to believe, it is to her advantage to do more than the foundation rule requires. The foundation should be laid in such a manner that the witness is brought back to the "real time" when the prior statement occurred. When the witness is returned to the "real time" of the prior statement, the confrontation becomes more effective, chilling, and more disorienting to the witness. The witness now senses that he is in trouble and, more importantly, that the cross-examiner is in control. On the other hand, it appears to the jury that the cross-examiner is being fair to the witness by completely establishing the prior statement.

In this foundation phase, the cross-examiner should always finish with what was said. In other words, finish with the inconsistency. Do not put the inconsistency before the orienting portions of the foundation of impeachment. Doing so would be similar to telling the punch line of a joke before the set-up.

§ 16.28   Foundation in a Civil Case

In the example below, a personal injury case, a foundation is laid before exposing an inconsistent statement on the fact in issue — the color of the car that ran the red light:

Q: Mr. Fraley, on February 12, 1981, you received a subpoena for your deposition?

A: Yes.

Q: You received it by certified mail?

A: Yes.

Q: You had never received a subpoena for your deposition before?

A: No.

Q: That subpoena directed that you go to the law office of Barney Frick?

A: Yes.

Q: It directed the exact time, 10:00 a.m.?

A: Yes.

Q: It directed the exact day, February 20?

A: Yes.

Q: It directed that you give testimony before a certified court reporter?

A: Yes.

Q: You knew what this testimony would concern?

A: Generally.

Q: You knew you would be asked questions about the car collision you saw?

A: Yes.

Q: On the 20th, you got up that morning and prepared to go to the deposition?

A: Yes.

Q: You had to take off work?

A: Yes.

Q: You had never been to that law office before?

A: No.

Q: You went to that law office knowing that you would be giving testimony about this case?

A: Yes.

Q: You knew that it was serious because you had received a subpoena?

A: Yes.

Q: You arrived just after 10:00 that morning?

A: Yes, just a little bit after 10:00. I was nervous and missed a turn and I was somewhat late.

Q: When you arrived a little after 10:00, you were nervous that you might be in trouble because you were late?

A: Yes.

Q: When you arrived I was there?

A: Yes.

Q: Mr. Frick was there?

A: Yes.

Q: The plaintiff was there?

A: Yes.

Q: The defendant, George, was there?

A: Yes.

Q: And there was a certified court reporter there?

A: Yes.

Q: She had a stenographic machine, didn't she?

A: Yes, just like on TV.

Q: That's right, Mr. Fraley, it all looked just like on TV: very official, didn't it?

A: Sure did.

Q: In fact, you were sworn just like you were today?

A: Yes.

Q: You raised your hand and swore before God to tell the truth that morning?

A: Yes.

Q: And it was your intention to tell the truth that morning?

A: Yes.

Q: It was not quite as scary as coming into court because it was only in a law office?

A: I was just as nervous.

Q: You knew that it was just as serious as your testimony here today?

A: Yes, I did.

Q: You took it that seriously?

A: Yes.

Q: You knew it was about this case?

A: Yes.

Q: You knew a lawsuit had been filed once you got your subpoena?

A: Yes, I figured that out.

Q: You knew that it was required that you give honest testimony?

A: Yes.

Q: You were told by both lawyers before you started to testify just how important your testimony was?

A: Yes.

Q: You were told at page 2 line 16 through 23 that it was important that you understood each of the questions and responded truthfully if you understood those questions?

A: Yes.

Q: I also told you that if you didn't understand a question, to say that you didn't understand the question, and not just guess at the answer?

A: Yes, you told me that.

Q: I spoke in such language that you could understand?

A: Yes.

Q: I was seated across the table from you, wasn't I?

A: Yes.

Q: My opponent, Mr. Frick, was on your side of the table?

A: Yes.

Q: The court reporter was at the end of the table taking all of the questions and answers down verbatim word for word?

A: Yes.

Q: At the end of the deposition, page 392 line 10 through 12, I asked you if you had understood all my questions, and you told me that you had?

A: Yes.

Q: In fact, you had understood all my questions, hadn't you?

A: Yes.

Q: And when I asked you at page 73, line 16 of the deposition, what the color of the car was, your answer was, "I don't know?"

A: That's what I said.

Of course the cross-examiner moves on with the cross-examination after these foundational chapters are completed.

§ 16.29 Foundation from a Criminal Case

The following example is from a criminal case to expose an inconsistent statement by a dishonest (not a mistaken witness) witness:

Q: On March 13, 1998, you were interviewed by Detective Sable?

A: Yes.

Q: He questioned you at the Aurora Police Department?

A: Yes.

Q: He questioned you about this crime?

A: Yes.

Q: With him was Detective Caplin?

A: Yes.

Q: You knew why you were being questioned?

A: Yes.

Q: You promised them you would tell the truth?

A: Yes.

Q: You were being questioned about the death of a man?

A: Yeah, Crown.

Q: Dickey Crown was dead?

A: As a bug.

Q: These detectives had your full attention?

A: Sure did.

Q: So, when they asked questions, you made sure to listen?

A: Right.

Q: And then you answered their questions?

A: If I could.

Q: And you answered truthfully.

A: As best I could.

Q: They asked you if you were watching the whole time as Crown was killed?

A: Yes.

Q: But what you told the Detectives Sable and Caplin that day is not what you swore to this jury today?

A: No, it wasn't.

Q: What you told the Detectives that day is this (Madam prosecutor, I am at page 27, line 10 of the transcript of the interview of March 13, 1998, question by Detective Sable: "Did you see your father hit him with the hammer?" Your answer, at line 14: "No, no, I wasn't looking, I was walking down the stairs when I heard a noise and I turned around and Crown was falling down the stairs."

§ 16.30   Foundation for the Witness Who Is Merely Mistaken

With a mistaken witness the cross-examiner approaches more gently, but still thoroughly. Tone, pace, and gestures can soften the questions, but the questions still completely establish the foundation:

Q: Mrs. Hernandez, on direct examination you told the jury the man who robbed you was, "Short, about five foot six?"

A: Yes.

Q: Now Mrs. Hernandez, you were robbed at about 10:30 at night?

A: Yes.

Q: By 10:35 you called the police?

A: That's true.

Q: By 10:40 the police arrived?

A: Yes.

Q: They asked you what had happened?

A: Yes.

Q: You wanted to tell them exactly what had happened?

A: Yes.

Q: You wanted to tell them as accurately as you could?

A: Yes.

Q: The whole event had just happened not more than ten minutes before that?

A: That's true.

Q: When Detective Martin asked you to give a description of the man, that detective was asking you about something that just happened?

A: Yes.

Q: You told him a description the very best you could?

A: Yes.

Q: What you told him ten minutes after it happened was the man who robbed you was about your height?

A: Yes.

Q: You are about six foot, one inch?

A: Yes.

Q: A tall woman?

A: Rather.

Q: You assured the detective the robber was about six foot, three inches?

A: Yes, I did.

Q: You honestly said six foot, three inches?

A: That's what I believed.

§ 16.31   Have the Fact Finder Visualize the First Statement

It is the prior statement that the cross-examiner is alleging to be the more accurate. As result, the cross-examiner should attempt to make the prior statement as visual as possible to the judge or jury. This is best done by giving the fullest development of the foundation material. The exact exposure of the inconsistency seldom requires more than one question. That question is too quick and too short to have the effect needed. The foundation material makes the prior statement more visual to the jury, giving the inconsistent statement itself the depth and texture needed by the jury to absorb its significance.

At this point, the cross-examiner has accomplished two of the three goals of the presentation of the impeachment: (1) exposure of the inconsistent statement; and (2) demonstration that the former statement was made under circumstances where the witness had the desire and opportunity to be accurate. The cross-examiner must now complete the impeachment by proving: (3) that the original perception was made under circumstances where the witness could be expected to be accurate.

§ 16.32   Step 7 — Maximize the Damage Caused by the Inconsistency

It is not enough simply to expose the inconsistent statement. The cross-examiner must now milk the situation to obtain the maximum value from the change of story. All this must be done without being tempted to ask why the story had changed. Certainly the jury is interested in knowing why the story has changed. The jury is always interested in the motivation of the witness. Motivation may be more safely discussed by the lawyer later in closing argument. Suffice to say that cross-examination of a hostile witness is not the time to ask why the story has changed. This is decidedly not the time for discovery by trial. No enemy words should be used in forming up the questions (see chapter 8, *The Only Three Rules of Cross-Examination*).

§ 16.33   Maximize the Damage in Stages

At this point, much has already been done to maximize the damage. The witness has been irretrievably bound to the current version on direct examination. The cross-examiner has spent a substantial number of questions leaving no room for the witness to equivocate or vacillate on the current version.

Just as importantly, a great deal of damage has been done by what traditionally was considered a mere foundation phase in exposing the inconsistent statement. By meticulously documenting the foundation process, by stressing the reliability of the prior statement, and by assuring the truth of the prior statement based on the circumstances surrounding it, the cross-examiner has already done much to maximize the damage.

§ 16.34 Maximizing the Damage of an Inconsistency by Employing the Chapter Method

Having exposed the inconsistency at this point in the cross-examination, the cross-examiner need only revert to the familiar chapter method of cross-examination (see chapter 9, *The Chapter Method of Cross-Examination*). The cross-examiner proves the reliability of the earlier version just as if the original version were a goal-fact to be established through conventional cross-examination techniques. Although the goal-fact has been revealed (of necessity), the cross-examiner must still put the fact into its context. To do this, the cross-examiner must begin at the top of the chapter that establishes that goal-fact. By using leading questions, all of the detailed facts will lead a jury to believe that the goal-fact was correctly perceived in the first instance.

In the last example, above, assume the cross-examiner was not confronted with an inconsistency but wanted to establish that the robber was tall. The cross-examiner would ask the questions in the chapter form. When the cross-examiner has already disclosed this goal, she might simply return to the top of the chapter and establish the facts that make the original version believable.

§ 16.35 Step 8 — Listen to the Direct Examination

The cross-examiner should be aware that inconsistencies occur not only before trial, but also during trial, direct examination, and earlier portions of cross-examination. Every time witnesses speak, they have the opportunity to produce inconsistent statements. Listening at all times is, therefore, a requirement. The cross-examiner cannot assume the story will remain the same.

It seems simple, but listening is the least favorite of the occupational necessities that the cross-examiner must perform. Some cross-examiners do not listen at all. Others do not listen well. In order to deliver consistently strong impeachments, the lawyer must become a consistently attentive listener. Trial lawyers are willing to practice courtroom speaking. However, those same lawyers are reluctant to practice courtroom listening. Listening is a distinct skill, and like other skills, it must be practiced. The ability to engage in focused listening in a courtroom setting is as much a trial skill as the ability to form appropriate questions.

While the prepared cross-examiner can come to court armed to expose inconsistencies in the previous statements of the witness (see chapters 5, 6, and 7), the cross-examiner must be especially vigilant to pick up on new inconsistencies or variations on inconsistencies created in the direct examination of the witness. If the cross-examiner does not "hear" the direct testimony, there is nothing to signal to the cross-examiner that an inconsistency has occurred. "Listening" and taking notes are two different things. Too many cross-examiners studiously spend direct examination taking notes, and as a result, they do not hear the direct testimony. They merely record it. Other cross-examiners spend direct examination planning their upcoming cross-examination. As a result, they cannot hear the direct testimony. If the cross-examiner is conferring with the client or colleagues, she cannot hear the direct testimony.

§ 16.36   Courtroom Listening Involves More Than Listening

The cross-examiner should listen not only with her ears, but also with her eyes. So often the nonverbal language of a witness (such as the averting of the eyes and the hesitancy of body movement that is inconsistent with the verbal language used) signals the uncomfortable stance of the witness. The words may fit, but the demeanor of the witness may not.

While listening to the direct examination the cross-examiner should also be cognizant of her own feelings. There is a feel to each witness's testimony. While cross-examination is a science and impeachment is a branch of that science, feeling or instinct should not be abandoned. The science of preparation, sequencing, and technique frees the cross-examiner to feel the texture, rhythm, and overall effect of the testimony. It is essential to take in the information with the lawyer's ears, eyes, and feelings to know that a new inconsistency has occurred. For instance, if the cross-examiner feels sympathy for the witness, it is a good bet that the fact finder is similarly feeling sympathy. If, in the mind of the cross-examiner the witness has come across as confused, in all likelihood the jury is feeling the same way. If the cross-examiner believes that the witness is being deceptive but making a good impression on the jury, the cross-examiner should factor those considerations into the style and methods of cross-examination. The jury may not appreciate that the witness is being deceptive. The cross-examination will need to begin at a lower pitch and move methodically through the chapters likely to cause the jurors to reconsider their impressions of the witness.

§ 16.37   Dealing With New Inconsistencies Occurring in Trial

This same identification process that is used to properly prepare and document inconsistencies prior to the start of trial applies to both the direct examination and preceding chapters of cross-examination. Every answer given by a witness, whether on direct examination or on previous chapters of cross-examination, may become inconsistent with a later answer of the witness. Unless the cross-examiner is in a trial in which daily transcripts are produced, and there is time to have those transcripts produced prior to impeachment, the cross-examiner must develop a method to keep track of the inconsistencies developed during trial. It is also essential that the witness be confronted in such a way that the witness cannot successfully suggest that he was not inconsistent on direct testimony or in his earlier cross-examination.

Because the cross-examiner is now listening during direct examination, and during all portions of the cross-examination (and is not distracted by taking notes, thinking of other sections of the trial, or chatting away with the client or colleague), the cross-examiner will be able to perform the required task of hearing and answer that creates a new opportunity for impeachment.

Assume that on direct testimony the witness has, for the first time, testified inconsistently with all of his pre-trial statements on an issue. It is a significant fact, and one that the cross-examiner intends to impeach upon. Upon hearing this new inconsistency, the attentive cross-examiner is alerted to the need to prepare an impeachment on this now occurring inconsistency.

§ 16.38   Assist the Fact Finder to Visualize the Moment the New Inconsistency Was Created

As soon as she hears the new version of a fact, the cross-examiner should make a mental note of the scene in the courtroom at that moment. Note first the exact time that it occurred. Next, scan the courtroom quickly; note the exact locations of the various participants, particularly if the participants are in odd positions. Finally, note any other occurrence that may bring the jury back to this exact moment when it is time to impeach.

Example:

Q: Sir, earlier in your direct testimony you said Bobby held a check in his hand when he told you to sign the contract?

A: Yes, I did.

Q: You said this in response to Mr. Kugen's question?

A: Yes.

Q: He said that this morning?

A: Yes, I think so.

Q: You will remember that you were not in the witness chair, but you were at the diagram in front of the jury?

A: Yes.

Q: You will remember that Mr. Kugen was standing beside you there?

A: Yes.

Q: You will remember that immediately after saying that, Mr. Kugen suggested you return to the witness chair?

A: I do.

The cross-examiner is making the jury visualize and re-experience the inconsistency given earlier on direct testimony. The same type of visualization may be employed when a new inconsistency arises in a preceding chapter of cross-examination. At times the cross-examiner may choose to impeach immediately on the new inconsistency. There are those instances, however, in which the cross-examiner chooses instead to finish her chapter and later return to the new inconsistency. In such instances, it is appropriate to do some setting of the scene of the moment of the new inconsistency.

As is true of all cross-examinations, this foundation should be laid one fact at a time. By performing it phrase by phrase, the foundation has greater impact.

§ 16.39   Effect on the Witness

As the cross-examiner assists the fact finder to visualize that moment on direct examination when the inconsistent testimony was given, this technique has a substantial effect on the witness. The witness senses or knows, depending on the witness's experience at testifying, that the cross-examiner is about to challenge that previous testimony. The time necessary to assist the fact finder to visualize the previous moment places the witness in an uncomfortable position of realizing that the earlier statement is about to be challenged but the witness is unable to defend the statement itself while he is asked detailed questions about the scene when the previous testimony was given. The body language of the witness will portray that the witness is uncomfortable. This uncomfortable body language will heighten the drama of the impeachment itself.

§ 16.40   Advantages for the Cross-Examiner When the Witness Changes His Story at Trial

In all other respects, an inconsistency occurring during trial will be handled like an inconsistency discovered before trial. However, it comes very late in the game, which is an added advantage. It offers the cross-examiner an opportunity to point out how many times this story could have been told, but was not. It, therefore, allows the cross-examiner to close the chapter or chapters exposing this new inconsistency with summary questions that give the history and context of the inconsistency:

Q: Four times we have discussed this case?

A: Yes.

Q: Four times — once on April 1st, 2001?

A: Yes.

Q: Second on June 17th, 2001?

A: Yes.

Q: The third on August 14th, 2001?

A: Yes.

Q: And the fourth time two days before this trial began; isn't that correct?

A: Yes.

Q: You never told me, you never stated, you never said at all what you testified to on direct examination (the car was green) on any of those four occasions, did you?

A: No.

Q: You never discussed it?

A: No.

Q: You never brought it up?

A: No, I didn't.

Q: You never said a thing, did you?

A: No.

§ 16.41 An Advanced Variation of the Eight Steps to Impeachment by Inconsistent Statement

Every technique can be varied, stylized, and improved upon. So too, the eight steps of impeachment by inconsistent statement can be modified. Instead of reviving the latest version, laying the foundation, and exposing the inconsistency, the cross-examiner can perform the steps in a different and equally dramatic order.

In this advanced technique, the cross-examiner ignores the existence of the version given on direct examination and begins the cross-examination on the issue as if to establish the earlier version as the only version. In essence, the cross-examiner proceeds as if there were no new version.

This is accomplished by performing the entire chapter on the point as originally written. The leading questions are presented in the order leading to establishment of the goal-fact. The cross-examiner marches the witness toward the goal-fact; as if oblivious to the fact that today's version of the goal-fact is inconsistent with the goal-fact originally sought.

The leading questions, as originally written, should produce the appropriate "yes" answers. (If they don't, so much the better, as a new denial of one of the questions simply results in yet another inconsistency to be wielded by the cross-examiner.) Of course, when the cross-examiner reaches the goal-fact, the witness will now deny its truthfulness. The lawyer is now at the point of the inconsistency.

The cross-examiner must ask the goal-fact *as if* it was not contradicted. The cross-examiner will examine as if there had been no inconsistency. However, when the witness denies the truth of the goal-fact and reiterates the new and inconsistent version, the cross-examiner will drop back into the steps of impeachment by inconsistent statement and establish the foundation facts, and continue sequentially to the announcement of the original version as if it were the first exposure of the inconsistency.

§ 16.42 Example of Advanced Variation

This example of the advanced technique is found in a criminal case. The defendant was indicted as part of a drug conspiracy. No drugs were ever found on him, though an informant testifies against him. On the stand is a DEA agent who intends to link the defendant to a drug transaction through his subjective interpretation of defendant's "suspicious activities." On direct examination, the DEA agent has testified for the first time that the defendant's actions in walking down the airport concourse were suspicious.

The cross-examiner begins the impeachment by ignoring the inconsistency and sticking to the chapter previously prepared to establish the original version:

Q: Mr. McCarthy got off about halfway through the deplaning passengers?

A: Yes.

Q: He walked to the center of the concourse?

A: Yes.

Q: He turned and looked up at the monitors?

A: No, he scanned the monitors.

Q: Scanning means looking?

A: You would have to make that determination.

Q: You couldn't?

A: I wouldn't know.

Q: He stopped in front of the monitors?

A: Yes.

Q: The monitors are hung from the ceiling?

A: Yes.

Q: A person looking at the monitors would need to look up?

A: Yes, they would if they wanted to read them.

Q: Mr. McCarthy looked up?

A: He did.

Q: He looked up at the monitors?

A: It appeared so.

Q: Moving on, Agent, isn't it true that if people are leaving the Pittsburgh Airport, it has been your experience that they continue down the concourse to the terminal?

A: Yes.

Q: If people stay on the concourse, it is because they have a connecting flight?

A: Yes.

Q: That is what Mr. McCarthy did?

A: Yes.

Q: He looked at the monitors?

A: Yes.

Q: And then after looking at the monitors he walked away from the monitors down the concourse?

A: Yes.

Q: If his gate is down the concourse, that's where he would have to go to get to his plane, isn't it?

A: Yes.

Q: You didn't know where he was going?

A: No.

Q: People catching a connecting flight in that concourse would make that same turn?

A: Yes.

Q: You know Pittsburgh is a hub?

A: Yes.

Q: You know it is a hub of U.S. Air?

A: Yes.

Q: You know that U.S. Air controls every single flight on concourse A?

A: Yes.

Q: He fit the profile of somebody catching another flight?

A: No, he was looking around constantly and scanning all the faces. He would speed up, then slow down. He would stop and then start again.

Q: In a pre-trial hearing of June 16, 2002, we discussed this very issue?

A: What issue is that?

Q: I asked you about Mr. McCarthy's actions?

A: Yes, you did.

Q: I asked those questions in front of this very judge?

A: Yes.

Q: The Assistant United States Attorney, Ms. Thomas, was sitting right where she is sitting today?

A: As I recall.

Q: I asked you about Mr. McCarthy looking at the monitors?

A: Yes.

Q: I asked you about his walking away from the terminal?

A: Yes, that came up.

Q: And I asked you at page 119, line 16 of that hearing, before this very judge and this very prosecutor: "He fit exactly the profile of somebody catching another flight?" and your answer, under oath, before this very judge and from that very chair, at page 119, line 18 was, quote, "yes."

A: That's true.

The impeachment on this point may now be considered complete. Counsel need not ask about the changes in the story. The rules of impeachment have been complied with. The witness has been confronted with the prior version, and the believability of the prior version has been established. However, the order of events is different; some would say more artful.

Though the witness's answer on this issue is exactly the one given on direct examination, it is inconsistent with former testimony. Instead of reviving the original and harmful version, exposing the inconsistency and then going back to shore up the pre-trial answer, counsel has, instead, inverted the process by ignoring the inconsistency. The cross-examiner performs the chapter toward the desired (but now unobtainable goal-answer) and intentionally puts the witness in a position where he must then announce the new version, and thereafter be impeached upon it.

§ 16.43   Handling of the Documents and Who Reads the Inconsistency

Generally the rules do not require the cross-examiner to hand the documents to the witness and show the witness the exact inconsistency. However it is often the better practice to permit the witness to have the inconsistency in front of him. This assures the jury that the cross-examiner is being fair in dealing with the witness. In addition, by requiring the witness to visually confront their own inconsistency (or, in the example of an audio, DVD, or videotape recording, to actually hear or see the inconsistency), the cross-examiner permits the witness to react visually to the contradiction in real time. Counsel might consider blowing up a key inconsistency or using an overhead to simultaneously show both the jury and the witness the inconsistency.

There is no fixed rule as to when to give the witness the documents if the cross-examiner is not required to do so immediately. A major factor in making that determination hinges upon the decision of whether the cross-examiner or the witness will read and expose the inconsistency. There are valid tactical reasons for each of the two techniques. Many lawyers are of the school of thought that lawyers should be in control at all times and should read the inconsistency so that they can give the inconsistency appropriate emphasis and tone of voice. This technique allows the cross-examiner to choose the tone, pace, and emphasis within the sentence.

The alternative technique, in which the lawyer requires the witness to read aloud the inconsistent statement, has the virtue of impeaching the witness out of his own mouth. For these lawyers, the disadvantage of losing control over voice and emphasis is compensated for by the impact of the jury witnessing the witness impeach himself.

Flexibility is the key. The circumstances of the impeachment, the complexity and length of the impeaching statement, and the demeanor of the witness are all factors that must be weighed in making the decision as to whether the witness or the lawyer should read the inconsistency.

A major consideration in determining whether the witness should read the inconsistency is whether the inconsistency is worth the time to have the witness read it. If the witness reads it, it takes longer. However, even if the witness is to read the inconsistency, the lawyer should always phrase the question in a strictly leading manner so as not to permit the witness to run on:

Q: A few moments ago, you told us that you recalled my client performed "adequately" on the straight leg lifting test?

A: Yes.

Q: But that is not what you said when asked that question in your deposition.

A: I believe it is.

Q: To be precise, at page 20, line 12 of the deposition, I asked you, "How did Julie do on the straight leg lifting test?"

A: Yes, I recall the question.

Q: Please read to the jury your answer at page 20, line 14.

A: "Well, she had some problems, actually some significant difficulty with that test. She scored quite weak."

In this manner, as little control as possible is turned over to the witness. The only role assigned the witness is to read his own words at precisely the point indicated by the cross-examiner.

§ 16.44   Requiring the Witness to Read the Inconsistency and Repeating It

In deciding who should read the impeaching passage, it is possible for the lawyer to have her cake and eat it too. Observe the following passage, which is an extended form of the previous example:

Q: A few moments ago, you told us that you recalled my client performed "adequately" on the straight leg lifting test?

A: Yes.

Q: But that is not what you said when asked that question in your deposition.

A: I believe it is.

Q: To be precise, at page 20, line 12 of the deposition, I asked you, "How did Julie do on the straight leg lifting test?"

A: Yes, I recall the question.

Q: Please read to the jury your answer at page 20, line 14.

A: "Well, she had some problems, actually some significant difficulty with that test. She scored quite weak."

Q: You answered the same question that you answered on direct examination differently at your deposition, didn't you?

A: Yes.

Q: You answered it at page 20, line 14, didn't you?

A: Yes.

Q: The question was put to you on line 12, wasn't it?

A: Yes.

(The lawyer then reads the question with appropriate emphasis along with the answers.)

As this example demonstrates, it is possible to force the witness to impeach himself and then again impeach the witness with the cross-examiner's choice of tone and emphasis.

Chapter 17

IMPEACHMENT BY OMISSION

SYNOPSIS

§ 17.01   Three Additional Steps Required for Impeachment by Omission

There are three separate and distinct steps for the technique of impeachment by omission. Each step is in reality a separate goal, requiring one or more chapters of cross-examination for its accomplishment. Successful, powerful exploitation of an omission requires accomplishment of each of the three steps:

1) Either by professional duty or by factual circumstances of the case, the person who is being impeached by his omission must have understood the need to be complete on important details;

2) The document, report, or hearing must have been an appropriate place (and hopefully *the* appropriate place) to speak of or note the important matters that were omitted; and

3) Under the factual circumstances of this case, at the time of the making of the document, report, or hearing, the matters were known and were important.

§ 17.02   Relationship of Impeachment by Omission to Impeachment by Inconsistent Statements

Impeachment by omission requires the same eight-step process as impeachment by inconsistent statement. However, the difference is that the exposing of the inconsistent statement (step 6) exposes the fact that before trial there was a lack of an answer on the critical area. That is, there was no factual information given prior to the version given in the direct testimony.

An impeachment by omission is far more dependent upon logic than many other forms of impeachment. Almost inevitably, the reason something <u>was said</u> was because it was believed at the time. The assertion of the fact had a value, a degree of conviction that is evidenced by its being said at all. Because there are so many explanations (many of them benign) as to why something <u>wasn't said</u> before trial, the cross-examiner must be extremely careful in establishing the value of the prior statement that contains the omission. Logically, the greater the significance of the omitted statement, the greater the prior opportunity to document that omitted statement. There is also a greater desire or need to document that omitted material so that it appears to the fact finder that if the event had occurred it would not have been omitted. This same logic renders the witness far less able to logically explain the absence of critical items within the document. Of course, the cross-examiner will not ask the witness to explain why the critical information was omitted.

The point of the impeachment by omission is to show that the current testimony is not deserving of belief. The chapter method is used to establish the logical reasons why the newly remembered material is unlikely to be accurate. Having performed those chapters well, the cross-examiner has done as good as can be expected with the facts. It is not for the cross-examiner to invite the witness to explain his way out of the problem.

§ 17.03   Equating or Translating in Impeachment by Omission

It should be pointed out that Step 5, equating or translating, is still necessary. In fact, Step 5 is now more important. The cross-examiner must take great pains to ensure the jury understands that the facts given on direct examination are not something that the witness ever spoke about prior to trial. In order to accomplish this, it is important that the new version (the direct testimony) be clearly defined or translated. Only after pinning down the exact meaning on the new material can the cross-examiner definitely prove that prior to trial there was never a statement or implication made as to those new facts. If the cross-examiner fails to require precision as to the new story, it leaves the witness with the ability to argue that, indeed, he did previously say something akin to his new story. The fault then falls back on the cross-examiner for failing to understand the previous words of the witness, rather than on the witness for failing to previously divulge this important information. The jury is left with a confusing picture at best.

§ 17.04 Translating in Impeachment by Omission — A Civil Example

The following example comes from a wrongful death case. The defendant, while driving in a residential area at night, struck a pedestrian crossing the road. The defendant's theory of the case is that he could not see the man in time to stop.

The investigating officer is called to the stand. In the original police report, the officer makes no mention of any unusual weather conditions, including any unusual darkness. There is a section in the report where the investigating officer could note any unusual weather or road conditions.

The officer testified on direct examination that the night of the incident was "quite dark." Because the cross-examining lawyer was not careful enough to equate "quite dark" (a very subjective term) with a less subjection description, the cross-examiner failed to eliminate any other similar statement in the report to "quite dark." The witness is left with room to explain the omission:

Q: Officer, you said on direct that the night was "quite dark?"

A: Yes.

Q: You filled out a police report involving this incident?

A: Yes.

Q: A portion of that report provides a place where you could note any usual weather or road conditions?

A: Yes, it does.

Q: Nowhere in that section do you note that the night was "quite dark."

A: No, I don't, but you have to see that I marked down that it was 12:32 a.m., a night, on page one.

Not only does the witness escape the omission and contradiction, but the cross-examiner is made to appear to the jury as someone who is intentionally picking an unnecessary and minuscule fight with a well-intentioned witness. Compare that result with the more careful cross-examiner who spends more time translating the new testimony before beginning the impeachment by omission (and therefore before the witness realizes how to tailor the answers to approximate something in a previous report):

Q: Officer, you said on direct that the night was "quite dark?"

A: Yes.

Q: You are a person accustomed to being precise?

A: I try to be.

Q: And you used the phrase "quite dark" because it seemed to you to be the appropriate phrase?

A: Yes.

Q: It was unusually dark for you to specifically say that in your direct testimony?

A: Yes.

Q: In fact, you chose the exact words "quite dark?"

A: Yes.

Q: You're meaning to tell the jury that it was unusually dark that evening?

A: Yes.

Q: You found it to be unusually dark when compared with other evenings?

A: Yes.

Q: Compared with other evenings during that time of year?

A: Yes.

Q: As you investigated this case, the factor that stood out in your mind was that it was unusually dark, at the scene of the accident?

A: Yes.

The phrase "quite dark" has now been translated to mean "unusually dark" during that time of year. The cross-examiner has tied the witness to a more objective and more descriptive word selection. The witness has less room to explain the omission.

§ 17.05   Equating Impeachment by Omission — A Criminal Example

In the following criminal law example, a "snitch" witness is explaining why he agreed to kill the defendant's wife. The theory of the defense is that the snitch committed the homicide for his own financial gain — as part of a robbery of a wealthy family.

The witness, on direct examination, must explain why he participated. He testified that a large part of his motivation for the crime was the defendant's threats to hurt or kill the snitch's family if he failed to carry out the murder plot. The witness vividly relates the Thanksgiving Day phone call in which the defendant voiced these threats. No mention of these threats is found in the grand jury transcripts or in the district attorney interview notes. The cross-examination begins:

Q: Now, yesterday (on direct examination), you said that there had been threats made on your family?

A: Yes, sir, there was.

Q: And those threats were part of your motivation to become a murderer?

A: Very strong part, yes.

Q: So, it wasn't greed that drove you to murder?

A: No.

Q: It was fear for your own family?

A: Ms. Hall, I was driven to the act by several factors.

Q: The threats on your family were a large part of it?

A: Yes, ma'am.

Q: These threats occurred during a telephone conversation with Don that was made from the Wurner residence on Thanksgiving?

A: Yes.

Q: According to you, during that conversation you said, "I can't guarantee it will be done?"

A: That's correct.

Q: And then Don threatened your family?

A: He said something to the effect of, "You've stretched me out long enough and I don't have the time to hire anyone else. I know where you live and I know where your kids go to school."

Q: And you said to him, "Are you threatening me?"

A: I said, "Are you threatening my family?" And he said to me, "I'll do what I have to do."

Q: You can remember it pretty clearly, I imagine, those threats on your family?

A: I've thought about it a considerable amount, yes.

Q: Burned into your mind, is it?

A: You might say that, yes.

Q: Don was threatening to kill your wife?

A: I took it that way.

Q: He was threatening to kill your children?

A: That's what I believed.

Q: That is about the worst threat he could make?

A: To me, it was.

Q: You were horrified?

A: Sickened.

Q: Sickened about the mess you were in?

A: And my family.

Q: Sickened about the fact that if you didn't commit a murder, your family could be murdered?

A: Yes.

Q: These threats were your worst nightmare?

A: My worst nightmare was that he would do it.

Q: So you murdered a woman?

A: At his instructions.

Q: Because of his threats?

A: Yes.

Q: Isn't it true that on December 11, when you testified under oath before the grand jury, you never said a word about any such threats?

A: I don't believe I did.

Q: And when the DA Investigator interviewed you on February 6 of this year to get you ready for trial, you never mentioned it to her?

A: I don't believe so. I was still very afraid for my family at that time.

Q: You testified under oath before the grand jury and when you talked to the investigator to get ready for trial you hid things?

A: No, sir, I wasn't trying to hide anything. It was a matter of Don, I'm sure, would be seeing these reports, and I was very afraid for my family's lives.

Q: You are here to accuse Don of hiring you to murder his wife?

A: Yes, sir.

Q: And you were afraid to drop in the allegation that he threatened you? That was what you kept out to save yourself?

A: Again, a lot of emotional problems at that time.

Q: Your emotional problems kept you from telling the grand jury what you came up with yesterday for the first time?

A: I didn't come up with it. It happened.

Q: You are telling us your emotional problems kept you from telling the grand jury or the prosecutor, "I'm being threatened, my wife is being threatened, my children are being threatened"?

A: The admission of an act of that tragic amount has — at the time I was seeing the investigator and the grand jury it was a most difficult few days.

Q: So, in those most difficult few days you decided not to tell them that your family's lives were being threatened by Mr. Frohlich?

A: I don't believe that I decided to not tell them anything.

Q: But you didn't tell them?

A: No, sir, I did not.

Q: In this call that was burned into your memory, this threat that motivated you to kill a mother of three, you remained silent under oath?

A: Yes, sir, I did.

Q: And on February 6, when you were getting prepared to testify, you again neglected to tell the DA's office about the threats?

A: Yes.

Q: On February 6 of 2002, DA Lucas and Ms. Thompson came down to Canon City to see you. That was a few days ago?

A: Yes, sir.

Q: And they went over your story with you again?

A: Yes, sir, they did.

Q: To make sure you were ready for trial.

A: They asked me how I was feeling and asked about it, yes.

Q: Isn't it true that on February 6, 2002, you never said any such thing about threats?

A: In February, I did say it, yes.

Q: That your life was being threatened by Mr. Frohlich?

A: Yes.

Q: That he had told you, "I know where you live, I know where your kids live"?

A: Yes, sir.

Q: That's in this statement?

A: I believe it is, isn't it?

Q: Let's go through it —

A: All right.

Q: — shall we?

A: May I?

Q: Certainly.

A: Doesn't appear to be here now.

Q: Isn't there, is it?

A: No, sir.

Q: Not one word of it?

A: Doesn't seem to be.

Q: When you say, "Doesn't seem to be." What you really mean is that the truthful answer is, "It isn't."

A: No, sir, it isn't.

Had the cross-examiner, in her haste to impeach by omission, skipped Step 5 of "equating or translating" and immediately confronted the witness with the fact that the witness had never previously said that the defendant had threatened his family, the witness could respond:

> "Well, I didn't say it just that way. I did say to the grand jury that I would never forget the Thanksgiving Day call from Don and that it was a 'troubling call.' But then we moved on to the plan for the murder, and nobody ever asked again."

But by using Step 5 the cross-examiner has gone a good deal of the way down the road to closing off the ability of the witness to deny the contradiction.

This example was selected in as much as there are such forms of testimony where there are no clear-cut, easy methods of equating or translating the direct testimony against the omission prior to trial. Unlike impeachment by inconsistent statement, there is no clear-cut fact testified to prior to trial. Since impeachment by omission is more an application of logic, greater care must be used to fashion factual chapters that show that even if the precise issue was not previously raised, logically the current version would have come out in some pre-trial setting if true.

§ 17.06　Exposing the Inconsistency When It Is an Omission

When the lawyer exposes the omission as an inconsistent statement, the foundation of Step 6 (what is thought of as orienting the witness to the prior statement, and what has now been discussed as a sanctifying the prior statement) must be done with greater care. The foundation requirements of who, when, where, and what each must be done with greater care than when dealing with impeachment by an inconsistent statement.

This foundation for impeachment by omission is in fact a bit bizarre. What is being attacked is not a new version of prior testimony, but new testimony where no prior testimony on the subject exists. Logically there is no specific prior version. What there is, at most, is a prior occasion where the witness could have offered and should have offered such testimony, but did not do so. When the new version of facts is set against silence, the impeachment is not a process of comparing apples to apples, or even apples to oranges. The technique of impeachment by omission is much more akin to comparing apples to air.

Witnesses can make up a new fact whenever they wish, even on redirect examination. The following is an example of a witness who has suffered great damage through a cross-examination chapter bundle designed to display a series of perks demanded by the witness as a condition of the sale of his business. The chapters had their desired effect; so on redirect examination his lawyer has offered the witness an opportunity to explain what appears to be his very greedy conduct. Now, for the first time, the witness has offered a completely new and self-serving explanation of his conduct. This is an excellent opportunity for the cross-examiner to engage in impeachment by omission.

Redirect examination of the plaintiff:

Q: Now, Mr. Holden, finally, you were asked about your desire to retain those items in that consulting agreement which the defendant's lawyer described as perks. Do you remember those questions?

A: Yes.

Q: Mr. Holden, that particular agreement was assignable and transferable to any party you might choose, wasn't it?

A: Yes.

Q: And Ms. Williams asked you about that, didn't she?

A: Yes.

Q: Did you have an intention when you entered into that consulting agreement that was the reason why you requested of the defendant what Ms. Williams calls perks?

A: Yes.

Q: And would you tell The Court and jury what that was?

A: As a result of the experience that I had — I had gone through, and was going through with my child, it was my intention to set up the foundation, which I did subsequently, that would serve the purpose with — that had the intended purpose of helping others who ran into the same kind of problem that I did or also being a value to teachers, parents, friends of people with problems, etc.

Even during my tenure in the franchise, the ability to use the franchise, the asset, whether we gave seats to people who supplied the managers with cars, different suppliers to the club, in many different ways, they liked it. They liked to travel with the team. They liked to have tickets to the games, be able to go down to the dugout, also tremendously valuable assets for auction purposes, being able to auction off so many seats to the World Series for the purchase of the charity, as you know.

So that was why it (the contract which contained the many perks) was assignable. They didn't know what the charity was going to be called at that point, nor did I know exactly what its first functions would be. But I knew what its intent was going to be.

What, in fact happened was, as we know, that (consulting agreement containing the perks) was canceled. But, in the process of it being canceled, the purchase price was increased by — the purchase price was increased by approximately two million U.S. dollars. And that later, in 1985, after I had been paid that, that $2 million was the initial founding seed money that I put into the Holden Substance Abuse Foundation.

Judge: Defense counsel, do you have any questions on these questions?

Recross of the plaintiff:

Q: So as I understand it, Mr. Holden, there was a plan all along that all of these requirements in the consulting agreement were there so you could give them to some charitable use?

A: Yes.

Q: That's a very vivid memory you have of how all the World Series tickets, all of the passes, all of the seats in the owner box, those were always in your mind clearly as part of a package you intended to present to charity?

A: Yeah. I didn't divorce myself from being a part of that because you would be a host to the — for example, if we held a charity action in Los Angeles, and people would bid on that, they wouldn't come unattended to (the defendant's) box. So I couldn't say that I wouldn't use a seat. I don't mean to say that.

Q: But, certainly, it was a well-constructed plan you had all along?

A: Ms. Williams, I don't know how well constructed it was.

Q: It's a very vivid plan you had?

A: Yeah. This was not a minor subject to me, Ms. Williams.

Q: I understand. It was a major subject to you?

A: My child's health? Yes.

Q: Let me read to you what you said under oath July 10-July 9, 2001. Page 292, Line 4.

A: Okay.

Q: Question by Mr. O'Conner. "Do you remember wanting to have some type of consulting agreement with the defendant and the team when you sold the team?" Your answer: "Yes. I remember that it was contemplated in the original agreement." Question: "Why did you want it?" Your answer:"I can't recall the exact reasons at this time." Question: "Would you remember any reasons?" Your answer: "No. Stated differently, I don't recall why my team of advisors and I believed that was how we arrived at this agreement." Question: "Do you remember what you wanted out of that consulting agreement?" Your Answer: "I don't understand the question." Question: "What were you going to do if it actually got signed?" Your Answer: "No, I don't remember." Question: "Do you remember whether you were going to get paid?" Your Answer: "No, I don't." Question: "Or how much you were going to get paid?" Your Answer: "No, I don't." Question: "Or any other perks you would have gotten?" Your Answer: "No, I don't remember."

Q: You didn't remember any of those things under oath, did you?

A: I didn't remember them then, no.

Q: And at page 353, line 4, "I'm looking at Exhibit 65 on page 2, section 2-B-1. Do you recall asking (the defendant) as part of this consulting agreement to agree to allow you — when I say 'you,' I mean holdings, to have exclusive use of box 209 with three parking spaces in the red area at the Stadium for all baseball games, including playoff games by the team?" Your answer: "No. I do not recall that." Page 354, line 2. Question by Mr. O'Conner, "Do you remember asking (the defendant) to agree to provide Holdens at no cost, two seats in the managers' section on all flights made by the (team) in connection with two seats in the owners' box and six seats in the stands for each away game played by the Bulldogs? Do you remember asking for that?" Your Answer: "I don't recall this." Question: You don't recall this? The document itself (the consulting contract containing all the perks) you couldn't even recall; is that right, Mr. Holden?

A: Ms. Williams, I didn't recall all of these things because it isn't what happened. I do recall what I did with the foundation.

Q: Why don't we summarize it this way. You were under oath, sir, for two full days, and never have you said anything remotely like what you just said about this consulting agreement?

A: I agree with that, Ms. Williams.

As can be seen, the more the witness claims to have a vivid memory of a very important event, the less likely it is that the event would have slipped his memory during the deposition. If jurors determine that a witness has intentionally misled them or has fabricated any portion of his testimony, it is likely that the credibility of the witness will never recover.

Just as in the impeachment by inconsistent statement, the cross-examiner will only identify the "what" as the last act in the foundation (and with impeachment by omission the "what" is always a zero or a blank). For example:

Q: Mr. Fraley, on February 12, 2001, you received a subpoena for your deposition?

A: Yes.

Q: You received it by certified mail?

A: Yes.

Q: You had never received a subpoena for your deposition before?

A: No.

Q: That subpoena directed that you go to the law office of Barney Frick?

A: Yes.

Q: It directed the exact time, 10:00 a.m.?

A: Yes.

Q: It directed the exact day, February 20?

A: Yes.

Q: It directed that you give testimony before a certified court reporter?

A: Yes.

Q: The subpoena told you about this wreck?

A: Yes.

Q: On the 20th you got up that morning and prepared to go to the deposition?

A: Yes.

Q: You had to take work off?

A: Yes.

Q: You had never been to that law office before?

A: No.

Q: You went to that law office knowing that you would be giving testimony about this case?

A: Yes.

Q: You knew that it was serious because you had received a subpoena?

A: Yes.

Q: You arrived before 10:00 that morning?

A: Actually I arrived just a little bit after 10:00. I was nervous and missed a turn and I was somewhat late.

Q: When you arrived a little after 10:00, you were nervous that you might be in trouble because you were late?

A: Yes.

Q: When you arrived I was present?

A: Yes.

Q: Mr. Frick was present?

A: Yes.

Q: The plaintiff was present?

A: Yes.

Q: The defendant George was present?

A: Yes.

Q: And there was a certified court reporter there?

A: Yes.

Q: She had a stenographic machine, didn't she?

A: Yes, just like on TV?

Q: In fact, you were sworn just like you were today?

A: Yes.

Q: That morning you raised your hand and swore before God to tell the truth.

A: Yes.

Q: And it was your intention to tell the truth that morning?

A: Yes.

Q: It was not quite as scary as coming into court because it was only in a law office?

A: I was just as nervous.

Q: That's right, you knew that it was just as serious as your testimony here today?

A: Yes, I did.

Q: You took it that seriously?

A: Yes.

Q: You knew it was about this case?

A: Yes.

Q: You knew a lawsuit had been filed, once you got your subpoena?

A: Yes, I figured that out.

Q: You knew that it was required that you give honest testimony?

A: Yes.

Q: You were told by both lawyers before you started to testify just how important your testimony was?

A: Yes.

Q: You were cautioned at page 2, line 16 through 23, that it was important that you understood each of the questions and responded truthfully if you understood those questions?

A: Yes.

Q: You were also told that if you didn't understand a question, to say that you didn't understand the question, and not just guess at the answer?

A: Yes, you told me that.

Q: I spoke in such language that you could understand?

A: Yes.

Q: I was seated across the table from you, wasn't I?

A: Yes.

Q: My opponent, Mr. Frick, was on your side of the table?

A: Yes.

Q: The court reporter was at the end of the table taking all of the questions and answers down verbatim?

A: Yes.

Q: At the end of the deposition, page 392, lines 10 through 12, I asked you if you had understood all my questions, and you told me that you had?

A: Yes.

Q: In fact, you had understood all my questions, hadn't you?

A: Yes.

Q: And then I asked you: "Is there anything of importance that happened that day?"

A: That's right.

Q: Your answer was: "No, I cannot think of any"?

A: Yes.

Q: I then asked: "Anything that stands out in your mind?"

A: Right.

Q: Your answer was "No"?

A: Yes.

§ 17.07   Impeachment by Omission on Professional Witnesses

As can be seen, the foundation for the document, report, or statement that is silent on a key point must be at least as complete as if the document were being accredited for purposes of introducing an inconsistent statement. A more thorough foundation is needed when examining professional witnesses. In such cases, their very professionalism and training must be invoked as logically supporting the notion that such important material, if true, would never have been omitted.

A good general question to set up the impeachment by omission of law enforcement agents, and expert witnesses is to ask, "You consider yourself a thorough officer?" Most witnesses believe they are being complimented and do not understand that something has been omitted from their reports. Even the most cautious witnesses find it difficult to tell a jury that they do not consider themselves to be thorough, fair, or interested in all the important facts of the matter.

After establishing that the professional training of the witness requires that witness to carefully note important facts, the cross-examiner should next establish the sanctity of the report in such a way as not to signal the witness the context of the upcoming impeachment. This is accomplished by first laying a very broad foundation for the proper process of creating the document at issue, before moving into an examination of the document itself. The scope of questioning must be very general at first because the witness can be expected to invoke all manner of excuses if he is first alerted that there is a significant omission in his reports.

For example, asking an officer if he has been on the force twenty years and then asking: "And you have filled out thousands of police reports?" will immediately trigger in the officer's mind that there must be an omission in this police report. A better approach is to discuss with the officer, through leading questions, the importance of documenting facts regardless of whether the facts help or hurt one side. Another excuse-stealing chapter is built around facts that show that the officer or witness had the desire and the time to be accurate. Each chapter has the effect of making it more logical that missing information would be in the report, if that information really existed.

§ 17.08 A More General Approach Is Required When Dealing With Professional Witnesses

Consider the following more general approach, dealing not so much with the word "thoroughness," but more with the concept of thoroughness and the word "professional." The cross in this area begins with a discussion of the process of police work and only later moves into the specific document:

Q: Officer, you consider yourself a professional?

A: Yes.

Q: Being a law enforcement officer is not just strapping on a gun? (No officer will deny this.)

A: No, not at all.

Q: It takes certain educational requirements?

A: Yes.

Q: And after those educational requirements have been accumulated, you have on-the-street training?

A: Yes.

Q: You are then sent to the police academy for refresher courses?

A: Yes.

Q: And you are taught at that police academy, both before and after training on the street, subjects dealing with the important aspects of being a law enforcement officer?

A: Correct.

Q: Being a law enforcement officer is more than just riding around in a squad car?

A: Yes.

Q: It is more than just physically making arrests?

A: Yes.

Q: It takes special training?

A: Yes.

Q: It takes special skills?

A: Yes.

Q: It takes special knowledge?

A: Yes.

Q: The mental or intelligence aspect of law enforcement is every bit as important as the physical aspect?

A: In my opinion, it is more important.

Q: Thank you, Officer, the mental is more important than the physical nowadays, isn't it?

A: Yes.

Q: Law enforcement officers around the country are connected with various computers?

A: Yes.

Q: The computers share with other law enforcement officers on a moment's notice various information?

A: Yes.

Q: It is through that information that you can exercise the mental aspect of law enforcement?

A: Yes.

Q: Modern law enforcement is much more about finding facts than it is about force?

A: Yes, indeed.

Q: Those facts are put into computers in a very specific way, are they not?

A: Yes.

Q: There are certain forms that have to be followed?

A: Yes.

Q: There are certain specific procedures that have to be followed?

A: Yes.

Q: Certain information must be put in there so that others can use it?

A: Yes.

Q: The facts have to be collected in a certain way so that others can rely on them?

A: Yes.

Q: The facts have to be done in a certain way so that other law enforcement agents can use those facts?

A: Yes.

Q: In addition to being reported under a certain procedure and in a certain manner, the facts must be accurate?

A: Yes.

Q: Above all else, the professional law enforcement officer demands accuracy of himself?

A: As best we can.

(At this point, an experienced officer may speculate that his report will be in question. The word "accuracy" will stimulate that speculation.)

Q: When you filled out your incidence report on this occasion, you knew that others would rely on it?

A: Yes.

Q: You knew that it had to be done in the correct manner?

A: Yes.

Q: Using the correct procedure?

A: Yes.

Q: And you followed those procedures?

A: Yes.

Q: You filled it out in the proper manner?

A: Yes.

Q: And you included in that report any and all facts and information that you knew to be important in this case?

A: Yes.

Q: You knew that others would rely on these facts and information and that all important facts and information should be included in the report?

A: Yes.

§ 17.09   Establish the Value of the Omission

There are a myriad ways to question an officer, a doctor, or an expert of any kind in order to set up the two essentials of impeachment by omission:

1) Because of their profession, training, or role in this case they, more than others, appreciate and agree with the need to be meticulous; and

2) The report or document about to be discussed is the correct place to put such information.

In order for impeachment by omission to be successful, the cross-examiner must separately establish a third concept: The missing information is of such value that it could not possibly be overlooked or omitted from this report.

The cross-examiner is advised to approach each of these three requirements as separate chapters of cross-examination, each requiring thorough, detailed presentations for the jury. In a sense, cross-examination by omission is a three-legged stool, and failure to establish any one of these legs results in a cross-examination that is unstable. Whichever leg is not firmly established will be seized by the witness as his excuse for the omission; i.e., "I thought it was just a preliminary report"; "I was going to mention it later"; or "I didn't realize at the time it was so important." Even if the witness does not dredge up the excuse, the impeachment by all omission is vulnerable to a redirect examination that suggests to the witness the need to explain the omission.

§ 17.10   Exposing the Omission

There are two powerful ways to expose the omission. While each one is useful, the second method has greater impact.

The first method (and surely a competent method) is to confront the witness with the report or document and say:

Q: And there was never a mention of that in your deposition (in your statement/report)?

A: No. (This answer of course helps the cross-examiner.) (This answer gives the cross-examiner the least amount of material to exploit.)

Or

A: I don't think so. (This answer gives the cross-examiner more to work with.) (Depending on the reaction of the jury, the cross-examiner can now more fully question the witness by going page by page through the report, paragraph by paragraph, or even line by line.)

Or

A: If you say so. (This is often the answer of a witness who knows that there is nothing in the report.) (The witness's answer communicates to the jury and the judge that the cross-examiner is correct and the witness was not. This has long-term benefits to the cross-examiner.)

§ 17.11 Exposing the Omission Dramatically

If the cross-examiner has been thorough and has firmly established the sanctity of the prior statement, report, or deposition, the jury will be left to wonder why this new and important material was not mentioned earlier. Again, it must be stressed that now is not the time for the cross-examiner to ask the explanation of the witness as to why the additional material wasn't previously mentioned.

A more dramatic way to expose the omission is presented below:

Q: Please show the jury where in your report (in your deposition/statement) you say that (cross-examiner inserts claimed, but omitted, material).

What happens inevitably, with even the most experienced witness is a fumbling through the material as the witness desperately tries to locate something that would show that there is not a complete omission. In the heat of cross-examination, no one can read that fast. The witness is now embarrassed and psychologically off stride because he knows that he must finally admit to the jury that it was not mentioned in any of the logical places. The fact finder is now factually equipped to draw the logical conclusion: The new statement cannot be found in the report where it logically should have been unless the fact or statement did not occur.

§ 17.12 How the Witness Copes in Real Time with an Impeachment by Omission

Witnesses are predictably uncomfortable when confronted by an impeachment by omission. In fact such chapters produce some of the most frustrating moments for a witness. Simultaneously, impeachments by omission are illuminating moments for the jury, as such chapters graphically demonstrate not only the fact of the contradiction, but also lay bare how this witness copes with his important omission. Often the witness greets with silence the completion of an impeachment by omission. The silence thus created has a predictably dramatic impact in the courtroom. The silence is read by the fact finder as the witness saying, "You caught me" (see chapter 21, *Creation and Uses of Silence*).

Silence is not the only possible response. Some witnesses will calmly look at the cross-examiner and state, "It is not in the report." The witness will often offer this reply without even looking at the report, the statement, or the deposition transcript. This response makes possible a different technique. After that answer and an appropriate silent pause, the cross-examiner might choose to follow up with:

Q: You know that it is not in the report, don't you?

A: Yes.

Q: You knew that before I started asking you about it?

A: Yes.

Q: You knew that before you gave your direct testimony?

A: Yes.

Q: You knew that when you were preparing for your direct testimony?

A: Yes.

Q: You knew there was nothing in your report that would say what you said on direct testimony?

A: Yes.

Or

Q: You knew that it wasn't in your report?

A: Yes.

Q: You won't even look at your report, will you?

A: No.

Q: You don't have to look at your report because you know that it is not in there?

A: Well, that is right, I think. I am really taking your word for it, counselor.

Q: Well, please look through the report and tell the jury if what I said is absolutely true?

A: OK.

At this point, the witness is now forced back into the report. A word of caution: This technique should be reserved for the witness perceived to possess power. In other words, these additional pointed questions by the cross-examiner should be used only with experts, professional witnesses, high-level corporate employees or any other witness who the jury perceives can handle themselves. Using this technique on a vulnerable witness will not be tolerated by the fact finder.

Both techniques maximize damage. In the prior example, while the witness is not forced back into the report and the long silence that accompanies it, the witness is shown to have intentionally contradicted his report in his direct testimony.

§ 17.13   Three Techniques That Put the Omission into Context

By placing the omission into the factual context of the case being tried, the damage to the witness is enhanced. Witness this cross-examination of a physician in a failure to diagnose cancer case:

Q: You have looked carefully through your medical records, and there is no statement about doing a hemocult test?

A: No.

Q: There is no statement about finding "no blood" in the stool?

A: No, there isn't.

Q: But that's exactly what you testified to on direct examination, isn't it?

A: Yes.

Q: Now, you have thoroughly reviewed the records?

A: Yes.

Q: You have looked at every page?

A: Yes.

Q: In 39 pages of medical records concerning your treatment of Mr. Moffitt, there is not one sentence of performing a hemocult test, regardless of the results?

A: No.

Or

Q: In the two and a half hours of questions and answers that you swore to in that deposition, not one of those words describes a hemocult test you claim to have run?

A: No.

Or

Q: In the nine months of records itemizing your care of Mr. Moffitt, not one time did you mention, refer to, or imply the existence of a negative hemocult test?

A: No.

Q: Two hundred seventy days of treatment records without a mention, but in April of this year, after this suit was filed, you suddenly remembered the test?

A: Yes, it's the truth. I did that test.

Each of these examples provides a technique to put into factual context the complete absence of testimony about a particular medical test. Although the cross-examiner knows that the deposition, the witness statement, or the records are long, thorough, and exhaustive, the jury does not necessarily know or appreciate that fact. The absence of a fact, expressed in a statistical context, must be exploited and exposed to the jury. The number of ways to put into context the opportunities missed by the witness to say exactly what he is now saying is limited only by the cross-examiner's reasonable creativity.

§ 17.14   Handling of the Documents for Impeachment by Omission

The American rules of impeachment do not require the cross-examiner to show the witness the documents upon which the witness will be impeached. Nonetheless the cross-examiner should always hand the witness the documents for purposes of impeachment by omission. There are few absolutes in the courtroom, but this is one of them. If the cross-examiner is correct, if there is nothing in the report that will help the witness (and, after all, this is what impeachment by omission is all about), the cross-examiner is only giving the appearance of being fair to the jury by giving the document to the witness. If on the other hand the cross-examiner withholds the documents that are allegedly silent on the key point being impeached, it appears to the jury that the lawyer is being unfair. The witness must have an opportunity to survey the document in order to verify the assertion of the cross-examiner that no such statement appears. The cross-examiner is not giving the witness anything to help himself. It is with the documents in hand that the witness looks and feels the most foolish. The witness is frustrated and must now cope with the contradiction.

Chapter 18

ADVANCED IMPEACHMENT TECHNIQUES

SYNOPSIS

§ 18.01   Mistakes, Lies, and the Human Condition

Trials are about the facts. The effect of a solid impeachment of an important witness can be so harmful to the overall credibility of the opponent's case that recovery is very difficult.

The word "lie" may have more euphemisms than any other word in the English language (fib, fudge, spin, selective memory, falsehood, perjury, false lead, figment of imagination, inaccuracy, whopper, craw fishing, fixing, shading, false witness, deceive, misrepresent, mislead, play pretend, fake out, stretch, make up, role play, prevaricate, and jolly pies [special thanks to Morven, Georgia, population 392, the only community in America that instantly recognizes this term as a euphemism for lies]).

This is not to say that every impeachment in the courtroom is based on a witness maliciously lying. Witnesses often unknowingly misrepresent the truth; they make mistakes. Many of those mistakes are honest errors. Whether intentional or unintentional, the skilled cross-examiner must be able to impeach effectively and efficiently when the facts are distorted.

§ 18.02   Believability of the Witness Involves More Than Just His Words

Witnesses make mistakes. Witnesses deceive. Witnesses change their stories. The mistakes, the deceptions, and the contradictions must be exposed. It is not only the fact of a mistake, deception or a contradiction that matters to the jury. It is the revelation of the mistake, deception, or contradiction in front of the fact finder that counts the most. It is often the spontaneous real time reaction and demeanor by the witness that tells the jury whether to believe the witness. These spontaneous reactions occurring in front of the jury are referred to throughout this chapter as "real time" reactions, meaning that no interpretation of them is required since the jury witnessed them as they occurred.

Both the impeachment itself and the method by which the witness handles the confrontation will guide the jury in its assessment of credibility. It is this appearance of truth that the jury will hold dear through consideration of the testimony of the witness. Does the witness openly admit the inconsistency, does the witness lapse into "I don't know" or "I don't remember," or does the witness deny that there is any inconsistency? This real time handling and coping with the confrontation is as important an aspect of the destruction of credibility as the impeachment itself.

Contradiction of the witness in front of the jury in real time is the most powerful and memorable method of attacking the credibility of a witness through cross-examination.

§ 18.03 The Types of Impeachment

The witness may be impeached by:

1. Bias;

2. Interest;

3. Motive;

4. Prejudice;

5. Inconsistency with another witness;

6. Inconsistency with physical evidence;

7. Inconsistency with things not done;

8. Inconsistency with common sense;

9. Omissions; and

10. Inconsistent statements.

Impeachment by bias, interest, motive, or prejudice takes many forms, in the sense that no particular legal or procedural foundation is required. By following the only three rules of cross-examination (chapter 8), the lawyer need only show the facts proving bias, motive, interest, or prejudice of the witness. The chapter method (chapter 9) maximizes the effect of this type of impeachment.

Impeachment by inconsistency with other witnesses, with physical evidence, or with things not done and things that do not exist may not require a foundation. However, there are recommended foundation phases that assist in giving these types of impeachments impact. Impeachment by inconsistent statements is the most frequent form of impeachment and it is the easiest for the jury to comprehend. Once learned, impeachment by inconsistent statement is the easiest method to create mistrust of the witness in the minds of the jurors. Impeachment by inconsistent statement requires the ability to lay a proper foundation, to handle documents, and to apply techniques to highlight or maximize the differences in testimony. Impeachment by inconsistent statement is treated in chapter 16, *Eight Steps of Impeachment by Inconsistent Statement*. Impeachment by omission requires the identical foundational obligations of impeachment by inconsistent statement, except the inconsistent statement is a blank: "It is not there," "It was not said," or "It did not occur."

§ 18.04 Mistaken Versus Dishonest Witnesses

Too often cross-examiners, when faced with an impeachment opportunity, fail to perceive the inherent difference between the mistaken witness with good intentions and the dishonest witness with evil intentions. The testimony of each may be identical, but the techniques and methods for revealing the inconsistencies and the voice and mannerisms that the lawyer uses are dramatically different.

The cross-examiner must first recognize that some witnesses are inconsistent not because they are intentionally fabricating, but because of honest errors. The tone of the cross-examination (both voice tone and word selection) therefore must be different for these two categories. The body mannerisms of the cross-examiner must be different (see chapter 22, *Voice, Movement, Body Language, and Timing*). The selection of words used in the questions must be different. The goals of each chapter of cross-examination must be different. For the mistaken witness, all will be softer. The tone is gentler. The words in these questions are less challenging. The goals of the chapter are not to show intentional deceit, but to reveal human errors.

With an intentional lie, a cross-examiner's tone may be harsher, the questions more pointed, and the word choices more severe. The goals of the cross-examination are more extreme. This witness must be shown to be falsifying.

§ 18.05   Witnesses Who Are Both Mistaken and Dishonest

The next step is to recognize that there are no strict delineations between witnesses who are mistaken and witnesses who intentionally deceive. There are those witnesses who intentionally deceive, but on certain points are simply mistaken. There are those witnesses who are honestly mistaken, but when shown their honest error refuse to admit the error and become intentionally deceptive.

By the same token, even those witnesses who intentionally seek to deceive the jury about certain issues will generally be honest about many other issues, and honestly mistaken concerning a third class of issues. The most dishonest of witnesses is honest most of the time. It is simply that the dishonest portion of the testimony is likely the most critical portion of their testimony. The cross-examiner must analyze the witness's placement on the spectrum from credible through mistaken to liar (see §18.06, below), but must also analyze each chapter of the cross-examination of each witness on that same spectrum. Only then can the cross-examiner begin to predict the likely overall impression that a jury will take away from the witness. It is through this analysis that the cross-examiner may choose not to impeach on certain issues where the witness is simply mistaken so that the impact of the intentional deceit can be maximized. Multiple other variations exist and must be consciously addressed before the beginning of the cross-examination (see chapter 3, *The Strategy, Preparation, and Organization of Cross-Examination*).

§ 18.06   Spectrum of Credibility to Lying

Credible→ Mistaken→ Lying

The law recognizes this spectrum of credibility. A basic legal instruction concerning credibility reads:

> If you (the jury) find a witness to be unworthy of belief, the jury may disregard that portion of the witness's testimony; however, if the jury finds that the witness has intentionally misrepresented evidence, the jury is authorized but not required to disregard all of the evidence provided by that witness.

As is true of the best legal instructions, this language tells jurors to act in a manner consistent with how people in a non-trial setting think. Common experience teaches that people make mistakes. The phrase, "I'm only human," is one that any person of maturity can identify. People are more forgiving of those who make mistakes rather than those who lie. This is particularly true if there are circumstances that allow an understanding of why a person would be mistaken. On the other hand, everyone becomes quite intolerant of even the merely mistaken person when their mistakes negatively affect other people's lives. Few treat intentional liars with the same respect or dignity accorded a mistaken person. A jury reacts the same way.

§ 18.07 At Times the Inconsistency May Be Substantive Evidence

Impeachment is, at times, a double-edged sword. Both edges cut the witness. The cross-examiner must be attentive to the fact that the inconsistency may be considered substantive evidence. Since that is true, the admission then has a dual purpose. Not only is the inconsistent statement used to impeach the witness, the prior statement is also considered substantive evidence.

This is an enormously important distinction. The prior statement does not merely establish that the witnesses changed his story. The prior statement stands as evidence of what the truth may be. It is incumbent upon the cross-examiner to show the jury any indication of reliability that compels it to believe that the prior statement is the more accurate rendition.

§ 18.08 Relationship of Theme to Impeachment

Impeachments should always occur consistent with the theory of the case. If the witness has testified in matters which are inconsistent with each other, but the latest statement in trial actually helps the cross-examiner, it is foolish for the cross-examiner to use the prior inconsistent statement to impeach the witness. By so doing the cross-examiner implies that the later, more helpful statement is inaccurate. It is therefore difficult to successfully impeach if a theory or theme of the case is not clearly established. This is a simple statement representing a simple concept, but to cross-examiners, who are by definition aggressive, it is an often violated concept. Too often cross-examiners see an impeachment and take it believing that every impeachment is a good impeachment. Such advocates use every impeachment whether or not it is helpful to the theory of the case. They impeach with a prior statement just because it is "fun" to expose the inconsistency.

"I want to hurt the witness" is neither a theory nor a theme. It is not the basis upon which a cross-examiner can impeach. There are guidelines to the relationship of theme to impeachment.

§ 18.09   Rule 1: Always Impeach Consistent with the Theory and Theme

The plaintiff's theory of the case is that the defendant was traveling too fast for conditions and thus caused the collision that resulted in the plaintiff's injury. Speed and conditions are essential to the theory. The defendant testified at deposition that he was traveling "the speed limit." The speed limit was 55 mph. He further stated: "I was traveling 45 to 55 mph." At trial on direct examination, after it has been established that it was foggy and raining at the time of the collision, the defendant testified on direct that he was going "slower than the speed limit," probably "35 mph."

Is the impeachment by inconsistent statement consistent with the theory? Yes. It is consistent with the theory that the defendant would now change his testimony to reduce the speed of his vehicle. Since the impeachment is consistent with the theory and theme of the case, the cross-examiner should impeach this new version of his speed through introduction of the inconsistent statement showing he believed he was traveling at a higher rate of speed.

Given the same theory of the case, assume that the defendant has testified on direct examination that he was going "10 mph over the 55 mph speed limit." "I had just passed someone." This is clearly inconsistent with his previous story of 45-55 mph. Would this new version of his speed be consistent with the theory of the case? Obviously, it would. In fact, it would be harmful to the theory to impeach this new version even though the statement at deposition is inconsistent with the direct testimony. As enticing as it may be to the aggressive cross-examiner, the lawyer must pass on this opportunity to impeach. The current version is consistent with the theory and, therefore, the lawyer must let it stand as the gospel.

§ 18.10   Rule 2: Do Not Impeach Contrary To or Against the Theory of the Case

In a hunting accident case, the theory of the case is that the defendant shot before first light in the morning and, therefore, could not have seen what he was shooting. This shot, which resulted in the plaintiff's death, was thus a negligent act.

At her deposition, a witness testified that she immediately ran towards the defendant when the shot was fired. She recognized the defendant as the person who fired the shot. Later in the deposition, when asked about the time of the shot, the witness testified that the shot was before daylight. The witness could not remember how much before daylight.

On direct examination, the defendant establishes through this witness that the witness did not know who had fired the shot because it was too dark to see.

The statement has two components. As to the lighting conditions, this direct testimony is consistent with the statement at deposition that the shot was fired before first light. As to identity, the statement is inconsistent with the witness having identified the defendant as the shooter.

The cross-examiner does not want to impeach that portion of the statement that relates to the time of day or to the visibility. Those portions of the direct testimony are consistent with the theory of the case. On the other hand, the cross-examiner would like to impeach on the subject of who fired the shot. If this witness is the only witness who can identify the defendant as the shooter, and if it is plausible that the shot could have come from another unidentified person, plaintiff's counsel could cross-examine and impeach concerning the identity issue. However, if other evidence will clearly establish the identify of the shooter, the cross-examiner is better off forgoing any cross-examination on the identification inconsistency with the witness. This is an example of the cross-examiner's recognition of a fact beyond change. If the evidence will undoubtedly establish that the defendant was the party who fired the fatal shot, even the possible impeachment of this witness on the issue of identity is of no value if the purpose of that impeachment is to try to challenge the fact beyond change — the identity of the defendant as the shooter.

Should impeachment in the topic of identity be required, the cross-examining counsel must hone in on the precise topic to be impeached and ignore other areas. The cross-examiner must be mindful that any impeachment of this witness, even if performed with surgical precision, has some harmful effect on the overall credibility of the witness. If this is the only witness who can establish the key "before dawn" aspect of the story, it may be necessary to forgo any impeachment whatsoever on the identity with this witness. There is too much to risk.

When making the critical decision on whether to impeach, the cross-examiner must weigh whether there is any dispute about the identity of the shooter. If the identity of the defendant as the shooter is a fact beyond change, it is certainly not worth the price of witness credibility (no matter how small) to impeach in order to better establish a fact well established by other witnesses.

§ 18.11 Rule 3: Use Common Sense When Impeaching on Matters Unrelated to the Theme

The decision to impeach on matters that seem unrelated to the theme is more complex than the first two rules. It requires a great deal more courtroom judgment and common sense. It requires judgment from the likely viewpoint of the jurors, not the viewpoint of the cross-examiner. It requires common sense from those beliefs held by everyday non-lawyers, not from lawyers:

1) When deciding whether to impeach on matters unrelated to the theory of the case, one must discern whether the matter is truly unrelated. Is there some connection to the theory of the case that can be used to assist the theory? Can the matter be related in a consistent way with the theory? If so, follow Rule 1. If not, see Rule 2. Is the matter contradictory to or against the theory of the case? If so, follow Rule 2. If neither, continue the analysis.

2) If the matter is clearly unrelated to the theory of the case, then the cross-examiner must decide if the impeachment would be distracting

to the jury and take attention away from the theory or theme of the case. If it distracts the jury, don't do it. If it does not, proceed with the analysis.

3) Is it big? Is the impeachment, although unrelated to the theory or theme of the case, of such magnitude or importance that the jury would perceive this witness in a generally less favorable light? In that instance it would be a worthwhile effort. Indeed, the theory of the case would be structured in such a way to make the impeachment relevant to the theory of the case.

The first goal is to examine the theory of the case to see if there is a way to make the big impeachment relevant to the opposing theories of the case. The risk that a judge will rule the matter collateral seems high. If there is a method to make that impeachment relevant to one of the two theories, it is important to discuss that link in the opening statement so that a judge might better perceive the tie between the big impeachment and an issue with in the case. If the seemingly unrelated matter is of such interest to the jury, then indulge the jury. This decision becomes a time-weighted decision. The advocate must keep in mind that time spent on a fact is the measure of importance of that fact in the courtroom. How much time will it take to perform this impeachment? What time of day is it? At what place is the trial on the time line of the presentation?

If the impeachment will require significant time and effort, it is ordinarily not worth the effort. If it is late in the day and the jury is tired, and this will be a concluding sequence, don't do it. Unless it is of such interest that it will be a concluding sequence that the cross-examiner will be satisfied to have the jury remember overnight, don't do it. Since it is not related to the theory or theme of the case, in all likelihood, it will not be of such importance.

§ 18.12   Impeachments Near the Close of the Evidence

As the trial nears closing the jury becomes impatient. It becomes eager to stop listening and start deciding. The jury has an innate sense of the momentum of a trial, and a judge even more so. As the momentum moves faster and faster toward the close of the evidence, both want the trial to be over. Be leery of impeachments on potentially collateral matters late in the case.

Whether to pursue a "late" impeachment depends, in part, on the perception of the cross-examiner as to which side is winning the trial. If the trial has gone badly, and the probability of losing is great, greater risk in cross-examination and impeachment is justified. Consequently, the cross-examiner should take every opportunity within reason to impeach in hope of developing favorable information. If the trial has gone badly and if it appears that the verdict is against the cross-examiner, there is very little risk in conducting a risky impeachment.

§ 18.13 Example of Unrelated Impeachment

An example is helpful in considering when to impeach on matters not directly related to the theory or theme of the case.

Direct Testimony: Long Blonde Hair

Police Report

Assumption 1: Long sandy colored

Assumption 2: Light brown

Assumption 3: Shoulder length

Assumption 4: Short dark hair

Assumption 5: Bald as a cue ball

This example has five distinct example variations contained within it, based on the five assumptions.

Assume that the direct testimony provides that eyewitness identification described the perpetrator as having "long blonde hair." Under that section labeled "police report" there are five different assumptions, giving five different examples of the inconsistent statement made by this witness to the initial investigating officer, so as to give us a spectrum of evidence to view for purposes of impeachment.

Assumption 1: "Long sandy colored hair" compared with "long blonde hair" could be argued to be an inconsistent statement. It just can't be argued successfully — at least not unless the entire lawsuit is about hair, hair color, and hair length.

Even if this inconsistency went directly to the theory of the case, in exercising the judgment of a juror and in applying common sense to this possible inconsistency, the cross-examiner should not impeach.

There just isn't enough difference between "sandy" and "blonde." There is no difference at all between "long" and "long."

Are the colors different? Yes, to a degree. However, the lawyer attempting to use this slight inconsistency may well undermine her own credibility rather than the credibility of the witness. That is the opposite effect desired. It is the antithesis of impeachment. The real test is whether a jury would fully characterize the two descriptions as inconsistent with each other. They would not.

Assumption 2: "Light brown" has a somewhat more pronounced inconsistency with "blonde." If this was the only inconsistency, the same analysis as in Assumption 1 would apply. However, because there is also the omission concerning the length of the hair, the cross-examiner is now faced with a decision. Should the cross-examiner impeach only on the omission concerning the length of the hair or should the cross-examiner impeach on the omission concerning the length of the hair and couple that with the possible inconsistency concerning the color? No hard and fast rules are apparent. It is a question of judgment — juror judgment.

Too often, however, a good impeachment can be rendered ineffective when coupled with a nit-picky or false inconsistency. It is better to err on the side of solid, easily differentiated inconsistencies than to couple them with an uncertain or less apparent inconsistency. Coupling strong impeachments with weak impeachments makes the strong appear weak.

Assumption 3: Shoulder length. Here there is an omission as to the color. This complete omission may be more significant to the average juror than the length of the hair. Color may be more visual than the length of the hair. The complete lack of testimony as to the color may be significant enough for impeachment, if the omission of the color of the hair goes to the theory of the case. In the event that this omission does not attach to the theory of the case, ordinarily this omission would detract from the cross-examination more than would be helpful and should not be attempted. But, again, it requires judgment.

"Long" is not synonymous with "shoulder length." It may well be that the cross-examiner must develop more specifically that the word "long" used by the witness in the direct testimony is different from "shoulder length." By laying a careful foundation, moving from the general to the specific, a more meaningful impeachment as to the length of the hair might be developed. This effort will only be worthwhile if the length of the hair affects the theory of the case. If it does not, the amount of time, effort, and the distraction on the jury's attention is certainly not worthwhile.

Assumption 4: Short dark hair. Here is an inconsistency on the color of the hair and a stronger, more definite inconsistency as to its length.

Dealing first with length of the hair, there is a clear contradiction where one description contains the word "long" and the other description contains the word "short." As these words are truly polar opposites, the witness will have a difficult, if not impossible, time explaining this contradiction.

Consequently, if an inconsistency concerning the length of the hair adds to the theory of the case, certainly this inconsistency should be fully developed. If it does not, the value of this inconsistency (since it is so specific) is still a worthwhile subject for impeachment if the witness needs to be generally impeached as to credibility.

While, at first, the difference between "blonde" and "dark" may have immediately suggested to the cross-examiner a direct contradiction, upon reflection the more-experienced cross-examiner would note that there are various shades of "blonde" and various shades of "dark." Therefore, the inconsistency is not as defined as the inconsistency concerning length of the hair. In this assumption (short dark hair), even if the color of the hair matters to the theory of the case, the cross-examiner should first impeach on the length of the hair, it being the most defined, and then move on to the color, in the hope that the witness would be defensive about having already been confronted about the length of the hair. By leading with the stronger inconsistency ("short" vs. "long") and only then moving to the relatively weaker inconsistency ("dark" vs. "blonde"), the credibility of the witness is already damaged and the willingness of the witness to explain or "fight back" is diminished (see chapter 12, *Employing Primacy and Recency* and chapter 11, *Sequences of Cross-Examination*).

In the event that either or both the length of the hair or the color of the hair is not directly related to the theme of the case, the cross-examiner must once again fall back on an analysis of whether the theory of the case is generally assisted by diminishing the general credibility of this witness.

Assumption 5: Bald as a cue ball. This assumption presents three different areas of impeachment, as well as a very dramatic and visual word choice to more strongly emphasize the inconsistency.

First, there is zero length of hair given.

Second, there is no color of the hair given.

Third, there is no hair given.

While the very dramatic testimony of "bald as a cue ball" is not in and of itself a fourth inconsistency, it may well be treated as such by the cross-examiner.

The lawyer must first develop that this description includes zero length of hair and no color of hair, and that in fact there is no hair ("bald") given in the police report. All three of these factors are directly contradictory to the three words used to describe the length of the hair on direct testimony. Thus, the cross-examiner can use the exact quote from the police report ("bald as a cue ball") to dramatically re-emphasize the inconsistencies.

§ 18.14 Impeachment on the Witness's Dramatic Word Selection

Visualize the fact that a very thorough impeachment has been done on the length, the color, and the lack of hair. At that point, the cross-examiner could then appear to be impeaching on the exact dramatic language:

Q: You didn't just say that he had no hair?

A: No, I didn't say it that way.

Q: You didn't just say that he was bald?

A: No, I didn't say that.

Q: You said that he was "bald as a cue ball?"

A: Yes.

Q: You have seen cue balls?

A: Yes.

Q: You know that they are smooth?

A: Yes.

Q: You know that they are glossy?

A: Yes.

Q: You know that they not only look smooth, but are smooth and cool to the touch?

A: Yes.

Q: You used the exact phrase "bald as a cue ball" to emphasize to the investigating officer just how bald this person was?

A: I guess.

Q: You used "bald as a cue ball" to make sure that the officer realized how bald this person was?

A: Yes.

Q: You used those words "bald as a cue ball" as the best way of describing what you saw?

A: Yes.

The phrase "bald as a cue ball" is not in and of itself an inconsistency. But whenever the inconsistency is stated in unusual, emotional, or dramatic words that come directly from the witness's mouth or written statement, it offers the cross-examiner another form of impeachment.

There are, in effect, four different inconsistencies. Each is well defined and should be easily accomplished. Moreover, because the witness used such descriptive language in the original report, the jury is easily persuaded to believe that the previous statement in fact took place and the description was considered by the witness when uttered. It is unlikely anyone could have put those words in the witness's mouth, or mistakenly put them into a report. The words carry an individualistic quality much like that of a signature. Because there is an unusual turn of phrase, the words self authenticate.

Consequently, the impeachment of this witness, whether or not it applies to the theory of the case, will in most cases be fruitful and effective for the cross-examiner, *so long as* destruction of the general credibility of this witness assists the theory of the case.

Judgment is critical as to when to impeach and how much emphasis to place on the impeachment. As can be seen from the five previous examples, there are few absolutes in making this judgment. It is a sliding scale depending on numerous factors to be applied to that specific factual setting, the specific theme of the case, and the specific witness.

Obviously some choices are much easier than others. All choices should be considered carefully.

§ 18.15   Impeachment as a Source of Theory and Theme

The concept that theories and themes of the case come from the important cross-examinations has been discussed (see chapter 2, *Developing a Theory of the Case*). It may truly be said that many theories and theme phrases are developed from the most telling of impeachments in the major cross-examinations. Not only do impeachments provide the trial lawyer with some of our most powerful theme lines, theme lines are regularly used to create impact in impeachments.

In chapter 25, *Trilogies*, the concept of trilogy will be developed. It is in impeachment, and particularly in maximizing the damage of impeachment, that trilogies, using thememic questions to emphasize the theory of the case, are most readily applicable.

Below is an example of how a theme phrase can be inserted into the impeachment. Once established during the impeachment, the theme line can then be re-emphasized as a theme and theory of the case. The example comes from a plaintiff's case where the "eyewitness" has apparently made an honest mistake in observing several factors contributing to the collision. There is an inconsistency between the pre-trial interview of the defendant and the direct testimony given at trial for the plaintiff:

Q: Immediately after the collision, you told the investigating officer that the light was red for the plaintiff?

A: Yes.

Q: But now that fact has changed?

A: Yes.

Q: You told my investigator three months after your collision that the light was red for the plaintiff?

A: Yes.

Q: But now that fact has changed.

A: Yes.

Q: You told me three days before trial that the light was red for the plaintiff?

A: Yes.

Q: But now that fact has changed?

A: Yes.

The theme phrase, "But now that fact has changed?" can be firmly established through a repetition in this, and perhaps another, chapter of cross-examination. Then, in closing argument, it can be used to refocus the jury on the inconsistency of this witness and how that relates to the theory of the case.

§ 18.16 Techniques for Maximizing the Damage of an Inconsistency

The basic steps of impeachment are necessary not only for foundation purposes, but also to create a dramatic effect that assists in maximizing the damage of the impeachment (see chapter 16, *Eight Steps of Impeachment by Inconsistent Statement*). First, the inconsistency is well-framed and highlighted by the wedding of the witness to the current version. Then the inconsistency is revealed, followed or preceded by the facts that bolster the believability of the prior version. Alhough these steps alone damage the credibility of the witness, there are additional techniques that maximize the damage.

Once an inconsistency has been exposed, never hesitate to maximize the damage of that inconsistency. Depending on the demeanor of the witness, the demeanor of the jury, and the status of the trial, the cross-examiner may wish to maximize the damage in a fast, efficient, lean method, or in a more painful, pointed, and withering style. In any event, the damage must be maximized to make the greatest impact on the jury.

§ 18.17   Make the Intentionally Deceitful Inconsistency Personal to the Jury

Assume that the witness has now admitted that the prior version of his testimony given before trial to the grand jury was contrary to his direct testimony. This inconsistency has been exposed. In an effort to wring more damage from that inconsistency, the cross-examiner can make the contradiction personal to this jury. This is done by putting the jurors in the shoes of the people who heard the first version:

Q: On February 12, 1992, you raised your hand to tell the truth?

A: Yes.

Q: You faced twenty-four grand jurors in this county and swore to tell the truth?

A: Yes.

Q: The grand jury sat in chairs just like this jury?

A: Yes.

Q: Those jurors needed to hear your testimony?

A: Yes.

Q: Your truthful testimony?

A: I suppose so.

Q: You suppose so? You thought perhaps that the grand jury wanted to hear dishonest testimony?

A: No, of course not, no.

Q: This very prosecutor asked you whether you had a meeting with Bobbie Rudolph on Friday afternoon, August 10, 2001?

A: Yes.

Q: And you told them you did?

A: Yes, I did.

Q: When you say you did, you mean you told that to the grand jurors?

A: Yes.

Q: But, in truth, you did not have meetings with Bobbie Rudolph on that Friday.

A: No. I didn't meet him, not that time.

Q: You did not tell the grand jurors the truth?

A: No.

Q: Exactly what you told them on February 12, 2002, is at page 29, line 16: "Answer: At that particular meeting he was leaving for the airport at that time and I'm dead positive it was that Friday." That was what you told the grand jurors?

A: Yes.

Q: You looked them in the eye, and you lied?

A: It wasn't the truth.

Q: First, you swore an oath to tell the truth?

A: I took an oath.

Q: Then you lied?

A: On that one issue I did.

Q: You promised that jury the facts, the truth, and then you delivered a lie?

A: As I say, on that one issue.

Q: You didn't take an oath that said you would lie on some issues?

A: Okay.

Q: True?

A: Yes, that's true.

Q: But today, when you swore on oath, you really meant it?

A: Yes, I do. I honestly do.

Q: Today, then, you wouldn't look this jury in the eye and lie?

A: No, absolutely not.

Q: Your promise to this jury to give the truth is different than your promise to that other jury?

A: To me, in my heart, it is.

This example is deliberately harsh. The primary prosecution witness is caught in a lie. That lie can be expressed in terms of an inconsistent statement. The value of the inconsistency is not the information itself, not even that the witness will lie, but the willingness of the witness to lie to *jurors*, to lie to citizens under circumstances parallel to the circumstances of these jurors. The technique makes the inconsistency personal to the jury.

§ 18.18   Make the Mistaken Inconsistency Personal to the Jury

The merely mistaken witness must, of course, be handled more delicately, although the technique remains the same. The same technique of personalizing the circumstances of the inconsistency should be used, but phrased in terms of error rather than deceitfulness.

In this example, a pediatrician is called as a prosecution expert to testify to the age of a vaginal tear she detected in a five-year-old girl she examined in a sex assault investigation. Her original medical report placed the age of the injury in a way favorable to the defendant. Now, before trial, she has changed her testimony. Nonetheless, she is a physician and her credentials are excellent. The cross-examiner's judgment is that a frontal assault on her credibility would create greater risks than necessary. As a result, the cross-examination is more tuned toward personalizing this change for the jurors, rather than exposing the willingness of the witness to lie to jurors:

Q: Of course you examined the nick quite carefully?

A: Yes.

Q: You noted an absence of echmosis?

A: Yes.

(The series of questions explaining echmosis is omitted.)

Q: An absence of echmosis is medically significant?

A: Yes.

Q: It tells you something about the age of an injury?

A: Yes.

Q: It can't tell you how long ago an injury occurred at a maximum?

A: No, it can't.

Q: But it can tell you how long ago an injury occurred at a minimum?

A: Yes.

Q: You can help us set a rough maximum from your knowledge of pediatrics?

A: Yes.

Q: At a maximum, this injury could have been several months old?

A: Yes.

Q: But your examination of the injury and your findings of a lack of echmosis, do help set a minimum?

A: Yes.

Q: Your exam was 7:15 p.m. on December 19, 2002?

A: Yes.

Q: You could tell this injury was at the very least more than 2 days old?

A: No, I think now that it could have been as little as 24 hours old.

(Impeachment begins.)

Q: Dr. Taylor, you knew on December 19, 2002, at 7:15 p.m. why you were examining this little girl?

A: Yes.

Q: You knew that her mother feared she had been sexually assaulted?

A: Yes.

Q: There is no more concerned person in the world than a mother looking after her child?

A: Pretty much true.

Q: And you knew that her mother was going to ask you had anything happened, what happened, when did it happen?

A: Yes.

Q: So you examined Brandy?

A: Yes.

Q: And we have already discussed your physical findings?

A: Yes.

Q: And then you brought Brandy's mother into the room?

A: Yes.

Q: She was looking to you for guidance?

A: Yes.

Q: She was looking to you for answers?

A: Yes.

Q: She was looking to you for the truth?

A: Yes.

Q: And you had no reason to hold back?

A: No, I wasn't holding back.

Q: You were a doctor looking at a medical problem?

A: Yes.

Q: You were not an advocate?

A: No.

Q: You had to call it the way you saw it?

A: Yes.

Q: You owed that mother the truth about her child?

A: Yes.

Q: And you told that mother your truthful findings?

A: Yes.

Q: Nothing added, nothing subtracted?

A: Yes.

Q: Just the truth?

A: True.

Q: On December 19, 2002, after a thorough and professional examination, you told Brandy's mother that at a maximum the injury could be months old?

A: Yes.

Q: You told her that at a minimum the injury was at least 2 days old?

A: Yes.

Q: You wanted Brandy's mother to know the truth?

A: Of course.

While the jurors probably have no experience equivalent to the physician, some have experience as concerned parents. It is intended that the scenario of a doctor speaking frankly with a parent strike a chord in the jurors to make them more responsive to the physician's earlier advice to the parent.

§ 18.19   Personalize the First Statement for the Jury

Assume an inconsistency between the current version and what the adult first reported to the police, hospital staff, or social services worker concerning what the child said about an assault or a personal injury. Under these circumstances, it is quite easy for the cross-examiner to show that a caring parent would remember and report every nuance of a child's allegation. The jurors are comfortable with the thought that, if they, in their role as parents heard their child complain of an assault or injury, would both remember its details and relate them fully and accurately to the authorities.

Another frequently used technique of personalizing the inconsistency to the jurors is to show that the witness, when reporting a fact, whether it is a traffic accident, a homicide, the description of a robber, or the scenario of a medical procedure, was willing and felt it necessary to be thorough. By showing that the reporting witness knew others in positions of authority would rely on his perceptions, the jurors view the witness who now changes the story as a dangerously erroneous or inconsistent person who cannot be trusted.

§ 18.20 Break the Inconsistency into as Many Separate Changed Facts as Possible

In a divorce case, the husband is seeking custody. On direct examination, the husband has graphically testified that he witnessed his wife hit their child with a coat hanger three times. The husband has testified by deposition that the wife is unfit for custody because of a mental disorder. He further testified by deposition that he did not see the alleged attack by the wife on one of the children with a coat hanger.

Assume that the husband has been irretrievably bound to his current direct testimony version and thereafter he has been bound to the deposition process and the necessity and opportunity to tell the truth.

Q: On March 13, 1999, at your deposition, page 123 line 12, you were under oath and the question was put "Did you see the attack?" and you answered "No?"

A: I said that.

Q: On March 13, 1999, under oath, no coat hanger was mentioned?

A: No.

Q: No "three hits" were mentioned on March 13, 1999?

A: No.

Q: No "picture that won't go away" was remembered on March 13, 1999?

A: No.

Q: No attack on your son was remembered on March 13, 1999?

A: No.

This is an example of a lean, fast-moving technique. The cross-examiner maximizes the damage in a very short burst of questions that quickly and efficiently highlight the number of inconsistencies contained within one "remembered" story. The questions begin with the word "no," just as the witness's answers to the deposition questions were "no."

§ 18.21 Treat Each Initial Story Fact as a Separate Impeachment

Assume that the inconsistency has been shown. On direct examination, the eyewitness to the collision testified that he saw the collision. At his deposition he testified as follows:

Q: Did you see the collision?

A: No, I didn't know it happened until later. I was on the corner, but it was noisy. There was a lot of traffic. I was not looking that way. I was talking to my girlfriend. She had asked me to buy her a drink. We were entering the Sheraton Bar.

In this technique, the cross-examiner won't simply impeach with the fact that the witness has previously testified that he did not see the collision. Instead, each fact contained in the first (true) story will be formed as a separate item of impeachment:

Q: You didn't just say in your deposition testimony that you didn't see the collision?

A: No.

Q: You testified that you didn't even know that it happened?

A: That is correct.

Q: You testified that you didn't know that it happened until later?

A: That is correct.

Q: You testified that you were not even looking that way?

A: Right.

Q: You testified that you were talking to your girlfriend?

A: Right.

Q: You testified you were talking to her and not looking in the direction of the collision?

A: Right.

Q: You testified it was noisy?

A: Right.

Q: You testified you didn't even hear the collision?

A: Right.

Q: You testified you were talking to your girlfriend, you were looking the other way, and you were distracted?

A: Right.

Q: You and your girlfriend were talking about going into the bar?

A: Well, she asked me to buy her a drink.

Q: That is correct, she was asking you to take her into the bar and buy her a drink?

A: Yes.

Q: You were entering the bar?

A: Yes.

Q: For all those reasons you said you had not seen the collision?

A: Right.

This technique is simply a converse of the previous technique. Instead of focusing on the new version, the cross-examiner instead focuses on the details contained in the original statement — details that are now in dispute. Each detail that has "disappeared" or been changed is handled as a separate item of impeachment.

§ 18.22 Looping Off the Inconsistent Version

For major inconsistencies that involve sufficient importance in the case, consider having the witness read the inconsistency first. Then the lawyer can loop (repeat) that inconsistency (see chapter 26, *Loops, Double Loops, and Spontaneous Loops*) back to the witness. The lawyer is forcing the witness to provide a "spontaneous" loop, which is not actually spontaneous because the cross-examiner has required the witness to read aloud from the transcript or document and thus can plan the loop in advance. Example:

Q: A few moments ago, you told us that you recalled my client performed "adequately" on the straight leg lifting test?

A: Yes.

Q: But that is not what you said when asked that question in your deposition.

A: I believe it is.

Q: To be precise, at page 20, line 12 of the deposition, I asked you, "How did Julie do on the straight leg lifting test?"

A: Yes, I recall the question.

Q: Please read to the jury your answer at page 20, line 14.

A: "Well, she had some problems, actually some significant difficulty with that test. She seemed quite weak."

Q: "Some significant difficulty" is the term you used, Doctor?

A: Yes, I did.

Q: The "significant difficulty" was in simply raising her leg, while keeping her knee straight?

A: That is the test.

Q: The "significant difficulty" was that she could no longer do with great effort what the average person can do with little effort?

A: Yes, well, in that particular test, she was having problems.

In this manner the cross-examiner maximizes the damage by ordering the witness to impeach himself before looping the inconsistency. The frequent reaction of a witness undergoing this form of impeachment is to answer in a monotone or barely audible voice in an attempt to minimize his prior statement. This alone speaks to the jury about the credibility of the witness and his real time coping.

§ 18.23 Serial Impeachment

In chapter 11, *Sequences of Cross-Examination*, there is a discussion of the need to spread impeachments throughout the cross-examination in order to better control the witness. However, there are those occasions in which a series of impeachments may be performed back to back as a method of highlighting the overall lack of credibility of the witness. This technique is termed serial impeachment. The effort here is to string together as many inconsistencies or inaccuracies as possible, regardless of their relative strength to show that the witness simply should not be believed because of the sheer number of inconsistencies.

The cross-examiner must be careful to develop only those inconsistencies that are not likely to be viewed as trivial. An inconsistency that is minor can still be real. But when two versions of a fact seem very similar, whether major or minor, the cross-examiner runs the risk of appearing unfair by suggesting that the answers are inconsistent. If one inconsistency out of ten is not fair, the impact of the other nine inconsistencies is diluted. For example, if an officer has filled out a standard motor vehicle collision report and made an error on the direction of north, the average jury, absent other compelling facts, will not consider that inaccuracy to be very noteworthy.

Add to that factual situation that the investigating officer has pointed north in the direction of south, has labeled the cross streets inappropriately (that is, Poplar Street is shown as Elm Street, and Elm Street as Poplar) and has inadvertently miscalculated the "military time" on the collision report, the jury may now be led to believe (by these multiple inaccuracies) that the witness is unworthy of trust:

Q: Officer, you have north pointing towards the top of this diagram?

A: Yes.

Q: While, in fact, the true direction of north is at the bottom of the diagram?

A: I guess that is true.

Q: That is true?

A: Yes.

Q: You have labeled the street that runs horizontally on the diagram as Elm?

A: Yes.

Q: And, in fact, that street is Poplar?

A: Yes.

Q: You have labeled the street running vertically on the diagram as Poplar?

A: Yes.

Q: When, in fact, that is Elm Street?

A: Yes.

Q: For this investigation, which you have called "thorough," you have even shown the wrong time of the day when this collision occurred?

A: Yes.

Perhaps none of these inaccuracies are critical to the issue of how the collision occurred, but when strung together they begin to lead the listener to question whether this witness can be trusted on any matters requiring accuracy.

§18.24 Serial Impeachment Leads to Spontaneous Loops

When the witness is confronted with one impeachment after another, even if they are relatively "small" impeachments, some witnesses feel the urge to explain why there have been so many inconsistencies. Experts particularly attempt to explain. This leads to the opportunity for the cross-examiner to spontaneous loop the unresponsive answer to the witness for effect (see chapter 26, *Loops, Double Loops, and Spontaneous Loops*). Example:

Q: You are a CPA?

A: Yes.

Q: You are a CPA who specializes in valuations?

A: Yes.

Q: You completed this report?

A: Yes.

Q: You completed all of the calculations in the report?

A: Yes, I did.

Q: In paragraph 7, there is a mathematical error that amounts to $1,014.00?

A: Yes, you pointed that out.

Q: In paragraph 13, there is a mathematical error that amounts to $9,056.00?

A: Yes, it is tied to the first error.

Q: In paragraph 15, there is a mathematical error that amounts to $17,389.00?

A: Yes, it is also related.

Q: And finally in paragraph 19, there is a mathematical error that amounts to $27,983.00?

A: Yes.

Q: You made those four errors just on the mathematics in your report?

A: It was one error compounded.

Q: You say the errors are compounded? (spontaneous loop)

A: Yes, they are related.

Q: You are telling this jury that one of your errors compounded at least four times to create a larger and larger error? (reloop)

A: Yes. (The cross continues.)

By the use of the spontaneous loop, the trial lawyer has maximized the effect of the serial impeachment.

In the next example involving an accident investigation reconstruction, the opportunities to spontaneous loop presents themselves multiple times:

Q: All of the accident investigation and reconstruction depends upon accuracy in the initial measurements, doesn't it?

A: Yes, sir.

Q: Kind of like the computer, if you put garbage in, you get garbage out?

A: Yes, sir.

Q: If the accuracy is wrong, then your conclusion is wrong?

A: It would be, yes, sir.

Q: In your diagram, you have twelve feet for the third lane, the lane Officer Predovich was traveling in?

A: Twelve feet, yes.

Q: Would you mark that, please?

A: Yes, sir.

Q: You marked all the rest of the lanes twelve feet too, right?

A: Yes, sir.

Q: Mark in all the twelves that you marked on your diagram. The only reason I'm asking you to mark twelve, that's what your diagram shows.

A: Yes, sir.

Q: And your report is based upon the diagram?

A: Yes.

Q: Now, what you said on the diagram was that from the median to the middle of her car was thirty-seven feet?

A: Thirty-seven feet.

Q: Would you mark it in?

(Witness complies.)

Q: That is absolutely wrong, isn't it?

A: What?

Q: It is not thirty-seven feet from the median to the middle of her car, is it?

A: No, it should be thirty-seven feet to the outside tire mark.

Q: That's not what you chose to mark on your diagram, is it?

A: No.

Q: It's thirty-seven feet, according to you, to the end of lane # 1, isn't that true?

A: According to that diagram, yes.

Q: So according to your diagram, Faye Predovich's car is over here in lane # 2?

A: According to my diagram it's in the center of that lane.

Q: OK. According to the diagram her car is here, but the feet are wrong, the measurement is wrong?

A: One of them must be, yes, sir.

Q: But you never looked down and said twelve, twenty-four, thirty-six, is different from thirty-seven to the middle, did you?

A: No.

Q: You just saw that today?

A: Just saw it today, sir.

Q: You do not have a more important case on your desk, do you?

A: No, sir.

Q: You had sufficient time to look at this diagram before she was charged with a felony?

A: Probably so, sir.

Q: In fact, you do not know even today that that first lane that you say is twelve feet is more than fourteen feet?

A: I won't argue with you, sir.

Q: In accident reconstruction, seconds and inches count, don't they?

A: Yes, sir.

Q: In accident reconstruction investigation, inches can make the difference, right?

A: They can.

Q: You do not have any idea today if any of these measurements are truly accurate measurements?

A: No, sir, I don't.

Q: Please mark the widths of these lanes.

(Witness complies.)

Q: Now, you are telling us you personally actually measured all these distances and widths?

A: I measured all of them.

Q: Would it interest you to know that your measurements are inaccurate on those too?

A: Sure.

Q: Would that be something that you would like to know?

A: Sure.

Q: And a foot or two, an inch or two makes a difference?

A: It could. Those are approximate for the accident report.

Q: These are rounded off, right?

A: Yes, sir.

Q: She is charged with a felony for driving misconduct, you are the only investigator on the scene, and you round off the numbers?

A: On lane widths, yes.

Q: Sometimes you rounded up and sometimes you rounded down?

A: Depending on the extra.

Q: So if I said to you today under oath what are the real measurements of these lanes, not the rounded off, you do not know them?

A: I can look, sir — check my notes.

Q: These are your rough notes, right?

A: Yes, sir.

Q: So the official report isn't as accurate as the rough notes?

A: That's correct.

Q: What the prosecutor gets as an official report has every single lane involved in this accident rounded off, guessed at?

A: Yes, sir.

Q: Nowhere in any of your courses did it say that was proper?

A: It doesn't.

Q: Nowhere did it even come close to say, look, when pressed for time, don't be accurate?

A: No, it doesn't say that.

Q: In all the books and in all the courses you've taken they have said to you, "For God's sake, be accurate?"

A: Nearly every one.

Q: It's the whole heart of investigation, isn't it?

A: The accuracy that is being expounded upon here by you and by the books is leveled very heavily on the tire marks and evidentiary data that is available. There is no excuse, and I don't intend to offer one as to why I screwed up on the lane widths. I did.

Q: The fact of the matter is that things in the field just aren't like they are in the book, isn't that the truth?

A: That frequently happens.

Q: So they told you to be careful and prudent in your measurements, and you were something other than careful and prudent?

A: On those lane widths, yes.

Q: And you were the man solely charged with this responsibility?

A: Yes, sir.

Q: You agree that's a gross deviation from the standards of conduct for an investigator and reconstructionist?

A: It probably would be.

As the witness gives unresponsive answers, the tone and the aggressiveness of the cross-examination can be amplified as the jury hears the unresponsive answers as excuses that can only negatively affect the credibility of the witness.

§ 18.25 The "Big Bang" Impeachment

Another technique of impeachment is built upon the use of a single important impeachment. If there is but a single large and important impeachment to be performed, the cross-examination must make special efforts to appropriately highlight the impeachment by focusing attention on this one area of the case. In setting up such a major impeachment, it is imperative that the cross-examiner use the opening statement as an opportunity to focus the attention of the fact finder on the coming impeachment. Having successfully performing the impeachment, the advocate should recapture that moment and its importance within the closing argument. In cross-examination, this one area of impeachment must be held up under a magnifying glass so that the jury appreciates every nuance of the change of stories on this issue.

Whether to conduct "serial" impeachments or the "big bang" impeachment is not a question of choice, but a question of availability. Cross-examiners do not create "big bang" impeachments. Facts either lend themselves to it or they don't. However, the cross-examiner is in a position to allow the fact finder to more fully appreciate the importance of the "big bang" impeachment. The cross-examiner is in a position to decide whether serial impeachments will be effective with a given witness. The cross-examiner can always withhold impeachment on any proffered or available inconsistency.

In accordance with the principles of primacy and recency (chapter 12), it is important to remember that if the cross-examiner is to perform a serial impeachment, the cross-examiner should start the string of impeachments with a particularly strong impeachment and finish the string of impeachments with another strong impeachment.

There are two reasons for this sequencing of the chapters of impeachment. First, the jury must be left with the impression that the multiple impeachments were for a purpose and involved important material. Second, the string of impeachments will affect the witness who must cope in real time with the realization that he has contradicted himself on many occasions. By saving the strongest impeachment for last, the witness will often realize that the worst contradiction has not yet been revealed. As a result the witness will often begin worrying about that upcoming contradiction. This will add to the anxiety of the witness and may cause the witness to visibly display that anxiety. Virtually any display of anxiety will further or weaken the credibility of the witness.

§ 18.26   More Than One Inconsistency on a Single Point

What does the cross-examiner do when the direct testimony is different from a prior deposition statement and is different from a statement taken in an interview? Each of the prior statements is different from each other as well; that is, there are three separate and distinct statements, all independently inconsistent with each other.

There are two basic techniques to handle this very advantageous scenario. The advocate is reminded that the proper goal of impeachment is not merely to show a change of stories, it is to invest an earlier statement with greater believability. When there are multiple statements from which to choose, the cross-examiner is searching for the statement that most assists her case or has the greatest propensity to undermine the opponent's theory of the case.

First, the cross-examiner can decide to impeach only with the most helpful inconsistent statement and not mention to the jury the other inconsistent statement. This is not an ethical decision, but a tactical one. Alternatively, the cross-examiner may chose to show to the jury both prior inconsistent statements and show that they are inconsistent with each other. Thus, all forms of the fact or event will be before the jury.

The rationale for the first method is to show the jury that the witness, when previously testifying, gave facts supportive of the cross-examiner's theory of the case and that this earlier version is to be believed in preference to "today's" version. The rationale for the second method is to show the jury that the witness has repeatedly told contradictory and inconsistent versions. Therefore the witness should not be believed at all on this issue.

Whether to exercise the first method or the second method is a question of judgment and common sense for the cross-examiner. Among the factors to be calculated are the credibility of the witness up to that point in the trial, the value of any one of the multiple available inconsistent statements to the cross-examiner's theory of the case, and the likelihood of convincing a jury of the "truth" of any one of the earlier versions. On the other hand, multiple impeachments of versions of a single story fit quite well inside a "serial" impeachment technique. It says to the jury: This witness changes lot of little things, and sometimes changes things more than once.

In exercising judgment on the appropriate technique, the cross-examiner must remember that if she does not cross-examine on both inconsistent statements, the opponent may choose to do so on redirect examination. However, this decision is more than a little problematic for the opponent, who may be seen by the jury as joining in the attack on the credibility of the witness the opponent put on the stand.

For example, in a divorce case, the husband is alleged to own an asset that the wife contends is worth $200,000. The husband has testified on direct examination that it is worth $50,000. Before trial, the husband submitted a loan application to a bank in which he claimed the asset was worth $250,000. In conversations with tax authorities, the husband testified that it was worth $75,000. To the wife on numerous occasions, the husband said that the asset was worth $100,000. To the wife's attorney at deposition, the husband testified that the asset was worth between $30,000 and $50,000.

The cross-examiner might choose to put in the bank document only — showing a value of $250,000. The cross-examiner might choose to put in the bank document ($250,000), as well as the statements to the wife ($100,000), to show his testimony of $50,000 is intentionally low. Or the cross-examiner might put in all the versions: Bank — $250,000; statements to wife — $100,000; husband's testimony — $75,000; deposition — $30 — 50,000. This latter technique permits the cross-examiner to argue not any one of the husband's estimates is more believable than the others, but that none are to be trusted since the witness is shown to be willing to say whatever is necessary, depending on the audience.

Amend the example and leave only the bank loan application ($250,000) and the IRS estimate ($75,000). The cross-examiner might still choose to introduce both in order to impeach the general credibility of the husband. However, the cross-examiner might well elect to impeach only with the bank loan document, trying to invest it with as many circumstances of reliability as possible, and argue that this husband is credible on this estimate. Under this scenario, the cross-examiner would never mention the IRS estimate of $75,000, event though it casts doubt on the husband's trial testimony of $50,000. Having ignored this second inconsistency, the cross-examiner leaves to the direct examiner the tough choice as to whether to introduce it in redirect. If so, the husband's own lawyer is pressing the husband to be less than credible in his own testimony. If not, the direct examiner must now seek out an explanation for the painfully inconsistent $250,000 value.

§ 18.27   When the Newest Version Is the Most Helpful: To Impeach or Not to Impeach

Assume that the unusual occurs: The most current version of the testimony, as given in direct examination, is more helpful than the previous version because the current version better fits the cross-examiner's theory of the case or has a greater propensity to undermine the opponent's theory of the case.

The cross-examiner should not impeach with a prior unhelpful or less helpful statement or omission. The cross-examiner who listens attentively to the direct examination (see § 16.35) will mentally register that the new version is inconsistent with prior statements. However, the value of the impeachment is outweighed by the value of the admission. Regardless of its impeachability, the new version, which is consistent with the cross-examiner's theory of the case, is more helpful as a credible statement. Not only must the impeaching version be ignored, all efforts must be directed toward supporting the new and more helpful version. The cross-examiner can gently assist the witness in explaining to the jury why the witness is able to make the statement that the lawyer wishes to support. It is unwise to alert the witness that he has made a previous inconsistent statement on that very topic. The cross-examiner should tie the witness to the current version of the fact.

The cross-examiner may feel some sense of frustration because the cross-examiner is passing up an easy impeachment but the temptation to impeach must be resisted.

The value of the prior inconsistency is far outweighed by the damage that the cross-examiner would do to the case by pursuing the impeachment. Inasmuch as the new version is more helpful to the cross-examiner, or more harmful to the direct examiner's theory of the case, the cross-examiner may presume the direct examiner did not see the change coming. If the new version was first stated on direct examination, the direct examiner probably was quite surprised and moved away from the area as quickly as possible. Now, on cross-examination, the technique to exercise is to completely bind the witness to the direct testimony version so that the witness cannot be "rehabilitated" by the upcoming redirect examination.

The opponent's purpose on redirect will be to lead the witness away from this new version and back to the earlier, more helpful version in order to guard against the ability of the direct examiner to redirect the witness back to his earlier version. The cross-examiner should use a series of leading questions to provide the witness with facts and circumstances that caused the witness to feel even more confident in the answer he has just given. The tone and manner of the cross-examiner should be matter-of-fact. The voice of the cross-examiner suggests, "Of course this is the truth." The effect of such leading questions is to bolster the witness both factually and psychologically so that the witness is more likely to resist the opponent's efforts at "rehabilitation" on redirect examination. Even if the opponent can successfully encourage the witness to repudiate the new version and adopt the previous and inconsistent version of facts, the damage cannot be undone. The jury will also resist this effort and see it for what it is. Most opponents will decline to try to rehabilitate.

§ 18.28 Making Use of External Inconsistencies

External inconsistencies come in four distinct varieties: inconsistencies between or among witnesses, inconsistencies between a witness and an item of physical evidence, inconsistencies between a witness and facts that are implied by the witness to exist but that that does not exist, and inconsistencies with things not done. To be sure, inconsistencies between a witness and things not done, and inconsistencies between a witness and things that do not exist, are actually inconsistencies by omission. An inconsistency between a witness and things not done or things that do not exist, makes use of the same rules and considerations that apply to impeachment by omission (see chapter 17, *Impeachment by Omission*).

As to any inconsistency between or among witnesses and inconsistencies between a witness and physical evidence, such inconsistency will be handled using techniques similar to those techniques employed in inconsistent statement impeachments rather than the techniques that apply to impeachment by omission.

As to all four types of impeachment, steps 1 through 8 of impeachment by inconsistent statements will apply (see chapter 16, *Eight Steps of Impeachment by Inconsistent Statement*).

When equipped with an inconsistency between witnesses, too often cross-examiners display the inconsistency to the hostile witness and then ask the hostile witness to explain why the inconsistency exists. This is a poor tactic. Witnesses who are invited to give explanations will often come up with explanations. Alternatively the cross-examiner may be tempted to ask the argumentative question, "Are you saying that witness Jones is lying?" This is also poor on many grounds.

Ordinarily, it is unwise to confront the witness with the fact that their testimony on a particular point is inconsistent with the testimony of other witnesses or with physical evidence or the lack of physical evidence that should be present according to the witness's testimony. It is safer and more effective to discuss the inconsistency in closing argument when the witness is no longer on the stand to explain. That does not mean that there are no techniques that may be used under the circumstances to highlight the inconsistency. In such circumstances, since both Step 6 (expose the inconsistent statement) and Step 7 (maximize the damage) will not be done, the process of tying the witness to the current version should be done in order to maximize the differences between the two versions.

However before engaging in this tactic, the cross-examiner must gauge who is likely to win the battle of credibility — the witness being tied to a version of a fact or the other witness or document that will be used to impeach the witness. Only if the contest is wholly and unquestionably stacked in favor of the other witness or the contrasting physical evidence should be cross-examiner engage in a Step 4 technique (tie the witness to the current version). If there is a true contest of credibility, the cross-examiner should forgo all techniques that support the witness being cross-examined and instead let the answer stand naked, without support. In contrast, the cross-examiner will do all possible to support and bolster the more helpful version given by another witness or piece of evidence.

§ 18.29　Using Charts to Maximize Damages by Inconsistencies

In maximizing the damage caused by the revealing of an inconsistency, charts are often useful. Consider Chart 1 below. During the testimony of witness Gayle, only that portion of the chart showing Gayle is shown to the witness and to the jury. It would show that witness Gayle testified that the red light was directed to the defendant, but that the defendant's speed was not excessive and that there were no other witnesses available to see the collision.

When witness Hank was called, Hank is only shown that line of the chart that shows that he testified that the red light was to the defendant, but that he did not know the speed of the vehicle and did not know if there are other witnesses.

Finally, when witness Miller is called, Miller is shown only that line of the chart that applies to him, which shows that the red light was not to the defendant, but that the defendant's speed was excessive and that there were no other witnesses that could view the collision.

Then in the plaintiff's second closing argument, the jury is shown all of the versions put together and shown that the plaintiff's case and the witnesses for the plaintiff are inconsistent with one another.

Chart 1

	Red Light	Speed	Other Witnesses
Gayle — Witness 1	Yes	No	No
Hank — Witness 2	Yes	?	?
Miller — Witness 3	No	Yes	No

In a criminal case example, a chart can be used equally well for differences with witnesses and the known and conceded physical facts. The defendant in this example is in his early twenties. He is six feet, two inches tall and does not have any facial hair or scars.

When witness Jordan is cross-examined, Jordan will be shown (as will the jury) (see Chart 2) the fact that he has testified that the height is six foot three, the age is thirty, the robber had a beard, and he is not sure if there was a scar visible or not.

When witness Houston testifies, he will be shown his line, which will confirm his testimony that the height was five foot seven, the age from thirty to thirty-seven, that there was only a mustache on the robber, and there was clearly a scar on the robber's face.

When witness Ryan was cross-examined, he would be shown that portion of the chart that shows that the robber was five foot seven, in his early twenties, had no beard, and had no scar.

In final argument, the chart can be used to illustrate the inconsistencies and discrepancies between the various witnesses, as well as to show the actual physical facts.

Chart 2

	Height	Age	Beard	Scar
Jordan	6'3"	30	Yes	?
Houston	5'7"	30-37	Mustache	Face
Ryan	5'7"	Early 20s	None	None
Physical Facts	6'2"	Early 20s	None	None

Each witness is not confronted with or even informed of the other witnesses' testimony because it would be improper to ask one witness to comment on another witness's testimony. On a more practical level, when one witness is confronted with contradictory testimony of another witness or contradiction by physical facts, it inevitably causes the witness to enter spontaneously into an explanation that is difficult or impossible to control on cross-examination.

Prosecutors can also make use of this technique. When a defendant or other defense witness testifies in a manner inconsistent with other witnesses or with the physical evidence, a chart displaying this inconsistency can be of great benefit during closing argument. A technique to bring alive this conflict in the evidence during the cross-examination is to ask leading questions to the witness being cross-examined designed to establish that the other witnesses were in a perfectly good position to observe the matter upon which they testified. The hostile witness should not be asked to comment on the substance of the inconsistent testimony, but can be placed in a position where he, in essence, vouched for the ability of another witness to accurately observe.

§ 18.30 Avoiding Offering Opportunities for the Witness to Explain

The jury wants to know why a witness has testified to one set of facts at a given time and then testified on a different occasion to a different set of facts. But the cross-examiner never offers a witness a "why" question on cross-examination. In matters of inconsistency, it is equally unwise to invite the witness to explain the situation that, on its face, hurts the credibility of the witness. The time and place to explain the witness's motivation to the jury is in the cross-examiner's closing argument. At that phase of the trial, the witness can no longer contradict the cross-examiner nor teach the jury. If the witness is asked why the story has changed, the witness inevitably has a perfectly reasonable and logical explanation. Whether the witness intentional deceives or is honestly mistaken, the witness will have an acceptable explanation for the jury. There is no need for the cross-examiner to seek it out. In any event, the cross-examiner is likely to hear more about this than he or she wished during the opponent's redirect examination.

In a simulated trial concerning the crime of the century, the assassination of President John F. Kennedy, an experienced cross-examiner, Vincent Bugliosi, was cross-examining a defense expert witness. The witness had testified in direct examination over twenty-five years ago and had not then been cross-examined. He had never told the Warren Commission, he had never told the Congressional Committee on Assassinations, and he had never told the Federal Bureau of Investigation about certain facts concerning John F. Kennedy's brain injury. The defense team, led by Gerry Spence, was offering this evidence as critical to the defense. After skillfully establishing that the witness had never testified to these facts and had failed to tell anyone about this evidence, including various government entities and the cross-examiner in a recent telephone conversation, Mr. Bugliosi asked the witness, in effect: "Why didn't you ever tell anyone this before, on what has to be the crime of the century?" The response of the witness, who had been in the military at the time of the assassination, was, in essence, "I had been ordered not to talk with anyone about the assassination and the autopsy."

Mr. Bugliosi skillfully attempted to extricate himself from this explanation of a twenty-five year silence. Unfortunately, the eyes of the jury were not watching and, it must be assumed, the ears of the jury were not listening. When it comes to motivation for change, the best the cross-examiner can do is break even. More often than not, it is worse. Save the subject of "why" until closing argument.

Chapter 19

CONTROLLING THE RUNAWAY WITNESS

SYNOPSIS

§ 19.01 The Fear

The question calls for a yes or no answer. The witness is entitled to give either answer. Instead, the witness responds with a narrative. The answer may be long or short. The answer may contain words that amount to "yes" or "no," or the answer may entirely evade the question being asked. In all of these events, the cross-examiner is confronted with a "runaway witness."

The chief problem of a "runaway witness" is his effect on the ability of the cross-examiner to paint the precise picture in each chapter goal. The more wordy the answer, the more the picture may be distorted or muddied by the inclusion of unnecessary information. The runaway witness is attempting to take over, if even for a moment, as the guide to the facts. The cross-examiner will ordinarily want to extinguish this behavior as it is the cross-examiner who is best able to communicate the most important facts to the jury.

The runaway witness often attempts to insert facts, descriptions, and interpretations of his choosing. This type of witness is not merely distorting the picture being painted by the cross-examiner; he is trying to paint a contrary picture of his own choosing.

The runaway witness ranks as one of the greatest fears of the cross-examiner. However, one of the greatest opportunities to the cross-examiner is when the witness is unresponsive. An unresponsive or runaway witness often appears without notice, and sometimes when least expected. That is part of the fear. The fear expands because once the runaway witness surfaces the lawyer is enmeshed in a battle to retain control of the cross-examination. Thoughts of opportunity are not present as the unprepared cross-examiner struggles to regain control.

Expert witnesses and professional witnesses (those witnesses who testify more often than anything else in their careers whether an expert or not) heighten the fear of the cross-examiner more often than other witnesses. In this age of *Daubert*, where experts and other professionals who testify must do so for a living, the cross-examiner is posed with greater challenges. These professional witnesses are purposefully unresponsive and have refined their skills to artfully dodge the cross-examiner's question.

§ 19.02 Definition of the Runaway Witness

A runaway witness is any witness who is unresponsive to the question put on cross-examination. This unresponsiveness may take many forms. The witness can answer the question on cross, but in such a way as to make the answer unintelligible. The witness can refuse to answer the question put on cross and answer a different question. The witness can answer generally the question on cross, but include many other answers to questions not asked. The witness can volunteer prejudicial information to dramatic effect. The witness (particularly the expert or professional witness) can object to the question posed and in some instances rule on his own objection, without ever answering the question.

Example:

Q: Professor, you never measured the circumference of the aluminum alloy tube?

A: I didn't consider it to be relevant. In fact, I don't consider it relevant now. I am sure that it is not relevant. What I did was . . .

§ 19.03   Establishing Control

At times the witness becomes non-responsive so quickly that control was not lost, but was really never established.

Below is an excerpt from a divorce trial, with the defendant called for purposes of cross-examination:

Q: Raise your right hand, please. Do you swear that the testimony you are about to give this court on the matter pending before the court is the whole truth and nothing but the truth, so help you God?

A: I do. I would like to also make clear, Mr. Dodd, that I was not—it is not manic depressant. It is psychothymic, and there is a big difference.

Q: Thank you. Is that in response to the oath or the question I did not ask you?

Caught totally by surprise, cross-examining counsel offers up an objectionable question. Worse yet, the only three rules (see chapter 8, *The Only Three Rules of Cross-Examination*) are not followed, therefore providing opportunity for another non-responsive answer:

A: The question you did not ask. I would just like to clear it up, that it was not manic depressant, it was psychothymic that I was dismissed for.

Q: The fact is you are still on Lithium?

A: Yes.

A quick return by the cross-examiner to the only three rules, and control is beginning to be established.

Such witnesses give trial lawyers a lot of sleepless nights and make other careers appear safer and wiser. Fortunately, there are a number of tried and true techniques that the skillful trial lawyer can use to subdue, and ultimately, control non-responsive witnesses.

Many of these techniques focus on the opportunity given the cross-examiner by the unresponsive answer. All are designed to re-establish control and re-focus the fact finder on the lawyer to guide and teach the lawsuit.

As shown in the example above, cross-examining counsel, even when experienced and confident in his own abilities, can react poorly to the unresponsive witness. Whether it is an ongoing argument with the witness, a childish remark to the witness, or unprofessional conduct (all of which probably could be said about the example), counsel "looks bad" to the jury, to the judge, to the opponent, and worst of all, to the witness. The lawyer's resort to one-upmanship, invariably leads to the unresponsive witness battling the unwary lawyer. In these moments of near panic, now more than ever, the lawyer must resist these ego-related impulses and rely instead on the techniques of control. The lawyer may well "one up" the witness, but that teaches nothing and distracts the fact finder from learning in real time the important facts that support the cross-examiner's theory of the case.

Empirical research has disclosed many techniques for stopping the runaway witness. With these techniques the cross-examiner will be able to stop or take advantage of even the most incorrigible witness's run-on answer. Many times, the most incorrigible run-on answer comes from the lips of the professional or expert witness. Some techniques work best against the professional or expert witness. Some of the techniques illustrated will be incorporated into the trial lawyer's repertoire of courtroom techniques to be used on a regular basis. Others would be used best on isolated occasions. Still others are better performed in a setting of a deposition or other non-jury setting.

It has been asked why there are so many different techniques to control the runaway witness. The answer is that there are many different types of runaway witnesses in many different settings. Different techniques are needed for different situations. But a deeper, more meaningful answer is found in the varied personalities and styles of cross-examiner's throughout the world. Some techniques come naturally for certain lawyers, while other lawyers struggle with those same techniques. Consistent with this statement is that some lawyers prefer to use certain techniques above others. It is a question of style and personality, as well as the circumstances under which the technique would be used. A wide selection of techniques is helpful for the variations of trial witnesses and situations.

§ 19.04 These Techniques Create Drama in the Courtroom So the Lawyer Does Not Have to Speak or Act Loudly

None of the techniques for controlling a runaway witness require or encourage the use of loud, argumentative, or offensive language. Grandiose gestures are discouraged. These techniques are designed to eliminate the feeling that such conduct is necessary.

When the trial lawyer eliminates offensive, inappropriate conduct as a method of controlling the runaway witness, the judge (see chapter 22, *Voice, Movement, Body Language, and Timing*) seldom cuts off the cross-examination. Opposing counsel is presented with less opportunity to object. Most importantly the jury does not observe rudeness, ugliness, and unprofessional conduct from the cross-examining trial lawyer. Inappropriate or emotional responses by the cross-examiner are often understood or misunderstood by the jurors as proof that the witness is doing damage to the cross-examiner's case. The techniques outlined below rely more on the skill, psychology, and self-control of the lawyer to contain the runaway witness. These techniques verify for the jury that the cross-examiner will not be dissuaded by such witness tactics, but will get to the truth of the matter despite such tactics.

Though some of these techniques allow for a voice that is different than the tone used in previous questions, each of the techniques can be delivered in any conversational voice. The techniques may be accompanied by a change of position in the courtroom, or a gesture, but such physical components of a particular technique rely less on confrontational body language and movement, and more on the change of tone or posture itself. All these techniques can be accomplished with a slower rather than faster rhythm in the questioning, though again, there may be occasions when the cross-examiner will change the rhythm as a method of enhancing a particular technique. The important thing to remember is this: The techniques so solidly confront the unresponsive witness, that the cross-examiner need not raise her voice, move with aggressive or confrontational gestures, or speak faster.

As the trial lawyer gains confidence in her ability to use these techniques to bring the witness back under control, the cross-examiner is likely to adopt a more assured and more self-disciplined tone of questioning. Because the cross-examiner is functioning as a teacher, rather than as an advocate, jurors are more inclined to view the runaway witness as an impediment to the orderly process of trial. The behavior of the witness is more akin to an interruption than an exploration of the facts. In teaching her theory of the case to the judge or jury, rudeness, loud voice, threatening movements, and rapid-fire questioning are all counterproductive to the cross-examiner. The techniques discussed within this chapter permit the cross-examiner to quietly and methodically reign in unresponsive and out-of-control runaway witnesses without distracting the fact finder from listening and absorbing the cross-examiner's theory of the case. By eliminating the opponents' objections and judges who interrupt cross-examinations because of the use of loud and ugly language and body language, there are fewer distractions during the cross-examination. Teaching is improved.

§ 19.05   Relationship of Techniques to the Only Three Rules of Cross-Examination

With one dramatic and seldom-used exception, the foundation of each of the techniques to control the runaway witness is fully grounded in the three rules of cross-examination (see chapter 8, *The Only Three Rules of Cross-Examination*). The cross-examiner cannot deviate from: (1) leading questions; (2) one fact per question; or (3) a logical progression from the general to the specific ending in one goal. Lawyers who have studied and become comfortable with those three building blocks of cross-examination understand how they are the major method of controlling the ability of a witness to evade the question. But all lawyers still experience discomfort when a runaway witness begins to flee from the question asked, so each lawyer must remind herself of the necessity of employing these three rules in those moments of discomfort. If the three rules of cross-examination are fundamental to the orderly presentation of evidence, they are even more important when the witness seeks to interrupt that orderly presentation. They are the basis for the more specialized techniques used to control the runaway witness.

§ 19.06 Behavior Is Molded by Consequences

Remember psychology 101 from college? Remember the maze that the little white rats were placed in? The rats learned that if they performed well they were rewarded with a food pellet, but if they performed poorly they received no reward or worse, negative feedback. This was the concept of the Skinner box introduced by psychologist B.F. Skinner. The concept remains true for all thinking organisms.

The people who take the stand as witnesses are thinking organisms. They have learned through innumerable experiences that good behavior will be rewarded and that bad behavior will be punished. Many witnesses do not understand what is expected of them as a witness. They need cues as to what is acceptable behavior in answering a leading question. Some witnesses know what is expected of them, but for their own purposes seek to ignore the rules of conduct implicit in a leading question format. As to both types of witness the cross-examiner using these techniques seeks to reward good conduct by giving positive reinforcement to the witness who answers "yes" or "no." Likewise, if the runaway witness is engaging in a form of conduct the lawyer wishes to discourage, the cross-examiner applies negative consequences to the runaway answer.

What is an acceptable means of rewarding the short, direct answer to a leading question? When the witness is responding with simple direct answers (preferably yes), rewards include a gentle encouraging nod of the head, a pleasant teaching voice and most important, efficient movement to the next question, the next subject matter, and the next chapter. Do not create an impediment to the "yes" answer. If the witness has agreed with the fact suggested by the cross-examiner, the witness has earned a reward. A change to a harsher tone of voice, a negative gesture, or a follow-up question that suggests that "yes" is a foolish, illogical, or undesirable answer, all serve to sanction the witness for agreeing with the cross-examiner. The cross-examiner would not punish her coworkers, her children, or her pets for doing what she wanted them to do. For the same reason she cannot afford to punish a witness for answering "yes."

On the other hand, when the witness becomes a runaway witness by using unresponsive answers, volunteering information, or by a myriad of other evasive devices, sanctions must be applied. The techniques that are discussed in this chapter apply those sanctions. Some of the sanctions are severe by courtroom standards. Some are more gentle and encouraging. With this said, let there be no misunderstanding: They are all negative stimuli. The techniques for controlling the runaway witness all employ negative feedback as a means of extinguishing unwanted behavior.

§ 19.07   Trials Provide a Difficult Environment in Which to Work

Every trial lawyer knows that good evidence presentations — particularly on cross-examination — are built methodically. Trial lawyers also know that a well-planned cross-examination chapter can get off-track very quickly. This is a demonstration of Murphy's asymmetrical principle:

Things go right gradually, but they go wrong all at once.

Such is the nature of cross-examining hostile witnesses. A witness who runs away can undermine a lawyer's methodical preparation, careful construction of individual questions, and thoughtful implementation of building those questions into chapters. Understanding this as the backdrop of the environment in which a cross-examiner toils daily, the need for techniques that are judicially acceptable, non-objectionable, simple to apply, and effective, cannot be overstated.

§ 19.08   Techniques That Don't Work

[1]   "Just Answer 'Yes' or 'No'"

Television, movies, and, unfortunately, some trial skill programs in law school have encouraged trial lawyers to fall back on the command, "Just answer my question 'yes' or 'no,'" as a method of controlling the runaway witness. This is *not* a valid controlling technique. First, most judges will not permit the lawyer to do that. They will inform the witness that they may explain their answer, even at length, if necessary.

More importantly, a lawyer's resort to using oratorical blunt force signals to the jury that the cross-examiner is not playing fair. The lack of choice given the witness suggests to the jury that the lawyer is trying to "trick" the witness. Non-lawyers resent this heavy-handed attempt to straitjacket the witness. To them it appears that the lawyer is attempting to "put words in the witness's mouth." A lawyer resorting to this method lowers both her personal credibility and the credibility of the leading question as an appropriate teaching device.

Inevitably the opposing attorney objects to the admonition that the witness "just answer 'yes' or 'no.'" The objection creates an unwanted break in the leading question and short answer technique. There is a break in the teaching of the cross-examiner's theory of the case. The objection is a distraction. More often than not, when objected to under these circumstances, the cross-examiner reacts poorly, emotionally, and overstates her position rather than responding calmly to the objection. This creates more distraction. The jury is often completely distracted from the importance of the question.

Expert witnesses have often been trained to respond to the lawyer directing them to "just answer yes or no" whether or not the opposing lawyer objects. Their response is along these lines: "I cannot adequately explain (teach) to the judge or the jury the full answer to your question with just a 'yes or no.'" Whether or not this is true, the response further aggravates the situation. Again, the net result is that the cross-examiner looks to be playing games.

Credibility is the paramount feature of the successful trial lawyer. When the trial lawyer loses her credibility, the case is lost. Credibility is severely damaged when the cross-examiner utters the words, "just answer my question with a 'yes or no.'" Don't do it.

[2] Asking the Judge for Help

[a] Court-Offered Help

In frustration, some cross-examiners will ask the judge to order the witness to "just answer 'yes' or 'no.'" Asking the judge to help in this way is an impractical way to control a runaway witness. Few judges are predisposed to favor trial lawyers over witnesses. The judge figures, correctly, that since the lawyer was the one who lost control, the lawyer should be the one to suffer the consequences. If the cross-examiner asks for help, the judge is likely to say something to make a bad situation worse. At best the cross-examiner will get, "I will permit the witness to give a full and complete explanation if the witness thinks that explanation is necessary for a complete answer." Who needs that help?

The judge, having been *invited* by the cross-examiner to participate, will often add their own commentary: "You want this court to direct the witness to answer that question? I have been on the bench 40 years and I cannot understand your question!" or "I think the witness is answering your question." Now the cross-examiner has a runaway witness and a runaway judge.

Trial lawyers should not be surprised with such responses from the bench. The purpose of the judge is not to assist the cross-examiner. The judge's refusal to help sends a message to the witness, opposing attorney, and jury. It is not a good message for the cross-examiner. The witness sees and hears the cross-examiner's frustration. In the event the bench does not sanction the witness, the witness is encouraged to do more of the same offending conduct.

The opposing lawyer now knows that the cross-examiner is not in control of the courtroom. This produces the confidence to make more objections, particularly speaking objections. Alternatively, opposing counsel may feign disinterest in the cross-examination. This apparent lack of interest signals the jury and the court that the cross-examination has degenerated into a personal battle of wills not having much to do with the search for truth. This in turn encourages judges to issue their favorite ruling: "Move it along."

During the process, the jury observes the change of dynamics from trial lawyer in control and directing the examination to witness controlling the trial lawyer. The jury notices that now the judge and opposing counsel are active participants. The cross-examiner's voice is no longer the voice of control. The scene is moving from clarity to chaos. The purpose of the cross-examination was to impact the opposing theories and of the case, either to promote the cross-examiner's theory of the case or to harm the opposing attorney's case. None of that is being accomplished now because there is confusion. All of this is caused *not by the unresponsive witness*, but by the cross-examining lawyer who is inartfully dealing with that witness. It is therefore essential that the cross-examiner undertake to control the witnesses on cross-examination. Do not invite the help of judges.

Of course, if the court offers help, the lawyer should certainly accept it. Should the court spontaneously instruct the witness to answer, the cross-examiner should accept the power of the bench. When the court voluntarily gets involved in the effort to control the runaway witness, the witness has hurt his credibility, which tells the jury that this lawyer is being fair in her questioning. Permit the court to volunteer; do not seek its assistance. The best way to accept the help of the power of the bench is to remain silent (see chapter 21, *Creation and Uses of Silence*). Do not restate the question unless prompted by the judge to do so, or the witness must admit that he does not know the question by asking for the question again. If the witness has to admit that he does not know the question, the witness admits to all (judge, jury, opposing counsel, and to the cross-examiner) that the witness was not listening to the question and was going to answer whatever question the witness chose to answer.

On the other hand, there are those witnesses who simply are unwilling to answer in a straightforward fashion. There are those judges who are skilled at spotting the evasive efforts of such witnesses and who will not tolerate this misconduct. Such judges often lose patience and take it upon themselves to instruct the witness to "just answer yes or no." Jurors will regard such an instruction from the court as a sign that the conduct of the witness is inappropriate. To the court, such a judicial instruction means that the witness has lost credibility. Such an instruction from a judge is the most powerful sanction that can be administered. The witness will likely now change his behavior and will answer questions more directly.

[b] "The Deal"

The Deal originates when the cross-examiner, early in the examination, suggesting to the witness that the cross-examiner will ask fair questions that need only a "yes" or "no" answer. In exchange for this type of questioning the cross-examiner advises the witness that yes or no answers will prove sufficient. "I am going to ask you a series of questions, each of which can be answered with a yes or no answer. If I do that, will you please provide me with a yes or no answer?"

The Deal is not a suggested method of controlling the witness. It is offered up by a lawyer who fears that somewhere down the road she will lose control of the witness. It is an attempt to control the runaway witness before the witness has run. The Deal sends all the wrong messages to the fact finders in the trial and to the opponent, who is made aware that the lawyer believes she will have trouble with the examination. Most importantly, the signal is sent to the witness that the lawyer fears this kind of conduct. If the witness is not friendly to the cross-examiner's cause, wouldn't the witness cause as much difficulty as possible by using this request against the lawyer?

When analyzed, this "deal" is nothing more than a sophisticated method of saying: "Just answer my questions 'yes' or 'no.'" Inexplicitly, the "deal" is most often heard when cross-examiner is dealing with more difficult witnesses. It is heard when a cross-examiner is beginning to question a child witness. It is heard when a cross-examiner is beginning to cross-examine an opposing expert or professional witness.

The Deal signals to the witness that the lawyer hopes to unduly confine the witness's answers. It also puts the judge on notice that the lawyer is attempting to cut off any explanation. Worse, it tells the jury that the lawyer is attempting to "put words in the witness's mouth." *Worst of all*, the offer of the Deal often generates an immediate objection, followed by a rebuke from the court on the witness's right to answer fully and fairly. As a result, the cross-examination begins at the worst possible credibility level. In an attempt to avoid the witness's digging a hole for the cross-examiner, she has dug the hole herself. The advocate has denied her own credibility before the witness ever answered a question. The Deal will not work; do not propose it.

§ 19.09 A General Technique That Assists All Other Techniques: Keep Eye Contact

When cross-examining a difficult witness, always maintain eye contact. Avoiding eye contact is interpreted as weakness. Life experiences verify this both in and out of the courtroom. People who will not make eye contact are uncomfortable and less than forthright. People who will not make eye contact are often afraid. If the cross-examining lawyer suspects the witness will become non-responsive or runaway in their answers, the lawyer must keep her eyes fixed on the witness when asking questions and when receiving answers. By directing the lawyer's full attention to the witness's eyes, she serves non-verbal notice that she will not put up with any nonsense or permit deviation from the question-and-answer approach she has been following. Control the runaway witness's eyes until the witness is off the stand.

By keeping eye contact with the witness, it is not suggested that it be an angry stare down by the cross-examiner. Fixed eye contact on the witness does not have to be unpleasant. The eye contact is telling the witness that the cross-examiner is completely focused and will not be deterred from getting answers to tough but fair questions.

When dealing with expert witnesses, eye contact is even more essential than when dealing with lay witnesses. Expert or professional witnesses look for any opening to advance the opposing lawyer's theory of the case. Keeping eye contact deters experts by giving the expert witness less psychological room to evade or embellish. Furthermore, there is a useful byproduct from this eye contact. If the expert witness is looking back into the eyes of the cross-examiner, the expert or professional witness is not looking into the eyes of the jurors as such witnesses are so often trained to do.

Of course, the trial lawyer must sometimes divert her eyes from the witness to look at notes and observe exhibits, charts, overheads, or other demonstrative aids. There techniques enable the cross-examiner to divert her attention while maintaining psychological control of the witness. The cross-examiner may take her eyes off of the witness after the answer has been given and before the next question is asked, or in limited circumstances even while the next question is being asked. In other words, the cross-examiner may put a question to the witness, receive an answer to that question, and then divert attention to a new task such as putting up an exhibit, or consulting notes. Because there is no question pending, there is no permission for the witness to speak. Eye contact should be maintained from the conclusion of the cross-examiner's question through the entire answer of the witness. When there is an interruption of eye contact between questions, cross-examiner should reestablish eye contact before posing the next question.

§ 19.10   Body Movement and Active Listening

When dealing with the runaway witness, the examiner must not only maintain eye contact, she must control her own body movement during the cross-examination. A question has been asked; the witness has hesitated and is now mentally debating whether to give the answer that will undoubtedly hurt the witness or to give a longer, less-responsive answer. At that point, all body motion must stop by the examiner. Constant eye contact and no movement is necessary to convince the witness that the only acceptable answer is a simple "yes," and that the cross-examiner is coiled to strike at the unresponsive answer.

One of the most important things for a cross-examining lawyer to do is to listen to the answer. The lawyer is experiencing many distractions: "loading" the next question, judging the reaction of the judge and the jury to the question, awaiting the answer, and hoping the opponent does not object. Sometimes the cross-examiner has the "aid" of an activist client, co-counsel, or an investigator at counsel table who wish to offer suggestions. These suggestions may be worthwhile, but the time to consult is between questions, not when an answer is pending. When the witness has a question pending, has hesitated in answering a question or has answered the question, but appears to be mentally debating whether to add more to the answer, all distractions must be avoided so that the cross-examiner may actively listen to the answer and observe the witness. The cross-examiner is not just using her ears, but her eyes and all other senses and feelings. Jurors and judges focus on the demeanor of the witness, the character of the witness, and the balance of power of the courtroom. Those attentive fact finders often get the real truth about the witness by observing any hesitations that precede or follow the initial answer. The trial lawyer has to be free to observe that conduct as well. The trial lawyer does this best by focusing completely and shutting out all other distractions and movement until the pending question is answered.

§ 19.11   Where and When to Use These Techniques

Controlling the runaway witness is not just to be sought in the trial. The skillful trial lawyer should not wait until the jury is empanelled to start conditioning the witness to give "yes" or "no" answers. Recall that behavior is molded by consequences. The witness can and should be conditioned during the pre-trial matters to give responsive answers. In order to encourage short answers and to discourage runaway answers, the cross-examiner should begin to exercise control over the witness at all pre-trial opportunities, in order to lessen the need to train the witness in real time in front of the jury.

The more the cross-examiner believes a witness will become a runaway witness, the more control the cross-examiner needs to employ in any pre-trial confrontation. The more the trial lawyer has properly trained the witness through pre-trial question-and-answer sessions, the less the witness is likely to fight the trial lawyer in front of the jury. A witness who has learned how to answer responsively has also learned that the responsive answer causes the lawyer to move on. The solemnity of trial sometimes serves to discourage narrative answers. In trial, most witnesses are more nervous. The stress of the trial environment coupled with the previous education of what works to get through the cross-examination experience, encourages the witness to provide short answers. Certainly this is less exciting for the trial lawyer, but that is a wonderful thing in trial. There will always be too much excitement in the middle of a trial for the cross-examiner.

§ 19.12 Depositions and Other Pre-trial Opportunities

In civil trial work, lawyers have the opportunity at temporary order hearings, motions hearings, and, most importantly, depositions and less formal interviews to "teach" witnesses by the use of controlling techniques that any answer other than "yes" will result in unpleasantness for the witness. Each witness is different and calls for different techniques to be used. For example, at a deposition, find a number of techniques that successfully control the witness. Reinforce them several times so that when that technique is used at trial, the witness is already conditioned to respond. If the advocate has conditioned and controlled the witness prior to the jury being empanelled, then control in front of the jury is much easier to maintain.

§ 19.13 Pre-trial Motion in Limine

There are witnesses (particularly expert and professional witnesses) who become so schooled in trial work that every answer is unresponsive. Every unresponsive answer is intentional and malicious. The ability to evade, and to insert harmful material is one of the reasons opposing counsel has hired them.

After confronting this type of witness at a deposition (and preferably a videotaped deposition), trial counsel may file a pre-trial motion in limine requesting the court to rule prior to trial that the witness shall be responsive to questions on cross-examination and not volunteer non-responsive information. This motion is best made using specific excerpts from transcripts and excerpts from videotaped depositions to illustrate the misconduct.

Even when trial counsel spends a great deal of time illustrating examples, most trial courts will rule that the motion will be "taken under consideration" or will be "reserved" until trial.

What then is the purpose of spending so much time preparing the motion? Because the judge has been forewarned. When the witness becomes repeatedly unresponsive, the court having been forewarned and having examples of what has happened at deposition, will turn on opposing counsel and direct him to control the witness. Often this is the situation in which a judge may order a witness to confine their answers to the question asked. The time spent on the motion is well worthwhile.

§ 19.14　Non-Jury Settings

The right to discovery through depositions translates into excellent opportunities to condition witnesses to answer responsively. In criminal work, the right to depositions is limited. With rare exceptions, depositions in criminal cases are permitted. As a result, in criminal work there is far less opportunity to confront the witnesses prior to trial. There are still opportunities, however, at motion hearings and preliminary hearings. Regardless of the venue, any question and answer scenario provides an opportunity to condition the witness through the use of techniques to control the runaway unresponsive answer.

Do not fear that pre-trial exposure of the witness to the techniques of control will allow the witness to "figure out" the techniques and avoid them at trial. None of the techniques involve trickery, sleight of hand, or unfair advantage. They are valid methods of preventing unresponsive answers. That is precisely why the techniques are so useful in front of a jury. The fact finder sees that the cross-examiner is only seeking to get at the truth in posing a series of questions that call for answers the witness is dodging.

§ 19.15　Opportunities Created for the Cross-Examiner from Unresponsive Answers

Trial lawyers fear unresponsive answers so deeply that substantial opportunities are missed when an unresponsive answer is given. When the trial lawyer is not actively listening to the answer, particularly when the answer is unresponsive, the trial lawyer misses opportunities. The reason that the trial lawyer is not listening to the answer is that the trial lawyer is distracted by her own fear of the unresponsive answer. Many times the unresponsive answer will provide two different types of opportunities for the cross-examiner.

The first type of opportunity enables the application of each of the techniques discussed below. That opportunity is to show to the fact finder, be it a judge or jury, that the witness is not being responsive. This elusive answering speaks to the character of the witness, as well as the interest, motive, and bias of the witness. By highlighting the elusive answer, the cross-examiner may undermine the witness's credibility.

The second type of opportunity offered by the unresponsive answer happens when the witness attempts to avoid assisting the cross-examiner's theory of the case. The witness will refuse to use certain words that are fair in describing what has happened. The witness will refuse to acknowledge certain tough, but fair questions. When a witness does this, he often poorly chooses the words to explain his position. Remember, the witness is now off the script. No one does that well — not trial lawyers, and certainly not witnesses.

Example:

Q: You heard the cars *smash* together?
(The trial lawyer has chosen a vivid but fair word to describe the collision.)

A: I don't know what I heard. I heard the sound of metal striking metal and then a thud.

The cross-examiner chose the word "smash" to describe the severity of the collision. In an effort not to agree with that descriptive word, the witness has chosen even more dramatic language: "metal striking metal" and "thud." If the trial lawyer is listening these new descriptive words can be used against the witness (see chapter 26, *Loops, Double Loops, and Spontaneous Loops*).

All of the techniques highlight the first opportunity that undermines the credibility of the witness. Some of the techniques go on the offensive and highlight the additional witness language. Look for the new opportunities when the witness adds to the answer. Do this by listening.

§ 19.16   Ask, Repeat, Repeat

The lawyer has asked a fair, clear question, in its simplest form, using commonly-understood words. The answer can only be "yes." In order to avoid giving the cross-examiner an answer, the witness has sidestepped with a non-answer.

Without taking her from the witness, the lawyer simply asks the question again, in exactly the same words and tone of voice and articulating each word. The pace of the question is slightly slower. If the witness is foolish as to again ignore the obvious "yes," the trial lawyer can slowly lean slightly forward without taking her eyes off the witness. The next step is to repeat the identical brief, simply constructed question, but even more slowly.

The successively slower repetition of the *identical words and tone* emphasizes to the witness, the court, and, most importantly, the jury that the witness is refusing to answer a short, straightforward, easily answered question. The forward body motion emphasizes that all are waiting for a response. Even the most evasive witness has great difficulty in evading the third posing of the question.

Some lawyers question whether a judge would permit the trial lawyer to ask the same question three times. In fact, this is a technique that maximizes the likelihood that the judge will voluntarily intervene and insist that the witness actually answer the question, in order to "move it along." Further, it is not redundant or repetitious to ask the same questions, if that question has not been answered.

Q: The car was blue? (In a situation where the witness knows the car was blue).

A: The car was traveling down the street, it started to go through the red light, I didn't even see brake lights . . . (babble, babble, babble) . . . and finally it did turn the corner and I still hadn't seen the brake lights.

Q: (Slower) The car was blue?

A: Well, it was going so fast when it went through the red light.

Q: (Slower still) The car was blue?

A: Yes, it was blue.

Q: The car was going south?

This technique is particularly effective with children and with expert or professional witnesses. It may be suggested that the emotional maturity of both groups is identical. In any case, children are intimately aware with having a question or a command directed a second time. This is particularly true when the second command is said slower, not louder.

The effect on an expert is just the opposite. He is stunned that anyone would repeat a question. He is an expert witness because he is at the top of his profession. How often is a surgeon asked the same question? How often is a tenured professor in chemistry asked the same question? In each instance, whether child or expert, the desired response is obtained.

It is worth a reminder: There was an offending behavior (an evasive answer) followed by a sanction (a repeat of the question), resulting in an appropriate behavior (a short responsive answer) followed by reinforcing positive stimuli (next question).

§ 19.17   Reversal, or Ask, Repeat, Reverse

This technique of repeat and reverse is a variant of the first technique. The lawyer asks the question. She then asks the identical question, but slightly slower and leaning forward. This gives the witness two opportunities to tell the truth before the lawyer reverses the question in the third asking.

For example, in a divorce case it is necessary to establish that the defendant-husband signed financial statements indicating a net worth of several hundred thousand dollars. The lawyer knows from prior depositions and interrogatories that the husband now contends that his net worth is really zero. He contends that the financial statements were exaggerated to obtain a bank loan. Undoubtedly, the defendant/witness has been warned by his lawyer that this subject will definitely come up at trial:

Q: Mr. Allen, you signed Plaintiff's Exhibit 10, your financial statement, as of August 1, 2000?

A: You have shown me so many documents, I am not sure. I know that I signed some financial statements and others I didn't sign. I was trying to borrow money to keep my family afloat for so long, I just wasn't sure what I was signing many times. They really don't mean anything.

Q: Mr. Allen, you signed Plaintiff's Exhibit 10, your financial statement, as of August 1, 2000?

A: She knew why I wrote that. Who signed it is beside the point.

Q: Mr. Allen, you did not sign Plaintiff's Exhibit 10?

A: (Mumble, mumble, mumble) I didn't say that. I signed it.

The third asking could also be phrased: "Mr. Allen, you did *not* sign Plaintiff's in Exhibit 10, your financial statement, as of August 1, 2000?"

It is a question of style and personality as to whether to truncate the reverse question or to emphasize the word "not" and restate the entire question on the reverse.

The technique of ask, repeat, reverse, is one of the most effective methods of controlling an expert witness. This is particularly true when the expert has reports, operative notes, letters, or any other type of documents. Because the document or fact, whatever it may be, will not go away, this technique is particularly effective.

§ 19.18 An Obvious and Indisputable Truth

This technique is best used when the witness will not confirm even the most obvious and indisputable truth. When used early in the cross-examination during confrontations with the witness over simple questions, it dramatically sets the scene for later use of the ask, repeat, repeat technique.

Ask, repeat, reverse is often used in establishing foundational answers that will be used on numerous occasions during the remaining cross-examination of the witness. A witness who has experience testifying recognizes the sound of a foundational question and knows that there is an upcoming potential problem for the witness. The witness is then more likely to resist the foundation. An example from a criminal case:

Q: Detective Brown, you signed the report of July 1, 1998?
An experienced criminal detective (a professional witness) hearing this question realizes that it is prefatory to an attempt to impeach the witness. In fact, experienced detectives will correctly predict that the cross-examiner intends to point out something that is "missing" from the report.

A: I sign many reports. I don't know if I signed this report. In fact, this report was done very hurriedly. You would have to understand that we are under such tremendous strain because of crime in the street and in America today, and the paperwork comes last.

First note that the question has not been answered. Instead, the witness has injected into the trial for the jury's benefit that (1) he is overworked; (2) that he must combat crime every day; (3) that he fears crime in the street, as do the members of the jury; and (4) that paperwork is not fun. No one would disagree with that.

All of these devices or dodges are offered in the hope that the cross-examiner will take the bait (see chapter 30, *Recognizing and Controlling Bait*) and never establish the foundation question. In the alternative, it invites the cross-examiner to abandon a slow meticulous foundation and jump ahead with the witness. (If this is done, the witness will best the cross-examiner later because no effective foundation has been set.)

The next question (identical to the first):

Q: Detective Brown, you signed the report of July 1, 1998?

A: Can I see the report? As I said, I have been very busy. I am also recovering from a hospitalization caused by another defendant on crack cocaine who attacked me while I was trying to make an arrest. It is very hard to keep up with all of the paperwork.

Again the officer attempts to steer the cross-examiner away from the foundation question and to inject emotional or sympathetic issues into the trial.

Q: Detective Brown, you did *not* sign the report of July 1, 1998?

A: I signed the report. Yes, I signed it. (Customarily this last admission is given with some exasperation. The exasperation stems from the realization that all of the efforts to steer the cross-examiner away from the focus of this question have failed.)

§ 19.19   Medical Malpractice Usage

In a medical malpractice case, the defense lawyer for the doctor has told the doctor that much of the case comes down to the defendant doctor's failure to include in his operative notes and his discharge summary reference to certain critical diagnostic procedures.

The defendant doctor knows that the expert witness for the plaintiff will specifically attack and criticize the defendant as falling below the standard of responsible care on the basis that those critical procedures did not occur because they were not referenced in the defendant doctor's operative notes and discharge notes. It is fair to predict that the verdict hangs on the jury's belief as to the accuracy of these notes:

Q: Dr. Torch, you dictated operative notes of June 24, 1999?

A: I am in the business of taking care of sick people. I am required to make certain notes about what I have done. I dictate them quickly after surgery. They are transcribed several days later. By the way, the hospital is terrible with this, and it sometimes takes three or four weeks to have my notes returned to me. Sometimes I sign them, sometimes I initial them, and sometimes I review them, but don't sign them. In comparison with all my other important duties, I just don't know. (By not taking the bait to other areas, the trial lawyer preserves this question and now highlights it for the jury.)

Q: You dictated operative notes of June 24, 1999?

A: As I said . . . (babble)

Q: You did not dictate those notes, Doctor?

A: No, no, I didn't say that. I just said that, well, I don't know. Do you have my notes there? Do I have my notes here? Oh, I see my notes. No, I didn't say that I didn't dictate it.

Q: In fact, Dr. Torch, you did dictate operative notes of June 24, 1999?

A: Yes, of course, I dictated them.

§ 19.20   Full Formal Name

A previously compliant witness has for the first time run away with an answer. This witness has thus far appeared to be trying to answer fairly. Jurors can sense the witness's apparent candor, so the lawyer has to rein in the witness without incurring the jury's hostility. Anything that changes the customary tone of questioning serves as a mild rebuke to the witness. The cross-examiner need not use a harsh tone or angry gesture to remind a witness of their obligation to answer the question. The use of the witness's full formal name represents a change in the style of the questioning and thereby provides a sanction:

Q: You failed to review the x-ray of her neck?

A: Well, any person this old, with bones so soft, x-rays can be difficult to interpret.

Q: Doctor Franklin Jeremiah Toth, you failed to review the x-ray of her neck?

A: Correct.

This technique depends on a childhood reflex. When someone calls out a full name in a public place, whether it is an airport, theater, or ballpark, that person does not just look up; he snaps to attention. The witness's eyes snap to connect with the cross-examiners. Years of human experience have taught that when authority figures use full names to address someone, the person is in trouble. The ingrained drive to avoid trouble with authority figures will ordinarily make the nonmalicious runaway witness resume safe "yes" and "no" answers. In reality, the full formal name makes the witness focus. That is all that is necessary with this type of witness.

§ 19.21   Embarrassment or Humiliation

[1]   Use of Formal Names

[a]   Application to Expert Witnesses

Always keep in mind that no witness wants to be embarrassed or humiliated. By calling the witness by his or her formal name and title, if there is a title (such as Doctor, Professor, Captain, etc.), the witness senses that humiliation and embarrassment is not far away.

There is no down side risk with this technique. There is no objection possible. There is no connotation or suggestion that the cross-examiner is in anyway denigrating the witness. The cross-examiner is merely making the question more formal. That added formality subtly changes the tone in the courtroom. The witness can be expected to be aware of that change of tone and to desire that the tone return to a more conversational mode. The short and honest answer of the witness should immediately be met with a return to the less formal tone of questioning so that the witness has fully experienced both the negative sanction and the positive reward.

Experts are accustomed being called by their titles, e.g. Doctor, Professor, etc., but they are unaccustomed to hearing their entire name with their title attached. Example: Evelyn P. Brown, III, M.D. FASC, you saw the blue car? Experts are very much like trial lawyers. Neither wants to be embarrassed.

[b] Child Witness

Since this technique is based on responses learned in childhood, it is extremely useful in stopping a child witness. The full formal name need not be spoken harshly or in an authoritative tone. In fact, it is better used in a quiet but firm voice.

§ 19.22 "Sir" or "Ma'am"

[1] Use

[a] Younger Witnesses

Once the formal name has been used, it is seldom necessary to use it again, even if the examination is a quite lengthy one. Simply starting the question with "sir" or "ma'am," as the case may be, will immediately bring back in line the unresponsive, but nonmalicious witness. Just as there is no down side risk for using the "full formal name" technique, there is no down side risk of objection or proper interruption to this technique. What would the objection be? "Objection, the cross-examiner is being polite." Use the "sir" or "ma'am" at the beginning of the question for maximum effect.

This is also a very effective technique when dealing with young people (not children), who are not used to being addressed as "sir" or "ma'am." By promoting them to the more formal and adult status of "sir" or "ma'am," the cross-examiner reminds them of the seriousness of the task at hand; they will then resort to more serious (i.e., more responsive) answers.

[b] Evolution of Politeness

It is an interesting geographic phenomenon that in the South where "sir" and "ma'am" are customarily and commonly used, even when addressing young people, that a frequently used "sir" or "ma'am" stills works and highlights the need to respond directly to the question in the courtroom. In other sections of the country where "sir" and "ma'am" are not used as commonly the effect is multiplied. Since the first edition of this book, the world has not gotten more polite. Consequently, the technique works better and better.

§ 19.23 Shorten the Question

Even when the cross-examiner is properly implementing the three rules of cross-examination (see chapter 8, *The Only Three Rules of Cross-Examination*), questions can be shortened to highlight the malicious non-responsive nature of the witness. The cross-examiner is using a leading question. She only has one fact in the question and the question is in logical order. Nonetheless, the witness refuses to responsively answer the question. In this circumstance, continue to eliminate words from the question until the witness is left with only the key word of the question.

Example:

Q: The car was blue?

A: The sun was in my eyes . . . I really wasn't paying that much attention. I was looking for my ride. . .

Q: Car . . . blue?

A: As I said, I was distracted. I wasn't paying as close attention as you might think. I am just not really sure.

Q: Blue?

A: Blue . . . yes, blue.

This technique isolates the essence of the question. It provides a substantial negative consequence to the unresponsive demeanor of the witness. It should be reserved for those witnesses who maliciously refuse to answer obvious questions. This technique highlights for the judge and jury that the witness is intentionally being obstructive. There is no need to use a loud or harsh voice. The technique is so powerful a soft tone produces a bountiful effect. In fact, this is one of those techniques harmed by use of a loud or harsh tone of voice. The power of the technique lies in the simplicity of the question. Any addition to the technique tends to make the questioning sound degrading.

§ 19.24 Physical Interruption

While effective methods for physically interrupting the runaway witness are numerous, ethically-appropriate circumstances in which to interrupt an answer are far more rare.

The method of interruption depends on the cross-examiner's personal characteristics, such as body size, gender, degree of aggressiveness, and overall personality. The right choice also depends on witness's behavior. The more offensive jurors find a witness, the more grandiose the physical interruption can be and still be tolerated by jurors. The lawyer must never show greater scorn for the witness than the jury has already shown. The jury must set the tone for the lawyer's disdain of the non-responsive witness. Whenever in doubt, the lawyer should underplay the amount of scorn shown. Err always the side of politeness.

§ 19.25 Ethical Note for Use of Techniques That Interrupt

It would be unethical for the cross-examiner to interrupt or cut off the answer of a witness. This consideration is over and above the evidentiary objection most likely to be heard. However, if the interruption is followed by the identical previously asked question, the ethical objection is eliminated. A different question is not asked. The same question is asked.

§ 19.26 Polite Interruption

The question is put to the witness. The witness becomes unresponsive. The witness's unresponsive answer would lead to a mistrial.

While ordinarily the cross-examiner should never verbally interrupt a witness, this is the exception to the rule. The cross-examiner must weigh the damage of a possible mistrial against an objection by the opponent.

Once the cross-examiner has decided that a polite interruption must be made, the interruption must be made quickly and before the harm that would result in a mistrial can be accomplished by the witness. The cross-examiner would then immediately address the court (preferably before the objection is even made) and ask to approach the bench with opposing counsel to explain the reason for the interruption.

Example:

Witness: . . . And then after the fall, the adjuster from the . . .

Cross-Examiner: I'm sorry. You must not have understood my question. Your Honor, may we approach the bench with opposing counsel to discuss a matter immediately?

Opposing Counsel: Objection. He is interrupting the witness.

Court: Approach the bench.

Note that the cross-examiner appears to put the onus on herself as she indicates there is a problem with her question. Normally the problem is not with the question, but with the unresponsive answer. Being polite is more important than being right in this instance.

§ 19.27 Pre-trial Use of Technique Particularly with Experts

The use of physical techniques receives strong reaction from an expert or professional witness in particular. The trial lawyer is well advised to test these techniques (prior to a jury trial) with the expert at a deposition, interview, or other pre-trial opportunity, rather than risk an overreaction by the witness in front of a jury.

§ 19.28 The Hand

A witness begins to answer the question with a long unresponsive answer. The lawyer simply holds up her hand like a traffic officer's stop signal. It sounds odd, but it works. Try it at a cocktail party on someone you don't like. (While it will stop the conversation, it will not improve the relationship.)

In a trial setting, the answer just trails off. Trial lawyers can tell when a physical interruption has been accomplished, since the answer ends with an ellipsis on the transcript:

Q: The aircraft tail was designed by Boeing?

A: The tail assembly was designed by Boeing, but you have to understand that it has many component parts, all of which . . .

The lawyer has silently interrupted. Now the witness is waiting to see what will next happen. The safest way to get back on track is to remind the witness gently of where the lawyer is in the questioning:

Q: Let me make sure we understand each other. My question is "The aircraft tail was designed by Boeing?"

A: Yes.

Of recent years, a new phenomenon has been observed in the use of this technique. Multiple expert witnesses are beginning to use "the hand" to control lawyers both on direct and cross-examination. The expert puts up a hand, which stops the direct-examining lawyer or the cross-examining lawyer from asking the next question. This permits the expert witness to add more to his answer, even after a long pregnant pause at the end of the original answer. Be forewarned. Don't let the witness's hand stop the next question.

§ 19.29 The Shaken Finger: Child Witnesses

When the witness begins to answer the question unresponsively and at length, the lawyer simply slowly shakes her index finger back and forth as she would at a naughty child. That simple gesture, with other appropriate body language to support it, makes the witness feel guilty. This technique works most appropriately when other techniques (particularly, the hand) have been employed earlier in the cross-examination. Now, when the witness continues to demonstrate that they have not learned the lesson of responding to the question asked, the shaken finger (naughty witness!) is appropriate.

This technique is also quite effective when cross-examining the child witness. Each cross-examiner has known the frustration of attempting to cross-examine a child witness when everyone in the courtroom is concentrating on whether the cross-examiner will attempt to trick, confuse, intimidate, or otherwise mishandle the child. Controlling the runaway child witness is a difficult undertaking. "The Finger" has been found to be extremely effective in use with a child witness. It seems less powerful or overbearing than many of the more sophisticated techniques.

The alleged child molestation victim is one of the most challenging witnesses that cross-examiners face. The charge itself is so inflammatory and the witness's testimony so readily accepted by the jury that control is essential, but the cross-examiner must be careful not to appear to be victimizing the child in the context of the jury trial:

Example:

Q: You never told your mother?

A: No, I never told her (sob, sob), but I was frightened of him. I was scared of him. He would put his hand on my . . .

Q: (Shaken finger) You never told your mother?

§ 19.30   Head Shake: Expert Witnesses and Child Witnesses

This technique is rather close in its mechanics to the previously discussed "the finger." When the witness begins to answer a question unresponsively and begins to volunteer, the lawyer shakes her head from side to side. This gesture silences the witness. The witness feels as though the trial lawyer believes that the witness is "too slow" to have understood the question. Often after the witness becomes silent, the witness will say, "Yes, the answer to your question is yes,"to prove that he did in fact understand the question and is not "slow." Just as the finger is effective with handling child witnesses, so too is the "shaking head." It is even more effective with experts.

§ 19.31   The Seat

This technique must be reserved for the witness who obviously is deliberately trying to evade the cross-examiner's questions. The witness is willful or maliciously non-responsive. Remember, physical interruption techniques can be used only when the jury, if they could participate, would resort to the same technique. This is a powerful technique because of its particularly aggressive and insulting nature and must be reserved for the witness who has clearly and completely worn out his welcome with the jury. This witness refuses to answer even the most simple, straightforward question and is now viewed by the jury as someone who is seeking to conceal the truth.

No one is immune to feeling humiliated when someone refuses to listen. The trial lawyer must communicate to the jury, the judge, her opponent, and the witness that she is refusing to acknowledge or listen to the non-answer.

The technique is simple. This technique works best when the lawyer has been following the principle to never take your eyes off a non-responsive witness. It will heighten the impression that this witness is behaving so badly that he/she should be ignored. If the cross-examiner has calculated correctly, and jurors consider this witness to be malicious and willfully nonresponsive, they will side with her. They may even emulate your conduct and turn their heads away from the witness. The jury has to have reached this level first before the lawyers.

Do this by walking slowly back to counsel table, sitting down and looking down at the table. Don't read anything. Don't look at anything. Just stare down at the table. Counsel perhaps holds her head in her hands. Witnesses babble and stutter to a full stop when confronted with this deliberate effort to offend. Because of the terribly aggressive nature of this technique, counsel is forewarned to use it sparingly.

§ 19.32   The Whole Body

This technique is reserved for only very unlikable, non-credible witnesses. In some rare criminal trials and some civil trials — divorce cases come to mind — the opposition uses a wholly reprehensible witness. This witness refuses to answer. Such a witness may resort to insults and abusive language in their non-responsive answer. The witness is so far out of line and uncooperative that he is seen as violating the decorum of the courtroom. Do not trade insults with the witness. It will only lower the cross-examiner to the level of the witness. Instead, visibly refuse to be bested or goaded by this outrageous behavior.

Such a witness is almost always maliciously non-responsive. He has determined that a non-responsive answer is better than a responsive answer. The trial lawyer must prepare the way for this technique by first fully discrediting this witness, by using prior bad acts, startling inconsistencies in testimony, or both (see chapter 11, *Sequences of Cross-Examination*). She will also have used several other control devices illustrated in this chapter.

While the witness runs on and on with a non-responsive or insulting answer, the lawyer should slowly turn her back on him. She looks above to simulate counting the holes in the ceiling's acoustical tiles. If this does not silence the witness, the lawyer slowly turns her head over her shoulder. She glances at the witness, as if to say, "Are you still talking?" She then returns to counting ceiling tiles. The witness's answer will soon taper off.

What is the judge doing while she is doing this? Interestingly, many judges permit this show of disdain. If the witness has behaved so badly as to deserve this conduct, in all likelihood, the judge was getting ready to issue a rebuke. The silence caused by this technique gives the judge just the right opportunity to tell the witness to answer the questions and stop the game playing. Some trial judges may interrupt this process:

Court: Ms. Hall, what exactly are you doing?

Ms. Hall: With all due respect, your Honor, this witness has not and is not now answering my question.

Court: Well, we will have none of this. You will ask specific, directed questions, and the witness, you will give specific, directed answers. Does everyone understand this?

Ms. Hall: Yes, Your Honor.

Witness: Yes, Ma'am.

Ms. Hall: You have been convicted of felonies in the past?

Witness: Yes, I have, but . . .

Court: That is enough. She asked you a specific question, and you have given her a specific answer. Now let's move it along, counselor.

§ 19.33   Use at Depositions — The Body and the Modified Seat

While the use of these techniques (the Body and the Modified Seat) at trial is limited, its use at depositions is more frequent. Depositions are less formal than trials. At a deposition, when a witness is maliciously running on with answers, the cross-examiner can turn her back to the witness, either while still sitting or by standing and turning her back to the witness. This often results in the dramatic stop of all testimony. The message is sent clearly to all.

§ 19.34   Objection: Non-Responsive Answer

The cross-examining lawyer has only one legal objection that can be used as a technique to control the runaway witness. The objection is stated as follows: "Objection, non-responsive answer." The objection that the witness is being non-responsive in her answer calls upon the court to become involved in enforcing the rules of witness examination.

It is, in a sense, inviting the court to assist in controlling the witness. Therefore, the cross-examiner should only use this objection when many other techniques have been used but have been unsuccessful in controlling the witness.

It is particularly helpful to use this objection when the court has nonverbally indicated to the cross-examiner that the court has tired of the witness not being responsive. The cross-examiner then takes the nonverbal cue from the court and gives the court an opportunity to volunteer to control the witness. The more malicious the unresponsive, rambling answer is, the more likely the trial court will accept the invitation to enter to help control, and the more likely that that entrance will be harsh and critical of the witness's behavior.

There are two substantial risks to this technique. First, once invited to participate in the cross-examination, the court may continue to be actively involved in the cross-examination. This is never a good thing. Too often the judge may see this objection as an invitation to referee the cross-examination on a question-by-question basis. The risk is that all continuity will be lost. This risk is substantial and must be weighed heavily by the cross-examiner when considering using this technique.

The second down side risk that the trial lawyer must weigh before using this technique is the likely response by the court. For this technique to work, the judge: (a) must be listening; (b) must know the rule of evidence; (c) must know that the objection belongs to the cross-examiner; and, (d) must be willing to enforce the rule. Weigh these factors carefully before the use of this technique.

When the technique is properly employed and the objection is sustained, the result is dramatic and lasting:

Cross-Examiner:	Objection, non-responsive answer.
Court:	Sustained.
Cross-Examiner:	I ask that the non-responsive answer be stricken from the record.
Court:	The answer will be stricken.
Cross-Examiner:	I ask that the jury be admonished to disregard the answer.
Court:	Jury is instructed to disregard the last answer.

As seen from this interchange, the court has delivered a very sharp rebuke to the witness. Even the strongest expert witness will wish to avoid a repeat of this scenario. Shorter, more honest answers will follow.

§ 19.35 The Court Reporter

While the judge is certainly the highest-ranking member of the courtroom staff, the jury views all court personnel as holding power. All members of the judge's staff are seen as "official" and are treated by the jury with special respect. Most importantly, the courtroom staff is seen as neutral. It is significant when it is perceived by the jury that they are using their power to aid one side or the other.

The technique: Having asked the witness a leading question and having received a rambling monologue, the lawyer may turn to the court reporter and ask, "Please may I have my question read back to the witness?" All action in the courtroom will halt as the reporter slowly articulates each word of the stenographic record.

Having the question repeated word for word by a court official and read back with great clarity intimidates the runaway witness and immediately brings a short, responsive answer.

If the lawyer has the misfortune to be working in a system in which tape recorders have replaced court reporters, some forewarning to the court clerk is required.

Judges also view this technique as employing official powers of the court. The judge believes the court reporter is an extension of the court. When using the court reporter technique, the judge seems to listen more intently to the read back and often visually, if not verbally, directs the witness to answer the question as read back. This is a very subtle way of having the judge volunteer to get involved by directing the witness to answer the question.

§ 19.36 Use at Depositions

The use of this technique at deposition has had a remarkable and dramatic effect on expert witnesses who are always prepared to give long, unresponsive answers to questions at the deposition. When the deposition is videotaped and the video camera continues to record while the court reporter reads back the question, the effect on the witness is profound. Witnesses not only respond to the question from the court reporter, but also respond better to questions that follow that recitation by the court reporter.

§ 19.37 Use of a Blackboard

Quite often the courtroom is equipped with a blackboard, white board, or other large writing surface. The blackboard can serve in much the same way as having the court reporter read the question back. If a witness is consistently unresponsive, and the question is short and to the point (see chapter 8, *The Only Three Rules of Cross-Examination*no boldface), the cross-examiner may simply write the question on the board during or after hearing the unresponsive answer. When faced with the written question, the witness often will stop the unresponsive answer. Even if the witness does not stop the unresponsive answer, he will recognize that he must eventually respond to the question.

If the cross-examiner is fortunate, the witness will see the question being written and respond to it. The lawyer can then highlight the answer by asking the witness if they are responding to the question she has written on the board. Inevitably the answer is "yes."

If the cross-examiner is very fortunate, the witness will ignore the question written on the board and finish her answer. This permits the questioner, while pointing at the words on the blackboard, to repeat the question. The graphic simplicity of the question on the blackboard requires the witness to provide a short, plain answer. Further, because it is time-consuming, the judge will often follow up the blackboard's use with a request that everyone "move it along." The witness gets the point of this indirect scolding, as does the jury.

§ 19.38 The Long Term Effect of Using the Blackboard Technique

Once the blackboard technique has been used, the witness is extremely sensitive to its reuse. If the trial lawyer desires to signal to the witness that the blackboard technique will be used again, the trial lawyer need only pick up the chalk and take one or two steps in the direction of the blackboard. The witness will stop the unresponsive answer he is currently voicing. The mere threat that the lawyer will return to the blackboard technique is enough to stop the witness.

§ 19.39 Use of a Poster

If a blackboard is effective, the poster is not only effective but also intimidating to the witness and the opponent. The poster further demonstrates to the jury and the judge the cross-examiner's thorough and complete and preparation for the trial.

Trial counsel knows the heart of her cross-examination. Trial lawyers are often quite able to predict at which point in certain cross-examinations certain witnesses will rebel or try to evade answering the critical questions. This is particularly true when dealing with expert witnesses. If the big question can be predicted, and the non-responsive answer is foreshadowed through discovery or pre-trial hearings, then an appropriate poster can be developed before trial. If there is no discovery, careful listening to direct examination questions can develop the material for the poster. The poster can be drawn during a recess. Then, when the predicted evasion comes to the big, critical question, cross-examining counsel can prop the poster on the desk. The critical leading question is already written on the poster in the identical language. This becomes a written form of the repeat technique.

An example comes from a typical personal injury case. The cross-examining attorney has questioned this witness at deposition. The witness has attempted not to answer a critical question at the deposition, but finally, and after a great deal of questioning, has admitted that she suffered from low back pain before the date of the collision. That pain was caused by an unrelated, on-the-job, lifting injury:

Q: You had injured your back four years before this collision?

A: My back really hurts now. It has hurt so long and it has hurt so much since your client hit me. I wasn't doing anything wrong. I was sitting there stopped at the red light.

Q: (The cross-examining attorney pulls out a poster prepared before the trial, with the identical question printed on the poster.)

There is a long pause. The cross-examiner points to the poster but does not repeat the question. (Whether to repeat the question verbally or only by body language is a question of style.) The witness spontaneously answers:

A: Yes, my back was hurt before the collision.

The witness also must think that the cross-examiner is psychic or has no social life to know ahead of time that the identical question would be asked and that the witness would be unresponsive. This sanction stays with the witness for a long time. The witness can be expected to want to avoid a repeat of this sanction. The likely consequence is a more responsive witness.

§ 19.40 "That Didn't Answer My Question, Did It?"

First Scenario

Q: The car was blue?

A: (Babble, babble, babble)

Q: That didn't answer my question, did it?

A: What was your question?

Q: The question is: The car was blue?

A: Yes.

Second Scenario

Q: The car was blue?

A: (Babble, babble, babble)

Q: That did not answer my question, did it?

A: Yes, I think it did.

Q: Repeat my question?

A: (If the lawyer is not lucky) I don't know it.

Or

A: (If the lawyer is lucky) . . . (long pause) I don't know it.

Or

A: (If the lawyer is very lucky) . . . I know it was something about a car. What was it?

This technique is confrontational. It is best reserved for use against an expert or professional witness. The jury must sanction this confrontation before it is used. The witness must have repeatedly refused, deliberately and maliciously, to answer straightforward questions.

Under any of the scenarios, the witness is taught to respond to the precise question asked.

§ 19.41   "My Question Was . . ."

This manner of controlling is less confrontational than the preceding technique. It has the same effect, particularly when used after the prior technique that is so confrontational.

The jury is reminded that the question was not answered. They are reminded of the very specific wording of your question. In that sense, this technique is much like a verbal blackboard and to the same effect. If analyzed, this technique is the "repeat" technique with a point on it. It is not as aggressive as "that does not answer my question, does it?" technique, but more aggressive than the simple "repeat" technique.

An additional benefit of this technique is that it points out to the jury the precise question that the witness is evading. Because of this, it is best to use this technique in situations where the cross-examiner is to draw additional attention to the factual assertion contained within the question. The jury receives a better understanding of the importance of the fact at issue, while the witness is sanctioned for the non-responsive or runaway answer.

§ 19.42   "Then Your Answer Is Yes"

This technique is easily understood by jurors. It can be used with any witness, whether that witness is a willfully non-responsive witness or just cannot help answering at length. The cross-examiner's tone can be adjusted depending on the circumstances. At the heart of this technique is the cross-examiner's ability to hear what amounts to "yes" hidden within a longer answer.

Quite often an expert witness will respond with a long and involved recitation rather than concede an important point to the cross-examiner. Because the expert knows that a straight denial will not hold up to further cross-examination, the witness seeks to camouflage the admission so that the cross-examiner will be deprived of its value.

Cross-Examiner: The securities and exchange commission has no jurisdiction over fixed annuities?

Witness: The securities and exchange commission has jurisdiction over instruments carrying a market risk. We have jurisdiction over many forms of annuities. In fact, we have jurisdiction over every type of annuity that involves market risk. While fixed annuities do not involve a market risk, per se, they have similarities with investment contracts that carry market risk. Indeed, we have jurisdiction over investment instruments that are essentially the same as fixed annuities.

Cross-Examiner: Then your answer is "yes," the securities exchange commission does not have jurisdiction over fixed annuities?

Witness: Yes.

Or

Cross-Examiner: You had the report that showed toxic levels of mercury in the dirt?

Witness: Well, while there was a report that showed those levels, there was no reason to believe them accurate, and in fact all the evidence to us indicated otherwise.

Cross-Examiner: So your answer is yes. You had the report that showed toxic levels.

Witness: Yes, I had the report.

This is best delivered after a long answer, without moving or taking your eyes from the witness's eyes and with a slight, helpful smile. Usually the affirmative response is quickly forthcoming.

The Nuremberg Trial

This technique has long been used by cross-examiners. An example can be found in Sir David Maxwell-Fyfe's cross-examination of Herman Goering during the Nuremberg Trials:

Maxwell-Fyfe: This order would be dealt with by your prisoner of war department in your ministry, wouldn't it?

Goering: This department, according to the procedure adopted for these orders, received the order, but no other department received it.

Maxwell-Fyfe: I think the answer to my question must be "yes." (Technique: Then your answer is yes?) It would be dealt with by the prisoner of war department, you ministry, isn't that true?

(Technique: Repeat.)

Goering: I would say yes.

§ 19.43   If the Truthful Answer Is "Yes," Will You Say "Yes"?

This is a variation of the technique just described. It should be reserved for the obstinate witness, particularly one being discredited. This technique should be employed when non-responsive answers are repeatedly given to very short, simple questions to which no witness contests that the fair answer is "yes." After a series of long, non-responsive answers, the cross-examiner can ask, "If the truthful answer is 'yes,' will you say 'yes'"? Obviously, the witness has to answer "yes" to the question.

Immediately follow by repeating the identical question that received the non-responsive answer. The witness will answer with a simple "yes."

Simple, Direct, Brief

It bears repeating that the lawyer's question must be simple, direct, and brief. There must be only one fact per question (see chapter 8, *The Only Three Rules of Cross-Examination*). If her question has too many facts in it, or if the fact is subject to interpretation or explanation, the downside effect of this technique is devastating to the cross-examiner and the cross-examiner's credibility. An example of how *not* to do it:

Q: If the truthful answer is "yes," will you say "yes"?

A: Yes.

Q: You were walking down the hill, you got to the bottom about ten minutes later, and made a right-hand turn on to the dock?

A: I know that you want me to say yes, but I cannot. I did go down the hill. It took at least ten minutes. It might have been fifteen minutes and therefore I cannot say yes. I don't really think it was a right-hand turn, it was more like a left-hand turn, which brings up the whole point that you are trying to get me to agree to something with a simple "yes" that wouldn't be true.

This same type of questioning can be accomplished successfully with shorter more specific questions:

Q: If the truthful answer is "yes," will you say "yes"?

A: Yes.

Q: You went down the hill?

A: Yes.

Q: You estimated that it took approximately ten to fifteen minutes?

A: Yes.

Q: There was a dock at the end of the hill?

A: Yes.

Q: You turned onto the dock?

A: Yes.

Q: That's the way it happened?

A: Yes.

§ 19.44 Story Times Three

Some witnesses seem unstoppable. They have been coached to tell a story, and they are going to tell their stories — usually dramatic and harmful stories calculated to destroy the advocate's case. This sort of witness will tell this story as often as possible and seems to have the uncanny ability to recognize the worst possible moments. Only in these dire circumstances is the following technique appropriate. Try multiple techniques first before reverting to this technique, because this is a technique of last resort at trial.

This technique is best used at deposition. There is no jury to be poisoned. No judge to interrupt. By requesting repeated recitations of the "story", all the emotion of the witness and the "story" is drained away. Control for individual questions that follow become much better.

Three quick scenarios are given to illustrate the devastating effect of "the story."

Criminal case: The criminal co-defendant who has agreed to testify against your client says at every opportunity, "Jones (your client) made me do it. He placed the gun to the officer's head and pulled the trigger. Then he laughed."

Civil case: An eyewitness to an intersection collision says whenever he can, "That may be true, but I saw your client's car go right through the red light."

Divorce case: The opposing spouse takes every opportunity to say, "She walked out on my sick child and me. She called from a bar and didn't even ask about the child. She asked me if I knew Fred B., who was with her."

The witness has repeatedly volunteered this story at critical times during your cross-examination. No matter what questions have been asked, the same story finds its way into the answer.

To defuse this situation, ask the witness: "You want to tell your story, don't you?" The answer will be "yes." Instruct the witness to tell it to the jury. Then instruct the witness to repeat it. After the retelling, instruct the witness to repeat it again. (Judges have been known to interrupt at this point with "I have heard enough of that story, now let's ask questions and give answers." Counsel can live with that.)

When the witness is finished with the third (progressively less dramatic) telling of the story, ask, "Have you told us your story? Do you want to tell us all one more time? No? Okay, let's go on." The witness will surely refrain from telling the story again. This is painful in the execution, but effective in stopping the long-term, chronic pain. It remains an effective technique for emotional witnesses at deposition.

§ 19.45　Elimination: Use of This Technique at Trial

This technique is particularly valuable to teach the witness before trial that it is painful, embarrassing, and even humiliating to be a runaway witness. It signals the axiom: "We can do this the easy way or the hard way, but we will do it." The technique comes in two forms. When used at a deposition the technique of elimination is longer and more time-consuming. When used in trial, the technique requires questioning that is more to the point. After experiencing the form at a deposition, few witnesses look forward to the trial form.

The question is asked, and the witness gives a non-responsive answer. The cross-examiner begins eliminating other possible factual variations. At some point during the process, the witness will offer to give the "yes" that was warranted by the original question asked. Do not let the witness off the hook. Continue with this technique until the witness insists on giving the response that you first requested.

Q: The car was blue?

A: Well, I only saw it for a moment. . . . (Minutes later the answer concludes without ever giving the color of the car.)

Q: The car was black?

A: No.

Q: The car was green?

A: No.

Q: The car was purple?

A: No.

Q: The car was yellow-green?

A: No, it was blue. It was blue.

Q: Thank you.

The more willfully, non-responsive the answer, the more outrageous the process of elimination:

Q: The car was blue?

A: Well, I only saw it for a moment and when I looked over . . . (Minutes later the answer concludes without ever giving the color of the car.)

Q: The car was black?

A: No.

Q: The car was green?

A: No.

Q: The car was purple?

A: No.

Q: The car was yellow-green?

A: No.

Q: The car was puce?

A: No.

Q: The car was burnt sienna?

A: No, no. Blue, blue, blue.

The more willful and undesirable the witness, the more persistent the cross-examiner can be with the technique of elimination.

Deposition Training

This is an excellent technique to train the witness in depositions (where objections do not stop the technique) not to be unresponsive. With the latitude given at depositions, the painful technique of elimination can be used to its full extent, and the witness recognizes that it is an unpleasant experience to be avoided in front of twelve perfect strangers at a jury trial.

Q: The car was blue?

A: Well, I really wouldn't say blue, it was more of a . . . (Minutes later the answer concludes without ever giving the color of the car.)

Q: The car was black?

A: No.

Q: The car was green?

A: No.

Q: The car was purple?

A: No.

Q: The car was puce?

A: No, the car was blue.

Q: The car was burnt sienna?

A: No. No. Blue. Blue.

Q: Well, you weren't sure before, let's make sure that we are absolutely concrete on this. The car wasn't hot pink?

A: No, I said blue. It was blue.

Q: But you were not sure before. Let's make sure that it was blue.

A: It was blue. It was blue. It will always be blue. It will never change from blue.

There is a trial form of the "elimination" technique. It involves a much shorter version, a much quicker rendition.

Example:

Q: That then was a lie?

A: I am not sure that I would call it a lie.

Q: It wasn't the pure truth?

A: No.

Q: It wasn't the whole truth?

A: No.

Q: It wasn't even partially the truth?

A: I guess not.

Q: It was a lie?

A: Yes.

It is the same technique that has been truncated for trial.

§ 19.46   Spontaneous Loops

A loop is the repetition of a key phrase (see chapter 26, *Loops, Double Loops, and Spontaneous Loops*). A spontaneous loop is a repetition of all or part of an unexpectedly good but unresponsive answer. This type of loop is called spontaneous because it happened without the trial lawyer expecting it. More often than not the cross-examiner will use a simple word or phrase from a long answer that the witness has volunteered (see chapter 26, *Loops, Double Loops, and Spontaneous Loops*).

Words of warning: First, to fashion effective spontaneous loops, the lawyer must *listen closely* to the witness's answers. The cross-examiner should use quoted language to get their point across. Second, the cross-examiner should only spontaneously loop quoted words or phrases that are *helpful* to her case. It dramatically undermines the case if the trial lawyer begins looping words or phrases that have no particular value to the theory of the case or words that may be harmful.

In a case about a Covenant Not to Compete Employment Contract, the cross-examiner is representing the employee attempting to invalidate the contract and the covenant not to compete, based on the over breath of the terminology of the contract. It is strictly and purely a technical legal argument.

Judges and juries dislike people who sign contracts but do not live by them. In the cross-examination of the employer, the cross-examiner was seen looping the wrong phrase, which was destined to impale his client, the employee, on the basic common sense concept, "If you sign a contract, you should keep your word and live by that contract."

Here is an example of how *not* to loop, and words that don't help:

A: We negotiated the contract for a long time. We both agreed verbally to it. We shook on it. We gave our word. Then it was reduced to writing. He had his lawyer look at it. I had my lawyer look at it when his lawyer had made some changes, but it was still the same contract. It is the contract to which we agreed.

Q: You gave your word?

A: Yes.

Q: My client gave his word?

A: Yes.

Q: You both gave your word?

A: Yes.

Q: As gentlemen?

A: Yes.

Q: As people who would keep their word?

A: Yes.

This is a classic example of what *not* to loop from the employee's point of view. The employer's attorney could but smile and realize that his point was being driven home successfully by his opponent and would ultimately win the case at the trial level. Why was this done? Because the lawyer heard a dramatic phrase in the unresponsive answer. Any dramatic phrase or words of impact tantalize the cross-examiner to spontaneously loop them. Only loop those phrases that help the cross-examiner's theory of the case or hurt the opponent's theory of the case.

Here is an example of the appropriate way to loop:

A: . . . and after the shooting we got into the car and drove away like any normal family would . . . (babble, babble, babble)

Q: Sir, you said that you were like any normal family. (Spontaneous loop of the phrase.)

A: Yes.

Q: Like any normal family you left town in the dead of the night?

A: Yes.

Q: Like any normal family you gave aliases to each normal family member, including the five-year-old?

A: Yes.

Q: Like any normal family, you stole license plates every other day, as the five-year-old watched?

A: Yes.

Spontaneous loops work to silence witnesses because they fear that their own words will return to haunt him. No person is so articulate, careful, or controlled that he doesn't use certain words and certain phrases that he later wished he could take back.

Whether the witness is a college professor with a doctorate in microbiology or a ruthless government informant trained in the art of lying, her non-responsive answer is likely to include words or phrases that the cross-examiner can use to discredit her. This is why the cross-examiner must listen to the entire answer carefully. Within it are often nuggets of golden opportunities.

§ 19.47   Combinations of Techniques

[1]   The Relationship of "Ask, Repeat, Repeat" to "Ask, Repeat, Reverse"

By using the "ask, repeat, repeat," the cross-examiner sets up the "ask, repeat, reverse" technique. The converse is also true. By using the "ask, repeat, reverse" first, the "ask, repeat, repeat" is also in a better position to train the witness. Experience has taught that "ask, repeat, reverse" with expert or professional witnesses is the more dramatic technique and should be used first to set up the "ask, repeat, repeat" thereafter.

[2]   The Relationship of Full Formal Name to "Sir" or "Ma'am"

Once the full formal name technique has been used, the "sir" or "ma'am" technique can be used thereafter with good effect. The full formal name technique enhances the use of "sir" or "ma'am" thereafter.

[3]   The Relationship of Shortened to Blackboard

The trial lawyer can effectively use the "shortened" technique for dramatic effect individually. But when used as a preceding technique to the blackboard technique — when the lawyer knows that she will be using the blackboard technique later in the examination of this same witness — the shortened technique dramatically increases the effectiveness of the blackboard technique. Save the blackboard for theory essential questions.

Once the blackboard technique has then been issued, the return to the "shortened" technique is equally effective.

[4]   The Relationship of Court Reporter to the Blackboard or Poster

When the trial lawyer has used the court reporter technique, the witness is extremely sensitive to the cross-examiner moving to the blackboard or the use of the poster technique. It is logical that the silent delay in setting up each of these three techniques creates fearful anticipation in the witness.

[5] The Relationship of "That Didn't Answer My Question, Did It?" to "If the Truthful Answer Is 'Yes,' Will You Say 'Yes'?"

Once the technique of "if the answer is yes, you will say yes" technique is used, a return to the "that doesn't answer my question" technique highlights that the witness has promised to say yes to truthful questions and has reneged or broken that promise. The effect is dramatically enhanced.

[6] The Relationship of "That Didn't Answer My Question Did It?" to "My Question Was . . ."

Once the very aggressive technique of "that doesn't answer my question does it" technique has been used, often times with an expert or professional witness, the less dramatic technique of "my question was . . ." is effective. The latter technique does not appear to be overly aggressive, but when used after the very aggressive former technique, it appears to the witness to be more aggressive than when used alone. It receives a prompt response from the witness.

[7] The Relationship of "Then Your Answer Is Yes" to "Ask, Repeat, Repeat"

As so eloquently illustrated by Sir David Maxwell-Fyfe's cross-examination of Herman Goering, once the witness has been prompted with "so your answer is yes" technique, that technique is significantly enhanced by following it with a repeat of the original question.

[8] The Relationship of the Hand to the Finger and the Head Shake

Once the hand is used, all following less dramatic gestures (finger, head shake) are enhanced. The less dramatic gestures signal the boundary of an acceptable answer. More sanctions will result if the witness does not confine his answer.

§ 19.48 Summary

No one welcomes non-responsive witnesses. But with these techniques in the cross-examiner's arsenal, the trial lawyer will no longer fear them. Through these techniques, such a witness can be controlled. The trial lawyer can also use a non-responsive answer as an opportunity to punish the witness, weaken his credibility, and teach him the virtue of a straight "yes" or "no" answer.

An effective cross-examiner can control a witness artistically and subtly by using these techniques. There is no need to raise one's voice, become ugly, or unprofessional. The fear in the stomach may remains, but it will appear to the cross-examiner's opponents, to the court, and, most importantly, to the jury that it is the cross-examiner and not the witness who is in control. Some unobservant lawyers will say that the cross went well because "the witness never fought her." This is naive. In many cases the witness is up for the fight, until he is trained that the only easy course through the trial is to give simple "yes" and "no" answers.

A cross-examiner who can control the runaway witness through these techniques experiences positive feedback. Because more control is exerted, the witness fights less. Because the witness fights less, the cross-examiner can concentrate on the three basic rules and experiment with the more advanced techniques.

Chapter 20

DEALING WITH THE "I DON'T KNOW" OR "I DON'T REMEMBER" WITNESS

SYNOPSIS

§ 20.01 Answers to the Inconsistent Statement

Often a witness who has been pinned down in an obviously harmful chapter, or whose honest answer will contradict his side of the case, or whose credibility will come under further attack, will decide the best course of conduct is to stop answering the leading questions. Of course, absent a valid privilege, a witness is not permitted to simply decline to answer the cross-examiner's questions. Instead, the witness will fall back on the answer, "I don't know" or "I cannot remember." The witness sees this as safer than any other answer. There are techniques that take advantage of such answers and punish the witness. There are techniques that take advantage of such answers when they are true.

§ 20.02 Three Steps to Recognition of the Cross-Examiner's Control

Do not be alarmed by this form of evasive answer. First, the witness is communicating that the lawyer has successfully confronted him. By refusing to further respond, the witness is no longer even attempting to exercise control over the cross-examination. The witness is conceding that the cross-examiner has a better knowledge of the facts than the witness. The witness is further telling the fact finder that it would be risky to rely on those things the witness claims to have remembered because the witness has demonstrated a complete lack of memory in areas of importance. "I don't know" or "I don't remember" are generally helpful answers. Second, do not believe that this dodge is a successful technique for the witness to extricate herself from the confrontation.

Third, do not become frustrated, angry, or loud with the witness. This will only tarnish the appearance of dominance now gained. It will also re-empower the witness. The cross-examiner's anger is the witness's victory.

A witness who in response to being confronted with an impeachment, inconsistent statement, or other telling point, claims "I don't know" or "I can't remember" is in a defensive posture. If the impeachment has been properly presented, the jury will not accept this defensive posture as a legitimate position. It is now the task of the cross-examiner to put into context what the witness is really saying. Then this shallow, elementary, transparent subterfuge of the witness will be shown for what it is — an evasion. In this way, the witness is doubly punished: once by exposure of the contradiction and once more by stripping away the bogus dodge.

§ 20.03   Differentiating and Using the Honest "I Don't Recall"

There are certain questions to which it is reasonable for the witness to say that he cannot remember or that he does not know the answer. If, after suitable probing, the witness holds to his claimed lack of knowledge, let it be. How much probing is suitable? The witness should not be able to later claim that he suddenly remembered a fact. On the other end of the spectrum, there are certain questions to which it would be absurd for the witness to say that he could not remember or did not know the answer. Those evasions must be vigorously pursued.

As an example, it would be absurd for the witness to suggest to the jury that he could not remember a document authored by the witness in the recent past concerning a matter of great importance to the lawsuit. One is expected to recognize one's own work when such work is material to one's life. Barring some highly unusual circumstance, people are expected to know their own primary business affairs.

§ 20.04   Spotting Circumstances in Which "I Don't Know" or "I Don't Recall" Are Likely Dishonest Answers

In a child custody case, the mother who suggests that she cannot remember that she wrote a letter to the father concerning the child's education and what school the child should attend in the upcoming school year is perceived by the jury as ridiculous. The jury does not hear that statement as, "I don't recall," but rather as, "I refuse to talk about it because it hurts me."

On the other end of the spectrum, a jury may well understand the fact that the witness may not understand Einstein's theory of relativity unless the witness is a nuclear physicist. Again, the reason is obvious — it is the very rare person who would know such a thing. It is neither normal nor necessary to possess such knowledge. As a result, the ordinary person is absolved from ridicule or impeachment when he confesses lack of knowledge in an area unrelated to his life or business.

Under certain circumstances and as to certain classes of people, the jury anticipates knowledge of even specialized matters. While the jury does not have that specialized knowledge, it still believes the witness should. The jury is skeptical of the witness who claims no such knowledge.

A high corporate officer may well not recall the contents of a memo on which he was copied where such memo is *facially routine*. Under such circumstances, even the handwritten initials on the memo showing that he received and read the memo will not cause jurors to disbelieve the assertion that he does not recall the memo or its contents. However, if the contents of the memo are highly unusual or relate to matters deeply important to the executive, a jury will be more skeptical of a denial.

For instance, if the executive is shown a memo about a product safety issue that is done routinely and is part of a general engineering study, the jury may believe that he does not remember even though he signed and initialed it. On the other hand, if the memo is about the corporation's liability as to a defective product and contains the executive's handwritten statement against interest, a jury would not believe that he does remember the matter.

§ 20.05 Determining What "I Don't Know" or "I Don't Remember" Really Means

The witness may be saying something useful when he uses, "I don't know." Too often, the cross-examiner accepts the "I don't know" or "I don't remember" answer without pinning down its real meaning. There are, in fact, two possible meanings:

1) The witness once knew the information being requested, but has now forgotten the facts; or

2) The witness never possessed the information. The witness never knew the facts.

The distinction *might* be important to the cross-examiner. Example:

Possibility 1:
I don't know = I never knew

Q: You do not know what the robber was wearing.
A: No, I don't know.
Q: You never got a good enough look to see the clothes?

A: No, not really.
Q: When you say you don't know — the fact is you never knew?
A: I guess so.

Possibility 2:
I don't know = I once knew, but don't know anymore

Q: You do not know what the robber was wearing?
A: No, I don't know.
Q: But you once knew?
A: What do you mean?
Q: At the time of the robbery, you saw the robber's clothes?

A. Yes.
Q: In fact, you looked right at them?

A:	Yes.
Q:	But now, you no longer recall the clothing?
A:	No, I don't.

Possibility 1:
I don't know = I never knew

Possibility 2:
I don't know = I once knew, but don't know anymore

Q:	What you once knew, you no longer know.
A:	Right.

Obviously, the distinction can be major. Cross-examining counsel need not stop after eliciting the "I don't know" answer, but can move on to further define the reason for the answer. That reason can then be folded into the impeachment mix.

The spectrum can generally be seen as outlined below:

Obvious lack of knowledge	Reasonable lack of knowledge	Absurd not to know

With that spectrum as a guideline, one very valuable cross-examination technique after having successfully confronted the witness and caused the witness to revert to "I don't know" or "I cannot remember," is to take the witness closer and closer to the absurd end of the spectrum with the witness insisting that the answer is not known or not remembered.

§ 20.06 Techniques for Showing That Such Answers Are Illogical and Therefore Not Credible

As discussed, such answers are frequently evasions. The witness has chosen to stop giving information because the information would work against his position in the case. There are techniques for demonstrating that such answers are illogical. And an answer that is illogical lacks credibility. The witness may not be required to remember what he refuses to remember, but he can be punished for his convenient failure of memory.

The methods for doing this are simple. Meticulously demonstrate either:

(1) This is the kind of information the average person (read: juror) would have if he was *in the circumstances of the witness*, or

(2) The witness is within that special group of people of whom such knowledge is expected.

Assume in a domestic relations case that the cross-examiner has successfully confronted and impeached the witness with statements concerning his earning potential. On direct examination, the witness testified that his earning potential is less than $20,000 per year. At the deposition, the witness testified that in 1991, the year before the trial that the witness had actually made and reported $30,000 for that year. When confronted with this statement, the witness attempts to evade using the, "I don't know" response:

Q: You had the earning potential for that year of $30,000?

A: I guess so.

Q: Well, that is what you made that year?

A: Yes.

Q: You were working up to your potential?

A: I don't know.

Q: You are not telling us that you earned more than your potential?

A: I guess not.

Q: $30,000 was, in fact, what your potential was that year?

A: I don't know.

Q: Your potential for 1992 is $30,000?

A: I don't know.

Q: Your potential to increase your income is greater?

A: I don't know.

Q: What you are telling this jury is that you don't know your earning potential now?

A: That is right.

Q: You don't know your potential for 1992?

A: That's right.

Q: And you don't know your potential for 1991?

A: That's right.

Q: And that is true even though you actually made $30,000 in 1991?

A: Yes.

Q: But you don't know any of those other things?

A: No.

Another method is to ask it this way:

Q: Your potential for 1991 was $30,000 a year?

A: I don't know.

Q: Well, in 1992, you received a raise?

A: I don't know. I cannot remember.

Q: You cannot remember if you received a raise in 1992?

A: No.

Q: You get a paycheck every other week?

A: Yes.

Q: You put it in your bank account?

A: Yes.

Q: And you live off it?

A: Yes.

Q: You have to live off it until you get your next check?

A: Yes.

Q: You got 26 paychecks in 1991?

A: Yes.

Q: You deposited them in the bank also?

A: Yes.

Q: And you lived off these checks?

A: Yes.

Q: Now, you cannot remember if your check is bigger than it was last year?

A: No.

Q: You cannot remember if the check you received last week was bigger than each of the 26 paychecks you got last year?

A: No.

Q: So you don't really know what your salary is?

A: No, not really.

In each case, the cross-examiner draws the witness closer and closer to the absurd end of the spectrum so that the jury will reasonably believe that the witness is not trying to remember and that he is using this as a device to avoid honestly answering the question.

Below is an example of a commercial case in which the cross-examiner applied the technique of showing that under the circumstances, the witness would be expected to remember what occurred and that therefore, the "I don't recall" answer is likely being used to conceal information harmful to the witness's side of the case. The circumstances are that the witness attended an important meeting in which a crisis concerning a failing investment was discussed. The witness simply cannot recall what occurred at the meeting:

Q: You were in California on business?

A: Yes.

Q: You received a call from the secretary to the President?

A: She did call me.

Q: She told you that the President of the Company wanted you to fly back immediately to attend a special meeting?

A: She asked me if I could fly back.

Q: She told you the meeting would begin at 9 a.m. the next day?

A: Yes.

Q: And you knew that in order to make the meeting you would have to cancel all your meetings on the West Coast?

A: Well, I couldn't be in two places at once.

Q: In fact, it was clear to you that you did not have a choice. You were to cancel your meetings and fly back immediately?

A: I would not have asked if I had a choice. When the President calls you, you go.

Q: Exactly. This was a directive. You were to be there no matter what it took?

A: I knew I had to be there.

Q: So you took the midnight flier and arrived at 5:30 a.m.?

A: Yes.

Q: And then you showed up at 9 a.m. for the meeting?

A: Yes.

New chapter: Who was at the meeting?

Q: The meeting was in the boardroom?

A: Yes.

Q: You had never been invited to a meeting in the boardroom?

A: No, this was the first time.

Q: When you got there you found that the President of the Company was there?

A: He was.

(Now, for purposes of brevity, the chapter will be summarized.)

The cross-examiner should place all of the other important people at the table. Then the cross-examiner should show with another chapter that the subject matter was an investment directly under the supervision of this vice president. Then the cross-examiner should construct another chapter showing that a package of materials was handed out to each member in attendance. The cross-examiner can then show the length of the meeting, that lunch was brought in, and that nobody took phone calls or left the meeting to attend other business, implying that this was a very important meeting.

Cross-examiner can then use a chapter that shows the content and quantity of materials that were passed out. The importance is to show that what was passed out must have been important to the decision.

Cross-examiner should use any other chapters that help show the importance and unusual nature of the meeting. In addition, it is important for the cross-examiner to establish that the subject of the meeting was something that would have been directly related to the responsibility of the vice president.

Having completed these chapters showing that by circumstances, by training, or by profession the subject matter of this meeting is something the witness should recall. The cross-examiner can now ask leading questions posing facts the cross-examiner has a good faith belief are accurate:

Q: The subject of the meeting was Middletown Widget Co.?

A: I don't recall if that came up or not. It may have.

Q: In fact, the meeting concerned whether Middletown Widget Company was about to fail?

A: I don't recall.

Q: The materials that were handed out included detailed financial materials showing financial projections for Middletown Widget Co.?

A: I don't know if that is accurate. I do not recall what was handed out.

Q: Middletown Widget Company was an investment that you were responsible for supervising?

A: Yes.

Q: And during this meeting you were repeatedly asked whether this investment was about to fail?

A: I don't remember one way or the other. I don't remember the details of the meeting.

Q: In fact, one of the subjects of the meeting was whether the other investors should be warned about the potential failure of Midwest Widget so that they could take actions to protect their investments?

A: I don't recall if that was a conversation or brought out during that meeting.

As can be seen, it is highly unlikely that the truthful response is "I don't recall." In fact, the more the witness cannot recall, the less likely it is that the answer is truthful. If there is any evidence that supports the leading question (and of course there is or the lawyer would not have asked such questions) the jury will be entitled to draw the inference from such evidence that the meeting progressed along lines suggested by the cross-examiner. In this scenario, the cross-examiner does not have another person in that meeting who can testify to what occurred. But if the cross-examiner puts together those few facts which are available, and can accurately paint a picture of an important meeting about a failing company, the denials of the witness will ring hollow.

Jurors will believe that a person in that position would recall the meeting and in fact would be willing to loudly deny the leading questions if the witness could honestly do so. But the witness cannot, so she is hiding behind the "I don't remember" answer. Yes, the witness can continue to assert a lack of knowledge. But with every ``I don't remember" answer the witness looks more foolish and deceptive. At some point the witness must make a choice. Continue to look foolish or begin providing honest responses that assist the cross-examiner's case.

§ 20.07 Application of These Two Techniques Lead to Likely Results

When these techniques are applied, there are two likely results. Both outcomes are good for the cross-examiner:

(1) The jury will not believe that the witness "does not know" or "does not remember," and will instead assume that the honest answer would include information harmful to the position of the witness.

(2) The witness will be discouraged from the further use of "I don't know" or "I cannot remember."

Let us first examine the consequences of a witness who persists in such non-answers. If the witness persists in claiming a lack of knowledge on important items, control of the teaching function is turned over to the cross-examiner. The witness is so concerned with being embarrassed that the testimony becomes completely secondary.

The witness is marginalizing himself. The witness is telling the jury that he is not the source of reliable information. If the jury concludes that the answer, "I don't remember," is dishonest the jury will assume that the honest answer hurts the witness. The jury will search for the likely information and will find it within the cross-examiner's leading questions. The cross-examiner has won the battle of facts as the witness has withdrawn from the battle.

Let us next study the second possibility. The witness realizes that he is losing credibility with every "I don't remember" answer. The witness can follow the logic of the leading questions that establish the circumstances that make it appear that the witness is hiding or denying information. Every "I don't remember" answer is a self-inflicted wound. The witness understands he is being made to look foolish. Under these circumstances, a surprising number of witnesses succumb to the pressure created by the cross-examiner and begin to truthfully answer the leading questions. Why does this happen? Happily for our system of justice, it is psychologically difficult for a witness to take the oath, sit on a witness stand, stare a fact finder in the eye, and repeatedly claim to have no memory of important information. There comes a point when the witness would rather look professional and competent by giving an answer, even if the answer hurts his side of the case rather than to continue to look unprofessional or foolish.

§ 20.08   "I Don't Remember" (Except What Helps Me)

When a witness uses the "I don't remember" on all issues or facts, except the one the opponent happens to need, the cross-examiner must highlight for the jury the improbability of this favorably selective memory. The witness will be shown to be nothing more than the wayward child, who when confronted about the muddy church clothes, remembers she did nothing to get dirty but can't remember how the mud got on the clothes. Just as the parent would quietly lead the child to say "I don't remember" until that response lacked any credibility, so too the cross-examiner uses the same method to discredit the witness.

In this example, a police officer testified that his partner went to the door of a house. The testifying witness remained at the squad car on the roadside. The distance from one to the other was approximately twenty yards. At the preliminary hearing, the officer was questioned as to whether he heard anything coming from the house or the porch area, and he testified "not really." The subject was then dropped.

Now, on direct testimony, this same officer testified that he heard some conversation from the porch area. He now remembers specifically that he heard his partner say something that included the word "police" before breaking down the door.

At trial, the two issues as to whether the officer on the porch made himself known to the inhabitants of the residence and whether the residents gave him permission to enter the front door is directly at issue. After the witness is confronted at trial with his preliminary hearing testimony of "not really" hearing any conversation from the porch area, and after being confronted with the physical facts that are inconsistent with his ability to hear what happened on the porch, the following transpired:

Q: You cannot tell this jury the exact words that were used in that conversation, can you?

A: No, I cannot remember.

Q: You cannot remember the whole conversation that you now claim you heard?

A: No, I cannot remember.

Q: You claim you now remember your partner using the word "police?"

A: Yes.

Q: But you cannot remember anything else about it?

A: No.

Q: You cannot remember what the inhabitants said?

A: No.

Q: You cannot remember if they said come in?

A: No.

Q: You cannot remember if they said stay out?

A: No.

Q: You just cannot remember anything about what the inhabitants said?

A: That is right.

Q: You cannot remember anything about what your partner said, other than that you claim he used the word "police" in whatever he said?

A: That is right.

Q: You cannot remember if he said, "Police, open up?"

A: No, I can't.

Q: You cannot remember if he said, "Police, I am going to kick down the door?"

A: (Pause) No, I can't.

Q: You cannot remember if he said, "Police, I am going to shoot down the door?"

A: Well, I don't believe he would say that.

Q: Officer, the question was, you cannot remember if he said, "I am going to shoot down the door?"

A: No, I really cannot remember what he said.

Again, taking the witness through so many facts that he "cannot remember" destroys the credibility of the witness. The reason the answer lacks credibility is the application of the technique demonstrating that under the circumstances of this case, and given the training of the officer, it seems highly unlikely that he could not hear the words of his fellow officer. The "I cannot remember" answer raises the question of whether the witness can remember anything in the context of his previous general denial at the preliminary hearing. The witness's credibility in remembering only one fact that is helpful to his partner at trial now seems improbable. Through the application of this technique, the "I don't remember" witness can be of substantial value and assistance to the cross-examiner.

Below is an example of the second technique, showing that a person with the special characteristics of this witness would be expected to know or remember those particular facts.

The defendant car driver, who is accused of being intoxicated, cannot recall the details of a two-hour period. After satisfactorily answering a series of detailed questions about the early evening hours, complete with details of a party she had attended, the people at the party, and the time she left, the questioning moves on to when she left:

Q: You left the party at about 10:30 p.m.?

A: I'm really not sure — yes.

Q: You would agree, though, 10:30 is the approximate time you left?

A: Well, I really can't be exact, but about 10:30.

Q: Okay, let's work backward. The collision was at 12:15 p.m.?

A: Yes.

Q: You already said that you left the party around 10:30?

A: Yes.

Q: That would leave approximately an hour and forty-five minutes unaccounted for?

A: Yes.

Q: It could be two hours?

A: All right, two hours unaccounted for.

Q: Just before the collision at 12:15 p.m., you were headed west?

A: Yes.

Q: You know you were headed west on Lattice Street?

A: Yes.

Q: But you do not know from where you were coming?

A: No.

Q: You had been gone from the party for one hour and forty-five minutes?

A: Yes, about that long.

Q: But you do not remember where you had gone?

A: No, I do not. I guess I just drove.

Q: But you don't remember where you drove?

A: No.

Q: You don't remember whether you stopped?

A: No.

Q: You don't remember why you might have stopped?

A: No.

Q: You don't remember where you might have stopped?

A: No.

The jury is shown that the witness has a remarkable memory of only certain events.

Similarly in a federal civil rights lawsuit a witness claims not to be able to recall that the plaintiff/former arrestee of the defendant had questioned the arresting officer on multiple occasions as to why she was being arrested. Yet the witness can still recall "literally word for word" that the officer advised the plaintiff on at least two occasions of her rights and claims to remember the officer's verbatim description of other, less important subjects.

In a criminal case, a ten-year-old girl recalls being sexually assaulted (fondled) by her babysitter. However, defense counsel knows from the preliminary hearing transcript that she can't recall multiple other events surrounding this incident. Here the cross-examiner will use, "You don't remember?" as a theme phrase to show that the child cannot remember very simple details, both before and after the alleged incident, and has only an overview or conclusory memory of the fondling incident itself. "You don't remember?" is used to illustrate that the event, in fact, did not occur:

Q: When your mother left, you were watching TV?

A: Yes, I was watching Disney.

Q: Tony (the defendant babysitter) wanted to watch MacNeil/Lehrer?

A: Some dumb news show.

Q: You didn't want to watch that?

A: No.

Q: And you told him so?

A: Yes.

Q: But he changed the channel anyway?

This chapter is fully developed, showing a great recall of many facts. The cross-examiner then moves to the fondling incident:

Q: Now you've told us that you wrestled with Tony?

A: Yes.

Q: And that when that happened Tony put his hand inside your underwear?

A: Yes.

Q: You were in your bedroom when you were wrestling with Tony?

A: Yes.

Q: Tony didn't shove you into your room?

A: No.

Q: Tony didn't put you in "time out" in your room?

A: No.

Q: Tony didn't want to watch TV in your room?

A: No.

Q: And Tony didn't want to play in your room?

A: No.

Q: You don't remember how come you were in your room?

A: I just was.

Q: You don't know when Tony came to your room?

A: No, I don't.

Q: And you don't remember why Tony ever came to your room?

A: I don't know.

Chapter 21

CREATION AND USES OF SILENCE

SYNOPSIS

§ 21.01   Silence as a Technique

Silence speaks louder than words, and often it speaks more eloquently to the jury. Silence is its own technique. It has different uses and, under differing circumstances, it has different meanings. The cross-examiner must resist the natural human instinct to fill the silence in a courtroom. Silence can accomplish what words cannot.

§ 21.02   Silence as a Timeout

Trial work is intricate. Whether on direct or cross, questions must be posed in a permissible style in accordance with rules. There are multiple rules: evidentiary rules, procedural rules, substantial law rules, and the written and unwritten rules of the judge trying the case. Answers given continuously change the balance of persuasion. The lawyer senses the attentiveness of the jury. The flow of information that the lawyer must process is immense. There are times during a cross-examination when the lawyer simply needs to take a timeout. It may be because the lawyer has received an answer she has to deal with in some detail or an answer so good she wants to let it "breathe." Or perhaps a chapter has concluded and the lawyer must collect her thoughts before beginning the new chapter. Because trials are so complex, there are hundreds of reasons for a moment's reflection.

§ 21.03   The Advocate Must Control the Courtroom

It is important that the advocate feel comfortable in the courtroom. Of course, comfort is a relative state of being. The advocate feels comfortable when she is in control. Yet there are times when the advocate can sense that events are not under control. If the cross-examiner wishes to take a moment to regroup, consider a new tactic, or take a moment for any other reason, the cross-examiner need not ask the judge for permission. Does the judge usually deny the request? Worse, what if she did? The lawyer doesn't need the permission of the opponent, the witness, or anyone else in order to gather one's thoughts or materials. If the examiner needs the time, the examiner should take the time. After all, the time taken is measured in seconds, not minutes. The question is *how* to take a moment in such a way so as to continually demonstrate that the lawyer has matters under control. There is a technique to take a brief timeout in such a way that the silence represents the examiner's power. The silence that occurs when the cross-examiner is regrouping for further cross-examination is a silence that disturbs witnesses. The cross-examiner can create additional witness anxiety. The objective is not to create witness anxiety, although that is certainly a byproduct. Anxiety in a witness is useful in that an anxious witness finds it more difficult to deceive. This phenomenon is further discussed in chapter 8, *The Only Three Rules of Cross-Examination*.

§ 21.04   Take a Moment/Take a Sip

Before rising to cross-examine, the advocate should partially fill a glass of water. Do not fill the entire glass, since the day will come when the glass will be knocked over.

Now, during the cross-examination, an unexpected answer comes that must be exploited. It may be so good that the lawyer must leap on it and push it to its boundaries (see chapter 26, *Loops, Double Loops, and Spontaneous Loops*), or so bad that it must be minimized efficiently. In either event, the lawyer has come to the conclusion that she needs a moment to think about her alternatives. At the same time, the lawyer doesn't want to stand at the podium looking as if she is stuck for words.

A short timeout may be created by walking over to counsel table and taking a sip of water. If additional time is needed, the lawyer can take a moment to pour another quarter glass of water and sip it. These normal actions reassure the jury that the lawyer remains in control and that the lawyer feels comfortable in the courtroom. Having created a timeout, and having regrouped, the lawyer is ready to return to the task.

§ 21.05 Silence to Create Drama for Things About to Happen, or "Sit Still Please, While I Reload"

Sometimes the advocate wishes to emphasize factual points about to be made in the cross-examination. A technique for focusing the attention of a fact finder on material about to be disclosed is to create silence before entering into that new chapter. This technique can also be useful in long cross-examinations. The silence serves to punctuate the material and give the jurors a moment of rest before the cross-examiner undertakes a new and important area.

It is equally effective in which the lawyer is engaging in a confrontational cross-examination. The confrontation may be a series of chapters designed to show the witness is mistaken, in which case the tone will be relatively gentle and understanding. Perhaps the confrontation will be built around a series of chapters designed to show that the witness has a motive, interest, or bias causing him to be less than honest. Here the tone may be less gentle (see chapter 22, *Voice, Movement, Body Language, and Timing*). Nonetheless, in any series of chapters that are confrontational, the emotional pinch of the cross-examination can prove wearing on the fact finder. As the emotional temperature in the courtroom rises, the cross-examiner runs the risk that the confrontational chapters begin to sound repetitive or unfair. By introducing silence at one or more points between confrontational chapters, the lawyer gives the fact finder time to breathe while simultaneously emphasizing that the amount of material available with which to challenge the witness is quite large.

In preparation for such a cross-examination, the necessary chapters of cross-examination must have been written. Within these chapters it is important to note the exhibits that may be used. Where possible, the source of the fact contained within a leading question has been noted (see chapter 10, *Page Preparation of Cross-Examination*). All sources, whether transcripts, exhibits, or prior statements, should be stored at counsel table. Where permissible, the cross-examination should be conducted from a podium or another part of the courtroom away from counsel table. If counsel is expected to cross-examine from a seated position at counsel table, the lawyer should place all materials necessary for impeachment on a separate part of the table away from the chapters of cross-examination that are directly in front of the lawyer. The key to this technique is to create physical space between the cross-examiner and materials that will be used for impeachment.

The cross-examiner will perform the cross-examination using the written chapters. At certain points there will be chapters that require a document. Perhaps the document is a transcript, a photograph, or an exhibit. At the point in the cross-examination where a source document is required (most often for impeachment), counsel returns to her table to retrieve the necessary source document. The necessary documents should not be buried in the file or in boxes. Instead, all sources and documents needed for the cross-examination should be laid out in an identifiable order on counsel table.

Example:

Q: Today you say that the first time you saw the truck, you were already within 50 feet of it?

A: Yes.

Choreography:

1) Cross-examiner says nothing, but momentarily permits her eyes to linger on the witness, then she moves to counsel table (no need to rush over);

2) An unhurried, studied look at the array of source materials;

3) Selection of the appropriate transcript;

4) Purposefully turn through the pages to the correct page and line;

5) Return to podium; (or other location from which the cross-examination was being conducted)

6) The casting of eyes upon the witness; and

7) Begin impeachment from the transcript or document.

This choreography takes several seconds. The silence between the last answer and the beginning of the impeachment has infused additional importance into the coming questions. The series of calm, purposeful movements has communicated to the witness and the jury that the cross-examiner is confident and in total control of the facts. The movement to counsel table followed by retrieval of the necessary transcript or document reinforces the witness's fear that any facts the cross-examiner requires may be retrieved instantly. This technique has the added benefit of keeping the area where the cross-examination is to be performed (podium or other favored area) uncluttered.

There is an additional benefit to keeping the source materials away from the area of the delivery of the cross-examiner. The lawyer's movement from the podium back to counsel table communicates her sense of control and freedom in the courtroom. Self-confidence is evident, both by the freedom and the purposefulness of movement.

In order to successfully employ this technique of silence, the advocate should refrain from the practice of taking to the podium a trial notebook containing virtually everything related to the chapters of cross-examination about to be performed. Instead, source material for impeachment or demonstrative purposes needs to be left a sufficient distance from the cross-examiner so that the lawyer's movement to retrieve the necessary document creates several seconds of silence. Even then, it is unnecessary to stack source materials on counsel table only to fumble through them. Instead, they should be arranged for easy access as circumstances justify. After the necessary document is retrieved from counsel table and used in the cross-examination, the cross-examiner will ordinarily want to take the source material back to the counsel table. This creates additional silence. The advocate should treat the source document with respect. It should not be dropped on counsel table or tossed into a pile. Any document used should be replaced in some systematic way so as to stress its importance. In addition, the orderly storing of materials necessary for cross-examination both implies and establishes another element of self-control and confidence within the cross-examiner. The fact finder can use the silence created to add attention to the point just scored. Remember, however, that the cross-examiner is aiming to create moments of silence, not minutes. The purpose is to highlight the material that can benefit from such highlighting. This technique is not for show, but for emphasis.

If the cross-examiner knows that, in all likelihood, she will need to use the source material again in an upcoming chapter, the prompt and orderly return of the material to counsel table is essential in order to recreate the mini-drama before a future impeachment.

§21.06 The Effect on the Witness

What does the witness do while the lawyer slowly and methodically creates this silence? The uninitiated witness may sit calmly at first, but will continue to follow the lawyer with his eyes. The witness who has been to the courtroom before will likely not be as calm. That witness is following the lawyer, but with a knowing sense that the lawyer is about to find the impeachment material.

In either case, the witness is silent. The witness is focused on the lawyer. That reinforces the focus of the jury and judge on the lawyer as well.

The witness's anxiety builds as the silence lengthens. The witness comes to realize that he is about to be impeached. There is a cumulative effect on the witness after the lawyer has completed this technique, and then returns to the technique for the next impeachment. The witness now realizes that the lawyer's silent trip to counsel's table ends with an unpleasant experience for the witness. That anxiety may manifest itself in the visual expression of the witness, the body language of the witness, and the tone of the witness when he finally answers. It may cause the witness to recant. Regardless of the witness's reaction, the lawyer continues to move in a self-confident and measured manner, conveying to all that she is in control.

§21.07 Silence to Paragraph Chapters: The Technique of Keeping Selected Chapters at Counsel Table

Some witnesses will require many chapters of cross-examination on several separate areas. In such a cross-examination it may prove useful to store at counsel table chapter bundles relating to separate issues, taking to the podium only the chapter bundle necessary for that portion of the cross-examination about to be performed. This technique is most useful in multi-chapter cross-examinations on distinctly separate areas of the case. There are, of course, multi-chapter crosses in which certain chapters follow each other with great rapidity — chapter bundles (see chapter 10, *Page Preparation of Cross-Examination* and chapter 11, *Sequences of Cross-Examination*). Example: In an identification case, defense counsel may cover chapters on height, weight, eyes, clothing, and other areas of description a chapter at a time, but several of the chapters may be completed in rapid order. They should be bundled together. One chapter should flow naturally to the next with little loss of time.

On the other hand, there are some impeaching cross-examinations where one particular sequence of chapters (a chapter bundle) may take a significant period of time. That set of chapters is often a whole story in and of itself. These chapters may be all the lawyer will need at the podium or presentation area. When counsel has completed this set of chapters, she can close it up, as she would a book that has now been concluded, take it back to counsel table, and place it in the stack of completed material. Then she may survey the table, as if to say to the witness, "I will now select my next arrow from my quiver." The effect on the judge and jury conveys complete organization. To the opponent, there is frustration knowing nothing can be done to stop the cross-examiner. Of course, the lawyer knows which chapter she is going to pick, and after a brief pause to locate the next needed chapter or bundle of chapters, she can select the material and bring it back to begin the next chapter or set of chapters on the witness.

This short break not only gives the lawyer a moment to change the focus of her thoughts, but allows the jury to digest what it has just heard, make conclusions about the value of the previous chapter, and appreciate that topics are about to be changed. In effect, the silence creates an editorial comment in the story. The jury understands that a chapter or chapter bundle has been completed, and that the cross-examination will now move into a new chapter or chapter bundle (see chapter 11, *Sequences of Cross-Examination*).

§ 21.08 The Effect on the Witness by Silence Between Chapters

When the lawyer closes the material at the podium or other location where the lawyer is delivering the cross-examination, the witness may well silently (or not so silently) breathe a sigh of relief that the cross-examination has ended. When the witness realizes that the lawyer has not ended the cross-examination, but has only gone to counsel's table to retrieve materials to deliver more cross-examination, there is a decided downturn in the effect and mood of the witness. This roller coaster of emotions destroys the confidence of the witness, creates more anxiety, and tires the witness dramatically. The witness feels helpless to stop the cross-examination. In fact, the only way the witness can likely accelerate the end of the cross-examination is to revert to short, affirmative answers to the lawyer's leading questions.

§ 21.09 Silence to Focus Attention on the Importance of Exhibits

Counsel is permitted to pace an impeachment or other dramatic moment by moving to counsel table and retrieving the appropriate exhibit: a photograph, a signed report, documents, or other tangible items. This technique is similar to the "sit still while I reload" technique. Counsel has the opportunity to leave the podium or presentation area and control more courtroom space by moving over to the table. Both techniques can be used either to highlight the importance of an exhibit for impeachment or to highlight the importance of an actual trial exhibit. When the lawyer efficiently plucks out the single exhibit needed precisely when she needs it, the lawyer further demonstrates her ability to control that witness. The cross-examiner also demonstrates mastery of the facts of the case, which in turn enhances the credibility of the lawyer with the fact finder. Now, having created an amount of purposeful silence while obtaining the necessary exhibit, the cross-examiner has highlighted the importance of the exhibit about to be used. The silence focuses all attention on the exhibit.

The technique creates additional opportunities to infuse drama into the cross-examination. The lawyer can pick up the document and hold it high at eye level, as if to say to the witness, "Now do you want to tell the truth?" The lawyer can pick up the document and hold it as if to say to the witness, "Look, what's the use in your dodging? I've got the proof right here." The document can be aimed at the witness as if it were an offering the witness wanted to ignore. Or, alternatively, it can be carried back to the presentation area and read from gently: "Let me remind you of your statement of February 7, 1986."

Silence transforms a document or transcript into a prop on the stage. The cross-examiner may even turn, holding the document in her hand in a very non-threatening fashion and simply stare at the witness. This tells a jury, "Look, I know the witness is wrong and the proof is right here in my hand." The cross-examiner can freeze the witness in his seat and softly correct him with, "That isn't what you said originally, is it?" or "Let's go over that paragraph of the contract," or "Doctor, let me show you the medical report."

The cross-examiner alone chooses the range of emotions brought to the courtroom through these techniques. Silence magnifies and highlights the emotion chosen. The lawyer never errs by underplaying her emotion. Overplaying the emotion creates multiple risks (see chapter 22, *Voice, Movement, Body Language, and Timing*). The importance of this technique is that it uses the silence to focus the jury on the facts being revealed. An additional benefit may be found in the emotional reaction shown by the witness. However, the reaction of the witness is secondary to the importance of the material. Silence is used as a technique to aid the fact finder in their appreciation of the facts produced by the cross-examination. The effect on the witness is always secondary. Counsel must recall that it is not necessary that the witness appreciate the facts being scored, only that the fact finder understand the importance of the facts being established.

§21.10 Silence as an Answer

Silence itself can serve as a dramatic answer. The use of silence as an answer focuses all attention on the question and the word selection that was carefully selected within the question. The silence shows the jury that any answer would hurt the witness and the witness is unwilling to give the answer.

For the cross-examiner, it is often predictable when the witness will either refuse to answer a question or be very slow in answering the question. One source of this predictability comes from the fact that most witnesses will not answer a question when they know that the answer requested by the cross-examiner in the leading question does not exist. Examples: a fact not listed in a report, an event not recorded, or a document that does not exist.

In order to derive the greatest impact from missing information, several preliminary chapters should be developed (see chapter 18, *Advanced Impeachment Techniques*). First, establish the existence of an appropriate document, hearing transcript, or occasion for which the material should be found.

For example, in a medical malpractice case, the defendant/doctor is cross-examined as follows:

Q: After the surgical procedure, you prepared a written report?

A: Yes.

Q: You do this after you perform every surgical procedure?

A: Yes.

Q: This is the protocol or standard method that you have been trained to use?

A: Yes.

Q: The report contains a description of every significant thing that was done during your surgical procedure?

A: Yes.

Q: It contains who was present?

A: Yes.

Q: What operating room that was used?

A: Yes.

Q: What was done in the surgery?

A: Yes.

Q: And what results were obtained?

A: Yes.

Q: Such a detailed report is necessary because a surgeon will perform hundreds upon hundreds of surgeries?

A: Many hundreds.

Next, establish the opportunity, ability, and desire to have correctly and completely either recorded or related the information that concerns that document, hearing, or occasion in a separate chapter:

Q: Doctor, the surgical report is a very important document?

A: Yes.

Q: It is done so that you can accurately recall what occurred during any one of your many surgical procedures?

A: Yes.

Q: It is used by other doctors, consulting doctors to know what was done during the surgery?

A: Yes.

Q: Those other doctors base decisions that they will make on that report?

A: Yes.

Q: Many times, consulting doctors have to rely on that report because you are not available to talk with them?

A: That is true.

Finally, establish the importance in a separate chapter of the specific information, showing that it is the very sort of information one would expect to find within the document or transcript.

Q: Doctor, we discussed the importance of the report?

A: Yes.

Q: And, of course, the information put in there is what makes the report so important?

A: Yes.

Q: It is a thorough description of the surgical procedure?

A: Yes.

Q: You describe where the incision was made?

A: Yes.

Q: You describe what appliances or foreign bodies were placed in the open wound?

A: Yes.

Q: You describe what sponges you place in there?

A: Yes.

Q: You describe what clamps you place in there?

A: Yes.

Q: You describe everything that goes into that open surgical wound?

A: Yes.

Q: Doctor, just as importantly, you describe everything that was taken out of the open surgical wound?

A: Yes.

Q: Each instrument, each appliance, and each sponge is individually noted as having been removed from the open surgical wound?

A: Yes.

Q: All of that is very important?

A: Yes, it is.

Q: It is important to make sure that nothing is left in the surgical wound?

A: That is true.

Now that the jury understands that the witness is claiming this information to be important, that the witness had every reason to put it in a document or relate it in a previous statement, and that there was every opportunity to do so, the absence of the information can be pointed out. That absence is its own chapter:

Q: Doctor, nowhere in our surgical report concerning the plaintiff do you show where sponge number three was removed from the open surgical wound, do you?

A: .... (papers shuffle)

As this technique demonstrates, silence can be a powerful answer. Sometime in our years of schooling, each of us can remember being called on by the teacher when we did not know the answer or could not find the right material. The resulting silence was embarrassing, perhaps even humiliating. The silence roared in our ears and showed in our faces. When impeaching by omission (see chapter 18, *Advanced Impeachment Techniques*), the lawyer can place the witness in the same position by asking the witness to locate the language or facts that were omitted from the document. The answer is silence.

Too often the cross-examiner hurriedly points out that the material is not there, and then rushes to the next question. Too often the cross-examiner dispels the silence by offering up the next question. In order for the silence to serve its purpose, the examiner must allow silence to linger in the courtroom until it has proven the central point — that the important information suggested by the witness on direct is to be found *nowhere* in the report.

Interestingly, the longer the lawyer permits the silence, the longer and more strenuously the witness will search for the missing information — even when the witness knows the information is not there.

There is a heavier silence in the courtroom as the witness slowly at first, and then more hurriedly, scans the document and appears perplexed by the omission in the document. This occurs whether or not the witness knows prior to trial that she will be impeached by omission. The witness feels compelled to look at the document, in hopes that the omitted material will magically appear. As the witness looks at the document, let the silence build. The silence is dramatic and becomes more defining. It highlights the fact that this important material will not be found.

There is sometimes an unusual witness who refuses to even look at the document. That witness stares at the lawyer, but says nothing. That silence coupled with the conduct hurts the witness not the lawyer. The witness defiantly acknowledges the truth.

§ 21.11 Silence and the Pouting Witness

If the witness refuses to search for the omitted information in the document, nothing requires the cross-examiner to hurry into the next question. By looking the witness in the eyes and holding the gaze, the cross-examiner can create the silence nonetheless. The jury will understand why the witness fails to even look at the document. After a moment, the cross-examiner may break the silence by questioning along these lines:

Q: You are not looking at the document?

A: No.

Q: And the reason you are not looking at the document is because "the note" is not there.

A: Right.

Q: It's not there because you never put it there.

A: I guess I didn't.

Should the cross-examiner want to spend more time on the lack of the note, she may do so at will. She simply takes the document page by page or paragraph by paragraph:

Q: Doctor, it is not on page 1?

A: No.

Q: It is not on page 2?

A: No.

§ 21.12 Silence in the Misleading Witness

Certain experienced and professional witnesses (often expert witnesses), when confronted with documents, reports, and treatises that do not contain the information requested in the report, have developed a misleading answer to the question.

Example:

Q: Nowhere in the report does it show that the chemical was weighed?

A: I don't know.

The witness knows full well that the report does not show the weight of the chemical. The witness is attempting to put the lawyer in a defensive position by testing the lawyer as to whether or not the lawyer knows with particularity and precision the content of the report. The cross-examiner has within her control a technique that will shift the anxiety back to the witness. The cross-examiner will go page by page, paragraph by paragraph, or line by line if necessary through the report with the witness eliminating any doubt and confirming that the chemical was never weighed. This effort by the witness to put the lawyer on the defensive will backfire if the lawyer responds with this technique. The more time used to show the jury that nowhere in the report is the chemical weighed, the more this technique highlights that fact of omission. The more time and effort the witness puts into dodging the question, the more damaging the omission is to the witness's credibility.

What if the report contains hundreds of pages? The judge and the jury will refuse to give the cross-examiner time to go page by page, paragraph by paragraph, or certainly line by line through such a voluminous report. Even if the cross-examiner was permitted that time, the effect on the fact finder would be severe boredom, and the drama that the cross-examiner hoped to create would have the opposite effect. The cross-examiner need only follow the following technique:

Q: Doctor, you say that you don't know if the report shows that the chemical was never weighed?

A: That is right.

Q: Doctor, when you step down from the witness stand, you may take a copy of the report with you and look through it page by page, paragraph by paragraph or line by line. If you find it, you will return to the courtroom and tell me?

A: I suppose so counselor.

This question can receive an objection, but more likely, the judge will favor the lawyer over the misleading witness who disavows knowledge that he should have.

§ 21.13   Completing the Moment: Silence as an Exclamation Mark

Silence can be used to highlight information that has just been elicited. The entire focus of this silence is to call attention and add emphasis to the fact *last* made (see chapter 12, *Employing Primacy and Recency*). It informs the jury that what was just said was of great significance and should not to be overlooked. In the theater, this technique is termed "completing the moment." Completing the moment must contain no motion, no action, and no distraction of any kind. This void of sound and action is the ultimate exclamation mark. This technique should only be used with a question of great value producing an answer of great significance.

For example, a customer at a nightclub is removed from the club. He is beaten up by the doorman. He goes home, arms himself and returns to the nightclub to see the manager. The doorman who had beaten him earlier refuses to let him in. After an angry interchange, the customer eventually shoots the doorman. The customer is charged with aggravated assault. The doorman is cross-examined:

Q: Kenny (the customer) came to the front door?

A: Yes.

Q: His face was bruised and bloodied?

A: Yes.

Q: You had done that to him?

A: Yes.

Q: You had beaten him up?

A: I removed him from the club.

Q: When he came back, he did not threaten you with his weapon?

A: That is true.

Q: He did not point a gun at you?

A: No.

Q: He did not even show you a gun?

A: No.

Q: He asked to see the manager?

A: Yes.

Q: He told you that he wanted to talk to the manager?

A: Yes.

Q: You didn't tell the manager that a customer wanted to talk with him?

A: That is true.

Q: And you refused to let him see the manager?

A: Yes.

Q: You refused, knowing that he wanted to talk to the manager about your beating him up?

A: Yes.

(Pause for effect at this moment. No movement.)

Another example of completing the moment: In a civil securities fraud case, the stockbroker employed by the defendant's brokerage house is cross-examined. The underlying facts have been produced through the chapter method. This summary chapter is done to summarize and focus on the previous chapters:

Q: For six years you handled the account of Ms. Kruelewitz?

A: Yes.

Q: For six years you had full discretion?

A: Yes.

Q: For six years on every trade you made a full commission?

A: Yes.

Q: You knew she was elderly?

A: Yes.

Q: You knew she was retired?

A: Yes.

Q: You knew she lived off her portfolio's earnings?

A: Yes.

Q: And then, on 12/6/91, you bought for her commodities futures?

A: Yes.

Q: A volatile, high-risk market?

A: Yes, but it was a good investment.

(Complete the moment by silence. No movement.)

As these examples show, "completing the moment" freezes the action by silence. The lawyer's entire gaze must be upon the witness. It is a focused look, but not a stare. Any movement, note taking, change of expression, or turn of the body will detract from the impact of this technique.

Keep in mind, it is termed completing the *moment*, not the *minute*. The lawyer's internal clock will tell her how long is enough. A few seconds is a powerfully long period when used in this context. Let it be clear that the questions used in conjunction with this technique do not have to be aggressive or loud since the impact is derived from the content of the chapter that is reinforced by the use of silence.

§ 21.14   Silence to End a Cross-Examination

Silence to complete the moment is most effective to complete not only the moment, but to complete a bundle of cross-examination chapters or an entire cross-examination. It may be used to highlight a chapter completed immediately before a recess, at the end of the day, or best of all, at the conclusion of the entire cross-examination. Conclude the cross-examination with a chapter containing a critical admission from the witness, and then freeze the moment by the use of silence. Then sit down. In all likelihood, the judge will be the person who next speaks, giving a stamp of approval to the use of silence.

A beautiful, blonde-haired, blue-eyed, 12-year-old little girl claimed to be the victim of sexual assault. The defense lawyer realized before the child ever took the stand that the cross-examination would be sensitive and difficult. In all likelihood the child would cry.

To heighten this terrible effect, the prosecution has dressed the child in as innocent a manner as possible. The child's demeanor (which appeared to be genuine) was timid, quiet, and tearful, without being hysterical.

What could be done with the witness that would help the defendant's theory of the case was to establish that she had not told the people closest to her about the alleged assault. Additionally, over a period of several days, her story changed. The cross-examination, which was relatively brief, ended with a trilogy (see chapter 25, *Trilogies*). The child responded to none of the final chapter's questions:

Q: When the police asked you what happened, you did not tell this story to the police?

A: (The child's face is pointed towards her lap, soft whimpering or crying can be heard just barely over the amplification system.)

Q: When your priest asked you, you did not tell this story to your priest?

A: (The child's position changes, if at all, just slightly.)

Q: When your mother asked you what happened, you did not tell this story your mother?

A: (The whimpering increased just slightly.)

The defense lawyer slowly, without taking her eyes off the witness, moved to counsel table, sat down and continued to look at the witness. It seemed like hours before the judge said, "We all need a break. We will take our noon recess now." It was only a matter of seconds before that interruption by the court and an even shorter period of silence between each question. But the meaning of the silence after each of the questions, heightened by the use of silence to end the cross-examination, made the sequence of non-answers into the focal point of the case.

Chapter 22

VOICE, MOVEMENT, BODY LANGUAGE, AND TIMING

SYNOPSIS

§ 22.01   Conveying Information Aside from the Pure Facts of the Question

A primary method by which information is conveyed to the jury is through the leading questions asked by the advocate. The cross-examiner conveys additional information through voice, movement, body language, and timing. These oratorical and physical cues assist the jury in understanding not only the facts, but also the importance the cross-examiner places on selected facts. These techniques aid the lawyer in establishing impact at selected points in the chapters and on selected chapters in the overall cross-examination.

Tone of voice, movement within the courtroom, body language, and timing are all techniques that can help the jury understand that the cross-examiner is establishing points that cannot reasonably be disputed. This is regardless of whether the cross-examiner is understanding of the weaknesses of the witness, whether the advocate is branding the witness a liar, calling him mistaken, or vouching for his honesty. Lawyers instinctively understand all of these elements and convey with their voices a great deal of emotion. It is therefore important that the emotion conveyed be conscious and consistent with the theory of that particular cross-examination, chapter, and overall theory of the case.

§ 22.02   The Magnifying Effect of the Courtroom

As a general proposition, the courtroom is a magnifying glass held over human behavior. In the courtroom, small voice changes, slight movements, and silences all take on additional meaning. While the jurors may from time to time tune out, they really can't go very far for very long. Their options are limited. They are not allowed to bring in books or begin a conversation with their neighbor. For the most part, the most interesting thing going on is right in front of them: the trial. Because the courtroom fosters this microscopic examination of often fast-moving or complex human events, the cross-examiner must realize that the emotions shown by the cross-examiner are highlighted and appear greater than life-size to the jury.

Consequently, the cross-examiner should always be aware that a moderate amount of any emotion shown by the cross-examiner will appear to the jurors to be a great amount of that emotion. The jury will hear a slightly scornful tone as a caustic and highly derogatory tone. A tear in the eye of the cross-examiner will convey very deep emotion to the jury. Bearing this in mind, the cross-examiner must use the courtroom magnification of emotion for conscious, well-directed use.

§ 22.03   Overuse of Emotion

Assume the cross-examiner faces a very hostile witness. Perhaps it is defense counsel facing a government informant, a prosecutor facing the defendant, a plaintiff's lawyer facing a defendant medical doctor, or an insurance defense lawyer facing a parent plaintiff who has lost a child. Assume the lawyer has the objective of completely discrediting the witness by showing her story to be fabricated. Clearly the content of the questioning will be pointed. Ordinarily the lawyer's voice rises, the words are quickened, the movements are sharper, and the entire scene conveys to the jury the lawyer's lack of respect and scorn for the witness. This may be effective, and, in fact, undoubtedly is effective in limited circumstances and for limited periods of time. A successful cross-examination synchronizes voice, movement, and timing.

On the other hand, there are times when this is not the optimal style. Juries have a difficult time listening to a highly emotional pitch. Withering crosses are great on TV, but they last only three to five minutes. Television judges don't interrupt and juries don't get offended. Real jurors can feel trapped when the emotional pitch of the courtroom becomes uncomfortable. Because the courtroom is a closed environment, levels of discomfort can be reached all too easily.

A sustained, high-pitched, heavy-handed, highly emotional cross-examination will wear down the jury's appreciation for what is being accomplished and overload their emotional circuits. It becomes a distraction, not a teaching aid. Perhaps of most importance, a highly emotional series of questions, unless quickly curtailed, will cause judges to cut off that line of cross-examination. Judges, after all, are only human. While they may (but probably don't) share the cross-examiner's disdain or scorn for a witness, judges are not likely to let the examiner keep beating on the witness with a sledgehammer. As the emotion builds, everyone gets uncomfortable. However, the only person the cross-examiner really wanted to make uncomfortable was the witness. There is a more effective and acceptable technique to achieve that end.

§ 22.04   Underplaying Emotion

Courtroom theatrics are overrated. The jurors want the facts. If they feel the lawyer is substituting emotion for fact, the jurors will begin to block out the factual importance of the leading questions. The emotional pitch distracts them. The lawyer must have confidence in her own ability to teach the case. It it is still possible to instill great drama at appropriate times within a cross-examination. The technique is to realize that virtually anything that sounds out of the ordinary will convey the impression that this information is critical to the jury's decision. Instead of becoming louder in her questioning, the lawyer can break out of an overly emotional, theatrical style by lowering her voice, slowing down her timing, and using non-threatening gestures and movements. This is not to diminish the usefulness of the powerful chapter of cross-examination with a single pointed gesture or a raised voice where appropriate. Where are these efforts appropriate? These techniques are appropriate when the cross-examiner wishes to plant a flag — to tell a jury that this information is very important to the contrasting theories of the case. There are significant advantages to being able to address important facts at any emotional pitch that will be tolerated and appreciated by the jurors.

The advocate will benefit from having multiple helpful non-distracting techniques to plant a flag or draw the attention of the jurors to a particular question and answer. The cross-examiner should understand that a small movement, a lowering of the voice, and the judicious use of silence can all be used to draw the attention of the fact finder to the fact or chapter of great significance. Armed with multiple techniques, the cross-examiner can make a concise, well-reasoned, intelligent decision on which technique to use, rather than be saddled with only a single technique from which to work. Much the same way that a racing bicycle has many gears, the adept cross-examiner must have many emotional levels of cross-examination from which to ply her craft.

Instead of jabbing the finger at the witness, the cross-examiner can use open-armed shrugs. Instead of continuously scowling at the witness, the cross-examiner can use some wide-eyed responses or a slight tilt or lowering of the head to show the jury that the answers are acknowledged as less than candid. By building breathing space between particularly powerful questions or chapters, the questions have greater impact and it is clear to the jury that the examiner is in control. Lies or contradictions may be revealed in a slower and more thorough fashion.

Imagine a cross-examination in which the lawyer revealed prior inconsistent statements that the cross-examiner believes were contrived by the witness at the time they were made. Assume that the witness is willing to concede that his prior statements on a particular issue were lies. The tendency of many cross-examiners is to force the jurors to pay great attention to these concededly important admissions through use of an angry tone, with finger pointed and eyes narrowed. The cross-examiner demands in an emphatic tone, "And that was a *lie?*"

Effective? Maybe. But how is this technique going to sound the third, fourth, and fifth times? Unfortunately, in this case, the content is diminished by the style. The lawyer overloads the jury's emotional attention span. That dramatic, harsh delivery will begin to grate on the nerves of the jurors. Furthermore, such a brutal style encourages a judge to limit these factual attacks either by an argumentative objection or on her own initiative.

What is the problem? The information within the questions is relevant and the issue of credibility is fairly before the court, but the method of cross-examination appears overbearing in the confined space of a courtroom. When the judge understandably steps in to tone down the lawyer, the message to the jury is that this questioning is unjustified. That is a bad message. What the cross-examiner really needs is the latitude to prove the lies of the witness without incurring the wrath of the judge, drawing an objection from the opponent, or causing discomfort among the jurors. Furthermore, the other real goal is to encourage the witness to continue to admit that he lied. Even if the lawyer is forbidden to put an emotional stress on that question, a witness repeatedly testifying that he has lied is a witness to be cherished and encouraged — not assaulted and discouraged.

§ 22.05   Gentler Is Stronger

If the identical words are used with a soft voice, a calmer tone, and conversational facial gestures, the lawyer can score just as many points and keep the jury fresh and willing to listen to the attack. The advocate may quietly ask: "That was a lie?" The lawyer may add to it a little hand shrug, as if to say there really is nothing unusual about this, that it is simply . . . another lie.

Quieter is louder in a courtroom. This may sound a bit too Zen for some advocates, but it is true. A lowered voice can instill far more drama with far less risk than the same question asked in a very loud and demanding tone. A matter-of-fact voice when coupled with very damaging admissions by a witness suggests to the jury that the facts clearly demonstrate the point. No additional emphasis is necessary. The strength of the cross-examination is not diminished by the lack of harshness; it is enhanced. The same subtle dramatic effect can be used on a witness who has changed her story: "But now the facts have changed?"

Even when the question being asked is not objectionable per se, if it is asked often enough and harshly enough the opponent is going to object as "argumentative" and the judge is going to sustain the objection. Judges simply don't like messy scenes in their courtroom. Judges all want to control their courtroom, and they have the right to do so. No one gets reversed for these types of rulings. Loud, harsh, ugly scenes suggest that the judge's courtroom is out of control. Judges don't like anything to be out of control, including lawyers who behave out of control. Overly emotional presentations sound out of control.

There are precious few cross-examinations that truly result in the destruction of a witness. The believability of a witness is seldom killed with a sledgehammer series of questions. The lawyer is more likely to destroy the credibility of a witness by letting the witness unravel slowly. The cross-examiner who is willing to quietly make point after points, establish a series of worthwhile goals, and efficiently impeach or show motive, interest, or bias will get greater results than a lawyer who has the same evidence but insists on using showmanship instead of technique. The picture of a repetitively harsh cross-examination or an examination performed in a consistently angry, incredulous, or accusatory manner is an ugly picture indeed. All people, jurors included, avoid ugly scenes.

§ 22.06 Picking the Appropriate Emotion

That is not to say that there can be no emotion within a cross-examination. It is just that the emotion and its level must be appropriate for the courtroom, witness, and theme of the case. As an example, an eyewitness must be cross-examined in a case in which the defense is misidentification occurring through human frailty. The lawyer is not alleging malice, misconduct, or subterfuge on the part of the witness. She is just simply pointing out that there are so many inconsistencies: The opportunity to observe was so brief and the witness was so unsure. A conviction based upon this evidence would be, if not a mortal sin, at least a grievous legal error. The cross-examination tone and style is characterized by understanding. The defense lawyer can appreciate how difficult the circumstances were by displaying to the jury and to the witness that it is all right to be mistaken. Mistakes happen. Reassure the witness that changing the story happens.

In pursuit of this theory, the lawyer must exhibit understanding of the human frailty of the witness. Punish the witness not in the slightest for discussing how difficult the circumstances were, how unsure he currently is, and how much he would like to change descriptions to make his memory fit the case now.

This eyewitness is frequently a victim and certainly innocent of any wrongdoing. Therefore, anything done by the cross-examiner that conveys punishment, disapproval, approbation, or disrespect will lead directly to the jury's disapproval of the cross-examiner. Using soft words and phrases to convey the lack of precision that is so characteristic of the witness's observation is far better:

Q: As I understand it, Ms. Jones, there were no street lights on the block in which this happened?

A: True. Yes.

Q: In fact (open-handed gesture), the street light (far-away gesture) is in the middle of the next block? (head cocked to the side slightly) (Pacing: slow, conversation, no emphasis on any words.)

A: A ways away.

Now, contrast that with an inappropriate voice and tone:

Q: Isn't it true (voice dropping) the nearest street light (scornful tone) is in the next block!!? (heavy emphasis, finger pointing at witness.)

Brilliant Cross? No. On TV maybe, but not in real life.

§ 22.07   Create No Disincentive to the Answer "Yes"

What the cross-examiner wants is for the witness to verify the leading question. The cross-examiner will do very well if witnesses will repeatedly say "yes." It may not be dramatic but it is efficient. When the cross-examiner punishes a witness for agreeing with the leading question the cross-examiner diminishes the likelihood that the witness will keep saying "yes."

The above example of a television-inspired method of cross-examination has managed to convey the information in such a nasty way that the lawyer has alienated herself and her client from the jury, encouraged the witness to resist the leading questions, caused the judge to prepare to pounce on the cross-examiner, and destroyed the utility of the factual message. Furthermore, that kind of questioning is unlikely to encourage a witness to admit other errors, difficulties, or uncertainties. This harsh form of cross-examination punishes the witness for admitting helpful facts. This makes no tactical sense. The lawyer wishes to encourage the witness to admit to inabilities to see things, not discourage. The pointed, accusatory technique incorrectly reinforces the witness's instinct to fight with the cross-examiner — to repel the perceived attack:

A: Well, yes, the light was in the next block, but I could see well enough!

The same is true of impeachment of the eyewitness with prior inconsistent statements. The cross-examiner needs to convey to the witness that it would be unnatural if the story didn't change. It is counterproductive to use a tone that criticizes. How could the story stay consistent since this witness never really had a good look at anything? Example:

Q: Mr. Littman, I understand your testimony to be that you now think the man who robbed you was about six feet tall?

A: Yes.

Q: And that is your best estimate today, isn't it?

A: Yes.

Q: Mr. Littman, the night this happened, you gave a statement to the police? (Classic impeachment follows, all done in conversational tone, no sharp movements or angry voice.)

A: Yes.

Q: Mr. Littman, you wanted to catch the man, didn't you?

A: Yes.

Q: You wanted to give the police as much help as you possibly could?

A: Yes.

Q: You wanted to be as accurate as you could?

A: Sure.

Q: So you told them what you saw as best you could?

A: Yes.

Q: You told them the man was about your height?

A: Yes.

Q: You told the police the robber was about five foot seven?

A: Yes.

The cross-examination is conducted with open-handed gestures and an understanding tone of voice conveying to the jury how natural it is that the first description was the best. The jury, not the witness, understood that the later description must be the product of a faulty recollection or some other problem yet to be revealed. In this way, the witness is reassured that maybe nothing terrible will happen by admitting changes in the story. In fact, the witness is pleasantly surprised to discover that cross-examining counsel asks rather easy, short questions and is quick to move on after receiving an affirmative answer.

Cross-examination is not an ego contest between the lawyer and the witness. It is simply part of teaching the case to the fact finder. A witness who is willing to answer "yes" to damaging questions should be encouraged, not discouraged in that course of conduct. If the witness learns that an affirmative answer will bring the wrath of the cross-examiner, the witness learns that he may as well try to evade. Teach witnesses consistently. Teach them that it is quite all right to admit damaging information. Teach them that a clear, clean admission will be rewarded through the lawyer moving on to the next topic. Have faith. The jury will understand the import of the admissions.

§ 22.08   Emotion Must Be Congruent with Purpose

Examine the business-like cross-examination of the accident investigation officer who was called by the plaintiff to put in surrounding details of the road wreck resulting in the death of the plaintiff's child. This officer went to the scene, did a routine investigation, discovered some facts of no great significance to the plaintiff, but some of which may be of assistance to the defense. This officer's testimony does not hurt the cross-examiner:

Q: Officer Maloney, you were in charge of collision investigation?

A: Yes.

Q: That means you keep outsiders away so that you can make sure the evidence is left alone?

A: Yes.

Q: The reason you're doing that is to make sure the Department of Transportation lab has a chance to get all of the evidence, and try to find out what happened?

A: Yes.

Q: You know how to do that right?

A: Yes.

Q: You did do that right, didn't you?

A: Yes.

Q: You roped it off?

A: Yes.

Q: You kept the people out?

A: Yes.

Q: You didn't let anyone touch or move things?

A: Yes.

All of this is done in a steady, conversational, business-like tone. The pace can be moderately faster (when compared with the previous example) since this witness is conversant with what is being discussed. This officer has been here before. No great pauses for effect are necessary because the jury can follow the train of thought. The witness is not being pushed or prodded. No emotional pitch is necessary.

The matter-of-fact manner in the cross-examiner's voice and movement shows the jury that it must have been done correctly as it is such a simple task being conveyed in a straightforward manner. Now, when something of significance is either found or not found in the roped off area, the fact that the area was properly protected by the officer will not be in dispute. The tone of voice and non-threatening body language are designed to put the officer at ease. The witness does not sense a trap because there is no trap. There is no need to evade or hedge on answers. The witness is encouraged as being sure of his answers, thus further reinforcing the picture being drawn by cross-examining counsel. The tone of this cross is congruent with this portion of the theory of the case. This officer did the job correctly. In order to non-verbally convey this, the cross-examiner's voice is reassuring and so are all the accompanying mannerisms.

§ 22.09   Emotion to Disguise Purpose

There are occasions when the cross-examiner purposely disguises the emotional content of the information in order to assure a flow of truthful information from a witness who might otherwise be inclined to modify or distort the testimony. Example: A woman meets an alleged rape victim shortly after an alleged rape. The witness describes a set of events and observations that are not unusual. The lack of unusualness is itself significant. The cross-examiner should question in a straightforward and non-threatening manner that conveys fairness. The cross-examiner does not want the witness to appreciate that this material is highly prejudicial to the claims of her friend and that in every question the cross-examiner is undermining the alleged victim's story. All the (leading) questions are therefore asked in an even-handed manner. No sharp gestures or other form of emotional highlighting is used. The cross-examiner conveys that these are easy questions and easy answers unworthy of great reflection:

Q: You were home when Sylvia walked in?

A: Yes.

Q: You were in the living room watching television?

A: Yes.

Q: She walked in the front door and talked to you briefly before she went upstairs?

A: Yes.

Q: It was a routine conversation?

A: Yes.

Q: There was nothing particularly memorable about it?

A: That is true.

Q: She wasn't crying?

A: No, she wasn't.

Q: She wasn't sobbing?

A: No.

Q: And in fact, she did not seem out of control?

A: Correct.

Q: The conversation appeared to you to be no different than any other ordinary conversation you have in the course of a day with a friend?

A: True.

Q: And if you would have seen her out of control, you would have remembered it?

A: Yes.

Q: If her clothes were torn or in disarray, you would have seen it?

A: I think so.

Q: But you didn't see it?

A: No.

Q: What you saw was Sylvia, the person that you knew quite well?

A: Yes.

Q: You and she talked?

A: Yes.

Q: A normal conversation?

A: Yes.

Q: And when the normal conversation ended, she walked up to her room?

A: True.

In this sequence, the lawyer's voice is at conversational level. Similarly, the timing of the questions is in line with a socially paced conversation. The tonal inflections are those of a normal conversation; there is no raised voice for effect. Gestures are neutral; the cross-examiner's body is not tense. This is not interrogation, but a conversation. The normalcy of the lawyer's manner conveys the message to the jury: "Look folks, there really isn't anything abnormal about that scene. As a result, it also means that there is something abnormal about the alleged victim's story."

The advocate is advised to save the emotional pitch for closing. Even then, a little goes a very long way. Underplaying an emotion by the lawyer permits the jury to feel more emotion. However, if the lawyer overplays the emotion, the jury may feel less and abandon the emotion completely. During cross-examination the normalcy of the voice and movements will convey to the jury the abnormal testimony when it is put into its proper context, which will be brought forth fully in the closing argument. It is not necessary or helpful that the witness understand the lawyer's important facts. It is only necessary that the jury understand.

§ 22.10   Underplayed Emotion as a Comment on Content

A relatively young man in his mid thirties, apparently healthy, has died in a house fire. Arson is suspected. His life was insured for $200,000. The widow made a claim for the proceeds of the life insurance policy. The insurance company declined to pay as it investigated the arson charge. The young man's widow did not appear to be shocked, traumatized, or even surprised by news of his death when she received it the following day on vacation. This reaction did not appear consistent with what a young wife's reaction would be upon hearing such news.

During the first trial, the cross-examiner was scornful, direct, and very pointed in her questioning. She was very harsh in her mannerisms. A mistrial was declared because the jury was evenly divided as to the verdict. Jurors described the cross-examination as harsh and insulting. This debriefing educated the cross-examiner.

In the second trial, the cross-examiner questioned the witness in a tone and manner more akin to: "I just don't understand." She used a quiet and almost confused tone — but the tone is underplayed. The cross-examiner seems generally to be inquiring and not in a disbelieving way:

Q: You had gone on vacation without your husband? (Said in a tone that implies: "I don't understand, don't married people vacation together?")

A: Yes.

Q: When you left him, he was healthy?

A: Yes.

Q: When you left him, he was happy?

A: Yes.

Q: When you left him, he was alive?

A: Yes.

Q: You had not called him the day before you were told of his death?

A: No.

Q: You had not visited him?

A: No.

Q: You had not gone home to see him?

A: No.

Q: This call to tell you of his burning to death came out of the blue?

A: Yes.

Q: With you when you got this terrible call was one of your girlfriends?

A: Yes, Sally Major.

Q: Ms. Major has already testified?

A: Yes.

Q: You didn't scream when you got the call?

A: No.

Q: You didn't start to cry?

A: No.

Q: You didn't start to sob?

A: No.

Q: There was no outward suggestion of what you call your "terrifying shock?"

A: No.

Q: You just put down the phone and said "He's dead?"

A: Yes.

Throughout this examination there was an "I just don't understand" tone. These questions were accompanied by a slight lowering of the eyelids, a little frown, a slight tilt of the head (slowly) as if to show confusion. That was the entire dramatic overtone needed. The cross-examination was conducted slowly with pauses between each short question to highlight the "confusion." There is almost a hesitation effect as each question was phrased.

§ 22.11   How to Conduct a Short Cross with Appropriate Emotion

A short cross-examination can still be a very important cross-examination. There may be only a handful of chapters to be examined upon. Within those chapters could be material deserving of appropriate emotion, tone of voice, movements, or pace of questioning.

The witness who is suspected of intentionally deceiving is under cross-examination. The cross must destroy the witness's credibility or the government prevails. The witness has already admitted to a string of prior misconduct (see chapter 11, *Sequences of Cross-Examination*).

The jury is now comfortable with the thought that this witness is a despicable person. It remains to be shown whether the jury will reject this witness's testimony on the issues at this trial. But at least the jury is now fully acquainted with the witness's bad character and propensity to lie. The lawyer can safely punish this witness quickly with her cross-examination. The jury will now permit this.

Having set up the witness's prior inconsistent statement that was designed to elude the police or serve the witness's own needs, the cross-examiner conducts this portion of the cross-examination in a normal tone of voice. She avoids pointing and confrontational gestures, using instead open-handed gestures. Her timing of the questions of cross-examination is slow, with pauses before the word "lie." A true question mark can be heard at the end of each question:

Q: And that . . . was another lie? (emphasis on "lie.")

A: Yes.

Q: It was a lie that *you* created?

A: Yes.

Q: You created it because it would help you?

A: Yes.

Q: You told another lie, because if somebody would *buy* it, if they would buy your lies, you could get out of trouble?

A: Yes.

Q: And if *lies* get you out of trouble, you're all in favor of *lies*? (voice dropping, on "you're all in favor of lies," finger pointing at witness, shaking finger, and slight snarl.)

Hypothetically, the opponent could raise the objection that this is a compound question. On a law school exam it might be. But, in the courtroom, where the pace has moved along briskly, and the witness has been defeated decisively and thoroughly, the government lawyer who has offered this witness truly does not want to object to this as a "compound" question. The gist of the cross is apparent. The ability of the witness to answer is so obvious. Such an objection would appear to the jury to be game playing. If granted, the cross-examiner could ask two damaging questions instead of one.

Should an objection be made to the last question as being a compound or multiple question, then the cross-examiner is invited to slowly and methodically cut through each one of the phrases:

Q: That was another *lie*? (voice and body emphasis on the word "lie.")

A: Yes.

Q: It was a lie that *you* created?

A: Yes.

Q: You created it because it would help *you*?

A: Yes.

Q: *You* told another lie?

A: Yes.

Q: If they would buy your lies, you could get out of trouble?

A: Yes.

Q: If *lies* get you out of trouble, you are all in favor of *lies*? (enunciate each word distinctly.)

A: Yes.

Q: You are all in favor of *lies* whenever you decide they will help you? (finger pointing at witness, shaking finger.)

§ 22.12 Emotions Appropriate for the "Sloppy" Witness

During the cross-examination of the officer who has failed to perform her job and has not collected the evidence that could have freed the client, the lawyer is going to question with a tinge of anger, tending toward betrayal. The lawyer does not call the witness names; there is no need for that. The witness was simply sloppy. Sloppy is something that citizens cannot afford in the criminal justice system. Sloppy police work makes for sloppy verdicts, and sloppy verdicts can convict innocent people.

The emotion to express in the cross-examination is the displeasure for the job done by the officer. Within limits juries are tolerant of human frailty. Furthermore, in general, juries respect police officers. Inefficiency, laziness, and sloppiness are less palatable to the jury. These traits are especially unpalatable when possessed by persons sworn to a duty. Jurors are intolerant of people who have a duty, and whose failure to perform that duty may cause harm or risk to others. It is this emotion the cross-examiner wants to build on:

Q: *You* were there to guard the scene?

A: Yes.

Q: You were there to make sure the evidence was *preserved*?

A: Yes.

Q: The point of preserving the scene is to make sure that the crime lab has a chance to get the evidence?

A: Yes.

Q: So that with the evidence, the lab can find out who did this?

A: Yes.

Q: Crime labs not only help convict the guilty, they can help *free the innocent*?

A: Yes.

Q: That knife was the murder weapon?

A: Yes.

Q: *You* could tell from looking at the victim that he was knifed?   *Alternate Emphasis*: *"knifed"*

A: Yes.

Q: *You* could tell from the knife that it had blood on it?   *"blood"*

A: Yes.

Q: Whoever knifed Jerry Botham held that knife?   *"held that knife"*

A: Yes.

Q: But *you* went over and picked it up?   *"picked it up"*

A: Yes.

Q: *You* picked it up by the handle?   *"handle"*

A: Yes.

Q: *You* picked it up with *your naked hand*?

A: Yes.

Q: And when *you* picked it up, *your* fingerprints and
your palm prints were laid over whosever fingerprints   *"whosever"*
and palm prints were there before?   *"before"*

A: Yes.

Q: So the crime lab could no longer *read* the fingerprints?

A: No.

Q: The fingerprints of the evidence *you* were to *guard*?

A: Right.

Now, in the first format, the lawyer's hands are not open in an understanding way, nor are they pointed, as would be done with the "lying" witness. But the entire hand is being used in perhaps a medium-speed, chopping motion. A single pointed finger has too much impact for this situation. The officer isn't deserving of the understanding that open hands and open shoulders would give. But a pointed finger may be too scalding. The advocate's body is leaning forward, both hands are going out at the same time for emphasis, and both hands are pointing toward the officer on the impact words. The lawyer's lips are tight. There is the slightest negative shaking of the head, eyes are narrowed slightly, and perhaps the fingers are going to the forehead.

The alternate format switches the focus off the witness and onto the actions themselves. If one were to adopt this cross-examination format, one would use a less aggressive voice, and be more demonstrative with their hands. That is, when talking about the officer's putting his fingerprints over the top of the murderer's fingerprints, the cross-examiner might use a grasping motion to simulate the officer's faux pas.

In this alternative approach, the cross-examiner is less attacking and more informative. The body is, therefore, more casual and less forward. The words are spoken simply, but not unkindly. The cross-examination becomes an explanation of poor police practice, not an indictment of the officer himself. The cross-examiner seems almost sorry that all this happened because, had the officer not screwed up, the defendant would today be free.

§ 22.13   Case-Specific Mannerisms

Voice, movement, body language, and timing must be appropriate for every examination performed. They must be appropriate not only for the tone of the examination, but also for the message (the theme) to be conveyed to the jury about the particular witness and the witness's place in the theory of the case. Because the goal with each witness differs, the method, style, and mannerisms in examining each witness may differ. Each cross-examination must be performed in a manner that assists the cross-examiner in obtaining the results desired in that particular cross-examination.

Lawyers must move away from artificial styles to a more conversational or natural approach to each subject and each cross-examination. In the end, the cross-examiner should learn to control the gestures, slow down the timing, soften the movements, and breathe more emotion into smaller, less theatrical questions. These are all conscious decisions, developed and verified before trial. By using these techniques there will be fewer occasions in which the cross-examiner will use angry words or tone. In addition, the jury's attention span is lengthened. Finally, the judge will have less need to intervene to "protect" the witness.

Chapter 23

DIMINISHING OR BUILDING THE POINT

SYNOPSIS

§ 23.01   Strengths and Weaknesses to the Theory of the Case

Both sides of every lawsuit have strengths and weaknesses to their case. Each side has its strengths: good facts, viable, believable chapters, strong issues, and powerful witnesses. Each side also has weaknesses: bad facts, missing chapters, weak issues, and seemingly indefensible witnesses. In fact, it is likely that the vast majority of cases that go to trial can be legitimately argued by the opposing parties, and that a verdict for either party will find adequate support in the record.

There are those few cases, both civil and criminal, where the opponent's facts are overwhelmingly persuasive. In such a case, the strategy of the opposing lawyer's case is simply that he has nothing to lose by trying the lawsuit.

Even in these "impossible" cases there are strengths for the lawyer's side, arguments that can be made, and facts that can be stressed. The lawyer may need to take greater risks since the challenge is "impossible."

§ 23.02   Relationship to the Only Three Rules and the Chapter Method

While both sides of a lawsuit have strengths and weaknesses, the differences are not measured on an absolute scale, but on the scale of perception. It is *the jury's* determination of the value of a point that determines its weight. Diminishing and building a point explores techniques of altering the fact finder's perception of the worth or value of a particular piece of information.

The method of diminishing or building a point builds on the fact-by-fact presentation of evidence and logical progression as set out in *The Only Three Rules of Cross-Examination* (chapter 8). Diminishing or building a point also depends on the advocate's use of the chapter method of cross-examination (see chapter 9, *The Chapter Method of Cross-Examination*).

§ 23.03   Jury Perception (Give Me a Fact, Any Fact)

Somewhere each of us has seen illustrations of principles of perception. One of the most frequently encountered is the one below:

<-------->

>-------<

Though the lines are identical, the lower line appears longer. Similarly, a skilled cross-examiner can make any point of a testimony appear more or less important.

§ 23.04   Methods

[1]   Overview

To diminish the importance of a fact, place it at the end of a series of greater nonfacts, that is, facts that would be of even greater significance *had* testimony been offered to support them. Placing the observed fact at the conclusion of this list makes the observed fact seem small in comparison to bigger facts that could have been or should have been presented.

Conversely, to build the significance of a fact, place it at the conclusion of a series of lesser facts, all of which were testified to by witnesses. By building up to the key fact through a series of questions, each fact taking on greater significance, when the final fact is exposed, and its significance under these circumstances cannot be overlooked. It is made to look larger.

The best way to illustrate the technique of diminishing or building a point is to take a fact in a lawsuit and give an example of how to diminish its value for one side of the lawsuit and, in the alternative, how to build the value of that same fact for the other side of the lawsuit. Assume that one lawyer is skilled in building and diminishing points, but her opponent is not. After reviewing the comparative examples below, make an objective determination as to which side of the lawsuit the jury will more likely decide *appears* stronger or weaker.

[2]   A Controlled Example

[a]   Description

In a theft from a motor vehicle case, a witness testified that she saw the defendant on the day and afternoon in question standing beside the blue car. Other testimony shows this car was entered. Items were stolen out of it. The issue became whether the defendant was the thief.

[b]   To Diminish the Fact and Mental Image

To diminish value of the fact testified to by the witness, begin by showing in very general terms what the witness saw. Then proceed to a "no" chapter of questioning as to specifics that the witness did not see, or things that did not happen. Conclude with a question that is consistent with the limited nature of what the witness saw and what the witness did not see ("You saw the defendant standing by the blue car?"). Example:

Q: You looked out your window?

A: Yes.

Q: You saw Bobby (the defendant)?

A: Yes.

Q: He was in a parking lot?

A: Yes.

The "no" chapter of questioning begins:

Q: He wasn't breaking into the blue car?

A: No.

Q: He wasn't trying to open the door of the blue car?

A: No.

Q: He wasn't trying to open the trunk of the blue car?

A: No.

Q: He wasn't breaking a window?

A: No.

Q: He didn't have a crowbar in his hands?

A: No.

Q: He didn't have a screwdriver in his hands?

A: No.

Q: In fact, he didn't have anything in his hands?

A: No.

Q: He wasn't looking around furtively?

A: No.

Q: He wasn't looking up and down the street?

A: No.

Q: He wasn't looking at the windows of the apartment building?

A: No.

And then a concluding question that reverts to a "yes" question:

Q: He was standing beside the blue car?

A: Yes.

By isolating certain facts, the concluding question makes the conduct that is observed seem unremarkable. It is diminished.

[c] Building the Fact and Mental Image

To build the significance of a fact testified to by the witness, begin very generally with what the witness saw, then slowly and thoroughly proceed with more and more specificity as to what the witness saw. Narrowly confine the specifics more and more to the issue to be proved. In building the fact, use all "yes" questions. Do not revert to a "no" question chapter:

Q: You looked out of your window?

A: Yes.

Q: You could see the parking lot?

A: Yes.

Q: It was a large parking lot?

A: Yes.

Q: The defendant was standing in the parking lot?

A: Yes.

Q: The parking lot is bigger than a football field?

A: Yes, it is.

Q: The defendant wasn't just standing in the parking lot, he was over in the northwest corner of the lot?

A: Yes.

Q: That is where the blue car was?

A: Yes.

Q: He was standing by that blue car?

A: Yes.

Q: He was standing beside the driver's door?

A: Yes.

Q: He was the only person standing by the blue car in the northwest corner of the parking lot?

A: Yes.

Q: And that was the only car that was broken into in that whole parking lot?

A: Yes, as far as I know.

The cross-examiner makes the point seem larger by eliminating other explanations. Furthermore, the cross-examiner has begun with a wider view of the scene, and has advanced the focus with each question until the critical fact is seen in a close-up. The defendant is the only person standing by the car that was broken into. The cross-examiner has made the point seem bigger by starting with the very general and moving to the very specific. The cross-examiner narrows the focus of the inquiry until the defendant standing beside "the only car that was broken into" becomes a significant important fact.

[3]   A More Subtle Example — Extent or Degree of Damage

[a]   Description

Many lawsuits are often tried over the extent or degree of damage. For example, in a personal injury case in which the defendant admitted to rear-ending the plaintiff, the issue becomes the extent of the injuries incurred. Or, in a commercial case in which the jury has found certain breaches of the contract, the amount of damage remains to be contested.

In this civil case, the plaintiff claims that she has incurred a soft tissue injury to her upper back and neck as a result of an automobile collision. The mental image to be diminished or built is the extent of that injury.

[b]   To Diminish the Fact or Mental Image

The cross-examiner may lessen the extent of the injury the plaintiff claims to have suffered as follows:

Q: Doctor, you examined the plaintiff?

A: Yes.

Q: You did your examination in your office?

A: Yes.

Q: You did x-rays of the plaintiff?

A: Yes.

The "no" line begins:

Q: The plaintiff had no broken bones?

A: No.

Q: The x-rays showed nothing out of the ordinary?

A: No.

Q: The plaintiff had no open cuts?

A: No.

Q: The plaintiff was not bleeding?

A: No.

Q: The plaintiff had no scars from previous cuts that had healed?

A: No.

Q: The plaintiff did not have scratches?

A: No.

Then the concluding question that reverts to a "yes" line:

Q: In your examination, what you found was that the plaintiff had a complaint of pain?

A: Yes.

What the cross-examiner is really saying to the witness and the jury is that this person's condition could have been much worse, but was not. The doctor must agree with that. The concluding question makes the jury believe that the complaint of pain is much more exaggerated than warranted.

[c] Building the Fact or Mental Image

The cross-examiner may increase the extent of the injury suffered as follows:

Q: Doctor, you examined the plaintiff?

A: Yes.

Q: You examined the plaintiff in your office?

A: Yes.

Q: Your examination was thorough?

A: Yes.

Q: You did x-rays of the plaintiff?

A: Yes.

Q: The plaintiff complained of pain?

A: Yes.

Q: The plaintiff complained of pain in her upper back and neck?

A: Yes.

Q: You took the complaint to be honest and genuine so you made x-rays of the plaintiff's upper back and neck?

A: Yes.

Q: The x-rays showed the bones of the back?

A: Yes.

Q: But x-rays cannot show the muscles, ligaments, and tendons of the upper back and neck, can they?

A: No, they cannot.

Q: X-rays cannot show pain, can they?

A: No.

Q: But you made x-rays because you were afraid that even the bones in the upper back and neck may have been hurt?

A: Yes.

Q: You had no objective way of x-raying muscles, ligaments, and tendons in that area of the back?

A: No.

Q: But what you had was a complaint of pain specific to the upper back that you considered to be genuine?

A: Yes.

Here the cross-examiner, by taking the doctor through the injury, and going from a very general focus to a much more narrowed or confined focus, and going from general medical statements to specific medical statements, makes the image appear larger. The more important the issue, the greater the amount of detail needs to be brought before the jury.

[4]   Example — Explaining the Client's Conduct

[a]   Description

In this context, the meaning to be applied to the conduct of a person from the facts observed can be greatly expanded or rendered harmless by the sequencing of the questions. The defendant in this divorce case is alleged to have committed adultery, but denies it.

[b]   Diminishing the Fact

The cross-examiner may portray the testimony establishing that the defendant was seen in the hotel lobby as innocuous conduct as follows:

Q: You saw the defendant five days prior to the filing of this divorce petition?

A: Yes.

Q: You knew the defendant because you knew both the plaintiff and the defendant as a married couple?

A: Yes.

Q: You did not see the defendant talking with any woman?

A: No.

Q: You did not see the defendant touching any woman?

A: No.

Q: You did not see the defendant having lunch with a woman?

A: No.

Q: You did not see the defendant going up in an elevator with a woman?

A: No.

Q: You did not see the defendant in a motel room with a woman?

A: No.

Q: You did not see the defendant having sex?

A: Of course, not.

Q: You did see the defendant in a hotel lobby?

A: Yes.

Q: He was near the front desk talking to the clerk?

A: Yes.

Q: You walked over to the front desk?

A: Yes.

Q: The defendant turned toward you?

A: Yes.

Q: The defendant spoke with you?

A: Yes.

Q: He excused himself to go to the men's room shortly thereafter?

A: That is true.

Q: What you saw was the defendant in a hotel lobby and he spoke to you?

A: Yes.

[c] To Build the Fact

The cross-examiner may stress the point that the defendant committed adultery as follows:

Q: You saw the defendant five days prior to the filing of this divorce petition?

A: Yes.

Q: You knew the defendant because you knew both the plaintiff and the defendant as a married couple?

A: Yes.

Q: You saw the defendant in a hotel?

A: Yes.

Q: He was at the front desk?

A: Yes.

Q: It was 2:00 p.m. in the afternoon?

A: Yes.

Q: He was talking with the clerk?

A: Yes.

Q: He had a pen in his hand?

A: Yes.

Q: There was a woman standing beside him?

A: Yes.

Q: As you walked up to him, he turned to look at you?

A: Yes.

Q: He appeared somewhat pale?

A: Yes.

Q: He spoke to you very quickly?

A: Yes.

Q: He turned and walked into the men's room?

A: Yes.

Q: The woman that he was standing beside watched him walk into the men's room?

A: Yes.

Q: So did the clerk?

A: Yes.

Q: They both looked at each other after he left?

A: Yes.

Q: Neither said a word?

A: True.

§ 23.05   Applications: Trials and Pre-trial

The ability to diminish or build a point is a critical technique in the trial of a case. Through these techniques, the lawyer creates for the jury the appearance of strength of her case and weakness of the opponent's case by the building or diminishing of value of certain facts. Creating a perception of the value of the facts is the critical purpose of the cross-examination. In a close case, that appearance could be the difference between winning and losing. If the cross-examiner has this ability and utilizes it in pre-trial hearings, non-jury pre-trial hearings, depositions, and even interviews of witnesses, the cross-examiner persuades or convinces the opponent and the witness of the strength of the cross-examiner's case and the weaknesses in the opponent's case. Witnesses become less sure of their testimony.

Many cases are settled under unreasonable terms because of the fear that the trial will result in a worse outcome. The lawyer who has the ability to build and diminish facts before the trial begins can create more fear. The value of spotting the likely trial chapters necessary to undermine an opponent's theory of the case will permit and advocate the ability to cross-examine at depositions and other pre-trial stages with great accuracy and effect. The facts that should be diminished or built are the facts that have the greatest impact on the opposing theories of the case.

Chapter 24

JUXTAPOSITION

SYNOPSIS

§ 24.01   Best Ways to Learn

Our common sense and our common life experiences teach us that people tend to act the same as they have in the past. In other words, "You can tell more about what people believe by what they do, than by what they say." While mutual funds must warn that past performance is no indication of likely future results, the opposite is largely true when it comes to people.

In developing techniques for cross-examination, the lawyer can use this wisdom to her advantage: "A leopard cannot change its spots." But this concept goes beyond common sense. It has scientific basis. It has a foundation in the rules of evidence.

On a second plane, the intellectual plane, Leon Festinger, a leading authority of cognitive development, determined that all learning is the result of contrasting and comparing. That is, the unknown is either similar to or not similar to what is known. If it is similar, distinguish characteristics that are not similar and reconcile characteristics that are similar. If it is not similar, it may be contrasted to what us known and determined in what way the two are dissimilar.

On a third plane, the Rules of Evidence acknowledged this concept. It is clear that the courts believe and have adopted common sense life experiences and Leon Festinger's learning concepts. For example, Federal Rule of Evidence 404 provides for the introduction of evidence of similar transactions in a case not involving those transactions. Many states have followed this trend of reasoning with statutory or case law authority for admission of such evidence in the state courts.

It is not limited to criminal acts, but is also applicable to civil transactions. The more bizarre or out of the ordinary the conduct, the more readily admissible the conduct. Because the conduct is unusual, it makes common sense that similar usual acts should show a pattern. For example, similarities in sex crimes or patterns of armed robbery were historically used by prosecutors to show the likelihood that the person committing the earlier crimes is the same person committing recent crimes. The pattern is alleged to be part of the proof. Certainly the trend continues towards increased admissibility of similar transactions with a blending into Federal Rule of Evidence 405 evidence as to habit.

§ 24.02   Compare and Contrast: One of the Best Ways to Teach

Because people can effectively learn best by contrast, the cross-examiner can use this contrasting technique to vividly illustrate the facts that support her theory of the case or which undermine the opponent's theory of the case. There are two types of juxtaposition. Event juxtaposition uses the two chapter method or the three chapter method to logically lead the listener (judge or jury) to a conclusion to which the cross-examiner knows the witness will not agree. Both the two chapter and three chapter juxtaposition techniques will be explained. But first concentrate on the purpose for the techniques. These techniques are designed to establish by inference that which a witness will likely deny. In that way, the credibility of the witness is undermined and the logical conclusion is still before the fact finder. Double loop (see chapter 26, *Loops, Double Loops, and Spontaneous Loops*) juxtaposition uses parallel facts in one chapter to explain why a witness may have made certain conclusions without that person having all of the adequate facts. Both types of fact juxtapositions require well thought out and written out chapters backed up by well thought out sequences of questions.

§ 24.03   Event Juxtaposition

An example will highlight the use of the juxtaposition as to events.

In a criminal case, a government informant with a prior felony conviction will readily admit his former prior felony conviction, but will deny unequivocally any involvement in the present crime. The use of juxtaposition by the cross-examiner can address this dilemma:

Q: In 1982, you were convicted of armed robbery?

A: Yes.

Q: You robbed John Findley?

A: Yes.

Q: He was your friend before the robbery?

A: Yes.

Q: You knew his family?

A: Yes.

Q: You had dined at his home?

A: Yes.

Q: You saw that he was rich?

A: Yes.

Q: Shortly thereafter you returned to his home?

A: Yes.

Q: You were disguised with a mask?

A: Yes.

Q: You went into his home uninvited this time?

A: Yes.

Q: You robbed him?

A: Yes, I did.

The cross-examiner will now immediately initiate an event juxtaposition chapter concerning the present crime for which the defendant is charged and in which the government informant declares he had no involvement:

Q: You know Dan Hale?

A: Yes.

Q: He is the victim in this case?

A: Yes.

Q: He became a friend of yours?

A: Yes.

Q: You came to know his family?

A: Yes.

Q: You had dined at his house?

A: Yes.

Q: You found out that he was rich, that he had money?

A: Yes.

Q: You robbed his house?

A: No.

Q: You were disguised with a mask and robbed his house?

A: No.

The answers to the last two questions are critical. The witness answers are "no". There are no verbal admissions. Nonetheless, the jury can better see the parallels between the two cases. That parallel logically infers the answers should be "yes". The jury can, then, better accept the argument that the "no" answers were indeed "yes." By adding silence after each "no" answer, the cross-examiner can highlight the lack of logic of the answer (see chapter 21, *Creation and Uses of Silence*).

The informant may well make a speech on redirect examination that the defendant was really the guilty party. The witness will say he did not know anything about the details or participate in the crime until after the fact. Nonetheless, the jury has been shown by parallel event juxtaposition chapters, and the homily that a leopard cannot change its spots, that they should infer that the witness is lying. While the cross-examiner cannot prove by verbal admission a "yes" answer, she can provide evidence to the jury that supports a "yes" conclusion by them.

Event juxtaposition works because of the parallels between the two chapters. The cross-examiner should provide as many detailed facts as possible in each chapter. The more factual similarities between the two chapters, the more likely that the fact finder will believe that the "no" answer is truly a "yes" answer. The fact finder can conclude that the witness is not telling the truth. This is the bonus that is often accomplished through the technique of event juxtaposition.

The key to the technique of juxtaposition is careful organization and pre-planning of the cross-examination or chapters necessary to show the similarities. The technique takes advantage of the organization skills of the cross-examiner by making clear to the jury the parallel natures of the known conduct of the witness and the *denied* conduct of the witness (see chapter 11, *Sequences of Cross-Examination*).

§ 24.04   Organization of Juxtaposed Chapters (Two Chapter Method)

One method to the organization of juxtaposed cross-examination chapters is to first highlight those specific facts from one chapter that require and will produce a "yes" answer. Then the cross-examiner must form the second juxtaposition chapter with as many factual parallels as possible to the first chapter. When drafting the two chapters to be juxtaposed, the cross-examiner must focus on detailed facts. The more parallel the facts of the two chapters, the more logical and believable the inference the lawyer seeks to draw that the conduct denied is the conduct that occurred. Although the second chapter will almost certainly produce predictable "no" responses to the critical concluding leading questions, the juxtaposition of the parallel fact situations causes more skepticism of the "no" answers than would have occurred in a conventional chapter format or a random chapter presentation.

Event juxtaposition requires two separate and distinct chapters of material. The jury must be given the opportunity to completely grasp the significance and conclusion of the first chapter before they are even introduced to the more important chapter. If mixed together as one much larger chapter, the highlighting of the parallel conduct is lost.

§ 24.05   Three Chapter Event Juxtaposition

Another method of juxtaposition is to extract material from both of the other chapters making a separate distinct third chapter. This third chapter should only be done after the two parallel chapters have been totally completed. The example below will highlight the juxtaposition of Chapter 1 against Chapter 2 and Chapter 3 (see chapter 9, *The Chapter Method of Cross-Examination*).

This is a form of chapter bundle. Event juxtaposition is equally applicable in civil cases: In a divorce case, the titling of a brand new Mercedes 560 SL in the name of the mother of the defendant husband is alleged by the wife to be an effort to defraud her out of her interest in the vehicle. The husband refuses to admit this. There is no independent proof that the husband did, indeed, purchase the expensive car.

There is, however, the prior conduct of the defendant husband titling a commercial tract of real estate in the wife's name in an effort to defeat potential claims of creditors early on in the marriage when the husband and wife relationship was solid. By the use of parallel juxtaposition, the jury can hear the "no" answers of the defendant but recognize the implication that this is a course of conduct that the defendant has used before.

First Chapter

Q: Early in your marriage, you loved your wife?

A: Yes.

Q: Early in your marriage, you trusted your wife?

A: Yes.

Q: A tract of commercial real estate was purchased early in the marriage?

A: Yes.

Q: It was very expensive?

A: Yes.

Q: That real estate was placed in your wife's name?

A: Yes.

Q: It was not placed in your name?

A: That's correct.

Q: There were no documents, legal or otherwise, that would connect your name to that piece of commercial real estate?

A: That's true.

Q: At that time, there was a lawsuit pending against you by a creditor?

A: Yes.

Q: That creditor had a potential claim against you?

A: Yes.

Q: You were concerned about having to pay the creditor money?

A: Somewhat concerned.

Q: You admit to this jury that you placed the commercial real estate tract of land in your wife's name, in part, to defeat that potential claim by the creditor?

A: Yes, yes, I will.

Second Chapter

Q: You love your mother?

A: Yes.

Q: You trust your mother?

A: Yes.

Q: A new 560 SL Mercedes has recently been purchased?

A: Yes.

Q: It is very expensive?

A: Yes.

Q: It was titled in your mother's name?

A: Yes.

Q: It was not titled in your name?

A: That's correct.

Q: There are no documents, legal or otherwise, to connect you with that vehicle?

A: True.

Q: Your wife has a lawsuit pending against you for divorce?

A: That's true.

Q: You know that your wife is claiming interest in all the assets and income of the marriage?

A: Yes.

Q: You are concerned about your wife's claims against the assets and income?

A: Of course.

Q: You purchased the new 560 SL Mercedes in your mother's name to defeat the claim of your wife?

A: No.

Third Chapter

Q: Early in the marriage you loved your wife?

A: Yes.

Q: You love your mother now?

A: Yes.

Q: Early in the marriage you trusted your wife?

A: Yes.

Q: You trust your mother now?

A: Yes.

Q: A commercial piece of property, which was very expensive, was purchased early in the marriage?

A: Yes.

Q: A new 560 SL Mercedes was recently purchased, and it was very expensive?

A: Yes.

Q: The land was placed in your wife's name?

A: Yes.

Q: The Mercedes was titled in your mother's name?

A: Yes.

Q: There is no paper trail to connect you with the commercial land?

A: That's true.

Q: There's no paper trail to connect you with the Mercedes?

A: That's right.

Q: When the commercial real estate was purchased, there was a lawsuit pending against you?

A: Yes.

Q: There is a lawsuit pending against you now by your wife?

A: Yes.

Q: When the real estate was purchased, the lawsuit provided that the creditor may have a potential claim against your assets?

A: True.

Q: The lawsuit that your wife has filed provides for a claim against the assets?

A: Everything.

Q: You were concerned about the creditor's claim against the real estate?

A: Some concern.

Q: You are now concerned about your wife's claim against the assets?

A: She is claiming everything.

Q: You placed the commercial real estate in your wife's name to defeat the claim of the creditor?

A: Yes.

Q: You placed the title to the new Mercedes 560 SL in your mother's name to defeat your wife's claim?

A: No.

Because the husband's conduct is so significant to the wife's theory of the case, the cross-examiner has chosen to use three chapters rather than two chapters to highlight the parallels involving the track of commercial real estate and the purchase of a new 560 SL Mercedes. The more important are the facts to be juxtaposed to the advocate's theory of the case, the more time and detail needs to be spent illustrating to the jury and judge the parallels between the two events. The more parallels, the stronger the inference that the conduct denied actually occurred. By adding a third chapter that highlights the contrast between the parallels fact by fact, the cross-examiner is leading the fact finder to the conclusion that the factual parallels are not merely coincidental, but the factual parallels exist because the conduct is exactly the same. The cross-examiner is, as always, aided by logic and common sense. To the extent that the witness appears to be illogical, or, to the extent the witness appears to be providing answers which contradict common sense, the less credible of the answer.

In commercial litigation, a common tactic used by witnesses who are executives is to claim no memory of important meetings, memos, or conversations. The careful cross-examiner can use juxtaposition chapters to show the parallel between meetings, memos, and conversations that the witness can remember clearly in precise detail against this claimed lack of memory on the critical meeting, memo, or conversation that formed a basis for the cross-examiner's theory of the case. Often, it is easy to show that the executive has an excellent memory of the memo or meeting that helps his side's theory of the case, but no memory of a meeting or memo on the same subject being used to attack his side's theory of the case.

§ 24.06 Double Loop Juxtapositions

Do not be intimidated by the title of the technique. With careful preparation, this technique is easily applicable in the courtroom. In chapter 26, loops and double loops are discussed as a means of emphasizing certain information for the jury. The concept of double loops is added to juxtaposition to make clear to the jury that there is great contrast between the two facts contained in the double loop. It is this contrast that will further highlight and emphasize the two facts for the jury. From the emphasis of these contrasting two concepts, the jury will be lead to certain logical inferences and emotional conclusions.

For example, in a personal injury case, the plaintiff was rendered unconscious at the time of the collision. The defendant was not rendered unconscious. Not only is there a question of the extent of the plaintiff's damages for the jury to consider, but there is also a question concerning certain conclusions that the investigating officer reached in her incident report immediately following the collision.

By the use of double loop juxtaposition, the jury will be led to conclude that the conclusions made by the officer were based, not on all the facts, but only on the facts provided by the defendant. Further, the plaintiff's damages will be highlighted in contrast with the lack of defendant's injuries.

Cross-Examination of the Defendant

Q: Bob Simms (the plaintiff) was knocked out by the force of the collision?

A: Yes.

Q: You were not knocked out?

A: Yes.

Q: You were conscious?

A: True.

Q: Bob was unconscious?

A: He was out.

Q: At the time of the collision, Bob was unconscious, but you were fully conscious when the investigating officer arrived?

A: Yes.

Q: Bob could not talk after the collision?

A: No.

Q: You could talk after the collision?

A: That's true.

Q: After the collision, Bob could not speak?

A: Yes.

Q: But you could speak?

A: True.

Q: After the collision, Bob could not walk?

A: That's true.

Q: But you could walk?

A: Yes.

Q: After the collision, Bob could not walk, but you could walk when the investigating officer arrived?

A: Yes.

Q: You could demonstrate?

A: Yes.

Q: But Bob could not demonstrate?

A: He was out.

Q: Bob could not talk with the investigating officer?

A: No.

Q: You could talk to the investigating officer?

A: Yes.

Q: After the collision, you could talk and demonstrate to the investigating officer, but Bob could not talk or demonstrate when the investigator arrived?

A: That's true.

Q: Bob did not talk with the investigating officer at the scene?

A: No.

Q: You did talk with the investigating officer and told your version of the events?

A: That's true.

Q: After the collision, at the scene, you were able to tell the investigating officer your version of the events, but Bob Simms could not?

A: That's true.

§ 24.07   Comparison of Event Juxtaposition and Double Loop Juxtaposition

In event juxtaposition, the cross-examiner is leading the witness through two parallel events, one that concludes with the witness agreeing with the factual goal of the cross-examiner. In the second juxtaposition parallel event chapter, the cross-examiner knows that the witness will not agree with the important facts of the chapter but that the denial of those facts by the witness will make the denial appear to be false. In that way, event juxtaposition contrasts the "yes" answer in the first parallel with the "no" answer in the second parallel event.

In the double loop juxtaposition chapter, the cross-examiner is contrasting two separate facts in an effort to have the jury conclude that there are good reasons that certain conclusions have been reached by others who did not know and could not know all the facts in the entire scenario.

In this method, the double loop juxtaposition receives all yes answers. The facts within the body of the questions are contrasted to show the disparity. By contrasting the example in § 24.03 with the example in § 24.06, the difference in the techniques is apparent.

Chapter 25

TRILOGIES

SYNOPSIS

§ 25.01   Trilogies — A Technique to Plant a Flag on Certain Sets of Facts

A case involves thousands of facts, and not all of them are of equal value. Trial work is dramatic for the lawyers, but, realistically, jurors experience moments of confusion or boredom. Even if a juror could concentrate on every question and answer, the advocate wants the juror to put greater weight on certain facts. It is important to have techniques that allow the lawyer to point out to the jury a very significant fact. The advocate needs a variety of techniques that ethically allow her to heighten the impact of a particular fact. The technique of trilogies is one such technique. It is designed to cause the fact finder to better hear the facts referred to in the trilogy, and to instantly recognize that they are facts of great importance in relation to the contrasting theories of the case.

Unfortunately in times gone by, lawyers attempted to cause jurors to sit up and take notice of a particular answer by using loud tones, great emotion, and dramatic gestures. Even if occasionally useful, such devices wear thin very quickly and have the propensity to turn off jurors. Courtroom dramatics are highly overrated and frequently objectionable.

A trilogy within a cross-examination is a much more sophisticated technique to draw attention to particularly important facts. The trilogy technique is borrowed from literature and history. The trilogy is an important and unobjectionable technique that allows the cross-examiner to build the drama and to make more memorable the chapter or chapters of cross-examination containing the trilogy.

§ 25.02   Trilogies Are a Literary Device

The trilogy technique is originally found in literature. Trilogies are now used in advertising, politics, and in other settings in which it is desired to convey a message in a memorable way. Trilogies have a cadence, a rhythm, a stirring that makes them more memorable than couplets, quadruplets, or other phrasing. It is this characteristic of rhyming that makes the trilogy phrase memorable.

Plato, in his *Republic*, Book IV, uses the trilogy "wisdom, courage, and temperance" as the virtues of a state. Aristotle, in his first book on politics, describes the person who is without a state as the "tribeless, lawless, heartless one." Both philosophers used trilogies throughout their works and described the power of the number three in their philosophical writings.

In a more modern political setting Roy Barnes, a trial lawyer, while serving a term as the Governor of Georgia used this trilogy to describe the plight of battered and neglected children:

> "We can only imagine how horrifying their world must be —
> **Neglected** by those meant to care for them,
> **Betrayed** by those meant to protect them,
> **Battered** by those meant to love them."

The Biblical phrasing of "the Father, the Son, and the Holy Ghost" forms a trilogy. "See no evil, hear no evil, speak no evil" is in the form of a trilogy. Kate Kedzie, in arguing the case for women's suffrage, said in one of her first public meetings:

> We are the forgotten people.
> We are *the abused,*
> *the trampled upon,*
> *the ridiculed,*
> because we are powerless. But my friends, the storm is rising and
> above it our voices will be heard. "Justice," we cry.

Vincent of Beauvais, in an allegory, spoke of Genghis Khan as having sent three demons ahead of him to destroy his enemies:

> "the spirit of fear,
> the spirit of mistrust,
> and the spirit of discord."

Abraham Lincoln, in the Gettysburg Address, an address of only three paragraphs, used two trilogies:

> We cannot dedicate,
> we cannot consecrate,
> we cannot hallow this ground. . .
> . . . and that government of the people,
> by the people,
> for the people
> shall not perish from the earth.

General Douglas C. MacArthur, in his address to the cadets of West Point, used the motto of the Military Academy when he said:

> In the evening of my memory, always I come back to West Point.
> Always there echoes and re-echoes
> Duty,
> Honor,
> Country.

"Veni, vidi, vici" (I came, I saw, I conquered), according to Plutarch, was written by Julius Caesar in a letter announcing the victory of Zela, which concluded the Pontic campaign.

Winston Churchill, a great statesman, a gifted orator and prolific writer, often used trilogies. In describing the most important lesson that life had taught him, he said: "Never give up, never give up, never ever give up."

When orators and writers have not used trilogies, common wisdom has reduced the sentiment to trilogies nonetheless. Winston Churchill used the phrase "blood, toil, tears and sweat" in his address to the House of Commons, May 13, 1940. Common wisdom years later turned it into a more memorable trilogy: "blood, sweat, and tears."

Select a classical writing, or review the transcript of a well-regarded speech, and chances are that within the body of that work will be found at least one trilogy, if not multiple trilogies. Trilogies cross cultural lines, from Plato to Churchill, to Haji Gullalai, Intelligence Chief of Afghanistan (1992).

> *"He [Mullah Omar] will be hanged. He sold out his country,*
> *he sold out our people, and he sold out Islam. He has no*
> *place to hide. . ."*

§ 25.03 Three Steps to Creating a Trilogy

In trial work, as in literature, trilogies are not discovered; they are created. The technique can be mastered and the trilogy created by following three simple steps:

1) Find a fact or concept of importance to the theory of the case;

2) Express it in three different ways or divide it into three separate parts; and

3) Express each of the three parts in three separate parallel statements (leading questions).

In cross-examination, the trilogy will be formed by using three separate leading questions, each constructed in parallel sentence form. Each will require verification of a single fact.

In a civil context in the cross-examination of a man who claims to love his family, it is extraordinarily easy for the man to answer the first question. Then he is locked into the successive questions that form a trilogy:

Q: You love your family?

A: Yes.

Q: *You love your family*, but you left town for three days to meet your lover?

A: Yes.

Q: *You love your family*, but you wouldn't pay for gymnastics for your little girl?

A: Yes.

Q: *You love your family*, but you spent the gymnastics money on your lover?

A: Yes.

In the criminal context, in a prosecution for assault, a trilogy can be formed this way:

Q: He was smaller than you, *but you hit him anyway?*

A: Yes.

Q: He was drunk, *but you hit him anyway?*

A: Yes.

Q: He wanted to stop fighting, *but you hit him anyway?*

A: Yes.

As can be seen in both examples, the factual answers to the questions asked assist the cross-examiner. However, the cross-examiner gains more power and creates a more vivid picture by requiring verification of the theme phrase, "You hit him anyway." In the civil example, the theme phrase, "You love your family, but . . ." and in the criminal example, ". . . but you hit him anyway," provides a refrain by which to remember the facts.

§ 25.04 Technique: Three Facts + a Theme Phrase = a Trilogy

There is a linking of the three facts and the use of the repetitious theme phrase; hence a trilogy is created by the three parallel questions.

In each example, the lawyer could have expressed the facts without the form of a trilogy. In the civil example:

Q: You left town for three days to meet your lover?

A: Yes.

Q: You refused to pay for the children's gymnastics?

A: Yes.

Q: You spent the gymnastics money on your lover?

A: Yes.

In the criminal example:

Q: You are six foot one?

A: Yes.

Q: Jimmy is smaller than you?

A: Yes.

Q: Jimmy was drunk?

A: Yes.

Q: You knew my client was a juvenile?

A: Yes.

Q: In spite of these things, you hit my client?

A: Yes.

In each case, the cross-examiner asked all of the factual questions and received an appropriate "yes" answer, but the cross-examiner had not achieved the emotional or persuasive impact that could have been gained through the trilogy presentation.

In this copyright infringement case, the defense lawyer wished to remind the jury that the plaintiff's business had not sold very many copies of its software. In cross-examination, defense counsel summarized some of the most important chapters on the unprofitability of the business with this trilogy:

Q: Few agents really try it?

Q: Few who try it ever buy it?

Q: Few who buy it ever renew it?

Of course such a trilogy is dependent upon the underlying facts. For this trilogy to work, the cross-examiner needed to have performed chapters of cross-examination that fairly demonstrated the facts recited and summarized in the trilogy.

§ 25.05 Theory, Theme Phrases, and Trilogies

A trilogy can be used not only to establish important facts that support the theory of the case, but also to emphasize those facts. Therefore, it follows that an excellent use of a trilogy is to establish the facts of importance to the theory of the case and to establish them in such a way that they create, embody, or utilize selected theme phrases.

For instance, when the theory of the case is that the opponent's witness is lying in order to gain assistance for himself, and a theme is that "Smith will lie to anyone at any time if it will help." The lawyer needs to establish situations in which Mr. Smith has lied and has gotten assistance from that lie. In order to create a trilogy, the lawyer needs to find three such situations and express this concept in three different but parallel forms:

Q: When lies will help, you use them?

Q: When truths will hurt, you ignore them?

Q: When facts don't work, you change them?

Of course, for this to be effective, the lawyer must have set up three factual situations in which the lawyer can show these three things to be true. That is, the lawyer needs a factual situation where the witness changed the facts in order to help himself, a situation in which the witness lied in order to assist himself, and a situation in which, had the witness told the truth, the truth would have hurt him. Then, having established those facts, the lawyer can summarize with the trilogy similar to the one above.

In a fight resulting in homicide, the lawyer cross-examined a witness about the actions of the deceased. The lawyer did this to set up the motivation for the defendant to come back later and start a second fight in which the deceased is killed by the defendant. The defendant is Tom and the victim is Vince. A theme phrase, "But that didn't stop Vince," was chosen before trial to support the theory. Questions to the prosecution witness concerning the earlier fight should emphasize that theme phrase:

Q: Tom was drunk, but that didn't stop Vince?

Q: Tom stopped swinging, but that didn't stop Vince?

Q: Tom was down, but that didn't stop Vince?

In this commercial case, the plaintiff's counsel reminded the jurors of the lack of care or oversight given by an investment advisor. The investment he was supposed to be monitoring experienced significant financial setbacks. A regulatory agency published reports that he did not review. Nor did he make any possible phone calls that could have put him in touch with people who would have told him about the financial problems. In fact, he made very little effort to stay on top of the declining fortunes of the investment.

Plaintiff's counsel built several chapters around documents that were available, people who could have been called, and methods for checking on the company. At the end of each chapter dealing with each of those specific facts counsel added the trilogy refrain:

Q: You didn't write?

Q: You didn't call?

Q: You didn't check?

Because each fact was true, they made perfectly valid leading questions and never called for a conclusion by the witness.

§ 25.06 Various Expressions of Trilogies

Since trilogies are used repeatedly in a cross-examination, it is useful to have a variety of methods to present a trilogy, so that its sound does not become stale. The trilogy just presented could be itself broken into six questions, rather than three, in order to create a variety:

Q: Tom was drunk?

A: Yes.

Q: But that didn't stop Vince?

A: No, it didn't.

Q: Tom stopped swinging?

A: Yes, he did.

Q: But that didn't stop Vince?

A: No, it didn't.

Q: In fact, Tom was knocked down?

A: Yeah, at one point.

Q: But even that didn't stop Vince?

A: No.

By stretching the trilogy into six questions, the lawyer has forced the witness to spend even more time describing painful facts. Remember time is the measure of importance in the courtroom. The lawyer has milked the facts for even more emotional benefit. Once again, trilogies are best when tied to a theme phrase.

A trilogy can take many forms. Often it is a tag line (theme phrase at the end of the sentence), or a prefix (theme phrase at the beginning of the question), but it can be both.

In a civil case where the defense is that the defendant did not cause the wreck despite certain undeniable physical evidence, the plaintiff's lawyer formed a trilogy in the cross-examination of the defendant as follows:

Q: *Even though* your car was across the center line after the collision, *you deny that you caused this wreck?*

A: Yes.

Q: *Even though* the gouge marks were across the center line, *you deny that you caused this wreck?*

A: Yes.

Q: *Even though* the skid marks were across the center line, *you deny that you caused this wreck?*

A: Yes.

In a civil case where the defendant refused to say whether he knew what caused the wreck, but would only say that he didn't know, trilogies can be used to equal effect:

Q: *After the collision,* your car was across the center line?

A: Yes.

Q: *But you don't know how the cars collided?*

A: No.

Q: *After the collision,* the gouge marks were across the center line?

A: Yes.

Q: *But you don't know how the cars collided?*

A: No.

Q: *After the collision,* you told the deputy what you saw?

A: Yes.

Q: *But you don't know how the cars collided?*

By the cross-examiner forming the question in such a way that the witness is required to admit certain facts in the first, third, and fifth question, and the witness is required to disclaim knowledge in the second, fourth, and sixth question, the jury is led to the conclusion that the witness is not trying to remember what occurred.

In a criminal case of assault on a police officer, the defendant's theory of the case is that since the DEA agents broke in on a no-knock warrant at midnight while wearing civilian clothes, the defendant thought the agents were burglars. Therefore the agents, by their own actions, placed the defendant in a situation where his gunshot response was reasonable. Cross-examination questions to the DEA agent:

Q: *You chose to break in — in the dark of night?*

Q: *You chose to break in* wearing blue jeans and leather jackets, not police uniforms?

Q: *You chose to break in* with no warning?

Or

Q: *You chose* not to announce yourself?

Q: *You chose* to disguise yourself?

Q: *You chose* to do it when John was asleep?

Or

Q: You broke in at midnight; *that was your choice, not John's?*

Q: You decided to wear blue jeans and leather jackets rather than uniforms; *that was your choice, not John's?*

Q: You chose to break down the door with no warning; *that was your choice, not John's?*

Or

Q: *You chose to break in* at midnight — all the better to surprise John?

Q: *You chose to break into* the house from many routes at once — all the better to surprise John?

Q: *You chose to break in* with no warning — all the better to surprise John?

§ 25.07   Good Facts Do Not Naturally Occur in Threes

It bears repeating that trilogies are not naturally found within the facts; they are developed from the facts. In a case in which discrediting an eyewitness is critical to the theory, the lawyer can find three facts the witness did not perceive, and get the witness to agree that he did not perceive them because, "It happened too fast," or that "It was too dark." A trilogy can be fashioned to bring that concept home to the jury. Perhaps the trilogy will not be powerful enough to carry the entire theory of the case, but it will serve the theory:

Q: It happened so fast you did not see his hands?

Q: It happened so fast you did not see his hair?

Q: It happened so fast you did not see his eyes?

Or

Q: It was too dark to see . . . (expressed in conjunction with three facts).

Or

Q: It was so dark you could not see . . . (expressed in conjunction with three facts).

There may be many things the witness could see, but by focusing on three things to which the answer is, "It was too dark," or "It happened so fast," at least the concept of not seeing is brought home to the jury.

In a self-defense case, the lawyer may break the fight sequence down into points at which the victim could have stopped. By finding any three points within a sequence of events at which the victim could have elected to discontinue the confrontation, the lawyer can create a trilogy:

Q: You came to the door, but you didn't stop?

Q: You went out on the porch, but you didn't stop?

Q: You ran down the sidewalk, but you didn't stop?

Or

Q: You could have stopped at your door, but you didn't?

Q: You kept going?

Q: You could have stopped on your porch, but you didn't?

Q: You kept going?

Q: You could have stopped on the sidewalk, but you didn't?

Q: You kept going?

This same trilogy can be refreshed in closing argument: "He could have stopped at the door, but he didn't; he just kept coming. He could have stopped at the porch, but he didn't; he just kept coming. He could have stopped at the sidewalk, but he didn't; he just kept coming." (Remember that trilogies work in closing argument as well as in cross-examination.)

The lawyer has only to survey the available facts and pull out three powerful facts that can be placed into a sequence of questions. Often the lawyer need only look at the conduct of the witness to find three things done, three things not done, three things said, three warning signs ignored, or three things omitted. Having found three facts of importance, the trilogy can easily be built. Witness a simple trilogy from a home defect litigation. The questions are asked of a developer:

Q: The soil engineer told you the soil was expansive?

Q: You didn't reengineer the slab to account for it?

Q: The soil engineer told you lawn watering close to the foundation would be a problem?

Q: You didn't reengineer the sprinkler system to account for it?

Q: The soil engineer told you water drainage from the roof would be a problem?

Q: You didn't re-engineer the gutters and downspouts to account for it?

§ 25.08 What to Do If There Are More Than Three Good Facts

As all of these forms indicate, the lawyer is taking a complex event and pulling out three individual facts, which she then expresses in parallel sentence form. All are tied together by a theme phrase that expresses the lawyer's aim or that goes to the theory of the case.

The lawyer may pick any three facts out of this whole scenario, so long as those facts validly require a "yes" answer, and so long as they can fairly be expressed in parallel sentences. Obviously, the lawyer must limit herself to three expressions of fact in order to have a trilogy. A reduction to two, or an increase to four will break the rhythm, thereby destroying the oratorical effect of the trilogy.

If the lawyer has more than three useful facts in a scenario, the lawyer can maintain the power of a trilogy by dividing the facts into two separate trilogies. The cross-examiner needs to complete a full set or trilogy, and then break away from the trilogy form with a separate question in order to have established the trilogy. The lawyer can then return to the trilogy form and do another full set of three, thus completing a second trilogy.

By way of example, if the lawyer is trying a case in which the inconsistent statements of a witness are the key to the case, the lawyer must construct trilogies designed to bring home to the jury that this witness is not credible. The reason he is not credible is because of the multiple changes in his story. In order to do this, the lawyer must first prove three separate inconsistent statements as to the description (for an example). They can be height, weight, moustache, hair, blue jeans, or any three factors that change the story that has been given on direct. Having proven three changes, the lawyer can now summarize with the trilogy:

Q: You saw the man's height?

Q: *Now it has changed?*

Q: You saw the man's build?

Q: *Now it has changed?*

Q: You saw the man's hair?

Q: *Now it has changed?*

Assuming that the lawyer has three more changes, she can ask a short leading question or a short series of questions to provide a mental break for the jury. Then she can return with another trilogy on changes:

Q: You saw the color of the gun, but now it has changed?

Q: You saw the masking tape disguise, but now it has changed?

Q: You saw the car he got into, but now it has changed?

In this manner, the lawyer has not destroyed the rhythm of a trilogy by expanding it beyond three. She also has not thrown away good facts beyond the initial three. The lawyer has instead searched to find six facts that she can mold into two separate trilogies. Be sure to break each trilogy into a separate group.

§ 25.09   Trilogies Can Be Shortened to Create a Different Sound

The lawyer can add flexibility to trilogies and create interesting staccato effects by shortening the trilogy or abbreviating it. The lawyer does this by announcing the trilogy phrase, and then quickly asking three very short leading questions — all of which are fashioned from the trilogy theme phrase:

Q: You were in close?

Q: Close enough to push him?

Q: Close enough to punch him?

Q: Close enough to kick him?

Or

Q: You were in close?

Q: Close enough to push him?

Q: To punch him?

Q: To kick him?

§ 25.10   Converting Loops to Trilogies

Loops are logically related to trilogies: both are flag-planting techniques. Loops take certain facts or phrases and use them repetitively for emphasis; trilogies are based on repetitive phrasing. As a practical matter, loops can often be converted into trilogies. Once a loop has been used, use it three times, particularly when a lawyer is beginning the use of trilogies.

In the following example, a loop is established and formed into a double loop; from the double loop a trilogy is formed:

Q: You knew the driver was injured?   *establish fact one*

A: Yes.

Q: The injured driver was trapped in the car?   *loop*

A: Yes.

Q: He was bleeding?   *establish fact two*

A: Yes.

Q: The injured driver laid trapped in the car bleeding?   *double loop*

A: Yes.

Q: The injured driver was screaming?   *trilogy*

A: Yes.

Q: The injured driver was moaning?

A: Yes.

Q: The injured driver was bleeding?

A: Yes.

In analyzing this portion of cross-examination, the lawyer commenced the sequence by establishing a loop. She then established a second fact that could be coupled with the first fact in a combination to form a greater impact. This created the double loop. The double loop was then reformed into a trilogy.

But a loop to a trilogy need not be a fancy maneuver. Witness this simple conversion of a powerful loop phrase into a useful trilogy. The cross-examination is of an expert who has testified to the theoretical lost profits from a failed business venture:

Q: Your assumption is that the dealers would pay $50 for the part?

Q: $50 per unit would be a very good price?

Q: A better price than they had ever been paid at wholesale?

Q: A better price than even their projections called for?

Q: A better price then they have ever been paid since then?

The intent of the trilogy is to communicate to the jurors that the assumptions of the expert are unreasonably optimistic. The expert would never agree with that conclusion, but if each of the trilogy questions is accurate, the expert can try to explain with a, "Yes, but . . ." answer, but the fair picture is just plain "Yes." By pulling together three separate methods of comparison of the assumed price to other factual measures, the assumption is shown to be a gross overstatement of the value of the product.

§ 25.11 Converting Verbs to Trilogies

When the lawyer is first beginning to utilize trilogies, it is often easier in cross-examination to use verbs to create the trilogy. In the above example, the verbs "screaming," "moaning," and "bleeding" were used with the same sentence construction preceding them.

As a practical matter, it is easier to think of synonyms for verbs quickly than to think of synonyms for nouns or adjectives quickly. When verbs are connected with theme phrases, a more sophisticated trilogy can be formed:

Q: You hit Johnny?

A: Yes.

Q: You kicked Johnny?

A: Yes.

Q: You beat down on Johnny?

A: Yes.

Or

Q: You hit Johnny, but he never got up?

A: Yes.

Q: You kicked Johnny, but he never got up?

A: Yes.

Q: You beat down on Johnny, but he never got up?

A: Yes.

§ 25.12   Trilogy Pyramids

Earlier in this chapter it was suggested that multiple trilogies can be created when the cross-examiner had more than three facts with which to work. However, the rhythm of a group of facts sounds best as a trilogy. The rhythm or cadence of a trilogy will not be improved by adding a fourth, fifth, and sixth sentence. At that point the technique loses its rhythm and rhyme and begins to sound like nothing more than a list. In order to keep the rhythm and memorable nature of a list of facts broken into multiple trilogies it is necessary to separate each trilogy by some factual questions that break up the list of facts and signal the end to each trilogy. A technique to create this break is to insert a thematic summary question or a short series of questions between the trilogies so that the trilogies will not run together. In this way, the jury can recognize the change in rhythm that signals the end of each trilogy.

By referring back to literature and history, it will be noted that a more refined treatment of multiple trilogies can be developed. These multiple trilogies can be quite persuasive and can augment the lawyer's oratorical skills.

Winston Churchill, in his speech to the House of Commons after the debacle of Dunkirk, used multiple trilogies:

> We shall go on to the end, we shall fight in France, we shall fight on the seas and oceans, we shall fight with growing confidence and growing strength in the air, **we shall defend our island**, whatever the cost may be, we shall fight on the beaches, we shall fight on the landing grounds, we shall fight in the fields and in the streets, we shall fight in the hills; **we shall never surrender**.

Here Winston Churchill created a trilogy, separated that trilogy by a theme phrase, created a second trilogy, and highlighted that second trilogy with another theme phrase related to the first theme phrase.

When this speech is viewed in light of the historic events of which Winston Churchill spoke, it can be seen that he was not urging his nation to fight, for they had done that. He was urging his nation to defend the island and to never surrender. The trilogies were designed to highlight the theme phrase of "never surrender." Therefore, the thematic conclusion was not to fight, but rather to never surrender.

§ 25.13   Trilogy Pyramids on Their Use of Law

If the cross-examiner has more than three facts with which to work, the cross-examiner can separate the trilogies, not with just any short question or short series of questions, but with thematic conclusion phrases. In a perfect world, if the cross-examiner can develop at least nine facts with which to create trilogies that all center around the same theme phrase, the trilogy pyramid would be formed.

§ 25.14 Trilogy Pyramid Defined

A trilogy pyramid is three trilogies separated by three thematic conclusion questions. Those three thematic conclusion questions then form a fourth greater trilogy of thematic conclusion questions.

Not only are trilogy pyramids extremely effective and persuasive in cross-examination, but they also form entire paragraphs with which to convince a jury in closing argument.

In a personal injury case where the defendant denies liability despite the presence of physical evidence to the contrary, the following trilogy pyramid was used. The questions are numbered so that the analysis that follows is more easily understood:

(1)   **Q:** The gouge marks were across the center line?

      A: Yes.

(2)   **Q:** The skid marks were across the center line?

      A: Yes.

(3)   **Q:** Your car was across the center line after the collision?

      A: Yes.

(4)   **Q:** But you deny that you caused this wreck?

      A: Yes, I do.

(5)   **Q:** You saw him (plaintiff) sprawled on the side of the road?

      A: Yes.

(6)   **Q:** You saw him (plaintiff) unconscious?

      A: Yes.

(7)   **Q:** You saw him (plaintiff) with his chest caved in?

      A: Yes.

(8)   **Q:** But you deny this wreck caused those injuries?

      A: That is right.

(9)   **Q:** He was knocked unconscious?

      A: Yes.

(10) **Q:** He had broken ribs?

      A: Yes.

(11) **Q:** He was bleeding?

     A: Yes.

(12) **Q:** But you deny his injuries were severe?

     A: Yes.

(13) **Q:** You deny all of those things?

     A: Yes.

Analyze the first trilogy — questions 1, 2, and 3. The repeating phrase is "across the center line." The second trilogy, questions 5, 6, and 7, each describe injuries of the plaintiff. These injuries are described by what the defendant "saw." The trilogy formed in questions 9, 10, and 11 further describe the severity of the injuries. The thematic conclusion questions, questions 4, 8, and 12, are all phrased with the phrase, "But you deny." Question 13 was a summary of the preceding trilogy pyramid to set it apart from the balance of the cross-examination.

With careful analysis, it can be seen that the thirteen questions all relate to one question. That is, the defendant denies all responsibility.

§ 25.15 Trilogy Pyramids and Experts

In both civil and criminal cases, the best method of cross-examination of the opposing expert is not to discuss the things the expert has done, but the things he has not done. First show the importance of the things to be questioned on, and then show that they were not done. By doing so, the lawyer may cast doubt on the credibility of the expert's ultimate judgment and conclusions. By placing the things not done into groups, the lawyer can more persuasively argue them to the jury, particularly if they are placed into trilogy pyramids.

For instance, instead of simply saying the expert did not take fingerprints, that same concept can be formed into a complete trilogy. Instead of simply saying the expert did not take hair samples, that same concept can be turned into a trilogy. Instead of simply saying the expert did not analyze other pieces of physical evidence, that concept of lack of analysis can be placed into a trilogy. Thus a trilogy pyramid can be formed:

Q: Officer, you did not take the time to dust for fingerprints?

Q: You did not take the time to try to lift the fingerprints?

Q: You did not take time to take fingerprints from the car?

Q: You did not take the time to do any of those things?

Q: Officer, you did not take the time to look for hair samples in the car?

Q: You did not take the time to take hair samples from George?

Q: You did not take the time to take hair samples from Virginia?

Q: You did not take the time to do any of those things?

Q: Officer, you did not take the time to take blood samples from the stains in the car?

Q: You did not take the time to take saliva samples from the stains in the car?

Q: You did not take the time to take semen samples from the stains in the car?

Q: You did not take the time to gather any forms of DNA evidence in this case?

§ 25.16 Trilogies Tie Closing Argument to Cross-Examination

Trilogies can either be revived in closing argument, or can be announced for the first time in closing argument as a dominant theme of the case:

She saw the man's height.

Now it has changed.

She saw the man's build.

Now it has changed.

She saw the man's hair.

Now it has changed.

The lawyer can also announce her trilogy as a thematic summary sentence:

> They say you can rely on her: The robber's height changed. They say you can rely on her: The robber's build changed. They say you can rely on her: But what she saw keeps changing. She was certain of the weight, but it changed; she was certain of the beard, but then it changed; and she was certain of the height; but then it changed.

The repetition of the material of cross-examination, headlined by a thematic phrase, revitalizes the information. It makes the jury visualize more vividly those portions of the cross-examination in which these costly admissions were obtained.

The theme phrase, coupled with the key facts of the cross-examination, dominates the closing argument by focusing the jury's attention on the oratorical device of the trilogy. Since it is the most memorable set of phrases of the trial, it becomes the most likely talking point in jury deliberations. Any time a jury talks about the most memorable parts of the cross-examination, it is working toward the desired verdict.

The trilogy in argument can also embody concepts of the case as much as individual facts. Observe this example taken from a case in which the plaintiffs were poor, uneducated, and had been inarticulate in describing their pain. Insurance defense counsel pointed out the verdict should not be very much, since the plaintiffs had done very poorly in describing their conditions. Besides, any verdict is likely to amount to a great deal of money in comparison to what they possessed. In contrast, plaintiff's counsel's trilogy rebutted in closing:

> Because they have less education, the defendants say they have less feeling. Because they can't explain their pain, the defendants say they don't hurt. Because they are poor, the defendants say their pain is cheap.

In a criminal case in which the prosecution uses a "snitch" who lied for personal gain on several occasions, a trilogy can capture the essence of many hours of cross-examination:

> When he needed money, he has lied. When he needed help, he has lied. When he has needed freedom, he has lied.

Another example:

> He has lied to judges — but the prosecution says you can trust him.

> He has lied to his customers — but the prosecution says you can trust him.

> He has lied to his wife — but the prosecution says you can trust him.

All of these examples use the trilogy in closing argument to summarize the character of the witness and to tie it back to individual facts proven on cross-examination.

Bobby Lee Cook (a great southeast lawyer) gave this closing argument in defending a man for shooting his former wife, who the defense alleged had humiliated him over a period of years after the divorce. Cook also had to explain why the ex-husband had driven to the middle of town and shot his wife in broad daylight on the courthouse steps where she worked without apparent provocation:

> What do we have, all of us, whether we are lawyers, farmers, or ditch diggers, what do we have that we hold dearest, except our homes, our children, our spouses, and perhaps most importantly . . . our dignity, our pride, and our self-respect. . . . (This) was a kind, decent, hardworking man.

§ 25.17   Trilogies in Opening Statements and Closing Arguments

This book is about cross-examinations, but the most important parts of cross-examinations are foreshadowed in opening statements and refreshed in closing arguments. In that sense, trilogies, along with other flag-planting techniques discussed in this book, should have a place in opening statements, cross-examinations, and closing arguments.

A trilogy in opening statement alerts the jurors to a critical aspect of the advocate's theory of the case. Using a trilogy in closing argument allows the jury to visualize that chapter of cross-examination that contained the trilogy. The cadence of a trilogy allows the jury to memorize the facts contained within the trilogy. As a result, a trilogy is a very useful as a method of communicating the theme.

Examples of the use of trilogies in opening statements and closing arguments abound.

Analyze this example from Edward Bennett Williams's closing in *United States v. Hoffa*. Mr. Williams summarized the lack of honesty of the government's witness using the following trilogy:

> From this man's lips, *we learned that he lies.*
>
> From this man's lips, *we learned that he deceives.*
>
> From this man's lips, *we learned that he falsifies.*
>
> What kind of man can lie while carrying a rosary, the symbol of *truth*, *honesty*, and *beauty*?

Note that in the second portion of the paragraph Mr. Williams used a second trilogy to vividly remind the jurors of the picture of the witness lying while carrying a rosary. As a result, Mr. Williams recapped his credibility attack on the witness and gave the jurors a vivid negative image by which to remember the witness.

Prosecutors often build their case using circumstantial evidence and do not have the words of the defendant to use in crafting a trilogy for opening statement or closing argument. That makes no difference. The circumstances themselves may be built into a powerful trilogy reciting the theme of the prosecution case. Witness this trilogy used by prosecutor in both the opening statement in closing argument of a white-collar case. The purpose of the trilogy is to summarize the actions of the defendant who, when he fell upon tough economic times, first tried to raise cash by selling items he owned then resorted to selling investments that belonged to his clients:

> He sold what his business owned.
>
> He sold what his family owned.
>
> And then he sold what he didn't own.

A newspaper reporter, writing about the fall of Enron (2003) opened his story with this trilogy:

> Out of cash.
>
> Out of credit.
>
> Out of time.

In another example taken from a commercial case, the defendant wished to communicate to the jury that the plaintiff had not sold his business because he was misled, but because he had gotten a very good price at a time when he very much needed the money. The trilogy defense counsel used in opening statement and in closing argument to remind the jury of these critical chapters of cross-examination was as follows:

Right price.

Right terms.

Right time.

§ 25.18   Trilogies Use Finesse

One of the attractions of the trilogy is that its power comes not from the lawyer's size, aggressiveness, or loud voice. Trilogy is a technique of finesse instead of force. As such, it exemplifies the type of technique that can be used on the most fragile of witnesses — children.

The case involved a sexual assault on a child. Despite a series of episodes that the child could now describe in great detail, the child had never mentioned a single one of these incidents to a single person until later, when the story was told to a neighbor. A trilogy was selected to close the cross-examination:

Q: You didn't tell the police?

A: (Silence with tears in her eyes.)

Q: You didn't tell your priest?

A: (More silence, with her eyes lowered to look at her lap.)

Q: You didn't even tell your mother?

A: (More silence, with stifled tears.)

(Silence by defense counsel — completing the moment.)

Q: No more questions, Your Honor.

The power of the trilogy stems from its content. Its form makes it memorable. Hence it is a more likely topic of discussion in the jury room. Better still, its power forces opposing counsel to try to defuse it. This means that opposing counsel will frequently waste his redirect or second closing argument combating the lawyer's use of trilogy in her cross-examinations or closing argument. Trilogies affect the balance of persuasion in the courtroom.

Chapter 26

LOOPS, DOUBLE LOOPS, AND SPONTANEOUS LOOPS

SYNOPSIS

§ 26.01   Loops as a Flag-Planting Device

The cross-examiner needs a variety of techniques that ethically and appropriately enable the advocate to call the jury's attention to a particular fact. While it is hoped that jurors will hear all the answers, the reality is that some answers matter more than others. There are those facts of such importance that they deserve highlighting. In essence, the lawyer wishes to "plant a flag" on that fact. Any trial technique designed to highlight a particular fact, whether the technique involves voice, movement, demonstrative aid, or oratorical device, is a flag-planting device. The techniques of looping, in all its various forms, are flag-planting techniques designed to call additional attention to a fact of importance.

§ 26.02   Three Looping Techniques

In the trial of a case, certain facts, phrases, and descriptions must be emphasized. Lawyers on each side of the case want to emphasize their strong points and their opponent's weaknesses. This desire to emphasize has led to the creation of loops. Loops emphasize certain facts and phrases in a subtle, but dramatic, ethical, and unobjectionable manner. There are three types of loops: the simple loop, the double loop, and the spontaneous loop. Each type of loop emphasizes certain words and phrases. However, each type of loop has special purposes and can be used more effectively in certain circumstances. Each is designed to add emphasis by permissible repetition, avoiding objections, and lowering the risk of bad answers. Historically, flawed techniques created objections and heightened the risk of bad answers.

§ 26.03 The Problems with Merely Repeating an Answer

Unaided by the technique of looping, lawyers often attempted to emphasize words and phrases by re-asking the question or by repeating the answer:

Q: You saw that the company's rating was downgraded?

A: Yes.

Q: There really is no question, you saw the company's rating was downgraded?

A: Well, now that I think about it, I got the whole report but I cannot recall if I actually read the part about the company being downgraded.

This technique is flawed, both tactically and legally. The second question in the example is objectionable as being "asked and answered" or "redundant, repetitive." Worse, the hostile witness immediately retreats having sensed that the cross-examiner is happy with the admission concerning reading about the downgrade. Having been signaled by the cross-examiner's second question that it is an important fact, and having been offered an immediate opportunity to soften the answer, the witness does so. Understandably the cross-examiner becomes frustrated. The witness now sees where the cross-examiner is going and knows what excuses must be offered in order to avoid giving the information desired by the cross-examiner.

Some lawyers engage in an equally dangerous but more amateurish technique. They pretend not to have heard the favorable answer. They will attempt to use their lack of comprehension as an excuse to repeat the question:

Q: Northwest canceled their order?

A: Yes they did.

Q: I am sorry, I didn't hear that. Did you say Northwest canceled their order?

At best this technique may work once in a trial. At worse, it offers the witness a chance to withdraw or modify the answer that so clearly helped the cross-examiner. This technique undermines the cross-examiner's personal credibility (lawyer pretends to be deaf) and still permits the witness to soften or withdraw the answer.

§ 26.04 Advantages of the Looping Technique

The cross-examiner needs a method of reinforcing a favorable fact while minimizing the ability of the witness to withdraw or modify the good answer. The technique of looping provides a subtle method of adding emphasis without encountering either of the drawbacks inherent in the old "re-asking" method. It does so by capturing the answer from the witness and reinforcing it rather than questioning it. The voice and phraseology of the cross-examiner will give no clue that the answer is extraordinarily helpful. It is the repetition of the fact that provides the emphasis.

§ 26.05   Simple Loop Formula

Looping is a method by which an important or favorable fact is re-emphasized by repeating the information to be highlighted in the body of the next question. At its most basic form it works like this.

Definition:

1) Through a leading question establish the desired fact or phrase;

2) Use the fact or phrase established within the body of the next question, but without re-asking the fact; and

3) Connect the looped fact or phrase with a question that contains an undisputed fact. Attach the looped fact to a safe fact in the second question.

§ 26.06   Analysis of the Formula

This is one of those very effective techniques that both looks simple on paper and is simple in practice. By repeating the helpful fact or phrase within the body of the next question or questions, the importance of that fact is re-established. Remember that the more time spent on a fact in the courtroom the more importance is attached to that fact. Time is a measure of importance. By precisely quoting the phrase used earlier by the witness within later questions, the jury is reminded that it was the witness who established the critical fact or agreed with the critical fact. The lawyer has neither misstated nor overstated the fact established. Furthermore, by reusing the critical fact within the body of next question, the lawyer does not take the risks that come with re-asking the fact.

Once the cross-examiner has learned to loop, the three-step process becomes automatic. The steps do not need to be memorized. In fact, they won't even be remembered. Instead, the process of repeating a very favorable fact within the succeeding question will become a natural instinct in the courtroom.

The fact or phrase to be looped should be an easily understood fact or phrase. The fact to be looped must be clear and concise. The looped fact should not be vague or unduly complex. The fact or phrase selected to be looped must be inserted as a predicate, or a given, into a new question that contains a fact not in dispute. By connecting the looped fact or phrase with a fact not in dispute, the witness has no basis upon which to deny the succeeding leading question. The fact asked in the new question was selected because it was beyond dispute. It is an "easy" question. Since the witness has already admitted in the prior question the "looped" fact or phrase, the witness cannot refuse to answer the question on that basis, either. Therefore, the witness cannot refuse an affirmative answer to the succeeding question or questions.

§ 26.07   Simple Loop Example

In a personal injury case where the plaintiff was ejected from the vehicle, the cross-examiner's goal was to use this fact to show the severity of the impact. However, the facts can objectively be interpreted as the plaintiff was thrown or fell with much less force from the car. Plaintiff's counsel needs to create a vivid picture, inasmuch as the plaintiff miraculously did not receive any permanent or disfiguring injuries. Damages (more precisely, the extent of damages) — not liability — are the critical issues that remain in the case:

Step 1:	**Q:**	The man was *hurled* from the car?
	A:	Yes.
Step 2:	**Q:**	After he was *hurled* from the car,
Step 3:		he landed on the highway?
	A:	Yes.

In Step 1, plaintiff's counsel uses a leading question to establish her desired fact that the plaintiff was "hurled" from the vehicle.

In Step 2, having gotten the witness to adopt this descriptive fact, plaintiff's counsel inserts the fact (loops it) into a "safe" (Step 3) second question. In this example, there is no question that the man was laying on the highway after he exited the vehicle.

Therefore, Step 3, attachment to an undisputed fact, was satisfied. The cross-examiner had previously established that the collision had occurred and that the man had been in the car involved in the collision. The only issue in the preceding question was how the man left the vehicle. The cross-examiner, through careful pre-trial analysis, had chosen the word "hurled," which the cross-examiner felt best illustrated the force of the collision. The lawyer chose a vivid but fair word.

§ 26.08 Looping Emotional Words

The goal of the cross-examiner is to loop powerful words and images tied directly to the cross-examiner's theory of the case.

An example from a domestic relations case: At issue was the cause of the separation. The defendant husband testified that the plaintiff wife was not upset by the separation and was not emotional when told. He testified that she might have had tears in her eyes, but that she certainly hadn't cried. An independent witness is called and examined by the wife's attorney on various other issues, but is cross-examined on the emotional impact to the wife on hearing that the husband was leaving, with a specific chapter goal to emphasize the emotional impact on the wife:

Q: Helen was *crying*?

A: Yes.

Q: She was *crying* when she turned to the defendant, Harry, and asked: "Why, Harry?"

§ 26.09 Looping Is a Learned Skill — Adjectives Are Easiest

Like most techniques in trial work, looping is a learned skill. The easiest words to loop are descriptive words, such as adjectives. They are easier for emphasizing concepts. An example of an adjective loop:

Q: The car was speeding?

A: Yes.

Q: The speeding car crossed the intersection?

A: Yes.

This is not to say that nouns, verbs, and other forms of words should not be looped. They can and will be after the cross-examiner has firmly established the technique of looping. For instance, "hurled" was looped, and it is a verb in that question.

The cross-examiner may loop phrases as well:

Q: This was undeniably a bad development?

A: Yes.

Q: After you learned of this *undeniably bad development*, you called your boss?

A: Yes.

§ 26.10   Multiple Simple Loops

The cross-examiner may use the loop technique repeatedly to build a consistent picture with the repetition of certain powerful or thematic words.

In a previous example, the cross-examiner emphasized the fact that the wife was crying while she asked the defendant about the cause of the separation. The word "crying" can be looped repeatedly by the cross-examiner to emphasize the severity of the emotional impact.

An example from an identification case: The defendant is charged with armed robbery of a fast-food operation. The manager was face-to-face with the robber and has identified the defendant. The manager is five feet eleven inches tall; the defendant is five feet nine. A goal of the cross-examination is to challenge the current testimony of the eyewitness that the defendant was the robber. As part of this challenge the cross-examiner wishes to show that on a prior occasion the witness described the robber as being a tall man. The lawyer begins by taking facts from the discovery and putting into context the factual situation in which the manager saw the robber:

Q: You were at work behind the counter?

A: Yes.

Q: And you looked up from work and saw the robber?

A: Yes.

Q: You judged him to be a tall man?

A: Yes.

Q: In fact that is how you described the robber to the police: "he was a tall man?"

A: That's what I told them.

Q: The tall man (loop) was no more than three feet away?

A: Yes.

Q: You looked the tall man (loop) up and down?

A: Yes.

Q: And you noticed you had to look up (loop) at him?

A: Yes.

Q: He was tall?

A: Yes.

Q: Taller (loop) than you?

A: Yes.

Q: And you're pretty tall (loop) yourself?

A: Yes.

Q: You're five foot eleven?

A: Yes.

The lawyer established the phrase "tall man," then integrated the phrase into the body of a subsequent question. The lawyer does not re-ask the witness whether the robber was "tall." That fact is simply put in as a given. It is a fact already established.

The simple loop highlights a fact of importance. This use of a simple loop is to emphasize that a product was failing:

Q: There was a marketing plan for the product?

Q: The marketing plan for this product called for sales of 600,000 units in the first quarter of 2003?

Q: Sales of this product barely made 200,000 units in the first quarter?

Q: The product was failing to even approach what you needed?

Q: He tried to put even more advertising dollars behind this failing (loop) product?

Q: You thought the failing (loop) product needed a brand overhaul?

Q: Eventually you brought together an entire team to discuss what to do about this failing (loop) product?

The simple loop of the term "failing product" cannot help but emphasize to the jury this fact of importance.

§ 26.11   Simple Loops for the Purpose of Labeling

Times have changed. The pace of life in and out of the courtroom has changed. Judges and juries are bombarded with an avalanche of facts, names, and new nouns everyday. "Twenty-four/seven" has become a way of life.

Listeners simply cannot remember people's names or the names of new products. The problem in the courtroom is magnified. The lawyers have learned the names of the witnesses by working on the case for hours, days, or even months. Jurors are requested to immediately memorize the names of the parties, witnesses, and lawyers. If this was not difficult enough, they are then expected to listen to questions about what one witness, whose name they can barely recall, heard another witness say to perhaps even a third witness. Questions refer to exhibit numbers or the names of important exhibits. Keeping up with may prove overwhelming. Jurors give up when overwhelmed. When they cannot follow the questioning they mentally shut down. If jurors become frustrated at their inability to link the testimony with the names or exhibit numbers being used, they are likely to stop listening. No theory can get through to a juror who has tuned out.

By labeling each important witness and each important exhibit, the trial lawyer makes the jury's job and the judge's job much easier. Looping is the technique that lends itself to this labeling process.

§ 26.12   The Technique of Looping to Label

The technique of looping to label is a simple and natural way of assisting people's memory in the courtroom environment. Looping labels can be used in any case, in any cross-examination, and in any questioning. Looping assists the memory anytime there is a need to label a fact, a witness, or a particular exhibit. The technique is simple: Find a descriptive but fair label that is consistent with the cross-examiner's theory. Use that label in place of the name of the witness, or the number of the exhibit, or the date of the event. Use the label consistently throughout trial so that both jurors and witnesses can easily equate the label with the person, event, or exhibit. In a self-defense case:

Q: You looked out the door and saw several boys?

Q: One of the boys had a stick in his hand?

Q: The boy was *quivering*? (establish)

Q: The quivering (loop to label) boy said, "Where's John? I want to see John."

Q: You looked through the screen and said to the *quivering* boy (reloop), "If you're looking for trouble, you found it."

Q: And the quivering boy (reloop) looked back at you, but said nothing?

This is a simple loop used multiple times. The phrase "quivering boy" is looped for the purpose of labeling. The repetition of the phrase is essential in creating within the juror's minds a vivid picture of the quivering boy. When the key phrase "quivering boy" is used in closing argument, the picture is revived and becomes more vivid. The previous testimony is more easily recalled by the jury. The label used ("quivering") is more memorable and consistent with the lawyer's theory than "defendant," "murderer," or even his name. When the jury deliberates, it is essential that the jury equate the phrase "quivering boy" with the defendant, not the fact that the defendant shot the witness five times.

§ 26.13   Loops to Label Exhibits

Trials have become more complicated. It seems every trial has hundreds of exhibits. Particularly in commercial litigation, the exhibits frequently number in the hundreds and often in the thousands. The most conscientious judge or jury cannot keep the exhibits straight. The lawyers who have dealt with the case for months and years before trial have a most difficult time keeping up with exhibits. Why is there a reasonable expectation that judges or juries could possibly do so?

Looping helps to label exhibits and eliminates the necessity of the judge or jury to memorize the exhibit number. Everyone begins to refer to the exhibit by the label loop. It is chosen to be consistent with the cross-examiner's theory.

In a commercial case a critical memo read: "I believe the brokers should contact their clients." After a meeting with his boss, the author of the memo changed the memo to read: "I believe the brokers should _not_ contact their clients." Understandably this memo was one of the most critical documents in the lawsuit brought on behalf of the clients who were not contacted about a failing investment. Of course the memo had an exhibit number, but there were hundreds of numbered exhibits. The memo had a date, but the date had no special significance. Instead, plaintiffs' counsel referred to the memo as the "_Not_ memo." The label stuck because the label was fair and because it was natural shorthand for the exhibit.

This "smoking gun" exhibit was marked sequentially as plaintiff's exhibit no. 136. It clearly was the brilliant Nova star of the plaintiff's theory of the case, but it was buried in the exhibits as exhibit no. 136.

Whenever the exhibit was referenced, it was called "the not memorandum." Whether it was on direct examination, cross-examination, or in closing argument, it was consistently called "the not memorandum." Not only was the label descriptive and vivid, but it was also completely consistent with the cross-examiner's theory of the case. Soon everyone in trial used the same description:

Q: The original version of the "not memo" was not distributed to the clients?

A: No.

Q: The original version of the "not memo" was not sent to the brokers?

A: No.

Questions to a separate witness should reuse and reinforce this label:

A: You did not keep your copy of the "not memo?"

Q: No need to.

A: In fact be made at a point to destroy your copy of the "not memo?"

A: I tossed it.

The label is so much more effective than an exhibit number or a date where neither the number nor the date had any special significance.

§ 26.14   Loops to Label Events

If the date of a particular event is important to the theory of the case, then a way to productively label and loop the label is to refer to the event by its date:

Q: At the September 28th meeting . . .

Or more vividly:

Q: After the merger the entire sales department was fired?

Q: They got the word by group e-mail?

Q: The e-mail was sent out on Saturday, May 26?

Q: You have heard that e-mail referred to as "the Saturday night massacre?"

Q: As a result of the Saturday night massacre . . .

Q: Within days of the Saturday night massacre . . .

§ 26.15   Loops of Undisputed Facts Critical to Theory

While the purpose of simple loops is always to accentuate a fact or phrase, the fact or phrase is not always the subject of dispute. Instead, the fact or phrase may represent a concept so central to the theory of the case, and so important to the cross-examination, that its mere establishment and repetition adds weight to the thrust of the cross-examination. They are words to remember, i.e., word choices that the cross-examiner believes will support the theory of the case in the most meaningful way possible (see chapter 2, *Developing a Theory of the Case* and chapter 8, *The Only Three Rules of Cross-Examination*).

What follows is an example of the establishment of the key adjective that will be used in the cross-examination of an expert witness:

Q: You told us in direct examination that you consider yourself an expert in accident investigation?

Q: You have taken classes at the Colorado Law Enforcement Training Academy on traffic accident investigation?

Q: But those courses were basic?

Q: The real training took place at the Institute of Police Traffic Management?

Q: There you took a two-week course called Technical Accident Investigation?

Q: The book they used primarily in their teaching was "The Northwestern University Book on Technical Accident Investigation?"

Q: It is considered to be the leading book in the field?

Q: You were taught out of it, you respect it, and in fact, it is *the Bible* of the industry?

Q: It is *the Bible* (loop) of Accident Investigation?

Q: One of the critical measurements in determining speed is from a skid coefficient to friction on the roadway?

Q: This is called the "drag measurement?"

Q: To determine the drag measurement, you use a drag sled?

(Chapter on drag sled usage and its importance in determining speed is measured from skid marks.)

Q: Now let's talk about what the Northwestern University Book, *the Bible* of Accident Investigation, says you ought to do?

Q: *The Bible* says multiple measurements are to be taken along the path Of the skid mark?

Q: *The Bible* says that multiple measurements must be taken in order to show a range of drag factors?

Q: *The Bible* says that it is critical to show a range of drag factors as different parts of the roadway have completely different coefficients to friction?

Q: Now that's what *the Bible* says?

Q: Let's compare how you did it to *the Bible*?

Q: You pulled the drag sled across the skid marks near the south end of the north median?

Q: That's not the way *the Bible* says to do it?

Q: You did not perform multiple drag tests over points along the skid?

Q: That's not the way *the Bible* says to do it?

Q: You did not run multiple tests at any point?

Q: Your calculations are based on a single drag test?

Q: That's not the way *the Bible* says to do it?

A: No, sir.

During cross-examination when the witness felt safe, the witness was happy to admit that the Northwestern University Book is "The Bible" of accident investigation. The selected phrase, "The Bible," can then be repeatedly looped as a label in impeachment to show a string of comparisons between the work done and the commandments of "The Bible." Having earlier accepted this characterization or label, it is now too late for the witness to deny or hedge on that key label.

§ 26.16   Using Loops in the Cross-Examination of Experts

Experts are always difficult to cross-examine. They are intelligent. They generally know their field of expertise. Most importantly, they are experienced in testifying. The looping technique is just as valuable in the cross-examination of the expert as it is in the cross-examination of a lay witness. Any time an affirmative answer is provided to a leading question, the fact proved in that leading question is capable of forming the basis for a loop. Neither the technique nor its usefulness is affected by the fact that the witness happens to be experienced at testifying:

Q: In 2001 he lost more than $2 million on his stock investments?

Q: A $2 million loss was an enormous loss in comparison to his net worth?

Q: This enormous loss resulted in . . .?

Q: As a result of this enormous loss . . .?

Q: On his financial statement, this enormous loss is reflected in a decrease . . . ?

A separate technique is to loop conclusory terms used by the opposing expert and pair of them with other facts that contradict the conclusory term. In the cross-examination of an independent medical examination expert who has testified dozens of time, the cross-examiner used simple loops:

Q: You needed to do a thorough physical examination?

Q: You needed to do a complete physical examination?

Q: You needed to do an unbiased physical examination?

Q: Your thorough, complete, and unbiased physical examination took less than twenty-five minutes?

The expert initially believed that admitting to "thorough," "complete," and "unbiased" was a trivial matter. The expert may well have thought it would help his posture in the eyes of the jury. But when those words were used in juxtaposition (see chapter 24, *Juxtaposition*) to the fact of "less than twenty-five minutes," the effect was terrible.

§ 26.17   Looping to Lock in a Disputed Subjective Facts

In spite of the use of leading questions, there are times when the witness's answer cannot be predicted. There are areas in which the witness has available a broad range of responses, all of which can be successfully defended by the witness against even a skilled cross-examiner. The most difficult words to force on a witness are nebulous, vague, or subjective words. Often, this is in the area of description: "pretty dark" versus "dark" versus "very dark"; "pretty quick" versus "almost immediately" versus "instantly." Words that describe a situation can also be disputed. Calling a meeting a "crisis meeting," referring to an accident as "horrific," asking the witness if an event "shocked" gives the witness wiggle room. If such a subjective term is the goal of the cross-examiner, she should insert it in a leading question early in the cross-examination. Once the witness has accepted such a term, he becomes more comfortable with the term if it is then used in relation to any other facts in the case.

There is a technique by which the cross-examiner can increase the odds of getting the witness to accept the cross-examiner's characterization of the subjective fact. This technique requires the cross-examiner to reverse the ordinary loop process. By inserting the hoped-for fact or phrase in a leading question that contains a second, unarguable fact, the witness is more inclined to quickly affirm — without fully considering the implications of the vague, subjective, or arguable phrase. Once rewarded with an affirmative response to this most desired fact or phrase (see chapter 8, *The Only Three Rules of Cross-Examination*; chapter 11, *Sequences of Cross-Examination*; and chapter 9, *The Chapter Method of Cross-Examination*), it is helpful to loop the response at least once, so as to permanently establish it in place and make backtracking by the witness more difficult later in the cross-examination or redirect examination. In the example below, the desired term is "instantly." The cross-examiner should first establish an easy (undisputable) fact:

Q: You heard the shot?

Q: You were standing outside the drug store when you heard the first shot?

Q: The first shot was followed instantly (instantly is very subjective) by shots two and three? (No question there were three shots?)

Q: Three shots instantly (looped) following each other caused you to run?

§ 26.18 Looping Subjective Emotional States

Whether it is a domestic relations case, a personal injury case, or even a victim's testimony in a criminal case, the emotional state of a person is often at issue. Even in the "white-collar prosecution" of Martha Stewart, a witness's emotional state was an issue. In a previous domestic relations example, the defendant husband testified that the wife was not particularly emotional. The wife testified that she was close to hysteria. The truth may lie somewhere in between, but the cross-examiner's job on behalf of the wife is to emphasize to the jury just how emotional this woman was at the time of the separation. One technique is to first try to gain an affirmative answer to the desired description of the emotional state. If the witness declines to adopt that description, the cross-examiner can follow up with some physical manifestations of the emotional state that will cause the jurors to mentally accept the subjective description that the lawyer first suggested:

Q: Your wife was close to hysteria when you asked for the separation?

A: She was somewhat upset.

Q: She was trembling?

A: Yes.

Q: She was weeping?

A: She was.

Q: As she was weeping and trembling, she asked you, "Why, Harry?"

A: Yes.

Q: You said to your trembling, weeping wife that you felt you needed to "move on?"

A: Yes.

Q: And as your wife stood there weeping and trembling you asked her how soon she thought she could go back to work?

A: Yes.

The cross-examiner has not gotten the witness to adopt the subject of description "close to hysteria." But the factually based descriptions of a weeping, trembling wife, shows the phrase "somewhat upset" to be understated. Another example:

Q: The man who robbed you was tall?

Q: Taller than you?

Q: You are five eleven?   *key fact*

Q: You could see he was a very tall man?   *establish*

Q: The very tall man was wearing a blue jean jacket?   *phrase loop*

§ 26.19   Chain of Loops

If the cross-examiner wishes to move a witness from point A to point Z in the story — where point Z is the sought-after testimony — it is often possible to move the witness along the path to admission of the key point by a series of loops. In this technique, the lawyer establishes a fact, loops that fact to the next fact, loops the second fact to the next fact, and continues to loop answers until the lawyer gets to the most desired answer.

Looping in this manner is really an extension of logic: If A, then B; if B, then C, and so on. The mass of facts connected with newly introduced fact drives and accelerates the momentum for the witness and the jury. The series of loops is a desirable method in such cases, as it very quickly moves the witness from A to Z while offering less room for the witness to evade. A civil example:

Q: You picked up a salad at McDonald's?

A: Yes.

Q: You were eating your salad as you drove?

A: Yes.

Q: As you drove, you changed the radio station?

A: Yes.

Q: As you changed the radio station, you looked down?

A: Yes.

Q: While looking down, you failed to see the stop sign?

A: Yes.

Q: Not seeing the stop sign, you drove straight into the intersection?

A: Yes.

Q: You drove into the intersection at about 25 miles per hour?

A: Yes.

Q: And at 25 miles per hour, you slammed broadside into Randy Garman's car?

Another example:

Q: You filled out a *bank loan application* at First National?

A: Yes.

Q: In the *application*, you told the bank that you *owned a house*?

A: Yes.

Q: You told them the *house you owned* was worth *$85,000*?

A: Yes.

Q: You told them that this *$85,000* house had a *$40,000 mortgage*?

A: Yes.

Q: The *$40,000 mortgage* never existed?

A: No.

Q: The *$85,000* value never existed?

A: No.

Q: You never *owned that house*?

A: No, sir.

Q: You lied to the bank about owning that house?

A: Yes.

Q: The *value*, the *mortgage*, the *house* were all lies?

A: Yes.

Q: They were lies you put into a *bank loan application*?

A: Yes, sir, they were.

Q: The *bank loan application* was a con?

A: Yes, sir, it was.

Q: To complete the *con*, you had to tell several *lies*?

Q: You needed to *lie* to complete the con?

A: Yes, sir.

A: Yes, sir.

Q: You needed the *con* to get the *money*?

A: Yes, sir.

Q: You were willing to take the *money* if somebody was foolish enough to believe the *con*?

A: I guess you could say that.

§ 26.20 Saving Impeaching Facts

When the witness makes an admission, repetition of the admission will be helpful in succeeding sentences. Attempting to require the witness to repeat the answer exposes the lawyer to objections (redundant, repetitive). It also drains the answer of its vitality. By using a loop, however, the lawyer can sustain interest and avoid objection:

Q: When you told the police that you had borrowed the money from loan sharks and were paying them 5% interest a week, that was not the truth?

A: No, it was not.

Q: You put that story together out of thin air?

A: Yes, sir.

Q: *Out of thin air*, you invented facts?

A: Yes, sir.

Q: *Out of thin air*, you invented people?

A: Yes, sir.

Q: *Out of thin air*, you invented conversations?

A: Yes, sir.

The lawyer is the one who chooses the phrase "out of thin air" to equate with "not the truth." Certain phrases lend themselves to greater memory by the jury. Certain word choices or selections (see chapter 8, *The Only Three Rules of Cross-Examination*) lend themselves to physical expression when verbalizing them.

Who cannot see the lawyer repeatedly using this phrase "out of thin air" in closing argument? Who cannot see the lawyer gesturing with her arms when using the phrase "out of thin air" each time that she uses it in closing arguments? Who doubts that the jury will remember the phrase "out of thin air" and the physical gesture when deliberating the veracity of this witness?

§ 26.21   Double Loops Technique

Simple loops can be quickly mastered. Once they are, it takes only minimal additional effort to learn the double loop technique. Double looping is a technique that can be used for two distinct purposes. The first, and the most frequently employed purpose is its use to juxtapose two inconsistent concepts (see chapter 24, *Juxtaposition*). That is, contrasting two dissimilar or inconsistent facts in a single question to promote a desired jury reaction. Two facts are pushed together to show the lack of logic inherent in a witness trying to verify both facts.

The second common purpose of the double loop technique is to use two or more looped facts in combinations to heighten an image and produce a result that will be much more memorable and more closely linked than the two facts alone.

§ 26.22   Double Loop Formula

1)   Establish first desired significant fact.

2)   Establish second desired significant fact.

3)   Loop both facts together in a third question and later questions.

4)   Always tie the double loop to a "safe" undisputed fact.

§ 26.23   Double Loop for Contrast

In the following example, the cross-examiner contrasts the size difference between the two combatants:

(Establish fact one.)

Q: Eddie is six one?

A: Yes.

(Establish fact two.)

Q: George is five seven?

A: Yes.

(Loop both established facts.)

Q: You saw six-foot, one-inch Eddie hit five-foot, seven-inch George?

A: Yes.

(Loop both again.)

Q: Six-foot, one-inch Eddie beat on five-foot, seven-inch George with his fists?

A: Yes.

The first two questions establish a great disparity in size. The double loop contrasts this disparity in the third question. Please note that the cross-examiner could have chosen not to double loop both facts in a fourth question. The cross-examiner chose to use the double loop in a succeeding question to emphasize the size disparity. This double loop many now be used repeatedly.

§ 26.24   Building the Double Loop

Example in a criminal snitch case:

Q: When you said, "I didn't do it!" to the police, you lied?

Q: You lied because the lie was better than the truth? (loop)

Q: You lied because the lie was more likely to help than the truth? (reloop)

Q: You lied because you hoped the lie would get you out of trouble?

Q: And when you lied to get out of trouble, you made up details? (double loop)

Q: And when you lied to get out of trouble, you made up events? (double loop)

Q: And when you lied to get out of trouble, you made up conversations? (double loop)

The cross-examiner loops the word "lied" as a simple loop several times and then ties that simple loop with another loop of "get you out of trouble." Once this second fact has been established, the cross-examiner double loops the word "lied" with the phrase "get out of trouble," and uses it several times to heighten the effect of the double loop. The double loop is intended to tie "lie" and "get out of trouble." In closing argument, the lawyer can argue that the snitch is in trouble, and the snitch lies to "get out of trouble."

It is obvious from this example how much emphasis can be placed on simple words or phrases that if used separately would escape the attention of the jury. When used repetitively, without running the risk of an objection, the key facts and phrases are emphasized to the jury.

§ 26.25   Use of the Double Loop to Juxtapose Inconsistent Facts

In an impeaching cross-examination, assume the witness has said something that is accepted as true. However, if examined in juxtaposition to other facts, the story casts doubt upon the original assertion. The witness has told a story or fact, often in direct examination, which in isolation appears reasonable, but when examined in context with other testimony of the witness, appears to be untruthful and illogical. In such cases, it is helpful to permit the witness to establish the first fact and later in cross-examination to perform a double loop that juxtaposes the first assertion and shows it to be implausible.

The double loop technique to juxtapose inconsistent facts is at the heart of the following example from a commercial case:

Q: You have told us that you were unaware of any facts that caused you any concerns about the financial health of this company?

Q: You knew the company had twice been downgraded by the rating services?

Q: You know the company had lost money for three consecutive years?

Q: This double downgraded, money-losing company caused you no concern?

Another example is drawn from a criminal case. The purpose is to cast doubt upon the credibility of a witness by allowing the jurors to see the inherent inconsistency between established facts and the position taken by the witness.

In the homicide case discussed, an eyewitness claims she was forced to prostitute herself to get money to feed her starving baby. The starving baby story is central to her version of events. She has testified to that on direct examination. There is no reason to believe that the witness is going to abandon such a central feature of her story. Hence, the lawyer should not be afraid to ask the phrase: "Your baby was at home starving?" Having established that phrase, perhaps at a very early stage of the cross-examination and having received a defiant "yes," the lawyer may later double loop it in juxtaposition to other inconsistent known facts of the case.

In reviewing the chronology of events set forth in the witness statement charts (see chapters 5, 6, and 7), the lawyer finds that after committing the first act of prostitution the witness went to a local fast food chain to eat a hamburger. Consider a loop of the phrase, "Your baby was at home starving," in juxtaposition with this new fact in an attempt to make the previous story of the starving baby appear unlikely: "Your baby was at home starving, and you sat down to eat a hamburger?"

The lawyer has double looped an answer from a previous chapter ("Your baby was at home starving") in juxtaposition to a newly established fact ("You sat down to eat a hamburger"), which has the effect of making less credible one of the two assertions by the witness. Since the two facts cannot logically exist simultaneously, and since one of the facts is uncontested (ate the hamburger), the jury is led to reject the double looped fact (baby at home starving).

§ 26.26 The Cross-Examiner Chooses Which Fact to Validate and Which Fact to Discredit

If a particular area of testimony of a witness will become less credible because of some other testimony of the witness, then a loop of the original testimony and a loop of the subsequent testimony (hence, a double loop), juxtaposing two irreconcilable sets of facts, will leave the jury to reflect upon which one is untruthful. The cross-examiner can elect which fact to strengthen and thereby tilt the scales as to which fact will be rejected. Contrast the fact to be discredited with an undisputed fact. It is a matter of selection by the cross-examiner.

Left to their own devices, some jurors might notice the two assertions and come to the opinion that they are in logical opposition. The science and techniques of cross-examination are used to make this possibility a certainty. The double loop of concepts in opposition accomplishes this goal.

There is one situation where it is entirely predictable which of the two assertions the jurors will accept. When a witness is confronted with facts that he admits to be true, and the witness gives an opinion (lay or expert), expresses a subjective point of view, or otherwise offers a nonfactual expression inconsistent with the admitted facts, the facts will prevail over the subjective or conclusory assertion of the witness.

The prepared cross-examiner juxtaposes these inconsistent facts and phrases from various parts of the witness's testimony and places them in one sentence, so that the jury can reach the desired conclusion as to the absurdity of the believability of both of these phrases. Often the witness notices that her story is inconsistent and begins to offer new excuses and more unbelievable testimony to attempt to reconcile these positions. The more unbelievable excuse creates more opportunities for more juxtaposed double loops.

§ 26.27   Use of the Double Loop to Highlight Contrasting Theories

The double loop is not only used to contrast inconsistent or irreconcilable facts, but it can be used effectively to show the jury the contrasting positions of the parties.

In a personal injury suit, where part of the insurance company's defense is that the collision just wasn't a big deal, the plaintiff's lawyer can use double loops to her advantage. In the cross-examination of the defendant driver:

Q: The man was unconscious?

A: Yes.

Q: The unconscious man was laying in the front seat bleeding?

A: Yes.

Q: The unconscious man that we are talking about is the plaintiff?

A: Yes.

Q: But you walked away from your car?

A: Yes.

Q: You weren't lying in the front seat bleeding; you walked away?

A: That's right.

Q: You ran the light?

A: Yes.

Q: And after you ran the light, it was you who walked away from your car, and it was the plaintiff who lay unconscious, bleeding in his car?

A jury may understand why the defendant believes the collision to be no big thing; the jury will also understand why the plaintiff considers the collision a major event. It is the plaintiff who benefits from the contrasts of the facts that the defendant walked away from the collision without a scratch while the plaintiff was rendered unconscious and bleeding. To heighten that contrast further, the cross-examiner may well add the phrase "without a scratch" to the description of the defendant walking away from the collision. Now that phrase, "without a scratch," can be used in a double loop contrast or juxtaposition later in the cross-examination.

In a civil case involving police brutality, plaintiff's counsel knows the officer will resort to the phrase "just trying to get the situation under control" from pre-trial testimony. Hence, the cross-examiner establishes it, loops it, and then ties it to loops of earlier testimony concerning the injuries to the plaintiff forming a double loop:

Q: You were just trying to get the situation under control?

Q: You used your 5-cell flashlight to help you get it under control?

Q: Specifically, you used your 5-cell flashlight to get Mr. Johnson under control?

Q: And after you got him under control you needed to call an ambulance?

Q: You needed to call an ambulance to look after his head injuries?

Q: His head injuries occurred when you were trying to get the situation under control?

§ 26.28   Use of Double Loops in Combinations

Experience teaches that one fact, one adjective, or one description may not convince the listener of the severity of an event, but that multiple descriptions combined may well have such an effect.

One of Johnny Carson's historically favorite comedy routines with Ed McMahon is an example:

Carson: It was really a big event.

McMahon: How big was it?

Carson: (Smiling shyly at the audience) It was so big that. . . . (The routine continues with multiple examples of how big the event was, beginning with gross distortions and ending with absolute, but hilarious, absurdity.)

The cross-examiner can double loop to place together multiple descriptions in one question or in a series of questions. This leads the jury to conclude that the event was significant. This is not to say that the witness will ever agree that the event was significant, but only that the witness will be required to agree to a list of facts that will ultimately lead the jury to conclude the event was tremendously significant.

In a personal injury case, the defendant has denied that the plaintiff was severely injured by the collision:

Q: The other driver was unconscious? (fact one)

A: Yes.

Q: He was unconscious and lying on the front seat of his car? (loop)

A: Yes.

Q: You walked over after the collision and looked in his window?

A: Yes.

Q: You saw that he was unconscious? (relooped)

A: Yes.

Q: You also saw that his shirt was soaked in blood? (fact two)

A: Yes.

Q: As you stood there looking through the window, you realized that this unconscious, blood-soaked man might die? (double loop)

A: I didn't know one way or the other.

§ 26.29 Expert Witnesses and Double Loops

Expert witnesses testify in jargon, conclusions, and subjective interpretations. The rules of evidence permit expert witnesses to give their opinions in these forms, but the rules also permit the cross-examiner to attack those statements in multiple ways. Undermining the factual basis of the opinion is a time-honored method. The double loop lends itself to this attack.

Q: Doctor, you said on direct testimony that Ray is doing "as well as can be expected?"

A: Yes.

Q: Ray has a shattered tibia?

A: Yes.

Q: Ray is doing "as well as can be expected" for a teenager with a shattered tibia?

A: Yes.

Q: Ray is doing "as well as can be expected" for a teenager with a shattered tibia who can never walk on uneven ground again?

A: Yes.

Q: Ray is doing "as well as can be expected" for a teenager with a shattered tibia who can never play football again?

A: Yes.

Q: Ray is doing "as well as can be expected" for a teenager with a shattered tibia who will always walk with a limp?

A: Yes.

When the expert is confronted with the double loop showing the incongruity of the conclusion, "as well as can be expected," against hard-edged facts the expert becomes uncomfortable on the stand. The opponent is placed in a position of not wanting to talk about "as well as can be expected" in his closing argument. The double loop comparison of the conclusion of the expert to the hard-edged facts changes the psychodynamic of the courtroom. That phrase has been poisoned for the opponent for the balance of the trial. When double loops are used in combination, the purpose is to irretrievably connect the two facts in the mind of the jury.

Q: The child was bleeding? (fact one)

A: Yes.

Q: Her mother was crying? (fact two)

A: Yes.

Q: The crying mother was holding her bleeding child? (double loop)

A: Yes.

§ 26.30 Creating the Double Loop for Use Against the Expert

Every expert must admit certain facts in order to be considered by the court an expert. Every expert must admit certain facts to be believed by the jury.

Those same facts that the expert admits, and in most cases embraces, can be compared to individual hard-edged facts that dramatically undermine the expert. The cross-examiner need not find the basic facts or admissions that the expert must show to be considered an expert. Those facts are obvious; they need not be sought out. Example:

Q: Doctor, you have assured us that you used "all of your professional skills" in operating on Ms. Babb?

A: Yes.

Q: You sliced into Ms. Babb's bowel with your scalpel?

A: Yes.

Q: Now, you were using "all of your professional skills" when you sliced into her bowel with your scalpel? (double loop)

A: Yes.

Q: You were using "all of your professional skills" when you completely overlooked the fact that you had sliced into her bowel with your scalpel?

A: Yes.

Q: You were using "all of your professional skills" when you overlooked the fact that you had sliced into her bowel with your scalpel and fecal material was leaking into her abdomen?

A: Yes.

§ 26.31   The Double Loop Technique Increases the Overall Value of the Good Facts Upon Which It Is Built

The technique of double looping illustrates that combining looped facts and phrases in a thoughtful manner, be it in juxtaposition or in combinations, makes the perception to be conveyed to the jury greater than the sum of the looped facts or phrases. The witness must continue to agree with the looped facts and phrases. Ordinarily the witness will never agree with the logical conclusion or perception to be deduced or to be felt by the jury based on the admissions by the witness of the looped facts and phrases. For this reason, the cross-examiner is better off not asking the witness to admit the logical conclusion. The double loop produces material for closing argument. It is at that time the cross-examiner can safely explore its significance, although the jury has well understood it at the time of its original airing.

Should the witness voluntarily try to argue out of the implications of the double loop, the jury concludes not only what the cross-examiner wishes for it to conclude based on the admitted facts, but the jury also concludes that the witness is being unreasonable and unbelievable in refusing to make that same conclusion. By the use of double loops, the cross-examiner is rewarded, not only in the sense that she has skillfully emphasized and re-emphasized important facts to her theory of the case, but by the undermining of the witnesses credibility. In a sense, double loops lead to double rewards.

§ 26.32   Spontaneous Loops

All of the loops shown thus far have been written and executed according to the cross-examiner's script. They were prepared pre-trial. There is nothing spontaneous about them, although simple and double loops sound spontaneous to the witness and the jury. These loops were planned; the lawyer carefully selected the words.

However, one of the most enjoyable and effective uses of looping occurs when a witness gives an unexpected answer, which has in it a wonderfully helpful fact that substantially advances the lawyer's theory of the case. The critical difference between spontaneous loops and simple or double loops is that the witness chooses the words.

In a pure spontaneous loop, it is the witness who has made that word choice in front of this jury and judge. The witness will never be able to disclaim that word choice, no matter how ill conceived or regrettable that word choice is. The spontaneous loop is based on the phrase that has escaped the lips of the witness. Forever in this trial, the witness will be charged with the responsibility of uttering it.

§ 26.33   Word Selection and Simple Loops Lead to Spontaneous Loop Opportunities

In the setting of a commercial litigation case involving two professionals dividing a practice, the more senior partner who maintained all of the books of the practice reacts to the well-thought out word selection by the cross-examiner and offers a more dramatic opportunity for a spontaneous loop:

Q: You had an extremely profitable practice?

A: Well, it was only the appearance of a profitable practice.

Q: It was the "appearance of a profitable practice," but it was a fake?

A: Yes.

Q: It was the "appearance of a profitable practice," but it was intended to deceive?

A: Yes.

Q: It was the "appearance of a profitable practice," but it was a believable lie?

A: True, I guess.

Whatever softening of the phrase "profitable practice" that the witness believed he could achieve by suggesting "it was only the appearance of" was dramatically reversed by the destruction of the witness's overall credibility. The witness ran from the planned loop and created the opportunity for the spontaneous loop.

§ 26.34   Why Spontaneous Loops Happen

Two events must occur for a spontaneous loop to happen. First, the witness must say something that helps the cross-examiner's theory of the case or uses a powerful word that may dramatize the cross-examiner's theory of the case. Why does this happen? Some witnesses are simply trying to tell the truth. The phrase is reasonable and the witness uses it innocently. Some witnesses are not trying to describe the events in a way helpful to the cross-examiner's theory of the case. But as Aesop has taught, no one can carefully select words to their advantage every time. Witnesses misspeak. Witnesses are under strain and misspeak more often than they normally would.

> The shaft of the arrow had been feathered with one of the eagle's own plumes. We often give our enemies the means of our own destruction.
>
> Aesop
The Eagle and the Arrow

The second event that must occur is that the cross-examiner must be listening. Listening is one of the most difficult skills for a cross-examiner. In the heart-thumping drama of a cross-examination, where goals must be accomplished and distractions avoided, it is difficult for the cross-examiner to listen. When the cross-examiner does listen and when the witness offers that powerful phrase, the opportunity for spontaneous loop has been created.

§ 26.35   Definition of Spontaneous Loop Technique

1) Listen. Any answer other than a "yes" or "no" may offer an opportunity for the cross-examiner. Listen with the cross-examiner's theory of the case in mind.

2) Lift. Extract any useful word or phrase from the answer.

3) Loop. Use the helpful factor phrase in the body of the next question.

4) Tie the spontaneous loop to a safe, undisputed fact.

Compare the definition for spontaneous loop with the definition of a simple loop. There is but one difference. The cross-examiner must listen for the spontaneous loop. All other steps to the spontaneous loop are identical to the simple loop.

§ 26.36   Examples of Spontaneous Loops

The plaintiff is thrown from the vehicle after a collision. A portion of the cross-examination of the defendant is shown:

Q: The impact hurled him (the plaintiff) from the car?

A: I wouldn't say hurled, more like tossed.

Q: It "tossed" him about 30 feet? (spontaneous loop)

A: Well, yeah.

Q: In fact, it tossed him up against a light pole?

A: True.

This example can be analyzed as follows: The lawyer selected the word "hurled" intentionally to loop. It was to illustrate the tremendous impact of the collision. It was to be looped throughout the cross-examination. It was used in place of a word such as "thrown," which was taken from the investigative officer's police report.

The defendant, an intelligent man, chose not to agree with that word choice. But even intelligent witnesses are placed off guard when they are confronted with well-thought out word choices designed to have an impact on the jury. The defendant, in hindsight, made a worse choice when he selected the word "tossed." Unquestionably, the defendant was thinking that "tossed" was a much less aggressive and violent type of throw when compared with "hurled." Unfortunately for the witness, the lawyer coupled the word "tossed" with the very frightening facts in the case. She got the benefit of the picture of a man tossed from his vehicle and the added benefit of a defendant who unfairly tried to minimize those facts in front of the jury.

§ 26.37   Spontaneous Loop Opportunities Come from Witnesses Who Are Unresponsive

The following is an example of looping from a spontaneous answer by a government informant. The questioning comes at the end of a series of chapters on the informant's prior felony convictions. This chapter summarizes previous chapters:

Q: Three times in ten years you have been convicted of felonies?

A: Yes, but they were never violent crimes, they were just "cons" (a phrase to loop spontaneously).

Q: You "con" people?

A: I didn't hurt people, I just deceived them (two phrases to loop spontaneously).

Q: And when you didn't hurt people, but you just deceived them, you did it to get their money?

A: Yes, I guess so.

Q: And when you didn't hurt people, but you just deceived them, you did it to get what you wanted?

A: Yeah.

Q: And when you didn't hurt people, but you deceived them, you did it to get what you needed?

A: Yeah. (Witness looks at prosecutor.)

In this example, the witness volunteers the word "cons." "Cons" is immediately looped. This in turn leads to an additional phrase to loop spontaneously. Spontaneous loops at first taunt the witness to volunteer again. Then they punish the witness for volunteering. Silence from the witness soon follows.

§ 26.38 Spontaneous Loops to Silence the Witness

Spontaneous loops silence the unresponsive or out of control witness (see chapter 19, *Controlling the Runaway Witness*). Spontaneous loops eventually threaten the witness so much that the witness will refuse to volunteer in any matter. Through spontaneous loops, the cross-examiner exercises control over the witness by punishing the non-responsive answer.

In the preceding examples, note how each time the cross-examiner effectively uses the spontaneous loop, the witness's answers become shorter and shorter until they are monosyllables. An example from a commercial case:

A: Counselor, you have to understand that net worth means "real worth."

Q: Sir, you said that net worth was "real worth," but what you call the "real worth" did not include the hidden bonds?

A: Well, yes.

Q: What you called the "real worth" was understated by $56,000?

A: Yes.

Q: What you have called "real worth" wasn't real?

A: Yes.

Q: It was unreal?

A: Yes.

Q: It was fantasy real?

A: . . . Yes.

§ 26.39   Spontaneous Loops — Selecting Power Words

Spontaneous loops of helpful facts volunteered by the witness, or facts that can be turned to the advantage of the cross-examiner, should always be utilized.

Do not loop power words that are detrimental to the cross-examiner's theory of the case, themes, or theme phrases. As seemingly obvious as this may appear, in the heat of the battle, the cross-examiner must instantaneously differentiate between helpful and unhelpful power words in light of her theory. The cross-examiner cannot simply listen for a power word and then spontaneously loop it. It is extremely important to listen to the witness carefully in order to effectively employ the spontaneous loop technique. It is even more important to analyze the power words heard in light of the cross-examiner's theory of the case.

In a self-defense case, the cross-examiner asked a witness who did not participate in the fight, but who was clearly a friend of the victim, the following:

Q: When Barry (the "victim") came through the door fast, he didn't say a word?

A: No, he just came barreling through the door and drilled the guy.

Q: The guy he drilled was Brian? (spontaneous loop)

A: Yeah.

Q: When Barry barreled through the door and drilled Brian, Brian didn't even have his hands raised? (spontaneous loop)

A: No, he didn't.

In the first question, the cross-examiner only wants the witness to agree that the "victim" came through the door fast. Instead the cross-examiner is rewarded with the dramatic phrasing and power words of "barreling through" and "drilled." The cross-examiner wisely chooses to loop "drilled" first and "barreled through" second. Why is this the wise selection? It is more important to the cross-examiner's theory of the case that the "victim" drilled (hit) the eventual defendant in a homicide case, than it is that the victim came through the door fast or "barreled through." When given a variety of power words, take the most critical to the theory of the case first. Then follow up with the other less critical words.

In a personal injury case, in attempting to set up a loop of the word "smashed," the plaintiff's lawyer asked the defendant:

Q: You smashed into Tony on his motorcycle?

A: I don't know what I hit. I just heard a thud and the sound of metal smashing metal.

Q: When you heard the thud, followed by the sound of metal smashing metal, you knew you had hit something? (spontaneous loop)

A: Well, yes.

Q: And when you looked up from the thud and the sound of metal smashing metal, you saw you had hit a man? (reloop)

A: I thought so.

Q: A man on a motorcycle?

A: Yes, apparently so.

Q: It was apparent because the man was lying in the street? (spontaneous loop)

A: Yes.

The cross-examiner was only looking for a "yes" to the word "smashed." "Smashed" was a pre-planned loop. The defendant, in an effort to avoid that word, offered a far more chilling description of the collision. Clearly, the thud and the sound of metal smashing metal is a much more graphic description than the single word "smashed." It deserves to be spontaneously looped immediately.

§ 26.40   Spontaneous Looping of Theme Phrases

After reading chapter 2, *Developing a Theory of the Case,* it should go without saying that whenever a witness offers any phrase on cross-examination that supports the theory of the case, the phrase should be spontaneously looped for emphasis in front of the jury.

The following example is taken from a commercial case. The plaintiff sold his business but kept a right of first refusal, which he claims allows him to buy back any portion of the business that the buyer might intend to sell to a third-party. The plaintiff alleges that the right of first refusal is so broad that transfers for no consideration from the buyer to his brother and sister trigger the right of first refusal. The defendant and his expert term such a transfer as a "convenience transfer." The defendant argues that this transfer for tax considerations falls outside of an arm's length transfer contemplated by the contract. Plaintiff has endorsed an expert witness on contract law. During the cross-examination of the plaintiff's expert he is asked the following questions:

Q: You have been involved in "convenience transfers?"

A: I have been involved in such brother/sister transactions.

Q: A brother/sister transaction is not the same as the sale of an asset?

A: There would be differences.

Q: There is nothing illegal about brother/sister transactions?

A: No, they are common.

Q: Brother/sister transactions are a common and perfectly valid way to move an asset between family members?

In this example, the cross-examiner is given two opportunities to spontaneously loop answers from the expert in such a way as to stress the theme of the defendant's case. Defendant's theory is heavily dependent on stressing that transactions among family members that do not involve arm's-length bargaining are common and are not to trigger a right of first refusal such as contained in this contract. The volunteered statements by the expert assist in establishing that theory of the case. Though the expert had no intention of offering such an opinion, the cross-examiner can use his answers.

A short example follows from a domestic relations case, in which the entire theory of the plaintiff wife was that she was "a good and loving mother." The lawyer for the plaintiff wife cannot really emphasize that the woman was particularly loving or supportive of the husband. Good wife — no. Great mom — yes.

The jury trial as to assets and alimony commenced after a non-jury trial when the court awarded the wife the minor children. Custody was no longer the issue — only money. The cross-examiner had managed to cross-examine the defendant at length concerning the fact that the plaintiff wife was a "good mother." It was effective and it obviously stayed in the mind of the defendant husband. In front of the jury, the following occurred:

Q: She was a good mother?

A: A great mother.

It was obvious from the look of the witness that the witness had hoped to cut short the line of cross-examination that would establish for the jury all of the wonderful things that the woman had done for the children during the marriage (see chapter 30, *Recognizing and Controlling Bait*). The cross-examiner does not take the bait, but spontaneously loops the phrase "great mother," using it in connection with individual facts.

Q: As a great mother, she did her best for the kids when times were tough?

A: Yes.

Q: As a great mother, she did her best to get the kids to study and to go to school?

A: Yes.

Q: As a great mother, she nursed her kids when they were sick?

A: Yes.

§ 26.41 Delayed Spontaneous Loops from Direct Examination and Discovery

Sometimes the witness has given an answer on direct examination that is either better than expected or phrased in such a way as to be of great use to the cross-examiner. Remember: what sets spontaneous loops apart from other loops is that the word choice is generated from the witness. The witness makes that choice, not the lawyer. In order to spontaneously loop the phrase or word in cross-examination, the lawyer must refresh it in the juror's minds by bringing it forward in the cross-examination immediately.

Return to the personal injury case earlier discussed. The insurance company calls an independent medical examiner whose job it is to minimize the plaintiff's pain and suffering claim. While trying to minimize the damages, the doctor says on direct examination, "He's doing absolutely as well as could be expected." Plaintiff's counsel, in cross, spontaneously loops this phrase:

Q: Doctor, you mentioned that Ray is doing "absolutely as well as could be expected?"

A: Yes, I did.

Q: He's doing absolutely as well as could be expected for a person whose tibia was shattered?

A: Yes.

Q: He's doing absolutely as well as could be expected for a person whose fibula has a metal rod in it?

A: Yes.

Q: He's doing absolutely as well as could be expected for a person who's got metal screws holding parts of his leg together?

A: Yes.

Q: He's doing absolutely as well as could be expected for a person who has gone through four separate surgeries?

Here the cross-examiner uses a delayed spontaneous loop from direct examination concerning the phrase "absolutely as well as could be expected." Note that a spontaneous loop does not have to be a dramatic or powerful phrase each time. It can be helpful or it can be in the theory of the cross-examiner's case. In this example, it is both helpful and in the theory of the cross-examiner's case. That spontaneous loop is then tied to facts already in evidence. The facts are so powerful that they recast the implications of the phrase "absolutely as well as could be expected" and make more vivid to the jury the tough job the plaintiff has ahead in his recovery.

The delayed spontaneous loop does not have to be taken just from the direct testimony of the witness at this trial. It can be taken from any statement made by the witness, even statements made pre-trial. In the example that follows, the government informant had described himself in an early statement to the police as an "honest man":

Q: You have told us that you are an "honest man?"

A: Yes.

Q: You told Mr. Smith if he would just co-sign a loan for you, you would pay him back right away?

A: Yes.

Q: That's the same "con" you had run on Bob Issacs?

A: Might have, yes.

Q: It's a con you've run before?

A: I've said those words before, yes.

Q: But you are an "honest man?"

A: In those particular instances, no, I was not, sir.

§ 26.42   Relationship to Other Techniques

Loops incorporate the concept of word selection that is basic to the foundation to cross-examination. Once a loop or double loop has been introduced into the cross-examination, opportunities for spontaneous loops increase as witnesses try to flee from the descriptive words used by the cross-examiner. By looping theme phrases, the cross-examiner emphasizes her theory of the case to the jury repeatedly. Simple loops, double loops, and spontaneous loops advance and emphasize all other techniques of cross-examination.

Chapter 27

CROSS-EXAMINATION WITHOUT DISCOVERY

SYNOPSIS

§ 27.01   The Scenario of the "No Discovery" Witness

The trial lawyer sits confidently at counsel table. The lawyer is relatively confident because she is prepared in a way that reduces her stress to an acceptable level. And then it happens.

The opponent calls the next witness. The cross-examiner does not know the witness. Maybe she does not even know why this witness is being called. Perhaps she does not even recognize the witness's name. Or perhaps she does know this witness but does not know why this witness is being called. The one thing she does know is this: she has no pre-trial discovery from or about this witness. Her stomach is in knots. Her confidence is fast evaporating. Anger, fear, and frustration engulf her.

This situation has intentionally been painted to be "as bad as it can be." The lawyer must now assemble a useful cross-examination and deliver it in just minutes. It can be done. It is not a test of willpower or spontaneity, but of science and technique. There are useful techniques to be employed in these situations.

There are certainly easier cross-examination scenarios, but there are tougher ones as well. Every lawyer has to confront the witness who is extremely destructive to her case, by being well prepared and capable of delivering testimony without a trace of bias. In these cases, the presence of discovery would not matter much. The absence of discovery is not the greatest obstacle to the trial lawyer's ability to successfully handle a witness. A witness is a package of pluses and minuses. With or without discovery, the lawyer is called upon to instantly assess the person, his testimony, the consistency of his testimony with other testimony or evidence, and many other factors. Discovery is simply one of the factors that provides or limits the immediate availability of certain techniques at the onset (and at the onset only) of cross-examination.

So, the cross-examiner must put herself in the necessary mindset. The opponent has called a witness. The lawyer has no discovery on this witness. That means there are no reports of interviews and no depositions. The trial lawyer must quickly prepare to cross-examine this witness.

§ 27.02 Control Your Emotions

First, the trial lawyer must recognize that she is angry and frustrated. She must get rid of that distraction if she is to do a competent job. She is in trial. She must postpone pondering questions such as: "Why did this happen?"; "Why are 'they' doing this to me?"; or "What did I do wrong to let this happen or not be able to fix it?" Now is the time to focus on something that will help handle this problem.

Anger, frustration, or self-doubt will betray the trial lawyer in many ways. If the lawyer concentrates on the wrong done to her, it will distract her from listening to the witness. During the cross-examination, the lawyer's unusually hostile demeanor will portray her as being either frustrated or angry. This will distract the listener (be it a judge or jury) from listening to the substance of the cross-examination and may give the impression to the fact finder that the direct examination was extremely damaging, even if it wasn't.

Negative emotions may cause the lawyer to show anger or uncertainty in the tone of her questions. The listeners — judge, jury and witness — will hear the cross-examiner using a less confident tone. Sensing weakness, the witness may often become emboldened to fight back. Feeling ill at ease with the facts, the cross-examiner will often resort to questions that center on generalities, opinions, legalisms, and conclusions. ("You were negligent, weren't you?" or "You looked after your own interests rather than the interests of your client?") The use of global language or conclusory questioning is in direct contrast to the most effective methods of cross-examining (see chapter 8, *The Only Three Rules of Cross-Examination*). When the cross-examiner becomes frustrated or angry, it is common to revert to this line of questioning.

In such circumstances, the lawyer must rely on the familiar techniques she has learned — short questions (Only Three Rules), grouped by subject matter (Chapters), and built upon logic. All are designed to cast doubt on the opponent's theory of the case, or to support her theory of the case. The one good emotional aspect that flows from the "no discovery" witness is the inevitable rush of adrenaline. It will make the cross-examiner quicker and better able to accomplish the task at hand: Analyze what the witness presents in some systematic way, in order to find areas in the cross-examination likely to be productive.

§ 27.03   Logic Provides Safe Questions

A big reason why the cross-examiner feels overwhelmed by the "no discovery" witness is that she has heard the axiom: "Ask no question to which you do not know the answer." This misunderstood axiom leads to an absurd mindset: "Lacking discovery I cannot guarantee what this witness will say to any of my questions, therefore I cannot safely ask any questions."

This reasoning is false and shortsighted. There are more ways to "know" the answer than by reading the facts in discovery. Even if the lawyer has no discovery about this witness, she may well already possess discovery about much of the subject matter of the testimony. She may be aided by the testimony of previous witnesses and by her interviews of her own witnesses and client. And undoubtedly, the cross-examiner is aided by logic and common sense. The trial lawyer may not be equipped to impeach the witness with a prior inconsistent statement, but she certainly knows the logical facts that flow from the witness's testimony. She also knows the facts that logically led to the information recited in direct examination.

The cross-examiner can add to her potential cross-examination all the questions to which answers are dictated by common sense. That is, the direct testimony of the witness should have been in accord with common sense, and the answers received in cross-examination should comport with common sense. The risk of an answer defying common sense is borne by the witness, not by the cross-examiner. Certainly, the witness can say anything by way of an answer, but that does not mean that anything will be believed. The cross-examiner may, therefore, safely ask leading questions containing facts that logically flow from the facts recited by the witness. If the witness denies the truthfulness of these assertions (answer: "no"), the cross-examiner may have to live with the "no" answer, but the witness will have to live with the lack of credibility occasioned by giving an illogical answer. The cross-examiner wins in this scenario.

§ 27.04 The Cross-Examiner's Advantage: The Witness Does Not Know the Cross-Examiner

Often, if the cross-examiner does not know the witness, the witness does not know the cross-examiner. The witness does not know the cross-examiner's style, mannerisms, or degree of preparation. As perceptive as trial lawyers can be, most are desensitized to how much witnesses learn about the trial lawyer as they observe the trial lawyer depose them, take testimony from other witnesses, or see the trial lawyer do other courtroom work. Witnesses perform discovery on the lawyer too. With the "no discovery" witness, the trial lawyer is an unknown factor to the witness. To the extent that the cross-examiner observes the witness during his direct testimony and before the witness knows the lawyer's intentions concerning cross-examination, the ability of the cross-examiner to observe and mentally prepare for the coming cross-examination far outweighs the ability of the witness to observe the lawyer and prepare for cross-examination.

If the cross-examiner is anxious about what the witness's answers might be, think how anxious the witness will feel about having no idea of what the questions might be. If the witness does not understand enough to be anxious about that lack of knowledge, so much the better. A witness who is unaware of the likely scope of cross-examination has precious little time to game plan what might be the good and the bad answers. The witness is on the receiving end of the questions, so it is worse for him. At the end of each chapter of cross-examination (see chapter 9, *The Chapter Method of Cross-Examination*), the cross-examiner will be mentally saying "no more questions (on that subject matter)" just before she turns the page and starts her next chapter. The witness can never say "no more answers" to a particular area of inquiry. The witness is seldom a courtroom veteran, and most witnesses do not enjoy the trial experience. In truth, the witness feels more anxiety than does the cross-examiner, especially when the witness has no prior experience with the cross-examining lawyer.

The cross-examiner has an entire repertoire of techniques at her disposal that the witness has not seen before. As a result, in the critical area of observation of the "opponent," the advantage lies with the cross-examiner. Through observation of direct examination, the cross-examiner has a fix on the style, confidence level, and emotional pitch of the witness, while the witness has little or no idea of the cross-examiner's approach.

§ 27.05 The Cross-Examiner's Advantage: The Witness Does Not See the Full Scope of the Case

A witness may understand his limited role in the overall case, but a witness rarely knows the roles played by all of the other witnesses on the witness's side of the case. Rarer still is the witness who fully understands the opponent's entire theory of the case. No witness fully understands all of the nuances of the competing theories of the case; but the prepared cross-examiner does. No witness can understand the strategic importance of the vast array of facts; but the prepared cross-examiner can. As a result, the witness cannot easily identify how a particular answer will aid the cross-examiner's theory or weaken the opponent's theory; but the prepared cross-examiner can recognize such an answer.

The cross-examiner has studied and dissected the case. No matter how little time the cross-examiner has had to prepare for the trial, that preparation is more global than the preparation of the witness. The cross-examiner understands the likely strengths and weaknesses of both sides. The cross-examiner understands the competing theories of the case. The witness does not. This knowledge of the contrasting theories of the case provides a monumental advantage for the cross-examiner.

Knowing the contrasting theories of the case means the cross-examiner possesses a broader and deeper knowledge of the important facts in the case and just as importantly, which facts are the most important ones to each theory of the case. Because the cross-examiner can quickly seize on a seemingly innocuous answer and understand how that answer helps or hurts a theory of the case. The "theory of the case" advantage goes to the cross-examiner. Since there are two theories of the case, the cross-examiner's advantage is doubled.

§ 27.06   The Cross-Examiner's Advantage: Witnesses Cannot Know How Their Testimony Fits in With Other Witnesses

Cases are built on facts. The cross-examiner knows far better than the witness what has been said and what will likely be said by the other witnesses. Not only does the cross-examiner know the previous testimony, she knows the demonstrative evidence and the exhibits. Because of that knowledge, the cross-examiner can quite easily recognize how the testimony of this witness may contradict another witness called by the opponent, or how it may support a witness who has been called or who will be called by the cross-examiner. There may be times when the witness testifies in opposition to an exhibit and does so confidently because the witness has not seen or does not recall all of the exhibits. But the cross-examiner knows the exhibits and can easily see how to use the witness's testimony. Likewise, the cross-examiner can make conscious, educated decisions on how to integrate the testimony available from this witness into the balance of the trial. A witness simply cannot have all of this detailed case knowledge available to him as he testifies. As a result, the trial lawyer enjoys a decided factual advantage over the witness in the ability to integrate the witness's answers into the case.

§ 27.07   "No Discovery" Seldom Means "No Information": The Name of the Witness Allows Database Discovery

An important issue in crafting a cross-examination is: what does the cross-examiner know (or reasonably believe) about the witness and his anticipated testimony? Even in the absence of any formal discovery, the cross-examiner enjoys several strategic advantages over the witness. Often she does have or can find some "discovery" to help her cross-examine the witness. She may not have formal discovery, but that does not mean she has no knowledge concerning the role of this witness.

The first step is to question the concept of whether she truly has "no discovery." Is there absolutely nothing known of this witness? Or pre-trial, did the trial lawyer know the name of the witness. She may have no formal discovery, but that does not mean she knows nothing and can learn nothing about this witness. If she knows even the name, she can run database searches and potentially find a great deal of useful information. The lawyer may investigate the witness using conventional techniques. The lawyer can simply ask her client: "Who is this person and where do they fit?" Anything that she already knows before the witness takes the stand assists her in forming her potential cross-examination chapters.

The opponent may identify witnesses by name in the opening statement. Take this opportunity to begin discovery on potential witnesses to be cross-examined. Now with computer databases so readily available, such as LexisNexis or the Internet, the time between hearing a witness's name in opening statement and the beginning of the cross-examination affords the computer-assisted cross-examiner additional methods of investigation. While the computer databases cannot tell the lawyer what the witness will say, such databases may reveal powerful facts useful in attacking the credibility of the witness. Such information could include unpaid judgments, tax liens, name changes, divorces, lawsuits by and against the witness, news articles mentioning the witness, articles written by the witness, and many more facts from public records. The witness seldom expects the cross-examiner to know any of these materials, so the early and appropriate use of such information often causes a witness to believe that the lawyer knows even more. This causes the witness to be more forthright during cross-examination.

Example: The plaintiff sues his former employer. At trial the plaintiff calls a former stockbroker of the employer to support plaintiff's theory. The credibility of this "no discovery" witness is one issue of interest to the cross-examiner. A quick database search by witness name brings up the following facts: the witness has several unpaid tax liens, and two unsatisfied judgments. None of these matters are disclosed in the U-4 form required to be filled out and updated by the witness/stockbroker. Armed with this basic knowledge the cross-examiner could perform several chapters demonstrating that the witness obtained his brokerage job with the defendant by omitting required information; that the witness has obtained a new brokerage job without advising his new employer or the government of the required information; and that in spite of earning an ample income, the witness has failed to file tax returns or pay the taxes owed to various government entities. Such chapters are only a beginning. Undoubtedly there will be a great deal more cross-examination on the details of the direct testimony, but armed with only the name, and using an inexpensive database search, the cross-examiner now has more cross-examination material available.

§ 27.08   "No Discovery" Seldom Means "No Information": Testimony of a Witness Can Often Be Anticipated

While it is reassuring to know who the witness is as a person, if the lawyer does not, there are still many avenues into a successful cross-examination. The most important information in cross-examination is knowledge of what testimony will be offered. Knowledge beyond "absolutely nothing" is some knowledge, and it is a starting point for the development of cross-examination. It is entirely possible that if the cross-examiner knows who is to be called, even with no formal discovery, she will know enough to perform several useful chapters of cross-examination. Perhaps there will be chapters (see chapter 9, *The Chapter Method of Cross-Examination*) relating to motive, interest or bias, based solely on the cross-examiner's knowledge of the need of this witness to support the opponent's side of the case. Does the witness have some business relationship with the defendant? Does the witness have something to gain if the contract is unenforceable? Is this witness engaging in the same type of conduct that has caused the brokerage firm to sue its former stockbroker? If the answer is yes, any of these are fertile areas for preliminary chapters demonstrating a motive, interest, or bias of the witness.

There are many trial situations where the lawyer lacks discovery, but still knows a great deal about the witness. There are temporary restraining order hearings in both commercial and family law contexts. There are criminal cases where the victim and defendant know each other, or certainly have a good idea about what the "no discovery" witness is going to say. There are temporary order hearings in divorces where the parties may not yet have been deposed, but certainly know an enormous amount about what the other party is likely to say.

If the lawyer does not know the person, but knows the subject matter of his testimony, she can assemble chapters based on what the client or others have told her about the issues. Only where there is absolutely nothing known about that witness — not the name, not character traits, not profession, not connection to the case, not connection to the other party, not connection to the opposing counsel — is the trial lawyer truly starting from zero. That is a rare event. But, even then there are techniques that will assist in formulating useful chapters of cross-examination.

§ 27.09   Opening Statement: An Opportunity to Discover Information About the Opponent's Theory of the Case and Identity of Witnesses

The opponent will probably give an opening statement. That opening statement is an aid to cross-examination. When the opponent gives the opening statement, it is an opportunity for the cross-examiner to "discover" more information about the opponent's theory of the case and specific information about witnesses that the opponent intends to call. Pay attention to the opponent's opening statement. The cross-examiner may well disagree with much of what is said by the opponent in opening statement. Nonetheless, the opponent's opening statement provides a solid foundation for the building of cross-examination chapters. Use it to identify more clearly and with more depth the opponent's theory of the case. A good opening statement tells the jury what the opponent intends to prove and how he intends to prove it. His opening statement tells the cross-examiner no less. Identification of the nuances and details of the opponent's theory of the case will alert the lawyer that witnesses that have not been discovered may be coming. Any amount of preparation time is precious time to prepare for the "no discovery" witness. Do not ignore this opportunity.

Take notes on the opponent's opening statement. The notes should identify the opponent's theory of the case, the theme, what the opponent considers his strongest points, and what methods will be used to attack the trial lawyer's theory of the case. Be especially mindful of any facts or testimony the opponent promised to the jury that the lawyer believes will not be proved or which are overstated. Then seek opportunities on cross-examination to use the opponent's witness to disagree with or fail to support opposing counsel's assertions made in their opening statement. Using this technique, the opponent's witness unknowingly attacks the credibility of opposing counsel's case.

Example: Plaintiff sues for breach of contract. Plaintiff knows that the defense will call a witness who will support some aspect of the defendant's case. Plaintiff had a romantic relationship with this witness. Plaintiff's counsel, in seeking to minimize the relationship, refers to it in opening statement as a "brief flirtation." Defense counsel need not wait until this defense witness is on the stand to challenge plaintiff's description of the relationship. Other witnesses called by the plaintiff may well be unaware of this description. There may be no discovery as to these witnesses. In fact, defense counsel may not know which people will be called to support the plaintiff. Nonetheless, defense counsel may draft chapters for the cross-examinations designed to show how close and long-lasting the relationship was. Now, when the plaintiff calls a business associate or close friend in support of some other proposition in the case, that witness may well be an excellent witness to the close relationship between the plaintiff and the anticipated defense witness. Furthermore, it is highly unlikely that this witness has been prepared by plaintiff to discuss the relationship between plaintiff and the defense witness. Through these chapters, used with witnesses who likely do not understand the implications of their testimony, it will be possible to paint the picture of a close and trusting relationship. It will become apparent to the fact finder that opponent's phrase "brief flirtation" is untrue. While these chapters would have been worthwhile to generally support the credibility of defense counsel's witness, their value is increased by the fact that they demonstrate that opposing counsel was not honest in this aspect of their opening statement. Use the opponent's statement to add chapters to cross-examinations to come.

§ 27.10 Opening Statement May Reveal the Facts Upon Which the Opponent's Case Is Built

The more detailed the opponent's opening statement, the more the cross-examiner will be alerted to the important details of the opponent's theory of the case and the prospective witnesses who will be called to build upon that theory (see chapter 13, *The Relationship of Opening Statement to Cross-Examination*). Even if no witness is named, the opponent has revealed the facts underlying the theory of the case.

There are opponents who deny the cross-examiner the opportunity to comprehend his theory of the case by limiting or waiving the opening statement. Perhaps he rationalizes that he does not want to "give away" his best facts. Perhaps he doesn't have a fully formed theory of the case. In either event, if the cross-examiner cannot comprehend the opponent's theory of the case, the strength of that case, the specific facts and specific witnesses that will support that theory of the case, neither can the fact finder. This situation is good news for the cross-examiner.

The opponent may have denied the cross-examiner discovery of his theory and witnesses, but he has paid too high a price to do so. The case is not won by confusing the opponent but by teaching the case to the fact finder. The correct technique is to use the opening statement to teach the fact finder. If an opponent makes a useful opening statement, he must simultaneously provide the cross-examiner with an excellent opportunity to "discover" what is coming. Similarly, trial counsel is not tempted to hide her theory of the case, witnesses, and the facts that will support her theory. The opening statement is a vital component in the process of teaching the case. It must not be abandoned or truncated. Let the opponent cope with how well she teaches, not how effectively she hides her theory.

Prepare for the "no discovery" witness by listening carefully to the opponent's opening statement for the themes of the opposing parties' case. A good opening statement may reveal several themes upon which the opponent will depend.

Example:

In a civil case alleging copyright infringement, plaintiff's opening statement revealed the following themes:

- We devised a computer program.
- It was very advanced.
- It had great market potential.
- The market for our program collapsed.
- As a result we lost millions of dollars in likely sales (damages).

None of these themes should come as a surprise to the defendant. However, in articulating these themes, the opening statement will likely reveal much of the factual support. Furthermore, within each of these broad themes, there are sub-themes that the skillful opponent will advance. Sub-themes may be thought of as the groups of or individual factual chapters the opponent will need to develop in order to prove his themes and thereby prove his theory of the case. These sub-themes are likely to become quite evident in opening statement. As a result, the necessary and available cross-examinations will also become evident.

Opponent's Theme:

- Our computer program had great market potential.

Sub-Themes:

- The 20 largest insurance companies were a prime market for our software.

- Four large insurance companies had already expressed an interest in our software.

- One large insurance company was already testing our software and preliminary results were favorable.

- Hundreds of individual copies of our software had already been sold to individual insurance agents.

By listening to the opponent's opening statement, the themes and sub-themes are easily identified and the testimony of prospective witnesses are better understood and prepared for in advance. The cross-examiner may not know which witness will be called to support any of these sub-themes. Nonetheless, as the topics can be anticipated, the necessary cross-examination chapters can be prepared.

§ 27.11 Identify Why This Witness Is Being Called: What Are the Goals of the Direct Examination?

When the opponent calls a witness who, by name and relevance, is unknown to the lawyer, the first objective is to identify the goal of the direct examination. To what purpose has the opponent called this witness? Obviously the opponent believes the witness will support the opponent's side of the case. No witness should be called to support the abstract notion that she is a "good witness." Each witness should be called to add a specific set of facts to the case. The cross-examiner need not fear witnesses who are called for appearance sake, but who know little or nothing that advances the opponent's theory of the case. In fact, it is exceedingly dangerous to call witnesses merely to get a good face before the jury. Such witnesses have little or no functional goals, and therefore have no anchor to cling to during cross-examination. They are prepared on so little of the facts of the case that they are actually far more vulnerable on cross-examination when they can be taken into areas where they cannot foresee how a particular answer helps or hurts their side's theory of the case.

A witness takes the stand either to build the opponent's theory of the case or to weaken the cross-examiner's theory of the case. The direct examination will reveal the specific purpose of the witness. The cross-examiner's job is to identify the purpose and then analyze what has to be done to further that purpose. Next, analyze whether the witness can be taken into different areas to assist the cross-examiner in her theory of the case.

The lawyer may discover that the principal purpose of a witness is to bolster a fact she had already concluded she could not successfully counter or did not need to counter. The witness is new, but the information is old and may not be in dispute. The opponent is just piling on. No cross-examination on that issue is needed. To cross-examine on that issue is to fight an unnecessary battle that the lawyer cannot or need not win. The opponent had one officer testify to the confession, now they have two. They had one executive testify that the company cares about its shareholders and would never deceive them. Now they have two executives saying the same thing. If the lawyer was prepared to cross-examine the first witness, the extra witness adds little or nothing new to the opponent's case. In fact, multiple people testifying about the same set of facts are likely to produce inconsistent testimony. To the extent that the cross-examiner has chapters that worked on the previous witness testifying to the same area, those chapters may safely be used again. To the extent that multiple witnesses provide inconsistent testimony as to any fact, chapters pointing out that inconsistency can quickly be drafted.

§ 27.12   The "Me Too" Witness: Do They Really Add Anything to the Case?

Many witnesses offer "me too" testimony. Yes, his testimony hurts, but the judge and jury have heard most of it before. The cross-examiner is not going to need many notes because the cross-examiner has heard it before as well. Those chapters prepared for the other witnesses that preceded or that will follow the "me too" witness are applicable to this witness. The cross-examiner actually has a greater advantage than the witness in these circumstances. The cross-examiner knows better than the witness how the other witnesses have or will testify to the same events. While listening to the direct testimony of this "no discovery" witness, the cross-examiner will be mentally comparing the rendition of events from this witness against the testimony of the other witnesses and the documents that the cross-examiner intends to use with the other witness for purposes of contradiction and consistency.

To this extent, the cross-examination of this "no discovery" witness gives the cross-examiner an extra opportunity to contrast inconsistencies between this witness and other witnesses. There is also a greater opportunity with this witness for the trial lawyer to highlight word selection and phrasing used by this witness that may be more favorable to the cross-examiner's theory of the case, compared with that of the other witnesses.

§ 27.13   Prepare for Likely Topics of Cross-Examination

Assume the worst: the lawyer knows absolutely nothing about this witness. The cross-examiner does not recognize the name of the witness or the reason why this witness is being called. The initial "discovery" must come from the direct examination. First, analyze why this particular witness is being called. What purpose does the opponent have for putting this particular witness on the stand? Once the lawyer identifies the purpose for which the witness has been called, she may well discover that she has prepared chapters (see chapter 9, *The Chapter Method of Cross-Examination*) on those topics, believing them to be useful for a different witness.

In other words, she is prepared for a witness in these chapters of cross-examination, but thought a different name would be attached to the anticipated testimony. As an example, many times the cross-examiner is prepared to cross-examine a certain relative of the opposing party in a domestic relations case, but the opponent puts on a different relative who has not been deposed and has not been interviewed. Similarly, in a commercial case, the cross-examiner may be prepared to cross-examine one of the attendees at a meeting, but the opponent decides to put up a different attendee who has not been deposed.

In the criminal context, the prosecutor often calls a detective who is not as prominently mentioned in the reports rather than the detective that has previously testified in a preliminary hearing or motion to suppress hearing where the more prominent detective was cross-examined. Because the cross-examiner was prepared for many of the same fact topics, the chapters prepared for one detective will generally work for another.

Prosecutors, domestic relations lawyers and others are confronted daily with relatives or friends of the defendant who are there to "support" the defendant. They have not been interviewed or subjected to pre-trial cross-examination. As an example, in the simple street crime case, where the criminal episode is relatively confined (a fight, a drug deal, a theft) the prosecutor knows what she is looking for in cross-examination, though she may not know whom the defendant will call. In the larger case, such as white-collar crimes and conspiracies, it is likely that the prosecutor has background on the key events, though she may have nothing directly from this witness. The fact topics are known; what is not known is this witness's precise statement on the topics. Using whatever she knows about the likely topic, chapters of cross-examination can be written on the likelihood that the opponent will call a witness in these areas. The same concept applies to a defendant cloaked with a Fifth Amendment right. The prosecutor may have no discovery, but well knows the case from the viewpoint of other witnesses. Cross-examination chapters can be written for the potential testimony of the defendant. The prepared cross-examination for the defendant will often serve as chapters for other defense witnesses as well.

In each of these circumstances, the cross-examiner is prepared to cross-examine the general species of witness and often can prepare cross-examination chapters for most of the important topics. The cross-examiner just is not going to be able to cross-examine the individual witness she envisioned. But the cross-examiner is largely prepared. The names of the witness may change, but the cross-examination does not.

When the "no discovery" witness is called, those chapters prepared for the general species of this witness should be at the forefront of the lawyer's mind. Although they may not be a precise fit for this witness they are very useful. In fact, they form the basis upon which to actively listen to the direct examination and the basis on which to modify trial counsel's chapters of cross-examination for this witness. Each individual witness is different and brings unique personality traits to the witness stand. However, by being prepared for the generic species of this witness (eyewitness, investigating detective, attendee at a meeting, relatives/friends of a party, recipient of a memo), the cross-examiner has preparation even though it might be said that the cross-examiner has no discovery.

§ 27.14   Evaluating the Pre-Testimony Behavior of the Witness; First Impressions

Additional "discovery" occurs as soon as the witness's name is called. Because the cross-examiner has no pre-trial information about this witness, she needs to be more focused than usual on the available "in trial" discovery. She begins learning when the witness is called to the stand. A trial lawyer observing the witness walk to the stand, can immediately learn the data on sex, age, race, features, confidence level, how the witness walks, dresses, and any other characteristics she can detect. Does the witness demonstrate that he knows the opposing party? Does he know the opposing lawyer? Is he carrying a book, a chart, or a file? The cross-examiner has started her discovery before the witness starts talking. Now the cross-examiner's task is to hear his story, read his character traits, and recognize what is available for cross-examination.

Once the witness takes the stand, the cross-examiner can continue to evaluate the character traits of the witness. Even before the witness starts to testify, the confidence displayed by the witness on the witness stand and the amount of comfort or discomfort that the witness shows as the oath is administered, tells the trial lawyer more about the witness. Some witnesses appear calm and ready to testify. Most witnesses look uncomfortable. The witness stand is not a friendly place, and very few people want the role as trial witness. By following the eyes of the witness, the trial lawyer can often determine if the witness has ever testified before, if the witness knows anyone in the courtroom, and if the witness truly wants to be in the witness chair. While it is true that these observations do not guide the lawyer to the chapters of the cross-examination, these observations can lead to an informed opinion as to the experiential, confidence, and emotional level of the witness. These factors, in turn, help the lawyer decide what tone she should adopt in the first moments of her cross-examination.

The moment the witness begins talking, the cross-examiner can begin to assess the "type" of witness that has been called. This assessment begins with the swearing-in process. Every trial lawyer during the course of her career has seen a witness raise his left hand rather than his right hand to take the oath. This act, or acts like this, and more importantly the witness's reaction to this embarrassment, tells the cross-examiner more about the witness. Is the voice loud and strong on "I do"? Is the witness seemingly proud to be testifying? Does the witness apparently look as if he wants to be here? If so, the cross-examiner is likely seeing the evidence of a committed witness. The witness is not neutral but partisan. The witness is somehow involved in the case and wants to help the side that called him.

If, on the other hand, the witness seems uncomfortable, uneasy about being called, has the look of someone who would rather be elsewhere, it is likely because the witness would rather be elsewhere. In this latter case it is less likely the witness is attached to the side that called him. Therefore, it is more likely that the witness will be more flexible or malleable in the answers he will give on cross-examination. So even before the testimony begins, observe the witness to see what the witness is demonstrating.

§ 27.15 Note Taking During Direct Examination: Three Elements

[1] Focused Listening

When the cross-examining lawyer lacks discovery and the direct examination testimony is previously unknown, often the trial lawyer tries to compensate by writing down as much of the direct examination as possible. This is a natural reaction. Since the lawyer on cross-examination had no prepared chapters, she compensates by taking more notes. The theory being: More notes = more discovery = more preparation for cross-examination. But the trial lawyer cannot effectively listen, observe, absorb the new material, and consider the impact of this witness on the fact finder, all while writing copious notes. The value of copious notes is almost always less than the value of focused listening accompanied by selective note taking.

[2] Selective Note Taking

The cross-examiner does not need to "learn" the entire direct examination. In almost all circumstances, the trial lawyer is concerned with only parts of the direct examination, so encyclopedic notes are counter productive. Only selective notes are required. The guiding questions are: (1) which areas are worthy of note taking; and, (2) how to actually take those notes. When faced with the task of cross-examining the witness without aid of pre-trial discovery, the cross-examiner takes selective notes solely to assist in the cross-examination of this or other witnesses or occasionally, the closing argument.

The cross-examiner will not want to repeat the full scope of the direct examination. Furthermore, the cross-examiner has the ability to select the areas to be covered in cross-examination. In fact, the cross-examiner may decide to ignore the entire direct examination and proceed into different chapters. The trial lawyer has the right to cross-examine only on parts of direct examination that interest her. She has the right to cross-examine on details never brought up by the witness. That is, the cross-examiner may question "in the gaps" of the direct testimony. In fact, there may be limited circumstances in which the cross-examiner declines to cross-examine at all.

[3] Identifying What Areas Are Worthy of Note Taking

Lawyering and court reporting are different professions. Trial lawyers and witnesses make a record. Court reporters preserve the record. But even an accurate record of what was said is often misleading, as the impact of what was said is vitally important and wholly absent from the transcript. There is no sound, movement, tone, or mannerisms in a transcript.

It is not unusual to read a transcript of a cross-examination that went particularly well for the cross-examiner, but the cold page reads as if the witness was doing just fine. The cross-examiner must concentrate on the vital information while hearing the tone, the hesitations, and while witnessing the faces, the mannerisms, the nuances of testimony that tip off areas where the witness seems to be evasive or confused, confident, or uncertain. If required to choose, the cross-examiner is better served by actively listening and taking fewer notes than by taking very complete notes and missing the opportunity to absorb the non-verbal information.

Freeing the lawyer from a legal pad also affords her the opportunity to track the impact of the witness on the trier of fact. The reaction of the listeners is more important than the trial lawyer's own reaction. In order to judge the impact of the testimony on the fact finder, the cross-examiner must observe the fact finder. When the cross-examiner does not have pre-trial discovery, listening, observing, and noting the reaction of the judge and jury to the direct is even more important to her and of greater help to her in deciding on the course of her cross-examination.

§ 27.16   Taking Notes on Direct Examination in a Chapter Format: One Chapter Per Page

A pivotal issue for the cross-examiner is how to effectively take notes during the "no discovery" direct examination. (For the layout of the trial notebook page, and a discussion of how to take notes during trial, see chapter 10, *Page Preparation of Cross-Examination*.) There are several useful systems. To be useful, any note-taking system must be efficient, meaning it must produce notes of immediate use in forming cross-examination chapters without inordinate time or effort.

Ironically, the note taking skills and techniques honed over years as a student are incompatible with the role as a trial lawyer. When a student is confronted with new information in a classroom setting, she handles it by taking extensive notes, and, later studying all of those notes in preparation for a final examination in which the lecturer asks questions based on what the lecturer said in class (the notes). In other words, the task is, "Can you repeat what the lecturer said?" In contrast, trial lawyers will seldom have the luxury of even an overnight recess to study up for the cross-examination and the cross-examination will certainly not be successful if it is merely a repetition of the direct examination. Furthermore, much of what is said in direct examination is not new and is not worthy of note taking. She needs only those notes that will help her with the cross-examination to come.

One easy system for efficiently tracking the direct examination is to take notes in a chapter form. (For the structure, makeup, and content of chapters of cross-examination, see chapter 9, *The Chapter Method of Cross-Examination*.)

Most direct examinations are conducted chronologically. Opposing counsel can be expected to take the witness chronologically through whatever topics the witness is expected to support. The opponent may not realize it, but this pattern is similar to chapter method of presentation. As a result, the cross-examiner has the ability to follow and organize the direct examination for note taking purposes.

In this system, effective note taking of a direct examination is a paper-intensive process. The cross-examiner is going to need many sheets of paper, but she is not necessarily going to take a lot of notes. For some unknown and ill-conceived reason, trial lawyers try to put as many notes on as many topics as possible on one sheet of paper. The result is a hodge-podge of note-crammed pages relating to every issue or topic raised on direct examination. This is not a system. It is a recipe for frustration. Encyclopedic notes on all the issues raised on direct examination are not in a form to be immediately useful in preparing a cross-examination.

In utilizing the chapter method of cross-examination preparation, the lawyer has grown accustomed to the fact that every cross-examination chapter deserves a separate page. No chapter will exceed a single page. Each chapter will be contained on the front side only of the page (see chapter 10, *Page Preparation of Cross-Examination*). There are good reasons to utilize the same system for note taking during every direct examination and especially during the direct examination of a witness for whom there is no discovery. For starters, one system is better than two systems. In times of stress, a single system is far easier to employ.

When faced with a "no discovery" witness, the cross-examiner needs a blank legal pad. As the direct examination proceeds, the cross-examiner can identify where the chapters break. In turn, the cross-examiner breaks down her notes of the direct examination into chapters. All notes on one chapter of the direct examination are on one page. On that page the cross-examiner notes potential issues for cross-examination. Through this process the cross-examiner is breaking the direct examination into its component chapters. Some of these chapters will lead to cross-examinations, and some of these chapters will be omitted from the cross-examination. By taking notes in this chapter method, the cross-examiner is better equipped to identify the likely areas of cross-examination, to take notes as to what those cross-examination questions might be, and even to order the pages of potential cross-examination in a sequence most helpful to the cross-examiner at the end of the direct examination.

What the cross-examiner needs most is not a full rendering of the direct examination, but only the key testimony on which to cross-examine, and the cross-examining lawyer's thoughts on what to do. Undoubtedly, the cross-examiner's notes on a single chapter will not fill the entire page. They will be truncated: abbreviated. But each chapter will be on a separate page. Leave the partially filled page as is. Lawyers should prepare their chapters of cross-examination one chapter per page to avoid confusion and make sequencing easier (see chapter 11, *Sequences of Cross-Examination*).

Remember the opponent probably will not understand the chapter method so she will tend to cover areas at the issue and event level, rather than at the more instructive and finer detailed chapter level. As a result, during the direct examination, the cross-examiner must be attuned to shifts in chapters within the issues. Recall, an issue may be large, but the chapters of cross-examination expose the helpful facts at a much finer level. The opponent may be asking about a meeting (event) while the cross-examiner understands that several important things occurred at the meeting (chapters). As each chapter is identified the cross-examiner should begin taking notes on a new sheet of paper. At the top of each page, counsel will note the title of that chapter, just as she would have done had she the opportunity to write out her chapters of cross-examination in advance (see chapter 10, *Page Preparation of Cross-Examination*).

Another advantage of noting one chapter per page is that at the end of the direct examination, the cross-examiner can very quickly discard unproductive material, add other chapters that may have been previously developed for other witnesses, and reorganize these several pages into a persuasive order and begin the cross-examination (see chapter 11, *Sequences of Cross-Examination*). This reorganizing of the newly noted, admittedly truncated, chapters takes just seconds. This time is well spent for the effect on the witness and opponent. Had the cross-examiner chosen to work from the non-system of pages of notes taken on the direct examination as it was unfolding, she would have had little opportunity to enhance chapters, eliminate chapters, or place chapters in a more persuasive order.

Why only put one chapter on a page? Why label the chapter name at the top of the page? Remember, some of these notes may prove useful in the cross-examination of other witnesses who are hours or days away from being called.

The problem with noting more than one chapter to a page is that the cross-examiner is led into cross-examining from a page of notes that relate to a great many chapters. That will inevitably cause the cross-examiner to follow the chronological order used by the opponent in conducting the direct examination. Chronological order almost always is a mistake on cross-examination (see chapter 11, *Sequences of Cross-Examination*). One of the biggest risks of following a strict chronological approach based on a page of notes taken during direct examination is that the cross-examiner will inadvertently wander into areas on which she never intended to cross-examine. Trying to cross-examine from a page containing notes on many chapters also leads the cross-examiner into a series of one or two question chapters. In other words, when the cross-examiner is looking at the one or two points she had time to write down during direct, she is led to think these are the only points worth making. In reality, if the cross-examiner has one or two points already outlined on a chapter, by logically considering the topic, and by recalling previous testimony and anticipated testimony on the same chapter, the cross-examiner is likely able to add facts that support the chapter goal. The lesson: one chapter = one page = one system = less confusion = more control of the cross-examination.

§ 27.17   The Concept of "Filtered Listening" — What to Take Notes On

As a first step to the process of note taking during direct examination, it is advocated that active listening is more beneficial than extensive note taking.

This is especially true when confronted with the no discovery direct examination. The cross-examiner must mentally filter the large amount of information that the cross-examiner is hearing and seeing. The purpose of the filters is to sift out only the direct examination testimony, which may be useful to the cross-examiner for possible cross-examination chapters.

This sifting is accomplished through a dual filter process. The cross-examiner should listen to the direct testimony with a critical ear, searching for material that may be employed in the coming cross-examination. As always, useful material is material that tends to strengthen the cross-examiner's theory of the case or material, which tends to weaken the opponent's theory of the case. Material that can be used to attack the credibility of that witness or any other witness of the opponent should be categorized as material which tends to weaken the opponent's theory of the case. Anything that fails this dual screening should be eliminated from further consideration for the immediate cross-examination.

(1) The filters must operate in real time so that the trial lawyer can apply them as the witness is testifying. An overabundance of notes is a hindrance to the speedy organization of an effective cross-examination. If this were a deposition, pre-trial hearing, or any other occasion when a transcript might be available, the cross-examiner might well spend significant time studying the answers in order to ferret out all the useful cross-examination material. But in trial, there is little time to contemplate all of the nuances of the direct testimony. In preparing the no discovery cross-examination, the decisions by the cross-examiner must be made rapidly. Studied reflection is a luxury not available in this setting.

(2) The filters must be easy to apply. Since there is little time to consider all the ramifications of the direct testimony, the filters must extract evidence that the cross-examiner already understands and can immediately employ.

(3) Finally, and most importantly, the filtering process must be something that the cross-examiner trusts, otherwise she will not use the filters with confidence.

§ 27.18 The "Dual Filters" Method of Note Taking

(a) The first and most important filter is the cross-examiner's own theory of the case. Testimony, or the gaps in the direct testimony that affects the cross-examiner's theory of the case, are worthy of consideration for possible immediate cross-examination. Does this testimony or gap in testimony help the cross-examiner's theory of the case? This is the most important and timely question for the cross-examiner to ask herself. If so, conducting a no discovery cross is an acceptable calculated risk.

(b) The second filter is expressed by this question: "Does this testimony contain material which can be used to weaken the opponent's theory of the case?" Testimony that hurts the opponent's theory of the case is worthy of consideration for cross-examination.

Having employed these two filters, the cross-examiner, comes away from the direct examination with useful notes that suggest cross-examination chapters. Not all notes on the direct examination are of equal value. How can these notes be quickly prioritized? One useful starting point for the organization of the coming cross-examination is to employ the resulting notes to create chapters that will be used in the following order: (a) testimony leading to chapters that support the cross-examiner's theory have the highest priority for use in cross-examination; and, (b) testimony leading to chapters that can damage the opponent's theory are the next priority.

There are several reasons for this technique of prioritization. The cross-examiner has only two types of information to listen for while experiencing the direct examination. Witnesses called by an opponent have almost certainly been prepared by the opponent. The opponent can be counted on to do a better job preparing the witness to defend the opponent's theory of the case. Furthermore, the witness ordinarily has a factual grounding in the opponent's theory of the case and is therefore better able to understand how their testimony bolsters the opponent's theory of the case. In contrast, the witness has less understanding of the cross-examiner's theory of the case and almost certainly has received less preparation in that area. By concentrating on making the witness a positive witness for the cross-examiner's theory of the case, the cross-examiner is focusing on areas in which the witness is less prepared. In addition, the cross-examiner knows her theory of the case better than she knows the opponent's theory of the case. The witness, in all likelihood, has not been prepared for a cross-examination that supports the cross-examiner's theory of the case, rather the witness has been prepared to withstand a confrontation or attacking cross-examination designed to hurt the opponent's theory of the case — the side of the case that the witness is prepared to support. Many cross-examiners instinctively think their first obligation, and perhaps their only obligation, is to "attack" the credibility of the witness or the testimony of the witness. Antiquated notions of cross-examination cause the lawyer to view attack as the principal focus of cross-examination. It is especially unwise to rely on attack as the principal goal for the cross-examination of the "no discovery" witness.

By listening for the potential chapters that are non-confrontational or informational (see chapter 11, *Sequences of Cross-Examination*), the witness is less prepared for that area of cross-examination and valuable information assisting the cross-examiner's theory of the case can be extracted without fight from the witness. Confrontational chapters are ordinarily more difficult to successfully accomplish. It is therefore better for the cross-examiner to accomplish what can be gained without a battle before wading into confrontational chapters. Difficult cross-examinations tend to exhaust the cross-examiner. Under the strain of a difficult cross-examination there is an understandable tendency to "get out" of the cross-examination. This is particularly true of "no discovery" cross-examination. Under these circumstances the cross-examiner leaves behind useful chapters of cross-examination that could have been accomplished with correspondingly less effort.

Example: In a domestic relations case, the cross-examiner is confronted with the elderly mother of the 50-year-old male defendant. The mother, while known to the plaintiff, was not deposed and was not interviewed. Why? Because the defendant had listed so many relatives, there was simply neither enough time nor money in the arsenal of the plaintiff to conduct depositions of every relative. It is also true that unconsciously the plaintiff's attorney thought that she could conduct a "you love your son" cross-examination if, in fact, the mother was put on the stand.

Opposing counsel put the defendant's mother on the stand to testify about certain specific personal property that was "inherited or gifted" to the son only (not the son and wife) from his family. This personal property was no small amount of assets as the antiques involved were valued at several hundred thousand dollars.

Instead of giving in to the instinctual temptation to conduct a confrontational "you love your son" type of cross-examination, the cross-examiner actively listened to the direct testimony in which the defendant's mother testified that she was in the home place of the plaintiff and defendant numerous times per week. The witness testified that she observed the location of the antiques and the manner in which the parties utilized them.

The cross-examiner began the cross-examination with a chapter that was consistent with her theory of the case. The plaintiff's mother-in-law admitted that when she visited the home of the plaintiff, she was always treated with respect, offered coffee, and shown the achievements of her grandchildren. The house was always in a clean state.

Each of these chapters was developed in length. All were consistent with the wife's theory of the case. The mother-in-law did not feel confronted. The mother-in-law felt like a proud grandmother not her son's advocate.

The cross-examiner also conducted chapters on the willingness of the daughter-in-law to share meals (when the mother-in-law had stopped in at lunch or dinnertime); that the meals were well prepared (but not as good as the mother-in-law's); and, that the daughter-in-law often sent with the elderly widowed mother-in-law plates of food for later consumption. The mother-in-law very readily, and without complaint, admitted all of the pertinent facts in these chapters. All were consistent with the wife's theory of the case.

What the mother-in-law did not understand was that the defendant/husband had already complained in his direct examination to facts that the plaintiff/wife was seldom at home, did not cook, the cooking was poor and of "fast food" variety when it was done, and that the house was never kept in a clean manner that he had been accustomed to in growing up in his mother's home.

Without confrontation, the cross-examiner was able to turn this "no discovery" witness into a formable witness that supported the cross-examiner's theory of the case and contradicted the defendant's previous testimony. While it could never be proven, it is believed that this successful cross-examination of the mother-in-law eliminated other relatives that the defendant/husband was to call. The opponent simply didn't call those witnesses. There would be a conflict between the mother-in-law's testimony and any relatives that would be called as that type of witness.

Another example: In a slander case, the plaintiff called a witness who was a neighbor of the plaintiff at the time the slander was published. The court permitted this witness to testify in substance that upon hearing the published slander about the plaintiff, the neighbor witness had thought less of the plaintiff. The witness admitted that she had socialized less with the plaintiff and his family until the plaintiff and his family moved from the neighborhood some months after the published slander. Despite objection, the neighbor witness also testified that the slander continued to bother the plaintiff. She also testified that it had stayed in her mind despite the passage of several years. She stated that when she had last seen the plaintiff at a social gathering, she had thought about the comments that constituted the slander and asked the plaintiff about them. She said the plaintiff appeared uneasy and distracted which she had presumed was caused by the plaintiff's uneasiness in seeing his former neighbor and being asked about the slanderous statement.

The neighbor witness had been offered on direct testimony for the purposes of establishing damages for the plaintiff of a massive amount. It was part of the direct examiner's theory of the case that the plaintiff had been damaged by the slanderous comments, that the plaintiff had been ostracized by the community, and that he continued to be ostracized by the community because of the slanderous remarks.

The cross-examiner began her first chapter consistent with the cross-examiner's theory — the plaintiff had no damages:

(Establish the witness saw the plaintiff often.)

Q: From what you said on your direct examination, I understand the plaintiff, Mr. McLeod, moved from your neighborhood some months after July '99 (the date of the publication of the slander)?

A: Yes, I don't remember the exact date, but several months later.

Q: Before they moved, they lived across the street from you?

A: Yes.

Q: Because they lived across the street from you, you literally saw them every day of the week?

A: Almost every day.

Q: You all lived so close that seeing them was an easy thing to do?

A: Yes.

Q: In fact, many times there was no plan to it, they either saw you or you saw them?

A: Often.

Q: You saw them when you both lived in the same neighborhood in passing but also at planned social gatherings?

A: True.

Q: In passing you may just say hello or you may stop and talk about the weather, the children, or things affecting the neighborhood?

A: Yes, we talked about many things.

New Chapter:

(Witness continued to socialize with the plaintiff after the "slander.")

Q: Socially, you would visit with them for barbecues or drinks or such as that?

A: Yes.

Q: You would host some of these gatherings?

A: Actually we did very little in hosting. Mr. McLeod often hosted gatherings, as did several of the other neighbors.

Q: You were invited to these gatherings by the plaintiff?

A: Yes.

Q: You went to those?

A: Yes.

Q: You chose to go to those?

A: Yes.

Q: You were invited by other neighbors to gatherings?

A: Yes.

Q: You knew the plaintiff would be present as well, in all likelihood?

A: Well, I didn't really know that.

Q: Well once you got to the gathering, you would see the plaintiff?

A: Yes.

Q: You would know that he was there?

A: Yes.

Q: You chose to stay?

A: Yes.

Q: You never left just because the plaintiff was there?

A: No.

New Chapter:

(After the plaintiff moved, continued socializing.)

Q: After the plaintiff moved away from your neighborhood, you continued on occasion to see the plaintiff socially?

A: Yes, but not as much.

Q: That's right, "not as much" because you just didn't live as close to each other in the same neighborhood?

A: Well yes, that is true.

Q: The plaintiff still invited you to social gatherings?

A: From time to time.

Q: You attended?

A: Yes.

Q: You obviously knew the plaintiff was going to be there?

A: Yes.

Q: You attended even though you knew the plaintiff was going to be there?

A: Yes.

Q: You made a special effort to get there because it wasn't just in the neighborhood anymore?

A: I suppose that is true.

Q: You had to drive further and you had to make more arrangements?

A: Yes, I suppose that is right. I just did it. Didn't really think about it.

Q: You not only attended these events, but you spoke with the plaintiff?

A: Yes.

Q: You shared a drink, whether it was alcohol or not?

A: I don't drink alcohol.

Q: Well you shared a nonalcoholic drink or whatever was being eaten?

A: Yes, I suppose we did.

New Chapter:

(Exposed family to the plaintiff.)

Q: You took your family?

A: Yes.

Q: Your spouse and your children?

A: We only took the children when kids of their age were invited.

Q: I understand. But on those occasions, you did take your children?

A: Yes.

Q: You took your children and your spouse knowing that you were not exposing them to bad influences?

A: No, I wouldn't do that.

Notice that the cross-examiner did not confront the witness on areas that seemed ripe for confrontation (i.e. "you are a friend of the plaintiff, therefore . . ."). Rather, she started the cross-examination on more informational chapters, guaranteed to undermine the opposing plaintiff's theory of the case concerning damages. She also strengthened her theory that there was slander, it was published, but there was no damage. The cross-examiner successfully cross-examined the witness where there was no discovery. The witness never showed an appreciation that he was supporting the defendant's theory of the case nor that he was undermining the plaintiff's theory of the case on damages.

In each of the examples, the question could be asked as to why the witness would volunteer or state a fact that was helpful to the cross-examiner's theory of the case or hurtful to the proponent of the witness's theory of the case. Witnesses see their role with tunnel vision. They want to present the facts that they have prepared with the other lawyer, which helps that lawyer's side of the case. But they don't understand in full depth the theory of the cross-examiner's case or the theory of the direct examiner's case. The lack of in-depth appreciation of the two opposing theories of the case relegates the witness to answer with truthful unprepared responses.

Some lawyers ask, "Why should I try to develop with an opponent's witness chapters that will help my theory of the case or hurt the opponent's theory of the case when I have my own witnesses who will testify to those facts?" Assuming the cross-examiner has the material with which to score the points, the answer is that the fact finder, be it a judge or jury, will more easily and more fully accredit statements and facts given by the opponent's witnesses. Admissions by the opponent's own witnesses are more valuable than those same facts and statements when made by witnesses on the cross-examiner's side of the case. No matter how articulate or erudite the cross-examiner's own witness, their testimony sounds self-serving. There is always an advantage to use the opponent's witnesses to establish or bolster chapters that the cross-examiner must put up in her own case. Think of these chapters, facts and statements as verbal requests for admissions. When the witness says "yes," that is proof beyond a doubt. In this way, much of the burden is removed from the cross-examiner's own witnesses.

The tone of these types of cross-examinations is often not hostile. In fact, the witness does not fight the cross-examiner as she establishes a chapter. The witness has already testified on direct examination in a manner congruent with that chapter. The cross-examination actually more fully builds upon the direct testimony rather than attacking it. As long as the cross-examiner by tone, word selection, or body language does not use an attacking posture towards the witness, the witness will not fight the cross-examiner. Often the cross-examination sounds conversational. It is more of a tone of "let's talk a little more about the things that you have already talked about" as opposed to "isn't it true" or "you must admit", or "you love your son, so (you will lie)" or "the plaintiff is your friend, so (you will lie)."

§ 27.19   Note Ideas for Potential Cross-Examination

Note taking by the cross-examiner is only a preliminary step in the process of creating cross-examination chapters. It is but a starting point. The notes tell her what was said, but the cross-examiner is left to develop a plan on how to use this information. The cross-examiner needs techniques that move her beyond the direct examination into the possibilities for her cross-examination. In moving from her notes to her cross-examination, the cross-examiner must recall that her cross-examination is not limited by the exact chapters covered by the direct examination — she is free to cross-examine on any area raised by the direct examination and on credibility. It is entirely conceivable that her cross-examination will cover facts never discussed anywhere in the direct testimony. After all, the direct examination was designed to tell the opponent's best story, not the entire story. The direct examination was designed to leave out entire sections of the case, and to omit harmful material even in the areas that were covered. It is the cross-examiner's job to add, to bring out new areas deserving of consideration, and to weaken, where possible, the points made by the opponent in direct-examination.

In addition, the motive, interest, or bias of a witness is always a fair subject for cross-examination. As the cross-examiner listens to the "no discovery" direct examination, she can add her own notes on motive, interest, and bias. The trial lawyer may not have known who was to be called, or what they would say, but she may well spot their motive, interest, and bias. The credibility of every witness is fair game for cross-examination. The witness may have testified to things they could not know, or to things that are both incredibly helpful to the opponent while being incredibly unlikely. Testimony that defies logic, the physical laws of nature, or common sense deserves to be cross-examined. In short, notes of direct examination do not mark the boundaries of potential cross-examination.

The cross-examiner's page layout must accommodate a separate set of notes — counsel's notes to herself containing observations about the direct examination and possible questions for cross-examination. These notes naturally evolve from what the lawyer is hearing. During direct examination, she recognizes facts she wants to accentuate in her cross-examination. She hears gaps in the testimony that she might exploit, she finds contradictions between this witness and another witness called by the opponent. The lawyer needs notes to herself on how to approach these chapters. When her notes directly relate to the notes she is making during direct examination, those notes can be put opposite her question notes. These "thought" notes are tactical thinking and are placed in the column for tactics (see chapter 10, *Page Preparation of Cross-Examination*).

The cross-examiner's notes of the direct examination were taken in chapters. So the notes on the lawyer's thoughts belong on the same page as the direct examination that spurred the lawyer's thoughts. Almost immediately after writing the notes, it will be her turn to cross-examine the witness. So what does the cross-examiner write in her cross-examination column?

(1) Note chapters that can safely be emphasized.

(2) Note chapters left out of the story that counsel can have the witness admit.

(3) Note entire chapters that witness will logically admit, even if not part of the witness's direct examination.

(4) Note logical inferences; since witness said x, he must admit y and z.

(5) Note contradictions with the facts, circumstances, witnesses, exhibits.

(6) Note facts relating to motive, interest or bias.

§ 27.20 The Testimony Begins: Keying-In on Voice Tone

[1] Tone Offers Clues

One of the critical assessments that the cross-examiner must make of each witness is the tone of the answers given by the witness. Whether or not there is discovery, the lawyer is always aware of the witness's tone of voice. Tone of voice gives her insight into the mind and character of the witness and when she has no discovery, she needs all the clues she can get. Tone often schools the trial lawyer on the confidence level of the witness. Is the tone assured? Is the tone objective? Is the tone laced with emotion? Is the tone uncertain? The lawyer can better understand the degree that this witness feels tied to the opponent or to his own story. The lawyer can thereby better judge the degree of flexibility the witness is likely to demonstrate. She begins to learn why the witness is here. She can now better understand the role the witness is expected to play by the opponent.

The witness's tone can be an incredibly important clue to the cross-examiner. Listen for voice tone changes as the direct examination proceeds. Some parts of the direct will sound as though they have been rehearsed. The lawyer may easily detect areas where there is a certain assuredness in the tone of the witness. The cross-examiner learns from this tone where the witness is within his testimonial zone of comfort.

[2] The Less Confident Tone as a Guide to Cross-Examination

A starting place is the witness's tone of voice betraying the witness's lack of confidence in an area. Almost every witness changes his tone when he becomes less confident about the subject matter of the questioning. This tone change often occurs when the witness is led into areas in which he does not want to go, or the witness unintentionally strays into areas where he did not want to be. When the trial lawyer hears this change of tone, she understands it as a signal that this area may be a fertile area for cross-examination. Wherever she picks up on a change of voice, it is vitally important that she focus on the witness, not on her note pad. Whenever a witness betrays in any manner a lack of confidence in his testimony, the cross-examiner should be especially observant of the witness's word choices, hesitation, and mannerisms. It is when the witness lacks confidence in an area that the lawyer is most likely to hear the "oops" testimony — the admission of confusion, the nonsensical assertion, the fact that does not logically fit. Perhaps the witness is in an area he does not want to discuss in detail. Perhaps his own uncomfortable role in the case is about to be revealed.

[3]   The Confident Tone as a Guide to Cross-Examination

A confident witness tone in a particular area of testimony gives equally valuable information on areas of potential cross-examination. How can very confident, direct testimony in an area be a guide to important and successful cross-examination? The answer lies in the immediate analysis of how that particular testimony impacts the two competing theories of the case. A witness may offer up information (whether or not sought by the direct examiner) which either directly aids the cross-examination theory of the case or which directly weakens the opponent's theory of the case. The cross-examiner, recognizing the witness's tone of certainty, may on cross-examination guide the witness first into a repetition of the useful material and then an elaboration of the topic. This cross-examiner's technique can be done in relative safety, even without benefit of pre-trial discovery. The confident tone ensures cooperation on cross. The witness will not back off this area where he is confident.

[4]   Taking Cues from Opposing Counsel's Tone

The cross-examiner can also receive important clues from the tone of the opponent conducting the direct examination. When the tone of the lawyer conducting direct examination betrays a lack of preparation or confidence, it is a sign for the cross-examiner that the script of the direct examination is uncertain, is not being followed, or is fraught with hazards for the direct examiner. The opposing counsel's change of tone is often attributable to the fact that the direct examiner knows that there is danger in asking questions in this area because the witness may not be supportive or the witness will go too far. Alternatively, the direct examiner may not know how the witness is going to answer questions or what details he will supply in areas where only the general answer is known. Once again, this is agreeable ground for possible cross-examination. The cross-examiner must carefully listen for nuances in the tone of the lawyer conducting the direct examination.

§ 27.21   Does the Testimony Conflict With Testimony of Other Witnesses?

The witness who is called to do nothing more than bolster another witness may well provide opportunities for effective cross-examination. First, has the witness said anything at variance with the other witness called by the opponent on the areas that he has addressed?

It is the rare witness who can testify about the entire case. Rarer still are "no discovery" witnesses who can testify about the entire case. Almost every witness is a niche witness. That is, he can testify about single events or issues. His testimony will not span the entire case. Most witnesses assume that if their testimony "sounds good" for "their side," it must be assisting their side. The flaw in this reasoning is that testimony can sound good but actually be quite harmful to the opponent. This occurs because cases are almost always far more complex than any one witness can envision. The testimony that protects one issue may simultaneously assist the cross-examiner on another issue.

The niche witness will instinctually protect his niche, his testimony, and what he has to offer. While the witness is trying to protect his testimony, he may testify to facts that may be destructive or contradictory to other niche witnesses, without realizing that he has done damage to the lawyer who has called him on direct examination. There is a technique to spot and exploit this weakness: listen for areas in which the witness is at odds with another witness called by the opponent. In cross-examination take this witness back into that chapter and cross-examine him so that he repeats and expands the portions of testimony that are at odds with testimony by another one of opponent's witnesses. This technique effectively attacks the credibility of both witnesses, each without notice as to why their testimony is being reinforced by the cross-examination.

§ 27.22 Keying Off of the Overly Precise Question

Is opposing counsel asking a very precisely worded question? This is often a signal that this lawyer and the witness have agreed that the witness can truthfully and safely answer the question if, but only if, the wording is very precise and very narrow. What is not being said may be very apparent to the cross-examiner, who may reveal the misleading nature of the direct testimony by pointing out the very narrow nature of the opponent's question, and then using a series of leading questions to flush out the hidden facts. Look for this most often with expert witnesses. When dealing with the expert, listen for what is *not* added to foundation questions or hypothetical questions on direct examination. It is often the precise question that leaves out a fact or qualifies a fact so dramatically that logic would leave the fact out, where the lawyer can attack on cross examination.

§ 27.23 Fact Fumbles

The cross-examiner is, of course, listening for the fumbles. Where is the answer that catches the direct examiner by surprise? When the cross-examiner hears or sees the surprise, she needs to immediately focus on the precise question and the precise answer it produced. The opponent is now in trouble and she must silently observe what facts can assist the cross-examination.

Most direct examinations, by nature, appear less goal-directed than cross-examination. Direct examination must be conducted using open-ended questions. As a result, direct examinations can more easily meander or go off on a tangent because of miscommunications between counsel and his witness. Facts that support the cross-examiner's theory of the case or hurt the opponent's theory fall out and the listening cross-examiner must pick up on them and build chapters based on these fumbles. By using the dual filter the fumbles will more easily be heard.

§ 27.24   Keying Off of Answers That Veer Off Course

A direct examination can appear to go off on a tangent. This usually happens either because the examining lawyer has taken the witness into unrehearsed territory or the witness has answered a direct examination question unresponsively. The direct examination may also go off the script when the witness continues to testify after the initial question has been answered. These occurrences are some of the most revealing times of the direct examination for the cross-examiner. The cross-examiner may recognize when this is happening by the words being said, or the tone exhibited either by the witness or the direct-examiner, or by the facial expressions of the witness or the direct examiner.

The unexpected tangential information and the proffered details that a witness gives to the direct examiner may well open up areas of cross-examination. These new areas of cross-examination can undermine the general impact of the direct examination just concluded. This happens because the jury has witnessed the direct examination go astray. They realize there was a slip-up or something that did not fit. When the cross-examiner takes advantage of the slip-up by pulling out more information in that area, the jury values this information highly. In essence, the testimony becomes more important because it leaked out. Listen for the details that are volunteered.

Example: The plaintiff has sued the defendant for damages arising out of personal injuries suffered in a car accident. The defendant's vehicle hit the back of the plaintiff's vehicle at a stoplight on a road that had a moderate slope. From the plaintiff's point of view, she was "slammed into" as she sat at the stoplight. From the defendant's point of view, she "drifted into" the plaintiff at "idle speed." Defense counsel seeks to minimize the impact. Because the slope of the road would affect the speed of the "drift," the plaintiff's lawyer had conducted an on-scene investigation that included the exact degree of slope of the road.

The defendant calls an eyewitness in an attempt to show that this was a low speed collision. The plaintiff had not deposed this witness because of the expense relative to the size of the likely damages. The effort to interview the witness had been unsuccessful. When called by the defendant the witness testifies that the collision was not a substantial collision. On direct examination, the opponent asked the witness about the speed of the defendant's vehicle when it collided with the rear end of the plaintiff's vehicle:

Q: How fast was Mrs. Rupert's car (the defendant) traveling?

A: Not too fast. The road is pretty much flat there at the light and she really just drifted into the plaintiff's car.

At this point, defendant's counsel has received the answer he was seeking — defendant's car "drifted" into the rear of plaintiff's car. But the witness has added an unasked fact: the slope of the road. The witness has testified erroneously concerning the slope of the road. Her tone was more hurried, but not dramatically so. Some damage has been done, but the misstep should be further exploited on cross-examination.

The cross-examiner heard the words concerning the slope of the road and also noted the abrupt shift of subject matter, the change in tone and pace of the direct examiner's words. She realized that the chapter concerning the slope of the road would be productive on cross-examination. This "no discovery" witness can be safely and easily asked now about "the road is almost flat there. . . ." One way to spot the miscommunication: the testimony is not tied up by the opponent. Instead the matter is dropped.

§ 27.25 A Cross-Examination Clue: Opposing Counsel Interrupts His Own Witness

The cross-examiner often sees interruptions by the examining attorney as he attempts to steer the witness back into safe or rehearsed territory. When the cross-examiner knows the opposing counsel is uncomfortable in an area, she needs to give the witness more room to deliver damaging material. This may be by objection. But realize the objection also creates an interruption. This interruption was designed to protect the lawyer. By allowing the witness to continue, the cross-examiner potentially opens up further areas for cross-examination.

There are at least two lessons to be learned when the direct examiner interrupts his own witness. First, is the lesson that the witness had either intentionally or unintentionally wandered into an area that the direct examiner did not want to pursue in direct examination. This tells the cross-examiner that this is an area that should be considered for cross-examination.

The second and less obvious lesson is that this is an opportunity for the cross-examiner to observe how the witness reacts to an interruption. Does the witness talk over the interruption? Is the witness submissive to the interruption? Is the witness frustrated by the interruption? Is the witness embarrassed that he has gone into an area into which the lawyer did not want him to go? All of these factors tell the cross-examiner which of the many methods available to control the runaway witness would be most effective in dealing with this witness (See chapter 19, *Controlling the Runaway Witness*).

This is often an overlooked lesson. Direct examination allows the cross-examiner to "go to school" on how best to control this witness. Assess the witness continuously to determine which method or methods available to control the runaway witness will work best if these are needed in cross-examination. Assess whether or not this witness is someone who is determined to say what he came to say regardless of what is being asked. Or, to the contrary, is this a witness who does not object to being confined into any area selected by the examiner. Is this a witness who will allow himself to be regimented back into areas that the lawyer wants to explore? The cross-examiner's understanding of the tenacity and personality of the witness better arms her for the cross-examination.

§ 27.26 Spotting and Exploiting Gaps in the Direct Testimony

Most direct examinations are conducted chronologically. Most trial lawyers adopt this form of direct examination because it is easier to convey the information, easier for the witness to follow, and easier for the fact finder who is unfamiliar with the story.

By moving through chapters of direct examination in chronological order, opposing counsel has also made it easier for the cross-examiner to follow and analyze the direct examination. The cross-examiner is better able to spot the gaps in the story. Is the witness skipping over certain information? Is the direct examination lawyer encouraging the witness to quickly move over some part of the story? Is there an event that logically should be talked about but which is being skipped? These are the kind of questions that the cross-examiner, who is actively listening to the direct examination, should be asking herself.

There are, at least, six types of gaps. As the direct examination progresses, the cross-examiner should be attuned to listening for each.

§ 27.27   Gap 1: The Conspicuously Missing Event

The most obvious gap is one in which there is a complete gap in the chronological presentation by the direct examination. As an example, a prosecutor was conducting the direct examination of a state trooper involved in the stopping, questioning, and testing of a suspect for driving under the influence. Methodically, the prosecutor took the state trooper through the reasons that the officer had activated his blue lights and stopped the vehicle. Methodically, the prosecutor took the officer through the initial contact with the defendant. Then, in one question, the officer is focused beyond the tests:

Q: What did you do after the defendant exited his vehicle?

A: I had him perform a series of field sobriety tests.

Q: After the field sobriety tests, what did you do?

The prosecutor then developed the handcuffing and arrest procedure. He covers the reading of certain rights. He takes the officer chronologically through the balance of his contact with the defendant.

The gap concerning the field sobriety tests suggests an opportunity for the cross-examiner to develop a productive cross-examination. The gap was created in the direct examination for a reason by the opponent. If the opponent thought there was good news in the field sobriety exam, the cross-examiner likely would have heard that testimony in detail.

§ 27.28   Gap 2: Lack of Details Gap

Similar to the "complete gap" is the "lack of details" gap.

In a medical malpractice case, one of the operating room nurses testified in great detail, including to the tenth of a milligram, to the administration of certain medicines to a hip replacement patient. She testified to the exact size of the orthopedic reamer/drill, as precisely as to the exact millimeter. However, when she was questioned on direct examination, she testified that a "small amount" of synthetic bone was placed in the hip. As to this part of the surgery the witness was asked nothing and offered no details. No exact measures, in fact, no discussion. The plaintiff contended that this "small amount" of synthetic bone is one of the reasons that there was no in-grow of the hipbone into the orthopedic device.

As soon as the cross-examiner notices this gap in the details, it becomes a potentially productive area for cross-examination. The witness omitted the details for a reason.

§27.29 Gap 3: Gaps in Timing of Questions

The tuned ear of the cross-examiner must be aware of the cadence or speed of questions and answers in direct examination. When there is a substantial increase in the cadence or speed of questions by the direct examining lawyer, this is a type of gap in the testimony. The direct examining lawyer is signaling to the witness to go faster in this particular area. This is frequently a tip off that this direct examiner has concerns about this area of testimony. Look at this material closely for cross-examination.

On the other hand, when the direct examiner reduces the speed of the questions, the cross-examiner must be attuned, not only to the speed, but also to the tone of the reduction of the speed. This slowing of questions on direct examination may be intentional by the lawyer conducting the direct examination. The direct examination lawyer may be emphasizing this material through the creation and use of silence (see chapter 21, *Creation and Uses of Silence*).

If the reduced speed of questioning causes the witness to testify in greater detail, the cross-examiner has likely discovered the strength of the witness and the primary reason he was called to testify. This also signals to the cross-examiner that this is where the witness is most prepared.

However, if the tempo of questioning slows down and the tone of the direct examination lawyer becomes less confident, that may well signal to the cross-examiner that the direct examination attorney is unsure of or concerned about the responses of the witness in that area of the direct examination. In each case, the speed or cadence of the questions has to be examined intently by the cross-examiner for possible inclusion in the cross-examination of those chapters.

§27.30 Gap 4: Stories Told Out of Order

The cross-examiner should be conscious of where the direct examination begins chronologically. The direct examination, after introduction of the witness to the fact finder, should start where it is easy for the fact finder to follow the testimony. When the direct examination attorney attempts to ignore facts, statements, or events that happened earlier than where the direct examination begins, it is an effort by the direct examination attorney to steer the witness away from those earlier facts and events. The cross-examiner must mentally process the previous testimony of the witness, the testimony of other witnesses on this point, and events for potential chapters on cross-examination.

§ 27.31   Gap 5: An Illogical Stopping Point

The cross-examiner must also listen for where the witness stops testifying, but the story keeps going. Does the testimony stop abruptly? Does the testimony stop before the logical end of the story? These occurrences signal to the cross-examiner that there may be potentially successful cross-examination chapters that post-date the testimony on direct examination.

§ 27.32   Gap 6: Covering the Entire Time, But Not the Entire Story

Perhaps the subtlest of gaps on direct examination occurs when the witness or the direct examination lawyer intentionally omits issues or events that occur simultaneously with those events to which the witness is testifying. An example: a witness gives direct testimony about a work place confrontation in a hostile work environment case. The witness is able to reconstruct through his testimony that he heard the defendant yelling at the plaintiff (Bobby). The witness testifies in some detail as to the words, the tone, and the volume of the defendant's voice during this confrontation.

The cross-examiner noted that the witness was never asked nor did the witness volunteer about what the plaintiff, Bobby, had said. There was no testimony about the words that Bobby used, the responses Bobby made to the defendant's comments, the tone that Bobby used, or the volume that Bobby used. There was no testimony about Bobby's utterances at all. The cross-examiner mentally book-marked and took a brief note on this gap on the issue of what Bobby had said for prospective use on cross-examination.

Whenever there is a gap in the testimony of the witness on direct examination, that gap is normally one that may produce favorable cross-examination material. Listen for the gaps in direct. Some gaps are witness-created. Others are direct-examiner created. The gaps in the direct testimony are often where the cross-examiner may produce favorable cross-examination material.

§ 27.33   Sourcing the Direct Examination

Just as was true for pre-written chapters (see chapter 10, *Page Preparation of Cross-Examination*), the cross-examiner needs a column on the page for cross-examination that she creates during direct where she would ordinarily have her "source" information. There may be no pre-trial source when there is no discovery on this witness. Even the "no discovery" witness may testify about an exhibit, and the lawyer may discover the exhibit is the source of the witness's testimony on a particular point. The cross-examiner must make a note of the exhibit number in the source column (see chapter 10, *Page Preparation of Cross-Examination*).

There is also another source for the cross-examination. That source for prior statements to be used in the cross-examination is the direct examination. If the cross-examiner attempts to impeach using testimony from the direct examination, it is not exact enough just to refer the witness to "your direct examination." It would be better that the cross-examiner had a more specific source.

If counsel were impeaching from a deposition, she would speak more specifically than "didn't you say in your deposition . . . ." Instead she would rather refer to the page number and line number of the deposition. Similarly, the cross-examiner may choose to refer to the exact time that the statement was made on direct examination. It takes literally microseconds to note the time that a witness has made a statement that will be used in cross-examination. If the noted material is too voluminous, and there is no opportunity to note the time, then don't bother. Just as the cross-examiner would be better off actively listening and observing than taking the first note, it is better to forego noting the time if that is a distraction to actively listening to the direct testimony.

§27.34 Get the Transcript: Tiny Transcripts Can Have Big Impacts

Occasionally during direct examination, a witness may say something so helpful or so impeachable that the cross-examiner wishes he had a transcript of exact words. This can be done, and can be done in time for cross-examination. The technique is to note, as closely as possible the exact wording of the question, the answer and the exact time. Then, at the first recess, counsel should ask the court reporter for a transcript of just that small block of testimony. The cross-examiner's ability to supply some of the exact words and/or the time will allow the court reporter to quickly search the transcript, find and type the needed passages. The cross-examiner is now armed with the exact words of the witness and can impeach or elaborate on them. The jury and judge love this technique. The cross-examiner must make sure the passage was worth the effort as this device makes the most highlighted chapter of the cross-examination.

§27.35 Sequencing the Cross-Examination: Safety and Control

The benefits of sequencing a cross-examination have been discussed in Sequences (see chapter 11, *Sequences of Cross-Examination*). Of all the reasons for sequencing chapters of cross-examination, the most important guideline with the "no discovery" witness is to keep control of the witness on cross-examination. Of course, the absence of pre-trial discovery tends to lessen counsel's ability to control the witness. The beginning of the cross-examination is more important than usual in that a lawyer's cross-examination of "no discovery" witnesses will tend to be shorter, and the witness will be more able to evade. Consequently, with the "no discovery" witness it is crucial that counsel begin the cross-examination with a "control" chapter. If the cross-examiner has solid chapters on motive, interest, or bias, she should lean toward using them at the start of the cross-examination. There is a safe sequence for the "no discovery" witness. The sequence is based primarily on control of the witness and safety for the cross-examiner. Because this is the focus of the sequencing, the cross-examiner's confidence will build as the cross-examination goes on. The confidence of the witness will recede for the same reasons that the cross-examiner's confidence goes up. There is always an inverse ratio between the confidence level of the cross-examiner and that of the witness.

Another way to look at sequencing of the cross-examination is that the cross-examiner is going to start with safety. The cross-examiner prioritizes what will help the cross-examiner's theory of the case and what will hurt the opponent's theory of the case. All else is eliminated. What is left is what is safest. What is safest is where to begin. It may well be that by doing these safe and productive chapters the witness will offer up answers that help in other targeted areas: bias, assistance to the cross-examiner's theory, harm to the opponent's theory, marginalization, or credibility. So much the better. The hastily planned and safe cross-examination has yielded more safe material — only now it is the opponent witness who is forced to work without discovery.

But assume no such impeaching chapters are available. Perhaps this is a disinterested witness or a witness about whom the lawyer knows too little to prepare an attack built on bias. In such cases, counsel can turn to another effective method of control: informational chapters. More often than not, this type of control chapter will also be a non-confrontational chapter that is designed to bolster or enhance the cross-examiner's theory of the case. The cross-examiner may pick up one or more statements made by the witness that support the cross-examiner's theory of the case. Counsel then elaborates on or cements those statements. In that sense, the trial lawyer is not confronting the witness on what was said on direct, but rather this first chapter of cross-examination is an extension of what the witness has said in his direct testimony. Since the witness was there already, taking him deeper into that chapter will be less dangerous.

If no motive or credibility chapters are available to the cross-examiner, or when these chapters are exhausted the cross-examiner can next turn to chapters that build upon aspects of the direct examination that hurts the opponent's theory of the case. Counsel has used the available motive, interest, and bias material, developed the material that helps her theory or bolsters her witnesses, and exploited the testimony that hurts the opponent's theory. Now the cross-examiner can consider chapters that marginalize the witness. Finally, the cross-examiner can use general credibility attacks that show inconsistencies between this witness and every other witness, inconsistencies with common sense or with documents, or internal inconsistencies in the testimony.

§ 27.36   Logic Based Cross-Examination

The cross-examiner is never restricted to only those questions to which she knows the answer. The cross-examiner may ask with confidence and with safety all leading questions (facts) that logically flow from testimony given by the witness. As an example, the witness has testified on direct examination that he saw the defendant at the scene of the crime, then, the cross-examiner can logically infer that the witness saw the crime scene and its contents. Note this is different than seeing the crime. The cross-examiner can logically infer that the witness then had the ability to see the details surrounding the crime scene. Undeniably, the witness can testify that he did not see other things, but the less the witness recalls of the scene, the less the jury will credit the original testimony. But what if the witness denies the leading questions that logically flow from the facts stated on direct examination? In that event, the cross-examiner will still have a good cross-examination chapter. Imagine a witness who says he saw only one fact but none of the related facts. Such testimony is inherently weak. Testimony that can be shown to be illogical loses its credibility, and as a bonus, the witness loses personal credibility too.

Just as admitted facts logically flow to other facts that should be admitted, certain emotions logically flow from facts. Where the admitted facts logically would produce a particular emotional, physical, or behavioral reaction in most people, the witness can safely be asked a leading question that suggests he experienced that emotion, had that physical reaction, or engaged in that appropriate responsive behavior. Show the witness the facts that would ordinarily produce surprise and the witness should admit being surprised. Show the witness a factual setting in which the normal person would inform their supervisor, and the witness can safely be asked the leading question, "You told your supervisor?" Certainly, the witness can deny the leading question, but in so doing, loses credibility. The witness comes off to the fact finder as "not normal." The technique of cross-examining from the known fact to the logical but unsourced or undiscovered fact is useful, easy, and safe. It is one of the foundations of cross-examination of the "no discovery" witness.

This logic-based cross-examination opens up broad factual areas in which to cross-examine logically and consistently with the cross-examiner's theory of the case based on fleeting direct testimony references.

Example: The "no discovery" witness (police officer) has testified on direct examination that he arrived at the scene of a collision moments after the cars had collided. The collision resulted in a vehicular homicide prosecution. The witness has testified that the defendant was being taken out of his vehicle, and that he observed the defendant to be unsteady on his feet, to be nearly hysterical, and that other on-scene persons had to verbally insist that the defendant not walk away from the scene of the collision.

Because the witness was at the scene and made the observations concerning the defendant, the witness can be cross-examined successfully and safely on areas that are consistent with the defense theory of the case. The following chapters suggest themselves. The witness should acknowledge that:

(1) It was dark;

(2) It was raining;

(3) There was no lighting at this particular intersection;

(4) The cars were terribly mangled;

(5) There was tremendous damage to the deceased's vehicle;

(6) He would be able to identify the tremendous damage to the deceased's vehicle;

(7) The defendant was also in that same collision and his car was also "totaled";

(8) The windshield of defendant's car was shattered;

(9) It appeared as if defendant had hit his head against the windshield;

(10) A head injury to the defendant was completely consistent with the amount of damage done to his vehicle;

(11) Defendant's hysterical behavior was consistent with head injuries;

(12) Defendant's loud boisterous conduct was consistent with head injuries;

(13) Defendant's being "unsteady" on his feet was consistent with head injuries; and

(14) Defendant's disorientation was consistent with head injuries.

All of these facts are consistent with the defendant's theory of the case. It is true that the witness could refuse to acknowledge any or all conduct resulting from head injuries by saying: "I don't know." Is that really a downside risk to the cross-examiner? The fact finder could accept these responses as illogical or likely untruthful. On the other hand, the cross-examiner could become more aggressive. She could attack the illogical lack of information more aggressively (see chapter 20, *Dealing With the "I Don't Know" or "I Don't Remember" Witness*). Which way the cross-examiner chooses to go is a courtroom judgment. However, because of the rule of logic, the material available to the cross-examiner greatly expands.

§ 27.37 Direct Examination Chapters Intended for the Cross-Examiner's Witnesses Can Be Used for Cross-Examination

If the trial lawyer has prepared chapters for the direct examination of her witnesses, those same chapters can be pressed into service as cross-examination materials. When analyzing the direct testimony of this "no discovery" witness, the cross-examiner has at her disposal all of those chapters prepared for her direct examination of her own witnesses. Those chapters can be utilized to take the witness on with chapters consistent or at least congruent with the cross-examiner's theory of the case. The technique is to listen for testimony that bolsters or agrees with testimony she will advance. She can then use her chapters to show that, in several respects, the opponent's witness supports her theory of the case.

What the cross-examiner has prepared for one witness (even her own on direct examination) gives aid to her cross-examination. Her technique is to use what has been prepared for a different witness. Those chapters designed to be effective with the general species of witness, whether on direct or cross-examination, serve as a basis, a starting point with which to actively listen to the direct examination. The cross-examiner is gauging which of her chapters will work, and which can be quickly adapted.

§ 27.38 Building Cross-Examination on Consistencies, Inconsistencies, and Contradictions

Whether the witness is a discovery or a "no discovery" witness, immediately upon hearing the direct testimony, the cross-examiner customarily recognizes how the direct examination of the witness fits into the context of testimony of other witnesses already heard by the fact finder, or to be heard by the fact finder. The cross-examiner will also be able to recognize how the testimony fits with the documents and demonstrative evidence. The fact that this witness was unexpected does not deter the cross-examiner from utilizing those same factors to her advantage with this "no discovery" witness.

A witness may also offer direct examination testimony that is internally inconsistent with some other portion of his or her own testimony. This is always a worthy subject for cross-examination. Counsel must avoid the temptation to ask the witness to explain the reasons for the internal inconsistency. Instead, separately and independently establish each fact and allow the fact finder to hear the contradiction. Of the two points in contradiction, the better technique is to firmly establish the weaker or more changeable testimony first, then follow up with the stronger or less changeable but contradicting testimony. In this way, the witness is less able to alter or amend his testimony when confronted with the inconsistencies. In other words, firmly lock in the testimony the witness is most capable of changing, then reintroduce the testimony that was already completely established. Leave to the opponent the risky business of explaining the inconsistency on redirect (see chapter 14, *Redirect and Recross Examination*).

§ 27.39 Using the Witness to Bolster the Cross-Examiner's Witnesses or Theory

Showing the consistency of this witness with helpful testimony that the cross-examiner intends to elicit during direct or other cross-examinations has the natural consequence of aligning this witness with the cross-examiner's theory of the case. The technique is to find items of importance within the direct testimony or within the logical cross-examinations that tie them to the cross-examiner's case. Inasmuch as the jury or judge has had the benefit of the lawyer's opening statement, the leading question will communicate that this testimony is a helpful admission by the witness. As the cross-examiner spots these helpful areas, she can cross-examine at greater length as she is in a safe area.

Showing this type of testimony of the opponent's witnesses favorably impacts the fact finder, while simultaneously discouraging the opposing lawyer from calling more surprise witnesses.

Recall, the witness has gone through no discovery process and as a result is far less able to appreciate the subtleties of the case. The witness is likely to testify with as much certainty on facts that help the cross-examiner's theory as on facts that helped the opponent. The witness simply does not recognize the danger. The cross-examiner can often find in the direct examination some testimony that contradicts other witnesses called by the opponent. Counsel has only to put the two witnesses' versions in opposition. As the witness discusses the fact in detail, the witness simultaneously damages the other witness, often with no recognition that this is happening.

The opposing lawyer knows this witness has been pulled out of the "no discovery" bag. If the cross-examiner can handle this witness effectively, a warning shot has been fired across the bow of the opponent for all other "no discovery" witnesses the opponent is considering calling.

§ 27.40   Comparison of Values to Conduct

A useful technique is to take a witness into areas in which the witness is likely to want to answer in a particular way, and then craft logically linking questions that cause the witness to adopt positions that seem helpful to the direct examiner's theory, but are actually helpful to the cross-examiner's theory of the case. Often this technique is built on a witness who wants to testify to abstract values or principles rather than facts. Once called to testify about certain values or principles, the witness cannot easily limit the testimony in that area. Thus, the witness can be made to embrace the logical extension of such values or principles, even when to do so will help the cross-examiner's theory of the case.

Example: A brokerage firm is accused of hiding negative financial information on a particular investment from investors. The defendant calls an executive to testify generally about the high-principled corporate culture. The executive testifies about the brokerage firm's philosophy about sharing information with its clients. This executive is called to say that the brokerage firm strives to be completely candid and helpful to its clients and that the company has no reason to deceive its clients. The direct is all very helpful. But the technique of comparing values to conduct will lead to an easy and effective cross-examination.

During that direct testimony, the executive is given the opportunity to tell the jury that A.B.C. is a conscientious, candid, and high quality stock brokerage firm. "Our brokerage firm is the best" seems like a perfectly safe area of testimony. The witness perceives no danger in this testimony niche and believes that presenting this testimony can do nothing but help defendant A.B.C.'s side of the case. His thinking is that the better the corporation looks generally, the better for the corporation's side in this case. It is very difficult for a witness testifying to abstract values to see the danger that comes from the comparison of these abstractions to the specific factual corporate conduct.

In this situation, the cross-examiner is faced with a "no discovery" witness called to offer new information. After identifying this information, the cross-examiner can see that it is not necessary to take on the witness in cross-examination by attacking the testimony. Instead, the motivation of the witness to protect his limited role of praising the corporation can be used by the cross-examiner to construct one or more chapters that helps the plaintiff's theory of the case. When the cross-examiner's theory of the case involves the failure of the corporation to communicate with the plaintiff about serious financial matters, the cross-examiner gains value by encouraging the witness to embellish on the ability, desirability, and willingness of the brokerage firm to communicate accurate financial information to its clients. The executive is set up to answer questions on cross-examination that assist the cross-examiner's theory of the case without realizing the destructive nature of those questions:

Q: Sir, you are Senior Vice President of A.B.C. Brokerage Firm?

A: Yes.

Q: You are proud of A.B.C. Brokerage Firm?

A: Indeed I am.

Q: You have told them that A.B.C. does not try to live up to minimum standards of integrity and service, but instead A.B.C. intends to live up to the highest standards of integrity and service?

A: Yes.

Q: In fact, that's what you advertise to your clients "count on A.B.C. for superior financial advice?"

A: Yes.

Q: As Senior Vice President with 28 years at A.B.C., your company exhibits fundamental, good character values, such as trustworthiness?

A: Yes.

Q: Your clients can count on, in fact should count on A.B.C. for accurate information concerning their investments?

A: Yes, they should.

Q: A.B.C.'s clients should depend on A.B.C. to have superior research on their investments?

A: Yes, we pride ourselves on our excellent research department.

Q: And your clients can count on your research department?

A: What do you mean?

Q: Well, if your research department came across bad financial news on a company your clients were heavily invested in, your research department wouldn't ignore the bad news?

A: No.

Q: They wouldn't hide the bad news?

A: Of course not.

Q: In fact, it would be completely foreign to A.B.C.'s culture and advertising to fail to disclose bad financial news?

A: It would be contrary to our culture.

Q: It would be wrong?

A: It would be wrong.

Q: Because full and fair disclosure of investment facts is the job of A.B.C.?

A: It's certainly part of the job.

Q: A.B.C.'s clients can count on A.B.C. to truthfully communicate the financial — whether it is good news or bad news?

A: Yes, we have been accused of giving too much information.

Q: You would err on communicating too much rather than too little?

A: Yes.

Q: That is what A.B.C. is supposed to do?

A: Yes.

Q: That is what A.B.C. does?

A: Yes.

Q: And if A.B.C. didn't do that, didn't tell investors the facts for better or worse, that conduct would be beneath the level you have set for A.B.C.?

A: Yes.

Q: That conduct would be beneath the level A.B.C. has set for itself?

A: Yes.

Q: That conduct would be beneath the level that your investors should reasonably expect from A.B.C.?

A: I would agree.

Q: Timely, accurate and candid communication is one of the corporate character traits that you say makes A.B.C. Brokerage special?

A: Just one of them, but yes.

Q: And to be accurate and candid, your communication should not add what is untrue, or omit what is true?

A: I would agree.

This "no discovery" witness unwittingly benefits the cross-examiner's theory of the case. The proud corporate executive has now established a high standard for the disclosure of financial information. He has cemented the "duty" issues. He has told the jury that investor reliance on A.B.C. for information is reasonable. He has even said that a failure to fully disclosure the financial facts is a breach of duty. This very bright, very high ranking corporate executive has bragged his firm into liability problems, all the while believing he was doing nothing more than what he had done on direct examination — convince the jurors that A.B.C. Brokerage Firm is a fair and honest company adhering to the highest standards, a company to be trusted to know the truth and to tell the truth.

§ 27.41   Impeachment by Inconsistent Statement

When the lawyer has pre-trial discovery of inconsistent statements, she can plan her impeachment as part of a scripted cross-examination. That pre-trial planned impeachment cannot exist at the time that the "no discovery" witness begins testifying. With no discovery, there is no pre-trial prior inconsistent statement. But even this limitation may evaporate once the witness begins testifying. The witness may say something on direct examination and later contradict himself, either within his direct examination or in the course of cross-examination. Realize then that even the technique of impeachment through use of prior inconsistent statements may become available during the course of a cross-examination of a witness where no pre-trial discovery exists.

When a witness says something on cross-examination inconsistent with what they have said on direct examination, there is an understandable tendency to impeach using the former statement. Often the impeachment begins with a phrase such as "didn't you say on direct examination . . .?" The cross-examiner should first examine which statement is more helpful, the statement made on direct examination, or the purportedly inconsistent statement made on cross-examination. It is the more helpful version of the facts that the cross-examiner needs to bolster, and it is the less helpful version of facts that should be weakened by further cross-examination.

If the better version of facts is the statement made on cross-examination, the cross-examiner may well choose to bolster that answer by providing the witness with other facts that logically support the new answer. As usual, cross-examination should be conducted with leading questions. However, the tone is also important. The cross-examiner should display by their tone and their attitude that this chapter is so clearly correct that there can be no question as to the accuracy of the witness's answers. In other words, by the form of the question and by the cross-examiner's attitude, the witness must be reassured and encouraged in the answer which most aids the cross-examiner. The "impeachment" of the less useful answer given on direct examination or on cross occurs through the gentle and detailed verification of the more useful answer, rather than through the more abrupt confrontation concerning why two different answers have been given.

§ 27.42   Credibility Cross-Examination

Certainly general credibility attacks that the cross-examiner may use on any witness may be applied to the "no discovery" witness as well. However, because this witness is "no discovery," the lawyer has the same problem: how to find the credibility attacks within the direct examination. To some extent, because the cross-examiner does not have a prepared script for this witness, the cross-examiner's creativity is not restricted, tied down, or scripted. With that said, counsel should concentrate on the basics of the general credibility attacks: bias, interest, and motive.

Example: The plaintiff alleged that the defendant had committed domestic violence upon her more than four and one-half years prior to the separation of the parties. The court permitted the opponent to call the wife's sister, despite the fact that she was not listed as a potential witness. The sister testified that on the night of this domestic violence, she had driven the wife to the hospital. Once there, the wife feared that her husband's career with the military would be damaged if she entered the emergency room. She and the children would be financially punished if that happened. She refused to go into the medical facility to be seen by the doctor.

This undiscovered witness (sister of the plaintiff) was offered to verify that she had in fact taken the wife to the hospital, and that the wife had in fact had numerous bruises, red marks, and a blackened eye. She was called to bolster the testimony of the plaintiff who had been rather successfully cross-examined earlier in the trial as to the severity of this domestic violence, the fact that wife had not seen a doctor, and the fact that this had gone unreported to anyone for years.

The plaintiff had also been cross-examined consistent with the cross-examiner's theory of the case, that she had been plotting for years to sue the defendant as soon as he had retired from the military, and his military retirement had begun to pay out. Rather than attack this sister/witness directly as to the veracity of the details that she testified, the cross-examiner attacked the witness's bias, interest, and motive, which was consistent with the cross-examiner's theory of the case:

Q: Mrs. Schubert, you testified that you carried your sister to the medical facility but she refused to go in?

A: Yes.

Q: You testified that you begged her to go in?

A: Yes.

Q: You testified that you told her that as time passed that she would forget how badly brutalized she was?

A: Yes.

Q: You testified that, in fact, you sat there with your sister in the car that night and wrote down details about what you testified today?

A: Yes.

Q: Your sister knew that you were writing those details down?

A: Yes.

Q: Your sister agreed that you would keep those notes?

A: Yes.

Q: In fact, you still have those notes, but your explanation is that you just didn't bring them to trial today?

A: Yes.

Q: Your sister always knew that you had those notes hidden in your home?

A: Yes.

Q: She always knew that you would be available to her with those notes?

A: Yes.

Q: When your sister filed this lawsuit, she discussed with you that you still had those notes?

A: Well, I don't know that she actually discussed that with me.

Q: But she knew that you still had the notes?

A: Yes, I am sure that she did.

Q: She knew that you were prepared to testify about what was on those notes?

A: Yes.

Q: Every night since those notes were made that your sister went home to her husband, she knew that you had those notes ready to use in a divorce trial against her husband?

A: I guess she did.

Q: Well the fact is ma'am, that she knew that?

A: Yes.

Q: She knew and you knew that those notes would be used if she ever filed this divorce action?

A: Yes.

Q: She knew that those notes were there available for her with great detail?

A: Yes.

Q: The details were to be used to convince a jury that this had occurred?

A: Yes.

Q: That was a secret that you and your sister shared?

A: Yes.

Q: You never shared that secret with her husband?

A: No.

Q: You never shared that secret with counselors?

A: No.

Q: You never shared that secret with ministers?

A: No.

Q: You never shared that secret with law enforcement?

A: No.

Q: You never shared that secret with the husband's military supervisors?

A: No.

Q: It was never shared with anyone?

A: No.

Q: Instead, you kept these notes for one purpose — waiting to be used when your sister asked for alimony and property division?

A: Yes.

§ 27.43   Marginalizing the Witness

The technique of marginalizing a witness certainly applies to the "no discovery" witness. As discussed, most witnesses are niche witnesses. They can testify to a rather small number of facts. If this "no discovery" witness cannot be used to support the cross-examiner's theory of this case, or be used to hurt the opponent's theory of the case, and cannot be attacked safely, or the facts upon which the "no discovery" witness testifies cannot be attacked, then the cross-examiner may consider marginalizing the witness by asking a series of chapters designed to illustrate to the fact finder that this witness knows precious little about the case.

In a case about a driver who had something to drink on the afternoon before a collision, whether it is a criminal case or a personal injury case, where the opposing lawyer has newly "discovered" this witness who observed the cross-examiner's client consuming alcohol earlier in the day, the cross-examiner chose to marginalize a witness by utilizing a series of chapters to highlight the lack of knowledge. Each numbered paragraph is the name of a chapter, not individual questions. There are many more detailed and supporting questions for each chapter.

(1) You saw Mr. Jones (the cross-examiner's party) for less than thirty-five minutes?

(2) That observation period was before 2:00 p.m. in the afternoon?

(3) You did not see Mr. Jones after that time, including and up to the time of the collision after 10:00 p.m.?

(4) You did not see what Mr. Jones had to eat in that eight-hour period?

(5) You did not see what physical activity Mr. Jones did in that eight-hour period?

(6) You did not see what liquids, including non-alcoholic beverages, Mr. Jones consumed in that eight-hour period?

(7) You did not see whether Mr. Jones napped in that eight-hour period?

(8) You did not see how Mr. Jones conducted himself in that eight-hour period?

(9) You did not see how Mr. Jones drove his vehicle in that eight-hour period?

These are but nine of the chapters used to marginalize the witness.

Often in commercial litigation, the corporate party will call a corporate executive as a spokesman for the corporation. This executive is often selected because he has the right look and sound and is nimble in his speech. It can even be the president or CEO, who makes a great appearance but who had little or nothing to do with the matter at issue. Such a witness can be marginalized by a series of leading questions designed to show that he was not at the key meetings, often because the decisions were being made below his level. He did not write or even receive the key memos at issue. This witness was not involved in giving the orders. He was not involved in performing the due diligence. He was not involved in testing the product.

It may well be that it wasn't the witness's job to do any of these things. That is certainly a very helpful answer to the cross-examiner as it helps to further marginalize the witness. The point of marginalizing the cross-examination is not to blame the witness for anything, but rather to take the witness out of the case. This form of cross-examination tends to be short and punchy. It is characterized by questions such as: "You were not assigned . . .," "You did not do . . .," "It wasn't your job . . .," and "You were not aware . . . ."

§ 27.44 Avoiding Any Unnecessary Risk in Cross-Examination of the "No Discovery" Witness

The most useful analysis identifies those chapters upon which the cross-examiner may productively examine the "no discovery" witness. To be thorough, an analysis as to what not to cross-examine must be made as well. Cross-examination is an anxious business. Cross-examination without benefit of pre-trial discovery produces greater anxiety principally because the cross-examiner intuitively and logically recognizes there is a greater risk. The cross-examiner understands the damage that has been done on direct examination, but fears even more the damaging testimony that an ill-conceived cross-examination may reveal.

The single most important technique to use in limiting or minimizing additional damage on cross-examination of the "no discovery" witness is to realize that the opponent has almost certainly directed his witness on direct examination into those areas in which the witness can do the most damage to the cross-examiner's theory of the case or do the most good for the opponent's theory of the case. Accordingly, before the cross-examination begins, the cross-examiner has probably heard the worst the witness has to offer.

Consequently, to minimize the risk of cross-examination of "no discovery" witnesses, avoid asking for a repetition or elaboration on the most damaging aspects of the direct examination. A frontal assault upon those damaging areas of testimony often produces greater damage to the cross-examiner. The witness repeats and makes worse the worse parts of direct. The cross-examiner becomes frustrated. Lacking details that are useful and could have been verified in discovery, the cross-examiner begins using more global terms, which, of course, are easily deniable by the witness (see chapter 8, *The Only Three Rules of Cross-Examination*). The damage is enhanced, and the foundation level rises.

Examples:

WEAK

Q: Your conduct was negligent?

A: I wouldn't agree.

BETTER

Q: The speed limit was 60 mph?

A: Yes.

Q: On a normal weather day 60 mph was as fast as you could drive?

A: I guess so.

Q: But this wasn't a normal weather day?

A: Not really.

Q: On this day it was snowing?

A: Yes. It was.

Q: In fact, it was snowing hard?

A: Yes.

Q: The road was icy?

A: In spots.

Another example: First, the cross-examiner tries to eat the entire subject in one gulp by putting before the witness an entirely conclusory statement.

WEAK

Q: Your software was never accepted in the marketplace?

A: I disagree.

BETTER

Q: You had been trying to sell your software for 3 years?

A: We weren't trying, we were doing it.

Q: Your biggest sale was 200 copies to one company?

A: Yes, but we hoped to sell more.

Q: In 1999 you sold less than 3,500 copies?

A: Yes.

Q: In 2000 you sold less than 3,500 copies?

A: Yes.

It is better to indirectly attack the witness (logic or motive, interest, bias) if an attack must be made. It is better still to take the witness into chapters designed to support the cross-examiner's theory of the case or hurt the opponent's theory of the case without a direct attack upon the witness. Only after control of the witness has been established are direct attacks advisable.

§ 27.45 Conclusion

The "no-discovery" witness presents the cross-examiner with additional challenges and stress. However, techniques exist for dealing with this situation — techniques that the cross-examiner already knows.

The cross-examiner has the advantage of being well prepared with respect to the case as a whole. Moreover, "discovery" is available in the opening statement and the direct examination. The cross-examiner must listen carefully for the opponent's theme in the opening statement and for statements representing what the witnesses will prove. With focused listening and selective note taking during the direct examination of the "no discovery" witness, the cross-examiner can plan the scope and content of the cross-examination.

Using her knowledge of the facts of the case, the opponent's theme, and the testimony of other witnesses, the lawyer can successfully handle cross-examination of the surprise witness with familiar tactics: the chapter method (see chapter 9, *The Chapter Method of Cross-Examination*), sequencing (see chapter 11, *Sequences of Cross-Examination*), and logic-based questions. Rarely is a "no questions" cross-examination the best solution. Normally, the witness is valuable to the cross-examiner.

Chapter 28

THE CRYING WITNESS

SYNOPSIS

§ 28.01   The Rising Tide of Helplessness

The crying witness is a special problem in cross-examination. Unlike the runaway witness, whose danger comes from overly broad answers, the crying witness harms the cross-examiner through his highly emotional demeanor. The outburst implies that any cross-examination is unfair and the resulting lack of answers to the cross-examination questions posed.

When a witness starts to cry, whether in a domestic relations case, a criminal case, a medical malpractice case, or any case, the cross-examiner may feel control ebbing away, followed by the strangling feeling of a rising tide of helplessness. The impulse to take some drastic measure seems irresistible. The most likely measure is to dramatically shorten the cross-examination. Such a solution must, however, be resisted.

The cross-examiner must control his or her own feelings of helplessness caused by the crying witness. The cross-examiner often fears that the emotions of the fact finders (the jury or the judge) will rise in sympathy for the witness. The cross-examiner will undoubtedly feel frustration, and occasionally even panic. In response, the cross-examiner concludes that there is "no good way out" of this situation. This fear causes the cross-examiner to forget those tactics designed to re-establish control, while coping with the additional emotional component that has been injected into the courtroom. Second, once the cross-examiner is under control, she can begin controlling the witness's emotions.

Many of the situations that work to re-establish control of the runaway witness (see chapter 19, *Controlling the Runaway Witness*) in which the cross-examiner repeats the question she previously asked, reinforces for the crying witness the fact that the cross-examination will not be stopped merely because the witness cries. The use of the witness' formal name, or the introduction of a question with the more proper "Sir" or "Ma'am" may also cause the crying witness to resume eye contact, pay closer attention to the question, and may thereby wholly or partially extinguish the crying behavior. When the cross-examiner judges that the crying conduct is blocking the cross-examiner's ability to establish an extremely important point, the use of the blackboard technique may be helpful. As discussed in chapter 19, *Controlling the Runaway Witness*, the cross-examiner can place a single, very important previous question on the blackboard and then call for an answer to that specific question. When using this technique with a crying witness, it is important that the gesture be under-played. That is to say, the cross-examiner should go about this business very quietly, and with no added physical gestures. This technique is so powerful that its misuse will cause added sympathy for the witness. Hence, the technique should only be used when the question is extremely important, when the anticipated answer can be clearly established, and when, in the judgment of the cross-examiner, the fact finder likely believes that the crying conduct is avoiding a fair but tough question.

§ 28.02 Cutting the Witness Off: An Unworkable Tactic

Often, the cross-examiner's first response is to attempt to cut off or speak over the witness. The cross-examiner may offer a tissue or a sip of water in an effort to look better in the eyes of the fact finder. Just as coffee produces a wide-awake drunk, tissues and water for a crying witness usually create a nose-blowing, water-sipping, but still crying witness.

When these first "sensitive" efforts have met with no great result, the cross-examiner often goes to the opposite extreme by very sternly questioning the witness in order to "force" an answer. This second method usually fails because the witness is still in an emotional state that leaves him unresponsive. As long as the crying continues, the witness is unintelligible and unable to respond to the techniques covered in chapter 19, *Controlling the Runaway Witness.*

The longer the crying episode, the clearer it becomes that the fact-finding process is being affected. On the other hand, the more the questioning is pressed by firmly pursuing the cross-examination, the more the cross-examiner fears exacerbating the out-of-control witness.

One thing is certain: The solution of "no more questions" is no solution at all. The witness has won. The cross-examination has ended, not because there are no additional facts needing to be covered, but because the cross-examiner has judged it too difficult to try to accomplish these factual goals. No cross-examination at all would have been better than a cross-examination ending with the witness crying and the cross-examiner being the culprit. But do not be mistaken: Forsaking cross-examination under these difficult circumstances is never advocated.

Clearly, a set of techniques is required to discourage, diminish, or stop the crying from occurring, or to deal effectively with the situation once it has occurred. If possible, the lawyer needs to prevent the crying witness. If that is not possible, she needs to put the cross-examination back on track as quickly as feasible.

§ 28.03   Foreseeing the Problem

When did this witness start crying? If the witness began crying in the opponent's case, the cross-examiner has ample notice of the problem. Similarly, the witness is much more fatigued by the crying long before the cross-examiner stands up to examine. Under the circumstances, the crying may well extinguish itself. If not, the best rule is to press ahead as the jury has witnessed an opponent make their factual way through the crying.

But what if the crying begins during the cross-examination? The cross-examiner must assess the degree to which the crying is affecting the ability to conduct a meaningful cross-examination. Witnesses cry to different degrees and with different effects. The witness who is crying hysterically, which will be called "wailing," requires a different approach than the witness who is attempting to stifle the cry and who could be characterized as "whimpering."

A "wailing" witness is either unable or unwilling to stop crying and signifies a loss of self-control. So long as this conduct continues, no cross-examination is possible. In effect, the witness has put up a tangible sound barrier and a visible emotional barrier to the process of cross-examination. No judge would permit an angry witness to refuse to answer cross-examination questions. But judges are tempted to allow the crying witness to engage in conduct that similarly truncates the right of cross-examination. In essence, the judge feels it is fair to order a witness to answer, but unfair to order a witness to stop crying. While the cross-examiner can certainly appreciate the difference in the situations, the result is often the same: loss of cross-examination.

In contrast, the "whimpering" witness may have some vestige of self-control left. Under these circumstances cross-examination can continue, though with difficulty. Cross-examination is possible as this witness can hear the questions and has sufficient self-control to interrupt their crying with a responsive answer.

Whether "wailing" or "whimpering," it is assumed in this discussion that the witness is sincere in the demonstration of emotion or at least appears sincere. Insincere crying is another matter and will be discussed later in this chapter.

§ 28.04 Pre-Trial Identification of the Highly Emotional Witness

Any pre-trial exposure to the witness should be used to gauge how the witness will likely react emotionally at trial. In the course of an informal interview or in the more formal deposition, the cross-examiner must allow (not prevent) witnesses to show the natural, emotionally-charged positions in their testimonies. In this way, the cross-examiner can gauge the level of the witness's emotions, so as to accurately predict just how emotional the witness may become at trial. Even the act of refusing an interview says something of the witness's emotional state. The form of the refusal, as expressed by the witness, gives the cross-examiner valuable clues. If a witness is highly emotional in declining the interview, or demonstrates he is affronted by the mere request for interview, that witness is signaling a greater propensity to act just as emotionally at trial.

Hence, a pre-trial interview, deposition, or court hearing should be used to not only gauge the emotional pitch of the witness, but also to train the witness that crying will not end the cross-examination. In fact, it will prolong the time on the witness stand. Those techniques a lawyer might use in trial to extinguish the crying behavior may be used in any available pre-trial questioning sessions. In this way, the witness can learn that it is to his advantage to control his emotional level. The trial lawyer can better gauge which techniques will have the best effect in controlling the crying behavior should it reoccur during trial.

If the witness shows any emotion before trial, it is reasonable to anticipate that that emotion will be magnified at a contested hearing or trial. A courtroom in trial is generally a quiet place. In this environment, the courtroom magnifies any emotion. This is certainly true when applied to the crying witness. A sniffle and choked voice are "heard" as a witness barely under control. A small whimper is "heard" as hard crying. A wailing witness comes across as hysterical. Trials have a way of putting people, not just testimony, under a microscope. Witnesses can sense this. Some witnesses will react by being more subdued, but some will react by becoming even more emotional, as the courtroom produces an added strain.

Whether in trials or in mediation or arbitration, this is an age of "less discovery." As a result, the witness will not be known personally to the cross-examiner prior to trial. In such cases, the cross-examiner is given a window to the witness during the direct examination and perhaps during breaks. But these observations are limited. Certain general observations may assist the cross-examiner.

When a child, an elderly person, or a relative of the person on trial (i.e., the defendant in a criminal case or either party in a civil case) testifies, heightened emotions can be anticipated.

Trial lawyers become accustomed to openly dealing with highly emotional issues. While this is necessary, the cross-examiner must be mindful and sensitive of the emotional impact of the chapters on which she is to cross-examine the witness. The more sensitive the material appears, the more likely the crying.

§ 28.05   The Importance of Identifying the Crying Witness Before Trial

Whenever the trial lawyer believes that a witness may become a crying witness, the lawyer needs to be prepared ahead of time to exert an added degree of cross-examination control. This is not to say that the trial lawyer cannot handle the unexpectedly crying witness without pre-trial preparation. However, pre-trial identification of this type of witness certainly makes dealing with this witness easier. Forewarned is forearmed.

For example, exhibits and demonstrative evidence are in greater need with the crying witness (see § 28.28, below). The drafting of exhibits and demonstrative evidence is handled much more easily prior to trial. Many families own and use video cameras, if not digital equipment, but cross-examiners continue to fail to videotape depositions and interviews. If the witness did not cry when the question was asked on the videotape, and if that witness cries to the extent that cross-examination becomes very difficult at trial, it may be possible to play the videotape showing that the witness did not find it necessary to cry when this matter was covered pre-trial. If, on the other hand, the witness cried during the pre-trial examination, the lawyer could better gauge what questions will produce the highly emotional response. Such a videotape can prepare the cross-examiner to deal with the emotional witness in ways a cold transcript can never hope to do.

§ 28.06   What Not to Do: Gestures That Verify the Right to Cry

When the crying begins, the cross-examiner should initially refrain from offering the witness a break, a tissue or hankie, or water. These seemingly helpful gestures signal that the witness has every reason to cry and can control the pace of the cross-examination. They signal that the witness can create a "time out." Yielding to the crying witness transfers control from the cross-examiner to the witness. Control that is transferred to the witness is as dangerous as control lost.

If a recess is requested by the attorney who first called the witness, or by the trial judge, no objection should be voiced. However, the cross-examiner should not initiate the request. The witness who repeatedly breaks down, thus requiring the witness's own lawyer to ask for a recess, will be perceived differently than a witness who is offered a time out by the cross-examiner. The offer of a recess by the cross-examiner is seen as recognition of the witness's "right" to be out of control. The exception is the witness who is so clearly out-of-control that no further questioning is possible. A judge will ordinarily be quick to grant the recess, and once the jury is out of the courtroom, the judge may voluntarily become involved in the effort to get the witness back to an emotional level where examination can continue.

§ 28.07   Using the Lawyer's Eyes and Body Language to Keep Control

Even in the face of terrible and prolonged crying, the cross-examiner must not avoid the witness's eyes when the witness looks up. The cross-examiner should remain neutral in appearance, both in body mannerisms and facial expressions. This is not an appropriate time for a stare down, or a withering look. The trial lawyer's appearance should be one of readiness, willingness, and intent to continue the examination as soon as the witness regains minimal composure. The examination must continue as soon as practical. The cross-examiner dare not wait for the witness to be completely unemotional. Remember, once the cross-examination is again underway, there is a momentum to the questioning. A witness who answers questions is a witness more willing and able to answer further questions. The cross-examiner must be ready to continue the cross-examination without apparent effect (positive or negative) from the delay caused by the crying.

Silence, particularly neutral silence, speaks more loudly than "time out" behaviors and has none of the downside risks (see chapter 21, *Creation and Uses of Silence*). The emotion for the cross-examiner to display is patience. By this attitude, it is demonstrated that the material of the cross-examination needs to be covered in order for the fact finder to fairly judge the matter.

The cross-examiner remains neutral so that the fact finder cannot infer ill will or malicious behavior on the part of the cross-examiner. But the cross-examiner must maintain eye contact with the witness in order to demonstrate readiness to continue the examination. It conveys to the witness that the cross-examiner is not afraid of the witness's emotions and is neither ashamed nor hesitant to ask tough but fair questions that provoke emotional reactions. The witness is thereby taught that crying will not stop the cross-examination from occurring. Perhaps not immediately, but inevitably, the cross-examination will be accomplished. This message must be consistently conveyed by attitude and conduct. The case will continue in the areas dictated by the cross-examiner. The message is conveyed by quiet neutrality and patience, not by impatient words or angry gestures. Eye contact is a key element of control of the crying witness.

§ 28.08   Behavior Is Molded by Consequences [The Cross-Examiner Should Consider Moving the Emotion-Producing Chapter to a Different Witness]

The cross-examiner can often foresee which witness is likely to cry, and the point at which he is likely to cry. In such a case, it may be possible to cover the emotion-producing material with a different witness. Of course, the cross-examiner must weigh whether the alternate witness can cover these chapters as well as the potentially crying witness, and whether the jury will attach the same credibility to the facts admitted by the alternate witness.

In a personal injury action, assume that liability is contested, but damages are substantial. Defense counsel alleges comparative negligence on the part of the plaintiff driver. There are two available witnesses to the alleged negligent driving conduct: another driver on the highway traveling several car lengths behind plaintiff's car, and the plaintiff's girlfriend who was riding in the passenger seat of plaintiff's car. Both witnesses may be able to offer the same information, but an emotional outburst is far more likely from the companion than from the stranger. The cross-examiner must weigh whether the fact finder is likely to be equally persuaded by the testimony of the driver several car lengths behind the plaintiff as opposed to essentially the same admissions made by a person closely tied to the plaintiff.

The cross-examiner should anticipate that some witnesses will inevitably cry. While it is certainly not the job of the cross-examiner to induce a witness to cry on cross-examination, the fact that it occurs is not a mark against the cross-examiner. In other words, cross-examiners are bound to encounter witnesses who will cry, and perhaps cry at appropriate times and in appropriate ways. The cross-examiner cannot always steer the cross-examination around that witness, or the chapters that are likely to produce crying. For that reason, a series of techniques to deal with the crying witness should be part of every cross-examiner's training.

§ 28.09   The Wailing Witness

When a witness is "wailing" (loud and prolonged crying, hysterical crying, out of control crying), the cross-examiner cannot ask questions or even be heard above the witness. The best resource of the cross-examiner is patience, combined with non-threatening, continued eye contact and no body movement. The cross-examiner should stand ready to continue the cross-examination, but give no indication to the fact finder or the witness of being negatively affected by the witness's behavior.

Just as a wailing child must soon come up for air, the wailing witness will do the same. Likewise, the witness discovers what all children discover when their continued crying does not result in being caressed and held. The crying (wailing) eventually stops. A crying witness stops, partially out of embarrassment, as the courtroom is silent and all present are watching a witness out of control. The crying also stops because 'wailing' is physically and emotionally exhausting. The cross-examiner may feel the wailing took forever to end, but patience is rewarded quicker than other techniques. The net result is that the witness is physically weaker. The cross-examiner may now resort to the techniques in chapter 8 — the use of short, leading questions, each containing one new fact per question. The object here is to put a fact before the witness so that a simple "yes" can provide the necessary answer. This method decreases the amount of work that the witness must do to answer the question, and allows the cross-examiner to make progress even with a witness who has minimal emotional control.

In the best-case scenario, the crying stops completely and the cross-examination may continue. In the worst-case scenario, the witness becomes a "whimpering" witness. Either scenario is preferred to the wailing witness.

There is another possible "stopper" to the wailing witness: either the opposing party's attorney or the court may suggest a water break, tissue, or recess. Once this witness-created recess has been offered and accepted one time, few judges will continue to offer it on a regular basis. Remember, all judges realize that they must "move it along" in order to complete the case and keep up with the caseload. The judge will understand that, as emotional as the testimony may be, the review of evidence must continue. The case must go on. Once a judge has called a full recess in order to accommodate the crying witness, the judge will be very reluctant to call a second recess. The cross-examiner may count on the fact that the judge will urge the witness to maintain self-control so that the case can continue. Judges have seen it all. They have had to cope with crying witnesses, crying family members, and highly emotional situations. Judges are acutely aware that the legal system cannot be subverted by emotional displays.

Similarly, once the cross-examiner's opposing counsel has requested a recess, or offered water or a hankie, the opposing counsel will not be as quick to ask for an additional recess if the witness resumes "wailing." Should the wailing continue, opposing counsel has the unenviable choice of permitting the wailing to continue or asking again for some type of "break" for the witness. This scenario wears thin. No matter how sincere the crying, the opposing counsel has vouched for the witness's need to continue to wail (and has thus become the dreaded enabler). Opposing counsel's credibility is now tied to a witness who, in essence, is avoiding answering the tough but fair cross-examination questions.

Consider the effects of the witness's continued wailing on the fact finder. Be it a judge or a jury, how many adults happily tolerate the sound of "wailing" for an extended period of time? It is discomforting, no matter how sympathetic the listener may be. The cross-examiner must always remember to exercise patience. Fact finders will better tolerate silence than they will a cross-examiner who feels compelled to ask questions in an effort to stop the wailing or who asks questions over the wailing. The parent who yells over a child's wailing, no matter how frustrating the wailing may be, makes the situation worse. A parent's patience is admired. The same formula attaches to the courtroom.

§ 28.10 The Whimpering Witness

When the cross-examiner has followed the suggestions above for dealing with a wailing witness, it must be admitted that the witness has halted the questioning, not the cross-examiner. Therefore, the cross-examiner lacks complete control. This reality is no reason for the cross-examiner to panic. The cross-examiner should understand that the loss of control was balanced by the exercise of patience. Demonstration of patience is itself an element of control. Once the wailing has been reduced to whimpering, or when the witness has only whimpered and not wailed at all, the cross-examiner is in a position to take complete control.

Once wailing has turned to whimpering, or before whimpering becomes wailing, the cross-examiner must move crisply and steadily to eliminate the whimpering.

§ 28.11   Slowing the Pace of Questions to Re-establish Control

After the crying has stopped or been reduced to whimpering, the pace of the questioning must be somewhat slower than the cross-examiner might like. Some cross-examinations present best at 45 rpm's. Rather than immediately resuming questioning at the desired 45 rpm level, the cross-examiner must be content to drop back to 33 rpm for the first several questions. This permits the witness to become composed and to "hear" the question.

It is a common mistake for the cross-examiner to resume questioning at too fast a pace after the crying has stopped. Once this occurs, the witness may become frustrated and fall back into the wailing mode as much out of self-defense as from genuine emotions. A questioning pace that is too slow (16 rpm) may encourage the witness to ramble. It is a question of adjustment. The cross-examiner must understand the multiple factors at work. She must use her trial judgment.

This reduced rate of questioning should last only a few questions in order to reorient the witness to the process of leading questions and short answers, and then the desired pace of questioning should resume.

§ 28.12   Beware of the Glazed Look

Either in or out of court, most lawyers have experienced the glazed look over the face of a person telling a story. The look on the face, particularly the glazed look in the eyes of the person telling the story, non-verbally but eloquently communicates the fact that the witness is seeing, hearing, and experiencing the situation again. An eerie sense of "the truth" surrounds this kind of retelling of the story. The witness is back "in the moment" of the emotionally-charged event.

Once the witness sees himself in the story (whether truthful or not), the witness will bring to the story the experience and emotion of being there. A glazed look acts as an early warning detector for the cross-examiner that wailing or whimpering may soon follow. As soon as the cross-examiner sees a glaze in the eyes or senses in the tone of the witness that the witness is reliving the event, the cross-examiner must immediately treat the witness as a whimpering witness and follow the guidelines for controlling a whimpering witness. It is easier to control the witness before the whimpering starts. By exercising the necessary techniques to forestall whimpering, the cross-examiner maintains control.

The following are methods to extract the witness from the full scope of the highly emotional event so that the witness can concentrate sufficiently to answer appropriate leading questions.

§28.13   Focus the Witness on Less Emotional Details

Certainly, the cross-examiner should always follow the three rules (see chapter 8, *The Only Three Rules of Cross-Examination*). However, when questioning a whimpering witness, the cross-examiner must concentrate on using the most minute and detailed facts in the presentation of one fact per question. As questions become more detailed, more concentration is required by the witness to remember the specific facts and to accurately answer the cross-examiner's questions. The more detailed the facts, the more detailed and focused the concentration required to answer the question. By increasing the concentration required of the witness, the witness is moved away from emotion. Broader questions offer opportunities for the witness's mind to drift and become more emotional.

In this example, the complaining witness is testifying to the circumstances surrounding an alleged assault. In an effort to break through the crying, the cross-examining counsel moves the witness into a block of questions seeking details of the physical setting of the assault, without directly referring to the assault.

Improperly orienting the witness:

Q: Before Darren tried to kiss you he was standing in the bathroom?

A: Yes. (Witness begins to sob more loudly.)

Q: And when you got close to him, he grabbed you and began kissing you?

A: Yes. (Witness begins crying to the extent that further questioning is quite difficult)

Compare this method of reorienting the witness:

Q: Darren was in the bathroom?

A: Yes.

Q: The door was open?

A: Yes.

Q: You could see him there tying his tie?

A: Yes.

Q: When you saw him tying his tie it was apparent to you that Darren was getting ready to leave?

A: I thought so. (Whimpering is beginning.)

Q: The bathroom is at the far end of the hall?

A: Yes.

Q: The bathroom is ten full strides from where you were standing?

A: About that many.

Q: The bathroom was twenty feet between you and Darren?

A: About that many. (The whimpering slows down.)

Q: You were standing in the living room?

A: Yes.

Q: You were within a step for two of your front door?

A: Yes.

Q: Darren was standing inside the doorway of the bathroom?

A: Yes. (The whimpering stops.)

Q: While you remained by the living room?

A: Yes.

Why is the whimpering more likely to stop? The witness is being required to respond to relatively precise distances rather than Darren. Furthermore, the witness is not introduced abruptly to the alleged assault, but to other facts not directly related to the assault.

§ 28.14   Distraction as a Method of Limiting Crying

[1]   Identify and Avoid, Where Possible, the Isolated Issue Likely to Cause the Crying

Undeniably, some portion of the case may justifiably lead the witness to cry. That does not mean the lawyer must always encounter that part of the case. It may be possible to cross-examine around that single issue. In order to do so, the cross-examiner needs to engage in a two-step approach.

[2]   Identify the Source of the Emotion

In order to distract the witness from the emotions that are causing the whimpering, the cross-examiner must find two answers: (a) the source or factual setting of the emotion; and (b) the type of emotion causing the crying. Too often, the cross-examiner over-simplifies the problem, concluding that "this case" or "this testimony" is upsetting to "this witness." The cross-examiner is better equipped to avoid the crying by analyzing what particular scenario within the case is upsetting to the witness or what emotion is causing the "upset." In order to better control the crying witness, the cross-examiner must understand whether it is fear, sorrow, guilt, or a variety of other feelings that is causing the emotional reaction.

Similarly, the cross-examiner will be assisted by analyzing which facts are leading to the emotional response. Once the cross-examiner understands the factual setting or picture that is driving the emotion, the cross-examiner can minimize discussion of that area. Once this is done, the cross-examiner can understand the etiology of the crying. She can attempt to distract the witness from that etiology by placing chapters surrounding the main tap of emotion, but not directly touching upon it.

[3] Out of Chronological Order

If the cross-examiner has fallen into a chronological cross-examination, the witness will often start to whimper or wail in anticipation of the emotion-provoking event that chronologically follows the questions asked. See chapter 11, *Sequences of Cross-Examination*, for the dangers of chronological cross-examination. By proceeding chronologically, the cross-examiner has inadvertently engaged the area of cross-examination likely to produce a highly emotional response. The crying is likely to commence when the witness first realizes that the highly emotional area is about to surface. If, instead, the cross-examination is not in chronological order, the cross-examiner has diminished the ability of the witness to foresee the point at which the highly emotional area will be introduced.

The cross-examiner should immediately initiate a chapter out of chronological order to distract and force the witness's thinking away from the chronologically expected events that encourage crying (see chapter 9, *The Chapter Method of Cross-Examination*). By moving out of chronological thinking, the witness is forced to pay greater attention to the details of the new and unexpected area of questioning. For this reason alone, the witness is unable to ramp up to manifest the emotion that results in crying. By disrupting the witness's emotional train of thought, the cross-examiner deprives the witness of the chronological lead-in to that emotion. Thus, the need to cry is eliminated.

If the defense lawyer in a personal injury case where a mother and infant child were involved in a collision cross-examines in a chronological manner, the mother will often begin to cry as the cross-examination nears the chronological point where the child's injuries occurred. On the other hand, if the defense attorney cross-examines out of chronological order, the mother is not given an opportunity to accurately predict when the questioning about the child's injuries will occur. The mother is thereby denied the lead-time to work up the emotion (no matter how sincere that emotion may be) and the mother is less likely to whimper or wail. Better yet, the cross-examiner may find that it is unnecessary to cross-examine on that part of the story at all, as the most emotionally charged chapters may be unnecessary, or they may be covered to the same effect through a less emotional witness (see chapter 9, *The Chapter Method of Cross-Examination*).

In essence, the cross-examiner may well be able to maneuver the cross around the area of heightened emotional content. If the true issue is how the accident occurred, the cross-examiner may move, in non-chronological order, through different chapters of the pre-collision story; she never falls into the highly emotional and non-productive discussion of the injuries.

On the other hand, damages or failure to mitigate damages may be at issue. Then, the collision itself, with all of its horrid memories and nuances may be lessened by cross-examining in non-chronological order using chapters on recovery, treatment, missed doctor visits or lack of need for medications.

§ 28.15   Direct the Witness Out of the Physical Surroundings Causing the Emotion

The glazed look or whimpering often occurs when someone is being questioned about the physical layout, lighting, and sounds surrounding the location of a traumatic event. When the physical layout is inquired into on cross-examination, and the witness shows signs of that glazed look of re-living the event or begins to whimper, it is time for the cross-examiner to remove the witness from those physical surroundings. The cross-examiner should ask questions that require the witness to shift focus to another locale, and/or describe the physical surroundings in a more structured way, perhaps using diagrams, or photos of the scene taken afterward where visual cues to the emotional facts no longer appear.

Take for example a case where a witness has been sexually assaulted behind a school gymnasium locker room in a storage area. The area behind this locker room is dark and cramped.

In achieving certain goals required for the defense, the cross-examiner deemed it necessary to question, in some detail, the location of the alleged assault. The poor lighting in the area of the "assault" helps the defendant's theory of the case — misidentification of the defendant. No cross-examiner looks forward to doing this chapter. This lawyer deemed it necessary. However, if the cross-examiner only questioned about that particular location, without references to distract the witness, the cross-examiner might well see the glazed look that leads to whimpering or wailing.

The following questions present a poor example:

Q: You say that it was behind the lockers?

A: Yes.

Q: It was dark?

A: Yes.

Q: There was only one light bulb at the very end?

A: Yes.

Q: It is a small area?

A: Yes.

Q: Old benches and chairs were stored back there?

A: Yes. (The witness's eyes glaze with tears streaming down her face.)

Compare this with the following series of questions that require the witness to make multiple comparisons of a description of the same area:

Q: You say that it was behind the lockers?

A: Yes.

Q: Not out in front of the bleachers?

A: No.

Q: It was dark?

A: Yes.

Q: Darker than at the other end of the gym?

A: Yes.

Q: There was only one light bulb?

A: Yes.

Q: The light was not as bright as the bulb at the top of the steps of the gym?

A: True.

Q: It is a small area?

A: Yes.

Q: The area in front of the lockers was larger?

A: Yes.

Q: Old benches and chairs were stored back there?

A: Yes.

Q: Old benches and chairs were also stored at the other end of the gym?

A: Yes.

In this sequence, the cross-examiner repeatedly requires the witness to mentally remove herself from the physical surroundings of the alleged assault and mentally compare the surroundings with other locations.

Remember, this technique does not require the cross-examiner to neglect an area deemed deserving of cross-examination. In the above example, a cross on the physical surroundings may well be essential to the defense. This technique is designed to create an atmosphere in which the witness must describe the physical surroundings without mentally placing herself within those physical surroundings. The questioning continues by forcing the witness to "see" other locations that are not emotionally heavy. By shifting her vision from location to location, the cross-examination shifts the focus of the witness away from emotionally laden facts. A beneficial byproduct of comparison is its effectiveness as a teaching model.

§ 28.16 Cross-Examining on Selected Aspects Within a Personal Relationship

Not all parts of a relationship are equally emotion laden. Moreover, it often happens that the aspect of the relationship of importance to the cross-examiner is not the aspect of the relationship likely to provoke a highly emotional response. Questioning a witness about a close personal relationship often provokes an emotional reaction. To distract and keep the witness from reacting emotionally, the cross-examiner should focus the cross-examination on only one aspect of a personal relationship at a time. To do this, the cross-examiner must differentiate between various aspects of a personal relationship. Witnesses do not categorize their personal relationships with other persons in that same analytical manner. By careful chapter and question selection, the cross-examiner must cause the witness to also reflect and react only to that limited aspect of the relationship rather than the entire personal relationship.

For instance, in a divorce and child custody case, the cross-examining lawyer must require the witness to concede the closeness, intimacy, and trust within a relationship between the other spouse and the children, without broaching the larger subject of the closeness (or lack of), intimacy (or lack of), or trust (or lack of) within the relationship between the divorcing parties.

Most spouses do not dissect the character of a person into "trust as it relates to the children." Rather, they look at a character only as to whether the person can be trusted generally. In order for the cross-examiner to develop the theory of the case that proves the father is the appropriate custodial parent, the wife should be questioned about the facts that prove her husband is a trustworthy parent capable and willing to properly make financial decisions regarding the children.

In cross-examining on this limited nature of "trustworthiness," the cross-examiner runs the risk of opening the emotional door for the witness to volunteer answers on other aspects of trustworthiness or more likely lack of trustworthiness on the part of the husband. The witness may well relate "trustworthiness" to her husband's adultery and breach of their wedding vows. This is certainly not the area the cross-examiner wanted to hear about. In order to avoid this witness migration on the selected area to a related area, the cross-examiner must narrowly confine the cross through the careful crafting of a goal-specific chapter.

Example 1 illustrates how the lawyer is attempting to win custody for her client. In order to do so, the cross-examiner is trying to establish, through the opposing spouse, that the husband has consistently and appropriately been attending to the financial needs of the children. In this first example, the questioning is so broad as to permit the witness to envision a highly emotional breach of trust that has occurred in the relationship, thus producing a highly emotional and unhelpful response.

Example 1:

Q: For eight years, you have seen your husband around the children?

A: Yes.

Q: Ever since the day the twins were born?

A: Yes.

Q: And you have seen your husband make financial decisions during those years for the welfare of the children?

A: Yes.

Q: You have learned to trust your husband's ability to make decisions?

A: No, I have learned that it is a mistake to trust him. I believed and trusted him, but I found that he was very good at fooling me. (Crying begins.)

Q: You trusted your husband's financial decisions regarding the children?

A: I trusted him and he destroyed my trust. (More crying.)

Q: But you trusted him *regarding the children*?

A: I will never trust him again. I shouldn't have trusted him then. (Continued crying.)

In example 1 above, the lawyer wanted to concentrate on the husband's character trait of "trust as it relates to the financial well-being of the children." But the questioning elicited responses from the witness concerning her husband's character trait of "trust as it relates to the husband's general trustworthiness."

The second example (a better cross) illustrates the need for more careful question selection to focus the witness on the more limited topic of "trust as it relates to the children."

Example 2:

Q: For eight years, you have seen your husband around the children?

A: Yes.

Q: Ever since the day the twins were born?

A: Yes.

Q: You have seen your husband make financial decisions during those years for the welfare of the children?

A: Yes.

Q: During that eight-year period of time, you and your husband banked with the same bank?

A: Yes.

Q: You had the same bank officer handle your bank business?

A: Yes.

Q: That bank officer assisted you and your husband in making financial decisions?

A: Yes.

Q: He assisted you in making financial decisions that affected the twins?

A: Yes.

Q: He assisted you in making good financial decisions regarding the twins?

A: Yes.

Q: You trusted your husband's financial decisions regarding the children?

A: Yes.

Q: You knew that you could trust your husband's financial decisions regarding the children?

A: Yes.

Q: You trusted your husband's financial decisions regarding the children more than the bank officer, who is not related by blood to the children?

A: Yes.

Throughout this sequence of questions, the witness is steered away from the unnecessary and emotionally laden area of "trust" in general. The questioning focuses the witness on the more limited but pertinent issue of trust as it regards the financial affairs of the children. The witness may even answer in such a way as to show impatience with such obvious questions. This series of questions avoids generating the emotional response permitted by the first series of questions, which failed to tightly focus the witness on a limited aspect of the issue of "trust as it relates to the children."

§ 28.17   Ask for Facts Not for Feelings

The cross-examiner may inadvertently promote crying by casting one or more chapters of cross-examination in terms that are highly emotional. One of the most frequent errors a lawyer makes is to label conduct for the fact finder where such label is likely to produce an emotional response from the witness. Cross-examination is built upon facts, and the fact finder can be trusted to apply the appropriate label. In the example below, the cross-examiner rightfully tackles an important subject, but unnecessarily promotes a highly emotional response.

The witness, a lawyer, has been called as an adverse witness by the plaintiff in an environmental dumping case. At issue is whether her firm knew of and participated in a cover-up of documents proving hazardous waste dumping by the defendant corporation. The court has ruled pre-trial that certain documents were improperly withheld from the plaintiffs. The court has ruled that plaintiff's counsel may call the participating lawyers (for purposes of cross-examination) and may inquire into the fact that such documents were withheld. Plaintiff's counsel, understandably, consistently uses the term "cover-up" within the cross-examination. By phrasing the questions in such a manner, the cross-examiner induces a highly emotional response — a crying denial of a cover-up.

This error intentionally places the witness into an emotionally-charged scenario — that she is part of a cover-up, that she has disobeyed her legal obligations, and that she has committed a fraud upon the legal system. By branding or labeling the conduct, the lawyer has openly suggested that this lawyer-witness has behaved in a fraudulent and despicable manner. The cross-examiner has invited a highly emotional answer compounded by crying. The combination of the motion and the crying could well cause a jury to believe the witness's denial that there was anything wrong with the conduct. The cross-examiner has in essence, put the professional and personal self-worth of the witness at issue and a jury that has nonverbally shown that it likes the witness will downplay their dislike of her conduct.

The cross-examiner need not frame the issue by asking, "Didn't you cheat?" or "Aren't you a cheater?" Instead, the cross-examiner may employ a series of questions that takes the witness and the fact finder away from the branding of the offending conduct and into a factual description of the offending conduct.

The cross-examiner must let the facts tell the story and thereby allow the fact finder to apply the appropriate label. To diminish the likelihood of crying, the tone should be neutral, not accusatory:

Q: XYZ Corp., including you, knew of the plaintiff's position — that XYZ dumped chemicals into the ground?

A: We were aware of that allegation in plaintiff's complaint.

Q: Exactly — you were aware of what plaintiff's wanted to prove?

A: If they could —

Q: As an experienced lawyer you knew there were several different ways the plaintiffs could go about proving XYZ Corp. had improperly dumped chemicals?

A: Hypothetically there would be different ways to try to prove it — if it were true.

Q: One way we could prove it would be through XYZ employees who witnessed the dumping?

A: Of course — if it had happened.

Q: If someone at XYZ saw it, then we could call those employees as our witnesses?

A: Hypothetically— if such a person existed.

Q: Since XYZ employs hundreds of people at the plant it would be impossible for us to find and interview all of them?

A: I suppose so.

Q: The plaintiffs would need to know which of these hundreds of employees witnessed the dumping?

A: If any dumping took place.

Q: And if plaintiffs can't identify which XYZ employees witnessed the dumping, we could never prove it happened?

A: I suppose so.

Q: The way we would have know which XYZ employees saw the dumping would be through the process of getting documents from XYZ that showed which witnesses witnessed the dumping?

A: Yes.

Q: On June 16, 2001, you received Exhibit 42 the XYZ internal investigative report on dumping?

A: Yes.

Q: Exhibit 42 disclosed the names of three XYZ employees who said they witnessed illegal dumping of chemicals on XYZ land?

A: That was their allegation — but we had no reason to believe it to be true.

Q: On January 23, 2003, your law firm, on behalf of XYZ Corp., received our request for production of all reports or documents?

A: We did get that request.

Q: Our request for production of documents called for a great many things including any document showing any potential witnesses to any possible chemical dumping by XYZ Corp.?

A: We did get that request.

Q: In response to our demand for documents, XYZ sent us some documents?

A: A great many documents as I recall.

Q: There was one document in particular you didn't send us — Exhibit 42, the investigative memo showing the names of the three XYZ employees who said they witnessed the illegal dumping of chemicals on XYZ land?

A: That was not disclosed.

Throughout this entire chapter no crying is heard. What has changed the demeanor of the (hostile) witness? The cross-examiner's tone is neutral. There is no pointed allegation against this witness. The witness is not branded a cheater. The facts are simply stated and the jurors are left to apply their own label to the conduct.

In addition, the phrasing of the questions is neutral. The questioning is about actions taken by or on behalf of XYZ Corp., not the actions taken by this individual lawyer. If the witness is likely to draw any favorable reactions from the fact finder, there is no benefit in trying to personalize the wrongful conduct to this witness. This lesson holds true in all types of litigation. The individual witness need not be blamed, so long as the blame comes to rest on the opposing party. Here, there is no need to personalize the blame with this witness, so long as the fact finder understands that the opposing party is to blame.

Finally, the cross-examiner attaches no judgment or conclusion to the facts. The cross-examiner has avoided any emotion-producing "summation" form of questions such as "So, you knew . . ." or "So, you intentionally . . . ." Such a summation of the evidence is unnecessary. The power lies in the recitation of the facts. The jury will appreciate that they are not being called upon to pass personal judgment on a witness that they might like or for whom they might feel sympathy. Instead, they are only asked to appreciate the factual significance of the facts that the evidence existed, the evidence was requested, and the evidence was not turned over. In context, the jury also understands that without benefit of this critical document, it was unlikely the plaintiffs would ever discover the most important eyewitnesses in the case. And the cross-examiner intentionally bypassed the emotional component of the situation and thereby diffused what could have been highly emotional witness. The cross-examiner asked for facts, not for feelings. She cross-examined on the conduct engaged in, not the character of the witness.

§ 28.18   Take the Witness Out of the Mood That Provokes the Crying

Every case generates a dominant emotion. It has been said in chapter 2, *Developing a Theory of the Case*, that the dominant emotion must be identified and utilized to ideally develop a theory of the case. As a corollary, for the lawyer to be most effective when cross-examining emotional witnesses, the cross-examiner should strive to take the witness out of the emotional mood that causes that witness to experience a highly emotional memory. Examples have been given on how to take the witness out of the mood by focusing on "out of chronology," "out of physical surroundings," or "out of the overall personal relationship."

The essential element of controlling the potentially emotional witness is to take the witness away from the emotional mood by very focused questioning in the areas in which cross-examination is required (i.e., the development of tight chapters), and careful phrasing of the questions that will move the witness away from the emotional context of the case. The cross-examiner must question with specific hard-edged facts that do not lend themselves to emotional generalizations by the witness about those facts.

In confronting the emotion-prone witness, the cross-examiner must strive for detail. "He never hurt you?" may seem like a factual question (the cross-examiner meant physically), but it invites broad and unpredictable response:

- "He hurt my dignity."

- "He hurt my feelings."

- "He beat me up physically and psychologically."

This causes emotions to fly. It would be better to ask:

- "He never pushed you?"

- "He never slapped you?"

- "He never kicked you?"

Or, even better:

- "You were not pushed?"

- "You were not slapped?"

- "You were not kicked?"

While "hurt" is subjective, "slap," "kick," and "push" are much more objective. They are more detailed. By selecting words with more precise definitions, the cross-examiner hems in the witness to a narrower range of likely responses. Simultaneously, the cross-examiner lessens the likelihood of dredging up emotions related to the entire upsetting experience by focusing the witness on very particular factual issues.

The phrasing of leading questions dependent on such hard-edged facts narrows the range of responses. It forces the witness either to answer within the commonly accepted meaning of the fact, or to lose credibility by stretching the fact to an unrealistic level in order to give an emotional response.

In another example, the cross-examiner may ask the eye witness/victim of an armed robbery, "You were *upset* during the armed robbery?" The cross-examiner is trying to establish a mood in which misidentification was likely. Because "upset" is a generality — really a combination of generality and conclusion (see chapter 8, *The Only Three Rules of Cross-Examination*), the witness is permitted great latitude in feeling a range of emotions when asked the question. This wide latitude allows room for feeling any one of several emotions that may cause crying, i.e., fear, anger, guilt for feeling fearful. On the other hand, the witness may be asked, "You were frightened during the armed robbery?" While "frightened" may also be a subjective term, it eliminates the much wider latitude of responses offered by the word "upset." When dealing with emotional issues, the cross-examiner must be especially vigilant in question and word selection in order to offer the narrowest and least emotion-laden facts.

§ 28.19   Fact Mastery — A Good Byproduct of Word Selection

There is a useful byproduct of carefully crafted questions based on hard-edged facts. The witness and the fact finder come to understand that the cross-examiner has a thorough understanding of the facts of the case. Of course, in a perfect world, each cross-examiner in each case does have a thorough understanding of all of the facts of the case. Alas, trial work is never a perfect world.

In order to discourage the witness from testing the bounds of the cross-examiner's knowledge of the facts, the cross-examiner must be especially precise in questioning on the facts the cross-examiner has mastered (see chapter 8, *The Only Three Rules of Cross-Examination*). When the cross-examiner shows a mastery of the facts of a specific area of the case, a signal goes out to the witness, and to the judge and jury, that the cross-examiner has added credibility to other aspects of the case. When leading questions in a particular area (chapters of cross-examination) demonstrate that the cross-examiner knows the critical facts in minute detail, the witness discovers that details can be "learned" from the cross-examiner's questions and he must therefore listen and follow each question carefully. This continuous process of asking the witness detailed questions takes away his ability to predict and prepare for the likely upcoming areas of the cross-examination, which often initiates an emotional reaction. By depriving the witness of the "work ahead time," the lawyer removes one of the initiators of the emotional response.

§28.20 Use Detailed Chapters Preceding and Following an Emotional Chapter

Certain chapters in cross-examination must be performed by the cross-examiner even though the cross-examiner realizes ahead of time that those chapters are emotionally laden. Human experience teaches us that *most* highly emotional outbursts do not just "happen out of the blue." Instead, the emotional response ramps up and is progressive. That is, once the witness begins to feel emotional, their response becomes more emotional as the emotional matter remains under consideration. By preceding an emotionally laden chapter with a chapter heavy in non-emotional, hard-edged details, the witness is diverted from thinking ahead to emotionally issues. The witness is required to think objectively and non-emotionally.

It is best that these preceding, hard-edged, non-emotional chapters have an independent value to the cross-examiner. The detailed facts within those chapters enable the cross-examiner to move through valuable material unencumbered by the crying likely to begin when the witness concentrates on the emotional chapter.

Once the emotional chapter has been concluded, a chapter to immediately follow the emotion-laden chapter with hard-edged detailed fact takes the witness out of the emotional frame of mind. At best, this transferring of the witness's mind set from non-emotional to emotional to non-emotional, leaves the fact finder with a question as to the sincerity of the emotion expressed. At worse for the cross-examiner, it mitigates and confines the emotional aspects of the testimony.

§28.21 Example of Detail Chapter Preceding Emotional Chapter

In a criminal trial, a prosecution witness was questioned about a drug transaction that ultimately resulted in the death of her boyfriend. Her boyfriend was killed in Atlanta, Georgia, after he and the witness flew from Las Vegas to Atlanta to conclude a drug transaction. During the direct testimony, the witness began to whimper when the prosecutor began questioning her about the flight from Las Vegas to Atlanta (apparently in response to her memory of the brutal slaying of her boyfriend in Atlanta).

In support of the cross-examiner's theory of the case, assume that it was necessary to inquire into the details of the drug transaction in Atlanta. This was obviously an area likely to produce crying. In an effort to distract the witness from the upcoming area of questioning, the cross-examiner first developed a series of questions about the flight from Las Vegas to Atlanta, forcing the witness to focus on details. This focusing prevented the witness from crying or showing any emotion during this chapter on the flight. This approach, in and of itself, produced a difference between the witness's emotional outburst on direct examination and her far less emotional responses on cross-examination.

In addition, by focusing the witness on details, the cross-examiner succeeded in tempering the witness's emotion as well as delaying and mitigating the emotion produced when discussing the drug transaction in Atlanta:

Q: You have told us that you flew from Las Vegas to Atlanta?

A: Yes.

Q: You flew on Delta Airlines?

A: Yes.

Q: Your ticket was purchased in your own name?

A: Yes.

Q: You had checked in alone?

A: Yes.

Q: You carried your baggage on board?

A: Yes.

Q: You were in seat 16B?

A: I'm not sure.

Q: It was a middle seat?

A: Yes.

Q: It was a seat far from where Mr. Patterson (the boyfriend) was seated?

A: Yes.

Q: Mr. Patterson was near the rear of the plane?

A: Yes, I think so.

Q: You landed in Atlanta at 1:32 p.m.?

A: Around 1:30.

The facts of this chapter are not of great factual importance. However, the chapter has psychological value. First, it grounds the witness in a rather clinical setting, entirely avoiding emotion-laden images. Next, the witness has learned that the cross-examiner has solidly researched details of the case. The physical appearance of the witness changed as she concentrated on the details of the flight. She presented a stronger posture and spoke in a firmer voice. She answered with facts that are certain and have no great emotional content. The witness adopted a studious demeanor as she concentrated on the significance of these facts. She did not understand the significance of seat 16B, but thought of that information rather than the slaying of her boyfriend several hours after landing in Atlanta.

By preceding emotion-laden chapters with chapters heavy in non-emotional details, the witness is diverted from thinking emotionally. If, in addition, these earlier chapters have independent value to the cross-examiner, then the added detail within them enables the cross-examiner to move through the valuable material unencumbered by the crying likely to begin when the witness concentrates on the upcoming emotional chapters.

In the example, the cross-examiner robs the girlfriend of time to emotionally reflect on the death facts by using a non-emotional, factually-detailed chapter.

§ 28.22 Hard-Edged Facts — Defined

Hard-edged facts are facts capable of being examined upon with precision. They are objectively verifiable and not dependent on the individual witness's subjective interpretation of a word or situation. When working to suppress emotional breakdowns, it is helpful to require the witness to answer questions based on hard-edged facts.

§ 28.23 Hard-Edged Facts and Emotion

[1] Dates

A witness will find it more difficult to become emotional when answering questions based on the hard-edged facts. It would be an overstatement to suggest that hard-edged facts preclude emotionalism, as the facts themselves may be emotion-laden (e.g., you saw three knife wounds in your husband's back). Hard-edged detailed facts assist in the control, but are not a universal salvation.

In a divorce case, the seemingly innocuous question, "You were married for twenty years?" may well lead to a tearful response. Why? The question fails to confine the witness to a particular factual setting, instead inviting the witness to generalize on innumerable memories of a twenty-year marriage, many of them emotion-laden.

On the other hand, the witness may be safely asked, "On the 9th day of July, 1983, you were married?" The hard-edged fact sought in that question focuses the witness to a particular date and offers a lesser degree of latitude for the witness's memory to wander.

[2] Hours and Minutes

In a personal injury case, the collision occurred on December 27, 2001. When asking about the collision, defense counsel is entering into an emotion-laden area. If the witness is asked if the collision occurred shortly after Christmas, a great deal of mental latitude is given by the question. If the specific date is asked, less latitude is given. Better if the question is phrased, "The collision occurred at 9:37 a.m. on the 27th day of December, 2001?" Less mental wandering is permitted.

Most witnesses are immediately defensive about exact times. This is true even though the exact time may well be undisputed. Inevitably, the witness responds, "About that time." This defensiveness aids the cross-examiner. The witness, who is reflecting defensively about the exactness of the question, has less latitude to reflect on emotional aspects of the general scenario.

[3]   Distances/Measurements

In a physical assault case in which the theory of defense is that the witness was too far away to accurately observe the identity of the initial aggressor, it is important for the cross-examiner to establish that the witness was far from the initial action. The witness is given too much emotional latitude by phrasing the question, "You were pretty far away?" Less latitude occurs with the question, "You were 57.5 feet away?" The witness may not know the exact measurement, but the question indicates that the cross-examiner does. Therefore the witness becomes somewhat defensive. Since the cross-examiner knows more detailed facts than the witness, the witness reflects less on the emotion associated with that fight, no matter how far away he was.

[4]   Proper Names and Titles

In a personal injury case, defense counsel noted during the deposition that whenever the parent of the injured child was asked about the physical therapy performed on the minor child, she became tearful. The sincere tearfulness was apparently caused by the parent's reflection on the pain that the minor child experienced every time physical therapy was necessary. Cross-examination was necessary because the physical therapy facts showed full range of motion at multiple sessions. The therapist was out of the country serving in the Middle East. By introducing the chapter on physical therapy with more detailed, hard-edged facts, much of the emotion could be taken out of the parent's responses concerning the physical therapy sessions.

The chapter begins:

Q: The physical therapist's name was Linda T. King-Lopez?

A: Yes, that was her name.

Q: She was a professional physical therapist, registered by the State of California?

A: I am sure that she was.

Q: Linda T. King-Lopez was also certified as a vocational rehabilitation therapist?

A: Yes.

Q: Therapist King-Lopez performed twelve sessions of physical therapy?

A: Yes.

Q: Therapist King-Lopez drew up a specific plan for each session?

A: Yes.

[5] Addresses

Just as in the simple use of a formal name and title, use of an exact address causes the witness to concentrate on the specific hard-edged facts of the question rather than any emotion associated with the question. The cross-examiner could ask, "The shooting occurred on Fourth Street?" or the question could be rephrased more specifically as: "The shooting occurred on the corner of Central and Fourth Street?" Answer: "Yes."

It would be better to ask, "It happened in front of 428 Fourth Street?" Answer: "Yes." In this example, the witness must concentrate on the specific facts requested. If the witness does not know those specific facts, so much the better as the witness must concentrate on those hard-edged facts in the hope of dredging up the correct address from memory.

[6] Defensive/Non-Inflammatory Facts

It must be understood that detailed hard-edged facts need not be non-inflammatory. Often cross-examination must be conducted in an area that is inherently emotionally inflammatory to the witness. The cross-examiner cannot and need not avoid highly emotional areas. The cross-examiner should infuse detailed hard-edged facts in a manner that causes the witness to concentrate on the hard-edged facts rather than on the inflammatory nature of the chapter. An added benefit is that the hard-edged facts may well make the witness defensive. A defensive witness cannot cry as readily as a witness relaxed with the facts.

Example:

In a murder case where the defense is self-defense, defense counsel wishes to point out that the weapon used was brought to the home by the sister of the deceased, who witnessed the shooting. The wife of the deceased was the shooter. There was "bad blood" between the wife of the deceased and his sister before the shooting. The sister of the deceased is now subject to cross-examination. She is hysterical with anger and sorrow over the shooting death of her brother.

The defendant used a gun taken from the purse of the sister of the deceased. The sister of the deceased is very defensive about this. (The witness is wailing. The judge has already taken one break, but before the cross-examiner can ask the first question, the wailing begins again.)

The cross-examiner, without taking his eyes from the witness, stands still and waits for the wailing to recede.

Q: The gun used to shoot your brother was a .38?

A: Yes. (The wailing starts to pick up steam.)

Q: You owned that gun?

A: Yes. (The wailing starts to become quieter, but anger is dripping from the answer.)

Q: You had bought this gun six years ago?

A: You had bought it for your own protection?

Q: It was for your defense?

A: That's right.

Q: It was what you called your "little protector"?

A: Yes.

Q: You called it that?

A: Yes.

Q: Your 'little protector' that you used for self-protection?

A: Yes. Protection. My protection. (Now there is almost hysterical anger in the answer, but no crying.)

§ 28.24   Emotional Consequences to the "I Don't Know" or "I Don't Remember" Witness

When following this analysis, some lawyers may reflect that when witnesses are questioned with detailed hard-edged facts, the "easy out" for the witness is to say, "I don't know" or "I don't remember" (see chapter 20, *Dealing with the "I Don't Know" or "I Don't Remember" Witness*). On deeper reflection, the cross-examiner is aided by these dodges.

By saying "I don't know" or "I don't remember" repeatedly, the witness is made defensive. Evasive answers themselves steer the witness away from the emotion of the chapter. This is a positive development for the cross-examiner, not a negative development, and one that should be exploited in order to deter emotional/crying responses in the witness.

In a personal injury case where a minor child was severely injured by a collision that occurred between the pickup truck in which she was riding as a passenger and a locomotive, the parent of the minor child was questioned as follows:

Q: The distance from the warning light to the intersection was 46 feet?

A: I don't know exactly how far.

Q: You know it is more than four car lengths?

A: About . . . I don't know for sure.

Q: The train whistle blew 3.5 seconds before the train entered the intersection with the road?

A: I'm not sure.

Q: It blew when you were more than 50 feet away from the tracks?

A: About . . . I don't know exactly.

Q: At your speed, it took 3.5 seconds to travel that distance?

A: Something like that . . .

Q: The locomotive had a halogen-energized headlight?

A: I don't know.

Q: It was bright?

A: I guess.

Q: The light shone more than 250 feet out in front of the locomotive?

A: I don't really know.

(No apparent emotion shown by the parent of the minor child injured by the collision at this point.)

§ 28.25   Specific Techniques to Control Crying

As pointed out earlier in this chapter, exhibits and demonstrative evidence are helpful in controlling the crying witness. In order to use these specific techniques to their optimum potential, pre-trial consideration preparation of the "props" is advised. Exhibits and demonstrative evidence require the witness to be stimulated by more than just questions that they hear. Exhibits and demonstrative evidence require the witness to use his eyes. When a witness is stimulated not only by having to listen, but also by having to observe, the witness must concentrate to a greater degree. This concentration suppresses the ability to cry at the same time.

The common theme of these techniques is the requirement that the witness shift concentration to something other than the emotion that the witness may be feeling. The more concentration required, the less emotional latitude the witness has in feeling and manifesting the emotion.

§ 28.26   Impeachments with Documents

Impeachments are wonderful things. They are to be polished, saved, and spent like small gems. Impeachment with documents is effective in stopping the crying witness. Because of this, such impeachment chapters (even small impeachments) must be carefully stored and utilized when necessary to control the crying witness.

The following example comes from a divorce case:

Q: Both of you agreed that he was going to move out?

A: Yes.

Q: You decided, you knew in your own mind that the marriage as man and wife was over?

A: No. I told him that if he would remain in therapy, get therapy on his own . . . (The witness begins to cry loudly).

After what seems like minutes, but is in reality approximately thirty to forty seconds, opposing counsel obtains permission from the court to offer a drink of water to the witness. The witness composes herself somewhat and is now whimpering with the ever-present hankie close at hand dabbing her eyes. During this entire time, the cross-examiner has not moved. The cross-examiner has not taken his eyes from the witness. The witness has on several occasions snatched glimpses at the cross-examiner to see if he is still looking at the witness. The cross-examiner is not staring in a menacing or aggressive manner, but is looking without distraction at the witness and, when the witness looks up, into the eyes of the witness.)

Q: Please look at your deposition transcript, page 36, line 15, ma'am.

A: I am sorry. I don't have a copy.

Q: Here is a copy of that particular page. I asked you this series of questions starting at line 15.

Q: But once he moved out, you really never thought you would reconcile as husband and wife?

A: I hoped that we could come back together as friends, but I wanted to go through with everything first.

Q: I understand about the "friends" part, ma'am, but as man and wife, you didn't feel . . .

A: I wasn't . . . no, I wasn't closed to anything.

Q: But you wanted to go through with the divorce?

A: Yes.

Q: You wanted to go through with the divorce?

A: Yes.

Q: Even if both of you got into therapy, you wanted to go through with the divorce?

A: Yes.

Q: Those were the questions and answers given?

A: I'm sorry, I didn't understand your original question. I was upset.

Q: The question was and is: You *were* going to get a divorce once your husband moved out?

A: Yes. (The whimpering has completely stopped now.)

This impeachment has been accomplished without the use of aggressive force, ridicule, or implication that the witness has intentionally changed her testimony at trial. But the crying stopped. Why? First, the witness was required to concentrate on the process of impeachment in which the previous answers were read back. This required the witness to mentally project back to the deposition. The deposition is unlikely to provoke an emotional reaction. At most, the feeling the witness must associate with her deposition is her apprehension at going to the deposition. That remembered sense of apprehension coupled with her slight change in testimony made the witness even more defensive, which assisted in stopping the crying. Second, the witness had to look at, if not read the document handed to him.

§ 28.27 Any Impeachment Requires the Attention of the Witness

The use of any document in aid of any impeachment requires the witness to concentrate on the document and is effective to help suppress emotional reactions. An impeachment based on the witness's own words (prior testimony) is most effective in stopping the emotions as it produces an overlay of defensiveness as to what the witness has previously said. There is a transfer of the witness's concentration from the present date and time to the date and time of the previous testimony.

§ 28.28 Make the Witness Use His Eyes

[1] The Use of Charts or Other Blowups to Draw Concentration

Many cases have a document, a photograph, or a piece of physical evidence that can be converted into a diagram, chart, or blowup. This allows the cross-examiner the opportunity to create demonstrative aids to be used as a "stopper" to a crying witness. If a witness must focus attention on a demonstrative aid because the witness knows that the fact finder (judge or jury) can also see that chart or blowup. The witness must concentrate on the demonstrative aid or appear to look uninterested or stupid in front of the fact finder. This will encourage the witness to stop whimpering or crying.

In the first example below, the cross-examiner improperly begins the chapter with a very broad question inviting a subjective and the emotional response:

Example 1:

Q: The fact is that you have enough money to support yourself?

A: No. No, I cannot make it. (The witness's voice is raised and shrill. The witness is beginning to whimper again.)

Using the techniques previously discussed, change the example to a questioning involving hard-edged or objective facts, coupled with the use of a demonstrative aid.

Example 2:

Q: Mr. Smith, you are familiar with your financial condition?

A: Generally.

Q: You have previously provided us with a summary of your financial records for the last year?

A: Yes.

Q: You have done that in the form of a sworn financial affidavit?

A: Yes. I have.

Q: Sir, let's look at this chart, which is a blowup of your financial affidavit.

A: Where is it?

Q: I am putting it on the easel now. It is fair to say that you are claiming $2,600 in expenses today?

A: I think so. Yes, I see it there. Yes. (The whimpering begins to taper off.)

Q: Of that $2,600, $540 is for medically related expenses?

A: I guess that is what it adds up to.

Q: Of that $540 a month in medical expenses, $200 a month is in prescriptions?

A: Yes.

Q: $100 a month in doctor bills?

A: Yes.

Q: And you are claiming $240 a month in physical therapist visits?

A: Yes.

Q: This adds up to $540?

A: Yes. (The whimpering has stopped completely as the witness continues to stare at the chart while silently doing the mathematical calculations.)

[2] Use of Documents to Focus the Witness on Less Emotional Material

When the cross-examiner places a document before a witness, that process requires the witness to use his or her eyes. Documents are always an adjunct to a pending question or line of questions. Of course, the witness must concentrate on the question itself. When a document is added to the cross-examination, the witness is called upon to divide her concentration between the document and the question relating to the document. The question calls for auditory concentration, while the document calls for visual concentration. The simultaneous use of the two senses diminishes the ability of the witness to remain in the emotional moment likely to produce a crying response.

The following occurred after the witness had tearfully explained why she had to go to Greenleaf, a psychiatric hospital, for an extended stay. The plaintiff's claim was that the stress of her job duties required her to be hospitalized for psychiatric care. The witness appeared emotional throughout her testimony:

Q: My question was, after you got out of Greenleaf Rehabilitation Center, you continued to drink?

A: Yes.

Q: And you continued to spend more than 10% of your take-home pay on alcohol, did you not?

A: (No response.) (The witness refuses to make eye contact and again begins to whimper more loudly.)

Q: You spent more than 10% of your take-home pay on alcohol?

A: I don't know if that is true. (The voice is trembling and the whimpering has increased.)

Q: Your take-home pay was $1,600 every two weeks?

A: Yes, I believe so.

Q: That is $3,200 a month?

A: Yes, about that much.

Q: You were released from Greenleaf Rehabilitation Center on October 10, 2001?

A: I believe so.

Q: Please look at check number 764.

A: That is my signature.

Q: I have marked this check as defense Exhibit 14.

A: Okay.

(Introduction of Exhibit 14)

Q: It's your check of November 9, 2001, to the Wagon Wheel Liquor Store?

A: Yes. (The whimpering begins to recede markedly.)

Q: You signed that check?

A: Yes.

Q: It was for $222.89?

A: Yes.

Q: You spent this money for alcohol?

A: Yes. (The whimpering stops completely.)

Q: Let me show you another one of your checks marked defense Exhibit 15.

A: Okay.

Q: Exhibit 15 is your check number 799 dated November 20, 2001?

A: Yes.

(Introduction of Exhibit 15)

Q: It is your signature on defense Exhibit 15, a check you signed to the Wagon Wheel for more liquor?

A: Yes.

Q: This time you wrote a check for $178.38?

A: Yes.

[3] Documents Containing the Signature of the Witness

Documents that show the witness's signature, no matter how benign, capture the witness's attention more than documents that the witness has not signed. Similarly, documents or exhibits that the witness has authored, also capture the witness's concentration to a much greater degree. In both instances, the witness understands that he bears personal responsibility for the document. As a result, his attention is more closely focused on its contents. Once the cross-examiner makes it clear that she will use a document authored by the witness, the witness very much wants to survey the document. Using this technique is likely to capture the attention and concentration of a witness and thus diminishes the likelihood of an emotional response.

[4] Surrogate Documents

When the cross-examiner is faced with a scarcity of documents or possible demonstrative exhibits, a blank document that has applicability to the case may sometimes be used. This "non-document," surrogate document, or exhibit containing blanks not filled in may help control the crying witness.

In a products liability case, the insurance defense attorney is faced with a plaintiff who arouses sympathy and who is willing to cry about his inability to obtain employment:

Q: Your position eleven months ago was that you are unable to work?

A: I am unable to work. I still am unable to work. I can't work. (Sob) (Sob) Look at my hands. (Author's Note: When the court reporter starts to put "witness sobbing" or "witness crying" into the record, the whimpering is approaching the wailing limit and is having an emotional impact on the courtroom.)

Q: There is no physical infirmity that stops you from working, is there?

A: No there isn't. Physically I can walk around. (The whimpering continues.)

Q: Your position is that your mental health counselor has not ordered you back to work and therefore you are not going to try to go to work?

A: My counselor doesn't have to release me to go to work. I am in this body. I know how I feel. (The sobbing and whimpering becomes more pronounced.)

Q: You have not tried any jobs in the last twenty months?

A: I don't believe anyone would hire me. (The sobbing increases.) I have an emotionally disturbed mind. (More whimpering.)

Q: You could have gone to the Labor Department?

A: Yes, but there was no reason.

Q: You could have completed this Labor Department Form LD-1?

A: I could have, but nobody would hire me anyway.

Q: This form is a form to apply for any available job?

A: I am not sure (witness pauses). Yes, I see.

Q: There is a place on the form for your name?

A: Yes.

Q: There is a place for your address?

A: Yes.

Q: There is a place for your medical history?

A: Yes.

Q: You have not completed this form?

A: No.

Q: You have not given your name?

A: No.

Q: You have not given your address?

A: No.

Q: You have not given your medical history?

A: No. (The questioning on this "non-document" continues until the whimpering is eliminated completely.)

§ 28.29 Physical Evidence

When a cross-examiner presents to a witness a piece of physical evidence, the likely response is studied concentration of the exhibit. Care must be taken that the exhibit itself does not produce a highly emotional response. In other words, in a wrongful death case, presenting the plaintiff family with their child's yearbooks is very likely to draw the unwanted emotional response. The physical evidence technique calls for the cross-examiner to make use of emotionally-neutral items of evidence.

The plaintiff's lawyer is cross-examining the defendant in a personal injury case. The defendant has tearfully and effectively denied responsibility for the collision. The tears that the defendant is shedding have been effectively described as tears concerning the injuries to the plaintiff, even though the defendant contends the plaintiff caused the collision through her own negligence.

Example:

(The defendant continues to whimper.)

Q: I hand you now what has been marked as Plaintiff's Exhibit 4, which is a piece of your car.

A: Yes, I saw this at the deposition.

Q: That's a piece of the headlight rim from your car?

A: Yes. (Whimpering tapers off.)

Q: Please examine it to make sure that this is your headlight rim.

A: Yes, I see it. It looks like the one that I saw before.

Q: It's a rim from a '92 Taurus?

A: Yes. (No crying.)

Q: That rim was located over one hundred yards away from where your car hit the other car?

A: I don't know exactly how far, but it was across the street and down the road a ways. (No crying or whimpering.)

The plaintiff's lawyer has eliminated the whimpering, but also proven that the collision was such that pieces of the car flew more than one hundred yards down the road.

§ 28.30   Causing the Witness to Focus on Sounds

All that can be said for making the witness concentrate visually on charts, blowups, documents, non-documents, or physical evidence can also be said for making the witness concentrate on sounds. Tape recordings are an excellent way to cause the witness to stop whimpering and sobbing. The witness must concentrate on the tape recording because it cannot be heard if he is whimpering and sobbing (particularly if the tape recording is played at a regular speaking level volume and not higher). The best recording is that of the witness's own voice. No one likes to hear his recorded voice. That alone produces defensiveness in the witness.

§ 28.31   Causing the Witness to Use Their Eyes and Their Ears

Videotapes and DVDs have changed the way trials are conducted. They are being used with increasing frequency in both civil and criminal trials, and in all forms of alternative dispute resolution forms. If making the witness concentrate visually is effective and if making the witness concentrate through sound is effective, then making the witness concentrate through sight and sound is even more effective in controlling the whimpering witness.

Just as documents that have been authored or signed by the witness capture the witness's most concentrated attention, exhibits and demonstrative evidence that include the voice and the image of the witness capture the concentration and attention of the witness like no other exhibit or demonstrative piece of evidence.

§28.32 Make the Witness Move

The need to perform physical tasks can impede crying. In most courtrooms, the witness box is elevated by at least one step. If the cross-examiner requires the witness to step down from the witness box to point to a chart, blowup, map, or chalkboard or to use any exhibit, the witness is forced to concentrate on physical tasks that will slow the flow of tears.

The mere movement out of the witness box requires the witness to concentrate. Whether whimpering or not, no one wants to embarrass himself or herself by falling down in front of others. The fear of embarrassment overrides the emotional display of whimpering.

Care must be taken not to appear unfair to the witness. A witness who is so out of control emotionally that he cannot reasonably be expected to engage in questioning should not be asked to step down and demonstrate anything. However, a witness who is under emotional control will preserve their self-control when asked to perform physical tasks that seem reasonable in the context of the questioning.

§28.33 Crying Leading to Excuse of Confusion

After a spell of legitimate crying, the witness will often further impede the cross-examination by alleging he is confused and does not understand the question. This excuse may be eliminated by requiring the witness to perform simple calculations.

Example:

A: I'm sorry, I am just confused. I don't understand what you are saying.

Q: Well, let's do the math. You claim expenses of $2,000?

A: Yes.

Q: If we subtract the house payment of $400 . . .

A: Yes.

Q: That would leave you with $1,600?

A: That's what the figures say. (At this point all whimpering and all confusion have stopped.)

Q: The numbers are correct, aren't they?

A: Yes, that's what the numbers add up to.

Q: And that's the truth?

A: Yes.

Questions requiring the witness to make simple calculations (basic addition and subtraction) can take the witness out of a state of claimed confusion.

§ 28.34   Insincere Crying

This chapter has discussed techniques to analyze and control the crying witness. Throughout, the assumption has been that the crying was sincere. The cross-examiner should always treat the crying witness as a sincere crying witness until the fact finder (jury or judge) has, through non-verbal communication, expressed to the cross-examiner that the fact finder has concluded that the crying is insincere. Even if the cross-examiner has concluded that the crying witness is insincere, it is not enough reason to change the cross-examiner's demeanor from neutrality to hostility. It is the likely perception of the fact finder that must be considered. Only in those rare cases where it is virtually certain that the fact finder has concluded that the crying is insincere, may the cross-examiner treat the crying as insincere. Only at that point, may the cross-examiner treat the crying conduct with any measure of disdain. Of course, if the fact finder has already concluded that the crying is insincere, the witness has already done grave damage to her credibility. In such circumstances, while it is tempting to show hostility or disdain, the safer course is to continue cross-examination with a relatively neutral tone and demeanor. The risk of offending the fact finder is so great, and the benefits of a change of voice and attitude are so small, the cross-examiner is well advised to treat all crying conduct as if it were genuine.

§ 28.35   Theory of the Case Enhanced by Crying

Thus far, it has been assumed that the cross-examiner's theory of the case would be enhanced by deterring the crying witness. However there are those times, those cases, and those theories of the case that are enhanced by a crying witness. By reversing the techniques shown in this chapter, the cross-examiner can cause the crying witness to become more emotional. Once the lessons are learned as to how to control the crying witness, certainly the lessons can be reversed to encourage the crying witness.

By reversing the techniques to encourage the witness to cry, the cross-examiner can achieve the desired result without using open-ended questions or daredevil risk-taking. For example, in a case where the defendant father is trying to show that the plaintiff mother is emotionally unstable to care for the minor children, it is to the cross-examiner's benefit to have the witness cry as often and as long as possible. The cross-examiner places the plaintiff mother mentally back into an emotional state, an emotional location, with emotional facts in an effort to have her cry in front of the fact finder:

Q: Ma'am, you were there when little Bobby got hit in the face with the baseball?

A: Yes, that was some six years ago.

Q: He did not receive any permanent damage?

A: No, but at the time we were afraid that he would lose his eye.

Q: You were there when the baseball was hit in his direction?

A: Yes.

Q: It was hit very hard?

A: Yes.

Q: He was not looking towards the ball?

A: No, he was very small. When children are that age, their attention span is not all that it should be. I know that he should have been paying more attention, but he wasn't. (The color of the mother's face is coming up to red. The speed of her breathing is picking up.)

Q: The person who hit the ball was bigger and stronger than Bobby?

A: Yes, he should have been paying attention. I know that it wasn't on purpose.

Q: The ball hit Bobby just above his left eye?

A: Yes. (A glazed look is settling over the mother's face.)

Q: You were right there on the side of the field, not thirty feet from Bobby?

A: Yes, I ran onto the field as soon as the ball hit him.

Q: Bobby dropped immediately onto his back?

A: Yes. (Whimpering now starts.) My first thought was that he was dead.

Q: You were the first one there?

A: Yes. He looked so small. (Crying begins now in earnest.)

By now moving directly into a more recent episode with the minor children that is less emotion-provoking, the cross-examiner can keep the crying witness in an emotional state that is undue in relationship to the factual content of the next chapter of the cross-examination. The cross-examiner's theory is served.

§ 28.36   Silence — A Tool for the Lawyer

No trial lawyer looks forward to cross-examining an emotional or crying witness. There are however techniques that can be used effectively to mitigate or eliminate a substantial portion of the emotional testimony.

The cross-examiner cannot use these techniques unless that lawyer has gained control of her own emotions before attempting to control the emotions of the witness. Perhaps the best technique for gaining that control over the cross-examiner's self is the use of silence (see chapter 21, *Creation and Uses of Silence*). Just as the cross-examiner must be patient in weathering the emotional outburst of the witness, it is even more important that the cross-examiner be patient in obtaining control of herself. That silence will be effective in front of a fact finder under the conditions of a highly emotional witness.

§ 28.37   Selecting a Tone That Diminishes the Likelihood of an Emotional Response

The tone of the cross-examiner's voice can have a substantial influence on the emotional pitch of the cross-examination. A quiet, business-like recita-

tion of very damaging facts will produce a lower emotional level in the courtroom than an accusatory or harsh tone used to introduce the same facts. If a
cross-examiner wishes to diminish the likelihood of a crying response, or is
attempting to extinguish the crying conduct already occurring, it is wise to
underplay her tone, rather than to use tone of voice as a flag-planting device.

But why should the cross-examiner give up a very useful tool — tone of
voice — in conjunction with important cross-examination material? There are
two steps in the process of deciding whether to refrain from using a valid
change of tone of voice in conjunction with material likely to provoke a crying
response. First, the cross-examiner must determine whether this is the point
in the cross-examination where the witness is likely to react in a highly emotional state. Next, the cross-examiner should calculate whether the build-up
to this highly emotional chapter is so obvious that the fact finder can also see
that the material is likely to provoke a crying response. If both of these judgments appear to be true, then the material about to be covered does not need
any additional emphasis. The completely valid technique of using a different
tone of voice to highlight material is unnecessary when, in the judgment of the
cross-examiner, the material has already been highlighted for the fact finder's
attention.

That is not to say that the cross-examiner should refrain from using a more
insistent tone of voice with every chapter of cross-examination likely to produce an emotional response. For instance, in commercial cases it often occurs
that the corporate executives for a defendant company are angrily (the anger
is often as emotional as crying) insistent that their actions were appropriate and guided only by the best interests of the plaintiffs, whether they are
shareholders, or customers, or even the other employees. The cross-examiner
need not forsake the techniques of selecting an appropriate tone of voice for
critical questions merely because the executive is likely to react emotionally to
chapters pointing out the alleged misconduct. Cross-examination, in its very
nature, draws out emotional responses. It is not the goal of the cross-examiner
to perform a bland cross-examination to excite no one. The lawyer underplays
a tone of voice in cross-examination only when the cross-examiner consciously
determines that a more neutral tone will be a more helpful tone. This being
said, when the cross-examination centers on highly emotional chapters likely
to produce a crying response from the witness, and when the cross-examiner
would prefer not to produce that response or to cope with the crying response
if it occurs, the cross-examiner is advised to perform such chapters in a neutral tone so that the tone of voice will not add to the emotion implicit in the
material.

§ 28.38 Use of Admissions of a Party-Opponent in Lieu of Highly Emotional Chapters

It has been previously discussed concerning the admissions of a party-op-
ponent at trial in lieu of certain chapters of cross-examination. This technique
applies in the setting of the crying and emotional witness.

There are times that the cross-examiner calculates that the answers given by the witness within a deposition or within answers to interrogatories are about as good as the cross-examiner is likely to receive. The cross-examiner may also conclude that the same questions, or impeachment using these answers, will likely produce crying. Where the cross-examiner does not wish to contend with that emotional outburst, she may choose to use the deposition answers or interrogatory responses of a party opponent as admissions of a party opponent rather than as impeachment material and in lieu of asking the identical questions in trial. This is one of many factors the cross-examiner will consider.

Chapter 29

COPING WITH OBJECTIONS

SYNOPSIS

§ 29.01   The Problem — Objections

The more experienced the lawyer, the more the realization that the standard of admissibility is a very flexible one. Relevancy is almost always a discretionary call and very much depends on the parties' theory of the case and the court's appreciation of those theories (see chapter 2, *Developing a Theory of the Case*). What is collateral to the case versus what is plainly relevant often depends on the ability of the court to understand the significance of the evidence. In other words, the more the advocate can give context to a chapter, the more the trial court can recognize the importance and relevance of facts to the case being tried. Objections often stem from the fact that the opponent does not recognize, or does not wish to recognize, the context into which a chapter of material is offered.

A second area of likely objection is the purely technical: Does the evidence offered comply with the applicable Rules of Evidence? As a brief example, most trial lawyers believe they know hearsay when they hear it. However, most trial lawyers are not as well studied as they might be with regards to the exceptions to the rule against hearsay. For instance, the Federal Rules of Evidence give the lawyer twenty-two reasons to except the evidence from the hearsay rule to get the evidence in front of the ears and eyes of the jury. But if those are not good enough, a twenty-third exception, the discretionary "other" exception used in the discretion of the court, gives even more latitude.

At times when the cross-examiner is working in a chapter the context of which the opponent does not understand, the opponent may mistakenly believe or harbor a hope that the cross-examiner is working in an area that the court will rule out of bounds. The opponent's objection may be based on relevancy or based on the cross-examiner's alleged failure to comply with some applicable Rule of Evidence. Sometimes a judge, caught off guard, can fail to understand why a chapter may be relevant and therefore can mistakenly rule with the opponent. Alternatively, the judge may need further factual development within a chapter in order to understand that the Rules of Evidence permit the line of inquiry. In any event, the risk is that the cross-examiner could be cut off from a fruitful line of inquiry. It would be unfortunate and unprofessional for the cross-examiner to allow this to happen.

This book does not deal specifically with the subjects of the Rules of Evidence or the foundations necessary to introduce evidence. These subjects are a part of the techniques of cross-examination to lay evidence before a fact finder in such a way as to minimize objections and to maximize not only the admissibility, but also the understanding of the facts contained in the chapters. It is therefore critically important for the cross-examiner to find ethical, professional ways to follow desired lines of cross-examination. This chapter discusses techniques that allow a cross-examiner to avoid unnecessary objections, and to fairly meet objections, all with the purpose of allowing the lawyer to continue cross-examining in areas relevant to the theory of the case. More importantly, these techniques permit the lawyer to go on the offensive when an objection is made and to expand the depth and breadth of cross-examination.

§ 29.02　Objections Represent Distractions to Teaching

All objections are distractions to the cross-examiner's efforts to teach her theory of the case, as well as to efforts to expose the defects in the opponent's theory of the case. Each of the techniques discussed are designed to minimize the distraction by the objection and, where possible, to discourage further objections. In the rare instance when the cross-examiner is baiting an objection, the cross-examiner's purpose is to eliminate objections that might occur later in the cross-examination when more significant chapters will be developed. However, the cross-examiner must never lose sight of the fact that the purpose of cross-examination is to teach the judge and jury. The purpose is not to show the opponent that the cross-examiner knows the rules of evidence better, is quicker witted, or is more skilled in handling objections. The true purpose of trial is to obtain the best possible outcome, not to win a game of one-upsmanship with the opponent or witness.

Distractions are not helpful to the teaching process. However, when the listener becomes irritated by the distraction, the person causing the distraction (the opponent) becomes the object of the negative emotion. These are times to take advantage of the opponent's overuse or misuse of objections.

§29.03 Following the Only Three Rules of Cross-Examination Eliminates Many Objections

If the lawyer is adhering to *The Only Three Rules of Cross-Examination* (chapter 8), fewer questions will need to be rephrased due to the opponent's objections. By following these rules of leading questions and cross-examining in a logical progression to reach a specific goal, few "form" objections will be left for the opponent to make. Compound questions have been eliminated. Every question is leading. About all the cross-examiner needs to worry about is an argumentative, hearsay, relevancy, or foundation objection. Each of these objections is easily handled.

§29.04 Objections Based on "Argumentative"

"Argumentative" objections are most often made in two instances. The more common circumstance giving rise to this type of objection is the cross-examiner's body language, tone, and volume of the question during cross-examination. The best "teaching" cross-examinations do not rely on a loud voice, do not require aggressive body language, and do not resort to a sardonic or sarcastic tone. Each of these techniques, in its own way, is a distraction to the learning potential of the fact finder. The words that the cross-examiner selects in her question bring the power to the question, *not* these artificial devices. The techniques described in this book and in this chapter are designed to work better with a calm demeanor, a business like tone, and a less aggressive volume. While there are places for a change of tone, an appropriate gesture, even a sarcastic tone, such places are few and far between. Such techniques are best used sparingly.

The second most common reason for an "argumentative" objection is the word selection made by the cross-examiner or the request by the cross-examiner that the witness adopt the cross-examiner's conclusion. The cross-examiner should not view an "argumentative' objection to the word selection as a sanction, but rather as a positive response acknowledging the power of the word that the cross-examiner has selected.

With this said, the cross-examiner should willingly rephrase the question, not by eliminating the vivid word description, but by breaking the vivid word selection down so that it is more clear to the fact finder that the vivid word selection was originally appropriate. The goal is to achieve understanding, to create the picture and, to communicate the information. Seldom is the precise word chosen by the cross-examiner the only word that can accomplish those goals. Example:

Q: She had suffered a massive amount of blood loss at the scene?

Opp: Objection, argumentative as to the word "massive."

Q: Your honor, I will rephrase.

Judge: Fine, do so.

Q: When you arrived at the scene, you saw blood on the carpeted floor?

A: Yes.

Q: The blood was surrounding Ms. Magic?

A: Yes.

Q: The blood was matted in her hair?

A: Yes.

Q: The blood was still coming out of her shoulder area?

A: Yes.

Q: As a trained EMT, you attempted to stop the blood loss?

A: Yes.

Q: You did that by direct pressure?

A: Yes.

Q: It was not easy to do so?

A: No.

Q: It was not easy because everything was slippery with blood already pumping out of her shoulder?

A: Yes.

Q: It was arterial blood?

A: Yes. . . .

Whether the cross-examiner returns to the word "massive," originally thought offensive, is now immaterial. The cross-examiner has slid off the objection and has expanded the admissibility and the factual detail of the cross-examination based on the objection made by the opponent.

Whenever the cross-examiner hears an objection made on the grounds of "argumentative," the cross-examiner should hear that as an opportunity to be more factually descriptive and more factually detailed and precise. It is an advantage to the cross-examiner, rather than a disadvantage.

A second form of the second most common reason for an "argumentative" objection is an objection lodged to the cross-examiner's nonfactual conclusion obtained within a chapter. In other words, the cross-examiner requests that the witness adopt the cross-examiner's conclusion. For instance, having factually demonstrated that the plaintiff used the defendant's product in a way never intended, or in a manner that was clearly dangerous, defense counsel might try to add, "That was a pretty stupid thing to do, wasn't it?" While the jury may well be thinking the same thing, the objection "argumentative" is likely to be sustained. Defense counsel should have left well enough alone. The facts of the chapter were sufficient; the conclusion is for the jury to determine. Again, the cross-examiner's adherence to the only three rules of cross-examination makes such a nonfactual, conclusory statement unnecessary and counterproductive.

§ 29.05 Objections Based on "Hearsay"

The Rules of Evidence are beyond the parameters of this treatise, but suffice it to say that an objection based on "hearsay" also gives the cross-examiner opportunities to get into more rich, precise detail in explaining one of the twenty-three exceptions to the hearsay rule. It is not difficult for an advocate to spot where one of her chapters will likely draw a hearsay objection. Having foreseen the objection, the correct technique is to determine in advance the likely hearsay objection and establish the facts needed to overcome that objection before asking the leading question likely to produce the hearsay objection.

In other words, part of the chapter must be the facts that establish the exception to the hearsay rule. The sequencing of the questions to fit into an exception is critical to avoiding the objection or to overcoming the objection, if it is made. If done in the wrong order, the judge hears what sounds like a request for hearsay, followed by the appropriate hearsay objection. In this scenario, the court is likely to sustain the objection. In response, the cross-examiner will often try to establish the exception that permits the answer. But at this point, the cross-examiner is swimming upstream. Judges do not like reversing their positions. An objection once sustained is more likely to be renewed and again sustained. It is far more productive for the cross-examiner to anticipate the objection. Then carefully lay a factual groundwork for the exception so that the opponent must weigh whether to lodge the objection. In this order, the judge will have already heard the best argument for admissibility available to the cross-examiner before ruling on the objection.

§ 29.06 Objections Based on "Relevancy"

There are those chapters or questions the relevance of which cannot be doubted, regardless of the opponent's objection. When cross-examining counsel is completely confident of the relevance of a line of questioning, counsel should press ahead with the response and anticipate a correct ruling that permits the lawyer to continue with her line of questioning.

However, there are those chapters or questions the relevance of which may not be immediately apparent. The better technique is to establish context for the evidence in light of the cross-examiner's theory of the case. By far the most scientific approach to the problem is to give an opening statement that makes clear to the court the theory of the case. Once the court understands the theory of the case, the judge is equipped to immediately compare a chapter to that theory. Seeing a logical relationship will allow the court to deny the objection based on relevancy. In fact, many relevancy objections are really disguised objections for an opponent who is saying, "I don't see how this chapter matters." When the opponent can recognize the relationship of the chapter to the matters in dispute, fewer relevancy objections are made.

By way of example, if the lawsuit is about the act of a corporation taken in the year 2004, then, in the abstract, a conversation or event that took place several years before appears to lack relevance. The time separation of a few years alone works against the cross-examiner. However if the conversation or event is foreshadowed in the opening statement so that its relationship to the case can be explained, the court knows why this evidence is being introduced. Once again there is a heavy price paid by lawyers who want to keep secrets from the opponent in opening statement. A secret kept from the opponent is a secret kept from the judge, and a surprised judge cannot be counted on to make an informed decision on a disputed item of evidence. It is far better to make clear through the opening statement, or through other chapters, why a particular chapter has relevance to the theory of the case. Then, if the opponent lodges a relevancy objection, the court is in a far better position to appreciate the significance of the material sought to be introduced.

§ 29.07　Rule 1: Be Willing to Rephrase Objectionable Questions

There are those questions in cross-examination in which the ruling is much more in doubt. Counsel may well have phrased a question poorly or phrased a question in a way that invites objection. Rather than pitch the relevancy fight at the sound of the first objection, cross-examining counsel may be better off "sliding off" the objection by use of the technique of voluntarily rephrasing the question. To reiterate, relevancy is often a discretionary call for a judge. Thus, the willingness to rephrase places the judge in the position of wanting to permit the testimony into evidence, so long as the question may be more properly phrased.

Judges always allow lawyers to rephrase questions. It eliminates the need to rule. Experienced judges prefer not to rule if no ruling is necessary. They have learned that the fewer the number of evidentiary issues available for appeal, the fewer the evidentiary grounds for appeal.

For example, if the opponent objects, claiming irrelevance, and the cross-examiner believes additional facts will assist in establishing relevance, it is a far better technique to ask to rephrase rather than to attempt to make a speaking objection that tries to place before the judge the facts that supposedly establish relevance. In such a situation, the cross-examiner might say, "Mrs. Jones, let me rephrase that question." Alternatively, the advocate might address the problem in this way: "Your Honor, I wish to withdraw that question and lay a better factual foundation." Now the judge has even less reason to become involved in the cross-examination or to rule on the objection.

What is the judge going to do when the cross-examiner voluntarily and quickly offers to rephrase or to lay better foundation? The court is unlikely to say: "No, you cannot rephrase the question" or "No, I will not allow any further foundation."

By offering to rephrase the question, or to establish additional factual points that will moot the objection, the cross-examiner has made it clear that she is confident in her abilities to properly admit testimony. The cross-examiner thereby lowers the emotional level of the courtroom by assuring the judge that the cross-examiner is mindful of the rules and is attempting only to do what is permissible. The primary thrust of this technique is to remove the necessity for the court to rule. The cross-examiner should rephrase the question or withdraw that question until additional supportive facts have been introduced. Often the rephrasing of the question discourages the opponent from renewing his objection.

In these gray areas, it is often most helpful to the cross-examiner to use the rephrase technique before resorting to providing the court with a clear-cut answer to admissibility. If a relevancy objection to the rephrase question is renewed by the opponent, the subject area is still open for debate on the relevancy issue. In effect, the cross-examining counsel has created a second opportunity to offer the testimony into evidence. If there is no objection after the cross-examiner rephrases, then the evidence is in. If a second objection is made, the cross-examiner may now argue the admissibility of this area of facts.

There is a pleasant by-product to this technique. The judge normally will smile at the lawyer who quickly and voluntarily agrees to rephrase the question. Judges who smile at a lawyer seldom hurt that lawyer's case.

§ 29.08 Rule 2: Acknowledge the Correct Use of the Objection

Occasionally, the cross-examiner must privately admit that the opponent has made an appropriate objection. The cross-examiner should be willing to act on that private admission; it is the professional thing to do. Juries like it and so do judges. It shocks the opponent. Maybe it will cause the opponent to think he should concede points when he has done something objectionable. But don't count on it.

There are many ways to gracefully concede a valid objection. If the objection is to a question that could be better phrased or in any other way is objectionable, but can be made not objectionable, accept the ruling or make the ruling unnecessary by withdrawing the question and beginning again.

If, on the other hand, the objection is valid because the question in its current form is inadmissible, counsel may elect to discontinue trying to put into evidence that particular testimony but continue to press a similar, but admissible, line of questioning. The cross-examiner should return to this similar line of questioning and highlight its difference with some changes of wording or sentence structure.

Example:

Q: Dr. Moffitt, looking at Exhibit 17, the letter from Dr. Bloom to Dr. Hutt, would you agree that it warns Dr. Hutt of the patient's deteriorating condition?

Opp.:   Objection your honor — calls for speculation, and the document speaks for itself.

Q: That's correct — it may call for speculation. Let me ask you this, Dr. Moffitt: Isn't it true that your state of mind when you read Exhibit 17 was . . . .

It may be argued that it is the same question just worded differently. However, now it is not objectionable.

When continuing the line of questioning in this manner, question the witness in a matter-of-fact voice. Do not be exorbitant with gestures, voice, or attitude. The idea is to do it quickly, concisely, and in a business-like demeanor. The opponent is put back because the cross-examiner has placed her opponent in the jury's eyes as someone who has "interrupted." Every trial lawyer is sensitive to that characterization. By moving along in a matter-of-fact voice and by doing so without hesitation, the point is made. The similar line of questioning has continued. The jury will now become irritated if the witness is further interrupted or not permitted to answer.

Remember, there may be multiple ways to prove a fact. If a single question within any chapter draws a sustained objection, the chapter should not be abandoned. The cross-examiner should work around the problem and continue with the chapter. If an entire chapter is ruled inadmissible (likely on relevancy grounds), the cross-examiner should endeavor to determine whether there is another chapter available or a chapter which could be quickly assembled that establishes much of the same facts, or that leads to the important inferences that the cross-examiner hoped to accomplish with the inadmissible chapter. The advocate is reminded that objections are sustained to particular questions, seldom to entire areas of questioning. It is unwise and unnecessary to assume that a sustained objection as to a particular question means that the court will not permit any questioning in that area. Of course, if a judge has ruled in limine, or has ruled in trial that a particular area, event, or conversation is inadmissible, it is the duty of counsel to obey that ruling. Chapters that seek to get into forbidden areas by subterfuge must be avoided.

§ 29.09 Rule 3: Baiting the "Foundation" Objection

The technique of baiting the foundation objection should be used in the event the cross-examiner has a feisty opponent who attempts to object whenever possible. The cross-examiner must be sensitive to the fact that objections are a matter of tactics. A trial is not a law school examination in which spotting an objectionable question earns a point for the objecting party. Offering an opponent the opportunity to make an unnecessary "foundation" objection is also useful in a cross-examination that will contain numerous "gray areas" that must be developed later in the cross-examination.

Early in the cross-examination, ask at least one or two questions that require a foundation. As to each of these questions lay the foundation meticulously. Preferably, it should be done in such a way that the jury vaguely understands the ritualistic nature of foundation questions. Soon thereafter, pose leading questions to which the answer will be "yes." Deliberately remove all foundation questions to this line of questions. Go right for the jugular. Do not set up the foundation at all, despite the only three rules and chapter method.

When the objection comes, say a silent prayer of thanks and acknowledge it gracefully. Then use this response: "Your honor, I did shorten my questions. I will more fully establish the foundation."

Now slowly, meticulously, inch by inch, small fact by small fact, establish the foundation. Do not leave out any possible foundation material. Discomfort your opponent by questioning in meticulous detail. Once the opponent has been punished with this intentionally meticulous foundation material, the opponent will be far less likely to object on foundation grounds in the future. This then gives the cross-examiner tactical choices and advantages as to when and in how much detail to lay future foundations. No doubt the attentions of the judge and the jury have been captured by this interaction. Both recognize, because of the earlier full foundation questions, that cross-examining counsel knows how to perform the ritual. Because counsel has now completely and accurately laid the foundation for this question, judge and jury know that no deception was involved in this statement. And because the eventual leading question was answered "yes," they know that the cross-examiner was being impeded in route to a goal she could easily establish.

Under these circumstances, the perception is that it is the cross-examining counsel who is trying to "move it along," and it is the objecting counsel who is throwing up unnecessary roadblocks to the establishment of the truth. Having fully established the necessary foundation, move to the precise "bottom line" question to which your opponent objected. The opponent can no longer object.

The cross-examiner just taught the opponent that it is not wise to object when she is cross-examining. As gray areas are developed, the opponent is gun-shy of further objections, even if the objections are not as to foundation.

§ 29.10 Rule 4: Moving It Along

Opponent: Objection, this is cumulative.

Examiner: Your honor, I think I can move this along fairly rapidly.

When was the last time that a judge resented a lawyer trying to "move it along?" If the lawyer is in a gray area and the cross-examiner perceives that it permits the court to make a discretionary call, a pitched battle is probably undesirable. It is better to offer to pursue it briefly. Keep the promise. Move it along. Cut to the bottom line and then leave the area entirely. Once the court becomes acquainted with the idea that the cross-examiner knows that the trial must be moved along, the court is more likely to permit brief forays into possibly tangential areas. Because the matter is handled briefly, the judge often views the call as having gone both ways. Cross-examining counsel cannot complain that she was not permitted to delve into the area, yet the opponent's objection was recognized by limiting the cross-examiner on this issue. There is something for everybody — be satisfied with it. Make the point, *do not* try to go back and fill in the rest of the chapter. Move on and move into an area whose admissibility cannot be questioned (see chapter 11, *Sequences of Cross-Examination*). The court sustains objections much less often with this method. This is a fact of life. Those lawyers who police themselves best are least policed by others.

§ 29.11   Rule 5: "Your Honor, I'll Tie It Up"

Opponent: This is a collateral matter and should not be inquired into on cross-examination.

Examiner: Your Honor, I am about to tie it up.

Judges permit lawyers to "tie up evidence." Lawyers who are skilled in the art of tying up evidence get far more borderline evidence before the jury. Further, the lawyer who has been conducting goal-oriented cross-examinations has built up her credibility with the judge. One of the first added benefits of the chapter method of cross-examination (see chapter 9, *The Chapter Method of Cross-Examination*) is that it produces a series of questions that move toward resolution or clarification of a definable fact issue. A judge who understands that the cross-examiner consistently questions toward a goal is far more likely to permit questioning in a hazy area on the assumption that the cross-examiner knows where she is going and has a plan on how to get there. Since the cross-examiner has always tied matters up in the past, she will be permitted more latitude in "gray" areas of inquiry. Of course, the cross-examiner must always tie it up. Never promise without clearly delivering on the promise.

If the lawyer has given a theory-driven, fact-intensive opening statement, this response is needed less often. That opening statement occurred because the advocate understood that the chapter's fact would be performed in order to support the theory of the case. Now the cross-examination is occurring through the chapter method. There are no one-question chapters. Every chapter establishes the factual context in which a leading question is asked. As a result, there are fewer occasions when a lawyer needs to reassure the court that she can "tie it up." More often the court understands how the desired testimony is tied to the theory of the case and to the chapter in which it is being asked.

§ 29.12   Rule 6: Tie It Up, Then Go Back

Opponent: This is a collateral matter and should not be inquired into on cross-examination.

Examiner: Your Honor, I am about to tie it up.

When confronted with this objection, do not meander toward the goal and do not speak in parenthetical points. If there is a reasonable risk that the court has lost patience with this line of inquiry or is on the fence concerning its admissibility, sacrifice greater context for admissibility. Everything but the essence should be eliminated. Cut to the bottom line and establish the goal-fact.

This is not to say that the lawyer must overlook forever the remainder of the prepared chapter and fail to give the jury the entire unabridged cross-examination of this line of questioning in due time. What this means is that the lawyer must incisively cut to the bottom question that will tie it up. Once the court has been shown that the subject can be tied up, the lawyer can properly return to that interrupted line of questioning. By establishing a bottom-line point for the court, the examiner has satisfied herself and the court that the evidence is subject to being tied up. The lawyer can now safely return to her line of questioning, to the question that was first objected to by the opponent, and pick up where the objection first interrupted the chapter.

Using this technique, the judge knows that the examiner has returned to where she was interrupted. More importantly, the jury knows. Perhaps most importantly, your opponent now understands that objections such as this will not distract the cross-examiner. Establish the point quickly and then returning to where the objection first began. By giving the jury the entire unabridged line of questioning of that matter and continuing through a reestablishment of the goal point, the opponent is taught a painful lesson. The opponent has permitted the examiner to give the abridged version and then the unabridged version of that line of questioning. The point has been made not once, but twice. The opponent now realizes that the point can be made quickly or slowly, once or twice, depending on whether the objection is made. Once performed, this technique discourages further objection.

This technique works best when a judge is impatient and wants the trial to "move along."

§ 29.13 Rule 7: Speaking Responses — Miniature Closing Arguments

Opponent: Objection, this is entirely collateral and should not be gone into on cross-examination.

Examiner: Your Honor, our theory of the case is premised in part on the fact that this witness has on multiple occasions mislead or lied to the plaintiff. To have a "thorough and sifting" cross-examination, permit me to present to the jury each of those instances. This instance is about misrepresentation of this witness's ability to the plaintiff.

If a speaking response to an objection is permitted by the court, the cross-examiner has the right to tell the judge where the cross-examiner is going with the line of questioning. If a speaking objection is not permitted, seek permission before replying. For example, "May I reply Your Honor?" Or, "May I be heard Your Honor?" If the matter is of great importance, and if the court frowns on speaking objections or speaking replies, respect the rules of the court but protect the ability to reply in this way: "May I be heard on this at the bench, Your Honor?" Always tie the response to the theory of the case. When countering the objection that a fact or line of facts is collateral or irrelevant, it is important that the court understands the relationship of that chapter to the theory of the case.

If the objection, whether or not stated directly, is that the cross-examination has gone on too long or in too great detail, the examiner's response should also include a key phrase known to the court as being the standard for cross-examination in that jurisdiction. For instance, in Alabama, the standard is "a thorough and sifting cross-examination." When this well-known phrase is included in the response, it encourages the court to rule using another well-known, if not well-worn, phrase, "Well, all right, this is cross-examination."

More importantly, where permitted, the speaking response is designed to acquaint the jury with this area of inquiry (a miniature closing argument). Do not make a speaking response until permitted by the court. Stop if the judge indicates enough has been said. The more liberal the judge on speaking responses, the more specific the speaking responses can be.

Opponent: Objection, this is entirely collateral.

Examiner: Your honor, this line of questioning goes directly to our theory of the case. That theory is that the plaintiff breached this contract by making it impossible for my client to be able to perform it. This line of questioning is designed to show that the plaintiff is a man of manipulative means and bent of mind who would have the audacity to manipulate this contract in such a way as to make it impossible for my client to perform. Then he sues my client.

Argumentative, you say? Yes, it is. This is the time to argue. Remember, it is a miniature closing argument. If the court permits speaking responses, push your speaking response as far as accuracy, ethics, and professionalism permit.

A word of caution: Never push the speaking response further than the cross-examination can establish. In other words, if the cross-examiner is going to use words such as "manipulative," the cross-examination had better show that the plaintiff is "manipulative." Remember the judge and jury are always weighing the lawyer's credibility. The advocate's passion and enthusiasm cannot be permitted to interfere with the advocate's credibility.

§ 29.14   Rule 8: Dealing With Objections Designed to Assist the Witness on Cross-Examination

[1]   Talking Objection That Suggests Answers to Witness

There are those lawyers who, having exposed their witnesses to penetrating, effective cross-examination, feel the call to come to their aid (much in the sense of an ill-timed cavalry charge). They often do so by voicing an objection that is designed not to engender a ruling, but to coach the witness. These objections, like trick-or-treaters, come in many costumes, but underneath are all based on childish motivations.

There are many forms of this objection designed to assist a witness, but they all have the same basis. The opponent is attempting to tell the witness how to safely answer (or evade) the question. The by-product of this objection is that it interrupts the cross-examiner's flow. Don't let it happen. Slide off the objection. Make the interruption a part of the cross-examination. The objection may suggest the witness "doesn't know" or "doesn't remember," or it may actually suggest lines of testimony. Each type of objection can be turned to the advantage of the cross-examiner.

A cross-examiner, in control, must expose these objections for what they are. By doing so, the jury is taught that the objection should not have been made. The cross-examiner stays calm. She knows the objection was improper and distracting, but she also knows techniques to punish the interruption and reward her theory of the case. Simultaneously, the cross-examiner's appropriate response warns the opponent against further frivolous or "coaching" objections. The witness is taught not to look for help from his lawyer. The witness is all alone.

[2] The Favorite Suggestion: "Only If the Witness Knows"

A frequent suggestion offered by way of objection is that the witness shall only answer "if he knows." This hint may be dealt with in a number of ways.

Technique 1:

Q: You recognize Dr. Clark as an expert in the field of pediatrics?

Opp.: Objection, Your Honor; only if she knows.

Q: Dr. Shaw, I have been asking you questions for more than forty-five minutes.

A: Yes, though it seemed longer.

Q: And before that my opponent asked you questions for about ninety minutes?

A: Yes.

Q: All this time you understood that we were both asking you what you knew?

A: Well, I suppose so.

Q: In fact, you never once thought that if you didn't know something, you should fake the answer.

A: Of course not.

Q: So, in fact, every question asked by both sides asks for you to answer using only what you know?

A: Yes, I suppose so.

Q: Now let's return to my question — What you knew about Dr. Clark was. . . .

The objection was designed to give the witness an "out" before answering. The cross-examiner shows that it is much too late for the witness not to answer. The witness will answer rather than appear illogical and foolish.

[3]   The Evading Witness: "I Don't Know"

When a cross-examination is successful, there are certain times when the witness will know the answer but not want to give it. This is particularly true with theme-related questions. This is absolutely true with very important concluding questions.

For example, in a divorce case, after the cross-examiner had taken the defendant wife through multiple instances of spending what would appear to the jury to be frivolous and rather outrageous amounts of money on clothing and jewelry, the cross-examiner brought the questioning to a conclusion by asking the witness the affect these purchases had on the marriage:

Q: When you spent $ 3,300 on shoes during the summer of 2002, you knew that your husband was struggling to make ends meet?

A: (A lengthy pause.)

Opp.: That question calls for my client to speculate. She has no way of knowing that answer.

Judge: The witness is instructed not to speculate. If you don't know, say you don't know.

A: I don't know.

Q: You don't know?

A: I don't know.

Q: You do know that you spent $ 3,300 on shoes in the summer of 2002?

A: Yes.

Q: You do know that your husband was managing the money?

A: Yes.

Q: You do know that he was working very long hours?

A: Yes.

Q: You do know that he told you that summer that he was having trouble making ends meet?

A: Well . . . he might have said that.

Q: Then, Mrs. Grey, you know that your spending $ 3,300 on shoes that summer was affecting his ability to make ends meet?

A: I'm not sure.

Opp.: She has already testified that she didn't know.

Q: I am cross-examining on the truthfulness of that very response. Your husband had complained to you that there just was not enough money to pay the bills?

A: Yes, he said something like that.

Q: Then, Mrs. Grey, if I understand it correctly, you knew that you had spent $ 3,300 on shoes the summer of 2002, and you knew your husband was complaining there wasn't enough money in the family budget?

A: Yes.

Q: What you didn't know was that spending $ 3,300 on shoes was making it hard to make ends meet?

A: Yes, I just don't know.

The point to be made is, don't let the witness off the hook just because her lawyer has suggested the witness doesn't know the answer. Often, claiming not to know the answer is worse for the witness than any answer the witness could give (see chapter 20, *Dealing With the "I Don't Know" or "I Don't Remember" Witness*). More importantly, when the witness says she doesn't know the answer, often the jury knows that the witness does know the answer but just doesn't want to answer it. The dodge of "I don't know" is exposed by carefully building up the known facts to show the obviousness of the desired, but evaded, answer to the original question.

The cross-examiner must avoid permitting the line of questioning to be stopped by the "I don't know" suggested by the opponent's objection. Following the technique described above, the objection actually permits the cross-examiner to re-establish the line of questioning, and to go through the line of questioning a second time. The jury hears the bad facts concerning the witness's conduct multiple times. Using this technique, the evidence is highlighted rather than suppressed. Whether the concluding answer is, "I don't know" or the answer that the cross-examiner wants is immaterial, so long as the jury understands the "I don't know" to be evasive. The jury hears the evidence and sees the evasive character of the witness.

[4] Coping With the Objection: "If He Remembers"

The same technique applies when the opponent suggests to the witness that the witness cannot (read: should not) remember. The phrase makes no sense in any event. Witnesses tell the facts they do remember. Implicit in every question is a request to relate what is remembered. Putting aside the absurdity of the suggestive objection, through appropriate cross-examination, this response can be a strong comment to the jury that the witness doesn't care to remember. That it is, in fact, an open and obvious deception.

In a medical malpractice case:

Q: Doctor, when the child was brought to the emergency room, both parents were there?

A: Yes.

Q: They both told you how terribly hard the child had struck her head on the concrete?

A: How hard? (pause)

Opp.: The doctor previously testified on direct examination and on this cross-examination that he doesn't remember those types of details.

Q: Your Honor, let me approach it a different way.

Judge: Proceed.

Q: You do remember the child coming into the emergency room?

A: Yes.

Q: You do remember the parents being there?

A: Yes.

Q: You do remember the fact that the child had struck her head?

A: Yes.

Q: You do remember she had a closed head injury?

A: Yes.

Q: You do remember from medical school training that the severity of the blow to the head is important?

A: Yes.

Q: You do remember from medical school that taking a history is important?

A: Yes.

Q: You do remember that if the patient is not conscious or cannot verbalize the history that you take that history from whatever reliable source is available?

A: Yes.

Q: You do remember that the parents gave a portion of the history?

A: Yes.

Q: You do remember they gave you the child's name?

A: Yes.

Q: You do remember they gave you her name because you asked for that information?

A: Yes.

Q: You do remember they gave you her age because it was important to your diagnosis and treatment?

A: Yes.

Q: You do remember they gave you her prior medical history because it was important to your diagnosis and treatment?

A: Yes.

Q: You do remember they told you how hard she hit her head because it was important to your diagnosis and treatment?

A: I guess so.

Q: Doctor, you do remember that the parents told you that the child struck her head very hard?

A: I guess so.

Notice the use of the tag phrase, "you remember." In this context, it is not used in violation of the principle of primacy (see chapter 12, *Employing Primacy and Recency*), but is designed to highlight or loop (see chapter 26, *Loops, Double Loops, and Spontaneous Loops*) the phrase used by the opponent "does not remember" in his objection. It simultaneously points out the absurdity of the witness not remembering the big fact when he remembers less important facts.

The opponent has made this objection to distract the jury from the cross-examination and to educate the witness "not to remember" certain critical admissions needed by the cross-examiner. Instead, the contrary occurred. The cross-examiner shall look forward to this type of objection in the future. It can be used to intimidate the witness thoroughly and to force the admission. It can be used to educate the jury that the witness and the objecting lawyer are both trying not to be helpful and intentionally not recall critical evidence. It silences objections.

The technique is to slide off the objection. Immediately revert to a series of questions, each containing one fact, and each requiring a "yes" answer. The advocate may use the phrase, "You do remember" in each of these questions. Work slowly and methodically up through the things remembered, taking them either in chronological order or order of importance to the case, leading up to the critical issue that the witness claims he can't remember. Along the way, punish the witness and your opponent with the phrase, "You do remember." The cross-examiner is spontaneously looping the phrase from the objection (see chapter 26, *Loops, Double Loops, and Spontaneous Loops*), and all the time making the bigger point of the fact that the witness claims he can't remember. The objection permits greater cross-examination, not less. However, keep in mind that use of the phrase "you do remember" can become as repetitive and boring a habit as any other tagline (see chapter 12, *Employing Primacy and Recency*). The phrase should be used in this scenario as part of this specific technique and then it should be discontinued.

[5]   Coping With the Objection: "The Witness Already Said . . . ."

In its most sophisticated form, this type of objection is designed by the opponent to educate the witness under cross-examination as to what story to give. The opponent attempts this either by repeating some portion of direct testimony or some portion of the answers given on cross-examination.

While the objecting lawyer understands that he is now testifying rather than the witness, the jury will hear it as an objection. Further, the witness is educated to repeat the litany delivered by the lawyer.

This is a *speaking* objection. In response, the cross-examiner might argue that was not what was said on direct examination or earlier in cross-examination. In the alternative, she might argue that the lawyer is improperly making speaking objections.

A third method is to handle it by sliding off the objection. For example, in a criminal case, the prosecutor attempts to save the witness by a speaking objection. The girlfriend/informant is now testifying against the former boyfriend/drug dealer. The girlfriend testified on direct that she was afraid of the boyfriend to explain why she did not talk with the police until weeks after her arrest and weeks after the defendant boyfriend's arrest. The defendant's theory of the case is that the girlfriend agreed to speak to the prosecutor only after her lawyer arranged for immunity for her testimony. Substantially into the cross-examination and as a concluding question to a chapter of questions on her failure to talk with the police, the following occurred:

Q: The fact of the matter is you waited two full weeks after the arrest to tell the police that your boyfriend was the drug dealer?

A: Yes, but, but . . . .

Opp.:   Your Honor, she has already testified that she was afraid of the defendant and that was why she did not notify the police right away.

The defense lawyer is trying to misrepresent to the jury.

Q: Your Honor, I am not misrepresenting anything to the jury. I am cross-examining the witness on that point. I will be glad to rephrase so that there will be no question of exactly what I am asking this witness.

Judge: Why don't you do that?

Q: Your lawyer said in his objection that you were afraid of your boyfriend?

A: Yes.

Q: And you are now telling us that you were afraid of your boyfriend and that was the reason you didn't tell the police about his drug activity?

A: Yes.

Q: And you are now telling us that you were afraid of your boyfriend from the time before the arrest until you finally went and talked with the police?

A: Yes.

There are two chapter paths to follow for the cross-examiner.

The First Path:

Q: Your lawyer was with you when you went to talk to the police?

A: Yes.

Q: You heard your lawyer discuss the fact that all charges against you would be dropped?

A: Yes.

Q: Your lawyer told the police that once the charges were to be dropped, you were willing to talk with them.

A: Yes.

Q: Your lawyer said that in front of you?

A: Yes.

Q: Your lawyer said now that the charges were dropped you were willing to tell that the cocaine was your boyfriend's (the defendant)?

A: Yes.

Q: You were present when your lawyer said that to the police?

A: Yes.

Now the point is "the lawyer" is a witness with a vested interest. His objections will not be listened to in the same light. It now appears to the jury that the opponent was misrepresenting facts to them. The issue is "your lawyer" now. The opponent has suffered substantial blemishes to his credibility.

The Second Chapter Path:

Q: Your lawyer didn't say in his objection that after your arrest, you and the defendant went home together?

A: No, he didn't say that.

Q: Your lawyer didn't say that you then moved home to your parents for two weeks?

A: No, he didn't say that.

Q: Your lawyer didn't say that you were away from the defendant for fourteen days with your daddy before you went to talk to the police?

A: No.

Q: Your lawyer didn't say that your parents have money and immediately got you to a lawyer?

A: No.

Q: Your lawyer didn't say that your parents kept you away from the defendant?

A: No.

Q: Your lawyer didn't say your parents wouldn't let you talk to him or him to you during that two weeks?

A: No, he didn't.

Q: Your lawyer didn't say that in spite of your parents feelings, that you snuck out to see Billy Bob, the defendant?

A: No.

Q: Your lawyer only said in the objection that you were afraid of Billy Bob, the defendant.

A: Yes.

Q: And you are now telling us that two weeks away from him and the three separate times that you were intimate with him, you were afraid of the defendant?

A: Well . . . I don't know.

The witness stares at her lawyer at the prosecution table with the message, "Help me, help me," in her eyes for the jury to see. The opponent will not help. His credibility has been tarnished.

The objection of the opponent can be used to open up a new line of chapters highlighted by the phrase, "Your lawyer." The lines of distinction between her defense lawyer and the prosecuting lawyer fade during this line of questioning.

To those lawyers who believe that there would be objections to the phrase, "Your lawyer didn't say in his objection," there are three responses. First, the objection may well hurt the prosecution more than no objection at all. Second, the judge is now in a position to have to comment on a previous objection by the opponent. Most judges would prefer not to be put in that position. Most judges would look at your opponent as having opened up this can of worms. Most judges would decline to require a rephrase. If the judge does so, rephrase it. Only use that phrase in the concluding question. If the prosecutor wants to object then, again the objection may hurt more than not objecting. Third, if necessary, replace the phrase "your lawyer" with "the prosecutor." Now the objection has been removed, but the tie between the witness and the lawyer remains.

[6] Spontaneous Looping Off of the Objection

A preferred technique of dealing with the objection that coaches an answer is to spontaneously loop off of the objection itself. This example comes from a lawsuit between a real estate developer and his architect. The developer sues for malpractice in design. The developer's project manager is being cross-examined concerning whose fault it is that certain change orders were not incorporated in the field drawings.

Q: You never called Mr. Greenberg's architectural office to see if there were any change orders in the brickwork?

Opp.: Objection, Your Honor; the witness has already testified that he had been told by the brick mason that he was working from the newest plans.

Q: You talked to the brick mason?

A: Yes.

Q: The brick mason said he was up to date?

A: Yes.

Q: Not Mr. Greenberg, the architect?

A: No.

Q: Because you never talked to Mr. Greenberg, the architect?

A: No.

Q: You never talked to Mr. Greenberg's wife and partner, Mrs. Greenberg, also an architect?

A: No.

Q: You never talked to any of his staff?

A: No.

Q: The brick mason was not with the architect's staff?

A: No.

Q: You never called the architect?

A: Not on the bricks.

Q: You never relied on their word?

A: Not on theirs.

Q: You relied on the brick mason?

A: Yes.

    Or

Q: You relied on the brick mason?

A: Yes.

Q: The brick mason does not work for the architect?

A: No.

Q: The architect did not select the brick mason?

A: No.

Q: The developer selected the brick mason?

A: Yes.

Q: The brick mason got paid by the developer?

A: Yes.

Q: The brick mason does not draw the plans?

A: No.

Q: The architect draws the plans?

A: Yes.

Q: But you called the brick mason?

A: Yes.

Q: Never the architect?

By spontaneously looping (see chapter 26, *Loops, Double Loops, and Spontaneous Loops*) the phrase "the brick mason" from the objection and contrasting it to "the architect," the cross-examiner expands her admissible scope of examination.

§ 29.15   Dealing With the Interventionist Judge

The techniques within this chapter are helpful and in most courtrooms. Judges differ on the degrees to which they will permit lawyers to ply their craft. Some judges no longer respect the value of cross-examination, nor appreciate the subtle application of technique. These judges are not disposed to permit counsel to have input into any objections by opponents. In the courtroom, where these objections will result in an argument with the judge in front of the jury, cross-examining counsel must tailor the use of these techniques to the style and level permitted by the judge. But the lawyer must try them first. No one knows how a judge will react to these types of techniques until they have been tried. No one knows how the judge will respond with this witness in this trial. Always try the techniques first. Always adhere to the ruling of the court. If the judge insists that these types of techniques to respond to objections not be used, then desist.

Show the court and your opponent that going back to the old-fashioned way of responding to objections is easy. Show the ethical and professional fortitude to abide by the ruling.

Chapter 30

RECOGNIZING AND CONTROLLING BAIT

SYNOPSIS

§ 30.01 Bait Defined

When the cross-examination is going well for the lawyer, a witness will often search for a way to derail the cross-examiner. One of the most likely strategies is for the witness to offer bait. Bait is a partially or fully non-responsive answer to the question. It is designed by the witness to take the cross-examiner out of the current chapter or away from the current fact being discussed and into another area selected by the witness.

Taken outside the context of a courtroom, this is nothing more than the witness changing the subject. In a normal conversation, people change the subject because they prefer to talk about another subject or are trying to hide from something in the present subject. The same is true in the courtroom.

No "changing the subject" assists the cross-examiner. The cross-examiner is teaching her theory of the case through carefully drafted questions, chapters, and sequence of chapters. She has made conscious and intelligent decisions on how to craft the question, how to build the chapter, and how to sequence the chapters (see chapter 8, *The Only Three Rules of Cross-Examination*; chapter 9, *The Chapter Method of Cross-Examination*; and chapter 11, *Sequences of Cross-Examination*). All of these decisions were made with the purpose of being able to teach the theory of the case in an understandable manner and with a minimum loss of control to the witness. With that said, logic dictates that any change in the scripted sequence chapter or question would be counterproductive to the cross-examiner. It is nonetheless very difficult for cross-examiners to avoid taking the bait.

It would be a mistake for the cross-examiner to believe that only intelligent, expert, or professional witnesses know to offer bait. Life experiences have taught each person that changing the subject is often a good ploy in a conversation gone wrong. Every witness has the potential to offer bait to the detriment of the lawyer.

It is, after all, the power of the prepared chapters and sequence of the chapters that caused the witness to want to offer the bait. Stay with that power. Resist the urge to take the bait.

§ 30.02   The Mindset of the Cross-Examiner

All cross-examiners are egotists. The more successful the cross-examination to date, the larger the ego expands. As the ego expands, the cross-examiner believes she can do no wrong. The cross-examiner believes that any new area offered by the witness is an area in which the cross-examiner can successfully attack the witness. There is an urge to show the witness that the cross-examiner is mentally nimble and prepared to delve into subjects mentioned by the witness. These types of decisions are based on ego and emotion, not on teaching the case well and reducing risk of loss of control to the cross-examiner.

By refusing to take the bait offered, the cross-examiner can teach the subject matter thoroughly and well. The cross-examiner can retain control. The cross-examiner forfeits nothing in doing so. If, in fact, the bait is something the cross-examiner can further exploit, there will be an opportunity to exploit it later. The key to refusing bait is not to ignore it completely, but rather to ignore it at the time when it is first offered. Deferred gratification is not what trial lawyers are known to relish instinctually.

§ 30.03   Taking the Bait

Nothing to gain, something to lose. The cross-examiner might say that she has been baited away from the designed order of the cross-examination, but that no real harm was done because the cross-examiner was baited into another fertile area for cross-examination. While this may *appear* true, in truth nothing has been gained and something was lost in the process of taking the bait. Compare the complete control of the witness by proceeding one chapter at a time (see chapter 9, *The Chapter Method of Cross-Examination*), to moving from one successful area of cross-examination to a new area suggested by the witness. It is through the thorough development of *each chapter* that the factual goals of the cross-examination are realized and taught effectively to the fact finder. The effect on the jury or judge is maximized through detailed exploration of facts in a selected context or chapter. While some jurors would love to observe the cross-examiner successfully track down the witness in areas that the witness has suggested, there is a loss of context and detailed presentation that produces a less effective teaching method. Cross-examination is not an ego-based endeavor, but rather a teaching exercise that allows jurors to mentally see the images sought to be portrayed by each chapter. Exploitation of the bait can still happen, but in a safer and more understandable order.

§ 30.04 Types of Bait

[1] Introduction

There are four different types of bait. The cross-examiner must refuse bait offered no matter *how* tempting it appears. Each type of bait will be discussed. They appear as structure or chapter bait, intra-chapter bait (or the witness jumping to the goal fact), new fact bait within a chapter, and new chapter bait.

[2] Intra-Chapter Bait

[a] An Example of Intra-Chapter Bait

The most obvious of the baits is the intra-chapter bait or the witness choosing to jump to the goal fact of the chapter. In this scenario, the witness recognizes that the cross-examiner is proceeding thoroughly in a detailed manner and in a logical progression to a specific goal fact. The witness realizes the inevitability of admitting the goal fact. The witness recognizes that there is drama and context being built by the cross-examiner in the progression toward the goal fact. As the witness realizes this inevitability, the witness either intentionally or intuitively decides to skip or jump to the goal fact. The witness drops down to answer or discuss the goal fact even though the cross-examiner has only proceeded a portion of the way through that chapter of cross-examination. Too many cross-examiners see the admission by the witness of the goal fact as a cheap victory and one to be immediately seized upon. It is a victory that did not require hard fighting or risks. The cross-examiner rationalizes that to accept the admitted goal fact is all that is necessary. The cross-examiner accepts the goal fact and moves to the next chapter.

While the reasoning of the cross-examiner can be understood, the fallacy of the reasoning is that the chapter has not been fully taught to the fact finder. The mental image that the chapter was designed to build was not thoroughly illustrated. Consequently, the teaching of the theory of the case that included the mental image of this chapter was not taught in a way that will be remembered as distinctly and easily by the fact finder.

The cross-examiner wishes to prove that the witness attended and now remembers an important business meeting. The cross-examination of that chapter begins:

Q: You were employed by Avco in the summer of 2004?

A: Yes.

Q: You were a branch manager?

A: Yes.

Q: You ran the Tallahassee, Florida, branch of that company?

A: Yes.

Q: You had people that worked for you?

A: Yes.

Q: And you, of course, worked for others?

A: Yes.

Q: Your immediate supervisor was Don Dismull?

A: Yes, it was Mr. Don.

Q: He was your district manager?

A: Yes.

Q: In August of 2004, you received a call from Mr. Don?

A: Yes.

Q: In that call, he informed you that there would be a meeting of every branch manager in his district.

A: Yes.

Q: That meeting included every branch manager in the state of Florida?

A: Yes, that is right, I remember that. In fact, he called it an important meeting, but I knew it was an incredibly important meeting for every branch manager in the entire state to meet in Orlando. We had never really done that before.

Q: That's right. It was an extremely important meeting?

A: Yes.

The cross-examiner having gotten to the goal fact moves to another chapter and accepts the bait offered by the witness within the chapter of "the important meeting." However, the cross-examiner has sacrificed a more detailed and precise picture that the chapter was designed to teach. Look at the way the chapter would appear had the bait not been accepted by the cross-examiner:

A: Yes, that is right, I remember that. In fact, he called it an important meeting, but I knew it was an incredibly important meeting for every branch manager in the entire state to meet in Orlando. We had never really done that before.

Q: In your experience as a branch manager, Mr. Don had never called such a meeting?

A: No.

Q: In fact, the state manager had never called such a meeting?

A: No.

Q: Mr. Don instructed you to bring copies of all of the computer disks for the last six months from your branch?

A: Yes.

Q: You had sent in all of that information to Mr. Don monthly for the last six months?

A: Yes.

Q: But he instructed you to bring copies of those disks for each of the last six months?

A: Yes.

Q: He made a specific point of that?

A: Yes.

Q: He told you that each branch manager would be bringing that information for their branch?

A: Yes.

Q: He told you that the meeting was going to be about those records?

A: I don't know that he told me that, but I certainly could figure that out.

Q: That's right. You could figure that out. It was clear that it was about the financial records for each branch manager for the last six months?

A: Yes.

Q: You had never been asked to bring those records personally before?

A: No.

Q: You had never been instructed to make sure that you had specific records for a meeting?

A: No.

Q: That was unusual?

A: Yes.

Q: Because they already had the records on a monthly basis?

A: Exactly.

Q: They already had the records, but they instructed each of you to bring your monthly records for the last six months to this meeting?

A: Yes.

Q: The meeting was going to be extremely important?

A: Yes.

Q: He told you this was not a meeting to miss?

A: He did.

Q: He even joked that there would be no excused absences even for illnesses?

A: He did.

Q: In fact, he told you: "Don't be sick for this one. This is too important?"

A: Yes, I remember that.

The cross-examiner has taught a more vivid image to the fact finder. Drama has been built. Each juror can better see the image the lawyer has painted. This uniformity of vision is crucial in the jury room.

[b] Solution to Intra-Chapter Bait or the Witness Jumping to the Goal Fact

Cross-examination is about teaching. The best method to teach the fact finder the theory of the case and how each chapter fits into that theory of the case is via a thorough presentation of the entire chapter. This is contrary to some methods taught to prior generations of lawyers. For many years it was taught that a cross-examination was a commando raid with the illusion that the cross-examination had the purpose of getting the witness to admit any goal fact as quickly as possible. The cross-examiner would then scamper away to a new area before the witness could say something damaging. If the lawyer is to teach, she must create the opportunity to teach. The purpose of the chapter method of cross-examination is truly to teach the goal fact, and teach it in a complete context so that the jury and judge can understand and appreciate how each chapter fits into the advocate's theory of the case. The jury need not try to memorize the goal fact. Rather, the goal fact is understood in its place in the entire story of the theory of the case. With this said, the solution to intra-chapter bait is simple. Refuse the bait. Thoroughly teach the chapter and reinforce the goal fact at the end of the chapter.

[3] Structure or Chapter Bait

[a] Introduction

Again, the witness is spurred to derail the cross-examination because of its effectiveness. The cross-examiner is doing well; so well, in fact, that the witness realizes that the cross-examiner is allowing few, if any, points to be scored by the witness. The witness has become frustrated by the thoroughness of the questions and the complete control of the facts demonstrated by the cross-examiner. It is at this time that witnesses will try to change the subject. Many times witnesses will try to change the subject by offering structure or chapter bait to take the cross-examiner away from the present chapter.

In this setting, the witness will offer a short and seemingly helpful non-responsive answer designed to lure the cross-examiner from the prepared order of chapters of the cross-examination into a different and perhaps totally unexpected area of cross-examination. The witness may attempt to lure the cross-examiner into an area in which the cross-examiner was previously unaware (new chapter bait — to be discussed below more thoroughly). More likely the witness will attempt to lure the cross-examiner into an area that the cross-examiner fully intends to develop in later cross-examination chapters (structure or chapter bait).

In structure or chapter bait, the cross-examiner sees the opportunity to "one up" the witness by immediately shifting the attack to the baited chapter. This is particularly tempting to a cross-examiner, as she reasons that this shift of attack is safe because the baited chapter is one that the cross-examiner has already prepared and had planned to question upon later in the cross-examination anyway. There certainly is an emotional feeling of power when the cross-examiner takes this bait and moves to the chapter suggested by the witness. The cross-examiner rationalizes that she is psychologically beating down the witness because she is demonstrating that no matter where the witness goes, the cross-examiner is prepared to follow and defeat the witness. Therein lies the fallacy of this thought process. The cross-examiner should never follow the witness. To do so only encourages the witness to offer more bait while simultaneously weakening the stance of the cross-examiner as the teacher of the facts.

The witness must be made to follow the cross-examiner, both in the questions and in the sequence of the chapters. To do otherwise forfeits the conscious intellectual building of the cross-examination and defeats effective teaching. The cross-examiner may well follow where the witness is taking her, but the jury and judge will not. Juries and judges do not know the theory of the cross-examiner's case as well as the cross-examiner. The cross-examiner must teach that theory in the easiest and most understandable method possible. That method is the chapter method (see chapter 9, *The Chapter Method of Cross-Examination*). The cross-examiner must resist the chapter or structure bait. By following the witness to the different chapter, the witness has almost certainly caused the lawyer to truncate the delivery of the current chapter. Furthermore, by leaping into a different chapter, the witness has destroyed the sequence of chapters the lawyer had designed. There is no method to effectively return to the truncated chapter. Judges will not easily permit a lawyer to go back to a previous chapter. More importantly, juries don't listen when the cross-examiner returns to material that appears to have already been taught. Even though the cross-examiner may be teaching more details that are important, once the subject matter has been inquired into during the first rendition of the chapter, juries and judges will not easily listen to the second telling of the same chapter. Judges are much more likely to sustain objections to "asked and answer" or "repetitive and redundant."

There is an additional downside to leaping to a different chapter with the witness. In all likelihood, there has not been performed the necessary foundational or subsidiary chapters necessary to give the full context and meaning to the different chapter that the lawyer is now about to perform (see chapter 11, *Sequences of Cross-Examination*).

As an example, in a divorce case, the cross-examiner has successfully cross-examined the defendant's wife on her lack of support of her husband, both in his profession and as a parent. The cross-examination has proceeded covering the years of the marriage.

Because the cross-examination has proceeded in largely a chronological order and sequence (this is not recommended) (see chapter 11, *Sequences of Cross-Examination*), the witness was able to anticipate the upcoming cross-examination. This is but one reason to avoid the chronological cross-examination. In a non-chronological sequence of cross, the witness is given no clue as to the order or subject of the chapters. The witness must spend more time concentrating on where he is and less time on where he is about to go. The cross-examiner is also less likely to take the bait in a non-chronological cross-examination since it represents a wholesale abandonment of the planned sequence and not just a deviation from the chronological history. The bait offered, therefore, is simply less attractive.

However, in this example, the cross-examiner has moved chronologically and continues to structure the cross-examination in a chronological order of "bad acts" of the defendant's wife. In this example, the witness successfully baits the cross-examiner to change the planned sequence:

Q: Now, Mrs. Brown, when Johnny was only seven years of age and playing Little League Baseball, you did not attend a game?

A: That is correct.

Q: You did not take the child to any of the practices that year?

A: That is correct, too.

Q: And when Johnny made the All-Star Team, you did not attend that game or the ceremonies, either?

A: That is true. I also failed to attend the Championship Game, in which he played that year and the following year.

At this point, the cross-examiner knows that there is substantial evidence to support the conclusion that the mother did not attend the Championship Game because of the excuse of attending an out of town business meeting. The cross-examiner believes she can prove this was a fake meeting designed to permit the wife to carry on an adulterous affair out of town. The cross-examiner had prepared the cross-examination on the "Championship Game" as a concluding chapter on lack of support of parenting in regard to Johnny's baseball activity and as a transition into a chapter on adulterous relationships. The cross-examiner, overly anxious to get to the more interesting "conduct" for the jury's listening pleasure, takes the bait:

Q: I am glad that you mentioned the Championship Game; you told your child that you could not go to the Championship Game because of a business meeting?

A: Yes.

Q: In fact, the business meeting excuse was a fake?

A: Yes.

Q: It was an excuse?

A: Yes.

The cross-examiner may feel proud of the job she has done in successfully taking the bait and turning it against the witness. However, while these are good questions that should be developed at some point, many additional points on the mother's disregard to the Little League career of Johnny have now been skipped. The lack of support of the mother year in and year out, day in and day out, has been skipped. As a result, the cross-examiner will either forget to present this evidence, or, if the cross-examiner attempts to return to these skipped chapters, these Little League chapters will be out of context and seem redundant to the jury and the judge. The return to this day in and day out conduct seems a downturn in the emotional context of the chapters after having heard about "adultery." In the example to follow, the cross-examiner resists the bait and further intimidates and controls the witness by brushing aside the bait.

A: That is true. I also failed to attend the Championship Game, in which he played that year and the following year.

Q: I am glad that you mentioned the Championship Game. You did miss that game, didn't you?

A: Yes.

Q: Let me mark my notes to come back to that point, but let's finish the rest of the season first. Agreeable?

A: If you say so.

The cross-examiner marks her notes two pages further in her cross-examination (that is two chapters later as each chapter has its own page) (see chapter 10, *Page Preparation of Cross-Examination*) and then returns to Johnny's

baseball season. Should the cross-examiner wish to make a dramatic and significant point of bookmarking the offered bait by the witness, the cross-examiner may elect to mark the blackboard in front of the jury with the words,
"Wife missed two championship games." When those chapters of cross are to
be developed, make a point of referencing the blackboard. The notes are there
for the jury to see, and perhaps anticipate. The witness, of course, will see the
note too. The most gentle and subtle method of book-marking a chapter to
which the cross-examiner will return is simply to mention that chapter in the
context of the chapter now being examined upon:

Q: Now before we get to the Championship Game, you will admit for this jury
that Johnny had sixty-three games that year, not including the All-Star
and Championship Games?

A: Yes, about that many.

Q: Johnny played in each of those games?

A: Yes.

Q: But you never attended a single game?

A: That's true.

Q: Johnny had three practices for every game that he played that year?

A: I understand that is correct.

Q: That's 189 practices?

A: Yes, that math is correct.

Q: But you never attended a single one of those practices?

A: No, I didn't.

Q: You never drove Johnny to one of those practices?

A: That is true.

Q: You never picked him up from one of those practices?

A: That's true.

Q: You cannot even tell this jury where he practiced?

A: I guess that is true, too.

Q: Now, while you were missing those games and practices, your husband
attended them, didn't he?

A: Yes.

Q: Your husband attended every one of those games?

A: Yes.

Q: Your husband attended every practice?

A: Yes.

Q: Your husband drove the child to those practices?

A: Yes.

Q: Your husband picked him up from those practices?

A: Yes.

Q: In fact, your husband even stayed and assisted the coach at practices when the coach needed help?

A: Yes, I understand that is true.

Q: And he did this when he was practicing law on a full time basis?

A: Yes.

Q: He was going to court, he was representing people, but he always had the time to take your child to the practices?

A: I don't know if he had the time.

Q: Yes, that's right; even if he didn't have the time, he made the time for Johnny?

A: Yes, I guess so.

The cross-examining lawyer has taken full advantage of the chapter. The chapter keeps its place in the sequence of the cross-examination and is developed thoroughly. The witness is more thoroughly cowed by the individually proved and highly detailed facts. The fact finder is more thoroughly schooled in the theory of the case.

To be sure, many jurors would love to hear the "more interesting" questions about sex. However, there will also be jurors that will be more offended by the complete lack of attendance at the child's practices and games. There will be some jurors who will be touched by the father's dedication to the child's activities, even while the father is working a full time schedule. Most importantly, whatever the effect of these chapters on the individual jurors, these chapters set up the "championships game" chapters in such a way to add significance to that chapter by foreshadowing that chapter.

The lawyer will still get to the "sex," but it will be more dramatic when the lawyer delivers those chapters to the jury. While some judges and juries may be more affected by one chapter than another, by sticking to the planned sequence of chapters and by developing each chapter fully, the cross-examiner ensures that the jurors will get the full measure of *all* the best material. The full measure of good cross-examination material should not be wasted.

[b] Solution to Structure or Chapter Bait

The solution to structure or chapter bait is the most obvious of all of the solutions to all different types of bait. The cross-examiner must realize that she is going to get to the chapter offered in the bait. The cross-examiner must be patient. By the cross-examiner exercising self-control, the cross-examiner will surely arrive at the bait and chapter and will perform that chapter in its full context and in the sequence that was carefully developed prior to trial. Absolutely nothing is lost by refusing this type of bait since the cross-examiner will eventually get there.

[4]   New Bait

[a]   New Exaggerated or Distorted Facts

A witness undergoing a largely successful cross-examination has little to lose by manipulating the facts. Facts can be exaggerated. Facts can be distorted. Facts can be completely made up. The witness will generally resort to these drastic steps using one of two types of strategies. The more common scenario is when the witness adds new facts to the chapter but does not fully change the chapter. The second method is by adding a new chapter of facts in an effort to bait the cross-examiner away from the entire chapter presently being performed. This new chapter bait is much more tempting to the cross-examiner because it appears that there is an entirely new and fertile area in which to cross-examine. It often appears to the cross-examiner that an entirely new avenue of impeachment has been opened. While this may be true, caution is advised. There are dangers in immediately chasing after a chapter that lacks any pre-trial preparation and thought.

[b]   Within a Chapter

Ordinarily when the witness baits the lawyer within a chapter, the unresponsive answer implies the existence of additional facts that are consistent with the cross-examiner's chapter. At first those facts appear to be helpful to the cross-examiner's chapter and theory of the case. The cross-examiner, at present winning the cross-examination and thinking that she is on safe ground, wades in only to find that the presumed safe area is a trap.

In an example from the criminal context, an immunized witness is on the stand. Not only did the witness receive immunity for criminal conduct identical to that for which the defendant is accused, but the witness also has been placed in the Federal Witness Protection Program. She has been given a new identity, a new home, and a new community in which to live. The government has provided her a job and other financial benefits. To complete the deal, she must testify against the defendant. The witness is cross-examined on motive, interest, and bias.

Q: Mrs. Bearden, you received immunity for your testimony?

A: Yes.

Q: That means that the prosecutor has dismissed all of the charges against you?

A: Yes.

Q: You don't have to fear going to trial?

A: That's true.

Q: You don't have to fear going to jail?

A: That's true.

Q: But you received more than just immunity, didn't you?

A: What?

Q: You are now in the Witness Protection Program?

A: Yes.

Q: And in that program you get a lot of extra things?

A: What do you mean? (This non-responsive answer is caused by the cross-examiner's use of the vague wording and a generality "a lot of extra things" (see chapter 8, *The Only Three Rules of Cross-Examination*).

Q: You get a new name?

A: Yes.

Q: You get a new home?

A: Yes.

Q: You get a new job?

A: Yes.

Q: You get extra money?

A: Yes.

Q: Just as long as you testify against the defendant in this trial?

A: Yes, and I get a lot of other things that you didn't mention, too.

At this point the cross-examiner understandably believes that the "other things" that the witness "gets" will be helpful to the cross-examiner's case. The cross-examiner takes the bait and plunges in.

Q: That's right, you get a lot of other things, don't you? (Or worse: "What else do you get?")

A: Yes, I get to be away from my real family, I get to never see my children again, I get to never visit my mother who is dying of cancer, I get to never . . . .

Q: Objection your honor, the witness is being unresponsive. Move to strike.

No matter what the judge's ruling is, the damage has been done. Worse yet, the answer is not unresponsive. The cross-examiner asked what the witness "gets," and the witness answered in an unexpected manner.

[c] Solution to New Fact Bait Within a Chapter

Should the cross-examiner refuse to take the bait implicit in the phrase "other things," the cross-examiner is not hurt in any way. The implication from this unresponsive answer is that there are other things consistent with the cross-examiner's case that the witness gets. This does not hurt the cross-examiner. It helps the cross-examiner. The cross-examiner should leave it alone. If the opponent dares to enter into this "other things" on redirect examination, the cross-examiner will have more time to reflect on whether or not it is a productive area for cross-examination. By refusing the bait, the cross-examiner loses nothing and risks nothing.

[5]   New Chapter Bait

[a]   Introduction

Some witnesses, particularly witnesses who have testified on more than one occasion such as professional or expert witnesses, will offer new chapter bait when being successfully cross-examined. This species of new bait lures the cross-examiner with the promise that there are substantial additional facts that will support the theory of the case offered by the cross-examiner.

New bait represents not only a change of sequence but also an invitation to tackle unexpected areas of inquiry. The witness has become frustrated because the cross-examiner is effectively and thoroughly controlling the chapters of cross-examination. The witness fully understands that the cross-examiner is determining the course of the cross-examination. Realizing this, the witness offers up something totally new in hopes that the cross-examiner will be intrigued and follow up on this unknown area.

The witness hopes that the cross-examiner will ask more questions about the "new" chapter so that the witness can take control of the cross-examination or at least loosen the control exercised by the lawyer. The witness knows that the cross-examiner knows nothing about the new chapter because that new area is a made up or exaggerated fact pattern. The witness also calculates that if the cross-examiner does not ask any more questions about the new chapter than perhaps the jury will believe that the cross-examiner is seeking to hide those other facts.

As an example, in a civil case, the plaintiff has alleged that the defendant failed to perform the contract. Discovery showed that the plaintiff called the defendant one time after the contract had been signed by both parties. From the plaintiff's standpoint, the defendant admitted in that telephone call that he had willfully failed to perform his duties under the contract. From the defendant's point of view, the discovery was at least damaging in that regard. No other telephone calls were mentioned in the discovery. Despite the fact that the plaintiff's lawyer asked the defendant on his deposition whether any additional "communications" were involved between the plaintiff and defendant after the contract was signed but before the lawsuit was filed, the defendant answered, "No." At trial, the cross-examination of the defendant on the one known telephone call is in progress:

Q: J.D. (the plaintiff) called you on the 31st?

A: Yes.

Q: The call was about the contract?

A: Yes.

Q: The call was about your failure to perform the contract?

A: Yes.

Q: J.D. was angry with you?

A: Yes.

Q: You told him that you were sorry?

A: Yes.

Q: You told him that it had not been completed?

A: Yes.

Q: You told him that you had no excuse?

A: That's true, but we talked about it again in a telephone call three days later.

Up to this point, the cross-examiner has thoroughly controlled the witness. She now mistakenly believes herself to be bulletproof on the issue, even though the cross-examiner knows nothing of the second call. Instead of ignoring this reference, the cross-examiner, even though armed with the denial of any further "communications," immediately plunges ahead into this new and unprepared area:

Q: And in that telephone call three days later, the contract was not discussed?

A: Yes, it was. That's when he apologized for being angry. He told me that he understood why I couldn't complete the contract, and not to worry about it.

By immediately taking the new chapter bait, the cross-examiner commits multiple serious errors: First, by phrasing the question this way, the cross-examiner communicates to the jury through her own personal credibility that in fact there was an additional telephone call. The jury is predisposed to believe this because the cross-examiner has been teaching the case successfully through leading questions and therefore is led to believe that this fact is also true. Second, the question also implies acceptance of the fact that the telephone call was made three days later. Third, the jury is led to believe that the call was between the plaintiff and the defendant. The cross-examiner knows none of these facts. However, by following the witness into this area she has vouched for the credibility of the witness concerning these facts.

The jury is left with only one remaining question on this issue: Whether the content of the seemingly admitted second telephone call between the parties made three days later involved the contract. Unfortunately for the cross-examiner that fact seems to be implied as well by the question. Even if the cross-examiner follows up with:

Q: Didn't you tell me at your deposition that there were no further "communications?"

A: I guess so, if you say so. I didn't know that you meant by "communications" another telephone call.

The cross-examiner is given a Hobson's choice. She can attack the definition by the witness of "communication," but in doing so reinforces that there were multiple communications. On the other hand, she can abandon this line of questioning with the unfavorable impression to the jury that there was in fact a second telephone conversation.

[b] A Solution to New Chapter Bait

In this example, the cross-examiner took the bait and inquired into these supposed facts. In the process, the cross-examiner had substantially undermined the good work that she has done on the first telephone conversation. The error is compounded by the fact that the chapter or chapters on the first (and only phone call) has now been truncated by the cross-examiner's abrupt shift to questions on the "second" phone call. Had counsel first completed the prepared chapter, she would have more firmly established the necessity of the witness to create a second phone call. She would have also more firmly established the improbability of the second phone call.

The prepared series of chapters on the first phone call would demonstrate motive, interest, and bias of the witness that would affect the credibility of the witness when he later attempts to convince the jury that there was a second phone call and he failed to mention its existence when deposed on "other communications."

In each situation, the cross-examiner must first complete all chapters dealing with the first (and known) subject matter. Next, the cross-examiner should do such a cross-examination as is necessary to expose the fact that the baited new chapter of "unknown facts" was never previously mentioned by the witness. Third, counsel should refuse the bait until and unless the opponent has the courage to investigate these new uncharted facts on redirect examination. As discussed in more detail below, it is the opponent who now has the Hobson's choice. The choices available to the opponent are to ignore the new uncharted facts on redirect examination or explore them through the use of open-ended questions. Neither is for the faint of heart. Both choices introduce risks to the direct examiner while giving the cross-examiner further time to consider strategies and options.

In a scenario where there is no previous deposition question and answer that would eliminate "other communications" on the contract, the choice faced by the cross-examiner is an easier one. The cross-examiner has no ability to launch into a cross-examination of the "you never said this before" chapter. The lawyer is now facing new factual bait for which there is no safe counter attack if it goes wrong. Leave it alone. The lawyer must do all of the damage planned with the prepared materials. The lawyer can then wait to see if the opponent takes the bait on redirect — no easy task.

[c] Ignoring New Chapter Bait Places Pressure on the Opponent

If the cross-examiner believes that the new information is truly new, then the opponent must think of it as new, too. Remember, the opponent did not bring out this information on direct testimony, for one of three reasons:

1) The opponent did not know about it;

2) The opponent knew about it, but chose not to bring it out because ultimately it was bad for the opponent's case; or

3) The opponent planned to sandbag or have the witness set up the cross-examining lawyer with the "baited" comment.

Understanding this analysis, the cross-examiner must make the only logical choice available: *"Save it for recross examination"* (see chapter 14, *Redirect and Recross Examination*). If the information is new to the opponent and if the opponent wishes to launch into this new information on redirect examination, the opponent's redirect examination will be exploratory at best. That is, the opponent will not know what the witness is going to say because it has not been rehearsed. The cross-examiner enjoys a significant tactical advantage under these circumstances: The opponent must wade into the new material using open-ended questions. It is now the opponent who is most at risk by inquiring into the unknown.

Analyze the example as if the cross-examiner had declined the bait contained in the non-responsive answer concerning the second telephone conversation. It is a brave opponent who would venture the question: "What happened in the second telephone conversation?" In all likelihood, the opponent fears the unknown more than the cross-examiner. After all, the cross-examination has been going badly for the witness. The opponent called the witness. What opponent wants to expose a witness who is doing badly to additional recross examination?

As pointed out, the opponent could have known about the second telephone conversation, but chose not to bring it out on direct examination for a reason. The reason generally is that ultimately the second telephone conversation would go badly for the opponent's case. Under those circumstances, the opponent will not bring it out again on redirect examination if the bait is ignored on cross-examination.

Finally, the opponent who has sandbagged or instructed the witness to set up the cross-examiner with the baited chapter may now choose to examine on the second telephone conversation. The dramatic effect hoped for by the opponent is lost since the cross-examiner did not go into the second telephone conversation on cross-examination. This leaves the cross-examiner in a better position to object that the redirect examination in this area is beyond the scope of the cross-examination. Even assuming the judge permits redirect examination in this area, the redirect examination of the second telephone conversation now looks to be an after-thought by the opponent. How important could be, the jury wonders, if the direct examiner passed it up on the first go around.

Normally bait offered by a witness that is not taken by the cross-examiner leaves an impression favorable to the cross-examiner — not to the opponent. Bait refused can therefore hurt the witness by implication. The burden is then placed on the opponent to begin new testimony in redirect. Trial is not a good place to begin discovery. Asking about the unknown is always dangerous on redirect examination. Asking about the unknown during cross-examination is even more dangerous. If the cross-examiner chooses to leave the new material alone, the danger shifts to the direct examiner who must decide whether or not to redirect on this unknown area.

§ 30.05   Declining Bait Creates Time for Cross-Examination Analysis

Whenever the cross-examiner refuses the bait, the direct examining lawyer has a difficult decision to make. The direct examiner can take the bait and question about it or refuse it as well. In the event that the opponent takes the bait, the opponent must choose to develop it on redirect examination. The cross-examining lawyer has now created time to consider the appropriate method in which to deal with the new information. The time that the redirect takes and the information developed in the redirect examination permits the cross-examiner to make a more intelligent decision. Having heard the new material the cross-examiner can make a more informed decision whether to recross on the new material. Perhaps the witness's answers have not substantially affected the cross-examiner's theory of the case. Perhaps the new answers have created a new conflict between this witness and another witness called by the opponent. Perhaps the new answers have created an opportunity to perform an impeachment by omission. In any event armed with the details of the new information and time to consider the new information the cross-examiner is in an infinitely better position to determine whether to engage in a recross examination on this limited area. The cross-examiner has gained at least some time in which to make fundamental decisions on the necessity, sequence, and style of recross. In this regard, see chapter 27, *Cross-Examination Without Discovery*.

Admittedly the redirect examination may only take moments, but those moments are longer than the microseconds between the bait and the decision to take the bait on cross-examination. Should the redirect examination take significant time, the cross-examiner gains that much more time to make intelligent decisions about the necessity, scope, and method of any recross examination.

Chapter 31

PRE-TRIAL APPLICATION — USE AT DEPOSITIONS AND PRE-TRIAL HEARINGS

SYNOPSIS

§ 31.01   Practicing the Skills

Practice does *not* make perfect. Perfection is not possible in trial work. Fortunately, perfection is not necessary. Practice allows the trial lawyer to ingrain the techniques of cross-examination so that those techniques feel natural in trial. Trial is the last place to learn a technique. It is the place to employ a technique previously learned. Every lawyer needs to practice trial skills and techniques. It is better to practice when a client's fate does not hang in the balance. So if cross-examination skills need to be practiced, and they need to be practiced outside of trial, where can they be practiced? The answer is that cross-examination techniques are easily practiced in all manner of pre-trial settings including depositions, preliminary hearings, motion practice, and any other setting in which a witness can be examined by leading questions.

§ 31.02   Breaking Out of Learned Behaviors; Applying Conscious Decisions

"The unexamined life is not worth living."

Socrates

Cross-examination techniques work best when they flow naturally. The more energy the advocate must spend on remembering the steps of a technique, the less effective the technique. It is for this reason that any complex technique should be avoided. Trial work is tough enough as is. The techniques of cross-examination are meant to be solutions. They should not create new problems. If a lawyer practices cross-examinations techniques in a haphazard way so as to develop an inconsistent approach to cross-examination, there may be some short-term benefit in an individual cross-examination. But the advocate will not have gained the long-term benefits that come from applying techniques in the everyday cross-examination of witnesses. Valid cross-examination techniques are not saved up for the tough cross-examinations. They should be used in every cross-examination so that the tough cross-examinations will feel easier. The lawyer cannot afford to have two sets of techniques: one set of techniques for practice and one set for courtroom work. Recall that the object of the book is not to equip the lawyer with techniques capable of occasionally producing a wonderful cross-examination, but to equip the lawyer with those techniques necessary to regularly produce predictably strong cross-examinations. In the pursuit of powerful and successful cross-examinations, a single technique that is used occasionally is inefficient. However, a scientific method or system of cross-examination dramatically raises the advocate's level of cross-examination for the remainder of the advocate's career.

To put this in the trial setting: No client wants his lawyer to develop new skills during his trial. Undoubtedly, we all learn from each trial but the good news is that advocates do not have to wait for trials in order to master cross-examination techniques. The classical view that cross-examination skills could only be developed during cross-examinations in trial led to trial lawyers using old techniques that were familiar and comfortable to them. The techniques were used even if they were incomplete or outmoded. The development of new and better cross-examination skills was sacrificed daily in an attempt to work with the techniques the lawyer has long used — whether or not they had proven successful. This criticism extends beyond the legal profession. Each person falls into familiar patterns or behaviors. Once behavioral patterns have been developed, it feels safer to repeat them than to learn new ones. All lawyers recognize that learning and practicing new cross-examination skills during trials is difficult.

However the practice of poor techniques, in actual trial settings, does not make for improved techniques. It makes for permanent imprinting of techniques *regardless of the value* of those techniques. Through practice, the lawyer essentially learns how to execute bad habits and unsuitable styles of cross-examination.

Sometimes lawyers find themselves relying, not on bad techniques, but on undeveloped or misunderstood techniques. Many experienced trial lawyers, who, when asked how they perform good cross-examinations, respond that they don't know because they only do what has worked over the years. Once a trial lawyer understands why a technique works, she can consciously select the appropriate technique, and with practice instinctively, reflexively, and appropriately apply the technique. The goal of pre-trial practice is to allow the practitioner to become comfortable with the technique before it is needed in trial. The lawyer can learn to perform the essential techniques of successful cross-examination so that they become ingrained responses at trial.

§ 31.03 More Cross-Examinations Mean More Learning Opportunities

The only method known to develop better cross-examination skills and to experiment with more advanced techniques, is to actually perform cross-examinations.

All forms of human endeavor rely on practice as the primary method of improving skills. Practice is the preferred method for raising one's abilities to perform difficult tasks upon demand whether one is a musician, athlete, or chef . Therefore, it is no surprise that practice and repetition are the preferred ways of honing a cross-examiner's trial skills.

The more hours the advocate spends cross-examining, the more opportunities she has to polish, refine, and improve her skills. Conducting more cross-examinations offers opportunities to learn better techniques. There are many excellent opportunities to develop cross-examination techniques without using jury trials as the primary classroom.

§ 31.04 When to Learn Better Cross-Examinations

In many professions (medicine, law, architecture, accounting, etc.), there has always been serious debate over how a new professional learns her trade. In trial law, the problems of training trial lawyers are exacerbated by considerable ethical considerations. New lawyers must be trained, but clients don't want or expect to be part of the training regimen. Everybody wants an experienced trial lawyer, but from where do they come?

A newly-trained accountant would not be asked to prepare and file the federal income tax return for IBM. However, perhaps that same young professional may be asked to contribute *work product* to the filing and preparation of that tax return. No doubt that activity will be overseen by a more experienced accountant who can assist with the preparation, organization, and compiling of the tax return. Such a strategy may well have been developed by an even more senior and experienced team of accountants.

More likely than not, the young professional would be given a portion, under supervision, of a much less demanding task to gain experience and practical training.

In the legal field, many activities, duties, and chores can be taught in this same manner. Even the least experienced lawyer can search a title with supervision. Drafting a will can be performed competently under the supervision of more experienced counsel. There is time to correct, improve, and make competent the drafting.

Unfortunately for citizens who must go to trial, inexperienced trial lawyers have traditionally developed their trial skills and techniques at the expense of their first few clients. There has not been, historically, time or training techniques to teach the skills in advance. The piecemeal learning process that may work for accountants or architects will *not* work for trial lawyers. One does not easily parcel out a jury selection here and a closing argument there. While it is possible to dole out a single cross-examination in the case, the changeover from one lawyer to another is not beneficial to the client.

§ 31.05 Learning in an Adversarial Environment

Learning in an adversarial context does not permit acquiring cross-examination skills in a gentle, nurturing environment. It is not just that the environment is stressful. The environment is adversarial. The opponent seizes every opportunity to better his case when the cross-examiner has difficulty with her case. The opponent may make objections. The opponent may suggest to the witness behaviors to frustrate the new cross-examiner. Stress alone is not the issue.

Skills needed for trial work are different from those needed for non-trial work. Once the trial begins, there is no luxury to check the title one more time or fix any mistakes. Trial work is akin to the medical specialty of surgery. Unlike their counterparts, however, inexperienced lawyers have no lifeless cadavers on which to practice courtroom techniques.

Additionally, a new surgeon practices her craft under the guidance of a more experienced surgeon. Certainly surgery is stressful. It requires a team of professionals to perform well, but it is not adversarial. No one walks in the operating room and shouts "objection" as the surgeon wields the scalpel. No one intentionally violates the sterile field in an effort to confuse, disrupt, or disorient the surgeon.

§ 31.06 Practicing the Chapter Method of Cross-Examination

Every cross-examination breaks into chapters. This is true in the shoplifting trial and the homicide trial. It is true in a contract case concerning furniture and in a contract case concerning a telecommunications satellite. If the lawyer is working on her own small case, it is imperative for her to prepare the entire case in the chapter method. Even, if the lawyer is an associate in a larger firm, or the second chair to a far more experienced lawyer, the lawyer can help the team while still improving her own skills. The lawyer need only accept the responsibility to outline all of the chapters for one witness or some of the chapters for an important witness. The act of creating chapters of cross-examination for another lawyer's use is substantially the same as preparing those chapters for her own use.

Similarly, if a lawyer must comb the discovery to build the chapters, the lawyer learns how to assemble facts to build logical progressions to specific goals. Preparation is the most underrated of cross-examination techniques. It is the least appreciated, but it is the most valuable skill a cross examiner can acquire. The more quickly a lawyer learns how to pull together facts to create chapters, the more naturally it will become. It will be easier to form chapters under the time pressures that eventually plague every lawyer. Preparation of cross-examination chapters, the amalgamation of facts, the spotting of facts beyond change, and development of theories of the case are decidedly not the grunt work of the trial profession.

§ 31.07 Trials Require Real Time Decisions

Some valuable learning can be accomplished by watching an experienced trial lawyer exercise her skills. Unfortunately, watching is no substitute for the highly interactive process of cross-examination. A person may carefully watch someone drive a car, but it won't teach her how to drive, or at least how to drive safely. When a driver must make a split-second evasive maneuver, all the watching is no substitute for practical experience.

Studying books, listening to lectures, and observing demonstrations of skills are all helpful, but they are not sufficient to educate a trial lawyer. They should all be practiced. Once inexperienced lawyers have even been exposed to the teaching of trial skills, they are obligated to practice and reaffirm those skills time after time. Trial skills are *not* like bicycle riding. A lawyer cannot get back on years later and be as good as new. Unused trial skills atrophy. To retain their condition, they must be regularly exercised. In an era where trials are becoming less numerous, a trial lawyer cannot count on a regular flow of trials in which to practice her skills. The solution is to employ trial cross-examination techniques in non-trial settings.

For lawyers who have a tremendous amount of experience in the courtroom, the techniques discussed here are equally applicable. All lawyers have developed certain bad habits that must be broken. Once a bad habit is established, it is much more difficult to break the bad habit. Beyond that, trial work has become a much more complex vehicle than it was even five years ago. It is now recognized that trial work is a specialty. Fewer non-trial lawyers go through the periodic charade of being a trial lawyer. Consequently, the opponents are better. They are more skilled and more experienced.

Another layer of complexity has been added with the advent of the professional expert witness. Courts are demanding higher expertise for witnesses who testify on expert issues. Witnesses are better prepared. They are more skilled in evading questions on cross-examination and being unresponsive.

There may well have been a time in American history when courts were not clogged, disputes remained small, and criminal sentencing acts were less draconian. In general, trials were frequent, less expensive for the litigants, and the preferred method of dispute resolution. In that era, it may well have been possible to hone one's trial skills by trying many cases. It is no longer the case. Trial lawyers must find places other than trial to practice and perfect their craft.

§ 31.08   Other Solutions

This is not to say that the legal profession has ignored this predicament. Clinical trial practice courses are now standard offerings in law schools in the United States. There is increased recognition of the need for trial skill teaching in the law school environment.

The difficulty with trial skills clinics in law schools are that they terminate for the young professional after graduation from law school and before the prospective trial lawyer ever has a chance to suffer through the rigors of a real, full blown trial.

State bar organizations and numerous other bar-related organizations offer trial skill programs (e.g., National Institute of Trial Advocacy, National Criminal Defense College). These after-graduation clinical programs are built on the recognition that the only way trial lawyers (whether inexperienced or experienced) can better their trial skills is by actually performing those trial skills.

One of the major drawbacks, no matter how well intentioned and effective these learn-by-doing techniques have become, is that they are by definition of short duration and usually of great expense. Young lawyers can seldom afford the tuition or the time away from their office. Experienced lawyers cannot imagine being away from their office for one or more weeks at a time. In fact, few professionals can afford the luxury of even two weeks away from their practice to attempt to master these necessary and important skills. Even if a lawyer could break away to go to a trial institute for two weeks, this is not enough time to firmly acquire and practice the cross-examination techniques that are fundamental to a controlled, planned cross-examination. The solution is to acknowledge that cross-examinations skills are best acquired and polished by regular use rather than by cramming for the final examination that trial represents.

This is not to say that every examination in a pre-trial setting must follow the only three rules of cross-examination, that every chapter must be prepared, or that every question must be sourced. Pre-trial is not trial. It is not mandatory that every question be leading. Especially in the deposition context, it would probably be erroneous to make every question leading. Nonetheless, there certainly will be times in every deposition, preliminary hearing, or *Daubert* hearing, in which it is not only proper but profitable to employ leading questions.

§31.09 Cross-Examinations Require Real Time Interaction

Cross-examination is the most interactive of the trial phases. Practicing cross-examination is more difficult than practicing opening statement or closing argument. Cross-examination is an interactive process. Witnesses vary in their styles, personalities, and idiosyncrasies. As a result, cross-examining a friend is a meager substitute for the true experience. While opening statements and closing arguments are important, their techniques are more easily practiced. Nobody is shooting back.

The principles applicable to public speaking or presentations in the business and professional community require skills that can be developed and utilized in opening and closing arguments. This is not to say that those skills are easily mastered. In comparison to examination, there are simply more opportunities of a non-trial variety to accomplish these skills.

In direct examination, the lawyer and the witnesses (who are often clients) can rehearse and properly prepare the questions and answers. Yet even among closely allied lawyers and witnesses, one soon finds that the answers given to the identical questions at trial are often very different than those rehearsed prior to trial.

§31.10 Real Witnesses Do Not Cooperate, Therefore Cross-Examination Rehearsals Must Build in a Lack of Cooperation

When it comes to cross-examination, the old phrase that "it is much harder to plow a field with the other person's mule" is apropos. There is the central fact that the witness is not cooperating with the examiner and that there is no cooperation for preparation or rehearsal. There are more non-cooperating parties involved in a cross-examination. The witness, the opponent, and often the judge will actively work to defeat the trial lawyer's efforts at cross-examining the witness.

Every player has an agenda. As a result, it is virtually impossible to accurately replicate the trial cross-examination experience. But it is possible to mentally replicate the lack of cooperation likely to be experienced in trial.

In preparing for trial, the veteran trial lawyer as much as the beginner benefits from envisioning where the conflicts are likely to occur. When the cross-examiner has sourced a fact (see chapter 10, *Page Preparation of Cross-Examination*), the cross-examiner has no fear of the possibility of denial. If denial occurs, it is followed promptly by impeachment. Where the cross-examiner must be most attentive in preparation is in those chapters, or those parts of chapters, where the facts are critical, but independent proof does not exist. These are the chapters that must be most carefully constructed. As part of that preparation the cross-examiner should envision the likely methods any witness may use to deny the leading question. What excuses will the witness give? What alternative facts might the witness insert? If the witness says, "No," are there methods of incorporating that answer rather then fighting it?

In other words, the practice of cross-examination requires the expectation of things gone wrong. Things gone right take care of themselves. Once the trial lawyer becomes accustomed to scenario planning for the problem areas and answers, those answers in trial no longer take the lawyer by surprise. The lawyer would be delighted with the "yes" answer, but has conceived of how to deal with other alternatives. Often the result of this exercise is the crafting of additional chapters that establish what seemed to be minor facts, all with the intention of blocking the escapes or excuses likely to be offered up by the hostile witness. Before the deposition, the advocate should concentrate on how the witness is likely to evade questions in particularly important chapters. She can then can ask more questions in those chapters and establish more facts so as to either block the likely excuse or evasion or fully appreciate exactly how the evasion will occur at trial.

To be forewarned is to be forearmed. The advocate must constantly keep in mind that it is impossible to form a bulletproof cross-examination of any duration. One of the objects of pre-trial preparation is to weed out chapters that will not work. Identifying the battles that cannot be won allows the cross-examiner to find the theory of the case so as to accommodate those weaknesses.

A tremendous amount of trial skill can be acquired by the acts of cross-examination preparation. Yes, the full interaction between the advocate and the witness can only occur when an advocate is under oath and facing cross-examination. But everything that allows a lawyer to create control of that cross-examination can be practiced and implemented before trial.

§ 31.11   Traditional Deposition Methods Employing Only Open-Ended Questions Do Not Train Well or Produce the Most Usable Results

Civil firms have long depended on the taking of depositions as a method of enabling the inexperienced advocate to learn cross-examination skills outside the courtroom. Properly used, depositions are an excellent method of acquiring cross-examination skills. However, in order to get the best value out of a deposition, both as a training and trial preparation tool, it is necessary to abandon the notion that depositions are purely discovery devices. This is especially important in a case where many witnesses live in diverse locations and cannot be compelled to attend trial. In those cases, depositions are often the trial, or at least the trial testimony of that witness. Asking exclusively open-ended questions at depositions automatically puts the witness in control of the flow of facts. Practicing how to ask open-ended questions does not produce aggressive and accurate cross-examiners.

Furthermore, the Rules of Evidence at a deposition are so phenomenally different than the Rules of Evidence at trial. The lawyer can easily be lulled into bad habits such as poor question formation, inadequate evidentiary foundations, and conclusory questioning. It is customary in civil practice to reserve objections other than the form of the questions until the time of trial. Further, most depositions are conducted in a discovery fashion of open-ended, direct examination-type questions. This lack of structure may be fine for discovery, but it is clearly a sin in trial.

While it is beyond the parameters of this book to discuss the myriad tactics of deposition practice, it must forcefully be stated that there is ample room in deposition practice for the use of leading questions, posed one new fact per question, with the facts organized in logical progressions to specific, identifiable goals. Clearly the deposition cannot be properly conducted until the advocate has developed a theory of the case. A deposition unaided by a theory is pure discovery, not even aimed discovery.

Where possible in depositions, the advocate is advised to establish through leading questions the facts the advocate wishes to use at trial. Those facts should be established in short questions, not through an invitation for an answer that might contain desired facts. Where possible, the lawyer ought to refrain from taking the most important depositions until document discovery has taken place so that the lawyer may appear at the deposition armed with the documents that can be used to gain admissions, impeach where necessary, and allow the lawyer to engage in detailed cross-examinations on the most critical aspects of the case.

§31.12 Hours of Pre-trial Experience Using the Techniques of Cross-Examination Develops the Cross-Examiner's Confidence Better Than Moments of Trial Experience

The techniques set out in this book are designed to develop the abilities of the trial lawyer. The techniques set out in this chapter are designed to instill confidence in the trial lawyer. Confidence is the intangible factor that marks not the experienced trial lawyer, but the capable trial lawyer. The advocate who has practiced the techniques of cross-examination instinctively feels more comfortable using those techniques at trial. That comfort level shows. Strangely enough it shows by a lack of unusual mannerisms rather than by the ostentatious display of ego or technique. In other words, confidence breeds a focused attitude in the trial lawyer. The most noticeable aspect about a trial lawyer comfortable with her techniques and her abilities is her lack of wasted energy.

The confident lawyer unconsciously, but continuously exhibits her confidence to the jury in many forms. The jury is more inclined and almost compelled to believe and trust that lawyer. Self-confidence is an attribute that motivates others. Use of the leading question technique alone displays great confidence by the trial lawyer. It tells everyone in the courtroom that the lawyer views herself as a master of the facts. By assuming the role of a teacher of the facts, rather than a student of the facts, the lawyer expresses her confidence that the facts of the case fairly lead to a verdict in favor of her client.

How does a trial lawyer gain mastery of the techniques to build confidence? The following sections discuss several methods in learning and polishing cross-examination techniques in all pre-trial stages in which witnesses can be examined under oath.

§ 31.13   Cross-Examining Real Witnesses Is the Best Practice for Cross-Examination Pre-trial Non-jury Hearings

The science and techniques appropriate for trial are likewise largely appropriate for pre-trial hearings. While there may be tactical reasons to elect to use open-ended questions in certain pre-trial proceedings, the general theories of teaching do not change. In fact, much of the ability to successfully cross-examine at trial is dependent on the cross-examiner's pre-trial adherence to the only three rules of cross-examination and the chapter method (see chapter 9, *The Chapter Method of Cross-Examination*).

If at a pre-trial hearing, deposition, interrogatory, or other discovery procedure, cross-examining counsel asks a compound question, the value of the resulting answer is markedly decreased value for impeachment at trial:

Q: Did you see the car coming down the highway at a high rate of speed, try to avoid hitting the truck, but then crash into the rear of the truck?

A: Yes.

Analysis: Yes to what fact? Because the questioning counsel has violated the rule of one fact per question, the resulting answer is ambiguous. If the witness apparently changes his answer to any *one* of the above facts during trial, the witness can explain that the pre-trial answer applied only to one or some, but not all of the facts contained in the question.

By adhering to the one-fact-per-question format, questioning counsel produces a usable transcript. Regardless of the content of the answer, counsel must require the witness to give a clear and unambiguous answer.

While trials have become less frequent, the questioning of witnesses in some pre-trial proceedings is more frequent. Criminal law has preliminary hearings. Civil law has pre-trial challenges to experts and numerous depositions. These forums, as well as any other pre-trial forum in which advocates confront witnesses, are ideal opportunities to practice the science and techniques of cross-examination.

There is not a skill in this book that cannot be applied in a pre-trial setting. While it is true there will be no jury to hear the spontaneous loop or to pick up on the theme, there is still a witness who is trying to dodge and deny. There is still a cross-examiner who needs to clarify, amplify, and impeach. Often, there is still a fact finder present who is learning facts and gauging credibility. For tactical reasons, a trial lawyer may elect not to try a particular technique at a pre-trial hearing (perhaps in order to save an impeachment for trial or to gain more discovery through open-ended questions). The fact remains that when the lawyer elects to use a technique, the method of presentation in a pre-trial hearing need not be different than that which would be used in trial.

As a result, this description of the practice and techniques in pre-trial settings is relatively short: *That which the cross-examiner would want to do in trial should be practiced in pre-trial settings.* The DEA agent on the stand at a motion to suppress statements can be led, looped, and impeached in the same style and manner as if a jury were present. In fact, a fact-finder is present.

While judges are fond of saying, "Counsel, this isn't trial," the fact is they comprise a jury of one. The elements of persuasion do not change. The trial lawyer hoping to better her skills as a cross-examiner is best advised to press ahead in the same meticulous manner, using the appropriate voice tones and movements, and applying the same techniques as if a jury were present.

§ 31.14 Cross-Examining Real Witnesses Is the Best Practice — Depositions

Civil lawyers are both blessed and cursed with a potentially large deposition practice. Too often, these affairs become tedious and unending: "And what happened next?" While these questions have their place, and while the use of a deposition to gain discovery is understood, there are almost always large parts of a deposition that should be conducted in leading questions performed one fact at a time, building toward establishment of a goal.

Whether the deposition is going to be used in lieu of testimony at trial or whether it is being taken for discovery purposes and to prepare the lawyer for the trial cross-examination, it is critically necessary that the cross-examining lawyer apply lessons found in chapter 8, *The Only Three Rules of Cross-Examination*, and question along the goal-oriented lines discussed in chapter 9, *The Chapter Method of Cross-Examination*. The lawyer should use the techniques of loops, spontaneous loops, establishment of theme, and other techniques. These techniques are all designed to establish control of the witness, and witness control is as critical to success at a deposition as it is in a trial setting. Furthermore, if the lawyer's goal is to create a transcript that can be used later for impeachment, precise answers to single fact questions are a requirement. A witness who can successfully evade at a pre-trial hearing or churns out damaging information in the form of non-responsive answers must be sanctioned at the preliminary proceeding, lest he learn bad habits and devices that he can use against the lawyer at trial.

Far better that the witness should learn to answer the question put to him truthfully the first time. It is better if the lawyer emerges from the deposition with particular, dependable answers, rather than with a mushy transcript worthless for impeachment purposes. It is far better to know the witness's answer than to know that the witness prefers not to answer. For all these reasons, the cross-examiner is advised to practice the techniques of cross-examination at every occasion in which cross-examination is called for, including depositions.

§ 31.15 Pre-trial Presentation Equals Trial Presentation

There is yet another reason to practice trial level techniques continually in non-trial settings. The pre-trial use of appropriate cross-examination techniques mentally trains and conditions the lawyer to rely upon those techniques as the foundation of trial cross-examination. At the time of trial, there is much confusion, anxiety, and interruption. There is less time for the cross-examiner to concentrate on how to do a task. Certain techniques, such as one new fact per question, building toward a specific goal, use of loops and spontaneous loops, all must become such a practiced part of the cross-examiner's repertoire so that they can be effortlessly formed in the trial setting. The easiest way to condition a mind to do these complex tasks successfully is to practice them at every opportunity.

The same is true with tone of voice, movement, impeachment, and other skills that are designed to have a particular impact on a jury. They are better through practice at a pre-trial level. The angry, harsh tone of voice that becomes offensive in front of a jury is equally offensive in a deposition or preliminary hearing. Better to practice more moderate tones of voice and changing tones of voice in a non-trial setting. Practice in a pre-trial setting gives the lawyer the comfort to perform the technique automatically and confidently in front of the jury.

§ 31.16 Use of Pre-trial Cross-Examinations to Train the Witness

Just as trial lawyers pattern their minds to the practice of techniques in pre-trial settings, so do witnesses. A witness learns what is expected of him, what he can get away with, what is safe, and what responses will be punished. It is dangerous to allow the witness to be in control at a pre-trial setting, since it encourages him to seek control during trial. The trial lawyer has a variety of techniques for bringing the witness back under control at trial (see chapter 19, *Controlling the Runaway Witness*), but the cross-examiner would be better off if these techniques were not needed because she had already taught the witness to respond honestly and directly to leading questions. Hence, the use of the only three rules of cross-examination at a pre-trial setting trains the witness to respond to that form of questioning when trial occurs. The short, closed-ended, one-fact-per-question method of building toward a goal programs a witness to deliver the short, responsive answer required of them at trial.

Again, it must be acknowledged that some pre-trial matters, whether motions to suppress, hearings challenging the admissibility of an expert's opinion, deposition practice, or preliminary hearings, are engaged for purposes not limited to discovery. In such an instance, it may be that many open-ended questions are asked. However, the answer, when favorable to the position of the lawyer, can be looped and reestablished in multiple closed-ended questions. The fact can be cemented in place and put in context. Finally, a transcript can be built with such clarity that any changes by the witness at trial can be impeached.

Lawyers are fond of saying that they are taking a "discovery" deposition. The jargon is well understood, but the translation may be inappropriate. Depositions need not be a wholesale fishing expedition in an attempt to see what the witness will answer about the case. It should be, in pertinent part, the establishment of answers already known to the cross-examiner that will be depended upon by the cross-examiner at the time of trial. Some part of what the witness says may be new. Much of what he says should be responses to leading questions.

Whether the deponent is an eyewitness to an auto accident, a doctor performing an independent medical examination of the plaintiff, or an accident reconstructionist hired by the defense, he can be handled through leading questions. In each instance, matters that can impeach witnesses at trial can impeach them at pre-trial hearings or even at depositions. If the witness is going to falter at the pre-trial hearing or deposition, it is better to find out now than at trial. The tests performed, the results obtained, things seen and not seen, all can be established through leading questions that rein in and pin down the witness. A well-choreographed cross-examination done in a chapter format establishing these facts through hostile witnesses at pre-trial hearings and depositions, may be the single greatest way to prevail in the case without the necessity of the trial. In that regard, the pre-trial hearing or deposition is nothing but an extension of the trial — it is part of the advocacy designed to prevail in the case. It should be given the same attention, sophisticated preparation, and execution of technique called upon at trial.

§ 31.17 Pre-trial Cross-Examination Preparation

It is ironic that lawyers will stay up nights and work weekends preparing for a trial, but seem less willing to put in an hour or two of preparation for a pre-trial hearing or deposition that could obviate the necessity of trial. The well-honed cross-examination that results in suppression of a statement or evidence in the criminal case may take a fraction of the time the trial would require. Damaging admissions made by the opponent's expert witness at a deposition can frequently lead to a favorable settlement. The facts established in a deposition may well cripple the opponent's theory of the case. In fact, it is easier to obtain useful admissions in a deposition of any trial because opponents ordinarily spend less time preparing the witness for deposition than for a trial. If the cross-examiner's goal is to prevail on behalf of her client, then pre-trial hearings and depositions must be accorded their just place as major events in the case. They are worthy of preparation and application of technique so as to arm the cross-examiner should trial occur.

In this light, time spent scientifically preparing and executing cross-examinations prior to trial is a better use of time than performing pre-trial matters in a cursory way. Lawyers who hear themselves doing trial-level cross-examinations at pre-trial hearings are hearing the sounds of success. When the lawyer hears herself spontaneously loop an answer, create a trilogy, establish a theme, control a witness, build a chapter, or establish a goal, she is hearing superb advocacy. Superb advocacy is always rewarded. The trial is not the primary showcase for the lawyer's talent. It is never a waste of talent and time to diligently cross-examine in pre-trial settings.

§ 31.18 More Rewards

It has already been pointed out that such diligent preparation and presentation may obviate the necessity of trial. Even alone, good advocacy is its own reward. The cross-examiner becomes accustomed to applying techniques under difficult circumstances. In this way, the techniques of effective cross-examination can become matters of rote. The cross-examiner gains confidence in impeachment by omission, impeachment by inconsistent statement, voice, tone and movement, and a host of other techniques. As she masters her techniques in non-trial settings, she gains added confidence in the courtroom. As a result of the confident employment of the fundamental techniques of cross-examination, the advocate is rewarded by witnesses who are more under control and juries who are more in tune with the facts that support the advocate's theory of the case.

As the lawyer's ability to teach complex facts to the jury grows, better verdicts are obtained. The lawyer's sense of integrity grows. As the courts learn that the lawyer is willing to depend on preparation and the application of ethical and understated techniques rather then trickery and overly emotional or abusive cross-examination styles, the courts grant more latitude to the lawyer in trial. The judge's respect for the lawyer's ability to ferret out facts and establish goals leads to broader parameters of cross-examination. For all of these reasons, the single best method for perfecting the science and techniques of cross-examination is to practice them at *all* pre-trial opportunities, regardless of the audience or format. The trial lawyer should learn a single system of preparation, customize it to fit her style and needs, and employ that system repetitiously.

Chapter 32

HOW TO MASTER THE TECHNIQUES WITHOUT TRIAL EXPERIENCE

SYNOPSIS

§ 32.01 Innovative Training Exercises

It is exciting to be a trial lawyer. There is a mystique to what trial lawyers do. But how can trial lawyers learn to do it better? Both client and employers are hesitant to give newer lawyers the opportunities they need to learn, refine, and polish cross-examination techniques.

Happily, the techniques of cross-examination can be learned and practiced outside of trial. Available are additional innovative teaching devices that allow lawyers to practice the fundamental skills of cross-examination. It is possible to learn how to be a good cross-examiner and become adept at the techniques of cross-examination even if the lawyer has little access to witnesses in a trial setting. These same exercises permit more experienced lawyers to identify and correct poor habits.

§ 32.02   Cross-Examining Inanimate Objects

Future surgeons practice on cadavers. Future dentists practice carving chalk. Trial lawyers can take a lesson from these practices. Trial lawyers need to search out other alternatives to witnesses.

The ultimate objective of any cross-examination should be for the jury to be able to visualize and otherwise understand the specific objective or goal of the cross-examiner in such a way as to make the objective unforgettable to the jury during deliberations. The jury must be on such intimate terms with the objective of the cross-examiner.

The cross-examination of inanimate objects is a training technique that can be practiced anywhere, at anytime. There is no need for another participant. Therefore the cross-examiner can practice this technique much like the swimmer who practices laps for hours at a time and the golfer who practices a swing repeatedly.

There are levels of difficulty in this training technique and, therefore, it is suggested that the participant begin with the simplest of inanimate objects, such as a bar of Ivory soap. There is something pure with this type of start.

Remove the soap wrapper. Now, by using strictly leading questions, developing one fact per question and progressing from the most general to the most specific, direct questions to the bar of soap. Assuming if the bar of soap could speak, it would have to utter the response "yes" to every question:

(1)   You are an inanimate object?

(2)   You are a three-dimensional figure?

(3)   You are rectangular in shape?

(4)   You are approximately four inches long?

(5)   You are approximately two and a half inches wide?

(6)   You are approximately one and a half inches deep?

(7)   You are white in color?

(8)   The edges of your sides are rounded?

(9)   There is the word "Ivory" pressed into you?

(10) There is the word "Ivory" on two of your sides?

(11) The word "Ivory" is on the sides with the dimensions four by two and a half?

The lawyer has to develop further the line of inquiry in regard to the other senses, with the final question being: "You are a bath size bar of Ivory soap?"

If the soap actually answers, stop — you've been speaking too long with inanimate objects.

This example produces an idea of what can be done with any simple inanimate object. What at first blush seems a useless exercise is, in reality, a superb method of ingraining the three rules of cross-examination: (1) leading questions only; (2) one new fact at a time; and (3) leading toward a definable goal. Lest the lawyer think these techniques to be easily mastered, just read the last trial transcript in chapter 33, *Analysis of Trial Techniques in Cross-Examination*, to gauge the number of violations of the three rules.

§ 32.03 Cross-Examining in the Office

The inanimate object practice technique can be turned into a game involving two people. Time in the office can be used to practice cross-examination techniques. This practice method does not require a second lawyer. Any person with an interest in the questioning process is fair game. This second person will play the devil's advocate and will assess whether the lawyer has put too many facts into a question, whether the lawyer is proceeding from the general to a very specific goal in a logical progression, and whether the lawyer has correctly formed the question in a leading manner. This person takes on the voice of the inanimate object — looking for an opportunity to say "no," to claim a lack of understanding of the question, and to otherwise voice the accurate responses of the inanimate object. Why bother? Because the greatest strength of the cross-examiner is derived from the cross-examiner's ability to command an absolutely unbroken string of "yes" answers to a series of tightly controlled factual inquiries. When the game becomes boring, the lawyer has internalized the basic techniques of witness control.

Any of the non-lawyers can be given a script of facts to follow. Take it from a case, take it from a former trial advocacy course, take it from a factual pattern that has been experienced in the practice, or simply make up the facts. But reduce them to writing so that all players are following the same script.

First step: practice short chapters of leading questions.

In much the same way that the lawyer cross-examined the inanimate object, the lawyer can cross-examine these living, willing witnesses. Of course, the cross-examiner wants to start as simply as possible with short chapters of cross-examination (see chapter 9, *The Chapter Method of Cross-Examination*) with short intermediate goals. Remember, the object is to make the fundamental rules of cross-examination instinctual, something that need not be thought of. As these skills develop, the cross-examiner will progress to more difficult factual scenarios, and use more advanced techniques. This exercise is one of the best for working on advanced techniques, such as loops or spontaneous loops.

While this practice method can be used by a single lawyer cross-examining a single witness, the addition of a second opposing lawyer substantially toughens the exercise. First, an adversary keeps the cross-examiner honest.

Not only would your adversary object to questions soliciting clearly impermissible evidence (hearsay as an example), but the opponent is also charged with the responsibility of objecting to violations of the three rules of cross-examination, i.e., objecting to non-leading questions, to sequences of questions that do not progress logically from a general topic to a more specific goal, and to questions that contain too many facts per question within them.

Second step: practicing techniques that block redirect examinations

In the second step of this cross-examination exercise, at the conclusion of the cross-examination, the lawyer who has cross-examined the witness must endure the redirect examination from the opponent. This will assist in teaching the lawyer how to foresee dangerous redirect examinations and how to apply techniques that close doors to render redirect examinations more difficult.

Third Step: play the role of a witness

The final step in this three-step process within the law office is for the lawyer to become the witness and the witness to become the lawyer. It does not matter if the witness who becomes the lawyer is not trained in the law. The importance of the exercise is that the lawyer will experience the cross-examination from the receiving end. Through this exercise, the lawyer will be able to watch from the witness chair the frustration of an examiner when the questions are not formed carefully enough, when the questions contain too many facts, and when the questions do not proceed from a general to specific goal. The lawyer, as witness, will be able to test methods of derailing a cross-examination. As a result, the lawyer will better understand the pitfalls that await the disorganized or inattentive cross-examiner.

§ 32.04   Expert Witnesses

Lawyers now practice trial work in the time of the professional witness. Professional witnesses are witnesses for courtroom veterans. Anyone who has ever cross-examined a medical doctor who has testified in numerous auto accident/personal injury cases knows the meaning of the term "professional witness." Worse still, in this *Daubert* age, is the expert who does nothing but testify. Such witnesses have become experts at being experts.

Law enforcement agencies have witnesses who have testified in numerous trial settings and become quite expert and professional at testifying. When officers or agents have a certain aptitude for testifying, they are encouraged and often used as the case agent or supervising agent. In this way, trial testimony becomes one of their primary duties.

The most clearly delineated professional witness is the "expert" witness. Be it in a products liability case, a car accident case, abused spouse syndrome criminal case, or a medical malpractice case, the expert witness is not only expert in the field of their education but an expert at testifying.

In medical malpractice cases, it is not unusual to have expert medical witnesses who have testified on the standard of care in the medical profession more than fifty times. How many trial lawyers can claim to have tried fifty jury trials? How many have done so in five years?

Professional witnesses bring to the witness stand the experience and knowledge of how not to answer difficult questions, or how to answer them in such a way that they are helpful to the witness and not harmful.

§ 32.05   Training as a Witness Helps Prepare for the Expert

It does not take long for the lawyer who acts as the witness to understand how a witness thinks and how easy it is for the witness to control the lawyer asking the questions, rather than for the lawyer to control the witness.

The lawyer will be surprised, however, at how quickly the lawyer or non-lawyer cross-examination in this exercise develops those basic skills of cross-examination. Then the lawyer will experience a new frustration, the frustration of the witness. This is true even when the cross is applied to the better-educated, better-trained lawyer who acts as the witness.

The process has three steps. The first lawyer conducts a cross-examination. The second lawyer conducts redirect examination. The first lawyer then plays the witness on cross-examination. For each lawyer working in the process, the procedure is completed.

§ 32.06   Using Professional Witnesses

As the trial lawyer develops confidence and skills through these exercises, the trial lawyer should contact doctors, psychologists, and other professional witnesses who, on a regular basis, are called upon to give depositions or to testify in court. Offer to help them to develop their witness techniques in a safe, secure, and relatively non-threatening environment of the law office. Professionals who want to learn to testify better will readily agree. Often, professionals will volunteer others who would appreciate the training. Even if the professional witness is only playing the role of a non-professional witness (for example, the victim of a mugging), it is helpful to have these better-educated and extremely competitive individuals as witnesses.

Develop trial skills first on inanimate objects. Progress to living, but non-speaking objects. Use the law office cross-examination techniques with relatively safe and controlled factual and witness scenarios and progress to the more educated, more intelligent, and more competitive professional witnesses. These exercises keep the edge sharp for those dry spells between trials that every lawyer experiences.

§ 32.07   Group Cross-Examination (The Exercise of Cluster Cross)

Just as in the cross-examination in the office training exercise, the exercise of cluster cross training sequence regards the lawyer as a participant in a group setting. That is, in the law office setting the lawyer plays both the role of the lawyer and the role of a witness to experience the emotions felt by the witness, i.e., to look at the courtroom from "the other side."

In this exercise, the lawyer is teamed with other lawyers who ask questions one at a time in rotation. The true learning concept of this exercise is based on the fact that no lawyer criticizes herself well enough to understand that she is her own worst enemy on cross-examination.

Often, the lawyer feels frustration and, at times, humiliation when the lawyer's twentieth question results in an answer that destroys the preceding nineteen questions. The lawyer is unwilling to search those questions for the fatal error, which often occurred at the tenth or eleventh question in that cross-examination.

Because one lawyer follows another lawyer in this sequence, and the goal is to eliminate all other lawyers from the game or exercise, each lawyer can "hear" the errors of other participants that she would not "hear" from her own mouth.

§ 32.08   Official Rules of Cluster Cross

The purpose of the exercise is to reinforce the basic rules of cross-examination and to refine and highlight the need for a detailed analysis of the progression of a particular cross-examination for the more advanced cross-examiner.

Obviously required are closed-ended questions, one fact per question, and questions that proceed from the general to the specific. Knowing when to sit down is also required.

The exercise requires each participant to listen and to be patient with questioning so as not to become too aggressive.

§ 32.09   How the Exercise Is Conducted

A participant asks one question, and then the rotation begins, with all other participants asking one question before returning to the first participant to ask a second question.

§ 32.10   Objections and Disqualifications

The instructor (if there is one) and all participants may object. If an objection is sustained, the participant who asked the question is removed from the exercise, and may not participate further unless the removed participant makes an objection that is sustained. If that participant makes an objection that is sustained, that participant re-enters the exercise.

The instructor (if there is one) rules on all objections. If there is no instructor, one participant is selected to make the rulings. There are no appeals. Some types of objections include:

(1) Failure to ask a leading question.

(2) Failure to have only one fact per question.

(3) Failure to proceed logically from point "a" (general point) to point "b" (specific point), the goal.

(4) Greed — when a participant does not logically follow the sequence of the preceding questions and takes too large a jump toward the objective (results with the next participant having no ability to ask a question that will receive a "yes" answer).

(5) Backsliding — when a participant is unsure of where to proceed, that participant often backslides. Instead of going to point "b," the participant backslides towards point "a."

(6) Delay of Exercise — when participants are unsure of the direction in which to proceed, they stammer, shift feet, and otherwise wiggle. It is in the discretion of the participants before the exercise begins as to what time limit will be placed on each question.

(7) Breaking Character — too often when frustrated, a participant will attempt to break character and discuss some point, either with other participants or the instructor. This is more clever than delay of game, but equally objectionable.

(8) Couch Potato Objection — when a poor objection is made from one of the participants, that participant suffers disqualification if the objection has no reasonable good faith basis.

(9) Lame — when the progression is so slow and so minuscule as to alienate the jury, the objection of "lame" is made. This objection should not be sustained normally, as it is much safer to proceed very slowly towards the objective, rather than becoming too aggressive and skipping ahead.

§ 32.11   Goal

It is essential that everyone agree on the exact and specific well-defined goal before the exercise begins. If the goal is not clearly defined, inevitable arguments will break out concerning whether a certain question leads to the prior established goal.

§ 32.12   End of Exercise

When a participant feels that more questions are unnecessary and would be counterproductive, the participant may state "no more questions." If it is felt that this is appropriate, the goal has been reached, and the remaining participants in the exercise have won. However, in the event that additional questions need to be asked, that participant who states "no more questions" is eliminated and the questioning continues in rotation with the remaining participants.

Conversely, if a participant should say "no more questions," and does not, that is subject to an objection and, if sustained, that participant who asks the "one question too many" is eliminated.

§ 32.13   Timing

The cluster cross-exercise should be used periodically throughout the teaching of cross-examination and that a limited, relatively straightforward, factual situation is recommended so that there can be clearly established goals.

§ 32.14   A Brief Example of a Cluster Cross

Instructor: The goal that we are to reach is to ask this witness to admit that she could not see the defendant at a bus stop on First Avenue as she walked up Main Street, an intersecting street. There was a building in between her line of travel and the bus stop. It did not have any windows or doors through which to see the defendant. The witness did eventually see a man walking away from her on First Avenue when she reached the intersection of Main Street and First Avenue, but his back was to her. On direct examination, she testified that she saw the defendant and described his face and other features.

For purposes of this exercise, it is imperative that the witness be controlled so she will not be able to testify that she saw him standing at the bus stop before he turned his back and started to walk away from her. Example:

Participant 1: You were walking on Main Street?

Answer: Yes.

Participant 2: You were walking on Main Street towards the intersection of First Avenue?

Answer: Yes.

Participant 3: You never saw the defendant while you were on Main Street?

Participant 4: Objection. Greed.

Instructor: Sustained. Participant 3 is out of the exercise.

Participant 4: As you walked towards that intersection you were on the sidewalk on the left-hand side of the street?

Participant 3: Objection.

Instructor: On what grounds?

Participant 3: There is only supposed to be one fact in the question. He asked two. Both the fact that there was a sidewalk and that the person was on the left-hand side of the street.

Instructor: That is true, but that is very close to "lame." Participant 4, you are now out of the exercise. Participant 3, you are back in.

Participant 5: You were walking on the sidewalk?

Answer: Yes.

Participant 6: The sidewalk that you were walking on was on the left-hand side of the street?

Answer: Yes.

Participant 7: . . .

Participant 6: Objection. Delay of exercise.

Instructor: She only waited eight seconds to start her question.

Overruled. Participant 6, you are out of the exercise.

Participant 6: I cannot believe that was only eight seconds; it seemed like more than an hour.

Instructor: I am sure that it would feel that way to a jury as well.

Participant 7: You were walking towards the intersection of First Avenue?

Participant 6: Objection. Backsliding.

Instructor: Sustained. Participant 7, you are out of the exercise.

Participant 6, you are back in.

Participant 8: There was a building to your left?

Answer: Yes.

Participant 1: That building has no windows on the bottom floor?

Answer: That is correct.

Participant 2: That building has no doors with windows in them on the bottom floor?

Answer: Yes.

Participant 3: That building blocked your view of First Avenue?

Participant 7: Objection. Failure to have only one fact in a question.

Instructor: I am not sure on this one.

Participant 7: The witness could see portions of First Avenue.

Instructor: Oh yeah, that's right. Sustained. Participant 3, you are out of the exercise. Participant 7, you are back in.

Participant 5: The building prevented you from seeing to your left and to the left of the building?

Answer: That is true.

Participant 6: You know there is a bus stop on First Avenue near that intersection?

Answer: Yes.

Participant 7: That bus stop is to the left of the building, to the left of that intersection?

Answer: Yes.

Participant 8: You could not see through the building to see the bus stop as you were walking up Main Street?

Answer: That is true.

The exercise continues.

§ 32.15   Advanced Techniques

As the participants become more skillful, more advanced techniques will be utilized. At times it is helpful to have a conference prior to the exercise and have the participants agree on certain words that will be emphasized and will be used in looping.

§ 32.16   Practicing Techniques in Non-Legal Settings

Too often the lawyer views cross-examination as only applicable to the courtroom or courtroom-like settings. Nothing could be further from the truth. Interviews employ the same skills required as the courtroom setting. Discussion of office procedure with partners and employees often require the same type skills. On a more broad-based view, talking with anyone at any time can be used to develop these skills.

For example, the lawyer meets an attractive member of the opposite sex at a holiday cocktail party. The lawyer wants to get to know that person, so she initiates a conversation. After introducing herself, to develop more information about this person, she begins to ask questions. Not only can she ask these questions in a direct examination format eliciting open-ended responses, but she can also develop cross-examination questions that are designed to give the listener as much information about her as she is asking about the listener.

As another example, from time to time, lawyers must purchase something, such as clothes or a gallon of milk on the way home from the office. They can use this opportunity as a quick experiment to practice one or more of the techniques for controlling the runaway witness.

The lawyer might ask why she would use this in purchasing a retail item. The answer is simple. These people are salespeople. Salespeople volunteer continuously. They never answer the question that you ask. They always want to give the customer more information than requested.

Go in a store to buy a pair of trousers. The customer is short of time, but wants to purchase a pair of trousers. Ask the salesperson for a certain brand. The salesperson does not have that brand and tries to steer the customer to another brand. Utilize the repeat, repeat, reverse technique:

Customer: Sir, do you have a pair of Bugle Boy jeans?

Salesperson: Well, actually those are not very much in style any more. What we prefer to sell is Jordache. They are much more popular and fit better.

Customer: You have a pair of Bugle Boy jeans?

Salesperson: As I was saying, we prefer Jordache, but if that is not good for you, Calvin Klein is excellent. Much better than Bugle Boy.

Customer: You don't have a pair of Bugle Boy jeans?

Salesperson: Yes, we have them.

In another example, assume that the lawyer is in a grocery checkout line. There must be some rule somewhere that grocery checkout people (except for the express lane) must talk to stay sane. Use this opportunity to find out if the lawyer can stop a runaway witness by the use of body movements, such as the hand technique, the finger technique, or the head shake technique. For example, the lawyer asks. "Isn't it a shame that the tomatoes are not as large or as firm as they once were?" The cashier responds by saying yes and discusses the weather, the time of the year, and the season. The lawyer simply raises his or her hand in a stop sign motion. As a result, the cashier stops the conversation and quietly continues to ring up the purchase. The cashier never voluntarily enters into conversation again with you.

In a final example, the lawyer returns home from work. It has been a long and difficult day. Her child's bicycle is in the driveway. She calls the child in to talk with him. This is a cross-examination that no one does well. Use it as an opportunity to spontaneously loop the child:

Lawyer: Matthew, you left your bike in the driveway, didn't you?

Matthew: Well, I don't know that it is in the driveway. See, what happened was, Dad called me and told me to come in right now and to stop what I was doing. Dad called me to get in this house right now. Dad called me and that is why I left the bike where it was. Then, I tried to tell him that I was going to get in trouble for where the bike was and he told me that he didn't care about that, that he wanted me in the house right that minute.

Lawyer: Then you realized when you left the bike in the driveway that you would get in trouble?

Matthew: Oh, boy. How much trouble, Mom?

This technique can be very hard on families.

§ 32.17   Use of Digital and Videotape Technology

It has been said that the development and proliferation of videotape and digital recording devices has had a revolutionary effect on the preparation of witnesses for trial. Digital recording and videotape offers equally dramatic opportunities to address the trial lawyer's preparation for trial as well.

Not only is the digital or video camera used to film crime scenes, accident scenes, clients wearing neck braces, children at play in lovely surroundings in custody cases, and numerous other evidentiary matters, this visual technology should be an essential means of preparing the lawyer for trial. How the lawyer uses her body movements, tone of voice, and the integration of these activities with the content of the questions can all be enhanced by the use of digital recordings or videotape.

Too often and for too long, trial lawyers stumbled about blindly thinking that they looked, moved, and spoke in a pleasing manner congruent with the theory of the case. After all, each had graduated law school and become relatively successful in an intensively competitive profession. In each of the previous training exercises, the video or digital camera can be used so the lawyer may review her body language, movement, tone, and the congruency of those activities with the theory of the case for that exercise.

Some may ask, "Why would I want to videotape myself asking a bar of Ivory soap what color it is?" While asking those questions, watch the lawyer's face. Are the lawyer's eyes clinched so tight out of nervousness and concentration that the lawyer appears to be in need of immediate vision correction? If so, the expression may be worse when the lawyer is questioning a living, breathing witness under the microscope of the courtroom setting.

When the lawyer asked the bar of Ivory soap a non-leading question and caught herself, did she visually react in such a way that everyone watching her would know that she somehow had made an error? If this were true while the lawyer was cross-examining a bar of Ivory soap, it would be more evident in the courtroom.

If this short discussion has not convinced the lawyer of the need for digital or video technology to enhance trial preparation and to learn vital trial skills, take ten minutes of time and record the lawyer performing a cross-examination. Play the tape back. Within this time, if she does not verify for herself that a digital recording or videotape is essential to development as a trial lawyer, dispense with it.

§ 32.18   Practice Does Not Make Perfect; Practice Makes Permanent

These exercises may seem sophomoric to experienced trial lawyers. They may seem beneath the lawyer. The fact of the matter is that each lawyer wants to become a better cross-examiner. That's why the book was written. That is why it was purchased.

Whether a lawyer analyzes cross-examination minutely or has a visceral feeling for cross-examination, she knows that she needs to do it better. Each of the exercises is designed to improve the cross-examiner. Each of the exercises is designed to permit the lawyer to cross-examine in a safe and comfortable setting. Pick those exercises that will best enhance the needed skills as a trial lawyer. Practice.

Chapter 33

ANALYSIS OF TRIAL TECHNIQUES IN CROSS-EXAMINATION

SYNOPSIS

§ 33.01   Introduction

In order to illustrate the operation of the cross-examination techniques discussed in this book, certain examples have been set out. In keeping with the spirit of this book, these materials are not representative of the work of any one particular lawyer. The authors have freely drawn upon the common trial experiences of a great many lawyers. In some instances, fact, events, witnesses, and cross-examinations have been created in order to illustrate a particular technique. In other instances, factual cases have been drawn upon as the inspiration for a particular illustration. Nonetheless, even in those situations, the names, dates, places, and events have been modified for teaching purposes, and the resulting transcripts should not be understood in the least as actual transcripts of cases, but should be accepted solely in the spirit in which they are offered — hypothetical illustrations of the science and techniques of cross-examinations that might be employed in a courtroom setting. The purpose of this chapter is to set out excerpts from cross-examinations that show the utilization of many of the techniques discussed elsewhere in the text.

The purpose of these illustrations is not to give the reader some sense of the sequencing of cross-examinations, but the employment of methods of witness control, and the use of techniques that can be pre-planned or spontaneously drawn upon as the personality of the witness directs.

§ 33.02   Transcript 1 — Cross-Examination of a Corporate Executive

The following materials are drawn from a commercial litigation case. The names have been changed. The case involved an allegation by a small dog food manufacturer selling its premium brand dog food under the name Purebred.

The Purebred Company had trademarked that name. One day the owner of that company discovered that the Acme Co. was marketing a premium brand dog food which prominently displayed the name Purebred on its packaging. In trademark law, such a case is called "reverse confusion." Instead of an unknown company poaching on the name developed by a market leader, in a reverse confusion case a company with great marketing power is charged with misappropriating the trade name of a much smaller company, and thereby causing the market to believe that the name belongs to the more powerful company.

The plaintiff wrote a letter asking the defendant to cease and desist. When the defendant continued to market its dog food without changing its packaging, the plaintiff brought suit for trademark infringement. The defendant denied all liability. Trial to a jury followed.

The witness whose cross-examination is excerpted was, during the time of the actions complained of, a sales executive for the defendant company. As might be predicted, the witness was not supportive of the plaintiff's claims. The cross-examination was difficult. The witness seldom answered leading questions with short answers, but instead frequently provided narrative responses of some length. The cross-examiner attempted to use the witness to explain the enormous marketing muscle of the defendant, how that marketing muscle was used to take advantage of plaintiff's trademarked name, how easy it would have been to discover plaintiff's trademark, and how even after discovering plaintiff's trademark the defendant persisted in its marketing campaign.

The reader is reminded that these transcript passages are incomplete, and have been heavily excerpted in order to further the goal of demonstrating certain cross-examination techniques. These passages do not purport to be a full recitation of the testimony and the reader should understand that these materials are not designed to fully or fairly set out the testimony or the positions of the parties to the law suit. Entire chapters have been omitted. Within the chapters that are included, certain questions, answers, objections and rulings have been omitted as they do not materially assist in a discussion of the techniques being employed.

Transcript	*Analysis*
BY CROSS-EXAMINER: Q: Mr. Vancine, I'd like to take you back to your work with the Acme company.	*Chapter: Background at Acme* This witness is a corporate executive employed by the defendant. He has been called by the plaintiff for purposes of cross-examination. These are introductory questions designed to place the witness in context within his corporate organization.
A: Yes.	

Transcript	*Analysis*
Q: You began with Acme in 1975?	
A: That is correct.	
Q: And Acme Pet Foods was formed about November 1 of 1988?	
A: Yes.	
A: Acme had purchased Acme-Star around 1963. The part of Acme-Star Foods which made pet food, primarily Kitty-Cat cat food and Jerky Savory, those brands, along with some recent acquisitions earlier in '88, became Acme Pet Products.	
Q: So by 1998, you became the vice president of sales of that part?	
A: Yes.	
Q: So by April '99, at least, we have your assurance that you would be the person most knowledgeable about sales of Generic Breed Formula?	
A: I would not say I would be the most knowledgeable, but it was under my area.	
Q: Well, the success of it would accrue to your benefit as sales manager?	At this point, only a few minutes into the cross-examination, it becomes clear that this will be a difficult witness.
A: I was the sales manager responsible for Outdoor Blend.	
Q: And the failure of it would be a black mark on you?	
A: Not following your question.	
Q: I just want to know, sir, could we have your assurance you followed very closely the successes and failures of Generic Breed Formula?	

Transcript	*Analysis*
A: I followed the success and failure of Outdoor Blend and particular brand, the success or failure of a flavor or an S-K-U would not be considered a major issue.	Notice how the witness has picked up on the word "failure" and is now using it in his own answers.
	The witness is offering bait. A SKU is simply an individual product within a group of products and is not the issue. The witness has used the word "major issue." The cross-examiner spontaneously loops the phrase and confronts the witness with the phrase, offering the witness the opportunity to deny a fact easily provable.
Q: So you're saying to us that the problems of Generic Breed Formula were not a major issue?	
A: They were a major issue.	The witness is cornered by the facts and concedes that the product line was a major issue.
OPPOSING COUNSEL: Objection, Your Honor. There's been no foundation set that there's been a problem with this brand. I know it's cross-examination, but there still has to be foundation set.	The opponent reacts to the poor word choice of his own witness and tries to bail him out, but the objection is lame.
THE COURT: Overruled.	
BY CROSS-EXAMINER:	
Q: Mr. Vancine, you watched the transition from Outdoor Blend to a piece of it called Outdoor Blend Generic Breed Formula?	

Transcript	*Analysis*
A: I don't follow what you just said. We had a brand called Outdoor Blend. In 1999 when it came on to me, one of the subsets of Outdoor Blend was Generic Breed Formula. It wasn't a — the verbiage you used I did not follow.	
Q: So Generic Breed Formula, though, is a name you do follow, isn't it?	
A: Yes, it is.	
Q: That name, Generic Breed Formula, that was first used by Acme in about December 20 of 1997?	*Chapter: History of Generic Breed Formula*
A: That could be correct. It was sometime around then, yes. Don't know the exact date.	
CROSS-EXAMINER: Could I have Exhibit 12.002?	Exhibit 12.002 means Exhibit 12 at the page carrying the Bates number 002. This is by far the easiest way to number documents. In this way there's no confusion as to what page witness is to view.
And is there a white notebook that I may make visible to the witness, please?	
Q: If you would turn in that notebook to Exhibit 12. Acme, when it wanted to — let me wait until you're there, sir.	The document shows the application for a trademark issued by the United States patent and trademark office to the defendant. Its importance in the case will become clearer as the the jury is taken through the various names used by the defendant for its dog food. All of this has been explained to the jury in opening statement.
A: Okay. I'm following you, yes.	

Transcript	*Analysis*
Q: When Acme wanted to protect its name for a dog food, it went to the United States government, didn't it?	The cross-examiner seeks to demonstrate that the defendant well understands and takes advantage of the right to legally protect its product names while ignoring the rights of the plaintiff.
A: I don't know what this document is. I have no idea what this is.	
Q: Well, let's look at it. United States Patent and Trademark Office?	Witness attempts to deny any knowledge of such things as trademarks. This is a form of the "I don't know" answer.
A: I'm a salesperson, sir, I wouldn't know.	One method of attacking the credibility of such an answer is to show that by circumstances, training, or profession the witness in all likelihood does know the answer. If the jury reaches this conclusion they will additionally conclude that the witness does not want to admit the facts because the truth would hurt the witness's side of the case.
Q: How many — tell the jury how many Acme Pet Foods have you been sales manager or connected to.	
A: If you're talking brands, I think the terminology is brands, Acme owns dozens and dozens of Acme — of brands of pet food.	This question and answer shows that by circumstances the witness should be well acquainted with trademarks.
Q: And do you know, if I lay out the dozens and dozens of Acme brands on this table, brands you've been working with for a career, we're going to find after the names, Kitty-Cat, Jerky Savory, Super-Dog, we're going to find trademark registration by Acme, aren't we?	This question and answer shows that by profession the witness should be well acquainted with trademarks.

Transcript	*Analysis*
A: I do not know.	
Q: You don't know, as the sales manager, you can say to us, I don't know that we've trademarked Super-Dog, I don't know that it's — it's a protected trademark Kitty-Cat; is that your testimony, sir?	The question and answer shows that by training the witness should be well acquainted with trademarks.
A: As the sales manager, I do not know which — what's trademarked and what's not trademarked.	The witness still insists that trademarks are a mystery to him. In fact he goes too far and suggests that he is incapable of determining whether a brand or a name is trademarked.
Q: But we could tell if we just wanted to look at the can or the package, we'd see the little trademark symbol, wouldn't we?	This answer permits the cross-examiner to demonstrate how easy it is to determine if a name has been trademarked — one need only look for the trademark symbol. The jurors are likely familiar with such a symbol and therefore disbelieve the witness's protestations that as a career sales manager for major corporation, with years of experience he cannot tell what is trademarked.
Q: Normally you'd see either a trademark or a registration symbol, that's correct.	The witness gives up. He has now told the jury that this entire fight was unnecessary.

Transcript	*Analysis*
Q: And after working for Acme for 26 years, you're telling us you never really looked to see if you were trademarking your names?	The technique is again to offer the witness the chance to stake out an unrealistic position. This is a very common technique, and it produces the very likely result: The witness declines to take the unreasonable position and therefore must take the position that the cross-examiner wanted to establish in the first place—the witness well knows how to figure out if something is trademarked.
A: That is not the question you asked me originally, sir.	The witness attempts to dodge the question by commenting on the question rather than by answering the question.
THE COURT: Wait a minute. Hold on. Hold on.	The court will not condone this conduct and admonishes the witness. The admonishment of a court will virtually always put the witness under tight control for some period of time. Many witnesses will not act out again throughout the course of the cross-examination. Others will behave for a period of time and then begin exploring the boundaries of unresponsive behavior.
Mr. Vancine, your role here is to answer questions, not ask them. So you will either answer a question or say you don't understand it. THE WITNESS: Sir, I'm trying — I apologize.	This witness can be expected to be under control for at least the next few chapters.

Transcript	*Analysis*
THE COURT: Your last response was flippant, and so it's not appropriate to say that isn't what he previously asked you. You either will answer the question or say you don't understand. Do I may myself clear?	
THE WITNESS: Yes, sir. I apologize.	
THE COURT: Let's have a new question asked.	
CROSS-EXAMINER: Certainly.	
BY CROSS-EXAMINER:	
Q: If you would look at page, document 12001, please, the first page of this. When Acme wants to protect its, its names like Generic Breed Formula, it protects itself from others using it by trying to trademark it. Were you aware of that?	
A: Again, don't understand your question.	The witness is unwilling to be directly evasive but is still willing to say he does not understand.
Q: I'll try it in other words. Is your testimony after a quarter century with this company that you're unaware that Acme tries to protect its trademarks from being infringed on by others?	And, the technique used is to offer the witness opportunity to take an unrealistic position. Again, the witness declines to take a position that will inevitability hurt his credibility.
A: I do understand that is what Acme does. Can I explain why I said I did not understand the question, Your Honor?	The witness concedes the point.
Q: Sure.	

Transcript	*Analysis*
A: There is two parts to your question. Part of it had to do with Generic Breed Formula. Part of it had to do with trademarks, and I didn't know what part of the question to answer. I know in general terms, yes, Acme does protect trademarks. I do not know specifically what's trademarked and what's not.	
	In his narrative answer the witness once again makes the cross-examiner's point that defendant understands the value of its trademarks and will protect its trademarks while showing no regard for the legal rights of competitors' trademarks.
Q: And the reason you know, as a sales manager, that Acme protects its brands — that's another name for trademark?	The cross-examiner establishes that "brand" as a synonym for "trademark." This concession, put in front of the witness as a throwaway line is really quite important.
A: I am not legal, but in my understanding, yes. But as legal person, I don't know for sure.	
Q: The reason you know that is it's important to you in sales to protect your brand from being used by other competitors?	The question is phrased in such a way that the witness must concede the reasonableness of efforts to protect a trademark from a competitor. The hypothetical question is posed away that positions his company as the company in the right rather than the company in the wrong. This phraseology will almost always elicit a "Yes" answer.
A: That is correct.	

Transcript	Analysis
Q: So it doesn't surprise you at all that somebody else who has a brand wants to protect it against Acme's infringing, does it?	Now, having gained the "Yes" answer to the hypothetical, the cross-examiner need only switch the positions of the parties, placing the witness's company in the wrong, and the plaintiff in the right. It is very difficult for the witness to deny the rightfulness of plaintiff's position, having just said that position would be appropriate if adopted by the defendant.
A: No, not at all.	The wording of the answer is clear and certain. With these words the witness has displayed weakness or vulnerability on this point. The cross-examiner pushes the point to its furthest extent.
Q: You'd do the identical thing if you found us using your name on one of our bags, wouldn't you? OPPOSING COUNSEL: Objection, Your Honor. It calls for speculation. the witness out. THE COURT: Overruled. I'll let the witness answer if he can.	Opposing counsel understands the danger of the answer of the witness and tries to bail The Court, having heard the previous series of answers of the witness on this important point allows the cross-examiner the room needed to fully develop the point.
OPPOSING COUNSEL: Second objection, Your Honor, isn't that the golden rule? THE COURT: Isn't what the golden rule? OPPOSING COUNSEL: That question. THE COURT: Overruled. I'll let him answer the question, if he can.	Opposing counsel tries a second tact. The objection is a non-starter.

Transcript	*Analysis*
THE WITNESS: If I, in my travels, see a mark on another package in a store that looks similar to a Acme product that could cause confusion, my responsibility would be to send it back to the local marketing person who would be responsible for the next steps. But as a salesperson, my only responsibility is if I saw something in the field that looked like it competed with one of our brands, I would send that sample back to the marketing person. What was done next was not in my area.	The witness has gotten the message and attempts to duck the question.
BY CROSS-EXAMINER:	
Q: You'd do your best to make sure Acme protected itself from people who infringed your brands.	The cross-examiner brings the witness back to the central concept that a company whose trademark is being infringed should be expected to protect itself and that his company would certainly do that if the shoe were on the other foot.
A: As I described was my responsibility.	
Q: And you say, did I understand you correctly, you weren't aware of a problem with Generic Breed Formula, or did I misunderstand you.	*Chapter: Problems with Generic Breed Formula*
A: In what aspect, sir?	
Q: That it sold badly.	The cross-examiner offers up a subjective description.

Transcript	*Analysis*
A: The sales were not bad. The sales were not up to the objectives set for the business.	The witness engages in a well understood evasive device. He redefines the issue. Sales were not bad; they were simply not up to business objectives. Now the cross-examiner must use hard edged facts to show the jury that "bad" is a much more accurate description then "not up to the objectives set for the business." If the cross-examiner can accomplish this, the witness will lose further credibility.
Q: Let's look at Exhibit 14. You'll have it in your notebook.	
Q: Now, Exhibit 14 — we can pick up a date on this down at the bottom, May 25, 1999. See that, sir?	The first place to look for facts that can back down the witness is within documents produced by the witness's company. It is exceedingly hard for a witness to argue with facts contained within his own company's records.
A: Yes, sir.	
Q: And, Mr. Vancine, this document comes from Mr. Barnaby.	The author of the document is identified. Now the cross-examiner must give the author credibility.
Tell the jury what your relationship was with Mr. Barnaby.	
A: Dave Barnaby was the product manager on Outdoor Blend at this particular point in time. He had been a product manager on our products at Acme.	
(Chapters discussing the relationships between marketing and sales are omitted.)	

Transcript	*Analysis*
Q: Make it simple for me. You're vitally interested in the sales of Generic Breed Formula?	After a series of battles concerning the roles of marketing versus sales, the cross-examiner brings the witness back to the topic of most importance — how bad were the sales of the product in question.
A: Yes, sir.	
Q: And that falls into your day.	
A: Yes, sir.	
Q: And Mr. Barnaby is going to come up with the campaign, with the marketing strategy for it?	
A: He'll — yes.	
Q: Mr. Barnaby would need to know accurately how well Generic Breed Formula is doing, wouldn't he?	Our further questions are designed to enhance the credibility of the author of the document about to be used.
A: Yes.	
Q: Well, let's look at Exhibit 14. First line. GBF sales — that's this whole line, isn't it?	*Chapter: What Marketing Said About Sales*
A: Yes, sir.	
Q: This is the line where you're trying to convince consumers to buy different, different dog food for each different dog in the house?	
A: Yes, sir.	
Q: Sales not high enough to support a 14-SKU line. Now, that 14-SKU line means you have seven types in two bag sizes.	This is a quote from the document which is now displayed on a screen with the important sentence highlighted. In this way jurors can immediately focus on the only part of the document the cross-examiner wishes to discuss at this time. The term SKU is used and must be translated for the jurors.

Transcript	*Analysis*

A: Yes.

Q: Second line. Experiencing SKU discontinue indications by retailers with more to come. Let's talk about what that line means. You know in sales what it means, don't you?

Another line out of the document is highlighted. This quoted language again shows that sales of the product line were poor.

A: Yes.

Q: What it means is that the people that are going to sell this to the consumer don't want to stock it that way. They don't want much of this stuff, do they?

The corporate speak is now rephrased into lay terms.

A: They don't want the — as it says in the first line, 14 items was too many for retailers to be carrying.

Q: And they're beginning — well, not beginning — by now, by May of 1999, you knew sales were going down on this, didn't you?

A: As I articulated a few minutes ago, the sales were not meeting the sales objectives for the line.

Q: You have goals, and you're failing to meet goals.

The word "failing" is the key to this question.

A: That is correct.

The witness agrees with that term.

Q: So failure would be the right word, wouldn't it?

Now the cross-examiner can look the important description "failing."

A: In that context, yes.

Q: And what you're hearing back is we're not only getting retailers discontinuing, but we think there's more going to come. This line is getting weaker all the time.

Cross-examiner further interprets the document. The word "weaker" is added to the picture.

Transcript	*Analysis*
A: Yes.	The witness accepts this description because his own company document says as much. Remember, at this point the cross-examiner has been using the witness to discuss the words of another corporate employee. Since the witness has to agree with the core or document, it becomes easy to place similar thoughts in the head of the witness. No witness in his position will want to say he was unaware of the problems with the brand. Not only will this make the witness look foolish, but now that the witness has seen the cross-examiner use against him the words of a corporate document, the witness cannot be sure what he may have said in the past.
Q: And you knew that, didn't you?	
A: Yeah, I mean I agree with you.	
Q: And the reason you knew it is you didn't need somebody up above you in marketing to say that. You knew it from the ground up from your own training and experience, didn't you?	*Chapter: You Knew There Were Big Problems Selling the Product* Now that the witness has committed to this knowledge, he can be further settled with understanding the bad news by a play to his own vanity and sense of self importance. By building up the position of the witness and his own professionalism the cross-examiner puts the witness in a position where he wants to know the problems with a product.
A: Yes.	

Transcript	*Analysis*
Q: Your salespeople across the country, including Ed Jackson, are telling you, we're not getting interest in this Generic Breed Formula idea?	The cross-examiner introduces the name of yet another corporate employee. The jurors have heard that name in opening statement and are aware that this former employee has also provided important facts against the corporation and in favor of the plaintiff.
A: No.	
Q: In fact, we're not only not getting interest, we're finding it tougher all the time to get the shelf space we need.	
A: No. To not — we are getting interest. I did not say — please, as I said before, it was not meeting the objectives. But to say there was no interest is not correct.	After much of the damage is done witness attempts to retreat to "not meeting objectives."
Q: Well, saying there would be no interest would mean there would be zero sales and we know that's not true.	
A: That's correct.	
Q: It's just not enough sales.	This definition is unlikely to succeed as too many facts have already been admitted.
A: That is correct.	The cross-examiner can now take on the distinction the witness wishes to draw between sales being "bad" versus sales "not meeting objectives."
Q: Oh. That's pretty important in sales, isn't it? That's pretty important concept, we're not selling enough of a product. That's the beginning of the death of a product.	
	This concept advanced by the witness, when taken to its logical conclusion shows that the product is in danger of dying. This is a far cry from sales merely "not meeting objectives."

Transcript	*Analysis*

A: If something's not done about it, correct.

Q: If something's not done, it's the death of Generic Breed Formula.

OPPOSING COUNSEL: Objection, Your Honor. That's argument with the witness. That's not a question.

Opposing counsel tries to warn the witness.

THE COURT: Sustained. I'll let you rephrase that in the form of a question, if you choose to.

Once the Court offers the cross-examiner a chance to rephrase, the court is signaling that the concept is relevant and important but that the form of the question must be changed. Counsel should always comply by rephrasing the question. If the question has been argumentative, part of the technique of rephrasing should be the use of a lower volume.

BY CROSS-EXAMINER:

Q: Once it's in the spiral down, if something isn't done to Generic Breed Formula, it dies?

The picture of this product in a death spiral is now accomplished.

A: That would be a correct statement, if nothing is done.

Q: And you lose your investment.

A: That would be correct.

The chapter is concluded.
Chapter: Urgent Action Required

Q: And let's now see if we have some sense of the urgency of this. Generic Breed Formula isn't a mature product that's been on the product for seven or eight years, is it?

Transcript	*Analysis*
	The following leading questions are designed to put in important dates so that the jury can have a context in which to understand that the very real and significant problems of this product are occurring within months of its introduction to the market.
A: No.	
Q: It's only been on the market for, how many months at this point, May of '99?	
A: Well, you had mentioned December 20 of '98, being the first time it was used. And it was around that time frame. So, you know, a little over a year, year and a half by the time we had gone in distribution.	
Q: And so in a year to a year and a half, it's already bad enough that what Mr. Barnaby says is restaging the line must occur now. Now. Right, Mr. Vancine?	The witness is reminded that he is hemmed in by the statements in Exhibit 14 authored by another executive of the defendant. The word "now" is quoted directly from the exhibit. The cross-examiner can point to it and the witness must either buy into that sense of urgency, or dispute the corporation's own document. Predictably, the witness will not pick a fight with the exhibit.
A: Yes.	
Q: And the word "now" turns out to be, as we go through this, immediately, as quickly as Acme could do it; isn't that right?	The concept that action must be taken "immediately" is added to the picture.
A: Yes.	

Transcript	Analysis
Q: And the reason it was an emergency is because there isn't even time to study this for another six months, sales are going down that rapidly?	The term "emergency" is added to the picture.
A: I'm trying to think back to that time frame. Sales were declining. Some of the S-K-Us were not doing well. Some of the individual items were selling okay and selling pretty good at that particular time.	So here we are, many pages and many chapters after the witness tried to minimize the problem with sales of the product.
	The witness tries to salvage what he can, but the picture is not very pretty. *Chapter: Restaging the Product*
Q: What's going to have to happen here, according to marketing, is we're going to have to restage the line, and that has a meaning in your business, doesn't it?	
A: Yes, it does.	
Q: Restage the line means we're going to have to do some kind of rethink, reprogramming, we're going to have to start over?	The term "Restaging" is very important. It is now defined for the jury.
A: It's not start over. But it is definitely reenergize, reinvigorate, do something different than what we were doing. What we were doing was not working on all the items.	

Transcript	*Analysis*
Q: And what you're going to do when we're all done with this — the next hour or so you and I spend together — what we're going to do at Acme is we're going to find a better name than GBF, aren't we?	The linkup is now made for the jury. Earlier chapters have demonstrated that the dog food marketed by the defendant under its trademarked name was failing. As part of the urgent plan to restage the product the defendant wanted a new name. It is the contention of the plaintiff that the name selected infringed upon the plaintiff's trademark.
A: That's part of what was done, yes.	Cross-examiner wants to show that the defendant wanted to get rid of the old name and pick a better name.
Q: And that better name that we're going to find to energize the product, that name's going to get filled in on the bag, isn't it?	The bags of dog food are the most important exhibits in the case. The plaintiff must win the case by showing that the defendant used the name of plaintiff's dog food as part of a larger name that the defendant plastered all over its bags.
A: Yes.	
Q: And the name is going to get filled in on hundreds of thousands of bags, would you say?	
A: That's probably an accurate number. I haven't done the math, but, yes.	
Q: The name you hope is going to sell this dog food is Purebred?	This is the defense position. The name of its dog food is Outdoor Blend. The dog food is specially formulated for purebred dogs and therefore it is fair use to put the word Purebred in big letters on the bags.
A: The name we were hoping to sell was Outdoor Blend Purebred.	

Transcript	*Analysis*
(Chapters dealing with the old name are omitted.)	
CROSS-EXAMINER: Exhibit 13, please. Thank you, sir.	*Chapter: When the Bag Is Laid on the Shelf, the Plaintiff's Trade Name Is Most Prominent* The cross-examiner now begins using the bags.
BY CROSS-EXAMINER: Q: Let's show the jury just how important to Acme Outdoor Blend was under Generic Breed. It's not up here at the top, is it?	The support and for the cross-examiner to establish the method by which bags of dog food are customarily stocked on a shelf. The bags are laid on their side so that the bottom panel is the most prominent.
A: No. Q: No. It's down here. At the very bottom in the corner. A: That is correct. Q: And of course you know how these things get stocked on the shelf at all the stores, don't you?	The cross-examiner demonstrates to the jury how the bag is stocked its bottom panel exposed.
A: Yes. Mostly like this. Q: Butt end, as it's called?	Another term requiring translation.
A: Correct. The butt end down. Q: And let's show the jury just how important thought the Outdoor Blend name was to selling it. When it's stacked on its butt end, Outdoor Blend falls to the bottom. A: Correct. Q: And it's the GBF that you're promoting, isn't it? A: Yes. I mean from my viewpoint, the word "terrier" is the prominent name on this end of the bag.	

Transcript	*Analysis*
Q: Certainly Outdoor Blend was prominent?	
A: I agree with you on that.	
Q: And these bags don't get created at random, do they?	
A: No.	
Q: You know that Acme considers itself a global expert in marketing?	*Chapter: The Defendant Is a Global Expert in Marketing*
A: If you — yes. Yes. That's an accurate statement. I've read that.	The purpose of this chapter is to show that the defendant has gigantic marketing muscle, and that once it has begun using the trademarked name of the plaintiff, the plaintiff is far too small to compete.
Q: You've read it in the press releases?	The witness knows not to deny this as the phrase "global expert in marketing" is taken directly from the defendant's own press release.
A: Yes.	
Q: You've read the press release. Would you look at 11B in your book, please?	The trial exhibit that uses this phrase is now placed before the witness and the jury.
Q: Sure. You're aware of 11B. It's the Acme press release, isn't it?	
A: Yeah, I'm just — it's dated August 4, 2000, so obviously it doesn't come straight to mind, but, you know, I believe I've read some of the things in here; but, you know, being two years old, I don't recall verbatim, but, yes. CROSS-EXAMINER: **Your** Honor, I move the admission of Exhibit 11B. THE COURT: Is there an objection?	

Transcript	*Analysis*
OPPOSING COUNSEL: Objection based on relevance, Your Honor. There's no mention of any of the brands or issues involved in this lawsuit.	
THE COURT: Let the Court take a look at it here.	
Is there something in here that you think is more relevant?	
CROSS-EXAMINER: Yes, Your Honor.	
THE COURT: What is it?	
CROSS-EXAMINER: Both in the first paragraph, the Court will find language concerning the power of Acme marketing. And on page 11.003, there is a discussion of Outdoor Blend, discussion of the acquisition of Outdoor Blend in the last paragraph.	
THE COURT: All right. Overruled, overruled. The Court finds that this document is relevant.	

(Exhibit 11B admitted.)

(Jury out at 12:08 p.m.)

(Recess at 12:09 p.m.)

(Jury in at 1:50 p.m.)

(Reconvened at 1:50 p.m.)

    THE COURT: You may be seated. All right. Let's continue with the cross-examination of the witness.

Transcript	*Analysis*
CROSS-EXAMINER: Your Honor, may I move the admission of certain exhibits by stipulation?	It is far less time-consuming to move in large groups of documents by stipulation. The time it takes to establish a foundation, even for an undisputed time, is significant and can lead to unanticipated problems. It is far better to put in as many documents as possible without the hassle.
THE COURT: Yes. You may proceed. CROSS-EXAMINER: Thank you, Your Honor. BY CROSS-EXAMINER: Q: We were talking about Exhibit 11B, Mr. Vancine. The power of Acme to market its brands is enormous, isn't it, sir? A: Yes.	The cross-examination begins where it left off before lunch — with an exhibit. Again, when confronted with a document authored by the witness's own company, the witness will ordinarily not fight the words of the document or any reasonable inference that can be drawn from those words.
Q: You were working for one of the most successful food and pet powerhouses in the world. A: Food worldwide. Pet food was primarily a United States-based business. Q: And if you intrude on the brand of another, you had the marketing power to buy shelf space; is that true, sir?	This line of questioning is again designed to show the overwhelming marketing clout of the defendant. This is important because of its usefulness in relation to several hoped-for instructions on both liability and damages.
OPPOSING COUNSEL: Objection, Your Honor. Argumentative.	

Transcript	*Analysis*
THE COURT: Overruled.	
THE WITNESS: There's two separate questions there. Did we have the marketing power to buy shelf space, yes, if shelf space is being sold. The first part of the question, I think is an assumption, and I'd rather — I don't have a response to the assumption.	
BY CROSS-EXAMINER:	
Q: Well, we're talking about your ability. Your ability was to go up against any other brand and put the clout of Acme behind it.	
A: I'm not trying to be argumentative. I'm just trying to answer your question. There are brands bigger than Acme and there are brands smaller than Acme and we did not have unlimited resources.	The witness attempts to show that Acme really isn't all that big. His problem is that the plaintiff really is all that small.
Q: But we were much smaller than Acme, aren't we?	
A: I don't know who "we" is.	
Q: The Purebred Company.	
A: Yes.	
Q: And you knew you had the financial muscle to do couponing. Right?	*Chapter: Couponing* "Couponing" has previously been explained to the jury. The plaintiff claims this is another method by which the defendant infringed upon the trademark of the plaintiff, and caused confusion in the marketplace.

Transcript	*Analysis*
A: Could I go back to the prior statement, sir? I was not even aware that the Purebred Company existed till the deposition I gave back in April 2, '01. S there are several parts to your question. Do we have the power to do couponing, yes. Did I know about the Purebred Company, that it would be attacking Purebred, the answer is no. I'm trying to separate the questions	
Q: I promise we will talk about your knowledge, sir. The question before you is you had the power to do the couponing.	The cross-examiner brings the witness back to the important point, that the defendant used coupons that infringed upon the plaintiff's trademark.
A: Acme has power to run couponing. Answer is yes.	

(Chapters that discuss particular aspects of marketing are omitted.)

Q: In short, the muscle of Acme in the pet food marketplace was such that you could throw millions of dollars into advertising and marketing support for your launch of Purebred.	*Chapter: Millions Spent on the Relaunch* The witness will first try to imply that millions of dollars were not spent on the marketing campaign designed to relaunch the product under the new name, but will have to withdraw his denial.
A: Could, being hypothetical, yes.	
Q: In fact, you did put millions of dollars behind the Outdoor Blend relaunch?	
A: That is correct.	
Q: What you spent for Outdoor Blend was in excess of $6 million in marketing support?	

Transcript	*Analysis*

A: In trade and marketing support.

Q: Now, I'd like you to look at Exhibit 11A, please. Do you recognize Exhibit 11A as being a press release from your company, Acme, dealing with the acquisition of Outdoor Blend?

Chapter: Defendant's Dog Food Was Intended to Be Direct Competitor to Plaintiff's Dog Food

A: Yes, that's — yes, I do.

The following facts are adduced in order to show that the defendant is competing directly against the plaintiff in the very markets where confusion between like names to products was likely to occur.

(Exhibit 11A admitted.)

   CROSS-EXAMINER: Let's go up to the top, if you could.

   BY CROSS-EXAMINER:

Q: March 28, 1996. Outdoor Blend is a premium pet food line. This was your first premium pet food line.

A: Yes.

Q: So now, as of 1996, if we're a premium pet food line, you're going to compete directly with us for the first time.

A: Yes.

Q: And who you're going to target, allows us to further build our business in the specialty food channels, pet stores, feed stores, and veterinary clinics. That was the game plan of Acme, wasn't it?

A: Yes.

Q: And if we're in these veterinary clinics, you become our direct competitor, don't you?

A: Yes.

Transcript	*Analysis*
Q: And if we're in feed stores, you're now our direct competitor.	
A: Yes.	
Q: And if we're able to get into pet stores, you're going to be our direct competitor.	
A: Yes.	
Q: Let's then put the size of Acme Pet Foods into overall Acme, if we could come down to Acme Pet Products has sales in excess of a billion dollars.	
A: Yes.	
Q: That's who we're going to be competing against now, isn't it?	The picture is vivid, the tiny company is competing against the giant.
A: Yes.	
(Chapters omitted)	*Chapter: How Quickly New Bags Could Be Printed If the Defendant Wanted To*
Q: We were talking then about the rush to restage into Purebred, the restage of Outdoor Blend products.	The central purpose of this chapter is to demonstrate that when the defendant wants to change the name on a bag, the defendant can get new bags into the market place very quickly. This will become very important in showing the reluctance of the defendant to replace bags using the plaintiff's name.
A: Yes.	
Q: And if we'll go to Exhibit 26, page 001. This is from you, this is from you to the marketing force.	The witness is about to be confronted with his own statements.
A: Uh-huh.	
Q: Is that yes, sir?	
A: Yes. Yes, it is.	
Q: And it's August 23, '99, you're ready to roll this new product out in all of its bags by the end of August.	
A: Yes.	

Transcript	Analysis
Q: From a dead stop to a completely new formula and a completely new bag, ready to roll out in 90 days?	
A: I don't know what work had been done prior to David Barnaby's memo, but based on the dates, that is correct.	
Q: Well, let's talk about this change that you're making.	
A: Uh-huh.	
Q: What is changing — and let me get this into perspective. You're going to be talking to your sales force.	These are questions designed to accredit the prior statement of the witness.
A: That is correct.	
Q: It's probably about as important a job as you have.	
A: No. At the time it was not.	As phrased, it is very difficult for the witness to deny that he wanted to be accurate, that he had a need to be accurate, and that he was accurate.
Q: Well, can I at least assume that you try to be accurate?	
A: Yes.	
Q: Can I assume you try to be honest?	
A: Yes.	
Q: That you said what you intended to say?	
A: Yes.	
Q: You communicated to the Acme sales force what you wanted them to know.	
A: Let me just, for the — I did not write this memo. It's my name on the memo. I agree with everything in the memo. I take responsibility for the memo, but I did not write the memo.	The witness is very worried because this memo to his sales force is a smoking gun. The witness tries his best to soften the blow.
Q: Well, you certainly read it before you allowed it to go to your sales force.	This is an easy method of stopping the witness. He must take responsibility or look totally incompetent.

Transcript	*Analysis*
A: Yes, I agree with that. Yes. I take responsibility for it.	
Q: And what you said is changing. The product line will — product name will change.	*Chapter: "The Product Name Will Change"*
CROSS-EXAMINER: Could I have that highlighted?	This is a smoking gun document and it is imperative that the most important language be highlighted for the jury.
Q: The product name will change from Generic Breed formulas to Purebred formulas. That's what you said?	This is a direct quote from the document, and shows that the witness advised his own sales force that the name of the defendant's product would change, and that the new name would be the name previously trademarked by the plaintiff.
A: Out of context, that's what I said. But that's just part of the overall letter. The letter begins by saying, This change to the Outdoor Blend Generic Breed Formula, and when I get to the product name, I'm talking about communication of the product benefit to the consumer. But the letter begins by addressing Outdoor Blend, and several times in here, we talk about the new package — the last point on that page says new packaging to better communicate Outdoor Blend branding. So out of context, yes, I say the product name, but within the form of the whole letter, it's part of the Outdoor Blend relaunch.	The witness must try to explain.

Transcript	*Analysis*
Q: Well, am I reading it correctly, you told the entire sales force, what is changing, the name is changing, and the name is changing from Generic Breed formulas to Purebred formulas?	The technique is to require the witness to admit that the words suggested by the cross-examiner are indeed the words used by the witness. Do not permit the witness to imply that there words have been misquoted. Instead the witness will frequently argue that while they said a particular thing, that is really not what they meant. The cross-examiner must have faith that the document will speak louder than the excuse.
A: That's one of the several points I told them.	
Q: And in fact, that's true?	
A: That's true.	
Q: It's now Purebred formulas?	
A: It's Outdoor Blend Purebred formulas as part of the Outdoor Blend branding stated on the bottom of the page.	
Q: And so if a consumer said who makes Purebred formulas, the truthful answer would be Acme makes it.	*Chapter: Likelihood of Consumer Confusion*
A: Well —	The purpose of this brief series of questions is to try to establish that a consumer asking for the plaintiff's product line name is likely to be directed to the defendant's product that uses that name as part of a larger name. There will be several other chapters designed to make this point as it is the likelihood of consumer confusion is critical to liability.

Transcript	*Analysis*
OPPOSING COUNSEL: Objection. Objection. That's a question asking this witness to speculate on what a consumer would say.	
THE COURT: Overruled.	
THE WITNESS: If I was to ask the customer whether we — who makes Allergy, who makes Digestive, who makes Purebred, they would say do you mean Outdoor Blend.	
BY CROSS-EXAMINER:	
Q: I asked you, if the customer asked you, if it asked your company, who makes Purebred formula, the answer is the Acme Company.	
A: We market and we sell it. We don't always make it.	Now here is a truly bad answer. Based on the facts already admitted, the witness will have a difficult time denying the underlying premise that the defendant is now using the plaintiff's trademarked name. Instead, witness chooses to fight on the grounds that the pet food in the offending bags may actually have been manufactured by a different company. This is hardly the issue in the case, and even if true provides no defense.
(Chapters omitted)	*Chapter: Purebred Is Trademarked by the Plaintiff*

Transcript	Analysis
Q: The word "purebred" as it relates to dog food is trademarked, isn't it?	The purpose of this chapter is to equip the jurors with the facts they need to award punitive damages. This is one of many chapters designed to aid in that attempt. The concept the cross-examiner wishes to highlight is that the defendant has willfully and wantonly disregarded the rights of the plaintiff.
A: As you say, I don't know.	
Q: Don't know, even as we sit here in trial, you don't know?	
A: I'm assuming it is, that's why I'm sitting here. THE WITNESS: It has a registered trademark — CROSS-EXAMINER: Please, there is no question in front of you, sir. THE WITNESS: Thank you. BY CROSS-EXAMINER:	
Q: We make Purebred formula dog food, the Purebred Company, don't we, sir?	
A: The Purebred makes Purebred dog food.	
Q: Do you see the Purebred with the registration mark?	
A: Yes.	
Q: Do you understand the legal meaning that we have the right to?	
A: I see that you have the legal right to Purebred. I'm not a legal person. But in my mind, if I see this in a store, the word "adult formula," the word "chicken meal and rice" is common use as I see it on a lot of bags. The word "purebred," I see the registered mark, so that's trademarked.	

Transcript	*Analysis*

Q: In your mind that's protected?

A: Yes.

Q: Now, let's talk about why it's getting restaged. The new formula is to take care of the number one consumer complaint. You know what the number one consumer complaint —

Chapter: Your Dog Food Gives Dogs Diarrhea

A: Loose stools, as I already stated.

The importance of this chapter is not that consumers were complaining that defendant's dog food causes diarrhea. What it means is that once the defendant has linked its dog food with the name of plaintiff's dog food, consumers might believe that it is the plaintiff's dog food causing the problem. This permits the plaintiff to argue that the value of its trademarked name has been decreased by the actions of the defendant.

Q: Your dog food gives dogs diarrhea?

A: Not all dogs. Some dogs were having that problem, yes, it was.

Q: Enough dogs that it was the number one consumer complaint?

A: Yes.

Q: The number one consumer complaint about the food you were putting in the bag was that it caused diarrhea?

A: Yes.

Q: And on this issue of transitioning, Generic Breed Formula, that's what the formula that's giving the diarrhea.

A: Yes.

(Multiple chapters omitted)

Transcript	Analysis
A: The way I count up more items is, as I was saying earlier I sell Outdoor Blend. I don't sell Purebred. In my mind, as I stated, if I can end up at the end of the day with more Outdoor Blend items in a store for sale than I had ahead of time, I'm ahead of the game.	This material is a fragment of a larger chapter. It shows the use of a spontaneous loop of a phrase used by the witness. Note the phrase "I'm ahead of the game."
Q: And then — well, you never got ahead of the game. It continued to go down. Sales continued to go down, didn't they?	Now the phrase is spontaneously looped to show that is a phrase completely inapplicable to the real state of affairs.
A: Yes, sales are down.	
(Multiple chapters omitted)	*Chapter: The Defendant Could Sticker Over the Plaintiff's Name*
Q: And the key next steps, produce the new formula in existing stickered bags. Tell us about stickering a bag.	This is a portion of a chapter designed to acquaint the jurors with the fact that the defendant had an inexpensive way of observing plaintiff's trademark. Once notified of the plaintiff's intention to sue, the defendant could have placed stickers over plaintiff's name on the bags. This chapter is important in showing the willful and wanton misconduct of the defendant, and its unwillingness to try to diminish the damages it was doing to plaintiff's trademark.
A: I'm trying to recall how this was done. It looks like this was done at the factory. The old bags were taken and stickers made and applied to them at the factory before they were shipped out to the customer.	

Transcript	*Analysis*
Q: But you certainly know that the Acme company had the ability to sticker bags when it chose to.	
A: Acme or suppliers, yes.	
Q: So that if you wanted to cover up Purebred, you always knew how to do it, didn't you?	
A: I believe so, yes.	
(Chapters omitted)	*Chapter: The New Dog Food Using the Plaintiff's Name Is Also a Failure*
Q: Now, we're into the new bags that have Purebred on them. And they're not going to be a successful product, either, are they?	This chapter is designed to show that again, the actions of the defendant had actually decreased the value of the plaintiff's trademark in the marketplace. This is a separate item of damages. This chapter and others that tied to it are part of the factual foundation for an expert witness later to be called by the plaintiff, who will try to quantify the diminished value of the plaintiff's trademark.
A: They have not lived up to expectations. Some of the items are selling pretty well and some are not.	
Q: The Outdoor Blend Purebred line is not a successful product line?	
A: I'd agree with that.	
Q: And what that means when you boil it all down is consumers don't like it?	
A: The — there is a niche of consumers that do like certain items. But the vast majority of consumers either are unaware of it or don't like it.	

Transcript	*Analysis*
Q: And so the people who become — the people who don't like it learn I don't like the Purebred dog food formula?	
A: The Outdoor Blend Purebred formula.	
Q: And the reason — you tried to figure out why is this product not being accepted by consumers, why is it failing. You wanted to know that, didn't you?	*Chapter: Why the New Product Is Failing*
A: Yes.	
Q: And you found out the changes to the product itself, just this continual change, was working against you in the marketplace.	
A: On some items, we found limited consumer appeal.	
Q: You found that going from seven S-K-Us to five worked against you in the marketplace?	
A: No. I do not.	
Q: You don't?	
A: No, I do not.	
Q: No. Well, let me give you your deposition and see what you said under oath.	The witness has testified inconsistently with a statement in his deposition. The cross-examiner will now engage in a routine impeachment by inconsistent statement.
A: Okay.	
Q: I'm going to take you to page 39 of your statements to us under oath.	The source of the impeaching statement has been noted in the page preparation of a chapter, so it is immediately available to the cross-examiner.
A: Yes.	
Q: April 11, 2001.	
A: Uh-huh.	

Transcript   *Analysis*

Q: Mr. Lewis was there
    asking you questions.
A: Uh-huh.
    THE COURT: Is that yes?
    THE WITNESS: Yes, sir.
    I'm sorry.
    THE COURT: Verbalize
    your answer.
    THE WITNESS: Yes, sir.
    BY CROSS-EXAMINER:
Q: And these lawyers were
    with you; is that right?
A: Yes, yes, they were, sir.
Q: You were asked, "Would
    you characterize the
    Outdoor Blend Purebred
    line as a successful product
    line." Your answer. "No."
    Why not. "Two things or I
    guess, three things. The
    line has never caught on
    with consumers." Right?
A: Yes.
Q: "Of the four parts of our
    solution center, canine, it
    is by far a small segment?"
A: Yes.
Q: "I think there are just a
    lot of different elements
    going on that consumers
    have not taken hold of."
    Right so far?
A: Yes.
Q: Mr. Lewis asked you,
    "What elements are those?"
    Your answer, "The product,
    as you know, is designed
    as a Generic Breed
    Formula to follow the
    seven groups of the
    American Canine
    Association. Not many
    consumers understand the
    groupings, so I think that
    has been an issue." That's
    what you told us under
    oath.
A: Yes.

Transcript	*Analysis*
Q: "I think another issue has been with the product itself. I think there is confusion on the different types of herbs and stuff in the product."	
A: Yes.	
Q: Right? "And we have changed the product."	
A: Yes.	
Q: And another reason you now give, and we have seven SKUs down to five.	This is the impeaching statement.
A: Yes.	
Q: That's what you told us under oath when you asked us what were the problems and why was it being rejected?	
A: Yes.	
Q: And that's the truth?	
A: Yes. I think that's consistent with what I just said.	
(Multiple chapters omitted)	
Q: Now, let's talk about this new name "purebred."	*Chapter: It Was the Job of the Marketing Department to Make Sure There Was No Trademark Infringement*
A: Yes.	
Q: You've been in marketing in the 1980s for Acme.	This chapter is in line with an instruction which will tell the jury that the ability of the defendant to find the trademark is a factor to be considered. The witness is only too happy to shift the blame to a different department. There is no reason for the cross-examiner to punish the witness if the witness is willing to punish someone else.
A: Yes.	

Transcript	Analysis
Q: And you had always met with the legal department of Acme to make sure that you were aware that you were not infringing on somebody else's trademark. A: Yes.	Take note of the ease with which the witness gives up this important information. One reason is that the leading questions are accurate. A second reason is that the witness can actually paint himself as a victim.
Q: That was always what you had done before, wasn't it?	The witness wants the jury to know that if it had been his job in marketing, he certainly would have looked for the trademark. It is the task of the cross-examiner to position the witness so that he feels comfortable making himself look better while making his company look worse. The technique is to use a very understanding voice, and to apply to the witness "of course you would have done it better."
A: In marketing, that was my job. Q: It is the job of marketing to make sure it does not infringe on somebody else's trademark. A: That's correct. Q: And you knew that in Acme because that's where you'd been working for 25 years. A: Yes, sir.	*Chapter: The Defendant Had Set Procedure to Determine If Name Was Trademarked, But Failed to Follow That Procedure*

Transcript	*Analysis*
Q: So if we suggest to the jury that there was a method within Acme that was recognized to make sure you weren't infringing on a trademark, you could say to the jury, I was well aware of that.	This chapter follows a chapter in which the witness has been very cooperative. The witness is not on the spot. Neither he nor his actions are being blamed. Instead, the witness is offered the opportunity to confirm how easy it would have been to avoid this problem if only other people had done their job.
A: Yes, there is a procedure.	
Q: And the procedure was if you're going to use it, you better make sure you've got a legal right to do it.	
A: Yes.	The further the witness cooperates, the further the cross-examiner can push that chapter. Questions that might not have been attempted earlier can be attempted in a chapter in which the witness feels comfortable.
Q: And of course if you'd have only known that we existed, you didn't know, right?	
A: I did not.	
Q: But if you'd have only known we existed through the trademark search, we wouldn't be here, would we?	
A: Probably. Again, I don't know.	
Q: You know from having been in marketing, if you had known about our trademark, you wouldn't have used it; isn't that fair to say?	
A: I would go with whatever recommendation legal had given me.	
Q: But you certainly wouldn't have blown by it and say I'm not going to look at it.	
A: That is correct.	

Transcript	Analysis
Q: And what you found out in all of your years working there is it's not tough to do a trademark search, is it?	*Chapter: It's Not Difficult to Do a Trademark Search*
A: No, it is not.	Compare this to where the witness was at the start of the cross-examination. Where before he tried to avoid any knowledge of trademark law, now the witness is willing to talk about how easy it is to do a trademark search.
Q: It's all on computers, you put in the name and you find out if somebody owns it already.	These answers are positively devastating to the defense. Why is the witness giving this up? First, the leading questions have to be accurate. In addition, the thrust of the questions is to cast the blame elsewhere. The witness is offered multiple opportunities to tell the jury that he could have done a better job, but that it was not his job.
A: In my days it wasn't that simple, but, yeah, I would imagine now it is; I don't know.	
Q: And of course when we're about to come out with Acme Purebred in 1998, you had that whole legal department there at Acme, didn't you?	
A: We were in Tennessee. The legal department was in St. Louis. But, yes.	
Q: You had the phone?	
A: I'm not disagreeing with you, sir, yes.	
Q: And you knew who to call?	
A: I did not, personally. The marketing department probably did, I did not.	
Q: And the marketing department would be David Barnaby.	
A: That is correct.	

Transcript	*Analysis*
Q: And it was his responsibility to check with the trademark, not yours?	
A: It's not sales' responsibility, but, yes, it would be the marketing department's.	
Q: And that would be David Barnaby?	
A: Yes.	
Q: If only you'd have known that there was a Purebred Company selling dog stuff, right, if only you'd have known?	
A: Is that a question, sir; I don't know.	The witness plays the game "is that a question?"
Q: It is, sir.	The technique: Assure the witness it is a question.
A: I don't know what the question is. Please repeat it.	The reply is predictable. The witness has focused on the evasion and must ask that the question be repeated.
Q: But in fact, you did know that there was a Purebred Company.	Notice how short the answers have become. Whether it is witness fatigue, or whether the chapters are now pointing away from this witness, for whatever reason, the answers are coming more cleanly than ever. This is the time the cross-examiner must push for the optimum gain. If risks are to be run, run them when the witness is in this answer mode.
A: Yes.	
Q: You personally did know that?	
A: Yes, I did.	
Q: You didn't know it was our company. You always knew, though, that there was a Purebred Company marketing food for dogs.	Since the answers are flowing so well, the cross-examiner begins to reach for even better answers.
A: Yes. Marketing treats for dogs.	

Transcript	*Analysis*
Q: In the same business you were in.	
A: There's a significant difference in our business between treats and food.	
Q: They were marketing Doggy Jerky.	
A: Yes, they were.	
Q: And that's a direct competitor to one of your products?	The cross-examiner is now on a role. Now is the time to try to establish as many elements of an instruction as can be quickly accomplished. A single "yes" here can avoid chapters' worth of material later. Furthermore, the helpful answers of this witness have the effect of shortening the cross-examinations planned for later witnesses. So many points are being conceded that the cross-examiner should consider moving chapters out of other witnesses and into this cross-examination, at least for as long as the witness stays in this answering mode.
A: That is correct.	
Q: And you knew that this Purebred Company was out there long before — you knew that long before you started marketing with Purebred on your packages.	
A: That is correct.	
Q: So if we start with I have no idea there was a Purebred Company, your answer would be that's not true, I personally, as the head of sales of Acme, knew there was a Purebred Company competing with Acme.	
A: Yes.	
(Chapters omitted)	

Transcript	*Analysis*
Q: But you now knew that there was a Purebred Company, a direct competitor, and that you go to Purebred on your bags, let's cover all the people you called up. Okay?	
A: Okay.	
Q: That list would be very short, wouldn't it. It would be zero.	
A: That's correct.	
Q: You didn't call legal and say, guys, we're putting Purebred on our bags, I know as your national sales — well, what was our formal title again?	
A: I was either general manager of sales or vice president of sales at that time, one of the two.	
Q: Vice president of sales of Acme, I know there's a Purebred Company in this dog food business. You didn't make that phone call, did you?	
A: No, I did not.	
Q: You didn't call Kramer.	
A: No.	
Q: Didn't call — didn't call anybody.	
A: No.	
Q: You just rolled it out.	
A: Yes.	
Q: Because it's a great name for a dog food, isn't it?	This is a theme phrase. The witness does not fully buy the theme phrase, but he certainly does not deny it.

Transcript	*Analysis*
A: Well, it's a great name, but there's more to it. In my mind Purebred on the label like that is not the same as Purebred in small print in a distributed by clause, and when I sold against Purebred Company at Costco and everything else and other companies, they weren't even printing Purebred on there.	
(Numerous chapters omitted concerning sales to pet food stores)	
Q: Mr. Vancine, you're at Exhibit 7, page 001. And we find here you getting a copy of this letter of January 5, 1990, written by your western division sales manager, yes?	*Chapter: It's Easy to Find the Plaintiff's Company* This chapter is based on a letter written to the defendant's company. That letter dates back to years before the lawsuit, and shows that the defendant's company could have, should have, and probably was aware of the plaintiff's company, even though plaintiff is small.
A: Uh-huh.	
Q: Please, sir.	
A: Yes. Yes.	
Q: Written by your western division sales manager trying to sell Acme Pet Food products to a particular company?	
A: Correct.	
Q: The Purebred Company?	
A: That is correct.	
Q: Of San Diego, California?	
A: Correct.	
Q: It really isn't that hard to find us if you want to find us, is it, Mr. Vancine?	This is the payoff line. It has some risk to it. The risk is lowered by the existence of the letter. When confronted with a document, a witness is far more likely to concede even a point they could argue.
A: No.	

Transcript	*Analysis*
(Chapters omitted)	
Q: January of 2000, we sent a cease and desist order. Nothing happened in sales?	*Chapter: Although Told to Stop Using the Plaintiff's Name, Defendant Continued to Do So*
A: I'm trying to think when we started to change to the word "breed specific."	
Q: Can I help you with that?	This is a simple interchange, begin it reinforces the credibility of the lawyer.
A: That would be very good, yes.	
Q: When you changed it was when, when one of your executives came to you and said, we can't call it Purebred anymore, we have to call it Breed Specific?	
A: That sounds correct.	
Q: And that was in about the summer. The summer of 2000.	
A: That could be correct. It sounds good.	
Q: And in fact, maybe I can help you with your deposition, all the way back in April of 2001 at page 17, line 3.	
A: Yes. Yes.	
Having looked at that transcript, does it refresh your recollection as to a conversation you had?	His question is designed to refresh the recollection of the witness concerning who told him that he was no longer to use the plaintiff's name. The person who told him is seated in the courtroom as the corporate representative.
A: Yes, it does.	
Q: Who was the conversation with?	
A: I would think it was with David Kramer.	

Transcript	*Analysis*
Q: Mr. Kramer is sitting right there, isn't he?	
A: Yes.	
Q: By August of 2000, you were told in sales, we can't use Purebred anymore on our bags.	*Chapter: The Defendant Recognized That the Name Belonged to the Plaintiff*
A: Yes.	
Q: And you were told, destroy some of our advertising materials for Purebred?	
A: To start using Breed Specific everywhere as we're reprinting POP material, as we're reprinting anything that sales had which had interaction with customers, to use Breed Specific.	
Q: And reason you were told you couldn't use Purebred was 'cause it was our trademark name.	Notice how the witness attempts to evade. He refers to the problem as a "legal issue" as if that were not a real issue.
A: Because of legal issues.	
Q: That you weren't allowed to use Purebred anymore.	
A: Yes.	
Q: Yes, you need to answer —	
A: I was told to stop using Purebred and go to Breed Specific.	
Q: You were told to stop for a reason, though, Mr. Vancine.	
A: No, it was a legal reason. It was for a legal reason.	The witness keeps attempting to minimize the problem by calling it a legal issue. The cross-examiner need only apply logic to obtain an extremely helpful admission.
Q: And the legal reason you were told we were not allowed to use Purebred, it belongs to a different company.	
A: Yes.	

Transcript	*Analysis*
(Chapters omitted)	*Chapter: Defendant Knows Not to Use the Name, But Continues to Do So*
CROSS-EXAMINER: 50B, please.	At this point the cross-examiner introduces a series of defendant's bags which continue to use the plaintiff's name. Previous chapters have explained how to decipher the packaging code on the bags. The exhibits now introduced show that the bags were filled and distributed after the defendants had said it would stop using the plaintiff's name. This is a critical point for punitive damages.
Q: Handing you 50B001. The large container of Purebred. December 30, '01. Which means to you, as a trained person in sales, this went into the bag December 30 of 2000, didn't it?	
A: Most likely, yes. CROSS-EXAMINER: 49D, please. BY CROSS-EXAMINER:	
Q: I'm going to give you 49D.003. Purebred on it. February 15, '02, which means February 15, of 2001, you're still putting Purebred out on the market, aren't you?	The leading question interpreting the packaging code coupled with the exhibit, easily establishes the conduct of the defendant and leaves the witness with no escape.
A: Most likely, yes. CROSS-EXAMINER: Could I have 89, please. BY CROSS-EXAMINER:	
Q: And these bags, you don't, you don't run one bag through your assembly line at a time, do you?	
A: That is correct.	

Transcript	Analysis

Transcript

Q: Let me give you 89.006.
CROSS-EXAMINER: Move
the admission of 89006,
Your Honor.
THE COURT: It will be received.
(Exhibit 89.006 admitted.)
BY CROSS-EXAMINER:

Q: Look at the back of it. This
one you're going to see
says use by June 30 of '02.

A: That is correct.

Q: And so if it went into the
bag June 30 of '01, that
was a full nine months
after your company said it
was going to stop using
Purebred, isn't it?

A: As I stated earlier, I don't
know what my company
received and I don't know
what my company said.
CROSS-EXAMINER:
Exhibit 55, please.

Q: Tell the jury the use-by on
this bag of Purebred.

A: December 3, '02.

Q: December 3, '02. Meaning
on December of 2001, 15
months after you got the
word to stop using
Purebred, your company is
still running assembly
lines putting this dog food
into Purebred bags and
putting it out through your
sales department
throughout the nation; isn't
that true?

Analysis

The next in a parade of bags
that shows that in spite of
the conversation in which the
witness was told the company
would stop using the name,
the bags kept getting filled
and placed on the shelves.

The cross-examiner
demonstrates that the bag fill
dates are getting closer and
closer to the trial date,
showing that the conduct of
the defendant continued
without cessation and that
only a jury verdict will stop
the conduct.

Transcript   *Analysis*

A: I don't know that for sure,
    but it appears that way. I
    don't know.

                                      (End of excerpt of
                                      cross-examination)

§ 33.03   Transcript 2 — Cross Examination in Commercial Case Alleging Breach of Contract

The following example is a commercial case alleging breach of contract. Names have been changed.

In 1980 Ryan Brown was doing well financially. He had sold his Alaskan mineral development company, Brown Enterprise, to Alaska Enterprise Investment Corporation (AEIC), a corporation owned by the State of Alaska. As part of that transaction, he obtained a coal commission contract which was likely to pay him more than $1 million a month for the next four years.

In February 1981, approximately four months after payments had begun under the coal commission contract, Mr. Brown purchased 100% of the Washington D.C. Bobcats hockey franchise, a team that was struggling financially.

Within Alaska there was substantial controversy and criticism concerning the coal commission contract. The perception among many was that AEIC had paid full value for the assets acquired, and that the lucrative coal commission contract constituted a form of further payment that was unjustified.

The coal commission contract gave AEIC the right to cancel the contract with 90 days notice. In 1981, the management of AEIC changed and in June 1981 the new management notified Mr. Brown that they intended to exercise the cancellation clause in the near future. Within months the coal commission contract was canceled.

In early 1984, Mr. Brown, in an extremely compressed time period, negotiated the sale of 60.8% of the hockey franchise to Paul Waterton. The price Mr. Waterton agreed to pay was believed to be the highest price ever paid to that date for a hockey team.

In 2000, 16 years later, Mr. Brown brought suit claming that the original sales contract was procured by fraud, entitling Mr. Brown to rescission of the sales contract.

It was Mr. Brown's theory of the case that he was an extremely reluctant seller of the franchise, that he only sold his remaining interest in the franchise because of health issues within his family.

It was the defendant's theory of the case that Mr. Brown was a willing and eager seller of his last remaining interest in the franchise, that he had sold the interest because of his dramatically changed financial circumstances, and that the family health issue, while possibly true, was not the precipitating reason for the sale. It was the position of the defense that in fact Mr. Brown had been willing to sell the team as early as 1982 when there was no family health issue. It was the defendant's theory that Mr. Brown sold the team because he could obtain the right price, at the right time, and on the right terms.

What follows are some of the chapters used at the beginning of the extensive cross examination of Mr. Brown. These chapters dealt with Mr. Brown's business activities in the period 1980–1984. The overall goals of these chapters were 1) to show Mr. Brown's financial motivations to sell his last remaining interest in the franchise and 2) to display facts that would effectively challenge the credibility of Mr. Brown and thereby affect his credibility throughout the remainder of his testimony.

The reader is reminded that these transcript passages are incomplete and have been heavily excerpted in order to further the goal of demonstrating certain cross examination techniques. These passages do not purport to be a full recitation of the testimony and the reader should understand that these materials are not designed to fully or fairly set out the testimony or the positions of the parties to the lawsuit. Entire chapters have been omitted. In fact, the chapters included constitute less than one quarter of the cross examination. Within the chapters that are included, certain questions, answers, objections, and rulings have been omitted as they do not materially assist in a discussion of the techniques being employed.

The reader will note that the cross examination of this well educated plaintiff seldom proceeded smoothly. In fact, the witness repeatedly answered that he could not specifically recall an event or conversation, but he declined to flatly deny or affirm the leading question. These materials are set out so that the reader can study the use and effectiveness of the techniques of cross examination under these difficult circumstances. Throughout the cross examination the reader is asked to fairly judge how the jury would likely react to the cross examination question and answers.

Transcript	*Analysis*
BY CROSS-EXAMINER: Q: Mr. Brown, let's talk for a moment about your business situation before you bought the Washington D.C. Bobcats.	*Chapter: Fall 1980, the Precursor to the Purchase of the Bobcats was the Sale of Brown Enterprise to AEIC*
Let's talk about what was going on in the months preceding that acquisition.	The jury is alerted that particular attention should be paid to the time preceding the purchase of the Bobcats. Because of a detailed opening statement, the jury understands the relationship between the witness's business problems in 1981 and his sale of the Bobcats in 1984.

Transcript	*Analysis*
Now, you acquire the Bobcats from the Burkequte brothers in February of 1981; is that right, sir?	
A: Yes.	
Q: Six months before that, in September of 1980, you had completed the business deal in Alaska.	*Chapter: A Controversial Aspect of the Deal Was the Existence of a Coal Commission Contract*
A: Yes.	
Q: As chairman of Brown Enterprise, and as an owner of many of the shares of Brown Enterprise, you made a sale of Brown Enterprise to AEIC, Alaska Enterprise Investment Corporation?	This chapter is designed to acquaint the jury with a particular part of the sale transaction. A portion of this transaction became very controversial, and led to the cancellation of a lucrative contract which the witness had been counting on to finance other business activities.
A: Yes, I did.	
Q: Now — and we call that AEIC, right? That's what everybody called it in Alaska?	An explanation of the unusual features of the sale are required.
A: Yes.	
Q: Now, AEIC was a very unusual company, wasn't it?	
A: In what way?	
Q: Its shareholders were all citizens of Alaska.	
A: Yes, sir. There were a number of, what we call "crown corporations" in Alaska; that is to say, corporations owned.	
Q: Every man, woman, child in Alaska received shares in AEIC. Please answer out loud, sir.	Do not allow witnesses to nod or give other nonverbal answers.
A: That's correct.	
Q: And you had sold your company to AEIC?	

Transcript	Analysis

A: Yes. They acquired Brown Enterprise.

Q: And the structure of this deal was front-page news in Alaska, wasn't it, Mr. Brown?

A: Yes.

Q: There was a lot of heat about your sale of Brown Enterprise to AEIC, wasn't there?

A: There was a great deal of interest in it.

A standard ploy: The witness understates the importance of an event. The cross-examiner should not become fixated on winning acceptance of his phrase. Instead, the cross-examiner should move from a subjective description to one or more objective facts that allow jurors to come to the conclusion suggested by the subjective description declined by the witness.

Q: Well, one of the people taking an interest in it was the Alaska Exchange Commission. Do you recall that, sir?

The cross-examiner spontaneously loops the phrase "an interest in it." A better spontaneous loop would have been "a great deal of interest in it."

A: Yes, I do.

Q: And they began hearings into the sale. You do recall that, don't you?

These facts are gleaned from newspaper articles obtained through a database search. It is increasingly common and important to conduct database searches on witnesses. The evidence gathered in this manner often comes as a surprise to a witness and therefore encourages the witness to be more forthcoming as the witness cannot gauge what facts the cross-examiner may have at her disposal.

A: Yes.

Transcript	*Analysis*
Q: And one of the aspects of the hearings was whether this marketing agreement that had been reached between you and AEIC was really fair to the people of Alaska?	
A: That was a question which they raised.	This answer is indicative of a style or strategy adopted by many witnesses. Facts stated in leading question are re-characterized by the witness to create a picture more to the liking of the witness. If the cross-examiner has hard facts with which to impeach, she should do so. If not, the cross-examiner must depend on the overall strength of the chapter as a method of allowing jurors to see through answers that are neither completely accurate nor fully inaccurate.
AEIC and I agreed prior to the beginning of that hearing to modify the coal-marketing contract, which they asked me to enter into, so that there was an out clause for them to be able to exercise.	The witness has jumped ahead in order to cut off the flow of damaging facts. As was discussed in chapter 30, *Recognizing and Controlling Bait*, the lawyer must decline the invitation. Instead the lawyer should pursue the chapter as planned.
Q: Let's go through it step by step, sir.	The cross-examiner declines the bait.
A: Sure.	
Q: What happened was the commission began hearings on whether this commission contract, the Alaska Exchange Commission began hearings on whether your commission contract was fair, yes?	*Chapter: The Coal Commission Contract*

Transcript	*Analysis*
A: I believe that's accurate.	Note the words: "<u>I believe</u> that's accurate." What is the likelihood that a businessman whose contract was under investigation by a quasi-governmental commission would be unsure of the reason for the investigation?
Q: And the commission contract gave you commission payments for four years?	This kind of detail can be very interesting to jurors if the opening statement has allowed them to see the relationship between a complex business transaction and the case they are to decide.
A: Yes.	
Q: Starting in about October 15 of 1980?	
A: I don't remember the start date, sir.	
Q: You recall it was before the end of 1980?	
A: Yes. I believe so.	
Q: Now, this contract was going to pay you more than $1 million a month projected over each month of the four years?	
A: It was not going to pay me. It was going to pay Brown Enterprise, and the employees that Brown Enterprise had, and their expenses to market the coal worldwide for the coal assets that I had sold them.	The witness knows that discussions of Brown Enterprise will entail admissions to many bad facts. The witness therefore tries to divorce himself from the corporate entity.
Q: Fair enough, Mr. Brown. Let's tell the jury who owned Brown Enterprise. You owned more than 90 percent of the stock in Brown Enterprise.	The cross-examiner can defeat this strategy by providing the jurors with facts that allow those jurors to reach their our own conclusion that the corporation and the individual are very closely linked.

Transcript	*Analysis*
A: I don't believe it was quite that high, but I was by far the largest single shareholder.	Wrong answer. If the cross-examiner has prepared correctly, then the answer to the leading question should be "Yes."
CROSS-EXAMINER: May I have the witness be provided with Exhibit A-5?	And of course, the cross-examiner should have a document to use for impeachment, and now that document is brought out.
Q: We obtained A-5 from your files.	The cross-examiner should remind the witness of the fact that in it is the witness's own documents that will trip him up.
A: Yes.	
Q: And it is appended with your balance sheet for Brown Enterprise, Limited. You find that at A-5 page 34.	Note how easy the impeachment becomes, because the fact has been sourced.
A: I do.	
Q: Projected bank loan documents of your company.	
A: Yes, sir. Do you recognize A-5 as containing part of the business plan of Brown Enterprise as it existed in 1980, '81, '82?	
A: Yes, I do.	
Q: And does it contain the financial situation of Brown Enterprise both in the body of A-5 and in the financial statements attached to A-5?	
A: I did not look at this before now, sir, but I believe that is an accurate statement.	The witness is now denying that he has seen a document, but must admit that the document is accurate.

Transcript	*Analysis*
Q: And if you will read to yourself, but not out loud, paragraph 15, small "i" and see if that refreshes your recollection of how much of Brown Enterprise you owned during this period of time, fall of 1980, 1981 and 1982.	The reason the witnesses asked to read it to himself is that the document is not yet in evidence. In fact, despite repeated efforts the cross-examiner will not get this document admitted as an exhibit. The repeated attempts and the repeated failure to get the document admitted became a standing joke among the lawyers. It is doubtful that the cross-examiner shared in the humor. However, any document or anything else can be used to refresh recollection.
A: Yes.	The document does indeed refresh the recollection of the witness.
Q: Does that refresh your recollection?	
A: Yes.	
Q: And, indeed, you were the owner of more than 90 percent of Brown Enterprise during this time Period?	The witness is easily impeached by his own document. There is a lesson for the witness. The cross-examiner suggested he owned more than 90%, and now the cross-examiner has proved he owned more than 90%. All of this impeachment could have been avoided had the witness only agreed with the fact correctly stated in the leading question.
A: This says 90 and a half percent.	The jury also learns that if the cross-examiner suggests it is true, it likely is true. No comment need or should be made concerning the success of the impeachment. The jurors understand the point. Move on.

Transcript	*Analysis*
Q: Now, you have told us that you were having financial difficulties. You admitted that earlier today. Do you recall that?	*Chapter: Financial Difficulties from Two Directions*
A: I said so, yes.	The witnesses conceded this in direct examination in an attempt to minimize the harmful effects. This again is an attempt to lower the cross-examiner to the bottom line which is merely conclusory. "Financial difficulties" can mean many different things to many people. The proper technique is to do the chapter that explains factually the financial circumstances so that the jurors can draw their own conclusion as to the severity of the witness's "financial difficulties."
Q: In 1980, the financial problems you have were that your chief investment was this company, Brown Enterprise, and it had two investments, Brown Oil and the coal commission contract; is that accurate, sir?	Is important to drop time references into leading questions in order to easily keep the jury oriented on the timeline. Because this is a compound question the cross-examiner has offered the witness multiple ways to avoid a direct answer.
A: Sir, I don't believe so. If I may — let me see if I understood what you just stated. What you said was this was my chief investment, and that in that investment, the two assets, or liabilities — two assets were the coal contract and Brown Oil U.S., correct?	
Q: No. I'm not saying that, Mr. Brown.	The cross-examiner created the problem. The cross examiner must fix the problem. The fix is to return to shorter questions.

Transcript	Analysis

A: Okay.

Q: Brown Enterprise was owned 90 percent by you. Its two primary assets were the coal commission contract and the oil company, called Brown Oil.

OPPOSING COUNSEL: Your Honor, may I object on Rule 402?

This is an area the opponent does not like. One of the most important aspects of an opening statement is that it allows a judge to understand why certain chapters are part of the advocate's theory of the case. This gives the court a much better vantage point from which to rule on relevancy objections.

THE COURT: Overruled.

THE WITNESS: That is correct. Those are the two primary assets of Brown Enterprise.

The cross-examination is back on track.

Q: (BY CROSS-EXAMINER) And what happened to create Brown Enterprise, was that in September, October, 1980, when you sold Brown Enterprise, the public company, to AEIC, you bought back some assets to create Brown Enterprise, the private company?

Chapter: Another Part to the AEIC Deal

A: Yes.

Q: And in order to do that purchase — well, the assets that you bought back were Brown Oil, the oil company in the United States?

A: Yes.

Transcript	*Analysis*
Q: And in order to afford this purchase, which was about $14 million, United States currency, you borrowed it from AEIC.	The cross-examiner must now explain a complicated business deal through a witness that is not particularly want to help. Patience and facts are all that are necessary.
A: I don't recall that.	The witness cannot recall borrowing $14 million. The reader should put himself in the place of the cross-examiner and fairly try to determine if the jury is accepting of that answer. This is not to say that the answer cannot be believed. In fact the cross-examiner must always fairly evaluate whether answers the cross-examiner believes to be inaccurate are being accepted or rejected by the fact finder.
Q: If you look at Exhibit A-5, page 7, paragraph 17, and see if that refreshes your recollection.	Leading question.
A: Yes.	Denial by the witness.
Q: You did. You borrowed back the entire purchase price of Brown Enterprise? THE COURT: I don't understand the question.	Impeachment. Again, the use of a document to refresh the recollection of the witness. Any question that cannot be understood should be rephrased. The court does a lawyer a judicially permissible favor by leading the lawyer know when a question has been phrased badly. Now that the lawyer has been warned, the lawyer can correct the problem. A lawyer should not feel any sense of anger toward the judge or witness who complains the question has not been understood. In fact, the person at fault is the lawyer.

Transcript	*Analysis*
CROSS-EXAMINER: Certainly, Your Honor.	
Q: (BY CROSS-EXAMINER) In buying back the oil company, you borrowed the money from AEIC to pay back to AEIC — in other words, you took out a loan from AEIC and said, I will pay for the oil company later, I owe you $14 million.	Rephrase the leading question. And if necessary, rephrase it a third way.
A: This doesn't say that, but —	
Q: Mr. Brown, you're saying you're unaware of Exhibit A-5?	This is another attempt by the cross-examiner to establish a foundation for admission of the exhibit. It will fail, but the facts contained in the exhibit will remain useful throughout the cross-examination.
A: I understand what Exhibit A-5, page 7 —	
Q: Let's just make sure we agree with what it is. This is a proposal you put forward through you and your agents to the Bank of Anchorage concerning your indebtedness to them?	These questions are all designed to accredit the document so that jurors will have confidence in the facts, and so that the witness will have less ability to deny facts contained in the document.
A: What are we — yes.	
Q: And, of course, you intended to be accurate with the Bank of Anchorage concerning your position?	
A: Yes.	This must be answered yes.
Q: And your position, financially, is stated in A-5?	
A: Yes. The position of Brown Enterprise.	This must be answered yes.

| *Transcript* | *Analysis* |

Q: (BY CROSS-EXAMINER) This describes in detail the financial problems emanating — stemming from the coal contract in 1981, and deals with the financial problems it caused for your company in 1981 and '82. Yes, sir?

A: I would like to hear that again, sir, please. I'm sorry.

Q: Certainly. This document was prepared by you and your staff because of your indebtedness to the Bank of Anchorage to the tune of more than $40 million?

If a witness wants to hear the question again, ask the question again. Nothing is lost by being polite to a hostile witness. The power is in the facts. Give the jury the facts.

A: I don't recall that number, sir, but I owed the bank — the Brown Enterprise owed the bank money, that's correct.

Note the oops answer, even the witness refers to Brown Enterprise as "I."

Again, the witness claims not to know if his company owed the bank $40 million. Nonetheless the jurors are getting a picture of the dimensions of the witness's indebtedness.

Q: And you had the debt to AEIC. That was another $14 million?

The cross-examiner is reminding the jurors of the other multimillion dollar debt proved up in an earlier chapter.

A: Well, whatever the figure was. For a minute, I owed money to AEIC.

Well, whatever . . .

Q: In the millions of dollars?

A: Yes.

Q: And this is the document you drew up, as you were unable to make the payments and were losing Brown Enterprise, the business you owned 90 percent of?

Hopefully now the picture is clearer: the witness was about to lose his business.

Transcript	*Analysis*
A: What do you mean by "losing," sir?	The witness who is clearly bright, well educated, and conversant with business terms needs help with term "losing" one's business. Cross-examiner loops the
Q: What I mean by losing, eventually the bank took it over. You couldn't make the payments. Do you recall that, sir?	term losing and defines it for the witness. At this point the reader should closely follow the answers of the witness to try to judge what impact they are having on the jury.
Note the use of "sir" as a method of trying to control the runaway witness.	
A: We voluntarily gave Brown Enterprise to the bank. So if you're taking —	
Q: Is that enough —	Notice that it didn't work. That is okay. If the cross-examiner has the facts and will stick to the facts the cross-examiner will emerge as the more credible person.
A: What you're saying here is taking out of context the discussions with the Bank of Anchorage, sir.	
Q: And these are the financial events going on in 1981, right after you buy the Bobcats.	Again, the technique is to put a reference to time inside the question to better assist the jurors in placing an event in the sequence.
A: What I'm looking at refers to 1982, in August.	Another time reference as it is critical that the jurors see that the financial situation of the witness is markedly deteriorating at the very time that he is going to need money to pay for the hockey team he has just purchased.
Q: (BY CROSS-EXAMINER) The sales commission contract was canceled March 31 of 1982. That was your last payment. Do you recall that, sir?	*Chapter: Cancellation of the Coal Commission Contract*

Transcript	*Analysis*

A: No. But that sounds approximately correct.

Q: You were notified in 1981, shortly after you bought the Bobcats, that the coal commission contract was being canceled.

A: If that's a question, I said I don't recall when in 1981.

Q: Do you recall it working like this? There was an agreement that AEIC came forward with that said will you accept a 90-day cancellation clause in your contract, and you had an understanding with that management that they wouldn't exercise it?

A: I didn't have an understanding that they wouldn't exercise — that they wouldn't exercise their right to cancel.

The witness did not believe his lucrative contract would be canceled.

Q: The management changed. And what happened is the new management came in and exercised the cancellation clause right after you bought the Bobcats.

But there was an uproar concerning the contract. New management took over. And the coal commission contract was suddenly canceled. But the witness had already bought the Washington D.C. Bobcats (on credit).

A: I already said, sir, I don't recall when that occurred. I agree with you that it did occur.

The chapter is concluded. Does the jury have the picture?

Q: And after that — well, let's go through, if we could, the payments you owed the Burkequtes.

Chapter: What You Owe the Burkequte Brothers/Payment Schedule

Transcript	*Analysis*
Q: And that payment schedule can be found at Exhibit I, page 2. Do you see it there?	This is an important exhibit. It shows the payment schedule. It is blown up on a board. The numbers are large and they are going to start coming due at the worst possible time, after the witness has suffered serious business setbacks.
A: Yes. CROSS-EXAMINER: I move the admission of Exhibit I, Your Honor. THE COURT: Received. CROSS-EXAMINER: I ask permission of The Court to display that in a blown-up form? THE COURT: You may.	The courtroom belongs to the judge. Ask permission. If the request is reasonable it will be granted.
Q: (BY CROSS-EXAMINER) On February 20, 1981, you purchased the Bobcats from the Burkequtes for $30,118,000. Do you recall that, sir?	Another time reference.
A: Thirty million, I recall. I don't remember the 118.	The lawyer is more precise than the witness. That is better than if the witness is more precise than the lawyer.
Q: And of the $30 million, that means that each one percent is being purchased for 300,000?	This method of computing the value of the team per 1% will become important as it provides an easy method of comparison for later sales of partial or complete interests in the team.
A: Roughly, yeah.	
Q: The payment schedule you had with the Burkequtes was that you would pay 8 million down at closing and you would owe them $22 million at 12 percent interest?	The payment schedule is now explained.
A: Yes. That's what this says.	

Transcript	*Analysis*

Q: But when you bought Brown Enterprise back from AEIC in the fall, right before this, you borrowed $14 million from AEIC on a four-year note at 12 percent interest as well.

Chapter: You Had Another Outstanding Loan When You Bought the Bobcats

The jury is reminded of the witness's other outstanding indebtedness.

A: Well, we have to go back to that exhibit, look at that.

Even the witness admits that the document not in evidence is the source of accurate facts.

Q: Certainly. It's A-5, page 7, paragraph 17. See if that refreshes your recollection. Do not read it out loud, please.

Notice how easily the cross-examiner confined to the right document, page, and even the paragraph in a very large list of exhibits. This is solely the result of sourcing the leading question. Again, The court has not admitted this document but it can always be used to refresh recollection.

Because the document is not in evidence, is improper to ask the witness to read from it.

Q: (BY CROSS-EXAMINER) Just months before buying the Bobcats from the Burkequtes, owing $22 million at 12 percent interest, you had bought the oil company from AEIC, owing them more than $14 million at 12 percent interest?

A: Yes.

Q: That was a four-year note?

A: Yes.

Q: And it was right after you bought the Bobcats that you learned the coal commission contract would be canceled?

Transcript	*Analysis*
A: Not — I have not agreed to that, sir. I do agree that it was canceled. I don't recall when.	A soft denial. The witness is not saying is wrong, only that he does not remember.
Q: And once you knew it was going to be canceled, you believed that your company, Brown Enterprise, would not be able to survive, because it was dependent on the flow of money from the coal commission contract to pay the expenses of Brown Enterprise.	*Chapter: Cancellation of the Coal Commission Contract Will Bring Down Brown Enterprise*
A: Yes. Unless there was enormous successes of Brown Oil, that's absolutely correct.	The witness agrees because those are the facts.
Q: And, in fact, you told the Bank of Anchorage, the cancellation of this coal contract is going to have a domino effect on your businesses.	
A: Actually, that's not what I said, sir.	
Q: (BY CROSS-EXAMINER) Isn't it true your company, Brown Enterprise, borrowed approximately $40 million from the Bank of Anchorage to finance Brown Oil?	*Chapter: Let's Not Forget About the Other $40 million Loan*
A: I don't recall the amount of the loan to finance Brown Oil, but it did — Brown — Brown Enterprise did borrow from the Bank of Anchorage for the purposes of financing Brown Oil.	The cross-examiner wants to remind the jurors not just of the amount that is owed but also who it is owed to: the Bank of Anchorage.

Transcript	*Analysis*
Q: Can you give us a dimension of what you recall? Do you think the $40 million is wildly inaccurate, sir?	If the cross-examiner has the facts, Sometimes a cross-examiner can offer the witness an opportunity to say that the fact is wrong. Most witnesses know they will be impeached if they say the fact is wrong, so they decline the opportunity to say the cross-examiner is wrong.
A: I don't think it's wildly inaccurate, but I think I have to say I don't recall.	As expected, the witness is unwilling to say that the cross-examiner has misstated the facts.
Q: Now the Burkequtes get security on the money you owe them, don't they?	*Chapter: The Sellers of the Team Have a Letter of Credit*
A: Yes.	Importance of the letter of credit is who issued it and what they can do if Brown fails to make the payments due the sellers.
Q: What the Burkequtes get was a letter of credit?	
A: Yes.	
Q: What a letter of credit means is that if you don't make any of the payments on principal and interest that are shown on Exhibit I, the Burkequtes can get it from the company that issues from the bank that issues the letter of credit?	The term "letter of credit" must be translated for the jurors.
A: Yes.	
Q: And the bank that issued the letter of credit for $31,600,000 was also the Bank of Anchorage.	The bank that can foreclose on the loan is the same bank to whom the witness already owes $40 million.
A: I don't recall that.	
Q: Who do you recall borrowing it from?	
A: I thought, frankly, the financing was done through Triad Bank and the United Bank of Washington D.C.	The witness cannot remember who financed the purchase of a professional hockey team.

Transcript	*Analysis*
Q: Would you look at Exhibit D-19, page 766 and 767?	The lawyer has sourced the answer and it is of immediate use.
CROSS-EXAMINER: Your Honor, I offer D-19. It's the closing binder for the sale of the Bobcats from Mr. Burkequte to Mr. Brown. THE COURT: Received. THE WITNESS: Sir, I have D-19. Where do you want me to go?	
Q: (BY CROSS-EXAMINER) I know it's very thick, because this is a closing binder on a deal, isn't it?	
A: It must — I don't know, but I haven't looked at it. THE COURT: Well, it's stipulated as that, Mr. Brown, by your lawyer, so you can accept that. THE WITNESS: Thank you, Your Honor.	
Q: (BY CROSS-EXAMINER) If you will, please, turn to page 766. You will find the page number at the bottom.	In an enormous binder with a great many documents cross-examiner can immediately take the witness to exactly the right page. Again, sourcing the leading question makes this very easy.
Q: D-19 is the closing binder with the documents from the sale from Mr. Brown to Mr. Waterton.	
A: I totally agree with that.	
Q: What happens, then, there was a cancellation of your loan — of your note to the Burkequtes, because Mr. Waterton had to pay the Burkequtes?	
A: Yes.	The witness is again shown to have a faulty memory and is easily impeached.

Transcript	*Analysis*

Q: And if you look at D-19, page 766, you will see that document is the cancellation of the $31,600,000 letter of credit issued by the Bank of Anchorage?
CROSS-EXAMINER: 766, first paragraph, please.
THE WITNESS: Yes.

The value of this simple impeachment is that it trains the witness on the dangers of denying that which is true.

The memory of the witness is shown to be inaccurate. The leading question of the cross-examiner is shown to be accurate. This is as it should be.

Q: (BY CROSS-EXAMINER) Okay. Now, let's get back to see if we are in agreement.
What happened was the Bank of Anchorage — that you were on the hook for the Brown Enterprise money — was also the bank that issued the $31 million letter of credit to the Burkequtes.

Chapter: If the Payments Are Not Made, the Bank of Anchorage Could Sell the Team
This is a rough form of a double loop. It is designed to remind the jurors that this bank is now the lender on two separate very large loans. One of those loans is about to go bad.

A: Yes.
Q: And what the Bank of Anchorage took as security was a provision from the NHL, and letters from your security agreement, saying if you missed payments, and they had to pay, that a trustee could be appointed to sell the team and pay back the bank?
A: I don't know that.
Q: You have no idea what security the Bank of Anchorage took on a $31,600,000 loan?
A: No, I don't. I'm not disagreeing with you, but I don't recall.

Note the witness is unwilling to agree, but unwilling to disagree.

Transcript	*Analysis*

Q: By the fall — no — so what the deal was with the Burkequtes, is that for the first two years, you could pay interest only on the $22 million you owed them?

Chapter: Structure of the Payments Due the Seller

Q: (BY CROSS-EXAMINER) So every quarter you owed the Burkequtes $660,000 on their note?

This is again an opportunity to use the exhibit board displaying the exact payments due every month to the seller.

A: Yes.

Q: And you owed AEIC principal and interest of $1 million every quarter?

This is a reminder of what other payments were due every quarter.

A: Yes.

Q: And you had the Bank of Anchorage loan, unrelated to the Burkequtes, of tens of millions of dollars.

This is a reminder of the third set of payments due on a third loan. Is the jury getting this picture?

Q: Now, the primary Enterprise of Brown Enterprise were the coal commission contract, which got canceled, and the oil company?

Chapter: The Financial Dominoes Begin to Fall
Back to the coal commission contract. Now the jurors can better understand how the cancellation of this contract begins a series of serious financial reversals.

A: Yes.

Q: And what happens when the coal commission contract was terminated? You didn't have the money to operate the oil company?

Q: (BY CROSS-EXAMINER) Without the coal commission Brown Enterprise, your contract, the oil company does company, did not have the not have the money it needs money to run the oil to keep operating. company.

A: It did not have the money to run the oil company on a continuing basis.

Enough for today.

Transcript	*Analysis*
THE COURT: Members of the jury, good morning. We are all very appreciative of the extra effort of your prompt arrival. We know it took a little more time than usual, but not as bad as they predicted. So we are ready to resume. Mr. Brown, if you will, please, resume the stand. Cross-Examiner, you may continue. CROSS-EXAMINER: Thank you, Your Honor. CROSS-EXAMINATION (Resumed) BY CROSS-EXAMINER:	
Q: Mr. Brown, in 1981, you bought the Bobcats in hopes of making money?	*Chapter: The Bobcats Were Supposed to Make Money, But They Lost Money*
A: Yes. I hoped we would make money.	
Q: You did not buy the Bobcats as a tax shelter?	This is a safe haven that must be taken away. If not taken away the witness could later try to say that losing money was perfectly acceptable as he had purchased the team as a tax shelter.
A: No. That was not my intent.	
Q: And in 1981, the hockey team did not make money; in fact, it lost money?	First your ownership — team losing money.
A: That is correct.	
Q: You mentioned that your memory was its loss was in the neighborhood of $1 million?	This is a quote from his direct examination. He has tried to convince the jury that the team only lost $1 million in its first year. These numbers going to prove to be wildly inaccurate.
A: That's my recollection.	The jury is reminded of the direct testimony in order to set up the impeachment from a document.

Transcript	*Analysis*
Q: And I wanted to clarify with you, if I could, sir, were you talking about a $1 million on a tax basis or on a financial reporting basis?	This question is just an extra precaution. The cross-examiner is prepared regardless of which answer the witness picks, but if the witness will pick one answer, the impeachment can be even more dramatic.
A: I can't answer that, sir, I don't know.	
Q: It was one of those two?	
A: I don't know if the tax-reported number and the actual loss were the same. That, I don't know.	
Q: I'm trying to determine, sir, whether the $1 million loss you're alluding to was a tax basis $1 million loss, or a financial reporting basis $1 million loss?	
A: I understand the question. And I'm not certain of the answer.	
CROSS-EXAMINER: May I have Exhibit U for the witness, please?	The witness is now set up for an impeachment by inconsistent statement contained in a document.
Q: (BY CROSS-EXAMINER) Do you have Exhibit U in front of you, sir?	
A: Yes, I do.	
Q: Do you recognize it as the report from your auditors?	
A: Yes.	
Q: For Brown Sports, Limited, for the year ending December 31, 1981?	
A: Yes.	
CROSS-EXAMINER: Your Honor, I move the admission of Exhibit U. OPPOSING COUNSEL: No objection, Your Honor. THE COURT: U is received.	A document is admitted.

Transcript	Analysis
Q: (By CROSS-EXAMINER) If you would turn, please, sir, to Exhibit U, page 4. Mr. Brown, do you see your accountant reported a net loss for Brown Sports, the Washington D.C. Bobcats for 1981 of $8,803,000?	Impeachment begins. This is the net loss, not the tax loss. This is a whole lot bigger loss and the witness has admitted to the jury. The reader should ask fairly what impression the jury will have at this point in the cross-examination. If the cross-examination is working, the credibility of the witness should be sharply diminished by this point. It is for the reader to determine whether they think that has happened.
A: Yes, I do.	
Q: Does that help your memory on that point, sir?	
A: I'm not sure what point you refer to. But if this is what we reported for tax purposes, I believe that this is a correct statement by Jim Russel.	
Q: Let us turn to U, page 8, if you could, sir. You mentioned the loss for tax purposes. That's a different kind of loss than a loss for financial purposes, isn't it, sir?	This is the tax loss.
A: Yes, it can be.	
Q: And, in fact — CROSS-EXAMINER: If we will go to the bottom, of U (8). Net loss.	The document is now up on a screen where all the jurors can see it. The particular line of significance is being highlighted so the jurors do not have to scan the entire document looking for the important fact.

Transcript	*Analysis*
Q: (BY CROSS-EXAMINER) U.S. income tax reporting the net loss for the Bobcats for tax purposes as shown at the bottom of U (8), it is $4,808,000?	Again, the document tells the story of losses far in excess of what the witness has previously claimed.
A: I don't see that on the sheet of paper I have.	
Q: Do you have U (8) in front of you, sir?	
A: Yes. I do now.	
Q: Do you see the net tax loss $4,808,000?	
A: Yes, I do.	
Q: Does that help your memory as to what kind of losses you experienced in your first year with the Washington D.C. Bobcats?	
A: I understand what this says. I thought it was around $1 million. It appears it was greater than that.	The witness knows he has been caught.
Q: I would like you, Mr. Brown, to help put that kind of loss into context in the 1981 time frame versus the numbers we are accustomed to now in the NHL.	Do the jurors believe that the witness was innocently mistaken?
	Chapter: Putting a Multimillion Dollar Loss into Context / 1981 The following facts are designed to remind jurors that these are 1981 numbers. An $8 million loss in 2004 might be less significant, but a loss of this magnitude when team revenues were so small is more significant.
In 1981, the entire team payroll would be about seven or $8 million, wouldn't it?	
A: I don't know.	
Q: In fact, the highest player you had in 1981 made $250,000 a year?	

Transcript	Analysis
THE COURT: I assume you mean the highest paid?	
CROSS-EXAMINER: Yes. Highest-paid player. Yes. Thank you, Your Honor.	
Q: (BY CROSS-EXAMINER) The salaries were nothing like they are today, were they, sir?	
A: That's correct.	
Q: And if we go, sir, to page U (4), we'll see some breakout on what it cost to run a team in 1981?	Use of a document to remind witness that cross-examiner has the facts.
CROSS-EXAMINER: If I could have the operating expenses section, please.	
Q: (BY CROSS-EXAMINER) Your total expenses to pay the team payroll and all the expenses of games for an entire season was only $9 million?	
A: And the total — yes, I got it.	
Q: And, in fact, if we take the entire revenues the Washington D.C. Bobcats could achieve, game admissions were the highest revenues, even higher than TV revenues in that era?	
A: Yes.	
Q: And for all of the games put together, Bobcats revenues were only $7,263,000?	
A: That's what this says.	The Chapter is concluded. The jury should have the picture that a $4 million or $8 million loss for a business this small was truly enormous.

Transcript	*Analysis*
Multiple chapters are omitted showing other aspects of the financial problems facing the witness.	
Q: (BY CROSS-EXAMINER) Now, you said in your direct examination, sir, that in 1982, you experienced serious cash flow problems.	*Chapter: Your Debt Structure in the Summer of 1982*
A: I did.	
Q: So there was a relationship between your activities on the personal side and your activities as the owner of Brown Enterprise, Limited?	
Q: And, in fact, that is one of the reasons that you talked to Coach Stout about finding someone who might buy a minority interest in the Washington D.C. Bobcats?	The witness has owned the team for only one season before he begins looking to sell a large stake in the team. This is extremely important because the witness's theory of the case is that he only parted with the team because of family issues occurring in 1984. A further part of the witness's theory of the case is that he so loved the team that he would have done anything to buy it back. Proof that he had some or all of the team on the market after one season is critical to the defendant's theory of the case that the team was sold for financial reasons and that the plaintiff/witness sold the team because he got the right price, with the right terms, at the right time.

Transcript	Analysis
A: That is one of the methods that I used to refinance myself, among others, not entirely the only one, that's correct.	
Q: So if I understand your testimony, it was a combination of your business investments and the cash outflow in them that caused this serious cash flow problem in 1982?	The cross-examiner has previously established the financial problems in 1981. The cross-examiner now establishes additional financial problems in 1982.
A: Yes.	
Q: Payments for interest on the Bobcats loan, as well as payments to AEIC and the Bank of Anchorage on the Brown Enterprise loan?	
A: That is correct. And through the undertakings that we made, including the option granted to Mr. Andrew and Mr. Borderland by the end of 1982, there were no cash flow problems.	The witness tries to tell the jurors that his financial problems were largely ended by default in 1982 through this transaction. The cross-examiner ducks the bait. We will get to this chapter later. It will not go well for the witness.
Q: I would like to talk about the Andrews/Borderland situation. But, first, when is it in 1982 that you first went to Coach Stout? How early in the year?	*Chapter: Asking Coach Stout If He Knows Anybody Wants to Buy Part of the Team*
A: I don't recall. But it would have been — my recollection would have been in the late — in the spring, late spring.	
Q: April, May time period, sir?	
A: I can't recall specifically, sir.	

Transcript	*Analysis*
Q: I would like to come back to that in a moment. But let's talk about the Fred Eves situation, if we could, sir.	*Chapter: Spring 1982, Learning Fred Eves Wanted to Buy the Team*
It is your statement that it was Robert MacKenize, your number one business advisor, who initiated the idea of selling the Washington D.C. Bobcats to Fred Eves in 1982?	This begins a critical chapter bundle. The cross-examiner will now establish that the plaintiff/witness was willing to sell the entire team as early as 1982, long before the supposedly family health issues surfaced.
A: It is my statement that he initiated with me. I don't know, as between Mr. MacKenize and Mr. Eves, who initiated that discussion.	The cross-examiner knows from the deposition of the witness that he will adamantly deny that he was willing to sell the team to Fred Eves. Pre-trial investigation has revealed a massive amount of evidence to the contrary.
Q: And did you give Mr. MacKenize the go-ahead to have conversations with Fred Eves in the spring of 1982 about selling your entire interest in the Washington D.C. Bobcats?	This series of questions is designed to allow the witness to dig as deep a hole as possible, always denying that the negotiations with Mr. Eves were serious.
A: I gave him permission to go ahead and discuss the possibility of the sale, not necessarily the entire sale of the Washington D.C. Bobcats. I did — having advised Mr. MacKenize and when I met with Mr. Eves that I was doing this because Mr. MacKenize wanted me to do it, but that I had no intention of selling the team. That is not what I wanted to do.	This is one of those chapters whose power only becomes apparent after the testimony of Mr. Eves.

Transcript	*Analysis*
Q: That's what I wanted to make sure I understand, Mr. Brown. You told your number one business advisor, Mr. Brown, before negotiations began, that you had absolutely no intention of selling all or any part of the Washington D.C. Bobcats in 1982?	Help the witness dig the hole.
A: Yes. I think the word I actually used was I had no interest.	
Q: Did no interest mean to you I'm not going to do this?	
A: It meant to me that this is something Mr. MacKenize really wanted to explore. It is my practice if one of the top men or women that I work with really thinks that I should look at something, that I honor and respect their views about that.	
In doing so, I didn't want to mislead anybody that this is something I was really not interested in. t	The witness paints a conclusory picture of being uninterested in the sale of the team. Facts will always trump conclusions.
Q: In that quest of yours to not mislead anybody, did you make it clear to Mr. MacKenize you had no intention of selling all, or any part, of the Washington D.C. Bobcats to Fred Eves?	This is a spontaneous loop of the witness's phrase "I didn't want to mislead anybody." If the jury believes that, the cross-examiner has not yet accomplished his job.
A: As I said, I said to Mr. MacKenize, I have no interest in this.	

Transcript	*Analysis*
Q: And did you make it clear in your interest in being candid to Fred Eves before the negotiation ever began that you had no interest in selling the Washington D.C. Bobcats to him?	The hole is very deep. Getting a witness to commit to the particulars is the best set up for an external impeachment. Any time the cross-examiner can get the witness to say a thing did occur or did not occur, that a statement was made, or a statement was not made, the impeachment is on firmer ground. Now a lawyer can call another witness who can say a particular thing is not true, or did not happen, or in some other way directly contradict the testimony of this witness.
A: Yes. I believe that I did.	The picture of a supposedly disinterested seller is painted.
Q: Now, you talked yesterday about a time when Paul Waterton was thinking about buying the team and he did something called due diligence. Do you know what that phrase means?	*Chapter: Fred Eves Begins His Due Diligence* The term is defined for the jury.
A: Yes.	
Q: Due diligence is a business phrase, isn't it, sir?	
A: Yes.	
Q: It is what buyers and sellers do when they're looking at each other to see if they're going to put a deal together?	
A: Usually.	
Q: But that's what it's for, to see if you're going to put the deal together?	
A: To see if there is a deal that can be done.	

Transcript	*Analysis*
Q: Now, after you told Fred Eves you had no interest in selling the team to him — by the way, you knew who Fred Eves was when he offered to buy the Washington D.C. Bobcats in 1982, didn't you?	*Chapter: Fred Eves Had to Be Taken Seriously*
A: I believe that he was the owner of ATC Investments	
Q: Actually, I'm not sure if at that point he had been. Did you recognize him as a part owner of the Omaha Corn-ears?	
A: No.	
Q: Did you know that he had owned and operated the Bronx Ball-handlers for 11 years?	
A: No, I did not.	
Q: Did you recognize him as an accomplished businessperson with the financial means to acquire the Washington D.C. Bobcats?	
A: I had no idea whether he had that capacity.	Is this believable?
Q: You had no idea whatsoever whether the man offering to buy the team had the money available to buy the team?	
A: Mr. MacKenize believed that he had the capacity to do so, but I did not know what that meant.	
Q: But you were not open to the possibility of selling the team to Fred Eves?	
A: I was not interested in it.	

Transcript	*Analysis*
Q: Now, one of the reasons Mr. MacKenize was discussing with you selling the entire Washington D.C. Bobcats was the serious cash flow problems you were experiencing?	*Chapter: You Needed to Sell Part of the Team / You Were Willing to Sell Part of the Team*
A: He believed, as I said, that I had too many eggs in one basket, and that he believed it would be prudent to reduce our exposure, financial exposure, to owning the Washington D.C. Bobcats, particularly in the light of facing a year that had a high probability of a players' strike.	
Q: That concept, too many eggs in one basket, that's another way of saying your investment in the Washington D.C. Bobcats was too big?	This is a spontaneous loop of "too many eggs in one basket"
A: No. I don't think I said that.	
Q: Well, that was the basket we were talking about, wasn't it?	
A: Yes. What I said was that we had too many eggs in one basket. That did not mean it was too big. It meant that if I could diversify the risk associated with the Bobcats, he believed that would be a good idea.	Boiling this phrase down, the witnesses admitting that he wanted to sell part of the team as early as 1982.
Q: In fact, in 1982, the only three baskets — well, there were only two baskets left by 1982, the Washington D.C. Bobcats and the failing Brown Enterprise?	The cross-examiner is trying to remind the jurors that the Washington D.C. Bobcats are the best asset left to be sold by the plaintiff.

Transcript	Analysis
A: No. That's not accurate, sir.	The witness partially denies this by redefining the question.
Q: Tell me what other businesses were providing you with any substantial income in 1982?	
A: You're making a distinction between assets and revenue. I had significant personal assets. And, in fact, during 1982, and including in 1983, I sold significant personal assets. If you will allow me to finish. Which meant two things. Number one, I was creating cash, and, number two, I was reducing expenses significantly.	
In fact, by the latter part, middle part of 1983, I had sold my principal residence in Alaska, other homes that I owned in the northwest, and the only home that I owned was my condominium at Washington D.C., because I intended to make the Bobcats the focus of my business activities.	In this runaway answer the witness admits excellent facts for his opponent.
Q: Let's divide this up and make sure we understand each other. You sold off your personal assets in an attempt to meet the demands of the failing Brown Enterprise Company?	
A: No. Not in an attempt to take care of my obligation. In fact, my obligations were resolved by the end of 1982, although, technically, the last payment was made in January of '83.	

Transcript	*Analysis*
Q: Well, your problems with Brown Enterprise were resolved in one way when you got off an airplane from a business trip and found that a subsidiary of AEIC had filed a petition for involuntary bankruptcy on Brown Enterprise; isn't that accurate, Mr. Brown?	This is a spontaneous loop of the witness's description that he has "resolved" the financial obligations of Brown Enterprise.
A: I don't know whether it's accurate the way you described it, sir, but we did receive that filing from AEIC, and we ultimately resolved that issue.	The cross-examiner has researched the issue and can point out that the loan got "resolved" by the witness losing his entire investment. The witness is forced to admit that a lender filed a petition for involuntary bankruptcy against Brown Enterprise. This is another example of the value of pre-trial investigation coupled with database investigation.
Q: How it was resolved was you lost your entire personal investment in Brown Enterprise in 1982?	Another spontaneous loop of the word "resolved."
A: That's correct.	
Q: That was many millions of dollars?	This chapter has gone about as well as it could possibly go all because the witness has tried to paint a financial picture that can easily be contradicted by facts known to the defense.
A: Yes.	
Q: And besides the many millions of dollars you lost personally in Brown Enterprise, you lost back to your creditors the principal business of Brown Enterprise, which was Brown Oil?	
A: Yes.	
Q: The plane you liquidated in 1982 was the Gulfstream, and that was liquidated, again, to try to meet the interest payments to the banks?	Cross-examiner can even tell the jury which assets of the witness had to sell to raise money. This kind of detail is designed to reassure the jurors that the cross-examiner knows the facts and will get them out, with or without the help of the witness.

Transcript	*Analysis*
A: Actually, to meet interest and principal.	End of the chapter.
Q: Now, this too many eggs in one basket concept, the eggs we are talking about, that means too many dollars in the Bobcats?	*Chapter: You Wanted to Sell the Entire Team to Fred Eves* A spontaneous loop of the witness's phrase "too many eggs in one basket."
A: Yes.	
Q: And your number one advisor was telling you in 1982 that it would be good to consider this sale of the Washington D.C. Bobcats?	
A: He was advising me that a partial sale of the Washington D.C. Bobcats would be one way of resolving ultimately our total cash flow problems.	
Q: Is it your testimony that the proposition put forward by Mr. Eves and the conversations with Mr. Eves were about selling a minority interest versus selling the entire interest you owned?	Helping the witness take another position that can be contradicted by documents and by witnesses. This is setting up an external impeachment.
A: My recollection is that it was unclear at the beginning of those discussions, at least to me, ultimately, as to whether or not — excuse me — it was a minority interest or an entire interest in the team. I believe that ultimately, it became clear to Mr. MacKenize and my other advisors that Mr. Eves was interested in acquiring the whole team.	The witness gives in. He cannot successfully maintain the position that he was unaware that the deal under discussion was a sale of the entire team.
Q: The whole team?	
A: And that transaction did not take place.	

Transcript	*Analysis*
Q: Well, it was a transaction you were not interested in?	The cross-examiner reminds the jury of the position taken by the plaintiff/witness: one of this should be happening because the witness had no interest in selling the team.
A: That's correct.	The reader should fairly reflect on the credibility of the witness at this point in the cross-examination. *Chapter: You Personally Met With Fred Eves*
Q: Mr. Eves flew out as part of his due diligence and met with you at the Bobcats' facility on Parker Street. Do you recall that?	
A: I met with him — how he got there, I don't know. But I met with Mr. Eves at Parker Street.	As part of his denial that the plaintiff/witness was willing to sell the entire team to Fred in 1982, the witness has denied any real involvement in the negotiation process. Knowing what Mr. Eves and other witnesses will say, the cross-examiner sets up a series of external impeachments. These impeachment's will only be completed when the other witnesses are called. However, the detailed opening statement has alerted the jury to the fact that the statements of the plaintiff/witness will all be contested.
Q: What you told us earlier at a deposition — do you recall telling us you think you just met Mr. Fred Eves in the parking lot of Parker Street and just said hello to him in passing?	The witness wants to minimize his contact with Mr. Eves. The cross-examiner should help the witness do this. In this way the Eves testimony will be clearly and unmistakably impeaching.
A: That's what I recall.	

Transcript	Analysis

Q: It is your recollection that that was the interchange between you and Fred Eves? You said hello to him in passing as he went to your facility?

A: That is what I recall.

Q: It's not true, is it, Mr. Brown, that you personally took Fred Eves through the entire Bobcats facility and showed him every part of it and discussed it in detail as part of his due diligence in getting ready to acquire the team?

A: I may have done that, sir. I don't recall it.

Q: You have a fishing trip in the spring of 1982 in which you brought all of the coaches of the Washington D.C. Bobcats and the management of the Washington D.C. Bobcats?

A: It's inaccurate what you said. So, no, I don't remember what you have said.

Q: My question was specific. Did you bring your coaches and your management to Marvine River Fishing Camp in early 1982?

A: You said did I bring all of them. The answer is no, I didn't, but some.

Q: Coach Stout was among them?

A: Yes.

Q: Now, could you place in time when the fishing trip was? How early in 1982?

A: Yes. Again, we run that fishing camp in June, just before Father's Day. It runs for a period of a couple of weeks.

Analysis:

The witnesses offered an opportunity to admit the facts that the impeaching witness will testify to. If the witness will admit them he will have impeached himself. If the witness continues to deny them he will later be impeached by others. And here again is the nondenial. Does the jury accept this answer?
Chapter: Bringing Fred to Meet the Coaches

The cross-examiner needs to establish a timeframe for the jury.

Transcript	*Analysis*
Q: So at this point, you had already talked to Coach Stout about the possibility of finding somebody to buy a minority interest in the Bobcats?	This is going to lead to a later chapter in which it will be shown that the witness was actually negotiating with two separate buyers at the same time.
A: I may well have done that. I don't recall.	Does the jury accept this answer?
Q: And didn't you invite Fred Eves — well, let me construct it with more detail. Didn't you have a conversation with Fred Eves in which he said to you, "If I'm going to buy this team, part of my due diligence is I'll want to meet the coaching staff and the management?" Do you recall that happening?	
A: No. I don't recall it. But it doesn't mean it didn't happen.	Is this the kind of answer that inspires confidence?
Q: And do you recall saying to Fred Eves the way you can check out the coaches and the management is to come oin us at the Marvine River Fishing Camp?	
A: I don't recall that. But, it's certainly a way he could have done it.	
Q: Well, do you recall Fred Eves coming out across the country to go to the Marvine River Fishing Camp?	
Q: Do you recall in approximately June of 1982 that you invited Fred Eves, personally, to come meet with the coaches and the management so he could do his due diligence on buying your entire interest in the Bobcats?	

Transcript	*Analysis*
A: As I said, I certainly invited Fred Eves there. I think he had a good time. I don't recall the words you're saying I said.	Will the jury accept this lack of memory? Does the jury believe that Fred to let was invited to the fishing camp to go fishing?
Q: How about the concept, Mr. Brown, that Fred Eves was invited by you to travel all the way to Alaska as part of his due diligence on buying your entire interest in the Bobcats?	
A: I don't recall him saying it as I said. It certainly would be for him to meet in an informal way some of the management, some of the coaches. I just cannot say I recall saying the words that you are saying I said. If I could, I would.	
Q: But do you recall now he was there, Fred Eves joined you?	
A: I told you I remember inviting him.	
Q: But you can't recall that you invited him as part of his checking out the team?	Is this believable? The reader should attempt to gauge the credibility of the witness at this point in the cross-examination.
A: No, I don't.	
Q: You just thought he was there for fishing?	
A: Sir, I don't know how to go further with this. I'm not saying that that isn't why Fred wanted to come to the fishing camp. I just don't recall saying the words that you're saying I said.	

Transcript	*Analysis*
Q: But if Fred Eves was coming to your fishing camp to do due diligence, to check out this acquisition, what you're telling us, he was checking out the acquisition, you had told him firmly you had no intention of doing —	This is a double loop. Fact 1. The buyer is doing due diligence. Fact 2. After having been told that the seller has no interest in selling What's wrong with this picture?
A: Those aren't my words, but — I mean I have said what I have said.	
Q: Do you recall, sir, telling Mr. Eves that the price for the Bobcats would be $54 million?	*Chapter: You Set the Price to Sell the Entire Team*
A: I do not.	
Q: Are you saying that conversation did not occur, or are you saying you just can't recall it?	
A: I'm saying I don't recall it.	Notice, the witness is offered chance to deny the truthfulness of a statement. His admission that he is unwilling to say the conversation occurred means that in a credibility contest with another witness that says the conversation occurred, this witness must lose.
Q: And if you would look at Exhibit A-2 — do you have in front of you A-2, sir?	But it isn't going to be just another witness that contradicts this testimony, other witnesses and documents will contradict the witness as well.
A: Yes, I do.	
Q: Do you recognize it as a contract for the sale of your entire interest in the Washington D.C. Bobcats to Fred Eves?	The cross-examiner cannot get this document in through this witness as he denies any knowledge of it. The document will come in through a later witness. It is a contract for sale of the entire team. It even contains the price and terms.

Transcript	Analysis
A: Yes.	
Q: Now in order to do due diligence on a business acquisition, the buyer is virtually certain to ask to see the financial records, isn't he?	*Chapter: July 4, the Buyer's Team Comes to Alaska to Close the Deal*
A: I would think so.	
Q: You wouldn't hand financial records of the Washington D.C. Bobcats out to people for no reason, would you?	
A: I didn't do this, sir, as I have said, nor was I a part of it. Now, obviously, if Mr. MacKenize who had a serious negotiation, which he did, I believe, with Mr. Eves, Mr. Eves would have wanted to see the financial records of the Bobcats.	The witness is trying to backpedal because the documents exist and the facts tell a different story.
Q: In particular, sir, I would like to talk about the July 4 weekend of 1982, July 4, I believe, was a Sunday, July 2, a Friday. Is it your testimony that you were unaware that Fred Eves sent an entire team, including lawyers, business executives, and accountants to Alaska to get ready to execute the purchase agreement with you?	Because of pre-trial investigation the cross-examiner has available a wealth of detail concerning this pivotal weekend. In hearing the facts contained in this chapter the reader should ask how likely it is that a prospective buyer would take these actions if, indeed, the team was not up for sale. The reader should also ask, how likely is it the plaintiff/witness would be unaware of these facts, or alternatively, would allow these things to take place if he were unwilling to sell the entire team.

Transcript	*Analysis*
A: It is my recollection that, indeed, Mr. Eves did send a team to Alaska. Mr. MacKenize had a team in Alaska, and that he did not believe it was a good idea to have these negotiations in the Washington D.C. Bobcat offices, with which I concurred. When you add to it to negotiate a purchase agreement, I cannot say that, because I don't know that, and I wasn't a part of those negotiations.	Is this believable?
Q: It is your testimony, sir, that in a deal that you had told both sides you did not want to do, and had no intention of doing, that both sides gathered lawyers, accountants, and executives in Alaska, your home, on the July 4 weekend of 1982 to get ready to sign a purchase agreement that you were unwilling to sign?	The question is built on the admitted facts and is designed to show how preposterous is the position of the plaintiff/witness. Is the reader persuaded? One must try to gauge how a jury is viewing this testimony in which many many of the leading questions are met with a partial denial such as "I don't recall" or "That may have happened" or "I am not saying that didn't happen, but . . ."
A: I cannot say what you have said, sir. I did not know the details of the negotiations. But it is my testimony that, indeed, both sides did send a team to Alaska and did whatever they did. And that I had advised both sides I had no interest in selling the team.	Another backpedal in the face of easily provable facts. Yes, the two teams were there, but no, I had no interest in selling.

Transcript	Analysis
Q: And, in fact, how the financial records got to Alaska was that you directed your attorney, Jane Douglas, of Kemper & Yan to pack up the Bobcats financial records and bring them to Alaska for the meeting?	Chapter: *You Directed That the Bobcats' Financial Records Be Brought to Alaska*
	A former lawyer for the plaintiff/witness has been deposed. She has been permitted to answer only those questions that the plaintiff believes do not implicate the attorney/client privilege or any other applicable privilege. A portion of her deposition will be read to the jury by the defense.
A: I don't recall that I told Jane to do that. But, if I did, I did. I believe it would have been Mr. MacKenize that would have done that, certainly knowing Jane Douglas would not have done that knowing that Robert would have had my authority to do that.	
Q: And, in fact, it was your request that this take place in Alaska so that the Washington D.C. press would hear nothing about it?	
A: I don't know whether it was my request, but certainly, whoever, came up with the idea, I would have agreed with.	

Transcript	*Analysis*
Q: And it was your request that this happen the July 4 weekend while you were in your home in Alaska.	The prospective buyer will testify in great detail concerning how difficult it was for him to round up his team of lawyers, accountants, and business executives to fly to Alaska on the July 4 weekend. He even recalls 20 years later how inconvenient it was for certain members of the team. It is that sort of fact and detail that vividly paints a credible picture.
A: I guess I have two problems. One, my request, and, two, I don't recall whether I was in Alaska or whether we were out of town.	
Q: Isn't it true, Mr. — Mr. Brown, you were waiting at your home while your negotiators tried to put together the final purchase agreement for your signature?	
A: Sir, I can only say what I have said. I do not recall that.	
Q: Let me turn to the conclusion of this. Do you recall that the Eves due diligence team wanted to compare the Bobcats' actual financial performance versus the projections you had provided them?	*Chapter: Eves Team Says "the Numbers Are Off/the Deal Is Off"*
A: No.	
Q: Were you aware that financial projections had been provided to the Eves team?	Witness claims he is unaware that his staff had provided financial projections to a possible buyer. What is the likely thinking of the jury? In this regard how much has it mattered that the picture of the witness is one of a very sophisticated businessman?

Transcript	*Analysis*

A: No.

Q: Were you aware that a comparison took place in Alaska of the actual financials to the projections?

A: No.

Q: Do you recall members of the Eves team coming to your home in Alaska to break off the negotiations?

A: That they came to my home?

Q: Yes.

A: No. I don't recall that.

Q: Do you recall any of them saying to you that the reason the deal was falling through was that your projected figures didn't match the actual figures?

A: No. I don't recall that.   The witness recalls none of this.

(End of excerpt of cross-examination)

§ 33.04   Transcript 3—Cross Examination in Personal Injury Case

The cross examiner represents a man driving a pickup truck pulling a four hundred gallon diesel fuel cell trailer on a two lane country road. An eighteen wheeler driven by the defendant loaded with eighty thousand pounds of gravel came up from behind the plaintiff at a much higher rate of speed.

A collision occurred, which exploded the diesel fuel cell and drove the pickup truck and driver into the ditch on the side of the road. The plaintiff experienced multiple injuries, including a herniated cervical disc and a rotator cuff tear on his left shoulder as a result of the collision.

Not all cross examination chapters are illustrated, but the first goal of the cross examination was to lock in liability on the defendant eighteen wheeler driver and eliminate any comparative or contributory negligence by the plaintiff driver. A second goal was to use the defendant truck driver to support as many elements of the plaintiff's case for damages and injuries as possible.

A third goal was to introduce as many facts as possible that support the influence that money was the root cause of the collision, and to prepare the jury for awarding monetary damages to the plaintiff.

Transcript	Analysis
Q: "... Now at the crossroads you had to come to a complete stop at the stop sign?	*Chapter: Accelerating with a Full Load*
A: Yes. I did.	
Q: You downshifted and came to a complete stop?	
A: Yes.	
Q: You knew that you had to start stopping hundreds of yards from the stop sign to be able to get your truck loaded with eighty thousand pounds of gravel to a complete stop?	Locking in time needed to decelerate to then compare danger of acceleration, and no time to declerate before collision.
A: I did. I saw the sign. I started to stop.	
Q: But you knew it took a long time to stop?	
A: Yes.	
Q: That's just the way it is when you are driving a truck with that much weight plus the weight of the truck?	
A: That's right. I had a full load.	
Q: Takes more time "with a full load"?	
A: Right.	
Q: From that stop sign, you began to accelerate?	Spontaneous loop.
A: Yes.	
Q: Started out in first gear, shifted to second and so on up through the gears?	
A: Yes.	
Q: With each shift your speed became greater?	
A: That's right.	
Q: When you are hauling a full load of that size, you cannot skip gears, you have to shift up through the gear tree?	

Transcript	*Analysis*
A: That's right. You tear up the transmission otherwise.	Spontaneous loop.
Q: From the dead stop at the stop sign to the time that you hit the back of Mr. Zeigler's trailer you continued to accelerate?	
A: Yes.	
Q: You never slowed down. You were always speeding up?	
A: Yes.	
Q: You were always shifting to the next highest gear?	
A: Yes.	
Q: Gearing faster and faster?	
A: Sure.	
Q: You have driven that road literally hundreds of times?	*Chapter: Know Road Had Turn-Offs to Left*
A: Yes.	
Q: It is two lanes?	
A: Yes.	
Q: Blacktop?	
A: Yes.	
Q: Traffic moving both north and south?	
A: Yes.	
Q: Fairly heavily traveled road?	
A: At times.	
Q: You know there are turnoffs to driveways and to crossroads through that section of Route 312?	
A: Yes.	
Q: Some of them are marked and some of them are not?	
A: That's right.	
Q: In other words, there are signs that say crossroad ahead?	
A: Right.	
Q: Some crossroads, particularly dirt crossroads, don't have signs?	
A: True.	
Q: None of the driveways have signs?	
A: That's right?	Spontaneous loops.

Transcript	*Analysis*
Q: And traffic can slow and come to a stop if someone is trying to a left-hand turn along there?	
A: That's true.	
Q: You knew all of that?	
A: I did.	
Q: Because of all those reasons, the speed limit is 55?	
A: That's right.	
Q: And that's a fair and safe maximum speed limit given all the conditions on that road?	
A: That's probably true.	
Q: Well our society believed that was the fair, safe, maximum speed limit?	Loop and trilogy.
A: Yes.	
Q: And you "probably" agree?	
A: I do agree.	Spontaneous loop.
Q: You completely agree?	
A: Yes.	
Q: That was the fair maximum speed limit?	
A: Yes.	Loop and trilogy.
Q: Now before you came around the turn, before you could see the pickup pulling the trailer, you new there was a pickup around that turn?	*Chapter: Warned of Slow Moving Truck*
A: I didn't know exactly where and I didn't know exactly what pickup truck, but I did know. Yes.	
Q: Not exactly, but you were warned?	Loop of theme word.
A: Yes.	
Q: And the way you were warned was that your front door or the truck ahead of you that you had been running with had gotten on the CB and told you that?	
A: That's right. Mike had called me.	

Transcript	Analysis
Q: And when Mike, your front door, called you, he said watch out there is a pickup truck pulling a trailer up in front of you, between us?	Loop.
A: Words to that affect.	
Q: And the words that he used was the pickup truck is pulling the trailer?	Spontaneous loop.
A: Yes.	
Q: And the words he used was the pickup truck is going slower than 55?	Loop.
A: Yes.	
Q: In fact, the words he used was, it is really just crawling along?	
A: Yes, I think those were his words.	
Q: Crawling was the word he used to warn you?	Double loop.
A: Yes.	
Q: As you received this CB warning, you are continuing to accelerate?	*Chapter: Warning Did Not Slow Him Down*
A: Yes.	
Q: You were approaching 55 miles per hour at that point?	
A: I wasn't looking at the speedometer, but it was about that speed.	
Q: You did not have to look at the speedometer because you are a professional truck driver? Right?	
A: Right.	
Q: As a professional you can judge your speed without looking at the speedometer? True?	Loop: Trilogy.
A: Yes.	
Q: In fact, a professional can judge your speed by the gear you are in?	Loop.
A: True.	

Transcript	*Analysis*
Q: A professional can judge it by the sound of the pull on the engine?	
A: Yes.	
Q: And you knew you were approaching 55 miles per hour?	
A: Yes.	
Q: You know you were approaching the fair, safe, maximum speed limit permitted on that road?	Loop from trilogy of previous chapter.
A: Yes.	
Q: And you are continuing to accelerate to that speed, even as Mike, your front door, warned you that a much slower pickup truck pulling a trailer was in front of you?	
A: That's true.	
Q: As you approached the Zeigler vehicle, you decided you were going to pass him?	*Chapter: Dangerous Pass*
A: Yes.	
Q: There was a passing zone there? True?	
A: That's right.	
Q: And you know along that stretch of the road, there are driveways to the left and crossroads both to the right and to the left?	
A: Yes, I have seen those.	
Q: You continued to accelerate as you approached Mr. Zeigler's truck and diesel trailer?	
A: Yes, I was running up through the gears.	
Q: And as you ran up through the gears, the speed continued to pick up?	
A: Yes.	

Transcript	*Analysis*
Q: Before you pulled out to pass around him, you checked your side mirrors, both to the left and to the right to make sure nothing was behind you?	
A: That's true. I do it before I pass anything.	
Q: But when you looked in those mirrors, you took your eyes off Mr. Zeigler's vehicle?	
A: Just for a moment.	
Q: And in that moment, you cannot tell this jury that Mr. Zeigler did not turn on his turn signal?	
A: No, I wasn't looking.	
Q: He was still just crawling along?	
A: Pretty slow.	
Q: Crawling — just like you were warned?	
A: Right.	
Q: But you had already started to pull out hadn't you?	Loop.
A: Yes.	
Q: You continued to accelerate pass 55?	Double loop of theme words.
A: Maybe a little past 55.	
Q: Well it was as little as 10 miles more than 55? 65 miles per hour?	
A: No more than 65 if that, but no more than 65.	
Q: So you continued to accelerate to a speed not more than 65 miles per hour and you started to pass Mr. Zeigler's vehicle?	Spontaneous loop.
A: Yes.	
Q: Pulling 80,000 pounds of gravel, a full load?	
A: That's what the load was.	
Q: A full load?	
A: Yes.	Spontaneous loop.

Transcript	Analysis
Q: You are pulling a full load — 80,000 pounds plus the truck at no more than 10 miles over the fair, safe, and maximum speed limit?	Spontaneous loop.
A: Yes.	
Q: Mr. Zeigler started to pull into the left-hand lane to make a turn into a crossroads just as you started to pass him didn't you?	
A: He did.	Multiple spontaneous loops and trilogy.
Q: Made the turn at a crawl?	
A: If you say so.	
Q: A crawl is the truth?	
A: Yes, counselor.	
Q: You slammed on your brakes?	
A: That's right.	
Q: But you knew it was too late already didn't you?	
A: There was no way that I was gonna stop.	Spontaneous loop.
Q: There is no way that you were gonna stop with a full load—80,000 pounds plus the weight of your truck at 65 miles per hour from slamming into Mr. Zeigler?	Loop. The witness shows frustration.
A: No.	
Q: And you knew all those facts when you pulled out to pass?	
A: Yes.	Spontaneous loop. *Chapter: Zeigler Did No Wrong*
Q: If you weren't going 65, you would have never hit Mr. Zeigler's slower moving vehicle?	
A: I guess that is right.	
Q: Well, if you were going the same speed as Mr. Zeigler you would not hit him?	
A: No.	

Transcript	*Analysis*
Q: If you hadn't tried to pass him, you would not have hit him?	
A: No.	
Q: And if you weren't going not faster than 65, you would've hit him?	
A: I see. That's true.	
Q: As you approached Mr. Zeigler, he was staying directly in his lane wasn't he?	*Chapter: Zeigler Innocent*
A: Yes.	
Q: He wasn't driving anywhere close to 55?	
A: No.	
Q: You can tell from his speed that he was gonna turn off or he could not drive any faster than he was driving?	
A: That's true.	
Q: You did not know which one it was did you?	
A: No.	
Q: You did not know if he was going to turn to the right or to the left did you?	
A: No.	
Q: But that did not stop you from trying to pass him did it?	
A: No.	
Q: The fact of the matter is that the speed of your truck combined with the acceleration of your truck, combined with the weight of your truck is what caused your truck to slam into Mr. Zeigler's vehicle?	*Chapter: Summary Chapter on Liability*
A: I suppose that's right.	
Q: Well, you don't suppose something in the road made you hit him?	Spontaneous loop.
A: No.	
Q: Mr. Zeigler didn't back into you?	
A: No.	

Transcript	Analysis
Q: Mr. Zeigler didn't pull into you?	
A: No.	
Q: You hit him square from behind because you couldn't stop that weight with those brakes at that speed?	
A: Yes . . .	
Q: When you got out of your truck, you went back to see if Mr. Zeigler was all right?	*Chapter: Injuries Immediate*
A: Yes sir, I ran back.	
Q: And when you ran back, you saw that he was holding his left shoulder?	Spontaneous loop.
A: Yes.	
Q: And he was complaining that his neck was hurting?	
A: Yes, I heard him say that.	
Q: He said that when you asked him if he was all right and he said his left shoulder and his neck was hurting?	Spontaneous loop.
A: That's true.	
Q: You're the one in fact who called the ambulance?	
A: Right.	
Q: And the reason you called the ambulance was he was hurt?	
A: That's what he said.	
Q: Well you knew you weren't hurt?	
A: No. I wasn't hurt.	
Q: You were protected by the big truck and 80,000 pounds of gravel?	
A: I guess so.	
Q: But Mr. Zeigler was the one who received the weight of that truck and the 80,000 pounds of gravel into the rear of his trailer at 65 miles per hour?	

Transcript	*Analysis*

A: That's true.

Q: And that weight was going more than 20 miles per hour faster than he was going?

A: Yes, I think that's right.

Q: It could have been as much as 35 miles per hour faster?

A: I am just not sure.

Q: You are not sure because you weren't looking at your speedometer, but you can't dispute that Mr. Zeigler was going much slower than you?   Spontaneous loop.

A: He was going much slower.

Q: And that you were accelerating every moment that you approached him?

A: That's true.

Q: The reason you called the ambulance was for them to come out and check Mr. Zeigler.

A: That's right.

Q: And you thought he was hurt enough to call an ambulance?

A: Well, I didn't know what to do.

Q: But the thing that you did do at that moment before talking to anyone else was to call an ambulance?

A: Yes.

Q: And the ambulance took him?

A: Yeah.

Q: During the time you waited with Mr. Zeigler, you found out that he was in the logging business?

A: That's true.

Q: That's why he was pulling the 400 gallons of diesel?

A: Right.

Transcript	*Analysis*
Q: You have driven trucks loaded with logs haven't you?	*Chapter: Zeigler Cannot Work at Logging Anymore*
A: Yes.	
Q: You have been in the woods where they were cutting the logs to pick up your trailers?	
A: I have.	
Q: You have seen that kind of work?	
A: Yes.	
Q: You have seen the kind of work that involves skidders and pullers?	
A: Yes.	
Q: Those are big machines that cut down trees and get the trees ready to load on trucks?	
A: That's right.	
Q: Mr. Zeigler told you that that was the kind of work he did?	
A: Yes.	
Q: Now that hard physical work isn't it?	
A: It is.	
Q: It requires a man's back and shoulders to steer those vehicles, to move those levers, and to do it over rough ground?	
A: It does.	
Q: There is a great deal of bouncing that happens in those vehicles and the vehicles not only bounce, but they shift around?	
A: Yes, sir.	
Q: It takes a good healthy man to do that kind of work? Doesn't it?	
A: Yeah, I suppose it does.	
Q: A man with a bad back would be hard-pressed to be able to do that kind of work?	

Transcript	*Analysis*
A: I guess that is right.	
Q: A man with an injured shoulder wouldn't be able to pull that steering wheel over those logs and over that rough ground out in the woods?	
A: I don't really know.	
Q: Well, sir, you pull a steering wheel ten/twelve hours a day in your truck over smooth roads don't you?	
A: Some of them are smooth and some are not.	
Q: The roads that aren't smooth the harder to pull that steering wheel isn't it?	
A: Yes.	
Q: So you know it would cause a great deal of pain to a man with a bad back and bad shoulder to pull a steering wheel eight hours a day out in the woods don't you?	Spontaneous loop.
A: Yes, I suppose it would. . .	
Q: You were working for J& J Trucking at the time of his collision weren't you?	*Chapter: It Is All About the Money*
A: Yes.	
Q: You weren't out on some personal mission?	
A: No.	
Q: You weren't out just going for a Sunday drive?	
A: No.	
Q: You were working?	
A: That's right.	
Q: And you were working to get paid?	
Q: That's right. That's why I do it.	
Q: And the way you get paid is by the load?	Spontaneous loop.
A: Yes.	
Q: The heavier the load, the more you get paid?	

A: That's right
legal limit.

Q: And the leg
80,000 pound.

A: Yes.

Q: That's maximum

A: Right.

Q: So it makes no financia
sense to you or to the
owner of the truck not to
load the truck completely,
to maximum weight?

A: That's right.

Q: That way, you are
maximizing the money you
can get from the maximum
load you are hauling?

A: That's right.

Q: You receive a percentage of
the load after it has been
delivered?

A: That's right.

Q: So the heavier the load,
the bigger your
percentage?

A: That's right.

Q: So the idea is to maximize
the load, which maximizes
your percentage?

A: Well my percentage stays
the same, but I get more
money for a heavier load.

Q: The idea is to maximize
that?

A: Yes.

Q: The more loads you can
make in a week, the more
money you can make in a
week?

A: That is generally true.

Q: Again, by maximizing your
loads you maximize your
money?

A: Right.

Q: So the idea is to run your
loads as fast as you can to
make as much money as
you can during the week?

Loop.

Loop.

Analysis

Loop.

anical
m?

t you can
s during the

you make
nical repairs and
entative repairs at
ght and on the weekends
when you are not
maximizing loads?

A: That's right.

Loop.

Q: That's so that you can
maximize the number of
loads per week?

A: True.

Loop.

Q: Understanding that there
are speed limits on the
roadway, the idea still is to
drive as fast as you can, to
make as many loads as
you can, every week.

A: That's right depending on
the speed limit.

Q: Well, sir, you do not drive
40 miles per hour in a
road that permits you
drive 55 miles per hour
that wouldn't make good
financial sense? Would it?

A: No, but I have driven 40
miles per hour in some 55
miles per hour road.

Q: But you did not choose to
do that, did you?

A: No.

Q: You had to do that right?

A: That's right.

Transcript	*Analysis*

Q: Because of weather, police radar, cause of traffic, but you didn't like driving 40 miles per hour because you knew it was costing you money?

A: That's true.

Q: The simple fact is the faster you go, the more loads you can make. The more loads you make per week, the more money you get paid for that week?

A: That's true.

Q: The formula that you want is the maximum weight per load, the maximum loads per week, to maximize your money?

A: That's it in a nutshell.

Q: Of course that nutshell means that you are driving your truck as fast as you can, as heavy as you can, and if a collision occurs, that will also maximize the damage? — *Loop plus trilogy.*

A: Well I never really thought about it maximizing damage.

Q: But that's the net result isn't it? Maximum damage because of maximum speed and maximum weight for maximum money? — *Spontaneous loop.*

A: Yes. Yes, I suppose so. — *Loop.*

Q: Hadn't thought of that before had you?

A: No.

Q: Weren't thinking of that the day you ran over Mr. Zeigler either did you? — *Witness adopts theme.*

A: No. — *Trilogy to finish chapter. (End of excerpt of cross-examination)*

INDEX

H

M

S